7TH EDITION

THE LAW AND BUSINESS ADMINISTRATION IN CANADA

J. E. SMYTH
Late Professor of Commerce
Faculty of Management Studies
University of Toronto

D. A. SOBERMAN
Professor of Law
Faculty of Law
Queen's University

A. J. EASSON
Professor of Law
Faculty of Law
Queen's University

Prentice Hall Canada Inc., Scarborough, Ontario

Canadian Cataloguing in Publication Data

Smyth, J. E. (James Everil), 1920–83
    The law and business administration in Canada

7th ed.
Includes index.
ISBN 0-13-511529-9

1. Commercial law — Canada.   I. Soberman, D. A.,
1929–   .   II. Easson, A. J.   III. Title.

KE919.S62 1995   346.71'07   C94-932192-3
KF889.S62 1965

Prentice-Hall, Inc., Englewood Cliffs, New Jersey
Prentice-Hall International (UK) Limited, London
Prentice-Hall of Australia, Pty. Limited, Sydney
Prentice-Hall Hispanoamericana, S.A., Mexico City
Prentice-Hall of India Private Limited, New Delhi
Prentice-Hall of Japan, Inc., Tokyo
Simon & Schuster Asia Private Limited, Singapore
Editora Prentice-Hall do Brasil, Ltda., Rio de Janeiro

ISBN 0-13-511529-9

Acquisitions Editor: Jacqueline Wood
Developmental Editor: Maurice Esses
Production Editor: Norman Bernard
Interior Design: VISUTronX/Jim Loates
Cover Design: Olena Serbyn
Cover Image: Tony Stone Images/Ken Whitmore
Page Layout: Jaytype

1 2 3 4 5   RRD   99 98 97 96 95

Printed and bound in the United States of America.

Every reasonable effort has been made to obtain permissions for all articles and data used in this
edition. If errors or omissions have occurred, they will be corrected in future editions provided
written notification has been received by the publisher.

$\mathcal{B}$RIEF TABLE OF CONTENTS

$\mathcal{C}$ONTENTS

v

PREFACE

Even before the first edition was published in 1964, the task of writing a book to provide a broad background to business law was a daunting challenge. Little could we predict the broad sweep of change — and growth — that quickly followed. In the second edition, in response to the suggestions of business law teachers, we added chapters on tort law and the law of negotiable instruments. In the third, we added an introductory chapter so that we could provide a better understanding of the increasing complexity of our legal system. In the fourth edition, we expanded existing chapters to include discussion of important developing areas, such as the implications of the Canadian Charter of Rights and Freedoms and consumer protection; nevertheless, we found it necessary to add one chapter on the rapidly growing area of professional liability. The fifth edition saw substantial changes in a number of areas, but they were accommodated without adding new chapters. In the sixth edition, once more it became essential to add a chapter on intellectual property. In writing the fifth and sixth editions, we were ever conscious of the scholarly and thoughtful contribution of J.E. Smyth both to the original concept of the book and his meticulous care in the first four editions. In preparing the seventh edition we are constantly reminded of his high standards, standards which we trust remain an essential characteristic of the text.

With the coming into force of the North American Free Trade Agreement and the completion of the Uruguay round of the General Agreement of Tariffs and Trade, the significance of international trade for Canada — already a very important part of our economy — is highly likely to increase. More than ever, Canadian businesses find themselves involved in international transactions as exporters, importers, or investors in joint ventures. We believe it is important that business students gain a familiarity with such transactions and have added a new Chapter 35 on this subject.

The law continues to change quickly, particularly in two areas related to the operation of a business:

    (i)   Employment law has seen many changes as a result of pay equity legislation, the impact of human rights codes, and now in Ontario with recently enacted employment equity legislation; these matters are considered in Chapter 23;

    (ii) Regulatory schemes, especially for protecting the environment, have increased substantially and influence many business decisions; for this reason we have rearranged the materials in the former Chapter 31 ("Management and Operation of a Corporation") into two chapters — a revised Chapter 31, "The Internal Affairs of Corporations", which sets out more fully the role of directors and the rights of shareholders, and a new Chapter 32, "The External Responsibilities of a Corporation", which includes a discussion of the rapid growth of environmental regulation and its importance to business decisions.

In preparing this edition, we have become painfully aware of a new paradox: while statute law and regulations are changing ever more rapidly, and technology — especially in computing and electronics — is changing the way we do business, the courts have become clogged with an enormous backlog of cases to be heard. Thus it may be that by the time the courts have considered important changes in regulations, or the effect technology may have on intellectual property matters or on contracts, typ-ically three to four years have passed — and there may be new regulations or further more significant changes in technology. The paradox makes it increasingly difficult to discern clear answers to such questions as, "Does a facsimile copy of a signed contract satisfy the requirement for "written evidence" under the Statute of Frauds?", or "Who owns the copyright to a message sent on Internet?"

We long ago discovered that subjects of little interest to one teacher are considered absolutely essential to another, and so it remains a continuing challenge to determine what materials might be deleted. For this edition, we have shortened discussion of some subjects and eliminated a few references. However, virtually all the changes in the law to which we have referred above are additions, not merely alterations, to exist-ing rules. And so, despite our efforts to reduce text, the seventh edition is somewhat larger than the sixth.

We are indebted to our colleagues in the Faculty of Law and in particular to Professor Donald Stuart for their advice and encouragement. Our special thanks to research assistant Darryl Aarbo for carefully checking statutory changes and current cases. We appreciate the feedback provided by all those who responded to a survey questionnaire about the sixth edition. We would also like to acknowledge the assis-tance given to us by Maureen Donnelly (Brock University), Dorothy DuPlessis (University of New Brunswick), Steven Enman (Acadia University), Sally Gunz (University of Waterloo), E. Michael Power, and Ernest S. Schmidt (Algonquin College) in their reviews of the manuscript of the seventh edition.

> D.A. Soberman
> A.J. Easson
> 1995

$\mathcal{E}$XPLANATION OF ABBREVIATIONS

Throughout the text and footnotes, references occur to reported decisions of the courts, to statutes, and to legal periodicals. Listed below are the abbreviations for frequently cited source materials.

Canada

REPORTS

A.R	Alberta Reports
B.L.R.	Business Law Reports
C.C.C.	Canadian Criminal Cases
C.C.L.I.	Canadian Cases on the Law of Insurance
C.C.L.T.	Canadian Cases on the Law of Torts
C.E.L.R.	Canadian Environmental Law Reports
C.P.R.	Canadian Patent Reports
C.R.	Criminal Reports
C.S.	Cour Supérieure (Québec)
D.L.R.	Dominion Law Reports
Ex.C.R.	Exchequer Court Reports
F.C.	Federal Court Reports
M.P.R.	Maritime Provinces Reports
N.B.R.	New Brunswick Reports
N.S.R.	Nova Scotia Reports
O.A.C.	Ontario Appeal Cases
O.A.R.	Ontario Appeal Reports
O.L.R.	Ontario Law Reports
O.R.	Ontario Reports
O.W.N.	Ontario Weekly Notes
P.P.S.A C.	Personal Property Security Act Cases
S.C.R.	Supreme Court Reports
W.L.R.	Western Law Reports
W.W.R.	Western Weekly Reports

STATUTES

Revised Statutes of

R.S.A.	Alberta
R.S.B.C.	British Columbia
R.S.C.	Canada
R.S.M.	Manitoba
R.S.N.B.	New Brunswick
R.S.Nfld.	Newfoundland
R.S.N.S.	Nova Scotia
R.S.O.	Ontario
R.S.P.E.I.	Prince Edward Island
R.S.Q.	Québec
R.S.S.	Saskatchewan

(Statutes for individual years are cited as S.A., S.B.C., S.C., S.M., S.N.B., S.Nfld., S.N.S., S.O., S.P.E.I., S.Q., S.S., respectively.)

S.O.R.	Statutory Orders and Regulations

PERIODICALS

C.B.L.J.	Canadian Business Law Journal
Can. Bar Rev.	Canadian Bar Review
Can. B.A.J.	Canadian Bar Association Journal
UBC L. Rev.	University of British Columbia Law Review
U.T.L.J.	University of Toronto Law Journal

JUDGES

J.	Justice
J.A.	Justice of Appeal
JJ.	Justices
C.J.	Chief Justice
A.G.	Attorney-General

United Kingdom

REPORTS

All E.R.	All England Reports
E.R.	English Reports (Reprint)
I.R.	Irish Reports
L.J. Ex.	Law Journal Exchequer
L.J.P.C.	Law Journal Privy Council
L.T.	Law Times Reports
T.L.R.	Times Law Reports

LAW REPORTS SERIES

Law Reports 1865-75

L.R.C.P.	Common Pleas
L.R.Ch.	Chancery
L.R.Eq.	Equity Cases
L.R.Ex.	Exchequer
L.R.H.L.	House of Lords
L.R.Q.B.	Queen's Bench

Law Reports 1875-80

C.P.D.	Common Pleas Division
Ex.D.	Exchequer Division

Law Reports 1875-91

App. Cas.	Appeal Cases
Ch.D.	Chancery Division
P.D.	Probate Division
Q.B.D.	Queen's Bench Division

Law Reports 1891-date

A.C.	Appeal Cases
Ch.	Chancery Division
K.B. or Q.B.	King's (Queen's) Bench Division
P. (before 1971)	Probate Divorce and Admiralty Division

Law Reports 1953-date

W.L.R.	Weekly Law Reports
Fam.	Family Division

STATUTES
(U.K.) at end of reference

JUDGES

B.	Baron
C.B.	Chief Baron
C.	Chancellor
L.C.	Lord Chancellor
V.C.	Vice-Chancellor
L.J.	Lord Justice
L.C.J.	Lord Chief Justice
M.R.	Master of the Rolls

United States

A.L.R.	American Law Reports
F.	Federal Reporter
F.R.D.	Federal Rules Decisions
N.E.	Northeastern Reporter
N.W.	Northwestern Reporter
N.Y.	New York Reports
P.	Pacific Reporter
U.C.C.	Uniform Commercial Code

Australia and New Zealand

C.L.R.	Commonwealth Law Reports (Austlalia)
N.S.W.R.	New South Wales Reports
N.Z.L.R.	New Zealand Law Reports
Qd.R.	Queensland Reports

PART ONE

THE LAW IN ITS SOCIAL CONTEXT

Like other major disciplines, law cannot be reduced to a simple set of rules and instructions that can be memorized and applied mechanically. We are all aware of the complexity and uncertainty in legal disputes. In order to gain an understanding of the legal system, we must learn something about its history and evolution, and theories that underlie its principles and rules. Chapter 1 provides an overview of the role of law in society and the continuing debate about its values.

Law provides the framework for virtually all business arrangements. Parties to a contract, investors in a corporation, owners of land and buildings, all desire reliability and predictability in their relations with others. The legal system provides much of that certainty. However, parties may disagree about their respective rights and obligations, and end up before the courts. The role of the courts is not only to settle disputes, but also to explain the rules, that is, to give reasons that justify their decisions. In turn, the explanations help others to adjust their relations and to avoid disputes. Thus, while only a very small proportion of business arrangements go before the courts, the courts play a much larger role in society, by providing reliable guidelines for business arrangements. Chapter 2 describes that role.

To the non-lawyer, the structure of the court system is confusing; an overview helps in understanding how disputes get before the courts and are ultimately resolved. Chapter 3 explains how the courts operate and how parties utilize them; we describe the court system in England — where ours originated — and those in Canada and the United States.

LAW, FREEDOM, AND SOCIETY

$\mathcal{L}$AW AND CONSCIENCE

It would be comforting to be able to provide a concise definition of "law". Unfortunately, no one has yet devised a satisfactory definition, even within hundreds of pages of text. Consider the following illustrations:

ILLUSTRATION A

Mary Brown was at home tending her sick eighteen-month-old baby. He had a high temperature caused by an undetermined virus. Suddenly she realized that the child had lapsed into a coma. Fearing that he was in a state of convulsion and might die, she rushed the child to her car and drove to the nearest hos-pital. Within a few moments she was driving 110 km/h in a 50 km/h zone. On arrival at the hospital the child was placed in emergency care, and the doctor commended her for having saved the life of her child. A police officer arrived on the scene and presented her with a summons for dangerous driving.

ILLUSTRATION B

James Black was just two weeks old and suf-fering from a generally fatal blood deficiency that could be cured only by means of a com-plete transfusion of his blood. His parents were members of a religious sect that pro-hibits blood transfusions, and they refused to give permission for transfusions. The obstetri-cian incharge of the hospital applied to the court to make the infant a ward of the Children's Aid Society so that permission for the transfusion could be obtained from the Society. After the court had made James Black a ward of the Society, but before the transfusions had been administered, his par-ents removed him from the hospital in breach of the court order.

Mary Brown drove her car far in excess of the speed limit — a speed limit designed to promote safety. She endangered the lives of other users of the streets, but she did so in order to save the life of her own child. She would not argue that the 50 km/h speed limit was unreasonable or unjust, but only that in the circumstances she was justified in break-ing the law or, possibly, that the law should not apply to that particular situation. On the other hand, the parents of James Black broke the law because they believed it was a bad law; in any event, it ought not to apply to them and their child against their religious beliefs. Mary Brown believed that she had the right to make every effort to save the life of her child; James Black's parents believed they had the right to risk the life of their child for their religious beliefs. In both cases, the law was apparently broken.

What then is "law"? Is it the same thing as "justice"? Why should we obey the law? Is it ever right to break the law? There are no clear answers to these questions. In most respects, the difficulties have remained unchanged over the centuries. Intelligent, moderate men and women generally agree that there are times when an individual is justified in breaking the law, although they would add that, generally speaking, the law should be obeyed. They would also agree that there are unjust laws, but even these ought to be obeyed because of the chaotic consequences for society if many people failed to obey them. Even while trying to get unjust laws changed by normal, lawful means, we should nevertheless comply with them.

Law and justice, then, do not always coincide. But, one may ask, "Is an unjust law really law"? In some circumstances, rare though they may be, a law has been argued to be so atrociously unjust that it need not be obeyed by anyone. To put the argument another way, such a "law" is no law at all, and should not bind us. If this is so, how can we distinguish an invalid law from a valid law? This question is one of the most perplexing ever raised. To shed a little light on it we will briefly examine the two oldest contrasting theories of law.

Natural Law

The most venerable theory is called *natural law.* There are two main streams within this philosophy. The older is based on religious belief. When a religion establishes a set of moral and ethical values, it necessarily prescribes rules of conduct based on these values. In ancient societies, the religious leaders were usually the holders of power and translated *their* religious rules into laws. Thus, law originated within religious teachings. Since religious precepts are considered by those who formulate them to be eternal and immutable truths, so too are the fundamental principles of law — natural law — based on them, even though detailed rules and their particular applications may vary as society changes.

The second view of natural law does not depend on a religious view of the world. Rather, it rests on the assumption that people are rational and that by applying their inherent abilities of reason and logic to their perception of the world will arrive at basic principles of justice. This position was taken by some of the ancient Greek philosophers, and although almost forgotten for many centuries, it was reasserted in the 17th century in an extreme form. The Dutch philosopher and lawyer Grotius stated that the truths arrived at by humankind would exist independently of God. Indeed, if God were not in total harmony with these principles, He would not be God.

Despite their differences about how we perceive the underlying principles, both views lead to the same basic view of law: fundamental, immutable moral principles are expressed in general legal principles, and may be further formulated in detailed rules for a particular society. One of the most eloquent expressions that combines these two views of natural law, based on the teachings of the 17th-century English philosopher John Locke, is found in the Declaration of Independence of the United States: "We hold these *truths to be self-evident:* that all men are created equal, that they are *endowed by their Creator* with certain unalienable rights, that among these are life, liberty and the pursuit of happiness." (Italics supplied.)

$\mathcal{L}$AWS OF NATURE AND LAWS OF HUMAN CONDUCT

Today, the word "law" has two distinct meanings. First, there are physical laws, laws of nature, that we learn in studying the natural sciences such as physics, chemistry, and biology. A primary example is the law of gravity. Second, we have rules governing our conduct. A law prohibiting stealing does not make it physically impossible for a person to steal; it says that one should not steal, and that one will be punished if found guilty of stealing. This is a *normative* law as opposed to a *physical* law. A person may break a normative law and risk the consequences; one cannot "break" the law of gravity.

This distinction, which seems so evident to us, was not recognized until comparatively recent times. As late as the 17th century, the expressions "natural law" (referring to human conduct) and "laws of nature" (referring to the physical universe) were used interchangeably. Laws describing natural phenomena, such as the movements of heavenly bodies, the seasons, biological reproduction, and the properties of various elements, were considered to be in no way different from laws governing human conduct, and all were considered to have been laid down either by the Creator or by an unchanging system of logic.

Paradoxically, natural law can, on the one hand, be a vehicle for reform and revolution or, on the other, give strong support to a highly conservative view of society, upholding the *status quo*. In the French and American revolutions, the battle cry was that the great principles of natural law (as exemplified in our quotation from the American Declaration of Independence) had been offended by man-made laws. In France the revolution used Rousseau's words: "Man is born free but is everywhere in chains". The laws that placed people in chains, therefore, were invalid. Natural law thus gave legitimacy to the revolutionary cry. Yet the same natural law has also been proclaimed in aid of the notion of divine right of kings to support an existing monarchy. A most striking (and unsuccessful) example is the claim of divine support made by the English monarchs in the 17th century before the revolution that deposed and eventually beheaded Charles I. The idea of divine right has been used to justify the maintenance of an aristocracy and to prescribe ranks of merit, and hence privilege, down to the lowliest serf; it has even been used to justify systems of slavery.

As we shall see, this two-edged sword of legal philosophy applies to other definitions of law as well as natural law. As an abstraction, legal philosophy tends to be neutral; partisans of different views of society inject their values into the philosophical system to give it the particular political cast of reaction or radicalism desired.

$\mathcal{N}$ATURAL LAW UNDER ATTACK—LEGAL POSITIVISM

A harmonious and unified view of the laws of nature and of humankind was a satisfying system for believers. By the 17th century, however, any semblance of unity in the Christian world of Western Europe was gone, and a variety of religious beliefs dominated different regions of the continent. Nation-states with diverse and conflicting national interests had arisen, and they amended their laws to suit their own interests. There was no longer one way to God, truth, and a righteous life. With each religious group heaping critical abuse on all others, skepticism grew among many of the thinkers of 17th-century Europe. As we have noted, some thinkers rejected faith in God and substituted the human ability to reason as the greatest single power in the world. They began to construct their own rational systems of moral conduct and of laws that should be based on them. Just as in the case of religious faith, however, rational systems lacked universal appeal. While some, like John Locke, asserted fundamental principles based on natural law, others were skeptical of the existence of any unchanging, basic rules.

The Scottish thinker David Hume made a particularly significant departure. It was Hume who first clearly distinguished between physical laws and normative laws. He made a further crucial distinction among normative rules themselves. He stated that some normative rules were "law" because they created a code of behaviour complete with sanctions for failure to live by that code. In contrast, other normative rules existed without sanctions for their breach. These were moral rules; failure to observe them might create annoyance or indignation in others, and a bad conscience in the wrongdoer, but no more than that. Hume's basic distinction, then, was between ascertainable rules that are binding, the law that "is", and rules that people "ought" to observe even in the absence of legal compulsion. His distinction was between the "is" and the "ought", or between *law* and *morals*.

What Hume called "law" has since become known as *positive law*. Those who insist upon a clear distinction between the "is" and the "ought" are called *legal positivists*. Legal positivism is concerned with ascertaining the body of law that "is", with describing those criteria or tools that can be used to distinguish positive law from all other rules. Some positivists disclaim any concern for what is good or bad about law because in order to assess the goodness or badness of a legal rule they would have to refer to a standard external to the law itself. Their concern is only with legal rules as such. They do not deny the importance of assessing the value of law, but say that is a task for the legislator, not the legal theorist.

How does one define law in a positivist system? The positivist asserts that law must come from a person or group of persons holding power over the general population. Those holding power can impose sanctions on individuals who break the law. John Austin, a 19th-century English legal philosopher, described law as "the command of a sovereign". He did not view the sovereign as merely a person called "the King". Austin described the sovereign in the England of his time as "the King in Parliament". The "command" of the sovereign was an act of Parliament duly passed by both houses and receiving royal assent from the monarch.

Austin's definition of law presents difficulties, some of which he acknowledged himself. For example, while his definition is relatively satisfactory when applied to a constitutional monarchy with a unitary system of government such as exists in England, it is much more difficult to apply to a federal country such as Canada or the United States, where as well as a national government, there are several governments at the provincial or state level. In the case of both Canada and the United States, his definition faces an added difficulty: lawful authority emanates from the Constitution, and a document can hardly be personified as a sovereign.

Modern legal thinkers have refined Austin's theory into more sophisticated 20th-century models. In place of a sovereign they recognize a basic law, a constitution habitually obeyed by the citizens of a country. This basic law enjoys a sufficient minimum level of acceptance by the general population just as long as they regard it as legitimate and binding.

The closed legal systems of positivists, however, do not provide a standard for measuring the minimum general level of acceptance required to come to the conclusion that a legal system effectively exists. To reach that conclusion an observer must make a decision based on personal values outside the logical system of the positivist. In unstable societies, the problem for the observer is sometimes very difficult to resolve. Thus, in the midst of a revolution when the old constitution has been denounced by many citizens and it may not be possible to ascertain whether anyone holds power, there might appear to be no law at all. In such a period, what happens to existing debts and obligations, or to people who commit acts normally considered criminal? How does the eventual victor become established as the lawful authority? Is it merely a nose-counting operation, so that a government exists again when the victor has sufficient (whatever that word may imply) acceptance to proclaim laws and administer sanctions? Positivist theories do not explain how a system of law re-emerges.

Suppose, for the purpose of examining the illlustrations below, that a positivist approach does provide a means of ascertaining what the law is in a stable society with a popularly elected government. It still does not, any more than does a system of natural law, answer the question, "When, if ever, is it right to break the law"? There is an adage that much learning in philosophy does not make a person good. In law, we have a parallel: much learning in legal philosophy does not provide easy answers to difficult moral questions about the law.

ILLUSTRATION A

Three men and a boy were shipwrecked in a small boat 1500 km at sea in the South Atlantic. What little food they had was exhausted within a few days. For the next six days they had no food whatever, and subsisted only on rainwater. All three men were married, with young families. Two of the men suggested that if no relief came someone should be sacrificed to save the rest. The third man dissented and the boy was not consulted. A day later, the two men suggested to the third that they should cast lots to determine who should be put to death to save the rest, but the third refused to consent. The proposal was not put to the boy, who at that time was very much weakened and lying helpless in the bottom of the boat. The three men spoke of their families and suggested that it would be better to kill the boy so that their lives could be saved. The first man proposed that if there was no vessel in sight by the next morning, the boy should be killed. On the following day, the two men offered a prayer for forgiveness for committing so rash an act, and then proceeded to kill the boy with a knife. The three men fed upon the body of the boy for four days until they were picked up by a passing ship. The first two men were charged with murder while the third was not charged with any offence.[1]

---

[1] *Regina v. Dudley and Stephens* (1884), 14 Q.B.D. 273.

ILLUSTRATION B

In 1944 in Germany a woman, wishing to be rid of her husband, denounced him to the authorities for insulting remarks he had made about Hitler while home on leave from the German army. The wife was under no legal duty to report his act, but what he had said was apparently in violation of statutes making it illegal to make statements detrimental to the government of the Third Reich . . . The husband was arrested and sentenced to death, apparently pursuant to these statutes, though he was not executed but sent to the front. In 1949 the wife was prosecuted in a West German court for an offence that we would describe as illegally depriving a person of his freedom . . . This was punishable as a crime under the German Criminal Code of 1871, which had remained in force continuously since its enactment. The wife pleaded that her husband's imprisonment was pursuant to the Nazi statutes and hence that she had committed no crime.[2]

Fifteen hundred kilometres at sea, in a small boat that could hardly be considered as part of the "national territory" of the home country of the shipwrecked men, is there any ascertainable positive law? (Indeed, should the law of any country apply?) Do these men constitute a miniature community that can make its own laws to suit its needs? If the law of one country is applied to them, should they be acquitted of any crime on the grounds that their dire circumstances justified their actions? If the law of a particular country does not apply, are there still immutable principles of justice that ought to be used to judge people's conduct, no matter where they find themselves? And if there are immutable principles, ought they ever to be applied to override the established positive law of a country? In the context of Illustration B, should the plea of the wife that her act was lawful under existing Nazi positive law fail because principles of natural law nullify the apparently valid positive law of an evil regime? If so, does the earlier law of Germany apply in the circumstances? Might it be argued in both cases that no positive law existing at the time had been broken, and that to punish either the men at sea or the wartime wife is to create *retroactive law* to deal with a situation after it has arisen? In most legal systems there is a strong aversion to retroactive law making something a crime when at the time the act was committed it was not a crime.

The above illustrations show that legal systems can be confronted with extremely difficult moral questions. No solution is entirely satisfactory, and reasonable people can strongly disagree about the appropriate disposition of a difficult case. Thus, it would be impossible to conclude that law and justice always coincide. There will always be disagreement in ascertaining what the law is in some situations, and even greater disagreement about whether its application has led to a just solution. Nor does legal philosophy help us decide whether it is ever right to break the law. At best, it can make the problem clearer and focus our minds on the central issue.

---

[2] Cited from H.L.A. Hart, "Positivism and the Separation of Law and Morals", (1958) 71 *Harvard Law Review*, p. 593 at pp. 618-9.

PURPOSES OF A LEGAL SYSTEM

We shall leave the relation of particular laws to justice, to examine the broader significance of a system of law. We have noted that most reasonable people would agree that, generally speaking, the law ought to be obeyed. What purposes are served when people obey the rules of a legal system? Whether looking at this question primarily as a legal matter or as a political and social issue, most people believe that freedom from violent conflict and the assurance of reasonably predictable and orderly relations among human beings are essential qualities of society. People need to feel free from the fear that arbitrary force will be used against them by their neighbours or the state. They should be able to rely with reasonable certainty on having normal expectations met, for example, that they will receive the agreed wages for their work, that they will be fairly compensated for injury caused by the fault of another person, and that a system of rules will be applied fairly to settle serious disputes. These are but a few of the expectations considered necessary, or at least highly desirable, in a society.

A legal system provides the broad framework for the detailed rules that create the essential qualities of a stable society. If individuals feel free either to obey or break the rules as they wish, then the rules will not secure the minimum standards of peace and predictability. We may conclude, therefore, that citizens generally ought to obey the law because in so doing they promote a reasonably harmonious society. If a legal system is to encourage the majority to accept this view, it must appear to them to be generally just, so that they are willing to make the following assumption about particular laws: that in the absence of other information a law is expected to produce just results. The assumption should be strong enough that if an unjust result seems to follow, the first step should be a careful re-examination of the process to make sure no mistake has been made along the way, and it was not the *application* of the law but the law itself that was unjust. A group of citizens may finally come to the conclusion, based on their own values, that the law really is a bad law and ought to be substantially altered or else repealed altogether.

CHALLENGING THE PURPOSES OF LEGAL SYSTEMS

In the above discussion, we make the basic assumption that a legal system is essential for a harmonious society. Our illustrations raise issues that do not contest this assumption. Rather, they are concerned with identifying and describing law and distinguishing it from other kinds of obligations. For this purpose, the illustrations contain highly emotional dilemmas that bring positive law into conflict with personal conviction based on moral or religious beliefs.

We can also, however, look at law primarily in an economic, social, and political context. From this perspective, some thinkers have attacked the very assumption that law is necessary or even desirable. Anarchists and Marxists in the 19th century were confronted with the unquestionable horrors of the Industrial Revolution that turned landless peasants into factory workers and subjected them to dreadful living and working conditions.

Those critics saw law as primarily a tool designed to perpetuate inequality and preserve privilege and power for the elite; law kept the proletariat in bondage.

Long before Marx, thinkers had considered what society would be like in a "natural state" without law and sanctions. In the 4th century, St. Augustine interpreted the Judeo-Christian account of the Fall of Man as supporting the need for law to restrain our baser instincts. Other views of humanity and law were proposed from time to time, but from St. Augustine through the Middle Ages and into the 18th century, the dominant view was that the legal order was needed to protect people from themselves. In the 17th century, the English philosopher Thomas Hobbes asserted that in a world with no enforced legal order, life would be "nasty, brutish and short". He argued that our natural propensities are aggressive and violent. A society based on brute force would be the very antithesis of a community where fairness and peace reign. People would live in constant fear, and their homes would indeed be castles.

There was some historical support for Hobbes' view. Looking back from the 17th century, Hobbes viewed the "Dark Ages" as a period of lawlessness and fear. To protect themselves against marauding invaders from the east and north, and gangs of brigands and pirates, men would pledge their allegiance to the most powerful in their midst. He would become their liege lord; in return for supplies and services, especially military service from his vassals, he offered protection from outsiders and settled disputes among the vassals themselves. Thus, the system of feudalism was born primarily to give life a measure of security and normality under the aegis of a feudal landlord. Eventually, in most European countries, the most powerful lord was able to obtain pledges of loyalty from lesser lords and proclaim himself king, even though his crown might be worn precariously. The prevailing theology of the Middle Ages aided these developments: St. Augustine's belief that laws administered with a firm hand were needed to keep the human tendency to greed and violence in check was interpreted as supporting the claim that those who demonstrated their God-given strength and courage — or their ruthlessness — were divinely chosen to become rulers.

Despite St. Augustine's dominant influence, another view of humanity survives dating from classical Greek times, that of innocent and benevolent creatures corrupted by an oppressive society with its system of laws and coercion. (Supporters of this view have never explained satisfactorily how innocent humanity created a corrupt society in the first place.) Although the view had been eclipsed by the doctrine of Original Sin, it persisted, and in the 18th century was reinforced by the coming of modern science. People began to explain many of the mysteries of the physical world, and leading philosophers of the time noted that the power of reason had apparently enabled humanity to arrive at truths independently of a theological base. Now, if people could solve many of the mysteries of natural science, why not those of their own nature and society? Humanity itself was exalted and idealized, contrary to the idea of Original Sin.

The benevolent view of humanity received fresh impetus from the Romantics at the beginning of the 19th century. The solution they proposed for society's ills was to abandon artificial urban societies and return to nature, to a simple rustic life where people could recapture the primordial state of innocence and happiness. Hobbesian ideas of the state and law and order were anathema to the Romantics. Romanticism also contained the seeds of anarchism. Anarchists did not want simply to flee the city: that would not solve the problem for the poor benighted souls left under the evil oppression of the organized state. Instead, they wished to destroy, stamp out entirely, this organized oppression, the state and its laws.

$\mathcal{M}$ARXISM

Marxism is closely related to anarchism. Marx was little concerned with humanity in the mythical "original state of nature"; yet he did assume that, once freed from the corrupting influence of a class society, people would be benevolent toward their fellows. Marx spent most of his time analyzing society in terms of property, power, and economics. Even scholars who disagree strongly with his values and conclusions will concede that Marx made a great contribution to the social sciences by emphasizing the relationship between the distribution of power and wealth in a society, and that society's prevailing ideas and values.

Marx observed that ownership of property — wealth — was the most important element separating the classes in society. The upper classes, though few in number, owned most of the wealth, and in industrialized countries, wealth consisted in large measure of factories and mines, the means of production. Thus, the upper classes controlled the means of livelihood and the very lives of the workers.

In the mid-19th century, the legal systems of countries in the process of industrialization — chiefly Britain, the United States, Prussia, and France — gave great protection to the owners of property in a variety of ways. In the first place, penalties for theft were very severe, frequently providing for capital punishment even when no violence was involved in the crime.

Second, taxes on income and wealth were either non-existent or negligible. Governments raised money mainly by means of taxes in the form of excise duties on goods, where the cost is passed on to the consumer of the goods, whether rich or poor. This form of taxation is now considered regressive by economists, because it throws a disproportionate tax burden on low-income people.

Third, most forms of labour unions were prohibited as constituting criminal activity "in restraint of trade". Legislators and courts held the view that agreements among workers interfered with the freedom of each individual worker to bargain with the employer. This "freedom" to bargain was considered sacred. As a result, workers were forbidden to organize and bargain collectively with factory owners about rates of pay and other working conditions. Because of the unequal bargaining powers of an individual worker and the owner of a factory, freedom to bargain was a myth: the worker either accepted the terms offered or had no work and no pay. At a time when there was no unemployment insurance or state welfare plan, refusing a job was tantamount to accepting starvation. Even the most partisan supporter of management today, although he might argue that the pendulum has swung the other way and that unions have more bargaining power than management, would recognize that 19th-century law concerning labour unions was so grossly unfair as to be barbaric. Working conditions reflected this situation: they were often unhealthy and dangerous, and the workers were paid a pittance.

Fourth, as we shall discuss in more detail later,[3] under the law of negligence, employers were virtually immune from legal action by employees for injuries suffered by them,

---

[3]   Chapter 23 under "Workers' Compensation".

whether in a mine, a factory, a railway yard, or an office. The employer reaped the benefits of the employee's efforts, but the employee took the risk of injury and disability without compensation.

The picture of society presented by these key elements in the legal system supported Marx's view that the legal mechanism of the state operated in large measure for the benefit of the property-owning classes. Most people today, with the benefit of the enlightened hindsight of the late 20th century, would probably agree with Marx's argument up to this point. But Marx went on to assert that the upper classes would never surrender any of their protection and privileges through persuasion or other forms of non-violent pressure. For Marx, the only way — indeed, the inevitable way — to change the situation was through the violent overthrow of the upper classes by a workers' revolution. A belief in the general inevitability of the historical process (including, in Marx's interpretation, the destruction of the legal system that protects the wealthy classes) is called historical determinism. But the events it predicted have not been realized. In the last two decades of the 19th century and in the early 20th century, many of the worst abuses and inequalities were reduced or eliminated by acts of Parliament and without revolution. The process has been a continuing, even accelerating, one.

The number of crimes for which capital punishment could be imposed was drastically reduced; they were limited almost entirely to crimes of violence against other persons and acts of treason. In the field of taxation, systems were introduced for taxing the incomes of individuals and corporations at progressive rates increasing as income increases, and in many countries, including Canada, Britain, and the United States, such taxes are now the principal source of revenue. Not only were labour unions made legal, but a separate system of labour law has been developed, with rules for recognition of unions, settling struggles between rival unions, and promoting peaceful settlement of disputes between unions and management. The system is far from perfect, but it does represent a genuine, substantial effort to create a fair system. Industrial law too has been drastically changed to provide compensation to workers injured on the job, and induce or even compel owners to improve safety and health standards on their premises.

Although the wealthy classes may not willingly give up their privileges, there is much evidence in many developed countries that they will not mount the barricades to defend them. Instead, in the process of bargaining with other segments of society, they will trade off many privileges in order to retain some benefits. In addition, even without being altruistic, intelligent people in a privileged position will often act out of long-term enlightened self-interest. For example, an employer who voluntarily improves working conditions or offers a generous profit-sharing plan to employees may well improve business profits. In an expanding economy such as Western countries have enjoyed since Marx's day, it has been possible for almost everyone to have more.

Marx believed that when the proletariat had overthrown the upper classes a classless society would be created, and the state and its system of coercive law would simply wither away, because law is needed only in an oppressive society. In the new classless world there would be no oppression, since everyone's natural needs would be provided for, thus creating in everyone a new willingness to share the goods of society with others. Even before the Bolshevik Revolution in Russia, many attempts had been made to create truly communal societies run on either anarchistic or Marxist principles. In these communities, usually established on farms remote from large cities, all things were owned in common: there was no private property, no formal government, no police, no coercion — at least in theory. Invariably they collapsed within a few months or years. The explanation given by believers in the commune is that although members joined with the best of intentions, they had been so corrupted by evil, class-ridden society that they could not escape their ingrained, dangerously selfish traits. It was their anticommunal faults that destroyed the communities.

Perhaps the problems of these idealistic societies were precursors of those of the communist world. In the U.S.S.R., far from withering away, the apparatus of the state seemed to be ever-expanding. There *was* an enormous centralized and impersonal bureaucracy from which the individual had to seek permission to do many of the things we in Canada do as a matter of course, if we so choose: change educational programs, change jobs, move from one part of the country to another, publish an article or a book, or leave the country.

The 1980s and early 1990s have seen radical changes in the Marxist world. Early in the 1980s, substantial economic reforms began in the People's Republic of China, permitting peasants to keep the benefits of surplus agricultural production. Productivity increased dramatically. Small enterprises began to flourish in the cities, and joint ventures with large firms in Western countries were encouraged. In the last few years China's economy has continued to expand rapidly despite the prolonged recession that has plagued Western countries and Japan.

In Eastern European countries there was a growing realization that the highly centralized, planned economies created after World War II were unable to respond effectively to changing economic and social conditions and to changing technology. The failures became apparent to both the citizens and leaders. We are now witnessing profound political and economic reforms in countries comprising the former Soviet Union and in Eastern Europe. We cannot know, of course, whether or not Marx himself might have modified his own views had he witnessed these events.

THE GOLDEN MEAN

The great Greek philosopher Aristotle recognized two broad categories of law which he called *retributive justice* and *distributive justice*, a classification that remains generally recognized today. Retributive justice is concerned with those rules that usually come to mind when the word law is mentioned — rules that prohibit acts considered to be injurious to others. Criminal law is the most obvious example. The government uses sanctions to enforce retributive rules and wrongdoers are punished. The illustrations earlier in this chapter about the shipwrecked men and the German wife were concerned with the breach of rules of retributive justice.

Distributive justice concerns the allocation of resources and wealth among the citizens of a society. These laws redistribute wealth by taking from those who have much and giving to those who have little and cannot adequately provide for themselves. This type of redistribution was once considered to be the province of charity, but now it is a part of government welfare schemes for those who are poor, sick, or disabled. Yet welfare, so narrowly defined, is but a small part of distributive law. Our laws provide far more important instruments of redistribution of wealth: a public system of education; prepaid medical care; unemployment insurance; subsidies and transfer payments by the federal government for regional development; transportation systems; and various types of equalization payments. Funds to sustain these programs are raised by progressive income tax and, as in unemployment insurance and medical care insurance, by compulsory premium payments; benefits are paid, for example, to those who are unemployed or who have incurred medical expenses, without regard to the source of contributions. Such schemes of redistribution are consistent with Aristotle's views.

Aristotle also believed that human beings were neither mainly greedy and brutish nor wholly innocent, well-meaning creatures. For Aristotle, the great danger lay in extremes. He saw humanity's greatest achievement as moderation in all things — the "Golden Mean". He recognized, in modern terms, that although human beings have a tendency toward greed and violence, they also have a conscience — a sense of right and wrong — and can be motivated by love and pity. Moreover, people have the power of reason and the ability to distinguish good from evil. Unfortunately, all do not have these qualities in the same measure, nor are all equal in intelligence and strength. Most important, not all people perceive things in the same way, nor do they have the same priorities. Even with an earnest will to do what is right and fair, two individuals will often disagree strongly about the merits of a dispute between themselves or between others. The reason idealistic communal societies fail is not that their members are imperfect converts to anarchism or Marxism, but because individuals do not share the same priorities and vary greatly in their strength and influence over others.

If this middle view of humankind is more accurate than either extreme, how are people to live in society when there will inevitably be honestly held, deep disagreement? They do not wish to abandon their freedom entirely to a Hobbesian absolute ruler in order to be saved from themselves, nor can they hope to live in a utopia entirely without rules. Human beings, then, must use their conscience, sense of justice, and power of reason to devise a system of rules that will resolve disputes and treat all people as fairly as possible in the distribution of society's benefits. As human beings learn by experience, and as conditions change, they will need constantly to revise the system in striving for justice.

JEREMY BENTHAM

The moderate, rational view of law and society has a strong appeal, but it is also deceptive, for it gives no criteria by which to judge whether laws are good or bad. There have been some remarkable attempts to set standards by which we should be able to assess the value of laws. The most influential effort, affecting much of the 19th-century law reform, was that of the great English reformer Jeremy Bentham at the end of the 18th century. Bentham developed the *principle of utility*, which asserted that the goal of society should be to increase the sum total of human happiness. The two factors by which happiness can be measured are pleasure and pain. By decreasing the amount of pain and increasing the amount of pleasure, the ends of society would be served:

> Utility therefore really meant no more than what served to increase human happiness, the sum of which was to be assessed by calculating the stock of pleasure and pain which resulted from a particular course of action. For this purpose numerical standards were adopted,

each man's happiness being considered the equal in value of that of any other man, so that the test of utility was what served the happiness of the largest possible number. Bentham's principle was aimed at "maximizing" human happiness according to the slogan "the greatest happiness of the greatest number". Although Bentham rejected natural law with scorn — for him natural rights were not just nonsense, but "nonsense upon stilts" — he was nothing if not a rationalist in the spirit of the Enlightenment... Ironically, Bentham's own principle that one man's happiness was of equal worth to another's, owed much to the widely established "natural" right to equality...

Despite a certain naiveté in his belief that happiness could be virtually quantified in almost arithmetical terms, Bentham's work laid a solid juridical foundation for much of the reform of the law which was one of the most crying needs of the early nineteenth century...[4]

While Bentham's philosophy was not entirely neutral, as Professor Lloyd has noted, it alone was not sufficient to bring about reforms. The insertion of Bentham's personal values and those of other 19th-century liberal reformers were needed to give his theories vigour and effectiveness. Reforms can never go beyond current values and perceptions of social evils, whatever philosophy is employed; almost one hundred years passed after Bentham stated his utilitarian views before some of the worst evils were ended by legislation.

SOCIAL ENGINEERING

At the end of the 19th century, the American legal philosopher Roscoe Pound was greatly influenced by the growth of the new social sciences, especially sociology. He saw emerging conflicts between constantly changing interests as a principal feature of society. As certain interests increased and grew dominant, their demands would be recognized through changes in the law. But the process was unsystematic and subject to chance events: some interests would gain recognition too easily, while others might go unheeded for too long. Pound envisaged law as a tool of "social engineering" to be used for consciously evaluating and adjusting competing interests.

... As the saying is, we all want the earth. We all have a multiplicity of desires and demands which we seek to satisfy. There are very many of us but there is only one earth. The desires of each continually conflict with or overlap those of his neighbours. So there is, as one might say, a great task of social engineering. There is a task of making the goods of existence, the means of satisfying the demands and desires of men living together in a politically organized society, if they cannot satisfy all the claims that men make upon them, at least go around as far as possible. This is what we mean when we say that the end of law is justice. We do not mean justice as an individual virtue. We do not mean justice as the ideal relation among men. We mean a regime. We mean such an adjustment of relations and ordering of conduct as will make the goods of existence, the means of satisfying human claims to have things and do things, go round as far as possible with the least friction and waste.[5]

Pound believed that most of society's ills were the result of ignorance. By scientific study of people's needs and expectations, and of prevailing values, more rational adjustments

---

[4] Lloyd, *The Idea of Law* (rev. ed.), pp. 98-9. Harmondsworth: Penguin Books, 1974.
[5] Pound, *Social Control Through Law*, pp. 64-5. New Haven: Yale University Press, 1942.

could be made to improve the lot of society. In many respects Pound's philosophy is a sophisticated child of utilitarianism: it rejects the absolute values of natural law and seeks to obtain its values, its criteria for change, from a scientific study of the community.

Pound's theory raised three important questions. First, does law influence the development of society (and if so, to what extent), or is it merely a reflection of changing values and other developments within society? Second, to what extent can scientific methods truly be used to improve the quality of lawmaking? Or are the social sciences really neutral but used by partisan groups to bolster a view to which they are already committed? Third, if scientific methods really can be effective in exposing society's ills and our own shortcomings in dealing with them, is there not the danger that they will in the process destroy important myths we need for our peace of mind? Suppose, for example, as some writers claim, that psychoanalysis of all judges would reveal that seemingly dispassionate judicial decisions are no more than the result of accumulated bias and other frailties of judges.

*L*AW AS AN INSTRUMENT OF SOCIAL CHANGE

The three questions above are related: if law is nothing more than a reflection of society's values, there is no point in seeking scientific methods to improve lawmaking. (Such a search would be pointless also for a totally committed Marxist who believes in historical determinism, since law will disappear after the revolution of the proletariat succeeds.) But most of us are keenly aware that, at best, the law reflects imperfectly the values of our society. Even in a totalitarian state, those holding power are unlikely to be able to make the law mirror their values completely. In a pluralistic democracy with many conflicting values, the law often reflects a contradictory mixture. Changes usually take place through a series of halting steps.

Occasionally, something approaching an "informed public will" becomes apparent and a major change does take place in accord with it. A remarkable example occurred in the history of universal medical care in Canada. In the 1960s, a relatively small but eloquent group of people persuaded the federal government that Canada needed and could afford a government-sponsored universal medical care scheme. However, implementation of the plan depended upon provincial cooperation and provincial legislation. Some provincial governments joined willingly, while others feared the cost to them would be overwhelming. Still others opposed the plan philosophically and politically. When the federal government used its fiscal powers to exert strong pressure on the recalcitrant provinces to join (through the threatened loss of substantial federal grants for failure to do so), these provinces found themselves unable to resist for long because their own electorates favoured the federal position. Thus, popular support for the medical care scheme permitted the federal government to sustain its pressure against sometimes bitter opposition. Although a number of provincial government members may strongly resent the methods employed by the federal government, none today would speak out seriously against the principle of universal medical care.

No doubt the conditions at the time of the main debate were ideal for the democratic process: the issue was one affecting everyone personally; eloquent advocates, both for and against, had outlined the problem in great detail; newspapers, radio, and television gave a good deal of time to the issue; not only politicians but doctors, economists, and lay people as well had ample opportunity to air their views. Fortunately, too, the question had little to do with conflicts among political personalities and the country was enjoying the kind of economic prosperity that made the plan feasible. Thus, the law changed to reflect public opinion.

A cynic might say that the medical care debate was no more than a happy accident, the exception that tests the rule; rarely does the law reflect society's values and real needs, because political expediency and chance dominate the legislative process. Responsible leaders of government have long recognized how difficult it is to prepare and carry out a program of legislative reform. Many events at home and abroad can change a government's fortunes and plans — its miscalculations of the public mood, political scandals, technological changes — and often lead to an election and change of government.

One way to overcome some of these difficulties is to announce, as much as several years in advance, that a particular problem needs intensive study, and to appoint a special study group staffed by experts to examine the problem with a view to making recommendations to solve, or at least alleviate, the difficulties. Following the British tradition, major studies in Canada are usually undertaken by royal commissions. When the cabinet announces a royal commission, it sets out the commission's terms of reference, appoints a chairman who is typically a respected politician or judge — perhaps a senator, or a specialist in the field to be studied — and several other commissioners to give political or geographic balance, depending on the nature of the problem. The commission then hires staff and also gives contracts for independent studies of specific aspects of its area of concern. Usually, it also holds a series of public hearings to receive the views of interested groups and individuals in various parts of the country. When all reports are in and the commissioners have settled on their recommendations, they submit their report to the government for publication and debate in the hope that statutory reform will follow.

Our cynic might well be most cynical of all toward royal commissions, saying that most royal commissions are nothing more than evasions, ways for a government to delay action on uncomfortable problems about which any decision is likely to cause it embarrassment. In two or three years, by the time the commission reports, the problem may have gone away — or become someone else's responsibility. Because of the time a royal commission takes, it frequently reports to a new government elected after it began its work, a new government that, as the former opposition, may have been against establishing the commission in the first place and have no interest in implementing any of its recommendations. Even when a government is not antipathetic, the commission itself, during its years of study, may have drifted away from political reality to the consideration of theoretical and impractical solutions, so that its recommendations are quietly filed and gather dust on library shelves.

The political process being the chancy thing it is, there is unfortunately much truth in criticisms of royal commissions. It is indeed difficult to systematically plan and implement legal and social reforms. Nevertheless, a number of such commissions have actually led to major reforms, and still others have changed our way of thinking about a problem and thus, though less directly, influenced changes in that area over a number of years.

The report of the Royal Commission on Health Services chaired by Mr. Justice Hall played an important part in the eventual introduction of universal medical care in Canada.[6]

No matter what one may think of royal commissions and other specialized research and fact-finding groups employed by government, their studies are likely to become ever more necessary and more common: as technical and environmental problems increase in complexity, lay people (members of Parliament and others) will need experts to make studies and translate them into as simple terms as possible before the necessary legislation can be passed to cope with these problems. Continuing attempts to minimize air pollution by internal combustion engines has led to extremely complicated legislation in Canada and the United States about the manufacture and operation of motor vehicles, legislation affecting producers of cars all over the world. The question has been further complicated by belated recognition of energy conservation as a major factor in the future design of all vehicles for transportation of both people and goods. Improving the purity of water resources, reducing noise levels, and protecting the ecology of the North are examples of other areas requiring increasingly sophisticated study and advice. Like it or not, we must rely more and more on scientific study before changing laws in the immediate future.

Conclusion

In this chapter we have discussed the two main streams of legal philosophy: law and conscience — the relation between law and the individual's convictions; and law and society — the legal system as a basic element in organized society. We have tried to raise those questions that we believe are most important. It would be impossible to discuss all the major works in legal philosophy in less than a very large volume. Those readers interested in further readings on the subject should refer to the bibliography at the end of the book.

Questions for Review

1. What basic element do different theories of natural law share?
2. Is an unjust law still law?
3. Distinguish a normative law from other kinds of laws.
4. What contradictory uses may be made of natural law?
5. Explain Hume's distinction between the "is" and the "ought".
6. What difficulty does Austin's definition of law present in a country like Canada?
7. How do modern positivists solve the problem of ascertaining what the law is in a time of revolution?
8. In the case of *Regina v. Dudley and Stephens*, would you acquit or convict the accused men? Why?
9. What is a retroactive law? What difficulties does it create?
10. What essential qualities must a legal system provide to a community?
11. When a law produces an unjust result, what is the first question that we should ask?

---

[6]   Canada, Royal Commission on Health Services, *Report*. Ottawa: Queen's Printer, 1964-5.

12. What view of law do anarchists and Marxists share?
13. Describe Hobbes' view of human conduct in a state of nature.
14. What was the chief significance of St. Augustine's beliefs for law in the Middle Ages?
15. Describe briefly four important aspects of 19th-century law that lent support to Marx's view of society.
16. What did Marx prophesy would happen to law after the proletarian revolution? What happened to communal societies founded on his thesis?
17. What is your own opinion of his prophecy as it applies to the former U.S.S.R. today?
18. Distinguish between retributive and distributive justice.
19. What quality or qualities do you think would prevent people from living in harmony with one another in the absence of enforceable laws?
20. Describe Bentham's principle of utility.
21. Can you perceive an element of natural law in Bentham's theory?
22. Describe what Pound means by "social engineering".
23. Do you believe that law is an entirely passive reflection of society's values? Explain.
24. It has been said that royal commissions and other government scientific studies of major problems do nothing but hoodwink the public. Discuss.
25. What is your opinion of the way in which universal medical care was implemented in Canada?
26. A common complaint of members of Parliament, especially if they are members of the opposition, is that the authority of Parliament is being eroded and displaced by government experts and administrative bureaucracy. Discuss.

CHAPTER 2

THE ROLE OF THE COURTS

$\mathcal{A}$s Arbiter of The Constitution

How effective is a statute in remedying a problem? After years of study, after the careful drafting of legislation, and after exhaustive debate in the legislature followed by final enactment, we might hope that at last the problem has been solved, or at least dealt with as best the present state of our knowledge will permit. But no — frequently the problem has just begun. If it is to be of any consequence, a new law must restrict or enlarge someone's activities, or lay down conditions for offering or taking away something of value.

When a new law begins to affect people's interests and they become unhappy about its application to them, they may complain to an official charged with administering the law. The matter may well end there: the administrator may change the ruling or give a satisfactory explanation to the complainants, or the complainants, though dissatisfied with the answer, may decide that it is not worth their while to take the matter further. If, however, they decide to press their grievance, they may well reach a point where asking informally for a remedy has become futile and a formal complaint must be made before either a court or an administrative board that regularly hears such matters. A serious dispute, though it may begin before an administrative board, is often appealed to a court and may even be carried, on further appeal, to the Supreme Court of Canada for final disposition. The statute itself may be attacked as unconstitutional. Before its effect is ultimately determined, then, the statute may have travelled a long way from its passage through Parliament.

In a federal country such as Canada or the United States, for practical purposes the Supreme Court rather than the legislature has the last word. To understand why this is so we must contrast our federal system with that of a unitary (non-federal) country like Great Britain, where there is a single supreme Parliament with complete jurisdiction over the entire country.[1] In theory the British Parliament can make, amend or repeal any law it wishes, although in practice its scope is restrained by custom, popular opinion, and the possibility of the government's defeat. The supremacy of the British Parliament is so pervasive that city and county councils are its creatures; it retains total power over them. In Canada, by contrast, we have two distinct levels of government, federal and provincial; under the Constitution Act, 1867,[2] each level has an independent existence and its own sphere of activity. Thus, unlike Britain's, our national Parliament cannot alter the structure of provincial governments. The division of legislative power made principally under sections 91 and 92 of the Constitution Act, 1867, allocates certain fields of jurisdiction to the federal Parliament and other designated fields (including power over municipalities) to each of the provincial legislatures. The Act gives residual powers to the federal government, so that all fields not expressly allocated to the provinces are within federal jurisdiction.

---

[1]   The supremacy of the British Parliament itself is now in question since the United Kingdom joined the European Community. The Treaty of Rome, which founded the Economic Community, very much resembles a constitution rather than a mere treaty: it established permanent institutions including a European Parliament, Council of Ministers, and Court of Justice. The issue is whether the Treaty is supreme and limits the laws of all member countries, including statutes passed by their legislatures. British courts have discussed the question without coming down firmly one way or the other, although there is quite strong support in some judgments favouring the supremacy of the Treaty of Rome. See Macarthys Ltd. v. Smith, [1981] 1 All E.R. 111; R. v. Henn and Darby, [1980] 2 All E.R. 166; Shields v. Coomes (Holdings) Ltd., [1979] 1 All E.R. 456.

[2]   This Act was formerly known as the British North America Act, but was officially renamed The Constitution Act, 1867, by the Constitution Act, 1982. Both of these Acts and all intervening amendments may now be referred to as the Constitution.

A constitution may not only allocate jurisdiction between levels of government, but may also prohibit government interference in certain areas, thereby removing them from the legislative power of both levels. (Though a prohibition of this type may exist in the constitution of a unitary country, we are here concerned only with federations.) In 1982, the Charter of Rights and Freedoms became part of the Constitution; it places limits on many aspects of government action and will be discussed later in this chapter.

Quite apart from any limits the Charter may place on the powers of both federal and provincial legislatures, there remains an inherent difficulty faced by all federations: problems faced by governments refuse to divide themselves into neat, clear-cut subjects for the convenience of federal and provincial jurisdictions. Many problems overlap both jurisdictions, and often both levels of government seem to have concurrent powers to regulate an activity. For example, the federal government has jurisdiction over radio and television broadcasting, and the provincial governments have responsibility for education. Who, then, has responsibility for educational television? Does it matter whether an educational television program is delivered in a taped cassette to be played over an internal closed-circuit system within a school, received through a telephone line, transmitted from a provincial government building to a cable-television system, or simply comes over the normal television network? The students in each instance watch the same program but, depending upon the method by which it reaches them, opinion differs about which government has power to regulate the content of the program.[3]

Problems of jurisdiction arose in the United States before Canada was founded. In the early 19th century, the Supreme Court of the United States held that neither the federal nor the state governments could have the last word on interpreting the U.S. Constitution; to give one level the power to interpret the document (doubtless in its own favour) would be to confer supremacy upon it. Instead, the court declared that it must itself be the final arbiter of the Constitution, the umpire between the two levels of government.[4] This position was accepted by the states and by Congress. In Canada, the Supreme Court has come to play the same key role as constitutional umpire.

ILLUSTRATION

The Canadian Parliament receives a report of a special study of abuses in the stock market that cause investors to lose their savings. In response, it passes a statute prohibiting certain kinds of advertising of securities as misleading, consequently making them criminal in nature. A broker who specializes in these transactions, claiming that his activity is lawful, carries on in defiance of the statute. He is charged with an offence under the statute and raises the following arguments in defence: (a) that the law is unconstitutional because it purports to make changes in an area that is exclusively within the jurisdiction of the provinces under the Constitution Act, 1867; and (b) that even if his first argument is wrong, the government as prosecuting authority has placed an unreasonable interpretation upon the statute and has applied it too broadly in charging him with an offence. He argues, in other words, that under any reasonable interpretation of the statute his activity would remain lawful.

---

[3] Federal and provincial governments are profoundly concerned about who controls the means of mass communication and education. There has been continual consultation and controversy in recent years. Both levels of government would like to resolve the conflict by mutual agreement rather than engage in a constitutional battle, with the attendant difficulties described in this section.

[4] Marbury v. Madison, 5. U.S. Reports, 1 Cranch, 137 (1803).

We can see from this illustration that a legislature faces a double problem whenever it attempts any type of reform. First, it must recognize that if its entire statute is ruled unconstitutional, it will be void and make no change at all in the law. (The broker in the illustration would then be subject to no new regulation whatever.) Indeed, even were the Supreme Court to interpret the statute in such a way as to avoid outright conflict with the Constitution, it might nonetheless restrict its application to areas under federal jurisdiction and thus so emasculate the statute that it would fail to accomplish the desired reform. In effect, the court would then be saying: "If these words were given a broad meaning, they would attempt to regulate activity beyond the jurisdiction of the federal Parliament. Clearly, Parliament could not have meant to do such a thing. If, however, we restrict their meaning to 'such and such', the regulation will be within federal jurisdiction and valid. We will assume that Parliament meant to do only what is possible under the Constitution, and accordingly find that these words have a restricted meaning." (Once again the broker would escape regulation, if his activity were outside federal jurisdiction.)

Second, and apart from the constitutional hurdle, courts have sometimes been criticized for interpreting statutes narrowly so as to interfere as little as possible with existing private rights. Accordingly, the courts' interpretation of a statute may in large measure frustrate an intended reform. (Again in this event, the broker might be saved by the narrow interpretation of the statute.)

A constitutional defeat in the courts is more serious than a narrow interpretation. Parliament cannot overcome a decision by the Supreme Court that a statute is unconstitutional unless the Constitution itself is amended — a process that requires a high degree of provincial agreement as well as the consent of Parliament.[5] However, if the problem is simply one of interpretation, the government can subsequently introduce an amendment to preclude future arguments of this kind. The trouble with relying on the ability to amend legislation is that except for emergencies or extraordinary pressure on government, the wheels of Parliament "grind exceeding slow", and a year or several years may pass in the normal course of events before an amendment is enacted.

When the Supreme Court nullifies legislation on constitutional grounds it can arouse strong feelings and sometimes vehement attacks, both on the judges as individuals and on the concept of a court that can have so much authority. A variety of cries can be heard: "The Court is a reactionary bastion standing in the way of badly needed reform"; "The Court is nine elderly lawyers, neither elected nor representative of the people, defeating the wishes of a democratically elected legislature"; "The Court has prevented one level of government from running roughshod over the jurisdiction of the other"; "The Court has stopped the government from making an unwarranted intrusion on individual liberties." Judges of the Supreme Court cannot escape making decisions that play a critical role in political, social, and economic change. As a result, the role and the personality of Supreme Court judges in particular, and of judges generally, have become subjects of great interest to legal theorists, sociologists, and psychologists, as well as to the practising lawyers who appear before them.

---

[5] A constitution, whether it is of a small social club or a large nation, almost always contains provisions for its own amendment. A "simple majority", that is, any number more than 50% (for example, 50.01%) may pass an appropriate motion to change any earlier motion or law also passed by a simple majority. But the provisions of a constitution are usually *"entrenched"*: only a "special majority" may amend them. Typically a special majority is two thirds or three quarters of the ballots cast, but sometimes there are quite complex special majorities, giving a specified group the power of veto. Unless *that* group, even if it comprises a very small minority, approves of a proposed amendment, the amendment will be lost.

$\mathcal{A}$s Interpreter of Legislation

The Literal Versus the Liberal Approach

We have seen how legislatures may take a long time to seek information and advice before passing legislation. When a court is called on to interpret that legislation, what information and advice, what evidence, will it permit to be brought before it? What will it consider? The long-standing English position has been that the meaning of a statute should be apparent on its face, so that it can be understood "on the run". After all, so this argument goes, a person reading a statute should be able to rely on its words alone, without looking further. If one does not understand a particular word or words, a standard dictionary should provide clarification, and if the word happens to be a specialized technical term, a standard technical dictionary or textbook should suffice. But that should be the limit of the necessary outside inquiry.

In theory, the English position is laudable: if it were necessary for a person to read other documents such as a multi-volume report of a royal commission in order to learn what a statute means, great hardship would ensue. The person would run the risk of misunderstanding the statute taken at its face value. Even if a large law library were available containing the needed material — something few people have — a lay person would not likely have either the time or the expertise to read and understand it.

In practice, however, the English approach leads to other difficulties. Most words do not have precise meanings, as mathematical symbols do. Frequently they are ambiguous, capable of different shades of meaning; sometimes they have several distinct meanings. A dictionary does not help solve such dilemmas. Furthermore, a statute rarely breaks entirely new ground; new laws almost always affect existing ones. (There are a few exceptions, such as a law to govern rights in outer space.) Most often a statute is passed with the express aim of changing existing law. In these circumstances it will not be possible to understand the new statute without first knowing what the law was before it was passed. An extreme example occurs when a legislature repeals an existing law.

ILLUSTRATION

New legislation begins with the following words: "The Widgets Act, Chapter 49 of the Statutes of 1981, is hereby repealed." What is the effect of these words? To understand them one must know what the law was before 1981 when it was changed by the Widgets Act, what change that act made in the law, and how the present repealing act changes the law. It may be less simple than it appears. Suppose that before the Widgets Act was passed the manufacture and sale of widgets was illegal. That Act set out rules for their legal manufacture and sale. Does the repeal of the Widgets Act make those activities illegal again, or does it make them entirely free from any regulation or prohibition?

It may be argued that it is foolish for a legislature to pass an act in such ambiguous terms, but statutes similar to the repealing act in the above illustration occur with disquieting frequency through inadvertence, perhaps as a result of hurrying through a backlog of legislation toward the end of a legislative session. The courts are then left with the problem, and they have had to devise methods of dealing with it. The English courts have conceded that it is often necessary to examine the state of the law before a statute was passed in order to determine what change has been made. The result is that a person cannot rely solely on the words of a statute, but if this fact is recognized, is the traditional English position not a myth?

Legislative History

How far should a court look into the circumstances surrounding the passing of a statute? Should it examine the report of a royal commission that led to the introduction of a bill in Parliament, the statements of the minister whose department was responsible for the bill, and the debates in Parliament itself? Should it, in other words, examine the *legislative history* of a statute? British courts have replied that no royal commission, government minister, or member of Parliament can speak for Parliament as a whole. (Indeed, two leading members of the Commons may have disagreed in debate on the meaning of a key phrase in a bill and yet both may have voted for the bill subsequently without their disagreement being resolved.) The view of the courts is that when Parliament passes a law it represents the "will" of Parliament as a whole. Thus the courts should resolve any ambiguities entirely from "objective" evidence: dictionaries, principles of interpretation already developed by the courts, and ascertainment of the state of the law at the time the statute was passed.

Until 1976, Canadian courts followed the British approach and refused to hear evidence of legislative history that purported to interpret the will of Parliament. In that year a substantial change in this position occurred in the *Reference Re Anti-Inflation Act*[6] decided by the Supreme Court of Canada. An important issue in the case was whether Parliament considered the inflationary situation in the autumn of 1975 to be a national emergency justifying use of the *emergency power* to pass the Anti-Inflation Act and thus to bring wage and price controls into effect. The court referred both to a government White Paper (a policy paper published prior to the introduction of new legislation) and to debates in the House of Commons as being necessary for reaching a proper decision. This use of legislative history seems to recognize a long-standing body of opinion that is in favour of examining all information available to a court in order to help it understand a statute, at least for the purpose of deciding whether it is constitutionally within the power of the legislature to pass it. According to this view, the courts themselves should be able to decide how much weight to give to various aspects of legislative history. In the United States, legislative history is customarily heard by courts and may often be very influential in their decisions.

The Brandeis Brief

In 1907, Louis Brandeis, a noted lawyer who subsequently became one of the most distinguished judges of the United States Supreme Court, prepared his *brief* (argument) for an important constitutional law case in a novel manner.[7] He amassed a great quantity of statistical information and expert testimony of factory inspectors and others to persuade

---

6   (1976), 68 D.L.R. (3d) 452.

7   *Muller v. Oregon,* 208 U.S. 412 (1907).

the court that the most up-to-date knowledge in health and social science should permit it to distinguish the present case from an earlier decision that invalidated a statute regulating hours of work. Rather than argue that the Supreme Court was wrong in its first decision, a difficult thing to do successfully, Brandeis argued that it would not be inconsistent for the Court to recognize the new information and distinguish a prior decision that it had made under different circumstances (even if the effect was to overrule the earlier decision): new circumstances demanded a new interpretation of the Constitution. The Court accepted Brandeis' argument and upheld the statute.

This type of argument, known as a *Brandeis Brief*, includes the submission of socio-economic evidence, and has become an important part of the United States process of constitutional argument ever since, frequently playing a decisive role. Perhaps the most famous decision occurred in 1954, when the Supreme Court reversed its earlier decision that "separate but equal" schooling facilities for black children did not conflict with constitutional guarantees given to all citizens.[8] The Court received exhaustive evidence about the inferior quality of education black children were in *fact* receiving under the purported equality of the dual education system in many states. There is no doubt that this information played a crucial part in the decision to order desegregation of public schools.

Canadian courts also admit appropriate "Brandeis Brief" evidence, subject to precautions about verification of facts and cross-examination of expert witnesses. After all, it may be argued that the state of the economy and social conditions at any particular time, as well as the results of scientific investigation, are as much "objective" evidence as the state of the law at the time the statute under consideration was passed. Thus, in the 1949 "oleomargarine case", the Supreme Court of Canada considered expert testimony that earlier beliefs about margarine being a nutritionally inferior product and a possible health hazard were mistaken.[9] As a result, legislation by Parliament under the federal power to enact criminal law prohibiting the manufacture and sale of margarine was held to be unconstitutional, since there was no longer any reasonable basis for considering the manufacture and sale of margarine to be criminal activity. The decision permitted the provinces to pass legislation to regulate the production and sale of margarine.

We have seen that specialized studies and expert technical advice have become increasingly important and more widely used in planning legislation; to a lesser extent, they are now used by courts called upon to examine the constitutional validity of legislation.

As Protector of Civil Liberties

The Various Meanings of "Civil Liberties"

The phrase "civil liberties" is difficult to define because it comprises a number of quite separate ideas related only by a general concern for the well-being of the individual citizen. Two other terms, "civil rights" and "human rights", are often used as synonyms. "Civil liberties" and "civil rights" are the older terms, and date from at least as far back as

---

8   Brown v. Board of Education, 347 U.S. 438 (1954), overruling Plessy v. Ferguson, 163 U.S. 537 (1896).
9   Reference re Validity of Section 5(a) Dairy Industry Act, [1949] S.C.R. 1, [1949] 1 D.L.R. 433.

the 18th century. They have referred traditionally to freedom of the individual in politics and religion. These terms have embraced freedom of expression (both of speech and of the press), freedom of association and assembly, freedom to practise and preach one's religion, freedom from arbitrary arrest and detention, and the right to a fair trial.[10]

We should note, however, that the term "civil rights" has a peculiar meaning in Canadian constitutional law. Section 92 of the Constitution designates "property and civil rights" as an area of provincial responsibility, and the provinces have relied on it in claiming jurisdiction over a wide variety of matters. The Supreme Court of Canada has generally taken the term as used in section 92 to mean something like "private rights" relating to the ownership of property, contract law, and family relations. Our concern in this chapter is not, of course, limited to this special usage.

Mainly as a result of the horrors of the Second World War — deportation, starvation, and genocide — there arose a greatly heightened awareness of human needs beyond the traditional freedoms we have already mentioned. United States President Franklin D. Roosevelt gave eloquent expression to these needs in his statement of "the Four Freedoms" in 1941.[11] They were developed in greater detail in the United Nations *Universal Declaration of Human Rights*, and the term "human rights and freedoms" came into general usage at that time. It is concerned in large part with Roosevelt's phrase "freedom from want" and the related idea of equal opportunity for employment and housing, without discrimination.[12] The idea has been further refined to include the assertion that it is society's responsibility to create jobs in order to make adequate employment available to wage earners in every household. It includes also the opportunity to receive publicly supported education and the right to reasonable minimum subsistence in food, shelter, and clothing, even when unemployed. In addition, Roosevelt's "freedom from fear" has been interpreted in part to mean freedom from discrimination based on sex, race, religion, and nationality, not only in housing and employment, but also in access to all public facilities and even to private clubs.

This expanded idea of human rights is not as recent as one might suppose; indeed, it is akin to Aristotle's concept of distributive justice. Since World War II, awareness of problems of social and economic welfare has helped to raise community standards in many parts of the world. Improvements depend mainly on the political and social climate within a country, changes in the perception of the role of government, and social legislation. Nevertheless, these reforms are frequently reflected in legal and constitutional changes such as those discussed in the next section.

---

[10]   These rights received international recognition after the Second World War. See United Nations documents *Universal Declaration of Human Rights* (1948) and *Covenant on Civil and Political Rights* (1966); *European Convention for the Protection of Human Rights and Fundamental Freedoms,* 213 United Nations Treaty Series 221 (1955); Luini del Russo, A., *International Protection of Human Rights,* Appendices A-E, Washington, D.C.: Lerner Law Book Co. Inc., 1971; Stein, E. and Hay, F., *Law and Institutions in the Atlantic Area,* Ch. VIII. New York: The Bobbs-Merrill Co., 1967.

[11]   Roosevelt, F.D., Message to Congress, January 16, 1941, as reported, for example, in Hardman, J.B.S., *Rendezvous with Destiny: Addresses and Opinions of Franklin Delano Roosevelt,* pp. 171-2. The four freedoms he identified were freedom of speech and expression everywhere in the world; freedom of every person to worship God in his own way everywhere in the world; freedom from want everywhere in the world; and freedom from fear anywhere in the world.

[12]   The federal government and all provinces have legislation prohibiting discrimination in housing and employment. See, for example: Human Rights Act, R.S.N.S. 1989, c. 214; Human Rights Code of British Columbia, R.S.B.C. 1979, c. 186; Human Rights Code, R.S.O. 1990, c. H-19.

Constitutional Protection

Canadian Charter of Rights and Freedoms

The legal base for the protection of human rights in Canada was profoundly altered by the Canadian Charter of Rights and Freedoms contained in the Constitution Act, 1982. Canadian courts were quickly confronted with a substantial number of challenges to federal and provincial statutes and procedures. As expected, the law with respect to the Charter has evolved very quickly and is likely to continue doing so at a hectic pace for at least a few years.

First, we should note that the Charter is *entrenched* in the Constitution: it cannot be repealed by an ordinary act of Parliament or of provincial legislatures in each of the areas where formerly they were able to pass and repeal laws at their will. Section 52 (1) states:

> The Constitution of Canada is the supreme law of Canada, and any law that is inconsistent with the provisions of the Constitution is, to the extent of the inconsistency, of no force or effect.

Repeal of the Charter can only be by way of amendment as provided for in the Constitution Act, that is, by consent of the Parliament of Canada and the legislatures of at least two-thirds of the provinces containing at least 50% of the population of all the provinces. We can see then that the Charter is much more difficult to change than is an ordinary statute.

Second, subject to the important qualifications in the following paragraphs, rights entrenched in the Charter cannot be infringed by ordinary legislation: to the extent that a statute offends a right in the Charter, it will be declared invalid. The legislature cannot interfere with those rights that are now founded on the "higher law" of the Constitution. This idea of rights based on a higher law was a major departure from British Parliamentary supremacy, and is more akin to the theory of the United States Constitution. The Canadian Bill of Rights passed by Parliament in 1960 was an ordinary statute, and attempts to claim that it had a higher standing than that failed. Canadian courts had only limited experience with the concept of entrenched individual rights before adoption of the Charter. Only in the one area of freedom of expression had a few judges suggested that there may be a fundamental right so important to the parliamentary system of government that no legislature could interfere. On the other hand, our courts have had wide experience in assessing whether a piece of legislation is within the competence of the federal Parliament or of provincial legislatures under section 91 or 92 of the Constitution, striking the legislation down when they have concluded that it is beyond the powers granted. The Supreme Court of Canada has shown that it is prepared to strike down as void statutes that offend the rights and freedoms guaranteed in the Charter.[13]

Third, the Charter includes section 33, which permits a legislature to override certain other sections. That is, if a statute states expressly that it "shall operate notwithstanding" those specified sections, a legislature may infringe some of the most important rights guaranteed by the Charter. Section 33 also contains a so-called "sunset" clause: the overriding section of the statute expires five years after it comes into force unless it is re-enacted by the legislature — and subsequently for each further five years. The reasoning behind these provisions seems to be as follows: the declaration of certain rights in our Constitution will give them great moral and political force; governments will rarely dare

---

[13]   See, for example: Regina v. Big M Drug Mart Ltd. (1985), D.L.R. (4th) 321, striking down the Lord's Day Act of Canada, as a form of compulsory religious practice; and A.G. of Québec v. Québec Association of Protestant School Boards *et al.* (1984), 10 D.L.R. (4th) 321, nullifying certain sections of Québec's Charter of the French Language, as violating minority language rights under s. 23 of the Charter of Rights and Freedoms.

to pass legislation expressly overriding the Charter, and very likely for only limited purposes — and they will have to produce strong reasons for continuing the override beyond the first five years. However, should the courts rule that certain desirable reforms offend the Charter, governments will not be thwarted: they can take the graver step of passing overriding legislation in order to pursue their policy goals. Only time will tell whether the legislatures will operate within these constraints or whether they will find it politically easy to circumvent the Charter and to use the override section at will.[14]

Fourth, none of the rights set out in the Charter is absolute: s. 1 states that they are all subject "to such reasonable limits prescribed by law as can be demonstrably justified in a free and democratic society". The problem of what amount to "reasonable limits" arises whenever a complainant claims that a right entrenched in the Charter, such as the freedom of expression, has been infringed.

In general, a statute is *presumed to be valid*, that is, to be within the power of a legislature passing it: a person attacking it must show why it is invalid. However, a person need show only that one of his constitutionally guaranteed rights has been infringed by a provision in a statute; the provision would then be *presumed invalid* unless the government could persuade the court that the infringement was "...demonstrably justified..." In other words, the burden would then be upon the government to establish that the section of a statute that interferes with constitutional rights is justified. It is difficult to predict in a general way how deferential the courts will be to the legislatures. In what circumstances will judges say, "Since the elected majority think this infringement is justified, we will not interfere" rather than "The will of the majority does not justify this interference with individual rights"?

The decision in *R. v. Oakes*[15] sets out a series of tests that the legislation must meet in order to justify itself under s. 1. First, the object to be served by the limit must be "of sufficient importance to warrant overriding a constitutionally protected right or freedom". That is, the object must not be trivial but "pressing and substantial". Second, the means chosen must be proportional to the importance of the objective and must impair the Charter right as little as possible in achieving the objective. Third, on an overview, when the effects of the infringement on rights are compared with the object that has been achieved, that object must on balance justify the infringement. This careful and somewhat laborious process had been undertaken by the courts a number of times, and usually they find that the legislature is justified.

---

14   After the proclamation of the new Constitution, the Québec government, having objected to the new Constitution Act, passed Québec Bill 62, entitled "An Act respecting the Constitution Act, 1982", S.Q. 1982, c. 21. The Act added a standard-form notwithstanding clause to all Québec statutes then in force in order to prevent the application of specified sections of the Charter to any Québec legislation. The legislature continued to add notwithstanding clauses to all new statutes until the election of a new government in December 1985. Subsequently, the new government declared that it would not systematically employ the clause in Québec legislation. In Alliance des Professeurs de Montréal v. Attorney General of Québec (1984), 21 D.L.R.(4th) 354, the Québec Court of Appeal declared Bill 62 invalid because it was too general; the court held that section 33 would be effective only if used specifically in each Act. Thus the Charter now applies to Québec legislation, just as it does to that of other provinces and of Parliament.

   In January 1986, the legislature of Saskatchewan passed "The S.G.E.U. Dispute Settlement Act", S.S. 1984-85-86, c. 111, ordering striking government workers back to work. In order to insulate the Act from application of the Charter, s. 9(1) of the Act states that "this Act is declared to operate notwithstanding the freedom of association in paragraph 2(d)" of the Charter.

15   [1986] 1, S.C.R. 103.

ILLUSTRATION

S. 2 states, "Everyone has the following fundamental freedoms:... (b) Freedom of thought, belief, opinion and expression, including freedom of the press and other media of communication". A toy manufacturer commenced an action claiming that a provincial statute, prohibiting advertising directed at persons under the age of 13, is unconstitutional because it infringes the manufacturer's s. 2(b) freedom.[16] Is such a provision prohibiting advertising an infringement of freedom of expression? And if it is, does the object the provision serves — pro-tecting children from being incited to buy or urge another person to buy goods—a pressing and substantial one? In the *Irwin Toy* case, the Supreme Court of Canada found that the provision did indeed infringe freedom of expression. However, it went on to hold that the objective was serious and pressing. It further held that the means chosen to restrict such ads (the setting of standards to assure that the ads remained available to adults) were minimal and proportional to the objective, and finally, that on balance the interference was justified.

The consequence of the Oakes test is to encourage legislatures to draft legislation that might impinge on a right or freedom guaranteed by the Charter with great care, seeking to minimize its effect on Charter rights.

Fifth, it has often been asserted that the Charter applies to governments and governmental activities, but it is still not entirely certain to what extent it will apply between private persons. In the private sector, the protection of human rights has been a matter for human rights codes, which have been passed by each of the provinces and by Parliament (to cover those activities that are under federal jurisdiction). These codes are not entrenched and may be amended from time to time by the legislature, or even repealed entirely, although complete repeal is highly unlikely. The Charter itself states that it applies "in respect of all matters within the authority of Parliament... [and]... of the legislature of each province". There is no doubt that these words make the Charter applicable to all statutes, to regulations under statute law, to municipal laws, to crown corporations, and very likely to government-funded institutions such as public schools and community colleges. It may even be argued that the words should apply to all corporations, whether they are giant enterprises such as Canadian Pacific or incorporated small businesses, since all corporations are creatures of government: a corporation cannot come into existence unless it is registered pursuant to statutory authority. So it could be claimed that incorporation amounts to a form of government action. However, the Supreme Court of Canada has refused to extend Charter applications to corporations and even to our publicly funded universities, because they are considered to be independent of the government.[17]

The Rights and Freedoms Protected by the Charter

We shall examine the most important protections given by the Charter, beginning with those rights and freedoms which may be overridden by Parliament or a provincial legislature through use of section 33.

---

16   Irwin Toy Limited v. Quebec (Attorney-General), [1989] 1 S.C.R. 927.
17   McKinney v. University of Guelph, [1990] 3 S.C.R. 229, at 266, "... the mere fact that an entity is a creature of statute... is in no way sufficient to make its actions subject to the Charter."

Fundamental Freedoms

2. Everyone has the following fundamental freedoms:
    (a) freedom of conscience and religion;
    (b) freedom of thought, belief, opinion and expression, including freedom of the press and other media of communication;
    (c) freedom of peaceful assembly; and
    (d) freedom of association.

Legal Rights

7. Everyone has the right to life, liberty and security of the person and the right not to be deprived thereof except in accordance with the principles of fundamental justice.
8. Everyone has the right to be secure against unreasonable search or seizure.
9. Everyone has the right not to be arbitrarily detained or imprisoned.
10. Everyone has the right on arrest or detention
    (a) to be informed promptly of the reasons therefor;
    (b) to retain and instruct counsel without delay and to be informed of that right; and
    (c) to have the validity of the detention determined by way of habeas corpus and to be released if the detention is not lawful.

[Sections 11 to 14 deal in detail with the rights of persons accused of crimes during Criminal proceedings against them.]

Equality Rights

15. (1) Every individual is equal before and under the law and has the right to the equal protection and equal benefit of the law without discrimination and, in particular, without discrimination based on race, national or ethnic origin, colour, religion, sex, age or mental or physical disability.

15. (2) Subsection (1) does not preclude any law, program or activity that has as its object the amelioration of conditions of disadvantaged individuals or groups including those that are disadvantaged because of race, national or ethnic origin, colour, religion, sex, age or mental or physical disability.

Three aspects of section 15 deserve comment:

(a) This section affected provisions of many federal and provincial statutes containing distinctions now likely to be considered discriminatory. Governments wanted time to review all legislation and prepare amendments deleting provisions considered to be unconstitutional; accordingly, section 15 came into force after a delay of three years, that is, on April 17, 1985.
(b) Subsection (2) permits "affirmative action" (or "reverse discrimination"), that is, programs aimed at assisting disadvantaged people such as the aged, handicapped or those who because of racial or ethnic background have lived in impoverished conditions. Without such a provision, it might have been possible for a person who was not a member of a disadvantaged group to complain that he or she was not receiving equality of treatment if a disadvantaged person were given an extra benefit such as special funding to obtain higher education or training for a job.
(c) As a result of intensive pressure by representatives of women's groups, the following section was added to the Charter:

28. Notwithstanding anything in this Charter, the rights and freedoms referred to in it are guaranteed equally to male and female persons.

We may note that section 28 is not subject to being overridden by Parliament or a legislature; it deals with equality of treatment between the sexes as does section 15(2), and it states that equality is guaranteed "notwithstanding anything in the Charter" including, presumably, section 15(2). Does this phrase then mean that affirmative action for the benefit of women offends section 28, so that a man may complain of unequal treatment if a woman is given special benefit?

The following rights and freedoms are also *not* subject to a legislative override:

Democratic Rights

3. Every citizen of Canada has the right to vote in an election of members of the House of Commons or of a legislative assembly and to be qualified for membership therein.

Mobility Rights

6. (1) Every citizen of Canada has the right to enter, remain in and leave Canada.
   (2) Every citizen of Canada and every person who has the status of a permanent resident of Canada has the right
       (a) to move to and take up residence in any province; and
       (b) to pursue the gaining of a livelihood in any province.
   (3) The rights specified in subsection (2) are subject to
       (a) any laws or practices of general application in force in a province other than those that discriminate among persons primarily on the basis of province of present or previous residence; and
       (b) any laws providing for reasonable residency requirements as qualification for the receipt of publicly provided social services.
   (4) Subsections (2) and (3) do not preclude any law, program or activity that has as its object the amelioration in a province of conditions of individuals in that province who are socially or economically disadvantaged if the rate of employment in that province is below the rate of employment in Canada.

Section 6(4) is an affirmative action provision permitting programs of employment that give preference to local workers in a province with higher-than-average unemployment in Canada.

Language Rights

Sections 16 to 22 make English and French the official languages of the institutions of the Parliament and government of Canada, and of the institutions and legislature of New Brunswick. Similar guarantees of the use of both official languages already existed and continue to exist in Québec under section 133 of the Constitution Act, 1867, and in Manitoba under section 23 of the Manitoba Act, 1870.

Minority Language Educational Rights

23. (1) Citizens of Canada
        (a) whose first language learned and still understood is that of the English or French linguistic minority population of the province in which they reside, or

(b) who have received their primary school instruction in Canada in English or French and reside in a province where the language in which they received that instruction is the language of the English or French linguistic minority population of the province, have the right to have their children receive primary and secondary school instruction in that language in that province.[18]

(2) Citizens of Canada of whom any child has received or is receiving primary or secondary school instruction in English or French in Canada, have the right to have all their children receive primary and secondary school instruction in the same language.

(3) The right of citizens of Canada under subsections (1) and (2) to have their children receive primary and secondary school instruction in the language of the English or French linguistic minority population of a province

(a) applies wherever in the province the number of children of citizens who have such a right is sufficient to warrant the provision to them out of public funds of minority language instruction; and

(b) includes, where the number of those children so warrants, the right to have them receive that instruction in minority language educational facilities provided out of public funds.

There are three features of Minority Language Educational Rights that should be noted:

(a) These rights are available only to citizens; landed immigrants or visitors, who are not citizens, may be required by the government of the province in which they reside to place their children in majority language schools.

(b) Citizens whose first language is neither English nor French may also be required to place their children in majority language schools (for example, persons born in Canada but who lived in Germany and whose first language is German and who subsequently returned to Canada).

(c) Section 59 of the Constitution Act, 1982, makes a partial exception for Québec:

59. (1) Paragraph 23 (1) (a) shall come into force in respect of Québec on a day to be fixed by proclamation issued by the Queen or the Governor General under the Great Seal of Canada.

(2) A proclamation under subsection (1) shall be issued only where authorized by the legislative assembly or government of Québec.

This section means that unless and until the legislature of Québec votes to bring 23(1) (a) into force, only anglophone citizens who received their primary education in Canada in English, or who already have one child who has received primary education in Canada in English, will have the right to have their children educated in Québec English language schools; thus, English-speaking citizens who are immigrants from, say, the United Kingdom, and who were educated there would not have the right to have their children educated in Québec English language schools, unless at least one child had started at an English language school in another province.

---

[18]   See, Québec Protestant School Board case, footnote 13.

Rights of the Aboriginal Peoples of Canada

The rights of aboriginal peoples are not guaranteed within the Charter itself, but section 25 states that nothing within the Charter shall take away from aboriginal rights. In addition, section 35 of the Constitution Act, 1982 — the section immediately after the end of the Charter — reads as follows:

35. (1) The existing aboriginal and treaty rights of the aboriginal peoples of Canada are hereby recognized and affirmed.

(2) In this Act, "aboriginal peoples of Canada" includes the Indian, Inuit and Métis peoples of Canada.

The Constitution Act further required the first ministers to meet within one year of the new Constitution taking effect to discuss, among other matters, those questions directly affecting aboriginal peoples. A number of meetings have since been held, including those leading up to the October 1992 referendum on proposed amendments to the Constitution; the amendments included extensive changes in aboriginal rights to self government. With the defeat of the proposals in the referendum and the election of a new government in October, 1993, the discussion of aboriginal issues has so far not contemplated further constitutional changes.

As can be seen from the above survey, the Charter is an extensive and complex document whose interpretation will determine the extent to which our rights and freedoms will be enlarged. The issues themselves are not new, however, and there is a long history of debate and judicial review that will carry over into the new era. Accordingly, it will be useful to examine one area, freedom of expression, as an example.

Freedom of Expression

The Interest of the Individual

The right to speak one's mind is a precious personal liberty, a means of self-realization. In countries that restrict this right for political or other reasons, the effect is demoralizing and intellectually stifling. A citizen with a lively interest in the community around him can, perhaps more readily than he realizes, find himself a member of a minority, dissenting vigorously from a popular sentiment or equally vigorously advocating an unpopular cause. Other citizens may take strong exception to his views and, indeed, try to suppress them. Only by his own willingness to tolerate offensive comment by others can he justify the right to free expression for himself.

As always, the exercise of a freedom cannot be totally unrestrained; it carries with it responsibilities and limits that may be imposed when those responsibilities are ignored. From the individual's point of view there are several restrictions on freedom of expression: the laws of *defamation, sedition, obscenity,* and *hate propaganda.*

A person may suffer injury not only by the actions of another (as when he is run down by a carelessly driven car), but also by the words of another (as when he is falsely accused of having stolen money). As we shall discuss in Chapter 4, a person who defames another by unjustifiably injuring his reputation becomes liable to pay compensation for the harm done. If the wrongdoer persists in communicating the defamatory statement, he may be ordered by a court to cease on pain of imprisonment for failing to comply. In the eyes of the law, it is one thing to give a critical opinion about another person but quite another to assert facts that are untrue. In practice, the line between opinion and fact is often difficult to discern, especially in the heat of emotional debate. "I don't think John Doe would be a courageous mayor" is a statement of opinion. "John Doe stole his partner's profits" is alleging a fact that if untrue would certainly be defamatory. But what is "John Doe is a thief"? or "John Doe would steal his grandmother's false teeth if he had the chance"? An outspoken critic has sometimes rued his words on finding himself the defendant in a lawsuit for defamation.

Although the law of defamation restricts a person's freedom of expression, it is justified because it helps protect another person's right to freedom from unwarranted and harmful statements. In the area of public debate on government policy and actions, as opposed to statements about specific individuals or groups, the law of defamation hinders freedom of expression very little.

The second restriction comes closer to being an interference with free criticism of the government. The uttering or publishing of a *seditious libel*[19] is an attack upon the government or the institutions of the country (for instance, on the judiciary or Parliament itself) that goes too far and becomes a crime. How far is too far? A placard proclaiming, "The McGrew Government a bunch of thugs. Down with McGrew!" may be vehement but it is not sedition. Nor would an election poster saying "Let's kick out the McGrew Gang!" be seditious. But the same poster carried to the doors of Parliament in front of a crowd armed with clubs and bricks might well amount to sedition. In other words, criticism becomes sedition when it grows so violent as to exhort others to act violently against the lawful government, and when that exhortation calls for immediate action.

It is only slightly less difficult to talk about the purpose of obscenity laws than about the meaning of obscenity itself. In a very general way, the purpose of laws against obscenity is to protect the general public, and more especially the very young, from all forms of communication — verbal, pictorial, or dramatic — that tend to "corrupt morals" or "outrage the moral sense of the ordinary citizen".[20]

This double standard leads to a paradox: there is no doubt that many people are outraged by certain books, magazines, paintings, and dramatic works; on the other hand, claims of objectivity for evidence that a particular piece of allegedly obscene material has had any ascertainable corrupting effect on a specific person or persons are highly controversial. Obscenity is usually associated with pornography and related to sexual conduct, but it has a wider meaning that includes extreme forms of violence and cruelty. One school of thought asserts that sexual obscenity is far less harmful, if indeed it is harmful at all, than obscenity relating to violence and cruelty. Many thoughtful and moderate people have concluded that no such thing as an identifiable, harmful piece of obscene work exists, but that the cumulative effect of obscenity over a period of years does exert a harmful influence on general community standards of moral conduct. Further, they believe that this is a serious problem: individual moral views are subtly changed for the worse by continued exposure to obscenity, especially during the formative younger years.

The issue of obscenity does not often involve material of a direct political nature. Usually it has to do either with profitable commercial pornography marketed by deliberately appealing to some people's taste for sensational or forbidden material, or with works

---

[19] Criminal Code, R.S.C. 1985, c. C-46, s. 59.

[20] See Criminal Code, s. 163.

defended as having literary or artistic merit in which the allegedly obscene material forms an integral part. The distinction between the two has frequently been debated before the courts. In the years since the Second World War, there has been a steady narrowing of the area prohibited by our obscenity laws, and a growing toleration of material that until recently would have been considered clearly obscene. The role of the courts has on the whole been to support this trend, so that our obscenity laws are now relatively insignificant restrictions on freedom of expression.

The main methods used to suppress obscenity are *censorship* and *seizure and prosecution*. Censorship is carried out by an administrative board before the works reach the public. The board members exercise their discretion about what to prohibit, to release subject to changing or deleting portions, or to pass freely.[21] The process is almost entirely outside the courts. Exhibitors of films and publishers of books usually abide by censorship decisions; to appeal to a higher authority of government, or to the courts, would endanger a continuing cordial relationship with the censors — people they must deal with regularly in earning their living. Prosecution, on the other hand, follows police seizure of offending material that has already reached the public. There may follow a lengthy trial at which the presiding judge or jury must decide whether the material complained of is or is not obscene. In view of the mixed and ever-changing views on this subject, the task is an extraordinarily difficult one.

The same developments that created increased awareness of human rights generally — the events leading up to the Second World War, the War itself, and its aftermath — also made Canadians aware of persisting racial discrimination in our society. A particular worry was hate propaganda that fostered and perpetuated many of the myths associated with racial discrimination. "In the early and mid-1960s, Canada was inundated with hate literature, much of it anti-Semitic and anti-black... [A]t that time... most of it was imported... "[22] As a result, in 1965 the Minister of Justice set up the Cohen Committee, which reported in that year.[23] "The Committee recommended that the Criminal Code be amended to deal with the advocacy of genocide and the defamation of identifiable racial groups." Two sections were then added to the Code.[24]

There has been one prosecution and conviction under these sections, that of teacher James Keegstra for "wilfully promoting hatred against an identifiable group" to his high-school classes, contrary to s. 281.2(2).[25] Ernst Zundel, a citizen of West Germany and landed immigrant in Canada, published material asserting that the Nazi Holocaust was a hoax and never occurred. He was charged and convicted, not under the racial propaganda provisions of the Code, but under s. 177, a section passed much earlier, that makes it an

---

21 See, for example: Motion Pictures Act, R.S.B.C. 1979, c. 284, s. 4; Theatres and Amusements Act, R.S.N.S. 1967, c. 304, s. 3, as amended by 1972, c. 54.

22 *Report to the House of Commons of the Special Committee on Participation of Visible Minorities in Canadian Society*, p. 69. Ottawa: Publications Canada, 1984.

23 *Report of the Special Committee on Hate Propaganda in Canada.* Ottawa: Minister of Justice, 1965.

24 R.S.C. 1970, c. C-34, ss. 281.1 and 281.2.

25 R. v. Keegstra (1985), 19 C.C.C.(3rd) 254. This report deals only with a pre-trial application by the accused to have the section of the Code declared unconstitutional. The application was rejected and the accused was convicted at trial (unreported). The only other reported case dealing with the hate propaganda sections is R. v. Buzzanga and Durocher (1979), 101 D.L.R.(3rd) 488, dealing with an unusual situation where members of a minority group attempted to ridicule hate literature by publishing some themselves. After an initial conviction, the Ontario Court of Appeal sent the case back for retrial, but it appears that the Crown discontinued the prosecution.

offence to "wilfully publish a statement... that he knows is false and that causes or is likely to cause injury or mischief to a public interest".[26]

Apart from the groups promoting racism themselves, there has been universal condemnation of the propaganda they produce. Nevertheless, there is heated debate about the merits of the criminal law provisions: many advocates of freedom of expression object in principle to the provisions in the Criminal Code and believe that there should be no restraints upon free speech. Others are critical of specific aspects of the provisions and wish to see them amended. As with the other restraints on freedom of expression, controversy about hate propaganda prohibitions is not likely to abate.

The Public Interest

Freedom of expression is the primary right, not only because it is essential to personal liberty to be able to speak one's mind, but also because it is a fundamental precondition of a democratic system of government. The right to criticize freely — to dissent publicly from the views and actions of the government — provides the only effective means of informing the populace about what government is doing (not just what it says it is doing), and assessing the extent to which its actions are good or bad. Former Chief Justice Lyman Duff of the Supreme Court of Canada said:

> ... it is axiomatic that the practice of this free right of discussion of public affairs, notwithstanding its individual mischiefs, is the breath of life for parliamentary institutions.[27]

Vociferous public reaction to government proposals has often led to important alterations or even to the abandonment of plans. A government that wins power with a large majority in one election has often suffered defeat in the following contest, when public anger, supported by a vigilant and critical press, radio, and television have illuminated its errors in judgment and insensitivity to social and economic needs.

In any form of totalitarian state, the first concern of the rulers is to suppress free expression as the most dangerous kind of heresy, a poison in the body politic likely to lead to rebellion. Repression invariably takes the same form: the government accuses its critics of deliberate misrepresentation of government policies and activities, and of reporting events in a distorted and inflammatory manner calculated to encourage breaches of the law and violence. Censorship, confiscation of newspapers and journals, and padlocking the premises of opposition media are usually accompanied by repression of opposition political parties and a ban on all forms of public assembly other than those sponsored by the government. The ruling clique makes self-righteous statements characterizing its critics as "criminal elements, enemies of the state". It promises that as soon as the "temporary" unrest and risk of insurrection pass, full civil rights will be restored.

Unhappily, examples of these practices abound throughout the world. It would be unwise to single out one or two examples: no doubt a number of readers would be upset that we had selected some while ignoring others they considered to be worse. In any event, it is well to appreciate that even nations that confidently regard themselves free from these forms of repression remain in danger of succumbing to them in times of crisis.

---

26   The trial is unreported. For a discussion of the issues, see Ryan, "The Trial of Zundel, Freedom of Expression and the Criminal Law" (1985), 44 C.R. (3rd) 334.

27   Reference re: Alberta Statutes, [1938] S.C.R. 100, at 133; [1938] 2 D.L.R. 81 at 107.

$\mathcal{A}$s Arbiter of Disputes between Private Parties

In this chapter we have considered the role of our courts in arbitrating constitutional issues, in interpreting and applying statutes, and in protecting rights and freedoms. Under a legal system such as ours, derived from the English common law, legislation has historically played only a small part in resolving legal disputes between private parties — individuals, corporations, or other organized groups not connected with the government. Despite the rapid increase in statutory law in recent years, there remain extensive areas of the law unaffected by legislation. In these areas, the courts apply principles that they themselves have developed in the process of rendering decisions in the past, and in novel situations they develop new principles. These activities of the courts are important and complex. We shall discuss the evolution and continuing importance of court decisions based on principles developed by the courts themselves in the next chapter.

$\mathcal{L}$egal Realism

While courts are mainly occupied with private lawsuits (motor vehicle accidents, family conflicts, and commercial disputes) and with criminal prosecutions, it is the constitutional cases that often decide the fate of important social reforms, and in the last few years of the 19th century they focussed the attention of American legal writers on the methods of the courts generally. Led by Oliver Wendell Holmes, the most influential legal thinker of the age and subsequently a great judge of the Supreme Court of the United States, a new, skeptical school of thought known as "legal realism" emerged.

Holmes stated that the chief concern of a lawyer when advising a client is to be able to predict which way a court is likely to decide a possible lawsuit. The thing that counts in making a prediction, Holmes asserted, is not to study what judges say but what they do. To understand this observation, one must first know something about the nature of a court decision.

A court renders its decision by giving *judgment* (making a formal order): let us say for example that the defendant has been found responsible for injuring the plaintiff (the complaining party) through careless operation of an automobile, and must pay x dollars in damages (compensation) to the plaintiff. This formal judgment is what courts do and, as far as the parties to the lawsuit are concerned, it is what counts. In many cases, especially if the case is of considerable importance, the court also gives *reasons for judgment*, aptly described as the judge's justification to the losing side for deciding against it. The reasons for judgment are published in an unending series of books called law reports, found in all law libraries and studied unremittingly by law students, lawyers, and other judges. Frequently the *reasons* for judgment are referred to inaccurately as the *judgment*. The reasons then are what the courts say. Traditional theory asserts that these reasons form a consistent set of principles from which it is possible to learn what the law is and, in turn, predict how the courts will act in future disputes.

The legal realists claimed that studying only the reasons for judgment as reported in law books creates a mythical view of the law and is harmful both to the practising lawyer (plus the client, of course) and to the cause of law reform. While not denying that general principles and specific rules enunciated by the courts do influence later decisions and *help* predict what may happen, the realists viewed these reasons for judgment as only a small portion of "the law in action". They claimed that at least two other elements are frequently more significant than the principles developed in preceding cases: (a) "facts" are more important than "law" — thus, the lawyer who establishes facts favourable to her client and so creates a sympathy for him is more likely to obtain a favourable decision than one who merely quotes favourable legal principles; and (b) the judge's personal bias is more important than "law" — his opinions, his political affiliation, and a host of other psychological influences. If a judge's moral views tend to be puritanical, therefore, he is more likely than his fellow judges to look with disfavour on a party whose conduct has offended conventional moral standards and, where the conduct was of a criminal nature, to give the accused a more severe sentence. The more extreme legal realists suggested that a judge's conscious or subconscious awareness of popular feeling, and perhaps even the state of his digestion, are likely to influence his decisions more than the rules on which he ostensibly relies.

The realists correctly emphasized that the great majority of lawsuits are decided conclusively at trial, that is, at the first hearing of the case before a single judge. A trial judge hears all the evidence and summarizes it in his *findings of fact* (part of the reasons for judgment); he also listens to the legal arguments of counsel for both sides before he decides what laws apply to the facts as he has found them, and then delivers judgment. It is at the trial stage where the court (the judge and possibly jury) encounters in person the principal parties to the dispute and their witnesses, where a sympathy or antagonism derived from a coincidence or conflict of cultural values is most likely to arise, and where lawyers have the greatest scope for playing on the emotions and prejudices of the court. Of course, if the loser is sufficiently unhappy with the trial judge's decision (sometimes both sides are dissatisfied), he may appeal to a court of appeal. To launch an appeal, however, is a costly and time-consuming process, and the appeal court must be persuaded — no easy task — to overrule the trial judge. Thus, most litigants choose not to pursue their cases further than the trial court.

Generally speaking, appeal courts accept the findings of fact of the trial judge and reconsider only his application of the law. Sometimes, especially in criminal cases, a court of appeal may accept an argument that the trial judge excluded important evidence supporting one side of the case, or that he admitted highly prejudicial and improper evidence against one side, or, more rarely, that the evidence does not support the judge's finding of fact. But since the judges sitting on the court of appeal have not had the opportunity to observe the demeanour of witnesses, assess the inflection in their voices, and draw conclusions about their credibility, they are hesitant to interfere with a trial judge's findings of fact; they are concerned mainly with what principles of law apply to them. It is precisely because of this generally limited role of appeal courts that the realists focussed their attention upon the trial judge and the fact-finding process. The personal prejudices of a judge are more likely to influence a court's decision when the decision is rendered by a single judge than when it is rendered jointly by two or more judges. It is therefore paradoxical that the trial judge, whose decision is only occasionally appealed from, presides alone, while appeal courts usually have three judges, at least two of whom must agree to render a new decision.

In the United States there is a particular reason why the fact-finding role of courts might tend to be neglected as a subject for study. Few trial judgments are reported (published) there, simply because of the vast number of trial court decisions; by contrast, virtually all court of appeal decisions are reported and so become available for study by the legal profession. This situation is different in Canada, where the law reports do include reports of decisions at trial. The number of lawsuits in Canada is much smaller not only because of population but also because Canadians are less litigious.

The tendency of the realists was to denigrate what judges say — the law in reported cases and in legal treatises — and emphasize the uncertainty, even the irrationality, in the trial process. If the law depends on the state of a judge's digestion it would seem that rules count for very little. But this is not true; the law in books affects a far greater portion of "the law in action" than the realists would admit. It influences and is frequently decisive in a host of legal transactions and relationships that never come before a court. For this reason most legal scholars, supported by the opinions of practising lawyers, reject the excesses of the legal realists.

There are two important areas where people use the law in books continuously without encountering the uncertainties of the trial process. First, parties to a continuing relationship use many legal rules merely as general guidelines. The parties do not stand on their strict rights because it is not in their interests to do so. Instead of fighting the case in a courtroom, each prefers to settle any disagreement by informal compromise as the best means of preserving an amicable and mutually advantageous relationship. Examples can be found in relations among partners and in the field of labour, where some enterprises have had decades of good relations between management and labour without resort to strikes, arbitration, or the courts. Second, very large areas of the law have highly developed, predictable, and generally fair rules, and people use them as a basis for resolving problems without going to court. Thus, a defaulting supply firm in a contract to deliver goods realizes full well that it has broken its agreement and may offer to supply different goods of higher quality to make up for its failure; the purchaser may accept willingly rather than resort to a lawsuit.

Even when disputes do go to court, many are decided in a predictable manner, simply because the side with the better case sues in order to enforce its rights against a stubborn defendant. This situation arises frequently in family disputes about the division of assets, or when a spouse sues for an allowance for support. (These decisions are rarely reported because they add nothing new to the evolution of the law.) These predictable cases aside, we are left with an area of genuine uncertainty where the reason for going to court is that either the facts or the law, or both, are acknowledged to be uncertain: the result here is indeed unpredictable. In these circumstances the very fact of uncertainty does increase the potential role of such other factors as a judge's bias. But this part of the law in action is much smaller than the legal realists would have had us believe, and they were unwarranted in using it to demonstrate that the law generally is uncertain.

Nevertheless, the legal realists have made a very important contribution. First and foremost, they made it a legitimate activity to study openly and in a scholarly and objective fashion those factors that are traditionally considered as non-legal — indeed, improper — but which in reality influence many legal decisions. Certainly, self-knowledge should help a judge overcome personal biases and become a better judge. As well, those responsible for selecting judges (in Canada, the federal and provincial departments of justice) may consider more openly the general character of a prospective judge, in addition to his or her legal abilities, both to ensure a better choice of individual judges and to achieve a balance of opinion on appeal courts.

In addition, the realists emphasized the importance of facts and the fact-finding process. They gave great impetus to more scientific consideration of the rules of evidence and court procedures to improve the processes and hence the fairness of the courts. In this respect the realists have been strongly influenced by the social sciences as a whole. Together with the writers in sociological jurisprudence, they have helped break down the barriers isolating law as an independent discipline with its own logic and language, and to place it centrally in society as a major instrument for good or ill. This practical accomplishment has far outweighed any contribution of a theoretical nature. Legal realism has taught us that a hardheaded assessment of such institutions as the courts is a beginning toward their reform.

It has been our goal in Chapters 1 and 2 to introduce the reader to legal theory and to demonstrate that law shares a common subject-matter with the other social sciences in its concern for the effective operation of an immensely complex modern society. The reader may even have been surprised to learn that the answers to the fundamental questions of law are not any easier to find than they are in economics or in sociology.

Questions for Review

1. How do the courts become involved in the process of legislative reform?
2. Why do British courts refuse to examine legislative history?
3. What is a "Brandeis Brief"?
4. Contrast a judgment with the reasons for judgment.
5. How does the role of an appeal court differ from that of a trial court?
6. Describe briefly the main contentions of the legal realists. Is there a conflict between the perception of legal realists and that of legal positivists?
7. How do statutes give rise to judge-made law?
8. What is the argument that justifies a power in the Supreme Court to override the will of Parliament?
9. Give an example of a legal problem that may arise from an attempt in a constitution to divide powers between levels of government.
10. Is it possible for a statute to be held to be constitutional and yet substantially fail in its purpose on constitutional grounds?
11. Is one more likely to be liable for defamation if one says to another person "Jane Brown stole a car last August," than if one says, "Jane Brown is a thief"?
12. Why is the constitutionality of a statute a more serious issue than its interpretation?
13. What arguments consistent with the protection of civil liberties can be made for some restraint on freedom of expression?
14. What is the usual form of political argument by which a suppression of free speech is justified?
15. Would you agree that a rule against any form of discrimination has universal validity, or do you think it should sometimes be waived with a view to helping disadvantaged minority groups (as, for example, in admission to universities)?
16. Should corporations have civil rights like individuals?

17. "There is another reason for democracy's commitment to the freedom of the individual — the belief that social progress is more likely to occur in an atmosphere where differences are permitted than in an atmosphere where differences are restricted. Many of the greatest human achievements were conceived in the womb of disagreement." (A.A. Borovoy, *The Fundamentals of our Fundamental Freedoms*, p. 4. Toronto: The Canadian Civil Liberties Education Trust, 1974.) Elaborate with one or two examples.

18. "We have a parliament to pass laws, a government to administer laws, and a police department to enforce laws. Ironically, these potent instruments for the restriction of liberty are necessary for the enjoyment of liberty." (Ibid., p. 5.) Comment on the meaning of this quotation.

CHAPTER 3

THE MACHINERY OF JUSTICE

Who Makes Law?

How can we know when rules are also laws? As we have noted, Hume defined positive law as a body of rules for the breach of which sanctions are imposed.[1] His definition is useful but not complete: the enforcement of rules must be the responsibility of government and not of private persons. Thus, a restaurant owner who makes a rule that men will not be admitted to dinner unless they wear neckties and jackets has not made a law. Nor are the rules of a private organization, say, a tennis club, considered law; a tennis club may impose effective sanctions such as fining or expelling a member who breaks an important club rule, but its rules amount to no more than a private arrangement among club members.

On the other hand, enforcement by government must not be interpreted too narrowly as a requirement. Austin's explanation of law as the command of a sovereign — even of an impersonal sovereign in the form of a written constitution — if taken too literally can mislead us. Many apparent forms of lawmaking seem unconnected with the sovereign. A legal positivist will argue, however, that Austin's definition is broad enough to include even the lowest levels of government and that regulations passed by the licence committee of a town council, for instance, can be shown to emanate indirectly from a sovereign. While it is true that the committee's authority can be traced back through municipal by-laws and the town's charter to arrive ultimately at the provincial legislature, as a practical matter the licence committee itself, acting on its own initiative, creates new law. Many lesser public bodies like licence committees are constantly changing existing law and making new law — and the volume of law generated in this way is growing ever more rapidly.

Substantive and Procedural Law

Dividing law into broad categories helps us to understand the legal system. The two most basic categories are *substantive* and *procedural* law.

Substantive law consists of the rights and duties that each person has in society. Some examples are the right to own property, to vote, to travel about the country unmolested, to enter into contracts, to sell or give away property; the duty to avoid injuring others, to perform contractual obligations, to obey traffic laws, customs regulations, and other laws. These substantive rules are further divided into the fields of *public law* and *private law*, referred to below.

Procedural law deals the protection and enforcement of these rights and duties. Thus, substantive rules decide which of two parties is at fault in an automobile accident, but it is through the rules of procedure that the injured party obtains a remedy against the wrongdoer. Procedural law prescribes the *machinery* by which the rights and duties recognized in substantive law are actually realized and enforced.

---

[1] See Chapter 1 under "Natural Law under Attack — Legal Positivism".

$\mathcal{P}$UBLIC AND PRIVATE LAW

Public law is concerned with the conduct of government and with the relations between government on one side and private persons (including organizations such as companies, clubs, or unions) on the other side. Public law divides into several categories, such as constitutional law, criminal law, and administrative law.

Private law comprises the rules governing relations between private persons or groups of persons. A person involved in a dispute may resort to the courts to have her rights against the other side decided by the rules of private law. These rules provide the fabric and substance of business law. Private law divides into a number of categories, the largest of which are contracts, torts, property, and trusts. In this book we are mostly concerned with contracts since they are the focus of business transactions. We cannot consider contracts in isolation, however, and from time to time in contract problems we shall encounter the law of torts, property, and, to a lesser extent, trusts. Frequently the term "civil law" is used to mean "private law". This usage creates unfortunate ambiguity, especially in a country like Canada, because, as we explain below, the primary meaning of civil law refers to a different legal system.

$\mathcal{T}$HE CIVIL LAW AND THE COMMON LAW

Two great systems of law have grown in Western Europe from the Middle Ages, and they have been inherited by most of the lands that the nations of Western Europe colonized.

The older of the two systems is called the civil law. It covers the whole of continental Europe and to a large extent Scotland, much of Africa, and the whole of South and Central America. In North America it applies in Mexico and to some degree in several of the southern United States, but particularly in Louisiana, which was French territory until early in the last century. When the English conquered French Canada, they guaranteed the people of Québec the continued use of French civil law in most areas of private law. To this day most of the private law of the province of Québec is civil law.

The other great legal system is called the common law and had its origin in feudal England at the time of the Norman Conquest. It covers the whole of the English-speaking world except Scotland and is a significant part of the law of many non-English-speaking countries that were part of the British Empire, notably India, Pakistan, Bangladesh, and the former colonies in Africa.

The civil law has its roots in Roman law. In the 6th century A.D., the famous emperor of the Eastern Roman Empire, Justinian, decided to codify the law of his vast domains. He brought together the leading jurists of the time and had them draft a comprehensive code based on the laws of Rome. This tome was a monumental contribution to law and became known as Justinian's Code. It was inherited by the whole of continental Europe and formed the foundation for most of its legal systems. A similar codification was ordered by Napoléon in 1804. This version, the French Civil Code, is best known as the Code Napoléon, and was adopted in or greatly influenced the development of codes in such countries as Italy, Spain, Germany, Switzerland, and Belgium.

In these countries the theory is that a court always refers to the code to settle a dispute. If the code does not seem to cover a new problem then the court is free to reason by analogy to settle the problem from general principles laid down in the code. In theory, a later court need not follow the earlier reasoning in a similar case; the second court may decide that in its view a just result of the law ought to be the reverse of the earlier decision.

Civil law theory could present practical difficulties. If in any system of law judges were continually to follow their own biases, values, and personal prejudices, and so contradict earlier decisions, the law would become a jungle. No one could learn what the law on a particular point is. It is a requirement of justice, therefore, that like cases be treated alike.

ILLUSTRATION

A contracts to build a house for B, but does not carry out the agreement. B sues A and collects money damages for the breach. X makes a similar contract with Y, and fails to carry out the contract. Y sues X for damages, but the suit is dismissed by the court. Either decision, examined entirely separately, might seem reasonable enough: some people might well believe that the builder was justified in backing out; others might favour the owner. But place the two decisions side by side, for example, in adjoining court-rooms on the same day. In these circumstances there would be two very unhappy litigants. A would complain because X in a similar situation escaped without paying any damages; Y would be angry because she obtained nothing while B got substantial damages for breach of a similar contract. A and Y would both feel unjustly treated, and most people would agree with them — the law should be either one way or the other, but not consist of two contradictory rules at the same time.

Equal and consistent treatment in like situations is one of the most important aspects of justice and hence of law as well. Judges must be interested in, and to some extent influenced by, what other judges have decided in similar cases, whether in civil law or in common law countries.

A second major attribute of law is predictability. Suppose, after the contrary decisions we have just discussed, P wishes to make a similar contract with Q. Q asks a lawyer whether the contract is a binding one — if P backs out will P be liable to pay damages to Q for any loss caused by P's failure to carry out the bargain? Q's lawyer would have to say, "Maybe yes, maybe no; it depends on whether the court prefers the result in the case of A against B, or that in X against Y." One can well imagine the state of confusion if this were the normal advice a client were to receive! If people are to be able to find out where they stand and to act with reasonable certainty, the law itself must be fairly predictable — a strong reason why like cases ought to be decided alike.

An important benefit of the concern that like cases be decided alike is the development by judges of principles that link like cases. These principles accumulate into a body of doctrine — a framework of predictable rules that serves as background for the vast majority of legal relations.

As a result, in civil law countries, judges do decide similar cases in the same way most of the time, although they are under no binding rule to do so. Today, in such countries as France and Germany, reports of decisions are regularly published so that lawyers and judges can learn what the courts are deciding, and how they are interpreting the Civil Code in modern disputes.

THE THEORY OF PRECEDENT

The common law judges of England discerned these twin needs of consistency and predictability as early as the 13th century. In fact, at certain stages the courts followed previous decisions slavishly, even when the results in new circumstances were nonsensical or manifestly unjust. This custom of following already-decided cases is called the theory of precedent — the doctrine of following precedents already established by the courts. The Latin phrase for the rule is *stare decisis* — to stand by previous decisions. Followed slavishly, such a system, while it has the merits of certainty and uniformity, becomes inflexible, reactionary, and stultifying.

Stare decisis has never been an ironclad rule. In the first place, words are at best relatively inaccurate vehicles for thought. This very vagueness of language permits judges to draw distinctions between similar problems and so refuse to follow obsolete precedents. Second, no two sets of facts are identical in every respect; even when the same parties are involved, the time must be different. Judges, when they feel it to be truly necessary, can distinguish the case before them from an earlier precedent by dwelling upon minor differences. In this way they are able to adjust the law rather slowly to changing circumstances and values. Nevertheless, the whole spirit of the common law system is bound to the theory of precedent. We look to past decisions to glean principles and to make new laws. Accordingly, a large part of the study of law is the study of decided cases.

Despite its internal flexibility, the theory of precedent hinders the law in accommodating the rapidly increasing rate of change in society. A decision that seemed quite acceptable in, say, 1938, may be entirely out of step with current social standards. The only way for a court to cope with a marked change may be to ignore *stare decisis* and directly overrule a prior decision. A prime example occurred in the school segregation question in the United States, as noted in Chapter 2, where the Supreme Court took account of social change and reversed its earlier interpretation of the United States Constitution.

There is a danger in overruling decided cases too freely, for to do so would undermine the needed consistency and predictability in law. The approach to this problem has been different in the United States, Britain, and Canada. The Supreme Court of the United States has never considered itself bound to follow its own previous decisions when the result would be manifestly unjust. In a reversal of its traditional position, the House of Lords (the English equivalent of the Supreme Court) has announced that it will no longer consider itself bound to follow its own decisions.[2] Its announcement is a clear recognition of the need for courts to depart from older decisions when contemporary standards call for change. The Canadian Supreme Court has not committed itself on this subject, but it seems highly likely that, following the example of the much respected courts of these senior common law jurisdictions, it too will accept this needed flexibility.[3] Accordingly, we may look forward to an increasing willingness on the part of our courts to disagree openly with past decisions.

An understanding of these significant limitations on *stare decisis* is important for those

---

[2] See announcement, [1966] W.L.R. 1234.

[3] See statement by Cartwright, J. in The Queen v. Binus, [1968] 1 C.C.C. 227 at 229: "I do not doubt the power of the court to depart from a previous judgment of its own . . ." It should be noted, however, that the court did not overrule itself in this case.

who will be proposing answers to the legal cases offered for discussion at the end of Chapters 4 to 35. It is a mistake to assume, when one finds an actual reported case with facts seemingly identical to those in the case under discussion, that the conclusion in the reported case is the most satisfactory one. It is much more useful to consider the case offered for discussion on its legal and social merits and then look at the reported case to see what light it may shed on the problem. Some of the reported cases have been severely criticized both by learned writers and by other courts in subsequent cases. They are cited because they offer an opportunity to discuss important problems.

Although both civil and common law reach the same conclusions in most areas of the law, there are some important differences. This book deals only with principles of the common law. Much of what is written here does not necessarily apply to the civil law of Québec.

$\mathcal{T}$HE SOURCES OF LAW

The Variety of Sources

The earliest source of our law is the body of decisions handed down by the judiciary and permanently recorded in England from Norman times to the present day. A second source consists of the statutes passed by Parliament and by provincial legislatures. The cabinet, in its formal role of adviser to the monarch, can also "legislate" within certain limited areas by issuing orders-in-council.[4] Every province has also passed statutes providing for the creation of municipal governments and their supervision. These statutes give municipalities the power to make law and to raise revenue for the benefit of their citizens. Municipal by-laws and regulations are thus a form of statute law. In addition to judge-made law and statute law, there is a vast area of subordinate legislation usually known as administrative law. It derives from authority granted by statute to various administrative agencies of government to make rules and regulations in order to carry out the purposes for which the legislation was passed.

Law Made by Judges

The Common Law[5]

As we have seen, the common law is based on the theory of precedent, which in turn depends on a constant flow of reported cases. An organized national system of courts was therefore necessary to enable the common law to develop: before a decision would influence judges in subsequent cases, it was necessary to have a judge with a recognized position in society and a court with a wide jurisdiction. Before the Norman Conquest the courts were mainly local, and varied greatly from county to county. William I gave England its first strong, centralized government, and thus laid the foundation for a national system of courts.

---

4 An order-in-council is issued by the Privy Council (in effect, the cabinet) in the name of the monarch, either in exercise of the royal prerogative or under authority of a statute.
5 Unfortunately, the term "common law" has three possible meanings: (a) common law as opposed to equity; (b) judge-made law (including equity) as opposed to statute law; and (c) all the law of a common law country as opposed to a civil law country.

The earliest decisions were, of course, without the benefit of precedent. Courts were often left entirely to their own resources in reaching a decision. It is not always easy to understand their reasoning, but there is no doubt that already established local customs played an important role at the outset. Evidence concerning a local custom would be admitted, influence the judge's decision, and then be incorporated in the common law. As the body of precedents increased, and as the courts developed into a settled order of importance, prior decisions exerted an ever-increasing influence.

Canon law and Roman law also influenced early judicial decisions in England. The Church created canon law when it had a separate legal jurisdiction and held its own courts in matters pertaining to itself, and to family law and wills. Roman law left its mark particularly in its distinction between possession and ownership of personal property. The influence of these systems of law was inevitable at a time when practically the only literate people were clerics, and scholars trained on the Continent. Still another force, feudal law, affected the common law concerning the ownership of land.

In the Middle Ages, trade was carried on almost exclusively by merchants who were members of guilds. Merchants used their guilds to solve disputes among themselves. They developed a set of rules and acceptable trade practices, and thus built a body of business customs known as the *law merchant*. They administered their rules speedily through their own courts. Only guild members came within the jurisdiction of these courts. The law merchant was developed and shared by all the trading nations of the medieval world.

The monopoly over trade held by merchant guilds eventually broke down, and persons who were not members increasingly entered commerce. The ordinary courts of the land were called upon to adjudicate in disputes between non-guild members. Naturally, they borrowed from the established rules of the law merchant. Our present law of negotiable instruments, for example, originated as a part of the law merchant.

Equity

The common law, by its very nature, has always looked to the past for its authority. In its very early stages of development, its judges often sought new remedies when aggrieved parties appeared before them. But as the body of previous decisions grew, the common law became increasingly strict. By the late 13th century, it had become very formal and was burdened with cumbersome procedure, much of it rooted in ancient customs and superstitions. An aggrieved person who came before the court had to find one of the ancient forms, called a "writ", to suit the particular grievance. If an appropriate writ could not be found, the court would not grant a remedy. As England developed commercially, these old writs did not provide relief for many wrongs suffered by innocent parties, and great hardship often resulted.

Aggrieved parties without a remedy in the common law courts began to petition the king, who, in the age of the divine right of the monarchy, looked upon himself as the fountainhead of all law and justice. The king considered the hearing of petitions an important duty to his subjects and often granted relief. But as the number of petitions increased, the king's chancellor (his chief personal adviser, usually a cleric) took over the task of administering them. The flow continued to increase and the chancellor delegated the work to vice-chancellors. Soon it was apparent that another whole system of courts was growing: the courts of the chancellor, or the *courts of chancery* as they became known. These courts were also known as *courts of equity*, and the rules of law which they administered are called the *principles of equity* or, simply, *equity*. Equity rivals the common law in its contribution to the legal system developed by our judges.

The approach of the chancery courts was at first different from that of the common law courts, since the medieval chancellor was an ecclesiastic as well as the general secretary of state. "Equity was a gloss on common law; it was a set of rules which could be invoked to supplement the deficiencies of common law or to ease the clumsy working of common law actions and remedies."[6]

The courts of common law limited themselves severely in the kinds of remedies they offered; they would invariably award only money damages to a party injured by a breach of contract. Yet sometimes money alone was not adequate compensation.

ILLUSTRATION

B owned two separate lots of land and agreed to buy the lot separating them from *S* in order to erect a large building on the three pieces once they were joined. *S* changed his mind and refused to convey the middle lot. If *B* sued for breach of contract in a common law court, he would be awarded only money damages, an inadequate remedy since his project would be frustrated.

By contrast, the courts of equity were prepared, if they thought fit, to decree *specific performance*, that is, to order the defendant to convey the land. If the defendant refused, he would be jailed for *contempt of court* until he relented and carried out the order. The threat of a medieval jail was highly persuasive!

Remedies available in the courts of equity were discretionary. The relative innocence of the petitioner and the hardship suffered determined whether the individual could hope for equity's special type of intervention. As equity developed, however, the principles upon which relief was given became almost as fixed as the rules of common law.

Merger of the Courts

For a long time, England had two rival sets of courts, the courts of common law and the courts of equity. In practice, a division of labour developed between them, since the advantages of equity were sought in cases where the common law remedies were inadequate. Equity dealt mainly with claims arising out of the administration of estates, the execution of trusts, and the foreclosure of mortgages, and in contracts it dealt with claims for specific performance, injunction, and the rectification and rescission of contracts. We shall examine the contracts remedies in Chapter 17.

In 1865, the British Parliament passed an act merging the two systems of courts into the single system we know today. The Canadian provinces passed similar acts shortly afterwards. For convenience, the division of labour has been preserved in England by having two divisions within the High Court of Justice: a Chancery Division and a Queen's Bench Division.

---

6   Jackson, *The Machinery of Justice in England*, (8th ed.), J.R. Spencer, ed., p. 7. Cambridge: The University Press, 1989.

The amalgamation of the courts of common law and equity did not mean the abandonment of the philosophy of equity. Every judge now is supposed to have two minds, one for equity and one for legal precedent. A judge may exercise the prerogative to apply an "equitable maxim" when it appears warranted in the circumstances. Equity thus provides a conscience for our modern common law; it prevents the law when applied to particular instances from straying too far from reason and fairness.

Statutes

The second main source of our law, statute law, consists of acts of Parliament and of the provincial legislatures and of by-laws passed by municipal governments. A statute overrides all the common law dealing with the same point. Although the volume of statute law is increasing rapidly, the common law still constitutes the bulk of our private law and, in particular, of the law of contracts.

Sometimes legislatures enact statutes to *codify* existing common law rather than to change it. This procedure explains, for example, the passing of the Bills of Exchange Act, the Sale of Goods Act, and the Partnership Act. Prior to the passage of these acts, the related law was to be found in a staggering number of individual cases. The acts did away with the labour and uncertainty of searching through the cases for the relevant law.

Courts are often called on to interpret a statute in order to decide whether it applies to the facts of a case, and if it does, to decide also on its consequences. Their decisions then form part of judge-made law and are often referred to in subsequent cases. Judge-made law and statutes are thus closely related. The traditional attitude of the courts toward the common law is quite different from their attitude toward statutes. While the common law is the creation of the courts themselves, statute law, as one writer put it, is "an alien intruder in the house of common law". The courts regularly use principles from earlier decisions, even though the facts may be quite different from the case at issue. On the other hand, the courts are less likely to apply the provisions of a statute unless the facts of the case at issue are covered specifically by the statute. This attitude of the courts is called the *strict interpretation* of the statutes.

Administrative Law

There are two main classes of legislation. The first and simplest consists of those statutes that change the law: they prohibit an activity formerly permitted or else remove a prohibition, thereby enabling people to carry on a formerly illegal activity. This type of legislation is essentially passive in that it provides a framework within which people may legally go about their business; it does not presume to supervise and regulate their activities, but leaves it to an injured party or a law-enforcement official to complain about any activity that has violated a statute of this kind and to initiate court proceedings.

The second class of legislation authorizes the government itself to carry out a program; to levy taxes and provide revenue for the purpose stated in the statute, such as building a hospital, paying pensions to the elderly, and offering subsidies to encourage a particular kind of economic activity; and to supervise and regulate the related trade or activity. Parliament itself has never carried out these activities, and is an inappropriate body to undertake any program requiring continuous supervision. It comprises a group of people from ridings across the country whose talents and interests vary greatly, and whose primary responsibility is to enact legislation. From early times in England, Parliament authorized the monarch to levy taxes, pay and equip the armed forces, and construct public works. Thus, projects *authorized* by Parliament were *executed* by the monarch and his officials — hence the term "executive" to describe the agencies of government that carry out Parliament's will. Translated into the terms of modern government, this process means that every government department, agency, and tribunal is established by the authority of the legislature in a statute. For example, the Canadian Radio-television and Telecommunications Commission was established under the Broadcasting Act, which sets out the purposes of that body and grants it regulatory powers to carry out those purposes.[7]

In exercising its regulatory powers and acting in its executive capacity, an administrative agency creates new law, which we defined earlier as "subordinate legislation". Some subordinate legislation sets down broad criteria regulating the type of guarantee that a licence applicant must supply to carry on a particular activity, and the amount and type of investment required as a precondition. Other subordinate legislation may be detailed and technical (fees for applications, location of transmitters) and may be only a single ruling on a particular application.

Important regulations, normally those setting out broad standards, require the approval of the cabinet in the form of an order-in-council. The agency itself drafts these regulations and the minister responsible for the agency brings them before the cabinet. Lesser regulations may be authorized by the minister, the head of the agency, or even a designated officer of the agency.

As we noted in Chapter 1, the growing complexity of society and government has increased the need for specialized knowledge and control in such areas as environmental protection, energy, transportation, communications, education, and welfare; and the list includes a growing number of business and professional activities that are believed to affect the public interest. As a result, government agencies, each with its own system of regulations and sanctions, continue to proliferate. Although administrative law is not a main area of direct concern in this book, we shall from time to time have to deal with law affecting labour relations, consumer protection, and the financing and operation of corporations, in which government agencies and their regulations play increasingly important roles.

The System of Courts in England

We have seen that the substance of the law is created by various institutions: the judiciary, legislature, and administrative agencies. A major part of business law continues to be formulated by the judiciary. Accordingly, we should be familiar with the system of courts and their rules of procedure.

Two reasons make it useful to begin by studying the English courts: first, much of our own law is derived from English case law, and these cases will be easier to understand if we are familiar with the structure of the courts that decided them; second, the English system affords a good starting place because England has a single government, and its system of courts is easier to grasp than the more complicated federal structure existing in Canada.

---

[7] Broadcasting Act, R.S.C. 1985, c. B-9, s. 5.

The Courts of First Instance

Courts of first instance are also sometimes called courts of original jurisdiction because it is in them that actions originate and trials take place. England has many different kinds of courts of original jurisdiction, each having certain types of grievances to decide. Their names differ from those of their Canadian counterparts, and to avoid confusion we shall not list them here, noting only their place in the English system of courts.

The Court of Appeal

The Court of Appeal is the next tier in the English judicial system. It is not a court of first instance; that is, actions do not originate in this court. Either of the parties to an action who is dissatisfied with the decision of a court of first instance may appeal to the Court of Appeal, where the decision will be reconsidered. The party who petitions for an appeal is called the *appellant*; the other party, the *respondent*. Trials are not held before the court, nor are witnesses called: the court does not entertain questions of fact because these were for the trial judge to decide. The Court of Appeal proceeds on the basis of a written record of the trial in the court of first instance. On appeal, lawyers for each side argue only questions of law, the appellant claiming that the trial judge erred in interpreting the law, and the respondent arguing to uphold the decision of the trial judge. The court may agree with the trial judge and dismiss the appeal, agree with the appellant and reverse the trial judgment, vary the trial judgment in part, or declare that the trial judge erred in failing to consider certain facts, and send the case back for a new trial in the lower court. The Court of Appeal usually hears cases in a panel of three judges, but occasionally five judges may hear a very important case.

The House of Lords

It is somewhat surprising to learn that the House of Lords, more widely known as the upper house of the British Parliament, is also the supreme court in Britain. Originally, any member of the House of Lords (members of the peerage) could sit with the House when it was convened as a court, but since the mid-19th century only great lawyers and judges who have been elevated to the peerage actually hear and decide appeals. The court usually consists of the Lord Chancellor and up to nine Lords of Appeal in Ordinary, who are full-time salaried judges. Parties dissatisfied with a decision of the Court of Appeal have one more chance before the House of Lords, the ultimate court of appeal and the highest court in the land.

THE SYSTEM OF COURTS IN CANADA

We noted in Chapter 2 that the division of legislative powers between the federal and provincial governments has inevitably led to disputes about which level has jurisdiction over the many problems that defy identification with the categories of the Constitution. Despite the inherent difficulties in federal constitutions, the division of powers in the Canadian Constitution has not fared badly. Some aspects of its treatment show great wisdom and have caused little or no trouble. Others appear rather odd at first sight, but can be explained by circumstances at the time of Confederation.

For example, the Constitution gives the provinces jurisdiction over the administration of justice — the organization and operation of police forces and the system of courts. At the same time, the Act gives the federal government jurisdiction over trade and commerce, banking, bankruptcy, and criminal law — matters frequently litigated before the courts — and also the exclusive right to appoint, and the obligation to pay, all county court and superior court judges.[8]

Why this peculiar division in the administration of the legal system? The explanation lies, at least in part, in the fact that at the time of discussions on Confederation in Canada, the United States had just been through a terrible civil war. Many Canadians believed that biased local state legislatures and locally elected judges (sometimes without any legal training) had fanned internal division in the United States by passing discriminatory laws and by frequently administering laws unfairly against "outsiders" (citizens of other states). The Canadian Constitution sought to avoid the problem of local bias by placing jurisdiction over matters peculiarly susceptible to local influence in the hands of the national government. Our Constitution also requires that only qualified lawyers be appointed to the county and superior court benches. Until retirement, they hold office conditional on good behaviour, and superior court judges can be removed only by "joint address", that is, a vote taken before both the House of Commons and the Senate. These provisions are designed to keep judges as unbiased and immune from local pressures as possible.

As in England, there are three tiers of courts: the courts of first instance, the intermediate provincial courts of appeal, and the Supreme Court of Canada. In the the late 1980s and the 1990s, the court systems in all provinces have undergone reorganization that has merged a number of the courts and simplified the court structure. The names and jurisdictions of the courts differ somewhat from province to province, but in general they follow the pattern set out below.

The Provincial Courts

The Courts of First Instance

INFERIOR TRIAL COURTS

Small Claims Court   The court handles disputes for smaller amounts of money. The maximum amounts have been increased in recent years in most provinces and vary considerably from one province to another. Its procedure is quite simple and informal, so that the cost of taking action is small.

Provincial Division   The court decides very little, if any, private law. It hears criminal cases of almost every type except for the most serious offences such as murder, treason, sedition, piracy, rape, and manslaughter. It may hold preliminary hearings in prosecution of these crimes to decide whether there is enough evidence to proceed to trial. No jury trials are held before Provincial

---

[8]   The Constitution Act, 1867, ss. 96 and 100. As we note below, in all provinces, these courts have been merged.

Division judges. If an accused person elects (as one may) to have a jury trial, the case must be heard in another court.

A division of the court also hears questions of domestic relations, but not divorce.

Youth Court

Children and adolescents who the government feels are too young to be dealt with in the ordinary criminal courts and require special care are brought before youth court judges. The organization of youth courts varies from province to province. In some provinces they operate as separate courts. In others, the family division acts as a youth court. Nova Scotia and Ontario have adopted a "two tier" model: 12 to 15-year-olds are dealt with in the family division, while 16 and 17-year-olds are dealt with in the regular adult division although they are subject to punishment as young offenders.

SUPERIOR TRIAL COURTS

Surrogate Court (or Probate Court)

This court supervises the estates of deceased persons. It appoints an administrator to wind up the affairs of anyone who dies intestate (without leaving a will), settles disputes over the validity of wills and division of assets, and approves the accounts of executors and administrators. Four provinces maintain separate probate courts,[9] while the remaining five common law provinces have merged them into the superior court system but with separate divisions.

General Division

The former District and County Courts have been merged in all provinces with the former higher level court, variously known as the High Court of Justice, Court of Queen's Bench, the Superior Court, the Supreme Court, and the Supreme Court Trial Division. It has unlimited jurisdiction in civil and criminal actions. The Court may also serve as a court of appeal from summary convictions made by magistrates or provincial judges for lesser offences.

Divisional Court

The Divisional Court, created in 1972, is peculiar to Ontario. It consists of the Chief Justice of the High Court and such other judges of that court as the Chief Justice designates from time to time. It sits in panels of three judges, more or less continuously in Toronto, and at various times throughout the year in several other centres. It hears appeals from various lower provincial courts and from various provincial administrative tribunals.

Intermediate Appellate Court

The Court of Appeal

Each province has one intermediate appellate court, called variously the Appellate Division, the Supreme Court *en banc* (the whole bench), and Queen's Bench Appeals, as well as the Court of Appeal. It performs the same function as the Court of Appeal in England.

---

[9]   Alberta, New Brunswick, Nova Scotia and Saskatchewan.

The Federal Courts

The Tax Court of Canada

The Tax Court hears appeals of taxpayers against assessments by Revenue Canada. The Court hears only tax appeals, and functions with relatively simple procedures. Either the taxpayer or the department may appeal its decisions to the Trial Division of the Federal Court. There new evidence may be submitted and the dispute retried, not as an appeal, but as in a court of first instance.

The Federal Court of Canada

The federal government maintains the Federal Court of Canada in two divisions, a Trial Division and an Appeal Division. Under a 1970 statute[10] reconstituting the former Exchequer Court of Canada, the Federal Court has received expanded jurisdiction, and certain kinds of actions that could formerly be brought in the provincial courts as well are now reserved exclusively for the Federal Court. The Federal Court has exclusive jurisdiction over such matters as patents, copyright and trademarks, disputes concerning ships and navigation, and many sorts of lawsuits against the federal government itself. There remains a large area of concurrent jurisdiction where a plaintiff may still sue in either a provincial or the Federal Court. For example, a person injured by the careless operation of a government motor vehicle may still sue in a provincial court.

The Supreme Court of Canada

The Supreme Court is the final court of appeal in Canada, the equivalent of the House of Lords in England. It consists of nine judges and hears appeals from both the provincial courts of appeal and the Federal Court of Canada. In addition, it has special jurisdiction under the Supreme Court Act[11] to rule on the constitutionality of federal and provincial statutes when they are referred to the court by the federal cabinet. In private actions the appellant must obtain special leave from the Supreme Court to appeal.[12]

THE SYSTEM OF COURTS IN THE UNITED STATES

Although both Canada and the United States have federal systems of governments, there are major differences between the constitutions of the two federations. In the United States, the individual states — at least theoretically — have more autonomy, and have the residual power that in Canada rests with the federal government. Again, although under the Constitution the Canadian government has the power to create a full system of three-tier federal courts throughout Canada, it has not done so, but has felt content to allow the provincial courts to decide cases of first instance (with the exception of the fields reserved

---

[10]   The Federal Court Act, R.S.C. 1985, c. F-7.
[11]   R.S.C. 1985, c. S-26, s. 53.
[12]   *Ibid.*, s. 40.

exclusively to the Federal and Tax Courts). On the other hand, the United States has set up a full system of federal courts that handle a large portion of litigation, although much less than the total handled by the state courts. Criminal law, for example, is a state matter, except in cases involving specific fields of federal jurisdiction, such as national defence, or in cases where an offence is committed in more than one state, such as moving stolen goods across state boundaries. The federal courts have jurisdiction in the following cases: bankruptcy; postal matters; federal banking laws; disputes concerning maritime contracts or wrongs; prosecution of crimes punishable under federal laws of the United States or committed at sea; actions requiring an interpretation of the U.S. Constitution, federal statutes and treaties; and disputes between citizens of different states.

The federal courts are organized in the familiar three-tier structure. The court of original jurisdiction is the District Court. There is at least one in each state and several in each of the more populous states. At the next level the country is divided into eleven judicial *circuits* with a Court of Appeals for each circuit. A particular Court of Appeals is often referred to by its number followed by "Circuit Court", e.g., Ninth Circuit Court. Finally, the Supreme Court of the United States hears appeals from the Circuit Courts and also acts as a court of first instance in a few special circumstances provided for in the Constitution. As a general rule, appeals end with the Circuit Courts of Appeals, and may be carried to the United States Supreme Court only at the discretion of the Supreme Court itself: it has usually limited itself to a review of decisions affecting basic human rights or constitutional rights and deciding important legal principles that have received conflicting treatment in different Circuit Courts.

Individual states have authority to create the courts they consider necessary, but in general the system of state courts follows the same pattern as that of the federal courts. Most states have a trial court, an intermediate appellate court, and a final appellate court. A few appeals are brought from the "final" state appellate court to the U.S. Supreme Court, when the appellant can convince the Supreme Court that a "substantial constitutional issue" is involved.

As a result, the great majority of cases commenced in the state courts can go no further than the highest state appellate court, thus permitting wide variations in decisions on the same matter among several states. By contrast, such inconsistencies have been rectified more often in Canada by the Supreme Court, whose decisions are binding on provincial Courts of Appeal.

We may note that in the United States judges in the federal court system are appointed, just as Canadian and English judges are. Many of the judges in the state courts, however, are elected by popular vote.

$\mathcal{U}$SING THE COURTS

Who May Sue?

Not everyone has the capacity to start an action. An adult citizen of Canada has the broadest capacity — virtually unlimited access to the courts for any type of action. Generally speaking, non-Canadians may also sue as freely as citizens. But as we note in Chapter 8 on the capacity to contract, during hostilities any person found to be an enemy alien loses the right to sue. A child is not permitted to bring an action alone but must be represented by an adult person. If a child begins an action, not knowing that an adult representative is required, and the error is discovered, the court will "stay" proceedings until a parent or guardian or a "next friend" is appointed. Children are presumed not to have the sound judgment needed to undertake the risks of court proceedings; they must rely on an adult person to act on their behalf. Similarly, an insane person cannot sue without a court-appointed representative.

Generally speaking, corporations (bodies incorporated by conforming to procedures under a statute) may sue and be sued, although foreign corporations may be subject to strict regulation and be required to obtain a provincial licence before bringing an action.

In each of the instances referred to above, action is brought by a "person", either for that person's own benefit or for the benefit of another person. For this purpose, a corporation is considered to be a legal "person" or "entity". An incorporated body is referred to as "it" rather than "they"; in other words, it is not thought of as a collectivity but as a single unit. Greater difficulties arise when an action is brought by or against an unincorporated collectivity, a group of persons such as a social club, a church, a political party, and perhaps most important, a trade union. In most cases, unincorporated groups are not recognized by the courts and may not sue or be sued. The position of trade unions varies: in some jurisdictions, it is possible to sue and be sued by a trade union, while in others it is not.

Standing to Sue

Suppose a careless landowner pollutes a stream that runs through a municipal park. If the municipality is reluctant to sue the owner, may an individual resident of the city sue on behalf of herself and all other residents for injury to the park? Suppose a board of censors bans a controversial film. May a resident of the province sue on behalf of himself and other residents who are denied the opportunity to view the film? Do individuals in these circumstances acquire "standing" before the court, and can they establish a right to be vindicated? Generally speaking, courts have been reluctant to permit actions by individuals when their rights are no greater than those of the rest of the public. The courts foresee a risk that especially litigious and cantankerous members of the public may choose to litigate many matters in which they have no direct interest. An ordinary citizen may be a member of several organizations including a trade union, hold shares in a company, vote as a taxpayer in a community, own land adjacent to public waterways, and be a user of a park and a movie fan. One can imagine many other roles in which an individual might be considered a member of a large group. The judiciary has worried that the courts could become clogged by such actions.

On the other hand, with growing awareness of damage to our environment through pollution and failure to practise conservation, with the growing complexity of pharmaceutical products, prepared foods, and mechanical devices sold to the public, the risk of serious injury to large groups of persons has grown. Effective means must be available to the public to protect itself from careless and unscrupulous enterprises, especially if no governmental body takes adequate steps to protect the public interest. Some recent decisions of the Supreme Court of Canada have recognized the right of a taxpayer to sue when he believes public revenues are being improperly expended, and the right of a movie viewer to bring an action when he believes his right to see a film has been taken away by a provincial censorship body.[13] This area is in a state of flux, and it is likely to be many years before satisfactory rules have been worked out by the legislatures and the courts to achieve a balance between the public interest and minimizing abuse of the judicial process.

Class Actions[14]

Suppose the owner of a car wishes to sue the manufacturer to recover loss caused by a serious defect in the car, and that the defect is known to exist in several thousand other cars of the same model. May the owner, indeed ought he to, sue not only on his own behalf, but as representative of a class — that is, on behalf of all the other owners — or must each owner bring his own lawsuit? If he fails in his action, will all other owners necessarily fail, or vice versa? Courts are reluctant to take away an individual's right to litigate his own claim. On the other hand, it would be unfortunate to clog the courts with hundreds, perhaps thousands, of repetitive claims in which all the salient facts and applicable laws had already been clearly established.

Again, there are no clear rules in this area. A court may first hear argument about whether an individual should represent a group in a class action and thus dispose of the matter for all members of the class at once. If the court so decides, then on handing down a judgment it makes the matter *res judicata* and the case cannot be brought before the court again to contest legal liability. In our example of the defective car, liability having already been established, other owners might then come forward to have the court assess the amount of damage if the parties could not themselves settle on an amount.[15]

Two provinces, Quebec with its civil law system and Ontario, have passed legislation to make it easier to bring class actions. In 1989, Ontario established a broadly based advisory committee to report and make recommendations for a new law. In response to the report, Ontario passed the Class Proceedings Act.[16] It permits either a plaintiff or a defendant to apply to a court to have himself and others in his group declared to be a "class". If the court agrees, it will appoint a representative for the class. The Act sets out the criteria the court must use in making its decision, and creates special rules for admitting evidence and awarding damages. There appears to be wide agreement that the Act is a major improvement, but it will take some time to see the results.

Procedural Law

We do not propose to instruct readers in procedural law. Most business people will gratefully concede that the intricacies of procedure are properly the province of lawyers. Nevertheless, an overall understanding of what the various steps in legal procedure aim to accomplish should help business administrators to work more effectively with their legal advisers. Moreover, business law students may be needlessly distracted in their study of cases by the occasional reference to procedure if they do not have a general idea of its function.

---

[13] Thorson v. Attorney-General of Canada (No. 2) (1974), 43 D.L.R. (3d) 1; Nova Scotia Board of Censors v. MacNeil (1975), 55 D.L.R. (3d) 632; Minister of Justice of Canada v. Borowski (1981), 130 D.L.R. (3d) 588.

[14] Kazanjian, "Class Actions in Canada", (1973) 11 *OHLJ*, 397.

[15] The difficulties in maintaining a class action in such circumstances are well illustrated by the decision of the Supreme Court of Canada in Naken v. General Motors of Canada Ltd. (1983), 144 D.L.R. (3d) 385. For comment, see Fox, (1984) 6 *Supreme Court Law Review*, 335.

[16] S.O. 1992, c. 6.

Just as most primitive religions were concerned more with ritual (tribal dances, sacrifices, witchcraft) than with theology, so primitive law was concerned more with procedure (use of the right words, form of writ and oaths) than with substance. Archaic procedure dominated the common law until the early 19th century, when England was swept by a great reform movement. The culmination was the passing of the Judicature Act by Parliament in 1873, unifying the courts and wiping out the last of the old common law procedure. The 1873 Act has been adopted by the common law provinces of Canada and modified to varying degrees. Even so, the rules of procedure remain an important part of the law; a well-defined procedure is necessary to permit the courts to work efficiently. Procedure has now been simplified, and the number of steps in legal proceedings greatly reduced.

Special procedures are still used to interpret wills, contracts, and other documents and to bring certain proceedings under statutes. Generally, however, the great bulk of litigation proceeds through the courts in one form, called an action, and in those provinces that follow the English procedure most closely an *action* is begun by issuing and serving a *writ* or a *statement of claim*.[17]

Settlement out of Court

Disagreements, injuries to persons and property, and breaches of a host of laws, all giving rise to legal claims, take place daily in vast numbers, but aggrieved parties litigate only a small proportion of these *causes of action*. Even when parties start court proceedings the disputes rarely go to trial. (In the City of London, England, fewer than one per cent of legal proceedings continue to trial.) Do all the remaining aggrieved persons simply abandon their rights? On the contrary, the great majority of serious grievances are resolved by *settlement*.

Settlement is an out-of-court procedure by which one of the parties agrees to pay a sum of money or do certain things in return for a waiver by the other party of all rights arising from the grievance. This process has always been important as it is speedy and definite, and avoids the expense of litigation. A party to a settlement also avoids the risk that the court will find against him. Since there are two sides to a story, and since the issues are rarely black and white, there is always some uncertainty in predicting which side the court will favour. Of course, the stronger one party's claim appears to be, the more advantageous a settlement it will demand, and usually obtain. Often a person starts legal proceedings to convince her adversary that she will not put up with delays or an inadequate settlement. As a result, many actions are settled soon after they are started.

Why then are the courts and the relatively small body of decisions resulting from an enormous number of disputes so important? There are two main reasons: first, the decided cases supply the principles by which aggrieved parties may gauge the relative merit of their claims, predict the outcome of a possible court action, and strike a value for their claims; second, the court is the last resort, the decisive tribunal when all compromise fails. It settles the issue when the parties themselves cannot.

Despite the obvious advantages of settling disputes out of court, the number of cases going to trial has increased steadily over the years, indeed much faster than the growth in

---

17 Several provinces have now simplified the process by abolishing the writ as a means of starting an action. The process now begins with issue of a statement of claim. For a good overview, see Watson and McGowan, *Ontario Supreme and District Court Practice*, 2nd ed. Toronto: Carswells, 1993.

population. There are a number of reasons suggested for more frequent resort to the courts, such factors as the higher general level of education and greater awareness of one's rights, especially since the Charter of Rights and Freedoms became part of our Constitution, the increased complexity of society and of the legal system generally, and the need for many new regulatory schemes. The large increase in the number of cases has led to a backlog causing very long delays in actually getting most cases heard. In the 1950s, cases were generally heard within a few months; rarely did a year pass without a case going to trial. In contrast, by the 1990s, delays of several years have become the norm. Even trials for relatively small claims that take little time to be heard, often wait many months and sometimes more than a year to be heard.

Delay often creates hardship: a plaintiff who has suffered serious injury may wait many years to be compensated; it may become much more difficult for witnesses to recall evidence; indeed sometimes one of the parties may die before the case is heard. As a result, new rules have been enacted to encourage settlement.[18] The rules penalize parties who do not accept a reasonable offer of settlement. Thus, if a party rejects a reasonable offer to settle from the other party and the court's subsequent judgment shows that the offer was a good one — it orders substantially the same remedy as the offer made — the first party will be ordered to pay the "costs" incurred by the other party.

Parties have themselves become increasingly aware of the advantages of avoiding court battles and, since the 1970s, often choose to utilize *alternative dispute resolution*. The procedures of alternative dispute resolution are discussed later in this chapter.

Procedure before Trial

A decision to start an action does not end matters; a trial does not follow automatically. After a decision to sue is made and a writ or statement of claim is issued by the court, it must then be served on the defendant. The initial process informs the defendant by whom and for what he is being sued, so that he can prepare to defend himself; the plaintiff cannot proceed with the claim until the notice has been served. It is axiomatic that as soon as one is served with a writ or statement of claim one should immediately consult a lawyer. It is a long-standing aphorism that "he who acts on his own behalf has a fool for a client". Lawyers have learned that people are so mesmerized by their own cause that they cannot properly evaluate their claims; in personal matters, one lawyer almost always has another lawyer as representative.

Once a plaintiff has formally commenced an action and served the required documents on the defendant, why should they not go to trial immediately? For one thing, court trials are expensive; the time of the plaintiff and defendant, their counsel (lawyer), the judge, and other officers of the court is valuable. It would be wasteful to use time in court to do things that can be done more quickly and cheaply out of court. It is worth some preliminary effort to discover exactly what the disagreement is about; otherwise the parties waste time arguing about some things on which they agree. The procedure followed after an action is started attempts to narrow the trial precisely to those matters on which the parties are at odds. The necessary steps are as follows:

(a) If the action was started by a writ, the defendant gives notice both to the clerk of the court and to the plaintiff that he intends to contest the action by *entering an*

---

[18] Rule 57 (18), B.C. Rules of the Supreme Court; Rule 14, Rules of Civil Procedure, Ont.; Rule 49, Rules of Court, N.S.

appearance. The plaintiff then delivers a statement of claim. (In the current Ontario Procedure an action begins with a statement of claim, thus eliminating the need for the first two documents, a writ and an appearance.) In the statement of claim, the plaintiff sets out in detail the facts that she alleges have given rise to her cause of action, and the damages suffered by her. The defendant replies with a *statement of defence*, admitting those facts not in dispute in the statement of claim and denying all others, and in addition setting out any other facts that the defendant intends to prove in court in support of his defence. The plaintiff may then deliver a reply countering the added facts alleged by the defendant and adding any further facts believed necessary to cope with the defence. Often the defendant will have a claim of his own arising from the same facts. He will then counterclaim as well as defend. In turn the plaintiff will defend the counterclaim. Both claims will then be tried together.

(b) The documents are assembled to form the main body of *pleadings*. Their purpose is to make clear exactly what each party intends to prove in court so that an adequate counter-attack can be prepared if available. The Hollywood element of surprise is contrary to the principle of law that each side should have sufficient notice to put its view of the facts before the court. If a party attempts to introduce surprise evidence, the court may refuse to hear it; or if it admits the evidence, it will usually delay proceedings to give the other side an opportunity to reply, and will also penalize the party with loss of costs. Pleadings often reveal an aspect of the claim of which the other side was unaware. For example, the plaintiff may claim to have an important receipt book in her possession. The rules of procedure compel the plaintiff upon demand to surrender it to the defendant for inspection. In some circumstances a party may demand further particulars of a claim so that it can be evaluated more clearly.

(c) Some provinces provide for various forms of *"examination for discovery"*, processes allowing either party to examine the other in order to narrow the issues further and to decide whether to proceed with a trial.

Once both sides have satisfied themselves that the action should go to trial, they ask court officials to place the case on the "docket" for the next sitting of the court.

The Trial

The trial is the culmination of the action. Parties bring their evidence of all facts in dispute before the court. In non-criminal actions the *burden* is on the plaintiff to prove her case. This she must do by bringing all the evidence of favourable facts before the court. Then she must be prepared to argue that these facts, once established, prove her claim in law. (Of course, counsel for the plaintiff must decide beforehand what facts she must prove in support of the claim.) The defendant, on the other hand, must attempt to establish his own version of the facts or at least to minimize the value of the evidence submitted by the plaintiff. The gap between the versions of the two parties is often astonishing. Sometimes the defendant will argue that even if the facts are as the plaintiff claims, they do not support her claim in law. For example, suppose the defendant had swerved his car off the road at night because of oncoming lights; the defendant might then state that although his conduct was as the plaintiff claimed, such acts did not constitute negligence but on the contrary had been quite reasonable under the circumstances.

Evidence is brought before the court by the examination of witnesses. Counsel for the plaintiff calls as witnesses those persons whose testimony is favourable to her client. Counsel for the defendant may next cross-examine those witnesses to bring out any aspects of their testimony that he believes to have been neglected and that may serve his client's position. Counsel for the plaintiff may then re-examine the witnesses to clarify any points dealt with in the cross-examination. Counsel for the defendant may also call witnesses of his own. Certain types of evidence are not *admissible* because they are prejudicial without adding anything to the facts in dispute or because they are *hearsay*; that is, they are words attributed by the witness to a person not before the court. The hearsay rule stems from a prevailing view that the credibility of oral evidence cannot be properly assessed when it is second-hand, and that one who is alleged to have made an assertion should testify in person and be subject to cross-examination and the scrutiny of the court. The rules of admissibility of evidence are intended to winnow bad evidence from good. Unfortunately, in the process they have become technical, more so in the United States than in Canada.

When the court has heard all the evidence, counsel presents the arguments in law favouring their respective clients. In simple cases the judge may give the decision at once or after a short recess, but in complicated and important cases the judge will usually reserve judgment in order to have time to study his notes of the facts and legal arguments, and to compare the opinions in decided cases and textbooks. When judgment is finally handed down, it is often delivered orally in the court; important cases are invariably given in written form as well, and are reprinted in the law reports.

Appeals

If either or both parties wish to appeal, they must make up their minds and serve notice within a time limit, usually thirty days or less.

As we have seen, most appeals take the form of a review by an appeal court of evidence forwarded to it from the trial courts. An appeal court also reviews proceedings of the trial court when it is contended that the trial judge erred in instructing the jury or in admitting or excluding certain evidence; in these instances the appeal court may order the case sent back to a new trial, directing the judge to correct the shortcomings of the first trial.

Costs

Who pays for the expenses of a court action? Quite apart from the time and effort of the parties who are adversaries in the court — their time away from employment and the lost energy — a lawsuit occupies the time of highly trained and expensive judges and court officials, lawyers, and their staffs.

In an important sense, the courts provide a public service, a forum for the peaceful settlement of disputes with the aid of government supervision and enforcement. Redress through the courts is an essential alternative to parties taking matters into their own hands, with the probable risks of violence. Our governments pay the costs of sustaining the court system, including the salaries of judges, registrars, clerks, and other employees, as well as the maintenance of court buildings. Litigants pay a very small portion of these overhead costs, through charges made for specific items such as issuing a writ or registering a judgment against a losing defendant in order to enforce a claim.

Litigants themselves pay the costs of hiring their own lawyers, although, as we shall see, an important development has been the system of *legal aid*, where the government pays for many legal services provided to low income litigants. A client pays a lawyer a *solicitor-client fee* — payment for time the lawyer spends in discussing the case with the client, helping the client decide whether to pursue or defend the action, and agreeing to be retained, that is, to represent the client in negotiations to settle or in action in court. As well, there are usually various expenses associated with a court case, such as time required to prepare for trial, court charges, travel costs when the case is heard or when evidence must be obtained at another location, and the usual array of out-of-pocket costs, all of which must be paid by the litigant. These direct costs of litigation are often substantial, especially if the original hearing is followed by an appeal, and, as we shall discuss below, they play an important part in an individual's decision whether to proceed with a lawsuit.

Suppose a person is sued and defends himself successfully, with the court dismissing the action brought by the plaintiff. Should the defendant be left with all the expense of defending an action that, as it turned out, was not supported by the court? Or suppose a party demands payment for an injury wrongfully inflicted on her, but for which the other party denies any liability; the aggrieved party then sues successfully. Should she have to bear the expense of recovering through court action a sum that the other party ought to have paid without making it necessary to go to court? Under English and Canadian law there is a principle that at least part of the costs of litigation should be shifted to the losing side by an award known as *party and party costs*.[19] In each province there is a published scale of costs, varying with the level of court in which the case is heard, for the preparation of court documents by the lawyer and for standard payment for each hour of preparation for presentation of a case and for each appearance or day in court. Accordingly, when a plaintiff wins a case for, say, damages in a traffic accident, the court will award "x dollars damages, plus costs", against the defendant; if the defendant successfully defends the action, the court will dismiss the claim "with costs", that is, party and party costs against the plaintiff. If the result of the action is a mixed one — for example, a plaintiff's claim succeeds in part and is rejected in part — the costs may be apportioned, or each party may be left to pay its own costs.

A solicitor-client fee is almost always greater than an award of party and party costs. Therefore, even when a client wins a case with an award of costs in her favour, these costs will ordinarily cover only a portion of the fee charged by her lawyer, so that the client will have to pay an amount over and above the costs recovered from the losing side. But she is considerably better off than the losing side with respect to the costs of the litigation; the loser must pay *both* party and party costs to the other side *and* a solicitor-client fee to his own lawyer, as well as, of course, the amount of the judgment.

Occasionally a client may believe that his lawyer has charged too high a fee for representing him in a court action and is unable to come to a satisfactory settlement of the disagreement about the bill. If necessary, he can have the matter referred to an officer of the court to assess the bill, that is, to set a fair fee for the service rendered in the action.

In quite rare cases, where a plaintiff has proceeded with an action without any reasonable basis for the claim, a court may find that the action is "frivolous and vexatious" —

---

[19] See Watson, Bogart, and others, *Civil Litigation*, 4th ed., Chapter 4. Toronto: Emond Montgomery, 1991.

undertaken primarily to harass the defendant — and order the plaintiff to pay costs greater than normal party and party costs in order to compensate the defendant for all expenses, including lawyer's fees.

The subject of costs raises the question of the economics of litigation: is it worthwhile to start an action? First, there is always a risk of losing; a plaintiff who loses is not only denied the remedy she seeks, but also must pay costs to the defendant and a fee to her own lawyer. Even if she seems certain of winning, it would generally be unwise to begin litigating a claim that would occupy the time of the courts and incur heavy expenses in retaining a lawyer in order to collect a paltry sum, or, conversely, to fight such a claim. Second, even apart from legal costs, often it would not be worth a client's time and effort to fight. For instance, a supplier of perishable goods such as potatoes might be offered payment of a reduced price by a buyer who claims that the potatoes had not arrived in as good a condition as promised. The supply firm might decide that it is not worth the trouble to sue for the difference in price of, say, two hundred dollars; nor for that matter would it wish to alienate the buyer, a good customer. It simply accepts the reduced price as full payment. On the other hand, if the supply firm has had several similar complaints from customers and is concerned that the carrier has been careless in transporting the potatoes, it may decide to claim against the carrier. If the carrier should deny liability, the supplier would find it necessary to sue the carrier and "join" the buyer in the same suit in order to obtain a ruling from the court about the degree of care that the carrier is bound to show as well as what amounts to satisfactory condition of the potatoes on delivery. In other words, a party may have additional reasons besides the actual recovery of an award of damages for bringing an action for a relatively small sum.

Contingent Fees

In the United States, most courts do not have a general power to award costs against a losing party. A party, whether winner or loser, is required to pay only his own lawyer's fees. It is argued that prospective litigants clog the courts with large claims even when the chances of success are poor; a plaintiff who fails does not risk having to pay the defendant's costs. However, the American system of costs "fails to compensate justly the winner whose claim has been vindicated, and it discourages the litigation of small claims."[20]

Under a contingent fee arrangement, "the lawyer agrees to act on the basis that if the client is successful the lawyer will take as a fee a certain percentage of the proceeds of the litigation, and in the event that the client is unsuccessful the lawyer will make no charge for the services rendered".[21] From a prospective litigant's point of view — especially in a case where there may be a fairly poor chance of winning but where any award made is likely to be for a large sum — a contingent fee arrangement may be the only practical way of bringing an action. A lawyer may take several cases and will be content to win one; the single contingent fee will cover his expenses in all the cases and leave him with substantial compensation for his work. For example, suppose a skier is injured very seriously on an open slope and complains that the accident was caused by an unmarked obstacle. Very likely, a court would find that she accepted the risks voluntarily or that she was author of her own misfortune through personal carelessness. On the other hand, on the small

---

[20] *Ibid.*, p. 265.
[21] *Ibid.*, p. 253.

chance that the court would find the resort owner liable for the injury, the skier might well find it feasible to bring an action if she was in a jurisdiction where a contingent fee agreement was available to her. She would probably not be able to afford the expense of litigation under the traditional Anglo-Canadian scheme for charging fees.

There are concerns about contingent fee arrangements: that they encourage unnecessary and even frivolous litigation; that they expose defendants to the costs of defending themselves against unmeritorious claims; that they encourage some clients to agree to unconscionably large percentage fees demanded by their lawyers; that they drive up the cost of settlements and court awards and thus affect insurance premiums. In Canada there has been growing acceptance of contingent fee systems, subject to supervision by the courts. Only Ontario expressly prohibits their use; the Barreau du Québec states that they are not allowed in Québec, but there appears to be no express prohibition. The remaining eight provinces permit contingent fees, subject to court supervision.[22] Although no statistics are available, it is generally agreed that contingent fees are used infrequently, and the traditional method of charging fees remains the prevailing one. A factor in reducing the demand for a contingent fee system in Canada has probably been the development of legal aid services described in the next section.

Alternative Dispute Resolution

The expense and delays involved in resorting to the courts have encouraged a new approach: today, many parties to disputes agree *not* to go to court and instead to use the private procedures of *alternative dispute resolution*, known as "ADR". The oldest form of ADR is arbitration — referring a dispute to an arbitrator who will *adjudicate* the matter; the arbitrator will hear the parties, much as in a court case but with less formality and more promptly, and will deliver a decision with reasons. Normally, the parties agree in advance to be bound by the arbitrator's decision, but under some plans, a party may appeal to the courts.[23] Arbitration is also used in public sector disputes, in such areas as labour relations, worker's compensation and international commerce (as discussed an Chapter 35).

An important aspect of ADR is *mediation*. In mediation, a neutral third party acceptable to both sides acts as mediator. The mediator has no power to make a binding decision, but assists the parties in reaching a settlement. She hears both parties present their positions, identifies and clarifies the issues and suggests middle ground that might be acceptable. At some point, the mediator usually meets separately with each side to explore the prospects of agreement and then brings them together again in the hope of reaching settlement. Mediation has a good record of success, but when it fails, the parties ordinarily resort to arbitration.

The advantages of ADR are:

Speed	— cases are resolved by mediation or arbitration much more promptly than through the courts;
Cost	— promptness in itself saves money, and in addition, since the parties themselves have chosen this method, they usually cooperate to avoid delays and keep the hearing as short as they can;

---

[22] "A slice of the settlement: contingency fees across Canada", Vol. 13, No. 9, October 1986, *National*, 12. Ottawa: The Canadian Bar Foundation.

[23] John C. Carson, "Dispute Resolution, Negotiation, Mediation and Arbitration in Ontario", (1993) 10:1 Business and the Law 1.

Choice of adjudicator	— unlike the courts, the parties can choose an adjudicator who they believe is especially suited to decide the issue because of his or her experience and expertise in the area of the dispute;
Confidentiality	— the parties can agree to keep the dispute private to minimize harm to their business through disclosure of confidential information or encouraging others to bring similar complaints;
Preserving on-going relations	— since ADR is usually less adversarial than litigation, it is less likely to foster antagonism between the parties, and will allow them to continue to work together afterwards.[24]

Legal Aid

Legal services, like all other services available in our society, require time and resources and cost money. Some services such as public education and police and fire protection have long been available without fee. Since the 1960s, basic medical and hospital services have also been provided to every resident in each province of Canada. The justification for provision of these services to everyone is broad: the well-being of every person contributes to general peace and prosperity; for the sake of fairness no one should be denied the essential benefits of safety, health, and basic education as a result of financial disadvantage. Our view of what basic services ought to be available to everyone has enlarged over the years, especially in times of prosperity when increasing productivity has created sufficient additional wealth for us to be able to afford more public services.

In the late 1960s, after our national health care system was well established, attention turned to legal services. Traditionally they had been available almost exclusively to those who could afford to pay, that is, to business and professional people. Low income earners could not afford legal services; what services they did receive were usually in the form of charity from lawyers who were willing to provide assistance free of charge to persons in dire circumstances. Ontario began a large-scale, publicly funded legal aid scheme in 1967, and most other provinces followed suit within a few years.

There are two different and, in some senses, competing models of legal aid, both used extensively in Canada. The Ontario model — sometimes known as the *judicare* model — has been adopted by several other provinces as the dominant method of delivering legal services. It has been described as follows:

> The purpose . . . is to ensure that, generally speaking, no person should be disqualified by lack of financial resources from having a lawyer represent him in either civil or criminal proceedings. Under the provisions of the Act, lawyers who have agreed to serve "legal aid clients" permit their name to appear on a panel in their county. A person qualifying for legal aid may select as his lawyer any lawyer whose name is on the panel. Qualification is predicated essentially upon two factors — lack of ability to pay for a lawyer and the nature of the case . . . The "legal aid lawyer" is guaranteed the payment of his fees and disbursements by the Provincial Government. The lawyer will be paid all of his proper disbursements but only 75 percent of his fees. The fees are calculated according to the tariffs contained in schedules . . . passed under the authority of The Legal Aid Act. The fees contained in the tariff are

---

[24] For a general overview, see, D. Paul Emond, *Commercial Dispute Resolution: Alternatives to Litigation.* Aurora, Ontario, Canada Law Book, 1989.

designed to represent average fees. The tariffs are strictly enforced by the Legal Accounts Officer who taxes every bill prior to its payment.[25]

The second model — known as the *community legal services* or *legal clinic* model — is well illustrated by the Saskatchewan scheme, described below:

> The Community Legal Services (Saskatchewan) Act, 1974 provides that legal services are to be delivered primarily by community law offices employing full-time staff lawyers. Area boards are to be incorporated to provide the services of the plan. Twelve boards have been elected from residents of the area who join the area legal aid society and each board has opened a community law office. Each board is empowered to advise the area staff on the legal need of the area residents, to establish committees to review financial refusals of eligibility, to negotiate area contracts with the provincial director, to establish information and counselling programmes, and to advertise the provision of legal services.[26]

Both models had their strident supporters in the first years of experimentation. Judicare and legal clinics were considered mutually incompatible: a province was thought capable of opting for only one or the other. Critics of the judicare model claimed it delivered only a watered-down version of middle class legal services, and did nothing to alleviate the social problems behind the legal problems of the poor. Critics of the clinical model feared, on the one hand, too much activism by clinics tackling political and social problems to the detriment of individual clients' specific needs for relief, or on the other hand, fear of governmental interference in individual clients' affairs. Each side claimed that the other had higher costs per case and was therefore less justifiable in economic terms. This latter debate still continues, but the earlier contest has much diminished. It is now generally recognized that both systems have some strengths and some weaknesses. Provinces committed to one system — Ontario in particular — experiment extensively with the other. As a result, we now have great diversity and continuing experimentation across the country. Alberta, New Brunswick, Newfoundland, and Ontario have predominantly judicare plans; Nova Scotia, Prince Edward Island, and Saskatchewan use community legal centres; while British Columbia, Manitoba, and Québec have mixed schemes utilizing both systems.[27]

Just as in health care, there is bound to be continuing development of delivery systems and changes in criteria for the availability of services, possibly going beyond that for the very poor. It is interesting to note that while modern legal aid plans had their origin in the United States of the early 1960s, Canada now appears to have gone much further; per capita expenditures on legal aid in Canada are between two and three times those in the United States.[28]

THE LEGAL PROFESSION

In England the legal profession is divided into two groups, solicitors and barristers. Solicitors are "office" lawyers. They spend almost all their time interviewing clients and

---

[25] Watson and Williams, *Canadian Civil Procedure*, 2nd ed., p. 2-70. Toronto: Butterworths, 1977.
[26] Zemans, "Legal Aid and Legal Advice in Canada", (1978) 16 *Osgoode Hall Law Journal*, 633.
[27] *Ibid.*, p. 666.
[28] *Ibid.*, p. 664.

carrying on the legal aspects of business and family affairs. They look after the drafting of wills, deeds, and contracts, the incorporation of companies, arrangements for adoption of children, and other domestic documents. They also prepare cases for trial, draft pleadings, interview witnesses, and make extensive notes for trial. In addition, they argue cases in some of the lower courts. Barristers take *briefs*, that is, cases handed to them by solicitors, to be presented in court. They also give opinions with respect to potential litigation and are consulted by solicitors on a wide variety of more complex legal issues such as corporate mergers and tax planning. They are a much smaller group and have their offices mainly in London around the central law courts.

In Canada, from very early times, lawyers became both barristers and solicitors. In the common law provinces, lawyers are qualified to carry out the duties of both professions and often do so, especially in smaller cities and towns. In larger cities, lawyers tend to specialize and to be either "office" lawyers or "litigation" lawyers. Under the civil law of Québec the profession is divided in approximately the same way as in England. Québec has *notaries* (solicitors) and *advocates* (barristers). In the United States the distinction has broken down completely. A lawyer is not called "barrister and solicitor" as in Canada, but is simply an *attorney*.

The legal profession is organized on a provincial basis in Canada. Each province has its own "bar" (barristers' society), and by provincial statute one must qualify as a member in order to practise law. Membership in one provincial bar does not permit a lawyer to practise in another province. A member in one province must meet the standards and pay the fees of the provincial bar in another province before practising in that province. A member of any provincial bar, however, may appear before the Supreme Court of Canada.

Questions for Review

1. What factors may discourage a litigant from appealing to a higher court?
2. What are the restrictions on appeals to the Supreme Court of Canada?
3. How does the operation of an appeal court differ from that of a trial court?
4. Why has subordinate legislation come to prominence?
5. What are the chief differences between the systems of courts in the United States and in Canada?
6. What are the advantages of a settlement over a court trial?
7. Motion pictures and television programs are responsible for a misconception about the way in which trials proceed. Explain.
8. What court procedures are designed to make the evidence received as reliable as possible?
9. Define appellant; respondent; counterclaim; counsel; bench; writ; settlement; pleadings; assizes; party and party costs.
10. Explain how a legal rule in one province may differ from that in another province.
11. How does a judge decide a case when there is no precedent available in earlier decisions?
12. A student is assigned a hypothetical case with a requirement that she offer an opinion about what the court's decision would be. She discovers that many of the facts are similar to those in an actual case reported in the law reports of thirty years ago. Is it sufficient for her to rely on the judge's opinion in the reported case?

13. One of the major purposes of private law is to settle disputes between businesses. How can the settlement of a particular private dispute make a contribution to the business community as a whole?

14. "Under a system of *stare decisis,* in which a court has frequently to say, 'Whatever the anachronism or inconvenience, we must abide by the established rule', it is extremely difficult for changing social needs to be met promptly and systematically." (Allen, *Law in the Making,* p. 352.)
    (a) Develop briefly the meaning of this quotation in your own words and explain the rationale or logic underlying the doctrine of *stare decisis.*
    (b) Explain how the courts have managed to apply this doctrine to permit some adaptation to changing social conditions.
    (c) Do the courts ever abandon the doctrine?

15. "I was never ruined but twice; once when I won a lawsuit and once when I lost one." How can a successful litigant lose?

16. Would you expect the Anglo-Canadian system of awarding costs to encourage or discourage litigation? Why?

PART TWO

TORTS

Most of this book is devoted to business arrangements, entered into by parties on a voluntary basis. Nevertheless, there are important aspects of the law that impose obligations on us without our agreement. For example, government regulation comprises an important area where duties are imposed; it will be discussed in appropriate chapters throughout this book.

In this part we discuss the law of torts: a manufacturer's goods may be defective and injure a consumer; a newspaper may publish a story that libels someone; a driver delivering goods may carelessly injure a pedestrian; an accountant's negligent audit of a business may be relied on and cause loss to an investor. In these and other situations, the party harmed may successfully claim a remedy against the wrongdoer. A business may itself suffer injury, for example, by a fire carelessly started on adjoining premises that spreads and damages its property, or because it receives negligent advice from its lawyer. All of these situations raise important issues of liability that are determined under principles of the law of torts.

In Chapter 4, we consider the essential characteristics of tort law that place a duty on everyone to take care and refrain from harming others by their actions. We shall concentrate on the most important tort — negligence, and shall also examine more briefly other torts — nuisance and "economic torts", and others that contain an element of deliberate conduct, such as defamation, deceit, assault and false imprisonment.

In our complex society there is a constant and increasing need for specialized knowledge about highly sophisticated activities, from engineering and medicine to navigation and valuation of assets. Those without a needed special skill have come to rely on "professionals"; it is accepted that in general it is reasonable to rely on them. Accordingly, those who hold themselves out as being qualified to perform these tasks are held to higher standards of care and skill than are the general public. Chapter 5 discusses the problems of professional liability.

The law of torts is a very broad subject and has an impact upon many aspects of everyday life. The aim of the following two chapters is to concentrate upon those aspects of tort law that most directly affect the carrying on of a business. In particular, a businessperson needs to be aware of the potential risks, and accompanying legal liability, associated with his or her activities as well as the remedies available when actions of others harm the interests of the business.

CHAPTER 4

THE LAW OF TORTS

Scope of Tort Law

The role of the law of torts is to compensate victims for harm suffered from the activities of others. Punishment is left to the criminal law when the particular conduct happens also to amount to a crime. For example, when a drunken driver collides with a parked vehicle, its owner may sue him in tort and the state may charge him with drunken driving.

The problem for tort law is to identify those actions that create a right to compensation. While the leading writers in the field cannot agree upon an entirely satisfactory definition of "tort", they have no difficulty in agreeing upon a lengthy list of torts. As our society becomes more complex the list of torts becomes longer and their importance increases.[1]

The basic issue for society, when dealing with such important causes of harm as automobile accidents, industrial accidents, and pollution is to determine who should bear the loss — the victim, the person whose act caused the harm, the group that benefits most directly by a common activity, such as all motor vehicle owners, or an even larger group such as taxpayers generally. Tort law is one important instrument for apportioning loss, along with such others as insurance and government compensation schemes.

Development of the Tort Concept

In the early stages of development, societies usually have very simple rules of liability for injurious conduct: anyone who causes direct injury to another has to pay compensation. No inquiry is made into the reasons for the injury or whether the conduct of the injurer is justified. Such liability for injury is called *strict liability*. There are records dating from the earliest times of the amount of compensation payable, according to the kind of injury and, sometimes, the importance of the injured party.

Gradually, the idea developed that a person ought not to be responsible for harm caused to another if he or she acted without *fault*.

ILLUSTRATION

A was driving his wagon down a road when a sudden clap of thunder caused the horses to bolt. *A* was unable to hold them back and the wagon ran down *B*, a passerby.

The old strict law, which would have held *A* liable for *B*'s injuries, was later modified to excuse *A* from liability in these circumstances. Both parties were equally innocent, so the loss was left to lie where it had fallen — upon the unfortunate victim, *B*.

---

[1] For a fuller discussion of the purposes of tort law, see especially Fleming, *The Law of Torts* (8th ed.), Sydney: Law Book Company, 1992. See also Linden, *Canadian Tort Law* (5th ed.), Toronto: Butterworths, 1993.

In addition, the courts began to consider the way in which the harm had arisen. At first, as we have noted, only direct injuries were recognized by the courts — running down another person or striking a blow. Gradually the courts began to recognize indirect or consequential injuries.

→ A is wrong
B got to recover damages.

ILLUSTRATION

A carelessly drops a log in the road , and does not bother to remove it although it is near sunset. After dark, *B*'s horse trips over the log and is seriously injured.

In early law, *B* would have been without a remedy. Eventually, however, the courts recognized that *A*'s act was as much responsible for the injury to *B*'s horse as if *A* had struck the horse by throwing the log at it. They allowed *B* to recover damages.[2] We can see then that early tort law changed in two ways: the law took into account the *fault* of the defendant; it also took into account *causation* — whether the defendant's conduct could be considered the cause of the harm. Both these developments present difficult problems, and continue to be energetically debated. We shall examine them more closely.

BASIS FOR LIABILITY

Fault

Fault, in the setting of tort law, refers to blameworthy or culpable conduct — conduct which in the eyes of the law is unjustifiable because it intentionally or carelessly disregards the interests of others. There is by no means universal agreement that fault is a sound basis for liability in all of tort law. As we noted at the beginning of this chapter, there is a general problem concerning the distribution of loss caused as a consequence of such activities as the operation of automobiles. Statistically, we know that each year there will be thousands of victims of car accidents. Should the victim or the victim's family have to bear the financial loss, or should it be borne by the driver or owner of the vehicle responsible for the accident? And should the right to compensation depend on the victim's ability to prove that some other person was at fault?

One justification for basing liability upon fault is a belief in its deterrent effect: people will be more inclined to be careful if they are made to bear the consequences of their carelessness. There is little hard evidence to support this theory, although it may be reasonable to suppose that large, highly publicized awards of damages have had an effect upon the standards and practices of manufacturers, surgeons, and similar persons affected by these awards. But the modern reality is that many of the activities where tort liability arises— driving a car, operating a factory or store, practising medicine — are covered by insurance. Carelessness is more likely to be deterred by the prospect of criminal penalties (for example, for dangerous driving) and of increased insurance premiums than by the possibility of being sued in tort.

---

[2] This example was discussed by Fortesque, J. in Reynolds v. Clarke (1726), 93 E.R. 747, and has been cited many times since by both the courts and leading writers as a classic statement of the law.

The defects of a compensation system based on fault are well known.[3] Accident victims who are unable to establish fault on the part of some other person go uncompensated and the costs and delays of litigation deter many other claims. These defects have led to suggestions that compensation should be provided in other ways. The most radical proposals would eliminate law suits for all personal injuries and compensate victims through a government scheme.[4] A step in that direction has been taken in Canada with the virtual elimination of fault as a basis for automobile accident claims, through a system of compulsory *no fault* insurance.[5] Another example of an alternative to the tort approach is found in the scheme governing workers' compensation in Canada.[6] Under this scheme, industrial accidents are seen as the inevitable price of doing business. Employers must contribute to a fund that is in turn used to compensate workers injured in industrial accidents, even when the employer is blameless and the injury is the result of the employee's own carelessness.

Strict Liability

Modern reforms tend to spread the burden of compensation widely, over society as a whole through government schemes, or over identifiable groups such as employers or automobile owners through compulsory insurance schemes. As already noted, early tort law took a narrow approach, imposing the burden of compensation upon the person regarded as having caused the injury regardless of whether he or she was at fault. This type of *strict liability* persists in some areas of modern tort law. A person who collects potentially dangerous things on his land, from which they subsequently escape, is liable for any resulting damage even if he was blameless in his care of them.[7]

ILLUSTRATION

A landowner stored water in a large cistern on his property. The cistern was accidentally punctured by a visitor's truck; the water flooded and damaged a neighbour's building.

The owner of the cistern is liable to compensate the neighbour. The risk of such damage is a burden the landowner must bear as the price for storing water on his land. (The truck driver may also be liable for the damage if he was at fault.)

Social Policy

Between comprehensive "no-fault" schemes, on the one hand, and strict liability on the other, there are many circumstances where liability based on fault is the fairest principle; in most areas of tort law, liability remains firmly on that basis. Whether liability should be based on fault or on other principles is an important question of policy, constantly changing as our social standards change. These social standards force the law to adapt in many ways, ranging

---

[3] For an interesting study, see Dewees and Trebilcock, "The Efficacy of the Tort System and its Alternatives: a Review of the Empirical Evidence", (1992) 30 *OHLJ* 57.
[4] A well known example of such a scheme is that introduced in New Zealand in 1974: see Ison, *Accident Compensation: A Commentary on the New Zealand Scheme*. London: Croom Helm, 1980.
[5] See Automobile Insurance, in Chapter 20, "Insurance and Guarantee".
[6] See Workers' Compensation, in Chapter 23, "The Contract of Employment".
[7] Rylands v. Fletcher (1868) L.R. 3 H.L. 330; Heintzman & Co. Ltd. v. Hashman Construction Ltd. (1973) 32 D.L.R. (3d) 622.

from direct legislative intervention, as in workers' compensation statutes, to more subtle influences on judge and jury in determining liability and the amounts of damages awarded.

Vicarious Liability

One area in which the law has responded pragmatically to the pressure of social needs is with respect to torts committed by employees in the course of their employment. An employer may be personally at fault for an act committed by an employee. For example, she may knowingly assign an employee to perform a dangerous task for which the employee is not trained. In such a case it is the employer personally who is at fault, and it may be that there is no fault on the part of the employee.[8]

But should an employer be liable when it is the employee alone who is at fault? Nineteenth century courts evolved a basis for making the employer liable for harm caused by the tortious acts of an employee when the acts arise in the course of employment. The employer is liable even when she has given strict instructions to take proper care or not to do the act that causes the damage. There are two main justifications. First, although an employee is personally liable for the torts he commits while acting for himself or his employer, employees generally have limited assets available to pay compensation for the potential harm they can cause — an engineer who operates a locomotive negligently may injure hundreds of passengers. Second, there is a strong argument based on fairness: the person who makes the profit should also be liable for the loss. Accordingly, the courts have developed the principle of *vicarious liability*, whereby an employer is liable to compensate persons for harm caused by an employee in the course of employment. The employee remains personally liable for his own torts, but the best chance for recovery usually lies against the employer.

A consequence of the development of vicarious liability has been that employers ordinarily insure themselves against such losses and take into account the cost of the insurance in pricing their products. We shall discuss an employer's liability further in Chapter 23.

NEGLIGENCE

Elements of an Action

By far the most important tort, and the one that best exemplifies the fault theory of liability, is negligence. The concept of negligence is quite simple: anyone who carelessly causes injury to another should compensate the victim for that injury. As it has developed in the courts, negligence has become a complex and sophisticated body of law, encompassing a wide variety of situations.

In establishing the right to recover compensation, a plaintiff must prove three things to the court's satisfaction:

(a) that in carrying on a particular activity the defendant owed the plaintiff a duty of care,

(b) that the defendant broke that duty by acting as he did, and

(c) that the defendant's conduct *caused* the injury.

---

8   See Edgeworth Construction Ltd. v. N.D. Lea & Associates Ltd. (1993) 107 D.L.R.(4th) 169.

All three requirements may create major difficulties for the plaintiff; lawyers debate all of them with great energy. The first element requires a policy decision or value judgment by the court — is the conduct complained of such that it *ought* to create a duty? The second question is a mixed question of policy and fact — did the defendant's conduct actually go so far as to amount to a breach of that duty? The third question is one not only of fact but also of philosophy.

Duty of Care

In order to establish liability in negligence a plaintiff must establish a duty owed by the defendant to refrain from the injurious conduct in question. In early tort law, it was enough simply to establish that a person had physically caused harm to another; if so he would be found liable. The question of his moral responsibility did not arise. As soon as we introduce the idea of fault, however, we must establish criteria for proving fault. The principal criterion is that an alleged wrongdoer, whom we shall here call A, should have realized his actions would do harm. Another way of putting it is to ask, "Should A have foreseen that his actions would cause harm?" or, since A cannot be expected to anticipate all the possible consequences of his action, "Would a normally intelligent and alert person — a reasonable person — have foreseen that A's conduct would likely cause harm?" But the plaintiff must go further: he must establish that the defendant owed a duty of care *to him*. As a general rule, the duty will arise only where the defendant could reasonably have foreseen a risk of harm to the plaintiff or to someone in the plaintiff's position.

ILLUSTRATION

A courier company that delivered packages for the Province of British Columbia undertook to deliver an envelope to a land registry office in Prince George. Unknown to the courier company, the envelope contained a document relating to land owned by the plaintiff. If delivered on time, the document would have enabled the plaintiff to sell its land. The courier company was unreasonably slow and delivered the document too late; as a result the plaintiff was unable to perform the contract of sale, and it suffered a loss of $77 000.

The Supreme Court of Canada held that the courier company was not liable to the plaintiff. It owed no duty of care to the plaintiff since it could not reasonably have foreseen that the delay would cause a loss to some third person, outside its relationship with its client, the Province.[9] Nevertheless, the courts have sometimes held that a duty of care is owed to persons other than the individual who is directly injured. For example, a negligent driver has been held to be liable to a parent who suffered severe nervous shock when she saw her own child, who was standing nearby, run down and killed.[10]

In recent years more and more duties have been imposed by statute, especially upon the operators of businesses - as we shall see further, in Chapter 32. In addition to statutory

---

9   B.D.C. Ltd. v. Hofstrand Farms Ltd. (1986), 26 D.L.R. (4th) 1.
10   Hinz v. Berry [1970] 1 All E.R. 1074.

penalties, breach of these duties may give rise to liability in tort to persons who are injured as a result. The courts have also shown increasing willingness to hold public bodies liable for the negligent performance of their statutory duties. Municipalities have been held liable to homeowners for issuing building permits for defective designs or for not carrying out proper inspections of construction works.[11] It now seems that a public body may be liable even where the statute imposes no duty but merely confers a discretionary power on it — for example, to maintain a highway — if it is negligent in the exercise of that power.[12]

Standard of Care

The law places a general duty on every person to conduct all activities taking *reasonable care* to avoid foreseeable injury to other persons and their property. It does not follow, however, that because harm may be foreseeable a particular activity must not be pursued at all; rather there is a duty in pursuing that activity to take reasonable care to avoid that harm. What then, constitutes a reasonable standard of care? It is often said that the standard demanded is that of the ordinary reasonable person, or "the person on the Yonge Street subway".[13] However, the standard necessarily varies according to the activity in question: the standard expected of a brain surgeon is that of a competent brain surgeon rather than the person in the subway.

In addition, the court must balance competing interests: on the one hand the court considers the degree of likelihood that harm will result and the potential severity of the harm, and on the other the social utility of the activity in question as well as the feasibility of eliminating the risk. It may be permissible not to take every possible precaution where the risk of serious damage or injury is very small, but where there is danger of a major catastrophe it would be unreasonable not to take every known precaution.

Increasingly, legislation not only imposes duties but also sets out the appropriate standard of care for particular activities. For example, safety standards for motor vehicles are prescribed by statute and such standards are frequently a good indication of where a court will set the negligence threshold. But it must be remembered that the tort of negligence is based on fault and the fact that a person may be guilty of breach of a statutory standard does not of itself make him civilly liable to a person injured as a result of the breach — at least if he can show that the offence occurred without fault on his part.[14]

Causation

For an action in negligence to succeed it is necessary for the plaintiff to show not only that a duty of care was owed to her and has been breached, but also that she has been injured as a result of that breach; that is to say; the breach of duty is the *cause* of the injury. Legal cause is a subtle subject about which whole volumes have been written.[15] The most extreme view of the theory of causation can link one act to every other act in the world.

---

[11] City of Kamploops v. Neilsen (1984), 10 D.L.R. (4th) 461; Rothfield v. Manolakos (1990), 63 D.L.R. (4th) 44.

[12] Just v. British Columbia (1990), 64 D.L.R.(4th) 445.

[13] Linden, *Canadian Tort Law, supra*, note 1, at p. 118.

[14] Sterling Trusts Corp. v. Postma and Little, [1965] S.C.R. 324; Regina v. Saskatchewan Wheat Pool, [1983] 1 S.C.R. 205.

[15] See, especially, Hart and Honore, *Causation in the Law* (2d.ed.), Oxford: Oxford University Press, 1985. For an interesting Canadian case, see Nova Mink Ltd. v. Trans-Canada Airlines [1951] 2 D.L.R. 241.

ILLUSTRATION

A breaks a china plate from a dinner set. The following day, his wife makes a special trip by car to a shopping centre to replace the plate. On the way she has a collision.

It could be argued that *A*'s carelessness in dropping the dinner plate the previous evening "caused" the accident. Had he not dropped the plate, there might not have been a collision. Yet in the eyes of the law *A* clearly did not "cause" the accident. In the first place, many intervening voluntary acts occurred to bring Mrs. *A* and the driver of the other car to the same place at the same time. Mrs. *A* might have chosen to go at another time, as might the other driver. The interposition of these voluntary acts removes any legal blame from *A*. Second, the accident might have occurred because Mrs. *A* or the other driver or both of them made mistakes in judgment. Had they driven carefully, no accident would have taken place.

For the most part the courts have avoided philosophical discussion and have adopted a common-sense approach. On the one hand it is clear that, no matter how blameworthy a person's conduct may have been, he will not be held liable for damage that he did not cause. In a famous case, a passenger in a small boat accidentally fell overboard into ice-cold water. The boat's operator was under a duty to try to rescue him but, although negligent in the attempt, was held not liable because even if he had used proper rescue procedures, the passenger would have been dead before he could have been reached.[16] Moreover, a person will not be held liable for consequences of his acts that are considered to be too remote. Generally speaking, the closer in time the inflicting of an injury is to a person's careless conduct, the less chance there is of significant intervening acts happening that would absolve the defendant, and the more likely the defendant is to be found the "cause" of the injury.[17]

Courts in the 19th century devoted much effort to identify the "proximate cause" of injury, and developed the *last opportunity* or *last clear chance* principle. The principle was based on the notion that, where an accident could be said to have been caused by two or more persons, the one who had the last chance to avoid the accident should be held entirely responsible. The principle depended on narrow distinctions that could result in injustice and has been largely discarded by modern courts. Thus, two or more persons who have quite separately contributed to an accident may be held liable: for example, an innkeeper allowed a customer to drink too much and then turned him out to walk home along a country road, where he was hit by a careless motorist; both the innkeeper and motorist were held to have contributed to the accident.[18] Nevertheless, in discussing the physical closeness or *proximity* of a particular act to a subsequent injury, we must eventually decide, as a matter of policy, at what point we cut off the process and pronounce that the actor is or is not responsible. The practical necessity of drawing reasonable limits for liability means that a court must decide to break the chain of causation at some point. In choosing that point, the court makes a social judgment.

---

[16]   Matthews v. MacLaren [1969] O.R. 137, affirmed sub. nom. Horsley v. MacLaren [1972] S.C.R. 441.
[17]   See, for example, Beecham v. Hughes (1988), 27 B.C.L.R. (2d) 1.
[18]   Menow v. Honsberger and Jordan House Ltd. [1974] S.C.R. 239.

Remoteness of Damage

Foreseeability is a major element, as we have seen, both in establishing whether or not a duty of care exists and in determining what is the appropriate standard of care. It reappears yet again when the question of the extent of liability for negligence is considered.

ILLUSTRATION

A carelessly throws a lit cigarette into a trash can. An explosion follows, causing serious injury to bystanders and damage to nearby property. A bottle of gasoline had been put into the receptacle earlier by an unknown person.

A has acted carelessly, has done something which he should have foreseen might cause damage or injury, and the actual damage is a direct consequence of his act, even though its nature and magnitude might have been wholly unforeseeable. Should A be held liable for all the consequences of his negligence? Until the 1960s the answer would seem to have been "yes".[19] In the "Wagon Mound" case,[20] the Privy Council attempted to restrict liability to those consequences which were reasonably foreseeable, so that the answer would then seem to have been "no". However, subsequent decisions in Canada and Britain have, by taking a broad view of what is foreseeable, largely restored the earlier position.[21] It is a well established principle that, when one person injures another, he "must take his victim as he finds him". He is fully liable even though the victim suffers a far more serious injury than might have been expected, perhaps because the victim had a pre-existing disability, allergy or an "egg-shell skull". Nor is this principle confined to cases of personal injury: when a teenager negligently started his father's snowmobile, with the result that it escaped from his control, sped across a school yard and collided with a gaspipe just outside the school, causing gas to escape into the school and explode, he was held liable for all damage. The damage was considered to be of a general type that might have been foreseen even if the extent of the damage was not.[22]

Economic Loss

As we noted at the opening of this chapter, the object of tort law is to compensate for loss suffered as a consequence of the wrongful act of another and, as we shall see, the remedy given in cases of negligence is a sum of money by way of *damages*. A plaintiff injured in an automobile collision may be compensated not only for his physical injuries and for the cost of repairing his car, but also for *economic loss*, wages lost due to an enforced absence from work, and the cost of renting a replacement car. But until quite recently the courts were unwilling to compensate for "pure" economic loss; that is, where there was no physical injury or damage to a plaintiff's person or property. However, that situation has changed dramatically over the past thirty years or so.[23]

---

19   Re Polemis [1921] 3 K.B. 560. See also: Cotic v. Gray [1981] 33 O.R. (2d) 356.

20   Overseas Tankship (U.K.) Ltd. v. Morts Dock & Engineering Co. (The Wagon Mound) [1961] A.C. 388; Overseas Tankship (U.K.) Ltd. v. Miller Steamship Co. Pty. Ltd. (The Wagon Mound No. 2) [1966] 2 All E.R. 709; MacMillan Bloedel (Alberni) Ltd. *et al.* v. British Columbia Hydro and Power Authority *et al.* (1973) 33 D.L.R. (3d) 538.

21   Hughes v. Lord Advocate [1963] A.C. 837; Regina v. Coté (1974) 51 D.L.R.(3d) 244 (S.C.C.).

22   Hoffer v. School Division of Assiniboine South [1973] W.W.R. 765 (S.C.C.). The father and the gas company that installed the pipe were also held liable.

23   For a survey, see Mactavish, "Tort Recovery for Economic Loss: Recent Developments", (1992/93) 21 C.B.L.J. 395.

Two types of case may be distinguished. In the first type, economic loss is caused without there being any physical damage at all. A classic example is the leading case of *Hedley Byrne v. Heller and Partners*,[24] in which the House of Lords established that financial loss suffered as a result of a negligent misstatement may be recovered. This subject is discussed further in Chapter 5.

In the second type there is physical damage, but not to the person or property of the plaintiff.

ILLUSTRATION

B negligently operated a tugboat and it collided with a railway bridge owned by *C*. The bridge was closed for several weeks for repairs. As a result, the railway company which was the principal user of the bridge suffered a substantial loss of profit because it had to re-route traffic.

The Supreme Court of Canada held that the railway company could recover its loss.[25] However, the decision was a narrow one: it turned in part on the close relationship that existed between the owner of the bridge and the railway company. Thus, while it is established that there *may* be recovery for pure economic loss in some situations, it is still far from clear when the courts will hold that a duty was owed to the plaintiff, or that the particular damage was not too remote.

Burden of Proof

Like plaintiffs in other actions, a plaintiff in a tort action must prove her case; in certain kinds of cases, however, she is in a peculiarly difficult position. A pedestrian knocked down by a car or a consumer poisoned by a dangerous substance in a jar of food may be unable to ascertain exactly how the defendant driver's or manufacturer's conduct contributed to her injury. For example, the car might suddenly have swerved out of control because of some hidden mechanical defect, or the poisonous substance might have been deliberately inserted into the jar after it had left the manufacturer.

The law takes these difficulties of proof into account. The injured party need only establish that the defendant's car or product physically caused the injury. The burden is then cast upon the defendant to exculpate himself. He is presumed to have been in breach of a duty owed to the plaintiff and also to be in possession of any information that might show him to be innocent of any breach. Once the burden has been shifted to him he will be found liable, unless he adduces the necessary evidence to satisfy the court that on balance he was not in breach of a duty to the plaintiff. This principle is commonly known as *res ipsa loquitur*, and may be translated as "the facts speak for themselves". It appears to have first emerged in a 19th century English case[26] in which the plaintiff, while standing in a street, was struck by a barrel of flour falling from the defendant's upper window. The not unreasonable conclusion was that, unless the defendant could prove otherwise, the most likely cause was the negligent conduct of the defendant or one of his employees.

---

[24] [1964] A.C.465.
[25] Canadian National Railway Co. v. Norsk Pacific Steamship Co. (1992) 91 D.L.R . (4th) 289. Contrast the earlier decision of that court in Rivtow Marine Ltd. v. Washington Iron Works (1973) 40 D.L.R. (3d) 530.
[26] Byrne v. Boadle (1863) 159 E.R. 294.

The Plaintiff's Own Conduct

Although the principles of liability for negligence are much younger than many other areas of tort law, they are old enough to have acquired certain rigid and undesirable features that have required statutory reform. Early in the development of the principles of negligence, the courts recognized that even if the defendant has been negligent, the plaintiff might properly be regarded as the author of his own misfortune. This defence seems reasonable enough: for example, if the defendant carelessly parks his vehicle in a dangerous place where it is hit by the plaintiff, but the defendant shows that the plaintiff could easily have avoided the collision had he been driving with a minimum of care, then it may not be unreasonable to excuse the defendant from liability.[27] However, the courts at first took a rather narrow and mechanical approach to the subject. If the defendant could establish even a small measure of blame on the part of the plaintiff, indicating that the plaintiff contributed in some measure to her own loss, the plaintiff would fail even if the defendant was mainly at fault.

In the 19th century, the courts attempted to ease the harshness of the *contributory negligence* rule by permitting the plaintiff to recover if, despite the plaintiff's negligence, the defendant nevertheless had the last opportunity or last clear chance to avoid the injury. This principle could itself be unjust in its application and, being based on a chain-of-events theory, it could not realistically be applied to "instantaneous" accidents such as most highway mishaps.

The way out of these difficulties was established by statutory reforms pioneered in Canada.[28] These statutes, known as *comparative negligence* or *apportionment of loss* legislation, required courts to apportion damages according to the respective degree of responsibility of the parties. The statutes do not set out in detail the basis for making the apportionment, but leave it to be decided by judges and juries according to their opinion of what is fair in the circumstances. And by applying an appropriate standard of care to the plaintiff as well as to the defendant, the courts have been able to give expression to changing standards within our society. For example, courts now commonly find that a person injured in a motor vehicle accident has contributed to some extent to her own injuries by failure to wear a seat belt.

A further problem arises when the victim is wholly blameless in the accident itself but her own *subsequent* conduct contributes to the *extent* of her original injuries. In some of these cases, the courts have decided that part of the damages were due to the plaintiff's unreasonable conduct and were therefore not recoverable — for example, in cases where a plaintiff refused to undergo safe and simple surgery and thus aggravated her condition.[29] This result may be justified either as a form of contributory negligence or on the ground that a plaintiff is expected to act reasonably to minimize any damage suffered. This ground is discussed further in Chapter 17.

The Relevance of Insurance

As mentioned earlier in this Chapter, the modern reality is that in many tort cases the actual loss will fall on an insurance company. Thus, in the case of automobile collisions,

---

[27]   Boulay v. Rousselle (1984-85) 30 C.C.L.T. 149 (N.B.). See also Wade v. C.N.R. [1978] 1 S.C.R. 1064.
[28]   Ontario passed the first statute in the field: Negligence Act, S.O. 1924, c. 32.
[29]   See Janiak v. Ippolito (1985) 31 C.C.L.T. 113.

both plaintiff and defendant are ordinarily insured against the loss that occurs. Suppose that A decides not to contract for collision insurance on her automobile and it is damaged in an accident caused by the negligence of another driver, B. Since A is expected to mitigate her loss, should it follow that she has contributed to the loss by failing to take out insurance against the risk? Can B successfully defend an action by A for negligence on the grounds that A might have avoided her loss with adequate insurance coverage? The answer is no. Courts do not admit evidence about the existence or amount of insurance coverage in negligence actions because their decisions must be based strictly on the merits of the dispute being tried, and be free from any suspicion that their judgment has been biased by a knowledge of the amount of insurance protection that the plaintiff has voluntarily chosen to purchase. Hence in our example the failure of the plaintiff to have insured her car against damage by collision would not be admitted as evidence and thus would not affect the amount of damages the plaintiff might recover.

Suppose, however, that in our example A had contracted for collision insurance. We need not worry that A will be compensated twice, once by her insurance company and again by the defendant. Ordinarily, when an insured party recovers first from her insurance company, the policy transfers to the company the injured party's right to pursue the claim against the wrongdoer. The insurance company "stands in the insured person's shoes"; that is, it becomes *subrogated* to the insured party's rights and may itself sue the defendant and collect. If in our example A recovers her loss, or part of it, by suing B, then to that extent she cannot recover from her own insurance company. In this respect, insurance provides protection to the extent that A cannot recover from B either because A is herself in part to blame or because B has insufficient assets to pay the claim.

SPECIAL ASPECTS OF NEGLIGENCE

Hazardous Activities

An assumption made in every case of negligence is that the injury sustained by the plaintiff would not have happened if the defendant had exercised reasonable care. However, some activities are inherently dangerous regardless of the care taken — for example, transporting high explosives. A strong argument may be made that in these circumstances, a person carrying on an inherently dangerous activity should be strictly liable for damage, regardless of fault. In other words, a person so engaged should charge for his services according to the degree of hazard, and should carry insurance to compensate for harm done to others. There is no reason why an innocent victim should suffer a loss caused by a dangerous activity carried on by another person for his own benefit. Although some United States courts have reached this conclusion, Canadian courts, in common with most other jurisdictions, still apply the principles of negligence. However, they have raised the standard of care proportionally as the danger increases. As a result, in many cases of hazardous activities the defendant finds the standard of care so high that it is virtually impossible for him to show that he has satisfied it. The effect is much the same as if he were strictly liable.

Product Liability

manufacturing → companies

Who should bear the loss in the following situations?

(a) *X* runs a small refreshment booth at a beach and buys her supplies from *Y* Bottling Co. Ltd. She sells a dark-green bottle of ginger ale to *A* who gives it to his friend *B*. *B* drinks half the contents and becomes violently ill. The balance is found to contain a decomposed snail. *B* is hospitalized and is unable to return to work for several weeks.

(b) *P* buys a *Q* Company sports car from *R* Dealer. On being driven away from the showroom, the car loses a defective front wheel and collides with a parked vehicle, injuring the occupant, *S*.

(c) *M* buys from the *N* Ski Shop a set of thermal underwear manufactured by *O* Company. The underwear contains a toxic acid and when it comes in contact with perspiration causes *M* to have a severe skin burn.

(d) *J* buys a bottle of cough medicine, manufactured by the *K* company, from her local drugstore. To try to get rid of her cold she drinks two stiff whiskies, takes a dose of the medicine, and goes to bed. During the night she has a heart attack. The cough medicine is extremely dangerous if taken with alcohol, but there was no warning to that effect on the bottle or package.

As we point out in Chapter 18, the retailer in each of our examples is liable to the buyer for breach of an implied undertaking that a product is not defective. But in example (a), *X* may well have insufficient assets to compensate for the loss. In any event, she sold the soft drink to *A* rather than to *B*, the injured party. Accordingly, *B* is not a buyer entitled to the protection of a contractual undertaking of fitness. Similarly, in example (b), the injured person, *S*, has no contractual relationship with *R* Dealer. In these circumstances, contractual remedies are not available. If the injured parties are going to be compensated, it must be by imposing liability in tort law or by providing a special statutory remedy. Since the manufacturing companies allowed the defective products to reach the market, public policy would seem to require that they should be liable.

Not until 1932 did the British courts recognize the duty of manufacturers to ultimate consumers of their products as an obligation in tort law; the House of Lords did so in the famous case of *Donoghue v. Stevenson*,[30] in which the facts were analogous to those in example (a). Example (b) is drawn in part from the United States case *MacPherson v. Buick Motor Co.*,[31] decided by the New York Court of Appeals in 1916, a decision that must have influenced the later House of Lords decision.

In the years since *Donoghue v. Stevenson*, its principle has been applied by the courts in a wide variety of circumstances to protect consumers and other members of the public who may be harmed. The increasing complexity and sophistication of manufactured products, and the resultant inability of consumers and even of intermediate distributors to detect dangers in these products, places manufacturers in a position of growing responsibility for the safety of consumers. On the whole, the courts have recognized this development and widened the application of the duty accordingly.

---

[30] [1932] A.C. 562.
[31] (1916) 111 N.E. 1050.

Simply to hold that manufacturers owe a duty of care to consumers and others who might be injured is only a partial solution to the problem. Normally, an injured party will have no way of proving that the manufacturer did not exercise reasonable care. Here, the principle of *res ipsa loquitur* comes to the aid of the plaintiff: if the product is defective, then it can reasonably be assumed that there has been negligence in some stage of its design, production, or inspection. The manufacturer is thus liable unless it can show that it has taken all reasonable precautions to prevent defective goods from slipping into the distribution system.[32]

In example (c), based on the leading case of *Grant v. Australian Knitting Mills*,[33] the manufacturing company was caught on the horns of the following dilemma: if the inspection process permitted such underwear to pass through undetected, the system was inadequate and the company was therefore negligent; if the inspection process was virtually foolproof, as indeed the manufacturer claimed, then surely one of its employees must have been personally at fault, making the manufacturer vicariously liable in any event. Accordingly, the present state of our law appears to make manufacturers liable for all product defects of which the present state of technology can reasonably be expected to make them aware. Courts will not accept as a defence the excuse that to eliminate the defect would add to the cost of production; a manufacturer does not have the right to market an inherently dangerous article where a method exists of manufacturing the same article without risk of harm.[34] Thus, manufacturers who choose to reduce costs by omitting necessary safety features, or by using a system of sampling inspection rather than inspecting every item, become responsible for harm that results. In the long run, the savings in production cost may be outweighed by increased insurance premiums for product liability.

Example (d) takes us a stage further. Even though a product is not defective in any way, there may be dangers if the product is not properly used; courts have ruled that manufacturers owe a duty to consumers to give proper warning of such dangers.[35]

Occupier's Liability

Common sense might lead us to assume that an occupier of land and buildings (owner or tenant) would be liable for injuries inflicted upon visitors to the premises according to the ordinary rules of negligence; a visitor should have a claim against the owner or tenant of a piece of real property for any harm caused by unreasonable conduct, such as creating or leaving unexpected hazards in places where they might injure an innocent visitor. Unfortunately, this area of the law became bound up with concepts of land law and, as we shall see in Chapter 26, land law developed from often rigid and irrational ancient common law concepts. Distinctions grew up dividing visitors on land and in buildings into several categories; the obligations of the occupier to take care vary according to the category to which the visitor belongs. The categories in descending order are *invitee,*

---

[32] U.S. courts have gone further. They tend to favour a principle of strict liability, under which the manufacturer impliedly warrants its products to be free of defects regardless of negligence. However, the end result is probably not very different.

[33] [1936] A.C. 85.

[34] Nicholson v. John Deere Ltd. (1989), 57 D.L.R. (4th) 639.

[35] Lambert v. Lastoplex Chemical Co. Ltd. [1972] S.C.R. 569 (inflammable laquer); Buchan v. Ortho Pharmaceutical (Canada) Ltd. (1984) 28. C.C.L.T. 233 (Ont.) (side effects of contraceptive pills).

licensee, and *trespasser.* The distinction between invitee and licensee was abolished by statute in England in 1957 and has also disappeared in some Canadian provinces.[36]

At common law, the highest obligation is owed to an invitee. An invitee is a person permitted by the occupier to enter for business purposes, where the occupier obtains some material benefit or has the probability of a benefit from the invitee's presence. For example, a customer entering a retail store is an invitee. Since the definition is highly artificial, the distinction between invitees and licensees is sometimes irrational. Courts have disagreed on whether an invitee of a tenant is also an invitee when passing over the landlord's premises in order to reach the tenant's premises.

ILLUSTRATION

A had been shopping at *B*'s milk store, in a shopping plaza owned by *C*. On his way back to his car he tripped over an uneven paving stone just outside the store, fell, and sustained injuries. He sued both *B* and *C*.

On similar facts it has been held that the plaintiff was an invitee of both defendants.[37] The owner of the plaza was negligent in its duty to maintain the sidewalk and the milk store had a duty to provide safe access for its customers.

We shall not attempt to discuss all the vagaries of this area of the law, but simply note that the duty owed by an occupier to an invitee is to take care to prevent injuries from hazards of which he is aware and also those of which as a reasonable person he *ought* to be aware. Thus, an occupier will be liable for an injury caused to an invitee by a hazard of which he had no knowledge, but would have known about had he taken reasonable care.

The licensee category includes all other visitors who enter with the express or implied permission of the occupier. Ordinarily a licensee enters premises for personal benefit, rather than for the benefit of the occupier. For example, a social guest is considered to be merely a licensee, even if his host expects ultimately to receive a business advantage as a result of the hospitality he has shown. The duty of an occupier to a licensee upon his premises is to remove concealed dangers of which he has knowledge; he has no liability for hazards unknown to him, even though a reasonable person in his place ought to have realized that a hazard existed.

In those provinces that have introduced occupiers' liability legislation, the distinction between invitee and licensee has disappeared and a common duty of care is owed by an occupier to all visitors lawfully on the premises. Essentially then, the general principles of negligence now apply.

A trespasser is one who enters upon premises unlawfully; he enters without an invitation from or the permission of the occupier and is either unknown to the occupier or, if known to him, would be refused permission. The duty owed in these circumstances is minimal: the occupier must not set out deliberately to harm the trespasser or recklessly disregard the possibility that his acts might injure a trespasser. Thus, he must not set out traps in an open field, or fire a gun in the general area where he knows a trespasser to be. It is sometimes said that even a trespasser is owed a duty of "common humanity".

---

[36]   Occupiers' Liability Act, 1957, 5 and 6 Eliz. 2, c. 31 (U.K.); R.S.A. 1980, c. O-3, s. 5; R.S.B.C. 1979, c. 303, s. 3; R.S.O. 1990, c. O-2, s.1 (a).

[37]   Snitzer v. Becker Milk Co. (1977), 15 O.R. (2d) 345.

OTHER TORTS

One Tort or Many?

Tort law is continually changing and expanding. New activities arise and increase in frequency to the point where they cause unreasonable harm to members of the public. The law eventually creates standards for carrying on these activities and grants remedies to parties injured by conduct failing to meet those standards. Today an aggrieved party need not find a "pigeon-hole" into which a complaint will fit in order to hold a wrongdoer liable for a loss. As a result, it is not possible to enumerate a definitive list of torts or a comprehensive description of all conduct for which the law imposes liability. Some writers attempt to rationalize a general principle of tort law: that all conduct that causes unreasonable harm to others is tortious and creates liability. But such a general principle is not very helpful without examining particular torts. For our purposes a discussion of specific areas of tort law is more useful. The torts discussed below by no means constitute an exhaustive list.

Some torts, for example, are examined in the context of other subjects; we shall discuss them as they arise and need mention them only briefly here. An outsider who incites a party to break an existing contractual obligation commits a tort known as *inducing breach of contract*. As we see in Chapter 9, any contract pursuing such a result is illegal as being against public policy. The tort of *deceit* takes the form of knowingly making a false statement with a view to inducing another to act upon it to his detriment. We discuss it in Chapter 11, under its alternative name of *fraudulent misrepresentation*, as it affects contract law. The tort of *conversion* consists in the wrongful exercise of control over goods, inconsistent with the ownership, or against the wish, of the party entitled to them. We encounter the tort of conversion in Chapter 19, when examining the liability of a seller who wrongfully disposes of goods which do not belong to him and of a carrier who disobeys instructions and wrongfully delivers goods. We meet it again in Chapter 33 when describing the liability of a buyer of goods under an instalment plan who wrongfully disposes of them before completing his payments.

The most ancient and familiar tort is that of *trespass*, the act of entering on the lands of another without consent or lawful right or, after a lawful entry, refusing to leave when ordered to do so by the owner. In less civilized and less well-policed times trespass was often an incitement to violence. Hence it was originally considered a crime, a breach of the peace. Now, however, an owner is restricted to fencing his lands and to using no more than reasonable force in ejecting a trespasser. He may also bring an action against the trespasser, but he will often get little more than nominal damages unless he can prove that actual harm was done to his property. A brief discussion of this tort arises in Chapter 27 in relation to the rights of landlord and tenant against one another, and again in Chapter 33 as a restraint on an unpaid seller in asserting the right to repossess goods while they are on the land of a defaulting buyer.

Deceit

If a person makes a false assertion of fact with knowledge of its falsity, or at any rate without an honest belief in its truth and with the intention to mislead some other person, the

misrepresentation is fraudulent and amounts to the tort of deceit. A victim who relies reasonably on the assertion and suffers a loss may recover from the wrongdoer. Liability for
misrepresentation, whether fraudulent or innocent, is considered further in Chapter 5.

The tort of deceit may also be committed when a person deliberately conceals or withholds information. For example, a bank allowed a customer to invest in a company that
owed a substantial debt to the bank. The bank's employees knew that the company was
on the verge of insolvency but did not disclose this fact to the customer. It was held that
the bank was guilty of fraud and liable to compensate the customer.[38]

Nuisance

Environmental Problems

A major problem confronting our society is pollution of the atmosphere and water
resources. In common law, the mere discharge of noxious substances into the atmosphere
or into water is not itself a breach of duty, either to the community at large or to individuals who may subsequently be harmed by those materials. A person who suffers injury as
a result may, of course, be able to establish liability in negligence. But it may be very difficult to establish that the conduct of any one person or industry has caused a harm. We
can see this difficulty in the buildup of carbon monoxide and other noxious substances
in the atmosphere from the operation of internal combustion engines in automobiles.
Those who breathe these fumes over an extended period of time may suffer serious injury
to health, but it is impossible to conclude that any one automobile is responsible for the
harm. For these reasons, effective control over pollution can be obtained only through
legislation that carefully defines standards limiting the escape of noxious substances and
that prescribes heavy penalties for failure to comply with those standards. Growing
awareness of the problem is now bringing about increased government regulation, as we
shall see in Chapter 32.

Public Nuisances

A small group of offences, known as public nuisances, includes such misconduct as
blocking public roads, interfering with other public amenities such as the use of market-
places or parks and, in a few instances, emitting dangerous substances in public places.
Actions against the wrongdoer may ordinarily be brought only by an organ of government on behalf of the public as a whole. Occasionally, an individual who has shown a
special injury considerably greater than that sustained by other members of the public in
general may successfully maintain an action for compensation against the wrongdoer.
These common law public nuisances are of limited significance today.

Occupiers' Rights

On the other hand, the common law has long recognized an occupier's right to the
normal use and enjoyment of his land, free from such interference as noxious fumes,
soot, contaminating liquids poured into rivers and streams or percolating through the
soil, and also such things as noise and vibration. The term "occupier" includes not only

---

[38]   Sugar v. Peat Marwick Ltd. (1989), 55 D.L.R.(4th) 230.

the owner of land but tenants as well. Since most members of the public qualify as owners or tenants of their homes, they may legally complain of *private nuisances*. A person who acquires land knowing that it is already exposed to a nuisance may nevertheless have a right to sue the offending party.[39]

Does the law give an occupier a right to absolute freedom from these various annoyances? The answer must be a relative one weighing competing interests in society. It turns on two main issues: the degree of interference with the occupier's use and enjoyment of the land, and the economic importance of the offending activity. These are questions that are difficult to resolve in the context of private litigation. Increasingly, they have become the subject of government regulation — an issue to which we shall return in Chapter 32.

The level of interference that a community as a whole already tolerates, and hence that individual members of it must tolerate as *reasonable use* (justified use not considered tortious), varies according to local conditions. The standard of reasonable use of adjoining lands in an industrial area such as Hamilton, Ontario, might be quite unreasonable and amount to tortious use in a holiday resort area such as Ingonish, Cape Breton. No matter what the local standard, however, an interference may be so severe as to rise above that level and be declared a nuisance.

Assault and Battery

One of the oldest torts recognized by English law is that of *trespass to the person*. Initially this tort consisted of direct and violent attack against the victim, a tort easily understood by both the citizen and the courts. The present-day legal terms are *assault* (the threat of violence) and *battery* (the actual physical contact), although the word assault is frequently used by itself in non-legal discussions to include the battery. Assaults are usually committed in the course of a crime; the attacker, if he is caught, may be fined or imprisoned. However, although he may be clearly liable, he frequently will have no assets for the victim to seize in order to satisfy a civil judgment. Accordingly, assault cases are rarely litigated as private actions and the details of this area of the law are of little practical importance. There is, however, one important exception. Since the essence of a battery is the unlawful touching of a person without consent, a surgeon who operates on a patient without consent commits a battery. This problem is discussed in the next chapter.

False Imprisonment and Malicious Prosecution

A more interesting aspect of trespass to the person is the tort of *false imprisonment*. (*False arrest*, a phrase often used in the same context, ordinarily includes a false imprisonment, but contains the additional feature of holding the victim with the intention that he be turned over to the police authorities for prosecution.) False imprisonment consists of "intentionally and without lawful justification subjecting another to total restraint of movement by either actively causing his confinement or preventing him from exercising his privilege of leaving the place in which he is".[40]

Physical restraint, or even the threat that it will be applied, is not necessary: it is enough that the victim be given the idea that disobedience of a command not to leave

---

[39] Belisle v. Canadian Cotton Ltd. [1952] O.W.N. 114.
[40] Fleming, *The Law of Torts*, supra, n. 1 at p. 27.

will lead to humiliation in a public place. A reasonable fear that a store detective or other employee might shout "Stop, thief!" would be enough restraint to amount to an imprisonment. Accordingly, there is a considerable risk in confronting a member of the public with the charge of a crime without very strong evidence. The policy of the law is not to encourage self-help remedies, such as citizen's arrest, except in very clear cases. For example, the store detective who arrests a suspected shoplifter when no shoplifting has in fact occurred at that time has no defence against an action for false imprisonment, even if he believed the suspect had stolen goods.

However, a private citizen who honestly makes a complaint to the police about a suspected crime is not liable for false imprisonment if the person is arrested by the police as a result of the complaint and the complaint turns out to be unfounded. Thus, if a store detective reports a suspected shoplifter to a police officer and the police officer arrests the alleged shoplifter, the store detective is not liable for false imprisonment, since he did not attempt to arrest the "shoplifter"; he merely reported his suspicions to a law officer. But if he did not have an honest belief that a crime had been committed he would be guilty of *malicious prosecution*. A charge of malicious prosecution is very difficult to prove, because in order to succeed the plaintiff must satisfy the court that the defendant acted from some improper motive, such as a wish to harass the plaintiff. Consequently, it is much less hazardous to report suspicious activity to the police and let them decide whether an arrest is reasonably justified, rather than attempt a citizen's arrest and learn too late that no crime has been committed.

Defamation

The tort of defamation is better known in each of its two forms, *libel* (written defamation) and *slander* (spoken defamation). Generally speaking, it consists of a statement that causes unjustified injury to the private, professional, or business reputation of another person. In defamation cases, the courts are not concerned with soothing mere injured feelings or redressing insults. They will not award damages unless the aggrieved party can demonstrate that the defamer has made serious allegations about his character, ability, or business reputation causing genuine and significant injury to the respect and esteem in which he is held by others. Such defamation requires *publication*, that is, "communication of the disparaging statement to someone other than the person defamed".[41]

A complete defence against a charge of defamation is that the alleged defamatory statements are true. The problem for a defendant in this instance is the difficulty of establishing, to the satisfaction of the court, the truth of the statements. The burden of proof makes it hazardous to make damaging statements in the vague hope of later being able to establish their truth.

The public interest requires that in some circumstances there shall be *absolute privilege*, a complete immunity from defamation suits. Words spoken in parliamentary debate, in proceedings in law courts and inquests, and before royal commissions are absolutely privileged; the aim is to promote vigorous and candid discussion without the inhibiting effect of defamation laws. As a result, even intentional and malicious falsehoods uttered in Parliament are completely immune from action in the courts.

In a variety of circumstances a person may have an obligation to disclose information or give an opinion about another. The obligation is rarely a legal duty, yet the effect of the

---

[41]   Fleming, *The Law of Torts*, supra, n. 1 at p. 536.

disclosure may be important both to the person receiving the information and the one about whom it is given. A letter of reference from a former employer, a teacher, or a bank manager may be solicited by an applicant with full knowledge that the letter will be frank and may contain some uncomplimentary statements. Yet the person supplying the letter would be hard pressed to prove everything he has stated. If he were in constant danger of having to defend his statements in a court of law, he would rarely be willing to give a letter of reference unless it could be couched in the most flattering terms. Obviously, such a situation would not be in the interests of applicants or of those who must rely on such letters to choose among applicants. The law extends a *qualified privilege* to anyone giving such information. Provided one gives it in good faith with an honest belief in its accuracy, one can successfully defend an action of defamation even if the statements prove to be untrue.

Qualified privilege arises in many other situations. Fair and accurate reports of proceedings in Parliament, courts, administrative tribunals, public inquiries and meetings enjoy qualified privilege. The common law also tolerates, as a necessary function in a democratic society, statements made as fair comment and criticism in matters of public interest. The basic requisite for a critic is to establish that he had an honest belief in his opinions.

Economic Torts

Finally, there is a group of torts sometimes referred to collectively as "economic torts" which, though rarely the subject of litigation, are nevertheless of importance to the business community. These torts fall into two main categories.

First, there are those torts that relate to the carrying on of business. Intentional *interference with contractual relations* is a tort whose origins can be traced back to the fourteenth century when, because of the shortage of labour resulting from the "black death", a statute was passed making it an offence to lure a servant away from his master. In modern times the action has a very limited application: if A induces B to break his contract with C, C will normally sue B in contract and A will not be liable to C unless she has acted unlawfully or maliciously.[42] *Unlawful interference with trade* is also a tort when, for example, A threatens B with violence if B continues to do business with C. Not only will B have an action against A for assault, but C may also sue for the interference with his business. Most of the law in this area, however, has been concerned with the activities of labour unions,[43] and now falls within the sphere of labour relations legislation.

The second category of torts relates to *false advertising* in relation to another's products. A person commits the tort of *injurious falsehood*, or *product defamation*, when he intentionally makes false and disparaging statements about the products of another person — for example, a business competitor. Rather than seeking to denigrate the goods of a competitor, a dishonest trader may try to cash in on their established reputation by passing off his own goods as those of the competitor, for example by using a deceptively similar label or form of packaging. Passing off is considered further in Chapter 25.

---

[42] In certain circumstances, the conduct of the parties may be reviewable under the Competition Act, R.S.C.1985, c.C-34; see Harbord Insurance Services Ltd .v. Insurance Corp. of British Columbia (1993) 9 B.L.R.(2d) 81.

[43] See Rookes v. Barnard [1964] A.C.1129.

EMEDIES

Since the purpose of the law of torts is to compensate an injured party, the usual remedy is an award of a sum of money by way of *damages*. The concept of damages is discussed in greater detail in Chapter 17, but since there are some differences in the principles that govern damages in tort and in contract a few observations will be helpful in this Chapter.

Generally, the purpose of damages is to restore the plaintiff, so far as is possible, to the position he or she would have been in if the tort had not been committed. The object of awarding damages is not to punish the wrongdoer, though *punitive* or *exemplary* damages may be awarded in rare cases, such as a brutal physical attack, a deliberate libel, or malicious false imprisonment.

Tort damages are often classified in two categories: *special damages* and *general damages*. Special damages refer to items that can be more-or-less accurately quantified — medical bills, the cost of repairing a car, or actual lost wages. General damages include more speculative items, such as future loss of earnings due to disability, and non-pecuniary losses such as awards for the "pain and suffering" of losing a limb, or one's sight. Obviously, it is impossible to put a money value on health and happiness, but the courts must attempt to do so. Unhappily, they have thousands of precedents to guide them.

In some cases, remedies other than damages may be available although they are rarely granted. Where a defendant has wrongfully converted the plaintiff's property, the court may order its specific *restitution* to the plaintiff, since to restrict the remedy to damages would in effect allow the defendant to compel a sale of the property. Courts may also grant an *injunction,* that is, it may order the defendant to refrain from committing further acts of a similar nature, under pain of imprisonment for contempt of court if he disregards the order. For example, an *injunction* may restrain the defendant from further trespassing on the plaintiff's land. Less frequently, courts grant a *mandatory injunction*, ordering the defendant to rectify a wrong, such as removing a fence blocking the plaintiff's right-of-way to his property.

Injunctions are sometimes granted in cases of nuisance. In such cases the court must carefully balance competing interests. Where a nuisance is so severe as to make the plaintiff's land unusable, to award only damages would be tantamount to expropriation of the land in return for the damage award. But where the interference is less extreme an injunction could restrain what might otherwise be a socially desirable activity and an award of monetary damages would be more appropriate.[44]

Courts are similarly wary of granting injunctions in cases of libel and slander, since such an order would effectively amount to censorship.

Questions for Review

1. What are the main purposes of tort law?
2. What must a plaintiff be able to prove in order to succeed in an action for damages for negligence?

---

[44] See K.V.P. Co. Ltd. v. McKie [1949] 4 D.L.R. 497. The Ontario legislature subsequently dissolved the injunction in that case and legalized the activity, granting the plaintiff compensation instead: K.V.P. Company Limited Act, S.O.1950, c.33.

3. What is the significance of shifting the burden of proof in certain kinds of negligence cases?
4. Is automobile insurance that provides protection against liability to third parties consistent with a doctrine of fault? Explain.
5. Is it correct to say that a person may sometimes be liable in damages to an injured party for the consequences of his tortious conduct, regardless of whether he could have foreseen those consequences at the time he acted?
6. Why is it necessary to resort to tort law in product liability cases?
7. Should a person who engages in transporting explosives, or in similar hazardous activities, be strictly liable for any injury that results?
8. By what logic can an employer be held liable for the negligent conduct of an employee who has been instructed not to act in the manner that caused the loss?
9. In determining liability for negligence a court will ask itself whether a reasonable person, given an opportunity to contemplate the probable consequences of the conduct in question, would have foreseen any danger in his or her conduct. It does not ask whether the defendant in fact foresaw any danger. Why would a court reject the latter question as a test for liability?
10. Why was the old contributory negligence rule a harsh one? In what way has our law now alleviated its severity and unfairness?
11. Why would a legislature ever dissolve a court injunction obtained in an action to restrain a nuisance? What alternative remedy might it provide then for the injured party?
12. What are the implications of sampling inspection for the liability of a manufacturer?
13. Distinguish between absolute and qualified privilege.

Problems

Problem 1
Prentice, an encyclopedia salesman, telephoned Hall and arranged to visit her at her apartment to show his firm's latest volumes. Entering the apartment building, owned by Newman, Prentice found the staircase lighting out of order. He attempted to climb the stairs in the dark, and fell on a loose step, breaking his leg. Hall knew of the faulty light and the loose step but had not thought to warn Prentice. Nor had anyone told Newman of either defect. What claim does Prentice have against either Hall or Newman?

Problem 2
Jones dictates a letter to her secretary addressed to Smith, her local Member of Parliament, accusing Smith of having accepted bribes for influencing government contracts. The secretary mails the letter to Smith. Jones' only evidence for the allegations is a conversation overheard at a cocktail party. Is Jones liable in damages to Smith for defamation?

Problem 3
The driver of an automobile is injured in an accident and brings an action against the other driver for damages for negligence. Of what possible significance may the fact be that the plaintiff was not wearing a seat-belt at the time of the accident?

Cases

Case 1

Brown is a farmer who raises chickens on a large scale. The baby chicks require a continuous supply of oxygen to survive and the necessary equipment for that purpose is connected to the electric power supplied to the farm. Brown had installed an auxiliary battery-operated power generator in the barn to be available as an emergency back-up. He had taken the further precaution of having a battery-operated power failure detector in his bedroom so that if the electrical power in the farmhouse failed, a warning signal would alert him to the potential danger of loss of electric energy to his operation.

Chauncey is a driver for Gardiner Transport Ltd. While driving the company's tractor-trailer on a night run, Chauncey allowed the vehicle to wander on to the shoulder of the road where the upper part struck overhead wires. As a result, electric power service in the area was interrupted for a period of five hours. The interruption extinguished the supply of oxygen to Brown's barn and several thousand chickens died. Unfortunately, Brown had temporarily disconnected the alarm detector in his bedroom and so on the one occasion he needed it, it was not in operation.

Brown brought an action for damages of $30 000 against both Chauncey and Gardiner Transport Ltd. to compensate him for the loss of his chickens. At the trial a witness estimated that 40% to 50% of chicken breeders used power failure detectors.

Discuss the merits of the plaintiff's case, with particular reference to each of the elements of a tort action. Explain with reasons what the court's decision would probably be.

Case 2

Chandler and Alfredo, buyers for another store, entered the shop of Park Avenue & Yorkville Fashions Ltd. and were recognized. The manager of the shop, Silverberg, became angry and in the presence of a number of customers accused Chandler and Alfredo of spying. There followed an exchange of insults. Silverberg called the shop detective, telling her to keep an eye on Chandler and Alfredo, and then telephoned the police, referring to Chandler and Alfredo as "suspicious characters". No one touched the two buyers, but they came to the conclusion that they would be detained if they were to try to leave. In due course three police officers arrived and escorted Chandler and Alfredo from the shop while Silverberg declared that he intended to press charges, although he did not specify what the nature of these charges would be. The two men were taken to the police station, but were released when they explained that they were in the store to check on prices being charged there.

Chandler and Alfredo brought an action against Silverberg for false imprisonment and Silverberg counter-claimed for damages for trespass. Discuss the relative merits of the claim and counter-claim.

Case 3

A passenger plane operated by Saltwater Air Lines Ltd., on a flight from Sydney to Dartmouth, deviated to the south of its normal path to avoid some clouds and give a smoother ride. In doing so the aircraft passed over a mink ranch operated by Scotia Mink Ltd. The noise of the plane caused panic among the mink and, because it was the whelping season, the female adults killed their young in large numbers. Animals valued at $10 000 were lost as a result of the incident. Scotia Mink Ltd. brought an action for $10 000 damages for negligence against Saltwater Air Lines Ltd.

The main building of the ranch had the words MINK RANCH painted in large white letters on a red roof. The evidence showed that the aircraft's altitude at the time was between 400 and 2000 feet and not in violation of the Air Traffic rules in the Regulations under the Aeronautics Act. The pilot and co-pilot were preoccupied with making an approach to the Dartmouth airport and had no opportunity to survey the ground beneath the plane.

It was also brought out in evidence that the Department of Transport in Ottawa had published and issued to all pilots and aircraft owners an information circular advising of the way in which mink ranches were to be marked to render them visible from the air, though the circular did not disclose the location of any mink ranches. The evidence showed that the pilots in this case had ignored the information circular.

Should the action succeed? Discuss the principles of tort liability that would seem to apply. Are your conclusions consistent with the objectives of distributive justice?

Case 4

Mrs. Rusholme engaged the firm of Saunders & Watts to refinish floors in certain rooms of a frame bungalow owned by her and her husband in Scarborough. She told Mr. Saunders that she and her husband would be away on vacation and that she would leave a key for the workers with her next-door neighbour. On the advice of her sister-in-law, who had had similar work done recently, she asked Saunders to leave the windows partially open for ventilation and to give the key back to her neighbour, who would close the windows when the floors were dry.

The Rusholmes' house was serviced by gas. Among the appliances was a gas stove in the kitchen with a pilot light that could be extinguished by a manual control. The downstairs floors of the house, including that of the dining room, were to be sanded; the dining room was next to the kitchen, with no door between the two rooms.

After sanding the floors, Saunders and Watts applied a sealer that they had bought from Standard Household Products Ltd. The label on each can of sealer contained the following warning:

DANGER — FLAMMABLE

Do not smoke. Adequate ventilation to the outside must be provided. All spark-producing devices and open flames (furnaces, all pilot lights, spark-producing switches, etc.) must be eliminated in or near working areas.

Avoid prolonged breathing of vapours. Wear a vapour cartridge mask. Replace cartridge before saturation.

On completing their work Saunders and Watts discussed what they should do about the doors and windows they had opened to allow the vapours to escape. Saunders recalled a reference to a recent case he had read about in the newspaper in which repairers who had left doors open after they had finished their work had been held liable in damages when thieves had entered and stolen valuable contents. The two men then closed all the doors and windows and left the key on the kitchen table beside the stove.

About eight hours after Saunders and Watts left, an explosion occurred in the house and it was seriously damaged in the ensuing fire. On returning from their vacation the Rusholmes found their home in ruins, and were dismayed to discover that they had neglected to renew the fire insurance policy, which had expired only a few days before they had left on their vacation.

The Rusholmes brought an action for damages against the firm of Saunders & Watts and against Standard Household Products Ltd.

Outline the legal questions raised by these facts and give your opinion of the probable outcome of the case with reasons.

CHAPTER 5

PROFESSIONAL LIABILITY

THE ROLE OF THE PROFESSIONAL

Who are professionals? They are people whose skills are described as having a significant intellectual content and draw on an underlying, developing body of theory
affecting the practice of their profession. Members of each profession are usually certified
to offer their services to the public under a system of licensing administered by one or
more governing bodies of the profession. Accordingly, clients view professionals as having
specialized knowledge and skills that the clients are prepared to pay for and rely on.

While the practice of a profession may require compliance with a code of standards,
those standards cannot be comprehensive enough to provide clear answers to all problems requiring advice. Ultimately, professionals must rely on their own judgment and discretion. Professional opinions are not infallible. Their value lies in assisting in clients'
decisions and in improving the probability that those decisions will be sound. Thus the
purchase of professional services reduces risk. Nevertheless, when a client pays for and
relies on professional advice and it turns out to be wrong, the question arises whether the
advice was given with sufficient care and skill. Is the professional liable for the loss or
harm suffered by a client, or even by someone else, who relies on the advice?

THE LEGAL DILEMMA

As in other areas of tort law, courts face a social problem in determining when liability for
professional incompetence or negligence arises. On the one hand, they are expected to
grant compensation to victims who sustain injuries that are often statistically inevitable. On
the other hand, if courts award damages to satisfy all demands for compensation, the
increased costs will likely inhibit many activities that are valuable to society as a whole. The
two social objectives of compensating innocent victims and of avoiding the discouragement
of legitimate activity compete with each other: the courts in defining liability must achieve a
tolerable balance. Fleming has commented on the nature of this problem as follows:

> The history of the law of torts has hinged on the tension between between two basic inter-
> ests of individuals — the interest in security and the interest in freedom of action. The first
> requires that one who has been hurt should be compensated by the injurer regardless of the
> latter's motivation and purpose; the second that the injurer should at best be held responsi-
> ble only when his activity was intentionally wrongful or indicated an undue lack of consider-
> ation for others ...[1]

Courts are faced with this task of achieving an acceptable balance when they are called
upon to determine when liability should arise for inadequate professional services. There
is, in theory, a persuasive argument to be made in favour of widened liability of professionals: in terms of distributive justice,[2] the benefits (or utility) gained by a plaintiff who

---

[1] Fleming, *The Law of Torts*. (8th ed.), Sydney: The Law Book Company, 1992, at 6.
[2] We have encountered the concept of distributive justice in Chapter 1 as one of the categories of law recognized by Aristotle.

recovers damages will exceed the losses (or reduced utility) of a professional defendant who has to pay them but can recoup his or her losses by increasing fees and by purchasing insurance protection to safeguard against liability. The argument assumes that an insurance system will spread the costs among so many clients or purchasers of insurance as to render them minimal. Unfortunately, this assumption has proven inaccurate and the costs have turned out to be much more than minimal. In a 1980 decision, Lord Denning dramatized the danger when he warned:

> ... Take heed of what has happened in the United States. 'Medical malpractice' cases there are very worrying, especially as they are tried by juries who have sympathy for the patient and none for the doctor, who is insured. The damages are colossal. The doctors insure but the premiums become very high: and these have to be passed on to the patients. Experienced practitioners are known to have refused to treat patients for fear of being accused of negligence. Young men are even deterred from entering the profession because of the risks involved ...[3]

In recent times the proportion of total gross national economic product accounted for by professional activity has increased significantly. With the rise in the general level of education, purchasers of professional services have also shown an increasing awareness of their rights and a greater willingness to pursue those rights in the courts. At the same time, the potential liability for economic harm caused by negligent conduct of professionals has increased considerably as a result of court decisions.

The combined effect of these developments has been to make professional liability an important topic for economic analysis. Awards of damages for professional negligence have led to extensive use of liability insurance; because of uncertainty concerning liability and the risk of heavy damages, insurance premiums are steadily increasing. Professional fees, in turn, must increase to cover insurance costs. As fees increase, clients expect more for their money, and when they are disappointed are more likely to sue. The process is something of a vicious circle.

DEFINING THE SCOPE OF THE PROFESSIONAL DUTY OF CARE

Contractual Duty

An agreement to provide professional services to a client contains a promise, whether stated expressly or not, to perform those services with due care. A breach of that promise is a breach of the contract for professional services, and the client may then sue for damages in contract. Does a client also have a tort claim for negligence? And would it matter whether the client sued for breach of contract or for negligence?

A complaint, whether it is based on contract or on tort, is still based on a breach of the duty of care owed to the client, but different results may follow from the two claims. At one time the courts appeared to favour the view that a professional's liability should be

---

[3]   Whitehouse v. Jordan [1980] 1 All E.R. 650, at 658.

governed by the duties owed under the contract.[4] This view limits a client's right to sue for the tort of negligence to special circumstances where the professional's conduct does not fall within his or her contractual obligations.[5] Subsequent decisions questioned this approach and suggested that a plaintiff may choose to sue either in contract or in tort. This approach has now been confirmed by the Supreme Court of Canada. In a case where a solicitor was negligent in arranging a mortgage that was later found to be void, the Court held that the client was entitled to sue in either contract or tort.[6] The common law duty of care is not confined to relationships that arise apart from contract and exists independently of the duty that is owed under the contract. The right to choose is important, since the rules governing the time limits for bringing an action might make it advantageous to sue in tort.[7] On the other hand, in a tort action a client's own contributory negligence may be raised as a defence.[8] However, if the client chooses to sue in tort rather than in contract the defendant may still rely upon any term of the contract that excludes or limits liability.[9]

A major part of this book is devoted to the law of contracts, including remedies for breach of contract, and subsequent chapters will discuss liability for breach of a contractual promise, including a promise to perform with due care.

Fiduciary Duty

Even apart from possible tort liability, a professional's duty is not entirely contractual. A principle of equity imposes a *fiduciary duty* of care on any dominant party in a special relationship of trust, such as usually exists in professional-client relations.[10] This fiduciary duty arises even when the professional donates services free of charge, so that no contract exists.

A fiduciary duty arising from a relationship of trust may sometimes impose a wider range of duty on a professional than is expressly stated in the contract. For example, a lawyer who entered into a business arrangement with a client of long standing, and failed to disclose his own precarious financial situation, was held to be in breach of his fiduciary duty to the client,[11] as was a bank that gave advice to a client regarding a proposed takeover without

---

[4] Nunes Diamonds v. Dominion Electric Co. (1972), 26 D.L.R. (3d) 699, at 727-28.

[5] See, for example, Beaver Lumber Co. Ltd. v. McLenaghan (1983) 23 C.C.L.T. 212 (Sask), where a seller of home building materials recommended an incompetent contractor.

[6] Central Trust Co. v. Rafuse (1986), 31 D.L.R.(4th) 481; B.G.Checo International Ltd. v. British Columbia Hydro & Power Authority (1993) 14 C.C.L.T.(2d) 233.

[7] The time limit for a tort action is normally calculated from the moment when the breach is *discovered*, rather than when it *occurs*, as is the rule in contract. In Central Trust Co. v. Rafuse the invalidity of the mortgage was not discovered until some years after it was executed. This difference in time limits is also important in cases of negligence by an architect or builder, where a defect may only be discovered many years after construction has been completed and it would be too late to sue in contract. See Brook Enterprises v. Wilding (1973) 38 D.L.R.(3d) 472.

[8] See Coopers & Lybrand v. H.E. Kane Agencies Ltd. (1985) 32 C.C.L.T. 1, and contrast Cosyns v. Smith (1983) 25 C.C.L.T. 54.

[9] Central Trust Co. v. Rafuse, *supra*; London Drugs Ltd. v. Kuehne & Nagel International Ltd. (1992) 13 C.C.L.T.(2d) 1. Concurrent liability is not restricted to professionals. In Morrison v. McCoy Bros. [1987] 3 W.L.R.301, it was held that a negligent truck repairer could be sued in tort as well as in contract.

[10] Nocton v. Lord Ashburton [1914] A.C. 932 at 943-58; Hedley, Byrne & Co. Ltd. v. Heller and Partners Ltd. [1964] A.C. 465 at 486. For an example concerning the duty of a bank to its customer, see Hayward v. Bank of Nova Scotia (1985) 32 C.C.L.T. 286.

[11] Korz v. St.Pierre (1987), 61 O.R.(2d) 609.

revealing that the bank, through one of its directors, also had an interest in the takeover and was thus in a position of conflict of interest.[12] Nor may an accountant use information obtained from a client to make an investment without the consent of the client.

A fiduciary obligation requires complete fidelity and loyalty to the other party, the beneficiary in the relationship. We shall examine this requirement again in later chapters when we consider such topics as undue influence, agency, partnership, and the duties of corporate directors.

Duty in Tort

A duty has meaning only in relation to the class of persons to whom it is owed. Defining the scope of a duty becomes essential whenever professional advice is relied on by persons other than the client who is paying for the services. Many people may rely on a professional opinion given to a single client, as for example:

(a) in the practice of professional auditing, when an auditor expresses an opinion on the fairness and accuracy of the client firm's financial statement;

(b) in the work of engineers and architects, when they recommend design specifications for structures that prove faulty and cause injury or loss of business to third parties;

(c) in assessments of credit worthiness prepared by credit analysts or bankers for their customers and which come to the attention of other lenders;

(d) in the estimates of business consultants engaged by a company to provide it with a valuation of the business or its shares, when the valuation is intended for the use of a third party;

(e) in the preparation of a will by a lawyer whose error causes a gift to an intended beneficiary of the client to be void;

(f) in the professional opinion given by one doctor to another on a consulting basis, concerning the patient of the second doctor.

Potential third party liability also exists for insurance agents and real estate agents. The contractual duty of a real estate agent is owed to the vendor of the property; that of an insurance agent is owed, frequently though not always, to the insurance company which arranges insurance. In the course of their work for their principals, however, these agents develop close relations with persons to whom they may refer as "clients", applicants for insurance and prospective purchasers of houses, respectively. While in a strict sense their commissions are paid by their principals, the persons with whom they deal in the course of their work provide them with the opportunity of earning the commissions. As we shall see below, they may become liable in tort to these persons.

It may come as a surprise to learn that the individual shareholders of a company do not have a contractual relationship with the auditor.[13] When shareholders vote to approve the appointment of an auditor at the company's annual meeting, they are acting collectively as one of the decision-making organs of the company, and are making a decision *for the company*. The contract by which the auditor is engaged is therefore a contract

---

[12] Standard Investments Ltd. v. Canadian Imperial Bank of Commerce (1985) 22 D.L.R. (4th) 410.
[13] Roman Corp v. Peat Marwick Thorne (1992) 8 B.L.R. (2d) 43.

between the auditor and the company as a separate legal entity: the shareholders are not parties to that relationship and any duty owed to them would be a fiduciary one.

THE EXPANSION OF PROFESSIONAL LIABILITY

Misrepresentation

As noted in Chapter 4, one of the most significant developments in the law of torts has been the extension of liability to negligent misstatements causing purely economic loss, as distinguished from those causing injury to persons or property.[14] As noted in our description of deceit in that chapter, wilful or fraudulent misrepresentation constitutes the tort of deceit, and damages have long been recoverable by the victim who relies on such statements. But fraudulent misrepresentation requires at least some guilty knowledge or wilful disregard of the falsity of information provided, whereas negligent misrepresentation requires only a breach of the duty of care and skill.

Until recent times, the courts drew back from holding persons liable for negligent misrepresentation except when there was a contract with the injured party or when they were subject to a special form of liability arising from their fiduciary duty, as when an accountant audits the accounts of a charitable organization without charging a fee, or when a doctor gives medical advice gratuitously. The reluctance of the courts to find persons liable for negligent misrepresentation in the absence of a direct contractual or fiduciary relationship extended especially to professional givers of financial advice and information such as accountants, bankers, trust company officers and stockbrokers, whose statements may reach large numbers of the public. Concern about the wide scope of potential liability was voiced by an English judge when he observed that "Words are more volatile than deeds, they travel fast and far afield, they are used without being expended."[15]

In a leading case in 1951,[16] the English Court of Appeal held that an accountant who carelessly audited a misleading financial statement, knowing that it would be shown to a prospective investor, was not liable to the investor for the loss caused by reliance on the audited statement. Suppose that a stockbroker was advising a client about the value of a company's shares while they were at lunch, and a stranger at the next table innocently overheard the advice. Would the stockbroker be liable to compensate the stranger for a loss suffered because, relying on the overheard advice, he invested in the company? The court feared that this kind of unexpected liability to third persons for advice given to and intended only for a client might make the risk so wide as to limit severely the reasonable freedom of professionals to practise their occupations. Lord Justice Denning, who dissented from the majority opinion in the above case, asserted that such risks were greatly exaggerated: the duty need not be owed to every conceivable person, but should be confined to a particular person or group whom the maker of the statement could reasonably expect to rely on it. However, the majority of the court feared that reasonable limits could not be set and that liability would thus become virtually unlimited.

---

[14] Negligent misstatements causing physical injury have long been actionable. For example, it would be a tort to assure an inquiring motorist that the road ahead is safe, while carelessly forgetting to say that there is a deep uncovered ditch across the road just over the brow of the next hill.

[15] Hedley Bryne v. Heller & Partners [1964] A.C. 465 at 534, per Lord Pearce.

[16] Candler v. Crane, Christmas & Co. [1951] 2 K.B. 164.

The *Hedley Byrne* Principle

Lord Denning's position was vindicated by the House of Lords twelve years later in the famous case of *Hedley Byrne v. Heller and Partners*, illustrated below:

Easipower asked Hedley Byrne, an advertising agency, to handle its account in placing ads in magazines and commercials on radio and TV. Since Hedley Byrne would have to extend credit to Easipower in arranging the advertising, it first decided to ask its own bank to obtain credit information on Easipower, and in particular about whether Easipower would be good for a line of credit up to certain limits. The bank manager made inquiries from Heller and Partners (Easipower's bankers) about Easipower's credit worthiness, without revealing Hedley Byrne's identity. Heller sent the following letter in reply:

CONFIDENTIAL

For your private use and without responsibility on the part of the bank or its officers

Dear Sir:

In reply to your inquiry we advise that Easipower is a respectably consti-tuted company, considered good for its ordinary business obligations. Your figures are larger than we are accustomed to see.

Yours truly,
Heller & Partners.

At no time did Hedley Byrne communicate directly with Heller, but its own bank did inform it of the full contents of the letter, including the disclaimer of responsibility. Hedley Byrne then accepted Easipower as an account and placed extensive advertising for it, running up a balance of many thousands of pounds. Shortly afterwards Easipower became insolvent and was unable to pay Hedley Byrne more than a small portion of the debt. Hedley Byrne sued Heller for the resulting loss, claiming it was caused by Heller's negligent misrepresentation of Easipower's credit worthiness.

The House of Lords found that although Heller neither dealt with nor even knew the identity of Hedley Byrne, Heller should have foreseen that its information would be used by a customer of the other bank. Accordingly, it owed that customer a duty to take reasonable care in expressing an opinion about the financial state of Easipower. On the facts, however, it held that the disclaimer of responsibility, clearly stated in the letter, absolved Heller of liability. In effect, the law lords said that Hedley Byrne could not rely on the information because of the disclaimer. Nevertheless, *Hedley Byrne* established the principle of liability to third parties for negligent misrepresentation.

The result seems to be that anyone who makes such a misstatement is liable for losses suffered by a wider group than those with whom he or she has a direct contractual or fiduciary relationship. There is little doubt that the decision widened the ambit of liability of people who give professional advice, but courts have exercised restraint and found limits which we are about to consider.

Practical Limits to the *Hedley Byrne* Principle

If the test of liability for negligent misrepresentation were to turn entirely on who could foreseeably be harmed, banks, public accountants and other financial analysts might be faced with an almost indeterminate liability. For example, the auditors of a company whose financial statements are widely distributed should be able to foresee that the statements may reasonably be relied on by many people unknown to them. They could be liable then to anyone who might happen to read the financial statements. The courts have stopped short of imposing so extensive a liability. They have limited the class of persons to whom public accountants owe a duty of care to those with whom they have a "special relationship". For this purpose, it appears that auditors have a special relationship only with those persons (not necessarily identified to them in person) whom they should know will have a specific use for the audited information. Hence, they owe a duty of care to persons whom they should have known were awaiting audited information to help in making decisions in particular types of transactions. It would seem by this test that eligible plaintiffs must not only be "foreseeable" in a general sense, but also more specifically "foreseen" in relation to a contemplated transaction. So when an auditor negligently prepared accounts for a corporation, knowing that they were to be shown to a potential purchaser of the corporation, the Supreme Court of Canada held that he was liable for the loss suffered by the purchaser.[17] But in a more recent case it was held that an investor who bought shares in a corporation, having studied its financial statements filed with the Ontario Securities Commission, could not sue the auditor who had been negligent in auditing the statements. Although it was foreseeable that an investor might rely on the statements, such a person was not within the class to whom a duty was owed.[18]

Liability for negligent misrepresentation is not restricted to financial information provided by professionals such as accountants and bankers. A municipality has been held liable for loss suffered by purchasers of land who relied on incorrect information given to them by the zoning department regarding permissible use of the land.[19] And an engineering firm that was negligent in preparing drawings and specifications for a provincial construction project was held liable for loss suffered by the construction company which had successfully bid for the contract in reliance on the specifications.[20]

Negligent Omissions

The duty to take reasonable care includes the duty not to omit essential steps in providing professional services. It embraces sins of omission as well as sins of commission.

---

[17] Haig v. Bamford (1976), 72 D.L.R.(2d) 68.

[18] Dixon v. Deacon Morgan McEwan Easson (1990), 64 D.L.R.(4th) 441. The statements showed a profit of $14 million when in reality there had been a loss of $33 million. A similar decision was reached by the House of Lords in Caparo Industries Plc. v. Dickman [1990] 1 All E.R.568. See also Canadian Commercial Bank v. Crawford, Smith and Swallow (1993) 15 C.C.L.T.(2d) 273.

[19] Bell v. City of Sarnia (1987), 37 D.L.R.(4th) 438.

[20] Edgeworth Constructions Ltd. v. N.D. Lea & Associates Ltd. (1993), 107 D.L.R. (4th) 169. Interestingly, the individual engineers employed by the firm, who prepared the drawings, were held not to owe a duty to the contractor.

ILLUSTRATION A

Fine's Flowers Ltd. sustained a serious loss from the freezing of flowers and plants in its greenhouse. The business had arranged its insurance coverage with the same insurance agent for many years and its insurance coverage and premium costs were extensive; it relied on the agent to recommend appropriate coverage and paid the necessary premiums without question. An inspector for the insurance company had advised the agent that the insurance policy with Fine's Flowers did not cover such matters as the failure of water pumps but the agent did not report this gap in insurance coverage to Fine's Flowers. As a result the company had no opportunity to arrange the required additional protection. The freezing conditions were caused by failure of a water pump which interrupted the supply of water to boilers that heated the greenhouse.

Since it was evident that the insurance policy provided no right of recovery from the insurance company, Fine's Flowers brought an action against the insurance agent for breach of his duty of care in failing to notify it of insufficient insurance coverage. The insurance agent defended on the grounds that such a duty of care was so broad and sweeping as almost to make him strictly liable, and that it was not part of his duty to know everything about a client's business in order to be in a position to anticipate every conceivable form of loss. The court nevertheless held that on the facts of the case a duty of care did exist, and Fine's Flowers succeeded in recovering damages from the agent. The grounds for recovery could equally be classified as negligent omission or breach of a special fiduciary relationship which had evolved between Fine's Flowers and its insurance agent.[21]

ILLUSTRATION B

Avery was being moved from Winnipeg to Regina by his employer. He located a real estate agent, Salie, in Regina and described the size and location of the house as well as the price and down payment that he was interested in. He also told Salie that he did not want to assume a mortgage with a high rate of interest or one that required early renegotiation. Subsequently, Salie telephoned Avery in Winnipeg to advise of a new listing that filled all his requirements. Salie had not checked the term of the existing mortgage directly but relied on data supplied, with a disclaimer of responsibility for accuracy, by the Regina Real Estate Board; these data showed a mortgage outstanding at 7.25% per annum with 21 years to run. Avery flew at once to Regina and made an offer on the house which was accepted by the vendor. Ten months after occupying the house, Avery learned that the mortgage was about to mature; he was obliged to refinance the mortgage at 10% per annum.

Avery brought an action against Salie for damages based on the present value of the additional interest he would have to pay. He succeeded in obtaining damages, but for a smaller amount than claimed because of uncertainties that might prevent the full loss claimed from occurring, such as the possibility that his employer might again move him and his family to another city.[22]

---

[21] Fine Flowers Ltd. v. General Accident Assurance Co. *et al.* (1974), 49 D.L.R. (3d) 641; affirmed (1978), 81 D.L.R. (3d) 139.

[22] Avery v. Salie (1977), 25 D.L.R. (3d) 495.

Setting Standards for Professional Services

The Nature of the Problem

Many goods and services are technical and complex, and an information gap often exists between those who buy them and those who sell. In dealings with the professions, a client is often unable to judge whether a practitioner is performing to an acceptable standard of care while the work proceeds. Much substandard professional work escapes detection because ordinarily several unhappy events must coincide before an actual injury or loss to a client results. But despite suffering no apparent loss, a client may not be receiving the quality of service bargained for, since the potential for better decisions and risk reduction is not being realized.

Hindsight and Foresight

One possible approach to the assessment of standards of professional services is simply to wait and see whether a client incurs any loss from relying on professional advice — a hindsight or *ex post* approach. This approach tends to turn professionals into insurers of their work and suggests that they will be strictly liable for all consequences of their clients' reliance upon it. In its extreme form, such an approach would make it impossible for most, if not all, professionals to continue to practise.

A second approach is to compare the quality of professional work done or advice given with standards prevailing in the profession at the time — a forward-looking or *ex ante* approach. The forward-looking approach requires other qualified professionals to give their opinions about whether the work in question has complied with acceptable professional standards. As well, it usually requires reference to a published code of conduct setting standards for that profession. This approach in its extreme form would seek to assess the adequacy of professional work without reference to the consequences of relying on it. Total disregard of these consequences would be unsatisfactory and unworkable, both for clients and for professionals, for it would ignore the economic reality that the effort and care devoted to a problem must have a relation to the value of the outcome.

Since we cannot ignore the costs and benefits of professional services, a modified version of the second approach suggests itself: professionals must form their opinions and advice in settings in which they cannot know whether their diagnosis will turn out to be inaccurate and their advice wrong. Frequently, however, they can reduce risks by putting more time and effort into their work. The problem is to decide just what degree of professional care is appropriate and economically justified in the circumstances. The professional who devotes the appropriate amount of skill and care would then meet the required standard in this modified version, even though the advice should turn out to be wrong. In this approach, foresight includes an element of awareness about the seriousness of harm that may flow from faulty professional advice.

Our courts are staffed by judges who are themselves members of a profession and aware of the dangers of being too influenced by hindsight. Lord Denning recognized the problem clearly:

> ... the judge required Mr. Jordan to come up to the very high standard of professional competence that the law requires. That suggests that the law makes no allowance for errors of judgment. This would be a mistake. Else there would be a danger, in all cases of professional men, of their being made liable whenever something happens to go wrong. Whenever I give a judgment, and it is afterwards reversed by the House of Lords, is it to be said that I was negligent? That I did not pay enough attention to a previous binding authority or the like? Every one of us every day gives a judgment which is afterwards found to be wrong. So also with a barrister who advises that there is a good cause of action and it afterwards fails. Is it to be said on that account that he was negligent? Likewise with medical men. If they are found liable whenever they do not effect a cure, or whenever anything untoward happens, it would do a great disservice to the profession itself.[23]

It is especially tempting to judge professional forecasts of company earnings with the benefit of hindsight. Liability for negligent misrepresentation, determined by whether or not the forecast proved to be incorrect, would effectively eliminate all published forecasts. The alternative is to judge forecasts on a forward-looking basis, on the reasonableness of the framework of assumptions within which the forecast was made, and on the thoroughness and care with which the data were obtained and the calculations made.

Hindsight was explicity rejected as the dominant factor in *Hodgins v. Hydro-Electric Commission of the Township of Nepean.*[24] Hodgins wished to add an extension with an indoor swimming pool to his house. Through his contractor, he sought the advice of the local hydro-electric commission on heating the addition. An employee of the commission, Runions, provided an estimate of the cost of heating by electricity. In reliance on the estimate, Hodgins specified electric heating for the extension. The estimate proved to be much below the actual costs. Hodgins sued the hydro-electric commission for negligent misrepresentation, on the authority of *Hedley Byrne*. In the Ontario Court of Appeal Mr. Justice Evans observed:

> ... the Court is required to consider the information available in 1967 to one in the position of Runions. The question then arises: Did Runions exercise reasonable skill, competence and diligence in the preparation of the cost estimate or did he not? In the opinion of the expert, Runions calculated the heat loss in the same manner as anyone similarly expert in the art would have done in 1967. In the light of that uncontradicted evidence, it would appear that Runions prepared his estimate according to the skill and knowledge available to those engaged in that particular field. If Runions met the standard then he was not negligent and no liability can be imputed to the defendant. That the estimate was incorrect is not questioned, but it is not sufficient that the plaintiff establish merely that Runions' estimate was wrong, he must go further and establish that the incorrect estimate resulted from a lack of skill, competence or diligence on the part of Runions... There was no failure on the part of the defendant to discharge the only duty in law which it owed to the plaintiff, which was to take reasonable care in the preparation of the cost estimate.[25]

---

23 Whitehouse v. Jordan, [1980] 1 All E.R. 650 at p. 658.
24 (1975), 60 D.L.R. (3d) 1.
25 *Ibid.*, at p. 4.

Who Sets the Standards?

The *Hodgins* case raised another important aspect of professional liability, that of arriving at the appropriate standard for judging professional conduct. The case was appealed to the Supreme Court of Canada, where Chief Justice Laskin agreed that the action should be dismissed. However, he added:

> In a case like the present, where liability is sought to be based on negligent misrepresentation, I do not think that it is invariably enough to defeat the action that the defendant has used the skill or knowledge known to him or to others in his field of endeavour.... In my opinion, the care or skill that must be shown by the defendant must depend, as it does here, on what is the information or advice sought from him and which he has unqualifiedly represented that he can give. He may assume to act in a matter beyond his then professional knowledge or that of others in the field and, if he does, he cannot then so limit the plaintiff's reliance unless he qualifies his information or advice accordingly or unless the plaintiff knows what are the limitations of the defendant's competence when seeking the information or advice.[26]

A professional must exercise the same degree of skill and possess the same level of knowledge as is generally expected of members of that profession: that is to say, he or she must live up to the standards of the profession. The courts will normally consider two types of evidence in determining what those standards are. Many professions publish a code of conduct for their members, or sets of guidelines to be followed in particular types of work. These can usually be taken as laying down an appropriate standard. Frequently, the courts also hear the testimony of practitioners who state what they consider a proper standard. Sometimes, of course, professional opinion is divided — for example, about the best medical treatment in a particular circumstance. In such a case it will normally be sufficient that the defendant has followed a well recognized practice, even though some other procedure might arguably have done better.[27]

Complying with normal professional standards, however, is not always an adequate defence. Established standards should not be allowed to become a means for protecting members of a profession from liability:[28] where there is other evidence that can be understood by an ordinary person, that evidence can be taken into account by a court even when it contradicts the testimony of experts.[29] As Chief Justice Laskin pointed out in the *Hodgins* case, sometimes a professional undertakes a task that is beyond the usual skills of his profession; he cannot then fall back upon the normal professional standard. The degree of skill and knowledge must be commensurate with the task undertaken.

Informed Consent

The setting of professional standards has a special application in the doctor-patient relationship. Many kinds of medical treatment — particularly surgery — involve risk-taking

---

26 *Ibid.*, at p. 5.
27 Belknap v. Meekes (1990), 64 D.L.R. (4th) 452.
28 See, for example, the decision of the Supreme Court of Canada in Roberge v. Bolduc, [1991] 1 S.C.R.374, in which a notary was held to have been negligent in conducting a title search despite having followed the common practice in the profession.
29 Anderson v. Chasney, [1949] 4 D.L.R. 71.

even when the procedure is carried out to the highest standards of care and skill; there may be a small chance that a patient will not respond well and will be worse off afterwards. We often hear about "complications" arising after an operation and that if they do not clear up the patient would have been better off without having undergone the ordeal. We shall assume that the doctor has not operated negligently and is not liable for poor performance. Nevertheless, a patient who has been harmed may complain that had the risks been explained, he or she would never have submitted to the treatment: the doctor in failing to inform the patient fully of the risks did not obtain a proper consent. In effect, the treatment was not authorized.

There are alternative ways of holding a doctor responsible for a subsequent harm should one of the risks occur: the doctor can be held negligent for not carrying out the duty to inform the patient; or, alternatively, to have committed a battery (an unwarranted invasion of the person) by performing the treatment without consent. Both approaches lead to liability if the doctor is found to have been in breach of a duty to the patient.

The modern tendency has been to hold a doctor liable in battery only when it can be said that there has been no genuine informed consent at all.[30] However, the courts have recognized a patient's right to full information about the risks inherent in a treatment and failure to inform fully normally amounts to negligence. When applying the principle, a court first considers whether the doctor disclosed every risk which he or she knew or ought to have known would be significant or material to the patient's decision to consent to the medical procedure. If the procedure is at the frontier of medical knowledge, and may, when performed, turn out unpredictably, the doctor must so inform the patient. However, the test applies only in relation to the standards and knowledge of the medical profession at the time the information is provided.

The court also considers a second question: would a reasonable person in the position of the patient, on a balance of probabilities, have decided against the procedure upon a proper disclosure of the risks? If the court is satisfied on the facts that the answer is "yes", then it is also saying that the failure to inform was not only a breach of duty but also caused the harm — and the patient will be awarded damages in compensation.[31] But where a physician fails to inform the patient of a minimal risk involved in a necessary treatment, and the court is satisfied that the patient would have consented to the treatment had the risk been explained, the physician will not be liable.[32]

if fails to inform & if done so patient would have said 'no' then doctor is liable.

CAUSATION AS A REQUIREMENT FOR LIABILITY

In the preceding chapter we defined the elements of tort liability and in so doing specified the conditions that must be met before damages will be awarded as compensation to an injured party: the court must find that the defendant owed a duty to the injured party; that the defendant was guilty of a breach of that duty; and that the breach of duty caused the injury. We have discussed the first two of these conditions in this chapter insofar as

---

30 See Norberg v. Wynrib (1992) 12 C.C.L.T.(2d) 1.
31 See Hopp v. Lepp (1980), 112 D.L.R. (3d) 67; Reibl v. Hughes (1980), 114 D.L.R. (3d) 1.
32 Kitchen v. McMullen (1990), 62 D.L.R. (4th) 481.

they affect the liability of a professional, and now turn to consider the special problems of satisfying the requirement of causation.

Professional relationships require the willing cooperation of the client, and his or her reliance on the advice of the professional. Causation becomes a question of reliance. As we have noted, in most instances a client purchases professional assistance on a complex technical question and has little or no basis for making an independent judgment about what course of action to follow. In some situations, it is possible that the professional opinion may simply coincide with the client's own inclination.

ILLUSTRATION

An investment company became interested in acquiring control of an apparently prosperous family company. The investment company commissioned a report on the prospective acquisition from a well known investment analyst. The report estimated the family company to be worth over $4 million and considered it to be a sound investment. Without having read the report, the directors of the investment company decided that they should move quickly; they heard rumours that there was another prospective purchaser. They purchased all the shares in the family company for $3.5 million. Subsequently, they learned that the major asset of their acquisition was almost worthless, and they had paid several times what the shares were worth.

Despite her negligence, the analyst should not be found liable, since her conduct was not in any way a cause of the loss. This hypothetical example is based in part on the decision in *Toromont Industrial Holdings v. Thorne, Gunn, Helliwell & Christenson.*[33] In that case, Mr. Justice Jessup said:

> What loss, if any, flows from the fact that the certificate of the auditors was wrong and that the auditors had been negligent in the audit? ... [T]he decision to purchase had already been made. The Toromont board and executive committee were eager to complete the purchase. They made little investigation and were worried about another prospective purchaser lurking in the background. I really do not think I can say that the purchase would not have been completed, or that the loss flowing from the negligence of the defendant is, in this case, the difference between the purchase price and the true value of the shares ... [N]o loss has been proved by Toromont flowing from the negligence of the defendant.[34]

Generally speaking, it is up to the plaintiff to establish that the misrepresentation led to the loss. As a matter of policy, legislatures sometimes wish to encourage compliance with the law by making it easier for plaintiffs to hold certain classes of defendants liable for their misconduct. Accordingly, they may relieve plaintiffs of the burden of establishing that they actually relied on a misrepresentation. Securities acts usually give buyers of securities a right to sue those responsible for disclosing corporate information in prospectuses when the information proves false and the buyer appears to have suffered a loss. These acts also give tenderers (sellers) a similar right in relation to information contained

---

[33] (1976), 14 O.R. (2d) 86.
[34] *Ibid.*, at pp. 94-95. (Some damages were awarded, however, on other grounds.)

in take-over bid circulars. For these types of disclosure, a person who buys or sells shares is deemed to have relied on the misrepresentation".[35] The statutes shift the onus to the misrepresentor who may then avoid liability by proving that the plaintiff had not relied on the misstatement.

THE ROLE OF PROFESSIONAL ORGANIZATIONS

Origins

Professions are, in some respects, the modern counterpart of medieval guilds. Guilds had their own standards of education and apprenticeship for admission, and their own courts for adjudicating disputes affecting the economic activities of their members. Modern professions are generally more concerned with offering expert opinions, diagnoses, and cost and value estimates than with the practice of crafts requiring manual skills, though both these elements are important in some professions such as medicine, dentistry, and architecture. Because of this historical background, the autonomy of professions, that is, their ability to determine and police their own specialized standards of compliance and behaviour, remains a jealously guarded prerogative.

Responsibilities and Powers

Today, most of the major professions — medicine, nursing, dentistry, accounting, law, engineering, and architecture — are governed by professional organizations established under, and to some extent regulated by, provincial statutes. A typical professional organization has a governing council composed mainly of elected representatives of the profession, but it may also have external lay representatives appointed by the government to provide an impartial voice in decision-making and to represent the public interest. Professional bodies have a number of special responsibilities:

(a) to set educational and entrance standards for candidates wishing to become full-fledged professional members;

(b) to examine and accredit educational institutions that prepare candidates for membership;

(c) to set and adjust standards of ethical conduct and professional competence on an ongoing basis;

(d) to hear complaints about and administer discipline to members who fail to live up to the established standards;

(e) to defend the profession against attacks that it considers unfair, and to look after the general welfare of the profession.

---

[35] See, for example: Securities Act, R.S.O. 1990, c. S-5, ss. 130(1) and 131(1).

The governing statute typically gives members of the organization the exclusive right to use a professional designation to identify themselves, and also usually gives members the exclusive right to practise their profession.[36] Anyone who identifies himself or herself as a member or attempts to practise when not accredited as a member may be — and usually is — prosecuted for committing an offence under the provincial statute.

Two important consequences flow from these powers. First, exclusivity gives these "self-governing" professions great power over the quality and cost of their services to the public; hence there exists a strong public interest in the affairs of the organizations. Second, the right to discipline gives the organizations great power over individual members; expulsion, or suspension for any extended period, may destroy a member's means of livelihood. As a result, economists have become very interested in the role of the professions, and especially of their governing bodies, in the economies of Western countries. In addition, researchers interested in the quality and accessibility of services and in administrative fairness in hearing complaints against professionals have investigated and written extensively about these problems.[37]

Discipline

Our concern is primarily with the last point, complaints against professionals and the role of governing bodies in policing the ethical conduct of members and maintaining their standards of competence.

Unfortunately, most professions have an inevitable minority of members who act in an unethical manner and harm clients. Such cases are often widely publicized. The response of governing bodies is uniform: breaches of good faith are severely punished by expulsion or suspension. (There may also be provision for some form of compensation to the injured client by the governing body itself.) These actions are quite apart from any criminal prosecution of the wrongdoer or from private (civil) liability actions discussed in the preceding sections of this chapter.

Perhaps the more pervasive and difficult cases are those arising from alleged breaches of professional standards of skill and care. In what may be considered isolated cases of negligence, governing bodies ordinarily leave the matter to the regular courts, where an aggrieved client may bring an action. However, in repeated cases of violations, or where the conduct of the professional has so grossly offended standards that the competence needed to remain in practice is called into question, the governing body will take disciplinary action in the same manner as it would for unethical conduct. Implicit in the task of maintaining standards is the obligation to take corrective measures to improve performance.

For the conduct of disciplinary proceedings against members, a professional organization usually has a standing discipline committee consisting of experienced members of the profession. In addition, the governing council usually designates one or more other members or a separate committee to act as "prosecutor" ; both the prosecutor and the accused member may be represented by lawyers at the disciplinary hearing. Ordinarily, the finding of a discipline committee takes the form of a recommendation to the governing council of the organization, which then acts on the recommendation to expel, suspend, reprimand, or acquit. Statutes usually provide for a further appeal to the regular courts.

---

[36] For example, the exclusive right to practise applies to medicine and law, but not to some areas of accounting.

[37] See, for example: Trebilcock, Tuohy & Wolfson, *Professional Regulation: A Staff Study*, prepared for the Professional Organizations Committee (Ontario: Ministry of the Attorney General, 1979).

Conflict of Duty Toward Clients and the Courts

A member of a professional body faces a dilemma when required to testify in court proceedings affecting a client or patient. On the one hand, the member is expected to reply to questions under oath when examined and cross-examined in court; on the other hand, the member's testimony may appear to be a breach of confidence in the professional relationship with the client. It appears that a member or student member of a professional organization has a duty to ask the court for a ruling before divulging any information obtained in a confidential capacity.[38]

A professional who learns that a client may be engaged in or is contemplating possibly illegal activities may well experience a further problem of interpreting her professional duties to the client. Needless to say, the professional must not assist the client (except to advise on possible illegality), and in dissociating herself from the client's activities may have to resign or terminate the relationship. It appears to be generally conceded, however, that a professional would not normally be obliged to reveal confidential knowledge to prosecuting authorities.

Implications of Professional Membership

The historical development of the professions, the present elaborate organization of their self-governing bodies, and the barriers to entry in the form of lengthy educational requirements and restricted availability of positions have created substantial prestige for those who are admitted as members. As a result, the sole fact of membership itself creates a representation to potential clients that a member possesses professional competence and skill of an order higher than might be expected of a person not holding membership. In other words, to offer oneself to the public as a member of a professional organization is to offer a standard of performance consistent with professional standards and to be accountable for failure to measure up to those standards. The corollary is that if a person is content to seek the advice or opinion of another who does not claim professional qualifications, the purchaser of the advice is not entitled to expect as high a standard of care (though a standard of care will still exist). In the words of Lord Diplock,

> ... the reference to 'such care as the circumstances require' presupposes an ascertainable standard of skill, competence and diligence with which the advisor is acquainted. ... Unless he carries on the business or profession of giving advice of that kind he cannot be reasonably expected to know whether any and if so what degree of skill, competence and diligence is called for, and ... he cannot be reasonably held to have accepted the responsibility of conforming to a standard of skill, competence and diligence of which he is unaware, simply because he answers the enquiry with knowledge that the advisee tends to rely on his answer.[39]

---

38   See Conkwright v. Conkwright (1970) O.R. 784.
39   Mutual Life & Citizen's Assurance Co. Ltd. v. Evatt, [1971] All E.R. 150. The implications of representing oneself as having expert qualifications have been dealt with in the comments of Chief Justice Laskin in the Hodgins case, quoted above in the section "Who Sets the Standards?"

Questions for Review

1. What factors, apart from judicial decisions, have probably contributed to an enlarged scope of professional liability?
2. Give illustrations of circumstances in which a professional may be held liable for negligence to someone other than a client.
3. To be held liable in damages for negligence, is it necessary for a professional to know the identify of the person injured?
4. Who turned out to be the principal defendant in *Fine's Flowers v. General Accident Insurance Co. et al.,* and why?
5. What crucial objection can be made to a "hindsight" approach to determining the adequacy of a particular professional practitioner's standard of care?
6. What problems does a "forward-looking" approach raise in determining whether a professional has exercised the required standard of care when a client suffers a loss?
7. Why is reliance on a negligent misrepresentation usually a necessary condition for liability?
8. In what respect may decisions of the courts put pressure on a professional body to codify its standards of professional conduct and competence?
9. How may a "civil rights" question arise in the activities of a professional organization?
10. The discipline committee of a professional organization regularly publishes its decisions in a newsletter circulated to members. The announcement identifies the member disciplined, the nature of the offence, and the penalty imposed. What professional purpose is served by this practice? Does the professional organization have any defence if the member (or former member) sues it for the tort of defamation?

Problems

Problem 1

Computniks Inc. hired Davinci as an architect to design its new office building. Davinci engaged Everest Consulting Engineers to design the foundation work and examine soil conditions. Everest was not a specialist in soils and after a preliminary inspection recommended deep soil tests by a geotechnical engineer to make sure that the underlying soil conditions could support the building. Davinci, without discussing Everest's recommendation with Computniks, decided that deep soil tests were not worth the cost and informed Everest that Computniks would not approve the expense. When a city building inspector subsequently asked for a soil report before approving construction, Everest supplied a letter describing its own superficial examination of the soil, which implied that there was adequate support for the building. It said nothing about its original recommendation for a more thorough deep test by specialists.

After construction, the building subsided and required $500 000 in remedial measures to make it safe and extend its life. Computniks sued both Davinci and Everest for damages. Discuss the grounds on which they might be held liable. What should be the result and why?

Problem 2

Miller suffered from rheumatoid arthritis, which caused a deformity in his right elbow, stiffness in the joint and numbness in his hand. He felt embarrassed in public because of the awkwardness in the use of his arm. He consulted Krauter, an orthopaedic surgeon, about obtaining relief through a surgical correction of the elbow. Krauter said she could cure the numbness in his hand and relieve the stiffness in his elbow, but she said that correcting the deformity would be complex and difficult, requiring the breaking of a bone in his arm and a long period in a cast; she thought it would be too difficult for him to cope with the procedure and recommended against it. At the time of this discussion, Krauter thought Miller was convinced by her advice to proceed only with curing the numbness and relieving the stiffness.

The following morning, however, when Miller had been prepared for surgery, he insisted on speaking to Krauter and said he would not let the operation proceed unless she was willing to correct the deformity as well. Krauter tried to dissuade him by saying he was being foolish and did not understand the consequences of his demand. Nevertheless, Miller refused to proceed and it seemed to Krauter that he had an obsession about having his deformity removed. Finally she agreed to perform the additional surgery, and Miller signed a consent form for it. Krauter did not try to explain that the surgical procedure for correcting the deformity might lead to additional stiffness in the elbow and thus undo much of the other corrective surgery.

Krauter then performed all the operations, and as a result there was additional stiffness in Miller's elbow. He sued Krauter for negligence in not informing him more fully of the risks involved in correcting the deformity, claiming that had he known about them he would not have consented. Discuss whether Miller should succeed in his action.

Problem 3

Eaton was shown a house by Cameron, a sales agent for a firm of real estate brokers. Eaton liked the location but said that the house would be satisfactory only if renovations were made to the kitchen, bathroom and basement, and if it were levelled to correct a slope in the living room floor. He asked, "Where can I find out about how practical it would be to do these things?" Cameron suggested obtaining a report from a qualified structural engineer. Eaton replied that he was not prepared to pay a large inspection fee. Cameron then recommended Jason, a contractor with whom she had had business deal-ings, and said that she thought she could persuade Jason to drive out from his office and prepare an opinion on the house without making any charge.

Cameron spoke to Jason, explaining that her client would not buy the house without a clear idea of the cost of putting it in satisfactory shape. Jason spent about one hour exam-ining the house and told Eaton that the house was sound and would take the necessary repairs. Eaton bought the house and hired a contractor to make the alterations.

The contractor discovered extensive dry rot and had to remove and replace some sub-floors and various joists and beams in bearing walls, and add adequate supports. As a result, the cost of the alterations was more than doubled. Eaton brought an action against Jason for his added costs. Jason argued that it had been understood that he was only to do a preliminary inspection and that in any event a large amount of rubble in the base-ment had prevented him from doing a complete inspection. He also pointed out that he was not a member of any professional engineering body.

Discuss the issues related to these facts and offer an opinion on the probable outcome of the action.

Cases

Case 1

Elwood Wayman is a prominent investment counsel in the business of designing, developing, and managing the private investment portfolios of busy, successful professional men and women. He is registered under the Securities Act. He also sends a monthly newsletter entitled *The Insiders' Forum* to each of his clients. Last April's edition of the newsletter included the following item:

Confidential and For the Use of Clients Only

> I recommend immediate purchase of the common shares of Monolithic Memories at any price below $20 a share. This company is soundly managed and has a potential limited only by the memory in its new computer.

On his way to work, M.B. Aye picked up a copy of this newsletter left behind by an earlier passenger on the subway train. He recalled that an acquaintance reputed to be very successful on the stock market had, only the day before, confided in him and two or three others at lunch that Monolithic Memories looked like a "hot prospect"; the coincidence of being reminded of it in this way seemed a lucky sign. As soon as he arrived at his office Aye decided to telephone Wayman as a last-minute check and managed to reach him. Aye said that he would be interested in buying the shares only if a capital gain could be realized quickly. Wayman confidently, "Yes, I still think it's an excellent buy. No doubt you'll double your money in three months. I hope we may have you for a client sometime soon."

Aye then borrowed $80 000, giving a mortgage on the stock-in-trade of his retail furniture store. He invested this money in 4000 shares of Monolithic Memories Ltd. Three months later, Aye read to his dismay that creditors of the company had petitioned for its bankruptcy. He also learned that the Securities Commission had suspended trading in the shares. Unable to repay his loan from the expected proceeds of the sale of the shares, he stood by helplessly while the finance company took possession of and sold a substantial part of his stock-in-trade; he had to close his business.

Aye then brought an action for damages against Wayman. In the course of the trial Aye's lawyer referred the court to the Securities Act, one section of which reads as follows:

> 38. (2) Future value. No person or company, with the intention of effecting a trade in a security, shall give any undertaking, written or oral, relating to the future value or price of such security.

Section 122 (1) (d) of the Securities Act provides that it is an offence to fail to comply with any provision of the Act.

Discuss whether, on the facts of this case, a court would be justified in applying the decision in *Hedley Byrne & Co., Ltd. v. Heller and Partners, Ltd.*, and offer an opinion on the probable outcome of the action.

Case 2

In March, 1988, Ivan Anderson left his job and took a position with A. Anderson Ltd., a closely held company owned and managed by his uncle, Archy Anderson. Archy and his wife tranferred a number of common and preferred shares in the company to Ivan in return for his leaving his other position and joining them. One condition of the transfer, set out in a letter dated March 18, 1988, was that should Ivan's employment with the company be terminated for any reason, his uncle would buy the shares back at fair value. "Fair value" was stated to be "the value as determined by a reputable firm of business consultants".

Ivan's employment with A. Anderson Limited was terminated on April 4, 1994. Some time later the company's secretary asked the business consulting firm of Carter, Benson, Randall and Co., to place a value on the shares held by Ivan Anderson, and gave them access to all the accounting records of the company. The consultants replied:

CARTER, BENSON, RANDALL AND CO.

Winnipeg, Manitoba

13 May, 1994

The Secretary,
A. Anderson Ltd.,
1500 Portage Avenue,
Winnipeg

Dear Sir,

Valuation of Shares — I. Anderson

1. We refer to your verbal request to place a value on the shares held by Mr. I. Anderson in your company in accordance with the letter of the 18th March 1988.
2. The shares held by Mr. I. Anderson in the company are as follows:- 1750 Common Shares of $1 each, 500 6% Non-Cumulative Preference Shares of $10 each.
3. In our view the fair value of these shares on the 4th day of April 1994 was as follows:-
   (a) The 500 6% Non-Cumulative Preference Shares of $10 each at a valuation of $2100.
   (b) The 1750 Ordinary Shares of $1 each at a valuation of $4750.

Yours faithfully,

(Signed)

On June 11, 1994 Ivan, in reliance on this valuation, transferred his shares to his uncle for $6850. About three months later, on September 10, 1994, a holding company was incorporated to acquire all the issued share capital of A. Anderson Ltd. After about a further four months the shares in the holding company were offered for sale to the public by a prospectus dated January 14, 1995. The prospectus included a report prepared and signed by the company's auditors. It placed a value on the company's share capital of $1 700 000. This value, if applied pro rata to the shares formerly owned by Ivan, would have made them worth not less than $35 000, that is to say more than five times the value put on them by the business consultants only seven months earlier.

Ivan felt that he had been unfairly treated and brought an action against the business consulting firm of Carter, Benson, Randall and Co., alleging that the valuation was misconceived and erroneous in one or more fundamental respects and was made on a wrong basis or bases. Among other things he said that the consultants had based their valuation on the last balance sheet for the year ended July 31, 1993 and had failed to take into account the great increase in the profits between July 31, 1993 and April 4, 1994. The profits had doubled in that time. He said that the consultants had included the goodwill at the book figure of $30 000, which was the figure at which it had stood since 1980, whereas it was worth far more. He also said that the consultants had failed to take into account the intention to "go public", which was known to them at that time.

Explain the nature of the legal problem or problems raised by these facts. Express an opinion, with reasons, about the probable outcome of the action.

Case 3

The Popular Furniture Company Limited was a small company turning out wooden furniture and doing contract work on interiors of offices and private residences. It required further financing and its manager and principal shareholder, Craftsman, approached the bank for a term loan. The bank manager had some reservations about Craftsman's abilities as a manager and agreed to approve a loan of $400 000 on the condition that an additional $300 000 of equity capital be invested in the company as well. The bank manager then introduced a local venture capitalist, Richman, to Craftsman.

Richman toured the plant of the Popular Furniture Company Limited and was impressed with its production efficiency. He told Craftsman that he would favourably consider buying new shares of the company that would provide it with an additional $300 000 in cash, if he were made a director, and if he were satisfied with the company's audited financial statements for the business year just ended.

In previous years McAdam & McCollum, a firm of practising public accountants whose partners were members of a leading professional accounting body, had done accounting for the Popular Furniture Company Limited. Craftsman got in touch with McAdam, explained the situation to him, and pleaded for an early audit of the company's accounting records. The accounting firm was very busy preparing income tax returns for clients at the time, but eventually sent Postwell, a junior audit clerk, to do the work. Postwell had been at the offices of the Popular Furniture Co. for the week during the spring of each of the past two years. As a closely held corporation, the company had contracted only for assistance in preparing its financial statements on a "non-audit" basis; that is, it had engaged the accountants to provide accounting services on terms that permitted them to accept company records as they stood and to dispense with the usual checks and verifications expected in a formal audit. No one told Postwell that the scope of her work this time would be any different from what it had been in the past; McAdam & McCollum had not asked for any increase in their fee.

Postwell prepared a set of financial statements in collaboration with the company's bookkeeper, which entailed some review of the accounting records for the purpose of ascertaining that the statements were plausible in the circumstances. McAdam & McCollum then delivered to Craftsman copies of these financial statements on their letterhead with the following report appended to them:

Auditors' Report

We have examined the records of The Popular Furniture Co. Ltd. for the year ended February 28, 1993 and have prepared therefrom the attached balance sheet as at that date and income statement for that year. Our examination included a general review of the accounting procedures and such tests of the accounting records and other supporting evidence as we considered necessary in the circumstances.

The accounts receivable are as shown by the records and we have not confirmed them by direct communication with the recorded debtors.

The inventories of materials and work-in-process were not taken by us or under our supervision and have been accepted as certified to us by Mr. Albert Craftsman.

Subject to the foregoing reservations we report that, in our opinion, the attached balance sheet and related income statement present fairly the financial position of The Popular Furniture Co. Ltd. as at March 1, 1993 and the results of operations for the year then ended in accordance with generally accepted accounting principles and as shown by the books of the company.

This was the first year in which the accounting firm had reported on the financial statements in this way. In the past, it had mailed the financial statements to Craftsman on plain paper, accompanied by a letter whose concluding paragraph read, "The attached financial statements have been prepared from the books and records and information furnished, without audit, and we are not able to express an opinion as to the financial position of the business."

The financial statements showed a profit for the year ended February 28 of $100 000 and an adequate working capital position as of February 28. Craftsman gave a copy of them, including the report of McAdam & McCollum, to Richman, who then invested $300 000 in a new issue of the company's shares and became a director and the chief executive officer of the company.

The company ran into severe financial difficulties in the following financial year, and went into liquidation. One of the facts that emerged was that during January of the preceding year, a department store had sent to the company an advance deposit of $200 000 in respect of a future shipment of furniture; the amount had been reported as sales revenue for the year ended February 28, without any shipment of the goods having been made so that they were also reported on the balance sheet as inventory as of February 28. As a result, what had been reported in the income statement as a profit should have been reported instead as a substantial loss, and working capital had been severely overstated on the balance sheet. The transaction with the department store was the first of its kind in the history of the company and Postwell had simply missed its significance in the course of her work.

After these unfortunate events, Richman brought an action against McAdam & McCollum claiming damages of $300 000, the amount of his lost investment in the company. At the trial Richman's lawyer referred the court to the following recommendations, among others, in the *Handbook* of the Canadian Institute of Chartered Accountants:

6020.18 Generally accepted auditing procedures in respect of accounts and notes receivable should include some form of direct confirmation of accounts and notes receivable by communication with debtors.

6030.09 Generally accepted auditing procedures in respect of inventories should include:
  (a) a review of the methods followed in the determination of quantities and values;
  (b) attendance by the auditors at the stocktaking, whether this is at the end of the financial period or at other times;
  (c) tests of the inventory quantities with confirmatory evidence such as rough count sheets, perpetual stock records, etc.;
  (d) tests of the pricing of the inventory items;

(e) tests of the clerical accuracy of the inventory.

8100.34 The public accountant's communication accompanying unaudited financial statements relating to a review engagement should clearly convey the limited nature of his involvement with the statements. The communication should be entitled "Accountant's Comments" and should:

(a) identify the financial statements;

(b) state who prepared the financial statements;

(c) indicate the source of the information used in the preparation of the financial statements when these have been prepared by the public accountant;

(d) state that a review was performed and briefly describe its nature;

(e) state that an audit has not been performed and disclaim an opinion; and

(f) not express any form of negative assurance.

8100.35 The communication should be phrased to avoid possible confusion with an auditor's report and accordingly:

(a) should not refer to the public accountant as auditor;

(b) should not use the word "report"; and

(c) should not include an opinion on the financial statements or any part thereof.

Offer an opinion about whether Richman's action should succeed; give your reasons.

PART THREE

CONTRACTS

In Chapter 3, we noted that, for business purposes, the largest areas of private law are contracts, torts, property and trusts. Contracts are the foundation of virtually all business arrangements, whether for employment, for the sale of goods, services or land, for the formation of a partnership or corporation or for the settlement of a dispute. An understanding of contract law is essential to an understanding of business arrangements. Hence, Chapters 6 to 17 are devoted to a comprehensive overview of contractual arrangements, from their formation, to a discussion of the various things that can go wrong, to their ultimate discharge, either by performance, by mutual agreement among the parties or by an aggrieved part resorting to the courts for a remedy.

Chapters 6 to 9 inclusive discuss the formation of contract — the various elements needed for the courts to hold that an arrangement is binding in law: Chapter 6, the procedures, formal or informal, followed by the parties; Chapter 7, the nature of a bargain and the elements required to make a promise binding; Chapter 8, who may bind themselves to a contract; Chapter 9, public policy and why certain bargains are found not to be binding. Chapters 10 and 11 consider the things that can "go wrong" — a court will conclude that what seemed like a valid contract does not bind the parties because there is a serious flaw. Chapter 12 discusses the requirement that certain contracts must be in writing, and the sometimes surprising consequences when such a contract is only oral. Chapter 13 describes the process of interpreting terms of a contract when parties disagree about what they mean. Chapter 14 explains the way rights under a contract may be acquired by persons who were not originally parties to it. Chapters 15, 16 and 17 discuss, respectively, the ways in which contracts come to an end, the consequences of breach by one party, and the remedies available to an aggrieved party.

CHAPTER 6

FORMATION OF A CONTRACT: OFFER AND ACCEPTANCE

THE ROLE OF CONTRACT LAW

We tend to think of law as a body of rules that constrain and control individual activity in the best interests of society as a whole. This tendency is natural enough, since it reflects the purposes of such important and familiar areas of law as criminal law and torts, where obligations are placed *involuntarily* on each member of society. Yet the law has another important role: it enables individuals to enter voluntarily into obligations by following legal rules established for the purpose.

Why do people enter into such obligations? Why not remain free of all obligations not imposed by law? The answer is simple enough: the ability to enter into obligations voluntarily *expands* a person's freedom of choice. A person who wishes to acquire certain advantages can bargain for them; one can agree to an obligation for the benefit of others in exchange for the advantage desired. In Chapter 2, we noted that many legal rules work as guidelines to form a background for voluntary legal relationships such as business partnerships. In this context, law is a facilitative process, a framework within which parties can decide upon and bargain for their own legal obligations. In a sense, it is an area where people make law for themselves and where they can express their individual preferences. Contract law is the prime example of law in its facilitative role.

We must not make this picture appear too idealized. As we shall see, there is often great inequality between parties to contracts in terms of bargaining power, expertise, and intelligence, and in some circumstances there is no opportunity whatever to bargain. Thus, many unfair bargains are made. Second, the rules of contract law are human rules subject to human frailties; sometimes they lead to unintended or unjust results. In a few instances, it seems beyond the ken of the legal mind to devise a fair solution for a manifestly difficult problem. On the whole, however, contract law responds well — perhaps better than most areas of the law — to the individual's needs and wishes, and it accommodates most relationships with a minimum of conflict.

THE NATURE OF A CONTRACT

Contracts generally begin with a promise, but not all promises become contracts. Although there may be a moral obligation to keep all promises seriously made, it does not follow that there will be a legal obligation. Contract law is concerned with legally binding promises. "The most popular description of a contract that can be given is also the most exact one, namely that it is a promise or set of promises which the law will enforce."[1] These words of a great English lawyer in the opening paragraph of his treatise on the law of contract, beg the question, "What types of promises will the law enforce?" Before we can discuss how the law "enforces" a contract, we need to decide whether there is a contract. Accordingly, we shall concern ourselves with two aspects of the definition through this and the following eleven chapters: first, an examination of the promise or promises that may form a contract, and second, an investigation of the resources available in the law to enforce them.

---

[1] Winfield, *Pollock's Principles of Contract* (13th ed.), p. 1. London: Stevens & Sons Limited, 1950.

THE NATURE OF AN OFFER

A contract does not come into existence until an offer has been made by one party and accepted by the other party. An *offer* is a tentative promise made by one party, the offeror, subject to a condition or containing a request to the other party, the offeree. When the offeree accepts the offer by agreeing to the condition or request, the offer is transformed into a contract. The promise is no longer tentative: the offeror is bound to carry out his or her promise while the offeree is bound to carry out the condition or request.

A mere invitation to do business is not an offer to make a contract. The display of a coat in a shop window does not amount to an offer to sell; a mail-order catalogue does not guarantee that the goods pictured or described will be delivered to all who try to order them. These are simply merchandising or advertising devices to attract customers and to start negotiations for a contract of sale. Perhaps the prospective customer, acting in response to the invitation, will make an offer which the merchant may in turn accept or refuse. On the other hand, the merchant may make an offer as soon as the customer shows interest.

Newspaper advertisements generally are presumed to be mere invitations to do business. An advertisement to sell goods at a certain price is an invitation to the public to visit the advertiser's place of business with a view to buying. Of course, a business cannot intend to sell merchandise to everyone who reads its advertisement. Its supply of goods is limited, and it cannot accurately predict the number of readers who will be seriously interested. If the advertisement were taken to be an offer and many people accepted it, the advertiser would be liable for breach of contract to all those who accepted its offer and to whom it could not supply the relevant goods. On the other hand, there is no rule that advertisements can never be offers; the courts have on occasion held them to be offers, when their wording reasonably favoured this intention. An advertisement to sell a fixed number of items at a fixed price to those who accept first, an offer of a reward for information or for the return of a lost object, or a reward to any person using a preventive medicine who still catches an illness, all may be valid offers. This group of advertisements forms only a very small proportion of newspaper advertisements; they are the exception rather than the rule.

When self-service supermarkets and drugstores arrived in England, the courts had to decide whether the display of merchandise constituted an offer and the act of the customer in taking the merchandise from the shelf amounted to an acceptance, or whether the display was merely an invitation to the customer to make an offer by taking the merchandise to the cashier.[2] The matter was of importance, because an English statute made it unlawful to sell certain chemical products unless the sale was supervised by a registered pharmacist. The court held that the statute was not violated because a registered pharmacist was at hand near the cashier with authority to refuse a customer's offer to purchase any drug. The judge said:

> The mere fact that a customer picks up a bottle of medicine from the shelves in this case does not amount to an acceptance of an offer to sell. It is an offer by the customer to buy, and there is no sale effected until the buyer's offer to buy is accepted by the acceptance of the price.[3]

---

[2] Pharmaceutical Society of Great Britain v. Boots Cash Chemists (Southern) Ltd. [1952] 2 All E.R. 456.
[3] *Ibid.*, per Lord Goddard at 458.

The Communication of an Offer

The form of an offer is not important as long as its sense is understood. The offeror could say, "I offer to sell you my car for $500", or, "I will sell you my car for $500", or even, "I'll take $500 for my car". All are equally good offers. In each instance the tentative promise is to sell the car if the buyer meets the condition of agreeing to pay the stated price.

We are accustomed to thinking of an offer as being communicated orally or in writing, but an offeror can also express an offer by conduct without words. Holding up one's hand for a taxi, raising a finger at an auction, and the gestures of floor traders at a stock exchange are examples that come to mind. As we shall see, an offeror may even communicate an offer by proceeding with performance to the knowledge of the party benefiting, though without any formal request having been made for the services rendered.

An offeree cannot accept an offer until first learning of it. This proposition has an unexpected twist. A person may find and return a lost article to its owner and afterwards learn that a reward has been offered for the return of the article. The finder is not entitled to the reward because she did not act *in response to* the offer of it. The offer must have been communicated before it can be accepted.

Crossed offers provide a further illustration of this rule. If A writes to B offering to sell her car for $1500 and B meanwhile has written a letter crossing A's letter in the mail offering to buy A's car for $1500, there is no contract. B was unaware of A's offer when he wrote, and accordingly B's letter could not be an acceptance; A was unaware of B's offer — A's letter, too, could not be an acceptance. Unless either A or B sends a subsequent acceptance, no contract will be formed.

Similarly, we cannot be obligated by people who do work for us without our knowledge. We are entitled first to receive an offer to do the work, which we may then accept or reject. A person for whom work has been done without his request, and without his knowledge, may well benefit from it; but as he has not accepted any offer to do the work, he has no contractual obligation to pay for it. In *Taylor v. Laird*,[4] Taylor had been hired to command Laird's ship; during a voyage he gave up his command but helped to work the vessel home in another capacity. Laird refused to pay Taylor for the different services. The court held that Laird was within his rights because he was not given the option of accepting or refusing Taylor's services.

Suppose, however, that goods or services are tendered to a person without his request but in circumstances where he has an opportunity to reject them. At common law, if he accepts the services or uses the goods, he is presumed to have accepted the offer and to have promised to pay the price. Unfortunately, this common law rule has proved to be inadequate in dealing with unconscionable selling practices that tempt consumers to obligate themselves to pay for unsolicited goods. Accordingly, many provinces have passed legislation to reverse the rule, at least as it relates to goods. For example, section 16 of the British Columbia Consumer Protection Act[5] states:

(2) Where unsolicited... goods are received, the recipient has no legal obligation to the sender in respect to them... unless and until the recipient expressly acknowledges to the sender in writing his intention to accept... [them].

---

4 (1856) 25 L. J. Ex. 329.
5 R.S.B.C. 1979, c. 64.

(3) In the absence of an acknowledgement... no action shall lie in the event of loss, misuse, damage, misappropriation or otherwise of the... unsolicited goods...

An Offer Made By Tendering a Written Document to the Offeree

Businesses that deal with the general public often present the terms of their offers in written documents handed to their customers, or they post notices containing terms on their business premises. Sometimes both methods are used together, the delivered document referring to the terms posted in the notice. Common examples are tickets for theatres, railways, and airlines, receipts for dry cleaning, parking space, watch repairs, and checked luggage, as well as insurance policies and bills of lading. Almost without exception, a person receiving any one of these documents is neither asked nor expected to read or approve of its terms. If he were to take time to read it and suggest changes, the offeror company would probably become very annoyed. It would say, "Take it or leave it." Thus, in fact, an offeree cannot change any terms of such a *standard form contract*: no real element of bargaining is involved. He *must* accept the offer as is or not at all. Often, as in a contract with a railway when there is only one practical means of transportation between two points, the offeree does not have the choice of refusing: he must accept if he is to make his journey. In these circumstances the offeror company has the tempting opportunity to disregard the interests of its offerees, the general public, and give itself every advantage; it rarely resists the temptation. On the other hand, the standard form contract is an indispensable tool. Imagine waiting in a queue at a railway ticket office while each would-be passenger bargains separately for each term in his contract!

> ... Too often, the standard form is presented as an evil. The form is a facet of the efficiency and standardization of modern business; in some situations a form may provide an accumulation of experience and a thorough job of drafting that could not be gathered for one deal alone. But the concentration of economic power, and in particular the rise of the large business corporation, has led to many situations in which bargaining power is grossly unequal. Power corrupts. Forms are often used in situations where contract in fact is distorted or denied. They are dictated, not negotiated.[6]

The public has two means of protection. First, if the business carried on by the offeror falls within one of the classes of business regulated by government boards or commissions, the terms of these documents will be subject to their approval. When these boards operate effectively, the public is usually well protected, and unreasonable and onerous terms are excluded. Second, in the vast range of unregulated activity the public receives whatever protection the courts can muster from the general law of contract. On the whole the latter form of protection is unsatisfactory, but unless we are to sanction government regulation of every niche of business activity, no other means is readily available. What protection can a court offer?

Courts begin by presuming that an unqualified acceptance of an offer is an acceptance of every term of that offer. Suppose, however, that the offeree in fact does not know that

---

[6] Risk, *Recent Developments in Contracts*, Special Lectures. p. 256. Toronto: Law Society of Upper Canada, 1966.

the offer contains a certain term. She purchases a ticket to attend a baseball game. The ticket contains a clause stating that the management reserves the right to remove the ticket-holder at any time without giving reasons. The ticket-holder does not know or suspect that the ticket contains such a term. Is she bound by the term? If she satisfies the court that she did not know of the term, then the court will inquire what steps the management took to bring the term to the attention of its customers generally. If it decides that the steps were insufficient, the ticket-holder will not be bound by the term; and if she has been wrongfully ejected from the baseball park, she will have the same remedy as if the term had not been on the ticket. On the other hand, if the court holds that the management had done what was reasonably necessary in the circumstances to bring the term to the notice of its customers, then the ticket-holder will be bound by the term whether she knew of it or not. The "ticket" cases always turn on their individual facts, and it is difficult to set down any firm guides of what is or is not sufficient notice. It should help us to understand the way the courts have reasoned on this matter if we look at some of the leading cases.

In *Parker v. South Eastern Railway Co.*[7] the contract was for the storage of a suitcase in the luggage room of a railway station for a fee. Parker deposited his bag and received from the attendant a ticket on the face of which were the words, "See back". On the reverse side of the ticket was a printed condition that the railway should not be liable for loss in excess of £10. The bag was lost, and Parker sued the railway for the value of its contents, £24. On appeal, the court decided that the issue was whether the railway had done what was reasonably necessary to notify customers of the term. The court ordered a new trial because the trial judge had not asked the jury to decide this question.

The fact that the ticket given in *Parker v. South Eastern Railway Co.* contained on its face the words, "See back" is important. If a ticket or other document given to the customer at the time of purchase contains a short and clear reference to other terms appearing either on the reverse side, or posted on a nearby wall in the form of a notice or sign, there is a greater likelihood that "reasonably sufficient notice" of those additional terms has been given. A sign in a parking lot in which the operator disclaims liability for loss or damage to car or contents may not in itself be reasonably sufficient notice to bind the owners of cars who park their vehicles there. We have to ask whether the ticket or voucher which a patron receives when he parks his car contains a clear reference to the sign and whether, in the circumstances, each customer ought to recognize the term stated on the sign as part of the contract he is making with the operator of the lot. A printed ticket or receipt which contains the words "subject to the conditions as exhibited on the premises" may serve to tie the sign in with each contract. The sign must, of course, be displayed prominently, but this in itself may not be sufficient; it must be brought home to the customer *at the time of the contract*. The operator of the parking lot, garage, or other place of storage cannot assume that he may exempt himself from liability merely by putting up a sign.[8] Lord Justice Denning has summed up the law on this subject as follows:

---

[7] (1877) 2 C.P.D. 416.
[8] Watkins v. Rymill (1883) 10 Q.B.D. 178. It may be more difficult for the operator of a parking lot to exempt himself from liability when the customer leaves the keys in the car at the request of the parking lot operator, because a bailment for storage and safekeeping is implied. See Chapter 21, *infra*. See also: Brown v. Toronto Auto Parks Ltd., [1954] O.W.N. 86; Samuel Smith & Sons Ltd. v. Silverman (1961), 29 D.L.R. (2d) 98; Hefferon v. Imperial Parking Co. Ltd. (1973), 46 D.L.R. (3d) 642.

People who rely on a contract to exempt themselves from their common law liability must prove that contract strictly. Not only must the terms of the contract be clearly proved, but also the intention to create legal relations — the intention to be legally bound — must be clearly proved. The best way of proving it is by a written document signed by the party to be bound. Another way is by handing him, before or at the time of the contract, a written notice specifying certain terms and making it clear to him that the contract is in those terms. A prominent public notice which is plain for him to see when he makes the contract would, no doubt, have the same effect, but nothing short of one of these three ways will suffice.[9]

An offeree may be willing to accept terms printed on a ticket or displayed on a poster on the reasonable assumption that the risk she may run relates closely to the bargain she has made, for instance, to the denial of any liability for damage to her car while parked in a parking lot. She would understand that the cost of parking would be higher if the car park had to insure against the risk of damage to her vehicle. But she would be surprised to find that the terms also exempted the car park company from liability for personal injuries suffered by her as she went to and from her parked car. Such special terms need to be brought directly to the attention of the offeree; indeed, she might then decide to park elsewhere. In other words, a court may well decide that there was adequate notice of usual, expected terms that the offeree chose not to read, but not of a surprising and therefore unreasonable term.

Our discussion in this section has been concerned with situations where the offeree receives a ticket, a policy, or some other form of notice of the terms of the contract but where she does not sign a document containing the terms. If the offeree signs a document, a strong presumption arises that she has accepted all the terms it contains; it becomes much more difficult for her to avoid the consequences. In recent years the prospects of persuading a court to disregard onerous terms imposed in a written and signed document have improved somewhat,[10] as we shall see in our discussion of misrepresentation and unconscionability in Chapter 11.

THE LAPSE AND REVOCATION OF AN OFFER

Lapse

An offer may lapse in any of the following ways:

(a) when the offeree fails to accept within a time specified in the offer;
(b) when the offeree fails to accept within a reasonable time, if the offer has not specified any time limit;

---

[9] Olley v. Marlborough Court Ltd., [1949] 1 All E.R. 127, at 134. Also quoted by Roach J., in Pickin v. Hesk and Lawrence, [1954] 4 D.L.R. 90.
[10] Tilden Rent-A-Car Co. v. Clendenning (1978) 18 O.R. (2d) 601.

(c) when either of the parties dies or becomes insane prior to acceptance. [11]

When an offer has lapsed, the offeree can no longer accept the offer. This result follows whether or not he realizes the offer has lapsed, for it has become a nullity.

Students of business law frequently have difficulty understanding how the courts determine what constitutes a "reasonable time", and the answer "It depends upon the circumstances of each case" may not seem helpful. The Supreme Court of Canada pointed out how the subject-matter of the contract may provide a clue for deciding whether a reasonable length of time has elapsed in an offer to buy or sell:

> Farm lands, apart from evidence to the contrary... are not subject to frequent or sudden changes or fluctuations in price and, therefore, in the ordinary course of business a reasonable time for the acceptance of an offer would be longer than that with respect to such commodities as shares of stock upon an established trading market. It would also be longer than in respect to goods of a perishable character. With this in mind the fact, therefore, that it was land would tend to lengthen what would be concluded as a reasonable time which, however, must be determined in relation to the other circumstances. [12]

The "other circumstances" which help to determine the length of a reasonable time include the manner in which an offer is made, and whether its wording indicates urgency. Often when a prospective purchaser makes an offer to buy property, she specifies that the offer must be accepted within twenty-four hours. The restriction is in her interest because it prevents the vendor from using this "firm offer" as a means of approaching other possible purchasers and bidding up the price.

Revocation

An offeror may be able to revoke (that is, withdraw) an offer at any time before acceptance, even when it has promised to hold the offer open for a specified time.

ILLUSTRATION

A Co. sends a letter dated January 15 to B offering to sell its warehouse to B for $800 000, stating that the offer is open only until January 19, and that it must have heard from B by then. B receives the letter on January 16, and immediately prepares a letter of acceptance. Before he mails his reply on the morning of January 17, A Co. changes its mind and telephones B saying that it wishes to withdraw its offer.

The revocation is valid because it has reached B before he has accepted. Accordingly, B can no longer accept A's offer.

In the above illustration, the offeror clearly revoked the offer before its acceptance: its personal communication of the revocation left no doubt about the offeree's knowledge of

---

[11] For a discussion of the effect of death upon the continuity of an offer, see Furmston, *Cheshire, Fifoot and Furmston's Law of Contract*, (12th ed.) pp. 63-64. London: Butterworth & Co. Ltd., 1981. "The truth would seem to be that the effect of death varies according to the nature of the particular contract. If...the offer is of a promise which is independent of the offeror's personality and which can be satisfied out of his estate, death [of the offeror] does not, until notified, prevent acceptance."

[12] Barrick v. Clark [1950] 4 D.L.R. 529, per Estey, J., at 537.

it. The legal position of the parties is less certain if the offeree merely hears rumours that the offeror has revoked, or hears that the offeror has made it impossible to carry out the offer because it has sold the property to someone else. The court will consider the offer revoked if it would be unreasonable for the offeree to suppose that the offeror still intended to stand by its offer.[13] Nonetheless, it is always poor business practice to make an offer to sell a particular item to one party and then sell it to another without having directly withdrawn the offer to the first party. Quite apart from damage to goodwill, the offeror risks an acceptance by the first offeree and inevitable breach when unable to fulfil both contracts.

An offeree may bind an offeror to keep its offer open for a specified time in one of two ways: (1) she may obtain a written offer under seal; (2) she may make a special contract called an *option* to keep the offer open. We shall consider the use of a seal in the next chapter. In an option, the offeree makes a contract with the offeror in the following general terms: the offeree agrees to pay a sum of money; in return the offeror agrees (1) to keep the offer open for a specified time (that is, not to revoke the offer) and (2) not to make contracts with other parties which would prevent it from fulfilling its offer (that is, to give the offeree the exclusive right to accept the offer). The exclusive right to such an offer may be very valuable to an offeree, even though she realizes she may eventually decide not to accept.

As an example, a manufacturer may purchase a number of options from property owners whose lots would, in the aggregate, provide a suitable location for a plant. The manufacturing company might offer $300 to Farmer A for the right to buy her farm within three months for $350 000 and obtain similar option agreements from other farms in the vicinity. In this way the company can determine at modest cost whether all the necessary property will be available and what the total cost will be. The manufacturer need not "take up" or exercise the options, that is, accept the offers to sell the farms; it would simply chalk up the price of the relatively small sums paid for the option agreements as the cost of a feasibility study for the projected plant. On the other hand, it would be within its rights to require each of the farmers who had sold it these options to sell at the agreed price, provided it accepts the offers contained in the options within the specified time. In this example, the farmers are in the position of offerors who for an agreed period of time are not free to withdraw their offers without being in breach of contract. There are really two contracts in contemplation: first, the option agreement itself and second, the actual sale that will materialize if the option is exercised.

$\mathcal{R}$EJECTION AND COUNTER-OFFER BY THE OFFEREE

In many business negotiations the parties make a number of offers and counter-offers, but until a specific offer by one side is accepted without qualification by the other there is no contract, and the parties have no legal obligation to one another. When an offeree receives an offer and, though interested, chooses to vary some of its features, he has not accepted;

---

[13] See *Dickinson v. Dodds* (1876) 2 Ch. D. 463.

rather, he has rejected the offer and made a counter-offer of his own. The initiative in bargaining may shift back and forth until one of the parties finds the last proposal of the other satisfactory and accepts it without qualification. Only then is a contract formed.

The making of a counter-offer amounts to a rejection of the original offer and brings it to an end. Further, the original offer does not revive if the offeror in turn rejects the counter-offer. The offeree can accept the former offer only if the offeror agrees to renew it; and this the offeror may be unwilling to do because of changed circumstances. The courts have held, however, that the offeree's merely inquiring whether the terms offered are the best he can expect does not amount to a rejection.

ILLUSTRATION

A wrote to B offering to sell her car for $2000. B replied by mail, "I will give you $1900 for the car." Two days later B wrote again to A saying, "I have been reconsidering. I will accept your offer to sell for $2000 after all."

There is no contract. B's counter-offer of $1900 brought the original offer to sell for $2000 to an end. While B has phrased her final statement in the form of an acceptance, she is doing no more than making a fresh offer of her own which A may or may not wish to accept. Perhaps someone else has offered A $2050 for the car in the meantime. If when A made the offer to sell for $2000 B had simply inquired whether this was the lowest A would go, the offer would have continued to stand. B would continue to be free to accept it within a reasonable period of time provided A did not withdraw her offer first.

The Elements of Acceptance

Its Positive Nature

Acceptance must be made in some positive form, whether in words or in conduct, with one exception which we note below. If acceptance is by conduct, the conduct must refer unequivocally to the offer made. One's conduct may happen to comply with the mode of acceptance set out in an offer and yet not constitute an acceptance. The offeree may habitually perform the act requested in the offer: she need not abandon her normal conduct to avoid accepting the offer. Suppose A always walks her dog around the park each evening, and B stipulates that A will have accepted B's offer to buy her car for $2000 if A walks her dog in the park the next evening. A need not abandon her normal habit the next evening to avoid having the contract foisted on her.

For the same reason, an offeror cannot stipulate silence as a mode of acceptance, thus forcing the offeree to act in order to reject the offer.

A sales representative for Ion Electric Supply Co. demonstrated a new high-speed Auto-analyzer for Glover, the owner of Speedy Car Repair Service. The price was $2500. Glover thought the device was useful but overpriced: "At $1500 I might consider buying it." The sales representative said that the price could not be reduced and removed the machine.

Two weeks later, an Auto-analyzer arrived with a letter from the sales representative as follows: "When I reported how impressed you were with our analyzer to the manager, he said it would be worth selling one even at a loss just to break into the market in your city. We know what an excellent reputation you have and it would be a good move to have our product in use in your shop. Our price is reduced, only to you, to $1750. That is below cost. If we don't hear from you in ten days we shall assume you have accepted this exceptional buy and will expect payment of our invoice."

There will be no contract even if the offeree, Glover, does not reply and simply allows the machine to sit idle; but he may well be bound if he takes the risk of using the machine, even to experiment with it.

Silence can be a sufficient mode of acceptance only if the parties have habitually used this method to communicate assent in previous transactions, or have agreed between themselves in advance that silence shall be sufficient, as where books are regularly delivered under a contract for membership in a publisher's book club.

Its Communication to the Offeror

Generally speaking, an offeree must communicate acceptance to the offeror. Some types of offers, however, can be validly accepted without such communication because the offeror asks only that the offeree perform an act, and implies that the act shall constitute acceptance. The offeror is bound to the terms of the proposition as soon as the offeree has performed whatever was required of him in the offer. The offeror may, in other words, dispense with notice to itself of the fact of acceptance.

This idea is illustrated by the decision in *Carlill v. Carbolic Smoke Ball Company*.[14] The Smoke Ball Company had placed an advertisement in a newspaper promising to pay £100 to anyone who used one of its smoke balls three times daily for two weeks and still contracted influenza. Mrs. Carlill used the smoke ball following the instructions supplied and contracted influenza. She sued the Smoke Ball Company on its promise to pay £100 — and succeeded. As a part of its defence the company pleaded that Mrs. Carlill had never communicated her intention to accept its offer. The court held that the offer had implied that notice was not necessary. All the company had asked was that readers should buy and use the smoke balls. Performance of the conditions set out was a sufficient acceptance without notification to the company.

The *Carlill* case also established that an offer may be made to an indefinite number of people who remain unknown to the offeror even after they have accepted. This result simply follows from the nature of the offer, a newspaper advertisement read by thousands of people. If the offer had been addressed to one particular person, then only that person could have accepted.

---

[14] [1892] 2 Q.B. 484.

The Moment of Acceptance

The moment that a contract is formed by offer and acceptance, each party is bound to its terms. A person may withdraw from a business arrangement only if he can show that the arrangement is still tentative, that is, has not yet "ripened into a contract". We must, therefore, be able to analyze business negotiations so that out of all that is said between the parties, we can identify a specific offer when it is made and the acceptance of that offer if and when it is given.[15]

The common business practice of *inviting tenders* illustrates the need for analyzing the various stages in a business deal to determine the point at which acceptance takes place. The purpose of inviting tenders may be to obtain firm offers from the tenderers for a fixed quantity of goods and services over a stated period, or it may be to explore the market of available suppliers and ascertain the best terms for proceeding with a project. When the object is to obtain firm offers, the most satisfactory tender will then become the basis for a contract between the inviter of the tenders and the successful bidder. This is normal practice when a government or company calls for tenders for the construction of a large project. A recent case suggests that when one party invites a tender from another, there may well be an implied contract that the first party promises, in return for the tenderer taking the trouble to prepare and submit its tender, to consider the tender and not ignore it entirely; if the first party fails to consider the tender it will be liable for damages.[16]

At other times, however, no intention to form a contract upon the receipt of tenders is implied; the procedure of inviting the tenders aims at accomplishing nothing more than a recognition of one supplier as the appropriate source of work to be done or goods to be supplied, as required over a future period. Thus, a municipal corporation may advertise for the submission of tenders by private trucking firms for the removal of snow from city streets during the coming winter. In these circumstances, the selection of the successful bid of a particular trucking company need not be followed up by a contract for the removal, for a given sum, of whatever snow may fall — it is not known how severe the winter may be or how much work will be required. The successful bidder is in the position of having made a *standing offer* and the municipality may avail itself of the offer by later placing specific requisitions for snow removal from time to time over the winter season. Each requisition so placed becomes an acceptance by the municipality of the standing offer of the trucking company; and to that extent the trucking company will have a contractual obligation to perform for the rate of remuneration specified in its bid. The trucker remains free, however, to withdraw from the standing agreement if it finds the agreement unsatisfactory, and it will have no liability to do further work after its revocation.[17]

The purchase of an automobile from a car dealer affords a further example of the importance of knowing when, precisely, a contract is formed. Car sales agents employed by a dealer normally have no authority to enter into contracts with customers. The management of the dealership retains the final word on both price and credit terms. Hence the role of a car sales agent is to persuade any prospective buyer to submit an offer at a specified price. When the sales agent takes the offer to the sales manager, the manager may strike out the proposed price

---

[15] In an English decision, the House of Lords resisted a tendency in some earlier cases to find that a contract is formed when the parties have substantially agreed on all the material terms, though the explicit acceptance of an offer remains outstanding: Gibson v. Manchester City Council [1979] 1 W.L.R. 294.

[16] See Blackpool and Fylde Aero Club Ltd. v. Blackpool Borough Council [1990] 1. W.L.R. 1195.

[17] See Great Northern Railway v. Witham (1873), L.R. 9 C.P. 16.

and insert a higher one with a request that the prospective buyer initial the change. The manager will have rejected the customer's offer by making a counter-offer. No contract is formed unless and until the customer accepts the sales manager's counter-offer.

TRANSACTIONS BETWEEN PARTIES AT A DISTANCE FROM EACH OTHER

When the parties are at a distance, an offeree may accept only in the way suggested by the offeror. An offer made by mail may reasonably be taken as inviting an acceptance by mail if no other mode of acceptance has been suggested. Understandably, a more efficient mode may be used: a fax or telephone call in response to a letter can be valid acceptance.

Contracts made through the post are so common in business that is it important to have a rule which clearly sets out how the time of acceptance is determined. The rule which the courts have adopted is that acceptance is complete when a properly addressed and stamped letter of acceptance is dropped in the mail. This rule is probably as practical and convenient as any alternative, when we consider that during the time required for a letter to reach its destination there must of necessity be a period of uncertainty in which the parties will not know whether a contract exists. The rule may be justified on the basis that an offeror who is prepared to use the mail to communicate an offer ought to be willing to have the same medium used for acceptance, and to take a chance that the post office will be efficient in bringing word of acceptance. An offeror who invites acceptance by mail must also be prepared to take the risk that the letter of acceptance may go astray; harsh though this may seem, it follows that the offeror would be bound by a contract without notice of its existence. Professor Waddams has explained the rule as follows:

> ... [T]he usual rationale is that it is the offeror rather than the offeree who could be expected to know that a communication [of acceptance] has gone astray, and to break the silence by enquiry. The offeror can guard against the effect of the rule by providing, expressly or by implication, that the offeree shall take the risk of loss or delay. This rationale appears sound. In case of loss or delay one of the parties must suffer and it seems appropriate to prefer the expectation of the offeree (that a contract exists) who expects no further communication, rather than that of the offeror (that a contract does not exist) since the offeror has by hypothesis manifested a willingness to be bound and could protect himself either by providing that acceptance must reach him or by enquiring into the silence of the offeree.[18]

An offer may, of course, invite acceptance by post although it was not sent through the mail itself. Whenever acceptance by mail constitutes a reasonable response to an offer, the acceptance is complete at the time of mailing.[19] Circumstances may, for example, make it reasonable that an offer made orally in the presence of the offeree be accepted by letter. The English courts have held:

> Where the circumstances are such that it must have been within the contemplation of the parties that, according to the ordinary usages of mankind, the post might be used as a

---

[18] Waddams, *The Law of Contracts*, (3rd ed.), p. 101. Toronto: Canada Law Book, 1993; also, Sibtac Corporation Ltd. v. Soo; Lienster Investments Ltd., Third Party (1978) 18 O.R. (2d) 395 at 402.
[19] The same principle applies when correspondence is sent by courier service: R. v. Weymouth Sea Products Ltd. (1983) 149 D.L.R. (3d) 637.

means of communicating the acceptance of an offer, the acceptance is complete as soon as it is posted.[20]

The "ordinary usages of mankind" govern the rules of acceptance to the extent that the offeror has not stipulated expressly how acceptance should be communicated. There is general agreement that the offeror has full power over the mode of acceptance. Thus if an offeror indicates a preference for acceptance by some means other than post as, for example, by telephone or in person, the offeree may still accept by post, but the offeror will not be bound unless and until the acceptance reaches him; further, it must reach him before the offer has lapsed. When the mode of acceptance specified is speedier than mail, the danger that the offer will lapse before a letter arrives is increased. In other words, the acceptance is not valid when dropped in the mailbox (as it would be if acceptance by mail were reasonably contemplated), but only when received. An offeror may invite acceptance by mail but stipulate that an acceptance will be effective only if received. An offeror may even state that acceptance will not be valid by letter at all. Such stipulations are effective, and unless the offeree accepts by complying with them he cannot bind the offeror.

The rule that applies to acceptance by mail has also been applied to acceptance by telegram: a telegram of acceptance is valid at the time it is delivered to the telegraph company. Except for these two modes of offer, however, an offeror will not be bound unless and until he receives the acceptance. When business people use instantaneous means of communication such as telephone, radio, or fax, the offeror must receive the acceptance before he is bound. In an English decision, the judge considered what would be the result if the telephone line were to go dead so that the offeror did not hear the offeree's words of acceptance. The judge concluded that the acceptance would be ineffective and that the offeror would have no contractual liability.[21] The common sense of this rule is that the offeree would know that the line went dead and that his acceptance might not have been heard. He must then verify that his acceptance was received.

The usual rule concerning the time of acceptance by mail differs from the rule concerning withdrawal of an offer. Revocation by mail is effective only when notice is actually received by the offeree, not when it is dropped in the mailbox. As a result, the offeree may accept and a binding contract be formed after revocation of the offer has been mailed but not yet received.

ILLUSTRATION

Chen, in a letter posted January 15, offered to sell his business to Baker for $70 000. The letter was received by Baker on January 17. On January 19, Baker posted her letter of acceptance, which did not reach Chen until the 21st. On January 18, however, Chen had decided to withdraw his offer and posted a letter to Baker revoking it. This letter did not reach Baker until January 20. Chen's revocation arrived too late. There was a valid contract on January 19 when the acceptance was posted. Chen was bound from the moment the letter was dropped into the mailbox.

---

[20] Henthorn v. Fraser [1892] 2 Ch. 27 per Lord Herschell, at 33. The law in Canada is probably accurately represented by this case, though there is some confusion caused by a Supreme Court of Canada decision on appeal from the Quebec courts where the post office is referred to as an "agent". See Charlebois v. Baril [1928] S.C.R. 88. See also Loft v. Physicians' Services Inc. (1966) 56 D.L.R. (2d) 481, where a letter posted in a mailbox but never received was held to be adequate notice to the defendant.

[21] Entores, Ltd. v. Miles Far East Corporation [1955] 2 Q.B. 327, per Denning, L.J., at 332.

Occasionally it may be important to know what is meant by the requirement that a revocation be "actually received". Is the revocation of an offer "received" if delivered to the place of business or residence of the offeree, or must it reach him in person? The general rule is that unless the offeror has knowledge that the revocation will not reach the offeree at his usual address, then delivery at that address establishes the fact and time of revocation, and the offeree is deemed to have notice from that time.

In contracts made by post, fax, or other long-distance communication, the offeror and the acceptor are often in different provinces or countries at the time. In case of a dispute it may be important to know where the contract was formed. If the law in the two places is different, as sometimes it is, the place where the contract was formed is one of the criteria for deciding which law applies. The general rule is that a contract is formed at the place where the acceptance becomes effective. This is determined by the moment in time when the contract is effective. Thus, when an offeror invites an acceptance by mail, the contract is formed at the moment the acceptance is dropped into the mailbox. Accordingly, it is formed at the place where the mailbox is located. When an instantaneous means of communication such as telephone or fax is used, the contract is not formed until the offeror receives the acceptance, and these contracts are formed at the place where the offeror receives the acceptance.

Unilateral and Bilateral Contracts

The Offer of a Promise for an Act

As we have seen in the *Carlill* case, an offer may invite acceptance simply by performaning its conditions without communicating acceptance. Indeed, we would not have expected Mrs. Carlill to have telephoned or written to the Smoke Ball Co. to inform it that she intended to accept its offer before she bought the smoke ball.

An offer of a reward is accepted by anyone to whom the offer is made if she performs the conditions stipulated, such as providing information or returning a lost article. If the reward is for providing information, the courts have decided that only the person who first gives the information will be deemed to have accepted and be entitled to the reward.[22]

In the above examples, the offers are part of a class of offers which require acceptance by performance of an act. Once the offeree has performed the act, he is not obligated to do anything more. All obligation now rests with the offeror to perform his half of the bargain. These contracts are often called *unilateral contracts*.

Some unilateral offers require the offeree to perform a series of acts over a long period, as for example in an offer to pay $2000 to the offeree if he will build and deliver a trailer to the offeror by a certain date. The offeree may accept only by actually delivering by that date, and until then there is no contract. We should note that an offeree may abandon performance at any time without being in breach. What would happen if the day before delivery the offeror revoked the offer? Strictly speaking, the offeror may always revoke

---

[22] Lancaster v. Walsh (1838) 150 E.R. 1324.

before acceptance, and early judges seemed to accept this view. It was apparent that the offeree might suffer considerable hardship, but the answer was "He knew the risk of revocation was present and accepted the risk." Since, however, parties often do not think about such possibilities, the hardship still occurs. Today, courts try to avoid this unfairness where possible by treating offers "as calling for bilateral rather than unilateral action when the language can be fairly so construed".[23] The advantage of treating an agreement as bilateral is that both parties are bound from the moment the offeree indicates the intention to perform.

Where the courts find it impossible to construe an offer as bilateral, they may still try to help the offeree by implying a *subsidiary promise* that the offeror will not revoke once the offeree begins performance in good faith and continues to perform. Thus, as soon as the offeree starts performance, a subsidiary contract is formed in which the offeror undertakes not to revoke while the offeree proceeds reasonably with performance. Accordingly, revocation will be a breach of the subsidiary contract. By this reasoning the court would probably hold that the offeror could not revoke in the preceding example of the trailer.[24] Of course, this subsidiary promise is merely implied, and its existence may be rebutted by an express term to the contrary. Thus if A offers to pay B $100 for the delivery of a typewriter to her son provided it is delivered at exactly 10:00 p.m. at a birthday party and provided A does not change her mind, A can revoke the offer before delivery.

The Offer of a Promise for a Promise

While unilateral contracts are important, they form only a small proportion of all contracts. Most offers require the giving of a promise, rather than the performance of an act as the means of acceptance. For example, if A Motors offers to sell a truck to B Co. Ltd. for $22 500 and B Co. Ltd. replies accepting the offer, a contract is formed though neither A Motors nor B Co. Ltd. has as yet performed anything. In effect A Motors has promised to sell the truck for $22 500 and B Co. Ltd. in return has promised to buy it for $22 500; the two parties have traded promises. If A Motors should refuse to perform its promise, then B Co. Ltd. would have a right to sue. Similarly, if B Co. Ltd. should refuse to perform its promise, A Motors would have a right to sue. The contract consists of the two promises and both parties are bound to perform. This type of contract is called a *bilateral contract*.

The most commonplace of all business transactions, the credit sale, is an example of the bilateral contract: at the time of the contract, and often for some time thereafter, the goods may be neither delivered by the seller nor paid for by the buyer. Again, a contract of employment comprises a promise by the employer to pay a wage or salary and a promise by the employee to work for a future period.

A characteristic of bilateral contracts is that each party is both a *promisor* and a *promisee*, since each has an obligation to perform for the other and each has a right to performance by the other. For the purpose of describing proceedings in a court action, however, we find it convenient to think of the party who alleges that she has not received the performance to which she is entitled as the promisee. The promisor, in his turn, may have one or more defences, which he offers to the court as a reason why his conduct

---

23   Dawson v. Helicopter Exploration Co. Ltd. [1955] 5 D.L.R 404, per Rand, J., at p. 410.
24   See Brackenbury v. Hodgkin (1917) 102 Atlantic 106, 116 Maine 399, and Errington v. Errington [1952] 1 All E.R. 149.

should be excused and why he should not be ordered to pay the promisee damages for breach of contract.

PRECISION IN THE WORDING OF AN OFFER

A vague offer may prove to be no offer at all, and the intended acceptance of it cannot then form a contract. If the parties enter into a loosely-worded arrangement, not having been specific in the terms of the offer, a court may find the agreement too ambiguous to be enforced. In *Taylor v. Portington*,[25] Portington wrote to Taylor offering to take a lease of Taylor's house for three years at a rent of £85 "if put into thorough repair" and the drawing-rooms "handsomely decorated according to the present style; paint is required both inside and outside although perhaps for some parts, one coat might be sufficient". Taylor replied accepting the offer. Later a dispute arose over the adequacy of the repairs, and Portington refused to proceed with his promise to rent the house. In the final hearing of the case, an appeal court ruled that the expressions Portington had used in his letter "imported uncertainty into what might otherwise have amounted to an agreement sufficiently definite for the court to enforce".

Other examples of lack of certainty in the terms of a contract are a promise to give a "fair" share in the profits of a business; a promise to "favourably consider" the renewal of the present contract "if satisfied with you";[26] a promise made by the buyer of a race horse to pay an additional amount on the price "if the horse is lucky".[27]

Uncertainty in the wording of the terms of a contract may be more apparent than real. It may be possible to adduce evidence of local customs or trade usage that gives a new precision to the terms. With the object of giving effect to contracts wherever possible, the courts have held (1) that anything is certain which is capable of being calculated or ascertained, and (2) that where a contract may be construed as either enforceable or unenforceable, they will favour the interpretation that will see the contract enforced. We shall examine these problems in greater detail in Chapter 13, when we discuss the interpretation of contracts.

THE EFFECT OF AN INCOMPLETE AGREEMENT

In *Friesen v. Braun*,[28] there was a lease of land for a term of one year from July 1, 1947. The lease included an option clause entitling the tenants to purchase the property for the sum of $1200 less the amount of rent received by the landlady up to the time the option was exercised. The option clause read in part, "The purchase money shall be paid as follows: On terms to be discussed and decided upon by the parties at date of acceptance."

---

[25] (1855) 44 E.R. 128.
[26] Montreal Gas Co. v. Vasey [1900] A.C. 595.
[27] Cuthing v. Lynn (1831) 109 E.R. 1130.
[28] [1950] 2 D.L.R. 250.

The tenants served a notice of acceptance of the option within the time specified and tendered the full sum in cash. The landlady refused the tender of payment, and the tenants brought an action against her for breach of the option clause. The court held that the option clause was invalid, and the tenants' case failed. One of the judges observed that "...an agreement which leaves one of the essential terms to be determined by the parties mutually at a future time is unenforceable." The same principle is expressed in the words, "The law does not recognize a contract to enter into a contract."[29]

We should, however, distinguish between a contract for the sale of goods and a contract for the sale of land in this respect. The Sale of Goods Act provides that the price in a contract of sale of goods "may be left to be fixed in manner thereby agreed, or may be determined by the course of dealing between the parties" and that "[W]here the price is not determined in accordance with the foregoing provisions the buyer must pay a reasonable price."[30]

Questions for Review

1. What is the relationship between a promise and a contract?
2. What must happen to an offer before a contract is formed?
3. How may an offer be made by conduct other than spoken or written word?
4. "We cannot be obligated by people who do work for us without our knowledge." Why?
5. What is the legal effect of a counter-offer?
6. What does it mean to "purchase an option"?
7. When does the selection of a successful bidder following an invitation for tenders normally create a contract?
8. Can the time of acceptance date from the time a letter of acceptance is mailed when the offer was not itself made through the mail?
9. When exactly is a letter withdrawing a previous offer effective?
10. What principles of law does the *Carlill* case illustrate?
11. Did the *Carlill* case concern a unilateral or a bilateral contract? Why? Under which type does a purchase on credit usually fall?
12. What is the effect of an agreement in which the parties state that certain terms will be discussed and agreed upon at a later date?
13. To what extent does the law protect the interest of the public in standard form contracts?
14. What is the difference between the revocation and the rejection of an offer? Between the revocation and the lapse of an offer?
15. What does it mean to say that the conduct of an offeree will constitute acceptance only if the conduct refers unequivocally to the offer? When might the offeree's conduct be "equivocal"?
16. Give an example of circumstances in which the rule "An offer must be communicated before it can be accepted" would operate.

---

[29] Von Hatzfeldt-Wildenburg v. Alexander [1912] 1 Ch. 284, per Parker, J., at 289. See also National Bowling and Billiards Ltd. v. Double Diamond Bowling Supply Ltd. and Automatic Pinsetters Ltd. (1961) 27 D.L.R. (2d) 342; Re Pigeon *et al.* and Titley, Pigeon, Lavoie Ltd. (1973) 30 D.L.R. (3d) 132. For a fuller discussion see Furmston, *Cheshire and Fifoot's Law of Contract* (10th ed.), pp. 34-38.

[30] See, for example: R.S.B.C. 1979, c. 370, s. 12; R.S.O. 1990, c. S-1, s. 9; R.S.N.S. 1989, c. 408, s. 11.

17. Is it also true that an acceptance must be communicated before a contract can be formed?
18. May a person withdraw a bid he makes at an auction sale before the fall of the hammer?

Problems

Problem 1
X offers to subscribe for 100 shares in Y Co. Ltd., which is issuing further stock. He makes his offer in June. He does not receive a letter of allotment (acceptance) from Y Co. Ltd. until the following November. Must he pay for the shares?

Problem 2
An amendment to existing criminal legislation makes it an offence "to manufacture, sell, or offer for sale" flick knives. The Sundries Shop exhibits a flick knife in its shop window. Its proprietor is prosecuted for violation of the statute. Should she be held guilty?

Problem 3
Flyte is the owner of the Brideshead subdivision. It comprises 20 lots, numbered 1 through 20. On September 1, Flyte telegraphed Ryder, "WILL SELL YOU ANY OR ALL OF THE LOTS IN BRIDESHEAD AT $15 000 EACH. DETAILS TO FOLLOW IN LETTER." Flyte then posted a letter to Ryder containing all of the necessary terms, including the required down payment and acceptable mortgage financing.

On September 2, after he had received the telegram but before he had received the letter, Ryder telegraphed Flyte, "ACCEPT YOUR OFFER WITH RESPECT TO LOT #1."

Has a binding contract been formed by Ryder's telegram? Can you think of circumstances in which this question could become the basis of a dispute between the parties?

Problem 4
Superior Used Cars Ltd. has as the most prominent display on its lot an immaculate, highly-polished model which rotates slowly on a raised circular platform under powerful floodlights. The price is on the windshield, $17 700. Walking home one evening, Williams noticed the display and stopped and asked a sales agent for a demonstration. The sales agent then proceeded to try to interest him in several other models which, she urged, were "really better" than the one displayed. When Williams persisted in wanting to see the one displayed, the sales agent replied that it was not actually for sale, but was being used as an advertising gambit. Has Williams any claim in contract?

Problem 5
Lambert purchased a car last year and placed her insurance with the Reliable Insurance Company, for whom Drake was the local agent. On July 29 last, Drake wrote as follows to Lambert, who was at her summer cottage: "As you know, your automobile insurance policy with us expires on August 15. We will renew this policy on the same terms unless notified to the contrary by you. You may sign the application form and pay after you return to the city."

On her way back from her holidays on August 16 Lambert struck and injured a pedestrian with her car. The pedestrian claimed $50 000 damages from Lambert, and on referring the matter to the Reliable Insurance Company, Lambert was informed that her policy of insurance had expired without renewal on August 15.

Describe Lambert's legal position.

Problem 6

A by-law of the City of Winnipeg prohibits the sale of horsemeat within the city limits for human consumption. The penalty for violation is a fine of $500 and costs or ten days in jail.

Lalonde operated a butcher shop, La Boucherie Franco-Canadienne, in St. Boniface, outside the Winnipeg city limits. Onasis, who owned a restaurant in Winnipeg, telephoned and asked whether Lalonde could deliver some horsemeat ("la viande chevaline") to his restaurant. Lalonde agreed to supply the meat. After the meat was delivered to the restaurant Lalonde sent Onasis an invoice for $17.65. Subsequently a patron of the restaurant who had ordered filet mignon complained that he had instead been served *filly* mignon.

The City of Winnipeg charged Lalonde with a violation of the by-law. What rule affecting the formation of contracts is relevant? What would be the result?

Problem 7

Moore, a resident of Oshawa, Ontario, read the following notice in the *Oshawa Herald*: "Those wishing to drive new automobiles to west coast contact P.T. Jones, 54 Totem Blvd., Vancouver. Expenses en route will be paid for." Moore wrote for information and received the following reply: "If you will deliver a V6 Pontiac Supreme four-door sedan to me by September 1, I will pay you $18 000 for it." When Moore read the letter she bought the car specified and set out for Vancouver. On arriving in New Westminster on August 15, she decided to telephone Jones to get the directions to 54 Totem Blvd. When Jones answered, he said: "Oh, it's you, Moore. I waited and waited to hear from you, and eventually bought a Cadillac I found on sale. I'm sure you can find someone else here to take the Pontiac off your hands."

If Moore were to sue Jones for breach of contract, would she succeed?

Problem 8

Evans wrote to Livingstone offering to sell him a farm for $168 000 on certain terms of credit. Upon receipt of this offer Livingstone immediately wired back: "SEND LOWEST CASH PRICE. WILL GIVE $45 000 CASH." Evans replied by telegram, "CANNOT REDUCE PRICE." Immediately on receipt of this telegram Livingstone wired his acceptance of $168 000. Evans refused to sell the land to Livingstone, claiming that Livingstone had rejected his offer and so terminated it. Has Livingstone any claim against Evans? (See *Livingstone v. Evans et al.* [1925] 4 D.L.R. 769.)

Problem 9

Schmidt saw an automobile which she liked in a dealer's premises. At her request the dealer promised to put the car aside and not to sell it until the next day when Schmidt was to return and tell the dealer whether she would buy the car. While on her way to the dealer's premises on the following day, Schmidt met her friend Williams. Williams told Schmidt that he had bought the automobile in question late the previous evening. Schmidt went to the dealer's premises and told him that she had come to take the car away. The dealer told Schmidt that the car had been sold to Williams. Is the dealer liable to Schmidt for breach of contract? (See *Dickinson v. Dodds* (1876) 2 Ch. D. 463.)

Cases

Case 1

Henwood wanted to buy from Foley a property in the village of Cataraqui some three kilometres west of Kingston. Henwood lives in Kingston and Foley lives in Cataraqui.

In May, Henwood went to Cataraqui to see Foley and offered to buy the property for $35 000. Foley refused the offer. On July 7 Henwood went again to see Foley, and this time Foley offered to sell the property for $40 000 and said he would hold the offer open for fourteen days at that price.

Early on the morning of July 8, another person called to see Foley and offered him $43 000 for the property. Foley accepted, subject to a condition for avoiding the contract if he found he could not withdraw from his arrangement with Henwood.

At noon on July 8, Foley posted a letter to Henwood stating, "Please take notice that my offer to you of July 7 is withdrawn."

This letter was delivered at Henwood's Kingston address the following morning about 10:30, but he was at work and did not see it until he came home for lunch at 12:30. That same morning, at Henwood's request, his lawyer had written to Foley as follows: "I am instructed by Mr. Henwood to accept your offer of July 7, to sell at the price of $40 000. Kindly have the contract prepared and forwarded to me." This letter was posted at 10:00 a.m. that morning (July 9). When Foley received it on July 10, he replied stating that the offer had been withdrawn.

Henwood brought an action for breach of contract against Foley. State with reasons what you think the court's decision would be.

Case 2

The Tomkins Well Co. Ltd. was hired by Norman Food Products Ltd. to drill a well for it on some property beside the sea; Norman Food needed a freshwater well for a factory it expected to have in operation there. In the negotiations the well company quoted a price of $28 per foot plus the cost of casing, but refused to guarantee that the well drilled would produce fresh water. Its representative did, however, say that they would probably be able to exclude any sea water by proper casing. The well was drilled at a cost of $4500 but produced salty water which could not be shut out and the project was abandoned.

Some time afterwards the well company returned its equipment to the property without the knowledge of Norman Food and drilled two more holes in an attempt to obtain a freshwater well; neither drilling was successful. The well company then billed Norman Food for $15 200, the total price for all the work done. Norman Food refused to pay that sum but offered to settle for $5000; when this offer was refused by Tomkins Well, the food company paid the sum into court, awaiting a judgment on the action brought by Tomkins Well for the total price.

In your opinion, what should be the result of this action? Would your opinion have been different if the well company had obtained a good freshwater well on drilling the third hole? (See *Trask Well Co. Ltd. v. Northern Food Products, Inc.* (1953) 31 M.P.R. 325.)

Case 3

On September 9, 1947, Clark in Saskatchewan wrote to Barrick in Ontario about buying Barrick's Saskatchewan farm. The parties exchanged several letters on the subject. The land was under lease so that a purchaser could not get possession until March 1, 1948, and in any case farming operations could not be carried on until spring.

Finally, by letter of October 30, 1947, Clark offered $14 500 cash for the property. Barrick replied as follows:

> Toronto, Ont.,
> Nov. 15, 1947.
>
> Mr. F.J. Clark,
> Luseland, Sask.
>
> Dear Sir:
>
> In reply to your recent letter, in which you offer $14 500 cash for the [land]...I have delayed answering in order to consult with those interested in the Estate and thereby be in a position to give something concrete.
>
> We are prepared to sell this land for $15 000 cash. If this price is satisfactory to you, the deal could be closed immediately by preparing an agreement for sale to be given you on receipt of the initial payment of $2000, transfer of clear title to be given you on January 1st, 1948 on receipt of balance of purchase price of $13 000. The present tenant Kostrosky's lease expires March 1st, 1948.
>
> Trusting to hear from you as soon as possible.
>
> Yours truly,
> R.N. Barrick

Clark was away when Barrick's letter arrived, but Clark's wife wrote on November 20 telling of his absence on a hunting trip and asking that the deal be kept open as she expected him home in ten days.

A new party, Hohman, became interested in the property, and on December 3 Barrick and Hohman contracted for its sale at $15 000. Clark returned home on December 10 and that evening mailed a letter to Barrick in which he accepted Barrick's offer. The following day Clark heard of Hohman's purchase and on that date wired Barrick as follows:

> RETURNED HERE YESTERDAY MORNING FROM BIG GAME HUNTING TRIP AIRMAILED LETTER TO YOU LAST NIGHT ENCLOSING TWO THOUSAND DOLLARS THIS MORNING TOWN GOSSIP CLAIMS WILLIAM HOHMAN HAS BOUGHT THE THREE QUARTERS PRESUME YOU RECEIVED MRS CLARK'S LETTER NOVEMBER TWENTIETH TRUST THAT REPORT IS NOT CORRECT WOULD APPRECIATE REPLY BY WIRE

Barrick replied that he had received an offer of $15 000 from Hohman which he had accepted on December 3, having had no reply from Clark, and noted that if Hohman failed to pay the $15 000 he would then be at liberty to sell to someone else. He concluded, "I am very sorry this hitch has occurred, and I shall return your $2000 immediately upon receipt of same."

Clark then sued Barrick for breach of contract.

Should Clark succeed? (See *Barrick v. Clark* [1950] 4 D.L.R. 529.)

Case 4

Daly, a United States citizen, entered into negotiations with Stevens of Vancouver with a view to arranging an investigation and staking of mineral claims at the head of the Leduc River in British Columbia. Daly had discovered evidence of deposits there some twenty years earlier.

On January 13, Daly wrote, "A large mining company in Boise is showing an interest. To protect my interest it will be necessary for me to arrive at some definite arrangement soon." Stevens replied on January 17, "Perhaps we can make some arrangement this summer to finance you in staking claims for which I would give you an interest. I would suggest that I should pay for your time and expenses and carry you for a 10% interest in the claims." Daly replied on January 22, "Your proposition appeals to me as being a fair one."

Soon after, Daly was called to active duty in the United States Naval Reserve Engineering Corps and was sent to the Marshall Islands. Correspondence continued with some difficulty, but on February 28 Daly wrote, "As I informed you in a previous letter, your offer of a 10% interest for relocating and finding these properties is acceptable to me, provided there is a definite agreement to this effect in the near future."

On March 5, Stevens wrote, "I hereby agree that if you will take me in to the showings, and I think they warrant staking, I will stake the claims and give you a 10% interest. The claims would be recorded in my name and I will have full discretion in dealing with them — you are to get 10% of the vendor interest. I can arrange to get a pilot here." Daly replied on April 12, "If you will inform me when you can obtain a pilot, I will immediately take steps for a temporary release in order to be on hand."

On June 6, Stevens wrote, "I was talking to a prospector who said he had been over your showings at the head of the Leduc River, and in his opinion it would be practically impossible to operate there, as the showings were behind ice fields which, along with the extreme snowfalls, make it very doubtful if an economic operation could be carried on. I now have so much work lined up that I doubt if I would have time to visit your showings and do not think I would be warranted in making the effort to get in there due to the unfavourable conditions. I must advise you, therefore, not to depend on making this trip, and suggest if you are still determined to go in, to make some other arrangements."

Daly did not reply. On his return from the Marshall Islands the following year, he did, however, follow up his interest in the property. He then discovered that in July, Stevens had sent prospectors into the area and, as a result of their investigations, had staked claims in his own name and later sold them to a mining development company. Daly brought an action against Stevens claiming damages for breach of contract. Should Daly succeed in his action? Explain.

Case 5

Early in August 1974, the Great Prairie Railway had constructed its line to the southerly boundary of K.C. Jones' land, near the town of Carmen, Manitoba. The railway company had not intended to enter Jones' land at all, but to terminate the railway just south of it. However, it ultimately decided to build across Jones' land up to the right of way of the C.P.R.

On August 9 the company opened negotiations with Jones through its right-of-way agent for the purpose of obtaining possession of the land necessary for the construction of its railway across his farm. Jones refused to give possession until the terms of sale of the right of way were fully settled. Jones finally handed the agent a detailed written statement of the terms upon which he would sell. The main terms were that the company was to be responsible for damage for trespassing or straying cattle as a result of its interfering with the fences, the company was to install proper railway fences and a level crossing when required to do so by Jones at the point he should indicate, and the price for the land taken was to be $1000 an acre.

When Jones handed these terms to the right-of-way agent for Great Prairie Railway, he notified the agent that if the railway took possession of the land, he would understand from that act that the company accepted and agreed to his terms. A few days later and without further communication with Jones, the company took possession and proceeded to construct the railway across Jones' land. About two weeks afterwards Jones was advised by letter from the right-of-way agent that the company did not propose to abide by the terms stated but proposed to proceed by expropriation. Jones, claiming that the railway company had accepted his offer, sued it for damages for breach of a contract containing the terms of his offer.

During the course of the trial the court was referred to the Railway Act, R.S.C. 1970, c. R-2, which reads in part as follows:

EXPROPRIATION PROCEEDINGS

Notice

156. Preliminary to proceeding to arbitration to fix compensation or damages, the company shall serve upon the opposite party a notice containing

(a) a description of the lands to be taken, or of the power intended to be exercised with regard to any lands therein described;

(b) a declaration of readiness to pay a certain sum or rent, as the case may be, as compensation for such lands or for such damages; and

(c) a notification that if within ten days after the service of this notice, or, where the notice is served by publication, within one month after the first publication thereof, the party to whom the notice is addressed does not give notice to the company that he accepts the sum offered by the company, either he or the company may apply to have the compensation fixed by arbitration as provided in this Act.

179. Upon payment...of the compensation...to the person entitled to receive the same, the [arbitration] award vests in the [railway] company the power forthwith to take possession of the lands...

What specific issue, in relation to offer and acceptance as a requirement for the formation of a contract, arises on these facts? Explain whether the the plaintiff or the defendant should succeed. What general issue of public policy issue is raised when a legislature grants powers of expropriation to various companies and other agencies?

CHAPTER 7

FORMATION OF A CONTRACT: CONSIDERATION, AND INTENTION TO CREATE LEGAL RELATIONS

$\mathcal{T}$HE MEANING OF CONSIDERATION

At the root of our idea of a contract is the concept of a bargain, that one party must pay a price, that is make some contribution, for the promise he obtains from the other party. In a unilateral contract the price paid for the promise of the offeror is the act done by the acceptor. In a bilateral contract, the price paid for each one's promise is the promise of the other. This price is called *consideration*. In short, consideration is "the price for which the promise [or the act] of the other is bought".[1]

When a party bargains for consideration, it usually brings him a benefit, such as a promise to pay him money or to deliver goods or render services to him; but it need not always confer a benefit directly upon him. So long as he bargains for an altered course of action or a promise of an altered course of action by the other party, he will have received consideration.

ILLUSTRATION

Adams, a creditor of Brown, threatened to sue Brown for the amount of an overdue account. Cox, a friend of Brown, then promised to pay Adams the amount due if Adams would refrain from suing, and Adams agreed.

If Cox failed to pay Adams as agreed and Adams sued him for breach of contract, Adams would succeed. To establish consideration Adams need only show that he adopted a different course of action, that is, that he forbore suing Brown, in return for Cox's promise. In this sense the "price" which Adams agrees to pay need not confer a direct benefit on the other contracting party, Cox.

$\mathcal{G}$RATUITOUS PROMISES

With some qualifications to be discussed later, consideration is essential to make a contract binding in law. A person may, of course, make a promise to another when the element of a bargain is completely absent. A promise made in the absence of a bargain is called a *gratuitous promise* and, although accepted by the person to whom it is made, does not constitute a contract and is not enforceable in law. A promise to make a gift and a promise to perform services without remuneration are common examples of gratuitous promises. Such "contracts" are void for lack of consideration, which is another way of saying that they never amounted to a contract.

The law does not hinder the performance of a gratuitous promise. It simply asserts that if the promise is not performed, the promisee has no remedy at law to compensate him for his disappointed expectations. As a matter of honour most people do, of course, perform their gratuitous promises.

Then what of a charitable donation? Charities seldom find it in their interest to sue those who have made subscription pledges. Their experience shows that they may rely

---

[1] Winfield, *Pollock's Principles of Contract* (13th ed.), p. 133.

upon their subscribers' sense of honour to a large extent; in their budgeting they are wise to discount the balance. They believe that people would become reluctant to give pledges if there were a probability of legal action to enforce them. Occasionally, however, subscribers have died before honouring large pledges, and charities have sued their estates.[2]

In looking for consideration in this type of subscription pledge, we have to ask, "What price did the charity pay for the subscriber's promise?" Our answer must be "None", if the charitable organization did not change its future course of action and incur additional expense in return for the promise. A sense of disillusionment and loss of faith in human nature on the part of its officers is not enough to constitute consideration. In some circumstances we might find consideration if the charity undertook a specific project, such as the construction of a building, in response to the subscriber's promise. The court must, however, be able to find an implied request from the subscriber that the charity undertake the project as the "price" of the subscription. When donations are for general funds, the charitable organization can make the pledges it receives legally binding only if it adopts the use of a seal on its pledge cards. We shall discuss the use of a seal in a later section of this chapter.

As long as the promise of a gift remains unperformed, the promisee is without recourse. But suppose the promise is performed and a gift is actually made: may the donor later change her mind and demand it back on grounds of lack of consideration? Generally speaking, no. Once she has voluntarily made the gift, it is no longer her property and she has no control over it. In exceptional circumstances the donor may show that she made the gift as a result of threats or undue influence, and the court may then restore it to her or award damages to the value of the gift. We shall consider the consequences of undue influence in Chapter 11.

Though a promisor is not bound by her gratuitous promise, once she undertakes the performance of it she is under a duty to carry it out without negligence. If, through her negligence, she injures the promisee or the promisee's property, she will be liable to compensate the promisee for the loss. A defence that the donor received no consideration for her promise will be of no avail. The standard of care is imposed upon her not by the promise but by the rules of the law of torts; indeed, she may be liable for any damages caused by her negligence whether the damage is done to the promisee or a stranger. Thus, a doctor who offers to give free aid to an injured person and negligently aggravates the person's injuries will be liable for damages. Similarly, a public accountant who gratuitously undertakes an audit for a charitable organization is liable for damages caused to the organization through her negligence. She is under no obligation to do the audit, but once she commences the work she must proceed with care.

Adequacy of Consideration

In developing the concept of consideration, the courts insisted that the consideration must always have some value in the eyes of the law; but they refused to concern themselves with whether the promisor made a good bargain. They took the view that it was not for

---

[2] See, for example: *Governors of Dalhousie College v. Boutilier*, [1934] 3 D.L.R. 593.

them to make a bargain for the parties, and if a party requested a grossly inadequate consideration for his promise, that was up to him. To assess the adequacy of consideration would require a personal value judgment; and the courts would have to relinquish their role of impartial arbiter if they were to concern themselves with adequacy. They might otherwise find themselves penalizing the business acumen of one of the parties and comforting the stupidity of the other. Much has been made of one judge's observation that a creditor can agree to accept a "canary or a tomtit" in settlement of his account if he chooses.[3] The adequacy of the consideration is not for the courts to determine.

This is not to say that a court will never be interested in the nature of the consideration. If, for example, the consideration is grossly inadequate for the promise and if other evidence points to fraud, duress, or undue influence exerted on the promisor, the court may hold that the promise is voidable at the promisor's option. Courts have become increasingly concerned with protecting the interests of consumers from unconscionable conduct.[4]

An important question of adequacy of consideration arises whenever parties to a dispute agree upon a settlement out of court. Suppose that subsequent to making a settlement one party should discover that she was mistaken about either the law or the facts: she promised to pay a sum of money to the other party when she really was not bound to pay anything. The threat of the other party to sue was without merit since he would have lost in court. Is his promise not to sue, therefore, worthless and hence not really consideration for the promise to pay something in settlement?

ILLUSTRATION

In an automobile collision between Juan Alvarez and Sally Brown, Brown's car suffers $800 damage. The parties engage in an extended argument by mail about which of them is responsible for the accident. Finally, after many months, Brown threatens to sue Alvarez unless Alvarez will agree to pay 75% of Brown's damages, that is $600. Alvarez promises to pay this sum in full settlement of all Brown's claims, and she agrees not to sue him. Subsequently Alvarez realizes that at the time he made his promise to pay Brown, more than twelve months had passed since the accident had occurred. The provincial Highway Traffic Act states: "No action shall be brought against a person for the recovery of damages occasioned by a motor vehicle after the expiration of twelve months from the time when the damages were sustained."

Alvarez now refuses to perform his promise to pay Brown $600. He states that since Brown could not have successfully sued him for damages, her promise under the settlement not to sue him is no consideration for his promise to pay $600. It is well settled, however, that Brown's promise not to sue Alvarez is good consideration for the $600 settlement, and she will succeed in an action against Alvarez.

Provided the promisee has an honest belief in her right to sue, giving it up is good consideration for the promisor's promise.[5] If this were not the rule, no one could ever be

---

[3] Jessel, M.R., in Couldery v. Bartrum (1881) 19 Ch. D., at 399.
[4] See Chapter 11. See also, Chapter 19: unconscionable consideration is now the subject of consumer protection legislation. See, for example: Business Practices Act, R.S.O. 1990, c. B-18, s. 2(b)(ii).
[5] Haigh v. Brooks (1839), 113 E.R. 119; Famous Foods Ltd. v. Liddle [1941] 3 D.L.R. 525, Fairgrief v. Ellis, [1935] 2 D.L.R. 806.

sure that a settlement was binding; subsequent information might upset a settlement made in good faith. Indeed, it could even be argued that until a dispute was actually decided by the courts, neither side could be sure that it had given anything of value as consideration for the promise of the other. Aside from being an intolerable situation for the parties, such a state of affairs would conflict with basic principles of the law: to discourage unnecessary lawsuits and to promote certainty in the law.

MOTIVE CONTRASTED WITH CONSIDERATION: PAST CONSIDERATION

Consideration is the *price* for the promisor's promise, however inadequate it may be in a financial sense. The reason for making such a promise, the motive, is irrelevant. Indeed, motive does not affect the question of consideration either way: it cannot change a gratuitous promise into a contractual obligation, nor can it transform a binding promise into a merely voluntary, moral obligation. A promisor's motive, whether it be gratitude, a sense of honour, duty, affection or charity, or even part of an unworthy scheme, does not affect the question of whether his promise is binding in law.

From an ethical point of view, we may say that it is wrong to break *any* promise seriously made and that every promisor has a moral duty to perform his promise. However, the doctrine of consideration would virtually cease to exist if every promise were legally enforceable simply because the promisor had a moral duty to do as he said he would. Although the doctrine of consideration has been attacked as causing unfair decisions in some instances (and undoubtedly it does, as we shall see), it has the virtue of being an external and objective test of whether a promise should be binding. In other legal systems, where moral obligation — called *moral cause* — may be substituted for the idea of a bargain, other difficulties arise in trying to probe into a promisor's motive in order to establish moral cause.

This point is illustrated in *Eastwood v. Kenyon*.[6] Eastwood had been guardian of Mrs. Kenyon while she was a child and had borrowed money, giving his promissory note, in order to finance her education and to maintain the estate of which she was sole heiress. On coming of age she promised that she would reimburse him, and after her marriage, her husband Kenyon promised Eastwood that he would pay his promissory note for him. This Kenyon failed to do. In bringing his action, Eastwood insisted upon Kenyon's moral duty to honour his promise, but his action failed because of lack of consideration. What price had Eastwood paid for Kenyon's promise? The court could find none. Kenyon's promise was not part of a bargain made with Eastwood. His motive, a sense of gratitude, a feeling of moral duty was strong enough to lead to a declaration of noble intent, though not strong enough to be binding at law when he failed to perform.

If a promise is made to reward a person who has previously done an act gratuitously or given something of value to the promisor, the promise is not binding. The promise is, in its turn, gratuitous, just like the benefit which the promisee had earlier conferred upon the

---

[6] (1840), 113 E.R. 482.

since

promisor; and as we have seen, gratuitous promises are not binding. Another approach is to say that the motive of the promisor was to return the kindness of the promisee, and, of course, motive and consideration are not the same thing. The benefit previously conferred upon the promisor is often called *past consideration*. But since there is no element of bargain, that is, of the benefit being performed *in return for* the promise, the expression is really a contradiction of terms, for "past consideration" is no consideration.

ILLUSTRATION

Adams saved Bodnar from drowning. Afterwards Bodnar promised to pay Adams $100 out of gratitude.

Bodnar may change his mind at any time before he actually pays Adams the money, and Adams will be helpless to enforce the promise. In saving Bodnar's life, Adams did not act in response to an offer to pay her for doing so. Bodnar's promise was made after the event and was therefore made for "past consideration". In the circumstances Adams did not pay any price for Bodnar's promise.

RELATION BETWEEN EXISTING LEGAL DUTY AND CONSIDERATION

Where *A* is bound by an existing contractual duty to *B*, a later promise by *B* to pay *A* something extra to perform the same obligation is not binding. The performance by *A* of his obligation is not good consideration for the later promise because he was already bound to perform — his failure to do so would have been a breach of contract. For example, a promise to members of a crew to increase their pay if they do not desert their ship is unenforceable.[7] There is an existing contract of employment between the crew and the employer which binds the crew to perform their duties faithfully. On the other hand, a term of such contracts is that the ship be seaworthy. If it proves unseaworthy, the crew are released from their obligation, and then, of course, there will be consideration for the promise to pay an extra sum if the crew stay with the ship.[8]

The problem often arises in the following circumstances: *A* may threaten to default on his obligation to perform and leave *B* to sue for the breach. If *B* is anxious to have *A* carry out his part of the bargain, he may agree to pay *A* more money. A typical example occurs when a construction firm discovers it has agreed to erect a building for too low a price, or runs into unexpected difficulties. The owner may be depending upon completion at a certain date, and should the firm abandon the job, the owner may lose valuable time, perhaps even putting herself in breach of other contracts, if she has leased out large parts of the building. Some U.S. courts have taken the view that the building firm is at liberty to abandon the job if it chooses, and pay damages. In this view a fresh promise to proceed, that is, not to abandon the job, is good consideration for an additional sum and the owner is bound to pay that additional sum on completion. Most courts, including all the

---

[7]   Stilk v. Myrick (1809) 170 E.R. 1168.
[8]   Turner v. Owen (1862) 176 E.R. 79.

English and Canadian courts, take the view that this conduct smacks of unfair pressure by the party threatening to abandon the contract. Accordingly, they hold that there is no consideration for the promise to pay an extra sum.[9]

While the doctrine of consideration can be used as a shield against economic blackmail, it hardly provides a justification for a blanket refusal by the courts to enforce any and every modification of existing contractual obligations. The underlying, but often unstated, reason why the courts have refused to enforce such "gratuitous" modifications is probably not so much the lack of consideration as the courts' unwillingness to support unconscionable conduct. As the common law stands, a supplier intent on economic blackmail can still exact a legally enforceable promise from its customer to pay an increased price by delivering a "peppercorn" or a paperclip (or any other item of negligible value) to him in return for the promise, or by insisting that the customer make his promise under seal (as discussed later in this chapter).

We can see that the doctrine of consideration is, at best, an imperfect instrument for achieving a socially or morally acceptable result. The question should be whether the contractual modification was an attempt to adjust the legitimate interests of the parties in changed circumstances and not to extort a higher price: not every modification of contractual terms amounts to an unconscionable exploitation of the promisor. For instance, a promisor may believe it is in his best interests to pay his promisee more in order to relieve the promisee from hardship and thus obtain a better performance. Thus far the Canadian courts have been reluctant to recognize this reality,[10] although a recent English case allowed a construction company to recover a promised extra sum for completion.[11] The court was satisfied that there was no economic duress; the construction company had not exerted undue pressure and both parties benefited from performance.

A related problem arises when a party to a contract promises a stranger to that contract to perform his existing obligations in return for a promise of payment from the stranger. Thus C may promise to pay A a sum of money to perform an obligation that A is already bound to perform under a contract with B. Suppose A, a construction firm, has promised to construct an office building for B. Is there consideration for a promise made by C, a prospective tenant, to pay A a sum of money if it completes the building on time?[12] A is already bound to B to construct the building on time: what further price does A give for C's promise?

This problem has seldom arisen in the courts, but when it does they seem to agree that A can enforce C's promise, and also that if A failed to perform, it would be liable to actions by *both* B and C.[13] We must therefore distinguish between the situation where the later promise is made by the promisee in the original contract, and where it is made by a stranger to that contract.

Another variation occurs when A's duty to perform is a public duty cast upon A by law, as for example where A is a police officer. If B promises to pay A for services as a police officer, the court is confronted with two problems — the question of public policy and of

---

[9] See Gilbert Steel Ltd. v. University Construction Ltd. (1976) 67 D.L.R. (3d) 606.
[10] See Reiter, "Courts, Consideration and Common Sense", (1977) 27 U.T.L.J. pp. 439-512, especially at p. 459.
[11] Williams v. Roffey Brothers & Nicholls (Contractors) Ltd., [1990] 1 All E.R. 512. For a useful commentary, see Halyk, "Consideration, Practical Benefits and Promissory Estoppel". (1991) 55(2) Saskatchewan L. Rev. 393.
[12] Shadwell v. Shadwell (1860) 142 E.R. 62.
[13] Scotson v. Pegg (1861) 158 E.R. 121; Pao On v. Lau Yiu Long [1979] 3 W.L.R. 435.

consideration. If police officers have been asked to do something which they are already bound to do or something which will interfere with their regular duties, the court will probably be concerned that the promise to pay them tends to corrupt public servants and will find the promise unenforceable. On the other hand, if the court finds that they have been requested to do something beyond their duties and not in conflict with them, it will probably find consideration and hold the promise to pay for the services binding. Thus, in *Glasbrook Brothers v. Glamorgan County Council*[14] a company agreed to pay for a special police guard during a strike and was held to be bound by its promise.

Gratuitous Reduction of a Debt

The requirement for consideration to make a promise binding can lead to other unexpected and unsatisfactory results, especially in business transactions. In the leading English case of *Foakes v. Beer*[15] a debtor owed a large sum of money and payment was overdue. His creditor agreed to take as payment a series of instalments of the principal and to forgo her right to interest if the debtor paid these instalments promptly and regularly. The debtor paid the full principal sum by instalments as agreed, but the creditor then sued for the interest. She succeeded, on the grounds that her promise to accept less than the total sum to which she was entitled amounted to a gratuitous promise to give away her right to interest, and thus did not bind her.

This rule is unrealistic. For a number of sensible reasons, a creditor firm (which we shall call *C*) may find it more to its benefit to settle for some reduction in the debt owing to it than to press its claim for payment in full. For one thing, such a compromise may avoid placing a debtor in bankruptcy where by the time all creditors' claims have been recognized, *C* might realize less money than if it had agreed directly to a reduction of its claim. Second, the proposed reduction may make it possible for the debtor to prevail upon friends to lend him enough money to take advantage of it, and make a fresh start. Third, the debtor may simply not have the assets to enable him to pay in full, so that a court judgment against him would not in any event realize more than the reduced amount. Finally, *C* may well need at least part of the sum owed it urgently for other commitments: it may be happier to take the lesser amount at once, even though it might later collect the full account with all the delays inherent in a legal action.

The rule in *Foakes v. Beer* may be avoided in several ways. In the first place, payment before the due date is sufficient consideration to make a reduction in the debt binding on the creditor if it so agrees. Thus if the debtor pays $600 one day in advance in settlement of a $1000 debt due the next day, the agreement to accept $600 will be binding. As we have seen, the court will not inquire into the adequacy of the consideration; if the creditor chooses to reduce the debt by $400 in order to receive it one day in advance, it may bind itself to do so.

Second, the rule in *Foakes v. Beer* applies only to payments of money. It does not apply to the transfer of goods or to the rendering of services. Since an individual may make a contract for a totally inadequate consideration if he so desires, he may agree to pay $1000 for a trinket,

---

14 [1925] A.C. 270.
15 (1884) 9 App. Cas. 605.

a cheap watch, or a package of cigarettes. Similarly, he may agree to cancel a $1000 debt upon receipt of any one of these objects. In effect, he is trading the debt for the object, and such an agreement is perfectly valid, provided he enters upon it voluntarily. The result of this reasoning creates a paradox: if a person agrees to accept $900 in full settlement of a $1000 debt, he may later sue for the balance successfully; if a person accepts $500 and a string of beads worth ten cents in full settlement of a $1000 debt, he will fail if he sues for the balance.

Third, the rule in *Foakes v. Beer* applies only to agreements between the creditor and the debtor. A third party, who is not bound to pay anything to the creditor, may offer to pay the creditor a lesser sum if it will cancel the debt. A creditor that accepts such an offer is bound by its promise and cannot sue the debtor afterwards.[16] The result is the same as if the third person had purchased the debt from the creditor.

ILLUSTRATION

A Co. Ltd. has an account receivable from *B* for $1000, and sells (assigns) it to *X* for $800. *A* Co. Ltd. no longer has any rights against *B*. It would not matter whether *X* was purchasing the account receivable as a business proposition and intended to hold *B* to her promise for full payment, or whether he wished merely to help the debtor. *X*'s motive is irrelevant. If he deals directly with the creditor, the debt for $1000 can be bought for $800.

The result would have been different, however, if *X* had lent $800 to *B* and *B* had then paid the $800 to *A* Co. Ltd. apparently in full settlement of the account of $1000. So long as *B* deals directly with *A* Co. Ltd., the source of the funds paid by *B* is irrelevant: *A* Co. Ltd. would not be bound by this settlement and could later sue *B* for $200 (apart from the statutory exceptions discussed below.)

Finally, as we shall see shortly, the rule in *Foakes v. Beer* is avoided if the creditor agrees in writing and under seal to reduce the debt.

The rule in *Foakes v. Beer* has been modified in British Columbia, Alberta, Saskatchewan, Manitoba, and Ontario by statute.[17] Under any of these acts, if a creditor agrees to accept part performance (that is, a lesser sum of money) in settlement of a debt, it is bound once it has accepted this part performance. On the other hand, it may be able to go back on its promise to accept a lesser sum of money before the sum is actually paid; the cases are unclear on the point.

*I*NJURIOUS RELIANCE (EQUITABLE ESTOPPEL)

There are times when a person makes a gratuitous promise to another fully intending to keep it but later finds it inconvient to perform. Meanwhile the promisee has quite reason-

---

[16] Hirachand Punamchand v. Temple, [1911] 2 K.B. 330.
[17] The Law and Equity Act, R.S.B.C. 1979, C. 224, S. 40; The Judicature Act, R.S.A. 1980, c. J-1, S.13(1); The Queen's Bench Act, R.S.S. 1978, c. Q-1, s. 45 (7); The Mercantile Law Amendment Act, R.S.M. 1987, c. M-120, s. 6; and The Mercantile Law Amendment Act, R.S.O. 1990, c. M-10, s. 16. For cases interpreting this section see Rommerill v. Gardener (1962), 35 D.L.R. (2d) 717 and others referred to therein.

ably relied on the promise and has incurred expenses he would otherwise not have made. What happens if the promisor subsequently defaults? According to the strict rules of common law, the answer is "nothing at all". The gratuitous promise remains gratuitous, the promise cannot be enforced, and the promisee suffers the burden of his expenses.

ILLUSTRATION

A, who has just ordered a new 90-hp. outboard motor, tells his friend B that he will give him his old 35-hp. motor as soon as the new one arrives. Before B can make use of A's old engine, he will have to make expensive modifications to his small boat. Instead, at A's suggestion he buys a new boat for $3000. Subsequently, A's brother reminds him that he had promised the old motor to him, and rather than promote a family quarrel, A tells B he cannot carry out his promise. B has no right in contract law to enforce A's promise.

Some parts of the United States have adopted a principle whereby A would be bound to carry out his promise.[18] Courts in these jurisdictions argue that since A by his conduct *induced* B to rely on his promise and B did rely upon it, to his injury, A must now honour his promise to prevent an injustice. This principle, known as injurious reliance, is based on rules similar to the tort rules concerning foreseeability of harm in negligence actions. The classic expression of the doctrine is as follows:

> A promise which the promisor should reasonably expect to induce action or forbearance of a definite and substantial character on the part of the promisee and which does induce such action or forbearance is binding if injustice can be avoided only by enforcement of the promise.[19]

Thus, although a promisor has not *requested* the acts of reliance of the promisee in return for his promise, inducement alone, as in the circumstances described above, becomes a substitute for the request. (If he had requested the act of reliance in return for his promise, there would be an offer, an acceptance, and consideration in all common law jurisdictions.) This position, as we are about to discuss, has been gaining more recognition in England and Canada.

When one person asserts as true a certain *statement of fact* and another relies on that statement to his detriment, the maker of the statement will be *estopped* (prevented) from denying the truth of his original statement in a court of law, even if it turns out to have been untrue.

---

[18] Ricketts v. Scothorn (1898) 77 N.W. 365.

[19] American Law Institute, *Restatement of Contracts*, Section 90, Washington, 1932.

ILLUSTRATION A

A has purchased a retail shoe business from X in rented premises owned by B. After a few months, A mentions to her landlord, B, that the business does not have an adequate sales area. She remarks that she would like to turn a back room into a display and fitting salon, but that the room contains a number of pieces of old furniture belonging to B that she would like to get rid of. B then says to A, "That furniture belonged to X and you acquired it when you purchased the business. You can do as you like with it." A replies, "I thought that the furniture was yours. That's what X told me." "No, it's yours," B answers. The tenant next door to A, is present and hears the conversation.

That evening, when B reports the incident to his wife, she becomes furious and reminds B that several antique pieces given to them by her grandmother are stored in the back room of the store. When B arrives at the shoe store the next morning he discovers that the furniture has been taken away to the city dump and compressed by a bulldozer. He then sues A for the value of the antique furniture.

B would fail because A can prove in her defence that B had asserted that the furniture was A's, and the court would estop B from asserting the true state of facts.

ILLUSTRATION B

Estoppel applies to an assertion of existing fact; but does it also apply to a promise of future conduct? Suppose that instead of stating the furniture was A's, B had replied, "I wouldn't mind seeing that ugly furniture of ours in the city dump, as long as you don't tell my wife. I promise not to interfere." The following morning, B's wife was shopping in the vicinity and saw the furniture being removed from A's premises. Before she could stop the workers, several of the best pieces were damaged beyond repair. B reluctantly sued A for the value of the destroyed pieces and the return of the remainder. B would recover the remaining furniture, but would he succeed in getting damages?

To answer this question, we must examine the original meaning of estoppel and its subsequent enlargement. For practical reasons, and generally until recent times, the courts restricted the use of estoppel to assertions of fact. When an assertion of fact has been made, its truth or falsity at the time of its assertion is an objective matter that can generally be determined by evidence. The essence of estoppel is reliance on facts as they were asserted to be at the time of the statement. Only if they were untrue at the time would the maker be estopped. The judges reasoned that the essential element of common law estoppel was missing when a person had made a promise of future conduct instead of an assertion of existing facts: a promise of future conduct was exclusively within the sphere of contract law and required consideration. The problem with their reasoning was that a person can act as much to his detriment on the strength of a gratuitous promise as on the strength of an assertion of fact that proves to be incorrect.

Sometimes a promisee may act on the strength of a promise when the promisor had no intention of keeping his word. The promisee can argue that she was acting on an assertion of *fact* by the promisor — that he was making his promise with the present intention of keeping it (which was not the case). This line of argument also presented difficulties. As we have noted, the common law courts resisted examining a person's motives; motives are not subject to proof by external evidence, except in those rare instances when a dishonest promisor gives himself away by his own admission. States of mind are notoriously difficult to ascertain at the best of times. In any event, the harm suffered by the promisee is the same whether the promisor originally intended to keep his promise and later changed his mind, or originally intended to mislead and never meant to keep his promise. While the question of intention is germane to the punishment of a wrongdoer in criminal law, it has little to do with the concern of contract law to seek external standards in order to determine when a promise is binding as a contractual bargain.

Whatever their problems with trying to adapt the idea of estoppel, the courts eventually found themselves unable to ignore the plea of an innocent party who had relied in good faith on a gratuitous promise only to find later that the promisor had changed his mind. In Illustration B above, A relied on B's implied promise that he would not demand the return of his furniture, and it can certainly be argued that A's reliance differs in its effect little, if at all, from his reliance on B's assertion in Illustration A that the furniture belonged to A. Solely on the grounds of fairness, the court would exercise its equitable jurisdiction to estop B from claiming that he was not bound by his gratuitous promise as it applied to the furniture already destroyed. Such reasoning appears to extend the idea of estoppel to promises. (The argument has been called *promissory estoppel* but the more common phrase is *equitable estoppel,* because the court is acting as a court of equity to override a common law rule.) The U.S. term "injurious reliance" and the English term "equitable estoppel" are essentially two sides of the same coin: injurious reliance looks at the situation from the point of view of the promisee, while equitable estoppel views it from the position of the promisor.

The English doctrine of equitable estoppel has not been carried as far as the U.S. doctrine of injurious reliance, at least in its present state of development. It appears to be limited to a *defence* against a claim by the promisor where a legal relationship already exists between the parties. The English courts have not permitted a gratuitous promisee to rely on equitable estoppel in order to make the promise to him a binding one. (Hence, in our earlier illustration of the gratuitous promise of an outboard motor, the promisee would not succeed in an English court.)

Although the doctrine of equitable estoppel originated over a century ago in the leading case of *Hughes v. Metropolitan Railway Co.*,[20] very little use was made of it for many years. In the Hughes case, a tenant under a 99-year lease of a large block of buildings was under an obligation to keep the building in good repair. The penalty for failure to honour a notice to repair given by the landlord (Hughes) would be forfeiture of possession.

---

[20] (1877), 2 App. Cas. 439.

Hughes served the tenant with notice that repairs were needed and the tenant had six months in which to make them. The tenant then suggested that perhaps Hughes might be interested in buying back the remaining years of the tenant's 99-year lease. Evidently the lease was a valuable one, as rents to subtenants had risen greatly over the long years of the master lease. Serious negotiation began when Hughes expressed interest in the proposal. All repairs were delayed with Hughes' acquiescence, as repairs would simply have increased the tenant's investment in the property and thus the sale price of the lease. After several months negotiations broke down, and the tenant then proceeded with the repairs. They were not finished within six months of the original notice, but were complete within six months of the termination of negotiations. Hughes sued for forfeiture of the lease, the effect of which would be to give him the remaining years free. In refusing Hughes' claim, the House of Lords stated that by entering into negotiation Hughes had impliedly agreed to a suspension of the notice, and he could not subsequently go back on his word and revert to his strict legal rights in the lease; the notice became effective again only on negotiations being broken off, when the tenant could no longer rely on Hughes' implied promise not to pursue his strict rights.

The *Hughes* case still illustrates the classic situation in which promissory estoppel arises: (1) some form of legal relationship already exists between the parties; (2) one of the parties promises (perhaps, indeed, by implication only) to release the other from some or all of the other's legal duties to him; and (3) the other party in reliance on that promise alters his conduct in a way that would make it a real hardship if the promise were not to be performed. If, in disregard of this promise, the promisor were then to sue to enforce his original rights, the promisee could successfully plead promissory estoppel as a reason the action against him should fail.

We should note, however, that the promise, because it is gratuitous, may be withdrawn. While its withdrawal cannot prejudice the promisee in respect of any reliance he has already placed on it, notice of withdrawal (or cessation of circumstances in which the promise is implied) may restore the promisor's rights to any future performance still owed by the promisee. Thus, in the *Hughes* case, the landlord was entitled, after the negotiations had broken down, once more to require repairs to be made within the six-month period provided in the lease.

The period immediately after the Second World War saw a flurry of cases in England in which Lord Denning sought gradually to develop the use of this doctrine.[21] More recently, Canadian courts have taken notice of it, and in particular the decision of the Supreme Court of Canada in *Conwest Exploration Co. v. Letain*[22] has pushed the doctrine quite far indeed; it can even be argued that the decision conceded that equitable estoppel might be used as a cause of action.[23] The facts were complicated, but the essential ones for our purposes can be summarized as follows.

---

[21] See, for example: Central London Property Trust, Ltd. v. High Trees House, Ltd., [1947] K.B. 130.

[22] (1964), 41 D.L.R. (2d) 198. See also: Re Tudale Exploration Ltd. and Bruce *et al.* (1978), 20 O.R. (2d) 593, per Grange, J. at 597 and 599.

[23] See, for example: Crabb v. Arun District Council, [1976] Ch. 179.

A held an option to purchase certain mining claims. Before the date of expiry of the option, B, the grantor of the option, impliedly agreed to its extension. (As in the Hughes case, it appeared to be in his interest to do so.) As a result, A did not hurry to complete the required task under the option before the original expiry date, but he did try to exercise the option shortly afterwards, and before B had given any notice that he wished to return to his strict legal rights. In an action brought by A asking the court to permit him to exercise his option, the court did not allow B to assert the original expiry date, and A's action succeeded.

The promise to extend the period was implicitly made during the original option period and thus while legal relations existed between the parties. On the one hand, therefore, it can be concluded that this decision amounts to no more than an application of the *Hughes* case. On the other hand, there is an opposing view that once the original option had expired, without an extension having been granted for additional consideration, there was then no subsisting legal relationship between A and B; they were as strangers. Thus, to permit A to succeed is to permit him to use equitable estoppel as a cause of action, as in U.S. cases of injurious reliance. It remains to be seen whether in future cases the Canadian courts will favour this second view.

The Effect of a Request for Goods or Services

When one person requests the services of another, and the other performs those services, the law implies a promise to pay. Although there is no mention of price, the implied promise is for payment of what the services are reasonably worth, that is, for payment *quantum meruit*.[24] Difficult though it may be when the services are not usual professional services with a recognized scale of fees, the court will nonetheless endeavour to find what is reasonable. A promise to pay will be implied in a request between strangers or even between friends, if the services are rendered in a customary business transaction. But such a promise is not usually implied when the services are performed between members of a family or close friends; the surrounding circumstances may show that although the services were requested, the parties expected them to be given gratuitously because of friendship, kindness, or family duty.

After services requested in a business relationship have been performed, the parties may agree on what they consider to be a reasonable price. If so, neither of them can later change his mind and ask the court to fix a reasonable price. In effect, each party has given up his right to refer the matter to the court by agreeing to a price.

---

[24] *Quantum meruit* means, "the amount one merits (for one's services)".

ILLUSTRATION

A asks lawyer *B* for legal advice. Afterwards, *A* asks *B* what her fee is and *B* suggests a certain sum. *A* refuses to pay it. In an action for payment for services performed, the court may give judgment in favour of *B* in the amount she requested or for some other amount that it deems reasonable.

If instead, *A* had agreed to the figure sug-gested by *B* but later changed her mind about paying, the court would not concern itself with what it considered reasonable: it would give judgment in favour of *B* for the amount earlier agreed upon. Only if the figure were obviously exorbitant might the court reopen the matter of what is reasonable.

The performance of services at the request of a party creates from that time an *existing obligation* to pay a reasonable price for them. When the parties later agree upon a fixed price, they have done away with the need for an implied price; and the subsequent payment of the fixed price satisfies all obligations owed by the party who requested the services. We must be careful to distinguish this position from that arising when a promise is made for a past consideration.[25] If, for example, *A* promises to pay *B* $100 because *B* has given her and her family an excellent dinner, *A* is not bound, since she is under no existing legal obligation at the time she makes her promise. If, however, *A* promises to pay *B* $100 because *B* has catered a dinner for her at her request, *A* would be bound; in fact, *A* was already bound to pay *B* a reasonable price, and she and *B* have merely agreed later upon what this price should be.

The principle of *quantum meruit* applies to goods supplied on request as well as to services rendered; generally, a court has less difficulty ascertaining the reasonable worth of goods than of services.

THE USE OF A SEAL

In medieval times, when few people could read or write, a serious promise or *covenant* was often recorded by a cleric. He would read the covenant over to the covenantor, who would then show his consent by impressing his coat of arms into a pool of hot sealing wax poured at the foot of the document. Usually the coat of arms was worn on a signet ring. By impressing his seal in this way, the covenantor adopted the document as *his act and deed*. To this day a document under seal is still called a "deed". After a time, other methods of sealing a document came to be used, including embossing the coat of arms directly on the paper. Today the usual method is to affix a small red gummed wafer to a document, but almost any mark identifiable as a "seal" will do, even the word "seal" simply written in.

A seal, however, must be affixed (or the word "seal" written) on the document at the time the party signs it. The word "seal" printed on the document in advance presents difficulties: it may simply indicate the place where the parties are to place a red paper wafer. In *Royal Bank of Canada v. Kiska*[26] the bank used a printed form of guarantee which included the

---

[25] Lampleigh v. Braithwait (1615), 80 E.R. 255.
[26] (1967), 63 D.L.R. (2d) 582.

word "seal" and also the words, "Given under seal at ..." and, "Signed, sealed and delivered in the presence of ..." The bank manager did not affix a red paper wafer, however, until some time after the guarantor had signed, and without the guarantor's instructions to do so. J. Laskin (later Chief Justice of the Supreme Court of Canada) commented:

> The respective words are merely anticipatory of a formality which must be observed and are not a substitute for it. I am not tempted by any suggestion that it would be a modern and liberal view to hold that a person who signs a document that states it is under seal should be bound accordingly although there is no seal on it. I have no regret in declining to follow this path in a case where a bank thrusts a printed form under the nose of a young man for his signature. Formality serves a purpose here and some semblance of it should be preserved ...[27]

A promise made properly under the seal of the promisor does not require consideration to make it binding. Historically, signing under seal was taken as an act of great deliberation. It is still considered so today. The seal says in effect, "I fully intend to be bound by this promise." Its presence means that the court will not, as it otherwise would, insist upon consideration to hold the promisor bound.

Although a seal is an alternative way to make a promise binding, it does not do away with any other requirements needed to make a promise enforceable. Other essentials for a binding contract (its legality, for example) remain the same.

The use of a seal may have a legal effect for offers, as well as for promises. When a business firm or public body invites tenders and requires them to be submitted under the seal of the tenderer, the legal effect is much the same as when an option is given: the tenderer cannot withdraw without being liable in damages.[28] Of course, any offer may be made under seal, and so rendered irrevocable, but a tender is a common example.

Certain documents, such as a deed of land and a mortgage, may require a seal even if there is consideration. These documents will be explained as they arise in later chapters.

An Intention to Create Legal Relations

Even when an apparently valid offer has been accepted and consideration is present, there may be no contract in law. Both sides must also intend to create a legally enforceable agreement. Of course, parties do not often direct their minds to the legal effects of their bargains, but the law presumes that the necessary intention is present in almost all instances where an agreement is seriously made. This presumption is especially strong in dealings between strangers, and in commerce generally. On the other hand, it is easier to rebut this presumption in arrangements between friends or members of a family, where it is often obvious that there was no intention to create legal relations. For example, claiming that a failure to show up for a dinner invitation would give the host a right to sue for breach of contract even though the host went to considerable trouble and expense would be highly unreasonable. Many domestic arrangements between husband and wife are on the same footing.

---

[27] *Ibid.*, at p. 594.
[28] See Sanitary Refuse Collectors Inc. v. City of Ottawa, [1972] 1 O.R. 296 at pp. 308-9.

In a United States case,[29] a farmer from whom a $15 harness had been stolen announced in the indignation and frustration of the moment, "I will give $100 to any man who will find out who the thief is." Thereupon someone present named the thief. When the informer sued to recover the $100, the court ruled that the farmer's statement was "the extravagant exclamation of an excited man" and could not be construed as a serious offer which, when accepted, would create a legal relationship.

We may note that the law *presumes* that the parties to a contract intend to be legally bound. The law takes this position because it is impractical, if not impossible, for a court to inquire into the state of mind of both parties at the time they made the agreement and to decide whether they truly had such an intention. Instead, the court uses the external or objective test of the reasonable bystander: if to such a person the outward conduct of the parties showed a serious intention to make an agreement, then in the eyes of the law a legally binding contract results.

The requirement that a promise must be seriously meant before it has legal consequences is important in interpreting the legal effect of advertisements. In *Carlill v. The Carbolic Smoke Ball Company*, considered in the preceding chapter, the company pleaded in defence that its undertaking to pay a £100 reward was no more than a "mere puff" and was not to be taken seriously. This defence might have succeeded, but for the fact that the company had included in its advertisement the statement, "£1,000 is deposited with the Alliance Bank, Regent Street, showing our sincerity in the matter." We shall discuss the possible legal effects of advertising further under the topics of misrepresentation in Chapter 11 and consumer protection in Chapter 19.

Even in a contract that would normally imply legal relations, the parties may include an express term that in the event of its breach neither party may sue the other. Such an understanding is usually recognized by the courts and is an effective defence to any action brought under the contract.[30] Terms of this kind now occur more frequently in certain types of contracts and particularly in franchising arrangements where the franchisee undertakes not to sue the franchisor in the event of disagreement. Since the franchisor often has the greater bargaining power, a franchisee may argue that the franchisor's insistence on the inclusion of such a clause is unconscionable and should be struck down, enabling the franchisee to sue. Unconscionability will be discussed more generally in Chapter 10.

Questions for Review

1. What is the consideration for the promise of the offeror in a unilateral contract? In a bilateral contract?
2. How may a gratuitous promise become enforceable?
3. Is there consideration for a promise to reward the promisee for performing what is already a contractual duty to the promisor? Does it make any difference if the promisee owes the contractual duty to someone other than the promisor?
4. Does the use of a seal answer for a failure to satisfy all essentials of a binding contract?
5. In what way may the common law rules about the need for consideration be unsatisfactory for business purposes? How can the defect be remedied?

---

[29] Higgins v. Lessig, 49 Ill. App. 459 (1893).
[30] Rose and Frank v. Crompton, [1925] A.C. 445.

6. Under what circumstances might a promised donation to a charitable organization be enforceable?
7. If past consideration were to be acknowledged as good consideration, what basic notion about consideration would be violated?
8. What is the nature of the obligation of a person who requests services?
9. Does a court ever concern itself with the adequacy of the consideration? If so, when?
10. What three essentials of a binding contract have we considered thus far?
11. A firm of public accountants has for years been auditing the accounts of a charitable organization without charge. It now appears that the treasurer of the organization has absconded with a sizeable amount of money and that an application of generally accepted auditing standards would have disclosed the defalcation in time to avoid the loss. Has the charitable organization any recourse against its auditors in these circumstances?
12. A supplier's invoice for goods has the following common term printed on it: "Terms — Net price thirty days; two per cent discount if paid within ten days." If the buyer pays the price less two per cent within ten days, can the supplier later sue successfully for the sum deducted?
13. Can there be consideration in a contract without the parties having expressly agreed upon what it is to be? Explain.
14. What question remains unresolved in the application of the concept of equitable estoppel by the Canadian courts?
15. A student asserts that consideration is present in most promises to donate money to charitable organizations because the promisor has an economic benefit from his promise in the form of a deduction from his taxable income. Is this reasoning correct? (Check the definition of consideration.)
16. A promises in writing to pay a sum of money to a university of which she is a graduate "in consideration for the subscriptions of other alumnae". Is that enough to make her promise binding? Explain.

Problems

Problem 1
MacGregor, who was having a private dispute with his neighbour, O'Toole, called upon an acquaintance of his, Smith, who happened to be a lawyer. In the course of a conversation about world affairs and the weather MacGregor casually mentioned his dispute, and wondered audibly whether a legal action against O'Toole for trespass and slander might not be feasible. Smith advised against it. Subsequently, MacGregor received a bill for $35 from Smith "for professional services rendered".

Has Smith contractual grounds for making this claim? Are there any additional facts it might be helpful to know before answering this question?

Problem 2
In 1939, Central London Property Trust, as landlord, leased for a period of 99 years an apartment building in London, England to High Trees House at an annual rental of £2500. By January 1940, many of the apartments had been vacated because of war conditions and the partial evacuation of the city. Central London agreed in writing to reduce the annual rental to £1250. High Trees House remained in possession and paid £1250

annually from 1940 through 1945. In 1945 the apartments in the building were again fully occupied. Central London then claimed from High Trees House (i) arrears of rent of £1250 for each of the six years 1940 through 1945 and (ii) acknowledgement of liability to pay rent at the rate of £2500 in future. Would either or both of these claims be likely to succeed if Central London were to seek to enforce them by court action? Give reasons.

Problem 3

Knight is the owner of Armour Heights Subdivision. On September 1, he offered in writing to sell Lot #3 in the subdivision to Archer for $15 000, and on September 2 Archer accepted the offer in writing and delivered her acceptance in person, by car. On September 4 Knight telephoned Archer to say that he had just learned that a shopping centre was going to be built in the subdivision near Lot #3, and that he would now have to have $22 000 for each of the lots, including Lot #3. Archer, equally excited by the news, agreed to change the price stated in the written contract from $15 000 to $22 000 and wrote her initials and the date opposite the change. Archer later tendered a cheque for $15 000 "in full settlement of the amount owing for Lot #3 per our agreement of September 2". Knight deposited the cheque and sued Archer for an alleged $7000 balance owing. Explain whether this action should succeed.

Problem 4

Charles Cameron owned substantial property but did not make a will because all his property was held jointly with his wife, Grace, and would pass to her as survivor. He did, however, ask Grace to make some provision for his brother, Donald Cameron, and his children, because they were so poor. Shortly after Charles died, Grace went to a lawyer and told him that she had promised her late husband to give certain things to his brother and that in case anything happened she wanted to get it in writing "so it could not be upset". Accordingly, she signed a document prepared by the lawyer promising that as soon as the business affairs of her late husband were settled she would give $10 000 to Donald Cameron to carry out her promise made Charles. The document contained a seal adjacent to her signature, and was delivered to Donald.

A misunderstanding subsequently developed between Grace and her brother-in-law, and Grace refused to pay him the $10 000. Donald sued her for the money.

State whether Donald would succeed in his action.

Problem 5

Sarah Binks, a prominent local citizen in the town of Crocus, undertook to contribute $500 000 towards the expansion programme of the local university. On the occasion when she signed the subscription card, the president of the university stated that the university would now be able to undertake the construction of an additional building, which it would name after her in recognition of her contribution. A picture of Sarah and the university president appeared in the *Crocus Daily Bugle* with a news item about her generous contribution to the university campaign.

Unfortunately, Sarah died shortly afterwards, before she had paid the amount. The executor of her estate, on instructions from her next of kin, advised the university that he did not propose to pay the amount. The university sued Sarah's estate for $500 000.

Examine the possible arguments for the plaintiff and the defendant, and state what you think the decision would be.

Problem 6

(a) Roberts was a business consultant and was recommended by a bank manager to Matsui. Matsui wished to buy the control of a business and was prepared to pay $100 000 or so if he could find a business which he regarded as satisfactory.

Matsui identified three companies in which he was interested, and at Matsui's request Roberts devoted most of his time from May to February of the following year investigating the three businesses. Roberts' rate of remuneration for performing these sevices was not discussed. Finally, after consultation with Matsui, Roberts managed to obtain an option for Matsui to purchase the shares of the A.C. Electrical Co. Ltd., one of the three companies identified by Matsui. When Matsui learned of Roberts' success in obtaining the option, he promised to pay Roberts $25 000 for his services. Roberts said that would be fine.

Matsui subsequently decided not to exercise the option, and refused to pay Roberts the $25 000. Roberts brought an action against him for this sum. In defence Matsui asserted that it was expressly agreed that if, as a result of Roberts' services or efforts, Matsui actually made a purchase, he would pay a suitable commission to Roberts but unless he made such a purchase, Roberts would be entitled to nothing. Roberts denied that Matsui's undertaking had been qualified in this manner. Faced with this conflict of evidence, the trial judge stated that he accepted the evidence of the plaintiff in preference to that of the defendant.

What is the main issue? Should Roberts succeed? (See *Roche v. Marston* [1951] 3 D.L.R. 433.)

(b) Suppose instead that the parties had discussed $25 000 as the appropriate fee before the services were rendered and then when Matsui learned of Roberts' success in obtaining the option, he was so elated as to promise him $5000 more. What issue would arise if Roberts found it necessary to sue Matsui for the $30 000?

Problem 7

Mrs. Pays owned a house in which she lived with Esme Pays, her granddaughter, and May Simpkins, a paying boarder. The three took part together each week in a fashion competition organized by a Sunday newspaper, the *Sunday Empire News*, in which readers were invited to place in order of merit eight fashions or articles of clothing. They sometimes discussed the possibility of winning in a way which assumed they would all share equally. The entries were made in Mrs. Pays' name, but there was no regular rule for the payment of postage and other expenses. One week the entry was successful, and Mrs. Pays obtained a prize of $750. May Simpkins claimed a third of this sum, but Mrs. Pays refused to pay it. May brought legal action to recover.

What is the main issue in this case? Should the action succeed? (See *Simpkins v. Pays* [1955] 3 All E.R. 10.)

Cases

Case 1

Harris N. Dealer was sole proprietor of a profitable computer data centre which he sold as a going concern to Alice B. Wheeler for the price of $80 000. The price was paid, $20 000 in cash and the balance in the form of a contract under Wheeler's seal and read in part as follows:

For value received Alice B. Wheeler promises to pay Harris N. Dealer the sum of sixty thousand dollars ($60 000) in ten years from April 1, 1987 together with interest at 16% per annum from April 1st 1987 payable monthly on the first day of May 1987 and on the first day of each and every month thereafter until payment of the principal sum on April 1, 1997.

After ten (10) days' default in any interest payment due under this agreement the whole amount payable shall become immediately due.

March 29, 1987.   Alice B. Wheeler [SEAL]

Dealer and Wheeler remained on friendly terms throughout the balance of 1987. Wheeler was somewhat dilatory in making her monthly payments of $800 interest, so that by the end of the year she had made six of the eight monthly payments required by then on dates more than ten days after they were due; Dealer had acquiesced in the arrangement without complaint, though the parties had never expressly agreed on any change in the due dates and Dealer seemed merely to have been indulgent with his debtor. Unfortunately, however, the parties had a serious personal disagreement early in 1988. On February 5, 1988, the January 1st interest payment then being 35 days overdue, Dealer wrote to Wheeler as follows:

This letter will serve to inform you that, an interest payment due under the terms of the contract dated March 29, 1987 being in default for more than 10 days, the whole amount under the contract is now due.

I hereby demand immediate payment of the principal amount of $60 000 and outstanding interest.

H.N.Dealer

Wheeler immediately paid the outstanding interest but refused to pay the principal sum. Dealer brought an action against her for $60 000.

Develop fully the arguments for both the plaintiff and the defendant. State with reasons, including reference to a relevant case or cases, whether the action should succeed.

Case 2

Krohm and Sterling incorporated Old Colony Silver Mines Ltd. for the purpose of acquiring mining properties and claims owned by them. They received 40% of the voting shares of the company as consideration for the transfer to the company of their interests. The remaining 60% of the shares were held by others who had bought them from the company for cash.

In the first year of the company's operations Krohm and Sterling personally advanced sums totalling $39 500 to the company to help it defray development costs. They received promissory notes from the company and the amounts were included in the company's general ledger in an account entitled "Notes Payable". By the end of the year it appeared that the company's prospects were good, but that to realize its potential the company would require additional outside financing.

At the first annual meeting of shareholders, Krohm stated that he and his fellow shareholder Sterling, for whom he was also speaking, had considered the company's financial position and concluded that it was imperative that the debt-equity ratio appearing on the company's balance sheet be improved if the company were to succeed in obtaining the additional financing it needed. He therefore wished the meeting to take note of the intention of both Sterling and himself to forgive the two promissory notes of Old Colony Silver Mines Ltd. in the amounts of $19 750 each. Sterling then spoke briefly to confirm Krohm's statement; the notes, he said, "would never be enforced". At this juncture, another shareholder rose to propose a motion of appreciation to Krohm and Sterling for "this most selfless, altruistic and loyal gesture". The motion was duly seconded and unanimously approved by the meeting, and recorded by the secretary in the minutes.

The next quarterly financial statements of Old Colony Silver Mines Ltd. omitted the notes payable to Krohm and Sterling from the company's liabilities as presented on its balance sheet, and showed the amount forgiven as an extraordinary item of income in the income statement, after operating profits for the quarter. Krohm and Sterling did not, however, surrender the company's promissory notes to it for cancellation, nor did they sign any statement acknowledging their expressed intention not to enforce the notes.

The company submitted its quarterly financial statements plus a cash flow projection to its bank in support of an application for a ten-year term loan. The bank evaluated its proposal but was unwilling to lend for so long a term, and the application was rejected.

A few weeks later Old Colony Silver Mines received from another mining company an offer of $300 000 for its individual assets. The offer required an undertaking from Old Colony Silver Mines that it would first pay all its debts out of the $300 000 before distributing any liquidating dividend to its shareholders. At a special general meeting of shareholders, Krohm and Sterling opposed the acceptance of this offer on the grounds that the company had not exhausted the possibilities for outside financing, but they were voted down. A resolution was then approved instructing Old Colony to accept the offer and proceed to distribute the proceeds of the sale to its creditors and shareholders in the course of winding up the company. At this stage Krohm and Sterling insisted that the sum of $39 500 they had previously lent to the company be first paid to them as creditors before any amount should be distributed to shareholders. The majority shareholders then passed a resolution directing the company treasurer not to pay these notes, in view of the statement made by Krohm and Sterling at the preceding meeting.

Krohm and Sterling then sued Old Colony Silver Mines Ltd., submitting their promissory notes as evidence of the company's indebtedness to them. Outline fully the defence which the company could offer, and then comment upon its validity.

CHAPTER 8

FORMATION OF A CONTRACT: CAPACITY TO CONTRACT

THE MEANING OF CAPACITY TO CONTRACT

Some types of people lack the ability, competence, or *capacity* in certain respects to enter into legally binding contracts. A contract may *appear* to be binding because there has been an offer made and accepted, and each side has given consideration. Nevertheless, as a matter of policy, the law may excuse one party from its obligations under the contract. We shall examine the reasons for this result and when it may occur.

MINORS (OR INFANTS)

Contracts Creating Liability for a Minor

In the law of contract a minor or infant is a person who has not attained the age of majority in his or her province. At common law this age was deemed to be 21, but it now varies according to the legislation in each province.[1] The general rule is that a contract of a minor is unenforceable *against* her but enforceable *by* her against the other side, whether or not the other person is aware that he is dealing with a minor. In consequence, a minor may often disregard contractual promises with impunity. When a minor owns considerable assets, her father or mother is ordinarily empowered to look after her affairs or, with supervision of the court, may make contracts concerning her property; if her parents are deceased or are unable to manage her affairs the court will appoint a guardian to do so.

The object of these rules is to protect minors, but if the rules had no exceptions they would defeat their purpose: businesses might refuse to rely upon any promise of a minor, causing her great hardship. A minor might require food or clothing in an emergency but be unable to find a merchant willing to sell her these things on credit. Accordingly, the courts have come to regard *necessaries* and *beneficial contracts of service* as exceptions.

Necessaries

A minor will be bound to pay a reasonable price for all necessaries she buys. Two criteria determine whether a particular purchase by a minor has been for necessary goods:

> (1) the goods must be necessary in relation to the minor's station in life;
> (2) the minor must not already have an adequate supply of them.

The first criterion was the issue in *Ryder v. Wombwell*.[2] The minor, Wombwell, had purchased on credit from Ryder a silver-gilt goblet and a pair of ornamental studs "made of crystals set in gold and ornamented with diamonds representing a horseshoe in which the nails were rubies". Wombwell was the younger son of a deceased baronet and moved in the highest society. He purchased the items as a gift for a friend, but refused to pay for

---

[1] For example: Age of Majority Act, R.S.B.C. 1979, c. 5 (19 years of age); R.S.N.S. 1989, c. 4 (19); R.S.M. 1987, c. A-7 (18); Age of Majority and Accountability Act, R.S.O. 1990, c. A-7, s. 6 (18).

[2] (1869), L.R. 4 Ex. 32.

them. Ryder's attempt to collect the price by legal action failed. The court ruled that although "necessaries" may vary according to one's position, the articles in question could not be necessary for a minor in any station of life, even one as exalted as that of Wombwell. "The burden lay on the plaintiff to give evidence of something peculiar making them necessaries in this special case and ... he has given no evidence at all to this effect."

The decision in *Johnstone v. Marks*[3] illustrates the second criterion. A tailor sued for the price of clothes supplied on credit to a minor who, in defence, pleaded infancy. The court held that the minor was entitled to produce evidence which showed that at the time of the purchase he was already well supplied with clothes. In dismissing the tailor's claim, Lord Esher said, "It lies upon the plaintiff to prove, not that the goods supplied belong to the class of necessaries as distinguished from luxuries, but that the goods supplied *when supplied* were necessaries to the infant."

The courts have in particular identified the following as necessaries: food, clothing, lodging, medical attention,[4] legal advice,[5] and transportation.[6] But "transportation" includes only the means of getting the minor to work, and does not include liability for the purchase price of vehicles required by the minor in carrying on a business.[7]

A minor's liability for necessary goods is not for the contract price, as such, but rather for a reasonable price on the same basis as *quantum meruit*, discussed in Chapter 7. In the absence of evidence that the minor has been exploited, the court usually regards the contract price as evidence of what a reasonable price should be.

Beneficial Contracts of Service

An infant is bound to the terms of a contract of employment when it is found to be for his benefit. Not every contract which associates a minor with a business venture will be deemed for his benefit, particularly when the minor is in business for himself[8] or in a partnership with others. The courts have largely restricted the kinds of business service contracts they will enforce against minors to contracts of employment or apprenticeship, and then only when they are considered to be beneficial and not exploitative.

It is remarkable how little litigation arises in practice as a result of attempts by minors to repudiate their contracts. An important non-legal sanction operates to persuade them, in spite of their opportunity to avoid liability, to perform their promises: if they should repudiate on grounds of incapacity, they would all but eliminate their chances of finding people willing to give them credit.

Contracts Creating No Liability for a Minor

A minor may always repudiate a contract for non-necessaries even where the non-necessaries are clearly beneficial to him. The purchase of a truck for use in his business may well be of great benefit to a minor; nevertheless, the truck is not a necessary.[9] We can only determine the nature of non-necessaries by reviewing the circumstances of cases

---

3 (1887), 19 Q.B.D. 509.
4 Huggins v. Wiseman (1690), 90 E.R. 669.
5 Helps v. Clayton (1864), 144 E.R. 222.
6 Cycle Co. v. Hargreaves (1898), 78 L.T. 296.
7 Mercantile Union Guarantee Corp. v. Ball, [1937] 2 K.B. 498.
8 *Ibid.*
9 *Ibid.*

that have decided whether a particular subject-matter was a necessary. A fairly large number of things have been held to be necessaries; beyond these things each case must be decided on its own facts, and the judges are reluctant to enlarge the group of necessaries. When a minor is living at home and supported by his parents, his purchases are less likely to be considered as necessaries than when he is on his own. The court assumes that a minor living at home is provided for.

Although there are no decisions on the point, it would appear that a minor will not be liable for necessaries which he has ordered but not yet received. Accordingly, he can repudiate a contract of sale before delivery of the goods.[10] The point is underlined in the Sale of Goods Act which defines necessaries for an infant in terms of goods sold *and delivered*.[11]

A minor who repudiates his liability for non-necessary goods may, if the goods are still in his possession, be required to restore them to the seller in whatever condition they may be at the time. In *Louden Manufacturing Co. v. Milmine*, Chief Justice Meredith said:

> Upon principle and the authorities cited ... it must be that if an infant avails himself of the right he has to avoid a contract which he has entered into and upon the faith of which he has obtained goods, he is bound to restore the goods which he has in possession at the time he so repudiates. If that were not so, a man might buy a farm for a large sum of money, give a mortgage upon it shortly before coming of age, then repudiate the contract, and insist upon holding the property. The authorities are all the other way, and establish that the effect of repudiating the contract is to revest the property in the vendor.[12]

Similarly, when the minor is a seller rather than a buyer in a contract for the sale of goods, he cannot repudiate the contract to recover the goods delivered unless he returns the money paid.[13]

There is nothing to prevent a minor from purchasing non-necessaries if he can find a merchant who is prepared to rely entirely upon the minor's honour for payment, or where he purchases goods for cash, is willing to trust him not to return them for refund.[14]

Ordinarily a seller cannot rely on a statement by a minor that his parents will pay for the purchase.[15] Authority to bind the parents may sometimes be implied from the fact that parents have paid the account for a previous purchase by their child without complaint. Apart from this possibility, a merchant needs express authority from the parents before being able to bind them.

Contracts Indirectly Affecting a Minor

A minor who has received benefit as a result of a contract for non-necessaries will not be able to recover money already paid, though he will be able to repudiate his remaining

---

10   Furmston, *Cheshire, Fifoot and Furmston's Law of Contract*, (12th ed.), p. 430-31.
11   See, for example: R.S.B.C. 1979, c. 370, s. 7, as amended, S.B.C. 1985 c. 10; R.S.O. 1990, c. S-1, s. 3 (1); R.S.N.S. 1989, c. 408, s. 5 (1).
12   (1908), 15 O.L.R. 53, at 54; McGaw v. Fisk (1908), 38 N.B.R. 354: Williston, A *Treatise on the Law of Contracts* (3rd ed.), Vol. 2, p. 35. Jaeger, ed. Mount Kisco: Baker, Voorhis & Co. Inc., 1959.
13   Williston, *op. cit.*, Vol. 2, s. 238, pp. 35-43. The right to repudiate may be lost when the infant comes of age.
14   Problems may arise for the minor if the goods have been used or damaged. This problem is discussed under the heading of "Rescission" in Chapter 17.
15   Hailsham, *Halsbury's Laws of England* (4th ed.), Vol. 24, p. 221. London: Butterworth & Co. Ltd., 1979.

liability. In *Valenti v. Canali*[16] a minor became tenant of a house under an agreement by which he was to pay a certain amount for the furniture in it. He paid part of the sum and gave a promissory note for the balance. He occupied the premises and had the use of the furniture for several months. Then he brought an action to have the contract rescinded and to recover the money he had paid. The court held that he could avoid liability on the note, but that he was not entitled to a return of what he had paid.

An adult can recover money lent to a minor only if the minor in fact used the proceeds of the loan to purchase necessary goods.[17] If he spends the borrowed money at the races, the lender cannot recover the debt. The voidability of minors' contracts is a part of the common law but can always be altered by statute. For example, the Canada Students Loans Act[18] provides that a guaranteed bank loan to a student "is recoverable by a bank from the borrower as though the borrower had been of full age at the time the loan was made".

A minor's freedom from liability in private law is limited to contract; he remains liable for torts such as negligence, assault, slander, libel, or deceit. If, however, the minor causes a loss while performing the very acts contemplated by the contract, the court will decide the case under the law of contract and not of torts, and the minor will escape liability for the consequences. The other contracting party will not, in other words, be permitted to circumvent the rules protecting minors in contract by suing for damages for a tort, where he would fail if he sued for breach of contract.

ILLUSTRATION

A minor hires a riding horse, undertaking as a term of the contract that she will handle the animal with care. In her exuberance she injures the horse by riding it too hard.

The owner of the horse may realize that if he sues the infant for breach of contract he will fail, since the subject-matter of the contract is a non-necessary. So he may think it clever to sue the infant for the tort of neglgence The owner will not gain by this tactic.[19] He will fail whichever approach he takes.

Suppose, however, that the infant had injured the horse by entering it in equestrian trials, something not at all contemplated in the contract. Since the minor's act that results in loss was outside the scope of the contract, the owner could then sue the minor for damages for negligence.

The Contractual Liability of Minors upon Attaining Majority

A minor's liability to pay for necessaries and beneficial contracts of service continues after she attains majority. In addition, she may *become* liable for obligations which could not be enforced against her while she was a minor. When she attains majority, this latter group of obligations becomes part of a class called *voidable contracts*, of which there are two types.

In the first type the minor acquires "an interest of a permanent continuous nature". She must repudiate such a contract promptly upon coming of age, or it will become

---

[16] (1889), 24 Q.B.D. 166.
[17] Hailsham, *op. cit.*, p. 175.
[18] R.S.C. 1985, c. S-23, s. 19.
[19] Jennings v. Rundall (1799), 101 E.R. 1419.

enforceable against her and she will be liable on it just as if she had entered into it after coming of age. This class of contracts is quite narrow but probably includes contracts in which the minor has purchased non-necessary goods, such as a car, which she promises to pay for by instalments over a period during which she becomes of age. The courts have decided that interests of a permanent or continuous nature occur in contracts for rights in land and in partnership agreements. A partner who is a minor is not liable for partnership debts contracted while she was a member of a firm and under age, but she will be liable for debts incurred by the firm after she attains full age if she does not repudiate the partnership agreement. In contracts of this nature, the minor loses the right to repudiate by not doing so promptly after becoming of age, or by accepting the benefits of the contract after that time.

The second and more common type of voidable contract does not create an interest of a continuous nature. It is not binding upon a minor unless she expressly ratifies the contract after attaining majority. In addition, some provinces require that to be enforceable, ratification must be in writing and signed by her.[20] Contracts of this class include a minor's promise to pay for non-necessary goods and a promise to pay for services previously performed at her request. A promise to pay for necessary goods not delivered to a minor by the time she becomes of age will also require ratification.

There is a small group of contracts that the courts have held by their very nature to be prejudicial and unfair to minors. Accordingly, they have declared that these contracts are completely *void* rather than merely voidable. The result of this distinction is that ratification by a minor after she attains majority is ineffective, and her promise to pay, merely gratuitous and unenforceable. In other words, in these circumstances there is never any contract capable of ratification. Examples are contracts that include forfeiture clauses and penalty clauses.[21]

OTHER PERSONS OF DIMINISHED CONTRACTUAL CAPACITY

The law protects a person of unsound mind or a person who is incapacitated through drink or drugs in the same way as a minor by making his contracts, except for necessaries, voidable at his option but enforceable by him against the other contracting party. An insane or drunk person is liable only for a reasonable price for the necessary goods.

In practice a drunk or insane person, upon becoming sober or sane, has a problem of evidence, which a minor does not have, in proving incapacity at the time of the contract. Proof of age is more readily established than the fact that one was so intoxicated or insane as not to know what one was doing.

The burden of evidence is the greater yet for the reason that the party seeking to avoid the contract must show not only that he was incapable of a rational decision at the time of the agreement, but also that the other party was aware of his condition. Unfortunately, if a person is so insane or drunk that he does not know what he is doing, his own observations about the other contracting party are unlikely to be reliable, and the necessary

---

[20] The Statute of Frauds: for example, R.S.O. 1990, c. S-19, s. 7; R.S.N.S. 1989, c. 442, s. 9.
[21] Beam v. Beatty (1902), 4 O.L.R. 554; Phillips v. Greater Ottawa Development Co. (1916), 38 O.L.R. 315.

evidence must then be adduced from all the surrounding circumstances.

As with voidable contracts generally, the party entitled to avoid must act promptly upon emerging from his state of incapacity. Unless repudiation comes within a reasonable time, the privilege is lost. It will also be too late to repudiate if, after regaining sanity or sobriety, the afflicted party accepts the benefits of the contract.

An increasing societal problem with respect to diminished contractual capacity is caused by an aging population. People are living longer and a higher proportion of them are becoming aged and infirm; frequently someone dealing with an aged person will be unable to tell whether she is simply physically frail or also suffers from diminished mental capacity, which might leave the contract open to subsequent attack.

CORPORATIONS

Since a corporation is a "legal fiction", a mere creature of the law, it has no physical existence — it cannot think or act or sign its name in the same way as a natural person can. But this kind of impotence is a mere technical handicap. The law could give corporations the capacity to make any contract or enter into any obligation that a natural person possesses, and many corporations acts now give this capacity. However, legislatures have not extended to all corporations the widest possible contractual capacity. Public corporations, such as municipalities and Crown corporations, are restricted in the range of their contractual activity because of the limited power conferred by the statutes creating them. Obligations which they purport to undertake but which are outside the ambit of the statute will, if challenged, be declared by the court to be *ultra vires* (beyond their powers) and, therefore, void. The promisee cannot enforce such obligations against the corporation. The legal consequences of *ultra vires* contracts are often complex and difficult.

In Canada, the determination of the contractual capacity of business corporations (limited companies) is further complicated because several methods of incorporation are in use, and each is subject to different rules about *ultra vires* transactions. We shall defer a discussion of this problem until we deal with corporations in Chapter 30.

We must wait also until we deal with the law relating to principal and agent in Chapter 22 to determine whether the person or persons purporting to act on behalf of a corporation have the power to bind it in contracts. The matter is especially important for a corporation because it is not a natural person and must make all its contracts through agents. When its officers do have the necessary authority, the corporation's signature is easily enough accomplished. Its name is signed to particularly important contracts and to formal documents, such as share certificates, bonds, debentures, deeds, and mortgages (and certified copies of any of these), by its officers' impressing the company seal with an embossing device.[22] For ordinary day-to-day business the signature of an authorized officer of the company will suffice.

---

[22] In most provinces it is no longer necessary for a corporation to have a seal, although it is still common practice to do so.

LABOUR UNIONS

To have a contractual capacity, a labour union must be regarded in law as a separate legal person. For the most part the legal status of trade unions remains equivocal, though the law varies significantly from province to province and is changing quite rapidly.[23] On the other hand, the legal status of corporations as employers is clearly settled. The discrepancy makes uncertain the enforceability of collective agreements between corporations and labour unions. However, most provinces do have statutes[24] that provide for an arbitrator in the event of a dispute arising out of the collective agreement. If an employer does not implement the decision of the arbitrator, the union may apply to a labour relations board for permission to prosecute, and for this purpose is vested with a separate legal status. If a union rejects the arbitrator's decision and causes an illegal strike, damages have occasionally been awarded against it; the enforceability of such decisions is currently a matter of debate. In those provinces where an employer may seek permission to prosecute a union for such a strike, the union's liability derives from a statutory provision and not from the contractual capacity of the union in general.

Despite their indefinite status, trade unions may bring actions or defend against them when they so wish. By a legal technique known as a *representative action*, a union may expressly or impliedly authorize one or more persons to represent it in court simply as a group of individuals having a common interest in a particular case. As a result, the officials of a trade union may bring or defend a representative action on behalf of its members.

MARRIED WOMEN

At one time a married woman had no contractual capacity, all her contracts were void, and she could not own property independently of her husband. All her contractual capacity and property were vested in her husband, and he assumed complete control of business affairs for the family.

Within the last hundred years a series of statutes has gradually conferred upon a married woman all the contractual capacity of an adult man. She may now hold or dispose of her property, earnings, and money, free from her husband's control. What is equally important, none of her property, unless it was conveyed to her by her husband with the object of defrauding his creditors, is subject to seizure for payment of her husband's debts.

Under family law reform legislation in the common-law provinces, parties may enter into their own "domestic" or "marriage" contract which provides in advance for the settlement of specific items of property in the event of separation; if they make no such contract, the provisions of the family law reform legislation will apply to such dispositions of property.

The creditors of a married woman may look only to her separate property as security for the debts she incurs from contracts made in her own name and from pledging her own credit. Over and above debts of this kind, a wife may have implied authority to make contracts for the purchase of domestic requirements in her husband's name, pledging his credit

---

[23] See Chapter 23 under "Legal Status of Trade Unions".
[24] See for example: Labour Code, R.S.B.C. 1979, c. 212, s. 93, as amended by Industrial Relations Act, S.B.C. 1987, c. 24; Labour Relations Act, R.S.O. 1990, c. L-2, s. 45; Trade Union Act, R.S.N.S. 1989, c. 311, s. 19(1).

for the purchases. These contracts belong to a discussion of the law relating to principal and agent, and we shall consider them again in Chapter 22.

ENEMY ALIENS

Ordinarily, an alien has the same rights as a citizen in making contracts and in all other matters of private law. An enemy alien, however, loses all contractual capacity during hostilities, apart from any special licence granted by the Crown. For the purposes of contracts an enemy alien is identified not by citizenship, but by the fact that either his residence or business interests are located in enemy territory.

Whenever there is the slightest suggestion that a contract made between an enemy alien and someone else is detrimental to the public interest, the contract will be held void as being against public policy, and the rights and liabilities created by it are wholly dissolved. In a few exceptional instances where the public interest is thought not to be affected, a contract may be regarded as being merely suspended for the duration of hostilities.

In the past the federal government has passed a number of statutes and orders-in-council after the outbreak of war describing the status of aliens in detail. It is necessary to refer to these when a party to the contract may be an enemy alien.

ABORIGINAL PEOPLES

In Canada, "Native Indians" living on reserves are still considered wards of the Crown. The property comprising the reserve is held by the Crown in trust for the benefit of the Indian band. It is not available as security for the claims of creditors, and any disposition of such property to an outside party is void unless the transaction has been approved by the Minister of Indian Affairs and Northern Development. Native peoples on reserves may manufacture and sell chattels to outsiders, although in the Prairie provinces, sales of produce must have the approval of a superintendent under the Minister. The legal position of Indians on reservations is set out in detail in the Indian Act.[25] Indians may be enfranchised after leaving the reservation, and their contractual capacity then becomes the same as that of any other citizen.

BANKRUPT DEBTORS

A bankrupt debtor, until he receives a discharge from the court, is under certain contractual disabilities. We will discuss these disabilities more fully in Chapter 34.

---

[25]   R.S.C. 1985, c. I-5.

Questions for Review

1. Does the fact that one of the parties to a contract is under age prevent him from enforcing the contract against the other (adult) party?
2. What is the purpose of the general rule concerning the enforceability of infants' contracts? What is the purpose of the exceptions to the rule?
3. What two criteria must we apply to determine whether goods which a minor has bought and received are of a type for which he must pay?
4. Are food and clothing the only things that may be necessaries for an infant?
5. If a minor operates his own business and enters into business contracts that are of benefit to him, are the contracts enforceable against him?
6. Are minors' contracts for non-necessaries always voidable when the minors attain majority?
7. What two types of minors' contracts must be distinguished for the purpose of determining the liability of the minors after they become of age?
8. What two points must be established before a person, intoxicated at the time of a contract, may avoid liability under it?
9. Under what circumstances may a contract voidable at the option of one of the parties cease to be voidable?
10. What is the nature of the legal problem that adds to the uncertainty of an action against a trade union?
11. When may the property of a married person be seized for payment of a spouse's debts?
12. How is the status of an enemy alien determined for purposes of contract?
13. Under what circumstances do Native Indians have restricted contractual capacity?
14. (a) When Jones was 17 years old, she took her stereo into the Mariposa Service Centre for an extensive repair job, which cost $175. If she does not pay, can the Mariposa Service Centre sue her successfully?
    (b) After Jones becomes of age, she picks up the repaired stereo and does nothing to repudiate her liability to the Mariposa Service Centre. Can the Mariposa Service Centre recover the money now?
    (c) Upon becoming of age, Jones tells the manager of the Mariposa Service Centre in a telephone conversation that she will pay the $175. Can the Mariposa Service Centre recover now?
15. Braun, while 17 years of age, orders a new suit of clothes which are necessary for him, in view of both his station in life and his present supply of clothing. The suit is to cost $275. Before the suit is quite finished, Braun changes his mind about the style and advises the tailor that he does not propose to accept or pay for the suit. Is he liable?
16. Kiang, a student 17 years of age, bought a suit of clothes for $250 and took it home. He then refused to pay the price, alleging it to be too high. The tailor sued for $250. It was established that the suit was a necessary article for Kiang, but he produced witnesses who testified that an identical suit might have been purchased elsewhere for $125. What will be the result of the action?
17. An adult lends a minor money which the minor spends on a necessary suit of clothes. If the minor fails to repay the debt, can the adult recover in a court action?

18. At 17 years of age Watson entered into a contract of employment with an oil company to enter its one-year training and familiarization program, including travel to various company properties, for promising young employees. Shortly after Watson went to work for the company, it proposed to send her, with an adequate living allowance, to its oil fields in the Northwest Territories for a few months as part of the training program. Is Watson liable for breach of contract if she refuses to go?

19. An adult lends a minor money which the minor spends on the midway at the local fair. Can the adult recover?

20. In what respects does our present law affecting the contractual capacity of minors seem illogical?

Problem

Sam West was a kitchen helper in a restaurant and 17 years of age. Having obtained his licence to drive, he went to Drive-Yourself Ltd., showed his licence, and signed for the hiring of a car. The contract contained clauses requiring the hirer to observe all laws regulating the use of motor vehicles, not to enter the car in any competition, to indemnify the hiring company for any fines imposed in respect of the operation of the automobile, and to return it in good condition.

West then gathered up seven friends and took them for a drive. While attempting to pass another car at 20 km/h above the speed limit, West lost control of the car and wrecked it against a stump. At the time there were three passengers in the front seat in addition to the driver, West.

Drive-Yourself Ltd. brought an action against West for the value of the wrecked car. What scope, if any, would the plaintiff company have for countering West's defence of infancy? Indicate with reasons whether its action is likely to succeed.

Cases

Case 1

For most of a year, Harrison acted as agent for the purpose of obtaining options on property on an island in British Columbia on behalf of the Western Development Company, which planned to develop the island industrially. These plans became known to the property owners on the island, and some of them, believing their holdings to be indispensable to the plan, sought to obtain prices much higher than the market value established there for farm or residential purposes.

Harrison obtained, for a consideration of $1, an option to purchase within one year the property of Mrs. Foy for $100 000. Harrison had negotiated the price with a Miss Foy and a widow, Mrs. Sheridan; he had offered $500 a hectare, which was the maximum he had been authorized to offer, and the two women had insisted upon $1000 a hectare; he had then reluctantly agreed to take an option at the price demanded, explaining that his principals would not likely take up the option at such an exorbitant price; Miss Foy had next insisted that a further $10 000 be added to the price for the barn; Harrison had agreed to that, too. It was only when the option agreement was prepared for signing that Harrison learned that he had not been dealing with the registered owner of the property, but with her daughters, both of whom resided there. He was informed that the owner,

Mrs. Foy, was a very old lady and was bedridden. Harrison was taken to the bedroom where he explained, carefully and accurately, the terms and effect of the option. Mrs. Foy appeared to understand what he was saying, nodding and smiling and from time to time saying, "Yes." At this juncture Harrison turned to Miss Foy, who was standing at the foot of the bed, and asked her, "Do you really think your mother understands the difference between an option and an agreement to sell her land?" Miss Foy replied, "Yes, I think she understands." Then Mrs. Sheridan asked Harrison if before getting her mother to sign he would wait until they could get the family lawyer to be present; Harrison, exasperated with the way negotiations had been proceeding, replied testily that he was not prepared to entertain any further delay or discussion of terms. He then asked Mrs. Foy to sign the option agreement. She did not sign her name but made a cross under the direction of one of her daughters who explained to Harrison that her mother used to be able to sign her name but that her hand was now too unsteady.

Harrison's principals did, in fact, elect to take up the option and sought within the year to obtain this property at the agreed price of $100 000; they had taken up the options on the adjoining properties and needed Mrs. Foy's property to complete the section of land they required. They were immediately met with the defence, on the part of the two daughters, that the option agreement was "not worth the paper it was written on" because Mrs. Foy was insane at the time of her signing. The principals brought an action to have the option agreement enforced. It was brought out in evidence that Mrs. Foy was, indeed, insane, a fact of which Harrison denied any knowledge at the time; it was also shown that the fair market value of the property as a farm at the date of the option agreement was about $70 000.

Express an opinion about the likelihood that the action will succeed.

Case 2

During the 1983-84 season Harvey ("Ace") Tilson played hockey for the Medicine Hat Broncos of the Western Junior Hockey League, and scored 30 goals and assisted on another 35 goals. In recent years many players in this league had been offered contracts to play professional hockey upon completion of their junior eligibility. They remain eligible to play in the league until the year in which they reach the age of 21.

In October 1982, Tilson signed a two-year contract with the Medicine Hat Broncos Hockey Club which was to terminate before the start of the hockey season in the early fall of 1984. However, at the beginning of training camp in September 1983, the manager of the Broncos presented Tilson and the other players with a new three-year contract. This contract contained a new set of standardized conditions of employment prescribed by the league and, by agreement among the clubs, was presented to all players in the league on a "take it or leave it" basis; the players understood that if they did not agree to waive their existing contracts and sign the new one they would not be able to play in the league and their professional prospects would be severely harmed. The new contract included the following clauses:

1. This contract supersedes all previous contracts between the Club [Medicine Hat Broncos Hockey Club] and the Player [Harvey J. Tilson].
2. The Club employs the Player as an apprentice hockey player for the term of three years commencing 1983 and agrees, subject to the terms of this contract, to pay the Player a salary of $50.00 per week plus an allowance for room and board of $135.00 per week, these payments to terminate at the last scheduled game of the Club each year.

3. The Player acknowledges that if his hockey skills and abilities develop to the degree that he is tendered and accepts a contract of employment with a professional hockey club, then the Club shall be entitled to compensation for its contribution to his development and, in consideration for such contribution by the Club, the Player agrees to pay the Club a sum equal to twenty (20%) per cent of his gross earnings attributable to his employment with such professional hockey club during a period of three (3) years beginning on the date at which he first represents and plays for that professional hockey club.

4. The Player agrees that during the term of this contract he will loyally discharge his obligations to the Club and that he will not play for or be directly or indirectly employed by or interested in any other amateur or professional hockey club. The Player agrees that the Club shall have the right, in addition to any other legal remedies which the Club may enjoy, to prevent him by appropriate injunction proceedings from committing any breach of this undertaking.

5. The Player acknowledges that if in breach of his obligations under section 4 the Player plays for any other hockey club, the Club will lose his services as a skilled hockey player and will suffer a loss of income from reduced paid attendance at hockey games and broadcasting rights and that a genuine estimate of the amount of this loss would be the salary that the Player can earn as a hockey player for any other amateur or professional club.

The manager of the Broncos advised the players to take their copies of the contract home and discuss them with their parents. He added that a signed copy must be in his hands by the beginning of the following week. Tilson's parents actively encouraged him to sign the contract, and Tilson returned a signed copy to the manager on September 5, 1983.

Tilson played for the Broncos in the 1983-84 season until March 21, 1984. On that day he became 18 years of age, the age of majority in Alberta. On March 22, 1984, in a letter to the club written by his lawyer, Tilson repudiated the contract "without in any way acknowledging the validity thereof." On the same day, in the company of his lawyer, he signed a Pan-American Hockey Conference contract with the Calgary Whippets Hockey Club Ltd. for three seasons commencing September 1 of each of 1984, 1985 and 1986 providing for annual salaries of $70 000, $80 000 and $90 000, respectively.

At the time, the 1983-84 season was almost over, and the Broncos had qualified for the playoffs and were favourites to win the Junior Cup. Tilson offered to stay with the team at his regular weekly salary and allowance during the 1984 playoffs if the Broncos Club would sign an agreement that Tilson's three-year hockey contract with it would expire when the playoffs ended. The Broncos refused and brought an action against Tilson, seeking an injunction to restrain him from breaking his contract or, in the alternative, damages of $150 000 representing the measure of its loss for being deprived of his services for the next two years.

Explain the legal issues raised in this dispute and offer with reasons an opinion about the probable outcome of the action. (For reference, see A. *Schroeder Music Publishing Co. Ltd. v. Macaulay*, [1974] 3 All E.R. 616; *Chaplin v. Leslie Frewin (Publishers) Ltd. and others*, [1966] Ch. 71.)

Case 3

Assume the facts of Case 2 above, with the exception that the Broncos Club did sign the agreement proposed by Tilson in March, 1984; that Tilson had played with the team during the 1984 playoffs; and that the Broncos Club had then brought its action against

Tilson. What line of reasoning might the Broncos use to support its argument that the March 1984 agreement was not binding on it? Would it be a good argument? Cite any relevant case or cases.

CHAPTER 9

FORMATION OF A CONTRACT: LEGALITY OF OBJECT

THE ROLE OF LEGALITY IN THE FORMATION OF A CONTRACT

We have seen that offer and acceptance, an intention to create legal relations, consideration, and capacity to contract are necessary, each of these elements, to the formation of a contract. In addition, the object of the contract must be "legal". In the absence of evidence to the contrary, the courts presume that business transactions neither offend the public good nor violate any law. Evidence may, of course, show that this presumption is wrong. If it does, the contract will at least be *void*, which means that in law it was never formed at all. In some circumstances the courts will stigmatize the contract by finding that it is also *illegal*.

THE DIFFERENCE BETWEEN A VOID AND AN ILLEGAL CONTRACT

No stigma attaches to the parties if their contract is void; they have just not succeeded in creating a binding agreement. If they have partly performed their undertakings, the court will do its best, taking all the circumstances into account, to restore them to their respective positions before the contract was attempted. It may order the return of money paid or of property transferred if the party complaining can show cause why it should be returned. Further, each party is released from the performance of any further obligations under the agreement. A court may find that only a *term* of a contract is void and that the remaining parts are valid. If it decides that the void term can be severed without doing injustice to the parties, it will uphold the remainder of the contract.

When a contract is not only void but also illegal, the court will refuse to aid a party who knowingly agreed to an illegal purpose. Not only may he not sue for money promised, but if he has transferred property to the other party, he will also be unable to recover it. If both parties are tainted with the illegal object, the fact that a court will assist neither of them has the effect of rendering the plaintiff impotent and thereby of assisting the defendant. The effect is summed up in the legal maxim that where both parties are equally in the wrong, the position of the defendant is the stronger. Given this attitude towards illegal contracts, it follows that no part of such a contract will be severed, leaving the remainder enforceable.

The law is not as helpful as it might be in providing an objective criterion for deciding when a given contract is illegal as well as void. Generally, the more reprehensible the object of a contract, the more likely it is that the contract will be regarded as illegal and a plaintiff's claim dismissed.

CONTRACTS AFFECTED BY STATUTE

Significance of the Wording of a Statute

Parliament or a provincial legislature may wish merely to deprive a particular type of contract of legal effect, or it may wish to go further and express positive disapproval. It can achieve the first object by providing in a statute that such agreements shall be void. To accomplish the second purpose it may describe the type of agreement as "unlawful" or "illegal" in the wording of the statute. It may even stipulate that performance of the agreement shall be a criminal offence, subject to prescribed penalties of a fine or imprisonment.

Agreements Void by Statute

Workers' compensation legislation, for example, states that any provision in an agreement between employer and employee purporting to deprive the employee of the protection of the Act is void.[1] Other statutes declare particular types of transfers of property to be void. In these instances the law says that despite the acts of the parties, the ownership does not pass from the transferor and that the property may be recovered from the transferee and applied according to the terms of the statute. Thus, the Bankruptcy Act contains a provision that if a person transfers property either by gift or for an obviously inadequate compensation and becomes bankrupt within one year, the transfer is void and the property is available to the trustee in bankruptcy.[2] The trustee may recover the property and apply it to the claims of the bankrupt person's creditors. The same statute provides that a transfer of property by an insolvent person to one of a number of creditors with a view to giving that creditor a preference over the others is "fraudulent and void" if it occurs within three months preceding bankruptcy.[3]

Some provinces have statutes which expressly state that all types of bets are void.[4] These statutes do not make betting a criminal offence — they do not prescribe fines or imprisonment for those who make bets.[5] They simply make it impossible for a winner to collect a bet through court action. Betting agreements have long been regarded by the courts as a nuisance, and not the kind of agreement deserving their attention when more urgent disputes await solution. Thus, the winner of a bet cannot enforce a promise (even in the form of a promissory note or a cheque) given by the loser to pay a wager, nor can a

---

[1] See for example: Workers' Compensation Act, R.S.O. 1990, c. W-ll, s. 18; R.S.B.C. 1979 c. 437, s. 13; R.S.N.S. 1989, c. 508, s. 21.

[2] R.S.C. 1985 c. B-3, s. 91 of the Bankruptcy and Insolvency Act, as amended by S.C. 1992, c. 1 and c. 27. S. 3 of the Act also provides, "For the purposes of this Act, a person who has entered into a transaction with another person otherwise than at arm's length shall be deemed to have entered into a reviewable transaction." Under s.100 a court may give judgment in favour of the trustee against the other party to such a transaction for the difference between the actual consideration given or received by the bankrupt and the fair market value of the property or services concerned. The provisions of the Bankruptcy Act are dealt with in more detail in Chapter 34.

[3] S. 95(1).

[4] See, for example: The Gaming Act, R.S.O. 1990, c. G-2, s. 4; Insurance Act, R.S.B.C. 1979, c. 200, s. 8. The early Gaming Acts of England which declare wagering contracts to be void are in force in the other provinces. See also: Halsbury, *The Laws of England* (3rd ed.), Vol. 20A (Canadian Converter), p. 221.

[5] Criminal Code, R.S.C. 1985, c. C-46, does, however, make certain betting activities illegal. It is a criminal offence to keep a gaming house (s. 201) or to operate a pool (s. 202) or a lottery (s. 206) unless within specified exceptions within the Act.

loser who has paid a wager recover it through the courts.[6] However, an innocent third person who purchases a note or cheque for valuable consideration, say a storekeeper who accepts the instrument in payment for goods, may be able to enforce payment.

A wager is an agreement between two parties in which each has at the time some probability of winning or losing. Organizations that manage lotteries and race tracks accept and redistribute money as a type of stakeholder, and it has been held that they are not a party to a wagering agreement. They do, however, remain legally accountable for performing their task as stakeholder.[7] For many years, provincial legislation has permitted the placing of bets at authorized race courses,[8] and there has since been legislation to permit the holding of lotteries.[9] With these important exceptions, wagers are generally simple agreements between individuals and are seldom if ever made between businesses. The subject would be of little interest to us, were it not for the fact that a number of contracts commonly regarded as being of a legitimate business nature have an element of speculation in them — insurance contracts, stock exchange transactions, and "futures" transactions in commodities. To be enforceable, these contracts must *not* be interpreted as wagering contracts.

Contracts of insurance form a large and important class of commercial transactions. In an honest insurance contract one does not, of course, *hope* that one will win the "bet" with the insurance company, but rather that should the feared loss occur, one will receive a measure of compensation. This fear of loss is expressed in the notion of *insurable interest*. For a person to have an insurable interest, he must have a financial benefit from the continued existence of the property or life insured or suffer some financial detriment from its loss or destruction. The insurance acts of the various provinces state that an insurance contract is invalid unless the party making the contract has an insurable interest in the property or life insured.

Statutes may simply declare where an insurable interest exists: for example, provincial statutes relating to life insurance provide that every person has an insurable interest in his or her own life, in the life of a child or grandchild, in the life of a spouse, in the life of another on whom he or she is wholly or in part dependent for support or education, in the life of an employee, or in the life of another person in which he or she has a financial interest. It would add nothing to the peace of mind of a person to learn that a stranger who stood to suffer nothing in the way of personal bereavement or pecuniary loss from his death was insuring his life with a life insurance company. There is an exception to the requirement of an insurable interest under the Uniform Life Insurance Act that has been passed by all the common law provinces. The Act waives the requirement if the person whose life is insured consents in writing to the placing of the insurance.[10] The statute makes all other policies void, even if an insurance company was willing to provide them, unless there is a legitimate insurable interest. Thus, a creditor may insure the life of a debtor for the amount of the debt, as a means of ensuring repayment should the debtor die; a landlord may insure the life of a tenant for an amount sufficient as compensation

---

6 By way of an exception, s. 3 of the Ontario Gaming Act permits a loser at "cards, dice, tables or other game" who has lost $40 or more at one sitting and who brings the action within three months to sue for recovery.
7 Ellesmere v. Wallace, [1929] 2 Ch. 1; Tote Investors Ltd. v. Smoker [1968], 1 Q.B. 509.
8 See, for example: Racing Commission Act, R.S.O. 1990, c. R-2.
9 Criminal Code, R.S.C. 1985, c. C-46, s. 207, as amended by 1985, c. 52, 1st supp. s. 3.
10 See, for example: Insurance Act, R.S.B.C. 1979, c. 200, s. 129(2)(b); R.S.O. 1990, s. I-8, s. 178(2)(b); R.S.N.S. 1989, c. 231, s. 180 (2)(6).

should the tenant die and the premises be unsuited to other occupants; partnership funds may be used to insure the lives of the partners and thus make available the money needed to buy the share of a deceased partner from the estate.

Often the person receiving the proceeds of an insurance contract (that is, the *beneficiary*) is someone other than the party making the contract. It is necessary only that the maker of the contract, not the beneficiary, have an insurable interest in the life or property insured. Thus a person frequently insures his own life, making a spouse or child the beneficiary.

Stock exchange transactions are among the more speculative business contracts. While they are no doubt often explained by a difference of opinion between the buyer and the seller about the future price of the shares traded, the essence of the contract is an actual sale of personal property. Bona fide contracts for the purchase and sale of shares are therefore valid and enforceable. If, however, the subject of an agreement is a wager about what the price of a particular stock will be at a specified future time, without an actual purchase or sale of the shares, the agreement is void.[11]

Whenever goods are purchased or sold for future delivery at a price agreed upon in advance, one contracting party may gain at the expense of the other because of price changes between the time of the contract and the time of delivery. Again, the speculative element in these contracts is incidental to a larger purpose, and the contracts cannot be impeached on the ground that they amount to wagers.

Agreements Illegal by Statute

Some statutes, as we have noted, have the effect of making agreements of a specified type illegal. An example is the Combines Investigation Act, discussed in a separate section below.

A number of other statutes do not deal directly with contracts but simply describe certain kinds of conduct for which they provide penalties. The most important of these statutes is the Criminal Code. Further examples are the Income Tax Act, which imposes penalties for false returns and evasion,[12] and the Customs Act, which exacts penalties for smuggling.[13] Any contract which contemplates such conduct is itself illegal, not because the statute directly says so (it may say nothing about contracts) but because the common law holds that when the *object* of a contract is illegal by statute, then the contract itself is illegal.

Provincial statutes and municipal by-laws require the licensing or registration of various classes of business and professional people, ranging from taxicabs and local building trades to moneylenders, trading partnerships, real estate agents, investment advisors and stockbrokers, optometrists, and public accountants.[14] It is a good defence to an action brought by any of them in the attempt to collect fees that the individual has not been properly registered. In *Kocotis v. D'Angelo*[15] an electrician sued for work done and materials supplied.

---

[11] Criminal Code, R.S.C. 1985, c. C-46, s. 83.
[12] S.C. 1970-71-72, c. 63, s. 239, as amended, S.C. 1980-81-82-83, c. 158, s. 58, S.C. 1988, c. 55, s. 182.
[13] S.C. 1986, c. C-1, ss. 110-116, 153-161.
[14] See, for example, the following Ontario statutes: Business Names Act, R.S.O. 1990, c. B-17, s. 7(1); Real Estate and Business Brokers Act, R.S.O. 1990, c. R-4, s. 3; Securities Act, R.S.O. 1990, c. S-5, s. 25; Health Disciplines Act, R.S.O. 1990, c. H-4, s. 100; Public Accountancy Act, R.S.O. 1990, c. P-37, s. 14; and others.
[15] (1958), 13 D.L.R. (2d) 69. But see Sidmay Ltd. et al. v. Wehttam Investments Ltd. (1967), 61 D.L.R. (2d) 358 for a case in which a mortgagor was required to honour his mortgage obligations even though the mortgagee was a corporation not authorized to lend on mortgages under the Loan and Trust Corporations Act (Ontario).

The customer pleaded in defence that the electrician was not licensed as an electrical contractor as required by the local by-law. The court held that the object of the by-law was to protect the public against mistakes and loss that might arise from work done by unqualified electricians and accordingly that the contract was unlawful. The court would not assist the electrician in his attempt to collect the account. A more recent decision asserts that a person in the electrician's position would now be entitled to recover for the materials supplied, though not for the fee for the services provided.[16]

On the other hand, an action brought *against* a person who has not been licensed will not fail on that ground: the defendant cannot claim that his own misconduct in not complying with a statute is a defence to an action by an innocent person. This result is an application of the general principle that a person (whether as plaintiff or defendant) will not be permitted to use evidence of his own wrongdoing for his advantage before the courts.

CONTRACTS ILLEGAL BY THE COMMON LAW AND PUBLIC POLICY

The Common Law

Over the years, the common law has condemned certain types of conduct and has granted remedies, usually in the form of damages, to parties aggrieved or harmed by that conduct. Generally the conduct is considered a private wrong or tort, and whenever a contract contemplates the commission of a tort, the contract is illegal.

Among the private wrongs or torts that may form the subject-matter of an agreement are slander and libel, trespass, deceit (fraud), and incitement to break an existing contract with someone else. In *Wanderers Hockey Club v. Johnson*[17] the plaintiff hockey club learned that Johnson had signed a contract to play for the 1912-13 season with another club managed by Patrick. It persuaded Johnson to enter into a second contract with it for the same season by offering him a higher salary. Johnson tore up his contract with Patrick, but as things turned out he failed to perform his new contract with the plaintiff, which then sued him for breach of contract. The action failed on the grounds that no cause of action can arise out of a wrongdoing; it had been obvious to both parties that the second contract could not be performed without breaking the earlier contract with Patrick.

An agreement may not have as its primary object the commission of a wrongful act but it nevertheless contains an undertaking by one party to indemnify the other against damages arising from any private wrong committed in the course of performance. In *Smith v. Clinton*,[18] the English firm of W. H. Smith & Son had agreed to print a weekly newspaper, *Vanity Fair*, for Clinton on the terms that they should have a letter of indemnity from Clinton against claims arising out of publication of libellous matter in the paper. In June 1907, an article was published containing statements libellous to Parr's Bank. W. H. Smith & Son settled the claim against them by paying Parr's Bank a sum of money. They in turn sought to recover the money from Clinton, but the action failed because the court refused to assist in the recovery of money to indemnify a wrongdoer.

---

[16] Monticchio v. Torcema Construction Ltd. (1980), 26 O.R. (2d) 305.
[17] (1913), 14 D.L.R. 42. See also: Fabbi *et al.* v. Jones (1972), 28 D.L.R. (3d) 224.
[18] (1908), 99 L.T. 840.

There is, however, an everyday arrangement in which the law makes an exception to the rule. A contract of insurance is neither void nor illegal because it proposes to indemnify a motorist for the damages he may have to pay to third parties as a result of his negligence in the operation of the vehicle; automobile insurance for public liability and property damage is valid. Other policies of insurance have been designed to protect professional people against the consequences of their negligence in the course of practice and such policies are also valid.

In addition, a person or a business may exempt itself from liability for negligence by the terms of a contract. Thus a railway or other carrier may state in its standard form contract for the shipment of goods (bill of lading) that it shall not be liable for damage to goods in excess of a stated amount, whether caused by the negligence of its employees or not. The temptation to stipulate for such exemptions is great, and as a result these contracts are often subject to government regulation.[19]

Public Policy

A contract may be regarded as illegal even though it does not contemplate the commission of a crime or of any of the recognized private wrongs. Public policy alone dictates the result. If the court decides that a particular contract is prejudicial to the interests of Canada, its relations with foreign countries, its national defence, its public service, or the administration of justice within the country, the contract will be declared illegal although its performance is neither a tort nor a crime in itself.

An agreement which has the perversion of justice as its object will be illegal on grounds of public policy. A promise to pay a witness either for appearing or for not appearing to give evidence in criminal proceedings is illegal.[20] In *Symington v. Vancouver Breweries and Riefel*,[21] the plaintiff made an agreement with the defendants (who were anxious to see one Ball convicted of illegal manufacture of alcohol) to give evidence that would assure Ball's conviction. A term of the agreement was that the plaintiff should receive from the defendants $1000 for each and every month of imprisonment called for in Ball's sentence. As a result of the plaintiff's testimony at the trial, Ball was sentenced to 12 months' imprisonment. The plaintiff received only part payment and sued for the balance. The action failed on grounds of public policy that the agreement tended to pervert justice. One of the appeal judges noted that Ball might have received a much longer term and that "no doubt the leniency of the court was disappointing". In summarizing, Mr. Justice Martin said in part:

> There is a peculiar and sinister element in this case which distinguishes it from all the others that have been cited to us, viz., that it provides for remuneration upon a sliding scale corresponding in amount to the amount of the sentence secured by the informer's evidence. This is so direct and inevitable an incentive to perjury and other concomitant nefarious conduct that it cannot be in the public interest to countenance a transaction which is dangerous to such an exceptional degree to the administration of criminal justice.[22]

---

[19] See, for example: National Transportation Act, S.C. 1987, c. 34, ss. 153-155.
[20] Collins v. Blantern (1767), 95 E.R. 847.
[21] [1931] 1 D.L.R. 935.
[22] *Ibid.*, at 937.

The arrangements by which a person accused of a crime may be released under bail are intended to be fair and humane.[23] However, they require that the party putting up the bail shall stand to suffer the forfeiture of the bail money should the prisoner abscond. Accordingly, a promise either by the accused or by a third party to indemnify the party putting up bail is illegal.[24]

The most common crime committed within the business world is embezzlement, the so-called "white-collar crime". It is often committed by persons without previous criminal record who succumb to temptation or personal misfortune and "borrow" funds without permission. On discovery, the embezzler usually repents and promises to repay every cent if he is not turned over to the police. In many cases, either through sympathy or in the hope of recovering the loss, the victim of the embezzler agrees to such an arrangement. As charitable as the motives of the injured party may be, it must be emphasized that the embezzler has committed a major crime for which the law demands conviction, though punishment may turn out to be lenient. In failing to inform the police of the commission of the crime, the victim is also in breach of the criminal law. Accordingly, an agreement not to carry out a duty to inform the police in return for a promise to repay the embezzled funds is an illegal agreement.[25] It should be remembered that a victim retains the right to recover the loss from an embezzler by suing for breach of trust or for wrongful conversion in tort.

In embezzlement cases, the victim does not himself contemplate committing a crime and may well be ignorant of the fact that failure to inform the police is wrong. Nevertheless, since the agreement tends to pervert justice, it is illegal. Indeed, the most an employer can do is to assure the embezzler that if restitution is made, he will testify to that effect as a mitigating factor in the court's assessment of the crime. The court considers restitution in these cases to be of great weight in arriving at a just punishment.

Agreements that promote unnecessary litigation are also considered to be attempts to obstruct the course of justice. They take up the time of the law courts when more serious matters are awaiting decision. A party may wish to stir up litigation because of its advertising value, on the theory that any kind of publicity is good publicity. In *Dann v. Curzon*,[26] a theatre manager promised to pay a party for intentionally creating a disturbance in a theatre and then suing the manager for assault. The party did create a disturbance and the summons for assault was dismissed. When the theatre manager failed to make the promised payment, the party sued him. The action failed on grounds of public policy.

In addition, agreements are illegal if their performance is sexually immoral. Those who have made a business of sponsoring such activities[27] or of publishing pornographic literature[28] have found the courts uncooperative in enforcing their supposed contractual rights.

---

23 See Friedland, *Detention Before Trial*. Toronto: University of Toronto Press, 1965; Criminal Code, R.S.C. 1985, c. C-46, ss. 763-771.

24 Herman v. Jeuchner (1885), 15 Q.B.D. 561; Consolidated Exploration and Finance Co. v. Musgrave, [1900] 1 Ch. 37.

25 See Turner, *Russell on Crime*, (12th ed.), pp. 339-41. Turner, ed. London: Stevens & Sons Ltd., 1964; also, U.S. Fidelity and Guarantee Co. v. Cruikshank and Simmons (1919), 49 D.L.R. 674; Keir v. Leeman (1846), 115 E.R. 1315.

26 (1911), 104 L.T. 66.

27 Pearce v. Brooks (1866), L.R. 1 Ex. 213.

28 Poplett v. Stockdale (1825), 172 E.R. 90.

AGREEMENTS IN RESTRAINT OF TRADE

Types of Restraint

Perhaps the most common reason for business agreements being challenged on grounds of public policy is that they may be in restraint of trade. The courts have long considered competition a necessary element of our economic life, and regard agreements that diminish competition as undesirable. Of the agreements that may be in restraint of trade, some are at worst simply void. Others are illegal, because they are prohibited by the Competition Act.

Though a contract contains a *restrictive covenant* (a term in restraint of trade) that is found to be against public policy, the term may not invalidate the entire contract. The courts may refuse to enforce the offending term while treating the remainder of the contract as valid.

The following classification of terms is helpful in sorting out the various effects of contracts in restraint of trade:[29]

(a) An agreement between the vendor and the purchaser of a business whereby the vendor undertakes not to carry on a similar business in competition with the purchaser.

(b) An agreement between employer and employee in which the employee undertakes that after leaving her present employment she will not compete against the employer, either by setting up her own business or by taking a position with a competing business.

(c) An agreement among manufacturers or merchants to restrict output or fix the selling price of a commodity or service.

The courts make an initial presumption that any term in restraint of trade is against public policy and void. But this presumption is not absolute. It may be *rebutted* (overcome) by the party seeking to enforce the covenant if it can demonstrate that it is a reasonable arrangement between the parties and does not adversely effect the public interest. We may note that public policy is virtually the sole consideration of the courts in judging type-(c) covenants. In types (a) and (b), the interests of the parties themselves are dominant.

Agreements Between Vendor and Purchaser of a Business

Often, an important asset of a business is its goodwill, that is, the trade and commercial connections that it has established through years of carrying on business under a particular name and in a particular location. The vendor of a business can only realize this value in a sale if he can make a binding promise to the purchaser that he will do nothing in the future to diminish or destroy the value of what he is selling. He can command a higher price for the business if he is free to covenant with the purchaser that he will not enter into any business that is likely to compete with the business he is selling: there will then

---

[29]   This basic classification has been adopted by leading English authorities on contract, viz., Furmston, *Cheshire, Fifoot and Furmston's Law of Contract* (12th ed.), pp. 407-413, and Guest, *Anson's Law of Contract* (26th ed.), pp. 325-39. Oxford: Clarendon Press, 1984.

be no danger of his attracting old customers and thus diminishing the value of the business being sold. After the sale, it is important that the law enforce reasonable undertakings of this kind made by the vendor, or else the purchaser, fearing he will be deprived of a valuable part of the asset he has purchased, will refuse to pay the vendor's price.

Accordingly, the law recognizes that both purchaser and vendor of a business may find a mutual advantage in a restrictive covenant, and that such a restraint need not be against the public interest. As well, the parties usually deal with each other on a more or less equal footing in striking a bargain both with respect to the price and the protection asked for by the purchaser. The vendor's covenant not to compete with the purchaser, as a term of an agreement for the sale of a business, may be enforced if it can be shown that the restrictions placed on the vendor are reasonable in view of the nature of the trade or practice sold. *& not against public interest*

Whether a particular restriction is so broad that it offends the public interest is for the court to decide. On the one hand, a clause forbidding the vendor ever to enter business again anywhere would, for most types of business, be more than is needed to protect the purchaser and would be considered to deprive the public of the benefits of the vendor's abilities: accordingly, it would be void. On the other hand, a term by which the vendor undertakes for a specified period of time (or perhaps even within his lifetime) not to set up business again within specific geographic limits that reasonably describe the area of competition may well be reasonable in the opinion of a court, and consequently valid. The size of the area and the period of time denied to the vendor vary with the nature of the business.

ILLUSTRATION

A dentist in Saskatoon sells his practice to a young graduate, promising that he will not practise again anywhere in Canada. The retiring dentist has a change of heart, however, and two years later sets up practice in the same city. The other dentist brings action to obtain a court injunction restraining him from doing so.

In these circumstances a restrictive clause which denies the seller a right to practise anywhere in Canada is in excess of what is neces-

sary to protect the interests of the purchaser. To argue that a covenant in restraint of trade is not against public policy, it is necessary to show at least that it is reasonable between parties. The scope of this covenant, in view of the nature of a dental practice, is unreasonable, and it is therefore void. The purchaser would fail to obtain the injunction, although if the covenant had been confined to the city of Saskatoon for, say, a period of three years, it would probably have been valid.

With rare exceptions, the courts have refused to take on themselves the task of narrowing to a "reasonable scope" the area within which the seller is not to set up business.[30] The basic objection to narrowing a covenant is that it discriminates in favour of one of the parties: it gives a purchaser who has demanded an unreasonable restriction the benefit of the court's opinion about the allowable maximum area not considered detrimental to the public interest. Accordingly, a helpful interpretation from the court ought not to be

---

[30]   See Goldsoll v. Goldman, [1915] 1. Ch. 292, and Attwood v. Lamont, [1920] 3 K.B. 571.

relied upon in framing the terms of an agreement. If a restrictive clause is held to be too wide, it is highly unlikely that courts will narrow it to a reasonable scope; the clause will be void and a seller who might otherwise have been bound by a reasonable restriction is free of the restraint. The lesson for the purchaser is that he should demand no more than a reasonable restriction, erring on the conservative side rather than demanding too much.

The case of *Nordenfelt v. Maxim Nordenfelt Guns and Ammunition Co. Ltd.*[31] illustrates how the nature of a business may be important in determining what is a reasonable restriction on its vendor. Nordenfelt had been a manufacturer of guns and ammunition. He transferred his patents and business to Maxim Nordenfelt Guns and Ammunition Co. Ltd. for £287 500 and covenanted that for 25 years he would not engage, except on behalf of this company, either directly or indirectly in the business of a manufacturer of guns or ammunition or in any other business competing or liable to compete in any way with the business of the company. Later, Nordenfelt entered into an agreement with other manufacturers of guns and ammunition, and the plaintiff company brought an action to enforce the covenant. The House of Lords decided that the clause could be broken into two parts: first, the promise not to engage in the manufacture of guns or ammunition, and second, the promise not to engage in *any other business* competing or liable to compete with the plaintiff company. The court held that the second promise was an unreasonable restriction and declared it void. But it also held it could sever the second promise from the first and that the first promise was a reasonable restriction. Accordingly, it granted an injunction to restrain Nordenfelt from working for any other business which manufactured guns and ammunition.

We can see, then, that although the courts will not save unreasonable restrictions by redrafting them or narrowing their effect, they will sever an unreasonable restriction from one that is reasonable — even if the restrictions occur in the same sentence — provided they are two distinct ideas and can be severed without changing the meaning of the reasonable restraint. In enforcing the restraint concerning guns and ammunition, the court pointed out that improved communications and transportation facilities had enabled orders to be directed to, and filled from, distant sources of supply, and had greatly broadened the market in which competition might be effective in certain lines of business. The decision, though handed down in 1894, recognized that the whole world had become a market in the ammunitions business. In expressing the opinion of the court, Lord Macnaghten set the law in its present mould:

> All interferences with individual liberty of action in trading, and all restraints of trade of themselves, if there is nothing more, are contrary to public policy and therefore void. That is the general rule. But there are exceptions: restraints of trade ... may be justified by the special circumstances of a particular case. It is sufficient justification, and indeed it is the only justification, if the restriction is reasonable — reasonable, that is, in reference to the interests of the public, so framed and so guarded as to afford adequate protection to the party in whose favour it is imposed, while at the same time it is in no way injurious to the public.[32]

---

[31] [1894] A.C. 535.
[32] *Ibid.*, at 565.

Agreements Between Employee and Employer

It is more difficult to convince courts that covenants between employee and employer restricting the future economic freedom of the employee are reasonable and not in restraint of trade.[33] Frequently there is no equality of bargaining power, and an employer is able to impose terms on an employee that the latter must accept if he wants the position. Later he may find that the covenant, if valid, makes it virtually impossible for him to leave his employer in order to accept another position in the vicinity: he would have to sell his house and become established in another city. In protecting employees by striking down unreasonable restraints, the courts at the same time serve a second public interest — they protect the mobility of labour and thereby encourage more efficient allocation of human resources.

We must distinguish agreements that try to govern an employee's means of livelihood *after* he leaves his present employment from those in which the employee undertakes not to compete directly or indirectly *while* he remains in the service of the employer. The law recognizes a full-time employee's primary duty of loyalty to the employer, and an absolute promise not to engage in any other business during the term of the employment is valid, whether that business competes with the employer or not. Similar agreements between partners that are operative during the life of the partnership are also binding.

A plaintiff seeking to enforce a restrictive covenant will usually ask the court for the equitable remedy of an injunction to restrain the defendant. A restrictive covenant may be enforced if it can be shown to be reasonable as between the parties and not injurious to the public.

The courts will more readily accept as reasonable certain restraints placed upon an employee who has access to valuable trade secrets or a knowledge of secret processes in his employment[34] or who has acted as the personal representative of the employer in dealings with the customers of the business.[35] In such circumstances, a promise by the employee not to work for a competing business or to set up a business of his own after leaving his present employment is more likely to be binding upon him, particularly if the employer has evidence that its former employee is acting in a way that is depriving it of its proprietary interest in trade secrets or customer goodwill.

Agreements among Existing Businesses

Agreements among two or more businesses to restrict competition among themselves are governed by statute as well as by the common law in Canada.[36] One of the most far-reaching provisions of the Competition Act (formerly the Combines Investigation Act) is the "conspiracy" section,[37] which makes it an offence, punishable by imprisonment for up to five years and a fine of up to $10 million, to conspire, combine, agree or arrange with

---

[33]   Mason v. Provident Clothing & Supply Co. Ltd., [1913] A.C. 724.

[34]   Reliable Toy Co. and Reliable Plastics Co. Ltd. v. Collins, [1950] 4 D.L.R. 499. For an interesting case that compares covenants both during employment and after termination, see Robinson (William) & Co. Ltd. v. Heuer, [1898] 2 Ch. 451.

[35]   Fitch v. Dewes, [1921] 2 A.C. 158.

[36]   See Nozick and Neff, *Competition Act 1992.* Toronto: Carswell, 1991.

[37]   Competition Act, R.S.C. 1985, c.C–34 (as amended), s. 45. The constitutionality of s. 45, which had been held by the Nova Scotia Supreme Court to contravene the Charter, was upheld by the Supreme Court of Canada in R. v. Nova Scotia Pharmaceutical Society (1992), 93 D.L.R. (4th) 36.

another person to lessen competition *unduly*. A conspiracy may be inferred by the court from the surrounding circumstances — an offence may be committed without there being any direct communication between the parties.[38] Conspiracies to fix prices, restrict output, standardize quality, allocate markets or customers, or prevent the admission of new businesses into the industry, for example, may have the effect of lessening competition unduly. It is not necessarily an offence, however, for businesses to exchange production and sales statistics and credit information, define product standards, agree to cooperate in research, or agree to restrict advertising. Because the essence of the offence is the "undue" restriction on competition, it may often be difficult to distinguish between those agreements or activities that are in violation of the Act and those that are permitted.

Competition may be reduced where two previously competing firms merge, or where one firm acquires control over a competitor. Under the former Combines Investigation Act certain anti-competitive mergers were a criminal offence.[39] The Competition Act adopts an entirely different approach. Mergers and acquisitions are "reviewable transactions" under Part VIII of the Act, and may be examined by the Competition Tribunal.[40] Parties proposing mergers and acquisitions that exceed a certain size must notify in advance the Director of Investigation and Research.[41] Where the Tribunal finds that a merger, or a proposed merger, is likely to prevent or substantially lessen competition it may dissolve or forbid the merger.[42]

Unfair Trade Practices

In addition to its concern with agreements between or among existing businesses, the Competition Act prescribes penalties for a limited number of unfair trade practices which might be employed by a single business with a view to enhancing its position in the market. Thus, it is an offence for a producer or supplier of goods, "by agreement, threat, promise or any like means", to attempt to influence upward or to discourage the reduction of the price at which its own dealers or anyone else will offer such goods for sale.[43] It is also an offence for a producer or supplier to refuse to supply goods or services to, or otherwise discriminate against, another business because of its low pricing policy. The prohibition is qualified by a provision that a producer does not violate the Act when it justifiably refuses to supply its product to a business; for example, if that business has been using the product as a *loss leader* (that is, selling it at less than its own cost), or as a bait to lure customers and then

unless justifiable

---

38 For instance, there may be a concerted practice in an industry where all producers repeatedly make the same price changes at the same time.

39 For a number of reasons, however, it had been almost impossible to secure a conviction under that act: see R. v. British Columbia Sugar Refining Co. (1960), 32 W.W.R. 577; R. v. K.C. Irving Ltd. (1978) 72 D.L.R. (3d) 82.

40 Established by the Competition Tribunal Act, R.S.C. 1985, c. 19 (2nd Supp.)

41 Competition Act, s. 114. Generally, the notification provisions apply only where the parties to the transaction have combined assets in Canada exceeding $400 million, and the transaction itself involves a transfer of assets $35 million in value: ss. 109, 110.

42 S. 92. In Alex Couture Inc. v. Canada (1990) 69 D.L.R. (4th) the Quebec Sup. Ct. held that s. 92 was invalid, since it infringed against the right of association, protected by the Charter. It is uncertain that this position would be upheld by the Supreme Court of Canada.

43 S. 61. See, for example, R. v. Shell Canada Products Ltd. (1990), 45 B.L.R. 231, where a fine of $200 000 was imposed in respect of threatening phone calls from a marketing representative to a dealer, despite the fact that there was no official company policy to keep prices up.

switch them to another, more expensive article, or because the business has failed to provide a level of services that its customers might reasonably expect.[44]

Other unfair practices forbidden by the Act include predatory pricing, discriminatory allowances, and misleading advertising.[45] *Predatory pricing* consists in the practice of selling an article at an unreasonably low price with a view to eliminating competitors. *Discriminatory allowances* take the form of rebates, discounts, or price concessions that are not also offered on proportionate terms to competing purchasers. No decisions have been reported on predatory pricing and discriminatory allowances, which may indicate that the sections are difficult to apply. We shall deal with the scope of the statutory prohibition of misleading advertising in Chapter 19 as a part of our discussion of the law relating to the contract of sale and consumer protection.

The Competition Act also identifies a number of other selling practices that may have the effect of diminishing competition and that, depending upon the circumstances, may also seem unfair to a buyer. These practices include (among others) a refusal to deal,[46] exclusive dealings, market restriction, and tied selling.[47] A *refusal to deal* occurs when a business requiring certain materials or services from a particular supplier is denied any supply. *Exclusive dealing* is an arrangement in which the supplier of a product to, say, retail outlets, requires these customers to deal only in that product or to refrain from dealing in other products specified by the supplier. In a *market restriction* a supplier requires its customers (e.g. dealers or distributors) to agree to sell the product in turn only to certain persons or within a specified geographical area. *Tied selling* takes place when a supplier requires, as a condition for supplying a product sought by a customer, that the customer also purchase some other article or service that it may not want. Affiliated businesses and franchises (such as a chain of fast food outlets) are exempted. The Act does not make these practices offences in themselves but it gives the Competition Tribunal the power to review complaints with a view to determining whether the particular practice has the effect of substantially reducing competition and, if so, to issue an order restraining the continuation of the practice.

The Act makes the directors and officers of companies personally liable if they authorize assent to, acquiesce in or participate in the commission of an offence by a corporation.[48] Although the usual practice has been to prosecute only the corporation for violations of the main provisions of the Act, section 65 makes it clear that proceedings may be brought against individual directors or officers whether or not the corporation has been prosecuted or convicted. We shall discuss the liability of corporations and their directors and officers for breach of regulation more fully in Chapter 32.

Questions for Review

1. Why may it be important to a party to a dispute to show that a void contract is not also illegal?
2. How can we tell whether the intention of the legislature is to make a certain type of agreement illegal as well as void?

---

[44] S. 61(10).
[45] Ss. 50, 51, 52.
[46] S. 47.
[47] S. 49. (See also s. 50 for other reviewable practices.)
[48] S. 65(4).

3. In what way does the Gaming Act inhibit wagering contracts?
4. What quality must an insurance contract possess to prevent it from being a wager and therefore void?
5. What kinds of business contract may have an element of wagering incidental to the main purpose of the transaction?
6. What exception is there to the rule that an agreement is illegal if it purports to indemnify a person against the consequences of his or her own wrongdoing?
7. What is the most help an employer can legally offer an employee who has been guilty of theft?
8. How is the public interest affected in an agreement that stirs up litigation? In an agreement in restraint of trade?
9. State the nature of the restrictive covenant that may occur in each of the following types of contract:
   (a) a contract for the sale of a business;
   (b) an employment contract;
   (c) an agreement between existing businesses.
10. In what ways may businesses "unduly lessen competition" by an agreement among themselves?
11. Review the facts of Case 2 at the end of the preceding chapter. Should Medicine Hat Broncos Hockey Club have sued Tilson and Calgary Whippets Hockey Club Ltd. jointly? For what reason?
12. What is the policy of the law that justifies a stricter view of restraints in employment contracts than in contracts for the sale of a business?
13. In a decision given in 1875, an English judge said, "If there is one thing which more than another public policy requires it is that men of full age and competent understanding shall have the utmost liberty of contracting and that their contracts when entered into freely and voluntarily shall be held sacred and shall be enforced by courts of justice." (Jessel, M.R., in *Printing & Numerical Registering Co. v. Sampson* (1875) 19 Eq. 462.) Explain how a conflict may arise between the attitude represented in this quotation and a willingness on the part of the courts to expand the types of contract that may be void or illegal for reasons of public policy.
14. In a pari-mutuel system, all the bets made on each horse in a race are registered on a machine which calculates the odds in such a way that the total amount of money paid in, less a percentage for expenses, is divided among those who bet on the winning horses. Is it possible for the organization that manages the pari-mutuel system to refuse to account for the money deposited with it, on the grounds that it is a party to a void contract? Explain.

Problems

Problem 1

Rhodes, a civil engineer, was hired by Nilsson Brothers, a firm of engineering consultants located in the borough of Park Forest. In her work, Rhodes acquired an expert knowledge of costs for the purpose of submitting tenders on various types of construction projects and the sources of supply of the necessary materials. She worked almost entirely in the offices of the firm: the partners handled most negotiations with the firm's clients.

Rhodes' contract of employment stated that for a period of five years after the termination of her employment she would not "engage in the professional practice of engineering either alone or in association with or as an employee of any persons within Park Forest or two miles thereof". Park Forest is a residential suburban borough in the largest metropolitan area in the province: there are two other firms of engineering consultants in Park Forest and some two hundred firms in the whole metropolitan area.

Within a few days of terminating her employment with Nilsson Brothers, Rhodes advised the firm's partners that she considered the restrictive covenant unenforceable and that she intended to open her own office as a professional engineer within Park Forest. Nilsson Brothers then sued Rhodes to obtain an injunction to restrain her from breaking the contract.

(a) Identify the legal issues and state the principles that would affect the decision (without coming to a conclusion at this point).

(b) What is the role of public policy in this problem?

(c) To what extent does the law recognize the respective interests of the employee and employer?

(d) Should the action succeed?

Problem 2

Dadson arrived at Pearson International Airport on a trip from Paris, and on leaving the building at the "Arrivals" level was approached by Carman, the owner and operator of a taxi licensed by the Municipality of Metropolitan Toronto. The airport is in Mississauga, where a by-law forbids taxis not licensed by the municipality to pick up fares in Mississauga. (Mississauga is outside the boundaries of Metropolitan Toronto.)

Dadson, unaware that Carman was not licensed in Mississauga, got in the taxi. On the way to her home in Mississauga, Dadson learned from notices posted inside the cab that Carman did not have a Mississauga licence.

When she arrived home safely, Dadson refused to pay for the ride. Carman sued Dadson in the First Small Claims Court of Peel County (Mississauga). Should the taxi owner succeed? Give brief reasons for your opinion.

Problem 3

Flanders & Co., a Montréal firm of wine importers, chartered the ship *Bacchus* from its owners, Swan Ltd., to transport a cargo of wine from Madeira to Montréal. The contract of charter party included a term to the effect that the charterer, Flanders & Co., should be liable for an additional $1000 for each additional day at the port of destination if the unloading of the ship were delayed for any reason. Unknown to either party, the wine was a prohibited product under the federal Food and Drugs Act because of a preservative used in its production.

When the ship reached Montréal, customs officers refused permission to unload pending determination of the cargo's compliance with the federal Act. The investigation and report from the government laboratory in Ottawa took ten days; it was determined by customs officials that it would be illegal to import the wine, and the cargo was finally transferred at dockside to another ship for shipment to New York.

When Flanders & Co. refused to pay the additional $10 000 caused by the delay, Swan Ltd., sued for the amount. What defence might Flanders & Co. offer? Would Swan Ltd. succeed? (See *Waugh v. Morris* (1873) L.R. 8 Q.B. 202.)

Cases

Case 1

Halton's elderly widowed aunt had been residing with him for many years as his house-keeper. She had very little money or other assets. Halton was successful in business and was content to support her. He paid amounts for her maintenance that approximately equalled the costs of a housekeeper's services.

Halton was approached in confidence by an agent of the Actuarial Life Insurance Company. The agent reminded Halton of his family obligation to arrange a respectable funeral for his aunt when she died. Halton then took out a life insurance policy on her life for $5000; it was clearly intended to reimburse him for his aunt's estate and funeral expenses. The annual premium was $225.

Halton paid the premium for seven years until his aunt died. The Actuarial Insurance Company then refused to pay the amount of the policy and Halton sued.

Discuss the legal arguments available to Halton and to the Actuarial Life Insurance Company. Bearing in mind that he might fail to recover the face value of the policy, what alternative claim might Halton make when bringing his action? (For reference, see *Harse v. Pearl Life Insurance Co.* [1904] 1 K.B. 558.)

Case 2

John Gifford and his friend, Karl Holtz, were enthusiastic followers of the commodities market, the market in which such products as wheat, cotton, tobacco, and coffee are bought and sold for future delivery. However, they did not have sufficient capital to engage in the market themselves, and so they played a game: they would "buy and sell" futures in various commodities under three-month contracts for delivery and then "settle" their fictional gains and losses on the delivery date. Karl did very well in the game and over a two-year period "earned" over $100 000 at John's expense.

One day John finally said to Karl, "I think I have a real winner here, the price of coffee is going to rise sharply in the next three months. At what price do you want to sell to me?"

Karl disagreed with John's prediction and replied, "I'll sell you $20 000's worth of coffee at today's price. The price is going to drop and you'll lose as usual."

"For once, not only am I right, I'm prepared to back up my words. Are you?" asked John. " Let's make this a real transaction. If the price goes up, you pay me the difference. If it goes down, I pay you."

"Okay, it's your funeral. It's a deal", Karl replied, and they shook hands on it.

Three months later, the price of $20 000's worth of coffee had risen by 30%, making John richer by $6000. When John demanded payment, Karl said he didn't have that much in the bank but grudgingly gave John three cheques for $2 000 each, one payable immediately and the other two post-dated one month and two months respectively.

John cashed the first cheque at Karl's bank at once. A month later, he used the second cheque to buy a used car from Grace Bukowsky. She has not yet presented it to Karl's bank for payment. John still has the third cheque.

Karl has heard from a friend studying law that the whole transaction might be "illegal". Give him your opinion with reasons.

Case 3

Culinary-Magic Corporation manufactures small household appliances such as toasters and electric frying pans, can openers and food processors. Last year it started a "cooperative advertising plan" with its retail dealers across Canada. The essentials of the plan were as follows: Culinary-Magic agreed to pay 50% of the cost of advertisements published by its authorized dealers advertising its products, provided that in the advertisements the products were suitably described to the satisfaction of the manufacturer and that the price designated in the advertisement was not less than the price specified by the manufacturer for use in such advertisements.

At the same time, Culinary-Magic sent out letters to all its retail outlets specifying suggested prices for each of its products, and advising them that, in its opinion, the sale of such articles could not be made at a price less than that specified and still permit the retailer a profit. The letters then stated that any retail store selling at a lower price could be considered by Culinary-Magic Corporation to be using its products as loss leaders and that it would have to reserve the right to decide whether it could continue to supply the articles to the offending store. As a follow-up, company sales representatives devoted considerable time in bringing retailers into line with others who had adopted the suggested prices.

The Attorney-General of Canada started a prosecution against Culinary-Magic Corporation for a violation of paragraphs (a) and (b) of subsection (1) of s. 38 of the Competition Act, S.C. 1986, c. C-23. The court was referred to the following parts of the Act:

38. (1) No person who is engaged in the business of producing or supplying a product...shall, directly or indirectly,
    (a) by agreement, threat, promise or any like means, attempt to influence upward, or to discourage the reduction of, the price at which any other person engaged in business in Canada supplies or offers to supply or advertises a product within Canada; or
    (b) refuse to supply a product to or otherwise discriminate against any other person engaged in business in Canada because of the low pricing policy of that person.

  (2) Subsection (1) does not apply where a person attempting to influence the conduct of another person and that other person are affiliated companies or... where the person attempting to influence the conduct of another person and that other person are principal and agent.

  (3) For the purposes of this section, a suggestion by a producer or supplier of a product of a resale price or minimum resale price in respect thereof, however arrived at, is, in the absence of proof that the person making the suggestion, in so doing, also made it clear to the person to whom the suggestion was made that he was under no obligation to accept the suggestion and would in no way suffer in his business relations with the person making the suggestion or with any other person if he failed to accept the suggestion, proof of an attempt to influence the person to whom the suggestion is made in accordance with the suggestion.

  (4) For the purposes of this section, the publication by a supplier of a product, other than a retailer, of an advertisement that mentions a resale price for the product is an attempt to influence upward the selling price of any person into whose hands the product comes for resale unless the price is so expressed as to make it clear to any person to whose attention the advertisement comes that the product may be sold at a lower price.

  (8) Every person who violates subsection (1)...is guilty of an indictable offence and is liable on conviction to a fine in the discretion of the court or to imprisonment for five years or to both.

(9) Where, in a prosecution under (1) (b), it is proved that the person charged refused or counselled the refusal to supply a product to any other person, no inference unfavourable to the person charged shall be drawn from such evidence if he satisfies the court that he and any one upon whose report he depended had reasonable cause to believe and did believe

   (a) that the other person was making a practice of using products supplied by the person charged as loss-leaders, that is to say, not for the purpose of making a profit thereon but for purposes of advertising;

   (b) that the other person was making a practice of using products supplied by the person charged not for the purpose of selling such products at a profit but for the purpose of attracting customers to his store in the hope of selling them other products;

   (c) that the other person was making a practice of engaging in misleading advertising in respect of products supplied by the person charged;

   (d) that the other person made a practice of not providing the level of servicing that purchasers of such products might reasonably expect from such other person.

In defence, Culinary-Magic Corporation established that retailers can advertise its products in any other manner and at any other price they wish without taking advantage of the cooperative plan; that retailers are at liberty to sell Culinary-Magic's products at any price they wish despite the price in a cooperative advertisement; and that it is quite usual for retailers to sell Culinary-Magic's products at less than the price in the cooperative advertising.

The prosecution established through evidence about the type of business relationship maintained between Culinary-Magic and its retail outlets ("dealers") that the dealers should be regarded as independent contracting parties relative to Culinary-Magic Corporation. There was no evidence that any of the dealers is a company affiliated with Culinary-Magic Corporation or is acting as an agent of it.

Discuss the merits of this prosecution and offer an opinion about whether it will succeed.

CHAPTER 10

GROUNDS UPON WHICH A CONTRACT MAY BE IMPEACHED: MISTAKE

THE RESTRICTED MEANING OF MISTAKE

A party sometimes discovers unhappily that a contract he has made is quite different from that intended — and he wishes to be freed from it. If there is a practical lesson to be gained from a review of the law on mistake, it is that the prospects for avoiding a contract on this basis are limited and precarious.

"Legal mistake" must not be confused with "mistake" in its more general, non-legal meaning. To say "I made a mistake going for a walk without my overcoat" or "She made a mistake agreeing to work over the weekend" is simply to say that a person, with hindsight, believes it was an error in judgment to have acted in a particular way. Such errors in judgment are not recognized by the courts as justification for avoiding obligations under a contract; to excuse performance on the basis of such mistakes would undermine certainty in contractual arrangements, so that parties would be reluctant to rely on them. An important element of contract law is that parties are entitled to rely on contracts they have made in arranging their affairs. In the words of a United States judge:

> Contracts are the deliberate and voluntary obligations of parties capable of contracting and they must be accorded binding force and effect. Those who enter into them must understand that they have a meaning and that they cannot lightly be tampered with.... The owner of property is supposed to know what it is worth and at least know what he is willing to take for his property. The purchaser may likewise exercise his free will and choice as to whether he will purchase property at a given price. After he has received the property, understanding that he is to pay a fixed price for it, he cannot be compelled to pay a different and greater price simply because the vendor was careless and negligent in the transaction of his own business [and had sold it for too little].[1]

ILLUSTRATION A

A leaves a note for B, stating, "I will sell you my car for $2400 cash." B delivers $2400 to A, and obtains possession and a transfer of the registration. A immediately realizes that he had made an error in his note; he had intended to write $2700 rather than $2400. However, B was unaware of the error; she simply thought the price was an attractive one. While in one sense there is a mistake, it is wholly on the part of A, and is one on which B reasonably relied: if a remedy were granted to A, either to increase the price of the car or to require its return, B's reasonable expectations would be defeated. A reasonable bystander reading the note and observing B's acceptance would conclude that there was a contract in the terms of the note as written. Accordingly, A would not have a remedy.

---

[1] Tatum v. Coast Lumber Co. (1909), 101 P. 957 at 960. See also: Scott v. Littledale (1858), 120 E.R. 304.

ILLUSTRATION B

L signs a five-year lease to rent a shop on a main traffic artery. He has misread a street map and believes that a city bus route uses the street, and that a bus stop is close to the shop. In fact the bus route runs along a	parallel route two blocks to the south. The landlord is completely unaware of the lessee's erroneous belief. Here also, the contract is binding on the lessee despite his innocent and mistaken assumption.

Two main types of mistake which may occur are *mistakes about the terms* of a contract and *mistakes in assumptions* about important facts related to a contract although not part of the contract itself.[2] Sometimes the court will grant relief on grounds we are about to consider, but frequently they will refuse to do so. The two illustrations above are examples respectively of the two types of mistake where relief would be denied by a court because, based on principles to be discussed, the mistaken parties would be found solely responsible for their own misfortunes. We shall also examine cases where relief will be granted.

Mistakes About the Terms

Words Used Inadvertently

As in our first illustration, one party may inadvertently use unintended words in stating the terms of a contract. If so, then we should ask how those words ought reasonably to have been understood by the other party. If, given all the circumstances, it was reasonable for the second party to rely on them and enter into the contract, then the contract will be binding on the first party in those terms. The consequences of the error will fall on one of the parties, and it seems only fair that it should fall on the one who caused the problem.

On the other hand, it may be clear to a reasonable bystander that the first party made a mistake in expressing the terms of the contract: the price may be absurdly low or quite unrelated to the range of prices quoted by both sides during negotiations. In such circumstances, a court would conclude that no reasonable person could have relied on such an offer as having been intentionally made; the attempted acceptance is akin to fraud ("snapping up an offer") and the contract is voidable by the first party. In *Webster v. Cecil*[3] the parties had been negotiating about the sale to Webster of land owned by Cecil. Initially Cecil had refused Webster's offer of £2000. Later Cecil wrote to Webster mistakenly offering the land for £1250. Immediately after he had mailed his offer, Cecil realized his error and wrote that the price should have been £2250, but his letter arrived after

---

2   It is important to note that problems relating to mistake are difficult to classify and analyse. Many different frameworks have been tried and none is entirely satisfactory in explaining the great diversity of problems that can and do arise. We believe that the approach adopted in this chapter, based in part on the work of G.E. Palmer, *Mistake and Unjust Enrichment.* Columbus: Ohio State U. Press, 1962, is simpler and yet more helpful than the analysis in earlier editions of this book. Lord Reid's observation is apt: "There was a period when ... hard-and-fast dividing lines were sought, but I think that experience has shown that often they do not produce certainty but do produce unreasonable results." (Saunders v. Anglia Building Society, [1971] A.C. 1004 at 1017.)

3   (1861), 54 E.R. 812.

Webster had posted his acceptance. Webster sued to enforce the contract and failed, the court finding that he could not possibly have believed that £1250 represented the intended offer price.

It may not always be easy to decide whether a party could have relied reasonably on words used in an offer. Perhaps he should have questioned the offeror to ask whether he really meant them; on the other hand, he could have believed that the offeror simply intended to make the offer so attractive the offeree would find it hard to resist accepting. After all, there may have been a change in the offeror's circumstances. What should the court do in the exercise of its discretion to grant relief? In this situation the court will want to consider the hardship suffered by either party should it decide against him. In *Paget v. Marshall*,[4] the court adopted an imaginative approach to deal with this dilemma. Paget had offered to lease out the third floor of a warehouse and a large portion of the second floor as well, reserving to herself only that portion of the second floor that was above a store she retained at ground level. Paget's brother explained these conditions to Marshall who found them satisfactory. However, after the lease was drawn up and signed by both parties, it was found to include the portion of the second floor that Paget had wished to keep for herself. Paget sued to have the lease corrected to exclude the second floor portion over the store. In giving judgment, Bacon, V.C., said:

> ...I must in charity and justice to the Defendant believe [him], because I cannot impute to him the intention of taking advantage of any incorrect expression...but...it is plain and palpable that the Plaintiff was mistaken and had no intention of letting...[her own premises]...the Defendant should have an opportunity of choosing whether he will submit...to have the lease rectified...or...choose to throw up the thing entirely, because the object of the Court is, as far as it can, to put the parties into the position in which they would have been if the mistake had not happened.... The Plaintiff does not object, if the agreement is annulled, to pay the Defendant any reasonable expenses to which he may have been put by reason of the Plaintiff's mistake....[5]

Perhaps not surprisingly, the defendant elected to keep the lease, as amended by the court, and to return to the plaintiff the portion over the store.[6]

Errors in Recording an Agreement

Sometimes parties may reach agreement — either orally intending later to turn it into written form, or first written informally and later to be put into a formal contract under seal — but subsequently one party discovers that the final written form does not accurately reflect the original agreement: a term may have been left out or important figures may be wrong. The party who stands to benefit from the mistake may insist that the final version represents the bargain and may resist any attempt to revert to the original terms. He may claim that the first agreement was too vague, or that it was subject to any further changes made before finally being *reduced* to writing or to a sealed instrument. Indeed, the defendant so argued, unsuccessfully, in the *Paget* case, above.

---

[4]   (1884), 28 Ch. D. 255.
[5]   *Ibid.* at 266-267.
[6]   It is interesting to note how the court disposed of the costs in the action. "...the Plaintiff is not entitled to costs, because [s]he has made a mistake, and the Defendant ought not to have any costs, because his opposition to the Plaintiff's demand has been unreasonable...", per Bacon, V.C., *Ibid.* at 267.

A party claiming that the arrangement was improperly recorded may ask the court for *rectification* of the contract. The request will succeed if the following conditions are met:

(a) The court is satisfied that there was a complete agreement between the parties, free from ambiguity and not conditional upon further adjustments.
(b) The parties did not engage in further negotiations to amend the contract.
(c) The change in the written document appears to be an error in recording, and is most easily explained as such.

In *U.S.A. v. Motor Trucks, Ltd.*,[7] the Government of the United States had agreed to pay a large sum of money in compensation for cancellation of war contracts at the end of the First World War. The payments were intended to reimburse a Canadian manufacturing company for equipment and buildings acquired to carry out the contracts. The sum to be paid was in settlement of all contractual obligations of the U.S. Government and, in return, the manufacturer agreed to give up all other claims under the contract and to transfer certain lands to the U.S. Government. Apparently inexplicably, transfer of the lands was left out of the final formal settlement. The manufacturer resisted the U.S. Government claim to the land on the grounds that it had originally consented to the inclusion of the lands while labouring under an "error as to [its own] legal rights". The Privy Council rejected the manufacturer's claim that the original settlement was not binding and accordingly ordered the final formal settlement rectified to include the lands. There was no evidence that the parties had engaged in further bargaining before the final formal settlement nor could the omission be explained except on the basis of an error.

It is not easy to establish the conditions necessary for rectification: if the terms were ambiguous in the original agreement or if the parties carried on subsequent negotiations, a court will be very reluctant to alter the final agreement. In another leading case, Lord Denning said, "In order to get rectification it is necessary to show that the parties were in complete agreement upon the terms of their contract, but by an error wrote them down wrongly."[8]

Misunderstandings about the Meanings of Words

Both parties to a contract may have agreed to the words actually used — neither party put them forward inadvertently nor were any of the terms subsequently recorded incorrectly. Nevertheless, the parties may place quite different meanings on the terms of the contract. In most instances, these disagreements can be treated as questions of interpretation. A court will decide which meaning is the more reasonable in light of the circumstances, including those things each party ought to have known about the subject matter of the contract and about the intentions of the other party. In some cases it will decide that the meaning given by an offeror to his own words was the more reasonable one. If so, the offeree will be bound on the terms as understood by the offeror. In other cases the court will decide that the offeror was imprudent to use the words as he did and that the

---

[7] [1924] A.C. 196. For more recent cases, see and compare R. v. Ron Engineering Construction Eastern Ltd. (1981), 119 D.L.R. (3d) 267; Belle River Community Arena Inc. v. W.J.C. Kaufman Co. Ltd. (1978), 87 D.L.R. (3d) 761.

[8] Rose v. Pim, [1953] 2 All E.R. 739 at 747.

offeree interpreted them more reasonably. In that event the offeror will be bound by the contract as the offeree understands it.

In *Lindsey v. Heron*,[9] the seller asked the buyer, "What will you give me for 75 shares of Eastern Cafeterias of Canada?" The buyer said he would make inquiries and then make an offer. Later in the day he replied, "I will give you $10.50 a share for your Eastern Cafeterias." The seller replied, "I accept your offer." The seller delivered the shares for his Eastern Cafeterias of Canada Ltd. and received a cheque in full payment. The buyer then realized that Eastern Cafeterias Ltd. and Eastern Cafeterias of Canada Ltd. were two different companies, and that he had the former company in mind when he made his offer to buy the shares. He stopped payment on his cheque. In defending an action by the seller, the buyer claimed that his offer to buy "Eastern Cafeterias" was ambiguous, as he could have meant either company. He argued that since he and the seller were talking about different companies in ignorance of the misunderstanding between them, there was never any agreement and no contract was formed.

This defence was rejected by the court. It held that in the light of the unambiguous statement of the seller when he referred to Eastern Cafeterias of Canada, the offer must be construed to refer to those shares. In giving the decision of the court, Mr. Justice Middleton said:

> I think that, judged by any reasonable standard, the words used by the defendants manifested an intention to offer the named price for the thing which the plaintiff proposed to sell, i.e., stock in the Eastern Cafeterias of Canada Limited. Had the plaintiff spoken of "Eastern Cafeterias", the words used would have been ambiguous, and I should find no contract, for each might have used the ambiguous term in a different sense; but the defendants, by use of these ambiguous terms in response to the plaintiff's request couched in unambiguous language, must be taken to have used it in the same sense.[10]

In rare cases the court is faced by an insoluble set of facts: both parties have been equally reasonable (or unreasonable) in the meaning they attributed to the words, and it would be unjust to hold one party to the other's interpretation. The classic example occurred in the case of *Raffles v. Wichelhaus*.[11] The contract was for the sale of cotton that was to arrive in England from Bombay on board the ship *Peerless*. By a remarkable coincidence two ships called *Peerless* were sailing from Bombay, one in October, the other in December. The seller believed that he contracted to sell cotton on the later ship; the buyer believed that he contracted to buy cotton on the earlier ship. A delay of two months in the shipment of a commodity subject to market fluctuations is a major difference in terms. Thus, when the cotton arrived on the later ship the buyer refused to accept it or pay for it. The seller sued for breach of contract, and the buyer pleaded mistake in defence. The defence succeeded because the court could not decide which ship *Peerless* was meant. A reasonable person would have been helpless to decide that the contract was for cotton on one ship rather than the other.

As suggested by Mr. Justice Middleton in *Lindsey v. Heron,* two parties, both equally careless, may use an ambiguous phrase, and the court will refuse to decide between the

---

[9]   (1921), 50 O.L.R. 1.
[10] *Ibid.* at 9.
[11] (1864), 159 E.R. 375. See also: Angevaare v. McKay (1960), 25 D.L.R. (2d) 521.

two conflicting interpretations. The practical result, then, is that the position of the defendant is the stronger: the party who tries to enforce the contract will fail. In *Falck v. Williams*,[12] a Norwegian shipowner communicated by cable with an Australian ship-broker arranging contracts of carriage for the Norwegian's ships from various ports in the Pacific. To save money, they used a code system in which single words stood for phrases or even whole sentences. The shipowner sent an ambiguous message in code. The court held it could equally have been interpreted that cargo was to be picked up in the Fiji Islands or at Sydney, Australia. The sender of the cable intended the ship to load in the Fiji Islands; the receiver understood the port to be Sydney. In rejecting the shipowner's action for breach of contract, Lord MacNaghten said:

> In their Lordships' opinion, there is no conclusive reason pointing one way or the other. The fault lay with the ... [appellant]: if he had spent a few more shillings on his message, if he had even arranged the words he used more carefully, if he had only put the word "estcorte" before the word "begloom" instead of after it, there would have been no difficulty. It is not for their Lordships to determine what is the true construction of ... [the] telegram. It was the duty of the appellant as plaintiff to make out that the construction which he put upon it was the true one. In that he must fail if the message was ambiguous, as their Lordships hold it to be. *If the respondent had been maintaining his construction as plaintiff he would equally have failed.*[13]

$\mathcal{M}$ISTAKES IN ASSUMPTIONS

About the Existence of the Subject-Matter of a Contract

We are here concerned with mistakes of a fundamental kind that radically change the nature of the parties' bargain. The most fundamental of mistakes is that about the very existence of the subject-matter. If at the time the contract was made the subject-matter, let us say goods in the hold of a ship at sea, had been destroyed unknown to either party, it is hard to imagine a sensible way to enforce the contract: is the buyer required to pay the price for goods that cannot be delivered? Is the seller liable for breach for non-delivery? In *Couturier v. Hastie*,[14] the parties had arranged for the sale of a cargo of corn believed to be *en route* from Greece to England. Unknown to them, the cargo had become overheated and was in danger of spoiling: the ship had to put into the port of Tunis where the corn had to be sold. An action by the seller for the agreed price for the cargo failed; the contract was held to be void.

This rule, as it applies to the sale of goods, has been incorporated in the Sale of Goods Act, which provides that "where there is a contract for sale of specific goods and the goods without the knowledge of the seller have perished at the time the contract is made, the contract is void."[15] Of course, if the seller was aware of the destruction of the goods, the attempt to sell them would be fraudulent and the buyer could recover damages by suing in tort for deceit.

---

[12] [1900] A.C. 176.
[13] *Ibid.* at 181 (authors' italics).
[14] (1852), 155 E.R. 1250, affirmed by the House of Lords (1856), 10 E.R. 1065.
[15] R.S.N.S. 1989, c.408, s. 9; R.S.O. 1990, c. S-1, s. 7; R.S.B.C. 1979, c. 370, s. 10.

About the Value of the Subject-Matter: Allocation of Risk

It becomes much more difficult to fashion solutions when the subject-matter of a contract is still in existence, but its qualities are radically different from those contemplated by the parties; one party may be paying far too much for what he will receive, or the other may be receiving far too little for parting with something that is much more valuable than he had realized. In either case one party may receive a windfall at the expense of the other. The willingness of a court to grant relief varies according to the factors discussed below.

Sometimes, it is generally recognized that the type of transaction is one in which the parties are aware of the possibility that the subject-matter may quickly rise or fall in value. Indeed, the contract can be thought of as one primarily allocating risk. Thus, *A* may be willing to pay $5 per share for 10 000 shares in a corporation she believes is about to make large profits, while *B* is content to accept $5 per share for them in the belief that the price is more likely to drop. If, unknown to either of them, the financial position of the company has already declined or risen sharply before the contract is formed, the court will not grant relief to the party adversely affected: the change of circumstance is one of the risks contemplated in the contract.

Frequently, however, it cannot so easily be inferred that the parties intended to accept a particular risk. The court may conclude it would be unfair to allow the bargain to stand, and will grant relief. In *Hyrsky et al. v. Smith*,[16] the plaintiffs purchased a parcel of land with the intention of developing it commercially within a few years. Foolishly, they did not have a qualified person carefully investigate the title to the property, as is the normal practice. As a result, they could be said to have taken some risk that the land was subject to "defects", that is, to claims by other parties. More than four years later, when the plaintiffs prepared to develop the land and the title was investigated, it was discovered that almost half the land purported to have been transferred to them had not been owned by the defendant. The remainder was too small to be developed commercially. The plaintiffs sued to have the contract set aside, the purchase price repaid, and the land returned to the defendant. The defendant resisted the claim on the ground that the plaintiffs had taken the risk of not investigating title. In response, Lieff, J. said:

> It is true that under our present-day system of conveyancing, the purchaser has ample opportunity to inquire and to inspect before he is compelled to close the transaction ....However that may be and notwithstanding the need for certainty and permanency in the law of ... [transferring land], these policy considerations must yield to the desirability of doing equity where there has been ... [a substantial error].[17]

Earlier he had said, "If the mistake as to quantity is so substantial that in essence it changes the quality of the subject-matter, then a proper case for rescission may exist." J. Lieff considered the possibility that the plaintiffs should be required to accept the smaller parcel of land owned by the defendant, but he concluded that this possibility was outside any risk that ought to have been assumed by the plaintiffs. Denying any relief to the plaintiffs would leave them with a piece of land too small for their purposes and leave the defendant with a windfall, a much higher price than the land was actually worth. Nor

---

[16] (1969) 5 D.L.R. (3d) 385.
[17] *Ibid.* at 392.

would it make sense for the court to order a reduction in price proportional to the land actually transferred to the plaintiffs; they would still have land they could not use. Accordingly, the court ordered the contract set aside as requested by the plaintiffs. However, it refused to award costs, because "had the plaintiffs searched the title as a prudent purchaser should have done, all of this litigation would never have arisen."[18]

In earlier cases, courts often seemed to ignore the question of whether a party could reasonably be held to the consequences of a particular risk, and instead tried to classify rather formally the kind of mistake that had occurred: was the mistake merely about a "quality" of the subject-matter or did it convert the subject-matter into something entirely different in "substance" from that which the parties had contracted for? If the latter, then the contract should be set aside. But "if it be only a difference in some quality", the contract should be left to bind the parties. This analysis tended to divert the court from the important issue of the reasonable expectations of each of the parties and the consequent fairness of upholding the contract or setting it aside. In a famous United States case, one cattle breeder owned a cow he believed to be infertile.[19] As such she had only a limited value for slaughter as beef; if she had been fertile her value as a purebred breeding cow would have been ten times the beef price. A second cattle breeder made inquiries about purchasing her. Although the evidence was rather confused, it seemed that he believed there was a chance that the cow could be made to breed, or at least he was willing to take a chance on her. As he was not ordinarily a buyer of cattle for butchering it was unlikely that he would buy a cow for slaughter. The parties agreed to a sale at the beef price, but before the buyer could arrange to pick up the animal the seller discovered that she was expecting a calf and refused to deliver. The buyer sued to claim the cow.

The court found in favour of the seller, asserting that "The thing sold and bought has in fact no existence." In other words, the difference between an infertile cow and a breeder was so great that it was almost as if the subject-matter did not exist, as in *Couturier v. Hastie,* above. There was, however, a vigorous dissent, in which the judge said, "The defendant thought she would not, but the plaintiff says he thought she could be made to breed ... each party took his chances."[20] If this was so, the majority decision appears to have been wrong in terms of the risks each party took.

Asking whether a party to a contract ought to bear the risk of a change in the subject-matter is simply another way of asking whether it would be unfair to deny a remedy when the change materializes. A 1971 judgment stated:

> ... if the Court finds that there has been honest, even though inadvertent mistake, it will afford relief in any case where it considers that it would be unfair, unjust or unconscionable not to correct it ...[21]

This broad approach, attempting to do justice and to minimize the effects of a mistake, is a commendable attempt to overcome earlier complicated and conflicting analyses of problems arising from a mistake in assumptions.

---

[18] *Ibid.* at 393.
[19] Sherwood v. Walker (1887), 33 N.W. 919.
[20] *Ibid.* at 925.
[21] McMaster University v. Wilchar Construction, [1971] 3 O.R. 801, per Thompson, J., at 810.

The Challenge of Achieving a Fair Result

Problems resulting from mistakes — situations in which one or both of the parties may have changed their position or foregone other opportunities — may be especially difficult for the courts to resolve.

In *Solle v. Butcher*,[22] a landlord had substantially renovated a building containing five flats. A surveyor, who had been the landlord's partner in the business of buying and renovating residential buildings, was himself interested in renting one of the flats. He investigated the rental status of the property and concluded that because of the renovations rent controls no longer applied: the flat that formerly was limited to an annual rent of £140 could now be rented for £250 at fair market value. On that mistaken assumption the parties entered into a seven-year lease. In fact, the property was still subject to rent control, although the landlord might have obtained permission for a higher rent than £140 had he reported the reconstruction of the flat to the rent control authorities and applied for and received consent to increase the rent before entering into a lease. Subsequently the parties ceased to be on friendly terms, and the tenant brought an action to recover his overpayments and for a declaration that £140 maximum could be collected for the remainder of the lease.

Both parties had believed they were dealing with a flat exempt from rent control while the flat was actually subject to controls — a serious mistake in assumption about the subject-matter of the contract, because the rent control acts made it impossible to enforce the lease at £250 per year. However, the court found that it would be unfair to hold the landlord to a seven-year lease at such a low, uneconomical rent as £140, and that it would also be unfair to the tenant to declare the lease void and force the tenant to vacate the flat. Instead, the court put the tenant "on terms". He was given a choice: either he could vacate the flat, thus bringing the contract to an end, or he could remain — but if he remained the court would temporarily suspend the lease, enabling the landlord to make an application to the rent control authority in order to charge the full rent that those authorities would permit for the remainder of the lease, subject to a maximum of £250 as originally agreed between the parties.

The technicalities involved in avoiding the prohibitions of the rent controls tested the ingenuity of the court in constructing a just solution — it required a particularly imaginative judge in the person of L.J. Denning to accomplish the task. A court's willingness to grant relief will be influenced by its ability to fashion a result that seems reasonably fair to both parties. If it cannot see its way clear to a solution within the exercise of its powers, it may simply refuse a remedy and leave the loss to lie where it has fallen.

Unforeseen Future Events

Parties to a contract sometimes fail to foresee a crucial change in circumstances under which performance is to take place. The contract may become physically or legally impossible to perform (as when new government regulations require a pharmaceutical product to be removed from the market as unsafe), or conditions may have so changed as to make the contract pointless (as when a party has purchased a seat to watch an entertainment that is cancelled). From the time such a contract is first formed until the unforeseen event occurs, there exists a valid, binding contract between the parties. However, a

---

[22] [1950] 1 K.B. 671.

court may find that such an event has frustrated the basic purpose of the contract and declare both parties to be discharged from the moment of the event. We shall defer our discussion of discharge by frustration until we deal with discharge of contracts generally, in Chapter 15. We should note, however, that frustrating events differ from mistakes in assumption in that mistakes concern the actual state of affairs at the time a contract is formed, while a frustrating event is one that takes place *after* formation, and could not be known to either party.

$\mathcal{M}$ISTAKE AND INNOCENT THIRD PARTIES

How the Problem Arises

A problem of mistake frequently arises in circumstances where the law would be quite clear if it affected only the original parties to a contract. One party is a rogue who practises deceit on a rather gullible — or at least imprudent — second party, and thus gains possession of goods or obtains a valuable signed document. It does not matter whether the mistake is one about assumptions (as where the victim is misled about the identity of the rogue) or one about the terms (as where the victim is misled about the terms of a document he signs). The rogue has practised a deceit and a court would willingly grant the victim relief. As we shall see, if the victim were to regain his senses quickly enough to pursue his remedies against the rogue, there would be no doubt that he could recover the goods or document from him. But alas, the rogue has usually profited from the deception and absconded. The contest that remains is between the victim and an innocent third party who has paid the rogue and in return acquired the goods or document that the rogue extracted from the victim.

Void and Voidable Contracts

To understand the law in this area we must consider the difference between *void* and *voidable* contracts, a subject that first arose in our discussion of infants' contracts. The distinction is important throughout the law of contracts. As we have said, to decide that a contract is void is to say that in law it was never formed at all: in this sense calling an agreement a void contract is a contradiction in terms — if it is void it is no contract. Nevertheless, through custom and convenience the term has long been used to describe agreements void from the beginning.

The results flowing from a declaration that a contract is void are logical enough and usually fair when only the two original parties are concerned: if A sells goods to B and the sale is declared void, it follows that ownership never passed from A to B; if B still has the goods, A recovers them and repays any part of the purchase price already received.

However, the consequences of finding a contract void are more far-reaching when A sells goods to B on credit and B resells the goods (which in law he does not own) to C, an innocent third party. The second sale is equally void because under common law B had no greater right to the goods than a thief would have, and cannot resell them. Consequently, the third party C does not acquire ownership although he has paid fair value for the goods and was unaware of the void sale between *A* and *B*. *C* must restore the goods to *A* and if he cannot, he will be liable to *A* (in the tort of conversion) for damages equal to their value. The common law recognizes no half measures: if *B* did acquire title (ownership) to goods under a contract with *A*, he could transfer title to a third party — *A* would have no rights against the third party and could claim damages only from *B*, the vanished rogue. In the absence of active participation in a fraud by the third party *C*, a common law court would not concern itself with the relative fault of *A*, in carelessly selling on credit to a rogue, and the third party in risking to buy from that rogue.

On the whole, declarations that a contract was void — with the harsh consequences that follow — are more unfair to third persons than to sellers of goods; after all, those who take the risk of selling goods on credit enable rogues to dupe innocent third persons. However, as we shall see, declarations that contracts were void were restricted by the common law courts to only a few situations, according to an abstract analysis that did little to take into account the fairness of the result.

The courts of equity took a much more flexible approach to granting a remedy to the victim of deceit. In situations where a common law court would refuse to declare a contract void and would leave the victim without a remedy, equity would declare it to be *voidable*, and would order that it be *set aside* or *rescinded*. This remedy became readily available for mistakes caused by wrongful misrepresentations, at least between the original parties to a contract; the court would set the contract aside, restore the property to the victim, and require him to return any benefit he might have received from the rogue (such as a down payment). While a court of equity recognized that at common law title had passed to the rogue, it would order him to restore both title and possession to the victim.

the rogue

ILLUSTRATION

A Co., the sole distributor of a certain brand of imported office machines, has received an advance sample of a revolutionary new word processor. *B* persuades *A* to sell and deliver the machine to her on the basis that *B* will test it and if it proves satisfactory will be prepared to buy at least 1000 units for her chain of retail electronics stores. In fact, *B* has lied: she has no chain of stores and intends to resell the machine to the highest bidder among several clients who may be interested in dismantling it and copying the innovations as quickly as possible. Fortunately, the next day one of the firms to whom *B* has offered the machine informs *A* Co. about *B*'s scheme. *A* serves *B* with a writ at once, demanding that the contract be set aside for deceit and the machine returned, on repayment of the purchase price by *A*. The court, in exercising its equitable powers, would grant *A* Co. its remedies.

On the other hand, equity recognized that new considerations of fairness entered the picture as soon as the rights of an innocent third party were affected. Equity drew back and would not deprive an innocent purchaser of goods obtained from the rogue. The party from whom the rogue obtained the goods was then limited to an action for damages against the rogue for the unpaid price of the goods or for the tort of deceit. Unfortunately, the rogue was usually penniless or had absconded and could not be found. Between the victim and the innocent third party, equity did not choose; it let the loss lie where it had fallen — invariably on the victim who parted with his property on the strength of the rogue's representations.

It is important to note that a third party, to receive this protection, must be *innocent* and have *paid value* for the goods. A victim's attempt to recover goods will not be frustrated by someone who buys from the rogue knowing about the rogue's fraud; equity will consider such a person as having no greater rights than the rogue himself. Thus, in our illustration above, if B had resold and delivered the word processor to one of her "clients", who intended to dismantle the machine and was aware of B's deception, A Co. could have recovered it from that client. If, however, the purchaser had innocently bought the machine for its own use, A would have had no claim against it. But innocence alone is not enough; the third party must have paid a price for the item. Equity will not permit a party who has received the machine as a gift, even without knowledge of the fraud, to retain it against A Co.

In summary, we can see that where a contract concerns only the two original parties, it may not matter whether the court declares it void or merely voidable. In either event, the court may order the return of property that has passed between the parties. But if the property has passed to an innocent purchaser, the original owner may recover it only if the original contract is declared void.

Mistake about the Identity of a Party to a Contract

The dire consequences of a finding that a contract is void are well illustrated by the English case of *Cundy v. Lindsay*[23] where the House of Lords decided that a mistake by the victim about the identity of the other party rendered the contract void. Lindsay, a manufacturer in Ireland, was persuaded to send goods on credit to a thief, Alfred Blenkarn. Blenkarn had signed an order for goods with an indistinct signature that appeared to be "Blenkiron & Co.", a reputable firm with offices on the same street but at a different number from that of Blenkarn. Lindsay did not check the street number but simply shipped the goods to Blenkarn, who then sold the goods to Cundy for cash and absconded. Cundy was unaware of the fraud. The facts came to light when Lindsay attempted to collect payment: he subsequently sued Cundy for the goods. Lindsay claimed that the sale to Blenkarn was void. The court accepted this argument. It held that as Lindsay intended to sell to "Blenkiron & Co." and only to them, Blenkarn obtained the goods entirely without Lindsay's consent. Thus, there was no contract between Lindsay and Blenkarn, and the ownership of the goods remained with Lindsay: Cundy was required to return them or pay damages. *is the victim of the 3rd party*

Unfortunately, the decision in *Cundy v. Lindsay* offends the general principle that between two innocent persons, both victims of a fraud, the loss should be borne by the more careless of the two. Lindsay had shipped goods on credit without a careful check of the street address of Blenkiron & Co., and it was as a result of this carelessness, however slight, that Blenkarn gained possession of the goods. On the other hand, Cundy was blameless. Between Cundy and Lindsay we should have expected that it would be Lindsay who would bear the loss, yet such was not the result. The decision that the contract was void led to a hardship upon Cundy. It is not surprising, therefore, that the courts attempted to limit the application of this case.

---

[23] (1878), 3 App. Cas. 459.

The year after *Cundy v. Lindsay*, in *King's Norton Metal Co. v. Edridge*,[24] a thief had once again obtained goods on credit. This time the fraud was more shrewdly executed: the thief, Wallis, sent an order using an impressive letterhead with the picture of a large factory and the name of a nonexistent firm, Hallam & Co., purporting to have international offices; he obtained goods from the plaintiffs, a firm of metal manufacturers. Wallis resold the goods and absconded. The metal manufacturers, claiming that their contract with Hallam & Co. was void, sought to recover the goods from the innocent purchaser; but the action failed. It was held that they must have intended to contract with someone, and since there was no "Hallam & Co.", it could only be with the writer of the letter, even though he was a very different person from the party they had in mind. Accordingly, the court held that the contract was only voidable for fraud and that title to the goods had passed to Wallis! The plaintiff could recover the goods from Wallis so long as he still had them, but meanwhile Wallis could pass title to an innocent purchaser. The decision is technically distinguishable from *Cundy v. Lindsay* because in the *King's Norton* case there was only one party with whom the vendor might have contracted (Wallis alias Hallam & Co.) and not two separate entities as in *Cundy v. Lindsay* (Blenkarn, and Blenkiron & Co.). Though an innocent party may perhaps be excused for failing to see the significance of this distinction, the *King's Norton* case has the virtue of limiting the application of *Cundy v. Lindsay* to fewer situations.

In *Cundy v. Lindsay* and the *King's Norton* case, the parties dealt by mail at a distance. The same difficulty about identity can occur when the innocent party and the rogue confront each other in person. Fortunately the inconsistency of the mail cases was eventually resolved in the personal contact cases. In 1918 in *Phillips v. Brooks*,[25] the English Court of Appeal held that the plaintiff jeweller intended to deal with the man who appeared in his shop, even though the man falsely identified himself as a reputable and wealthy member of the community whom the jeweller knew by name, but not in person. The contract was voidable and not void. As a result, a subsequent innocent purchaser from the rogue was able to maintain his right to keep the fraudulently obtained pearls, despite the jeweller's claim that he intended to deal only with the reputable named person and not the rogue who had appeared in his shop.

After some contradictory decisions, the English Court of Appeal in *Lewis v. Averay*[26] confirmed the reasoning in *Phillips v. Brooks*. In the later case, a rogue had obtained a car, paying for it with a bogus cheque, while impersonating a well-known English movie actor. The Court held the contract was merely voidable and protected an innocent purchaser who acquired the car from the rogue.

Canadian courts have followed the reasoning in *Phillips v. Brooks*. In one case,[27] the facts were very much like those in *Lewis v. Averay*. In another case, the Supreme Court of Canada held that a car-rental company had "consented" to the rental of a car to a rogue who gave a false identity.[28] On this basis, it would appear that innocent subsequent purchasers are better protected when the first transaction takes place face to face than when the transaction takes place through the mail.

---

[24] (1879), 14 T.L.R. 98.
[25] [1918-19] All E.R. 246.
[26] [1971] 3 All E.R. 907.
[27] Ellyatt v. Little, [1947] 1 D.L.R. 700.
[28] Terry v. Vancouver Motors U-Drive Ltd. and Walter, [1942] 1 W.W.R. 503.

Mistake about the Nature of a Signed Document

Non Est Factum

A third party may be affected by a mistake when a person is persuaded to sign a document that has been misrepresented to him either innocently or fraudulently. The victim may raise the plea known as *non est factum* ("it is not my doing"). If the court accepts the plea, it is good even against third parties who believe they have acquired rights under the document. In this respect the effect of a successful plea of *non est factum* is similar to the result in *Cundy v. Lindsay*: an innocent third party may suffer. The plea originated in medieval times when most people could not read or write. A person would bind himself to a written document by making a mark or impressing his family seal, but he had to rely on the honesty of the literate party who presented the document to him. If he were later sued for breach of the terms of the document, he could plead that it was not his deed, because of a serious misrepresentation. In medieval times the result was reasonable. The result would still be reasonable today if it were limited in application to illiterate and blind persons and those who read and write only in a foreign language — persons who must rely on the honesty of others.

Unfortunately, the plea of *non est factum* was later extended to literate persons who were simply duped into signing documents without reading them. As harsh as the result is from the point of view of innocent third parties who rely on the document without knowledge of the misrepresentation, the signer could nonetheless escape liability.

For more than one hundred years there was great uncertainty about the rules governing a signer's liability for a mistakenly signed document. At one point the courts limited use of the defense of *non est factum* to persons who had not been careless; if the signer had been careless he would be bound by his careless act.[29] Unfortunately, this sensible rule was subsequently restricted by an English court to cases where the document was a negotiable instrument such as a cheque. In all other cases a careless signer might still escape liability.[30] As recently as 1956, the Supreme Court of Canada followed this rule.[31]

 In 1971, in *Saunders v. Anglia Building Society*[32] the House of Lords returned to the rule that a careless signer could not avoid liability by pleading *non est factum*. Despite the fact that the plaintiff was a widow 78 years of age who had just broken her glasses, the court found her careless in signing a deed she had been unable to read, and thus bound by subsequent dealings in the property transferred in the document. In 1982, in *Marvco Color Research Ltd. v. Harris*,[33] the Supreme Court of Canada decided to overrule its 1956 decision and to follow the House of Lords decision in the *Saunders* case. Mr. Justice Estey said:

> This principle of law is based not only upon the principle of placing loss on the person guilty of carelessness, but also upon recognition of the need for certainty and security in commerce [of those persons who rely on signed documents].

---

[29] Foster v. Mackinnon (1869), L.R. 4 C.P. 704.

[30] Carlisle and Cumberland Banking Co. v. Bragg, [1911] K.B. 489.

[31] Prudential Trust Co. v. Cugnet (1956), 5 D.L.R.(2d) 1.

[32] [1971] A.C. 1004.

[33] [1982] 2 S.C.R. 744.

...the application of the principle...must depend on the circumstances of each case....The magnitude and extent of the carelessness, the circumstances which may have contributed to such carelessness, and all other circumstances must be taken into account...before a court may determine whether estoppel shall arise... so as to prevent the raising of this defence.[34]

It seems then that a person who relies on a document that he did not personally see signed still takes some risk: the signer might be blind, illiterate, or at least unable to read English — or perhaps rarely, might be literate but found by a court not to have been careless.

MISTAKES IN PERFORMANCE

What happens when a party "overperforms" an existing obligation by paying more money than in fact is owed? When it performs in a mistaken belief that an obligation existed, as when an insurance company pays a claim and then discovers that the loss arose from a risk not covered by the policy? When someone simply pays the wrong person? When the "lucky" recipient knows that the payment does not belong to him, the answer is straightforward: he cannot "snap up" a benefit that belongs to another person, and a court will order him to restore it. The question becomes more difficult when the recipient honestly but mistakenly believes that he is entitled to the benefit. A gradually expanding development in this area of *quasi-contract* (so called because the obligations may not arise as a direct result of contractual relations between the parties) has been the concepts of *unjust enrichment* and *restitution*; if, given all the circumstances a court finds that it would be an unjust enrichment to allow the recipient to keep the benefit, it will order restitution by finding a duty implied by law to repay it.

We must be careful not to oversimplify the law in this area by substituting a lay person's intuition about what is "unjust" when a sophisticated analysis of the commercial context is needed. For instance, as we have seen in Chapter 7, if a benefit is accepted in an honest and not unreasonable belief that it is tendered in settlement of an outstanding dispute, the party receiving the sum will not be regarded as having been unjustly enriched even when it later appears that he could not have enforced his claim by court action.

Questions for Review

1. What two main types of mistake are distinguished in this chapter? Identify a reported case that illustrates each type.
2. In what circumstances may neither party have a remedy for mistake about the terms of a contract?
3. What is meant by "snapping up an offer"? What is the remedy?
4. What conditions must be satisfied before a court will order rectification? Under what circumstances is a court unlikely to grant such a remedy?
5. What criticism can be made of the old legal rule that a court will recognize only

---

[34] *Ibid.* at 787-89.

mistakes that affect the "substance" of the subject-matter but not those merely relating to its "quality"? What were the courts trying to accomplish in creating these categories?

6. Who may raise the defence of *non est factum*? What problem does this raise for third persons? Describe the main restriction in raising the defence of *non est factum*.

7. You have just purchased some expensive second-hand dining-room furniture for cash. Unknown to you, the person who sold it to you had himself just bought it on credit from the original owner by representing himself to be another person with good credit standing. Which rule would you prefer: (i) a rule that mistakes about the identity of the other contracting party render the contract void; (ii) a rule that such mistakes render the contract voidable? Explain. Which cases are relevant?

Problems

Problem 1

Brown was the owner of a service station located on a two-lane highway. She learned that a new, four-lane freeway would bypass her service station, and then put the station up for sale. Seferis purchased the property from Brown for $125 000 and two months later learned that the highway on which it was located would be superseded by the new freeway, to be constructed within the next four years. Seferis then commenced action to have the contract set aside. Should he succeed? (See *Bell v. Lever Brothers, Ltd.*, [1932] A.C. 161 per Lord Atkin at 224.)

Problem 2

Boucher, acting as an agent for an undisclosed principal, secured an option on a farm belonging to Wright. By the terms of the option agreement Wright undertook in return for a payment of $200 to hold open for six months an offer to sell the farm for $60 000 and not to dispose of it in the meantime.

After Boucher had obtained this and similar options on adjoining property, he disclosed that he was acting for Canada Steel Car Co. Ltd., which would build a large plant in the district. As the company was an important one, the value of the property in the area was generally enhanced. When Canada Steel Car Co. Ltd. tried to exercise its option, Wright refused to convey her property according to the agreed terms. Canada Steel Car Co. Ltd. then brought an action against her for specific performance. In defending the action, Wright claimed that Boucher's failure to disclose the name of the purchaser induced her to sell at too low a price. Discuss the merits of this defence.

Problem 3

In negotiations preliminary to the sale of Argentine hare skins by Messrs. Colin & Shields to Hartog, the parties had discussed price on the basis of price per skin, the way in which Argentine hare skins are generally bought and sold. Afterwards Colin & Shields wrote to Hartog offering to sell to him 10 000 Argentine hare skins at $10\frac{1}{4}$ pence per pound. There are approximately three pieces to a pound of Argentine hare skins. When Colin & Shields realized they had mistakenly quoted a price in terms of pounds instead of pieces, they attempted to withdraw their offer, but by this time Hartog had already mailed his letter of acceptance. Colin & Shields refused to deliver the skins on the basis of "per pound" price. Hartog sued for damages for breach of contract of a sale of goods. Should he succeed? (See *Hartog v. Colin & Shields*, 1939] 3 All E.R. 566.)

Cases

Case 1

Powelson was interested in purchasing a commercial building owned by Samuelson and early in January told Samuelson that he would like to take an option on it for a period of six months. Powelson prepared a form of written option agreement in which he set the sale price at $200 000: both parties signed the agreement and Powelson paid Samuelson the agreed sum of $5000 for the option. It was dated January 24 and stated in part, "The term of the option is to be for 171 days from the date hereof, expiring at the hour of 11:50 p.m. on the 24th day of July, next."

On July 23 Powelson gave Samuelson written notice that he was exercising the option to purchase. In the meantime, property values had increased and Samuelson refused to convey the property, claiming that the option period of 171 days from the date of the document had expired on July 14. Powelson brought an action asking for rectification of the option contract and for specific performance.

Outline the arguments for each of the parties in this dispute and indicate whether the action should succeed.

Case 2

H. Golightly is a professional football player who has played for the Toronto Mercenaries ("Mercs") for the past three football seasons. The Toronto Mercs are a member of the Eastern Conference of the Trans-Canada Football League. Golightly lives in the southern United States during the off-season.

Golightly had an exceptionally good season last year and was in a good bargaining position for negotiating his salary for this season when he met with Rusty Trawler, the general manager of the Mercs last January. The parties discussed salary possibilities for the next two seasons in a tentative way but adjourned their meeting with a view of coming to final terms in early April.

In February, the Trans-Canada Football League had its annual meeting in Vancouver. At that meeting it was decided to increase the number of regular games scheduled to be played in the Eastern Conference from the usual 14 over many previous seasons to 16, commencing with the current season. By contrast, the Western Conference already had had a schedule of 16 games for several seasons; this decision brought the Eastern Conference in line with the Western Conference. It received wide publicity in the news media of the various cities with teams in the Eastern Conference.

Last April 3, Golightly telephoned Trawler from Biloxi, Miss. and they agreed to meet on April 6 in the offices of J. Berman, Q.C., Golightly's solicitor in Toronto. The meeting between Golightly, Trawler, and Berman lasted about three hours. Eventually it was agreed that Golightly should be paid $105 000 for the current season and $135 000 for the following year, plus further amounts for playoffs and bonuses; two separate contracts were signed to cover the two seasons. At the time, neither Golightly nor his lawyer, Berman, had any knowledge that the number of league games in the Eastern Conference had been increased to 16. In fact, the parties did not refer in any way to the number of games in their meeting in Berman's office. Trawler made no mention of the increased schedule. The contracts simply stated:

> The Player agrees that during the term of this contract he will play football and will engage in activities related to football only for the Club and will play for the Club in all its Conference's scheduled and playoff games ...

The contract also contained a clause to the effect that the player could be traded to a team in the Western Conference.

It was not until later, when Golightly reported for training, that he learned about the increase in the schedule. He then claimed that he would not have agreed to the salaries of $105 000 and $135 000 respectively had he known about this change; he would have bargained for more. On Berman's advice, he brought an action to have these contracts set aside with a view to their renegotiation.

Express an opinion, with reasons, about whether this action should succeed.

Case 3

Last year the Department of Public Works of the City of Saint John called for tenders for the construction of a water and sewage treatment plant according to detailed specifications. The Department issued as part of its required conditions for the submission of tenders a statement entitled "Information for Tenderers", one part of which read:

Tender Deposit

1. A deposit of $150 000 in the form of a certified cheque payable to the Department of Public Works, Saint John, must accompany each tender submitted.
2. Tenders must be submitted on or before 3:00 p.m., 4 July 1982.
3. Tender deposits will be returned to all tenderers other than the successful tenderer immediately following the selection of the successful tender.
4. A tenderer may withdraw or qualify its tender at any time up to the official closing time by submitting to the Department a letter bearing the appropriate signature and seal, as in its tender. The Secretary of the Department will mark thereon the time and date of receipt and will place the letter in the tender box. No telegrams or telephone calls will be considered.
5. The tenderer guarantees that if, following submission of its tender before the Department opens and considers all the tenders submitted, or before it has been notified that its tender has been recommended for acceptance, it withdraws its tender, the Department may retain the tender deposit for its use, and in compensation for the consequential necessity of having to invite and consider other tenders.
6. The tender deposit of the successful tenderer will be returned after the successful tenderer delivers to the Department a performance bond and accepts an offer by the Department to perform the work tendered for, on the terms set out in the tender.

In all, eight tenders with accompanying deposits were delivered to the Department of Public Works before the deadline on July 4. One of the tenders was submitted by Roberts Construction Co. It stated that the company was prepared to undertake the construction of the water and sewage treatment plant, as specified by the Department, for a price of $2 750 000.

Hudson, an employee of Roberts Construction Co., delivered the company's tender to the Department in person on the morning of July 4, and remained for the opening of the tenders at 3:00 p.m. At that time she learned that her employer's tender was much the lowest of the bids; in fact, the next lowest was for $3 400 000. From her prior experience, she felt that there must be something radically wrong and at 3:30 p.m. she phoned the general manager of Roberts Construction to report what had happened. On checking his copy of the tender he replied, "We're too low. I see now that we forgot to include two big items of overhead." At 4:10 p.m. on the same day, the general manager despatched a telex addressed to the Department of Public Works which read:

> Today we submitted our tender for the water and sewage treatment plant project and unfortunately, due to the rush of compiling our figures, we neglected to include in our price an amount of $750 000 for indirect labour and depreciation of equipment. Our lump sum tender should therefore be for $3 500 000 instead of for $2 750 000. Due to this unfortunate error we would appreciate being given the opportunity to show to you our estimate indicating the error, and request that we be permitted to withdraw our tender without penalty.

The Department of Public Works insisted that the Roberts Construction Co. had submitted the successful tender and sent the company a formal offer to engage it for the project at a price of $2 750 000. Roberts Construction refused to accept the offer. The Department then refused to return the deposit of $150 000 and Roberts Construction brought an action against it for a judgment ordering the return of the deposit.

Discuss with reasons the probability that this action will succeed.

CHAPTER 11

GROUNDS UPON WHICH A CONTRACT MAY BE IMPEACHED: MISREPRESENTATION, UNDUE INFLUENCE, AND DURESS

Misrepresentation and Torts

As we have noted in Chapters 4 and 5, a misrepresentation may amount to a tort when it is made fraudulently[1] or negligently.[2] A victim who relies reasonably on the assertion and suffers loss may recover from the wrongdoer. However, if a person makes an assertion neither fraudulently nor negligently but nevertheless it proves to be false, no tort has been committed and one who suffers a loss in relying on the statement has no claim in tort against its maker.

ILLUSTRATION

Andrews asks Barton, a stockbroker acquaintance, whether *X* Corporation is in sound financial condition, and Barton replies that she believes it to be very sound. Andrews then buys $25 000 worth of shares in *X* Corporation. Unknown to either Andrews or Barton, the company's president had just been charged with embezzling $2 000 000 and the company was insolvent at the time of Barton's assertion. Andrews' newly acquired shares are worthless and he has lost $25 000, but unless Barton should have known of *X* Corporation's difficulties, Andrews will have no claim against her.

A person who innocently makes a misstatement and later learns that it is false is under a duty to inform the other party of the true situation if it is not already too late to avoid injury. An innocent misrepresentation becomes fraudulent or negligent if the party responsible fails to correct it when in a position to do so.

Misrepresentation and Contracts

Misrepresentation most often occurs during preliminary bargaining that precedes formation of a contract. If a misrepresentation is "material", that is, if it is a statement that could reasonably be expected to influence the decision of a party hearing (or reading) it in favour of entering into a contract, a court may set the contract aside at the request of the innocent party. If a misrepresentation is fraudulent or negligent, it will grant damages as well as order rescission. However, when a misrepresentation is innocent, damages are not available as a remedy and an aggrieved party's remedy is restricted to the right to rescind. As we shall see in Chapter 17,[3] the right to rescind is limited by the rules developed by the courts of equity. In particular, if an aggrieved party cannot restore the subject-matter of the contract to the other party — for instance, because goods have been resold, consumed, or even have deteriorated substantially — the former will lose the right to rescind. Hence a party who has received less than fair value because of innocent misrepresentation may be left without any remedy.

---

[1] See section in Chapter 4, "Deceit".
[2] See section in Chapter 5, " Misrepresentation".
[3] Under "Equitable Remedies". Also: Waddams, *The Law of Contracts* (3rd ed.), pp. 413-21.

An aggrieved party may claim that a misrepresentation was actually a term of the subsequent contract. If the court accepts the claim, the party will be entitled to a remedy based on breach of contract. At one time, the courts distinguished sharply between pre-contract representations and express terms of a contract.[4] However, in recent years, they have been more willing to consider representations as having been incorporated into a subsequent contract and having become part of the contractual obligation of the maker of the statement. If a statement is an important inducement to enter into a contract, if the aggrieved party has suffered a substantial loss, and if there would otherwise be no remedy for an innocent misrepresentation because rescission is unavailable in the circumstances, a court may feel pressed by reasons of fairness to find that the statement has become a term of the contract. If a misrepresentation was made shortly before or at the time of entering into a contract, a court finds it easier to consider it a term of the agreement.[5] So too, courts have occasionally found statements about goods and services in advertisements and sales promotion material, read by a party before making a contract, to be incorporated in its terms.[6]

Remedies for breach of contract are separate from, and frequently more extensive than, remedies allowing for rescission for misrepresentation.[7] A general rule is that a plaintiff will not be granted a remedy he does not claim. If he sues for damages for fraudulent or negligent misrepresentation but does not also ask for rescission of the contract, he can secure only damages; if he fails to prove the fraud or negligence, he receives nothing. Since it can be difficult to predict whether a court will find one set of remedies or the other to be appropriate (occasionally it may find both available and give the aggrieved party a choice), a party may seek each remedy in the alternative with the choice left to the court.

CONSEQUENCES OF MISREPRESENTATION IN CONTRACTS

When a right to rescission for innocent misrepresentation exists, the party who relied on the misrepresentation must, upon learning the facts, renounce the agreement promptly; if she allows an unreasonable length of time to elapse without repudiating, or else takes further benefits under the contract, she will lose her right to rescind. If she has sustained out-of-pocket expenses in the performance of the contract, or has paid money to the other party before becoming aware of her right to rescind, she may be entitled to a money award known as an *indemnity* or *compensation* as a supplement to rescission.[8] Such loss must arise directly out of the performance of the contract, and the indemnity does not cover nearly as wide a variety of loss as does an award of damages.

In *Corbeil v. Appell*,[9] Appell hired a sales agent to arrange a sale of Appell's business. The agent represented to Corbeil, a prospective purchaser, that the gross receipts were from $35 to $40 daily. Corbeil asked if there were any records showing this daily

---

4   For example: Heilbut, Symons & Co. v. Buckleton, [1913] A.C. 30.
5   Dick Bentley Productions Ltd. v. Harold Smith Motors Ltd., [1965] 2 All E.R. 65. See also: Esso Petroleum Co. Ltd. v. Mardon, [1976] Q.B. 801.
6   Goldthorpe v. Logan, [1943] 2 D.L.R. 519; Murray v. Sperry Rand Corp. (1979), 96 D.L.R. (3d) 113.
7   See Chapter 17, sections on "Implications of Breach" and "Damages".
8   Whittington v. Seale-Hayne (1900) 82 L.T. 49.
9   [1950] 1 D.L.R. 159.

turnover, and the agent replied that Appell had no records but that the former owners of the business did have such records. Corbeil was introduced to the former owners, who did not produce any records but who confirmed in a general way the information given by the sales agent about daily gross receipts. Corbeil then purchased the business, delivering his car to Appell at the agreed value of $1000 as a down payment, and began to operate the business as of February 2, 1949. When he discovered that its revenue did not approach the amount indicated, he repudiated the purchase by letter dated February 8, 1949. He then sued for recovery of his car and damages for loss of its use, alleging fraud. The court held that fraud was not proved by these circumstances but that the contract might still be rescinded for innocent misrepresentation. The purpose of rescission is to restore the parties as nearly as possible to their position before they entered into the contract. Hence Corbeil was entitled to the return of his car and also to *compensation* for its loss of value by depreciation through use or accident.

In contracts for the sale of land, the right to rescission for innocent misrepresentation is lost once the transaction is completed and title to the property has been transferred. There are two main reasons for this rule. Purchasers are expected to "search the title", and to satisfy themselves by inspection of the property that it is as represented in the contract; if they are not satisfied they are expected to exercise a right to rescind *before* the time for completion of the transaction. Second, there is the danger that an outstanding right to recission would not be apparent to a third party who investigated the ownership of the land and relied on it, for example, to extend credit on the security of the mortgage. Only rarely will a court grant rescission after completion when a misrepresentation is not fraudulent.[10]

*O*PINION VERSUS FACT

A false assertion is a misrepresentation only if it is made as a statement of fact. Mere statements of opinion do not amount to misrepresentation and give no remedy for those who rely on them. The attitude of the law is lenient towards sellers who rhapsodize about their wares. A bookseller's claim that "this is the best textbook in its field" would leave a disillusioned purchaser without any remedy.

We can see most clearly the distinction between an expression of opinion and one of fact by contrasting two statements. If A says to B, "That property is worth at least $50 000 today", her remarks are no more than an expression of opinion. But if she says instead, "That property cost me $50 000", she has made a representation of fact.

Unfortunately, it is not always so easy to distinguish between statements of fact and opinion. Suppose a merchant wishing to sell some foreign goods says, "In my opinion these goods can be imported under the lower tariff rate in section ___ of the statute." It later appears that they cannot be imported under that section. In these circumstances the court might hold that the seller merely gave his opinion. But if in the view of the court the merchant is an expert in marketing these goods, or has purported to be one, the court may conclude that he made a misrepresentation; in this context an expert opinion is equivalent to a statement of fact.

---

[10] For an exception, see Northern & Central Gas Corp. Ltd. v. Hillcrest Collieries Ltd., (1975) 59 D.L.R. (3d) 533.

The phrase *assertion of fact* normally implies a representation in words, whether oral or written. However, conduct not expressed in words may constitute an assertion of fact. If a prospective buyer asks to see goods of a certain specification and in response a seller shows him some goods, the seller may by her conduct have asserted the fact that the goods meet the buyer's specifications.

Signed Documents and Misrepresentation by Omission

The act of signing a document, as we have noted in Chapter 6, creates a presumption that the signer has had notice of all its terms. Recent decisions have indicated that the presumption can be rebutted when a party (often a consumer) is expected to sign a document hurriedly and without an opportunity to read or understand it and when the other party has good reason to suspect that the signer may not fully comprehend the implications of signing the document. In the words of Professor Waddams (quoted with approval in a 1978 decision of the Ontario Court of Appeal):

> These cases suggest that there is a special onus on the supplier to point out any terms in a printed form which differ from what the consumer might reasonably expect. If he fails to do so, he will be guilty of a 'misrepresentation by omission', and the court will strike down clauses which 'differ from the ordinary understanding of mankind' or (and sometimes this is the same thing) clauses which are 'unreasonable or oppressive'. If this principle is accepted the rule about written documents might be restated as follows: the signer is bound by the terms of the document if, and only if, the other party believes on reasonable grounds that those terms truly express the signer's intention. This principle retains the role of signed documents as a means of protecting reasonable expectations; what it does not allow is that a party should rely on a printed document to contradict what he knows, or ought to know, is the understanding of the other party. Again this principle seems to be particularly applicable in situations involving the distribution of goods and services to consumers, though it is by no means confined to such situations.[11]

When a document is not signed, a party may not have the burden of rebutting a presumption about having had notice of the terms, and may therefore be able to avoid liability more readily as discussed in the "ticket" cases in Chapter 6.

Contracts Requiring Utmost Good Faith

In a number of circumstances, the concept of misrepresentation has been enlarged to include a failure to disclose pertinent information because one of the parties has access to vital information not available to the other. When the relationship between the parties leads to a special measure of trust being placed in one party by the other, it becomes

---

[11] Waddams, "Contracts Exemption Clauses Unconscionability Consumer Protection" (Comments), (1971) 49 *Can. Bar Rev.*, p. 578 at 590–591; cited in Tilden Rent-A-Car Co. v. Clendenning (1978), 18 O.R. (2d) 601 per Dubin, J.A. at 609.

unconscionable for the one to withhold information he knows to be material to the other's decision about entering into the contract.[12] The party "in a superior position of knowledge" then has a duty to inform the other so that he may have an idea of the risks he would be taking under the proposed contract. The facts of each case will determine the court's view. Although the courts have gradually widened the ambit of this duty, it would be a serious mistake to suppose that any contract will require the utmost good faith simply because one party knows something the other does not.

An important type of contract requiring *utmost good faith* is the contract of insurance: the party seeking insurance must disclose to the insurance company all pertinent aspects of the risk he is asking it to assume so that it may make an informed judgment about whether to provide the insurance coverage requested and fix a rate commensurate with the risk. A person who is applying for life insurance, for example, must disclose everything about her state of health that will be of value to the insurer in deciding whether to accept or reject her application. An insurance company can avoid its obligation to pay the insurance money to her estate or beneficiaries if the insured person withheld such information when applying for the insurance. Similarly, an applicant's failure to disclose that she has been refused life insurance by other companies constitutes a breach of good faith and hence a misrepresentation.

The requirement of the utmost good faith in applying for fire insurance is governed by statute in each of the provinces.[13] In *Sherman v. American Institute Co.*[14] the policy-holder, when applying for fire insurance, failed to disclose that he had had a previous fire and that the insurance company affected had then refused to continue the insurance protection. The insured property was damaged by fire again, and on these facts coming to light the insurance company refused to pay the insured. It was held that the insured's conduct constituted a fraudulent omission within the terms of the Insurance Act: the insurance company was not obligated to pay the insurance money.

Public liability insurance presents a special difficulty: an insured may have failed to disclose important information, justifying the insurer in refusing to pay a claim; however, an innocent third party, say a passenger injured by the negligence of the insured, would be unable to claim from the insurer. If the insured did not itself have sufficient assets to pay the passenger's claim, the innocent passenger would be the one to suffer the loss as a result of the insured party's non-disclosure *and* negligence. Accordingly, there may be a strong public interest in requiring that insurance to cover harm to third parties be binding, despite the breach of utmost good faith by the insured. The insurer would itself then have to take greater precautions to investigate the safety of the insured's operations before agreeing to insure. A recent decision of the Supreme Court has left the law in this area uncertain.[15]

Another type of contract in which one party typically has special access to information is a subscription for the purchase of shares or bonds in a corporation. The promoters or directors naturally know more about the corporation's affairs and prospects than do the investing public from whom they are soliciting subscriptions. The corporation usually

---

[12]   Lloyd's Bank Ltd. v. Bundy, [1974] 3 All E.R. 757 at 765.
[13]   See, for example: Insurance Act, R.S.B.C. 1979, c. 200, s. 220; R.S.O. 1990, c. I-8, s. 148; R.S.N.S. 1989, c. 231, Sched. to Part VII, s.1.
[14]   [1937] 4 D.L.R. 723.
[15]   Coronation Insurance Co. v. Taku Air Transport (1991), 85 D.L.R. (4th) 609.

gives the investing public information about a new issue of shares or bonds in a statement issued called a *prospectus,* or sometimes in other documents such as circulars, letters, or notices published in newspapers. All these documents present tempting opportunities for misrepresentation of a corporation's financial position by non-disclosure.[16] The various statutes comprising our corporations and securities legislation now require a disclosure of information in such documents in sufficient detail that directors, simply by omitting pertinent information, are more likely to be liable for violating the statute than for violating the common law.[17] As we shall see in Chapter 32, the securities acts of most of the provinces require that in many instances prospectuses be approved by the provincial securities commission or another government body before the shares can be offered to the public.

We have noted that generally a buyer of goods must take them with their defects unless some fact about their quality has been misrepresented. Certain qualifications to this doctrine of *caveat emptor* are discussed in Chapter 18 on the sale of goods. For example, *caveat emptor* applies only to quality or condition of the goods, not to ownership. A seller implies that he has the right to sell goods and to transfer full ownership free from any claims, simply by offering the goods for sale. Failure to disclose an outstanding claim will entitle the buyer to rescission. Although the buyer's right to rescind arises from a breach of an implied term rather than from a duty to disclose, the result is the same as if utmost good faith about ownership had been required of the seller.

A purchaser of an interest in land has, if anything, less protection against undisclosed faults of the property. If the vendor has made no representations, the purchaser must take it with all its faults.[18] Even if the vendor's ownership is subject to the claims of other persons, he need not disclose these claims. In the absence of representations by the vendor, the law presumes that the vendor offers to sell only the interest he has in the land. The purchaser can protect himself only by making a thorough investigation of title. In some cases, however, a court may imply a representation if non-disclosure amounts to fraud. For example, *A* purports to sell a piece of land to *B*, when in fact she occupies it only as a tenant, and is not the owner. The court would find that A impliedly represented herself as owner, and grant rescission to *B*.

The requirement of utmost good faith almost invariably exists in a continuing business relationship. Partnership depends on mutual trust, and accordingly, partners owe a general duty of utmost good faith to each other in all their transactions. Similarly, directors and officers owe a duty of good faith toward their corporation.

---

[16] See Gower, *The Principles of Modern Company Law* (4th ed.), p. 379. London: Stevens & Sons Ltd., 1979. "Contracts to acquire securities, whether from the company itself or from an existing holder, are not within the traditional category of contracts under which there is a positive duty to disclose all material facts. Nevertheless the difference between them and fully-fledged contracts uberrimae fidei [utmost good faith] is perhaps more apparent than real. Especially is this so when the content of the prospectus is prescribed by law."

[17] See, for example: Securities Act, R.S.O. 1990, c. S-5, s. 1(1) para. 25, 56, 122.

[18] In recent years the courts have gradually increased protection to purchasers with regard to serious defects that it would be impossible for them to discover. See, for example, Sevidal v. Chopra (1987), 64 O.R. (2d) 169, where the court held that the vendor had a duty to disclose that radioactive soil had been found on the property after the contract was made but before completion date.

Undue Influence ✓ — *voidable contract*

Undue influence is the domination of one party over the mind of another to such a degree as to deprive the latter of the will to make an independent decision. A contract formed as a result of undue influence is voidable at the option of the victim. The victim may avoid the contract only if he acts promptly after he is freed from the domination. If he acquiesces or delays, hoping to gain some advantage, the court will refuse to assist him.

Generally, undue influence arises where the parties stand in a special relationship to each other; one party has a special skill or knowledge causing the other to place confidence and trust in him. Typical examples of this relationship are doctor and patient, lawyer and client, minister and parishioner, parent and child. Sometimes undue influence arises when one party is temporarily in dire straits and will agree to exorbitant and unfair terms because he is desperate for aid.

ILLUSTRATION

A whaling ship three years at sea sailed into a thick fog near the Bering Strait and ran upon rocks. The coast was barren and the ocean navigable only two months in the year: winter was expected within two or three weeks. Another ship came along, res- cued the crew, and bought the cargo of whale oil at a bargain price, to which the captain of the wrecked ship readily agreed. The owners of the wrecked ship later suc- cessfully repudiated the contract for the sale of the whale oil.[19]

A party alleging undue influence must satisfy the court that the circumstances were such that domination was probable. He may do so relatively easily if a special relationship existed: the law presumes that undue influence was exerted in contracts advantageous to the party in the dominant position, as for example in a contract between a doctor and a patient in which the patient promises to sell the doctor an asset for a small fraction of its value. The absence of a special relationship makes it rather more difficult for the party alleging undue influence to make his case, but he still may be able to show, for example, that he was in a desperate state of misfortune at the time of the contract.

Once the alleged victim shows that circumstances likely to lead to undue influence existed, the burden shifts to the dominant party. If he is to save the contract, the dominant party must prove that undue influence was *not* exerted by him. He will often find the task of proving the lack of undue influence almost impossible. The courts are concerned that these circumstances should not be used as a device to exploit the weaker party. Sometimes the advantage taken of weakness on the other side is referred to as "fraud" or "constructive fraud", but as Lord Selborne has put it:

> Fraud does not here mean deceit or circumvention; it means an unconscientious use of the power arising out of these circumstances and conditions; and when the relative position of the parties is such as *prima facie* to raise this presumption, the transaction cannot

---

[19] Post v. Jones (1856), 60 U.S. 618.

stand unless the person claiming the benefit of it is able to repel the presumption by contrary evidence, proving it to have been in point of fact fair, just and reasonable.[20]

The most important factors in determining whether there is undue influence are the degree of domination of the stronger party, and the extent of the advantage he has received (that is, the unfairness of the bargain). The degree of domination is often difficult to ascertain. Domination involves questions of personality; by contrast, unfairness can generally be measured against the market value of the goods or services traded in a contract and is more easily judged.

Undue influence is somewhat more difficult to prove between husband and wife than in the other relationships, because the law presumes that at various times each party may well desire to confer a benefit on the other without exacting a good "price" in return. However, undue influence may arise, especially if a husband is a businessman and has persuaded his wife, who has had little or no business experience, to pledge her separate wealth as security for his business transactions. Two cases illustrate how undue influence may be found in the husband-wife relationship. In the first, a broker to whom a sum of money was owing either suggested or acquiesced in a misrepresentation by a husband; the husband obtained promissory notes from his wife and made them payable to the broker. The wife later avoided her liability on the notes.[21] In the second case a wife surrendered to a bank all her extensive separate estate in settlement of her husband's debts, in a series of transactions extending over a period of eight years. She was a confirmed invalid who had never had any advice that could be called independent, and had acted in passive obedience to her husband. The only lawyer with whom she had any dealings was the solicitor of the bank and of her husband. The transfers of her property were set aside and recovered for the benefit of her estate.[22]

Sometimes a person chooses of his own free will to confer a benefit on another by contract, but subsequent events bring a change of heart and a claim of undue influence; or the promisor may die, and his executor or heirs may then try to avoid the contract on grounds of undue influence. After the benefit has been promised but before it is actually conferred, the allegedly dominant person, relying on the contract, may enter into further obligations. He may, for example, make a contract with a builder to erect a house on a piece of land, relying on an earlier contract in which another person undertook to sell him the land at a very low price. If a court set aside the contract for the sale of the land because of undue influence the dominant party would have to break the second contract for the construction of the house, and would become liable for payment of damages to the builder.

To avoid such risks whenever undue influence is a possibility, the dominant party would be wise to ask the other party to obtain independent legal advice about his rights and duties before making the agreement. Not only will the suggestion to get advice tend to refute undue influence, but testimony of the independent lawyer, not associated with the transaction, that he explained the nature of the transaction and that the other party freely and with full knowledge made the commitment, will usually be conclusive evidence against the claim. A lawyer confronted with a situation where undue influence may

---

[20] Aylesford v. Morris (1873), L.R. 8 Ch. 484, at 490.
[21] Cox v. Adams (1905), 35 S.C.R. 393.
[22] Bank of Montreal v. Stuart, [1911] A.C. 120. See, also, Bertolo v. Bank of Montreal (1986), 57 O.R. (2d) 577.

exist will almost always send the weaker party to some other completely independent lawyer. The circumstance often arises when a husband brings his wife to sign documents in which she is to guarantee proposed loans for her husband's business. The lawyer will usually suggest several lawyers' names and ask the wife to choose one at random. She will then visit the other lawyer alone with all relevant documents, have them explained carefully, pay the lawyer for his time, and return with a certificate signed by the lawyer stating exactly what took place in his office. Although this procedure seems overly cautious, it is inexpensive and may save the husband or the creditor untold difficulties if later the possibility of undue influence is raised. And occasionally, after receiving independent legal advice, a wife may well have second thoughts and refuse to sign the documents.

A situation that invites undue influence often arises in contracts of loan. The borrower may be in a financial crisis and desperate for money: he agrees to any exorbitant rate of interest at the time. Later he finds that he cannot repay the debt because the interest is so high: it is all he can do to pay the interest regularly. The result of these loans is almost a form of bondage. The common law remedies discussed above are available, of course, but many jurisdictions have recognized that loans present a special problem and have passed statutes to provide additional remedies. Among the most important acts are the federal Small Loans Act,[23] which regulates the maximum rate of interest chargeable on loans up to $1500, and the federal Interest Act,[24] which sets out the method by which interest must be calculated in various types of loans. Several of the provinces have passed acts providing for the relief of debtors generally from highly oppressive transactions.[25]

Undue influence may also arise through fear of prosecution of a near relation.[26] Parents may be prepared to go to great lengths to save their child from prosecution for a misdemeanour, and sometimes a person in possession of the necessary evidence has elected not to press for prosecution following a promise of money from the parents. The matter is very close to the criminal offence of blackmail even though no express threat may have been made; presumably such activities would not come to light until the parent dies and the executor refuses to pay, or until the child dies and the possibility of prosecution ceases.

Undue influence is often an issue in disputes not involving contracts: it is frequently raised when a gift has been made and the donor wishes to recover the gift, and perhaps most often when a bequest has been made under a will. Generally speaking, the principles governing undue influence in these circumstances are the same as in contract.

Courts seem somewhat more willing than formerly to recognize a category of unconscionable contracts, whether as an application of the law relating to undue influence, as an extension of the concept of utmost good faith, or as a separate basis of complaint under the larger rubric of "constructive fraud". In an English case on this question, Lord Denning said:

> Gathering all together, I would suggest that through all these instances there runs a single thread. They rest on 'inequality of bargaining power'. By virtue of it, the English law gives relief to one who, without independent advice, enters into a contract on terms which are

---

[23]   R.S.C. 1985, c. 46, s. 347.

[24]   R.S.C. 1985, c. I-15, ss. 4 – 10.

[25]   See Unconscionable Transactions Relief Act, R.S.M. 1987, c. U20, s. 3; R.S.O. 1990, c. U-2, s. 2; Money-Lenders Act, R.S.N.S. 1989, c. 289, ss. 4, 5.

[26]   Kaufman v. Gerson, [1904] 1 K.B. 591.

very unfair or transfers property for a consideration which is grossly inadequate, when his bargaining power is grievously impaired by reason of his own needs or desires, or by his own ignorance or infirmity, coupled with undue influences or pressures brought to bear on him by or for the benefit of the other. When I use the word 'undue' I do not mean to suggest that the principle depends on proof of any wrongdoing. The one who stipulates for an unfair advantage may be moved solely by his own self-interest, unconscious of the distress he is bringing to the other.[27]

We must emphasize, however, that although inequality of bargaining power has become an important consideration before the courts, by no means has it replaced the need for sophisticated legal analysis and careful understanding of the business setting of transactions. Courts insist first on a clear understanding of the problem under consideration; only then will they apply, with restraint, the general principle of unconscionability. And for good reason: it is essential that courts do not lightly upset normal habits of reliance on bargains seriously made. The mere fact that with hindsight a contract looks like a "bad deal" does not make it unconscionable.

Duress

Duress consists in actual or threatened violence or imprisonment as a means of coercing a party to enter into a contract. The effect of duress is similar to that of undue influence: the contract is voidable at the option of the victim. The threat of violence need not be directed against the party being coerced — it may be a threat to harm the victim's spouse, parent, or child.

A situation closely resembling duress arises when one party has possession of the goods of another and wrongfully refuses to return them unless the owner promises to give the wrongful possessor some benefit. Suppose A had arranged a month's holiday and stored her antique sports car at a garage for $100, paid to the garage owner before leaving. While A was away the garage owner sold his business to B without informing him that A had prepaid the storage charge. When A came to pick up her car B demanded a further $100. After paying the $100 under protest, A obtained her car. If she wishes to sue B for the return of the money, she need not rely on duress; she can more easily prove that there was no right to the payment. There was in fact no contract at all with B. Since the payment was certainly not a gift, A would recover her money. In addition, if B's conduct had deprived A of the use of the car, she could recover damages for his wrongful possession. Accordingly the remedies available are adequate to protect A without using duress as a cause of action.

Historically, duress was a concept recognized by the common law courts and was narrowly construed by them. Today duress is still strictly confined by the courts to the circumstances described above. In contrast, the concept of undue influence was developed by the courts of equity to fill a gap and give remedies in circumstances not covered by the concepts of fraudulent misrepresentation and of duress. As a result, the concept of undue

---

[27]   Lloyds Bank Ltd. v. Bundy, *supra* note 12, quoted with approval in McKenzie v. Bank of Montreal (1975), 55 D.L.R. (3d) 641 at 652.

influence is wider ranging and more flexible than the other two concepts and, as Lord Selborne noted, includes circumstances that would not otherwise be called fraud.

Questions for Review

1. What is the difference between innocent and fraudulent misrepresentation?
2. Under what circumstances may it be important for a victim of misrepresentation to show that it was fraudulent?
3. In what circumstance will a court consider the adequacy of consideration as relevant?
4. In what respect is the application of the rule "let the buyer beware" (*caveat emptor*) modified in our law?
5. Which claim provides the broader remedy to a victim of misrepresentation — damages or "compensation"?
6. Under what circumstances does a victim of misrepresentation lose the right to rescind?
7. "The act of signing a document creates a presumption that the signer had notice of all its terms." How can this presumption be rebutted?
8. Why does the law recognize a separate category of contracts requiring "the utmost good faith"?
9. If a person sues for damages for fraudulent misrepresentation and the court decides that the misrepresentation was innocent, will it nonetheless set the contract aside? Why should the court adopt this position?
10. What is the difference between undue influence and duress?

Problems

Problem 1

Wong purchased a car from Botswell Motors Ltd. relying on a representation of a sales agent that the car was new except for some minor use as a demonstrator. Botswell Motors Ltd., however, gave no warranty about satisfactory performance of the car for any period. Two days after his purchase Wong took the car to a mechanic, Morris, because of trouble with the gearshift, and learned that the car was not new but had been repainted. In fact, the car had first been sold to a taxi business and Botswell Motors Ltd. had taken it back because of alleged defects.

Three weeks after he bought the car Wong wrote a letter to Botswell Motors Ltd. claiming rescission of the contract and offering to return the car on repayment to him of the payments he had made to date on the price. Botswell Motors Ltd. refused. Wong continued to use the car for a further four months, incurring more expense at Morris' garage because of the gearshift, and continuing to plead with Botswell Motors to take the car back. He then commenced action against Botswell Motors. What remedies, if any, are available to Wong?

Problem 2

Smart was Hull's lawyer for many years. Smart not only handled legal matters for Hull, but gave him important advice on business matters as well. At one stage, Hull owed Smart about $8500 for professional services and Smart suggested to Hull that the account could be conveniently settled in full if Hull would transfer his new 33-foot sailboat to Smart. Hull demurred at first, but realizing how indispensable his relationship with Smart had been and how important it was that Smart should continue to respect the confidential nature of his private business affairs, he transferred the sailboat to Smart.

A few months later Hull's daughter, who greatly enjoyed sailing, returned from graduate studies in Europe and persuaded her father to sue for recovery of the sailboat. Explain how the onus of proof will operate in the resulting legal action, and indicate the probable outcome.

Problem 3

Matheson told Eastman, the owner of a large number of rented houses, that he wished to buy a house containing an extra suite suitable for renting. Eastman showed Matheson one of his houses with a separate basement suite. Matheson liked it and signed a contract to purchase the property from Eastman. Unknown to Matheson the suite was unlawfully rented, because no permit had been obtained to build the suite; nor could a permit be obtained, because the ceiling was lower than the local by-laws allowed. Eastman was aware of these facts when he showed Matheson the house and also knew that Matheson was ignorant of them. He also realized that Matheson believed the house was being offered as a house with a rentable basement suite, although Eastman had done nothing more than show the house to him after Matheson had made his initial inquiry. Upon learning the true facts, Matheson sued for rescission of the contract and for damages.

Give the argument for both sides and state what the decision should be. (See *Graham v. Legault* [1951] 3 D.L.R. 423.)

Problem 4

Mrs. Goodfellow had hairs on her face that she wanted removed. She saw an advertisement in a newspaper that read as follows:

HAIRS removed safely and permanently by ELECTROLYSIS.
No marks. No scars. Results guaranteed.
AGNES LOTT. 120 Brandon Blvd., Edmonton.

Goodfellow went to the Brandon Blvd. address, consulted with Lott, a registered nurse, and was accepted for treatment without any physical examination. She then submitted to a series of ten weekly treatments by electrolysis, for which she paid $25 a visit. The results were unsatisfactory. At the end of the treatments hair continued to grow on her face as before. Subsequent medical diagnosis confirmed that an organic disorder made electrolysis an ineffective treatment for hair removal in her case.

Goodfellow sued Lott for damages for breach of contract and in the alternative for damages for fraudulent misrepresentation. Explain which, if either, of these causes of complaint would provide a valid basis for the recovery of damages. (See *Goldthorpe v. Logan*, [1943] 2 D.L.R. 519.)

Cases

Case 1

In response to an advertisement offering a free trial lesson in modern dancing, Galt, a graduate nurse, entered into a contract with the Modern Dancing Studios for 15 two-hour lessons for $350. Before she had taken all the lessons, the dancing instructor,

Valentino, told her that she would become a wonderful dancer if she would go on and that if she agreed to more lessons she would "probably get the bronze medal for dancing". On St. Valentine's Day he gave her a rose, and in the course of a lesson whispered in her ear how wonderfully she danced. She eventually signed a second contract to take another 35 hours of dancing lessons for $650. A new instructor was then assigned to her, and all compliments and personal attention ceased. Galt brought action for rescission of the contract and return of the $650.

On what ground might such a contract be avoided? Should the action succeed? (For references, see *Greisshammer v. Ungerer and Miami Studios of Dancing* (1958) 14 D.L.R. (2d) 599; *Gaertner v. Fiesta Dance Studios Ltd.* (1973) 32 D.L.R. (3d) 639.)

Case 2

Irving Lambert advertised his Mercedes car for sale for $16 500. A rogue introducing himself as Ron Glover called on Lambert in the evening, tried the car and said he liked it. They then went to the apartment of Lambert's fiancée, where in the course of general social conversation the prospective purchaser represented himself as being connected with professional football, where R.A. Glover was a well-known coach. He said he would like to buy the car and take it away that night and wrote a cheque for $16 500 which he signed "R.A. Glover". When Lambert asked for some identification he brought out a pass to the local stadium bearing the name of R.A. Glover, a photograph of himself, and an official-looking stamp. Lambert then transferred his passenger motor vehicle permit to him and allowed him to take the car. Two days after Lambert deposited the cheque, his bank advised him that it had been forged and was worthless.

A few days later, Maria Agnelli, who had advertised for a car of this type, received a visit from a man who said he was Lambert and produced a motor-vehicle permit bearing Lambert's name and address. Agnelli bought the car for $14 800. Within the next three or four days, Agnelli discovered that the usual driver's manual was missing from the glove compartment and telephoned Lambert to ask for further information about the car. Both parties then learned the truth.

Lambert brought an action against Agnelli for return of the car. Discuss with reasons the probability of this action's succeeding.

Case 3

On arriving at Vancouver Airport, Mr. Clemson, a frequent traveller, rented a car from Tilford Car Rentals Ltd., as he had done many times before. The clerk asked him whether he wanted additional collision insurance coverage and, as usual, he said, "Yes." The clerk added a fee of $10 a day for this coverage. She then handed the contract to Clemson and he signed it in her presence. She was aware that he did not read the terms of the contract before signing it.

Clemson's signature appeared immediately below a printed statement which read, "I, the undersigned, have read and received a copy of above and reverse side of this contract." On the back of the contract, in small type and so faint on Mr. Clemson's copy as to be hardly legible, there was a series of conditions, one of which read:

> Notwithstanding the payment of an additional fee for limitation of liability for collision damage to the rented vehicle, customer shall be fully liable for all collision damage if vehicle is used, operated or driven off highways serviced by federal, provincial or municipal governments and for all damages to vehicle by striking overhead objects.

The clerk placed Clemson's copy of the contract in an envelope and gave him the envelope and car keys. He got in the car, placed the contract in the glove compartment and drove to a nearby shopping plaza to buy a gift. While driving in the plaza parking lot, he collided with another car, causing damage of $2500 to his rented car. The car rental agency claimed that he was personally liable for repairs under the terms of their contract. Clemson refused to pay for the car repairs and Tilford Car Rentals Ltd. sued him for breach of contract.

Outline the nature of the arguments available to Tilford Car Rentals Ltd. and of the defences available to Clemson. Express an opinion, with reasons, about whether the action is likely to succeed.

Case 4

GasCan Ltd. is an integrated oil refining and distributing company that sells its products through a chain of service stations. It owns the land on which the service stations are located and leases them to tenants through its real estate department. As is normal in these arrangements, tenants agree to buy all their gasoline and other products from GasCan.

GasCan wanted to find a tenant for one of its service stations that had become vacant. Barcza expressed an interest in leasing it. The manager of GasCan's real estate department told Barcza that the company's sales division had made a forecast of the estimated annual sales of gasoline at the station: 900 000 litres. Barcza made a rough cash flow projection and signed a five-year lease of the station at a rental of $10 000 a year.

The company's estimate proved to be entirely wrong. The annual volume of the service station proved to be only about 200 000 litres. It appeared that the real estate department of GasCan had consulted with the sales division and that between them they had honestly but foolishly made "a fatal error". A new clerk in the sales division had checked sales made by the former tenant, but had assumed that the figures were in gallons whereas they had already been converted to litres. He converted them a second time, making the figures four and a half times higher than they should have been.

Barcza, who was an experienced and diligent station operator, tried hard to make a success of the business, but there was nothing he could do to raise gasoline sales close to the estimate. Over a three-year period he lost money steadily and finally became insolvent.

What remedies could Barcza seek in an action against GasCan Ltd.? What defences would GasCan raise? Who should succeed? Explain.

Case 5

X. Turpi Company Ltd. was in financial difficulty and was being pressed by its bank to reduce its loan. As a "solution" to this problem the company's general manager had duplicate invoices prepared for some sales and reported this sales revenue twice in the accounts: the bank continued to extend credit for a further month on the strength of the falsified financial position.

At this point Good, the company's accountant, realized what was going on, refused to prepare further financial statements for the bank, and resigned. She then went to the bank manager and reported these matters to her.

The financial position of the X. Turpi Company Ltd. continued to deteriorate. In a desperate move, its officers (including the general manager) approached a local enterpreneur, Rich, to urge him to invest some capital in the company. They showed him a list of the inflated accounts receivable. Rich then went to the company's bank to inquire about its present standing with the bank. The bank manager told him that there was no risk because the company's receivables were comfortably in excess of the bank loan, and suggested that the company's problem was merely a temporary lack of financing. Rich then guaranteed the company's bank loan and deposited $60 000 in marketable shares as security for his guarantee.

In the course of his regular examination, the auditor for X. Turpi Company Ltd. discovered the falsification in the accounts and insisted on their correction as a condition for expressing an unqualified opinion on the fairness of the company's financial statements. On learning the facts, Rich spent several days at the company's office in the hope of straightening out its tangled affairs. He interviewed several present and former employees, including Good. He then sought to recover the $60 000 in marketable securities he had pledged to the bank. The bank manager advised him that the bank had already sold the shares and applied the proceeds to the liquidation of the company's bank loan.

Rich brought an action against the bank for damages equal to his loss. In defence, the bank pleaded that it owed no duty to him because he was not a customer of the bank. Should his action succeed?

Case 6

Virginia McGraw inherited a fruit farm in the Okanagan Valley when her aunt died five years ago. Two years ago, she befriended Val Lawton, a used-car sales agent, and allowed him to operate the fruit farm on the understanding they would live there together when they were married.

Lawton operated the farm at a loss but concealed the mounting debts from McGraw by intercepting her mail. He did his business at the Tower Bank, where from time to time he filed statements of largely fictitious assets as a basis for increasing loans. His main assets seem to have been an affable and suave appearance, McGraw's affection for him, and his long friendship with the bank manager.

The bank took possession of McGraw's car when finally Lawton defaulted on his bank loan: he had offered her car as collateral security, asserting that it was his. The bank manager soon learned that the car was in fact owned by McGraw but refused to return it to her until Lawton's loan was repaid. McGraw was sympathetic when the matter was explained to her at the bank, and she then applied to her credit union to borrow enough money to repay the bank and recover her car. Three weeks later she returned to the bank with her fiancée and the money required to get her car back. Before handing over the keys to her, the bank manager asked her to sign "this bunch of papers". He advised her that her signature was required "as a matter of formality only". She then signed the papers and was given the car keys.

Six months afterwards, the bank claimed from McGraw a half year's interest on a mortgage on her fruit farm, and she then discovered that the mortgage document had been among the papers she had signed at the bank. The bank proposed to use the mortgage in substitution for other amounts still owed by Lawton.

At this point McGraw broke off her relations with Lawton and on the advice of her lawyer sued the Tower Bank. In her action she asked to have the mortgage set aside and, in addition, claimed $1000 damages in tort as compensation for costs incurred from the wrongful seizure of her car and the loss of its use.

Explain with reasons whether, in your opinion, this action should succeed.

CHAPTER 12

THE REQUIREMENT OF WRITING

The Distinction between Substance and Form

The Types of Contract Affected by the Statute of Frauds

Essentials of a Written Memorandum

The Effect of the Statute on Contracts within its Scope

The Doctrine of Part Performance

Evidence Required by the Sale of Goods Act

Consumer Protection Legislation

THE DISTINCTION BETWEEN SUBSTANCE AND FORM

Contractual duties, like all other obligations in law, are abstract concepts. Although we speak of the formation of a contract, we mean it in a legal, not in a physical sense. The parties must, of course, have agreed to the terms of their contract. The contract may exist only in their recollection of the spoken words, or it may be recorded in a written document, on a magnetic tape, or stored in a computer. Thus the *substance,* the terms of the contract, may have a variety of physical *forms* or even no form at all, other than in the minds of the parties. The distinction between the substance of the contract and the form in which it is known to the parties is crucial: we must not confuse the two. For the purpose of this chapter the following categories of form are important:

(a) contracts whose terms are entirely oral;
(b) contracts some of whose terms are oral and some in writing;
(c) contracts whose terms are entirely in writing, whether all in one document or spread through several ocuments, such as a series of letters.

The terms of a contract remain the same whatever form they may take, but from a practical point of view it is almost always advantageous to have them in written form. In good business practice some record is kept of even the simplest transaction at the time it is made. Of course, the more complicated a contract becomes, the greater will be the convenience of a written record. Human memories are fallible, especially when burdened with many details, and common sense tells us that it is better to trust to written records than to mere memory whenever a contract is complicated or will take effect over a long time. Many disputes may be avoided by keeping accurate records. At this point we must distinguish between records kept as good business practice and the legal significance of these records. Records that are a valuable aid in business may not satisfy the legal requirement of writing, which we are about to discuss. Furthermore, as we shall see, a business record may even assist the other party in enforcing its claim if it should obtain possession of the record.

In disputes before the courts, written evidence of a contract will aid a judge in determining what the terms are and in resolving a conflict of testimony by the parties, each with a different recollection of the contract. But written evidence does not resolve all problems. Even when a court has ascertained the exact words of the contract, the words themselves may be open to several interpretations, and the court must decide their meaning in the particular contract before it. We shall discuss the interpretation of contracts in the next chapter.

At common law, once the terms are ascertained, a contract is equally effective whether it is in writing or merely oral. However, in 1677 the English Parliament passed a peculiar act known as the Statute of Frauds. It was passed apparently for special reasons arising out of the turmoil of the times and was concerned mainly with ownership and the transfer of ownership in land. After the civil war and the restoration of the monarchy, Parliament wished to settle title to real property by eliminating perjured testimony in suits concerning land — hence the use of the word "frauds" in the title of the Statute.[1]

---

[1] See Furmston, *Cheshire, Fifoot and Furmston's Law of Contract* (12th ed.), pp. 200 ff. For a recent discussion, see Fridman, "The Necessity for Writing in Contracts Within the Statute of Frauds", (1985) 35 U.T.L.J. 43.

Two sections in the Statute particularly affected contracts, and almost immediately after they came into force judges were unhappy about their effect on this area of the law. The Statute was poorly drafted and did not accomplish its vague purposes. Unfortunately, it became so much a part of the law that it was re-enacted or adopted virtually unchanged in most common law jurisdictions, including those of Canada and the United States. A notable change in the law occurred when England amended the act in 1954: British Columbia and more recently Manitoba have passed major amendments.[2] In the remaining common law provinces the Statute is in force in its original form.

The effect of the Statute of Frauds is to render certain types of contracts *unenforceable* unless they are in writing. Unfortunately, the types of contract selected do not make sense to us today. Parties to oral contracts are often able to avoid their obligations solely because these contracts have been held to come within the scope of the Statute: the contracts might be perfectly valid in every other respect. It has often been said that by defeating the reasonable expectations of parties, the Statute of Frauds promotes more frauds than it prevents. For this reason the courts have striven to limit the application of the Statute wherever possible. The results have not always been logical, but the Statute has certainly been hemmed in by exceptions.

The problem of deciding whether a contract is affected by the Statute of Frauds arises only when an otherwise valid contract has been made. The mere fact that a promise is in writing as required by the Statute does not make the promise binding. There is no contract even to be considered unless all the requirements for the formation of a contract, as discussed in earlier chapters, are fulfilled.

THE TYPES OF CONTRACT AFFECTED BY THE STATUTE OF FRAUDS

A Promise by an Executor or Administrator to Answer Damages out of His Own Estate

The executor or administrator of an estate may discover that a debt owing by the deceased is due at a time when it is not convenient to pay it out of the estate assets, possibly because these assets have not been sold for cash. The executor may promise the creditor to pay the debt out of his own money if the creditor does not press the claim, knowing that the estate will reimburse him later. However, unless the executor has made the promise in writing and signed it, the creditor will not be able to enforce it.

This class of contract is relatively unimportant because it applies to a narrow group of circumstances. We deal with it first only to consider the types of contract affected by the Statute of Frauds in the order listed in the Statute.

A Promise to Answer for the Debt or Default or Miscarriage of Another

In attempting to limit the application of the Statute, the courts have distinguished between two similar types of promises, a promise of *guarantee* and a promise of *indemnity*.

---

[2] Statute of Frauds, R.S.B.C. 1979, c. 393, s. 4; R.S.M. 1987, c. F-158.

A guarantee is a promise to pay only if the debtor defaults: "If he does not pay you, I will." The creditor must look to the debtor for payment, and only after the debtor has defaulted may the creditor claim payment from the guarantor. In contrast, a person who makes a promise to indemnify a creditor makes herself primarily liable to pay the debt. Accordingly, when the debt falls due the creditor may ignore its claim against the party who benefited from the indemnity and sue the person who gave the promise to indemnify. "Give him the goods and I will see that you are paid", would usually be a promise to indemnify.[3] A promise by a purchaser of a business to its employees to pay back-wages owed by the former owner would also be a promise to indemnify.

The courts have applied this part of the Statute of Frauds *only* to guarantees. A guarantee must be made in writing to be enforceable, but a promise to indemnify is outside the Statute and is enforceable without being in writing.

Even the class of guarantees which falls within the Statute has been narrowed: the courts have excluded those guarantees incidental to a larger contract where the element of guarantee is only one among a number of more important rights and duties created by the contract. In *Sutton & Co. v. Grey*,[4] Sutton & Co. were stockbrokers and members of the London Stock Exchange with access to its facilities. Grey was not a member, but he had contacts with prospective investors. The parties made an oral agreement by which Grey was to receive half the commission from transactions for his clients completed through Sutton & Co. and was to pay half of any bad debts that might develop out of the transactions. A loss resulted from one of the transactions. Sutton & Co. sued Grey for half the sum according to the agreement. Grey pleaded that his promise to pay half the loss was a guarantee and was not enforceable against him because it was not in writing. The court ruled that the whole arrangement between Sutton & Co. and Grey had been a much broader one than merely guaranteeing the payment of a debt owing by a particular client, and that the Statute of Frauds should not apply. The agreement was thus enforceable, and Sutton & Co. obtained judgment against Grey for half the loss.

A further illustration of this approach concerns the liability of a *del credere agent*. Not only does he arrange the sale of his principal's goods, but he also guarantees payment by the buyer. If the buyer defaults the agent must pay for the goods. For this additional protection the seller pays the *del credere* agent a higher commission than an ordinary sales agent would receive. The courts have held that the main element of a *del credere* contract is the agency relationship and that the promise of guarantee is merely subsidiary. Accordingly, an oral contract for the services of a *del credere* agent (including his guarantee of customers' debts) does not come under the Statute and is enforceable.

In amending the Statute of Frauds in recent years, England and British Columbia have retained the requirement of writing for contracts of guarantee. In addition, British Columbia has done away with the judge-made distinction between indemnity and guarantee by requiring that both types of promise be in writing.[5]

In contrast to the restricted meaning given to the words "debt" and "default", the courts have given the word "miscarriage" a wider meaning. They have interpreted a

---

[3] As Furmston points out in *Cheshire, Fifoot and Furmston's Law of Contract* (12th ed.) at p. 205 it is the intention of the parties and not their language that determines whether the promise is a guarantee or an indemnity.

[4] [1894] 1 Q.B. 285.

[5] Law Reform (Enforcement of Contracts) Act, 1954, 2 & 3 Eliz. 2, C. 34, S. 1 (United Kingdom), and Statute of Frauds, R.S.B.C. 1979, c. 393, s. 4. Manitoba has simply repealed the entire Statute of Frauds, R.S.M. 1987, c. F-158.

promise to "answer for the miscarriage of another" to mean "to pay damages for injury caused by the tort of another person", for example by that person's negligence or fraud. Thus, to be enforceable, the promise, "I will pay you for the injury B caused you if B doesn't settle with you", must be in writing. On the other hand, the promise, "I will pay you for the injury B caused you if you will give up absolutely any rights you have against B", is a promise of indemnity and need not be in writing to be enforceable.[6]

An Agreement Made in Consideration of Marriage

This section has always been interpreted as applying not to a promise to marry but to related matters, such as arrangements about assets brought into the marriage as common property. In some provinces the section has been repealed,[7] but in any event it has been superseded in all common law provinces by extensive family law reform legislation. Although the legislation varies substantially from province to province, generally speaking it recognizes a wide variety of enforceable arrangements in marriage and in cohabitation relations.[8] A provision common to all the legislation is a requirement that these arrangements, since they are expected to apply to relationships over a long time, must be in writing to be enforceable.

A Contract Concerning an Interest in Land

Unlike most provisions of the Statute, this provision has received general approval as a necessary protection of property interests. The special qualities of land, in particular its virtual indestructibility, are discussed later, in Chapter 26. These qualities make it important that we be able to ascertain readily the various outstanding interests and claims against land. It is important, therefore, to have written records of transactions affecting interests in land verified by the signatures of the parties and available over long periods for inspection by interested persons. To this end we have systems of public records where interested parties may "search" and discover who owns or claims to own the interests that may arise in land.

We must distinguish between contracts concerning land to which the Statute applies, and others too remotely connected with land to be under the Statute. The courts have held that agreements to repair or build a house and to obtain room and board are outside the Statute, while agreements to permit taking water from a well, to lease any land, house, or other building or an apartment are within the Statute. Thus, an oral agreement to rent an apartment will be unenforceable, while an oral agreement to repair the apartment will be enforceable. We discuss the enforceability of leases again in Chapter 27.

England and British Columbia have retained the requirement of writing for contracts concerning interests in land.[9]

---

[6] Kirkham v. Marter (1819), 106 E.R. 490; Read v. Nash (1751), 95 E.R. 632.

[7] For example: S.B.C. 1958, c. 18; S.O. 1978, c. 2, s. 88.

[8] For example: Family Relations Act, R.S.B.C. 1979, c. 121, s. 48; Family Law Act, R.S.O. 1990, c. F-3, s. 52; Matrimonial Property Act, R.S.N.S. 1989, c. 275, s. 23.

[9] Law of Property Act, 1925, 15 & 16 Geo. 5, c. 20, s. 40 (United Kingdom), and Statute of Frauds, R.S.B.C. 1979, c. 393, s. 1, as amended by Law Reform Amendment Act, S.B.C. 1985, c. 110, s. 7.

An Agreement not to be Performed by Either Party Within One Year

The purpose of this part of the Statute is clear enough: Parliament did not wish to trust to memory the terms of a contract that would be performed over a long period. Unfortunately, the choice of a definite cut-off date, one year, does not accomplish this purpose — if indeed any provision, no matter how carefully drawn, could accomplish it. The injustice of allowing a wholly oral contract extending exactly one year to be enforced while not allowing the enforcement of a similar contract lasting a year plus a day became evident to the judges immediately after the Statute was passed. Again they tried to cut down the effect of the Statute. They held that the Statute did not apply to a contract, though it might well extend beyond a year, unless the terms of the contract specified a time for performance clearly longer than a year. The effect of this ruling is to exclude from the Statute contracts for an *indefinite* period.

ILLUSTRATION

Ajax Co. Ltd. hires Singh as supervisor for setting up an electronic data-processing system without setting out a schedule. Although the parties expect the project to take longer than a year, it is not certain to do so. Accordingly the contract is outside the Statute and need not be in writing.

On the other hand, if a contract is by its terms to extend beyond one year, it is governed by the Statute although it may be brought to an end in less than one year.

ILLUSTRATION

In an oral contract, the Trojan Co. Ltd. has hired Bergsen as general manager for two years, provided that either party may bring the contract to an end by giving three months' notice to the other. Bergsen has been working for the company for some months when he receives one month's notice of dismissal. He will be unable to enforce the term entitling him to three months' notice.

The courts have further interpreted the Statute not to apply even though *one* party will necessarily require more than a year to perform provided that the contract also shows an intention that the *other* party will wholly perform within a year.

ILLUSTRATION

Grigorian agrees to repair promptly a leaking roof on Brown's warehouse for $3000, the money to be paid in two annual instalments of $1500 each. Grigorian completes the repairs within five weeks. At the end of the year Brown refuses to pay the first installment, claiming that their oral agreement is unenforceable because payment could not be wholly performed within one year. Grigorian can enforce the contract. The court has again excluded the Statute where it can find the slimmest reason for doing so, in this case because the parties intended that one of them, Grigorian, should complete performance within a year, and did so.

Where the obligations of one party clearly extend beyond the year, the intention that the other should wholly perform within one year must be clear from the terms of the contract or from the surrounding circumstances: it is not enough that the party *might* perform within one year. Hence, an oral promise by A to pay B a sum of money in three years' time if B will tutor A's daughter in accounting until she obtains a professional qualification will not be enforceable, unless it can clearly be shown from the surrounding circumstances that the tutoring was to be done within the succeeding few weeks or months and *not* to continue beyond one year.

The provision of the Statute of Frauds concerning agreements not to be performed within one year illustrates better than any other the extremes to which the courts have gone to prevent the Statute from working an injustice. They cannot invariably circumvent the Statute, however, and injustice often results when the plaintiff fails only because the Statute of Frauds bars him. It may be hoped that the remaining provinces will follow the lead of British Columbia in amending the Statute.

Ratification of Infants' Contracts

Contracts requiring ratification by infants upon coming of age (that is, contracts that are not for a permanent interest in property) must in some jurisdictions be ratified in writing to be enforceable.[10] The requirement of writing does not, however, apply to the class of minors' contracts that are valid unless disaffirmed: for these contracts, mere acquiescence is sufficient to bind infants after coming of age.

Essentials of a Written Memorandum

We have discussed the classes of contract affected by the Statute of Frauds. Suppose now, that a contract falls clearly within its scope. What must the memorandum contain in order to satisfy the Statute and permit a party to maintain an action upon the contract? The Statute requires a "note or memorandum" of the contract "signed by the party to be charged" or the party's authorized agent.[11]

The memorandum must contain all the essential terms of the contract, including the identity of the parties. If the contract is for the sale of land, for example, the memorandum must name the parties, adequately describe the subject-matter (the land), and set out the consideration to be given for it.

---

[10] See, for example: Statute of Frauds, R.S.O. 1990, c. S-19, s. 7; R.S.N.S. 1989, c. 442, s. 9; also Chapter 8 of this book.

[11] Courts have had to consider whether new forms of transmitting documents such as *telex* (now virtually obsolete) and *facsimile* (or *fax*) satisfy the statutory requirement of being in "writing". In Rolling v. William Investments (1989), 63 D.L.R. (4th) 760, the Ontario Court of Appeal decided that a facsimile transmission of acceptance of an option was a satisfactory acceptance, even though when the parties made the agreement in 1974, they "could not have anticipated delivery of a facsimile of the [accepted] offer by means of a telephone transmission...The court concluded:

> Where technological advances have been made which facilitate communications and expedite transmission of documents we see no reason why they should not be utilized. Indeed, they should be encouraged and approved. [The defendant] suffered no prejudice by reason of the procedure followed.

Subsequent decisions of the Canadian courts have assumed that facsimile transmissions are sufficient to satisfy the writing requirement of the Statute of Frauds.

ILLUSTRATION

A gives *B* a signed offer to purchase Summerhill. *B* accepts by signing. The offer to purchase simply states the price to be $50 000 and does not say how the money is to be paid. In previous conversations the parties had agreed orally that payment should be $20 000 in cash and $30 000 by way of a ten-year mortgage. The memorandum is insufficient: the method of payment is an essential term and it has been omitted.

If *A* and *B* had previously agreed that the whole price should be paid in cash, then the memorandum would be sufficient, for by naming the price to be paid, without more, they imply that it should be paid in cash at the time the property is transferred.

The Statute of Frauds makes an exception for contracts of guarantee by stating that the consideration for that type of promise need not appear in the writing.[12]

The memorandum need not be wholly within a single document; several written notes may be taken together to satisfy the requirements of the Statute. No problem arises when one or more of the documents refer directly to the others. The plaintiff will have considerably more trouble if there are no cross-references within the documents. The courts have gone as far as to hear evidence that a signed letter beginning with "Dear Sir" was contained in a particular envelope that bore the name and address of the plaintiff, and in this way to link the two pieces of paper as a sufficient memorandum.[13] The court justified its decision on the grounds that even without oral evidence, it could reasonably assume that the letter was contained in an envelope: it admitted oral evidence merely to identify the envelope. Thus, the court did not have to rely solely on the testimony of the parties — something it rarely if ever will agree to do. In the words of Baron Blackburn:

> If the contents of the signed paper themselves make reference to the others so as to show by internal evidence that the papers refer to each other, they may be all taken together as one memorandum in writing ... but if it is necessary, in order to connect them, to give evidence of the intention of the parties that they should be connected, shown by circumstances not apparent on the face of the writings, the memorandum is not all in writing, for it consists partly of the contents of the writings and partly of the expression of an intention to unite them and that expression is not in writing.[14]

ILLUSTRATION

A wrote to *B* on May 4 offering to pay $10 000 for *B*'s computer and at the same time stating the terms in detail. *B* wrote back in a signed letter addressed to *A*, "I will accept your offer of May 4." The agreement is enforceable by either party. The two letters may be taken together as providing the necessary written evidence because they relate to each other and contain all the terms.

---

12 See, for example: R.S.B.C. 1979, c. 393, s. 5; R.S.O. 1990, c. S-19, s. 6; R.S.N.S. 1989, c. 442, s. 8.
13 Pearce v. Gardner, [1897] 1 Q.B. 688.
14 Blackburn, *A Treatise on the Effect of the Contract of Sale*, p. 47. London: W. Benning & Co., 1845, as quoted in North Staffordshire Railway Co. v. Peek (1863), 120 E.R. 777, per Williams, J., at 782.

The Statute requires that the note or memorandum be signed by the party to be charged — the defendant — and only that person, not the plaintiff. The plaintiff's signature is irrelevant; if the defendant has not signed, the plaintiff's signature on the document does not help and he cannot enforce the contract against the other party.

The courts have been lenient in prescribing what amounts to a sufficient signature; it need not be in the handwriting of the defendant. A printed name will suffice as long as it is intended to validate the whole of the document. A letterhead on an invoice is designed to verify the sale of the goods described below, without a signature and is sufficient; but a letterhead on stationery would probably not be sufficient if the written contents indicated that the letter was to be signed and it was not signed, as when the letter ends with "Yours truly" and no signature.

The Effect of the Statute on Contracts Within its Scope

What do we mean when we say that an oral contract affected by the Statute of Frauds is *unenforceable*? The courts have said that an unenforceable contract still exists even though one or both of the parties is unable to obtain a remedy under it through court action. Is this not the same as saying it is void? The answer is a definite "no", for although no action may be brought on the contract itself, it may still affect the legal relations between the parties in several ways.

First, a party may sometimes be unable to recover a down payment made under an unenforceable contract.

ILLUSTRATIONS

P orally agrees to buy Blackacre from *V* for $50 000 and gives a down payment of $5 000, the balance to be paid in 30 days.

(a) Suppose that *P* then sees a more suitable property and refuses to pay the balance. The Statute of Frauds applies and *V* cannot enforce the contract. On the other hand, *P* cannot by court action require *V* to return the payment. Although the contract is unenforceable, it is still valid and existing. *V* may retain the payment by claiming that it was properly owing and was paid under the contract.

(b) Suppose instead it is *V* who refuses either to complete the sale or to return the payment. *P* can sue successfully for the return of the payment. The court in these circumstances will not permit *V* to repudiate the contract and yet keep the payment received under its terms.

In the above illustrations we can see that the court will not permit the party who repudiates the contract to gain a further advantage, in case (a) by allowing *P* to recover her payment after her own breach, and in case (b) by permitting *V* to retain *P*'s payment after his breach. If the contract were found instead to be void, the problem of breach would not arise; there cannot be a "breach" of a void contract. Thus, if the contract had been void for, say, uncertainty (so that the requirement of offer and acceptance was not met), *P* could recover her payment whether it was she or *V* who refused to complete the transaction.

Second, a party who has accepted goods and services under a contract that is unenforceable because of the Statute will not be permitted to retain the benefit received without paying for it. Suppose that under an oral bilateral contract A promised to do certain work for B over 18 months, and B promised to pay A $60 000 on completion. Since the contract would not be performed by either party within one year, it would be "caught" (affected) by the Statute. Before A commenced work, B could repudiate with impunity and A would have no right to sue B. But if after A began working, B had repudiated and refused to give A access to B's premises where the work was being done, A could sue B *quantum meruit* for the value of the work done to that point: although B could still repudiate the oral contract (and A would have no right to enforce the contract in court), B had nevertheless requested the work to be done and would be liable to pay a reasonable price for it, as was explained in Chapter 7.

Suppose, however, that A completed the work as agreed, with B's acquiescence. The court would view B's original promise to pay for the work as a continuing offer of a unilateral contract, which A accepted by completing performance. No contract was formed until A completed performance and at that moment the price became immediately payable. In this view of the facts, the contract is clearly completed in less than a year after its formation, and it is not caught by the Statute. A could therefore sue B successfully for the agreed price of $60 000 — another example of the lengths to which the courts will go in their reasoning to prevent the Statute from working an injustice. At the same time, we should note that the agreed price would bind *both* parties, as it would in any enforceable contract. A could not refuse B's tender of $60 000 and sue *quantum meruit* simply because A believed the work to be worth more than the agreed price. The enforceable oral contract, now outside the Statute, governs the price A may recover.

Third, a written memorandum may come into existence *after* the contract has been formed and the memorandum will still satisfy the Statute. As long as the memorandum comes into existence before the action is brought on the contract, it will provide the necessary evidence.

ILLUSTRATION

P agrees orally to buy Blackacre from V. P then refuses to complete the contract, and V sends her a letter outlining the contract and demanding that she carry out her obligations. P replies by letter saying that she has decided not to go through with the contract referred to in V's letter and that she is not bound since the contract is not in writing. Even though the statements in P's letter were intended as a denial of liability, the two letters taken together would amount to a sufficient memorandum to satisfy the Statute and make the contract enforceable.

Fourth, a defendant who is sued upon an oral contract must expressly plead the Statute as a defence to the action. If he fails to plead it, the court will decide the case without reference to the Statute. The plaintiff will then succeed if he establishes that the contract, though oral, was validly formed.

Fifth, an oral contract may effectively vary or dissolve a prior written contract even though the oral contract could not itself be enforced. An oral contract within the Statute is effective as long as a party does not have to bring an action to have it enforced.

ILLUSTRATION

P agrees to buy Roselawn from *V* under a written contract containing a promise by *V* to give vacant possession on a certain day. Subsequently, *V* has unexpected difficulty in removing his tenants; he informs *P* that he will not be able to give vacant possession. *P* then finds another property equally suitable to her and available with vacant possession. Rather than get into a dispute, the parties make a mutual oral agreement to call off the contract: *P* releases *V* from his promise to transfer Roselawn with vacant possession in return for a release by *V* of *P*'s promise to pay the purchase price. Afterwards *V* succeeds in removing his tenants and sues *P* to enforce the original written contract. *P* may successfully plead that the subsequent oral contract validly terminated the written contract.

Nonetheless, the oral contract cannot be sued upon directly. Suppose that in addition to terminating the prior contract *V* had orally agreed to give *P* an option on another property in settlement of *V*'s default in not giving vacant possession. Although the oral contract effectively dissolved the prior written contract, *P* could not sue upon the promise to give an option because otherwise the court would be enforcing an oral promise for an interest in land.[15]

Finally, as we have seen, a party to a contract who has signed a memorandum can himself be sued, whereas he cannot sue the other party who has not signed a memorandum; if the contract were void, neither party would have any rights under it.

$\mathcal{T}$HE DOCTRINE OF PART PERFORMANCE

We have examined how the courts struggled to cut down the scope of the Statute of Frauds, severely limiting the circumstances in which it would apply. Nevertheless, even a strict interpretation of the Statute did not prevent it from thwarting a large number of contracts in the common law courts. The courts of equity (often known as courts of conscience) were prepared to go further within their own jurisdiction. In disputes concerning the sale of land plaintiffs often sued in these courts because of their special power to grant the remedy of specific performance if they felt the circumstances warranted it.[16] Within a few years after the Statute of Frauds was passed, the courts of equity developed and applied the doctrine of *part performance* to contracts concerning an interest in land: if the plaintiff could show that he had begun performance of the contract in reliance on it, the court would accept that performance as evidence of the contract in place of a written memorandum. The courts of equity and common law are now fused and our modern courts still employ the doctrine in cases concerning an interest in land.

Not every act of performance under a contract qualifies as a substitute for a written memorandum. The following conditions must be satisfied before the court will enforce the contract:

(a) As we have seen, the contract must be one concerning land.

---

[15] See *Morris v. Baron*, [1918] A.C. 1 for a similar result.
[16] See Chapter 3 and Chapter 17.

(b) The acts of performance must suggest quite clearly the existence a contract. Thus far in Canada, it seems that they must clearly indicate a contract respecting the land in question; they must not be ambiguous and just as readily explained as part of a quite different transaction. Thus, a payment of a deposit on the price of land, by itself, while certainly an act of part performance, is not a sufficient substitute for writing: the payment could refer to almost any kind of contract between the parties — a contract for the sale of goods or for services to be rendered.[17] (Illustration (b) on page 250 shows that the purchaser may at least obtain the return of the deposit.) However, if a plaintiff has taken possession of the land with the acquiescence of the defendant and has begun to make improvements on it, the court will consider this a sufficient act of part performance to satisfy the Statute. It would be extraordinary for an owner to allow a stranger to enter on his land and make improvements unless there were a contract in relation to the land to explain this behaviour.

(c) The plaintiff, not the defendant, must perform the acts, and must suffer a loss by the performance if the contract is not enforced. The plaintiff's performance in reliance on the oral contract and the defendant's refusal to carry out the contract combine to create a hardship that equity recognizes and seeks to remedy.

Once an act of part performance is accepted by the court as sufficient evidence, the contract will be enforced. Even though the act of part performance does not disclose all the terms of the contract, the court will enforce the contract according to the terms orally agreed.

Rawlinson v. Ames[18] illustrates how the doctrine of part performance works. Ames entered into an oral contract for the lease of a flat to which Rawlinson, the landlord, was to make certain alterations. During the course of the alterations (performed by Rawlinson), Ames inspected them and offered suggestions. On completion of the alterations she refused to move into the flat, claiming that as the agreement was for an interest in land and required to be in writing and signed by her, it was unenforceable against her. However, as plaintiff, Rawlinson was able to offer evidence of his part performance in lieu of a written memorandum, and succeeded in his action for breach of contract.

$\mathcal{E}$VIDENCE REQUIRED BY THE SALE OF GOODS ACT

For over two hundred years from its enactment, the English Statute of Frauds contained a provision requiring contracts for the sale of goods priced at £10 or more to be evidenced by a written memorandum or by one of three types of conduct. In 1893, this provision was repealed and replaced by a similar one in the new Sale of Goods Act. When the Canadian provinces adopted the Sale of Goods Act, they followed the English example.

---

[17] See *Ross v. Ross, Jr. et al.* (1973), 33 D.L.R. (3d) 351. In England, however, shortly afterwards the House of Lords held that it is sufficient that the acts of part performance merely indicate the existence of a contract: *Steadman v. Steadman*, [1976] A.C. 536. In that case the court held that payment of arrears of maintenance by a husband to his wife was sufficient part performance of a contract to transfer land to him. The court admitted evidence of the full terms of the oral contract and ordered specific performance.

[18] [1925] 1 Ch. 96.

What is a sale of goods for the purposes of the Act? The question is not always easy. Is, for example, a contract in which a carpenter agrees to provide materials and erect a garage a contract for the *sale of goods* or a contract for *work and materials*? If it is one for work and materials, it is enforceable without satisfying the requirements of the Sale of Goods Act. If it is one for the sale of goods, to be enforceable it must comply with those requirements. The problem of defining a sale of goods is also important for other provisions of the Act, and we shall consider it again in Chapter 18.

The various provinces have translated the £10 minimum into different amounts varying from $30 to $50.[19] Otherwise the wording has remained the same as the English wording. When a number of items are purchased at one time, the *aggregate* price of the order is the deciding amount for the purposes of the Act. In *Baldey v. Parker*,[20] Parker bargained for various articles in Baldey's linen shop. A separate price was agreed on for each, and no single item was sold for £10 or more, though the aggregate was much more than £10. Later a dispute arose about discounts, and when the goods were delivered, Parker refused them. Baldey brought an action against Parker for breach of contract, claiming that: the price of the articles should be considered item by item; the amount of each sale was not large enough to come within the Act; accordingly the contract, though oral, was enforceable. The court rejected the seller's contention and held that the total value governed the contract, making it unenforceable.

The Sale of Goods Act states: "The price in a contract of sale may be fixed by the contract or may be left to be fixed in a manner thereby agreed, or may be determined by the course of dealing between the parties."[21] In other words, the Act permits consideration to be determined in other ways than by stating a fixed price. With this exception, the Sale of Goods Act has the same requirements for a written memorandum as does the Statute of Frauds.

Unlike the Statute of Frauds, however, the Sale of Goods Act states expressly that a party to a contract for the sale of goods who cannot produce the required memorandum may still enforce the contract if he can show one of the following kinds of conduct:[22]

(a) "acceptance" and actual receipt of the goods by the buyer;

(b) part payment tendered by the buyer and accepted by the seller; or

(c) something "by way of earnest" given by the buyer to the seller.

(a) We have placed the word "acceptance" in quotation marks because the term has a special meaning in the Act. It means any conduct on the part of the buyer in relation to the goods that amounts to recognition of an existing contract of sale. The buyer will have "accepted" the goods when he does anything tantamount to admitting that he has a contract with respect to them, and will thus make the contract enforceable. Although he may be neither satisfied nor willing to keep the goods, yet if he does anything that acknowledges them as the goods ordered, he will not be able to claim that the contract is unenforceable. For example, proof that the buyer has inspected the goods or sampled them to

---

[19] The amount is $40 in Nova Scotia, New Brunswick, and Ontario; $50 in Newfoundland, Manitoba, Saskatchewan, and Alberta; $30 in Prince Edward Island.

[20] (1823), 107 E.R. 297.

[21] See, for example: Sale of Goods Act, R.S.B.C. 1979, c. 370, s. 12; R.S.O. 1990, c. S-1, s. 9; R.S.N.S. 1989, c. 408, s. 11.

[22] R.S.O. 1990, c. S-1, s. 5; R.S.N.S. 1989, c. 408, s. 7.

see if they are what he ordered will establish his "acceptance". Of course, he may still protest against the quality of the seller's performance; if the goods are not according to the terms of the contract, he may obtain remedies for breach of the contract. A buyer's remedies are examined later, in Chapter 19.

(b) There may even be doubt whether a buyer has made a part payment; the courts have to decide each case on its own merits. One point is clear: a part payment that will have the effect of making the contract enforceable must be a separate act subsequent to the formation of the contract. Thus, if the buyer agrees to set off a present debt owed to him by the seller as the equivalent of a deposit on the goods, the court will not regard this arrangement as a part payment. In the words of Baron Alderson,

> "... [the buyer] must have done two things; first, made a contract, and next, he must have given something ... in part payment or discharge of his liability. But where one of the terms of an oral bargain is for the seller to take something in part payment, that term alone cannot be equivalent to actual part payment."[23]

ILLUSTRATION

A orally offers to sell his typewriter to B for $150. B accepts orally and then hands A a deposit of $10, which A accepts. The act of handing A the deposit immediately after the contract was formed is a sufficient act of part payment subsequent to the contract and sat- isfies the provisions of the Act.

Suppose, instead, B replies, "I'll buy the typewriter at that price if you will deduct the $10 you owe me from the price and consider it as a deposit". If A agreed to these terms, there would not be sufficient part payment.

We must contrast a sale of goods (moveable, tangible property) with a sale of an interest in land (including buildings). Part payment is acceptable evidence as a substitute for a written memorandum in contracts for the sale of goods, but may be insufficient in contracts for an interest in land.

(c) "Earnest" differs from part payment in that it is not deducted from the price to be paid. Rather it is a token sum (or article) given to seal the bargain. Although the giving of something by way of earnest was common at one time, it is now rarely if ever done, and the reference to the practice remains as a relic in the Act.

Both the Sale of Goods Act and the Statute of Frauds may apply to the same contract. They will both apply, for example, where there is an oral agreement to sell goods that are to be delivered and paid for by instalments over a period exceeding one year. The evidence may satisfy the requirements of the Sale of Goods Act if the buyer accepts some of the goods or makes part payment, but it does not comply with the Statute of Frauds because it is an oral contract that neither party can wholly perform within one year. Accordingly, it is unenforceable because of the Statute of Frauds, but not because of the Sale of Goods Act.

The requirement of a written memorandum in the Sale of Goods Act is open to the same criticism as the comparable provision in the Statute of Frauds. In 1937 the English Law Revision Committee complained:

---

23   Walker v. Nussey (1847), 153 E.R. 1203 at 1205.

A man who by an oral contract buys or sells £10 worth of goods cannot...[subject to the special conduct accepted in lieu of a memorandum] enforce the bargain, yet a man who orally contracts to do work or to sell shares or to insure property...can enforce his bargain, and have it enforced against him *however great the amount involved.*[24]

In 1954, when the English Parliament amended the Statute of Frauds, it also repealed the section in the Sale of Goods Act requiring special types of evidence to enforce contracts for the sale of goods, and British Columbia followed suit in 1958.[25] The requirements are still in effect for the other common law provinces in Canada.

Many other legal aspects of a contract for the sale of goods exist besides questions of evidence. We shall turn to these later, in Chapters 18 and 19.

CONSUMER PROTECTION LEGISLATION

A growing concern for the protection of consumers in our increasingly complex market for goods and services has resulted in a recent flurry of legislative activity. All the common law provinces have passed statutes varying both in name and application.[26] These statutes are novel in that they are concerned with the protection of only one party to a consumer contract, the buyer. An example is the Ontario Consumer Protection Act, which covers not only goods but also services. The significant sections of the Act with regard to the requirement of writing are section 1, paragraphs (c) and (f) which state, respectively:

"buyer" means a person who purchases goods for consumption or services under an executory contract and includes his agent, but does not include a person who buys in the course of carrying on business or an association of individuals, a partnership or corporation.

"executory contract" means a contract between a buyer and seller for the purchase and sale of goods or services in respect of which delivery of the goods or performance of the services or payment in full of the consideration is not made at the time the contract is entered into;

and section 16, which states:

(1) Every executory contract...shall be in writing and shall contain...[detailed information about the subject matter of the contract, details of credit arrangements and costs and any warranty or guarantee given].

(2) An executory contract is not binding on the buyer unless the contract is made in accordance with...[subsection (1) among other requirements] and is signed by the parties and a duplicate original copy thereof is in the possession of each of the parties thereto.

---

[24] The Law Revision Committee (U.K.), *Sixth Interim Report,* 1937 (Reprinted 1955), Cmd. 5449, p. 9 (authors' italics).

[25] Law Reform (Enforcement of Contracts) Act, 1954, 2 & 3 Eliz. 2, c. 34, s. 1 (United Kingdom), and Statute Law Amendment Act, 1958, S.B.C. 1958, c. 52, s. 17.

[26] See, for example: Consumer Protection Act, R.S.B.C. 1979, c. 65; R.S.O. 1990, c. C-31; R.S.N.S. 1989, c. 92.

These sections are intended to give consumers wide protection in the form of complete disclosure by sellers. Although there are few reported decisions interpreting them,[27] the provinces have passed detailed regulations and set up agencies to hear consumer complaints as well as to investigate or even negotiate on the consumer's behalf. We will discuss consumer protection legislation in more detail in Chapter 19.

Questions for Review

1. What does it mean to say that a contract "comes within" the Statute of Frauds? What are the types of contracts so affected?
2. Explain the criticism that "on the whole they [the provisions of the Statute of Frauds and Sale of Goods Act requiring written evidence] promote rather than restrain dishonesty." (The Law Revision Committee, (U.K.) *Sixth Interim Report,* 937.)
3. For what reasons might a defendant who is sued on an oral contract caught by the Statute of Frauds not plead the Statute in defence?
4. Give examples of oral promises that are enforceable.
5. In what ways may an unenforceable contract differ from a void one?
6. When a contract must be evidenced by a written memorandum to be enforceable, what facts about the agreement must the memorandum contain?
7. Even though certain types of conduct may sometimes provide sufficient evidence of a contract, in what respects does a written memorandum still have a practical advantage?
8. State which of the following contracts are affected by a statutory requirement that would permit the promisor to plead that the contract cannot be enforced against him or her because evidence of the terms is not available in the required form:
   (a) *A* and *B*, the purchaser and vendor respectively of a piece of land, agree by telephone to call off the sale.
   (b) *C* enters into an oral contract with *D*, a contractor, to build a house for *C*.
   (c) *E* is the proprietor of a business that requires a bank loan. *E*'s father, *F*, tells the bank manager that if the bank will approve the loan and *E* does not repay it, he (*F*) will.
   (d) *G*, having just graduated from university, goes to work for a large Canadian manufacturing firm. In the exchange of letters between *G* and her employer, nothing is said about the duration of *G*'s employment.
   (e) *H* agrees orally to buy a talking parrot from *J*, who has taught the bird to talk. Its price is $100.
9. Are there any circumstances in which an oral contract for the sale of goods may still be enforceable?
10. In *Baldey v. Parker,* if the plaintiff had succeeded, would the application of the Sale of Goods Act have been narrowed or broadened?
11. What does the doctrine of part performance achieve? What points must a plaintiff establish to become entitled to its benefit?

---

[27] See, for example: Household Finance Corp. Ltd. v. McEllim *et ux.* (1970), 75 W.W.R. 187, where a husband and wife were joint signers of a promissory note. Only one copy of the detailed information on credit was given to the husband; the plaintiff (lender) thought this was sufficient. The action was dismissed against both parties because the wife had not received her own copy of the credit information.

12. Review the facts in Case 5 in Chapter 6. Would the Statute of Frauds affect your decision?

Problems

Problem 1

On January 15, Tonino made a lease with Logan, signed by both parties, in which Logan agreed to rent her apartment to Tonino at $600 a month for three years, commencing February 1. In March of the same year Tonino and Logan agreed orally that Tonino would pay an additional $15 a month rent upon the completion of certain alterations and repairs to the premises within three months. Logan completed the alterations and repairs in April, but Tonino refused to pay anything but the $600 a month specified in the lease. In August, Logan sued Tonino for the additional rent.

What points must the court settle in reaching its decision, and what should the decision be? (See *Donellan v. Read* (1832), 110 E.R. 330.)

Problem 2

After being interviewed for a position with Passmore, a lawyer with an established practice, Bidgood, who had just recently been called to the bar, received a letter stating: "I offer you a starting salary of $2000 per month. As we discussed in our conversation, in accepting this offer you agree that for a period of two years after termination of employment you will not engage in law practice within a one-mile radius of my office. If you find this offer satisfactory, please come to the office next Monday morning."

Bidgood reported for work and remained in Passmore's employ for several years. The parties mutually terminated the employment, and Bidgood immediately started a law practice across the street. Can Passmore enforce the promise not to compete? (See *Reeve v. Jennings,* [1910] 2 K.B. 522.)

Problem 3

Pearce offered to buy Greenacre from Vincent for $45 000 and gave Vincent a deposit of $5000. Vincent accepted orally and promised to arrange a formal transfer of ownership in two weeks. Several days later he discovered that an exit to a new super-highway was to be built along the front of Greenacre, substantially increasing its value. It appeared probable that the purchaser, Pearce, had known about the exit but had not told Vincent. Vincent refused to transfer the land unless Pearce would pay an additional $20 000, and also refused to return the deposit.

Pearce brought an action for specific performance or in the alternative for the recovery of her deposit. What should be the result?

Problem 4

The manager of Jiffy Discount Stores ordered a carload of refrigerators from Colonel Electric Company by telephone. When the refrigerators arrived at the warehouse, the transport employees and Jiffy's employees began unloading them. When about half of them were unloaded, the manager arrived and asked to examine one. An employee uncrated one refrigerator, and after looking it over, the manager stated it was not the right model and ordered the transport employees to take them back. The refrigerators were returned to Colonel Electric Company, and the company sued Jiffy Discount Stores for breach of contract. It was proved that the manager was mistaken, and the refrigerators did conform to the telephone order. What should the result be? (See *Page v. Morgan* (1885), 15 Q.B.D. 228.)

Problem 5

In October 1986, Nikolis approached Knowles to discuss the purchase from Knowles of a woodland lot outside the city of Fredericton. Knowles agreed to a price of $22 000, the transaction to be completed on December 1, 1986. Upon payment of a $2500 deposit by Nikolis, Knowles gave him the following receipt:

October 12, 1980

> Tomas Nikolis
>
> Received twenty-five hundred and ... xx/100 dollars ($2500) for purchase of woodland approx. 25 to 30 acres. Balance $19 500. Completion date, December 1, 1986.
>
> (signed) Jennifer A. Knowles.

Shortly afterwards, Knowles showed Nikolis the property and walked with him over the lines of the property on three occasions. On one of these occasions they were accompanied by Mrs. Nikolis. Since, however, Knowles was not sure about the actual area she had agreed to sell, she suggested having a survey made. Nikolis then arranged for a surveyor who, with Knowles' consent, blazed and cleared the property lines for about two days. Knowles refused to pay the survey costs of $200 and Nikolis paid them.

On December 1, Nikolis went to Knowles' house to pay her the balance of the price. Knowles said that the boundaries identified by the survey were different from what she had thought they were, and that she would not sell the woodland lot.

Nikolis brought an action for specific performance or for damages in the alternative. Indicate with reasons whether the action should succeed.

Problem 6

Carter left a position where he was earning $48 000 a year to accept a position as general manager of Buildwell Limited at the same annual salary. All negotiations leading up to his appointment were carried on orally between Carter and Webster, the president of Buildwell Limited. Both parties assured each other in various conversations that the employment would last "for life"; they agreed that each year Carter would receive a bonus, and that if he was not satisfied with it he could terminate his employment, but that the company could not terminate his employment unless he "did something wrong".

Over the succeeding few years Carter's salary was increased from $4000 to $5000 per month, and he received in addition annual bonuses of up to $4000. A letter to Carter announcing his last bonus was signed by both the president and vice-president of the company and included the words, "And we want you to know that with all the experiences we are going through in connection with the business, your efforts are appreciated."

Shortly afterwards Webster died, and immediately the company dismissed Carter without explanation, paying him one month's salary. Carter then attempted to go into business for himself but without success. He sued Buildwell Limited for wrongful dismissal, claiming breach of his employment contract. Can Buildwell Limited successfully plead the Statute of Frauds? (See *Campbell v. Business Fleets Limited*, [1954] 2 D.L.R. 263; *Shaver v. Hamilton Cooperative Creameries Ltd.*, [1937] 1 D.L.R. 489.)

Cases

Case 1

In February, Baldwin Co. Ltd., a woollen manufacturer, contracted to sell 500 pieces of blue serge to Martin Bros., tailors, at a price of $40 000, as stated in a written memorandum signed by both parties. After 220 pieces of the cloth had been delivered, a dispute arose between the parties: Martin Bros. complained of delay in delivery, and Baldwin Co. Ltd. complained of failure to pay for the goods delivered. Baldwin Co. Ltd. sued Martin Bros. for the price of the goods delivered, and Martin Bros. counterclaimed for damages for non-delivery.

In August, before the case came to trial, the parties orally agreed to a settlement and to substitute for the original contract a new one, in which Martin Bros. would have an additional three months to pay for the goods and have an option of buying the remaining 280 pieces at the prices in the earlier contract. The following November, Martin Bros. paid the amount due on the original 220 pieces of cloth and placed an order for the remaining 280 pieces under the option agreed to in the substituted contract. Baldwin Co. Ltd. refused to deliver these pieces, the agreed price being no longer profitable to them. Martin Bros. then brought an action against Baldwin Co. Ltd. for damages for breach of contract (failure to deliver). Should this action succeed?

Case 2

John Brown, a retired widower, stated to Mrs. Adele Barber, that if he could find a suitable house and if she would move into it as a housekeeper, help operate it as a rooming house, and take care of him, he would give her the house on his death. Mrs. Barber agreed. Mr. Brown purchased a house that he operated as a rooming house until his death five years later. During this period Mrs. Barber served as housekeeper, making the necessary food and other household purchases and turning over to Mr. Brown the balance of the board money received from the tenants. She received no remuneration for her services other than her own board and an occasional allowance for clothing.

Mr. Brown made no provision in his will for Mrs. Barber, and following his death Mrs. Barber brought an action against the executors of his estate for specific performance of his promise. In evidence, Mrs. Barber offered the testimony of her two daughters, her son, and her son-in-law, who were present at the time of the original conversation between her and Mr. Brown. The executor contested the action.

(a) What legal considerations are relevant to a decision in this case? State whether Mrs. Barber's action would succeed.

(b) Suppose that instead of remaining in the house until Mr. Brown's death, Mrs. Barber and Mr. Brown had decided to part company after Mrs. Barber had served as his housekeeper for three years. At that time Mr. Brown wrote and signed a memorandum to Mrs. Barber that stated, "I hereby promise to pay you $5000 in consideration for the surrender by you of any rights to my house according to our earlier agreement." When Mr. Brown failed to pay the $5000 to Mrs. Barber, she sued him for this amount. What defence might Mr. Brown offer? Should Mrs. Barber succeed?

Case 3

Janice Kelly, a student in her third year of Commerce & Business Administration, looked after banking arrangements for her older brother Paul, who was in the hairdressing business, and Paul helped Janice with her tuition and living expenses. Paul Kelly owed the bank a business debt of $6000 payable on demand, and as collateral security the bank held some mining shares registered in Paul's name. The bank pressed Paul to repay the loan, and suggested that the shares would have to be sold if repayment were not forthcoming.

At this time Paul persuaded Janice to go to the bank and sign a form of guarantee to a maximum of $4000 of his indebtedness. Janice signed a printed form presented to her by the bank at the foot of which there appeared the word "(SEAL)" in a place reserved for affixing a red gummed wafer, though none was in fact placed there until afterwards by the bank manager. A customer in the bank at the time, whom Janice knew, also signed as a witness. The printed form included the proviso, "The Bank may deal with the principal debtor, Paul Kelly, and with all his securities as it sees fit."

One year later, Paul failed to respond to a demand by the bank that he repay the loan, and the bank asked Janice to make good her guarantee. Janice went to the bank to protest that she had been led to believe the shares in the bank's possession were sufficient to repay the loan. The bank manager said that the shares had since declined in price and were worth only $1800. Janice then became upset, and, in the belief that without her signature the guarantee would not be enforceable, tore a strip from the bottom of the guarantee bearing her signature and swallowed it. When the bank officers present told her that her conduct had been foolish and futile because the witness could still prove that her signature had been on the document, Janice tore off a further portion of paper on which the witness's signature appeared and swallowed that too. At this stage, the police were called in. Janice was told that she would go to jail if she did not immediately sign another guarantee to replace the mutilated one. She eventually did so, and this time a red paper wafer was affixed when she signed.

Janice paid ten monthly instalments of $50 each in reduction of the claim against her, but refused to pay any more. The bank sued her for the balance owing. It produced both the remnant of the first document and the second document as evidence of the guarantee.

(a) Discuss the validity of the defences available to Janice Kelly in these circumstances.

(b) Identify the major issue in the case.

(c) Indicate, with reasons, the probable result of the legal action.

CHAPTER 13

THE INTERPRETATION OF CONTRACTS

THE RELATIONSHIP BETWEEN FORMATION AND INTERPRETATION OF CONTRACTS

We have examined the various elements necessary to form a valid contract. An understanding of them is essential to an understanding of contracts. But the large majority of disputes, both in and out of court, are over the meaning of the contract, not about its formation. Indeed, very often the reason a party disputes the formation of a contract is that he disagrees with its interpretation by the other party.

ILLUSTRATION

Smith offers to build a set of cabinets for Doe for $1000, and Doe accepts. The next day Smith appears and asks where the lumber is. Doe says, "You are supposed to supply it." Smith replies, "My price was for the work only, not for the materials."

At this point the dispute may take one of two different courses. The first alternative is that either party may claim that the offer was too vague because it omitted an essential term indicating who should supply the lumber: such an offer is not capable of acceptance, and accordingly no contract is formed. The second alternative is that each side will concede that the agreement "to build a set of cabinets for $1000" is valid, but Smith will claim that the proper meaning is that Doe should supply the lumber, and Doe will claim the contrary.

The problem of *construing* or *interpreting* the contract is the subject of this chapter. We are not dealing here with fraud or deceit, though each party believes passionately that his is the only sensible interpretation of the contract and that the other party must be dishonest to suggest that there is any other. Often a lawyer's most difficult task is to show the client that the view held by the other side has some merit. Only then may the lawyer broach the possibility of a compromise or, if the dispute goes to court, be in a position to counter the arguments of the other side.

A cynic may observe how strange it is that the interpretation by each party invariably favours itself. We may answer this remark in two ways. First, contracting parties do not always find themselves in conflict on questions of interpretation: in the vast majority of contracts no dispute arises because the parties have understood each other closely enough for their bargain to continue to be to their mutual advantage. Second, even where there is disagreement, each party might well have rejected the terms at the outset had he realized they would be construed less favourably towards him. Words are at best inefficient vehicles for communicating thoughts: they can be ambiguous without the parties' realizing it, and people tend to give themselves the benefit of the doubt even when they sense a possible ambiguity. Hence disagreements about interpretation of contracts are not surprising but rather are a common risk in business arrangements.

When parties appear before a court to have a question of interpretation settled, the court seeks the most reasonable meaning that can be attributed to the words in the circumstances. This is no easy task. The difficulties courts experience with problems of interpretation are responsible for much criticism of the law. Learning that his "sensible and just" interpretation has been ignored, the losing party often blames the law, the judge, the dishonesty of his opponent, and his lawyer. The winning party regards the legal proceedings as superfluous, and a waste of her time and money, since they merely confirm the meaning of the contract that she accepted from the outset. To the outsider the dispute appears as a mere quibbling over words — an unlikely approach to justice. Yet the litigation is caused because the parties could not agree on the meaning of the words they themselves used, and the dispute has to be solved by the court. These difficulties may arise even in relatively simple contracts. In complicated and important contracts, prevention through the use of legal advice in drafting the terms is likely to be far cheaper than the cure. Of course, lawyers themselves are not immune to the inherent problems of language, but their training and experience make them especially aware of the areas of danger.

To return to our illustration of the cabinets, the misunderstanding might have been avoided had Doe asked Smith, "Does your offer include supplying the lumber?" She might also have asked, "When shall I pay you: in advance, in instalments, or after the work is completed?" It is understandable but unfortunate that people do not always think about all the questions, even all the important ones, which may affect their contracts. The list of possible questions is a long one, and while the parties can reduce the chances of a later dispute over interpretation by carefully discussing the implications of their contract before its formation, they cannot always eliminate such a dispute.

THE INTERPRETATION OF EXPRESS TERMS

What precisely did Smith promise when he agreed "to build a set of cabinets for $1000"? In attempting to answer such a question, lawyers have often argued that there are two approaches to the interpretation of words: the *strict* or *plain-meaning* approach and the *liberal* approach.

The plain-meaning approach restricts interpretation to the ordinary meaning, the dictionary meaning of a word. In fact, however, few words have a "plain" or "ordinary" meaning. A glance at a dictionary will show how many words have two or more completely different definitions. In addition, the meaning of words changes from time to time and place to place, or the context of the words in a contract may make it obvious that they have been used in a special sense.[1]

The liberal approach, by contrast, looks to the purposes of the parties in drafting their agreement — what did they intend to say? It stresses the circumstances surrounding the contract, the negotiations leading up to it, the knowledge of the parties, and any other relevant facts. It minimizes the importance of the words actually used. The liberal approach also has its limitations. In its extreme form, it too may lead to unsatisfactory results by inviting endless speculation about what the parties may have intended but never expressed. The particular words one chooses to use are a part of one's conduct in relation to the contract, and in law, conduct (including words) must continue to serve as the primary guide to one's intentions.

---

[1] See Chafee, "The Disorderly Conduct of Words", 20 Can. Bar Rev., p. 752 (1942). See also our discussion of the interpretation of statutes in Chapter 2 on the role of the courts as interpreters of legislation.

As a result there are not really two distinct approaches to interpretation, one of which is used to the total exclusion of the other: rather than choosing directly between them, a court will simply emphasize one approach more than the other. In other words, the court must decide in relation to the circumstances of each case how far it should look beyond the words used to explain their meaning.

In our illustration of the cabinets, Smith promised "to build" them. Does "to build" include "to supply materials"? Literally, "to build" means only "to construct", but in practice it usually includes "to supply materials". When a contractor undertakes to build a house, the price usually includes the price of materials. In the illustration, the words themselves are not conclusive either way; there is an ambiguity. The court will then more willingly look outside the contract to the surrounding circumstances as a means of clearing up this ambiguity. For example, it will hear evidence of any past transactions between the parties to learn whether materials have been included in previous building contracts between them. It will hear evidence of the negotiations leading up to the contract: perhaps Smith had quoted different prices varying with the kind of lumber to be used; perhaps Doe had made it clear earlier that she wanted an inclusive price. Any of these facts, if established in court, would support the claim that "to build" in this contract meant "to supply materials" as well as labour.

The difficult judicial problem of achieving a balance between the plain-meaning and liberal approaches to the interpretation of the words used by parties in their contract has been commented on by one of the great authorities on contract law:

> ... [I]t can hardly be insisted on too often or too vigorously that language at its best is always a defective and uncertain instrument, that words do not define themselves, that terms and sentences in a contract, a deed, or a will do not apply themselves to external objects and performances, that the meaning of such terms and sentences consists of the ideas that they induce in the mind of some individual person who uses or hears or reads them, and that seldom in a litigated case do the words of a contract convey one identical meaning to the two contracting parties or to third persons.[2]

There is an inaccurate but widespread belief that when the two principals in a dispute give conflicting evidence in court and there are no other witnesses, the court will not accept either account but will apply the popular maxim, "One person's word is as good as another's." Normally reputable individuals have sometimes been tempted into making extravagant or distorted statements on the false assumption that a court has no choice but to accept their story on an equal footing with their opponents' testimony. True, a court is reluctant to accept direct testimony of one party rather than the other, and will seek corroboration if possible from a third party or from the actions of the parties in relation to the contract other than those disclosed in their own testimony. As a last resort, however, a court will choose between them. It will base its decision on the credibility of the parties themselves, taking all the circumstances into account — in other words, it simply decides which story seems more reasonable. With their experience in this type of problem, judges, though certainly not infallible, develop an intuitive ability for assessing the credibility of witnesses.

---

2 Corbin, *Corbin on Contracts* (One Volume Edition), Pt. 3, Ch. 24, sec. 536, p. 499, St. Paul, Minn.: West Publishing Co., 1952.

The dictionary definition of the words used, their meaning in the context of the contract, the surrounding circumstances of the contract, and the judge's ability to weigh the evidence are all means by which the court endeavours to interpret the express terms of a contract. Another important aid in deciding the meaning of words is evidence of special usage of words in particular trades and in particular areas of the country. In our illustration, Smith might produce expert witnesses who testify from their experience that in the carpentry trade standard usage of the word "build" means labour only. Or he might show that in that part of the country the word always had that meaning. In *Brown v. Byrne*, Mr. Justice Coleridge said:

> What words more plain than "a thousand", "a week", "a day"? Yet the cases are familiar in which "a thousand" has been held to mean twelve hundred, "a week" a week only during the theatrical season, "a day" a working day. In such cases the evidence neither adds to, nor qualifies, nor contradicts the written contract; it only ascertains it, by expounding the language.[3]

Evidence of special usage is not, however, conclusive: a court may well decide that the word was used in a general rather than a special way, perhaps because the user of the word was aware that the other party was not familiar with trade usage. In general, the courts construe words most strongly against the party who has suggested them, in order to prevent him from being able to select, among two or more possible meanings, the one that turns out to be to his advantage.

There are no hard and fast rules of interpretation. At one time the courts were quite mechanical in applying ancient canons of interpretation, but today they try to look for the most reasonable interpretation in the circumstances — an approach that requires flexibility and common sense. For a business person to be able to predict the decision a court is likely to reach if the meaning of a contract is challenged, she must know what a "reasonable interpretation" of it would be. Her personal interest deprives her of the ability to reach an objective conclusion about the reasonable meaning of the contract. She needs unbiased advice. The court, in searching for the objective meaning of words, seeks the advice of the mythical reasonable person — the personification of an informed, objective bystander. The business person's imperfect approximation of this legendary figure[4] must be her lawyer. If she finds her interpretation of a contract challenged, she should immediately obtain legal advice. By doing so she will have the benefit of an unbiased external opinion, when it will be of most help to her. Her protection will be twofold: if her interpretation of the contract is correct, she will learn how best to enforce it; if it is incorrect, she may avoid a costly breach of contract.

A court must render a decision, difficult though it may be, and the best available solution often is not entirely satisfactory. Frequently, the easier course would be to declare an agreement unenforceable because of an ambiguity in its wording; but if the courts took this attitude they would not be performing the role assigned to them in the community. Instead they lean towards keeping an agreement alive rather than brushing

---

[3] (1854), 118 E.R. 1304 at 1309.

[4] For an amusing account of all the attributes of the "reasonable person" see Herbert, *Uncommon Law,* London: Methuen & Co., 1948, in the fictitious case of Fardell v. Potts.

it aside as being without force at law. Equivocal words are assigned the meaning that makes a contract enforceable, if at all possible. Lord Wright, one of the most respected of English judges in commercial law, has given a classic statement of the rule in a House of Lords decision:

> The object of the court is to do justice between the parties, and the court will do its best, if satisfied that there was an ascertainable and determinate intention to contract, to give effect to that intention, looking at substance and not mere form. It will not be deterred by mere difficulties of interpretation. Difficulty is not synonymous with ambiguity, so long as any definite meaning can be extracted.[5]

THE PAROL EVIDENCE RULE

The Meaning of the Rule

Before a deal is made, the parties very often engage in a process of bargaining and negotiation, offer and counter-offer, with both of them making concessions until finally they reach a suitable compromise. The bargaining may be carried on orally or in writing. In important contracts, the parties usually put their final agreement into a more formal document signed by both sides. One party may later discover that the document does not contain one or more terms she believed were part of the agreement. Of course, the omission may have been due to a mistake in writing down the terms actually agreed upon — a typing error, for example. The equitable remedy of rectification, as explained in Chapter 10, may then be available. Where, however, there is no clear evidence that the term was omitted by error — as when the complaining party admits that she read the document over and approved it — she will be held to the contract as it is written.

According to the parol evidence rule, a term previously agreed upon between the parties but not included in the final form of the contract will not later be permitted to add to or contradict the contract. In this context the word "parol" means *extrinsic to* or *outside of* the written agreement.[6] The rule applies both to an oral agreement that has been reduced to writing and to a written agreement that has been set out in a formal document under seal.

The parol evidence rule operates to exclude *terms* that one party claims should be added to the contract. It does not exclude evidence about the formation of the contract such as its legality, the capacity of the parties, mistake, duress, undue influence, or fraud. In other words, it does not affect evidence of any of the circumstances surrounding the contract: it operates only to exclude the introduction of terms not found in the written document. As an example, we have seen that a court will admit oral evidence to prove that one of the parties made a material misrepresentation.

Sometimes parties agree to omit a term from the final form of the contract, still intending it to be part of their whole agreement. They are most likely to do so when they are

---

[5] Scammel v. Ouston, [1941] 1 All E.R. 14 at 25.
[6] For a more extensive discussion of the meaning of the parol evidence rule, see Cross and Tapper, *Cross on Evidence* (7th ed.), pp. 695ff. London: Butterworth & Co., 1985.

using a standard form contract, such as a conditional sale agreement, a short-term lease, a mortgage, or a grant of land. One party may persuade the other to leave a term out because it will be confusing or because his employer may object to it.

ILLUSTRATION

Sung leases a word processor with accounting capability to Jeans, Inc., a small but prosperous manufacturing company. An attractive part of the deal for Jeans, Inc., is the promise by Sung that her company will provide without further charge a new software program for inventory and accounts receivable records. Sung explains that the contract contains no reference to this new software program because it is in its final stage of development and has yet to be publicly announced; her company plans to introduce it with an advertising campaign.

The manager for Jeans, Inc. signs the contract without a term referring to the provision of the new software. The equipment is delivered but the program promised proves to be a failure and is never released by the word processing company.

Jeans, Inc. would be unlikely to succeed in an action against the word processing company for breach of Sung's oral promise. It is doubtful that it would be entitled to rescission for misrepresentation since Sung did not state as a fact that the program was fully developed and available at the time the contract was formed.

Though a party may suffer hardship, the courts have been reluctant to relax the parol evidence rule in these circumstances because they fear that any relaxation would tempt parties who are unhappy with their contracts to claim that favourable terms discussed during negotiations but not agreed upon are part of their contracts. The courts worry that they would create serious difficulties for the business community if they showed any disposition to upset written agreements deliberately made. For this reason, it is not wise to allow any term of importance to be omitted from the final written form of an agreement. If the term is important and the other side insists on excluding it from the final document, it is better to break off negotiations than to enter into the contract with the term excluded.

The Scope of the Rule

We have seen that once the parties have reduced their agreement to a document intended to be in its final form, the parol evidence rule appears to preclude either of them from offering evidence of other terms not in that final agreement. In some circumstances, at first sight the rule seems to apply, but the courts have concluded that the written document was not intended to embody the *whole* contract; they have therefore admitted evidence of its oral terms. In the preceding chapter we learned that the terms of a contract may be partly in writing and partly oral. If a party can show that the writing was not intended to contain the whole oral contract but was merely a part of it, then she may introduce evidence of those terms of the contract that are oral.[7]

---

[7] DeLasalle v. Guilford, [1901] 2 K.B. 215, is an extreme example of the lengths to which the courts will go in avoiding the parol evidence rule on these grounds.

ILLUSTRATION

A, the owner of a fleet of dump trucks, agrees orally with *B*, a paving contractor, to move 75 000 cubic feet of gravel within three months from Harrowsmith to Yarker for $15 000 and to provide any related documents that *B* may require for financing the project. To finance her paving operations *B* applies for a bank loan, and the bank requests evidence that the paving work can be started immediately. *B* therefore asks *A* to sign a statement to the effect that he will deliver 25 000 cubic feet from Harrowsmith to Yarker within the next month for $5000. Soon after *A* starts to make the deliveries, he discovers that he has quoted too low a price per cubic foot. He claims that his agreement with *B* has been reduced to writing and that he need move only the 25 000 cubic feet referred to in the writing.

The parol evidence rule does not apply. The written document for the bank was not intended to be a complete statement of the contract. Rather it was drawn up as part of *A*'s performance of his obligation under it. Accordingly, *B* may sue *A* for damages if *A* refuses to perform the balance of the contract, and for this purpose *B* may offer evidence of the terms of the original oral agreement.

There are two further circumstances where the rule by definition does not apply. First, it does not hinder the interpretation of express terms already in the contract. As we have seen in the preceding section, the court does accept evidence to explain the meaning of the words used in a written contract — to determine the meaning of the word "build" in the contract to build cabinets, for example. As one English judge has put it:

> There cannot be the slightest objection to the admission of evidence… which neither alters nor adds to the written contract, but merely enables us to ascertain what was the subject matter referred to therein.[8]

Second, the rule does not exclude evidence of an oral agreement that the parties may reach *after* they have entered into the written agreement. The subsequent oral agreement may change the terms of the written agreement[9] or, as we have seen in the preceding chapter, even rescind the prior contract altogether.[10] In either event, the court will hear evidence of the subsequent oral contract.

Collateral Agreement

An argument often made by a party is that there was a collateral agreement (sometimes called a collateral term) — an entirely separate undertaking upon which the parties were agreed and which they did not incorporate in their written contract, probably because the written contract seemed an inappropriate place for it. Such a collateral undertaking, the argument runs, may be enforced as a separate contract quite independent of the written document. Allowed much scope, this argument would easily circumvent the parol evidence rule. The acceptance of a claim for a collateral contract by a Canadian court seems to depend upon whether a separate consideration can be found for the collateral promise.

---

[8] Macdonald v. Longbottom (1863), 120 E.R. 1177 at 1179.
[9] See Johnson Investments v. Pagritide, [1923] 2 D.L.R. 985.
[10] Morris v. Baron, [1918] A.C. 1.

ILLUSTRATION

A offers to sell his residence, Rainbow End, to *B* for $90 000. *B* replies that she will buy Rainbow End for that price only if *A* will repair or replace a damaged, electronically operated garage door. *A* agrees to this request, and the parties draw a written contract for the sale of Rainbow End but do not mention the garage door in it because they believe they should not do so in a formal contract. *A* fails to perform his promise regarding the garage door.

The consideration for the garage door repair or replacement is the payment of the $90 000 purchase price for Rainbow End, and thus the promise to include the item appears as an integral part of the contract: unless the promise is mentioned in the written agreement, it is likely to be excluded by the parol evidence rule.

If, instead, *B* had agreed to pay *A* an extra $750 for the garage door, there would be a separate consideration for it. In effect there would be two separate contracts: a written contract for the sale of Rainbow End for $90 000 and a collateral oral contract for the repair of the garage door for $750. Because there would then be a separate consideration, the court would very likely consider the oral agreement outside the scope of the parol evidence rule and would enforce it.

Condition Precedent

We come next to a surprising historical exception to the parol evidence rule: the effect of a separate understanding about a *condition precedent*. A condition precedent is any set of circumstances or events that the parties stipulate must be satisfied or must happen before their contract takes effect. It may be an event beyond the control of either of them, such as a requirement that a licensing board approve the transfer of a business. And it need not be in writing. If the party alleging that a condition precedent was agreed on and not met can produce evidence to support the claim, a court will recognize it despite the existence of a complete written form of contract, and declare the contract void. The courts are prepared to recognize and enforce a condition precedent agreed to orally even when the subject-matter of the contract falls within the scope of the Statute of Frauds or the Sale of Goods Act.

ILLUSTRATION

B offers to sell a car to *A* for $4000. *A* agrees orally to buy it provided he can persuade his bank to lend him $3000. The parties agree orally that the contract will operate only if the bank makes the loan, and that otherwise the contract will be void. They then make a written contract in which *A* agrees to pay *B* $4000 in ten days and *B* agrees to deliver the car to *A* at that time. The writing does not mention that the contract is subject to *A* obtaining the bank loan.

The bank refuses to lend the money to *A* who then informs *B* that the sale is off. *B* sues *A* for breach of contract and contends that their oral understanding about the bank loan is excluded by the parol evidence rule.

The parol evidence rule does not apply, and *B* will fail in his action. In his defence, *A* may show that there was an oral understanding suspending the contract of sale unless and until he could obtain the necessary bank loan.

The courts will admit evidence of an oral understanding about a condition precedent even when the written contract includes an express term that the parties' rights and duties are governed exclusively by the written terms. Once a court accepts a contention that the parties did indeed intend to suspend the operation of their contract subject to a condition precedent, then the whole of the contract is suspended, including any term attempting to control the admission of such evidence. In support of this view, a court has said:

> This assertion as to the whole being in writing cannot be used as an instrument of fraud; the plaintiff cannot ignore the means by which he obtained the contract sued upon, falsify his own undertaking, and, by the help of the court, fasten an unqualified engagement on the defendant.[11]

Summary

In practice it is normally difficult to convince a court that the parol evidence rule does not apply: usually, when one party has misunderstood the effect of an agreement, and his later evidence about the alleged oral terms is in sharp conflict with the evidence of the other party, the court will limit the contract to the written terms. Accordingly, it is hazardous for a contracting party to count on the possibility of an exception to the rule, either at the time a contract is being formed and put in writing or at a later time when he must decide whether to go to court over a difference of opinion about the interpretation of the contract.

IMPLIED TERMS AS A METHOD OF INTERPRETATION

Read

We have noted that the parties to a contract cannot think of all those possibilities that may turn out to be a source of disagreement between them after their contract is formed. When we discussed the interpretation of express terms above, we were considering one of the approaches the courts use in trying to resolve such disagreements. A second approach to the problem is for the court to consider whether the intention of the parties can only be given effect by acknowledging the existence of a term that is implied. An *implied term* is one the parties have not expressly included in their agreement but which, in the opinion of the court, they would *as reasonable people* have included when they made their contract had they thought of the possibility of the subsequent difficulty arising. Thus, in our illustration of the contract to build cabinets the court might choose to concentrate upon the meaning of the express words "to build", or it might instead consider whether the contract taken as a whole implies a term that the carpenter is to supply the lumber necessary to build the cabinets. Sometimes, as here, the distinction between these two approaches is more apparent than real: the meaning of the word "build" is likely to be an important factor in deciding whether a term can reasonably be implied. In other instances the *type* of the contract will determine whether a term should be implied. Contracts for the sale of goods contain an implied term that the goods will be suitable for the purpose for which they have been purchased if that purpose has been made known

---

[11] Long v. Smith (1911), 23 O.L.R. 121, per Boyd, C. at 127.

to the seller and it is in the course of the seller's business to supply such goods;[12] but a contract for the sale of land carries with it no such implied term.

Implied terms are usually the result of long-established custom in a particular trade or type of transaction. They exist in almost every field of commerce and came to be recognized among business people because they made good sense or because they led to certainty in transactions without the necessity of spelling out every detail. In time, the courts fell into line with this business practice: when a party failed to perform in compliance with an implied term, the courts would recognize its existence and enforce the contract as though it had been an express term.

ILLUSTRATION

A asks B, a tire dealer, to supply truck tires for his five-ton dump truck. B then shows A a set of tires and quotes a price. A purchases the tires. The sale slip merely sets out the name and the price of the tires. Later A discovers that these tires are not safe on trucks of over three tons' capacity, and claims that he is the victim of a breach of contract.

On these facts there was no express undertaking by B that the tires would be safe for a five-ton truck or any other type of truck. Nevertheless, the court would hold that in the circumstances there was an implied term that the tires should be suitable for a five-ton truck. It would say that in showing A the tires after he had made his intended use of them clear, B, as a regular seller of such tires, implied that they would be suitable for A's truck.

We still, of course, have a problem of knowing in what circumstances the courts are likely to regard an implied term as an appropriate interpretation of a contract. As a general rule, they will imply terms reasonably necessary to give effect to a contract when otherwise the just expectations of a party would be defeated. This approach applies to all kinds of contracts, but in some fields, especially the sale of goods, insurance, partnership, and landlord and tenant relations, a large and complex body of customary terms has grown up. In many jurisdictions these customary terms have been codified in a statute which sets out in one place all the rules previously established by the courts for a particular field of law. Thus the court's decision in the illustration above follows a specific provision in the Sale of Goods Act.

A case which is often cited on the subject of implied terms is known as *The Moorcock*.[13] The defendants owned a wharf and jetty on the river Thames, and the plaintiff owned the steamship *Moorcock*. The parties agreed that the ship should be loaded at the defendants' jetty, the plaintiff paying for the service. While the ship was docked there, the tide ebbed; the vessel came to rest on a hard ridge beneath the river mud and was damaged. Its owner sued and recovered damages on the ground that the defendants must be taken to have implied that the facilities were reasonably safe for the ship at low tide, a necessary provision for carrying out the contract. In giving his opinion Lord Justice Bowen said:

---

[12] The various implied terms in a contract of sale are discussed in Chapter 18.
[13] (1889), 14 P.D. 64.

> I believe if one were to take all the cases, and there are many, of implied warranties or covenants in law, it will be found that in all of them the law is raising an implication from the presumed intention of the parties, with the object of giving the transaction such efficacy as both parties must have intended that at all events it should have. In business transactions such as this, what the law desires to effect by the implication is to give such business effi-cacy to the transaction as must have been intended at all events by both parties who are business men ...[14]

These famous words have been quoted and misquoted innumerable times by both judges and lawyers. The doctrine ensures that a court will not permit the legitimate and reasonable expectations of the parties to a contract to be defeated simply because the con-tract does not deal expressly with a serious contingency that affects the basis of the trans-action. On the other hand, the court will not go further than is necessary, and will not make a new contract for the parties. Nor will it imply a term that is contrary to the expressed intent of the agreement. Lawyers are sometimes inclined to resort to the *Moorcock* doctrine when all else has failed for their client. Consequently, the courts insist that the case for implying a term be made clearly. Parties should, therefore, consider care-fully what assumptions underlie the performance of a contract and bring as many of the important possibilities as they can think of into the open, so that they may reach an express understanding about the terms. Courts have become more cautious than formerly about finding an implied term on the authority of the *Moorcock* decision. In the words of Lord Justice Jenkins:

> I do not think that the court will read a term into a contract unless, considering the matter from the point of view of business efficacy, it is clear beyond a peradventure that both par-ties intended a given term to operate, although they did not include it in so many words.[15]

A Canadian decision illustrates the tendency of the courts to restrict the circumstances in which they will find an implied term on grounds of business efficacy. In *Douglas Bros. and Jones Ltd. v. MacQueen*,[16] the owner of certain property in Nova Scotia hired the plain-tiff to dig and drill a well at $3 per foot plus the cost of pipe. The plaintiff drilled a well to the depth of 385 feet, but the operation closed when the owner refused to pay for the work done and materials supplied because no water had yet been found. In defence of an action for the value of the work done and materials supplied, the owner claimed that the contract contained an implied term that he should have to pay only if clear water was obtained. The court rejected this argument. It held that the contract contained no implied term to this effect either from trade custom or for reasons of business efficacy. Accordingly, the owner was liable for the work done and the materials supplied.

As a general rule, when parties deal explicitly with a matter in their contract, they pre-vent a court from finding an implied term that deals with the same matter in a different way. If they have been very diligent in canvassing all foreseeable possibilities of future dis-pute, a court may conclude that they have intended to deal in a comprehensive way with all future eventualities, so that no further terms should be implied.[17] The parties may

---

[14] *Ibid.*, at 68.
[15] Sethia (1944) Ltd. v. Partabmull Rameshwar, [1950] 1 All E.R. 51 at 59.
[16] (1959), 42 M.P.R. 256.
[17] See Cooke v. CKOY Limited (1963), 39 D.L.R. (2d) 209.

seek to reduce the risk of such a finding by including a further term to the effect that express terms are not intended to be comprehensive; but they may still find a general reluctance by courts to find implied terms.

Questions for Review

1. What is the difference between the *plain-meaning* and the *liberal* approaches to the interpretation of contracts?
2. What kinds of evidence may help a court to decide upon the meaning of an ambiguous term in a contract?
3. What is a common explanation for parties' omitting an agreed term from the final written expression of their contract?
4. What does the word "parol" mean in "parol evidence rule"?
5. What is the difference between an express term and an implied term?
6. What is a condition precedent?
7. Suppose that at the time a contract is formed some of the terms are stated in a letter and other terms are agreed upon orally. Will the parol evidence rule operate to exclude any later testimony about these oral terms?
8. In a written contract A promises to pay B $1000 if B will bring a truckload of certain cases from Vancouver to A's residence in Thunder Bay. B does so. A fails to pay B the $1000, and B sues. In defence A offers evidence that B knew that the cases contained liquor and that their importation into Ontario was in violation of the Liquor Control Act (Ontario). Will such evidence be admitted? If so, how may it affect the court's decision?
9. In what types of contract are implied terms of special importance?
10. What was the principle declared in the *Moorcock* case?
11. How do the courts justify the parol evidence rule? Do you agree with them?
12. "... it is now generally recognized that a party to a contract is held to assume an obligation not because he voluntarily consents to be bound, but because the law attaches that consequence on the basis of his manifested conduct, with or without his consent." (Fleming, *The Law of Torts* (5th ed.), pp. 2-3.) Cite a case mentioned in the text that might be used as an illustration of this idea, and explain why.
13. "The normal contract is not an isolated act, but an incident in the conduct of business or in the framework of some more general relation ... " (Furmston, *Cheshire and Fifoot's Law of Contract* (8th ed.), p. 122.) Show how the idea expressed in this quotation is applied in the interpretation of contracts.
14. By what logic can one reconcile the doctrine of the implied term with the parol evidence rule, when oral testimony is required to establish the circumstances necessary for the operation of an implied term?
15. What did Lord Wright mean in his judgment in *Scammel v. Ouston* when he said, "Difficulty is not synonymous with ambiguity"?
16. In a conversation between an engineer and a professor, the professor contends that some understanding of how legal disputes arise is essential for the successful administration and management of a modern business. The engineer replies that she cannot see why; in her experience it is much more important to know the reputation of the person with whom one is transacting business than to rely upon a detailed

drafting of a written document, and that business depends much more upon the goodwill of the parties than upon the right to take court action if a contract is broken. Discuss the extent to which the engineer's argument is valid, and suggest some of the weaknesses in her position.

17. What may Corbin have meant when he wrote, "Implied promises are also express promises, symbols of expression always including acts and other conduct of the parties in addition to written or spoken words."? (*Corbin on Contracts,* One Volume Edition, p. 531.)

Problems

Problem 1

Mercer worked part time in Sayers Department store for several years. She was a good sales clerk and was asked to work full time — 37.5 hours per week. The employment was entirely oral. Since Sayers remained open six days a week for a total of 68 hours, Mercer's work schedule varied; sometimes she worked evenings and Saturdays, at other times just weekdays.

Two years later the province of British Columbia allowed Sunday shopping. Sayers decided to open on Sundays and required Mercer to report for work. She refused to do so claiming the requirement was not part of her employment contract. Sayers then dismissed her for breach of contract because she refused to obey a reasonable order of her employer. Mercer defended, claiming that since Sunday work was not part of her contract, Sayers had no right to make such an order. Explain whether you believe she is correct. (*Merilees v. Sears Canada Inc.* (1986), 32 D.L.R. (4th) 539.)

Problem 2

Fitzgerald had sold a large quantity of oil to the federal government to be shipped from Ontario and delivered at Halifax. He then made an oral agreement with the Grand Trunk Railway to carry the oil to Halifax in covered cars. (At the time it was apparently common to carry oil both in open and in covered cars.) A term of the oral agreement was that the oil would be carried in two shipments. The first shipment of oil was delivered to the railway, and the agent gave Fitzgerald a bill of lading for the oil shipped. The bill of lading did not state that the oil would be carried in covered cars. The railway shipped the oil in open cars, and as a result it was destroyed by weather.

Fitzgerald sued the railway for loss resulting from the breach of the oral agreement. The railway defended by claiming that the contract had been reduced to writing and the writing did not include a term that the oil should be carried in covered cars. Should Fitzgerald succeed? (*Fitzgerald v. Grand Trunk Railway* (1880) 4 O.A.R. 601. This decision discussed other issues, in particular the negligence of the railway, but they are not relevant to the above problem. See also, *J. Evans & Son v. Andrea Mezario* [1976] 2 All E.R. 930.)

Problem 3

Campbell offered to buy from Pym a three-eighths share in a machine invented by Pym provided that two engineers, Ferguson and Abernethie, were prepared to recommend the invention. They arranged a meeting to be attended by all four men at which the engineers might examine the machine and have Pym explain it to them. Confusion arose about the time of the meeting, and after several of the men had departed and returned, a meeting was held with one of the engineers, Abernethie, absent. The other engineer, Ferguson, approved of the machine, and the meeting agreed that as they were together and might find it troublesome to meet again, an agreement should be drawn up and signed which, if Abernethie later gave his approval, should be the final agreement. The agreement for the purchase of the three-eighths share was set out in the writing and signed by Campbell: it made no reference to the necessity for Abernethie's approval of Pym's invention.

Abernethie later refused to recommend the purchase of an interest in the machine when he saw it. Campbell then refused to proceed with the purchase. Pym sued Campbell to enforce the contract as written. Should he succeed? (*Pym v. Campbell* (1856) 119 E.R. 903.)

Problem 4

To assist John Lees & Sons in buying cotton on credit from Haigh, Brooks gave the following guarantee to Haigh:

> Messrs. Haigh:
>
> In consideration of your being in advance to Messrs. John Lees & Sons in the sum of £10 000 for the purchase of cotton, I do hereby give you my guarantee for that amount on their behalf.
>
> (signed) John Brooks

When the question of the validity of Brooks' guarantee arose at a later time, the court had to interpret the meaning of the words "in consideration of your being in advance". If the words "being in advance" meant "already being in advance" or "already having a sum owing to you from past credit purchases by John Lees & Sons", the guarantee would have been given for a past consideration (assuming, at any rate, that its purpose was not to obtain Haigh's forbearance from suing). If, on the other hand, the words "being in advance" meant "becoming further in advance", the debt to be guaranteed was a future debt, and there was consideration for the guarantee because Haigh, without the guarantee, might not have supplied goods to John Lees & Sons.

If no further evidence is offered to clarify the meaning of these words, what rule will the court follow in choosing between the two possible meanings? (*Haigh v. Brooks* (1839) 113 E.R. 119.)

Cases

Case 1

Atkinson advertised her house for sale and Kirby made a written offer to purchase it for $124 000. The parties discussed the offer several days later, and Atkinson said that she would also like to sell her furniture. After discussion about the amount of furniture for sale and its price, Atkinson accepted in writing Kirby's offer to purchase the house. The offer had made no reference to the furniture and simply required Kirby's certified cheque for $8000 as an immediate payment on account of the agreed price for the house if Atkinson accepted. In fact, Kirby gave Atkinson a cheque for $24 950, the excess being the price they had agreed upon orally for the furniture.

When Kirby occupied the house, he found that Atkinson had taken the grand piano with her. He sued for breach of contract, alleging that in their oral agreement about the furniture they had specifically included the grand piano, and that he had even tried it out in her presence. In defence, Atkinson pleaded that she had never intended to sell the piano, and that in any event evidence of the oral agreement about the furniture would be inadmissible.

With what issues must the court deal before reaching a decision? Should Kirby's action succeed? Give reasons for your opinion.

Case 2

In July, Saunders and Dimmock entered into a partnership for carrying on a grocery and butcher business on Dundee Street East in Toronto. They dissolved the partnership two years later, agreeing that Saunders would continue to operate the business by himself. Dimmock wrote out an agreement dissolving the partnership, and included in his covenant as retiring partner that he would not "during a term of five years from the date hereof commence and carry on a butcher and grocery business, neither directly nor indirectly, nor ... work as an employee in such business within a radius of one-half mile from the said premises at 346 Dundee Street East, in the City of Toronto."

Shortly after, Dimmock opened a grocery and butcher business at 258 Dundee Street East, less than a half-mile away, and operated it as sole proprietor. Saunders brought an action to restrain Dimmock from continuing to break the covenant. In defence Dimmock admitted that the half-mile restriction on employment was a reasonable restraint. He further conceded that if the restriction on carrying on business (owning a business) were also limited to one half-mile, it would be a reasonable restraint, but he argued that the words "half-mile" applied only to *employment* and that there was no geographic limit to his covenant not to *carry on business*. Therefore, the first half of the covenant was void because it was an unreasonable restraint, and accordingly he was free to carry on business as owner. Did Dimmock break the contract?

Case 3

Henry Doubt operated a business as a merchant tailor in Port Perry. He sold all the interest and goodwill of his business, stock-in-trade, and fixtures to Stone for $200 000 and covenanted with Stone that he would,

> ... neither for himself nor for any other person or company engage in the cutting or manufacture or repair of gentlemen's clothing, either tailor-made or ready-made, or in the merchant tailoring business in the village of Port Perry, or within eight miles of the said village, as long as the purchaser [Stone] shall carry on the business of tailor in the said village. But it is expressly understood that [the vendor is] not barred from the sale of ready-made goods or conducting a general store; also [the vendor] may act as a journeyman tailor, but not as either cutter or salesman in a merchant tailor business.

About a year later, Doubt bought out another business in Port Perry which sold ready-made clothing, gents' furnishings, shoes, rubbers, furs, hats, and caps. He had on hand a stock of fifty or more ready-made suits purchased by him from the manufacturer in Hamilton. To fit a particular customer it was sometimes necessary to lengthen, shorten, let out, or take in part of the suit. Occasionally, none of the clothing on hand would fit a customer, who would then be shown samples of cloth from which to select the material and a chart of different styles of suits made by the manufacturers from which he might make his choice. Doubt would then take the customer's measurements and forward them on a standard form to the manufacturers, who maintained a much larger assortment of goods and styles, sizes and patterns than a small retailer such as he could afford. In special instances, when the customer was quite "out of proportion", the manufacturer would have to make a suit up especially for him. Doubt sold about three hundred suits a year, of which about ten on the average had to be ordered from the manufacturer.

After Doubt had carried on the new business for three years, Stone sued him for damages for breach of contract. The court heard evidence from Mr. Walters, another retailer in the same business as Doubt, establishing that the practice followed by Doubt was customary. It was also established that the term "repairing" in the tailoring trade applies to damaged or worn goods. List the strongest points in Doubt's defence with reasons.

Case 4

Chénier sold the surface and minerals in her land in Alberta for $104 000 to Werner under an agreement for sale (an instalment sale that reserved the ownership in the property of Chénier until a specified amount of the price was paid). Werner defaulted payment, thus giving Chénier the right to recover possession by court action. Chénier started proceedings, but they were not yet complete when it became apparent that the land was very valuable. Werner entered into a petroleum and natural gas lease with Imperial Oil Ltd. and received a cash bonus of $110 000, which he intended to use to settle his debt to Chénier. About the same time Chénier, anticipating the recovery of her property by court order, entered into a similar lease of the same property with California Standard Oil Co. At the time Chénier gave her lease to California Standard Oil Co., she told the company's agent that her ability to lease the property depended upon a favourable outcome of her pending court action against Werner and that she could give the lease only if the company's agent would give her a signed statement acknowledging that she (Chénier) did not have any right to lease the mineral rights until the court action against Werner went through. The agent gave her a statement to that effect, and Chénier and California Standard Oil Co. entered into a lease of the mineral rights that made no reference to the proviso signed by the company's agent and, furthermore, contained a paragraph stating that the lease contained the whole of the agreement.

Werner tendered the balance of the purchase price to Chénier, but she refused it and proceeded with the court action. The court dismissed Chénier's petition for recovery of the property. She was, therefore, unable to lease the property to California Standard Oil Co. and that company sued her for breach of contract. Should the action succeed?

Case 5

For a number of years John Conrad Kent operated a very successful "pop" radio station, CROC, in Calgary. At the same time, a separately owned station in Edmonton, CRED, was languishing. Its policy of broadcasting classical music and book reviews to a small but higher-than-average-income audience was attracting very little advertising revenue. Finally, the desperate owner and principal shareholder of CRED Radio Limited approached John Conrad Kent to inquire whether he would act as a consultant in the operation of CRED. Soon afterwards the parties made a contract, in the form of the following letter:

C.R.E.D. RADIO LIMITED

Edmonton, Alberta,
15 December, 1985.

Mr. J. C. Kent,
400 Foothills Road,
Calgary.

Dear Mr. Kent,

This letter will confirm our recent discussions in which you expressed a willingness to act as a consultant to this Company on the terms set out below. If these terms continue to be acceptable to you, please acknowledge your agreement at the bottom of this letter and return one of the two enclosed copies to us.

1. You are to give us upon request such services and advice as we shall require and will consult with us in Edmonton at such times as may be reasonably required and are consistent with your duties elsewhere.

2. We are to pay you as remuneration for such services 40% of the operating profits of the Company. Operating profits shall mean the gross revenue from whatever sources before deducting your remuneration but after deducting all other operating and financial expenses, including depreciation expense and licence fees and taxes other than corporation income tax.

   Company's auditors shall prepare and deliver a statement of operating profits to you and to us as promptly as possible after 31st December each year, which statement shall be binding upon the Company and you. Payment of your remuneration shall be made by the Company within 30 days after the receipt of the auditor's statement.

3. Your employment shall be effective from 1 January, 1986 and shall continue until terminated in the events and in the manner following:

   (i) Should the Company become bankrupt or go into voluntary liquidation, your employment shall forthwith be terminated without notice.

   (ii)   In the event that the Company's broadcasting licence be cancelled for any cause whatever, your employment may be terminated forthwith by the Company by written notice to that effect.

   (iii)   In the event that the annual net profits of the Company for the three business years preceding the year in which such notice is given, have been on the average less than $20 000, your employment may be terminated by the Company at the end of the current business year by 6 months' written notice. "Net profits" shall mean the operating profits of the company as defined above after deducting your remuneration and corporation income tax.

Yours truly,
C.R.E.D. RADIO LIMITED
Rosanna Smith, President.

Approved and accepted:
John Conrad Kent.
21 Dec. 1985.

Kent had a free hand in the management of CRED, in making staff changes, in program planning and in policy making. He introduced radical changes that resulted in a complete turnover in the station's audience. To banish its former image, the station's call letters were changed to CROL. At first, Kent went to Edmonton at least once a month and spent two or three days at the radio station; his visits were less frequent after the station was operating profitably, but he was always available and never refused his advice or presence when requested. Over the six year period ending 31 December 1991, operating profits of CROL Radio Limited were $950 000.

At hearings of the Canadian Radio-television and Telecommunications Commission in October 1991, criticisms were made about CROL's program format and its non-local "absentee" form of management. As a result, the C.R.T.C. approved a renewal of the station's licence for only one year instead of the usual three years.

In January 1992, Kent moved to St. John's, Newfoundland to work with off-shore oil-drilling interests there. CROL Radio Limited then decided to terminate its contract with him. It sent him a letter stating that his services would no longer be used after 30 June 1992.

Kent protested that he was still available to perform the contract; that when the contract was being negotiated he had resisted a suggestion that it contain a provision for termination on reasonable notice and would have refused to sign a contract containing such a term; and that none of the specific events had occurred at which the contract might, by its express terms, be terminated. He sued for breach of contract against CROL Radio Limited, claiming damages of $400 000, his estimate of the present value of his annual earnings from the contract for the balance of his expected active business career.

Develop a line of argument for the defendant company, CROL Radio Limited, and speculate on Kent's chances for success in his action.

CHAPTER 14

PRIVITY OF CONTRACT AND THE ASSIGNMENT OF CONTRACTUAL RIGHTS

$\mathcal{P}$RIVITY OF CONTRACT

When parties make a contract, they create a small body of law for themselves by the terms they agree to. It seems reasonable that the scope of a contract — its power to affect relations — should be confined to the parties who created it: persons outside the contract, who had no say in the bargaining for its terms, should have neither rights nor duties under it.

In theory this reasoning seems sound, and in fact it represents the general attitude of the common law as well as of other systems of law. But in practice many situations arise where the purposes of justice generally, and of business convenience in particular, require that a contract be allowed to affect persons outside it. In the law of contract, a person who is not a party to a contract is called a *third person* or *third party,* or sometimes a *stranger* to the contract. In this chapter we are going to explore the effect of contracts on third persons. In other words, we are to examine the "sphere of influence" of contracts.

The general rule is that a contract does not confer any benefits or impose any obligations on a stranger to the contract. To succeed in an action in contract, the plaintiff must therefore be able to prove *privity of contract* with the defendant, that is, to show that they are both parties to the same contract.

ILLUSTRATION

A, a carpenter, owes $1000 to *B*. *A* offers to renovate *C*'s kitchen if *C* will promise to pay off *A*'s debt to *B*. *C* accepts the offer, and *A* completes the renovation. As a third party to the contract for renovation *B* cannot enforce *C*'s promise; there is no privity of contract between them.[1]

Consequently, if *C* fails to pay *B*, *B* cannot sue *C*, but may still sue, or say he intends to sue *A* for the debt *A* owes him; *A* may then sue *C* for his failure to carry out his promise to pay *B*, and will recover damages to $1000 plus any costs he suffered if *B* actually sued him.

An additional argument sometimes made against permitting a third person to sue on a contract is that he has not given consideration for the promise. Whatever the validity of this argument, it does not make the result any more satisfactory for the third person. Suppose in our illustration that *B* also signed as a party to the contract between *A* and *C* to renovate the kitchen. There would now be privity of contract between *B* and *C* because *C* would have made his promise of payment to *B* as well as to *A*. However, *B* still could not sue because he would not have given consideration for *C*'s promise. Not only must consideration for a promise be given by some party to the contract, it must be given by that party who is trying to enforce the promise.

We have seen in the preceding chapter that a consumer who purchases goods from a merchant receives the benefit of an implied term that the goods are reasonably suited for the purpose for which they are sold. Thus, if a person buys a can of salmon that turns out to be poisonous and seriously injures her, she may recover damages for breach of the implied term that the fish was suitable to eat — provided, of course, the merchant has sufficient assets or

---

[1] Price v. Easton (1883), 110 E.R. 518.

insurance to pay her claim. But in any event, members of her family who were also injured by eating the salmon cannot recover damages against the merchant: the merchant's contract was with the buyer, and only the buyer can sue successfully for breach of contract. Other members of the family have no privity of contract with the merchant and no rights under the contract.

Since they have no rights against the merchant what about suing the manufacturer? This action would seem reasonable since it is the manufacturer who has caused the product to be poisonous; the merchant has no way of knowing that sealed goods are not up to standard. But the buyer of the salmon contracted only with the merchant; she has no contract with the manfacturer and no right to sue it for breach of contract.[2] Fortunately, as we have noted in Chapter 4, both the consumer and her family do have a remedy in tort: they may sue the manufacturer for negligence. In perhaps the most famous case of the century, *Donoghue v. Stevenson*,[3] the House of Lords decided that manufacturers are liable in tort for damages caused by their products when the products are most likely to be used without intermediate examination.

> While in a shop, the plaintiff drank ginger beer poured from an opaque bottle into her glass. She drank one glassful, and when more ginger beer was poured from the bottle a decomposed snail also came out. The plaintiff became violently ill. Since a friend had bought the beverage for her there was no privity of contract between her and the shopkeeper. Nor could she sue the shopkeeper in tort, for he had not been negligent: the bottle had come from the manufacturer sealed and he had merely opened the bottle as is usual and passed it on to the consumer. The plaintiff sued the manufacturer for negligence.

The court held that manufacturers of goods used without intermediate inspection are under a high duty of care to make their products safe. It held that if the defendant company had not lived up to this standard, that is, if it were negligent in permitting the snail to get into the bottle, it must pay damages for the loss suffered.

A comparable question is whether a landlord owes a similar duty to persons who use premises occupied by a tenant. This time the answer is less satisfactory. A landlord has no liability to repair business premises unless the lease contains an express promise to do so.[4] Even when there is an express promise, its benefit extends only to the other contracting party, the tenant, and not to a third person such as an employee of the tenant. An employee injured because of the landlord's failure to repair as promised cannot maintain an action against the landlord for damages; there is no privity of contract between a tenant's employee and the landlord.[5] The courts have also held that there is no duty upon a landlord in tort, either to the tenant or to others, to repair unfurnished premises. As explained in Chapter 4, the tenant as occupier of the premises owes a duty of care to others who enter. In contrast to the liability of a manufacturer, a landlord may leave premises occupied by the tenant in disrepair without fear of being held liable in tort for injuries suffered by the tenant or by its employees or customers.

---

[2] The idea of a "collateral warranty" that we shall shortly refer to in Shanklin Pier, Ltd. v. Detel Products, Ltd. is still regarded as a special concession in particular circumstances.

[3] [1932] A.C. 562.

[4] This common law rule may, however, be altered by statute. For example, the Residential Rent Regulation Act, R.S.O. 1990, c. R-29, s. 94 provides that in respect of residential tenancies only, a landlord is responsible for providing and maintaining the rented premises in a good state of repair and fit for habitation. See also: Landlord and Tenant Act, R.S.M. 1987, c. L70, s. 116(1); Residential Tenancies Act, R.S.N.S. 1989, c. 401, s. 6(1).

[5] Cavalier v. Pope, [1906] A.C. 428.

The privity of contract rule can also have harsh consequences when it prevents a third person from enforcing a contract the whole object of which was to benefit him. Yet this was the decision in *Tweddle v. Atkinson*.[6] There the contract was between the respective fathers of a young married couple: the father of the husband promised the father of the bride that he would pay £100 to the married couple, and in return the father of the bride promised that he would pay them a further £200. The father of the bride died before he had paid the £200, and his executor, Atkinson, refused to pay it. The husband, Tweddle, brought an action to enforce the promise but failed because he was a stranger to the contract between the two fathers. The court rejected the argument that the plaintiff's kinship to one of the contracting parties made him something more than a "stranger" to the contract.

Novation

Novation occurs when the parties to a contract agree to terminate it and substitute a new contract. There are two types of novation: (a) The parties may change the subject matter of the contract. For instance, car dealer B may inform A that he cannot deliver the car A has ordered without a lengthy delay. They agree to cancel the contract and substitute a new one: for a favourable price offered by B, A buys a car that B has in stock. (b) One of the parties to the contract "leaves" and another replaces her. For example, M has a contract with Q to obtain advertising for her business. M arranges to sell her business to N, who wishes to continue the advertising arrangment with Q. M,N and Q meet and agree that: M and Q terminate their contract, each giving up all future rights under it; and N and Q sign a new contract under the same terms as the terminated contract between M and Q. In (b) above, novation substitutes a stranger for an existing party to the contract. The new party may sue or be sued on the new contract, and the former party no longer has any rights or obligations; the result is consistent with the rule requiring privity of contract. This subject is discussed further in the next chapter.

Vicarious Performance

A promisor cannot escape his liability to the promisee by imposing a substitute for himself without the consent of the promisee. In other words, he cannot transfer or "assign" his liability, even if he can find someone willing to assume the liability for him. The promisee may, of course, consent to a new contract with a change of parties, but then the arrangement is not within the terms of the original contract — it is novation.

There are nevertheless many circumstances in which a party may obtain someone to carry out his actual duties for him, though he remains accountable to the promisee for proper performance. Performance of this type is known as *vicarious performance*; an

---

6 (1861), 121 E.R. 762. The court based its decision on the rule that consideration must move from the promisee and that since the husband, Tweddle, could not show that he had given any consideration, his action must fail. But our definition of consideration also implies that the plaintiff to an action (in this case, Tweddle) must be a party to the contract; since he was not a party, he could not have given consideration in any event.

employee of the promisor performs vicariously (that is, on behalf of the promisor). Vicarious performance must be distinguished from personal performance. In vicarious performance the promisor assumes the role of the employer and engages someone to undertake the work for him. If the work is not done satisfactorily, the promisee will seek a remedy for breach of contract against the promisor, and not the promisor's employee. In turn, the employee can look only to the employer (and not to the promisee) for payment for the work he has done. The performance of the original contract is accomplished by means of a second contract, a contract of employment. The results are consistent with the rule of privity of contract.

Suppose, however, that in performing the contract an employee commits a tort: he negligently damages a valuable instrument belonging to the promisee. As we noted in Chapter 4 on Torts, the promisee may sue both the employer for vicarious liability and the employee personally. Of course, since the employer ordinarily has a "deeper pocket" than its employee, the promisee will choose to sue the employer.

Employers often protect themselves from such liability. For example, carriers and storage companies usually insert exemption clauses to exclude or limit liability for negligence. By allocating the risk of loss to the promisee, an exemption clause lowers a storage company's costs and allows it to reduce its price to the promisee, which in turn obtains its own insurance against loss. While such an exemption clause may protect the storage company from liability for negligence,[7] its employees are not parties to the contract; under the traditional privity rule they were unable to claim its protection. A recent decision of the Supreme Court of Canada has reversed that position and granted protection to employees, provided they can show that the clause was intended to be for their benefit and the damage occurred in the course of their employment.[8]

A promisor may employ a third party to perform the work vicariously if it is of such a nature that the personal performance of the promisor was not the reason why the promisee entered into the contract. The party entitled to performance generally cannot complain if someone other than the promisor turns up and does the work equally well. In fact, in many contracts the understanding is that by their very nature they must be performed by a large number of persons who are not parties to the contract: contracts for the construction of buildings, the manufacture of goods, and the transport of people, for example.

ILLUSTRATIONS

(a) *A* Co. Ltd. contracts with a public accountant, *B*, to have its accounts audited. *B* sends *C*, a senior accountant, to carry out the audit program. May *A* Co. Ltd. object? This is a type of work that can be carried out competently by a qualified accountant and ordinarily would not require *B*'s personal performance unless *A* Co. Ltd. had expressly bargained for it. Consequently, the vicarious performance by *C* is permissible and *A* Co. Ltd. is not entitled to reject the tender of such performance. (We may, of course, assume that a final review of the audit would always be made by *B*.)

---

[7] For a fuller discussion of the effect of exemption clauses, see Chapter 16.
[8] London Drugs v. Kuehne & Nagel International (1992), 97 D.L.R. (4th) 261.

(b) If C does such an inadequate job that he fails to detect a material error in the accounts and as a result A Co. Ltd. suffers a loss, A Co. Ltd. must look to B for damages for breach of contract. In addition, if C's poor work amounted to negligence, he would be personally liable to A Co. Ltd. in tort, and B would also be vicariously liable in tort for C's negligence

(c) Suppose instead that C performs satisfactorily and B dies insolvent without paying C his salary. Could C successfully bring an action for his wages against A Co. Ltd. as the beneficiary of the services he has rendered? There is no contract between C and A Co. Ltd. on which he may base his action. The arrangement has involved two contracts, one between A Co. Ltd. and B, by which A Co. Ltd. remains liable to pay B's estate, and one between B and C, but none between C and A Co. Ltd. C's action would fail.

A common example of vicarious performance occurs when goods are shipped to a destination that requires the services of a number of carriers. Thus, a shipment by rail from Toronto to New York City may be made by Canadian National Railways and the New York Central. The shipper contracts with a carrier whose franchise area includes the point of shipment and that carrier arranges for completion of the shipment with connecting carriers who operate outside its area of franchise.

Sometimes a party has its obligations performed vicariously when it should have performed personally, but the other party may have no opportunity to protest until the work is finished. In this situation, the promisor is guilty of a breach of a term in the contract (the implied or express promise to perform personally). The promisee may sue for damages to compensate for whatever loss he can show resulted from vicarious, rather than personal, performance.

TRUSTS

The following example introduces the idea of a trust. Suppose a mother wishes to provide for her son in the event that she should die while he is still an infant. In her will, she leaves a fund to be invested in securities, and directs that the income is to be used to care for her son. Since she requires someone to administer the fund and to pay the money out for his care, she also appoints a *trustee* and directs the fund to be paid over to him and be left under his control.

Suppose the mother then dies and the fund is handed over to the trustee. If the trustee refuses to pay the income out for the benefit of the son, what rights has the child as *beneficiary* of the trust? The old common law courts took the position that the trustee was the sole legal owner of the property, and refused to recognize the interest of the beneficiary in the fund. To redress this injustice, the courts of equity recognized that the trust fund was set up by the mother for the benefit of the son and not of the trustee. In effect, equity decided that the son was the true owner — the *beneficial owner* — of the fund. Equity developed procedures by which a beneficiary could compel a trustee (possibly a trust company) to carry out its duties faithfully. As we have noted in Chapter 3, the conflict between the courts of equity and the courts of common law was settled when the courts were amalgamated: the equitable principles recognizing beneficial interests in trusts prevailed in the new courts.

The trust concept has important applications in business. A trust is created when the creditors of a business convince the court that their debtor is no longer capable of paying its debts as they fall due. The court will order that the property of the bankrupt debtor be transferred to a trustee in bankruptcy for realization and distribution to the creditors. Another example occurs when a corporation transfers the title to its fixed assets to a trustee for the bondholders as security for the repayment of money borrowed by an issue of mortgage bonds; a corporation may pay annual instalments to a sinking fund trustee who will use the money to redeem and cancel a part of the bonds payable by the corporation.

A trust has been defined as "any arrangement whereby property is transferred with the intention that it be administered by a trustee for another's benefit."[9] In this definition and in all of the examples given above, the trust is created by the transfer of some kind of *property* to the trustee. How, then, is the concept of a trust related to contracts and the rights of third parties? The beneficiary of a trust is in a position analogous to that of a third party to a contract, being neither the person who created the trust nor the person who is appointed to administer it; yet the beneficiary has been given a means of enforcing the trust in his favour. In time the courts of equity developed an ingenious extension of the idea of the trust: they noted that the legal right to demand performance of a promise in a contract is a thing of value — a type of property, in other words. The next step was to say that a promisee who has extracted a promise for the benefit of a third person can sometimes be regarded as a trustee for the third person of the benefit of that promise. The way was then open for permitting a third party to enforce the contract in his or her favour. A trust of this kind is called a *constructive trust*. When a court accepts this argument the strictures of the privity of contract rule are avoided.

ILLUSTRATION

A, B, and *C* enter into a partnership agreement, a term of which states that if one of the partners should die his widow would receive a share of the future profits of the firm. On the death of *A*, the surviving partners *B* and *C* refuse to pay a share of the profits to *A*'s widow. Would she be successful in enforcing the term? The facts here are based on the case of *Re Flavell*,[10] where the court held that while the widow was not a party to the partnership agreement, the agreement had created a trust in her favour. It decided that her husband as promisee of the term in the partnership agreement had become a trustee of her interest. On his death his executor became the trustee in his place, and the executor was successful in obtaining the share for the widow.

Unfortunately, parties to a contract are not likely to be aware of the subtleties of a constructive trust, nor are they likely to create a trust expressly to ensure that a third party beneficiary will have rights enforceable in court. In an action by a third party to obtain a declaration that a trust was created, the court often must proceed only by inference from the contract: in many cases the party who intended to confer the benefit has died or is

---

9   Black's *Law Dictionary* (6th ed.). St. Paul, Minn.: West Publishing Co., 1990.
10 (1883), 25 Ch. D. 89. For an interesting modern case, see Beswick v. Beswick [1968] A.C. 58.

unavailable to give testimony of his intentions. As a result the courts have had considerable difficulty in deciding when a constructive trust has been created; even when the facts have been ascertained, it is hazardous to predict the decision.

One of the main obstacles to finding a constructive trust is the rule that once created, a trust cannot be revoked by those who created it without the consent of the beneficiary. Before a court will find a constructive trust, it must be satisfied that the contracting parties intended that the benefit for the third party should be binding on them *without the possibility of later revision or revocation by them.* The courts have been reluctant to infer such an intention between contracting parties.[11] As a result, the constructive trust has not become a reliable means for avoiding the privity of contract rule.

The difficulties inherent in this branch of the common law would seem to require revision by statute. As long ago as 1937, a Law Revision Committee in England proposed as a solution that a separate statute be enacted that provides:

> ... where a contract by its express terms purports to confer a benefit directly on a third party, the third party shall be entitled to enforce the provision in his own name, provided that the promisor shall be entitled to raise as against the third party any defence that would have been valid against the promisee. The rights of the third party shall be subject to cancellation of the contract by the mutual consent of the contracting parties at any time before the third party has adopted it either expressly or by conduct.[12]

The proposal has not been enacted in England or in any of the Canadian provinces. In several of the United States the courts have for many years followed a rule like that recommended by the Law Revision Committee.

Exceptions to the Privity of Contract Rule

Insurance

When one insures his life, he enters into a contract of insurance with an insurance company. This contract or *policy* may indicate that the insurance money is to be paid to a specified person, a spouse, say, who is not a party to the insurance contract. Each of the provinces has a statute that gives a beneficiary a right against the insurance company to enforce the insurance contract according to its terms.[13] Similarly, in a contract of automobile insurance, the company may promise to indemnify not only the owner but also anyone driving with his consent. If a person driving with the owner's consent injures a pedestrian and is required to pay damages, he may in turn sue the insurance company for indemnity against his loss, even though he was not a party to the insurance contract.[14]

---

[11] See Re Schebsman, [1944] Ch. 83.

[12] Law Revision Committee (U.K.), *Sixth Interim Report,* 1937 (Reprinted 1955) Cmd. 5449, p. 30.

[13] See, for example: Insurance Act, R.S.O. 1990, c. I-8, s. 195; R.S.B.C. 1979, c. 200, s. 146; R.S.N.S. 1989, c. 231, s. 197.

[14] See, for example: Insurance Act, R.S.O. 1990, c. I-8, s. 239; R.S.B.C. 1979, c. 200, s. 234, as amended by 1980, c. 50, s. 46.1.

The Undisclosed Principal

A further modification of the rule requiring privity of contract occurs when one of the contracting parties, unknown to the other, proves to be only an agent of someone else: the person for whom the agent was acting, known as an *undisclosed principal,* may sue or be sued on the contract. The subject is sufficiently complex that we shall defer a discussion of it for separate consideration in Chapter 22.

Contracts Concerning Land

The idea of privity of contract does not apply generally in land law. If the owner of land leases it to a tenant who promises to pay rent and keep the property in good repair, and the owner subsequently sells it, the tenant must perform the promises for the new owner. The value of the land on the market would be substantially lowered if the tenant could ignore promises made to the former owner. Similarly, the new owner must respect the tenant's rights to remain on the property until the lease expires. Otherwise tenants would always be in jeopardy of being evicted when land is sold. Accordingly, persons who acquire interests in land are often subject to earlier contracts relating to the property and can often take benefits under them.

There has been some debate about whether liabilities arising out of the chartering of ships may affect subsequent purchasers of ships in a similar manner.[15]

Special Concessions to Commercial Practice

Courts have sometimes been prepared to enlarge the sphere of a contract so that persons who are closely associated with a business transaction, though not strictly a party to it, may nevertheless find themselves subject to its terms.

In *Shanklin Pier, Ltd. v. Detel Products, Ltd.*[16] the owners of a pier consulted Detel Products, Ltd., paint manufacturers, about the best type of paint to use in repainting the pier. Detel recommended one of its paints as suitable and promised that the paint would have a life of seven to ten years. Shanklin then made a contract with a firm of contractors to do the work requiring them to use the paint recommended by Detel. The contractors purchased the paint from Detel. The paint proved unsatisfactory; it lasted only about three months. Shanklin sued Detel for breach of warranty regarding the quality of the paint.

We should note that there was an express contract between Shanklin and the contractors and another between them and Detel, but there was no express contract between Shanklin and Detel. Nevertheless, the court found that there was an *implied collateral contract* between Shanklin and Detel on the following terms: Detel warranted that its paint was suitable for the pier if Shanklin in turn required the contractors to purchase the paint from Detel. In the result, Shanklin recovered extensive damages.

In applying the principle of the *Shanklin Pier* decision, a Canadian court has found that a manufacturer of farm machinery made a representation to farmers in the form of a "collateral warranty" when it published a promotional sales brochure used by dealers for the

---

[15] See Lord Strathcona Steamship Co. v. Dominion Coal Co., [1926] A.C. 108, and Port Line Ltd. v. Ben Line Steamers Ltd., [1958] 2 Q.B. 146.
[16] [1951] 2 K.B. 854.

purpose of inducing farmers to buy its product.[17] Accordingly, a farmer recovered damages from the manufacturer for breach of a warranty. Mr. Justice Reid of the Ontario High Court of Justice said:

> I can see no legal basis for differentiating between dealer and manufacturer in relation to collateral warranties. The manufacturer initiated the affirmations; it was the manufacturer who apparently prepared and certainly published the brochure. The dealer would perforce have to rely on the manufacturer.[18]

In *Pyrene Co. Ltd. v. Scindia Navigation Co. Ltd.*[19] Pyrene sold certain aircraft tenders to a department of the Indian government on the terms that the Indian government should arrange for their shipment from London to India and that the goods should be at the risk of Pyrene until they were loaded on board ship. The Indian government then contracted with Scindia as carrier to ship the goods, and it was a term of that contract that the carrier should not be liable for damages in excess of £200. As a result of the negligence of Scindia in loading one of the tenders, it was damaged to the extent of £900, before it crossed the ship's rail. Since the goods were at Pyrene's risk, it had to make good the loss to the Indian government. Pyrene then sued the carrier for negligence to recoup its loss of £900. In defence the carrier claimed that Pyrene was bound by the term of the contract of shipment with the Indian government restricting the carrier's liability to £200. Since Pyrene was a stranger to the contract of shipment, it claimed that the rule requiring privity of contract meant that it was not bound by the term restricting liability, and that it should recover the full £900. The court ruled, however, that the effect of the whole transaction, and in particular of the agreement that the Indian government should arrange for shipping, was to make Pyrene a participant in the contract of shipment. Accordingly, it could not recover more than £200 damages.

These cases illustrate the growing sensitivity of the courts to the substance of commercial transactions and an inclination to grant appropriate remedies.

THE NATURE OF AN ASSIGNMENT OF RIGHTS

We have seen that apart from land law an assignment of liabilities to a third person is not possible. An assignment of contractual rights is, however, a common form of business transaction. It is, in fact, the most important and long-established concession to commercial practice that our courts have recognized. Historically, such assignments became enforceable only as the courts became more willing to relax the privity of contract rule.

---

[17] Murray v. Sperry Rand Corporation *et al.* (1979) 23 O.R. (2d) 456; 96 D.L.R. (3d) 113.
[18] *Ibid.,* at p. 466. See also: Andrews v. Hopkinson [1957], 1 Q.B. 229; Brown v. Sheen and Richmond Car Sales Ltd., [1950] 1 All E.R. 1102.
[19] [1954] 2 Q.B. 402.

ILLUSTRATION

A Ltd., a building contractor, has erected a building for *B*. Under the terms of their contract, *B* still owes *A* Ltd. $10 000, to be paid one month after the completion of the building. *A* Ltd. has purchased $12 000 worth of materials from *X* Corp. In settlement of its debt to *X* Corp., *A* Ltd. pays $2000 in cash and assigns in writing its rights to the $10 000 still owing by *B*. *X* Corp. then notifies *B* that she should pay the money to it rather than to *A* Ltd. when the debt falls due.

In the above illustration, the contractor *A* Ltd. is the *assignor* of its right to the payment of $10 000. It has assigned the right to *X* Corp., its assignee, for a valuable consideration. The consideration is *X* Corp.'s promise to accept the assignment in satisfaction of the balance of its claim against *A* Ltd. Given proper notice, the promisor *B* must perform for the assignee *X* Corp. instead of for the original promisee *A* Ltd.

As we noted in our discussion of constructive trusts, contractual rights are often valuable and may be considered a type of personal property along with the ownership of goods. The main difference is that tangible property, such as goods, may be possessed physically — it has a concrete existence; whereas a right to demand performance of a contract has no concrete existence — it is valuable only insofar as it is enforceable in the courts. The rights to tangible property that may be possessed physically are known as *choses in possession;* the rights to intangible property, to those things that have value only because they may be enforced by action in the courts, are called *choses in action.* There are many types of choses in action, including such things as patents, copyrights, stocks, bonds, rights to collect the proceeds of an insurance policy in the event the risk should occur, rights of action against persons who have caused injury, and rights under contracts generally.

A willingness to accept the ownership of choses in action as a form of personal wealth is an important mark of a modern industrial society. Choses in action give people the opportunity to retain valuable assets, say, their accumulated savings, and at the same time, through the ownership of shares and bonds, to put those assets to work as capital at the disposal of companies; in other words, this device links personal saving to business investment. In some less developed countries, it has been a major problem to persuade wealthy residents to abandon their preference for investment in gold, jewels, and real estate and to accept a portfolio of mortgages, shares, and bonds as an alternative form of property. This problem affects the development of active capital markets.

In this chapter we are concerned with the assignment of rights arising under contracts generally: a discussion of the specific features of such choses in action as mortgages, shares, bonds, and negotiable instruments is reserved for later chapters.

There is a similarity between an assignment of rights (choses in action) and a sale of goods (choses in possession). In an assignment the subject-matter is the transfer of contractual rights; in a sale the subject-matter is the transfer of ownership in goods. Although we might have expected the law to give equal recognition to each of these transfers, this was not so in the old courts of common law. They ruled that choses in action were personal rights and could not be transferred as could choses in possession. The rule grew steadily more inconvenient and obsolete as commerce increased. The courts of equity, on the other hand, were much more flexible; they recognized the efficacy and fairness of enforcing assignments of contractual rights. Equity required only that a clear intention to assign a benefit be shown either orally or in writing by the assignor, and then it would permit the assignee to recover from the promisor. Because of the conflict between the rules of the common law courts and those of equity, the courts of equity required in every action by an assignee of contractual rights that he make the assignor a party as well. The action then had three parties — the assignee, the assignor, and the promisor.

*E*QUITABLE ASSIGNMENTS

A basic principle of law is that a court will not decide a dispute unless all the persons directly affected by its decision have been made parties and have had an opportunity to argue on their own behalf. Thus, if an assignor assigns part of her rights only, she remains vitally interested in the result of an action by the assignee against the promisor: if the court should decide that the promisor is not bound to perform any part of his obligations, its decision would adversely affect the assignor as well as the assignee.

ILLUSTRATION

B has a claim against *A* for $10 000 under a contract. At the same time, *B* owes $6000 to *X* Finance Co. *B* assigns $6000 of her account receivable from *A* to satisfy *X*. Subsequently, *X* sues *A* for the $6000. If the court were to decide that *A* was not bound to pay anything on the debt because, say, the contract between *A* and *B* was within the Statute of Frauds and there was an insufficient memorandum of it, *B* would be affected, for she could not claim her remaining $4000 of the debt either. The court requires that *B* be made a party to the action by *X* so that she may take part in it.

In an assignment of part of a debt, both the assignee and the assignor are equally anxious that the court find the debtor (that is, the promisor) liable. Accordingly, the assignor *B* must have her own chance to argue and to adduce evidence. For example, it might well be that she would have in her possession a memorandum sufficient to comply with the Statute of Frauds, and her evidence might be decisive in holding the debtor liable.

Similarly, in an action brought by *B* against *A*, the court would require that *X* Finance Co. also be made a party.

Let us assume that the assignor assigns only part of its rights and the promisor is willing to perform his obligation, but he does not know what part he should perform for the benefit of the assignee and what part for the benefit of the assignor.

ILLUSTRATION

A owes $100 000 to B Inc., due in twelve months. B Inc. needs short term financing and borrows $80 000 from X Bank, repayable in one year, giving X Bank a *conditional assignment* of its account receivable from A as security for repayment of the loan. B Inc. and the bank have agreed that as long as B Inc. pays the interest on its loan every three months, the bank will not be entitled to notify A of the assignment; but if B Inc. fails to pay the interest or fails to pay the $80 000 on the due date, the bank may advise A to pay it that sum plus unpaid interest, in reduction of his debt to B Inc. In other words, the assignment is conditional upon the default of the borrower, B Inc.. If at the end of the year, the bank notifies A that B Inc. has assigned his account and demands that A pay the bank, A cannot afford to do so until he has verified the default and the amount owing. He must check with B Inc. Suppose B Inc. claims that it has paid the bank $60 000 of the debt. A is in a quandary: he is aware of the competing claims and fears that if he pays one party and guesses wrong, the other may sue him successfully and collect the amount in dispute a second time. In such a case A should hand the sum claimed by the bank over to the court as custodian and let B Inc. and the bank settle their dispute before a judge.

An equitable assignment also occurs when the subject of the assignment is an aggregate of book debts whose balances fluctuate over time.

ILLUSTRATION

Fribble Corp. owes $160 000 to Tower Bank under a demand loan. Fribble is required to make regular monthly payments on the loan and to provide the bank with half-yearly financial statements. It reported substantial losses six months ago and was slow in making two subsequent interest payments. The bank threatened to call the loan unless it received additional security. Fribble then gave the bank a conditional assignment of its accounts receivable, including several large accounts, some of them running to tens of thousands of dollars. Fribble receives frequent payments on these accounts from its customers, and also ships its products to them from time to time so that the account balances fluctuate substantially. Fribble promised to make its monthly interest payments without fail; otherwise the bank would call the loan and notify Fribble customers of the assignment.

In these circumstances the assignment is conditional, not only because it depends on a future event (default by Fribble), but also because the value of the accounts receivable varies according to the state of accounts between Fribble and each of its customers at any given moment.

In each of the above illustrations, all the parties have a vital interest in the assignment, and it is necessary that all should be bound by the same court decision. Thus, the requirement of equity that the assignor as well as the debtor(s) should be made parties to the assignee's action is a just one in cases where the assignor retains an interest in the contract.

STATUTORY ASSIGNMENTS

In many business transactions an assignor does not wish to retain any rights under the contract assigned. He assigns it wholly and absolutely to the assignee and has no further interest in it. If later the assignee wishes to sue the promisor, the requirement of making the assignor a party may be inconvenient and may even cause considerable hardship; the assignor may be out of the country for a time, or he may have died (in which case it would be necessary to make his personal representative a party). In any event it increases the expense of the action by bringing in a party who has no real interest. In 1873, when the British Parliament amalgamated the courts of common law and equity by passing the Judicature Act, they included a section remedying this defect. The section permits an assignee to sue the promisor to a contract without the assistance of the assignor provided (a) the assignment was absolute (unconditional and complete), (b) the assignment was in writing, and (c) the promisor received notice in writing of the assignment. Most of the provinces of Canada have since passed similar statutes.[20] Assignments that comply with these requirements have become known as *statutory assignments*. All other assignments are today called *equitable assignments*. We should note, however, that the statute did not create any new type of assignment. It merely provided a streamlined procedure for hearing actions on assignments that meet the requirements laid down by statute.

An assignment must meet the statutory requirement of being complete and unconditional if the assignor is to be excused from further participation. Since the requirements do not always suit the convenience of business, many assignments remain equitable rather than statutory. An assignment is *not complete* if the assignor retains an interest in the contract, as where a balance remains to be paid to him after the assignee is paid. An assignment is *not unconditional* when the amount assigned varies according to the state of accounts between the assignor and his debtor, as where the balance of the account assigned fluctuates because the assignor continues to sell goods or services on credit to the debtor (the customer) or the debtor reduces the balance assigned by making payments on account to the assignor. In neither of these situations is the assignment "absolute"; in the first, the assignor retains an interest and in the second, the balance assigned is not fixed and may need to be verified from the assignor's records. The statute says that the assignor's direct participation may be dispensed with when these circumstances do not exist.

The need for writing in support of the statutory assignment is also reasonable. If the assignment were oral, the assignee would ordinarily have to call the assignor as a witness anyway, to prove that the assignment was actually made. As we noted in Chapter 3, evidence given by other persons of what the assignor said is *hearsay,* and for this reason the court will not allow such evidence when the assignor himself is able to testify. A written assignment signed by the assignor is as good in most cases as his personal appearance in court. It may be tendered to the court, and only if there is a rare allegation of a serious fraud, such as forgery, will further evidence be required to prove the assignment. The

---

[20] See, for example: Conveyancing and Law of Property Act, R.S.O. 1990, c. C-34, s. 53; Law and Equity Act, R.S.B.C. 1979, c. 224, s. 32; Judicature Act, R.S.A. 1980, c. J-1, s. 21; R.S.N.S. 1989, c. 240, s. 43(5). The statutory provisions are somewhat different in certain provinces. See, for example: Choses in Action Act, R.S.S. 1978, c. C-11, s. 2 and the Law of Property Act, R.S.M. 1987, c. L90, s. 31(1) and (5).

requirement of notice of assignment in writing similarly is helpful and simplifies proving that the promisor knew of the assignment. It is good business practice and common sense to send written notice by registered letter when important rights are in question in any transaction.

Notice to the Promisor

The Effect of Notice on the Promisor

All assignments, whether equitable or statutory, require notice to the promisor. Notice to the promisor is not, of course, the same thing as requiring his consent. Indeed, a debtor ignores a notice of an assignment at his peril. Confronted with a demand for payment from one who claims to be an assignee, the debtor should, of course, require proof of the assignment to protect himself against a possible fraud, but once he has had an opportunity to satisfy himself that there has been an assignment, he must make further payments to the assignee. If he still persists in making payment to his original creditor, he can be sued by the assignee and required to pay the amount a second time.

ILLUSTRATION

Brian Wholesalers Ltd. buys a large quantity of goods on credit from Akron Manufacturing Co. and defaults payment. It offers to pay by assigning to Akron certain accounts receivable owed to Brian by retail merchants with excellent credit ratings. Akron agrees to this settlement and takes an absolute assignment of the debts, the largest of which is owed by Woolridge's Department Store. Akron sends a notice, signed by an officer of Brian, to Woolridge's

stating that the account has been assigned to it, and encloses a request that Woolridge's pay Akron. Woolridge's inadvertently ignores the notice and request, and pays Brian, which shortly afterwards becomes bankrupt. Akron sues Woolridge's for payment of the debt again.

In these circumstances Akron would succeed in its action; Woolridge's paid Brian at its peril after receiving valid notice of the assignment.[21]

The Effect of Notice from Contending Assignees

Recognition of the assignability of contractual rights is an important modification of the doctrine of privity of contract: someone other than the original party to a contract may emerge to claim the benefit of rights the contract has created. Indeed, more than one person may claim to be the assignee of the same right. Mercifully, the promisor need perform his obligation only once. In order to determine who is entitled to his performance, the court must ascertain the validity and extent of every right claimed against him by various contending assignees.

An unscrupulous creditor can gain a temporary prosperity by assigning to two different persons for valuable consideration the right to collect the same debt. The debtor is then faced with demands for payment from two sources. Which of the two innocent

---

[21] See Brandt's Sons & Co. v. Dunlop Rubber Co. Ltd., [1905] A.C. 454.

assignees is entitled to payment by the debtor? And which has only an action against the assignor for fraud? The cases are unanimous in deciding that the assignee who first gave notice to the debtor is the one entitled to payment. This rule, like the rule that the debtor must at least receive some notice of assignment before it affects him, offers the only fair treatment to the debtor. Otherwise a debtor would be in a very insecure position, never being sure when he makes payment that someone else to whom he should have paid the money may not turn up later.

When there are two assignees of the same debt, the one who receives his assignment from the assignor first may delay in notifying the debtor, so that the second assignee succeeds in notifying the debtor first. The second assignee is then entitled to payment by the debtor, unless he knows of the prior assignment at the time of the assignment to him. If he knows of the prior assignment, he is a party to the fraud, and cannot take payment ahead of the first assignee without becoming liable to him.

THE ASSIGNEE'S TITLE

One of the most important rules affecting assignments is that the assignee can never acquire a better right to sue the promisor than the assignor himself had. In legal terms, the assignee "takes subject to the equities". The result is that a person who acquires a right under an assignment takes it subject to any right arising between the original parties before the promisor receives notice of the assignment. In suing the promisor, the assignee may be met by any defence that the promisor could have put up against the assignor, the party with whom he originally contracted. Consequently, if a person takes an assignment of rights under a contract originally induced by the fraudulent misrepresentation of the assignor, the assignee will have no better chance to enforce his claim than if he had been the perpetrator of the fraud himself. In other words, if a debtor is the victim of fraudulent misrepresentation, the contract remains voidable at his option despite any assignment of the contractual rights. The debtor cannot, however, sue the assignee for damages for the tort of deceit: he must sue the assignor, the person actually guilty of the fraud.

We should contrast the position of a person who obtains title to goods by fraud with that of a person who obtains contractual rights by fraud. We have seen that in spite of his fraud a person may obtain title to goods so that, in turn, he may pass on valid title to a subsequent innocent purchaser. The innocent purchaser may retain the goods against the claim of the person fraudulently persuaded to part with his goods.[22] In contrast, a person who obtains contractual rights by fraud does not, by assigning these rights, give an innocent assignee the right to enforce them against the defrauded promisor. An innocent assignee of a chose in action is in a much more vulnerable position than an innocent purchaser of goods.

Fraudulent misrepresentation is not, of course, the only defence a promisor may use against an assignee: mistake, undue influence, duress, and a right to set off a debt owed by the assignor to the promisor are all effective. The promisor may also defend by showing that he received no consideration for his promise. The right to set off a debt requires further explanation:

---

[22] This result follows because fraud makes the contract voidable, not void. See Chapter 10 and King's Norton Metal Co. v. Edridge (1897), 14 T.L.R. 98; Lewis v. Averay, [1971] 3 All E.R. 907.

ILLUSTRATION

A is employed by B at a salary of $275 per week, payable at noon Saturdays when the business closes. On Thursday, A borrows $80 from B. On Saturday, A fails to appear at work on time. When he telephones an hour late an argument ensues, and B informs A that he is fired and tells him not to bother coming back. On Monday, A sues B for $275 in the small claims court. B may set off both the $80 loan and the $25 A would have earned had he appeared at work on Saturday morning. A obtains a court judgment for $170.

Suppose, instead of suing B, A had assigned his claim for salary to his neighbour X for $250. X would take it subject to the equities between A and B, and even though X did not know of B's loan to A and of A's failure to work on Saturday, B would be able to set off these amounts in an action by X. Thus X would recover $170 from B, the same amount as A could recover.[23]

Until an assignee gives the promisor notice of the assignment, acts of either the assignor or the promisor or their agents may prejudice the assignee's rights. Thus, it is important for an assignee to give notice as soon as possible. If he delays, his rights may well deteriorate.

ILLUSTRATION

Williams owes Mehta $300. Mehta assigns the debt to Young on May 1. Young neglects to notify Williams, and on May 11 Williams pays Mehta $125 on account, unaware of the assignment. Because of her failure to notify Williams, Young, the assignee, may now recover from Williams only $175 and must look to Mehta for the $125 already paid.

When a creditor, a building contractor, say, assigns rights to partial payment before it has completed performance, the assignee may be subject to an additional risk. Even when the assignee has given notice to the debtor (the party entitled to completion of the project), the debtor may be able to use defences based upon developments after the time of notice. The assignor's (builder's) subsequent failure to complete performance may cause the debtor damages which he can set off against the assignee's claim. In other words, an assignee's rights under a contract as yet incomplete are imperfect, and subject to proper completion of the contract.[24]

A general assignment of book debts is an important business device for securing credit. The common law provinces each have statutes making such assignments void against the assignor's creditors unless the assignment is registered in a public office where its terms are available for inspection. The purpose of these statutes is to protect prospective creditors:

---

[23] Provincial legislation may provide that an assignment of wages, or any portion, to secure payment of a debt is invalid. See, for example: Wages Act, R.S.O. 1990, c. W-1, s. 7(7); Assignment of Wages Act, R.S.S. 1978, c. A-30; Labour Standards Code, 1972, R.S.N.S. 1989, c. 246, s. 89. In the authors' opinion, the reference is to amounts of wages coming due in future and not to wages already owing at the time of assignment. The policy underlying such a rule seems to be to prevent a creditor from depriving an employee of the means of livelihood, diminishing the employee's incentive to work and so undermining the employment relationship.

[24] Young v. Kitchen (1878), 3 Ex.D. 127.

they may inspect the registry to discover whether some assignee has a prior claim against the assets of a person who has applied to them for credit. We shall consider the reasons for providing public notice more fully in Chapters 26 and 33.

Assignments by Operation of Law

Upon the Death of a Party

When a person dies, the law automatically assigns his or her rights and obligations under outstanding contracts to a personal representative. If the deceased person leaves a will naming a representative, the representative is called an *executor.* If he or she fails to name an executor in the will (or the executor refuses to assume the position) or else leaves no will (that is, dies *intestate*), the court will appoint a personal representative called an *administrator.* There is no obligation for a representative to perform a contract requiring personal services; the skill of the deceased cannot be demanded of the representative. We need only think of the executor of a deceased violinist to understand the reason for this rule.

The task of an executor or administrator is to pay all just claims against the deceased's estate, to complete performance of any outstanding contractual obligations of the deceased not requiring personal skill, to pursue all claims the deceased had against others, and then to distribute the assets according to the will — or in the case of an intestate person, distribute them to the heirs according to statutory provisions.[25]

Bankruptcy

A person carrying on business. who becomes insolvent, may realize that his position is hopeless, and may voluntarily apply for bankruptcy proceedings to avoid further loss to his creditors and injury to his name. As well, creditors may commence bankruptcy proceedings against even a reluctant debtor by petitioning the court for an order known as a *receiving order.* If the creditors satisfy the court that their debtor is insolvent, the court will declare him bankrupt and appoint a licensed trustee to take charge of his property. It is then the duty of a licensed trustee to liquidate the assets and to settle the creditors' claims.

We shall deal with bankruptcy again in Chapter 34. We raise the topic at this point simply to explain the relationship between a bankrupt person and the trustee in bankruptcy. The proceedings require an assignment to the trustee of the bankrupt person's assets, including his contractual rights as well as his liabilities.[26]

Assignments resulting from death and from bankruptcy proceedings started by creditors differ from other assignments in that they are involuntary; they take place "by operation of law". One's affairs are seldom completely in good order when either of these

---

[25] The way in which the estate of an intestate person will be distributed to the heirs is set down in provincial statutes. See, for example: Estates Administration Act, R.S.O. 1990, c. E-22; Intestate Succession Act, R.S.N.S. 1989, c. 236, c. 153; Estate Administration Act, R.S.B.C. 1979, c. 114, Part 7.

[26] A licensed trustee may, however, with the permission of inspectors appointed by the creditors, disclaim any lease of property of the bankrupt debtor. Bankruptcy and Insolvency Act, R.S.C. 1985, c. B-3 (as amended), s. 30(1)(k).

events occurs, and an assignment achieves an artificial extension of the assignor's legal existence until his affairs can be wound up.

NEGOTIABLE INSTRUMENTS

Their Nature and Uses

A negotiable instrument — for example, a draft, promissory note, or cheque — is a written contract containing a promise, express or implied,[27] to pay a specific sum of money to the order of a designated person or to "bearer".

Generally speaking, a negotiable instrument arises from a contract that precedes it: a buyer delivers a negotiable instrument in payment for goods or services received. But delivery of the instrument does not complete the promisor's obligation. If he does not honour the instrument when it falls due and is presented to be paid, the promisee has the choice of suing under the original contract or for failure to honour the instrument. Often a promisee chooses to sue on the negotiable instrument, because the procedure is somewhat simpler.

The unique aspects of the law of negotiable instruments arise when a promisee assigns an instrument to a third party.

Negotiability Compared with Assignability

The process of assigning a negotiable instrument is known as *negotiation*. A promisee or payee of an instrument may negotiate it in one of two ways: if the instrument is payable to bearer, he need only deliver it to a third party; if the instrument is payable to his order, he must endorse his name upon it and then deliver it. Negotiation is really a special type of assignment in which the new *holder* of the instrument acquires from the transferor the rights that the instrument has to convey.

Chapter 24 of this book examines the law affecting negotiable instruments in more detail. Since, however, negotiation is a special application of assignments, we can better understand both concepts by reviewing their differences here. In a sense, negotiation is a privileged type of assignment that, for reason of business convenience, is released from certain of the restrictions that apply to an ordinary assignment of contractual rights. It therefore differs from an assignment of rights generally in the following important respects.

Notice to the Promisor

We have seen that notice plays two important roles in assignment generally: first, written notice is necessary before an assignee may take advantage of a statutory assignment; second, notice protects an assignee against the consequences of payment by the promisor to the assignor or other assignees. Notice, however, is of no consequence in the transfer of a negotiable instrument — indeed, it is irrelevant. This result stems from the fact that

---

[27] According to the wording of a cheque, the drawer does not directly promise to pay its amount, but he does promise by implication that sufficient funds will be available in his account to pay it when it is presented.

the promisor in a negotiable instrument is liable to pay only one person, the holder of the instrument for the time being. Thus, even if he receives notice of the assignment, neither he nor his bank will pay the assignee unless the assignee presents the instrument. The promisor pays his debt only once — to the holder of the instrument for the time being *and* in exchange for the instrument. In effect he pays for the return of his negotiable instrument. "The idea of 'embedding' legal rights in a document, such that the abstract rights move in unison with the physical certificate, has been very potent in commercial law, especially in regard to debt obligations."[28]

ILLUSTRATION

Steele receives his monthly pay cheque of $2500 from Union Foundry Co. Ltd. He negotiates it to Comfy Furniture Mart for $2000 worth of furniture and $500 cash. Steele then tells his employer that he has inadvertently destroyed the cheque by throwing the envelope containing it into a fire, and he persuades the company to pay him a second time. When Comfy Furniture Mart presents the original cheque for payment, the foundry company must honour it even though the furniture dealer gave no notice of the assignment.

If instead Steele had assigned to the furniture dealer a claim against the foundry for arrears of wages (a contractual right not represented by any negotiable instrument) and if the furniture dealer did not immediately notify the foundry of the assignment, the foundry could defeat the claim of the furniture dealer, as assignee, by establishing that it had already paid Steele before receiving notice.

Defences of the Promisor

An assignee for value of a negotiable instrument may succeed in an action against the promisor where the assignor himself would not have succeeded. For example, even when a party is induced to undertake liability on a negotiable instrument as a result of fraud or undue influence, he may be sued successfully by a subsequent innocent holder who has given consideration for the instrument to the party guilty of the fraud; yet the rogue could not himself enforce the promise in the instrument.[29] A defrauder may thus transfer enforceable rights under a negotiable instrument much as he can pass valid title to goods to an innocent purchaser. Similarly, a person who has given a negotiable instrument in payment for an illegal consideration loses the defence of illegality against an innocent holder of the instrument for value. By contrast, in an ordinary assignment of rights, the assignee never acquires a better right than the assignor had; the debtor retains his defences against the assignee.

---

[28] Baxter and Johnston, "New Mechanics for Securities Transactions", (1971) 21 U.T.L.J. 358.
[29] But see The Bills of Exchange Act, R.S.C. 1985, c. B-4, restricting the rights of finance companies to assert the status of a holder in due course.

ILLUSTRATION

Bacchus contracted with Hermes for the illegal transportation of liquor into Ontario and gave Hermes his cheque for $2000 for services rendered. The police discovered and confiscated the liquor, and Bacchus then asked his bank to stop payment on the cheque to Hermes. In the meantime, Hermes had used the cheque to pay a debt to an innocent trade creditor, Argus, who knew nothing of the circumstances under which the cheque had been obtained. Argus learned that payment of the cheque had been stopped when he attempted to cash it at the bank. Argus sued Bacchus on the dishonoured instrument.

Bacchus might have used the defence of illegality in an action brought against him by the party with whom he contracted — Hermes. But he must pay the holder of the cheque, Argus, if (as appears probable) Argus can prove he took the instrument unaware of its illegal origin and gave value for it.

By contrast, if Hermes' claim for $2000 against Bacchus had remained simply in the form of an account receivable, no one to whom Hermes might have assigned the debt would have obtained a better right to collect it than Hermes himself had.

Form of Action

A holder of a negotiable instrument can sue in his own name; it is not necessary for him to join in the action any of the other parties who have signed the instrument.

Commercial Importance of Negotiability

For hundreds of years, merchants have found it to their mutual advantage to recognize negotiable instruments as a special class of readily assignable promise, free from the formalities and many of the risks of an ordinary assignment of contractual rights. Business experience has shown that negotiability has a convenience far outweighing the probable cost of its abuse. As we have noted, one of the ways the law restricts the possibility of abuse is by the rule that before a holder of a negotiable instrument can enforce it in the face of such defences as fraud, undue influence, duress, and illegality, he must have been unaware of the origin of the tainted instrument, and he or some previous holder of the instrument must have given value for it.[30]

Modern banking practice is based upon the relatively secure position of an innocent holder for value of a negotiable instrument. Banks, as innocent holders for value, are able to cash cheques or accept them for deposit without exhaustive inquiry into the background of the transactions out of which they arose: for example, they are entitled to collect the amount from a drawer even if his cheque originated as a result of fraud, undue influence, duress, or as a result of an illegal transaction. Without such a rule, banking facilities would be much less accessible to business and the public generally.

Currency

The familiar Bank of Canada note is a special type of instrument authorized by statute and designed to circulate with maximum ease of transferability. We shall refer to it again briefly in Chapter 24.

---

[30] In fact, the requirements are somewhat more technical than we can conveniently describe here: the holder must be a *holder in due course*. See *infra*, Chapter 24.

Questions for Review

1. Define the following terms: assignee; vicarious performance; novation; constructive trust; beneficiary; chose in action.
2. Under what circumstances may a promisor obtain the services of another to perform his obligation?
3. What are the chief respects in which the privity of contract rule has been modified?
4. Apart from law, what objection might an employer have to an employee assigning a part of his salary in payment of a debt?
5. By what legal rule could the old courts of common law refuse to enforce the rights of an assignee of a chose in action?
6. A fraudulently sold to B shares in a company that proved to be non-existent.
   (a) B signed an agreement for the purchase of the shares in which he promised to pay A $300. A assigned this debt to C.
   (b) B gave his promissory note for $300 payable to the order of A. A endorsed the note over to C.
   (c) Instead of promising to pay money, B delivered to A his stereo system in payment for the shares. A sold the stereo to C.

   In each of the above unrelated instances C was an innocent third party who gave consideration to A. What are C's rights?
7. A debtor owed his creditor $200. The creditor assigned her right to collect this debt to another person, X. The assignee, X, delayed in sending notice to the debtor that he was now the party entitled to payment. The debtor, before receiving any notice of assignment, paid his original creditor $125 on account. How have X's rights been affected?
8. Anderson, a skilled mechanic, agreed to do some car repair work for Bartlett. Anderson was busy when the car was delivered for repair and gave his friend Gauche the work to do, without consulting Bartlett. Gauche sent Bartlett a bill for the repair work. Bartlett refused to pay. Is he justified?
9. "If it were asked what discovery has most deeply affected the fortunes of the human race it might probably be said with truth the discovery that a debt is a saleable commodity." (McLeod, *Theory and Practice of Banking* (5th ed.), I:200.) Explain and elaborate on this quotation.
10. (a) Give a brief example illustrating the operation of the rule: "The successive assignees of an obligation rank as to their title, not according to the dates at which the creditor assigned his rights to them respectively, but according to the dates at which notice was given to the party to be charged." (*Anson's Law of Contract* (26th. ed.), p. 401.)
    (b) Explain the reason for this rule.
    (c) Why is this rule irrelevant for negotiable instruments?

Problems

Problem 1

King, a building contractor, completed the construction of a house for Harris. At completion Harris owed King a balance of $5000. King then borrowed $2700 from a moneylender, Jackson. In consideration for this loan, King assigned to Jackson as much of his account receivable from Harris as should be necessary to repay the sum borrowed plus interest and any further sums for which he might become indebted to Jackson. Is Jackson, as assignee, entitled to sue Harris without the assistance of King's testimony? (See *Jones v. Humphreys*, [1902] 1 K.B. 10.)

Suppose, instead that King had borrowed $7500 from Jackson and in partial settlement assigned the whole of the $5000 due to him from Harris. Are these changed facts in themselves sufficient to entitle Jackson to sue Harris without joining King in the action?

Problem 2

Rigoletto, an operatic singer of great renown, was engaged to give a concert in Montréal. A hall was rented, a stage crew hired, and much advertising undertaken. The day before he was to perform, Rigoletto sent word to Montréal that he intended to send his understudy, Tremolo, to sing in his place. The reason given for the change in plans was that one of Rigoletto's friends was leaving on an extended trip and Rigoletto wished to attend a farewell party in her honour. Tremolo was not, of course, nearly as well known as Rigoletto, but a noted music critic had recently observed that he was quite as good.

Can Rigoletto's sponsors in Montréal sue him for breach of contract? Give reasons.

Problem 3

Leeder sold his taxi business to Fisher, covenanting neither directly or indirectly to carry on or be engaged in another taxi business within five miles of the place of business for five years from the date of sale. The agreement contained the usual clause extending the benefit of the contract to the "assigns" (assignees) of the parties. Before the five years had elapsed, Fisher resold the taxi business to Pivnick, and Leeder entered into another taxi business within the five-mile area. Pivnick brought an action against Leeder for an injunction to restrain him from operating a competing business within the five-mile area. Should Pivnick succeed? (*Pivnick v. Leeder* (1932) 41 O.W.N. 143.)

Problem 4

On January 15 Benson, a contractor, agreed for $195 to install frozen-food cabinets in Ross' grocery store. During the period January 1 to 31 of the same year, Benson purchased groceries on credit from Ross to the value of $235. Benson had also borrowed money from Kilby, and on January 31, he assigned to Kilby his claim of $195 against Ross, in repayment of his loan. Kilby notified Ross of the assignment on February 2. Ross refused to pay Kilby. Is he entitled to do so? (See *Burman v. Rosin* (1916) 26 D.L.R. 790.)

Would it make any difference if Benson had instead purchased all the groceries on February 1, after he had assigned the debt due to him by the grocer but before Kilby had notified the grocer?

Are your conclusions just and reasonable from the point of view of Ross? Explain. What might a prospective assignee learn from a study of this problem?

Problem 5

B. Flatt and F. Major made a $50 wager about the spelling of *Cavalleria Rusticana*. Flatt lost and he gave Major his cheque for $50. When Major attempted to deposit the cheque in her bank account, she learned that Flatt had instructed his bank to stop payment on it. What are Major's rights?

Would it make any difference if Major had cashed Flatt's cheque with her corner druggist and the druggist was then confronted with Flatt's stop-payment order?

Cases

Case 1

Glashov purchased on credit from Brown a building for business purposes. In their agreement Glashov covenanted that he would insure the property and assign the insurance to Brown, the vendor, as security for the amount that remained owing on the purchase price.

Glashov insured the property with the Standard Insurance Company but neglected to inform the company that the proceeds in the event of a claim should be paid to Brown. The building was later destroyed in a fire.

Immediately after the fire, three of Glashov's trade creditors sought payment of their claims and agreed to accept from him an assignment to them of the proceeds of the fire insurance. The trade creditors gave notice to Standard Insurance Company at once, before the amount of the loss had been established and before that company had admitted any liability under the policy. Brown, after learning what had happened, informed the insurance company that she wished to claim the insurance money due, and supported her claim by showing to the company the terms of the agreement for sale. The insurance company paid the money into court for settlement of the dispute.

What is the nature of the trade creditors' argument that they should have the insurance money instead of Brown? What possible defence or defences might Brown offer against this claim? To whom would a court order the payment of the insurance money?

Case 2

York Bridge Co. Ltd. undertook construction work for the City of Toronto in July. A month later, when the construction work was partly completed, York Bridge assigned to Southern Ontario Foundries & Steel Co. Ltd. the amount of $6800 due to it in respect of work completed by that time. When it took the assignment, the management of Southern Ontario Foundries & Steel was aware that the claim its company was acquiring arose from an as yet uncompleted contract. Southern Ontario Foundries & Steel immediately notified the City of the assignment but delayed in pursuing its rights when the City was slow in paying.

York Bridge abandoned the contract in the following September, and its non-performance caused a loss to the City of Toronto of $25 000. When Southern Ontario Foundries & Steel then attempted, as assignee, to collect $6800 from the City, the City defended by claiming it no longer owed money for the construction work because the damages it had suffered from the breach of contract exceeded the sum owing for the part of the work that had already been done. Southern Ontario Foundries & Steel contended that the sum of $6800 was due and payable at the time the City had been notified of the assignment.

Explain the issues raised by these facts and the applicable rules of law, and express an opinion whether Southern Ontario Foundries & Steel should be able to recover $6800 from the City of Toronto. Explain also whether this would appear to be an equitable or a statutory assignment and indicate the significance that the type of assignment would have in this case. (For references, see *Young v. Kitchin* (1878) 3 Ex. D. 127; *American Bridge Co. v. City of Boston* 202 Mass. 374, 88 N.E. 1089.)

Case 3

Norton responded to a campaign for funds by the National Association for the Preservation of Wildlife (N.A.P.W.) by signing the following statement, which she gave to a canvasser for N.A.P.W.:

$250.00   Charlottetown, 2 Nov. 1990

To assist in the purchase of conservation area sites and in consideration of the subscriptions of others, I promise to pay to the Treasurer of the National Association for the Preservation of Wildlife the sum of two hundred and fifty dollars, payable $100 on 1 Feb. 1991 and $150 on 1 Aug. 1991.

(Signed) Joan I. Norton

This and other similar agreements permitted the Associations to acquire property for use as conservation areas.

In order to obtain cash immediately from some of the pledges made to it, including Norton's, N.A.P.W. sold (assigned) them to Simpson for an undisclosed cash sum. Simpson's secretary telephoned Norton to advise her of the assignment of her promise and Norton confirmed that she had made the pledge. Norton failed, however, to pay either of the instalments to Simpson. Simpson brought an action against Norton for payment of the $250.

Express, with reasons, an opinion about the probable outcome of this action.

CHAPTER 15

THE DISCHARGE OF CONTRACTS

The Ways in Which a Contract May Be discharged

To discharge a contract means "to cancel the obligation of a contract; to make an agreement or contract null and inoperative".[1] In this chapter we shall consider four ways in which the discharge of a contract may occur: by performance, agreement, frustration, and operation of law. In addition, a contract is sometimes said to be "discharged" by its breach, but this topic is reserved for separate treatment in the following chapter.

Discharge by Performance

The Nature of Discharge by Performance

Performance is the type of discharge expected when parties make their agreement. A contract is at an end when the parties have performed their respective obligations satisfactorily. For a contract to be fully discharged, performance must have been completed by both parties and not merely by one of them. A bilateral contract, formed by the offer of a promise for a promise, goes through three stages: first, when neither party has performed its promise; second, when one but not the other party has performed; and third, when both parties have performed. Only at the final stage is the contract discharged by performance. In a unilateral contract, formed by the offer of a promise for an act, the first stage never exists and the second takes place in the very formation of the contract: the last stage is still necessary for discharge by performance.

Performance may take several forms, depending on the contract. It may be services rendered, goods delivered, a cash payment made, or any combination of these.

Tender of Performance

Occasionally a party attempts to perform, but the other party refuses to accept the performance. An attempt to perform is called a *tender* of performance, whether accepted or rejected by the other party.

If a seller properly tenders delivery of the goods and the buyer refuses to accept them, the seller is under no obligation to attempt delivery again and may immediately sue for breach of contract.

A debtor who makes an unsuccessful but reasonable attempt to pay will be free from further liability for interest on the amount owing and generally will not have to pay court costs if he is later sued for the debt. To be sure of this result, he should offer the money in the form of *legal tender*. Legal tender consists of Bank of Canada notes (or "bills" as we call them) and coins to the following limits: silver coin to $10, nickel coin to $5, and coppers to 25¢.[2] A creditor is legally within its rights in refusing to accept payment in silver of a debt of, say, $100: it may also refuse any negotiable instrument, including even a cheque certified by a bank. In practice payment is normally made in a form that is not legal

---

[1] Black's *Law Dictionary* (6th ed.), p. 463.
[2] Currency and Exchange Act, R.S.C. 1985, c. C-52, s. 8 as amended by R.S.C. 3rd Supp. c. 35, s. 12.

tender, and the majority of business debts are now settled by cheque. Only when there is a risk of dispute does a legally correct tender of payment become important. The debtor will then make a formal legal tender of cash to the creditor to avoid any later claim that he was unwilling or unable to meet his obligations.

ILLUSTRATION

S agrees in writing to sell $10 000 worth of flour to B, cash on delivery. Before the date of delivery the price of flour rises substantially. S becomes anxious to discover a means of avoiding the contract; and, hearing a rumour that B is in financial difficulties, he uses the argument that B may be unable to pay as a pretext for notifying B that he is terminating the contract. B, of course, wishes to go through with the sale at the agreed price. She takes the contract to her bank and borrows sufficient cash (in legal tender) to pay the purchase price. She then tenders the money to S in the presence of a witness. If S does not deliver the flour and B sues him for breach of contract, S cannot claim in defence that B was unable to pay.

If a creditor is foolish enough to refuse a legal tender of payment, any subsequent action to recover the money will be at the creditor's own expense. On the other hand, the debtor is not discharged of her debt by having had her tender of payment refused. She will still have to pay it, but no interest will accrue after the date of tender. If the debtor tenders payment in a reasonable fashion (though not strictly speaking in the form of legal tender), a court may, at its discretion, award the costs of any subsequent litigation against the creditor.

There is a legal maxim that the debtor must seek out her creditor. She is not excused from tendering payment because her creditor is slow or diffident about asking for it: the onus is on the debtor to find and pay her creditor.

DISCHARGE BY AGREEMENT

Waiver

A contract may be discharged prematurely because the parties agree between themselves not to perform it. A *waiver* is an agreement not to proceed with the performance of a contract already in existence. If neither party has performed fully at the time both agree to call off the bargain, there will automatically be consideration for the waiver of each party: each still has rights and obligations outstanding, and a promise by one party to waive its rights is sufficient consideration for its release from obligations by the other.

On the other hand, if one party has already fully performed its part, but the other has not, it receives no consideration for its waiver of the other party's duty to perform. To be enforceable, its promise to release the other party should be under seal.

Atwater agrees to install a sound system in the Kent Theatre for $3500. Kent's right under the contract is to receive the benefits of the work and its obligation is to pay for it. Atwater's right is to receive the price, and his obligation is to do the work required. Consequently, if they should mutually agree to call off their contract before Atwater completes the work, there is consideration for the waiver. Atwater now promises to abandon a claim for payment; Kent Theatre promises in return to abandon a claim for services. Each party's promise is a price paid for the promise of the other.

But suppose that Kent has paid Atwater the $3500 and that to date Atwater has only partly built the system. At this stage any undertaking by Kent that it will "require neither completion of the work nor a return of any money" will be without consideration and therefore not binding unless under seal.[3]

Of course, neither party can impose a waiver on the other. A party who fails to perform without securing a waiver of the other, commits a breach of the contract. As we shall see in the following chapter, the consequences of breach are quite different from discharge by agreement.

Substituted Agreement

Material Alteration of the Terms

If parties agree to a material alteration of the terms, one that goes to the root of the contract, they have in effect agreed to discharge their original contract and replace it with a new one. Minor changes in the terms do not have this sweeping effect. As we noted in the preceding chapter under "Novation", to bring a substituted agreement into existence, a major alteration of the original agreement must be made with the consent of all parties.

In *Thornhill v. Neats*[4] a building contract required the contractor to pay a penalty if he did not have the work done by a certain date. Before its completion the contractor and the owner agreed that additional work should be undertaken by the contractor on the same project. The change made it impossible to complete the building by the date originally set. In settling a dispute about the total price of the project, the court held that the new agreement had discharged the old and that the penalty clause had disappeared with it.

Accord and Satisfaction

Sometimes a party finds it cannot perform its obligation according to the terms of the contract. It may offer the promisee a money payment or some other substitute if the promisee will discharge it from its original obligation. For example, a seller may find that it cannot obtain certain imported goods to fill an order and may offer other goods of equal quality, perhaps at a lower price, if the buyer will release it from its original promise. Accord and satisfaction often takes the form of a compromise out of court. Before a money settlement was agreed on, one of the parties may have been preparing to sue the other.

---

[3] This statement remains subject to the discussion in Chapter 7, concerning the "Gratuitous Reduction of a Debt", and "Injurious Reliance", at pp. 158-164.

[4] (1860), 141 E.R. 1392.

The distinction between a material alteration of the terms and accord and satisfaction is as follows: in a material alteration the parties are basically preoccupied with the new arrangement, and the discharge of the old contract is incidental — they may not even direct their minds to this problem; in accord and satisfaction the parties are directly concerned with the discharge of an existing contract — the new arrangement is for that very purpose.

A party may concede liability for damages though it and the other party still differ about the amount of the damages it should pay. The party admitting liability may tender payment of an amount in settlement but the other may refuse it on the grounds that it is insufficient. The first party may then pay into court the amount it has offered. If the other party proceeds with an action for damages and the court awards it no more than what has already been tendered in settlement, it will have to pay the court costs as the penalty for its insistence upon litigation; and the defendant will not be liable for interest on the sum due from the time it tendered the settlement. On the other hand, if the damages awarded are greater than the sum paid into court by the defendant, the judge may apportion the court costs between the parties, or if the amount of the defendant's tender was unreasonably low, the judge may order the defendant to pay all the costs.

Novation

As noted in the preceding chapter, novation is another method of discharge: a replacement of one of the parties discharges the original contract and substitutes a new one. A common example of novation arises when a party purchases a going business and assumes its outstanding liabilities as a part of the purchase price for the assets acquired. If the creditors accept the new owner as their debtor, either by an express agreement with it or by applying to the new owner for payment of their claims against the former owner, the liability of the former owner will be discharged and replaced by that of the purchaser. In the words of Mr. Justice Fisher:

> Where the business of a partnership is taken over by a new company [new owner] and the creditor of the partnership applies to the new company for payment, his claim is admitted and they promise to pay the debt, that is sufficient in my opinion to make the new company liable, as slight circumstances are sufficient to show an adoption by the creditors of the new company as their debtor.[5]

There must, however, be evidence of consent to the novation on the part of both the creditors and the new owner.[6] The evidence need not be in the form of an express agreement; it may be discovered by examining the conduct of the parties. A business is not permitted to deny liability if it has assumed all liabilities under a pre-existing contract and has acted upon that contract.[7]

In good business practice neither the vendor nor the purchaser of a business relies upon implied novation with creditors. The two parties to the sale agree upon what debts the new owner should assume and then call in the creditors to obtain their express consent to the substitution of a new debtor. In addition, to protect itself, the purchaser of a

---

[5] Re Star Flooring Co. Ltd., [1924] 3 D.L.R. 269 at 272.
[6] Toronto Star v. Aiken, [1955] O.W.N. 613.
[7] See Pacific Wash-A-Matic Ltd. v. R.O. Booth Holdings Ltd., (1979) 88 D.L.R. (3d) 69.

business makes a careful examination of public records, requires the vendor to provide a declaration setting out the names of all its creditors and the amounts owing to them, and publicizes the sale. We shall examine the statutory reasons for these procedures more fully in Chapters 33 and 34, which discuss creditors' rights.

A Contract Provides for its Own Dissolution

At the time the parties draw up their contract, one of them may foresee the possibility of some event affecting its ability or willingness to perform. If the other party is agreeable, they may include an express term to allow for this eventuality. Alternatively, there may be a similar term implied by trade usage or by the surrounding circumstances of the agreement. The term may be a condition precedent, a condition subsequent, or an option to terminate.

Condition Precedent

In Chapter 13 we noted that a condition precedent is a future or uncertain event that must have occurred before the promisor's liability is established. (The "occurrence" may be a "non-event", that is, a condition that the thing *not* happen before the time stipulated.) In that chapter we were concerned with the interpretation of contracts and the operation of the parol evidence rule, so that in our references a condition precedent was the result of an oral understanding. It may, of course, be a term in a written contract.

ILLUSTRATION

A Co. Ltd., located in Moncton, writes to *B* in Winnipeg offering him a good position. *B* replies by letter that he will take the position if A Co. Ltd. will first find satisfactory living accommodation in Moncton for his family. A Co. Ltd. accepts *B*'s counter-offer by mail. The employer's act of finding the specified living accommodation is a condition precedent.

Alternatively, *B* might reply that he will take the position if his wife, who works for a different firm, is *not* offered a promotion for which she has already applied. The failure to receive the promotion is a condition precedent.

Some have argued that a contract never even comes into existence when there is a condition precedent, and that to be capable of discharge a contract must first have existed. Yet there is a real sense in which a contract is formed from the time of the offer and the acceptance, even though a condition precedent is not resolved until later. A contract subject to a condition precedent does have a binding force from the outset, and the parties are not free to withdraw from their promises unless and until the condition precedent becomes impossible to fulfil. The arrangement is therefore much more than an outstanding offer that can be revoked prior to acceptance. Accordingly, if immediately after *B* received A Co. Ltd.'s acceptance he changed his mind and took a position with a different company he would be in breach of contract.

A contract may contain a series of conditions precedent; for example, an owner stipulates that as work progresses in a construction project it must be approved at specified stages by a designated architect or engineer. If, after any stage of the work is completed, the architect or engineer shows dissatisfaction with the quality of performance, the obligation to pay for that stage and for further work under the contract ceases. The approval of the architect or engineer is a condition precedent to payment for the preceding stage and for continuing with all remaining stages. When a party agrees to do work on these terms, it exposes itself to the judgment and reasonableness of the architect or engineer. Unless it can show that there has been fraud or collusion between the architect or engineer and the party for which it is to do the work, it is subject to the verdict reached; and it cannot claim a breach of contract if the work is brought to an end prematurely because the architect or engineer, acting in good faith, refuses to approve what has been done.[8]

A promisor is in an even more difficult position if it gives the right to approve or disapprove of performance to the promisee itself rather than to a third party such as an engineer or architect. The promisee's opinion of what is satisfactory is far more likely to be prejudiced in its own favour. The courts have held that a promisee given such a power can withhold approval and avoid liability under the contract. It does not matter that the promisee's judgment is unreasonable, or that the judge or jury believe that in the circumstances they themselves would have approved of the performance: so long as they find that the promisee is honestly dissatisfied, the promisor has no rights against it.[9]

Condition Subsequent

A condition subsequent is an uncertain event that brings a promisor's liability to an end if it happens. Liability is established when the contract is formed but one of the parties has reserved for itself an "out" in certain circumstances. A buyer of ticket for a baseball game has the benefit of a term in his contract that if the game is rained out before a stated inning he will be given a ticket for another game.

ILLUSTRATION

Norton is the holder of a baseball season's ticket which, because of some of his habits known to the management, was sold to him on terms that he must watch his conduct at the games.

Norton attends a game and his conduct is an annoyance and nuisance not only to the operators of the ball park but also to other fans and to those selling tickets. He has a loud, booming voice and insists on telling other fans things they do not want to know, and by moving about he obstructs the view of others. The management informs him that it is cancelling his season's ticket and tenders him a refund for the remaining games. Norton sues the management for breach of contract.

The contract has contained a term relating to a condition subsequent — Norton's objectionable conduct. It is therefore discharged by agreement rather than by breach, and Norton's action will fail.[10]

In contracts for the shipment of goods an "act of God" (the raging of the natural elements) may be a condition subsequent if it results in the destruction of the shipment. When a railway, trucking line, airline, or marine shipping company accepts goods for shipment, it undertakes to be liable for any damage if the goods arrive at their destination

---

[8] Hailsham, *Halsbury's Laws of England* (4th ed.), Vol. 4, 610, para. 1194.
[9] Truman v. Ford Motor Co., [1926] 1 D.L.R. 960.
[10] See North v. Victoria Baseball & Athletic Co., [1949] 1 W.W.R. 1033.

in a poorer condition than they were received by the carrier; but there is also a term discharging the carrier from this liability if the goods are destroyed by an Act of God. If the goods are only partly destroyed, the contract is not discharged completely; instead the carrier is absolved from liability to the extent that the damage was caused to the goods by an act of God and must deliver them as they are. Such a term is in fact implied by trade custom, but most carriers take the added precaution of expressly stating the term in their bills of lading. Accordingly, it is wise when shipping goods at the owner's risk to buy insurance against such loss.

Option to Terminate

A contract may include a term that provides that one party or perhaps both will have the option of bringing the contract to an end before its performance has been completed, usually by giving notice. The operation of the term results in discharge by agreement because the means of discharge have in fact been agreed upon in drawing up the contract. For example, a contract of employment of indefinite duration usually contains an option clause, either express or implied, entitling the employer to dispense with the services of an employee on giving the required notice, as explained in Chapter 23. Again, many mortgages have an option clause entitling the mortgagor to pay off the principal sum before maturity by tendering an additional payment of interest.

A further example may occur in a contract for the purchase of a business. A buyer may insist on a proviso allowing it to rescind the agreement if a current audit of the financial statements of the acquired business should result in the auditor being unable to give an unqualified opinion on their fairness. In these circumstances an auditor's qualified opinion (or unwillingness to express any opinion) would give the purchaser an option to terminate the contract.

DISCHARGE BY FRUSTRATION

Effect of Absolute Promises

The English common law originally held a party responsible in every instance for a failure to perform his promise — even when the failure had not been his fault. Of course, a party could avoid such consequences, if he foresaw them, by insisting at the time of agreement upon an express term absolving him from liability under stated circumstances. In fact, the argument for holding a party responsible was that he could have provided for the event in the contract but did not do so. Of course, as a practical matter it is not possible to foresee all eventualities. In any event, the economic cost of administrative time and legal advice involved in adding extensive lists of exemptions that would excuse performance only in rare circumstances would normally exceed the benefits of such a procedure.

As the next section will explain, the courts now excuse persons for failure to perform their contracts in a wide variety of circumstances where they are not at fault. Nevertheless, courts remain reluctant to excuse performance in some types of contracts; historically, they have regarded these kinds of contracts as inviolable regardless of the reason for which they could not be performed.[11] Tenants' covenants in commercial leases to keep the property in repair and to pay rent are promises of this kind, with the result that tenants have found themselves liable for damages caused by fire, storms, and enemy action, and liable for rent for the duration of the lease when the property was no longer of use to them.[12] However, in extreme cases where the whole point of the contract has disappeared, courts have become more willing to yield:

> I adopt the reasoning of Lord Simon in *Cricklewood v. Leighton's*[13] ... and accept his conclusion that there is no binding authority in England precluding the application of the doctrine of frustration to contracts involving a lease of land. I believe the situation to be the same in Ontario.[14]

It still remains open to a party to express his promise in such an absolute and unconditional way as to rule out any reservation for his benefit and thus forgo the defence of frustration.[15]

Several of the provinces have enacted legislation to overrule the common law and provide that the doctrine of frustration applies to tenancy agreements for residential premises.[16] The legislation does not, however, extend the doctrine to leases of commercial, as opposed to residential, premises.

Doctrine of Frustration

As we have seen, a primary consideration in our law is that contracts in general should have binding force and effect: for the courts to condone a failure to perform on slight pretext would be to create uncertainty in business affairs. The doctrine of frustration qualifies this general proposition. Accordingly, judges have given much thought to the problem of defining the scope of the doctrine and the instances in which it can be applied.

The courts have offered a variety of explanations for the doctrine of frustration. In *Davis Contractors Ltd. v. Fareham,* Lord Radcliffe said:

> Frustration occurs whenever the law recognizes that without default of either party a contractual obligation has become incapable of being performed because the circumstances in which performance is called for would render it a radically different thing from that which was undertaken by contract. It is not hardship or inconvenience or material loss itself which calls the principle of frustration into play. There must be as well such a change in the significance of the obligation that the thing undertaken would, if performed, be a different thing from that contracted for.[17]

In another case, Mr. Justice Goddard said:

---

11 It is tempting to compare absolute liability for contractual promises with strict liability in tort law, discussed in Chapter 4. We should note, however, that their historical development and the policy underlying them vary greatly.

12 Paradine v. Jane (1647), 82 E.R. 897; Redmond v. Dainton, [1920] 2 K.B. 256; Foster v. Caldwell, [1948] 4 D.L.R. 70.

13 Cricklewood Property & Investment Trust, Ltd. v. Leighton's Investment Trust, Ltd., [1945] A.C. 221.

14 Capital Quality Homes Ltd. v. Colwyn Construction Ltd. (1975), 9 O.R. (2d) 617, per Evans, J.A. at 629. The application of the doctrine of frustration to these cases still remains limited: see Victoria Wood Development Corp. Inc. v. Ondrey (1977), 14 O.R. (2d) 723.

15 Budgett & Co. v. Binnington & Co., [1891] 1 Q.B. 35; Hills v. Sughrue (1846), 153 E.R. 844.

16 See, for example: Landlord and Tenant Act, R.S.M. 1987, c. L-70, s. 90; R.S.O. 1990, c. L-7, ss. 87 and 88.

17 [1956] A.C. 696 at 729.

> If the foundation of the contract goes, either by the destruction of the subject-matter or by reason of such long interruption or delay that the performance is really in effect that of a different contract, and the parties have not provided what in that event is to happen, the performance of the contract is to be regarded as frustrated.[18]

Lord Sumner put it this way:

> It is really a device by which the rules as to absolute contracts are reconciled with a special exception which justice demands.[19]

A decision that a contract has been discharged by frustration may be viewed, then, as a practical and reasonable solution to be imposed authoritatively by a court under circumstances that were not anticipated by the parties.[20]

The simplest cases are those where performance becomes literally impossible, which explains why they were the ones first used by the courts to develop the doctrine of frustration. In *Taylor v. Caldwell*[21] the producer of a concert hired a music hall, but it was destroyed by fire before the scheduled date of the concert. The producer sued the owner for damages to compensate for losses sustained in having to cancel the concert. The court held that the contract had been discharged by frustration and refused to award damages. Had the court found instead that the contract had been broken by the owner of the music hall, it would have ordered him to pay damages.

In *Robinson v. Davison*[22] Robinson had engaged Davison, a pianist, to give a concert on the evening of January 14, 1870. He incurred expenses in preparing for the concert. About 9:00 a.m. on the morning of the 14th he received a letter from Davison stating that a sudden illness would prevent her from performing. Robinson had further expenses in cancelling the concert. When he sued for damages for his loss, the court held that the contract had been discharged by frustration, and the action failed.

The doctrine was carefully developed in a number of later cases where performance remained physically possible but would have a very different meaning for the parties from that intended when they made their agreement. *Metropolitan Water Board v. Dick, Kerr & Co.*[23] was such a case. In July 1914 in England, the contractors Dick, Kerr & Co. agreed to construct certain reservoirs for a local water board within six years at a specified price; they started work immediately. In February 1916, the Minister of Munitions, acting under wartime statutes, ordered the contractors to cease work. Most of their plant and materials was then sold under the Minister's directions. After the war ended, the water board insisted that the contractors should resume their work under the original terms, but the contractors refused to comply. Prices and conditions of supply were then drastically different from what they had been in 1916. The court held that the contract had been discharged by frustration and the water board failed in its action.

On the other hand, hardship is not a sufficient excuse for failing to perform. The mere fact that contractual obligations prove to be more onerous than anticipated will not, by itself, discharge a contract by frustration. It follows that a business that finds itself, as a

---

[18] Tatem Ltd. v. Gamboa, [1939] 1 K.B. 132 at 139.
[19] Hirji Mulji v. Chong Yue Steamship Co., [1926] A.C. 497 at 510.
[20] The theories underlying the doctrine of frustration are discussed in Furmston, *Cheshire, Fifoot and Furmston's Law of Contract* (12th ed.), Chapter 20; and in Guest, *Anson's Law of Contract* (26th ed.), Chapter 14.
[21] (1863), 122 E.R. 309.
[22] (1871), L.R. 6 Ex. 269.
[23] [1918] A.C. 119.

promisor, deprived of the most convenient or inexpensive method of performance, is not excused if other means remain by which it may reasonably perform. To excuse a promisor in these circumstances would, in the words of Lord Wright, be "to impair the authority of written contracts... by lax or too wide application of the doctrine of frustration. Modern English law has recognized how beneficial that doctrine is when the whole circumstances justify it, but to apply it calls for circumspection."[24]

Lastly, we note that for a contract to be discharged by frustration its performance must become impossible or purposeless *after the agreement was made*, for reasons beyond the control of the parties. We must distinguish this situation from one in which performance was impossible or purposeless at the very time the agreement was made. If the subject-matter has ceased to exist at the time of the agreement, the agreement is void for mistake, as Chapter 10 has shown: it is not discharged by frustration.

Self-Induced Frustration

A party to a contract cannot wilfully disable itself from performing and then claim successfully that the contract has been frustrated. Such *self-induced frustration* is a breach of the contract. In many circumstances the distinction between true frustration and self-induced frustration is readily apparent.

ILLUSTRATIONS

(a) A Co. contracts to transport earth for B. Upon realizing that it has made a bad bargain, A Co. sells its sole dump truck and claims that it cannot fulfil the contract because of frustration. We have no difficulty in deciding that A Co. has broken the contract.

(b) A Co. contracts to transport earth for B in an isolated northern community. Shortly after the contract is made, its truck (the only available one in the area) is stolen and wrecked. The contract is discharged by frustration, and A Co. is freed from its obligation to perform.

(c) A Co. contracts to transport earth for B. Its dump truck breaks down because of an employee's negligence, and there will be a long delay in its repair as the parties are in a small northern community. Because the situation is attributable to A Co.'s negligence, it will be liable for breach of contract.

Not every degree of fault or irresponsibility, however, will bar a party from claiming that the contract has been frustrated. As Lord Russell said in his judgment in a leading House of Lords case:

> The possible varieties are infinite, and can range from the criminality of the scuttler who opens the sea-cocks and sinks his ship, to the thoughtlessness of the prima donna who sits in a draught and loses her voice.[25]

Perhaps the most subtle variation of the problem arises when the frustrating event is only partly in the hands of the promisor.

---

[24] Twentsche Overseas Trading Co. v. Uganda Sugar Factory Ltd. (1945), 114 L.J.P.C. 25 at 28. See also: Graham v. Wagman (1976), 14 O.R. (2d) 349: "... I have never heard that impecuniosity is an excuse for non-performance of a promise." per Weatherston, J. at 352.

[25] Joseph Constantine Steamship Line Ltd. v. Imperial Smelting Corp. Ltd., [1942] A.C. 154 at 179.

ILLUSTRATION

A Inc., a firm of building contractors, makes a contract to erect a house for *B*. Before it begins actual construction, *A* Inc. follows the usual procedure of applying for a building permit from the municipality where the house is to be built. It is informed that the town has just passed a by-law requiring any contractor intending to build within the town limits to deposit $40 000 in cash to ensure compliance with all local regulations. *A* Inc. refuses to make the deposit on the ground that it was not part of the contract and that the hardship involved would make it uneconomical for it to go through with the contract. Has the contract been frustrated? There appears to be no easy answer; the courts must decide each case on its own facts.

The Effect of Frustration

Until now, we have assumed that frustration discharges the contract and frees both parties from the duty of further performance. In the simple situation where neither party has performed at all, a complete discharge of both is a fair settlement. But often the circumstances are not so simple, and discharging both parties may lead to injustice. When, for example, performance is spread over a period of time and is to be paid for on completion, a frustration of the contract before its completion may cause serious hardship for the performer or his estate. The harsh results in the old case of *Cutter v. Powell*[26] serve as an illustration. A seaman was to be paid on completion of a voyage from Jamaica to Liverpool. He died en route when the voyage was nearly three-quarters complete. An action by his widow to recover a proportionate part of his wages failed on the grounds that he had not performed as promised.[27]

Early decisions concerning frustration were harsh in another respect: the frustrating event was considered to terminate the contract and future obligations under it from the time of the frustrating event, but any performance already due was still enforceable. In the unhappy case of *Chandler v. Webster*[28] the plaintiff rented a room to view the coronation procession of Edward VII. The price was £141 payable at once, though the plaintiff paid only £100 and owed the remaining £41. Subsequently the contract was frustrated because the procession was cancelled. The plaintiff not only failed to recover his £100, but the court held that since the remaining £41 was due and owing before the frustrating event occurred, he was still liable for that sum too! The solution in this decision was to let the loss lie where it had fallen at the time of the frustrating event. → where all the $ was due.

The 1943 decision of the House of Lords in the *Fibrosa* case[29] altered the rule in *Chandler v. Webster*; it permitted a purchaser that had made an advance payment on equipment to recover its money, since it had received no benefit from the other party before the frustrating event took place. This solution seems eminently reasonable from the purchaser's point of view — but is it always so from the point of view of the other party? While a seller may not have delivered any of the fruits of its labour, it may well

---

[26] (1795), 101 E.R. 573.
[27] The harshness of this rule has since been mitigated to some extent by the doctrine of substantial performance, discussed in the next chapter.
[28] [1904] 1 K.B. 493.
[29] Fibrosa Spolka Akcyjna v. Fairbairn Lawson Combe Barbour, Ltd., [1943] A.C. 32.

have done considerable work towards the completion of the contract at its own expense; according to the *Fibrosa* decision the buyer can still demand the return of its deposit in full. In fact, in the *Fibrosa* case the defendant company had partially built expensive, custom-built machinery, and not only was it unable to require the buyer to share in its loss, but it had to return the entire deposit it had received.

It follows from the *Fibrosa* decision that if a seller cannot succeed in retaining a deposit on the grounds that it has incurred expenses, it certainly cannot recover these expenses from a buyer that has made no deposit. On the other hand, the judgment stated that if the seller had conferred even the slightest benefit on the buyer (for example, if the seller had delivered a small advance shipment of spare parts), the seller could retain the whole deposit. The common law did nothing to apportion the loss between the parties: it was a matter either of retaining the whole of the deposit or of returning it entirely.

At this point it became apparent that only legislation could correct the law. In 1943 the English Parliament passed the Frustrated Contracts Act in an attempt to remedy the inequities. Subsequently, the provinces of Prince Edward Island, New Brunswick, Ontario, Manitoba, Alberta, and Newfoundland have passed similar acts with some improvement on the original English Act.[30] British Columbia passed its own act to the same effect but with major differences discussed below.[31]

On the occurrence of a frustrating event, the acts provide for the allocation of losses between parties where money was paid on account by one party to the other or was due but had not yet been paid.

> If, before the parties were discharged...[a party] incurred expenses in connection with the performance of the contract, the court, if it considers it just to do so having regard to all the circumstances, may allow him to retain or recover, as the case may be, the whole or any part of the sums paid or payable.[32]

In neither of these situations may the performing party retain or recover any money in excess of the payment made or already due, even when its loss has been greater. The other party may recover any amount by which its payment exceeds the performing party's allowed loss. In addition, the acts authorize a court to award the performer a just proportion of any valuable benefit *received* by the other party regardless of whether a deposit has been paid.

Unfortunately, when a party has expended time and money in performance of a contract, but the other party, which was eventually to have received the benefit of the work has (a) made no deposit, and (b) has not yet received any benefit — except in British Columbia — the first party is still without remedy and must bear the loss wholly itself.[33] The British Columbia Act states, " a 'benefit' means something done in the fulfilment of contractual obligations whether or not the person for whose benefit it was done received a benefit."[34] Thus, expenditures made by the first party can be taken into account, and to

---

[30] Frustrated Contracts Act, R.S.P.E.I. 1988, c. F-14; R.S.N.B. 1973, c. F-24; R.S.O. 1990, c. F-34; R.S.M. 1987, c. F-190; R.S.A. 1980, c. F-20; R.S. Nfld., 1990, c. F-26.

[31] Frustrated Contracts Act, R.S.B.C. 1979, c. 144.

[32] Frustrated Contracts Act, R.S.O. 1990, c. F-34, s. 3(2).

[33] The point may be illustrated by the facts in Appleby v. Myers (1867) L.R. 2 C.P. 651. Even if the Frustrated Contracts Act had been passed at that time it would not presumably have altered the decision.

[34] Frustrated Contracts Act, R.S.B.C. 1979, c. 144. s. 5(4).

the extent that the other party has received no benefit from them, the loss is divided equally.[35] This solution seems fair to both parties.

The Sale of Goods

Where the Sale of Goods Act Applies

In a contract for the sale of goods where we might expect the doctrine of frustration to apply we must first consult the Sale of Goods Act to see whether it deals directly with the particular situation. The Act states:

know it

> Where there is an agreement to sell specific goods and subsequently the goods without any fault of the seller or buyer perish before the risk has passed to the buyer, the agreement is thereby avoided.[36]

Three conditions must be present for this section to apply. First, the goods must be *specific*, that is "they must be identified and agreed upon at the time the sale is made." Second, the risk must still be with the seller, that is, the seller must still be responsible for their safety. Third, the cause of the frustration must be the perishing of the goods.

ILLUSTRATION

A sends a fax to *B* offering to sell "the carload of number one flour sitting at our rail siding for $10 000, risk to pass to you on delivery of the shipping documents in seven days' time." *B* accepts by return fax. Three days later a shunting locomotive on adjacent tracks is derailed and knocks over the freight car containing the flour. The contents are spilled out and ruined by rain, frustrating the contract.

Both parties are immediately discharged from liability under the contract: *A* cannot sue for the price, nor can *B* sue for failure to deliver. *B* can recover any deposit it has made. *A*'s only remedy is against those responsible for the accident.

In the above illustration, all three elements mentioned in the Sale of Goods Act are present: the Sale of Goods Act applies and consequently the Frustrated Contracts Act does not.[37] If any one of these elements is missing, the Sale of Goods Act does not apply.[38] The Frustrated Contracts Act applies in the provinces having the Act; in the remaining provinces the parties are left with the common law position up to and including the *Fibrosa* case. We may now discuss the position of the parties in each of these circumstances.   *know it*

In Provinces where the Frustrated Contracts Act Applies

The application of the Act is more easily understood if we begin with some illustrations.

---

[35] Ibid, s. 5(3).
[36] R.S.B.C. 1979, c. 370, s. 11; R.S.O. 1990, c. S-1, s. 8; R.S.N.S. 1989, c. 408, s. 10.
[37] Except in British Columbia where s. 1(b) of the Frustrated Contracts Act states expressly that the Act applies even in these circumstances.
[38] See, for example: R.S.O. 1990, c. S-1, s. 2(2)(c).

ILLUSTRATIONS

(a) *A* sends a fax to *B* offering to sell "one thousand sacks of number one flour from our warehouse stock for $5000, risk to pass to you on delivery of the shipping documents in seven days' time." *B* accepts by return fax. Three days later, the warehouse and contents are destroyed by fire without any negligence on *A*'s part. The goods are not specific because they have not been segregated from the larger stock and earmarked for the buyer. *(1) not true*

(b) *A* sends a fax to *B* offering to sell "the carload of number one flour sitting at our rail siding for $10 000, risk to pass to you on delivery of the shipping documents in seven days' time." *B* accepts by return fax. Three days later, the government requisitions all of *A*'s flour, including the carload sold to *B*, in order to help feed the victims of a flood disaster. Here the contract is frustrated by an event *other* than the perishing of the goods. *(3) not true*

In neither of the above cases does the Sale of Goods Act apply. Under the Frustrated Contracts Act, if *B* had made a deposit and sued for its return, the court would consider whether *A* had incurred any expenses towards the completion of the contract and would take them into account in determining how much of the deposit *B* would recover. If *B* had made no deposit, *A* could only recover the value of any benefit already conferred upon *B*.[39] Thus, if *A* had delivered one sack of flour to *B* as a sample, it could recover the price of that sack, but no more.

Second, the Frustrated Contracts Act states that the courts shall give effect to any special provisions made by the parties in anticipation of a frustrating event.

ILLUSTRATION

Sale of Goods Act wouldn't apply b/c (2) not true.

A sends a fax to *B* offering to sell "the carload of number one flour sitting at our rail siding for $10 000, risk to pass to you upon acceptance of this offer. Delivery in seven days' time." *B* accepts by return fax. Three days later the flour is destroyed in a derailment accident. The risk has passed to the buyer when the frustrating event takes place.

In the above example, the parties have agreed expressly that the risk should pass to the buyer, which seems to indicate that the buyer would be liable for any loss caused by a frustrating event after the risk has passed. The buyer must then pay the price to the seller. While both the Act and the express terms of the contract indicate this result, there are no reported cases directly on point. Ordinarily, buyers arrange to insure valuable goods not in their possession when the risk passes to them.

Where the Common Law Applies

We may consider the above three illustrations again as if they had occurred in a province not having the Frustrated Contracts Act. In Illustrations (a) and (b) the *Fibrosa* decision applies. If *B* had made a deposit, it could recover it in full regardless of whether or not *A* had incurred

---

[39] Except, as already noted, in British Columbia, where the court could give recovery for part or all of the expenses incurred, whether or not a benefit was conferred.

any expenses towards the completion of the contract. If, however, *B* had received the slightest benefit, such as one sack of flour as a sample, it could recover none of its deposit.

The *Fibrosa* case did not consider situations where the seller had conferred a benefit upon the buyer (for instance, by an advance delivery of part of the goods) and where no deposit had been made. In these circumstances the older cases would likely govern: both parties would be immediately discharged by the frustrating event, and the seller would have no right of recovery against the buyer for the goods already delivered when, by the contract, none are to be paid for until all are delivered. This result conforms to the law as stated in *Cutter v. Powell* and shows the value of the Frustrated Contracts Act in avoiding a harsh result.

The result in the last illustration is the same under the common law; the common law rule as well as the statute respects the intention of the parties as contained in their contract of sale.

Where the Source of the Goods is Destroyed

Another way in which frustration may affect the sale of goods arises when the source of the goods, rather than the goods themselves, is destroyed. In a contract of sale containing no terms about how the goods shall be produced, the destruction of the *source* of the subject-matter will not frustrate the contract. If, for example, the parties do not specify where the goods shall be made but the factory expected to be the source is destroyed by fire, the supplier will probably not be excused from liability for failing to deliver goods according to the contract.[40] The supplier must either purchase them elsewhere for delivery to the buyer or pay damages for non-delivery. On the other hand, if the parties specify a particular source and the source is destroyed, the contract will be frustrated, and the buyer cannot demand delivery. In *Howell v. Coupland*[41] the contract was for the sale of 200 tons of potatoes to be grown in a particular field. The crop failed. When the buyer sued for damages for non-delivery, the court held that the contract had been frustrated, and the action failed.

The general rule is that a frustrating event must defeat the common intention of both parties. A contract of sale is not frustrated when the seller only (and not the buyer) has a particular source of supply in mind and that source fails. In *Blackburn Bobbin v. Allen*,[42] the buyer had ordered a quantity of Finnish birch timber to be delivered at Hull, England. He presumed not unreasonably that the seller would supply him from existing stocks in England and was unaware that the seller had to obtain it directly from Finland. The outbreak of World War I made it impossible to fill the order. In an action for damages for non-delivery, the English Court of Appeal held that there had not been frustration and that the action should succeed.

An interesting 1968 Ontario decision falls between the *Howell* and the *Blackburn Bobbin* cases.[43] In that decision, a trucker in Parkhill contracted with a Toronto corn merchant to

---

[40] See Twentsche Overseas Trading Co. case, above. But see also Dow Votaw, *Legal Aspects of Business Administration* (3rd ed.), p. 165, Englewood Cliffs: Prentice-Hall, Inc., 1969. The author notes that in the United States "there is an increasing trend in the courts towards implying an agreement that goods are to be manufactured in a particular factory which the parties reasonably understand is to be the source of the subject-matter of the contract."

[41] (1876), 1 Q.B.D. 258.

[42] [1918] 2 K.B. 467.

[43] Parrish & Heimbecker Ltd. v. Gooding Lumber Ltd., [1968] 1 O.R. 716.

deliver a quantity of corn to shipping points in the Parkhill area specified by the corn merchant. The parties appeared to have understood that the trucker was to purchase the corn from certain Parkhill farmers when the crop matured. Unfortunately, the trucker was unable to obtain the required quantity of corn because of a local drought. The corn merchant sued for damages for failure to deliver according to the contract. The Court of Appeal agreed with the defendant trucker that if the source of the goods formed a term of the contract the failure of the crop would have amounted to a frustrating event excusing the trucker from performance. The majority of the court found that the contract had not expressly stated that the corn should be from a particular source and it was unwilling to find an implied term to that effect. It held that the trucker should have obtained the corn from other suppliers and that it was accordingly in breach of contract. In dissent, Mr. Justice Laskin (as he then was) took a more liberal view of the defendant's obligations. He said, in part:

> I cannot agree that these contracts should be viewed in the absolute terms in which the majority [of the court] has treated them. I think it is clear that the original attitude of the common law that a contract duty is absolute has been considerably modified over the past one hundred years as we have come to recognize that mutual assumptions by parties that underlie their commercial relations cannot be ignored, and that, in the enforcement of a contract, allowance must be made if a failure of those assumptions supervenes, without fault of the contracting parties, after the contract has been made...

> It is ... material to the basis on which these contracts were concluded that the price to be paid by the defendant for the corn obtainable from the farmers was a price fixed by the plaintiff and the plaintiff also fixed the trucking charge that would be paid to the defendant for the transportation of the corn to the specified destinations set out in the written confirmations. It seems to me, therefore, that in the circumstances it would be changing the fundamental character of the contract to require the defendant ... to obtain the grain from some other area and at the same time insist that it accept payment on the basis of a price and trucking arrangement which contemplated that the grain would come from the area about which the representatives of the parties had reached an understanding.[44]

DISCHARGE BY OPERATION OF LAW

The Bankruptcy and Insolvency Act operates to discharge a bankrupt debtor from contractual liabilities after the processes of bankruptcy have been completed. The debtor is discharged, however, only if he qualifies for a certificate stating that the bankruptcy was caused by misfortune and without any misconduct on his part.[45]

A debt or other contractual obligation that has been neglected by a creditor for a long time becomes _statute barred_, that is, the creditor loses the right to bring an action on it. Each province has a Limitations Act setting out the time at which a creditor loses its

---

44 _Ibid._, at pp. 719-20.
45 R.S.C. 1985, c. B-3, s. 145.

remedy.[46] The Limitations Act "bars" (rather than completely discharges) a right of action if the promisee fails to assert it within the time specified. In so doing, it gives effect to the legal principle that the public interest requires a definite end to the opportunity for litigation. The effect of the statute is really to banish the right of action from the courts rather than to pass a death sentence upon it. The distinction is important because a claim may be rehabilitated and made enforceable by certain conduct of the promisor, as we shall see in Chapter 34.

Questions for Review

1. Define the following terms: accord and satisfaction; condition precedent; condition subsequent; waiver; tender of performance.
2. Is a debtor freed from liability if the creditor refuses payment? For what reasons might a creditor refuse payment?
3. How may a creditor prejudice itself by being unreasonable about the form in which payment must be made to it?
4. Suppose a party, guilty of breach of contract, offers to settle for a given amount of money, and the other party refuses it. What steps should the first party take?
5. What problem may arise for a party who receives the benefit of a waiver of a contract already performed by the other side?
6. In what respect does the arrangement known as accord and satisfaction involve a discharge of a contract?
7. How can you explain the fact that there have been legal disputes over contracts that have been discharged by agreement?
8. The principles of mistake and discharge by frustration may both relate to contracts in which the subject-matter is nonexistent. How do these principles and their remedies differ?
9. Give an example of a promise to which the doctrine of frustration will not apply.
10. May a contract be frustrated even though the promisor might still be able to perform it?
11. Does an unforeseen difficulty or expense constitute frustration?
12. What might be the undesirable consequences of extending the applicability of the doctrine of frustration to a wider variety of circumstances?
13. How may a contract for the sale of goods be frustrated?
14. What contribution does the Frustrated Contracts Act make to the law governing discharge by frustration?
15. In what respect may bankruptcy bring about the discharge of contracts?
16. (a) Gilbert owed Sullivan $100. Sullivan pressed Gilbert for payment and in a moment of irritation Gilbert tendered the entire sum in 25¢ pieces. Need Sullivan accept this payment? Would it make any difference if Gilbert had instead tendered payment in the form of a certified cheque?
    (b) Suppose Sullivan claimed that the amount was $125 instead of $100 as offered by Gilbert. Gilbert deposited $100 with the proper court official, and Sullivan

---

[46] See, for example: Limitation Act, R.S.B.C. 1979, c. 236; Limitations Act, R.S.O. 1990, c. L-15; Limitation of Actions Act, R.S.N.S. 1989, c. 258. For an explanation of the policy considerations underlying limitations, see "Adverse Possession" in Chapter 26 and "Limitations of Creditors' Rights" in Chapter 34.

sued him for $125. The court awarded Sullivan only $100. Who should have to pay the court costs, Gilbert or Sullivan? What would be the result if the court had instead given judgment for $115?

Problems

Problem 1
Smith, the owner of a steamship, received from Nugent a valuable horse to be carried from London to Aberdeen. During the voyage the ship sailed into rough weather, and the horse, being very frightened, struggled violently, suffered injuries and died. It was shown that the accident could not have been prevented by any amount of foresight and care that could reasonably have been expected of Smith.

Should Nugent succeed in an action against Smith for damages to compensate him for this loss? (*Nugent v. Smith* (1875) 1 C.P.D. 423.)

Problem 2
Urban Construction Co. contracted with Mandel to build a small two-storey office building for $240 000. The contract contained a clause stating that the agreed price would be reduced by $500 for every business day the building was not completed after April 1. The price was to be paid on completion of the building.

During construction, Mandel asked Urban Construction Co. to alter certain specifications so that a complete air-conditioning system might be installed at a later time with a minimum of inconvenience and so that there would be an additional washroom on the second floor.

The building was completed April 17. Urban Construction Co. refused Mandel's tender of a cheque for $243 500 (comprising $240 000 less $6500 for 13 business days, plus $10 000, the agreed price for the extra work). Urban Construction Co. brought action for $250 000, the full price without deduction.

Examine the validity of the arguments Mandel might use in defending the action.

Problem 3
Howard rented a room to Kennedy along the route scheduled for the procession of the Royal Family for the day on which they would appear in Halifax. The agreement was in writing and the rent for the room was for a substantial sum, payable at the time of the procession. In the meantime Howard redecorated the room for the occasion. Later it was announced that the route of the Royal Family through the city was changed and would not pass Howard's building. Kennedy then refused to pay the rent for the room, and Howard sued for the amount. Should Howard succeed? How would it affect the outcome if at the time Kennedy undertook to rent the rooms she had paid a $100 deposit? (See *Krell v. Henry* [1903] 2 K.B. 740.)

Suppose that the place in which these events occurred had been Saint John, New Brunswick instead of Halifax, Nova Scotia; would the result be different?

Problem 4
In 1954 the Dryden Construction Co. contracted with the Ontario Hydro Electric Power Commission to build an access road seven miles long from its Manitou Falls generating station to provincial Highway No. 105. The contract contained the following clause:

> The contractor agrees that he is fully informed regarding all of the conditions affecting work to be done and labour and materials to be furnished for the completion of the contract and that his information was secured by personal investigation and research and not from the Commission or its estimates and that he will make no claim against the Commission ...

In fact, the area over which the road was to be built was under heavy snow at the time and the temperature was very low. The description of the property proved to be inaccurate, there being much more muskeg than indicated. After these facts came to light, the contractor claimed to be excused from the contract, alleging that it had been frustrated and that what was required amounted to an entirely different contract.

Is there a binding contract to build the road? (*Dryden Construction Co. Ltd. v. Hydro Electric Power Commission of Ontario* (1957) 10 D.L.R. (2d) 124. This decision was reversed on other grounds not concerning frustration: (1960) 24 D.L.R. (2d) 529.)

Cases

Case 1

Maritime National Fish Ltd. operated five trawlers, each of which was fitted with an otter trawl for catching fish and could operate only with this equipment. The fish company owned four of the trawlers and chartered the fifth, the *St. Cuthbert,* from Ocean Trawlers Ltd. for one year from October 25, 1932, at the rate of $591 per month.

At the time the parties entered into the charter agreement they were aware of an amendment to the Fisheries Act (Canada) that required the licensing of all fishing vessels using an otter trawl; the legislation was intended to be a method of controlling the extent of this type of operation and of conserving the fisheries resources of Canada. Operators of boats using an otter trawl were required to apply for a separate licence for each boat.

In 1933 it became government policy to reduce the number of licences granted, and Maritime National Fish was advised that it would be granted licences for only three of the five trawlers it was operating. In April 1933, the fish company applied for licences for three vessels without naming the *St. Cuthbert* as one of them. It then informed the *St. Cuthbert's* owner, Ocean Trawlers, that the agreement for charter had become impossible to perform on and after April 30, 1933, and that it would not make further payments from that time. Ocean Trawlers sued the fish company for the value the charter for the period May 1 to October 25, 1933. Should the action succeed? (*Maritime National Fish Ltd. v. Ocean Trawlers Ltd.* [1935] A.C. 524.)

Case 2

Watson was employed as a clerk by Kilby, Farmer & Co., wool merchants, for forty years. During this period he was not covered by any pension scheme and neither he nor his employers made any contribution to a pension plan. In the January prior to his retirement he received the following letter from his employers:

> Dear Mr. Watson:
>
> Upon your retirement on June 30, next, we have decided to grant you a pension of $3600 a year, payable by monthly instalments.
>
> You are at liberty to undertake any other employment or enter into any business anywhere in the world on your own account except in the wool trade, and the only

other stipulation we attach to the continuance of this pension is that you do nothing at any time to our detriment.

Wishing you every happiness and success in the future, we remain,

> Yours sincerely,
> (signed) S. Holmes
> for Kilby, Farmer & Co.

Watson received his full salary to June 30 and after that a payment of $300 a month. Several years later Kilby, Farmer & Co. ran into financial difficulties and sent Watson the following letter:

Dear Mr. Watson:

In going through our accounts we were greatly surprised to find that an allowance of $3600 was being paid to you, whereas drastic steps have had to be taken of late to reduce business expenses, which have become excessive in relation to present-day values of wool and pressures of foreign competition in the textile business generally.

After due consideration we have come reluctantly to the conclusion that this allowance must be discontinued as from June 30, next. Will you please therefore take note of our decision. We remain,

> Yours sincerely,
> (signed) P. Moriarty
> for Kilby, Farmer & Co.

After Kilby, Farmer & Co. stopped paying the pension, Watson, then 78 years old, sued the firm for breach of contract.

Outline the possible defences of Kilby, Farmer & Co. and state with reasons whether Watson's action should succeed.

Case 3

Gilman Steel Ltd. is a large fabricator of reinforcing steel. It makes its product from steel bars purchased from steel mills in accordance with engineers' specifications for particular projects. Universal Construction Corp. is an apartment construction company.

In September 1988, Gilman and Universal signed a contract for the supply of fabricated steel at a price of $253 per tonne for use in three apartment buildings to be built consecutively by Universal at different sites.

At the first building site deliveries were made and paid for as agreed and construction of that building was completed. Then in July 1989, steel mill companies announced increases in the price of unfabricated steel, to take effect in two stages. The price to Gilman would increase on 1 August 1989 by $8.50 per tonne and a second increase of a then-unspecified amount would become effective as of 1 March 1990.

In the changed circumstances, Gilman suggested a new contract for the second and third apartment buildings. Universal agreed to reconsider because it found that it would not require as much fabricated steel for the remaining two buildings as it had initially contracted for. The parties signed a new contract for the supply of fabricated steel at a price of $257 a tonne, a price that only partially passed on the increase to Gilman. Universal had thus agreed to pay a higher unit price for a smaller quantity of steel. The parties did not include in the contract a clause providing for an escalation of price because Universal expected to complete the remaining buildings before the next round of price increases in March 1990.

Construction of the second apartment building began in August 1989 and Gilman made numerous deliveries of steel. Universal accepted all steel delivered and regularly paid the amount billed by each invoice at $257 per tonne. The second building was completed in January 1990 and construction of the third was started.

On 1 March, while the third apartment building was still far from completion, the steel mills announced the anticipated second price increase. Officers of Gilman, hoping to agree on another new contract, met with a senior officer of Universal. They asked Universal to consider a new contract since construction had not progressed as expected. Universal agreed to accommodate Gilman on the understanding that Universal would be given favourable consideration in the supply of steel for the construction of additional apartment buildings.

Gilman then prepared an agreement dated 1 March 1990 and mailed it to Universal. It was a duplicate of the preceding contract in July except that the price of the steel was increased. Universal did not sign or return the document but it did accept deliveries of steel invoiced at the new rates without protest. Universal adopted a new method of payment, however, after 1 March 1990. It no longer paid by cheques based on the invoice amounts but in round figures that tended at first to overpayment; however, by the end of the construction this procedure led to a net balance of some $25 000 owing by Universal.

As construction of the third apartment building neared completion, the comptroller of Gilman asked for payment in full of the account. Universal informed him that it expected some new mortgage money to become available enabling it to pay the account in full soon. At about the same time officers of Universal met with Gilman's officers to discuss a contract for the supply of steel for a new apartment complex. Universal reminded Gilman that it had twice agreed to new contracts and asked whether Gilman could offer a good price. Gilman made an offer and Universal said it would consider it. The meeting was conducted and concluded in an atmosphere of goodwill without complaint about the March price increase. Shortly afterwards Universal decided that the new offer was not attractive enough to accept and indicated for the first time that it would not pay the portion of the past due account that represented the increase in the March 1990 agreement.

Gilman Steel Ltd. sued Universal Construction Corp. for the balance owing according to its invoices.

(a) Outline the nature of the defence or defences available to Universal.

(b) Explain the nature of the argument or arguments that could be advanced for the plaintiff.

(c) Indicate with reasons what the court's decision would likely be. (If you perceive any difference between what the law is and what it ought to be in a case of this kind, set out your reasoning separately from your prediction of what the decision is likely to be.) (Reference: Reiter, "Courts, Consideration and Common Sense", (1977) 27 U.T.L.J. 439. The above case is adapted from an illustration in this article at pp. 447-50. For the purpose of the analysis of this case as required above, agreement or disagreement with Professor Reiter's conclusions is less important than an awareness of the issues raised by the case and discussed in his article.)

Case 4

Parker's Automatic Laundry Services Inc. installed coin-operated washing and drying machines in an apartment building owned by Mountbatten Estates Ltd. under a five-year contract dated 1 June 1985. The contract gave Parker's the exclusive right to install and maintain any laundry machines in the building. No one other than the employees of the laundry service company would be permitted to repair, remove or replace any of the machines. A clause in the contract read:

> In the event the Proprietor [Mountbatten] sells or assigns its interest in the said premises, such Successor shall be fully bound by the terms of this agreement and before the Proprietor sells or assigns it shall obtain the consent in writing of the grantee or assignee to the terms of this agreement.

In return, Mountbatten was to receive 20% of the gross receipts collected from the use of the laundry equipment.

Six months later Mountbatten sold the apartment building to Baldoon Holdings Ltd. for $2 500 000. The lawyer acting for Baldoon drew up the agreement of sale, one clause of which read:

> The Vendor [Mountbatten] warrants to the Purchaser [Baldoon] that the 10 washing machines and 10 clothes dryers located in the apartment building have been placed there by Parker's Automatic Laundry Service Inc. pursuant to an agreement dated 1 June 1981, a copy of which is attached hereto.

Following its purchase of the apartment building, Baldoon continued for a time to operate the building much as before and retained the same manager. Parker's made the first quarterly payment to Baldoon three months after its purchase. At that time Baldoon approached Parker's with a view to purchasing the ten washing machines and ten dryers and operating them itself, as owner of the building. Parker's refused and Baldoon then instructed Parker's to remove its machines within two weeks. When Parker's failed to do so, Baldoon moved the machines to a locked storage area in the basement of the apartment building and replaced them with new washing machines and clothes dryers of its own.

Parker's Automatic Laundry Services Inc. brought an action against Baldoon Holdings Ltd. for breach of contract. Indicate with reasons what the result of this action will likely be, leaving aside the question of what the amount of damages should be, if awarded,

Case 5

Diehl owned some land on which she planned to have a house built that would be suitable for her retirement the following year. She made a contract with Summers, a building contractor, to build a house for $80 000, the price to be paid in full on completion. The contract contained an unqualified promise by the contractor to complete the house at that price. When the house was about three-quarters finished, Diehl stored some expensive furniture in a completed part and took out a $20 000 fire insurance policy on the furniture.

Two weeks later, before the house was completed, lightning caused a serious fire that did considerable damage to both the building and the furniture. Summers learned that Diehl would receive about $16 000 in insurance money. When Diehl asked him to go ahead and complete the house, Summers said, "I believe I'm no longer bound to go on and if you do not pay me the insurance money I will ask a court to declare that the contract has been frustrated. I'm willing to compromise if you will pay me the insurance money." Diehl protested that she had lost considerably from the destruction of her furniture but finally said, "All right, go ahead and do the work."

When the house was completed Diehl paid Summers $80 000 but refused to pay anything more. Summers sued her for $16 000 on the ground that he had been led to believe he would receive this additional sum and would not otherwise have completed the contract.

At the trial evidence was submitted that in contracts of this kind builders frequently require an undertaking by the owner to insure the building during its construction against loss by fire and have the insurance company include a clause agreeing that in the event of a claim it would pay the insurance money first to the builder "insofar as his interest may appear." A copy of the written contract between Summers and Diehl was produced and showed that the contract did not include a term of this kind. The parties testified that neither of them had insured the building itself, as distinct from the contents. It was acknowledged that the contractor, Summers, would have had an insurable interest and could have insured the house himself to the value of the contract.

Develop the arguments for each of the plaintiff and the defendant, and offer an opinion about whether the action should succeed.

Case 6

The Canada Paper Corporation carried on a pulp and paper operation near the town of Rainy River. In 1905 Canada Paper entered into an agreement with the Government of Ontario under which Ontario would transfer to Canada Paper certain property with all water power facilities and in return Canada Paper would provide hydroelectric power to the town of Rainy River "to such extent as the Town may require at a fixed price of $14.00 per horsepower per annum." The agreement contained no provision about its duration. Canada Paper paid the entire capital cost of the power project.

Hydroelectric power was first supplied to Rainy River in 1911 and continued to be supplied until 1978 when Canada Paper protested that it could no longer afford to supply the town with power. During this period the town's population had increased by five times; power consumption per capita increased by 133 times. At the same time, Canada Paper had expanded its papermaking facilities and needed almost all the power produced from the power generating facilities. In addition, because of inflation the price of $14.00 per horsepower per annum was very low. The town bought the power at the cheap 1905 price and sold it to its citizen users at attractive prices that still yielded it a large profit.

In 1978, Canada Paper tried to renegotiate the contract with Ontario, but Ontario refused to make any change because of political pressure from the town. Canada Paper then gave Ontario notice that it would terminate the contract, effective in 1981.

Ontario commenced proceedings to enforce the contract. Describe the arguments that Canada Paper might use to defend the action, and offer an opinion about whether they are likely to succeed.

CHAPTER 16

THE EFFECT OF BREACH

*I*MPLICATIONS OF BREACH

In our discussion of the ways in which a contract may be discharged, we noted that breach is sometimes described as a method of discharge. This statement must be qualified in two ways: first, not every breach may discharge a contract; second, in any event breach does not discharge a contract automatically (as does frustration or completed performance, for example). Even when a breach is sufficient to discharge the contract, it will be discharged only if the party that suffered the breach elects to treat it as doing so.

An injured party cannot elect to treat every breach as discharging the contract and freeing it from its own obligation to perform. The breach must be of either the whole contract or an essential term of the contract, so that the purpose of the agreement is defeated and performance by the aggrieved party has become pointless. Breach of a minor term may entitle an aggrieved party to damages, but does not entitle it to abandon its obligations. If it does so, it is at its peril, and the other party may in turn sue it successfully for failure to carry out its promises.

ILLUSTRATIONS

(a) *A* agrees to sell 10 000 bags of potatoes to *B* Wholesale Grocers and to deliver them in yellow paper bags with green labels. Through a mistake, the labels are printed in blue rather than green. The management of *B* may feel annoyed and believe that their merchandise display will not be as effective. *B* may sue *A* and collect damages for such loss as it can show the breach has caused it. But it cannot reject the potatoes without itself committing a breach that might make it liable for heavy damages.

(b) *A* agrees to sell 10 000 bags of potatoes to *B* Wholesale Grocers and to deliver them to *B*'s warehouse on Wednesday in time for *B* to distribute them to its supermarket chain for a weekend special. *A* makes no delivery until late Friday afternoon. By this delay *A* has committed a breach of an essential term of the contract — delivery on Wednesday. *B* may reject the potatoes and discharge the contract, freeing itself from any obligation to pay for them. In addition, it may sue *A* for damages caused by failure to deliver on time. In the alternative, *B* may accept the potatoes if it decides it still wants them. In this event the contract is not discharged: *B* is liable to pay the price for the potatoes, subject to a deduction for damages caused by the failure to deliver them on time. If *B* should accept the potatoes and then refuse to pay for them, *A* could sue *B* for the price, and *B* could counterclaim for its damages.

Thus we see that breach itself does not discharge a contract: if the breach is of a minor term, the contract is still binding on both parties; if the breach is of a fundamental term, the party committing the breach is still bound, but the injured party may then elect to discharge the contract and free itself, or else affirm the contract so that it continues to bind both parties.

We should note also that a major term may be broken in a minor respect. Suppose, in our illustration above, that *A* delivers on time but is short by five bags. The *quantity* to be delivered is a major term, but delivering 9995 bags of 10 000 promised would be only a *minor breach* of that term and would not entitle *B* to reject the shipment. If however, *A* had delivered only 5000 bags there would be a *major breach* and *B* could elect to reject them.

It is not always easy to determine whether a term of a contract is essential to it or of lesser importance, or whether the breach of an essential term is a serious one. Nevertheless, in any dispute concerning a breach, the first task is to try to determine to which class the term in question belongs.

We must note an unfortunate development in terminology concerning essential and non-essential terms: for a variety of reasons stemming from 19th-century developments in contract law, essential terms became known as *conditions* and non-essential terms as *warranties*. These names are unfortunate because "condition" may easily become confused with "condition precedent" (where the word "condition" means a happening or event rather than a term of an agreement) and "warranty" may be confused with its special meaning in a sale of goods (where it means a guarantee of quality of the goods or of their ownership — usually an essential term). Despite the confusion, the use of "condition" and "warranty" to distinguish essential from non-essential terms has now become so common that we cannot ignore it. We must therefore take care to ascertain the meaning of these words each time we meet them.

How Breach May Occur

A party to a contract may break it by (a) repudiating its liabilities expressly; (b) by acting in a way that makes its promise impossible to perform; or (c) by either failing to perform at all or tendering an actual performance that is not equivalent to its promise. We shall discuss each of these ways in turn.

Express Repudiation

An express repudiation is a declaration by one of the contracting parties to the other that it does not intend to perform as it had promised. The promisee is entitled to treat the contract as being immediately at an end, find another party to perform and sue for whatever damages it sustains in delay and higher costs because the original contract will not be performed. Before substituting a new party to proceed with performance, it is prudent for the promisee to inform the repudiating party that it is treating the contract as terminated at once and is reserving its rights to sue for damages for breach.

A promisee may, on the other hand, continue to insist on performance. If it chooses this option and does not receive performance by the latest time promised in the contract, it is still entitled to damages for breach of contract but it takes a chance that intervening events may provide the promisor with an excuse for not performing.

Avery v. Bowden[1] shows what can happen when a promisee insists upon performance. A ship was chartered to sail from England to Odessa to pick up a cargo at Odessa. On reaching Odessa, the ship's master requested his cargo, and the charterer's agent refused to give him one. By custom a charterer was entitled to a period of grace to provide a

---

[1] (1855), 119 E.R. 647.

cargo. As soon as the charterer repudiated the contract, however, the ship's master could have treated himself as freed from further liability and sailed immediately for England. Instead, he elected to wait out the usual grace period and continue to demand a cargo. Before the period expired, war broke out between England and Russia, and it became impossible to complete the contract. The ship's owner was unsuccessful when he sued the charterer for damages caused by the futile trip: the contract had been discharged by frustration and not by breach. The court noted that the decision would have been different had the ship's master elected to treat the express repudiation as an immediate breach of contract.

Whenever breach occurs in advance of the time agreed on for performance, it is known as *anticipatory breach*. Suppose that A Co. has contracted with B Ltd. for the delivery to A Co. in six months of manufactured materials at an agreed price. A week after the contract is formed, B Ltd. discovers that it has agreed to a price that is much too low and informs A Co. that it will not deliver the materials as promised. B Ltd. has committed an anticipatory breach of its contract with A Co. and A Co. need not wait until the delivery date to sue B Ltd. The courts have recognized that, as a promisee, A Co. is entitled not only to performance of the contract in six months' time but also to a continuous expectation of performance in the interim between formation of the contract and its performance. (In *Avery v. Bowden*, the charterer's repudiation was also an example of anticipatory breach.) The concept is a basic one; it asserts that a contract exists and has legal effect from the time of its formation, and not just from the time of its performance.

Repudiation may also occur after performance has begun. In *General Billposting Co. v. Atkinson*[2] Atkinson had been employed under a contract containing a clause that he should not work in competition with the company for a given period after the termination of his employment. Atkinson was dismissed without cause in breach of his employment contract. He recovered damages for wrongful dismissal, and then began to work within the district as a self employed billposter. General Billposting sought an injunction restraining him from competition but failed. The court held that the company had, by its repudiation of the employment contract, entitled Atkinson to consider his own contractual obligations at an end.

[handwritten margin note: non-competition agreement part of initial agreement.]

[handwritten margin note: since contract was dismissed this non-comp. agreement no longer applied]

In these examples, repudiation takes the form of a declaration affecting the performance of the whole of the contract. There are business situations, however, in which one party repudiates only a minor term of the contract. As we have seen, such a breach does not entitle the other party to abandon the contract and declare it discharged. A wise manager will notify the other party that the firm is unable to perform exactly as promised as soon as he or she is aware of the situation, so that the other party may take immediate steps to reduce any loss that the breach may cause.

---

[2] [1909] A.C. 118.

A Co., a wholesale distributor of electronic equipment, has agreed to supply *B* Co., a chain of retail stores selling home entertainment components, with a large quantity of new cassette recorders, along with sample demonstration cassettes of spectacular sound effects and advertising for the new product. Several days before delivery, the manager of *A* Co. discovers that the tape recorders are in stock but that the demonstration cassettes have not arrived and appear to have been lost in shipment. Knowing that *B* Co. plans to feature the new product, *A* Co.'s manager would be wise to notify it at once of the expected breach of this minor term. *B* Co. may then arrange in advance for an alternative supply of good demonstration tapes. If *A* Co. were to deliver without prior indication of its inability to supply the tapes, *B* Co. might suffer a greater loss for which *A* Co. would be liable.

One Party Renders Performance Impossible

Under this heading, an act constituting a breach of contract includes only a wilful or negligent act of the promisor and not an involuntary response to forces beyond its control. Performance may be rendered impossible by an involuntary act but only a deliberate or negligent act is tantamount to repudiation: although not declared by the promisor in so many words, it is nonetheless implied. It is a form of the self-induced frustration we referred to in the preceding chapter. As with express repudiation, conduct that makes performance impossible may take place either before or during performance.

A agrees to sell her Ferrari sports car to *B* for $30 000, with car and registration to be delivered in three weeks. A few days later, *X*, unaware of the agreement between *A* and *B*, offers *A* $35 000 for the car. *A* accepts and delivers the car to *X* that day. *A* is in breach of the contract with *B* at the moment she makes the sale to *X*, and *B* may sue her as soon as he learns of it. *A* will not be permitted to argue that she can still deliver the car on time by buying it back from *X*; *B* is entitled to a continuous expectation of *A*'s prospective performance until the day agreed for delivery arrives. The result would be the same if *A*'s agent negligently sold the car to *X*.

Failure of Performance

Types of Failure

Unlike the other two types of breach, failure of performance usually becomes apparent only when the time for performance arrives or during the course of performance. A failure may be of various degrees: it may be a total failure to perform, it may be a grossly inadequate performance, or it may be a failure in a minor particular. It may also take the form of a satisfactory performance of all but one of the terms of the contract or of only part of a main term. The extent of a failure always has an important bearing on the nature of the remedies available to the injured party.

The problems created by failure of performance arise typically when the party guilty of the breach is required either by the terms of the contract, or by usual trade practice, to perform its part first. We have then to decide whether the injured party is excused from performance of its own part of the bargain. The question arises often in contracts calling for the delivery of goods by instalments when the quantity delivered fails to meet the amount called for in the contract. The issue is whether what is left undone amounts to a sufficient breach to free the injured party from its part of the bargain, or whether the breach is minor and entitles the injured party only to damages, while the agreement still continues to bind it. Partial delivery may be merely inconvenient, or it may be completely unsatisfactory.

ILLUSTRATIONS

(a) A contract of sale calls for the delivery of 6000 tons of coal in 12 monthly instalments of about 500 tons each. One of the terms is that the buyer will provide the trucks to take the coal away. In the first month the buyer sends sufficient trucks to take away only 400 tons. The buyer's default would not likely be sufficient to discharge the seller from its obligation to stand ready to providethe remaining 5600 tons over the following 11 months.[3]

(b) A seller is required by a contract of sale to deliver 150 tons of iron per month but delivers only 21 in the first month. Its default is very likely sufficient to discharge the buyer, which may then turn to another source of supply and sue for damages rseulting from the breach.[4]

Often, an innocent party is left in a quandary. If there is real concern about the seriousness of continuing defective performance, it is wise to seek legal advice before claiming to be discharged of one's own obligations; otherwise one risks being held liable for wrongful repudiation should a court find that the seller's default was only a minor breach.

In a contract where one party is to perform by instalments, the other may consider itself freed from liability only if it can offer convincing affirmative answers to each of these questions:

(a) Is there good reason to think that future performance will be equally defective?
(b) Is either the expected deficiency or the actual deficiency to date important relative to the whole performance promised?

The Doctrine of Substantial Performance

The courts have grown more willing to recognize substantial performance by the promisor, though defective or incomplete in some minor respects, as sufficient to bind

---

[3] See Simpson v. Crippin (1872), L.R. 8 Q.B. 14, where in a similar situation the buyer took delivery of only 158 tons in the first month, and yet the seller was held to the contract.
[4] Hoare v. Rennie (1859), 157 E.R. 1083.

the other party to its part of the bargain. The doctrine of *substantial performance* asserts that a promisor is entitled to enforce a contract when it has substantially performed, even though its performance does not comply in some minor particular with the requirements of the contract. The promisor's claim is, however, subject to a reduction for damages caused by its defective performance. The effect of the doctrine is that a promisee cannot seize upon a trivial failure of performance to avoid its own obligations.[5]

When the Right to Treat the Contract as Discharged is Lost

Two situations may occur where a breach of an important term, that would ordinarily give an aggrieved party a right to treat its obligations as discharged, entitles it only to damages. In the first, the aggrieved party may have elected to proceed with the contract and accept benefits under it despite the breach. In the second, it may have received the benefit of the contract and not learned of the breach until performance was complete.

ILLUSTRATIONS

(a) *A* chartered a ship from *B* for £1550, for a voyage from Liverpool to Sydney. The contract specified that the ship should have a cargo capacity of at least 1000 tons. The vessel proved incapable of carrying that amount of cargo, but *A* allowed it to load what it could and made an advance payment on the freight. Subsequently, *A* refused to pay the balance, claiming the contract to have been discharged for breach of a major term. In an action by *B* for the balance of the price, the court noted that while *A* could have treated the contract as discharged, refused to load the ship and sued for its loss, *A's* acceptance of performance by the smaller ship foreclosed the earlier option. Instead it had to pay the agreed price, less any counterclaim for damages it could establish.[6]

(b) *A* Farms purchased seed from *B* Nurseries, described by *B* as "common English sainfoin". After it was sown, it proved to be "giant sainfoin", an inferior type. However, *A* could not have learned of the breach until after the seed had been planted and came up, a time when it would be too late to reject the seed and treat the contract as discharged. *A's* only remedy was to sue for damages for the breach.[7]

These illustrations show that the right to consider a contract at an end may depend upon an aggrieved party still being able to reject the substantial benefit of the contract. If it cannot, it will remain bound to perform its obligations, subject to a right to claim damages.

Exemption Clauses

Their Purpose

In many types of transaction one party may run a risk that failure to perform on its part, sometimes even in a relatively minor respect, will cause substantial harm to the interests

[5] Dakin & Co. Ltd. v. Lee, [1916] 1 K.B. 566.
[6] Pust v. Dowie (1863), 122 E.R. 740 and 745.
[7] Wallis v. Pratt, [1911] A.C. 394. In a contract of sale the buyer's remedy is confined to money damages "where a contract of sale is not severable and the buyer has accepted the goods or part thereof", by virtue of the Sale of Goods Act. See, for example: Sale of Goods Act, R.S.O. 1990, c. S-1, s. 12(3); R.S.B.C. 1979, c. 370, s. 15(3); R.S.N.S. 1989, c. 408, s. 13(3).

of the other party. (We shall discuss the extent of that liability in the next chapter.) A party running these risks has several alternatives when striking a bargain: (a) it may obtain insurance against the risk and raise its price accordingly; (b) it may be a "self-insurer", that is, charge a higher fee and build up a reserve fund to pay any claim that arises later from harm to a customer; (c) it may insist on an *exemption clause* in the contract, in effect excluding itself from any liability for the risk and transferring the risk of harm to its customer. As we noted in our discussion of the ticket cases in Chapter 6 on Offer and Acceptance, the last alternative is often the most attractive.

There are several reasons why exemption clauses are widely used. In the first place, they permit a supplier of goods and services to keep its prices low, since it need not increase them to protect itself against the risk of liability to its customer. Second, if it is sued for damages despite the exemption clause, it will completely disclaim liability and thus seek to avoid the difficult question of the extent of its liability for the harm done. Finally, if it is in the position of using a standard form contract (especially if it is a detailed printed form with many other terms) it will in most circumstances have a distinct advantage over its customer; the customer may be quite knowledgeable about competitive pricing and drive a hard bargain, but will usually have little or no expertise in legal issues. Frequently, a customer will gladly accept a lower price without realizing the implications of an exemption clause.

Exemption clauses may make good sense and work reasonably well when the bargaining power and knowledge of the law is relatively equal between the parties. For example, one party may willingly assume a risk in return for a lower price; it may already have adequate blanket insurance coverage. Or the activity may be extremely hazardous; a charter airline may be unwilling to fly a client into northern mountain regions in winter except at the client's own risk. Generally speaking, however, the party preparing the standard form contract drafts exemption clauses clearly to its own advantage, and the courts have developed techniques to cut this advantage down in egregious cases.

Attitude of the Courts

When an exemption clause appears in a document that a customer does not sign — such as a ticket or receipt or a sign displayed on a wall — the first defence against it is to deny adequate notice of the term. If this defence succeeds, then the term is not considered to be part of the bargain between the parties.

Even if a person signs a document, in the circumstances described in Chapter 10 on Mistake, he may plead *non est factum;* if successful, the entire document including any exemption clause it may contain is void. As discussed in Chapter 11, a person may not be bound by a clause that is so unexpected and unfair that a reasonable signer would not think the contract contained such a term. This result is more likely if the contents of the document were misrepresented to the signer. A recent decision of the Ontario Court of Appeal has further enlarged the protection: for exemption clauses that absolve a defendant from liability for negligence, or limit its liability to a small portion of the harm suffered,

> ... *the defendant must establish* that it has specifically drawn the onerous limitation clause to the plaintiff's attention or has accurately stated its legal effect to the plaintiff *before* he signs the contract.[8] [emphasis added]

---

[8] Trigg v. MI Movers International Transport Services (1992), 84 D.L.R. (4th) 504, per Tarnopolsky, J.A., at 508.

This decision shifts the burden to the defendant to demonstrate that it adequately informed the plaintiff. However, where a person signs a contract that does not contain an unexpectedly onerous clause, he will be bound by all its terms contained; so too, with a document he is not expected to sign, if he actually knew or should reasonably have known its terms.

When adequate notice has been given, what effect does an exemption clause have if, apart from the clause, the party who has drafted it fails in some significant way to perform the contract as agreed? Exemption clauses are typically drawn in very wide terms. A supplier of machinery might exempt itself from all liability for defects in the product supplied, for any negligence of its employees, and for any guarantees implied by custom or trade usage — except for guarantees expressly set out in the contract, such as replacing any defective parts for three months. Courts have taken the view that exemption clauses should be very strictly construed against the party that draws them because they permit parties to evade legal responsibility ordinarily placed on suppliers of goods and services.

Even so, the courts respect the theory of freedom of contract, and in the absence of special rules (such as exist for common carriers) or special statutory protection (as in consumer protection legislation), they will not make a new contract for the parties to protect the one in a weaker position. If an exemption clause squarely excludes liability for the breach that has occurred, the injured party — subject to the discussion that follows — has no remedy. Thus, if one day after an express guarantee expires a piece of machinery breaks down for the first time, the supplier is not liable, even if at common law it would, in the absence of the clause, have been liable under an implied warranty of fitness.

Exemption clauses are strictly construed by the courts, in ways that are not at first apparent. Thus, a clause exempting a supplier from liability under the contract has been held not to exempt it from liability in tort.[9] Similarly, if a clause exempts a carrier from liability for negligence by its employees, the carrier will escape vicarious liability; however, the customer who has suffered injury or loss may still sue employees personally for their negligence unless, as decided in a recent Supreme Court of Canada case, the employees can show that the clause was clearly intended to protect them as well.[10] Again, if a warehousing firm agrees to store goods in building A, but for its own convenience stores them in adjoining building B, and they are lost under circumstances that would have been covered by an exemption clause had they been in building A, the firm will be liable because it has performed a different contract from that agreed between the parties.[11]

Fundamental Breach

The most difficult cases arise when on very careful scrutiny the exempting clause appears to protect the supplier of goods or services, but where, apart from the clause, a breach has been so serious as to defeat the purpose of the contract. In the absence of the clause, the aggrieved party could immediately have treated the contract as discharged, and sued for damages. In a number of cases in recent years courts have been reluctant to allow defendants to shelter behind exemption clauses. In some instances they have labelled the

---

[9] White v. John Warrick & Co. Ltd., [1953] 2 All E.R. 1021.
[10] London Drugs v. Kuehne & Nagel International (1992), 97 D.L.R. (4th) 261, discussed in Chapter 14, Privity of Contract, under "Vicarious Performance". Traditionally, employees are third parties who are unable to claim the benefit of an exemption clause in the contract between carrier and customer. The London Drugs case provides some relief for employees.
[11] Lilley v. Doubleday (1881), 7 Q.B.D. 510.

default as a fundamental breach and have applied a hard rule using the following reasoning: if a breach is so serious that it amounts to a non-performance of the contract, it goes to the "core" of the bargain between the parties; to treat an exemption clause as excusing one party entirely from performance would be repugnant to the very idea of a binding contract; therefore, the clause must be struck down and the aggrieved party given a remedy in order to preserve the idea of a binding bargain. This rather doctrinaire line of reasoning means that once a court "identifies" a fundamental breach it treats any exemption clause as ineffective to excuse that breach.

The above approach was seriously questioned in a 1964 judgment of the English Court of Appeal, when Pearson, L.J. said:

> As to the question of "fundamental breach", I think there is a rule of construction [interpretation] that normally an exemption or exclusion clause or similar provision in a contract should be construed as not applying to a situation created by a fundamental breach of contract. This is not an independent rule of law imposed by the court on the parties willy-nilly in disregard of their contractual intention. On the contrary, it is a rule of construction based on the presumed intention of the contracting parties. It involves the implication of a term to give to the contract that business efficacy which the parties as reasonable men must have intended it to have. This rule of construction is not new in principle but it has become prominent in recent years in consequence of the tendency to have standard forms of contract containing exceptions clauses drawn in extravagantly wide terms, which would produce absurd results if applied literally.[12]

This statement was generally approved by the House of Lords in the *Suisse Atlantique* case.[13] Although the law lords decided that the facts did not raise the issue of fundamental breach, they took the opportunity to discuss the subject exhaustively. The result appears to be that an exemption clause may effectively protect a defendant from liability for fundamental breach if in all the circumstances it ought to be inferred that the parties have so agreed. This opinion of the House of Lords was followed by the Supreme Court of Canada in a case where the defendant telegraph company failed to deliver a telegraphed tender, and the plaintiff contractor lost a construction contract it would otherwise have won.[14] The Court held that despite its failure to perform, the telegraph company was protected by the broad exemption clause printed on the telegram form. Subsequently, the House of Lords also allowed a very broad exemption clause to protect a defendant against liability for a deliberate act of destruction by one of its employees.[15]

The principle stated in the *Suisse Atlantique* case is a sensible one, especially in transactions between businesses that agree to apportion the risks of a contract through the use of an exemption clause. For instance, a contractor for a large construction project may obtain insurance coverage at a better price than would be possible if each of its subcontractors had to take out separate policies. The subcontractors are thus able to make lower bids by exempting themselves from liability, with the agreement of the contractor. In these circumstances, if a court were to hold an exemption clause ineffective to protect a

---

[12] U.G.S. Finance Ltd. v. National Mortgage Bank of Greece, S.A., [1964] 1 Lloyd's Rep. 446 at 453.

[13] Suisse Atlantique Société D'Armement Maritime S.A. v. N.V. Rotterdamsche Kolen Centrale, [1967] 1 A.C. 361.

[14] Linton v. C.N.R. (1974), 49 D.L.R. (3d) 548. Four of the justices dissented vigorously, protesting that the effect of the majority decision was to leave the telegraph company substantially without any obligation.

[15] Photo Production Ltd. v. Securicor Transport Ltd., [1980] 2 W.L.R. 283.

subcontractor, it would be defeating the bargain freely entered upon by the parties.[16] We should note, however, that courts continue to examine these clauses very carefully, and to interpret them as not protecting the defendant when it would appear manifestly unfair to give protection.

POSSIBLE CRIMINAL CONSEQUENCES OF BREACH

A breach of contract may be criminal when a party breaks the contract with the knowledge that the action will endanger human life, cause bodily injury; expose valuable property to damage; deprive the inhabitants of a place of their supply of light, power, gas, or water; or delay or prevent the operation of a train by a common carrier.[17]

THE BUSINESS SIGNIFICANCE OF BREACH

The vast majority of contracts are performed not because there are legal rules and courts to enforce them, but because the contracts make sense to the parties themselves. The parties must have seen a mutual economic advantage in forming their contract in the first place, or they would not have done so; the same advantage in most instances survives throughout the duration of the contract to provide each with an incentive to complete it. Few parties will ever enter into a contract if they seriously suppose that they may later have to seek one of the remedies for breach through court action. Of course, the expected advantages from the bargain do not always materialize, and the benefits for one of the parties may turn out to be losses; we cannot know how frequently such a party may be persuaded, even if reluctantly, to perform because of a knowledge that the sanctions available to the other party would make breach at least as expensive as performing the unprofitable contract. The remedies for breach that we examine in the next chapter seem to play this type of supportive role, encouraging in a small minority of instances the performance of contracts and so assisting the other party to attain its expectations. To borrow from the words of Professor Macneil, "... contracts are fundamentally mechanisms of cooperation and only mechanisms of conflict when things have gone wrong.... The law has thus to deal largely with pathological cases."[18]

---

[16] For a full discussion of the problems raised with respect to the allocation of risk, see Waddams, *The Law of Contracts*, 3rd ed.) pp. 312-25. In particular, at pp. 320-22 there is an interesting discussion of Harbutt's Plasticine case, where the court disregarded an exemption clause protecting a defendant and as a result there was further litigation against an insurer that contested the unexpected liability of the defendant. See Harbutt's "Plasticine" Ltd. v. Wayne Tank & Pump Co. Ltd., [1970] 1 Q.B. 447, and Wayne Tank & Pump Co. Ltd. v. Employers Liability Assurance Corp. Ltd., [1974] Q.B. 57.

[17] Criminal Code, R.S.C. 1985, c. C-41, s. 422.

[18] Macneil, "Whither Contracts" (1969) 21 *Journal of Legal Education* 403, at p. 408; reproduced in Swan and Reiter, *Contracts, Cases, Notes & Materials*, (4th ed.), p. 863. Professor Macneil goes on to say, however, that "... the rule of the pathological case governs the healthy case too."

Questions for Review

1. Why does the interpretation of an exempting clause require some reference to the other terms of the contract?
2. In what respect does the express repudiation of a warranty differ in its effect from the express repudiation of a condition?
3. Under what circumstances is a party who is the victim of a breach of condition limited to money damages as a remedy?
4. In a contract between two companies for the delivery of goods by instalments, one of the deliveries is short in the quantity specified. What tests may we apply in deciding whether the buyer can regard itself as discharged from its own obligations?
5. On May 16, A Ltd. contracts to deliver goods to B by May 31, with payment due on June 30. On May 23, B closes up his business and moves to another district. Has any breach of contract occurred before May 31?
6. By what reasoning can a company present a large balance of accounts receivable as a current asset as of its balance sheet date when those balances are not payable by its customers until some time after the balance sheet date?
7. Contrast the doctrine of substantial performance with the doctrine of part performance.
8. What do you think Professor Macneil meant when he wrote, "The most important support for contractual relationships is not a sanction at all, but a continuation of the exchange motivations which led the parties to enter the relationship in the first place."? ("Whither Contracts", (1969) 21 *Journal of Legal Education,* p. 403 at p. 410.)
9. Explain the following observation of Professor Fuller: "Expectations of future values become, for purposes of trade, present values. In a society in which credit has become a significant and pervasive institution, it is inevitable that the expectancy created by an enforceable promise should be regarded as a kind of property, and breach of the promise as an injury to that property." (Fuller and Perdue, "The Reliance Interest in Contract Damages: 1", (1936) 46 *Yale Law Journal,* p. 52 at p. 59.)

Problems

Problem 1

Shaw contracts with Universal Travel Services for an advertised three-week conducted tour through western Canada, including five days at Banff. The itinerary includes a stop at Mount Eisenhower. Instead of visiting this mountain, Universal Travel Services takes its patrons for a brief visit to Mount Assiniboine. Is Shaw entitled to treat her contract as discharged?

   Suppose additionally that Universal Travel Services, instead of accommodating its patrons for five days at Banff, booked them into a small hotel in Calgary for that period. What alternative remedies are available to Shaw? What further information would be useful for determining the remedy most likely to compensate her adequately?

Problem 2

O. Leander owns extensive greenhouses in which she grows flowers and plants for retail florists. On October 25, Jason, a retail florist, agrees to supply Leander with 1000 poinsettias for the Christmas trade, the plants to cost $1.00 each and to be available between

December 10 and December 20. Jason requests delivery on December 11. At that time Leander advises him that she will not perform the contract, since she can obtain $1.25 each for the plants elsewhere. Jason refuses to pay more than $1.00 a plant and continues to insist upon delivery. On December 16, an extreme cold spell arrives, Leander's heating system breaks down and all the poinsettias she has on hand freeze. Jason then purchases the 1000 poinsettias from another wholesale florist but has to pay $1.30 a plant.

Has Jason any remedy? Discuss the arguments in his favour and the defences that Leander might offer. Would it make any difference if the contract had provided instead that the plants should be available between December 10 and December 15?

Cases

Case 1

Fowler Engineering Co. agreed to supply Supreme Soap Co. with a specific machine for the manufacture of soap-chips from liquid soap. The essential terms of the contract were as follows:

> *Fowler agrees:* To supply the machine and supervise its installation; to supervise the installation of all motors and pipes supplied by Supreme Soap; to test the machine and put it in good working order.

> *Supreme Soap agrees:* To supply all necessary motors and pipes and labour; to pay $10 000 on delivery of the machine by Fowler; to pay the balance of $15 000 on completion of the installation.

When the machine was fully installed but had not yet been tested, Fowler demanded payment of the balance of $15 000. The manager of Supreme Soap Co. refused to pay until the machine had had a trial run and had proved satisfactory. Fowler said it did not want payment held up just because there might be some minor adjustments. Both parties were adamant. Supreme Soap Co. then employed another engineering firm to test the machine. The machine did not operate satisfactorily, although it was agreed that the defect could be remedied for about $250. The test also indicated that a different type of equipment would be better for the purposes of the soap company.

Supreme Soap Co. brought an action for return of the $10 000 deposit and for damages for breach of contract including the value of the floor space occupied by the machine, the value of the materials and labour it had supplied towards its completion, and the fees of the other engineering firm employed for the trial run. Fowler Engineering Co. counterclaimed for the balance owing on the price. What should the result be?

Case 2

The Town of Crestwood Heights contracted with the Ajax Construction Co. for the construction of a storm relief sewer. A term was that Ajax Construction Co. should conform to the decisions and adopt the methods of an engineer appointed by the town to supervise the project. As designated sections of the project were completed to the satisfaction of the engineer, the town was to pay for the work done.

Immediately after the work was begun, the engineer appointed by the town insisted upon a different grade for the sewers from that proposed by the construction company and demanded a jointing compound of better quality. An unfortunate conflict of personalities developed between the engineer and the manager of the construction company.

The company refused to comply with the engineer's demands and removed its equipment from the project, insisting as a condition for resuming work that the engineer be replaced. The town replied at once that abandonment of the work at this stage constituted a serious threat of property damage to homeowners in the event of a heavy rainfall, and that unless the work was resumed within two days the town would have it completed by other contractors. There were a number of inconclusive meetings between the mayor and other representatives of Crestwood Heights and the manager of Ajax, but they failed to resolve their differences. The meetings took place sporadically over a period of about a week. Without further notice to Ajax, the town hired another contractor with equipment available in the district, and the project was completed. The town brought an action against Ajax for $10 000, that figure being the extra sum paid to the second contractors over the contract price to complete the work Ajax had agreed but failed to do. Ajax claimed, as one of its defences, that the town failed to give it notice that a new contractor had been hired.

The following is an extract from the evidence at the time of the trial when the judge questioned Miller, the manager of Ajax Construction Co.:

> *His Lordship:* But you have already said when you signed the contract that you would agree that the engineer's ruling shall be final and binding?
>
> *Mr. Miller:* That's quite possible, but to my mind that contract is an unfair contract from beginning to end.
>
> *His Lordship:* That may be.
>
> *Mr. Miller:* That's not for me to judge.
>
> *His Lordship:* No, but it is for me.

Further evidence indicated that, while there might be room for a difference of opinion about the adequacy of the work done by Ajax Construction Co., the engineer engaged by the town had nevertheless acted in good faith in insisting on a different type of performance.

What should the court's decision be? (For reference, see *Rickards (Charles), Ltd. v. Oppenheim*, [1950] 1 K.B. 616; [1950] 1 All E.R. 420.)

CHAPTER 17

REMEDIES FOR BREACH

TYPES OF REMEDIES

In the last chapter we discussed the remedy of termination, that is, the right to treat the contract as discharged as a result of breach. In addition, the injured party may have several other remedies available, depending on the type of breach and the subject-matter of the contract. They are as follows:

(a) damages;
(b) equitable remedies — specific performance, injunction and rescission;
(c) *quantum meruit.*

DAMAGES

The Purpose of an Award of Damages

An award of damages aims to place the injured party in the same position as if the contract had been completed. The award is intended only to compensate an injured party for the loss caused by failure to perform, not to punish the party liable for the breach. Of course, knowledge of the fact that it will have to compensate another party usually deters a party from committing a breach it can avoid. In this respect, the purpose of an award of damages in contract is similar to that in the law of torts, that is, compensation and not punishment. The simple fact of liability also acts as an economic deterrent.

The consequences of an economic approach may in some instances seem surprising. One can imagine circumstances in which a party to the contract could increase its total profits by deliberately breaking a contract.

ILLUSTRATION

X Inc. contracts to supply 100 000 widgets at $2.00 each to Y Corp. It expects to earn a profit of $20 000 on the contract. Shortly afterwards, X Inc. receives an offer to supply a different item to Z Ltd. at a profit of $60 000 but if it accepts Z Ltd.'s offer it cannot possibly also produce the 100 000 widgets for Y Corp. X Inc. learns, however, that a competing manufacturer can supply widgets of equal quality to Y Corp. at $2.25, that is, for $25 000 more than its own price. In these circumstances it could be to the economic advantage of X Inc. to forego its profit of $20 000 on the contract with Y Corp. and pay that company $25 000 in damages for breach, while earning $60 000 on the new contract — a net gain of $15 000.

Such a strictly economic analysis of the purpose of damages leads to a controversial view of the nature of a contractual obligation:

A starting point for analysis is Holmes's view [as expressed in his "The Path of the Law"] that it is not the policy of the law to compel adherence to contracts but only to require each party to choose between performing in accordance with the contract and compensating the other party for any injury resulting from a failure to perform.[1]

This perception of contractual liability is morally neutral. It has been controversial precisely because it disregards any moral element in the legal obligation to perform one's promises.

We should note also that the arithmetic in our illustration above oversimplifies the nature of the decision that must be made. Additional intangible costs of a decision to break a contract are risk of harm to continuing good relations with the affected customer[2] as well as to one's general reputation for honouring commitments.

Mitigation of Damages

A business that has sustained a loss as a result of breach of contract is expected do what it can to mitigate the extent of the loss: the damages it can recover at law will not include what it might reasonably have avoided. In this respect, mitigation in contract law is analogous to the principle of contributory negligence in the law of torts. Thus, a business that has contracted to sell perishable goods and had them rejected upon tender of delivery will only prejudice itself by continuing to insist upon their acceptance. It must try to dispose of them at the best obtainable price as quickly as it can, if it wishes to recoup the resulting loss in an action for damages. Similarly, when a business has agreed to buy goods and the seller fails to deliver, it should move to replace the goods from other suppliers as soon as possible. The same rule applies when a contract of employment is broken by the employer. An employee in suing for damages for wrongful dismissal should be able to show that he or she made every reasonable effort to find suitable alternative employment as a means of mitigating personal financial losses.

In other words, an aggrieved party can recover only for such losses resulting from the breach *as it could not avoid by acting reasonably.* All the more so then, a party that acts in a manner that aggravates and increases the resulting loss will be denied recovery for the alleged additional damages. A byproduct of the mitigation rule is that it removes the incentive for conduct that is wasteful of economic resources.[3]

Prerequisites for an Award of Damages

Any damage arising from breach of contract, to qualify for recovery, must "flow naturally from the breach". This general principle has been interpreted to mean that a loss resulting from breach must be within the foreseeable boundaries of what the parties would have expected as a likely consequence of a failure to perform — assuming they had thought about the possibility of breach when they drew up their contract. Damages will not generally be awarded to compensate an injured party for some unusual or unexpected consequence of breach.

One of the leading cases on this point is *B.C. Saw Mill Co. v. Nettleship.*[4] A carrier failed to deliver a vital piece of machinery promptly to the sawmill as instructed by an

---

[1] Posner, *Economic Analysis of Law* (2nd ed.), p. 88. Boston: Little, Brown & Co. 1977. The analysis in the preceding   paragraph is based on Posner.
[2] The existence of this intangible cost is recognized by Posner, *ibid.,* at p. 67.
[3] See Waddams, *The Law of Contracts* (3rd ed.), pp. 514-24.
[4] (1868), L.R. 3 C.P. 499. See also: Cornwall Gravel Co. Ltd. v. Purolator Courier Ltd. (1978), 18 O.R. (2d) 551; Hadley v. Baxendale (1854), 156 E.R. 145; Koufos v. C. Czarnikow, The Heron II, [1969] 1 A.C. 350.

employee of the mill; the result was that the sawmill had to suspend operations until the part arrived. The carrier had not been told about the special nature of the machinery when it agreed to transport it. The owners of the sawmill failed to recover damages as compensation for the loss of time. If the carrier had been told of the importance of the item it would presumably have been liable for the loss — unless it exempted itself from liability and suggested that the sawmill insure the shipment against risk of delay or loss. Or it would have placed the item in a special category of freight to ensure greater care in delivery, and charged a higher rate for its services.

Sometimes a party does enter into a contract with knowledge of special liability if it fails to perform. In *Hydraulic Engineering Co. v. McHaffie Goslett*,[5] an engineering company had to make a machine to be delivered by a given date. Under a subcontract, it arranged with the defendant firm to manufacture a part of the machine. The engineering company had made it clear that the entire machine had to be completed for its customer within a specified time. The subcontractor did not manufacture its part until after the agreed date, claiming it had no employee competent to prepare patterns for it. Because of the delay the buyer from the engineering company refused to accept the machine. The engineering company successfully sued its subcontractor for damages including the loss of profit on the main contract and the expenditure incurred uselessly in making the machine.

In general, a seller or manufacturer of goods has a better idea of the consequences of late supply to the buyer than does a carrier of the goods. A supplier is more likely to know the needs of its customer in order to sell to it: a carrier usually knows only that the goods are to be picked up at one point and delivered to another, according to the terms of the contract of carriage.[6]

A breach of contract may spark a chain of events that results in a significant "consequential" loss for the promisee. To an outsider, the logical relationship between the breach and the type of loss may be a tenuous one. The critical test, however, is to ask whether, from the past business dealings between the parties and the actual and supposed knowledge of the promisor *at the time of the contract,* not at the time the breach occurs, its managers should reasonably have expected such a loss to be a result of breach on the defendant's part. If so, damages may be awarded against it to compensate for the loss.

THE MEASUREMENT OF DAMAGES

Expectation Damages

We have just noted that the relevant time for determining whether damages were foreseeable is the time of making the contract and not the time of subsequent breach. Similarly, the relevant time for determining the amount of damages that were foreseeable is also the time of making the contract. There is an important distinction between the assessment of damages for tort and the assessment of damages for breach of contract: in tort, the only conceiveable time for measuring damages is the time of wrongdoing, that is, the moment the tort is committed. In contract the reason for referring to the earlier moment of formation is

---

[5] (1878), 4 Q.B.D. 670.
[6] See Victoria Laundry (Windsor) Ltd. v. Newman Industries Ltd., [1949] 2 K.B. 528, per Asquith, J. at p. 537.

that a promisor becomes liable to uphold the promise and the promisee becomes entitled to a continuous expectation of performance from that moment until the time for performance arrives; it is on the basis of his reasonably foreseeable liability that the promisor has bargained for the price.

Should a court include in its award of damages for breach an amount equal to the *expected profits* on the aborted transaction? The answer is yes, because that result is implicit in the objective of placing an aggrieved party in the position it would have enjoyed had the contract been performed. An award of *expectation damages* for breach of contract often contrasts sharply with the measurement normal in tort, where recovery is limited to harm suffered as a result of the tort.

ILLUSTRATION

While examining a set of sketches in an art gallery, Jansen recognizes Took, a magazine art critic, and asks him what he thinks of the sketches. Took replies, "I like this one. I'm certain it is by Tom Thomson." As a result, Jansen immediately buys the sketch from the gallery at the asking price of $500. Took's assertion was a negligent misrepresentation and Jansen soon discovers the sketch is worth, at most, $100. If it had been a genuine Thomson its value would have been at least $5000.

In a tort action against Took, the measure of damages would be Jansen's loss, the $400 extra she paid above the market value of the sketch. However, she could not recover the potential profit of $4500 that she could have earned on resale, had Took's representation been true.

On the other hand, suppose Took was the gallery owner and sold the sketch to Jansen describing it on the bill of sale as a work by Tom Thomson. In these circumstances she could sue for the expectation loss of $4500.

Why should there be this difference in the basis for recovery of damages? The main reason is the high value we place in our society on being able to rely on contracts from the moment we make them. If a contract breaker were liable only to pay compensation for losses actually suffered by the other party (such as out-of-pocket expenses), it could often ignore its obligations with relative impunity: the other party may not yet have made any actual expenditures, even though it may have forgone the opportunity to make a similar contract elsewhere. Indeed, the "opportunity cost" — the lost chance of making a similar contract with a different promisor — is an important reason for using expectation loss as a measure of damages. Many, if not most, business arrangements would otherwise lack an adequate sanction in law: a "deal" would not be a deal in any binding sense. In other words, the liability for expectation damages provides the essential background remedy for an effective system of contract law.[7]

Contracts for the sale of goods provide a useful illustration of the approach taken by the courts in measuring expectation damages when one party is in breach. Suppose, first, that a buyer is in breach by refusing to accept delivery of the goods purchased. In an

---

[7] See Waddams, *The Law of Contracts* (3rd ed.), pp. 479-80. Also, West Coast Finance Ltd. and Booth v. Gunderson, Stokes, Walton & Co. [1974] 2 W.W.R. 428 at 434-5, and [1975] 4 W.W.R. 501.

action for damages,[8] the first thing that we need to know is whether the seller's supply of goods exceeds the demand for them, that is, whether the seller can supply goods to all prospective customers. If so, the buyer's breach results in the seller's losing the profit on one sale, regardless of the resale of those same goods to a second buyer: the seller would still have made the second sale even if the first buyer had accepted the goods, and thus would have made two sales instead of one. Accordingly, the seller may recover damages from the first buyer amounting to the lost profits on their contract of sale.

However, when the seller's supply is limited so that it could not have filled a second order if the first buyer had accepted the goods, the seller's damages will be measured by first, its additional expenses in taking reasonable steps to find a second buyer; and second, any loss in revenue as a result of having to accept a lower sale price in order to dispose of the goods. The seller may sustain no damages at all if it resells for the full contract price (or more) without additional selling expenses.[9]

Suppose, instead, a seller breaks its contract by failing to deliver on time. If the buyer can obtain the goods elsewhere, the damages will be those reasonable expenses incurred in seeking an alternative supply and any additional price the buyer has had to pay above the original contract price. Of course, if the buyer obtains an alternate supply for the same or a lower price than that in the original contract, there will be no damages.

These principles for measuring damages are based on the premise that when buyer and seller agree on a price and time for delivery, each has taken into account and therefore assumes the risk of changes in the market price between the time of making the contract and the time of delivery. Whether the price goes up or down in the interval, the seller must deliver and the buyer must accept delivery of the goods at the agreed time — or pay damages for failure to perform; they allocated the risk of change in price between them when they made the contract.

Consequential Damages

Consequential damages are in a sense secondary, one stage removed from the immediate effects of breach. Nevertheless they may be both serious and reasonably foreseeable, so that a defendant will be liable to compensate for them. In our example of a seller that fails to deliver goods on time, suppose the buyer is unable to obtain suitable replacements from another source in time to use them for the purpose it intended, for instance, to resell them or to utilize them as components in another product. The seller will be liable for those kinds of damages that it knew or ought to have known would flow "naturally" from the breach, that is, were reasonably foreseeable by the seller at the time the contract was formed. The measure will be the lost profits on any resale transactions and may include damage claims against the buyer by its own customers as a result of its unavoidable default on contracts with them.

---

[8] As we shall see in Chapter 18, the Sale of Goods Act provides special rules which set out when title to goods passes to a buyer before delivery. (See section on "Title to Goods".) If title has passed, a seller may sue for the price instead of for damages.

[9] In one sense, the first buyer's breach enabled the seller to make the second sale. See Apeco of Canada Ltd. v. Windmill Place (1978), 2 D.L.R. (3d) 1.

ILLUSTRATION

A Dairies Ltd. makes a written contract with *B* to supply *B*'s restaurant with ice cream twice weekly, on Tuesdays and Fridays. *A* Dairies fails to deliver on a Friday at the beginning of a hot summer weekend. Other suppliers are busy servicing their own customers and refuse to supply ice cream to *B*. *B* runs out of ice cream Saturday morning and cannot obtain a fresh supply until Monday. *B*'s loss is not the extra cost of obtaining ice cream elsewhere; it is the loss of profits on ice cream sales over the weekend.

A seller's breach of contract may consist instead in a delivery of defective goods. In these circumstances, other tests must be applied to assess the damages that would place the buyer in the same position as if the seller had performed the contract.

ILLUSTRATION

A supplier delivered sugar for the manufacture of beer. It turned out that the sugar contained arsenic, which made the beer unsaleable. In an action against the supplier of sugar the brewery was awarded damages based on the selling price, rather than the cost, of the beer that had to be destroyed.[10]

Consequential damages may arise from breach of a wide variety of contracts, not just the sale of goods. For instance, failure to repair the heating system of a concert hall as promised in time for a performance in midwinter could lead to the cancellation of the program, making the heating contractor liable for the losses due to cancellation, as well as for damage to the building by frozen pipes, since both are foreseeable harms.

General Damages

This term describes an estimated amount that a court may award over and above specific losses, for harm that cannot be quantified in precise monetary terms, but that the court believes necessary to compensate the aggrieved party fairly. Thus if a surgeon undertook to improve the appearance of a professional entertainer by performing plastic surgery on her nose, but the result was to disfigure the nose and give it a bulbous appearance, a court would have to decide what general damages, over and above specific out-of-pocket medical and hospital expenses, would compensate the plaintiff for the effects of this failure on her state of mind and professional morale. A U.S. court has in fact awarded general damages for breach of contract in such circumstances.[11]

Reliance Damages

example:

Suppose that a management consultant contracts to spend three months in advising a manufacturing firm on the reorganization of its operations. The contract term is to start two weeks later and in preparation for the project, the consultant spends the time assembling

---

10   Holden Co. Ltd. v. Bostock & Co. Ltd. (1902), 18 T.L.R. 317.
11   Sullivan v. O'Connor (1973), 296 N.E. 2d 183. Damages of $13 500 were awarded. For a recent Canadian decision, in which the plaintiff sued unsuccessfully in tort, see, Lokay v. Kilgour (1985), 31 C.C.L.T. 177.

and preparing materials and reading the latest literature on the specialized business of the client firm. Just as she is about to start the consulting project on site, her client cancels the contract, saying it has decided to make no changes for the indefinite future. Fortunately, the consultant is able to take advantage of another consulting opportunity that can be easily substituted at the same fee. She could not, therefore, recover expectation damages for the fee she would have received if the manufacturing company had not cancelled contract. However, she has still lost the time, effort and expenditures involved in two weeks' preparation. Now it is merely wasted effort, effort that was not needed for the substituted job and which could have been used more productively. In these circumstances the consultant may recover as reliance damages the costs of all expenditures and wasted effort that were reasonably made in preparation for the first job.[12]

damages incurred on your behalf to carry out the contract which the other party breached.

Liquidated Damages

Parties to a contract may agree in advance to terms stating an amount to be paid in damages if a breach should occur. The actual loss from breach may bear no relation to the agreed sum: it may turn out to be far greater or less. Nevertheless, if the terms were a genuine attempt by the parties to estimate a loss, they will conclusively govern the amount of damages recoverable. Such a provision for liquidated damages can provide an economic incentive both to the promisor to perform (and so avoid incurring liability for the stated amount) and to the promisee to minimize its actual loss (since it will be entitled in any event to the stated amount and any savings will accrue directly to it).

We must distinguish between a genuine attempt to anticipate or "liquidate" the consequences of a breach of contract and a *penalty clause*. If a term in the contract specifies an exorbitant amount, out of all relation to the probable consequences of breach, a court may find that it is intended merely to frighten a party into performance. Accordingly, the court will hold that it is a penalty clause and will disregard it in awarding damages based on an assessment of the actual loss suffered.

A sum paid as a deposit on the formation of a contract, to be forfeited on failure to perform, is a common type of liquidated damages provision, but it is treated somewhat differently. Partly because the money has already been paid as a guarantee of performance and partly because of a long history of deposits being forfeited, courts are reluctant to overturn such provisions even when they seem harsh. They are rarely recoverable. If, however, the sum is described as a part payment or a down payment, the courts will more readily examine whether its forfeiture would be a penalty.

At the other extreme, a term limiting liquidated damages to a very small sum may be tantamount to an exemption clause. For instance, if a term states that $1 shall be payable as full compensation for breach, the issue for a court may be whether there has been a fundamental breach making the clause ineffective, as discussed in the preceding chapter; it is clearly not a penalty. We should note also that any clause that limits the maximum recovery but also allows a lesser recovery according to the damage suffered can never be a penalty clause, although it may amount to an exemption clause.

---

[12] Anglia T.V. v. Reed, [1971] 3 All E.R. 690; Lloyd v. Stanbury, [1971] 2 All E.R. 267.

Nominal Damages

Occasionally a court may award nominal damages to acknowledge a breach of contract where the loss sustained by the promisee is negligible. A court award of $1 will at least establish the validity of the plaintiff's claim where a question of principle is at stake. In general, when the amount in dispute is nominal, the likelihood that a "successful" plaintiff will still have to pay or share court costs discourages litigation.

$\mathcal{P}$ROBLEMS IN MEASURING DAMAGES

Mental Anguish

We have noted the economic significance of contract law, and in this chapter, of damages for breach. There is, however, a range of contractual interests that are, at least in part, non-economic — illustrated in the preceding section by the case involving plastic surgery. We noted in an earlier chapter on tort law that courts have come gradually to recognize pain, suffering, nervous shock, and humiliation as harms for which they will grant limited recovery. The courts have now begun to follow this trend in contract, by recognizing mental distress resulting from breach as a form of non-economic harm entitled to compensation. A gradual increase in the number of cases is evidence of the trend.

Mental anguish may often occur when an employee is wrongfully dismissed, especially after long years of service. Apart from direct financial loss, for which he or she is entitled to compensation, the dismissed employee may feel humiliated and suffer a serious loss of confidence. Until as recently as 1976 courts refused to allow any compensation for such upset but in that year, an English court reversed this stand by awarding damages for mental anguish when an employer first urged the plaintiff employee not to accept an attractive position with another firm and a few months later wrongfully relegated him to an inferior position.[13] In the same year, a Canadian court awarded damages for loss of reputation in an action against a union by two of its members who had been wrongfully expelled.[14] Subsequently, Canadian courts have expanded the mental distress element of liability for wrongful dismissal.[15]

There are a large number of contracts, such as those for holiday travel and accommodation, that involve substantial sums of money but are not intended to confer an economic benefit on the vacationer. Unless courts take into account disappointment caused by the loss of an anticipated holiday, a vacationer would be without remedy apart from the return of any money paid. A return of that money would hardly be ample compensation to a vacationer who discovers at the airport that there is no flight nor any possibility of arranging an alternative holiday at the last minute. In 1973, an English court held, in the words of Lord Denning, "that damages for the loss of a holiday may include not only the difference in value between what was promised and what was obtained, but also damages for

---

13 Cox v. Phillips Industries Ltd., [1976] 1 W.L.R. 638.
14 Tippett *et al.* v. International Typographical Union, Local 226 (1976), 71 D.L.R. (3d) 146.
15 In Bohemier v. Storwal International Inc. (1982), 40 O.R. 264, affirmed 44 O.R. 302 (C.A.), an employee, not in management, was awarded $1500 for mental distress (in addition to other damages). In Pilato v. Hamilton Place Convention Centre (1984), 45 O.R. 652, the Court awarded $25 000 in damages for mental distress for the severe and unfair manner in which the plaintiff was dismissed.

mental distress, inconvenience, upset, disappointment and frustration caused by the loss of the holiday."[16] This reasoning has been followed by Canadian courts.[17] A different example of recovery for mental distress arose in an action against an airline for breach of contract in transporting the plaintiffs' dogs.[18] The plaintiffs recovered damages for mental suffering endured when they learned that their dogs were suffocated while being carried in the baggage compartment of an airplane.

Apart from recent claims arising from wrongful dismissal, the relatively modest amounts that Canadian and English courts have awarded as damages for mental distress in actions for breach of contract[19] suggest that they are hesitant to give great economic weight to highly subjective reactions that vary widely from person to person; they seem to have resolved their uncertainty by awarding damages, but only for limited amounts. In proposing a limit to the amount a plaintiff in a British Columbia case could recover for pain and suffering, the Supreme Court of Canada has indicated that the purpose of recognizing mental distress in an award of damages is "to substitute other amenities for those that have been lost, not to compensate for the loss of something with a money value ... [and] to provide more general physical arrangements above and beyond those directly relating to the injuries, in order to make life more endurable."[20]

We have noted that a U.S. court awarded general damages for mental distress to a professional entertainer for the "wasted" pain and suffering she experienced when plastic surgery was unsuccessful.[21] The plaintiff also claimed compensation for disappointment in not obtaining the anticipated enhancement in her beauty. The court declined to include such expectation damages as being too speculative. It relied on the opinion of noted authorities in contract law to the effect that, "[T]he reasons for granting damages for broken promises to the extent of the expectancy are at their strongest when the promises are made in a business context, when they have to do with the production or distribution of goods or the allocation of functions in the market place ..."[22]

Cost of Performance versus Economic Loss

The U.S. case, *Peevyhouse v. Garland Coal & Mining Company*,[23] provides a striking example of the difficulty of deciding on the appropriate criteria for measuring damages in circumstances that fall outside traditional categories of economic loss. Owners of a farm containing coal deposits leased it to a mining company for five years. The operation was strip mining, in which coal is scooped from open pits on the surface, scarring the land. The owners insisted on including a term in the lease that the company would restore the surface at the expiration of the lease by moving earth to level the pits. At the

---

[16] Jarvis v. Swan Tours Ltd., [1973] Q.B. 233. The quotation is Lord Denning's explanation of that decision in Jackson v. Horizon Holidays, [1975] 1 W.L.R. 1468 at 1472.

[17] Elder v. Koppe (1975), 53 D.L.R. (3d) 705; Keks v. Esquire Pleasure Tours Ltd., [1974] 3 W.W.R. 406.

[18] Newell v. C.P. Air (1977), 74 D.L.R. (3d) 574.

[19] $500 for each of the two expelled union members; £125 for mental distress from loss of a holiday in the *Jarvis* case and £500 in the *Jackson* case; $500 for mental distress of the owners of the suffocated dogs.

[20] Lindal v. Lindal (1982), 129 D.L.R. (3d) 263, per Dickson, J. at 272 and 273.

[21] Sullivan v. O'Connor (1973), 296 N.E. 2d. 183.

[22] The reference is to Fuller and Perdue, "The Reliance Interest in Contract Damages: 1", (1936) 46 *Yale Law Journal* 52, especially at pp. 60-63. The authors offer as justifications for expectation damages "the loss of opportunity to enter other contracts" and "a policy in favor of promoting and facilitating reliance on business agreements".

[23] (1963), 382 P. (2d) 109 (Okla). See also: James v. Hutton & J. Cool & Sons Ltd., [1950] 1 K.B. 9.

end of the lease the company vacated without restoring the land and the owners sued for damages.

Breach was admitted by the company. However, the court was faced with the following dilemma: the cost of restoring the land as promised would be $29 000, but the market value of the farm would increase by only $300 as a result of the restoration. The owners claimed damages of $29 000, measured by the "cost of performance", and the company countered that it was liable only for damages of $300, measured by the "diminution in economic [market] value" caused by the breach. The majority of the court held that:

> ... under the "cost of performance" rule plaintiffs might recover an amount about nine times the total value of their farm. Such would be unconscionable and grossly oppressive damages, contrary to substantial justice ... also, it can hardly be denied that if plaintiffs here are permitted to recover under the "cost of performance" rule they will receive a greater benefit from the breach than could be gained by full performance ...[24]

Accordingly, the court found that an award of $29 000 to the plaintiffs would have given them a windfall of $28 700; it awarded damages of only $300.

The position taken by the majority of the court is supported by the following economic analysis: it encourages parties to decide whether to perform or break their contracts in strictly economic terms. Thus it would discourage the coal company from committing $29 000 of labour, materials, and equipment to a project that would result only in an increase of $300 in value. If, instead, "cost of performance" was used to measure the damages, the company might have chosen to perform in order to avoid litigation.[25]

On the other hand, this strictly economic analysis ignores the owners' subjective interest in having the farm restored. For sentimental or esthetic reasons — suppose the farm had been in their family for generations and they occupied an adjacent farm — they may have bargained expressly for restoration. Was it legally impossible for them to bargain successfully for such a promise? Suppose that after losing their case, the owners nevertheless decided to proceed with restoration, and they paid a contracting firm $29 000 in advance to do the job. Could the contracting firm, having accepted the money, then refuse to perform, offering to pay damages of $300 as the measure of its breach? The *Peevyhouse* decision suggests that it could.

Even the economic argument can be stated differently: the approximate cost of restoration was known more or less accurately when the lease was entered into; this cost must have been taken into account in setting the price for access to the coal; the owners would probably have charged a higher price for the coal had they realized that the company could not be made to pay the cost of restoration; they could then have done the restoration using the extra revenue. In this sense, it is the company that has obtained a windfall of $28 700 in not having to pay the cost of what it had originally promised to do as part of the price of the lease.

It can be seen then that the *Peevyhouse* decision is debatable. The court was not unanimous in its opinion, and an opposite view was taken by another U.S. Court.[26] While economic analysis is an important tool in both the understanding and the application of

---

24 (1963), 382 P. (2d) 109, per Jackson, J. at 113.
25 See Posner, *Economic Analysis of Law*, 3rd ed., p. 109.
26 See Groves v. John Wunder Co. (1939), 286 N.W. 235, 123 A.L.R. 502. This decision is questioned by Posner, *ibid.*, pp. 90-91.

contract principles, it does not provide the exclusive basis for analysis. The legitimate expectations of parties may include non-economic interests which are also entitled to the protection of the law.

EQUITABLE REMEDIES   *not strictly monetary.*

Reasons for the Intervention of Equity

The old common law courts gave money damages as the sole remedy for breach of contract. But there are circumstances where money damages alone seem quite inadequate. For example, suppose a purchaser wishes to construct a large factory and for that purpose enters into contracts to buy adjoining lots from five different vendors. If one of the vendors, who owns a crucial middle lot, repudiates the agreement to sell, the purchaser will be left with four lots, now of no use, and will be unable to proceed with building. Damages suffered by the purchaser may be very large, perhaps many times the sale price of the lot the vendor refuses to transfer. The most sensible remedy would be to order the vendor to transfer the lot to the purchaser on payment of the purchase price. And that is exactly what the old courts of chancery (equity) did. They recognized the inadequacy of the common law remedy and intervened to grant one of their special remedies, that of *specific performance* (discussed below). Failure to comply with an equitable order places a defendant in "contempt of court" and can lead to a fine or imprisonment.

Reasons for Denying a Remedy

Equitable remedies are discretionary; that is, the court decides whether in view of all the circumstances there are good reasons to depart from the ordinary common law remedy of damages. However, the principles governing the exercise of this discretion have become well settled and a remedy is granted almost as a matter of course to a plaintiff that does not offend any of the established principles. The following are among the more important requirements of equity:

(a) A plaintiff must come to court with "clean hands", that is, he must not himself be found to have acted unethically; if there is an element of sharp practice on his part, the court will leave him, at best, with his claim for money damages.

(b) If, after learning of the defendant's breach, a plaintiff delays unreasonably in bringing an action, perhaps lulling the defendant into believing that no action will be brought, a court will deny an equitable remedy.

(c) As we noted in Chapter 10 on mistake, a court will refuse to intervene on equitable principles when to do so would affect an innocent purchaser.

(d) A court will not grant a remedy in equity when the plaintiff has not paid a substantial consideration for the defendant's promise; if the promise is simply given under seal or in exchange for a nominal sum, money damages alone will be awarded.

(e) Finally, a plaintiff must ordinarily be a party against whom the remedy would be awarded were he the defendant instead; for example, because a court will not grant an equitable remedy *against* an infant defendant when a contract is voidable at his option, neither will it grant that remedy *in his favour* as a plaintiff. This insistence on symmetry is an ancient principle and hard to justify on grounds of fairness.

Specific Performance

A judgment for specific performance is an order requiring a defendant to do a specified act, most often to complete a transaction. When the subject-matter is land, the court orders the vendor to complete and deliver all documents necessary to the transfer of ownership, and to vacate the premises so that the purchaser may take possession on payment of the purchase price. In situations where the court might be obliged to supervise a defendant, specific performance will not be granted. It follows that performance that depends on the personal skill or judgment of a defendant does not lend itself to an order for specific performance. Thus, an artist who repudiates a contract to give a concert will not be ordered to perform; to do so would be to invite a disgruntled performance. The plaintiff will have to be content with an award of money damages.

The remedy of specific performance is most often applied to contracts for sale of land. Courts granted specific performance originally on the argument that each piece of land is unique, and that consequently money damages are an inadequate remedy. Though we may doubt the validity of this reasoning when it is applied to a lot in a large subdivision, the principle is firmly established that, when requested, specific performance will be granted almost as a matter of course in contracts for the sale of land.

It may seem surprising that a vendor of land is entitled to specific performance just as is a purchaser. The reasons are, first, that the general principle giving parties mutual remedies wherever possible should be followed; and second, that damages may well be an inadequate remedy to a vendor. If damages were awarded, she would still be left with the land; she would have the problem of looking after the land, paying taxes, and maintaining buildings, and would have to find another purchaser in order to rid herself of these burdens. Therefore, the court may order the purchaser to specifically perform the contract, that is, to pay the vendor the full sale price and accept the land.

By contrast, courts will not ordinarily grant specific performance of a contract for the sale of goods — damages are considered adequate compensation. On a rare occasion the court will grant specific performance of a contract for the sale of a chattel having a unique value. Antiques, heirlooms, rare coins, and works of art are possible examples. Shares in a corporation may also be considered property for which specific performance is an appropriate remedy, especially when a plaintiff's primary purpose is to obtain a controlling or substantial interest in the firm.

Injunction

An injunction is a court order restraining a party from acting in a particular manner; in relation to contract, it restrains a party from committing a breach. For the remedy to be available, the contract must be found to contain a *negative covenant,* a promise not to do something. However, the covenant need not be stated expressly as a prohibition but may simply be a logical consequence of an express promise. Thus an *express promise* by a tenant to use leased premises for office space would likely be construed to contain an *implied promise* not to use them for a night club; the landlord could obtain an injunction prohibiting their use for a night club.

Sometimes a court may grant an injunction when it would not order specific performance, although the effect of the injunction may be almost the same as that of an order for specific performance. The reason is that the court does not have the problem of continuing supervision when it grants an injunction; it simply orders the defendant to desist from committing further breaches. Thus, when a hotel-keeper promised to buy all the beer he required exclusively from one source of supply and then purchased some elsewhere, the court granted an injunction restraining him from making further purchases from other suppliers.[27] The court did not say, "You must buy all your supply from this source, and we will see that you do." Instead, it said in effect, "In future you must not buy from any other source, and if we hear of your doing so, you will be in serious trouble."

Contracts of the kind just described are common, and breach can lead to serious consequences for both supplier and buyer. In the typical case the supplier is the one that seeks an injunction. However, in a 1974 case, the position was reversed. In *Sky Petroleum Ltd. v. VIP Petroleum Ltd.*[28] the buyer contracted for a long-term supply of petroleum products at fixed prices for its chain of service stations and promised to take all its requirements from the one supplier. The contract was entered into shortly before the 1973 energy crisis. The crisis created a shortage of fuel and a sharp rise in prices; during the crisis the supplier claimed that the buyer was in default in payment and by alleging breach it tried to free itself from the obligation to continue delivering to the buyer's stations. Because of the severe shortage, the supplier's conduct would have left the buyer without any source of supply and forced its business to close before the dispute could be heard by the courts. The buyer asked the court to take the exceptional step of granting a temporary injunction prohibiting the supplier from refusing to continue to deliver petroleum products to it, in effect compelling specific performance by the suppliers in the interval before the full trial of the dispute. The court granted the injunction to prevent the bankruptcy of the buyer before it had a chance to present its case.

Thus, in some circumstances a court will grant an *interlocutory* (temporary) injunction to restrain immediate harm being done by a breach of contract, pending formal resolution of the dispute at trial. Courts are reluctant, however, to grant even a temporary injunction of this kind in personal service contracts.

In contracts of employment, granting an injunction at the request of an employer against a former employee may have unacceptable consequences. If an injunction prohibits an employee from working for any other employer, it may leave the person with the harsh alternatives of returning to work for the plaintiff in an atmosphere of hostility, or being without any means of earning a living. Accordingly, a court is reluctant to grant an injunction against an employee who has promised exclusive services to one employer but has broken the contract by working elsewhere. Injunctions have been granted, however, when an employee in possession of trade secrets of great value left his employer in breach of his contract of employment and went to work for another in the same line of business,[29] and when a singer had promised her exclusive services to an employer for a

---

[27] Clegg v. Hands (1890), 44 Ch.D. 503.
[28] [1974] 1 W.L.R. 576.
[29] Robinson (William) & Co. Ltd. v. Heuer, [1898] 2 Ch. 451.

limited period only and expressly undertook not to sing anywhere else.[30] The granting of such injunctions is best regarded as an exception to the general rule that a court will not grant this remedy where the subject-matter of the contract comprises personal services and where the effect would be to leave the employee no alternative but to work for the original employer or remain unemployed.

Rescission

To this point, we have assumed in our discussion of remedies for breach that an aggrieved party should as nearly as is practicable be placed in the position he would have been in *had the contract been completed*. This assumption is appropriate in most cases, but there are some situations where another approach may be more advantageous to a plaintiff, where he would prefer to return as nearly as he can to the position that would have existed *had the contract not been made at all*. In other words, he would prefer to have the contract rescinded.

If a breach is serious enough to discharge the plaintiff from his own obligations, he may elect rescission, provided that it is feasible to return the parties substantially to their pre-contract positions. An aggrieved party must choose between an action for damages to obtain the benefit of the contract and one for rescission to return him to the position that would have been if a contract had never existed at all; he cannot have both remedies since they are directed toward contradictory purposes. Rescission is often denied if the subject-matter of the contract cannot be returned by the plaintiff to the defendant, as where it has been consumed or incorporated into other goods or sold to innocent third parties. If goods to be returned have been damaged or have deteriorated in value a court may refuse to order rescission and instead leave a plaintiff with the remedy of damages.

When rescission is available, it may sometimes be more beneficial for a plaintiff than an action for damages.

ILLUSTRATION

Glenn Construction Inc. agrees to erect a warehouse for Hoyt Equipment Ltd. for a price of $1 000 000, payable in four equal instalments at specified stages of construction. When the work is half completed and the second instalment is due, Hoyt defaults payment because of financial difficulties and requests that Glenn cease work, effectively repudiating the contract. Since the making of the contract, construction costs have risen much faster than anticipated by the parties. In fact, it appears that had Hoyt not repudiated and Glenn had to complete the project, it would have cost Glenn $1 085 000 rather than an expected $900 000, causing a loss of $85 000 instead of a profit of $100 000. We shall assume that because of the increase in prices, the current value of the work completed by Glenn at the time of breach is $575 000.

If Glenn sued for breach of contract it could collect damages of $250 000 for the missed instalment, but nothing for loss of profits because there would have been none.

---

[30] Lumley v. Wagner (1852), 42 E.R. 687; also Warner Bros. Pictures v. Nelson, [1937] 1 K.B. 209.

On the other hand, if Glenn sues for rescission of the contract, that is, elects to treat the contract as if it had never existed, it follows that Glenn can make no claim under the terms of the contract itself and would even have to account for the $250 000 received as the first instalment. However, the work done by Glenn was at the request of Hoyt and created a substantial economic benefit. These circumstances would allow Glenn to claim against Hoyt on a *quantum meruit* basis, as discussed earlier in Chapter 7, because valuable services were performed without a price having been settled by a binding agreement between the parties; although there was an agreed price in the contract, it has no effect once the contract is rescinded — it ceases to exist along with the rest of the contract. Accordingly, the price will be set by the court at the fair market value of the work. As a result, Glenn may obtain judgment for $575 000 less the first instalment received of $250 000, leaving a balance of $325 000. Thus, by seeking rescission and suing *quantum meruit* Glenn may obtain judgment $75 000 higher than the sum it would recover if it sued for damages under the contract.

The question arises, "Is Glenn merely being returned to the position that would have existed if the contract had never been made when it receives the market value of $575 000 for the work done, presumably including some element of profit?" In reply, it should be said that it is not possible to turn the clock back, place Glenn precisely in its pre-contract position, and enable it to seek an alternative contract and earn normal profits; the firm has lost that opportunity. Thus, payment of a normal profit margin on work done *quantum meruit*, by valuing the work at fair market value, can be viewed as reasonable compensation for the *opportunity cost,* that is, the lost opportunity.

Any advantage in suing *quantum meruit* on the facts of this case disappears if we change one important factor: suppose construction costs had not risen beyond those contemplated by the parties when they made the bargain. Glenn could then have expected a $100 000 profit on completion and would be entitled to that sum in addition to the $250 000 missed payment if it had sued for expectation damages.[31]

Perhaps the most common claim for rescission occurs when durable goods — equipment, machinery, or consumer products such as refrigerators or television sets — fail to perform as required in a contract of sale. A buyer who is unhappy with his acquisition rarely wants damages for the diminished value of the goods, or even a replacement of the same brand; he would much prefer to return the goods and get his money back. Since substantial use or deterioration of the goods while in the hands of the buyer may disentitle him to rescission, the remedy is often unavailable.

A less common but nonetheless important situation where rescission may be the preferred remedy arises in the sale of a valuable asset, such as land, when the purchaser defaults.

---

[31]   Indeed, if construction costs had risen less than expected, the current market value of the work completed to the time of breach would probably also be lower, and a *quantum meruit* claim could provide a smaller sum than the amount of the missed instalment.

V agrees to sell Blackacre to *P* for $325 000, receiving a down payment of $25 000, the balance to be paid in quarterly instalments of $25 000. *P* is unable to make payment at the time for the first instalment, when he was also expected to take possession of the property. If *V* were to try to hold *P* to the contract, she would be entitled to some damages for the late payment, but she would have to give possession to *P,* and would remain uncertain about *P*'s ability to meet future instalments. In these circumstances, *V* may well prefer to minimize her risks by obtaining rescission — returning *P*'s down payment and retaining possession of Blackacre.

*Q*UANTUM MERUIT

We have already discussed in Chapter 7 how a *quantum meruit* claim arises for a valuable benefit conferred at the request of a promisee. We have also examined how *quantum meruit* may be utilized by a contractor who elects to rescind a contract when the other party repudiates before the contractor has completed performance. In either case, if the parties cannot agree on a price, the contracting firm may have the court assess the claim on the basis of the fair market value of the benefit conferred.

A different question arises if the contractor decides to abandon the project before it is completed. Is it entitled to recover for the work done? In the absence of an express agreement to make progress payments, the normal presumption is that nothing is due until completion, and that a contractor that abandons after part performance, for whatever reason, cannot recover anything. There appears, however, to be one situation in which a worker who has abandoned a contract may still recover for the value of what has already been done. Blackburn, J. discussed the matter in *Appleby v. Myers* and stated as follows:

> Bricks built into a wall become part of the house; thread stitched into a coat which is under repair, or planks and nails and pitch worked into a ship under repair, become part of the coat or the ship; and therefore, generally and in the absence of something to show a contrary intention, the bricklayer, or tailor or shipwright is to be paid for the work and materials he has done and provided, although the whole work is not complete. It is not material whether in such a case the non-completion is because the shipwright did not choose to go on with the work.[32]

*M*ETHODS OF ENFORCING JUDGMENT

What happens when a party obtains a judgment for damages? How may he enforce his claim? When a plaintiff obtains judgment for a sum of money, he becomes a *judgment creditor,* and the defendant a *judgment debtor.* If the judgment debtor is sound financially, the force of the court judgment is usually sufficient: she will raise the money and pay it

---

[32] (1867), L.R. 2 C.P. 651 at 660-1. Note that in this case the court did find an express agreement that no payment would be due until the whole work had been completed.

voluntarily. If, however, she is recalcitrant or in financial difficulty and unable to raise the money readily, the judgment creditor must then move to enforce payment. We must be clear that a judgment debtor is not considered a criminal. She cannot be imprisoned for debt as she once could, provided she does not attempt to commit a fraud, such as absconding and taking her assets with her. (Some jurisdictions provide for detaining a fleeing debtor temporarily to extract the assets she is escaping with.) There are legal procedures by which a judgment creditor may seize as much of the debtor's property as is necessary to satisfy the judgment. If the assets are insufficient, the creditor is without further remedy for the time being. He may wait in the hope that the debtor will obtain more assets in the future so that he may seize them as well. Generally speaking, however, the creditor gets whatever he can soon after the judgment is obtained and writes off any expectation of further satisfaction at a future date.

The most usual procedure when the judgment debtor does not pay promptly is to register the judgment with the office of the sheriff of the county or district where the debtor resides, and request the sheriff to *levy execution* against the assets of the debtor to satisfy the judgment. An *execution order* gives the sheriff authority to seize and sell various chattels and arrange for a sale of the debtor's lands after an appropriate period of grace.[33] More complicated procedures are necessary to seize a bank account, the contents of a safety-deposit box, or an income from a trust fund. A creditor may also obtain a *garnishee order* against a debtor's wages. The order requires the employer to retain a portion of the debtor's wages each payday and surrender the sum to the creditor to be applied against the judgment.

Besides money damages, a court may make two other types of money awards for breach of contract. As we shall see in Chapter 19, a seller may be awarded the price of goods sold instead of damages for non-acceptance. And a lender of money may recover the amount of the debt by court action. Each of these awards is analogous to a decree of specific performance in which the performance is to take the form of a payment of money owed, except that the judgment debtor's failure to pay will not amount to contempt of court; a judgment creditor is left to the usual remedies described above.

Questions for Review

1. How may a term that fixes a sum for liquidated damages amount, in effect, to an exempting clause?
2. When may a worker sue *quantum meruit* and recover the value of what he has done when he himself has abandoned the contract?
3. Why might a court be willing to grant an injunction when it would refuse to order specific performance?
4. Can a party injured by breach of contract sue the other party for both expectation damages and rescission? Why or why not?
5. Illustrate how the mitigation rule can avoid a waste of economic resources.
6. Are there any circumstances under which a court may be prepared to compensate a type of loss that does not appear to "flow naturally from the breach"?
7. Why might a promisor be anxious to have an exemption clause protecting it from consequential damages?

---

[33] For a description of property exempt from seizure, see, for example: Execution Act, R.S.O. 1990, c. E-24, s. 2; Court Order Enforcement Act, R.S.B.C. 1979, c. 75, s. 65.

8. Why are nominal damages seldom awarded?

9. Explain the argument that there is no necessary economic virtue in a legal system dedicated solely to trying to compel the performance of contracts.

10. By what reasoning may a court be willing to award general damages but not expectation damages in a contract for plastic surgery?

11. Explain what you think the authors Fuller and Perdue meant in the following quotation: "If a contract represents a kind of private law, it is a law which usually says nothing at all about what shall be done when it is violated. A contract is in this respect like an imperfect statute which provides no penalties, and which leaves it to the courts to find a way to effectuate its purposes." (Fuller and Perdue, "The Reliance Interest in Contract Damages: 1", (1936) 46 *Yale Law Journal*, p. 52 at p. 58.)

Problems

Problem 1

The Complicated Machinery Co. Ltd. manufactures and assembles heavy equipment for industry. It accepted an order for a large machine from the Northern Paper Co. to automate certain processes, one of the terms being that the machine was to be completed by October 31 of the same year. The contract further stated that if the machine was not completed by October 31, the Complicated Machinery Co. Ltd. would pay the Northern Paper Co. "liquidated damages" at the rate of $500 a week for the duration of the delay. The manager of Northern Paper Co. had said in a letter accompanying the offer: "Until the machine is in full operation it is hard to say what our savings will be. Five hundred dollars a week is a rough guess."

Complicated Machinery Co. Ltd. failed to deliver until December 26, eight weeks late. It billed the paper company for the full price less $4000 (eight weeks at $500). The paper company discovered that the machine actually saved $1200 weekly in production costs. It therefore tendered as payment the full price less $9600 (eight weeks at $1200). Which party is correct and why?

Problem 2

Jones contracted with the Martin Floor Covering & Tile Co. to have her kitchen floor tiled. Before entering into the contract, Jones asked the manager of the company whether, once the job was started, the workers would be left on it without interruption until it was completed. The manager replied: "Why, of course. We never pull anyone off a job until it's finished." Jones then said: "All right, but I would not go ahead with this work on any other terms." → major term. it has been expressed & agreed to.

After the work was begun, the workers, under the direction of the company, were transferred to an "emergency job" at a new house that had to be completed by the end of the week because the owners were moving into it from out of town. As a result, the Jones family were unable to use their kitchen for a week and had to eat in restaurants.

The workers returned the following week and finished tiling the kitchen floor in the Jones home. Jones then refused to pay for the work done. The Martin Floor Covering & Tile Co. sued Jones for the price agreed on for the job. Jones counterclaimed for damages to compensate her for the cost of meals for all members of her family at Winston's Gourmet Restaurant for ten days, $850, taxi fare each night to and from the restaurant, $140, and $50 for dental costs incurred as a result of one of her children falling on the restaurant stairs.

Examine the arguments for the defendant and the plaintiff and state, with reasons, what the probable decision would be.

Problem 3

The plaintiffs were millers at Gloucester. Their mill was stopped by a break in the crankshaft of the steam engine by which the mill was worked. It was necessary to send the shaft as a pattern for a new one to Greenwich where the steam engine had been manufactured. The plaintiffs sent one of their servants to the office of the defendants, a common carrier; the servant told the clerk that the article to be carried was the broken shaft at the mill and asked when the shaft would be delivered at Greenwich. He was told that if it was received by noon any day, it would be delivered at Greenwich on the following day.

The next day the plaintiffs delivered the shaft to the defendants before noon, and paid £2 4s for the service. The carrier's clerk was told that if necessary he should make a special note to speed the delivery. In fact, the delivery was delayed through the fault of the carrier, and as a result the plaintiffs received the new shaft several days late. The working of their mill was delayed, and the plaintiffs lost profits of several hundred pounds.

The defendants acknowledged some liability for having failed to deliver the shaft within a reasonable time and offered to settle for £25; the plaintiffs refused, claiming a much larger sum for profits lost. The defendants then paid the £25 into court, and the plaintiffs sued. Should they succeed? (See *Hadley v. Baxendale* (1854) 156 E.R. 145.)

Problem 4

In November, Tanton agreed orally with Marsh to cut and haul to Marsh's mill approximately 500 000 board feet of lumber at a price of $20 per thousand delivered to the mill. The contract also stated that on its completion Tanton should be reimbursed for the cost of the construction of camps and roads necessary for the lumbering operations.

In January next, after Tanton had delivered 200 000 board feet to the mill, he found himself in financial difficulties and unable to pay his employees. At the time Tanton had been paid up to date for the logs delivered, but had not been paid for the camps and roads he had had to construct for the purpose. Tanton told Marsh that he was quitting and that he considered the contract as having been frustrated by his inability to pay his men. He then sued to recover the value of the work done in the construction of camps, roads, and bridges during the lumbering operations up to January.

Should Tanton succeed? (See *Tingley v. McKeen* [1954] 4 D.L.R. 392.)

Problem 5

Two students are trying after class to see what they can make of the legal significance of exemption clauses.

> *Harvey:* Exempting clauses are a cop-out. A promisor manages to put one in a contract and then is obligated to do nothing — only the other party is obligated.

> *Lise:* But maybe the other party got a lower price because of the exemption clause.

> *Harvey:* Often that's not so. Suppose the other party is a new Canadian and the exemption clause is in a standard form contract he's unfamiliar with?

> *Lise:* But that must depend on whether the parties had equal bargaining power. Isn't that what the instructor said? One of the parties doesn't have to be exploited. Suppose the contract is between two established businesses?

Harvey: Then I still say there's no consideration on one side. What price does the business protected by an exempting clause pay for the other's promise?

Lise: The business may not be opting out of all its obligations. Then there's still consideration. Don't you remember, "It is not for the courts to concern themselves with the adequacy of consideration"?

Harvey: But suppose we're talking about a fundamental breach. Then what we have in effect is a total failure of consideration, even if technically we could find a little bit of consideration still there. Since you're quoting legal aphorisms, "The law does not concern itself with trivialities", either.

Lise: I think you have to assume business people know what they're doing and that such one-sided contracts are the exception. Maybe with a novice, yes, but with an established business, no.

Harvey: I'm beginning to get worried. Suppose a court decides an exemption clause should-n't count because the breach is fundamental. If its reasoning is that there was a total failure of consideration, maybe there won't be any contract at all. Will that give the plaintiff what he wants? I thought he was suing for damages for breach.

Lise: Maybe we should go ask the instructor.

Comment briefly on Harvey's last point. Would the remedies available to the plaintiff business be different if the court found that there was no consideration instead of there being a claim for damages for breach of contract?

Problem 6

On June 30, Sinkiewicz, a professional football player, signed a three-year contract with the Mariposa Football Club Ltd. The contract contained the following clause:

The Player promises and agrees that during the term of this contract he will not play football or engage in activities related to football for any other person, firm, corporation or institu-tion, except with the prior written consent of the Club, and that he will not during the term of this contract engage in any game or exhibition of basketball, baseball, wrestling, boxing, hockey, or any other sport which endangers his ability to perform his services hereunder without the prior written consent of the Club.

In July of the following year Sinkiewicz accepted an offer from another professional football club, the Orillia Wildcats, and moved to Orillia intending to play with that club for the coming football season. He also arranged to play hockey in Orillia after the foot-ball season ended.

After learning about Sinkiewicz's breach, the officials of the Mariposa Football Club sued for damages and for an injunction restraining Sinkiewicz from continuing to break his contract. The Mariposa Club alleged that it had sustained irreparable injury in having to locate another player of Sinkiewicz's calibre, and that it had in the past spent consider-able money in training Sinkiewicz as a professional football player. In defence, Sinkiewicz testified that he would be unable to earn his livelihood if prevented from playing football and hockey. Discuss the legal issues the court will consider in reaching its decision. (See *Detroit Football Club v. Dublinski* (1957), 7 D.L.R. (2d) 9.)

Cases

Case 1

Brown, a painting contractor, made an oral contract with Hilton to paint the interior of Hilton's house for $1600, to be paid on completion of the work. Brown ran into difficulty when he painted the walls of the living room because the paint was sucked into the wall by the porous plaster. He had the same problem when he applied a second coat, then realized what was causing the trouble and applied what is known as a "sealer", so that the next coat might adhere properly. Leaving the living room until the sealer was dry, he began painting the dining room.

At that point, Hilton inspected the work and complained to Brown that the colour of the paint was not the colour she had selected. Brown became very annoyed and emphatically announced he would quit the job. She urged him not to abandon the work without first seeing her husband, but in a huff he removed his materials and equipment. When he abandoned the work, Brown had still to finish painting the living room and had not begun to paint several other rooms in the house. It also appeared that the woodwork had been painted without having been sanded, and would have to be repainted. Brown brought an action against Hilton for $890, claiming $230 for materials and $660 for 55 hours work. Should he succeed?

Case 2

Hunter owned a resort hotel at Twillingate Harbour, Newfoundland. During the summer he contracted with Burns, a plumbing and heating contractor, to enlarge the heating system of the hotel. The proposed work required moving the existing furnace, adding to the present network of ducts, and providing additional hot-air outlets in various specified rooms. The total price of the work and parts required was $15 000 and payment was "due on the full completion of the work".

By August 15, Burns' employees had proceeded to the point that the furnace had been relocated and the main trunk line of ducts had been installed; one or two branch lines to individual rooms had also been constructed. The work remaining to be done comprised about one third of the total — running most of the branch lines to various rooms and installing heating outlets there. On August 16, a fire broke out and the entire hotel building and contents were destroyed. Burns brought action against Hunter for $10 000, representing the value of services and parts supplied to the time of the fire.

The Frustrated Contracts Act, R.S.Nfld. 1990, c. F-26, included the following provisions:

> S. 3(2). This Act does not apply to
> (c) a contract for the sale of specific goods where the goods without the knowledge of the seller have perished at the time when the contract is made or where the goods without any fault on the part of the seller or buyer perish before the risk passes to the buyer.
> S. 4(3). Where before the parties were discharged 1 [sic] of them has by reason of anything done by any other party in connection with the performance of the contract obtained a valuable benefit other than a payment of money, the court where it considers it just to do so having regard to all the circumstances may allow the other party to recover from the party benefited the whole or any part of the value of the benefit.
> S. 4(7). Where it appears to the court that a part of the contract can be severed properly from the remainder of the contract, being a part wholly performed before the parties were discharged or so performed except for the payment in respect of that part of the contract of

sums that are or can be ascertained under the contract, the court shall treat that part of the contract as if it was a separate contract that had not been frustrated and shall treat this section as applicable only to the remainder of the contract.

Discuss the relevance, if any, of these statutory provisions. Should Burns succeed? Can your conclusion be justified in the light of good business practice?

Case 3

On September 2, the Department of Government Services published an invitation to submit tenders for the supply of materials for construction of a large administrative building. Its advertisement specified that tenders were to be delivered on or before 3:00 p.m. on November 6 at the office of the Contracts Officer of the Department of Government Services in Ottawa.

Buttonville Brick, Inc. prepared an estimate of the cost of supplying brick for the project and then made out a tender for delivery to the Department of Government Services. The tender was for the supply of all the brick required at a price of $556 000 — a price on which the company could expect to earn a profit of about $75 000.

On the morning of November 5 Buttonville's manager, Hodson, telephoned Bulldog Couriers Inc. to inquire whether it could deliver an important document in Ottawa by noon of the following day. He said, "A lot is at stake for us — maybe $100 000 — and if you can't deliver our envelope by tomorrow noon, either I or one of the other people here is going to have to drive directly to Ottawa with it." Hodson was assured there would be no problem with delivery.

Bulldog sent a station wagon at once to pick up the envelope. Buttonville Brick completed a bill of lading on a form supplied by Bulldog. It read,

BULLDOG COURIERS INC.

BILL OF LADING

Date: Nov. 5, 19__

Received at the point of origin on the date specified, from the shipper mentioned herein, the goods herein described, in apparent good order, except as noted (contents and conditions of contents of packages unknown) marked, consigned and destined as indicated below, which the carrier agrees to carry and deliver to the consignee at the said destination. For other terms, see reverse side.

Point of origin	Destination
Buttonville Brick Ltd.	Contracts Officer,
100 Industrial Lane	Department of Government Services
Buttonville Ontario	100 Drive, Ottawa

Contents	No. Pcs.	Weight	Charges
"Envelope— tender"	"1"	"400 g."	"$15.00"

"Deliver before 12 noon Nov. 6."

Declared value

(Maximum liability $3.00 per kg. unless declared valuation states otherwise. If a value is declared see conditions on reverse hereof.)

(signed) "Bernard Colley	(signed) "S. Hodson
for Bulldog Couriers Inc."	for Buttonville Brick Ltd."

On the reverse side, the bill of lading stated:

VALUE

Unless otherwise specifically agreed to in writing the carrier will not transport any goods declared to have a value in excess of $250. Enquiries for such service should be directed to the carrier's closest regional office.

APPLICABLE LAW

It is agreed that every service to be performed hereunder shall be subject to the laws relating to the terms and conditions to be contained in bills of lading applicable in Ontario under the Public Commercial Vehicles Act.

The van that took the envelope to Ottawa on its regular run was delayed because of a mechanical breakdown and the envelope was not delivered to its destination until 3:21 p.m. on November 6. As a result, it was rejected as an eligible tender. The contract was given to another bidder who, as it turned out, had submitted a bid of $590 000 — $34 000 more than Buttonville's. Buttonville sued Bulldog Carriers, Inc. for consequential damages of $75 000.

At the trial the following excerpts from the Public Commercial Vehicles Act (as it then applied) were cited:

12n (1). Except as provided in the regulations, every holder of an operating licence ... shall issue a bill of lading to the person delivering or releasing goods to the licensee for transportation for compensation.

(2). A bill of lading shall contain such information as may be prescribed and shall include an acknowledgement of receipt by the carrier ... therein described and an undertaking to carry such goods for delivery to the consignee or the person entitled to receive the goods and shall be signed by, or on behalf of, the issuing carrier ... and by the consignor.

(3). The conditions set out in Schedule A shall be deemed to be a part of every contract for the transportation of goods for compensation ...

SCHEDULE A

1. The carrier of the goods herein described is liable for any loss thereof or damage or injury thereto, except as herein provided.

5. The carrier is not liable for loss, damage or delay to any of the goods described in the bill of lading caused by an act of God, the Queen's or public enemies, riots, strikes, defect or inherent vice in the goods, the act or default of the shipper or owner...

7. No carrier is bound to transport the goods by any particular public commercial vehicle or in time for any particular market or otherwise than with due despatch, unless by agreement specifically endorsed on the bill of lading and signed by the parties thereto.

9. Subject to paragraph 10, the amount of any loss, damage or injury for which the carrier is liable, whether or not the loss, damage or injury results from negligence, shall be computed on the basis of,
   (a) the value of the goods at the place and time of shipment including the freight and other charges if paid; or
   (b) where a value lower than that referred to in clause a has been represented in writing by the consignor or has been agreed upon, such lower value.
10. ... the amount of any loss or damage computed under clause a or b of paragraph 9 shall not exceed $1.50 per pound [approximately $3.00 per kilogram] unless a higher value is declared on the face of the bill of lading by the consignor.

Develop arguments for each of the plaintiff and defendant in this action and express an opinion about the probable outcome.

PART FOUR

SPECIAL TYPES OF CONTRACTS

Your study of contract law in the last twelve chapters shows how pervasive is the use of contracts in almost every aspect of business. Some types of contracts have developed in areas that are particularly important to business and deserve to be examined separately. We have selected a number of them for discussion in this part.

Although service industries have grown rapidly in recent years, the production and sale of goods remains central to our economy and to almost all retail business. In Chapter 18 we discuss the nature of sales contracts and their legal effects, particularly regarding ownership of goods and the risks assumed by the parties to a contract. The first half of Chapter 19 considers the consequences of breach and the remedies available, for example, if a buyer fails to pay or a seller delivers defective goods. The second half of the chapter is devoted to the protection of consumers through regulation of sellers and granting new statutory remedies to buyers.

Chapter 20 discusses insurance law, an important aspect in the operation of every business and particularly so in transactions that involve the transfer of valuable property. The general purpose of insurance is to protect a person from losses resulting from a foreseeable risk. The chapter considers the necessary elements of a valid insurance contract, the limits of the availability of insurance and the way insurance is utilized by businesses. The latter portion of the chapter deals with the related topic of guarantees, that is, where a third person promises to perform a contract if the promissor should default.

In Chapter 21 we consider the legal consequences of a common occurence in business — when an owner, for a variety of reasons, may arrange for an asset to be put in the possession of another person — a bailment. A bailor may give possession of an item to a bailee in return for a fee, for example when a bailee rents a car from a car rental company. Conversely, a bailor may pay a bailee to accept an item, for instance, to repair it, or she may lend the item as a favour, without either party paying the other.

Chapters 22 and 23 consider respectively two essentail business arrangements. The first chapter explores agency arrangements, the means by which an enterprise operated by more than one person authorizes others to make binding contracts on its behalf. Sales persons, purchasing agents, managers, all are individuals who make contracts binding their principals. We consider the consequences of agents exceeding their authority and the remedies of third parties. In the second chapter we concentrate on the employment relationship, the respective rights and duties of employers and employees and effects their conduct may have on third parties. We also examine the various laws that regulate the employment relationships, such as workers compensation, pay equity and human rights.

Chapter 24 examines negotiable instruments — cheques, promissory notes and bills of exchange — their nature and role in business transactions, and the remedies available when one or more parties to an instrument defaults payment.

CHAPTER 18

THE CONTRACT OF SALE:
ITS NATURE AND EFFECT

THE SALE OF GOODS ACT

History

When the term "contract" is used, the type of contract that probably springs most readily to mind is the contract of sale. Yet in the long history of the common law, the law of sale of goods is a relatively recent development. The economic activity of medieval England was mainly agrarian, and much of the law was concerned with rules for holding land. Not until the late 18th century, when England had become the world's first industrial power, did the law governing the distribution and sale of goods become the subject of frequent decisions in the courts. In succeeding years, general principles began to emerge from the decisions of the courts, and in the latter part of the 19th century these principles were well established. By this time the body of case law was immense. Lengthy and learned treatises were written in attempts to digest and rationalize the cases into a logical pattern. In 1893, the British Parliament simplified the case law by codifying it into a comprehensive statute called the Sale of Goods Act. All the common law provinces in Canada have since adopted this Act, almost word for word.

The Sale of Goods Act resembles the Partnership Act (which we shall discuss in Chapter 29) in that it made no attempt to change the law: its purpose was to set out succinctly the law as it then existed, with clarification where necessary to resolve conflicts between competing principles. In particular, the cases decided before the Act was passed had recognized a number of important implied terms that formed a part of every contract for the sale of goods, unless those terms were inconsistent with the purposes of the contract or were expressly excluded by the parties. Such terms were codified: they are now implied under the Sale of Goods Act just as they were implied by case law before the Act was passed. We shall discuss these implied terms in the next section of this chapter.

Ownership and Possession

The words "ownership" and "possession" signify to the legal historian and jurist some of the most difficult analytical problems in the whole of law. A sophisticated system of law separates the two concepts. We recognize the distinction in everyday activity, as when we lend possession of an object to a friend yet retain ownership of it. We correctly assume that if a friend refused to return our car, we would have a remedy in the courts against that person, to protect our ownership or *title*. We have seen also in our discussion of mistake in Chapter 10 that in English law, the distinction between possession and ownership of goods is carried to its logical conclusion, since the owner may recover stolen goods from a subsequent innocent purchaser.

The separation of ownership and possession occurs frequently in contracts for the sale of goods: when the contract is a sale that passes title to the buyer immediately, possession often remains with the seller or with a carrier for some time afterwards; and, as we shall see, under instalment sales contracts, a vendor often retains title to goods as security for payment of the price, while possession passes to the buyer. Transactions other than sales, such as pledges, consignments, and rental arrangements, also separate ownership from possession. In this and the succeeding chapter we shall often refer to the passing of title independently of possession, and to a change in possession without a transfer of title.

Definition of Goods

In this and the next chapter we shall discuss mainly contracts governed by the Sale of Goods Act; we must therefore discover the limits of the Act's application. For the Act to apply, the subject-matter of the contract must be "goods". As we shall see in Part Five, property is divided into two main classes — real property and personal property. Real property is confined to interests in land. All other property is called personal property, which in turn has two categories — choses in action, and goods or *chattels*. We have already discussed the nature of choses in action in Chapter 14 in relation to the assignment of contractual rights. In contrast to choses in action, which obtain their value because they represent binding obligations, goods derive their value intrinsically, that is simply because people want the goods themselves, for the utility or satisfaction they furnish.

When discussing the requirement of writing in Chapter 12, we noted that a distinction must be made between contracts for the sale of goods and other contracts, for instance those for work and materials. The distinction is not always an easy one to make. For example, in contracting to have a house constructed, a boat built, or a central heating system installed, the buyer agrees to pay for a finished product as well as for the labour that produced it. The court's task is to decide whether it was the work or the materials that constituted the essence of the contract: if the final value is mainly the result of the skill and labour that have gone into its preparation the contract will be one for work and materials and not for "goods" as defined by the Act.[1] All other goods come within the definition of goods in the statute. In practice, however, the distinction is usually less important than it might seem, since many of the legal principles that apply to contracts for work and materials are much the same as provisions in the Sale of Goods Act.

Types of Contract of Sale

In the Sale of Goods Act, a contract of sale "is a contract whereby the seller transfers or agrees to transfer the property in the goods to the buyer for a money consideration, called the price ..." Money must form a part of the transaction; it follows that a straight barter of goods where no money changes hands does not come within the statute.

The Sale of Goods Act distinguishes between a *sale* and an *agreement to sell*. In a sale, the seller transfers ownership or title in goods to the buyer at the moment the contract is made. In an agreement to sell, the transfer is deferred until a future time; that time is either a specified date, or an indefinite date that depends on the fulfilment of a particular requirement. The Sale of Goods Act applies to both sales and agreements to sell. An agreement to sell may be formed even when the goods are nonexistent. A contract to sell goods to be manufactured in three months' time, or to sell a crop at a stated price per bushel when it has grown in a certain field, are examples of agreements to sell. An agreement to sell is a binding contract just as are other contracts containing promises of future conduct.

We should distinguish a contract of sale from a transaction known as a *consignment*. A consignment is a shipment of goods from one business to another: the shipper is the *consignor* and the recipient the *consignee*. There are two common varieties of consignment. First, the consignor may ship the goods in performance of a contract of sale; here, the con-

---

[1]   The examples mentioned — a house, a boat and a central heating system — have all been held to be contracts for "work and materials"; see Hodgkinson v. Hitch House Ltd. (1987), 60 O.R. (2d) 793. By contrast, a restaurant meal has been held to be "goods": Gee v. White Spot Ltd. (1986), 32 D.L.R. (4th) 238.

signor is a seller and the consignee a buyer. Second, the consignor may ship the goods to an agent (consignee) who will offer them for sale at his new location. In this instance ownership in the goods does not pass between the consignor and consignee: if the consignee sells them, the title passes directly from the consignor to the purchaser. Expensive items displayed in the window of a jeweller's shop, for example, may not be part of the jeweller's own stock-in-trade, but be simply held on consignment from a manufacturer or wholesaler.

Required Evidence

In Chapter 12 we discussed the circumstances in which a contract of sale may be unenforceable for lack of a memorandum in writing, or alternatively, for lack of evidence of certain conduct by the buyer. Please review the relevant sections of that chapter before continuing.

Terms in a Contract of Sale

Conditions and Warranties

In Chapter 16, we noted the unfortunate confusion caused by the use of one word "condition" in entirely different senses. The Sale of Goods Act has used "condition" to mean a major or essential term of the contract, the breach of which, if he so elects, relieves the injured party from further duty to perform the contract. It uses "warranty" to mean a minor or non-essential term, the breach of which does not relieve the injured party from the bargain — he must perform his side but may sue for damages. We shall use the two words in this chapter with the same meanings as those given by the Act. Some terms implied by the Act are conditions and others are warranties; we must be careful to note which terms fall into each class.

In the remainder of this section we shall discuss the more important terms of a contract of sale implied by the Sale of Goods Act, and also those terms that are usually expressly agreed upon by the parties.

Statutory Protection for the Buyer: Limitations on *Caveat Emptor*

Scope of *Caveat Emptor*

We encountered the Latin maxim *caveat emptor* (let the buyer beware) briefly in Chapter 11 in our discussion of fraudulent misrepresentation. We should be sure to understand the phrase. As a learned Irish judge pointed out, "*Caveat emptor* does not mean in law or Latin that the buyer must 'take chance'; it means that he must 'take care'."[2] In other words, he must be reasonably cautious when buying goods in circumstances where a buyer can, and usually does, exercise personal judgment. *Caveat emptor* is, however, not a rigid rule but a flexible general principle, subject to limits put on it by common sense and customary business practice.

Caveat emptor applies where the goods are in existence, and are specific items that may be inspected by the buyer, and where the seller has made no misrepresentations about

---

2   Wallis v. Russell, [1902] 2 I.R. 585, Fitzgibbon, L.J., at 615.

them. In these circumstances *caveat emptor* is a sensible rule: the buyer has the opportunity of exercising her judgment by examining the goods; if she distrusts her own judgment or has doubts, she may choose to bargain for an express term stating that the goods have a particular quality she requires.

ILLUSTRATION

Hard-Sell TV Ltd. advertises: "Used TV sets for sale. 17-inch to 23-inch sets all one price $50. Take your choice." Adams enters the store and asks a sales clerk to show her a 17-inch portable she can use in her basement recreation room. The sales clerk leads her to the sets and says: "Here are all our portables. Some are pretty good buys. See for yourself."

Adams examines several and finds one that appears to be in good condition. She turns it on and gets quite a good picture from the local station. When she asks whether the set is connected to an outside antenna, she is told that it is not. Adams says: "Well, it looks pretty good to me. I'll take it. Here's the $50. Just place it in the back seat of my car." When Adams gets the set home and attaches it to her outdoor antenna, she finds she can still bring in only the local station, whereas the living room set brings in a number of other channels.

Adams has no recourse against Hard-Sell TV. Had she wished an undertaking that the set would bring in other channels she needed to request it. At the price of $50 it is very unlikely that the seller would have agreed to give that undertaking.

Caveat emptor encourages buyers to take care and to determine that the goods are what they want before they contract to buy them. On the other hand, there are special circumstances in which the principle, if not qualified, would invite abuse by unscrupulous sellers. For example, a buyer must sometimes rely to some extent upon the knowledge or expert judgment of the seller, or by mutual consent a buyer may sometimes place special confidence or trust in the seller. Accordingly, a series of implied terms to protect buyers were evolved in the decided cases and are now found in the Sale of Goods Act.[3]

Seller's Title

Caveat emptor applies to the qualities of goods, not their ownership. Inspection by the buyer normally does nothing to indicate who owns the goods. In offering to sell goods, the seller impliedly represents that it has the right to do so. The Sale of Goods Act states (s. 13):

In a contract of sale, unless the circumstances of the contract are such as to show a different intention, there is

(a) An implied condition on the part of the seller that in the case of a sale he has a right to sell the goods, and that in the case of an agreement to sell he will have a right to sell the goods at the time when the property is to pass;

(b) An implied warranty that the buyer will have and enjoy quiet possession of the goods; and

---

[3] Although the wording of the various provincial Sale of Goods Acts is virtually the same, the numbering of sections differs considerably. For simplicity of reference in the remainder of this and the next chapter, we shall prefix each section quoted with the number used in the Ontario act, R.S.O. 1990, c.S-1.

(c) An implied warranty that the goods will be free from any charge or encumbrance in favour of any third party, not declared or known to the buyer before or at the time when the contract is made.

ILLUSTRATION

Alberti purchases a second-hand refrigerator from Blake. It later turns out that Cowan and not Blake was the owner of the refrigerator. Cowan retakes possession of the refrigerator from Alberti.

In the contract of sale between Alberti and Blake there was an implied undertaking by Blake that he had a right to sell the refrigerator, that Alberti should have quiet possession of it (that is, not have physical possession of it interrupted), and that it would be free from any encumbrance in favour of a third person. None of these requirements was satisfied. Alberti is therefore entitled to recover money damages from Blake for breach of an *implied condition of title*. We should remember, however, that the practical value of Alberti's right to sue Blake depends upon whether Blake can be located and, if so, will have enough assets to satisfy a court judgment: for this reason, a prospective buyer ought to take every reasonable precaution to ascertain that the seller has title before entering into a contract of sale.

Description

The Sale of Goods Act sets out the circumstances in which there is an implied term as to description, as follows (s. 14):

> Where there is a contract for the sale of goods by description, there is an implied condition that the goods will correspond with the description, and, if the sale is by sample as well as by description, it is not sufficient that the bulk of the goods corresponds with the sample if the goods do not also correspond with the description.

The word "description" applies to a generic characteristic of the goods (for example, that blouses offered for sale are cotton blouses instead of, say, nylon blouses) and not to words of praise about how good the blouses are (for example, that they will last a lifetime).

ILLUSTRATION

Weiss purchases from Powell, a seed dealer, some seed described as "Rose of Heaven Petunias". When the seed grows, they turn out to be "Pride of Barcelona Onions". Weiss may sue Powell for damages based on breach of an implied term to the effect that the goods shall correspond with the description, whether Weiss has inspected a sample of the seeds or not.

Suitability and Quality

The Sale of Goods Act makes two exceptions to the general rule that the buyer must exercise care as to the suitability and quality of the goods (s.15):

Subject to this Act and any statute in that behalf, there is no implied warranty or condition as to the quality or fitness for any particular purpose of goods supplied under a contract of sale, except as follows:

1. Where the buyer, expressly or by implication, makes known to the seller the particular purpose for which the goods are required so as to show that the buyer relies on the seller's skill or judgment, and the goods are of a description that it is in the course of the seller's business to supply (whether he is the manufacturer or not), there is an implied condition that the goods will be reasonably fit for such purpose, but in the case of a contract for the sale of a specified article under its patent or other trade name, there is no implied condition as to its fitness for any particular purpose.

2. Where the goods are bought by description from a seller who deals in goods of that description (whether he is the manufacturer or not), there is an implied condition that the goods shall be of merchantable quality, but if the buyer has examined the goods, there is no implied condition as regards defects that such examination ought to have revealed.

Part 1 offers protection to a buyer who has a particular purpose in mind for the goods. To have the advantage of this provision the buyer should declare this purpose specifically if it is not one of the general uses to which such goods are customarily put. It is not necessary, however, to state a purpose in so many words if it is obvious. Thus, when buying a dozen buns in a bakeshop, one need not announce to the clerk, "I propose to eat these, and so they must be edible." The essential requirement for Part 1 is that the buyer shall have relied upon the seller's skill and judgment.[4]

ILLUSTRATION

Slack buys 30 m of clothesline wire from a hardware store and uses it as a cable for a homemade elevator in his barn. The wire breaks with him in the elevator, causing him injury and shock. He sues the hardware dealer for damages.

Slack will not succeed because (a) he did not expressly state the particular purpose for which he intended to use the wire, and so did not rely on the seller's skill and judgment, and (b) his damages were not of a kind that were a likely consequence of normal use of clothesline wire.

A Canadian court has held that a contract for work and materials is also subject as a matter of common law to an implied condition of fitness, analogous to the condition of fitness implied in contracts for the sale of goods as described above.[5]

In *Baldry v. Marshall*, the court had to consider circumstances in which a buyer might lose the protection afforded by this part of the section because he had referred to the article by its trade name. Lord Justice Bankes said:

---

[4] Chapronière v. Mason (1905), 21 T.L.R. 633; McCready Products Ltd. v. Sherwin Williams Co. of Canada Ltd. (1985), 61 A.R. 234.

[5] A.G. of Canada v. Laminated Structures & Holdings Ltd. *et al.* (1961), 28 D.L.R. (2d) 92, per Macdonald, J., at 100-1. For an English case on this point, see Dodd v. Wilson, [1946] 2 All E.R. 691. See also: Atiyah, *The Sale of Goods* (8th ed.) pp. 20-28. London: Pitman, 1990.

The mere fact that an article sold is described in the contract by its trade name does not necessarily make the sale a sale under a trade name. Whether it is so or not depends upon the circumstances ... In my opinion the test of an article having been sold under its trade name within the meaning of the proviso is: did the buyer specify it under its trade name in such a way as to indicate that he is satisfied, rightly or wrongly, that it will answer his purpose, and that he is not relying on the skill or judgment of the seller, however great that skill or judgment may be?[6]

Part 2 of this section states when a seller is responsible for the quality of goods in their *general* uses. Under this part, to establish a breach of condition by the seller, the buyer need not show that he relied on the seller's skill and judgment.[7]

ILLUSTRATION

Payne purchases some canned peas at the Pure Food Grocery Store. The peas poison her and she loses wages for one week while recovering from the incident. Payne successfully sues the Pure Food Grocery Store for damages.

The contract of sale has been broken by the store because of the implied condition that the article should be of merchantable quality. The Pure Food Store may in turn recover from the manufacturer or wholesaler who supplied the canned peas because their contract of sale contained a similar implied term.

The word "merchantable" needs explanation: to paraphrase an Australian decision, goods of merchantable quality should be in such a state that a buyer, fully acquainted with the facts and having found the goods in reasonably sound condition, would buy them without reduction below the current market price and without special guarantees.[8]

In practice it is often uncertain which part of section 15 is the more relevant to a buyer's complaint, as the two parts tend to overlap in their application. Professor Waddams has commented, "It is not inappropriate that a buyer who buys goods for their usual purpose and finds them unfit should be entitled to complain both of their general unmerchantability and also of their unfitness for his own purpose."[9]

Sale by Sample

The last of the implied terms recognized in the Sale of Goods Act is set out as follows (s. 16(2)):

In the case of a contract for sale by sample, there is an implied condition

(a) that the bulk will correspond with the sample in quality;

(b) that the buyer will have a reasonable opportunity of comparing the bulk with the sample; and

---

[6] [1925] 1 K.B. 260 at 266-7.

[7] Wren v. Holt, [1903] 1 K.B. 610.

[8] Australian Knitting Mills Ltd. v. Grant (1933), 50 C.L.R. 387, per Dixon, J. at 418; also Bristol Tramways v. Fiat Motors, [1910] 2 K.B. 831, per Farwell, L.J. at 841.

[9] Waddams, *Products Liability,* (3rd ed.). p. 81. Toronto: Carswell Co. Ltd., 1993.

(c) that the goods will be free from any defect rendering them unmerchantable that would not be apparent on reasonable examination of the sample.

ILLUSTRATION

The plant supervisor at High Grade Printing Company examines a sample of choice quality paper supplied by Universal Paper Co. Ltd. and approves its purchase. When the paper is used in one of the fine books printed by High Grade, it turns yellow a month afterwards so that the entire run must be done over again. High Grade sues Universal Paper for damages for its loss. In defence, Universal Paper pleads that the paper supplied was exactly the same as the sample on which the purchase was based, and that a chemical test of the sample would have revealed the defect.

The printing company should succeed in its action if it can show that the defect would not have been apparent in the sample on an ordinary examination, and that an ordinary examination in this business would not include a chemical test.

Exemption Clauses

The Sale of Goods Act contains the following provision (s.53):

> Where any right, duty or liability would arise under a contract of sale by implication of law, it may be negatived or varied by express agreement or by the course of dealing between the parties, or by usage, if the usage is such as to bind both parties to the contract.

As a result, a seller may insist that a contract of sale shall contain an express term exonerating it from the liability normally imposed by implied terms. A prospective buyer may, of course, refuse to enter into a contract containing such an exemption clause; if he agrees to the clause, he loses the protection afforded a buyer by the Sale of Goods Act.

In the belief that the terms implied by the Act are fair and equitable, the courts have zealously restricted the circumstances in which a seller may absolve itself of liability under the Act. Clear and direct language must be used to contract out of statutory protections.

ILLUSTRATION

Syncrude ordered 32 gearboxes from Hunter, a manufacturer, to drive its conveyor belts in the Alberta tar sands project. Syncrude provided specifications of what the gearboxes were required to do and Hunter designed them to meet those specifications.

The contract contained an express term guaranteeing the gearboxes for a period of two years. When the period had expired the gearboxes developed faults that were found to be due to faulty design. Syncrude could not succeed in an action on the express term, but the Supreme Court of Canada held that the implied term of fitness under s. 15 of the Sale of Goods Act could still be relied on. The existence of an express warranty was not inconsistent with the statutory warranties.[10]

---

[10]   Hunter Engineering Co. v. Syncrude Canada Ltd. (1989), 57 D.L.R. (4th) 321. See also Fording Coal Ltd. v. Harnischfeger Corp. of Canada (1991), 6 B.L.R.(2d) 157.

If the words used do not precisely describe the type of liability disclaimed, the courts have reason for finding that the implied liability is still part of the contract. Thus, if a seller includes an express term that "all warranties implied by statute are hereby excluded", the seller will avoid liability under all those implied terms that are *warranties* but not under those that are *conditions*. Moreover, if the seller expressly promises that the goods shall be of a certain quality or type, an exemption clause that refers only to *implied* terms will not free it from obligations under this *express* term.

ILLUSTRATION

Allan agrees to purchase a car from Lambeth Motors Ltd. In the contract the car is described as "a new, 90-h.p., 6-cylinder sedan". There is also a clause, inserted by the seller, that "All conditions, warranties, and liabilities implied by statute, common law, or otherwise are hereby excluded." After taking delivery, Allan discovers that the car is not new and has only four cylinders, and he sues for damages.

The exempting clause refers only to implied terms. The undertaking that the car is new and has six cylinders is an express term in the contract of sale. The seller has, therefore, failed to exempt itself from liability and must pay damages.[11]

The courts have declared, moreover, that a seller cannot so completely exempt itself from liability that it may default on its bargain with impunity. Consequently, the courts would not give effect to an exemption clause that gives a seller immunity from action if it delivers goods entirely different from those contracted for by the buyer or if it delivers goods to which it does not have good title.[12] In effect, the courts have held that a contract for the sale of goods would be deprived of all meaning if a seller's obligation were merely to deliver the goods, "if he felt like it". (We have already discussed the doctrine of fundamental breach in relation to exemption clauses in contracts generally in Chapter 16, and must keep in mind the policy of the courts in giving effect to an allocation of risk expressly agreed between the parties.)

With respect to consumer sales, some provinces now prevent sellers from exempting themselves from liabilities under the implied conditions and warranties in the Sale of Goods Act. In these jurisdictions, the implied conditions and warranties continue to apply and provide a remedy for breach even when a customer has signed a contract expressly exempting the seller from liability. We shall discuss consumer protection legislation in the next chapter.

Payment

Many contracts of sale set out the time of payment expressly, and in others it may be implied from the terms of the contract and the particular circumstances. Where the contract itself gives no guidance about when the buyer is to pay, the courts assume that delivery and payment are concurrent conditions; the transaction is presumed to be a cash

---

11 Andrews Bros. Ltd. v. Singer & Co. Ltd., [1934] 1 K.B. 17.
12 Pinnock Brothers v. Lewis and Peat Ltd., [1923] 1 K.B. 690; Karsales (Harrow) Ltd. v. Wallis [1956] 2 All E.R. 866; Canadian-Dominion Leasing Corporation Ltd. v. Suburban Superdrug Ltd. (1966) 56 D.L.R. (2d) 43.

sale. But this presumption may be rebutted by the circumstances in which the contract is made. For example, where payment from a customer is accepted by credit card, the buyer is normally entitled to delivery of the goods immediately, before payment by the credit card company.

The courts interpret the time set for payment as a warranty unless the parties have expressed themselves otherwise. Consequently, a seller is not entitled to rescind the contract of sale and have its goods back, simply because payment is not made on time. It must be content with an action for the price of goods. But the parties often agree otherwise. A seller may insist on a term entitling it to retake possession in the event of non-payment. This provision is characteristic of the instalment sale, to be considered separately in Chapter 33.

Delivery

The terms in a contract of sale relating to delivery are mainly of three kinds: terms relating to quantity to be delivered; the time of delivery; and the place of delivery. We shall deal with them in turn.

A term specifying the quantity of goods to be delivered is a condition. If the term is broken, that is, if the seller delivers a substantially different quantity, the buyer is free to reject the goods. His right to do so exists whether a greater or lesser quantity is delivered than promised. The buyer may, of course, choose to treat the contract as not having been discharged by breach of condition and take all or part of what is in fact delivered. If he does so, he must pay for what he takes at the contract rate.

The time specified for delivery is also usually a condition, so that if the goods are not delivered on time the buyer may rescind the contract. He is free to look elsewhere for the goods he needs as soon as he learns they will not be available. If the parties agree that the goods are to be delivered as soon as they are available without specifying a time, then delivery is to occur within a reasonable time taking into account all the circumstances. What is a reasonable time for delivery may vary according to the place of delivery: delivery may occur at the seller's place of business, the buyer's place of business, or some intermediate point.

Often a commodity wholesaler or importer keeps its goods stored in the warehouse of a storage company, and a firm buying the goods may wish to leave them there until it has arranged to store them itself or until it has resold them. In these circumstances, where the seller and buyer do not arrange a physical delivery of the goods, when does the delivery take place? The Sale of Goods Act states (s. 28(3)):

> Where the goods at the time of sale are in the possession of a third person there is no delivery by the seller to the buyer unless and until such third person acknowledges to the buyer that he holds the goods on his behalf ...

Thus, delivery takes place when the warehouse firm sends a notice to the buyer that it is holding the goods on the buyer's behalf.

The place of delivery is normally either the seller's place of business or wherever the goods happen to be located at the time of the contract. The parties may, however, express a different intention, or their intention can be implied from trade custom. Thus, when we order goods from a department store and give the clerk our address, the agreed place of delivery is our residence.

An offer for sale sometimes states, along with the asking price, the terms of delivery. It may, for example, quote wheat at so much per bushel *f.o.b. Winnipeg,* or steel at so much for a shipment per tonne *c.i.f. Hamilton.* There are other forms of quotations, but f.o.b. and c.i.f. are the most common. The place mentioned in an f.o.b. quotation is often the city where the seller carries on business, though it need not be. F.o.b. means that the seller will place the goods at that location "free on board" the type of transport specified by the buyer. The seller's duty of delivery is complete when it arranges the kind of transportation requested and delivers the goods to the place of business of the carrier.

When a c.i.f. (cost, insurance, freight) price is quoted, the seller undertakes to arrange insurance in the name of the buyer, ship the goods, and send an insurance policy, bill of lading, and invoice for the total price to the buyer. This type of price quotation tells the buyer what the total cost of the goods will be when they arrive at the place named in the quotation, usually the buyer's place of business. The seller's duty of delivery is not complete until it has arranged insurance and freight, delivered the goods to the carrier, and tendered the necessary documents to the buyer "so that he may know what freight he has to pay and obtain delivery of the goods if they arrived or recover for their loss if they are lost on the voyage."[13]

A *c.o.d.* (cash on delivery) contract differs from the f.o.b. and c.i.f. contracts in that the seller's duty of delivery is not complete until it tenders the goods at the buyer's place of business or residence.

Risk of Loss

If buyer and seller do not expressly agree when the risk for loss caused by damage to or destruction of the goods will pass from the seller to the buyer, it becomes necessary to imply such a term from the contract as a whole. In f.o.b. and c.i.f. contracts it is reasonably implied that the goods remain at the risk of the seller until it has delivered them to the carrier, and in c.o.d. contracts, until the seller or its carrier has delivered them to the buyer. Parties may not think to include an express term concerning the passing of risk, and it may often be impossible to discover an implied term on the subject from the terms of the contract. Such an omission, though unfortunate, is understandable, since the great majority of contracts of sale proceed without any loss occurring between the time of making the agreement and the receipt of the goods by the buyer.

When a loss does occur, however, it is possible that both parties may disclaim any interest in or responsibility for the goods. The reason for their disclaimers is that the risk of loss follows the title to the goods unless the parties have agreed otherwise: the party that has title ordinarily suffers the loss. The courts and legislatures must provide rules for resolving their dispute when the parties have not provided their own. A first approach is to consult the general rules evolved to determine who has title under the Sale of Goods Act.

---

[13] Biddell Brothers v. E. Clemens Horst Co., [1911] 1 K.B. 214 per Hamilton, J., at 220.

TITLE TO GOODS

Specific Goods

The first four rules set down in the Sale of Goods Act (s. 19) for the passing of title relate to *specific goods,* that is, to goods in existence and identified and agreed upon as the subject-matter of the sale at the time the contract is formed. These rules apply unless a contrary intention of the parties can be inferred from their conduct or from customary trade practice. Accordingly, we must always read the rule in the context of each transaction.

Rule 1

Where there is an unconditional contract for the sale of specific goods in a deliverable state, the property in the goods passes to the buyer *when the contract is made,* and it is immaterial whether the time of payment or the time of delivery or both is postponed.

ILLUSTRATION

Maple Leaf Appliances Ltd. is having its annual January sale. Late on a Saturday afternoon, Haag buys a new television set displayed on the floor and pays for it by a cheque postdated five days later. The set is to be delivered on Monday. The parties never discuss which of them is to take the risk of loss before the set is delivered.

On the Sunday, burglars break into the seller's premises and steal the television set. Haag stops payment on the cheque. Maple Leaf Appliances sues Haag for the price of the set.

According to traditional analysis, title and risk are assumed to pass to the buyer at the same time and the action would succeed; since title passed to Haag on Saturday the loss would be his. This traditional analysis is based on a typical transaction between two businesses; the purchaser would generally have insurance coverage for newly acquired goods. It bears little relation, however, to a modern consumer sales transaction. On the one hand, a consumer would think of the television set as being "his" when he left the store and would object if the store were to re-sell it. On the other hand, he would assume that the retailer remained entirely responsible for the set until it was safely delivered. In other words, in the mind of a typical consumer, title to the set and risk of loss or damage would be separate concepts. This separation is not unreasonable but the extent to which the courts will recognize it remains uncertain.

If Maple Leaf Appliances had delayed delivery without Haag's request or consent and the theft had occurred instead on Monday night, so that the loss might have been avoided if the set had been delivered to Haag as agreed, Haag would not be liable to pay for the set.

Rule 2

Where there is a contract for the sale of specific goods and the seller is bound to do something to the goods for the purpose of putting them into a deliverable state, the property does not pass until such thing is done and the buyer has received notice.

During the same January sale described in the preceding illustration, another customer, Oliveira, agrees to buy a second-hand television set that Maple Leaf is displaying, but a term of the agreement is that Maple Leaf will replace the picture tube. It has not done so when the set is stolen. The title has not passed to Oliveira, and she is not liable for the price.

Even if Maple Leaf Appliances had replaced the picture tube shortly after Oliveira left the store, she would not have the title unless she had also been *notified* that the replacement had been done before the set was stolen. Often, when a seller undertakes to deliver the goods, it will not communicate separately with the buyer to say that the goods are now in a deliverable state but will simply deliver them. In these circumstances, the required notice to the buyer is satisfied by delivery, and the title passes at the time of delivery.

Rule 3

Where there is a contract for the sale of specific goods in a deliverable state but the seller is bound to weigh, measure, test, or do some other act or thing with reference to the goods for the purpose of ascertaining their price, the property does not pass until such act or thing is done and the buyer has received notice.

McTavish, Frobisher & Co. agrees to buy a pile of beaver skins from Peter Pond, a trapper, at $6.50 per skin. Before Pond counts the skins, most of them disappear mysteri- ously. Here, the title has not passed to the buyer, and in the absence of any special agreement between the parties, the loss is Pond's.

Rule 4

When goods are delivered to the buyer on approval or on "sale or return" or other similar terms, the property passes to the buyer:

(a) when he signifies his approval or acceptance to the seller or does any other act adopting the transaction;

(b) if he does not signify his approval or acceptance to the seller but retains the goods without giving notice of rejection, then, if a time has been fixed for the return of the goods, on the expiration of such time, and if no time has been fixed, on the expiration of a reasonable time, and what is a reasonable time is a question of fact.

We can see from this rule that a buyer may accept goods and acquire ownership without having expressly communicated that intention to the seller. As our discussion of bailment in Chapter 21 will show, a prospective buyer who has custody of goods on approval owes a duty of care in looking after them: a possibility of liability therefore exists, but since there is as yet no agreed price under a contract of sale the amount would be fixed by the court.

Unascertained Goods

The Sale of Goods Act sets out a separate rule for deciding when title passes in goods that are *unascertained* at the time of the contract. The extreme example of unascertained goods occurs when they have not yet been produced, that is, when they are *future goods;* but goods may also be unascertained even when they are in existence, provided they have not yet been selected and related categorically to a particular contract. Goods are ascertained once they have been set aside or earmarked and agreed upon as the subject-matter of the sale. When unascertained goods are the subject of a contract, by definition the contract must be an agreement to sell, for title cannot pass to a buyer until the goods are ascertained. Nor can the parties effectively insert a term in their agreement purporting to pass the title before the goods are ascertained.

Rule 5

(a) Where there is a contract for the sale of unascertained or future goods by description and goods of that description and in a deliverable state are unconditionally appropriated to the contract, either by the seller with the assent of the buyer, or by the buyer with the assent of the seller, the property in the goods passes to the buyer, and such assent may be expressed or implied and may be given either before or after the appropriation is made.

(b) Where in pursuance of a contract the seller delivers the goods to the buyer or to a carrier or other bailee (whether named by the buyer or not) for the purpose of transmission to the buyer and does not reserve the right of disposal, he is deemed to have unconditionally appropriated the goods to the contract.

ILLUSTRATION

Prentice orders from Hall's automotive supply store four truck tires, size 750 × 20. Hall has a large number of such tires in his stockroom. Later in the day, a clerk removes four of them from the rack where Hall keeps his stock. He sets them aside in the stockroom, attaching a note, "For Mr. Prentice". The clerk's act of separating the tires from the larger bulk does not amount to an unconditional appropriation of the goods. If the contents of the stockroom were to be destroyed in a fire, the loss of the tires would still be the seller's because title has not yet passed to the buyer.

Unconditional appropriation of goods to a contract does not take place until a seller can no longer change its mind and substitute other goods for delivery to the buyer. In other words, some act must be done that conclusively determines what goods are appropriated to the contract. It seems that nothing less than delivery of the goods — or at least an act that virtually amounts to delivery — will constitute unconditional appropriation. If Prentice had left his truck at Hall's garage and Hall had installed the tires, that would amount to delivery; title and risk would have passed to the buyer at the time of the fire.

A buyer's assent to appropriation can be presumed from his prior order. Accordingly, title may pass to the buyer even before he receives notice of the unconditional appropriation, as above, when the tires were installed. In this respect, then, the rule for unascertained goods differs from some of the rules we discussed earlier for specific goods.

Rule 5 above refers to the possibility of a seller "reserving the right of disposal". We shall consider this right in the following section when we deal with the bill of lading.

The Effect of Agency

When a business ships goods to its agent for the agent to sell, the effect of the consignment is to give the agent (the consignee) the appearance of ownership in the eyes of the public. Consistent with this appearance, statutes in the various provinces give the agent the same authority to deal with the goods as their owner has.[14] The agent may therefore validly pass title to anyone who purchases the goods in good faith, even though the sale may be on terms forbidden by the owner (the consignor). The agent, as a consignee of goods, may also pledge them as security for a loan, binding the owner to the transaction. We shall encounter the law on this point again in Chapter 22 on agency.

A similar though more complex problem arises when a seller gives a buyer possession but retains the title as security for payment, as it does in an instalment sale. We shall discuss the effect of an instalment sale in Chapter 33.

THE BILL OF LADING

Its Purposes

A bill of lading is an essential part of many commercial sales transactions and important to the remedies of the seller, as we shall see in the next chapter. In recent years, however, the written bill of lading has increasingly been replaced by computer transactions.[15] A broadly similar result, to that discussed below, is now achieved through a process known as Electronic Data Interchange.

We can best understand the nature of a bill of lading by considering its purposes:

(a) it is a receipt issued and signed by the carrier, acknowledging that specified goods have been delivered to it for shipment;

(b) it provides evidence of the terms of the contract between the shipper and the carrier to transport the described goods to a stated destination; and

(c) it may be evidence of title to the goods.

For the first two of these purposes the bill of lading may be either a *straight* or an *order* bill of lading; to serve the third purpose, it must be an order bill of lading.

---

[14] See, for example: Factors Act, R.S.O. 1990, c. F-1, s. 2; R.S.N.S. 1989, c. 97, s.2; Sale of Goods Act, R.S.B.C. 1979, c. 370, s. 58; R.S.O. 1990, c. S-1, s. 25; R.S.N.S. 1989, c. 408, s. 28. See also: Criminal Code, R.S.C. 1985, c. C-46, s. 325 for the circumstances under which a factor or agent does not commit theft by pledging or giving a lien on goods or documents of title to goods that are entrusted to him for the purpose of sale.

[15] See Kindred, "Trading Internationally by Electronic Bills of Lading", (1992) 7 Banking and Finance Law Rev. 264.

Straight Bill of Lading

By the terms of a straight bill of lading the shipment is consigned directly to a designated party. When a seller employs a straight bill, it usually consigns the goods to the buyer.[16]

A straight bill of lading states the name and address of the party that is to receive an *arrival notice* once the goods reach their destination. Anyone holding the arrival notice and representing the consignee named in the bill of lading is entitled to obtain possession of the merchandise. It is not necessary to present a straight bill of lading to prove title, and a consignee may obtain possession of goods at the point of destination without surrendering the bill to the carrier.

Order Bill of Lading

An order bill of lading is made out to the order of a specified party that, as a result, has title to the goods in the course of transit. The named party in the bill of lading may then transfer title of the goods to someone else by endorsing it. An order bill of lading operates in a manner similar to a negotiable instrument.

The customary practice is for a seller to consign a shipment to its own order. By having the bill of lading made out to in this way, a seller can retain the right of disposal during transit. It can thus withhold title from the buyer until the buyer makes satisfactory arrangements to pay for the goods. The seller, or its agent, then endorses the bill of lading over to the buyer so that the buyer may obtain the goods from the carrier.

Alternatively, the seller may endorse the bill of lading in blank, that is place only its endorsement on the document, unaccompanied by any words specifying the party who is next to have title. An *endorsement in blank* has the effect of giving any bona fide bearer of the bill of lading the right to receive the goods.

An order bill of lading is a useful device for transferring ownership in goods independently of their physical possession. The purchase of goods is often financed while they are in transit, as the buyer may be unwilling or unable to pay for them in advance of delivery, and the seller unwilling to ship without some assurance of payment. The party financing the transaction (the seller's or buyer's bank, for example) may hold the bill of lading as security for payment by the buyer. This device makes it easier to find parties to finance purchases of goods. Since the order bill of lading serves this purpose, sellers use it more often than the straight bill of lading in international trade, where the need for payment to be secured is greater.

Questions for Review

1. Is the sale of every type of chattel necessarily governed by the Sale of Goods Act?
2. Distinguish two types of consignment.
3. In what respects may the price in a contract of sale be important?
4. What are the obligations of a seller in a contract for the sale of goods?
5. Have the parties any control over the terms implied by the Sale of Goods Act?
6. Is there any difference between specific goods and ascertained goods?
7. Is the purchase of a portrait from an artist a contract of sale of goods or a contract for work and materials?

---

[16]   In international transactions the shipment may instead be consigned to a bank that is financing the buyer.

8. Is a contract for the sale of a prefabricated cottage a contract of sale of goods or a contract of sale of real property?

9. If a buyer and seller agree expressly that title is to pass at a specified time in advance of delivery, and the goods are destroyed in the interval between the passing of the title and the delivery date, who sustains the loss?

10. State which of the following terms are conditions and which are warranties: time of payment; time of delivery; an implied term as to description.

11. Assume all the facts in the illustration for Rule 1 under "Title to Goods" at page 383 except that the dealer had agreed to deliver the same model of television set "from our stock". Would the buyer then be liable for the purchase price?

12. Farmer *A* wanted to sell his goat for $10, and farmer *B* agreed to buy it. *B* put $10 on the table, and *A* suggested a glass of beer to celebrate the deal. While they were drinking, the goat ate the ten dollars. (News item, May 13, 1961.) Who owns the goat?

13. *A* makes a contract of sale with *B* to buy goods that have yet to be manufactured. When the goods are finished, *B* consigns them to *A* under a straight bill of lading. If the goods are damaged in the course of transit, who must sustain the loss (or attempt to recover from the carrier)? Why?

Problems

Problem 1
Ajax Co. Ltd. had 25 000 barrels of oil stored in a large tank on its premises. Barnsworthy Corp. agreed to buy 1000 barrels of the oil. Before Ajax had the opportunity to draw the 1000 barrels from the tank for delivery to Barnsworthy, the tank developed a leak, and 5000 barrels were lost before the leak was discovered and repaired. Ajax then refused to make delivery to Barnsworthy, claiming that the oil that had leaked out of the tank included the 1000 barrels purchased by Barnsworthy and that the loss was accordingly Barnsworthy's. It refused to pay, and Ajax sued it for the price. Should the action succeed?

Would the result be different if the oil had instead leaked out of Ajax's delivery trucks after they had been loaded with exactly 1000 barrels of oil and had been despatched to Barnsworthy's address?

Problem 2
Smith purchased a motor car from Goral, a dealer, who had purchased it from a third party. The contract between Smith and Goral contained an express term that the car "is, to the best of the seller's knowledge, free from any charge or encumbrance". It was later seized from Smith by the Crown as having been forfeited under the Customs Act for unlawful importation into Canada, that is, without the payment of customs duty. Neither Smith nor Goral was aware of the outstanding claim for duty, and they were innocent of the unlawful importation. Smith brought an action against Goral to recover the purchase price he had paid for the car.

State whether Smith should succeed.

Problem 3
Jonah and his wife went food-shopping in one of the supermarkets of Pause & Purchase Groceries. His wife had taken three one-litre bottles of Swinger Cola from the shelves and

placed them in the shopping cart he was pushing, when there was an explosion and a piece of glass struck Jonah in the left eye. One of the three bottles in the cart was shattered, with the bottom and some jagged sides remaining upright. The other two bottles were intact.

Jonah suffered a scarred cornea and permanently impaired vision in his left eye. He brought an action jointly against Pause & Purchase Groceries Ltd. and Swinger Cola Ltd.

Explain whether the plaintiff in this case would have any remedy under the Sale of Goods Act. Discuss also the nature of any other type of liability that might form the basis for the action. Indicate the probable outcome ignoring the question of the amount of damages.

Cases

Case 1

In December, Winnipeg Seafoods Ltd. orally agreed to purchase from Lakehead Fish Wholesale Co. 1000 five kilogram boxes of frozen Lake Superior herring at $1.40 per kilogram. The fish was then in the cold storage warehouse of a third party, the Bailey Co. of Thunder Bay. The Bailey Co. operated as a storage company that processed and stored fresh fish. At the time it held some 1500 boxes of this type of fish in storage.

Because Winnipeg Seafoods was short of storage space, it did not want the fish shipped to it but to have it remain in the warehouse at Thunder Bay. Lakehead Fish then arranged with Bailey to transfer the storage account to the name of Winnipeg Seafoods in respect of the 1000 boxes; and Lakehead Fish sent an invoice for $7000 to Winnipeg Seafoods. The invoice indicated that the merchandise was in storage at Bailey's in Thunder Bay. Immediately afterwards, Bailey sent its invoice to Winnipeg Seafoods for one month's storage charges, payable in advance. Winnipeg Seafoods did not pay either of these accounts. The price of frozen herring started to fall in the middle of January. The fish was held in storage until the end of January and then processed to prevent spoilage. On February 2, Winnipeg Seafoods returned the invoice of Lakehead Fish with an accompanying letter to the effect that it had decided to "cancel the order". Lakehead Fish then sued Winnipeg Seafoods Ltd. for the price of the fish, $7000, or in the alternative for damages for non-acceptance. Should it succeed?

Case 2

Dawson was in the business of land clearing, which required three heavy-duty tractors. He could earn gross revenue of $900 a day.

A sales agent for Vincible Tractors Ltd. sold Dawson a Model MX8 tractor for this work for the price of $32 000. The sales agent persuaded Dawson that this model was the one that would best do the work he wished to do with it. The document setting out the terms of the contract of sale stated in its opening paragraph, "Thousands of profit-making hours have been built into this equipment." It also contained the following clause:

GUARANTEE

The Vendor warrants the tractor described herein to be free from defects in material and workmanship under normal use and service, the Vendor's obligation under this warranty being limited to making good any parts which examination shall disclose to the manufacturer's satisfaction to have been defective, provided that such parts shall be so returned to the factory within six months after delivery of such tractor and that at the time of such return the tractor claimed to be so defective shall not have been operated in excess of 1500 hours.

The new goods herein ordered are sold under the above warranty and under no other warranty or condition, express or implied, all conditions and warranties implied by law being expressly negatived.

After delivery, the tractor was used from 18 to 20 hours a day by three skilled operators for six days a week. It worked well for a few weeks but then, while still under warranty, began to fail under the heavy pressure of work. Dawson had to return it repeatedly to the tractor company's nearest service depot for repairs. He had to take it from his place of work some 40 miles into Nanaimo on 20 occasions in its first year and, after the first six months, he ran up a bill for about $2500 for repairs required to keep it in operation. After about 1700 hours of work, it became clear that the tractor was basically useless for the purpose for which it had been purchased, being unable to develop enough power to do this type of work. The Model MX8 tractor had, in fact, been designed for loading gravel.

When Dawson refused to pay for the repairs, Vincible Tractors sued him for $2500. Dawson counterclaimed for damages of $10 000 representing his net earnings lost while the tractor was in the company's hands being repaired. What should be the outcome of this action?

Case 3
Prince was in the children's clothing department in King's Department Store looking over a rack of small girls' clothing on hangers, containing blouses, jumpers and two-piece outfits of a blouse and jumper. She admired a two-piece outfit priced at $19.92. The price was stated to be for both items and was on a tag pinned to the blouse. Prince then looked at a jumper, a one-piece outfit without blouse, with a price tag of $11.54. A security officer of the store, saw her remove the blouse from the two-piece outfit, take the price tag of $19.92 off and discard it, and put the blouse on another hanger. She then put the single jumper with its price tag of $11.54 "over top the blouse", to quote the security officer, and took the two garments on one hanger, as though they were a two-piece outfit, to the counter where she paid $11.54 to the person at the cash register.

Prince was apprehended as she left the store building and was charged with theft of the blouse under sections 322 and 334 of the Criminal Code. At trial her lawyer argued that she had bought the blouse in a contract of sale in which title had passed to her. Discuss the merits of this defence.

For references see The Criminal Code, R.S.C. 1985, c. C-46:

> **322.** (1) Every one commits theft who fraudulently and without colour of right takes, or fraudulently and without colour of right converts to his use or to the use of another person, anything whether animate or inanimate, with intent,
>
> > (a) to deprive, temporarily or absolutely, the owner of it or a person who has a special property or interest in it, of the thing or of his property or interest in it, ...
>
> (2) A person commits theft, when, with intent to steal anything, he moves it or causes it to move or to be moved, or begins to cause it to become movable.
>
> (3) A taking or conversion of anything may be fraudulent notwithstanding that it is effected without secrecy or attempt at concealment.

334. Except where otherwise prescribed by law, every one who commits theft is guilty of an indictable offence and is liable to imprisonment for a term not exceeding two years, where the value of what is stolen does not exceed two hundred dollars.

...

362. (1) Every one commits an offence who

(a) by a false pretence, whether directly or through the medium of a contract obtained by a false pretence, obtains anything in respect of which the offence of theft may be committed or causes it to be delivered to another person;

...

380. (1) Every one who, by deceit, falsehood or other fraudulent means, whether or not it is a false pretence within the meaning of this Act, defrauds the public or any person, whether ascertained or not, of any property, money or valuable security .

(b) is guilty

(i) of an indictable offence and is liable to imprisonment for a term not exceeding two years ...

CHAPTER 19

THE CONTRACT OF SALE: REMEDIES OF THE PARTIES, AND CONSUMER PROTECTION LEGISLATION

REMEDIES OF THE SELLER

Lien

The primary objective of a business selling goods is to recover the contract price. One way of ensuring recovery is to withhold delivery until payment is made. While the goods remain in an unpaid seller's possession the seller has a lien on the goods whether or not title has passed to the buyer: the seller has a claim or charge on them for their agreed price, and can refuse to part with them until the debt is satisfied. Once the seller delivers the goods to the buyer, however, it normally loses this special right to possession unless the buyer obtains them by theft or trickery. The right of lien is based upon possession and is extinguished when possession passes in good faith to the buyer.[1]

Not every contract of sale creates a right of lien for the seller. The remedy exists only in the following situations:

    (a) where the contract does not state that the buyer is to have credit, so that payment may be required upon delivery; or

    (b) where the goods have been sold on credit, the term of credit has expired without payment being made, and the seller still has possession of the goods; or

    (c) where the buyer becomes insolvent before delivery.

In (c), a seller who refuses to deliver is excused only if it can show that the buyer is insolvent. A seller should be sure of the facts before exercising the right of lien; otherwise it takes the risk that the buyer may subsequently sue for breach of the promise to deliver. It is not enough simply to hear that the buyer's financial position is questionable — it is necessary to be more specific, and to show that the buyer is definitely unable to meet current debts as they come due. Otherwise the seller must still deliver as promised, and becomes an unsecured creditor of the buyer for the price of the goods.

A seller may waive its right of lien — and rely on the buyer's credit — in two ways. It may waive the right by implication, as in the usual credit sale, simply by agreeing to deliver before payment is due. Second, it may voluntarily deliver the goods before it need do so.

Stoppage *in Transitu*

If a buyer becomes insolvent after an unpaid seller has delivered goods to a carrier, the seller may still have time to order the carrier to withhold them from the buyer. If given notice in adequate time, the carrier is bound to obey these instructions. If the carrier delivers to the buyer in spite of notice, it is liable for damages for conversion.

The right of stoppage *in transitu* is an extraordinary one because it allows a seller who may have neither title nor possession to goods to exercise control over them. Like the right of lien, however, the remedy disappears once the goods are delivered.

We have seen that a business may dispose of goods it has bought but not yet received if it holds an order bill of lading endorsed in its favour, or in blank, and assigns the bill of lading to a customer or creditor. After the seller exercises a right of stoppage *in transitu*, however, the buyer can no longer pass good title by means of a bill of lading to anyone who knows that stoppage *in transitu* has occurred. On the other hand, a buyer can pass

---

[1] An exception to this rule applies where an unpaid seller repossesses goods under the provisions of the Bankruptcy and Insolvency Act; this exception is discussed below, under the heading "Repossession".

good title to an innocent assignee who is unaware that the right is likely to have been exercised and who has given value for the instrument.

Lamb's Woollen Mills Ltd., Lancaster, England, ships a large order of women's sweaters to Byers Importers of Halifax, Nova Scotia. Since Byers is an old customer, Lamb's Woollen Mills forwards to it an order bill of lading for the goods, endorsed in blank. While the goods are still in transit, Lamb's Canadian agent learns that Byers is insolvent and notifies the carrier not to deliver the goods to Byers. In the meantime Byers resells the goods to Premium Department Stores Ltd. by assigning the bill of lading. The officers of Premium Depart-

ment Stores Ltd. are unaware of the exercise of the right of stoppage *in transitu* or of Byers' impending bankruptcy.

In these circumstances Premium Department Stores obtains the right to possession of the goods from the carrier. Lamb's ranks only as a general creditor of Byers, and in subsequent bankruptcy proceedings would share in the available assets in common with the other general creditors. The available assets would of course include the money paid by Premium Department Stores for the sweaters.

A seller takes the same risk in exercising a right of stoppage *in transitu* as it does in asserting a right of lien. If, as matters turn out, it has mistakenly assumed that the buyer is insolvent, the buyer may sue it for damages for non-delivery.

Repossession

As stated above, once possession passes in good faith to a buyer, the seller loses the right to repossess the goods even if the buyer fails to pay for them. An important exception to the rule was introduced in 1992 by an amendment to the law of bankruptcy.[2] Where a seller has delivered goods to a buyer and the buyer, before having paid in full for the goods, becomes bankrupt or insolvent, the seller may make a written demand for the return of the goods. The demand must be presented, within thirty days after the goods were delivered, to the trustee in bankruptcy or receiver appointed to manage the debtor's affairs. The right to repossess applies only to goods that were delivered in relation to the buyer's business, not to consumer goods. The goods must still be in the possession of the buyer, must be identifiable, and be in the same condition as they were when sold. If the price has been partly paid the seller has a choice between repossessing a portion of the goods in proportion to the amount still owing, or of repossessing all of the goods and refunding the amount already paid. The right of repossession ranks above any other claim to the goods, except those of a subsequent purchaser who has bought the goods for value and in good faith, without notice of the unpaid seller's claim.

Resale

After exercising a right of lien or of stoppage *in transitu* under the Sale of Goods Act, an unpaid seller may give notice to the buyer and resell the goods to a third party; the new

---

[2] Bankruptcy and Insolvency Act, R.S.C. 1985, c. B-3, s. 81.1, as added by S.C. 1992, c. 27.

purchaser obtains good title to them.[3] Although not expressly authorized under the Bankruptcy and Insolvency Act, it seems that an unpaid seller who repossesses goods under the Act also has the right to resell them. The right of resale is especially helpful when the goods are perishable, but is not confined to such emergencies.

The right of resale extends to other circumstances and is not limited to a lien or stoppage *in transitu*. It arises whenever a buyer commits a breach by refusing to accept goods.[4] Resale is then the means by which a seller mitigates its loss.

If the seller has made a diligent effort to obtain a good price on resale but obtains a lower price than that promised in the original contract, it may sue the original buyer for the deficiency.

Damages for Non-Acceptance

We have used the contract of sale to illustrate the measurement of expectation damages in Chapter 17. Our discussion assumed that the title to the goods had not passed to the buyer at the time of the buyer's breach. We saw that a critical factor in determining the appropriate amount of damages is whether the seller is in a position to supply more goods than prospective customers might order: if so, the seller's damages are measured by the profits lost due to the buyer's breach; if not, damages are generally measured by any deficiency in the resale price of the rejected goods compared with the original contract price.

ILLUSTRATION

Read examines a used accordion for sale in Crescendo Music Stores Ltd. She agrees in writing to buy it for $600 provided the bellows are repaired and gold monogram initials are affixed to it. Before the repairs are made, Read informs Crescendo that she has decided to take up the saxophone instead and refuses to accept the accordion. Crescendo sues Read.

The appropriate action is for damages for non-acceptance because the title has not passed to Read at the time of her repudiation. If the music store has more used accordions in stock than it has customers wanting to buy them, it has sustained damages equal to the profit it would have made had Read purchased the instrument as she promised.

If the store has no other used accordions and is able to resell the accordion, but for less than $600, it has sustained damages equal to the difference between the two prices. If the repairs and changes had been made, but Read had not been notified before she repudiated the contract, title would still not have passed to her, and the seller might have a claim for additional damages equal to its expenses. That would depend on whether the required changes had enhanced the value of the instrument: Crescendo should be able to recover the cost of affixing the gold monogram, but not that of repairing the bellows.

---

[3] See, for example: R.S.B.C. 1979, c. 370, ss. 44(1)(c) and 51(2); R.S.O. 1990, c. S-1, ss. 38 and 46(2); R.S.N.S. 1989, c. 408, ss. 41(1)(c) and 49(2) and (3).

[4] Guest A.G. (ed.), *Benjamin's Sale of Goods* (4th ed.), p. 156. London: Sweet & Maxwell, 1992.

Action for the Price

When title has passed to the buyer, a seller is entitled to its full price whether the buyer has taken delivery or not. If the buyer rejects goods after title has passed, he is rejecting what is his own.

ILLUSTRATION

Anderson buys a compact disc player on display at Burton's Appliance Store. The player is tagged "sold" with Anderson's name on it, and Anderson signs a form identifying the purchase and stating its price. On his way home Anderson sees another model in the window of Modern Electronics Ltd., and decides that he would prefer it. He refuses the delivery of the player by Burton's and Burton sues him for the full price of the machine.

The action will succeed. At the time Anderson attempted to repudiate the contract of sale, title had passed to him. If Burton's sues for the price, however, it must be willing and able to deliver of the compact disc player.

The conclusion in this illustration is based on the Sale of Goods Act. However, it has been criticized because a seller's right to sue for the full price may sometimes be hard to justify when the seller is left with the goods: if the buyer is a consumer the seller, as a dealer in the rejected goods, is normally in a better position to resell them. Accordingly, when a seller does not succeed in delivering the goods it is arguable that its recourse should be limited to an action for damages even though title may have passed to the buyer. In jurisdictions in the United States that have adopted the Uniform Commercial Code, a seller may sue for the price only when the buyer has accepted the goods or when the seller is unable after a reasonable effort to resell the goods at a reasonable price; in virtually all other circumstances, a seller may sue only for damages for non-acceptance, regardless of whether title has passed.[5]

Many retail businesses make it a practice for reasons of goodwill to waive contracts of sale upon the customer's request and, even when the goods have already been delivered, to take them back. The waiver of the original contract revests title in the seller so that it may then transfer the title to another buyer.

When a seller does sue, it often sues for the price or, in the alternative, for damages for non-acceptance. This strategy is appropriate when the seller would prefer a simple action for the price (as it normally would), but when it is not clear whether title has passed to the buyer at the time of repudiation. If the court decides that title has passed, the seller will recover the price. If the court decides that title has not passed, the seller will still recover damages for non-acceptance.

Retention of Deposit

In a contract of sale, as in any contract, the parties may provide that in the event of breach the party in default shall pay the other a specified sum of money by way of liquidated damages. As we have seen in Chapter 17, the court will enforce such a term if the

---

[5] For a discussion of the problems created by the rule that the seller is entitled to sue for the price where the buyer has rejected the goods, as long as title has passed, see Atiyah, *The Sale of Goods* (8th ed.), Chap. 26. London: Pitman Publishing, 1990. See also Uniform Commercial Code (U.S.), sec. 2-709.

amount specified is a genuine estimate by the parties of the probable loss. Depending on the circumstances, an amount paid by a buyer as a deposit may be treated as liquidated damages in the event of his default. In many contracts of sale the reason why the seller demands a deposit is to protect itself at least to that extent in the event of the buyer's non-acceptance; here the intention is clear that the deposit shall be forfeited upon breach by the buyer.[6]

However, we must distinguish between a *deposit* intended primarily to provide a sanction to induce performance of the contract by the buyer, and a *down payment*, agreed upon primarily as a part payment of the purchase price and unrelated to the seller's probable loss in the event of breach by the buyer. If the title to the goods has already passed to the buyer at the time the buyer repudiates, the seller is entitled not only to retain the down payment, but to sue for the balance of the price. If title has not yet passed, the seller is entitled to retain out of the down payment any damages for non-acceptance that it can prove and is accountable to the buyer for any remaining surplus.[7] If the seller can prove damages that exceed the down payment it may retain that sum and sue for additional damages.

$\mathcal{S}$COPE OF THE SELLER'S LIABILITY

Misrepresentation

The Common Law

We have considered the remedies for misrepresentation in Chapter 11; a review of that chapter is worthwhile at this point. We noted there that when a misrepresentation is innocent, the only remedy–rescission–is often impossible or at least impractical for the buyer; and to have the more extensive remedies available for misrepresentation, the buyer must establish either fraud or negligence.

The type of statement that comes within the definition of misrepresentation has two important characteristics for our present purposes. First, the statement must be part of the preliminary bargaining, and not be incorporated as a term in the contract of sale — if it were embodied in the contract, the buyer's recourse would be for breach of contract. Second, the statement made by the seller must be made as a statement of fact — the law provides no remedy for a buyer induced to enter into a contract by a mere expression of opinion, or commendation of the goods.[8]

Advertising can be misleading but still not amount to misrepresentation as we have defined it. While the common law may seem inadequate in this respect, several factors help both to explain this state of affairs and to minimize potential abuse. In the first place, most businesses act in a reasonably responsible way when dealing with the public, and any general rule sufficiently comprehensive to control and punish every type of deception would

---

[6] See Stockloser v. Johnson, [1954] 1 Q.B. 476. If the contract provides for a non-refundable deposit but the deposit has not been paid, for example where the purchaser has stopped payment on the cheque, the vendor is entitled to recover the agreed sum: Vanvic Enterprises Ltd. v. Mark, [1985] 3 W.W.R. 644.

[7] Stevenson v. Colonial Homes Ltd. (1961), 27 D.L.R. (2d) 698.

[8] In our discussion of negligent misrepresentation in Chapter 5, we noted that the expression of a professional opinion, as with expert opinion generally, may be regarded as a "fact" in the mind of the person influenced by it.

obstruct unduly the course of legitimate business. In the second place, no legal rule is an adequate substitute for a buyer's own care. A seller's superior position results largely from its knowledge about both its products and the limits of the law, and the only effective way for the buyer to minimize this advantage is to seek the knowledge for himself. Third, the common law can be, and has been, superseded by statute law in specific areas of abuse.

Legislation

Federal statutes that regulate representations generally are the Weights and Measures Act[9] and the National Trade Mark and True Labelling Act.[10] Other statutes not only govern the representations that can be made about particular products, but also provide for inspection of the industry and regulation of the quality of goods sold. The best known of these statutes is the Food and Drugs Act, which prescribes penalties for the sale of any article of food or any drug that is adulterated or that is manufactured, packaged, or stored under unsanitary conditions. The Act also provides in part:

> No person shall label, package, treat, process, sell or advertise any food in a manner that is false, misleading or deceptive or is likely to create an erroneous impression regarding its character, value, quantity, composition, merit or safety.[11]

An identical provision applies to deception in the sale of drugs. There are separate federal statutes regulating the sale of meat, livestock, fruit, vegetables, and honey.

Sellers must also take into account the growing body of legislation, both provincial and federal, regulating advertising. We shall deal with misleading advertising in our discussion of consumer protection legislation in the final section of this chapter.

Breach of a Term

Generally, a breach of a condition entitles the injured party to discharge the contract as well as to sue for damages for any loss suffered. The Sale of Goods Act, however, sets down circumstances where a buyer will *not* be entitled to terminate the contract and return the goods, even though the seller has been guilty of a breach of condition. The Act (s.12(3)) reads as follows:

> Where a contract of sale is not severable and the buyer has accepted the goods or part thereof, or where the contract is for specific goods the property in which has passed to the buyer, the breach of any condition to be fulfilled by the seller can only be treated as a breach of warranty and not as a ground for rejecting the goods and treating the contract as repudiated, unless there is a term of the contract, express or implied, to that effect.

This section means, first, that the buyer must keep the goods and be content with damages where the broken contract of sale does not contemplate delivery by instalments (is not severable) and the buyer has indicated an intention to keep the goods or treated them in a way inconsistent with the seller's ownership of them.

The section seems to contemplate a second situation where the right to repudiate would be lost when the contract is for specific goods, the property in which has passed to

---

[9] R.S.C. 1985, c. W-6.
[10] R.S.C. 1985, c. N-18.
[11] R.S.C. 1985, c. F-27, s. 5(1).

the buyer even though the goods are still in the seller's possession. However, when the seller has committed a breach of condition by allocating unsatisfactory goods to fill the contract such a result would seem surprising: it is difficult to see how title would pass to the buyer in that situation, short of the buyer's acceptance of the goods. Courts avoid applying this part of the section and sometimes even seem to ignore it as inappropriate to modern selling practices.[12]

ILLUSTRATION

A sales agent for Agrarian Implements Ltd. shows to Macdonald, a farmer, a catalogue containing pictures of various types of agricultural equipment that his firm has for sale. The agent tells Macdonald that they have just taken into stock "one brand new" combine of a type pictured in the catalogue. Macdonald agrees to buy it and signs the necessary papers.

When the combine is delivered, a neighbour of Macdonald recognizes it as one with which the same sales agent had earlier given him an extensive demonstration, and which the sales agent had referred to as "a demonstrator model that we could let you have at a bargain". Macdonald at once ships the combine back to Agrarian Implements and the company then sues him for the price.

The combine was a specific article at the time Macdonald agreed to buy it. Nevertheless, he is entitled to treat the contract as discharged and refuse to accept the combine. Agrarian Implements has been guilty of breach of the condition as to description (that the combine was new), and the courts have reasoned that title did not pass to Macdonald.[13] If, however, Macdonald took delivery of the combine and used it for farm work, he could not subsequently, upon learning that it was not new when he bought it, insist upon a right to return it. He must be content with damages.

In addition, even when the goods are specific and title has passed to the buyer at the time of sale, if the seller fails to deliver on time the buyer may later refuse to take them and may terminate the contract. The section concludes by stating that it does not apply where there is a term of the contract, express or implied, to the effect that the buyer can treat a breach of condition as grounds for rejecting the goods. When the parties specify a time for delivery, the courts may find that such an intention is implied.

In *Leaf v. International Galleries*[14] we can see the possible consequences for the buyer when the seller is guilty of a breach of condition but the buyer has accepted the goods. Leaf purchased a painting of Salisbury Cathedral that the seller, International Galleries, represented to him as a painting by Constable. When Leaf attempted to resell the picture five years later, it was discovered that it had not been painted by the famous English artist. Leaf tried to return the picture to International Galleries and recover the purchase price. The court held that the Sale of Goods Act section quoted above applied, so that Leaf did not have the right to treat the contract as being at an end. Since he did not sue for damages, as he might have done, his action failed. It is interesting that the court regarded the representation as having been incorporated into the contract of sale as a term; its decision does not answer the question whether, had the case been treated as one of either innocent

---

12 See Waddams, *The Law of Contracts* (3rd ed.), p. 407-8.
13 See *Varley v. Whipp*, [1900] 1 K.B. 513.
14 [1950] 2 K.B. 86.

misrepresentation or mistake, the equitable remedy of rescission might still have been available at that late date.

Wrongful Withholding or Disposition by the Seller

When the title to goods has already passed to the buyer, a seller who refuses to deliver them according to the terms of the contract is guilty of a tort: the buyer may sue the seller for damages for *wrongful detention*. She may also obtain a court order for their delivery. If, however, the seller has transferred the goods to a third party, it will have disposed of goods that do not belong to it; the buyer may sue for damages for the tort of *conversion*, that is, for converting the buyer's goods to its own use or purposes.

$\mathcal{C}$OMMON LAW REMEDIES OF THE BUYER

Damages for Breach of Contract

In Chapter 17 under the heading "Expectation Damages", we discussed the measure of damages available to a buyer when the seller fails to deliver. If delivery is merely delayed through the seller's fault and the buyer accepts the goods, the measure of damages is the value the goods would have had for the buyer if they had been delivered on time over their actual value when delivered.

A seller may be guilty of breach for other reasons than non-delivery: for example, failure to perform any of the implied terms as to title, description, suitability and merchantability, or compliance with sample; or failure to perform an express term as to the quality or capability of the goods. Damages sustained by a buyer from the seller's breach of a term may sometimes, as we have seen, be greater than the price of the goods; to recover the loss the buyer must take the initiative and claim it from the seller. When the damages amount to less than the contract price, the buyer may choose to tender to the seller the price less the amount of the damages; if the seller refuses the tender and sues for the full price, the buyer may defend by claiming to set off its damages against the price. To reduce the risk of having to pay court costs, the buyer should promptly pay into court the amount tendered to the seller.

Rescission

As we have seen, rescission is a remedy available either for misrepresentation or for breach of a condition. It is limited in its application to situations where it is still possible to restore the parties substantially to the positions they had before the contract was made; the remedy is further restricted by the provision in the Sale of Goods Act considered in the preceding section under "Breach of a Term". Nevertheless, rescission provides a possible remedy for a buyer when the seller fails to deliver goods that have been prepaid in whole or in part.

Specific Performance

The Sale of Goods Act gives the court discretion to order specific performance of a contract for the sale of goods, that is, to order the seller to deliver the goods to the buyer. Generally the court does not grant this remedy when a seller refuses to deliver because money damages are nearly always an adequate remedy. Where the goods have a unique value for the buyer, however, the court may exercise its discretion in his favour and order specific performance.

Damages in Tort

As explained above, a buyer may sue the seller for damages for the wrongful withholding or disposition of goods after title has passed. As we have seen in Chapter 4, a buyer may also obtain damages for deceit or for injuries sustained in using goods that were negligently produced.

Consumer Protection Legislation

Background

The concept of consumers as a class of people to be protected by the courts and legislatures is a relatively recent one. Indeed, it is probably still too early to call consumer protection a "concept"; it remains not much more than a label under which we may group diverse legislative schemes for protecting individual buyers of goods and services from injury, from receiving less than fair value for their money, and from being held to contracts that they have been unfairly induced to enter into. Specific laws to remedy abuses by merchants and moneylenders may be found in ancient codes and from time to time since the Middle Ages there has been activity by governments to give relief from harsh treatment by creditors.

Until the late 19th century, specific measures probably sufficed. Retail trade was carried on by relatively small local merchants who dealt directly with customers in an ongoing relationship: if sellers did not treat their customers fairly, customers would go elsewhere. Goods were simpler and most buyers could gauge the quality of what they bought, be it a suit of clothes, a bag of flour, a wagon or a horse. Even in this simpler trading environment, there was opportunity for misleading conduct and sharp practice, as well as fraud. The available remedies were more or less adequate: actions for the tort of deceit in cases of fraud, and remedies for failure to supply goods of merchantable quality and reasonably fit for the purpose for which they were bought. We have considered these remedies in Chapter 4 and in the preceding chapter.

Several modern developments have made these simpler remedies inadequate. First, the concentration of manufacturing and distribution in the hands of very large enterprises has virtually ended any equality of bargaining power between individual buyers and sellers. In the words of Lord Denning:

> ... the freedom was all on the side of the big concern...The big concern said "Take it or leave it". The little man had no option but to take it.[15]

Second, many manufactured goods have become so complex that even a competent retailer with a well-trained staff cannot detect defects or, if they are discovered, remedy them — the goods can only be returned to the manufacturer when a customer complains. The electronic calculator and quartz watch are good examples.

---

[15] George Mitchell (Chesterhall) Ltd. v. Finney Lock Seeds Ltd. [1983] 1 All E.R. at 113.

Third, economies of distribution dictate that many goods formerly shipped in bulk and divided by quantity at the retail level are now shipped in sealed packages that cannot be examined either by the retailer or the shopper until taken home and opened for use. This marketing system applies to everything from a package of wood screws to many items of fresh and frozen food. The result may be that the goods (sometimes) reach the consumer at lower prices, but there is no opportunity for assessing the quality of a product or its suitability for the consumer's intended use.

Fourth, a highly developed system of advertising through the mass media creates expectations of product performance that play an important part in inducing consumer purchases and is often more influential than the retailer with whom the consumer deals.

Fifth, in the purchase of expensive goods such as cars, large appliances and furniture, the use of credit has become the norm. Sophisticated and complex schemes for determining the cost of borrowing make it difficult for the ordinary buyer to understand the effective rate of interest being charged.

Finally, our increasingly urbanized society has transformed many families into consumers of housing services supplied by corporate owners of large apartment blocks.

Our legislatures have not developed a systematic theory or policy about consumer protection, and legislation has grown in response to specific, perceived problems, generally without much thought to the broader consequences of regulation. The current movement toward consumer protection really began in the 1960s.[16] Since then each Canadian province, as well as the federal government, has actively pursued legislative reform with little if any consultation, although with some copying of the legislative efforts of the pioneers in each field. This rather chaotic approach is not unique to Canada; other Western countries have taken a similar *ad hoc* approach to protecting consumers.

We should note that virtually all consumer protection statutes apply both to the sale of goods to consumers and to the sale of services such as home repairs, carpet cleaning and the preparation of income tax returns.

Some of the provisions of consumer protection legislation can best be understood in the context of discussions of other topics. Thus we have dealt with the requirement of written evidence of the terms of consumer sales contracts in Chapter 12 ("The Requirement of Writing") and with the prohibition of exempting clauses in consumer sales contracts in Chapter 18. We shall deal with changes in the law affecting residential tenancies in Chapter 27 ("Landlord and Tenant") and with restrictions on the repossession of goods purchased under instalment contracts in Chapter 33 ("Legal Devices for Securing Credit"). The purpose of the present section is to provide an overview of the main categories of consumer protection. We have identified the following five classes of consumer protection legislation, and we shall examine them in turn:

(a) regulation of misleading advertising;
(b) regulation of quality standards affecting labelling, safety, performance, and availability of servicing and repairs;
(c) regulation of business conduct towards consumers;
(d) disclosure of the effective cost of credit; and
(e) supervision of businesses that deal with the public through licensing, bonding and inspection.

---

[16] There are isolated earlier examples of consumer protection legislation; for example, provisions against false and misleading advertising were introduced in the Criminal Code as early as 1914.

Misleading Advertising and Other Representations of Sellers

The law affecting misleading representations by sellers of goods and services is steadily becoming more codified. The trend reflects the increasing political strength of the consumer movement and a skepticism about the ability of the courts to adapt and apply the common law to new and shrewd misleading selling practices. The danger inherent in this trend, however, is that it will pit the ingenuity of legislators against the schemes of what may be a relatively small percentage of sellers in an ever more complicated legal game. In any event, it marks the end of the era of *caveat emptor*.

The federal Competition Act contains a section[17] that begins with a general prohibition of misleading representations made for the purpose of promoting the supply or use of a product or of any business interest. More specifically, the section makes it an offence to make false or misleading representations about the qualities of a product, or the "regular" price at which it is sold. When reading the section we should also bear in mind that the Act defines the word "product" as referring equally to goods and services. The section is as follows:

52. (1) No person shall, for the purpose of promoting, directly or indirectly, the supply or use of a product or for the purpose of promoting, directly or indirectly, any business interest, by any means whatever,

(a) make a representation to the public that is false or misleading in a material respect;

(b) make a representation to the public in the form of a statement, warranty or guarantee of the performance, efficacy or length of life of a product that is not based on an adequate and proper test thereof, the proof of which lies upon the person making the representation;

(c) make a representation to the public in a form that purports to be

(i) a warranty or guarantee of a product, or

(ii) a promise to replace, maintain or repair an article or any part thereof or to repeat or continue a service until it has achieved a specific result

if such form of purported warranty or guarantee or promise is materially misleading or if there is no reasonable prospect that it will be carried out; or

make a materially misleading representation to the public concerning the price at which a product or like products have been, are or will be ordinarily sold; and for the purposes of this paragraph a representation as to price is deemed to refer to the price at which the product has been sold by sellers generally in the relevant market unless it is clearly specified to be the price at which the product has been sold by the person by whom or on whose behalf the representation is made.

An offence against this section carries a possible maximum penalty of five years imprisonment. However, an accused person may escape conviction by establishing that the act or omission giving rise to the offence was the result of an error and that reasonable precautions and due diligence had been taken to prevent such an error occurring.[18]

Subsequent provisions of the Act make various other types of selling practices an offence. The Act prohibits the publication of the results of testing the product and of

---

[17] Competition Act, R.S.C. 1985, c. C-34, s. 52, as amended. (Subsequent references to this Act in footnotes of this chapter will be to section numbers only.)

[18] The constitutionality of this "reverse onus" provision was upheld by a narrow majority of the Supreme Court of Canada in R. v. Wholesale Travel Group Inc. (1991), 84 D.L.R.(4th) 161.

testimonials of users that cannot be corroborated and have been used without the permission of the testing agency or user.[19] A section dealing with *double ticketing* states that where prices marked on products have been changed by the addition of a higher price, and each of the amounts is visible on the product or its package, the seller can charge only the lower amount.[20] The Act also prohibits *bait and switch selling:* it is an offence to advertise a product at a bargain price when the seller does not supply it in reasonable quantities.[21] The tactic here is to use the advertised price of an article in short supply to promote another, higher-priced article. Further sections prohibit *pyramid selling* and *referral selling,* that is, schemes in which customers are promised rebates for identifying persons to whom further sales are made.[22]

The Act also prohibits the practice (sometimes claimed to be inadvertent) of advertising an article or service as being for sale at a lower price than that actually asked of the customer. The relevant section reads in part as follows:

> 58.1 (1) No person who advertises a product for sale or rent in a market shall, during the period and in the market to which the advertisement relates, supply the product at a price that is higher than the price advertised....
>
> (3) This section does not apply
>
> (a) in respect of an advertisement that appears in a catalogue in which it is prominently stated that the prices contained therein are subject to error if the person establishes that the price advertised is in error;
>
> (b) in respect of an advertisement that is immediately followed by another advertisement correcting the price mentioned in the first advertisement...

The above provisions illustrate the overlap of federal and provincial jurisdictions in the Constitution Act, 1867; *both* levels of government seem to have concurrent powers to regulate these types of selling practices. The regulation of trade and commerce and the criminal law fall within the federal prerogative; property and civil rights in the province (including generally all contracts for goods and services) come within provincial legislative authority. One writer describes the ambit of the Act in these terms:

> Nowhere else in Canadian federal law is there a Statute of such day-to-day importance afflicted by such a glaring degree of constitutional uncertainty. This is unfortunate since, one way or another, the Canadian businessman needs to know what the rules are so that he may seek to comply. He can presume that the existing criminal provisions, and any reasonable additions thereto, will stand constitutionally and he will govern himself accordingly; as for the rest, he is in the realm of guesswork, faced with a moral impetus to comply with a law in force but knowing that major change, for example, in his distribution set-up, may be very costly and may subsequently prove unnecessary with the constitutional failure of the provisions in question.[23]

---

[19] S. 53.

[20] S. 54.

[21] S. 57(1) and S. 57(2)

[22] S. 55 (as amended by S.C. 1992, c.14) and S. 56. The amended S.55 now refers to pyramid selling as "multilevel marketing".

[23] Flavell, *Canadian Competition Law: A Business Guide.* p. 36. Scarborough; McGraw Hill Ryerson, 1979. The Act was then known as the Combines Investigation Act. For further consideration of the overlap between federal and provincial legislation see Nielson, "Reflections on Recent Federal Proposals for the Rationalization of Trade Practices Regulation in Canada", (1992) 21 C.B.L.J. 70.

Since 1965, all provinces have passed various forms of protection legislation dealing with misleading advertising. The earliest versions gave government agencies the power to prohibit such advertising on pain of fines against sellers who continued to mislead. Eventually, new remedies were given directly to consumers who were affected by the misleading statements. For instance, Ontario's Business Practices Act declares it to be an "unfair practice" to make "a false, misleading or deceptive consumer representation" which may include a wide variety of representations about the "sponsorship, approval, performance characteristics, accessories, uses, ingredients, benefits or quantities" that the goods or services do not have.[24] There follows a long list of examples of deceptive representations. The Act also describes an "unconscionable consumer representation" as a type of unfair practice that includes such conduct as simply asking a price that "grossly exceeds the price at which similar goods or services are readily available to like consumers."[25] A consumer subjected to an unfair practice may terminate the contract and "where rescission is not possible ... the consumer is entitled to recover the amount by which the amount paid under the agreement exceeds the fair value of the goods or services received under the agreement or damages, or both."[26] In addition, the court is expressly authorized to award exemplary or punitive damages against the wrongdoer.[27] Similar statutes have been passed in other provinces.[28]

Regulation of Labelling, Product Safety and Performance Standards

The federal Parliament has legislated extensively in prescribing public health and safety standards that the sellers of consumer products must meet. We shall review briefly the requirements of the most important of these statutes.

The Consumer Packaging and Labelling Act;[29] sets out comprehensive rules for packaging and labelling consumer products, including requirements for identifying products by their generic names and stating the quantity of the contents. The Act also provides for standardized package sizes to avoid confusion. The list of products sold in standardized packages is added to from time to time by federal regulation after consultation with affected industries.

The Textile Labelling Act[30] requires labels bearing the generic name of the fabric to be attached to all items of clothing. The federal care-labelling program encourages manufacturers to include recommended procedures for cleaning and preserving the fabric. In view of the pervasive use of synthetic fibres, these labels give us important information.

The Hazardous Products Act[31] divides products into two classes. Part I lists products considered so dangerous that their manufacture is prohibited in Canada. The list includes such items as children's articles painted with liquid containing lead. Part II lists products that must be manufactured and handled in conformity with regulations under the Act, and includes such items as bleaches, hydrochloric acid, and various glues containing potent solvents. The Minister of Consumer and Corporate Affairs has broad discretion in

---

[24] Business Practices Act, R.S.O. 1990, c. B-18, s. 2(a)(i).
[25] *Ibid.*, s. 2(b)(ii)
[26] *Ibid.*, s. 4(1).
[27] *Ibid.*, s. 4(2).
[28] For example: Trade Practice Act, R.S.B.C. 1979, c. 406; Unfair Trade Practices Act, R.S.A. 1980, c. U-3.
[29] R.S.C. 1985, c. C-38.
[30] R.S.C. 1985, c. T-10.
[31] R.S.C. 1985, c. H-3.

banning products deemed to be a threat to public health or safety, and has exercised it when manufacturers have failed to comply with a request from the Consumer Affairs Branch to correct defects in such products as infants' car seats.

The Food and Drugs Act[32] is a comprehensive statute regulating many aspects of foods and medical and cosmetic products, since virtually all of them, if improperly processed, manufactured, stored or labelled, may adversely affect consumers' health or safety. Provisions deal with such matters as conditions of sanitation in production, measures to prevent adulteration of food and medicines, the listing of ingredients contained in products, and the dating of products having a shelf life of less than 90 days.

The Motor Vehicle Safety Act[33] provides for the adoption of regulations setting national safety standards for motor vehicles whether manufactured in Canada or imported. It also requires manufacturers to give notice of defects in vehicles to the Department of Transport and to all purchasers of the defective vehicles.

Provincial statutes provide further protection for consumers. As we have noted in this and the preceding chapter, implied terms under the Sale of Goods Act with respect to merchantability and fitness are made binding on sellers in contracts with consumers; sellers cannot escape liability by requiring buyers to sign exemption clauses.[34]

This approach, of imposing liability on sellers by inserting compulsory terms in consumer contracts, has been taken further in the Saskatchewan and New Brunswick statutes.[35] Both acts, although in somewhat different ways, turn precontractual representations into "warranties" under a consumer contract and give consumers contractual remedies for breach, in place of confining the remedy to rescission for misrepresentation. Both statutes also create implied warranties that consumer products "will be durable for a reasonable period of time". A third important change to the common law made by these acts extends liability for breach of warranty to third persons who were not parties to the consumer contract, such as members of the buyer's family. It is necessary only to show that the harm to the person "who suffers a consumer loss ... was reasonably foreseeable at the time of the contract ..."[36] In addition, the Saskatchewan statute adds a new dimension to the liability of sellers of consumer products. It creates an implied warranty:

> where the product normally requires repairs, that spare parts and reasonable repair facilities will be available for a reasonable period of time after the date of the sale of the product.[37]

Regulation of Business Conduct towards Consumers

As a response to the excesses of high-pressure door-to-door selling methods, most provinces have enacted legislation giving a buyer the right to rescind certain types of contract of sale.[38] Unfortunately, there has been virtually no cooperation among the various governments and

---

[32] R.S.C. 1985, c. F-27.

[33] R.S.C. 1985, c. M-10.

[34] For example: Consumer Protection Act, R.S.N.S. 1989, c. 92, s. 20; R.S.O. 1990, c. C-31, s. 34(2). See also: R.S.B.C. 1979, c. 370, s. 20.

[35] Consumer Products Warranties Act, R.S.S. 1978, c. C-30; Consumer Product Warranty and Liability Act, S.N.B. 1978, c. C-18.1.

[36] S. 23 of the New Brunswick Act. See also s. 5 of the Saskatchewan Act.

[37] S. 11(8) of the Saskatchewan Act.

[38] For example: Consumer Protection Act, R.S.B.C. 1979, c. 65, s. 13, as amended by S.B.C. 1980, c. 6, S.B.C. 1985, c. 52; R.S.O. 1990, c. C-31, s. 21; Direct Sales Cancellation Act, R.S.A. 1980, c. D-35, s. 6, as amended by S.A. 1981, c. 44, s. 2.

the resulting provisions vary in the extent and nature of the remedies they provide for the buyer. The legislation was inspired by an act in the United Kingdom giving consumers a *cooling-off period* after door-to-door sales.[39] A buyer may terminate the contract during this period by giving written notice to the seller. Upon doing so, he or she has no further obligation under the contract and may recover any money already paid.

In these statutes the cooling-off period varies from two to ten days. In some provinces it is based on the time when the contract is entered into; in others, from the date on which a written memorandum of the contract is received by the buyer. The legislation applies to both goods and services but in some provinces it does not apply to sales under $50. Some of the provincial securities acts also contain a provision for a cooling-off period in the purchase of new shares and bonds issued by a company.

A cooling-off period is a departure from the common law approach to contracts. As our courts have developed the concept of contract, rights and liabilities of the parties are established at the time a contract is formed, and afterwards it is too late for one of the parties to change his mind and repudiate without being in breach of contract. This principle is consistent with the view that both parties to a contract should in general be able to rely on its performance from a clearly ascertained point in time. A statutory provision for a cooling-off period is an encroachment on this principle, justified by a need to control the exploitation of consumers by door-to-door sellers.

High-pressure selling can take the form of sending goods not ordered by the consumer, hoping to induce the recipient to pay for them. Consumer protection statutes expressly state that use of the goods by the recipient does not amount to an acceptance of the seller's offer. Accordingly, a recipient of *unsolicited goods* may use them without becoming liable for their price. The purpose of the provision is to discourage sellers from sending unsolicited goods to consumers, and it seems to have been quite effective. The rule may or may not be the same, depending upon the jurisdiction, for *unsolicited credit cards*. As a means of discouraging the practice, a province may go so far as to provide that the recipient of an unsolicited credit card who has not acknowledged any intention to accept it may nonetheless use it to purchase goods without incurring liability to the issuer of the card! Other provinces state that no liability can be created until the recipient either uses the card to make purchases or accepts its terms in writing.[40]

A standard form consumer contract may contain a term asserting that the lender or seller has some form of self-help remedy should the consumer default. For example, the contract may authorize the seller to repossess the goods from the consumer if instalment payments are not kept up, or to sue for the entire balance due under the contract if the consumer defaults in one instalment payment. Consumer protection statutes in some provinces state that the seller's remedy of *repossession* is lost once the buyer has paid a specified proportion (for example, two-thirds) of the purchase price,[41] and other statutes limit the circumstances in which a seller or creditor can enforce an *acceleration clause*.[42] A further example occurs in

---

[39] Hire-Purchase Act, 1964, c. 53, s. 4 (U.K.)

[40] For an example of legislation imposing the former result, see Consumer Protection Act, R.S.B.C. 1979, c. 65, s. 32; and of legislation imposing the latter result, see Consumer Protection Act, R.S.O. 1990, c. C-31, s. 36 and R.S.N.S. 1989, c. 92, s. 23.

[41] For example: s. 23 of the Ontario Consumer Protection Act.

[42] For example: Personal Property Security Act, R.S.O. 1990, c. P-10, s. 18; Consumer Protection Act, R.S.M. 1987, c. C200, s. 33; Residential Tenancies Act, R.S.O. 1990, c. R-29, ss. 5-7, 69.

the law of landlord and tenant, where some provinces have abolished a landlord's self-help remedy of seizing a residential tenant's goods for arrears of rent.[43]

Many merchants who sell durable goods to consumers on the instalment plan, "discount" their consumer credit contracts to finance companies. Typically, a merchant assigns the contract to a finance company and receives immediate payment of a sum that is less than the full amount to be paid by the buyer. The buyer then receives notice of assignment and makes the instalment payments to the finance company. The general rule about assignment of contractual rights, as we have seen in Chapter 14, is that an assignee "takes subject to the equities" and acquires no more enforceable claim than the assignor had. There is little doubt that a merchant can more readily (and probably more cheaply) find an assignee to buy its instalment receivables if the assignee acquires rights against the buyer that are *not* subject to any complaints the buyer (consumer) may have about the goods.

Merchants and finance companies found a way around the general rule about assignments by using a negotiable instrument: a buyer was required to sign a promissory note for the balance of the purchase price plus finance charges, and this note, along with the conditional sale contract, was endorsed by the merchant to the finance company. The finance company thus became a holder in due course of the note, immune to any "personal defences" the buyer might have against the merchant. Until the matter was corrected by legislation in the late 1960s, a consumer might be liable to a finance company with no opportunity to refuse to pay for the goods if they proved defective or if the dealer refused to perform its warranties. We shall refer to this matter again in later chapters.[44] By an amendment to the Bills of Exchange Act, finance companies became subject to consumers' defences against sellers.[45]

Another way around the rule was to use the contract of sale itself to waive the consumer's rights by a rather special kind of exempting clause: the consumer was asked to sign a standard form contract of sale containing a clause (sometimes referred to as a *cut-out clause*) agreeing that any assignee of the contract (for example, a finance company), when seeking to enforce the debt, would not be subject to the defences that the debtor (consumer) might have against the assignor (dealer). Most consumer protection acts now state that an assignee of a consumer credit contract shall have no greater rights than the assignor and is subject to the same obligations.[46]

The social wisdom of these legislative attempts to protect consumers against exploitative contractual arrangements imposed on them (such as self-help remedies inserted by sellers or creditors) has proved to be a controversial topic. Much legislative intervention on the side of consumers is justified by demands for a more equitable economic system: consumers are perceived as typically having much less bargaining power than businesses with which they deal. Legislators believe they have a mandate to prohibit unconscionable selling and credit practices. Some writers have challenged the assumptions underlying this point of

---

43   For example: Landlord and Tenant Act, R.S.O. 1990, c. L-7, s. 84; Residential Tenancy Act, S.B.C. 1984, c. 15, s. 48.

44   See Chapter 24 ("Negotiable Instruments") under the section "Consumer Bills and Notes", and Chapter 33 ("Legal Devices for Securing Credit") in the discussion of conditional sales contracts.

45   R.S.C. 1985, c. B–4, s. 191.

46   For example: Consumer Protection Act, R.S.B.C. 1979, c. 65, s. 3(1), as amended by S.B.C. 1980, c. 6; R.S.O. 1990, c. C–31, s. 31; R.S.N.S. 1967, c. 53, s. 20B.

view.[47] Consumer protection regulation is seen by some as paternalistic, overruling consumer preferences and substituting the government's view of what is in the consumer's best interest. Such regulation also doubtless adds to the cost of doing business. Is this cost absorbed by sellers and lenders in reduced profits or is it passed on to consumers in the form of higher prices? However, the normal contractual rules that leave the initiative to consumers in obtaining relief generally do not provide effective consumer remedies. Experience has shown that consumers are often unaware of their legal rights and, in any event, hesitate to take legal action to enforce such rights as they do know about. Consequently, the higher cost of special rules for consumer protection may be justified if the effect is to give fairer value to the large majority of consumers rather than to benefit the small number who are sufficiently well-informed and energetic to enforce their common law rights.

Disclosure of the Actual Cost of Credit

Consumer protection statutes of the 1960s, which dealt with door-to-door sales, also contained disclosure requirements for all contracts where a buyer of goods or services or a borrower of money repays the debt by instalments. They require sellers and lenders to give their customers a detailed statement of the terms of credit in dollars and cents and in percentage terms as an effective annual rate of interest, as well as any charges for insurance and registration fees. A customer is not bound by the contract if the seller fails to comply with the requirements.[48]

The purpose of this legislation was to make the costs of obtaining credit clearer to the prospective debtor, who would then find it easier to compare offers of credit and to shop prudently for the lowest effective rate of interest. However, it seems likely that the requirements benefit mainly those who are better educated and able to look after their own interests but are of little or no assistance to poor and ill-educated persons who are often charged unconscionable rates of interest because they are unable to evaluate competing offers of credit or lack the confidence to make inquiries. In other words, "truth in lending" offers a middle-class solution to a lower-class problem. It has sometimes been argued that if legislatures want to be more effective there are other ways of helping: they may set up bureaus to make credit advice available on a personal basis in poor areas, and perhaps even make loans available directly at reasonable rates.

Regulation of Businesses by Licensing, Bonding and Inspection

Consumer protection through licensing of businesses has been a method long in use. We have discussed the licensing of many professions in Chapter 5. Licensing is also used to regulate the providers of a variety of goods and services. A familiar example is the inspection and licensing of restaurants by municipal authorities to ensure sanitary conditions in the preparation of food.

Consumer legislation affecting door-to-door sales, to which we have already referred, led not only to cooling-off periods but also to the registration of door-to-door sellers. In addition, consumer protection acts may enable regulatory boards to suspend or revoke

---

[47] For a concise review of the literature see Ramsey, "Consumer Law and the Search for Empowerment", (1991) 19 C.B.L.J. 397.

[48] For example: Consumer Protection Act, R.S.B.C. 1979, c. 64, s. 26, as amended by S.B.C. 1980, c. 6; R.S.O. 1990, c. C–31, s. 31.

registration and to hear complaints.[49] All provinces prohibit door-to-door traders from continuing to sell unless they are registered so that the sanctions, if actively pursued, can be very effective.

Collection agencies—accused from time to time of using high pressure tactics and harassment to collect outstanding debts —are also subject to similar registration requirements.[50]

After some highly-publicized failures of travel agencies in the 1970s, in which consumers who had paid for holiday packages lost their money, some provinces passed legislation to license travel firms in much the same way as door-to-door sellers and collection agencies.[51] In addition, they required travel agents to be bonded in order to guarantee consumers against loss of prepaid travel and accommodation, or established Travel Assurance Funds to accomplish the same purpose.

Questions for Review

1. Compare the remedies of a buyer who is the victim of (a) fraudulent misrepresentation by the seller, and (b) breach of a term by the seller.
2. Is a buyer entitled to consider the contract at an end whenever the seller is guilty of a breach of condition?
3. When does the seller sue the buyer for damages for non-acceptance, and when does it sue for the price of the goods?
4. What use may an order bill of lading have that a straight bill of lading does not have?
5. If a seller tenders delivery of a larger quantity than the contract specifies and the buyer refuses to accept any part of the goods, may the seller sue successfully for damages for non-acceptance?
6. What are the rights of a seller that, before shipping goods that it has agreed to sell, learns that the buyer has a reputation for paying accounts slowly?
7. Describe some of the ways in which the common law and statute law in Canada prevent deceptive advertising.
8. A newspaper advertisement reads:

SPECIAL! SPECIAL!

For limited time only: $2.98

Regular price: $12.00

What facts would determine whether this advertisement is legal? What statute is relevant? What sanctions may be applied if the advertisement constitutes an offence under the statute?
9. In what respect, if any, does consumer protection legislation relating to unsolicited goods alter the common law rules for the formation of a contract by offer and acceptance?
10. Is the case for consumer protection regulation open-ended — the more the better? What constraints, if any, are there on the effectiveness of regulation?

---

[49] For example: Consumer Protection Act, R.S.O. 1990, c. C–31, s.5; Direct Sellers Act, R.S.S. 1978, c. 28, s. 4.

[50] For example: Collection Agencies Act, S.N.S. 1975, c. 7; R.S.O. 1990, c. C–14; Debt Collection Act, R.S.B.C. 1979, c. 88.

[51] For example: Travel Agents Act, R.S.B.C. 1979, c. 409; Travel Industry Act, R.S.O. 1990, c. T–19.

Problems

Problem 1

John Silver stops at the Admiral Benbow Inn and has a couple of bottles of ale. The ale contains arsenic and Silver becomes ill. He threatens to sue the owner of the inn. The owner protests that she has nothing to do with the contents of the bottles of ale she sells. Silver then threatens the brewery with legal action but it dissuades him by pointing out that the presence of the arsenic was not its fault because the poison was contained in sugar it had used in the brewing process. Silver then threatens to sue the sugar manufacturer but it claims that the fault lies with the manufacturer of acid used in the production of the sugar. Silver demands satisfaction from some quarter. Discuss his legal rights.

Problem 2

On December 30 Watson agreed to buy a set of cooking utensils for $400 from Never-Burn Pots & Pans Ltd. She signed a document and made a required cash payment of $150. The document stated that the set would be delivered "on or about January 15 next" and stated that "this contract is not cancellable". The contract made no reference to either party's rights to the cash payment in the event of breach. When the utensils were delivered to Watson on February 15, she refused to accept the articles and requested the return of the cash she had paid. In a letter to Watson dated February 18, Never-Burn Pots & Pans Ltd. stated, "We agree to cancel the contract as you requested, but according to the terms of the contract your failure to accept delivery means that you have automatically forfeited all the moneys paid thereunder." Watson sued to recover the $150 she had paid.

Examine the arguments available to each side and offer an opinion about the likely outcome. Does consumer protection legislation modify the position under the common law and if so, how?

Problem 3

On April 29, Christner agreed with Glassford, a sales agent of Mason & Risch Ltd., piano manufacturers, to buy a piano for $2700. On May 28, Christner telegraphed to Mason & Risch as follows:

> Dear Sir: This is to notify you that I hereby cancel my order for a Mason & Risch piano ordered through your local agent.

Christner also wrote Glassford a letter to the same effect.

Mason & Risch nevertheless shipped the piano to Christner, and when he refused to accept it, brought an action against him for the full price of $2700 or in the alternative for damages for non-acceptance. At the trial Christner's lawyer questioned an employee of Mason & Risch as follows:

> Q. What did you do about the selection of an instrument?
> A. We took it up immediately with the factory and had an instrument selected for Mr. Christner, and as soon as it was finished it was shipped.
> Q. Before it was finished did you get anything out of the way or out of the ordinary?
> A. I think we got a telegram from Mr. Christner and a telephone message from Mr. Glassford about it.

Evidence established that the manufacturer's profit on the sale of such a piano would be approximately $750.

What should be the court's decision?

Problem 4

VanDine purchased a second-hand Oldsmobile from True-Blue Auto Dealers under a contract that contained the following clause:

> No condition or warranty that the vehicle is roadworthy or as to its age, condition, or fitness is given by the seller or implied herein.

VanDine had inspected the car and found it to be in excellent condition, but it took her three weeks to arrange all the financing. The car was then delivered by the seller to VanDine's house late at night and left outside the garage. When VanDine inspected it the next morning, she found that it had the same serial and engine numbers and licence plates but had been badly damaged and stripped. It had evidently been towed to her place. The new tires had been taken off and old ones put on; the AM/FM radio had been removed; the chrome strips around the body were missing; the cylinder head was off the engine; all the valves were burnt; and there were two broken pistons.

VanDine had agreed to pay $4750 for the car but the mechanic at her neighbourhood service station estimated that it would cost her a further $2300 to restore the car to its former condition. VanDine immediately returned the car to True-Blue Auto Dealers. The finance company to which the dealer had assigned the contract then brought an action against VanDine for the amount due under it.

Discuss the legal issues raised by these facts and, with reasons, suggest a verdict.

Cases

Case 1

Wilson, a sales representative for Edible Meat Packers Ltd., persuaded Fowler, who operated a large mink ranch, to buy a quantity of Antarctic whale-meat in place of the Newfoundland whale-meat he was currently using for feed. The meat was from the first cargo of Antarctic whale-meat that Edible Packers had put on the market. When the whale-meat arrived in a refrigerated freight car, Fowler went to the freight yards to inspect it and did not like its appearance. He refused to take or pay for it unless he received a written assurance from Edible Meat Packers that it was safe. He received a letter to the effect that Edible Meat Packers had made a series of tests on its make-up and feeding qualities, and that the test feedings had obtained good results.

Fowler took delivery of the whale-meat and in the afternoon included it in a ration he placed on top of the cages where the mink could eat it as they required. Early the next morning Fowler went to his cages and found all the mink dead.

Fowler sued Edible Meat Packers for $25 000 in damages, the value of the mink that had been poisoned. It was established by expert evidence at the trial that the whale-meat had caused the death of the mink.

Give your opinion, with reasons, about the likely outcome of this action.

Case 2

In early December, Wendy Coates, the proprietor of the Sartorial Shop, contracted with the *Willowdale Weekly Advertiser* to insert the following advertisements on the dates mentioned:

December 15

Sartorial Shop's Pre-Christmas Clearance of coats, suits and dresses. 25% off. Your opportunity for Real Savings.

December 28

Sartorial Shop's Annual Post-Christmas Clearance Sale. Entire stock of coats, suits and dresses. 1/2 off. Your opportunity for Real Savings.

Through an error, the *Willowdale Weekly Advertiser* inserted the latter advertisement in the December 15 issue instead of in the December 28 issue. Coates immediately notified James Pressman, the owner of the paper, and insisted that as she was obligated now to sell her stock at a reduction of 50 per cent instead of 25 per cent, Pressman should be liable in damages for 25 per cent of the selling price of all articles sold out of stock before Christmas. Pressman offered to correct the mistake by a front-page story explaining the error, window signs, and any other measures available to him. Coates refused to have the matter corrected, however, stating that such a correction would appear to her customers as an attempt to avoid her liability to sell according to the terms of the advertisement, and that her customer goodwill would be lost and her integrity impugned. She proceeded to sell her stock to record crowds at a 50 per cent reduction in price.

Subsequently, Coates sued Pressman for $6000 as damages for breach of contract for advertising services. State with reasons whether the action should succeed.

Case 3

Koenig, who lived at Niagara-on-the-Lake, read the following advertisement in a Toronto paper:

Owner moving to California next weekend. Sacrificing 10-m. cabin cruiser. Very seaworthy. Sleeps 4, 2 cabins. Fantastic buy for cash.

Koenig then made an appointment by telephone with the vendor, Foote, to see the boat in Toronto. He inspected the boat and asked various questions about the type of construction, age, and whether it was a good family boat. Foote told him that the boat was about twenty years old and that he had used it for three or four years as a family boat. When Koenig inquired about its seaworthiness and how it handled in rough weather, Foote replied he had been out when the waves were ten feet high, and "it came through O.K." Foote told him that the hull tended to be spongy in the water but dried out in the winter, and that it was "in good condition in my opinion". Koenig asked further about the hull, and Foote replied that it was made of ash and had been repaired. Koenig took up a few floor boards to check for water in the bilges, and Foote told him that it shipped quite a bit of water when under way but that the pump was ample to take care of it. Koenig said that he was inexperienced about boats and asked Foote for tips on the care of the boat; Foote replied that there was nothing to do except, perhaps, some work on the valves and rings of the engine. The parties then agreed upon a price of $8700. Koenig asked if Foote would help deliver the boat to Niagara-on-the-Lake. Koenig, Foote, and two of Foote's children took the boat across the lake, running into some heavy seas en route. On arrival Koenig paid Foote the $8700.

Koenig left his new boat docked at a marina and on returning three days later learned that the pump had been working continuously. The boat was hauled out of the water, and he discovered that the hull was in very bad condition due to dry rot; the estimate for necessary repairs or rebuilding was for $3400.

Koenig sued Foote for damages for fraudulent misrepresentation or in the alternative for breach of contract. State with reasons whether you think this action should succeed.

Case 4

Medusa Electric Ltd. assembled hair dryers for a large national department store. It approached Perseus Products Inc. about the possible manufacture and supply of motors for the hair dryers. Medusa Electric specified the type of motors it required by sending Perseus Products a sample hair dryer completely assembled with a motor included. It did not indicate in any way what type of lubricating oil the manufacturer of the motor should use, nor did it provide any information about the nature of the composition material used in the plastic fan to be attached to each motor in assembling the hair dryers. (The plastic fan was to be supplied to Medusa Electric by another manufacturer.)

Perseus Products then manufactured its own model of the motor provided in the sample hair dryer and submitted it to Medusa Electric for testing. The lubricant used by Perseus Products was of the best quality and one customarily used by it in the manufacture of motors for other customers. On July 4, Medusa Electric gave a written purchase order for 10 000 motors to Perseus Products. The latter company then returned a written confirmation on its letterhead that stated:

> We will repair or replace at no charge if defective material or workmanship is demonstrated within one year of shipment. However, we do not guarantee suitability of our product for your application.

Shortly afterwards, Medusa Electric asked that the splines attached to the shaft in the motor be modified to give more "bite" when attached to the fan. Perseus Products then submitted a further model of the motor with a modified spline approved by Medusa Electric. It then proceeded to manufacture and deliver the 10 000 motors. Medusa Electric used the motors in the assembly of the hair dryers sold to the department store.

Following the sale of the hair dryers by the department store, nearly half were returned by dissatisfied customers under the store's "satisfaction or money cheerfully refunded" policy. An investigation of the defective hair dryers revealed that when the shaft with the splines was attached to the fan, tension was created that brought about cracking in the fan, making many of the dryers inoperative. To make matters worse, some oil leaked down the shaft and came in contact with the fan; the oil reacted with the particular plastic of which the fan was made, causing further cracking.

The department store refused to pay Medusa Electric for the hair dryers and Medusa Electric sued Perseus Products for the damages it had sustained.

Formulate the main question or questions to which the court must find an answer and then indicate with reasons whether the action is likely to succeed.

CHAPTER 20

INSURANCE AND GUARANTEE

THE NATURE OF INSURANCE

In its simplest terms, a contract of insurance is a method for shifting a risk of loss; that is, a method of purchasing protection against a possible loss. Not only does insurance *shift* the risk of loss from the person purchasing the protection, it also *spreads* the risk among a number of parties who have agreed to take a share in the risk.

ILLUSTRATION

Fifty farmers in a county agree at a meeting to form a contract of mutual fire insurance with one another: each promises to pay 1/50th of any loss suffered by fire by any other of the 50 in return for the promises of the others to pay collectively the whole of any loss suffered by him through fire (less his own 1/50th). Thus, when farmer A sustains a loss of $100 000, each of the other 49 will pay him $2000 for a total of $9800.

Such an agreement contains all the usual elements of an insurance contract, but it would have two great disadvantages: (a) it would require the farmer who suffered the loss to collect 1/50th from each farmer, an impractical task; and (b) the potential loss each farmer could suffer would vary greatly according to the value of his property, and the relative safety of the property because of its construction, use, or proximity to fire-fighting equipment. A farmer whose property consisted of $400 000 worth of fire-resistant buildings would not be happy to exchange his promise with a neighbour who had $1 000 000 worth of hazardous buildings; he would be taking a much greater chance of having to pay his neighbour $20 000 in a total loss than of receiving from him only $8000 in a less likely total loss of his own buildings.

The two disadvantages in the above illustration may be overcome in the following ways: (a) the money can be collected *in advance* to form a fund available to pay claims for losses suffered, and used for investment until it is required to pay claims; and (b) the *amount* of money collected from each insured can be so calculated that it bears a direct relationship to the risk being assumed, that is, the total possible amount of loss and the probability of that loss occurring. The insurance business proceeds on just these principles. However, instead of a group of risk-bearers getting together and agreeing on a cooperative basis to insure one another, an insurance company operates independently as a central agency for insuring risks and administering the funds collected. The insurance company calculates the payment required to insure a particular risk on the basis of experience with the type of risk in question, as summarized in actuarial tables. The amount it charges is also calculated to produce a surplus: it aims for an excess of money received for insuring risks over amounts paid out in claims and amounts set aside as reserves to meet unexpectedly large claims. The surplus may be paid out in dividends to shareholders or, in the case of a mutual insurance company, returned to policy holders.

We see, then, that insurance achieves a pooling of risks so that a large number of lucky participants subsidize the losses of a relatively few unlucky ones, and that typically an insurance company acts as intermediary in this process. Indeed, the need to spread the risk operates even among insurance companies themselves. When an insurance company contracts to provide insurance protection for a particularly large single risk — say, accepts a fire-insurance application on a $50 000 000 plant — the insurance company may re-insure a part of this risk with one or more other insurance companies. In the event of a claim, the loss is then spread among a number of insurance companies. Some international financial institutions, notably Swiss concerns, have specialized in providing re-insurance of this kind for smaller insurance companies.

INSURANCE TERMINOLOGY

An *insurance policy* is written evidence of the terms of an insurance contract. The insurance company providing the protection is called the *insurer;* the party contracting for the insurance protection is the *insured.*[1] The *premium* is the price paid by the insured for the insurance coverage specified in the policy. The premium may be paid in a single sum, but more usually it is paid yearly or at some other shorter interval throughout the term of the insurance.

The four basic aspects of an insurance contract are the nature of the risk covered, the amount for which it is insured, the duration of the protection, and the amount of the premium. The terms of a policy may require the insurer to pay the insurance money, in the event of a claim, either to the insured or to the insured's estate or to some other person designated as *beneficiary*. When an insured requires supplementary coverage, that is, wider protection than is available under the insurer's standard form policy, additional clauses are incorporated in the contract by attaching them to the policy in a separate insertion called a *rider*. When the parties agree to a change in the terms of an existing insurance contract, they may do so without rewriting the entire policy, by attaching a separate paper or *endorsement* to the face of the policy.

An *insurance agent* acts for a principal, the insurer, to arrange insurance contracts with persons seeking protection for themselves or for beneficiaries. In practice an insurance agent often renders a service to the insured as well, by offering advice about the appropriate coverage. The result has caused confusion about the role and responsibilities of the agent; English courts have held that an agent who fills in an application form for the insured acts as agent for the insured rather than for the insurer, but this view has not been followed by the Supreme Court of Canada.[2]

An *insurance broker* generally acts for the insured rather than for the insurer. As we shall see, a business is exposed to many types of risk and, accordingly, will often find it worthwhile to consult a specialist in insurance problems — a broker — who will determine the coverage required, and arrange insurance with the companies best suited to provide it at a minimum cost to the insured. However, the distinction between an agent and a broker is not always a clear one and it is possible in some cases for an agent/broker to be considered to be acting as agent for both the insurer and the insured.[3]

---

[1] In life insurance we must distinguish between the *insured* and the *life insured* when the subject of the insurance is the life of someone *other* than the party contracting for insurance.

[2] Newsholme Brothers v. Road Transport and General Insurance Co. Ltd., [1929] 2 K.B. 356, and Blanchette v. C.I.S. Ltd. (1973), 36 D.L.R. (3rd) 561.

[3] For a fuller discussion see Tuytel, "Agents' and Brokers' Liability: taking Stock a dozen Years after *Fine's Flowers*", (1991) 3 *Canadian Insurance Law Rev.* 115.

An *insurance adjuster* is an expert in the appraisal of property losses and offers these services to insurance companies for a fee. When a claim has been made, the adjuster gives an opinion to the insurer about whether the loss is covered by the insurance contract and, if so, what the amount of the loss is.

Generally speaking, insurance falls into two classes — *personal* insurance and *property* insurance. Personal insurance includes life insurance, hospital and medical insurance, accident and sickness disability insurance, and workers' compensation. All other types of insurance are property insurance. Life insurance is unique in that the risk insured against is certain to materialize sooner or later, though in the case of *term* insurance, it may not occur during the period covered by the policy.

$\mathcal{S}$TATUTE LAW REGULATING INSURANCE

Each of the provinces has one or more statutes regulating the practice of the insurance business within its borders. The main purposes of these statutes are to protect the public by requiring responsible operation on the part of insurance companies and others in the business, to protect both parties by making certain terms mandatory, and to provide a series of implied terms that apply when the parties have not expressly dealt with their subject-matter. Among other matters, the statutes do the following things: authorize the appointment of a superintendent of insurance who oversees the operations and financial responsibility of licensed insurers within the province; specify licensing requirements for insurers, agents, brokers, and adjusters; describe the terms that must be included in insurance policies; outline the nature of risks not covered unless expressly included in an insurance contract; define the extent to which an insurer may limit its liability; state the effect of misrepresentation on the contract, and the effect of suicide on life insurance; set out the conditions for an insurable interest; give formal recognition to the rights of beneficiaries and assignees; and prescribe the nature of the proof to which an insurer is entitled before it must pay a claim.

In addition to these provincial statutes, the federal Insurance Companies Act[4] provides for compulsory registration of federal and foreign insurance companies desiring to carry on insurance business in Canada, and also for voluntary registration of provincial insurance companies. Its aim is to ensure financial stability in the insurance industry by providing a system of inspection and by requiring statements and returns from these companies. The Act describes the types of securities in which the companies may invest their funds, the amounts of assets they must maintain in Canada, and the methods of computing minimum required reserves. It also sets out the means by which an insurance company may be federally incorporated.

In the next three parts of this chapter we shall describe briefly those types of insurance that are most commonly encountered in business.

---

[4] S.C. 1991, c. 47.

INSURANCE ON BUSINESS PREMISES AND OTHER ASSETS

Fire Insurance and Insurance Against Damage by Natural Elements

While fire insurance affords protection against loss by fire damage to buildings and contents (inventory, fixtures, and equipment), it is important to understand that the liability of the insurer sometimes does not extend to a variety of losses incidental to the fire, nor to fires attributable to certain specified causes. Thus, a fire insurance policy may not cover some of the following types of risk:

(a) losses of books of account, business papers, money, and similar items;

(b) theft of money or merchandise during the fire;

(c) loss of property belonging to others, kept on the premises;

(d) medical expenses of persons injured by the fire;

(e) loss of profits caused by suspended business operations while the property is being restored;

(f) increased hazard from a subsequent change in the nature of business operations or from subsequent vacancy of the premises;

(g) fire loss resulting from explosives kept on the property;

(h) damage caused by a fire used for heating or industrial purposes under the control of the insured;

(i) damage caused by riots, or invasion, of which the fire may be a part; or

(j) damage intentionally caused by the insured.[5]

An insured should check precisely which risks are covered in the insurer's standard policy and may be able to obtain protection against additional risks by having special terms inserted to that effect in the policy and paying a higher premium.

In most instances an insurer is liable either for the cost of repairing damaged property or for the value of the destroyed property. Value takes into account the condition of the property immediately before destruction. One may purchase insurance for full replacement value, but this higher protection is more expensive. In any event, one is wise to review the replacement value from time to time in order to make sure that protection is adequate; inflation or changes in building by-law requirements may make existing insurance inadequate.

When a debtor mortgages insured property to a lender as security for a loan, the lender (mortgagee) should see that the policy contains a *mortgage clause*. This clause requires that in the event of a claim the proceeds shall be paid first to the mortgagee "as his interest may appear", with the balance payable to the insured, and that insofar as the mortgagee has an interest, the insurance shall not be invalidated by any act or neglect of the insured.

In addition to fire insurance, an insured may arrange supplementary coverage against loss by water (rain, snow, or flood), wind, and earthquake. Farmers commonly buy insurance against damage to their crops by wind, storm and hail; and also participate in government-supported schemes to insure against crop failure caused by drought or blight.

---

[5] This exclusion may prevent recovery for damage intentionally caused by any other person whose property is also insured under the policy; see Scott v. Wawanesa Mutual Insurance Co. (1989), 59 D.L.R.(4th) 660, where the fire resulted from arson committed by the son of the named insured.

Businesses often make extensive use of plate-glass, which is costly to replace. Fire insurance covers the cost of replacement if the breakage is caused by a fire, but not otherwise, and the glass may be broken by such occurrences as automobile accidents, burglary, or a nearby explosion. Most businesses take out plate-glass insurance to protect against these risks.

Automobile Insurance

A business normally insures against loss of, or damage to, its vehicles; it also insures against injury to third persons and their property caused by the operation of those vehicles. Such insurance against third party liability is now compulsory and most provinces have introduced a compulsory system of "no fault" automobile insurance. This type of system provides for automatic compensation of automobile accident victims, regardless of who is to blame for the accident.

An automobile insurance contract typically contains a *deductible clause* stating that the insured shall pay the first $250 (or some higher amount) in respect of each claim. A deductible feature gives the insured a greater incentive to take care of the insured property and, by eliminating a large number of small claims, makes the insurance much cheaper.

Credit Insurance

A business may obtain protection against bad-debt losses by insuring the collection of its accounts receivable with a commercial credit insurance company. The insurer's assessment of the credit-worthiness of the customer-debtors whose accounts it insures determines the cost of the insurance. The risk of loss may be greater if the debtor resides outside Canada. A government agency, the Export Development Corporation, sells insurance to Canadian exporting businesses to protect them against the inability to collect the accounts of foreign customers.

A form of credit insurance may also be obtained by selling accounts receivable to a *factor*. A factoring business sometimes discounts book debts *without recourse* — that is, if the accounts it buys prove uncollectable, it has no recourse against the business from which it bought them.

Marine Insurance

This type of insurance protects against loss of a ship, its cargo, or equipment caused by perils at sea, including sinking, stranding, burning, collision, contact with sea water, and even piracy and mutiny. Marine insurance may be written for a specific voyage or a fixed period of time, depending on the nature of the risk. Although marine insurance is primarily intended to cover loss or damage at sea, it may also cover transportation by inland waterway or even by rail and road, as for example where part of a journey is by sea and part by land.

Marine insurance is one of the oldest forms of insurance and has developed somewhat independently from other forms. Certain rules or principles apply that are not found in other branches of insurance; for example, a marine insurance contract may include a *lost or not lost* clause by which the insurer becomes liable for a loss that, unknown to the parties, may already have occurred at the time the contract is written.

Marine insurance for perils at sea is often referred to as *wet marine* to distinguish it from *inland marine*. Inland marine insurance, also commonly called *general* insurance, covers many hazards to personal property situated on land and not covered by ordinary insurance contracts, such as damage to a contractor's equipment or farm implements from any cause other than natural deterioration.

Fidelity Insurance

Fidelity insurance protects against losses caused by the fraud or theft of employees of the insured. The policy is called a *fidelity bond,* and the insurer is usually called a *bonding company*.

Theft Insurance

Theft insurance provides protection against the unlawful taking of personal property of the insured. The policy may limit the liability of the insurer to a relatively small amount (well below the total amount of the policy) for losses of cash, negotiable securities, and jewellery — items easily carried off and disposed of by thieves — to encourage their proper safekeeping.

More limited and, hence, less expensive protection may be obtained by restricting the insurer's liability to loss by *robbery* (taking by force) or *burglary* (theft by unlawfully entering the insured's premises).

INSURANCE ON THE OPERATION OF A BUSINESS

Business Interruption Insurance

As we have seen, insurance payable for damage caused to business property by a fire does not neccessarily include compensation for the loss of profits that ensues when a business firm is unable to operate for a time following the fire, or for the costs of moving to temporary quarters. Business interruption insurance protects an insured business against these risks by paying compensation as follows: (a) an amount equal to the loss of profit; (b) expenses that necessarily continue even when the business is not operating; (c) money expended to reduce business losses (for example, the cost of moving to temporary quarters or overtime wages to hasten repairs).

The cost of this insurance varies with the rate of net operating profit estimated by the insured, the variety of expenses classified by the insured as fixed charges, and the maximum period for which the coverage is sought. The insured may also choose to insure the payment of all employees' wages and salaries for the same period as the business interruption or for some shorter maximum period. The policy may terminate compensation as soon as the damage caused by the fire has been repaired, or it may extend compensation until business profits return to normal.

Life Insurance on Lives of Key Officers

A business has a considerable investment in the training and development of its management, and in the event of the premature death of one of its officers must often incur further expense in training and developing a replacement. For this reason it has an insurable interest in its executives and may insure their lives. The insurance premiums are a business expense, and the proceeds of the insurance paid on death belong to the business.

In a partnership, each partner's interest in the firm is a part of the partner's personal estate and becomes payable to the estate after his or her death. To assist in settling with the estate of any one of them who may die, partners frequently carry life insurance on one another's lives. This form of insurance provides a fund enabling the surviving partners to pay to the estate the value of the deceased partner's share in the firm. A partnership may thus avoid the risk of having to liquidate valuable assets to raise the money needed for settlement. Similar arrangements are also common in small corporations, where principal shareholders insure each others' lives for the same purpose.

Public Liability Insurance

Businesses continuously face possible liability for injury to members of the public or their property. The harm may result from defective equipment or the negligent acts of proprietors or employees in the ordinary course of business. The liability of an employer for employees' torts is discussed in Chapters 4 and 23.

Examples of this type of risk are the possibility of injuries to customers in a retail store; to passengers in a train, bus, ship, or plane operated by a common carrier; to theatre patrons, through panic in a fire or riot; and to pedestrians or motorists and their property in accidents with business vehicles. Various forms of insurance are available to indemnify a business for the liability it may incur in many situations. As we saw in the preceding section, automobile and marine insurance normally protect against liability to third parties. Manufacturing and distributing companies may also obtain *product* insurance to protect against liability to members of the public who sustain injury in their use of the product sold.

Practising members of a profession may, and in some professions are required to, obtain *professional liability* insurance to indemnify themselves for losses payable to clients or patients as damages awarded against them for negligence. Similarly, the directors of corporations may obtain liability insurance as protection against the possibility of actions brought against them by shareholders or creditors for breach of their duty of care, diligence and skill.

A bailee, such as a carrier, repairer, or warehousing firm, may be liable for loss or damage to property in its care, and consequently may seek insurance protection. A bailee may decide to insure only its own liability, or may insure for the full value of the goods so that in the event of a total loss the customer will be fully compensated. The cost of additional insurance is ordinarily passed on to the customer. We shall discuss the liability of a bailee in the next chapter.

Rather than issue a variety of policies, each providing protection for certain types of activity or against specific risks, the modern tendency has increasingly been to issue *comprehensive general liability* insurance. Because of its broader scope such insurance tends to be expensive, though it may well turn out to be cheaper than purchasing a whole series of separate policies insuring against specific risks. The great advantage to the insured lies in the comprehensiveness of the coverage; unexpected risks are insured against rather than falling between the cracks of two or more separate policies. The insurer, however, may find that it will have to pay for unanticipated liabilities, such as those resulting from pollution and "toxic torts", for example, where a building of the insured is found to have asbestos insulation.[6]

---

[6] See Dolden, "The Comprehensive General Liability Policy: Responding to Modern Business Rules", (1990/91) 2 *Canadian Insurance Law Rev.* 11.

INSURANCE FOR EMPLOYEES

Hospital and Medical Insurance

The premiums for this type of insurance are sometimes a joint responsibility of employer and employee, with the employee making contributions through regular payroll deductions. Although the employer may contribute towards the premiums, claims are payable by the insurer to the employee. A plan of this kind may also include group life insurance coverage for employees.

Workers' Compensation Insurance

As we shall see in Chapter 23, an employer's liability to employees for injuries sustained in the course of employment has now been resolved over a wide area by statutes providing for compulsory workers' compensation insurance. A provincial government is in effect the insurer, though it delegates the administration of the insurance to a workers' compensation board. Employers to whom the legislation applies must make payments — in effect, premiums — to the board on behalf of their employees, who are beneficiaries of any claims made.

THE NEED FOR COMPLETE INSURANCE PROTECTION

The complexity of potential liability for many businesses is such that they cannot rely on their own resources to decide on insurance coverage. They need the advice of a specialist in the field such as an experienced insurance agent or broker.

ILLUSTRATION

"Some years ago there was a very prosperous manufacturing concern in a western Ontario city engaged in metal work. Their rented premises formed part of a large block. Their policies were placed through their auditor who sold insurance on the side. One day an employee was drawing off a gallon of varsol from a 48-gallon drum. Nearby was a large vat filled with paint through which an endless chain carried metal stampings. It was a warm, humid day and the employee had forgotten to turn off an open gas jet only a few feet away from the varsol. As he stood there he was suddenly paralyzed by the sight of a blue flame creeping towards him along the floor. It reached the open bucket; a tremendous explosion followed that quickly ignited the paint in the open vat. So intense were the flames that the workmen did not bother to use the doors; they got out through the windows. By the time the local brigade brought the fire under control, the place was a shambles. Valuable machinery was destroyed. Stock belonging to others and in process was ruined. The building was seriously damaged, and the fire had spread to the manufacturers on both sides, damaging their stock and equipment and merchandise."[7]

---

[7] Edson L. Haines, "Business Risks and Insurance Coverage", from *Counselling the Average Businessman*, p. 240. Special Lectures of the Law Society of Upper Canada. Toronto: Richard De Boo Limited, 1954. In the actual case, the insurance policy had included a restriction on the amount of inflammable liquid that could be kept on the premises, so that even the validity of the insurance contract was in question.

We may assume that the fire was caused by the negligence of the manufacturing concern, either through faulty precautions of management or the carelessness of the employee acting in the course of employment. What then are the potential losses in a situation like the one described?

(a) Injuries sustained by employees and others;
(b) loss to the landlord of the factory building and of revenue from it;
(c) loss to adjoining businesses of equipment, merchandise, and, if their operations were interrupted, of profits;
(d) losses sustained by the manufacturing concern itself resulting from being put out of business for some time. It will not only lose its profits during that period but will still remain liable for salaries under employment contracts. Other fixed costs such as municipal taxes will also continue to accrue.

The manufacturing concern will have liability to third parties in respect of the first three of these types of loss. It may have liability for injuries to employees who are not covered by workers' compensation. The landlord and adjoining occupiers will probably have their own insurance to cover losses of types (b) and (c), respectively, but to the extent that their claims are paid by their insurers, those insurers will become subrogated to their rights against the manufacturer.[8]

Various forms of insurance policies and riders are available to protect manufacturers in circumstances of the kind described — comprehensive general liability insurance, composite mercantile fire insurance on equipment and goods of others, and business interruption insurance, for example. A business that operates as a tenant may either contract directly for fire insurance coverage in relation to the part of the building it occupies, or arrange with the landlord to be added to the landlord's policy as an insured party. For each business operation the nature of the risks should be discussed and the appropriate insurance coverage decided, in consultation with an expert in the field.

$\mathcal{S}$PECIAL ASPECTS OF THE CONTRACT OF INSURANCE

Offer and Acceptance

The Offer

In the formation of a contract of insurance, a proposal by an insurance agent is usually just an invitation to do business, and not an offer. The eventual offer is made ordinarily by the party seeking the insurance protection — the prospective insured — on signing the application form. What, then, constitutes acceptance by the insurer? We need to know so that we can tell when the insurance is in force.

Life Insurance

With life insurance, the applicant's offer is not accepted until the insurance company delivers the policy; moreover, it is a condition precedent to delivery of the policy that the

---

8   The issue of subrogation is dealt with later in this Chapter, at p. 429.

first premium shall have been paid by the insured.[9] But it may take some time for the head office of an insurance company to prepare the policy for delivery: is the insured protected in any way in the interval between signing the application form and taking delivery of the policy? The answer depends upon the wording of the application form and related form for acknowledging receipt of the premium. Many life insurance companies include an *interim insurance* provision as a term in the receipt form given for the payment of the first premium. This provision gives the insured protection from the time of signing the application, provided that the first premium accompanies the application and that medical information or the results of any medical examination would be acceptable to the company on the terms proposed in the application. Such interim insurance expires once the insurer delivers the policy to the insured.

Property Insurance

Making contracts for property insurance is typically less formal than for life insurance. An agent dealing in property insurance may have an agency contract with each of a number of insurers. Each such contract gives the agent authority to sign and deliver policies and renewal certificates and generally to bind the insurer concerned; a business seeking property insurance can obtain the desired protection immediately, before paying the premium or receiving a policy. The agent need only prepare a memorandum or *binder* for the agency's records as evidence of the time and nature of the request for insurance. When immediate protection is required, an insured should be satisfied that the agent has an agency contract with the proposed insurer.

Renewal of Policy

Property insurance is written for a limited period (usually for one year). A common practice is for an insurance agent to prepare a renewal policy or memorandum and send it to the insured shortly before the current policy expires; the agent takes this method of reminding clients that their insurance protection is about to cease if not renewed. But unless there is evidence of an agreement between the agent and the insured that they intend the mere delivery of a renewal policy or memorandum to create a new contract of insurance, or such an agreement can be inferred from their past dealings with one another, the agent's act of delivering the renewal policy amounts to no more than making an offer to the insured.[10] No contract is formed until the insured communicates acceptance, and as the offer is open at most for a reasonable length of time, the insured cannot wait indefinitely to express assent.

Since an insurance agent normally acts for the insurer and not for the insured, any question of the agent's making a contract of insurance for the insured without the latter's authority, and subject to the insured's ratification, will rarely arise.[11] And even if the agent acts outside the scope of his actual authority, the insurer will be bound unless the insured knew of the lack of authority.[12]

---

[9] See, for example: Insurance Act, R.S.B.C. 1979, c. 200, s. 131; R.S.O. 1990, c. I-8, s. 157; R.S.N.S. 1989, c. 231, s. 182. In subsequent footnotes in this chapter, references to B.C., Ont., and N.S. will be to these statutes.

[10] Luke's Electric Motors & Machinery Ltd. v. Halifax Insurance Co. (1953), 10 W.W.R.(N.S.) 539 at 542-3; de Mezey v. Milwaukee Mechanics' Insurance Co., [1945] 1 W.W.R. 644.

[11] An insurance agent may still owe a duty of care to the insured to obtain suitable insurance: see discussion of Fine's Flowers Ltd. v. Central Accident Assurance Co. (1978), 81 D.L.R. (3rd) 139, in Chapter 5, under "Negligent Omissions".

[12] Wendeb Properties Inc. v. Elite Insurance Management Ltd. (1991), 53 B.C.L.R.(2d) 246. The question of apparent authority of an agent is discussed in Chapter 22.

Legality of Object

Wrongful Acts of the Insured

In our discussion of legality of object in Chapter 9 we noted that insurance is available against the consequences of the negligence of an insured person, or an insured business and its employees, but that the courts refuse on grounds of public policy to enforce a contract of insurance when the claim arises out of a criminal or deliberate tortious act of the insured.[13] Before a court will disallow a claim on this ground, however, the insurer must show that the loss was the reasonable or probable result of the wrongful act.

Insurable Interest

Chapter 9 has also distinguished an insurance contract from a wager by the fact that the insured has an insurable interest, so that the contract shifts a genuine risk of loss from the insured to the insurer. In that chapter, we defined an insurable interest as the measure of loss suffered by the insured from damage to or destruction of the thing insured. We did not say anything, however, about the time at which the insured must have the insurable interest. The answer depends upon whether the insurance is on property or on a life.

When a contract is for property insurance, as we noted in Chapter 9, under "Agreements Void by Statute", the insured must have an insurable interest at the time the contract was formed or the contract is void. Moreover, since the purpose of insurance is to indemnify for loss suffered, the insured must still have an interest at the time the claim arises; otherwise there will be no loss to be recovered by the insured.[14] The question of what constitutes an insurable interest can be a source of difficulty. In a leading English case, the House of Lords held that a shareholder who owned most of the shares in a company had no insurable interest in its principal asset, a quantity of timber destroyed in a fire; the loss was solely that of the company itself.[15] However, the Supreme Court of Canada has more recently held that a sufficient insurable interest exists where an insured can demonstrate a relation to, or concern in, the insured property so that damage to it will cause a loss to the insured.[16] Thus, a person who owned all the shares in a company was held to have an insurable interest in the property of the company, because damage to that property would necessarily reduce the value of his shares. The Court's reasoning suggests that any person holding a substantial proportion of a company's shares would have an insurable interest in its property; it is unclear whether a holder of only a small proportion would be found to have an interest.

When the contract is for life insurance, the person buying the insurance must either (a) obtain the written consent of the person whose life is to be insured, or (b) have an insurable interest at the time the contract is formed, though not necessarily at the time of death of the person whose life is insured.[17] Thus, if a creditor has insured the life of its debtor for the amount of the debt and that sum proves to be more than the balance owing at the time of the debtor's death, the policy is valid and the creditor remains entitled to the full

---

[13]   Beresford v. Royal Insurance Co., [1938] A.C. 586; Acklands Ltd. v. Canadian Indemnity Co. (1985), 8 C.C.L.I. 163.

[14]   Howard v. Lancashire Insurance Co. (1885), 11 S.C.R. 92.

[15]   Macaura v. Northern Assurance Co., [1925] A.C. 619.

[16]   Kosmopoulos v. Constitution Insurance Co. (1987), 34 D.L.R. (4th) 208.

[17]   See, for example: B.C., s. 129(2)(b); Ont., s. 178(2)(b); N.S., s. 180(2)(b).

value of the policy.[18] This arrangement, however, is not as common as one where a creditor requires its debtor to obtain life insurance, pay the premiums, and make the creditor a beneficiary for the amount of the debt. If at the death of the debtor the amount owing is then less than the value of the policy, the balance is paid to the debtor's estate.

Terms of the Contract

Standard Form

Chapter 6 referred to an insurance policy as an example of a standard form contract since it is prepared unilaterally in advance by one of the contracting parties (the insurer). To offset this advantage for insurers, the courts subject such contracts to a strict interpretation of the words they contain: they construe words most strongly against the party using them, as we noted in Chapter 13. They take the attitude, for example, that clauses exempting an insurer from liability in specific circumstances must be stated in clear and unambiguous terms in order to be binding.[19]

Utmost Good Faith

In our discussion of misrepresentation in Chapter 11 we noted that an insurer may avoid liability if it can show that the insured did not exercise the utmost good faith in the application for insurance. In one respect, the requirement of utmost good faith on the part of the insured has traditionally been particularly strict: an insured may be unable to collect for a claim even when it has arisen from causes unrelated to facts that the insured should have disclosed, but did not disclose. However, some recent Canadian decisions have mitigated the rule. For example, a statement by the insured that a nightwatchman would be present on the premises every night was held not to be material when the loss occurred in the afternoon.[20] And the insured need not disclose information of a general nature that should be well known to the insurer: an asbestos manufacturer was not required to inform its insurer that there were health risks related to working with asbestos, so long as the likelihood of exposure to asbestos was disclosed.[21]

An insurer may insert terms in an insurance contract in order to extend the obligation of the insured even beyond that imposed by the requirement of utmost good faith. The application form signed by the party seeking insurance may contain a provision that the applicant warrants the *accuracy* — not merely the *truthfulness* — of any declarations made. If in these circumstances an applicant for life insurance replies in the negative to the question, "Have you any disease?" and proves later to have had a disease of which he or she was unaware and which was perhaps not even revealed by a medical examination, the insurer may avoid its liability. Wording of this kind amounts to an abuse of the standard form contract by the insurer, and whenever such wording has been used the courts have insisted on strict proof by the insurer that the question was answered inaccurately.[22]

---

18   Dalby v. The India & London Life (1854), 139 E.R. 465.
19   See, for example: Indemnity Insurance Co. v. Excel Cleaning Service, [1954] 2 D.L.R. 721, per Estey, J., at 730.
20   Case Existological Laboratories Ltd. v. Century Insurance Co. (1982), 133 D.L.R. (3rd) 727.
21   Canadian Indemnity Co. v. Canadian Johns-Mansville Co. [1990] 2 S.C.R. 549.
22   See Furmston, *Cheshire, Fifoot and Furmston's Law of Contract* (12th ed.), p. 292-93.

The Insurance Act limits to two years the insurer's right to rescind life insurance contracts on grounds of inaccurate statements or non-disclosure by the insured.[23] This limitation does not extend to fraudulent statements made by the insured or to erroneous statements about the insured's age.

Promptness of Notice

Insurance contracts other than for life insurance contain a statutory term that the insured shall notify the insurer promptly of any change that is material to the risk and within the control or knowledge of the insured. Such a term then gives the insurer the option of either cancelling the insurance and returning the unexpired portion of the premium, or of informing the insured that the insurance will continue only on payment of an increased premium. Prompt notice by the insured in these circumstances is a condition precedent, so that the insurer is absolved from liability under the policy if it does not receive such notice.

Such insurance contracts also contain a term requiring the insured to notify the insurer promptly of any loss that occurs. Failure to give notice promptly may free the insurer from liability to pay the claim.

Assignment

Life Insurance

A life insurance policy of the type that accumulates a cash surrender value is an item of property — a chose in action — which the insured may assign for value, for example, by giving a conditional assignment of the policy to a bank as security for a loan. If the insured defaults on the loan, the bank is entitled to the cash surrender value up to the amount due on the loan.

The insurer's consent to an assignment of life insurance is not necessary, although the insurer is entitled to notice. The risk of the insurer is not affected by an assignment of the benefits of a life insurance contract. The consent of the beneficiary, however, is necessary for a valid assignment where the insured has deliberately chosen to make an irrevocable designation of that beneficiary.[24]

Property Insurance

As contrasted with life insurance, property insurance is not assignable without the consent of the insurer; in fact, novation is necessary. The reason for this rule is that an assignment substitutes a new person as the insured, and the personal qualities of the insured may be pertinent to the risk assumed by the insurer. When a person sells a house or an automobile, there is usually unexpired insurance on the property. It is not possible simply to impose a new owner of the property on the insurer; the new owner may have habits affecting the property that alter the risk of insuring it. A purchaser must therefore renegotiate the insurance with the insurer, possibly at different premium rates. On the other hand, *after* a risk materializes and an insurance claim is established, an insured may assign the claim (say, to creditors) without the consent of the insurer.

---

[23] See, for example: B.C., ss. 134-7; Ont., ss. 183-6; N.S., ss. 185-7.
[24] See, for example: B.C., ss. 141-2; Ont., ss. 190-1; N.S., ss. 192-3.

Subrogation

The principle that an insured may not recover more than the amount of his loss does not mean that he may not claim against the insurer because he happens also to have a right of action against the person who caused the loss. Thus, if a storeowner has obtained fire insurance for his premises and suffers a loss as a result of a fire negligently caused by his neighbour, he can recover from his own insurance company without having to sue the neighbour. On the other hand, he cannot recover twice over: if he were subsequently to sue the neighbour and recover damages that, when added to his insurance compensation would give him a sum in excess of his loss, he would hold that excess in trust for his insurer. As a result, so long as he is fully insured, he will have no incentive to sue his neighbour.

If that ended the matter, many wrongdoers would escape liability for their careless acts. However, under a general principles of insurance law, when an insurer has paid a claim it is entitled to "step into the shoes of the insured", and sue the person liable for the loss. This right of *subrogation* does not apply to all cases but, unless it is expressly excluded, it will generally be presumed to apply.[25]

CO-INSURANCE

Since it is common knowledge that few fires result in a total loss, a person or business applying for fire insurance may well think of saving premium costs by insuring the property for only a part of its total value. Fire insurance companies, concerned that such a practice might decrease their revenues substantially, often insert a clause in the insurance contract stating that an insured that does not purchase coverage of at least a stated percentage of the value of the property (usually 80%) will become a co-insurer, along with the insurance company, for any fire loss that results. The insured would not then recover the total loss from the fire, even though the loss itself was less than the face value of the fire insurance policy.

The amount of the claim is calculated from the formula

$$\frac{\text{actual amount of insurance carried}}{\text{minimum coverage required}} \times \text{ amount of loss}$$

subject to the proviso that in no circumstances will the insurer pay more than the amount of the loss itself or more than the face value of the policy.

ILLUSTRATION

A building owned by *X* Company Ltd. is insured for $80 000, but the insurance contract contains an 80% co-insurance clause. The building is damaged by fire to the amount of $30 000. The depreciated replacement value of the insured property at the date of the fire is $150 000. The insur-

ance company will then pay

$$\frac{\$80\ 000}{80\% \text{ of } \$150\ 000} \times \$30\ 000 = \$20\ 000$$

and *X* Company Ltd., as insured, must absorb $10 000

in a total loss of $30 000

---

25   See M.G. Baer, "Rethinking Basic Concepts of Insurance Law", in *Insurance Law*, p.210. Special Lectures of the Law Society of Upper Canada. Toronto: Richard de Boo, 1987.

We can see from the above illustration how a co-insurance clause provides the insured with an incentive to insure its property for an amount greater than it otherwise might be inclined to do. If the amount of the policy does not meet the requirements of the co-insurance clause, the insured must actually share with the insurer any loss that occurs.

UARANTEE

The Nature of a Guarantee

A guarantee usually arises in one of three common business situations. First, a prospective creditor may refuse to advance money, goods, or services solely on the prospective debtor's promise to pay for them. Second, a creditor may state that it intends to start an action against its debtor for an overdue debt unless the debtor can offer additional security to support a further delay in repayment. Third, a prospective assignee of rights under a contract may be unwilling to buy these benefits if it has nothing more to rely on than the undertaking of the promisor in the original contract.

In each of these circumstances further assurance, sufficient to satisfy the creditor or assignee, is often supplied by a third party who promises to perform the obligation of the debtor if the debtor should default in performance. The debtor is then called the *principal debtor*, and his obligation is known as the *principal* or *primary debt*. The person who promises to answer for the default of the principal debtor is called the *guarantor* or *surety*, and her promise is a *guarantee* or *contract of suretyship*.

ILLUSTRATIONS

(a) Crown Autos Ltd. agrees to sell a Super-Cyclone sports car to Tomins provided her uncle, Gilmour, will guarantee payment of the instalments. Gilmour agrees to assist his niece, and both join in signing an instalment-purchase agreement whereby Tomins promises as principal debtor to make all payments promptly, and Gilmour promises as guarantor to pay off the debt if Tomins defaults payment.

(b) Arthurs purchases a delivery truck from Bigtown Trucks Ltd. under an instalment agreement. After Arthurs has made over half his payments, he defaults because of business difficulties. Bigtown Trucks Ltd. threatens to retake possession of the truck. Arthurs states that if Bigtown Trucks Ltd. takes the truck his business will lose all chance of recovery. He asks the company to give him an extra six months to pay if he can obtain a satisfactory guarantor. The company agrees, and Arthur's friend Campbell signs a contract of guarantee, promising to pay the balance in six months if Arthurs fails to do so.

(c) Perez buys a commercial freezer from Quincy and gives a promissory note payable in 60 days for the full purchase price. Quincy is in need of cash and takes the note to her banker who agrees to give her cash for it less a 5% charge. Quincy endorses the note in favour of the bank, that is, she places her signature on it when assigning it to the bank, and thereby guarantees payment if Perez should default.

We may note three important characteristics of a guarantee. First, a guarantor makes a promise *to the creditor*, not to the principal debtor. A promise made to a debtor to assist in the event of default is not a guarantee, and since the promise is not made to the creditor, the creditor cannot recover on it. Second, a guarantee is a secondary obligation arising only on default of the primary debt. For this reason it is a *contingent* liability in contrast to the absolute liability of the principal debtor. A creditor has no rights against the guarantor until default by the principal debtor.[26] Third, a guarantor's duty to pay arises immediately upon default by the principal debtor. The creditor need not first sue the debtor. Strictly speaking, the creditor need not even notify the guarantor of the default before starting an action to enforce the guarantee. As a practical matter, however, the creditor always does make a demand on the guarantor before suing. Of course, when giving a guarantee, a guarantor may stipulate as a condition precedent to liability that the creditor must first have sued the debtor and have failed to recover, but it is unusual for a guarantor to do so.

In Chapter 12 we noted that the Statute of Frauds applies to a contingent promise to answer for the *miscarriage* (that is, the tort) of another. Such promises are generally described as guarantees.

ILLUSTRATION

Jenny Williams tries to rent a launch from Boat Rentals Ltd. but is refused because of her youth. Williams' father, a reputable businessman, informs the manager of Boat Rentals Ltd. that if the company will rent the launch to his daughter he will be responsible for any damage caused by her negligent acts if his daughter does not herself reimburse the company for any such damage. Boat Rentals Ltd. accepts his offer.

In the above illustration, the guarantee is rather like a contract of auto collision insurance, in which the father is the counterpart of an insurer and the boat-rental firm of the insured. If Williams' father had undertaken absolutely (without reference to a failure by his daughter to make good the loss herself) to assume any costs of his daughter's possible negligence, his promise would have been an indemnity and even more like a contract of auto collision insurance.

We have seen (in Chapter 12) that the distinction between guarantee and indemnity is important with respect to the requirement of writing in the Statute of Frauds. The distinction is also important in that the liability of a guarantor depends on the continuing existence of the liability of the principal debtor, whereas the liability under a promise of indemnity stands alone. Thus, if a person guaranteed the debt of a consumer debtor and the obligation was not binding under consumer legislation (for example, for failure to deliver a written statement of the terms of credit) the guarantor would not be bound to pay either. On the other hand, a promise of indemnity is independent of any obligation of the person who benefits from that promise. Thus, if *A* said to a seller, "If you will supply *B* with a 20-inch portable colour television set, I promise to pay the price", *A*'s liability would not depend on whether *B* has contracted a binding debt; so long as the seller carried out *A*'s wishes, *A* would be bound to indemnify it.

Continuing Guarantee

A continuing guarantee covers a series of transactions between a creditor and its principal debtor. A guarantor may, for example, agree to guarantee *X* Co.'s account with supplier *Y*

---

[26] See Chapter 12, for the distinction between a guarantee and an indemnity; an indemnifier promises absolutely to pay the debt of another person.

up to an amount of $5000. In a series of purchases by *X* Co. and payments by it, *X* Co.'s indebtedness to *Y* will fluctuate considerably; at any given date during the currency of the guarantee, the guarantor is contingently liable for the debt owing if it is less than $5000 and for a maximum of $5000 if the debt exceeds that sum — as it may well do whenever *X* Co. purchases a large shipment from *Y*. A continuing guarantee is often given for a specific length of time, and debts contracted afterwards, even if below the maximum amount, are not the liability of the guarantor. In any event, the death of a guarantor ends liability with respect to further transactions, although the guarantor's estate remains contingently liable for the debt existing at death.

A guarantor may limit liability under a continuing guarantee until a specified date: if the principal debtor has not defaulted by that date, or has defaulted but the creditor has not yet started an action to enforce the guarantee, then the guarantor's liability terminates for existing obligations as yet unpaid. The variety of terms of a guarantee are virtually limitless, and they depend only upon the ability of the parties to reach agreement.

Consideration

We have said that a guarantee is a promise, and we know that a promise is not enforceable unless it is given either under seal or for a consideration. Occasionally a guarantor does make the promise under seal, but generally does not. What then constitutes the consideration for a guarantee?

The consideration is clearest when the guarantor receives an economic benefit — when she obtains a higher price as an assignor of an account receivable, because she is willing to guarantee payment by the debtor. More frequently the guarantor does not receive any economic benefit for her promise: but as we have already noted (Chapter 7), consideration need confer no economic benefit on a promisor. We should recall that the essential element of our definition of consideration is simply that the promisee pays a price for the promise of the other party. This price may be the doing, or forbearing to do, of some act (or the promise to do so) by the promisee at the request of the promisor, although without any tangible advantage to the promisor. The creditor gives sufficient consideration for the promise of the guarantor, therefore, by performing some act or forbearing to do some act at the request of the guarantor. And the guarantor's request need not even be express; it may be implied from the circumstances.

ILLUSTRATION

Creely threatens to sue Dobbs for his past-due debt. Dobbs asks for 60 days more to raise the money, but Creely refuses to give the extra time unless Dobbs obtains a guarantee from his affluent cousin Guara. Dobbs takes a form of guarantee to his cousin, explains the situation, and requests her signature. Guara signs the guarantee and mails it to Creely. Creely forbears to sue Dobbs for 60 days. When Dobbs defaults payment again, Creely sues Guara. She defends on the ground that she has received no consideration for her guarantee.

Guara's defence will fail. The court will accept the argument that she impliedly requested Creely to forbear to sue Dobbs for 60 days, and that he gave consideration by complying with this request. Accordingly, Creely's action will succeed.

Similarly, when a person guarantees a contract by which the debtor obtains goods or services on credit, it is usually quite easy to imply a request by the guarantor to the creditor that the creditor enter into a contract it would otherwise have refused.

Discharge of Guarantee by Acts of the Creditor

A guarantee relates to the performance of a specific promise and no other. Sometimes a principal debtor and his creditor agree to a material change in the scope of the debtor's promise without obtaining the consent of the guarantor. If the change is one that might prejudice the position of the guarantor, her liability ceases. This principle also applies where the principal debtor does not consent to the change: a bank, having agreed in return for a guarantee to give a family company more time to pay off its arrears, made a demand for immediate payment; the result was that the company became bankrupt. Because the bank's breach of its agreement substantially increased the guarantor's risk, the Supreme Court of Canada held that the guarantor was completely discharged.[27]

In *Holland-Canada Mortgage Co. v. Hutchings*[28] a group of fifteen citizens jointly guaranteed a loan to a charitable organization so that the organization might obtain necessary funds. Subsequently the loan was renewed, and the interest rate increased from 7% to 8% per annum. Some of the guarantors, learning of the change, refused to give their assent and so were released. The remaining guarantors were not told of these developments, however, and when the loan was defaulted they were sued on their guarantee. The court held that they were not liable, first, because of a material change in the terms of the contractual obligation they had guaranteed and, second, because they had not known of the withdrawal of many of the joint guarantors with whom they had expected to share their liability.

By contrast, an arrangement between the creditor and principal debtor that in no way prejudices the guarantor does not discharge the guarantee. For example, a director guaranteed a mortgage debt of his company, and when the company defaulted a reorganization plan that reduced the amount of the mortgage was agreed to by the company and the creditor. The reorganization did not discharge the guarantee, although the guarantor's liability was reduced proportionally to the overall debt reduction.[29]

What happens, then, when a creditor agrees to give the principal debtor a longer time in which to pay the account? May such an agreement so prejudice the rights of the guarantor as to release her? The answer is that a guarantor will usually be released when the principal parties agree to an extension of time without her express consent. A creditor can keep a guarantee alive and enforceable, however, if it makes its promise to extend the time in a written memorandum that includes the words, "subject to reserving rights against the guarantor". It may seem strange that the creditor and debtor, in a contract between themselves, may thus affect the guarantor's rights; but the creditor has in effect made its promise to the debtor contingent upon the guarantor's willingness to let the debt remain outstanding. The creditor is then really saying to the debtor, "We agree not to require payment until [say] May 31, but you must understand that the guarantor may choose to intervene at any time before then, pay off your debt to us, and having thereby become subrogated to our rights, bring an action against you before May 31."[30]

---

27 Bank of Montreal v. Wilder (1986), 32 D.L.R.(4th) 9.
28 [1936] 2 D.L.R. 481.
29 Guardian Trust Co. v. Gagliardi (1990), 64 D.L.R.(4th) 351.
30 See Bristol & West of England Mortgage Co. v. Taylor (1893), 24 O.R. 286; Levy Bros. v. Sole, [1955] O.W.N. 989.

Rights of the Guarantor upon Default

Defences

A guarantor may generally defend an action by the creditor upon any grounds that would be open to the principal debtor. Thus, if a debtor has a good defence because of the misrepresentation of the creditor in selling the goods, the guarantor may take advantage of this defence. A guarantor may also set off against the creditor, in reduction of the debt, any claim the debtor has against the creditor, as when the debtor has performed services for the creditor for which it has not yet been paid.

If the principal contract is void, as for example in the case of a prohibited loan to a corporation, then any purported guarantee will also be a nullity.[31] It is uncertain whether a guarantor can plead the principal debtor's infancy as a defence on the grounds that if, as guarantor, she were to pay the debt to the creditor, she could not herself succeed in an action to recover it from the principal debtor.[32] However, as we saw in Chapter 8, the general rule is that a contract made with an infant is not void, but merely unenforceable against the infant and might not necessarily prevent the enforcement of a guarantee.[33]

Subrogation

We noted earlier in this chapter that an insurer, upon paying a claim made by an insured, becomes subrogated to the rights of the insured and may pursue any remedies that the insured would have against the party responsible for the loss. Similarly, a guarantor who pays off the creditor becomes subrogated to the rights of the creditor against the debtor and the debtor's assets. She may sue the debtor for the amount she has paid the creditor and for any expenses she has incurred because of the debtor's default; and if the creditor holds shares or bonds or other property pledged as security for the debt, the guarantor is entitled to have these assets transferred to her in mitigation of her loss.[34]

A guarantor may choose to pay off the creditor and become subrogated to its rights as soon as the debt falls due: she need not wait for the creditor to make a demand or to sue. The guarantor may wish to act even when the creditor is content to wait because it believes the guarantor is financially sound and able to make payment. The guarantor may have ascertained that the debtor is failing and wish to take action before the debtor becomes insolvent — if she waits until the creditor demands payment, it may no longer be worthwhile suing the debtor.

Requirement of Writing

Chapter 12 has shown that a contract of guarantee must be in writing and signed by the guarantor to be enforceable against her; and we noted that this requirement has been

---

[31] Communities Economic Development Fund v. Maxwell [1992] 1 W.W.R. 193.
[32] See *Report on the Age of Majority*. Toronto: Ontario Law Reform Commission, 1969, pp. 44-6. The argument in favour of enforcing such guarantees is that it would be unconscionable for the guarantor to have persuaded the creditor to lend to the minor and then to plead the debtor's infancy when the minor defaults.
[33] In William E. Thompson Associates Inc. v. Carpenter (1989), 61 D.L.R.(4th) 1, the principal debtor's obligation was held to be unenforceable because the interest rate exceeded the maximum permitted under the Criminal Code. Nevertheless, the guarantee of repayment of the principal sum only was held to be severable and enforceable.
[34] See Royal Bank of Canada v. Dickson (1973), 33 D.L.R. (3d) 332 at 343-4.

retained even in England and British Columbia, where the Statute of Frauds has been largely repealed.[35] The merits of requiring written evidence of a guarantee have been stated cogently by some of the members of the English Law Revision Committee in its *Sixth Interim Report*, 1937, as follows:

> We realize that most guarantees, such for instance as those given to a Bank, will, whether the act [Statute of Frauds] is repealed or not, always be contained in a written document; but, if oral contracts of guarantee are allowed, we feel that there is a real danger of inexperienced people being led into undertaking obligations that they do not fully understand, and that opportunities will be given to the unscrupulous to assert that credit was given on the faith of a guarantee which in fact the alleged surety had no intention of giving. A guarantee is in any case a special class of contract; it is generally one-sided and disinterested as far as the surety is concerned, and the necessity of writing would at least give the proposed surety an opportunity of pausing and considering, not only the nature of the obligation he is undertaking, but also its terms. The contract often gives rise to many questions, e.g., whether it is to apply to the whole of a debt or to a portion only, and if the former, whether it is to be limited in amount or to a certain period.

Questions for Review

1. What is the consideration received in an insurance contract by the insurer? By the insured?
2. X throws some old papers in her bedroom fireplace and realizes too late that the papers included some correspondence of great value as a collector's item. She claims the value of the destroyed material under her fire insurance policy. Will she succeed?
3. D is persuaded to buy an automobile on the assurance of his friend, E, that E will assist him in meeting the payments. D fails to pay for the car, and the seller, S, sues E. Will S succeed?
4. What test can we apply to distinguish a wager from an insurance contract?
5. Black purchases a life insurance policy, naming his wife as beneficiary. Afterwards Black is shot and killed while attempting to hold up a bank. Can Mrs. Black collect the insurance money?
6. Explain the circumstances in which the following persons may have a right of subrogation: an insurer; a guarantor.
7. Business interruption insurance usually protects against particular types of loss that result from destruction of or damage to business property. Give two examples.
8. What kinds of agreements between the creditor and the principal debtor will operate to release the guarantor?
9. X learns that he has a serious disease and applies for life insurance without disclosing this information. He is later killed in an automobile accident. Has the insurer grounds for refusing to pay the claim?
10. Explain briefly why the law affecting the assignment of an insured's rights is not the same for a contract of property insurance as for a contract of life insurance.

---

[35] In Alberta the requirement is more stringent; a guarantee by an individual must also be acknowledged before a notary public: Guarantees Acknowledgement Act, R.S.A. 1980, c. G-12. Only in Manitoba is there no requirement for a guarantee to be in writing: Act to repeal the Statute of Frauds, S.M. 1982-83-84, c. 34, s. 1. 1980,

11. "The recognition of a guarantee in law is only another means of avoiding the privity of contract rule to meet modern business convenience. A person may guarantee a debt without even talking to the debtor." Discuss the validity of this statement.

12. Why do we need legislation to specify terms of the insurance contract and regulate the conduct of companies and individuals engaged in the insurance industry?

13. A owns a building worth $550 000 and takes out two fire insurance policies for $400 000 each, one with the Ajax Insurance Company and the other with the Hercules Insurance Company. In the event of a fire, could she collect $400 000 from both companies?

14. What justification has an insurer for including a term requiring notice of a claim within a very short period?

15. Is it correct to say that there is no consideration in a contract of guarantee unless the guarantor receives an economic benefit for her promise?

16. Good Groceterias Limited recently lost one of its stores in a fire. It insured the stores over the years with Pyro Fire Insurance Company, without changing the coverage against losses by fire. When it first insured the store in question, the property had an actual value of $500 000, but at the time the loss occurred the replacement value of the property had increased to $750 000. Good Groceterias' policy with Pyro Fire included the following clause: "This company shall not be liable for a greater proportion of any loss or damage to the property described herein than the sum hereby insured bears to eighty per cent (80%) of the actual cash replacement value of said property at the time such loss shall happen." State the amount that Good Groceterias could recover from Pyro Fire Insurance under each of the following, unrelated assumptions:

   (a) The loss amounted to $360 000 and the insurance carried was $360 000.
   (b) The loss amounted to $660 000 and the insurance carried was $500 000.

Problems

Problem 1

Hastie Jr., aged 17, rented a car from Road Rentals Ltd. It was a term of the contract that he should be responsible for any damage caused to the car during the period of its rental. While taking some friends for a drive on the Trans-Canada Highway he missed a curve and demolished the car in a collision with a rock-cut.

Hastie Jr. failed to make good the loss to Road Rentals Ltd. and the company threatened to commence legal proceedings against him. At this stage Hastie Jr.'s father phoned the manager of Road Rentals Ltd. and promised that he would pay the cost of the wrecked vehicle if the company did not proceed to sue his son. The company then instructed its lawyer not to take action. Shortly afterwards, Hastie Jr. was killed in another automobile accident, and Hastie Sr. then refused to pay Road Rentals Ltd. The company brought action against Hastie Sr. for damages equal to the value of its automobile.

What arguments, if any, may Hastie Sr. offer in defence? What should be the results of the action?

Problem 2

While driving her truck on an icy road, Martin collided with another truck owned by Sawchuk. The two trucks became enmeshed and required the services of two tow-trucks to pry them apart. Despite the fact that the tow-trucks were operated with great care, as the metal separated an accidental spark set fire to Martin's truck, causing further extensive damage to it. The damage caused to Martin's truck by the initial collision was $2400 and by the subsequent fire, another $4100.

Martin was insured under a standard automobile policy which, in addition to insurance for public liability and property damage, provided coverage against loss of or damage to the vehicle due to collision or upset with $250 deductible for each separate claim. The policy also included a rider providing comprehensive coverage from any other cause; this comprehensive coverage was not subject to a deductible clause. The portion of the insurance contract relating to collision reads in part as follows:

> The Insurer agrees to indemnify the Insured against direct and accidental loss of or damage to the automobile caused solely by collision with another object, either moving or stationary, or by upset. Each collision or upset covered hereby shall give rise to a separate claim in respect of which the Insurer's liability shall be limited to the amount of loss or damage in excess of $250. Breakage of glass and loss caused by missiles, falling objects, fire, theft, explosion, earthquake, windstorm, hail, water, flood, vandalism, riot, or civil commotion shall not be deemed loss caused by collision or upset.

The rider providing the additional comprehensive coverage stated simply:

> The Insurer agrees to indemnify the Insured against direct and accidental loss of or damage to the automobile from any cause other than collision with another object, either moving or stationary, or upset.

State with reasons what amount, if any, Martin is entitled to recover from the insurance company.

Problem 3

On January 2, Oswald Kirkham lent John Lough $10 000 for one year at 15% interest per annum. Lough signed a promissory note in favour of Kirkham, and Lough's friend William Mahon endorsed the note as guarantor of the loan. In December following, Mahon was called away on urgent business to Australia and could not be reached when the note fell due. Lough defaulted on January 2 and requested a six-month extension from Kirkham. As consideration for the extension, Lough agreed to name Kirkham as beneficiary of a life insurance policy. Although neither Lough nor Kirkham could contact Mahon to get his consent, Kirkham granted the extension. In the agreement of extension he expressly reserved his rights against Mahon as guarantor; Kirkham believed that by keeping Mahon bound to the terms of the original agreement, Mahon would not in any way be prejudiced by the extension. On his return several weeks later Mahon was disturbed to learn of the extension, but took no action.

When the extension expired, Lough's business had become insolvent, and Kirkham sued Mahon on his guarantee. In defence, Mahon claimed:

(a) that the original guarantee was void because he had received no consideration for his promise, and

(b) that in any event the subsequent material alteration extending the time for payment without his consent extinguished his liability as guarantor.

In reply Kirkham claimed:

(a) that his making the loan to Lough was good consideration to Mahon, and

(b) that by Kirkham's reserving his rights against Mahon, Mahon's rights continued to be governed by the original agreement and were not affected by the extension, so that on learning of the extension Mahon could have paid the debt off and sued Lough immediately. By waiting, Mahon voluntarily took the risk that Lough would become insolvent, and cannot therefore blame Kirkham for the present state of affairs.

Whose argument is the better?

Cases

Case 1

Szabo, a tobacco farmer in southern Ontario, applied to Carter, an insurance agent, to obtain fire insurance protection on his barn and contents. The agent suggested a fire policy with Courtland & Tillsonburg Insurance Company.

Szabo's barn contained an apparatus called a steamer in which steam was created by means of natural gas lighted under a boiler of water. The fire policy contained the following clause under a heading "Barn Warranties":

> No steamer will be left operating unattended either day or night but will be banked if coal or wood operated or entirely shut off if oil operated during the night and at times when an operator is not in the building, and no open fires will be used and no smoking will be permitted in the building.

Tobacco farmers in the area were generally familiar with a practice that permitted them, upon written confirmation from the insurance company, to obtain lower premium rates by assenting to warranties of this kind that restricted or affected their use of the insured property. Szabo discussed the significance of the clause for his type of operation with Carter. Carter told him that the clause applied only to coal, wood, or oil steamers and not to gas steamers and said, "All you need do to comply with the contract so far as this gas steamer is concerned is to turn it off at nights and be sure to sweep out the barn." Szabo then contracted for fire insurance at the favourable rate available to insured parties who were able to comply with the Barn Warranty clause. No confirmation was requested from the insurance company, as it was considered unnecessary.

One winter morning, having started the steamer operating, Szabo left the barn for 15 minutes to get some breakfast. While eating, he saw fire coming through the roof of the barn; the building, valued at $200 000, was totally destroyed. The Courtland & Tillsonburg Insurance Co. contested Szabo's claim on the grounds that he had left the building unattended in breach of the condition subsequent stated in the policy. Szabo replied that the clause referred to was subject to the interpretation explained to him by Carter. Szabo sued the insurance company for the amount of the policy.

Offer, with reasons, an opinion about whether this action is likely to succeed.

Case 2

Calgary Features Limited required additional financing if it was to exploit some apparently attractive opportunities. Its directors decided to assist the company by raising the sum of $500 000 on their own credit. The company then applied for a loan with Merchants' Bank, on the terms that a guarantee would be signed jointly by all the directors. The guarantee was on a standard form provided by Merchants' Bank and included the clause:

> This guarantee shall be binding upon every person signing the same, notwithstanding the non-execution thereof by any other proposed guarantor.

Four directors signed the guarantee in the office of the bank manager in Calgary. Then one of them sent it to Edmonton, where four other directors signed it together. They noted the absence at the time of the signature of D. Fowler, the company's president (also a director), and agreed among themselves that they were signing only on the condition that the guarantee would not be delivered to the bank until Fowler had signed as well.

When the guarantee was returned to one of the directors in Calgary, she gave it to the bank manager with instructions that it was not to be treated as having been delivered to the bank as an operative instrument until Fowler had signed. In the end, Fowler refused to do so because he did not want to diminish his own line of credit at the bank. Nevertheless, the bank manager advanced the company $500 000 and the company gave the bank its promissory note for that amount.

Calgary Features Limited subsequently defaulted on the note and Merchants' Bank claimed the sum owing from those directors who had signed the guarantee. They refused to pay on the grounds that the guarantee would not operate unless and until all directors had signed. Merchants' Bank sued them to enforce the guarantee.

Explain whether this action should succeed.

Case 3

Premium Motors Ltd. sold Ralston a car on credit under a contract with a term providing that on the purchaser's signed declaration of good health, should he die before completing the required payments, any balance owing would be considered paid. For this purpose Premium Motors Ltd. had a separate insurance contract with Standard Form Insurance Co. to pay any balance owing by a deceased debtor. At the time of the purchase, Ralston also signed an application form for the related insurance in which he replied, "No" to the question, "Have you any disease?"

Three months after making this purchase, Ralston died of a heart condition. Mrs. Ralston was the executrix and main beneficiary of his estate. A few weeks later, a sales representative for Premium Motors called on Mrs. Ralston, and assuring her that by the terms of the contract no further money would be owing on the car, persuaded her to trade it in on a more expensive model. Mrs. Ralston signed an offer to pay the agreed price for the new car less the full current value of the trade-in car. The sales representative took the offer to the sales manager, who accepted it.

Standard Form Insurance Co. refused to reimburse Premium Motors Ltd. for the amount of the unpaid balance of the first car on the grounds that Ralston had given inaccurate information in applying for the insurance. Premium Motors Ltd. then requested this additional amount from Mrs. Ralston and, when she refused to pay it, brought an action against her.

Discuss the legal issues raised by these facts and state whether the action should succeed.

Case 4

Stanley Motors Ltd. operates a truck assembly plant in Vancouver. Three months ago, it sold three light school buses to the City of Guadalajara, Mexico. The agreed price for each bus was $35 000 f.o.b. Vancouver, with the purchaser to make all arrangements for shipment from Vancouver to Guadalajara. On the advice of Stanley Motors Ltd., the City of Guadalajara then entered into a contract of carriage with Georgia Motorship Lines Ltd. It was a term of this contract that the carrier should not be liable for damages in excess of $5000 including any damages attributable to the negligence of its employees.

While employees of Georgia Motorship Lines Ltd. were getting the buses ready for loading at dockside in Vancouver, a mast supporting the tackle equipment broke. A bus fell from a great height onto the dock and was demolished. The accident was the result of the operation of the loading equipment by employees of the carrier. Since the bus had not yet been placed on board ship, Stanley Motors Ltd. concluded that under the terms of its contract of sale it could not hold the City of Guadalajara liable for the price.

Stanley Motors Ltd. carries a basic manufacturer's policy with the Western Mercantile Insurance Company. This policy provides coverage against damage or loss to buildings, equipment, parts, materials, work in process and finished-goods inventories, and includes a transportation floater rider that extends the normal coverage to damage to finished products en route to customers while still at the risk of the insured. Stanley Motors Ltd. therefore claimed its loss under this policy.

Western Mercantile Insurance Company agreed to pay this claim, but also commenced action in the name of the insured against Georgia Motorship Lines Ltd. for damages of $35 000. Georgia Motorship Lines Ltd. offered to settle for $5000 but denied liability for any amount in excess of that sum, on the grounds that Stanley Motors Ltd. was bound by the term in the contract of carriage with the City of Guadalajara restricting its liability to $5000.

Offer an opinion about whether this action should succeed.

CHAPTER
21

BAILMENT

THE NATURE OF A BAILMENT

Definition

A bailment is a transfer of possession of personal property on the understanding that the party receiving the property will return it at a later time or dispose of it as directed. The transferor of the property, usually its owner, is called the *bailor* and the party that receives the custody of it, the *bailee*. The concept embraces a wide variety of economic and social activities. Familiar examples of bailment are: leaving an article with a railway for shipment; giving stocks and bonds to a bank as security for a loan; leaving a radio with a repairer; storing furniture in a warehouse; and lending a lawnmower to a neighbour.

Compared with Sale

A bailment is different from a sale. A sale transfers ownership, and as Chapter 18 has shown, need not require a change in possession. By contrast, a bailment does not alter ownership but does require a change in possession. Furthermore, the subject-matter of a bailment need not be a chattel: it may be a document representing legal rights, such as a share or bond certificate, bill of lading, or title deed. If one takes diamonds to a jeweller to have them made into a necklace or takes a share certificate to a broker to have it registered in the owner's name, the transaction is a bailment rather than a sale.

Compared with Trust

A transfer of property to a trustee for the benefit of one or more persons does not create a bailment. The creation of a trust gives legal ownership to the trustee and the beneficiary acquires an equitable interest in the subject of the trust. Thus a receiving order transferring ownership of the assets of a bankrupt debtor to a trustee in bankruptcy for the benefit of creditors is not a bailment; nor does the transfer of property to an executor under a will constitute a bailment. We should also note that the subject-matter of a trust may be real property as well as personal property, whereas bailment is confined to personal property.

Compared with Debt

A deposit of money in a bank or trust company creates a creditor-debtor rather than a bailor-bailee relationship.[1] By contrast, a deposit of specific items of personal property for safekeeping with a bank or trust company does create a bailment. The difference has important consequences if the recipient becomes bankrupt. A bailee has no title to articles entrusted to him: the articles do not form part of his assets available to creditors, and must be returned to the bailor intact. Thus, a bailor is better off on the insolvency of the bailee than a creditor is on the insolvency of its debtor; the creditor must await its share in the available assets of the debtor, along with the other creditors. That share is likely to be substantially less than the amount owing.

---

[1] For a case illustrating the importance of distinguishing between these relationships, see Royal Bank of Canada v. Reynolds (1976), 66 D.L.R. (3d) 88.

Non-Contractual Bailments

We should also note that a bailment can occur without any contract between a bailor and bailee. The essential elements of bailment are delivery of possession without the intention to transfer title and with the intention that the property shall be returned to the bailor. All these elements may exist without a contract, as when the owner of an article lends it gratuitously to a friend. Thus, a bailment is created when one person lends another a car or a typewriter. The intention that the object shall be returned need not be stated expressly between the parties but may be presumed from the circumstances. Similarly, if a customer leaves a coat behind in a restaurant, the restaurateur becomes an involuntary bailee of the coat and cannot refuse to return it at the customer's request.

General Classes of Bailments

Gratuitous Bailments

These bailments may be for the benefit of the bailor or the bailee, or indeed for the benefit of both parties. Examples of those for the benefit of the bailor occur when a pet is left with a neighbour during vacation, a lawn-mower is left with a friend who has offered to repair it, or valuables are left in a relative's office safe. Examples of bailments for the benefit of the bailee are the lending of a car for a trip, or a movie projector for a home showing. Examples of bailments for the benefit of both parties occur when a car is left with a friend for safekeeping but the friend has permission to use it from time to time, or when a loan of a camera is made in the hope that the borrower will buy it if satisfied with its performance.

Bailments for Value

By their very nature, bailments for value are of benefit to both parties: one party obtains the service desired and the other receives payment. Thus, both the rental of a car and the delivery of a camera to a repairer are bailments for the mutual benefit of bailor and bailee. We should note, however, that in the car rental the bailee receives the benefit from the change in possession of the chattel (obtains the use of the car), whereas in the delivery of the camera to the repairer, the bailor receives the benefit from the change in possession (the repairer can then make the repairs requested by the bailor).

LIABILITY OF A BAILEE

Liability under Contract and Tort

Sometimes bailed goods are lost, damaged, or destroyed while in the possession of a bailee. The question then arises whether the bailee is liable for the loss suffered. When the bailment is the result of a contract, the contract contains terms, either express or implied by trade custom, setting out the duties and liabilities of the bailee for the goods in its possession. Thus, a warehouse firm is not customarily obliged to insure goods stored with it against loss by fire; [2] but when it has expressly contracted to do so and fails, it is liable to the bailor for the insured value of the goods if they are destroyed by fire. As we noted in Chapter 13, in discussing the interpretation of contracts, parties do not and indeed cannot foresee all the possibilities of harm that may arise. All bailees are, however, under a duty to take care of property bailed to them. The standard of care required by the law of torts applies in circumstances not covered expressly or impliedly by the bailment contract, and the standard applies also to gratuitous bailment involving no contract at all. The required standard of care does vary, however, according to the type of bailment.

The laws of contracts and torts further intermingle when a contract of bailment includes a term that the bailee shall not be liable for damage to the goods while in his custody, even when the damage is caused by negligence in the course of performing the contract. The courts construe this type of exemption clause very strictly against the bailee, just as we have seen them do against the seller in a contract of sale. [3] If the goods are damaged for any reason not related to the actual performance contemplated by the contract, the bailee is not protected by the exemption clause. Thus, in the English case of *Davies v. Collins*, [4] an army officer took his uniform to the defendants to be cleaned. The defendants gave him a receipt in which they disclaimed all liability for damage arising in the course of "necessary handling". The uniform was never returned, and when the officer sued for its value, the defendants pleaded the exemption clause. It was established, however, that the loss arose when the defendants had sent the uniform to someone else for cleaning; the court found that the wording of the contract required personal performance by the bailee. Thus the damage had not taken place during "necessary handling" as contemplated in the exemption clause; the exemption clause did not apply. Accordingly, the defendants were held liable for the loss.

Although the law of bailment has elements of both tort and contract law, bailment is a distinct relationship governed by its own rules. For example, when goods are damaged or lost while in the possession of a bailee it is often difficult for the bailor to ascertain exactly how the harm occurred. Since a bailee is better able to establish the facts, the law of bailment places on the bailee the burden of showing that he was not negligent; he must offer some reasonable alternative explanation accounting for the loss. Consequently, it is easier for a bailor to sue under the rules of bailment than under the ordinary rules of tort. Also, we have already noted that a relationship of bailment may exist without any contract between bailor and bailee. The relationship may exist between a bailor and a *sub-bailee*, even when there has been no contract or communication between them.

---

[2] But the warehouse firm's failure to install alarm and sprinkler systems may amount to failure to exercise due care of the goods: Hogarth v. Archibald Moving & Storage Ltd. (1991), 57 B.C.L.R.(2d) 319.

[3] See Baldry v. Marshall, [1925] 1 K.B. 260, as discussed in Chapter 18.

[4] [1945] 1 All E.R. 247.

ILLUSTRATION

Leonore Punch took her diamond ring, worth $11 000, to Savoy Jewellers in Sault St. Marie for repair. Savoy was unable to do the repair, so they sent it to Walker Jewellers in Toronto. It sent the ring by registered mail and stated the value for insurance purposes as $100. Apparently, this was normal trade practice.

Since there was a postal strike when Walker had repaired the ring, it decided to return the ring to Savoy using a delivery service operated by Canadian National (CN). Again, the value was declared as $100. The contract between Walker and CN limited CN's liability for loss or damage to the declared value of $100. The ring was never delivered to Savoy. CN admitted the ring

might have been stolen by a driver but it had not made a thorough investigation.

Punch sued Savoy, Walker, and CN. The court found that Savoy was a bailee, and both Walker and CN were sub-bailees. All three owed a duty of care to Punch, and the burden on each of them was to show it was not responsible for the loss, or for not adequately insuring the ring. In addition, the clause in the contract between CN and Walker limiting CN's liability could not be relied on by CN against either Savoy or Punch, since they were not parties to the contract.[5] All three parties were found liable to pay Punch.

The Standard of Care

Generally speaking, the standard of care is least exacting upon a bailee when the bailment is both gratuitous and for the benefit of the bailor, as when A permits B to store her car in A's garage. The standard of care is most exacting on a bailee when the bailment is gratuitous and for the benefit of the bailee, as when one borrows a friend's car and obtains its use as a favour. A gratuitous bailment for the benefit of both parties is, at least in part, for the bailee's benefit and it would appear that the higher standard of care applies.

The standard of care for bailments of value falls between that of gratuitous bailments for the benefit of the bailee and of those for the benefit of the bailor. In addition, two special classes of bailee are subject to very high standards of care because they deal with the public generally. These are common carriers and hotel- or innkeepers, whom we shall discuss later in this chapter.

These variations in the standard of care make good sense. When a bailment is gratuitous and for the benefit of the bailor, the bailee should not be under a particularly high duty towards the bailor for, after all, the bailee is doing the bailor a favour. Thus, when a bailee allows a bailor to store her car in the bailee's garage, the bailee is not under as high a duty of care as a warehousing firm being paid to store the bailor's car would be.

When a bailment is the result of a contract the standard of care required of a bailee varies according to the type of goods bailed and the scope of the promise to look after the goods. In interpreting both express or implied promises of the bailee, the courts will consider all the circumstances. A bailee for value is expected to take the same care of goods

---

[5] Punch v. Savoy Jewellers Ltd. (1986), 26 D.L.R. (4th) 546. See, however, London Drugs Ltd. v. Kuehne and Nagel International Ltd. (1992) 13 C.C.L.T.1, in which the Supreme Court of Canada held that employees of a warehouse firm, sued personally for negligently damaging goods stored in the warehouse, were entitled to the protection of a clause in the storage contract limiting liability to a stated amount.

as a prudent and diligent person should take of goods belonging to those with whom he transacts business — a standard of care that is at least as high and probably higher than he might choose to apply to his own goods.

A bailee who borrows goods for personal benefit is under a very high standard of care in looking after the goods. The bailor receives no valuable consideration for this kindness, and so it is fair that in such circumstances the bailee should compensate the bailor when damage to the goods results from even slight carelessness on the bailee's part.

The standard of care must be couched in general terms to permit the necessary flexibility for coping with the innumerable situations that may arise. Mr. Justice Compton provided a good example of a general statement when he distinguished the standards of care required in a gratuitous bailment for the benefit of the bailor, and a bailment for value:

> What is reasonable varies in the case of a gratuitous bailee and that of a bailee for hire [value]. From the former is reasonably expected such care and diligence as persons ordinarily use in their own affairs and such skill as he has. From the latter is reasonably expected care and diligence, such as are exercised in the ordinary and proper course of a similar business, and such skill as he ought to have, namely, the skill usual and requisite in the business for which he receives payment.[6]

The nature of the goods bailed may also be important. If the property is very valuable and easily damaged, lost, or stolen, the standard of care required, even of a gratuitous bailee in a bailment for the benefit of the bailor, may be quite high: he must take greater care with expensive jewellery than with a bicycle stored in his garage. In the words of a Canadian judge, "The substantial question must always be, whether that care has been exhibited which the special circumstances reasonably demand."[7]

Remedies of a Bailee for the Value of Services Rendered

Damages and *Quantum Meruit*

In a contractual bailment the bailee, as a party to a contract, has the usual contractual remedies for breach by the bailor. Because of the character of bailment, rescission is rarely practical or even possible: it is too late to rescind a contract for storage or safekeeping or for the shipment of goods once the bailee has performed his duties; in most cases a worker cannot undo repairs already made to goods. Consequently, the main concern of a bailee is to receive compensation for services rendered.

When a bailee has completely performed his part of a contract, as when a warehousekeeper delivers up goods that have been stored with him, his remedy is an action for the contract price of the bailment services. Occasionally such an action may not be possible, as when a carrier has contracted to transport goods in several instalments and the bailor (shipper) delivers only part of the goods for shipment. The carrier may then sue *quantum meruit* for the value of the services he has performed and also for damages compensating

---

6   Beal v. South Devon Railway (1864), 159 E.R. 560, per Compton, J., at 562.
7   Fitzgerald v. Grand Trunk Railway (1880), 4 O.A.R. 601, per Moss, C.J.A., at 624.

the loss of profits he has sustained because the bailor failed to deliver all the goods for shipment. We have discussed these remedies for breach of contract in Chapter 17.

Lien

An important additional remedy available to a bailee for non-payment by a bailor is a lien on the bailed goods in its possession. A lien is a right to retain possession of the goods until the bailor pays what is due for the services. The right is obviously a valuable one, for the bailor cannot repossess the goods until it has paid the sum due. Generally, a right of lien arises only when the services have been performed and payment is already due. If payment is not due when the goods are to be redelivered, no lien exists, and the bailee is under a duty to return the goods.

ILLUSTRATION

Pliable Plastics Ltd. has very little storage space for its manufactured products. It enters into an arrangement with Stately Storage Limited whereby Pliable Plastics delivers its products for storage on a daily charge basis, and when they are sold, picks them up again for delivery to the buyer. Storage charges are billed and become payable every three months.

Stately Storage has no lien upon the goods stored with it until the end of the three-month period and until it has billed Pliable Plastics. If, after two and one-half months have passed, Pliable Plastics sells a portion of the stored goods, Stately Storage must surrender the goods on demand to Pliable Plastics or to a buyer who presents proper documents. When three months have expired and Stately Storage bills Pliable Plastics, Stately Storage has a lien for all the accrued storage charges upon the goods remaining in the warehouse at that time.

The right of lien was originally a common law right and was limited to bailees who performed services in the nature of repairs or improvements to goods bailed with them. The common law recognized a similar right of lien for the benefit of innkeepers and common carriers, who are under a duty to accept goods from anyone so long as they have space for them. Professional people like lawyers and bankers also have a common law right of lien over documents in their possession when they have performed services related to the documents. Even though they may have a common law or statutory right of lien, many businesses acting as bailees for value expressly provide for the right as a term in their contracts with customers. In addition to common law liens, various statutes create liens in other types of bailment. We shall discuss these rights of lien as they arise in the remaining sections of this chapter.

In our discussion of the rights of an unpaid seller in Chapter 19, we saw that a lien is a possessory remedy: an unpaid bailee loses his lien on the bailed goods as soon as the bailor obtains possession of them without deceit or fraud.

The Right of Sale

As we have noted, the right of lien is valuable to a bailee because the bailor usually needs to recover her goods and to do so must first pay off overdue charges. If, however, the bailor is unable to pay off the charges, as when she becomes insolvent, the bailee is left with goods he cannot use because he has no title to them, and yet he has the burden of storing them. Various statutes give bailees with a lien upon goods stored with them an additional right to sell the goods. Other bailees, who do not have the statutory right to sell bailed goods, may acquire the right to sell as a term of the bailment contract just as they may acquire the right of lien.

The provisions of the statutes vary in detail, but generally speaking they require, first, that a certain time elapse after payment falls due; second, that advance notice be given to the bailor of the bailee's intention to sell; third, that the sale be advertised; and fourth, that it be held by public auction. The proceeds of the sale are used, first, to reimburse the bailee for his costs of holding the sale, and second, to pay the overdue charges for his services; any surplus belongs to the bailor. We shall note the right of sale as it occurs in the remaining sections of this chapter.

STORAGE AND SAFEKEEPING

Liability

A warehousing firm that accepts goods for storage, a parking-lot operator who rents parking space and retains the car keys, a bank that rents a safety-deposit box — all are bailees for storage or safekeeping, and all are under a duty to take care of the goods stored with them.

The Judicial Committee of the Privy Council has described the liability of a bailee for value who has custody of goods in these terms:

> They [the bailees] were therefore under a legal obligation to exercise the same degree of care, towards the preservation of the goods entrusted to them from injury, which might reasonably be expected from a skilled store-keeper, acquainted with the risks to be apprehended either from the character of the storehouse itself or of its locality; and that obligation included, not only the duty of taking all reasonable precautions to obviate these risks, but the duty of taking all proper measures for the protection of the goods when such risks were imminent or had actually occurred.[8]

The express or implied authority that a bailment contract gives the bailee for dealing with the bailed goods may affect its liability for them. Thus, a warehousing company may or may not have implied authority to subcontract for the storage of the goods with another warehouse — the nature of the goods may be a determining factor. The English courts have held that in a contract for the storage of furniture it is implied that the bailee shall perform the contract himself and that sub-bailment amounts to a breach of contract.[9] The terms of a contract may reduce liability; for example, if the bailor overrides a warehouse keeper's usual discretion in handling the goods by directing where the goods are to be placed, the liability of the warehouse keeper will be restricted to complying with those instructions.

When storing goods with a warehouse, a bailor receives as evidence of the contract of bailment a document called a *warehouse receipt*. The document identifies the goods stored

---

[8] Brabant & Co. v. King, [1895] A.C. 632, per Lord Watson at 640.
[9] Edwards v. Newland, [1950] 1 All E.R. 1072.

and acknowledges that they are being kept in storage and are deliverable to the bailor's order. Ordinarily, a bailee must return to the bailor the exact goods stored. When, however, the goods stored are *fungible* (that is, replaceable with identical goods also in storage), the bailee's liability is discharged when he returns to the bailor goods of the exact description in the warehouse receipt. For example, when a quantity of grain of a specific grade is stored in a grain elevator in bins containing other grain of the same grade, the elevator company is bound to deliver not the exact grain that was bailed with him, but an equivalent quantity of the same grade.

A contract for parking an automobile in a parking lot, even when the car owner locks the car and keeps the keys, has frequently been regarded as an example of a bailment for storage. This interpretation has been challenged in an Ontario case in which the operator of a parking lot exhibited signs and included terms on parking receipts to the effect that "charges are for the use of parking space only", and further disclaimed liability for damage to the vehicle or its contents.[10] The court regarded the parking-lot operator's disclaimer of liability as a definition of the relationship contracted for, rather than as an exemption clause in a contract of bailment. It held that the relationship was one of licensor and licensee. According to this interpretation, the parking-lot operator was under a much lower standard of care as a mere licensor of space.

Remedies

As we have already noted, at common law a bailee did not obtain a lien upon goods unless he had performed some repair or improvement on them. Thus, a warehousing firm did not obtain a right of lien on goods stored with it unless it had specifically bargained for the lien. This is still the law in England today. In Canada, however, we have legislation passed by all the common law provinces, giving a warehouse a right of lien on goods stored with it for the amount of its charges. The statutes state that "every warehouseman has a lien on goods deposited with him for storage whether deposited by the owner of the goods or by his authority or by any person entrusted with the possession of the goods by the owner or by his authority."[11] The statutes require a bailee to give the owner notice when the owner's goods are bailed with it by some other party. Thus, a warehouse will advise a buyer (as owner of the goods) that the seller has delivered certain goods to it for the buyer's account, in compliance with the method of delivery stated in the contract of sale.

The statutes further provide that "a warehouseman may sell by public auction in the manner provided in this section any goods on which he has a lien for charges that have become due."[12] The warehouse must give notice to the person who is liable as debtor for the charges for which the lien exists, to the owner when the owner is a different person from the person liable to pay the charges, and to any other persons known by the warehouse managers to have a claim on or an interest in the goods. The notice must contain a statement that unless the charges are paid within the stated time, the goods will be

---

[10] Bata v. City Parking Canada Ltd. (1973), 2 O.R. (2d) 446.
[11] See, for example: Warehouse Lien Act, R.S.B.C. 1979, c. 427, s. 2; Warehousemen's Lien Act, R.S.N.S. 1989, c. 499, s. 3. In Ontario the former Warehousemen's Lien Act has been repealed and replaced by the Repair and Storage Liens Act, R.S.O. 1990, c. R-25. S. 4(1) which gives a similar lien to a "storer" of goods.
[12] R.S.B.C. 1979, c. 427, s. 4; R.S.N.S. 1989, c. 499, s. 5. In Ontario, a storer has a similar right: Repair and Storage Liens Act, R.S.O. 1990, c. R-25, s. 4(7).

advertised for sale and sold by public auction at a time and place specified in the notice. The statutes set out the details of the type of advertisement and the way in which the sale is to be held. The aim is to give adequate protection to the bailor or owner while giving the bailee a reasonably prompt method of obtaining payment.

WORK ON A CHATTEL

Liability

Bailment is often a normal consequence of contracts made for the maintenance of various kinds of business equipment, as when a truck is delivered to a garage for repair, when an electronics firm receives business machines for servicing, or when a laundry picks up factory uniforms for cleaning. A repairer who works on these articles on his own premises is a bailee for value. In accepting the work, the repairer undertakes to do it in a workmanlike manner employing the skill he professes to have, and also to have it done by the time he promises. Failure to do these things is a breach of contract on his part; depending on the circumstances, a breach may entitle the bailor not to pay for work already done or to sue for damages. A bailor is also entitled to the return of the chattel. The standard of care required of a worker towards chattels bailed with him is similar to that required of a warehousing company.

Remedies

Ordinarily, by leaving an article for repair, a bailor gives the repairer implied authority to order the parts necessary to carry out the repairs and include the cost of parts in the charges. A bailor who wishes to limit expenses may make it a term of the contract that the repairer shall not make repairs beyond a stated sum, or may prohibit the repairer from proceeding with the repairs at all if parts and labour exceed a specified amount.

If the parties do not expressly agree on a time for payment, a bailor is normally bound to pay for the work on its completion, although the usage in a particular trade may vary this rule. If a bailor fails to pay for the work done under the terms of the contract, a repairer has the usual contractual remedy to sue for the price agreed upon in the contract. If a bailor instructs the repairer to abandon the work before it is completed, or otherwise repudiates the contract, the repairer may claim remuneration in an action for *quantum meruit*, to obtain a reasonable price for the service already performed, and may also sue for damages for the loss of profits that would have been earned had the work been completed.

As we noted earlier in this chapter, the common law gives a repairer a lien for the value of the work done upon goods left with him. The common law right does not extend, however, to the right to sell the goods; the repairer may do no more than withhold them. Some of the provinces give an additional statutory right to the repairer to sell the goods when the repair charges are three months overdue.[13] These statutes apply safeguards similar to those required of a warehousing firm in selling bailed goods.

---

[13] See, for example: Repairers' Lien Act, R.S.B.C. 1979, c. 363, s. 2; R.S.N.S. 1989, c. 277, s. 45; Repair and Storage Liens Act, R.S.O. 1990, c. R-25, s. 3(3).

TRANSPORTATION

Classes of Carriers

The law distinguishes three types of carriers. A *gratuitous carrier* is anyone who agrees to move goods from one place to another without reward. A *private carrier* is a business that undertakes on occasion to carry goods for reward, but reserves the right to pick and choose its customers and restrict the type of goods it is willing to carry: it is a carrier whose decision whether to accept a request for its services is in each instance "guided ... by the attractiveness or otherwise of the particular offer and not by his ability or inability to carry, having regard to his other engagements."[14] A *common carrier* is a business that holds itself out to the public as a carrier of goods for reward. The essence of its status is that it does not discriminate among those who request its services, nor does it reserve the right to refuse an offer of goods for shipment when it has the means of shipping them. It may, however, be a common carrier on the terms that its services are restricted to a certain area and to those kinds of goods that are suitable for carriage by its equipment. Most railway and steamship companies are common carriers, as are some trucking companies and even gas and oil pipeline companies. Airlines may repudiate the status of a common carrier by reserving the right to refuse goods.

A carrier's liability for damage to goods in the course of transit depends upon the type of carrier it is. A carrier is a bailee that always has *some* responsibility for the goods under its control. Even a gratuitous bailee must exercise at least the diligence and care to be expected of a reasonable person in handling his or her own property. The duty of care required of a private carrier is somewhat greater. It owes a degree of care commensurate with the skill reasonably expected of a competent firm in its line of business; the amount of care that the reasonable person should apply to his or her own property is irrelevant. The liability of a common carrier is still greater, although it may take advantage of certain recognized defences that we shall examine.

Liability of a Common Carrier

A common carrier undertakes to indemnify the shipper (the bailor) against loss, whether the loss occurs through the carrier's fault or not. The carrier is therefore an insurer as well as a bailee. The historical reason for this special liability was to prevent the practice, once frequent in England, of collusion between carriers and highwaymen: the highwayman would "rob" the carrier of the shipper's goods and the carrier would plead that it was not its fault that the goods were taken. Although these reasons seem amusing when applied to the modern railroad, steamship, and trucking companies, there is eminent good sense in the rule itself: its practical effect is to relieve the shipper of any burden of producing evidence that it was the common carrier's want of reasonable care that caused the damage to the shipper's goods en route. In most circumstances it would be impossible for it to adduce this evidence. The shipper need only prove (1) that the carrier received the goods in good condition, and (2) that the carrier delivered them in bad condition or failed to deliver them at all. The burden is then on the carrier, if it is to avoid liability, to establish

---

14 Belfast Ropework Co. v. Bushell, [1918] 1 K.B. 210, per Bailhache, J. at 215.

that the cause of the loss was within one of the recognized defences available to common carriers. It is not enough for it to show that it was not negligent. Its only defences are an act of God, an inherent vice in the goods, or default by the shipper.

Defences Available to a Common Carrier

We encountered the idea of an act of God in Chapter 15, where we identified it as an example of a condition subsequent. This legal concept somewhat unkindly attributes a special class of misfortune to Providence. Lord Mansfield explained the term as follows:

> I consider it to mean something in opposition to the act of man: for *everything* is the act of God that happens by his permission; everything by his knowledge. But to prevent litigation, collusion and the necessity of going into circumstances impossible to be unravelled, the law presumes against the carrier unless he shows that it was done by the King's enemies or by such act as could not happen without the intervention of God as storms, lightning or tempest.[15]

It follows, then, that fire is not an act of God, unless caused by lightning, and that a common carrier, unlike other bailees for value, is liable for damage to goods caused by fire, even when there is no negligence provable against it.

A shipper may challenge a common carrier's defence by showing that the carrier acted irresponsibly. In the words of Mr. Chief Justice Cockburn:

> If by his default in omitting to take necessary care loss or damage ensues, he [the common carrier] remains responsible, though the so-called act of God may have been the immediate cause of the mischief. If the ship is unseaworthy, and hence perishes from the storm which it otherwise would have weathered; if the carrier by undue deviation or delay exposes himself to the danger which he otherwise would have avoided; or if by his rashness he unnecessarily encounters it, as by putting to sea in a raging storm, the loss cannot be said to be due to the act of God alone, and the carrier cannot have the benefit of the exception.[16]

Nevertheless, there is a wide variety of occurrences that may amount to acts of God and thus absolve the carrier of liability. If the shipper wishes protection against these risks, it may obtain it by a separate insurance policy.

A common carrier may also avoid liability for damage to goods if it can show that the goods had the seeds of their own destruction within them at the time of shipment: that they had an *inherent vice*. Thus, goods may have been in a combustible condition or have had latent defects that rendered them more susceptible to breakage than is typical of goods of their category. This defence by the carrier also includes inadequate packing of the goods by the shipper and is a good defence whether or not the carrier was aware of the inadequate packing.[17]

A common carrier can offer a third defence, that the shipper has been guilty of a breach of duty. A contract for the transportation of goods includes an implied promise on the part of the shipper that the goods are safe to carry; the term exists whether or not the shipper is aware of the danger.[18] It is possible, therefore, for the shipper itself to be in breach of contract and so to release the common carrier from its part of the bargain.

---

[15] Forward v. Pittard (1785), 99 E.R. 953, at 956-7 (authors' italics).
[16] Nugent v. Smith (1875), 1 C.P.D. 423, at 436.
[17] Gould v. South Eastern & Chatham Railway, [1920] 2 K.B. 186.
[18] Burley Ltd. v. Stepney Corporation, [1947] 1 All E.R. 507, at 510.

Indeed, if the goods cause damage to the carrier's equipment, for instance by exploding, the carrier may successfully sue for damages. Another example of default by the shipper arises when it declares less than the full value of the goods to the carrier. It may do this in order to pay a lower freight charge than it would have paid had it declared their true value. In these circumstances, the carrier is not released from its duty, but its liability is limited to the declared value.

Contractual Terms Limiting Liability of Carriers

A common carrier may, and frequently does, limit the amount of its liability when the shipper does not declare the value of the goods. Notice of this limitation in liability is printed prominently across the shipping document and repeated in detail on the reverse side. Thus, a bill of lading commonly states, "Liability limited to $50.00 unless higher value is declared by the shipper and inserted herein." This term requires the shipper to declare a higher value when necessary and to pay a correspondingly higher rate for the greater liability undertaken by the common carrier. Terms of this kind limiting the liability of carriers who operate interprovincial or international routes must be approved by the Canadian Transport Commissioners and thus there is some public control over the extent to which common carriers may contract themselves out of their special liability.[19] Terms limiting liability when subject to public control often make good sense between the parties: the common carrier bases its freight charges on all the terms of the contract and the other contracting party (the shipper) knows the extent to which it should contract separately for insurance. While these terms are a type of exemption clause, they seek to limit rather than eliminate the carrier's liability.

As with other types of contract, the courts have been unwilling to construe an exemption clause as freeing a party to a contract from liability for default when the default amounts to a total failure to carry out the contract.[20]

Remedies

All carriers, whether common carriers or not, have the usual remedies for breach of contract when a shipper is in default. There is, however, a distinction between common carriers and other carriers with regard to the right of lien. A common carrier, because it is bound to accept goods for shipment so long as it has space available, cannot question the credit of the bailor who tenders the goods to it. Thus, to protect the common carrier, the common law gives it a lien on goods shipped for the amount of unpaid freight or express charges on those goods. Although some doubt exists, the general opinion is that the common law does not give a private carrier a similar lien. Of course, the private carrier may, and usually does, acquire a right of lien on the goods as a term of the contract of carriage.

Neither the common law nor any statutes of general application give either common carriers or private carriers the right to sell goods retained under a lien. Both types of carriers, however, usually stipulate for an express right to sell the goods in case of default.

---

[19] The Railway Act, R.S.C. 1985, c. R-3, s. 341.
[20] Firchuk v. Waterfront Investments & Cartage Ltd. [1970] 1 O.R.327. See the discussion in Chapter 16, at pp. 374-7.

Hotelkeepers or Innkeepers

Definition of an Innkeeper

A distinction similar to the distinction between private carriers and common carriers exists between hotelkeepers or innkeepers and others who also offer various forms of accommodation to the public. The traditional word "innkeeper", like the more modern term "hotelkeeper", or simply "hotel", refers to a person or firm that maintains an establishment offering lodging to any member of the public as a transient guest. For this purpose, a hotel differs from a boarding-house keeper, who may pick and choose whom he or she is willing to accommodate, and also from a restaurant owner, who does not offer lodging to guests. The proprietor of a tourist home or motel that does not offer restaurant facilities is apparently not an innkeeper.

Liability

Businesses other than hotels or inns offering accommodation to the public are under a duty to take reasonable care of the belongings of their guests and patrons. Like warehousing firms, they are liable for damage or loss caused by their negligence or the negligence of their employees. Under the common law, however, innkeepers are under a much higher liability. They are liable as insurers for the *disappearance by loss or theft* of their guests' goods. The historical reason is similar to that for the liability of a common carrier — to prevent collusion between the innkeeper and thieves. There is, however, an important difference between goods bailed to a common carrier and goods left in the room of a hotel guest: the bailor of goods to a common carrier gives them over completely to the care of the carrier, whereas the hotel guest shares the responsibility with the hotel, since he or she has control over the goods from time to time when occupying the room. Accordingly, a hotel may avoid liability if it can show that the disappearance was due to the carelessness of the guest. It may be difficult to decide the cause of the loss in any given case. Leaving a door unlocked in a small country hotel may not amount to negligence, and the hotel might be liable if the guest's goods were stolen. The same act of leaving a hotel door unlocked in a large metropolitan hotel after flaunting expensive jewellery might well amount to carelessness that absolves the hotel.

For a similar reason, the considerations that make a common carrier an insurer of *physical damage* to goods bailed with it do not necessarily apply to a hotel: the guest may be in a position to ascertain whether there was negligence on the part of the hotel. Accordingly, a hotel is liable for damage to the goods of its guests — as distinct from its liability for their disappearance through loss or theft — only if the damage was caused by the negligence of the hotel's employees. What should happen, however, if the goods of a guest are totally destroyed in a fire? Surprisingly, there appears to be no clear answer to whether the hotel is an insurer or, like a warehousing firm, is liable for loss by fire only if its employees were negligent.

The Innkeepers (or Hotelkeepers) Act

A hotel may limit its liability as an insurer for the loss or theft of the goods of guests by complying with the provisions of the Innkeepers Act or Hotelkeepers Act in its province.

The various provincial Acts are largely based on the English Innkeepers' Liability Act, 1863. Depending upon the province, the legislation either reduces a hotel's liability to a maximum amount varying from $150 to $40, or eliminates its liability as an insurer entirely.[21] The hotel does not have the benefit of this protection "where the goods have been stolen, lost or injured through the wilful act, default or neglect of the innkeeper or a servant in his employ", or "where the goods have been deposited expressly for safe custody with the innkeeper". If the hotel refuses to accept the goods of a guest for safe custody it loses the benefit of the reduced liability under the statute and is subject to the full common law liability of innkeepers.

The various statutes require the hotel to display conspicuously a copy of the section of the Act that limits liability in order to take advantage of the section. If a hotel fails to comply with this requirement, it loses that protection.

Remedies

A hotel, like a common carrier, owes a duty to the public generally. As we have seen, it is restricted in its right to refuse guests. Accordingly, the common law gave it a lien over the goods of guests for the value of its services. The right was only a lien, however, and did not include the right to sell the goods. Boarding-house keepers and proprietors of restaurants had no such right to a lien.

This appears to be the law today in England. The Innkeepers Acts of the various provinces, except for Newfoundland, extend the right of lien to boarding-house keepers and lodging-house keepers on the goods of their guests.[22] The Acts also give the right to sell the goods of guests by public auction if their bills remain unpaid for a specified period. The requirements of notice and advertising vary from province to province. There appears to be no right of lien or sale for a restaurant proprietor either by common law or under the Innkeepers Acts.

$\mathcal{P}$LEDGE OR PAWN

While these two terms have the same legal significance, a pawn has a colloquial usage that restricts it to transactions with a pawnbroker. A pledge or pawn is a bailment of personal property as security for repayment of a loan. The borrower is the *pledgor* and the creditor the *pledgee*. The subject-matter of a pledge may be goods left with a pawnbroker, for example, or share certificates left with a bank. As with other forms of bailment, the basis of the transaction is that the title to the thing bailed remains with the borrower (bailor), although the possession passes to the lender (bailee).

A pledge is a bailment where the change in possession is for the benefit of the bailee. It requests possession of the pledgor's personal property as security for the loan it has made to the pledgor. In agreeing to lend the money, it gives valuable consideration for the pledge. Accordingly (as we noted above under "Liability of a Bailee"), as a bailee for value

---

[21] See, for example: Hotelkeepers Act, R.S.B.C. 1979, c. 182, s. 3; Innkeepers Act, R.S.O. 1990, c. I-7, s. 4(1); R.S.N.S. 1989, c. 229, s. 4.

[22] R.S.B.C. 1979, c. 182, s. 2; R.S.O. 1990, c. I-7, s. 2; R.S.N.S. 1989, c. 229, s. 3.

it must exercise such care as is reasonable in the ordinary and proper course of its business. A bank is expected to store negotiable bonds in its vault and is liable for their loss if they are left out of the vault and stolen.

A pledgee obtains a lien on the personal property pledged with it. The pledgor cannot recover possession of the goods until it repays the debt for which they are security. In addition, by pledging the goods, the pledgor gives authority to the pledgee to sell the pledged goods upon default. Such authority to sell is implied if not stated expressly in the contract of pledge. The lender (pledgee) may reimburse itself out of the proceeds of the sale for any costs incurred as a result of the default and for the amount of the unpaid loan. The surplus, if any, belongs to the borrower. If the property does not bring enough in the sale to liquidate the debt, the borrower remains liable as an ordinary debtor for the deficiency.

The rule is different for pawnbrokers, where the legal effect is governed by provincial statute. A pawnbroker may obtain absolute ownership of the pledged goods after retaining them for a specified period, sending notice of a last opportunity to redeem to the pawner and publishing a final notice in a newspaper.[23]

*H*IRE OR USE OF A CHATTEL

Examples of a bailment for hire or use are renting an automobile, leasing heavy construction equipment for building purposes, and leasing a postage-meter machine or electronic data-processing equipment for office use. In bailments for hire or use of a chattel the change in possession is for the benefit of the bailee; the bailor's benefit is in payment for the use of its property.

The standard of care required of a bailee that hires equipment is to take such care as a prudent person would exercise in the use of his or her own property. In *Reynolds v. Roxburgh*,[24] the defendant had rented a portable steam engine from the plaintiff to power a wood-cutting saw. The engine exploded immediately after it was put into use, and the plaintiff sued the defendant for the value of the destroyed engine and boiler. He alleged that the defendant had not tested the steam gauge and safety valve before running the machine. The court applied the rule that "the hirer of a chattel is required to use ... the degree of diligence which prudent men use ... in keeping their own goods of the same kind"[25] The court held that this standard of care did not require the bailee to test the safety gauge and valve. Accordingly the defendant was not in breach of his duty as a bailee for hire and was not liable to pay for the destroyed steam engine.

In bailments of this kind where the bailee has relied on the skill and judgment of the bailor to supply an article suitable for the bailee's requirement, and where it is the business of the bailor to supply such articles, the bailor impliedly warrants that the equipment is reasonably fit for the purpose for which it was hired.[26] Some doubt exists as to whether this liability is limited to defects of which the bailor ought to have been aware; but if a strict analogy is drawn with the corresponding implied term in a contract of sale, a bailor, like a

---

[23] See for example: The Pawnbrokers Act, R.S.O. 1990, c. P-6, ss. 20-22.

[24] (1886), 10 O.R. 649.

[25] *Ibid.*, per Armour, J., at 655.

[26] Griffith S.S. Co. v. Western Plywood Co., [1953] 3 D.L.R. 29.

seller, should be liable even if the offending defect in the chattel is something it could not have detected. We may note that in *Reynolds v. Roxburgh* the explosion of the steam boiler killed one man and severely injured another, so that while the point was not raised in the case, the liability of the bailor as well as the bailee might have been in dispute.

If a business contracts to hire a chattel for a given period it will be liable for the whole rental, even if it finds that it has overestimated the time it needed to use the equipment. (In the same way, a tenant of a building is liable for rent for the full period of the lease whether he occupies or uses the premises or not.) A bailor may, of course, agree to take equipment back ahead of time and to reduce the rental charges: when she does so, she is consenting to a discharge of the original contract of bailment and to replacing it with a substituted agreement.

A variation in a contract for the hire of a chattel is a contract of hire with an option to purchase. The bailee hires the chattel on the understanding that he has an option to purchase it by instalment payments, and if he does so, the title to the chattel will pass to him when the instalments are completed. Frequently, these arrangements state that any sums already paid for the hire of the chattel may be applied against the price if the hirer decides to buy. Meanwhile, the contract creates a bailment, and the hirer has no contractual obligation to pay the purchase price. The "hire-purchase agreement" is widespread in England in consumer sales but not in Canada, although it is used in lease/purchase arrangements for automobiles. In Canada, the usual device for purchasing articles "on time" is the conditional sale agreement which, as we shall see in Chapter 33, also creates a type of bailment for value.

The essence of a contract for the hire and use of a chattel is the surrender of possession by the bailor in return for a fee. Since a bailor already owns the chattel the remedy of lien has no application. Its claim is to recover the contract price for the hiring or to sue *quantum meruit* for the value of the benefit received by the bailee. A bailor may, of course, also sue for the return of its property if the bailee is in breach of the bailment contract or retains the property beyond the end of the rental period.

FINDERS

A person who finds a valuable object is not bound to take possession of it, but once he does so he becomes a bailee for the owner, and must exercise the degree of care to be expected of a bailee where the bailment is gratuitous and for the benefit of the bailor (the owner).

Sometimes, of course, the identity of the owner of an object is unknown: the question then arises of whether the finder is entitled to keep or sell it. Is there simply a bailment, or has ownership been acquired along with possession? In these circumstances, a finder generally acquires a good title against everyone except the owner; but the rule has been qualified so that it applies only to goods found in what the court regards as a "public place". As a result, in many instances a finder will not be entitled to keep the object as against a person who owns or controls the "private" place within which the object was found, even though that person may have been unaware of its existence.

A court may consequently have to decide whether the area within which the object is found can fairly be described as a "public place", or whether it can be said to have been within the "control" or "custody" of someone else. One or two examples will illustrate these difficulties. Suppose someone finds a $100 banknote on the floor of a retail shop: is a store where the public is invited a "public place", and if so, are some parts of the store more "public" than others?[27] Or, suppose the owner of an antique desk gives temporary possession of it to a repairer, who finds a valuable ring in a secret compartment that is unknown to the owner: can the finder be said to "control" or to "have custody of" the desk in which the ring was discovered?[28]

Although the question of the rights of a finder arises quite frequently, it is fraught with conceptual difficulties that tend to make the facts of each case more decisive than the legal rules themselves.[29]

Questions for Review

1. How does a bailment differ from a sale?
2. What important statutory rights does a warehousing firm have?
3. Why does a common carrier require a shipper to state the value of goods delivered for shipment?
4. Distinguish a private carrier from a common carrier.
5. What does the defence of *inherent vice* mean?
6. State whether there is a bailment in each of the following circumstances and if so, what standard of care is required of the bailee:

   (a) *A* takes his friend *B* on a motor trip. *B* insists on paying for the gasoline.
   (b) *C* finds an old wallet lying on the sidewalk. She picks it up, sees that it contains no money, and throws it back on the sidewalk.
   (c) *F*, on her way to the theatre, takes her car to a parking lot. The attendant asks her for the keys, and *F* leaves it to the attendant to find a space for the vehicle.
   (d) *G*, a student, borrows a book from the university library.
   (e) On a warm winter day *H* goes to the *J* Restaurant for a meal. On leaving the restaurant afterwards, he inadvertently leaves his hat and overcoat behind.

7. Give an example of a condition subsequent in a contract of bailment.
8. In which type of bailment does the bailee owe the greater duty of care: a gratuitous bailment for the benefit of the bailor, or a gratuitous bailment for the benefit of the bailee?
9. In what respect is the liability of a common carrier greater than the liability of a warehousing firm?
10. Under what circumstances does a bailor owe a duty of care to a bailee?
11. Assuming that there is no term in the contract of bailment requiring the bailee to insure the goods against loss by fire:

    (a) is a warehousing firm liable if such loss occurs?
    (b) is a common carrier liable?

12. Why is a pledge a more valuable right than a lien?
13. For what type of harm does a hotel have the liability of an insurer towards its guests?

---

[27] See *Bridges v. Hawkesworth* (1851), 21 L.J. Q.B. 75, where a customer was held to be entitled, as against the shopkeeper, to banknotes dropped on the main floor of the shop by some unknown person and found there by the customer.

[28] See *Cartwright v. Green* (1803), 32 E.R. 412, where the court decided in the negative.

[29] For an attempt to state the general rules, see *Parker v. British Airways Board* [1982] 1 All E.R. 834.

14. Jones took her outboard motor to Martin's Marina and Repair Centre for its annual overhaul and storage. Since considerable repairs and parts were needed, Jones left a deposit of $500 with Martin. Shortly afterwards, before making any repairs, Martin went bankrupt. What are Jones's rights in the bankruptcy proceedings?

15. What types of bailee have an obligation that is in conflict with their freedom of contract?

16. Is there a special reason for giving a common carrier a lien on goods shipped?

17. How does the history of the common law help to explain the special liability of a common carrier or a hotel?

Problems

Problem 1

Walcot arrived at the Red Lantern Hotel on a Saturday afternoon, checked in, and handed the bellhop a bag containing negotiable securities worth $12 000. He said nothing to the bellhop, who placed the bag under a counter at the bar, as he had often done on Walcot's previous visits. Walcot then had a business meeting with others in the bar of the hotel; once or twice he called for the bag and either deposited in it, or withdrew from it, some business papers.

When Walcot returned that evening to pick up the bag and take it to his room, he discovered that it had been stolen. Walcot sued the hotel proprietors for $12 000. At the trial Walcot testified that he had told the bellhop on his previous visit and on other occasions that the bag was important and "to be sure to keep an eye on it" and that he always tipped the bellhop at the end of his stay at the hotel. The bellhop testified that Walcot had never said anything to him about the importance or contents of the bag. After hearing the examination and cross-examination of these witnesses, the judge found the testimony of the bellhop more credible than that of Walcot.

What additional facts might the court wish to establish before reaching a decision? What would be the main legal issue in the case? Express, in relation to any additional facts assumed, an opinion about the likely decision of the court.

Problem 2

Rowan drove her car onto a parking lot operated by Lee. When she paid a deposit of $1.50 and turned her car over to Lee's employee, she received a parking receipt. The ticket contained on its face the following clause:

> Charges are for the use of parking space only. The company assumes no responsibility for loss through fire, theft, collision or otherwise to the car or its contents, whether due to negligence or otherwise. CARS PARKED AT OWNER'S RISK.

The parking-lot employee then volunteered to park the car for Rowan: in the process, he ran it into the side of another car already parked, causing considerable damage to both cars.

Rowan brought an action against Lee for damages for negligence or, in the alternative, for breach of the contract of bailment. Offer an opinion about whether her action should succeed.

Suppose that the owner of the other car in the collision also brought an action against the parking-lot owner for damages to her car. Would the result in that action necessarily be the same as that in the action brought by Rowan?

Problem 3

Mrs. Hubbard inherited a number of valuable pieces of furniture, china, and glassware. Not having room in her home for them, she had the Bailey Storage Co. pack the articles in steel-banded boxes and take them to its warehouse. Subsequently, the storage charges fell into arrears to the extent of $400. Bailey Storage sent Hubbard notice of its intention to sell the goods at public auction if the charges were not paid by a specified date. At the last moment Hubbard persuaded the manager of Bailey Storage not to dispose of the goods in this way, but to deliver them to Scrawley, an antique dealer and auctioneer to whom she promised she would give authority to sell the goods; she urged that Scrawley's experience in handling such articles would make it possible to realize much more from their sale. As soon as the goods were delivered to the auctioneer, however, Hubbard claimed personal possession of them, asserting that Bailey Storage had forfeited its warehousing firm's lien. Bailey Storage claimed possession of the goods. The auctioneer, afraid of liability for delivering the goods to the wrong person, kept them in custody and insisted that the matter be resolved by reference to the court. Before any court action commenced, the goods were stolen from Scrawley's premises one night when an employee inadvertently left a door unlocked. Is Scrawley liable and, if so, to whom? (For reference, see *Heriteau v. Morris Realty Ltd.,* [1944] 1 D.L.R. 28.)

Cases

Case 1

Shaw, an automobile dealer, arranged with Dr. DiLemma, a customer of long standing, to lend him a 1995 Mercury over the Thanksgiving weekend, with a view to a possible trade-in of the doctor's 1990 Thunderbird if the doctor was satisfied with the new car.

DiLemma drove the Thunderbird to Shaw's garage and left it there. Over the holiday one of Shaw's employees, an apprentice mechanic, came back to work on his own car. Normal procedure when employees wished to work in the garage for their own purposes was for them to obtain specific permission; the mechanic had attempted to telephone Shaw for permission but kept getting a busy signal. Nevertheless, he went to the garage and parked his car next to DiLemma's Thunderbird. While working on his car, the apprentice put a five-gallon can of gasoline in the trunk. He then noticed a piece of sheet metal hanging down from the back and undertook to cut it off with an oxyacetylene torch; a tremendous explosion followed.

On returning from his cottage with the Mercury the following day DiLemma saw the burned-out shell of his Thunderbird in the main building of the garage. Shaw refused to accept responsibility for the damage done to the Thunderbird. He contended that as no sale had been effected, the Thunderbird belonged to the doctor at the time of the explosion and had been left on his premises voluntarily. Dr. DiLemma then brought an action against Shaw for damages. Should he succeed? Identify the main issues and offer reasons for your opinion.

Case 2

On November 1, following a good day's business at her retail cheese shop, Alys Riesmann took her day's cash receipts to the Hi-Rise Bank and, since it was after banking hours, deposited them in the night depository there. When arranging for the use of this facility, she had previously signed a standard form document of the bank containing the following clause:

> The Bank shall be under no responsibility whatever in respect of any property placed in the depository but on the contrary the use of the depository shall be at the risk of the undersigned.

The next morning the head teller at the branch where Ms. Riesmann had deposited her money removed the contents of the depository and placed them on the counter for sorting, in full view of anyone looking through the window of the bank. Soon afterwards, before the teller had noted the amounts for credit to individual depositors and before the bank had opened for business, robbers broke through the window, held up the head teller and took the money, including that deposited the night before by Riesmann.

When Riesmann received her bank statement at the end of the month, she noticed that the deposit of November 1 had not been credited. On inquiry, she was advised that the money had been stolen and that the bank, in accordance with the exempting clause in her contract for the use of the depository, was not prepared to accept liability for it. Riesmann then brought an action against the bank for the amount of her deposit.

Outline the legal question that must be resolved in this dispute, and offer with reasons an opinion about the probable outcome of the action.

Case 3

In January Maud Bradshaw acquired a new, silver-blue mink jacket that cost her $3500. In April she took it to Collier Fur Co. for storage during the summer months. The proprietor said that although he did not have his own storage facilities, he had arrangements with another firm that had a good vault. Bradshaw replied that it was immaterial to her where the jacket was stored as long as it was properly looked after. Collier Fur Co. then gave her a document setting out the transaction and sent the jacket to Tidy Cleaners & Dyers Ltd. where it was stored. The document read in part as follows:

> In consideration of the payment of $75.00 insurance and storage charges, Collier Fur Co. agrees to accept the garment described above for storage and further agrees to insure same against loss or damage by fire, theft or moths for the season of 1995. Unless advised within five days from the date of this receipt, valuation of the garment as shown here will be accepted by both parties as correct and just and not subject to further alterations. Liability of Collier Fur Co. in any event is not to exceed the valuation of the garment as stated in this receipt.

For the purpose of determining the insurance and storage charge Bradshaw set a valuation of $2000 on the jacket, and this amount was inserted in the agreement.

When Bradshaw requested the jacket in the fall, Tidy Cleaners & Dyers Ltd. could not produce it; it had been either lost or given to another customer by mistake. Bradshaw sued Collier Fur Co. for damages of $3500 for breach of contract or, in the alternative, for negligence. Collier Fur Co. admitted liability for only $2000 and tendered that sum in settlement by depositing it with a court official. What should the court's decision be?

Case 4

The general manager of Maritime Steel Ltd. requested by telephone that Fundy Towing Co. Ltd. pick up a cargo of steel bars at Sydney and deliver them to the steel company's plant in Saint John. On previous occasions these parties had contracted by an exchange of letters, all of which included clauses to say that Fundy Towing was not liable for any loss of or damage to cargo as long as its tugboat was kept in seaworthy condition. On this occasion, they said nothing about such a term in their telephone conversation. They did, however, undertake to confirm in writing the terms agreed to in their conversation, though both neglected to do so.

Fundy Towing loaded the steel on a scow at Sydney. The scow was then linked by a tow-line with three others and towed as the rearmost scow behind a new tugboat. It was not possible for the master of the tug to keep the last scow in view. Going under a bridge in Saint John harbour, the last scow collided with the pier of the bridge. The load of steel was spilled: some was lost and much of what was recovered was so twisted that Maritime Steel incurred considerable expense in restoring it to a usable condition.

Maritime Steel sued Fundy Towing for damages for breach of contract, claiming the value of the steel lost, depreciation in the value of the steel recovered, salvage expenses, and loss of profit. Evidence was produced to show that the master of the tug, a person of considerable experience, had not followed a course in the centre of the opening under the bridge, and that the accident had been caused by a tow-line between the scows that was rather longer than usual.

What are the issues in this case? Should the action succeed? Give reasons for your opinion.

CHAPTER 22

PRINCIPAL AND AGENT

$\mathcal{T}$HE NATURE OF AGENCY

As we shall use the term, *agency* is a relationship in which one person, known as an *agent*, is authorized to bring another party for whom she acts, known as a *principal*, into contractual relations with third parties. Agency may be created by the terms of an employment contract in which an employer as principal delegates to an employee as agent the task of negotiating and making some or all of its contracts. However, the functions of agency and employment may be entirely separate: an agent need not be an employee at all. Thus, a person may be a commission agent, that is, one who sells on behalf of the principal to third parties. She may be under no duty to sell the principal's goods, nor be bound to keep herself available for her principal, but may simply receive remuneration in the form of commissions for whatever contracts she makes on behalf of her principal. A person may also volunteer gratuitously to act as an agent. A promise to do so is not binding, but once a person begins an undertaking to act as an agent in a particular transaction, that person is bound by all the duties of an agent under contract.

Sometimes the term "agency" has the larger connotation of a general representative capacity so that it encompasses a wider variety of activities than entering into contracts on behalf of a principal. It is in this larger sense of the term that an auditor is sometimes spoken of as an "agent" for the shareholders of a corporation: her function is to review the accounts and report to the shareholders on the fairness of the corporation's financial statements, but she has no authority to enter into contracts for either the corporation or its shareholders. Similarly, the so-called real estate "agent" does not have authority, as such, to sell the property of a client — her role is to introduce prospective purchasers, and the client contracts directly with the purchaser. In this chapter, most of our references will be to instances in which an agent's role is to enter into contracts for her principal.

In discussing the law of principal and agent we must keep in mind two levels of relationship: first, the relation between principal and agent, usually expressed in the form of an *agency agreement*; and second, the relation between the principal and third parties with whom the agent makes contracts on the principal's behalf. A contract setting out the relation between a principal and its agent should clearly define the limits of the agent's authority: how far she can go in making a contract with a third party without obtaining further instructions from the principal. An agency agreement may confer upon an agent a very wide and general authority to make contracts, or an authority narrowly restricted to making a specific contract, or any degree of authority between these extremes.

The agency relationship is widely used in business affairs. A corporation can enter into contractual relations only when its officers and employees act as agents on its behalf, whether the contracts be for hiring employees, purchasing goods and services, or selling its product. In partnership, too, agency plays an important role. Each partner is presumed by law to be an agent of the other partners, with very wide authority to act on behalf of the firm; often the partnership agreement concerns itself with the limits to be placed on this authority. Lawyers frequently act as agents for their clients in the purchase or sale of land and buildings. Stockbrokers are agents for clients who place orders with them to buy or sell shares. Insurance agents act on behalf of their principal, the insurance company, to negotiate contracts of insurance. Auctioneers and commission merchants in possession of goods have authority to sell them for their principals. *Del credere* agents, as we have seen in Chapter 12, not only make contracts for their principals but also guarantee performance by third parties.

Any person who has the capacity to contract may engage an agent to contract on his behalf. An agent's power to contract on behalf of her principal is limited to the capacity that the principal possesses. Accordingly, if a minor engages an agent, the contracts made for him by the agent are as voidable at his option as if he had made them personally.

While a principal must be competent to contract, an agent need not be capable of contracting in her own right. An agent may be a minor and yet bind her principal in contracts with third parties. However, the agency agreement itself would be voidable at the option of the minor.

WAYS IN WHICH AN AGENCY RELATIONSHIP CAN BE ESTABLISHED

By Express Agreement

An agency agreement may be oral, written, or in writing under seal; any definite arrangement between principal and agent, whatever its form, is an express agreement to create the agency relationship. If an agency agreement is to extend beyond one year, it must be in writing to be enforceable in provinces where the relevant section of the Statute of Frauds continues to apply; as we have seen, it does not apply in British Columbia and Manitoba. In any event, it is desirable for each party to have a copy of the agency agreement in writing and signed by both of them in order to minimize future misunderstanding about the scope of the agent's authority and other terms of the arrangement.

An agent should always have authorization in writing if she wishes to issue promissory notes, accept drafts, and draw cheques in the name of her principal, and she should sign them in a way that makes it clear that she is acting in a representative capacity; otherwise she may be personally liable on the instrument.[1]

A *power of attorney* is a special type of express agency agreement. In the usual and strict sense of the term it refers to a grant of authority under the seal of the principal. An agent who does not receive authority under seal can be authorized to do all acts on behalf of the principal except sign documents under seal. Accordingly, whenever the parties envisage that the agent may need to sign and seal documents in the course of her service, the principal gives authorization under seal in a power of attorney. A power of attorney, for example, is given to an agent who is expected to carry through a real estate transaction to its completion. Sometimes an agent's written authority is called a power of attorney although it is not under seal, but this description is not strictly accurate.

A contract of agency, like any other contract, frequently contains implied terms; these terms may supplement the express authority in the contract. Thus, when a principal expressly authorizes an agent to make a purchase, say, of Irish linen in Belfast, the agent would also have implied authority to make a contract for shipment of the goods to Canada.

By Ratification

Sometimes a person purports to act as an agent knowing she has no authority but hoping that the proposed principal will later adopt the contract. Subsequent adoption by the

---

[1] See Bills of Exchange Act, R.S.C. 1985, c. B-4, s. 51(1).

principal is called *ratification*. The need for ratification may arise for either of two reasons: first, because the person purporting to act as agent is not an agent at all for the principal whom she identifies; or second, because she has only a limited authority and has exceeded it. If a principal does not ratify, questions of reliance by third parties and estoppel may arise. These issues will be discussed in the next section of this chapter.

When a principal does ratify, the effect is to establish the contract with the third party retroactively, as if the agent had possessed the needed authority at the time she made the contract. The principal, agent, and third party are then in the same position with regard to the contract as if the agency agreement had existed from the beginning.

A named principal need not state his ratification expressly. It may be implied from the fact of his assuming the benefits of the contract. Moreover, ratification cannot be partial: a principal cannot accept the benefits without also reimbursing the agent for her costs, nor can he ratify only those aspects of the transaction that prove to be to his advantage but refuse to ratify the balance of the contract. A principal must also ratify within a reasonable time to be able to claim the benefit of a contract.[2]

Not all contracts made by an agent without authority may be ratified by the principal; in some circumstances the court will not recognize the ratification. In the first place, when an agent purports to accept an offer "subject to the ratification of my principal", the later ratification will not be retroactive. This apparent exception is simply an application of the rules of offer and acceptance: a conditional acceptance by an agent is not acceptance at all. The offeror may revoke the offer at any time before acceptance. In these circumstances the eventual "ratification" of the principal is really only an acceptance of the original offer.

Second, in jurisdictions that have not revised their corporations legislation to overrule the common law, a corporation, after it comes into existence, is unable to ratify contracts made for it by agents or promoters before it was incorporated. The historical reason given for this rule is that an agent cannot make a contract on behalf of a principal if at the time the contract was attempted the principal could not have made the contract on its own behalf. On this basis, even if the corporation after coming into existence acquiesces and acts under the contract, it cannot obtain any rights against the third party or be liable to it.

ILLUSTRATION

A and *B*, promoters of the *C* Co. Ltd., enter into a contract for the supply of office equipment before the corporation is incorporated. After its incorporation, *C* Co. Ltd. uses the office equipment but fails to pay the suppliers. If the suppliers sue *C* Co. Ltd., it may defend successfully on the grounds that it was impossible for it to ratify the contract, not having been in existence when the contract was made for it.[3] The suppliers may, however, sue *A* and *B* for damages for having warranted that they had authority to act when they did not.[4] In addition, since no contract was formed, title to the office equipment did not pass and the suppliers may now repossess it. The supplier would also likely succeed in a *quantum meruit* claim for any benefit *C* Co. Ltd. actually received from use of the equipment.

---

[2] Metropolitan Asylums Board Managers v. Kingham & Sons (1890), 6 T.L.R. 217.
[3] Kelner v. Baxter (1866) L.R.2 C.P 174.
[4] Delta Construction Co. Ltd. v. Lidstone *et al.* (1979), 96 D.L.R.(3rd) 457.

This result can be avoided if, after incorporation, C Co. Ltd. expressly contracts with the suppliers for the purchase of the office equipment; such a contract will relieve the promoters of liability and make the corporation liable at common law. However, the corporations acts of most Canadian jurisdictions now permit a corporation simply to adopt a contract made on its behalf before it was incorporated. We shall refer to this matter again briefly in Chapter 31 ("The Management and Operation of a Corporation").

Third, a principal cannot ratify a contract made for him if, at the time he purports to ratify the act, he could not have made that contract himself.

ILLUSTRATION

A arranges on behalf of P, but without P's authority, to insure P's buildings against fire loss, with the entire insurance payable to P. The buildings burn down, and P announces its ratification of the contract of insurance.

The ratification will not be effective because at the time P attempts to ratify, the buildings are already destroyed, and it would be too late for P itself to insure them.[5]

Another aspect of this third point is that a principal cannot ratify when the rights of an outsider are affected.

ILLUSTRATION

A, without authority from P, purports to accept T's offer to sell a large quantity of canned goods to P. Subsequently, before the delivery date, T learns that A had no authority. Because the market is uncertain,

T is afraid to wait for P's ratification and makes a contract to sell the same goods to X. Ratification by P will now be ineffective because an outsider, X, has acquired rights to the goods.

This illustration raises a further problem. Suppose the market value of the goods is rising rapidly at the time T learns A had no authority to buy them. Can T revoke its offer to sell, and retain the goods for later sale to another party at a higher price? The answer turns upon the legal significance of A's acceptance. If A's acceptance is ineffective until ratification by P, then T can revoke its offer before that time. If, on the other hand, A's acceptance creates a binding contract, we are confronted with the paradox that T is bound while P, not yet having ratified, has a choice to bind himself or not. This situation arose in *Bolton Partners v. Lambert*[6] where T's offer was accepted by A on behalf of P but without authority, and T then attempted to withdraw the offer before P's ratification. The court held that the revocation was ineffective and T was bound by P's subsequent ratification.

The decision has been followed in a few English cases although it has been criticized.[7] In *Fleming v. Bank of New Zealand*[8] Lord Lindley noted that the decision in the *Bolton* case

---

[5] See *Portavon Cinema Co. Ltd. v. Price and Century Insurance Co. Ltd.*, [1939] 4 All E.R. 601, at 607.
[6] (1889), 41 Ch. D. 295.
[7] See Fridman, *The Law of Agency* (5th ed.) p. 87. London: Butterworth & Co. Ltd., 1983.
[8] [1900] A.C. 577.

"presents difficulties", and suggested that the court might reconsider the authority of the case in the future. These misgivings are reflected in the position taken by courts in the United States, where revocation is held to be effective if it precedes ratification. The point has not often come before the Canadian courts, but in one case the court referred to Lord Lindley's statement and impliedly disapproved of the decision in the *Bolton* case.[9] As a result it is questionable whether the *Bolton* decision applies in Canada. Even if it does apply, it is subject to the important qualifications that ratification must not prejudice the rights of an outsider, and that the principal must ratify within a reasonable time.

Finally, a principal cannot ratify if at the time the agent made the contract, she failed to name her intended principal or at least mention the existence of a principal whose identity can then be ascertained. This rule prevents a person from entering into a contract simply in the hope that she may subsequently find a principal to ratify and so relieve her of her rights and duties. An undisclosed principal cannot afterwards ratify a contract made without his authority. On the other hand, as we shall see, when a contract is made with the authority of an undisclosed principal, the principal may intervene and enforce the contract, or may be held liable on the contract once the third party learns of his existence and identity.

By Estoppel

When one party allows another to believe that a certain state of affairs exists, with the result that the other relies upon such belief, the first party will be prevented from afterwards stating that the true state of affairs was different.[10] This rule of law is called *estoppel*: a party is *estopped* from stating the actual facts when he has induced another to rely on an entirely different version. The rule has relevance to the law of agency when a principal acquiesces in a person acting as his agent and a third party relies on that acquiescence.

Agency by estoppel arises when the agent's authority is merely apparent, and not real. An agent may acquire apparent authority from a past manner of transacting business by the principal or from trade custom. The circumstances may make it appear to third parties that an agent has authority to make the bargain when, in fact, she does not have any real authority for the purpose: there exists no understanding between the agent and her principal, express or implied, granting this authority.

Occasionally, a person may appear to have authority though she is not an agent at all; much more frequently an agent does have some real authority but her apparent authority exceeds her real authority. An agent may exceed her real authority by venturing into sideline activities, or she may act within the limits usually ascribed to agents of her type but in violation of a special restriction placed on her activities by the principal. In either of these situations the principal may be unhappy about a contract made for him and may object to performing the contract. When may the principal legally refuse to perform and when will he be bound by the contract?

The test is whether the third party should have been on notice about the agent's abuse of authority — or at least had reason to be suspicious — or whether it could reasonably assume from the kind of business in which the agent is engaged that the agent had authority for the contract in question. A third party is expected to act with a reasonable

---

[9] Goodison Thresher Co. v. Doyle (1925), 57 O.L.R. 300.
[10] See discussion in Chapter 7, under "Injurious Reliance (Equitable Estoppel)".

measure of business acumen, experience, and common sense according to the circumstances. Presumably a third party should first check with the named principal about the agent's authority if the proposed contract is not within an area ordinarily entrusted to such agents, or if its consequences are of relatively great importance for the principal and the third party. An agent does not, for example, usually have authority to borrow money in the principal's name or to commit the principal to new lines of activity. Further, an agent authorized to sell goods is not necessarily authorized to accept the purchase money, particularly where payment to the agent is not customary trade practice or where the principal has sent an invoice to the third party requesting payment. If the third party pays the money to the agent and the agent absconds, the third party may have to pay the money over again to the principal.[11]

On the other hand, it would be impractical or inconvenient in day-to-day business for third parties to have to check an agent's authority in every instance. A presumption of authority is established by trade usage for various types of agency. A principal that seeks to restrict abnormally his agent's authority takes the risk that the agent will have, in the eyes of third parties, an apparent authority exceeding her real authority and may make contracts in excess of that authority. The principal will be estopped from denying liability on contracts made for him within the range of that apparent authority. It is sometimes said that a principal "clothes" his agent with apparent authority: what frequently happens is that the principal provides the material and the agent cuts the cloth according to a somewhat more daring style than the principal had specified. In any event, third parties are entitled to judge by appearances — the clothes will make the man, or woman.

The moral for a firm that especially restricts its agent's authority is to be sure that the third parties with whom the agent is likely to deal receive actual notice of the restriction.

A principal may also be estopped from denying liability on contracts with third parties because of conduct known as *holding out*. If a business has represented someone to be its agent, either by words suggestive of that relationship or by acquiescing in similar contracts made for it by that person in the past, it will not be permitted to deny the existence of an agency. If it holds someone out as its agent, it will not be permitted to assert that no actual agency agreement with that person exists.

ILLUSTRATION

Pickering authorized a broker, Swallow, to buy hemp for him. After the purchase Pickering left the hemp on deposit at a wharf in Swallow's name. Swallow, without any authority, sold the hemp and delivered it to the buyer. The buyer became bankrupt, and the trustee, Busk, acting for the bankrupt buyer obtained title to the hemp.

Pickering claimed that he was not bound by the contract of sale made by Swallow and should be able to recover the hemp from Busk. The court held that Pickering's conduct in leaving the hemp in the broker's name had given the broker apparent authority to sell as well as to buy. Accordingly, Pickering failed to recover the hemp from Busk and could only claim as a creditor of the bankrupt concern. As we shall see, he might also have had a claim against Swallow for breach of their contract of agency.[12]

---

[11] Butwick v. Grant, [1924] 2 K.B. 483.
[12] Pickering v. Busk (1812), 104 E.R. 758.

A question of apparent authority may also arise when an agency agreement ends. If an agent continues to enter into contracts for the principal, and third parties have had no notice of the termination, the principal is bound by the contracts. The matter is of practical importance, as we shall see, when a partner retires from a partnership firm, since partners customarily act as agents for the partnership in contracts with outside parties such as suppliers.

The transaction known as a *consignment* may for some purposes create an agency by estoppel. As we noted in Chapter 18, the effect of a consignment is to transfer physical possession of goods from their owner, the consignor, to a consignee. While the consignor continues to own the goods, the transfer of possession gives the consignee the appearance of ownership and implied authority to sell the goods as agent for the consignor. The Factors Act states that a mercantile agent (for example, a retail shopkeeper or commission merchant) who holds articles for sale on consignment may effectively sell the goods or use them as security for a loan even when she exceeds her authority.[13] The third party (the buyer or lender) thus obtains valid title to the goods against the consignor, provided the third party accepted the goods innocently and in good faith, that is, without knowledge that the owner had forbidden their sale or pledge.

By Necessity

As a general rule, English law does not recognize agency by necessity. We can think of circumstances where one person enters into a contract on behalf of another without authority and where the party receiving the benefit of the contract has a moral duty to ratify. But legal systems do not compel moral conduct in all situations: our law does not make a party who benefited from the altruism of a neighbour liable to compensate the neighbour. "Liabilities are not to be forced upon people behind their backs any more than you can confer a benefit upon a man against his will."[14] Thus, no agency by necessity is created when a person orders the repair of a neighbour's roof that has been severely damaged by a gale while the neighbour was away on holiday. The party requesting the repair of the roof remains personally liable if the owner subsequently refuses to pay for the work. Whether the owner may have preferred less extensive or costly work, or whether he is content with the job and we would think him honour-bound to pay, he is not legally bound to do so.

The courts have recognized only a few exceptions to the general rule that denies the creation of agency by necessity. The owner of a barge salvaged at sea is bound to compensate the rescuer.[15] A carrier of perishable goods usually has authority as an agent by necessity to dispose of them at a reasonable price if it is unable to communicate with their owner for instructions.[16] And at common law, agency by necessity was also established when a husband failed to provide for the maintenance of his wife and family. However, family law reform legislation, designed to safeguard the rights of deserted

---

13   See, for example: Sale of Goods Act, R.S.B.C. 1979, c. 370, s. 58; Factors Act, R.S.O. 1990, c.F -1, s. 2; R.S.N.S. 1989, c. 157, s. 3. Note that the Factors Act retains a now obsolete definition of *factoring*. When the act was passed, a *factor* was one who sold merchandise shipped to him on consignment by the owner and, generally, received a commission based on the amount received from sales. In recent years factors have abandoned their selling and merchandising function and have concentrated on credit and collection activities.

14   Falcke v. Scottish Imperial Insurance Co. (1886), 34 Ch. D. 234 per Bowen, L.J., at 248.

15   The Five Steel Barges (1890), 15 P.D. 142 at 146.

16   Couturier v. Hastie (1856), 10 E.R. 1065.

spouses, seems to have abolished agency by necessity and replaced it with more general rights to claim financial support.

THE DUTIES OF AN AGENT TO THE PRINCIPAL

Obedience and Diligence

As in so many other special types of contract, custom and trade usage have introduced a series of rights and duties for both agent and principal as implied terms of the agency agreement. Any of these implied terms may, of course, be incorporated expressly in an agency agreement or may be excluded by an express term or even by the special circumstances surrounding a particular agency agreement. The breach of any term concerning duties, whether express or implied, gives the aggrieved party the usual remedies against the other for breach of contract. For example, an agent may have private instructions restricting her authority, and if she exceeds that authority but acts within her apparent authority, her principal will be bound by the resulting contract. Nevertheless, the principal will be able to recover from the agent any loss that results from the breach of duty.

The courts generally regard notice to an agent as being the equivalent of notice to the principal: what an agent knows, the principal is deemed to know. An agent, therefore, has a duty to be diligent in keeping her principal informed about all important developments affecting their relationship. Keeping in close touch with her principal will also give the agent the advantage of learning any new information that may have come to the principal and will assist her in carrying out her duties.

Competence

An agent may promise to act for her principal without receiving payment for her services. Before performing such a gratuitous promise she may withdraw. Nevertheless, if she does proceed to act on behalf of the principal, she is bound to use reasonable care, diligence and skill.

ILLUSTRATION

P purchases a piece of land by instalment payments. His friend, A, undertakes to make the payments while P is out of town. P also gives A the money needed to make the payments. A negligently pays the money to the wrong person. P may hold A liable for the loss. Since, however, there is no consideration for A's promise to perform the services, P's action against A must be in tort and not for breach of contract.

In other agency relationships in which an agent is to be paid for her services, the amount of skill that the principal can expect depends on the nature of the agent's task and her known competence for the purpose. An agent ought not to agree to represent a principal in complicated and technical transactions for which she is not qualified, but she has a better chance of avoiding liability for the consequences if she can show that the principal was fully aware of her modest qualifications.

Personal Performance

Because of the high degree of confidence and trust implicit in an agency relationship, the general rule is that an agent cannot delegate her duties. An agent's usual terms of reference include the personal exercise of her judgment, skill, and discretion on the principal's behalf. For this reason, there are relatively few situations in which an agency agreement can properly be performed vicariously by a sub-agent. Moreover, the agent who wrongfully delegates her responsibilities is guilty of a breach of duty to her principal.

There are some circumstances where the nature of the agency relationship or trade usage will give the agent an implied authority to delegate all or part of her duties. Thus, when a stockbroker agrees to buy or sell shares, the broker will have implied authority to make the actual purchase or sale through a sub-agent on the floor of the stock exchange. Again, when a bank acts as agent for its customers, it may sometimes require the services of other banks to represent it in countries where it has no branches itself. Indeed, whenever a corporation is appointed as an agent, it must perform through sub-agents, namely its directors or employees. Finally, a principal may give express consent to performance by a sub-agent, or may subsequently ratify that type of performance.

When an agent has implied authority to perform through a sub-agent, there is generally privity of contract only (a) between the principal and the agent, and (b) between the agent and the sub-agent: in other words, no privity of contract exists between the principal and the sub-agent. Accordingly, the principal may recover from the agent for the consequences of an improper performance by the sub-agent, but has no claim in contract against the sub-agent. The agent may in turn recover from the sub-agent.

When do contracts entered into by a sub-agent make the principal liable to the third party? The third party may enforce the contract against the principal if the sub-agent has express authority to act for him, or makes contracts that the principal subsequently ratifies, or acts in circumstances where the principal is estopped from denying his authority. Of course, the circumstances in which an estoppel may arise are more limited in view of the general rule against delegation noted in the first paragraph of this section. If a sub-agent fails to bind the principal, the third party may sue the sub-agent for breach of warranty of authority.

Good Faith

The duty of good faith arises from the fact that parties are in a special relationship of trust, a *fiduciary* relationship, of which principal and agent is only one example. The law also imposes a duty of the same high degree of good faith and loyalty on members of a partnership and participants in joint business ventures,[17] as well as on members of professions in their relations with clients and patients.

An agent normally receives a fee or commission for her services. Any money that comes into her possession in respect of contracts made for the principal belongs to the principal. She must keep separate records so that she can account to the principal for this money. It is desirable that the money should be put in a separate bank account. If the agent becomes bankrupt, property in her possession belonging to the principal would not then be confused with assets available for the claims of the agent's creditors.

---

[17] See Jirna Limited v. Mister Donut of Canada Ltd. (1971), 22 D.L.R. (3d) 639; Lac Minerals Ltd. v. International Corona Resources Ltd. (1989), 61 D.L.R. (4th) 14.

A stockbroker is both an agent and a trustee for her client (the principal) when she holds money and securities for the client with authority to buy and sell stocks and bonds for the client's account. Any profit the broker realizes from selling securities at a higher price than their cost, or any advantage she secures from buying stocks or bonds at an especially favourable price, accrues to the client. She must account to the client for such profits: her remuneration is limited to a broker's fee.

Good faith requires that an agent place the interest of her principal above all else except the law. She should inform the principal of any information coming to her attention that might influence the principal's decisions. If she has been authorized to buy property at a certain price and learns that it can be obtained for a lesser sum, she is bound to inform the principal. If she buys at the lower price she must pass on the savings to the principal. The duties of a patent attorney to her client also illustrate the rule. For a fee, a patent attorney undertakes to make application on behalf of an inventor to patent an invention. If the patent attorney's work in this connection suggests further refinements or improvements in the invention, she has a recognized duty to give her client (the inventor) the benefit of her ideas: she must not try to exploit them to her own advantage by an independent application for a patent in her own name.

In most circumstances, an agent is not acting in good faith when she serves two principals in the same transaction. The two principals in a business transaction have conflicting interests, as each will want to get the best possible bargain. The most common breach of faith by an agent consists in accepting a commission from a third party as well as from her principal. Such conduct is tantamount to taking a bribe to secure something less than the best possible bargain for the principal.

In a section entitled Secret Commissions,[18] the Criminal Code provides that an agent commits a criminal offence when she corruptly demands or accepts any remuneration from a third party in the conduct of her principal's business affairs. The third party that offers such a bribe or kickback is equally culpable. The section applies when the double agency proceeds "corruptly". We may assume that an agent can act legally for both parties if they are aware of the arrangement and have given their consent. However, ordinary business prudence dictates that a principal should hire his own separate agent to represent him in business transactions.

In *Andrews v. Ramsay*,[19] a real estate agent had agreed to assist in selling property on a commission basis. Subsequently, the agent accepted a commission from the purchaser. The court held that he was liable to his principal not only for the return of his regular selling commission but also for the commission he had received from the third party. Probably, had he chosen, the principal might also have avoided the contract of sale with the third party on grounds of fraud: a third party that offers a payment in these circumstances is as guilty as the agent and is a party to the fraud.

In *Salomons v. Pender*,[20] a real estate agent arranged a sale of land for the owner to a corporation in which the agent was a director and shareholder. The court held that he was not entitled to a commission because he had also an interest in the business of the other contracting party.

---

[18] R.S.C. 1985, c. C-46, s. 426.
[19] [1903] 2 K.B. 635.
[20] (1865), 195 E.R. 682.

An agent's loyalty to her principal is also compromised when she makes herself the other party to the contract without prior notice to, and approval of, the principal — by buying property from, or selling to, the principal. In such a case, an agent places her own interest in conflict with that of her principal. She will be concerned to get the best of the bargain for herself and not for her principal. In *Robinson v. Mollett*[21] a client gave a broker an order to buy tallow. The broker already held some tallow on his own account, and simply sent this tallow to the client. The court held that the client did not have to accept or pay for it. There was no evidence that the broker had obtained either the best tallow or the best price for the principal. Indeed, there is a presumption in these circumstances that the broker would obtain as much personal profit as possible. Again, in *McPherson v. Watt*[22] a solicitor agreed to sell property for a client and then decided that he would like to own it himself. He bought it ostensibly in the name of someone else. The court held that he could not enforce the purchase.

Occasionally a stockbroker may receive independently, from different clients, an offer to buy and an offer to sell the same shares. If she is a member of a recognized stock exchange, she will be subject to the rule that before she can match the sale, or any part of it, she must first make the offer to buy and the offer to sell available to all other members of the exchange. Only in the event that there is no response will she have the opportunity of selling one client's shares directly to the other. The rule was devised to prevent the manipulation of stock prices by contrived transactions, but it serves also to ensure that the broker will get the best available prices for clients.

The Duties of the Principal to the Agent

Commission

While both parties to an agency agreement have a strong interest in how an agent's fee is to be determined, perhaps surprisingly, they sometimes do not deal expressly with the matter. In the absence of an express term about remuneration, an agent is entitled to a reasonable fee to be determined by reference to the fees of other agents who perform comparable services. A request by a principal for services of a kind for which an agent would normally expect to be paid implies a promise to pay a reasonable fee — another example of *quantum meruit*.

The terms on which a principal retains a real estate agent raise special problems about the principal's liability to pay a commission. Placing property for sale with a real estate agent is essentially an offer to pay a fee to the agent in return for a strictly defined service. The prospective seller's offer to pay a commission will ripen into a contract only when the agent does what she has been engaged to do. Many agreements between prospective sellers and real estate agents state that the agent is entitled to commission when she introduces a prospective purchaser who is "ready, willing, and able to purchase" — the fact that the sale is not completed by reason of the seller's refusal to perform will not deprive

---

[21] (1874), L.R. 7 H.L. 802.
[22] (1877), 3 App. Cas. 254. See also Aaron Acceptance Corp. v. Adam (1987) 37 D.L.R. (4th) 133.

the agent of this right.[23] The seller may, however, withdraw his offer at any time before a satisfactory purchaser is introduced, and will not be liable to pay commission. He might even sell the property on his own, and he will not be liable to pay the real estate agent a commission unless the real estate agent was instrumental in introducing the purchaser to him. Real estate agents do, however, often urge a client to sign an *exclusive listing agreement* to operate for a stated period: the client undertakes to pay a commission on any sale of his property during the period whether it is sold by the client himself, the agent, or any other real estate agent. A client is not, of course, obliged to enter into such a contract, but if he does he will be bound by its terms.

Sometimes a prospective seller insists that the listing agreement contain a term that the agent is not entitled to commission unless and until a sale is completed. Such a term governs the rights of the agent; she is not entitled to her commission even when she introduces a suitable purchaser whose offer the seller refuses.

A number of provinces have statutes rendering a contract to pay commission to a real estate agent unenforceable unless it is in writing and signed by the prospective seller of the property. In these provinces, when an agreement for an agent's services is entirely oral, the agent does not acquire an enforceable right even though she may have introduced a willing and able purchaser to the client.[24]

Costs

Even if an agency agreement does not say so directly, there is implied a term that the principal will reimburse the agent for all reasonable expenses incurred within the scope of her real authority. The principal is under no obligation to reimburse the agent for unauthorized acts unless he ratifies them. An agent's ability to claim reimbursement in a court action may, as a practical matter, depend upon her having kept proper accounts and records to substantiate the claim.

LIABILITY OF PRINCIPAL AND AGENT

When an agent makes a contract on behalf of her principal with a third party, the question arises as to who is liable on the contract — the agent or the principal? The answer depends upon a number of factors; was the agent acting within the scope of her authority in making the contract, and was the identity or existence of the principal disclosed to the other party? There are three possible solutions: (a) the principal alone is liable on the contract, (b) the agent alone is liable, or (c) either principal or agent may be held liable.

The Principal Alone is Liable on the Contract

An agent incurs no liability on contracts made for her principal when the agency relationship is functioning as intended. Having brought the contract into being, the agent steps out of the picture: the principal is liable for performance and is the one able to enforce it

---

23 Columbia Caterers & Sherlock Co. v. Famous Restaurants Ltd. (1956), 4 D.L.R. (2d) 601.
24 See, for example, Real Estate and Business Brokers Act, R.S.O. 1990, c. R-4, s. 23; Real Estate Agents' Licensing Act, R.S.A. 1980, c. R-5, s. 25; Real Estate Brokers' Licensing Act, R.S.N.S. 1989, c. 384, s. 23.

against the third party. Further, an agent has no liability to the third party even when she acts outside her real authority so long as she acts within her apparent authority and thus binds her principal; but she may, as we have seen, be liable to the principal for breach of the agency agreement.

To ensure that she has no liability in contracts made for her principal, an agent should indicate that she acts as agent and should identify the principal.[25] The following are examples of signatures that accomplish this purpose:

> "The Smith Corporation Limited
> per W.A. Jones"
> or
> "W.A. Jones
> for The Smith Corporation Limited."

The identification of her principal is a part of the process by which an agent can make it clear to the third party that she is acting only as agent. If an agent does not name her principal, it may be more difficult for her to prove that the third party regarded her as merely an agent: she adds to the risk that the third party may be entitled to look to her for the actual performance of the contract.

Sometimes, however, an agent may persuade a third party to enter into a contract with an unidentified principal. She may describe herself as agent for a party that does not wish for the time being to disclose his name. If the third party is prepared to contract on these terms, it waives its recourse against the agent and limits it to a party whose identity it does not know.[26] An agent may negotiate on such terms in order to obtain options for the purchase of individual pieces of land intended for assembly into a large block. The reasoning is that if the prospective purchaser is a large developer, the disclosure of his identity and purpose might induce owners to hold out for much higher prices. In this situation, although the principal was not named in the contract, it was nevertheless made on his behalf and with his authority, and he alone is liable on, and entitled to enforce, the contract.

A principal does not discharge his liability by handing over the contract price, or goods, to his agent for transmission to the third party; if the agent absconds with the money or the goods, the principal remains liable.[27]

The Agent Alone is Liable on the Contract

When an agent categorically describes herself as a principal though she is in reality acting for an undisclosed principal, the agent alone has rights and liabilities relative to the third party. The principal can neither sue nor be sued on the contract.[28] If the agent describes herself (incorrectly) as the "owner" of a building or a ship, the third party is entitled to regard the operation of the contract as confined to itself and the agent.[29] The agent must, however, do something more than merely fail to disclose the existence of a principal; she must also contract on terms that she herself is the real principal.

---

[25] See Hills v. Swift Canadian Co., [1923] 3 D.L.R. 997.
[26] See QNS Paper Co. v. Chartwell Shipping Ltd. (1984), 62 D.L.R. (4th) 36.
[27] Irvine & Co. v. Watson & Sons (1880), 5 Q.B.D. 414.
[28] Note, however, that the principal may still acquire rights under the contract as an assignee from the agent.
[29] Humble v. Hunter (1848), 116 E.R. 885. Contrast the decision in Watteau v. Fenwick, discussed below.

Either the Principal or the Agent May Be Held Liable on the Contract

Sometimes a person who is in fact an agent makes no mention of her status, and deals with a third party without representing herself as either principal or agent. The third party is entitled to sue the agent on the contract. This is fair, since it may have been influenced by the personal credit and character of the agent.

What are the third party's rights when it discovers the existence and identity of the principal? If the contract was one which the agent had authority to make, the third party has the option of holding *either* principal *or* agent liable for performance of the contract, but not both. If the third party sues and obtains judgment against the agent before it learns of the real principal, it has no rights against the principal.[30] If, however, the fact of agency emerges during litigation, the action may be discontinued and fresh proceedings taken against the principal.

Once a third party elects to sue the principal, the principal may treat the contract as being made with him and has all of the defences of a contracting party.

ILLUSTRATION

A buys goods on credit from *T* Ltd. without disclosing that she is acting for *P* Co. Upon *A*'s default in payment *T* Ltd. learns that *A* was in fact *P* Co.'s agent, and sues *P* Co. for the price. *P* Co. is entitled to counterclaim if the goods are not according to the contract or if *T* Ltd. has been guilty of breach of any other term in the contract of sale.

An undisclosed principal has contractual rights as well as liabilities: he may normally intervene and enforce the contract against the third party.[31] To succeed, however, he must show that the contract was made with his authority. If the agent had no real authority, the undisclosed principal cannot ratify the contract and enforce it. But can the third party hold the principal liable?

ILLUSTRATION

A was employed as manager of an alehouse by *P*, a firm of brewers. *P* had expressly forbidden *A* to purchase certain articles for the business, even though the normal practice of the trade was to give managers such authority. *A* contracted to buy such articles from *T*, without disclosing that he was *P*'s manager. On the licence above the door of the alehouse, only *A*'s name appeared, suggesting that he was the owner rather than a mere manager. When *T* discovered the agency relationship, he sued *P* for the price of the goods.

The English Court of Queen's Bench held the brewery firm liable[32] on the basis that the contract was one that a manager would normally have power to make and was thus within his apparent authority. The fallacy of this reasoning, however, has been pointed

---

[30] Kendall v. Hamilton (1879), 4 App.Cas. 504.

[31] An undisclosed principal is not permitted to enforce a contract that is essentially personal in nature; for example, a contract to purchase shares in a family corporation. See Collins v. Associated Greyhound Racecourses [1930] 1 Ch. 1.

[32] Watteau v. Fenwick [1895] 1 Q.B. 346.

out by several commentators[33]: if the principal was not disclosed, how could the agent have *apparent* authority to contract on his behalf? In a recent Canadian case,[34] the court declined to follow the English precedent.

ILLUSTRATION

A Co. was a management company controlled by the owner of a shopping mall. It had entered into a contract to rent an electronic sign from *T* for use in the shopping mall. In 1983, *P* Co. acquired the ownership of the mall; *A* Co. continued to manage the mall as its agent. *T* was unaware of the change of ownership. In 1985, *T* entered into a new contract with *A* Co. to renew rental of the sign. At the time, no mention was made of *P* Co.'s ownership. The contract was one which *A* Co. had no authority to make. *P* Co. refused to honour the contract and was sued by *T*.

The British Columbia Court of Appeal held that *P* Co., the undisclosed principal, was not liable on the contract. The agent had no authority, and the plaintiff had no knowledge of the principal's existence. The plaintiff's right of recovery was against *A* Co. only.

Liability for Misrepresentation

When an agent acting within her apparent authority is guilty of fraudulent misrepresentation in making a contract, even though the principal did not authorize the misrepresentation and may even have forbidden it, the third party may rescind the contract. Furthermore, the third party may successfully sue the principal as well as the agent for the tort of deceit;[35] the principal may suffer a loss because the contract will not be performed or because he must pay damages, or for both reasons. If the principal was innocent of the fraud, he may in turn successfully sue his agent for damages to compensate for the loss, but if he participated in the misrepresentation he is a co-conspirator and has no rights against the agent.

More generally, it appears that a principal is vicariously liable for torts committed by his agent while representing him — in much the same way as an employer is vicariously liable for torts committed by an employee in the course of employment. Thus Fridman states as one of his conclusions:

> An agent acting within the scope of his apparent authority will make his principal liable for torts committed by him, even if his acts were prohibited by the principal, or were not for the principal's benefit, though the same might not be true if the third party had notice or warning of these facts.[36]

As we have seen in Chapter 4, the actual tortfeasor (in this case the agent) remains liable for her torts, even though the principal is liable as well.

An agent may also be liable to a third party for negligent misrepresentation. For example, Canadian courts have held that a real estate agent, though engaged and paid by the vendor, also owes a duty of care in the statements she makes to the purchaser.[37]

---

[33]   See the comments of Fridman, (1991) 70 *Can. Bar Rev.* 329.
[34]   Sign-O-Lite Plastics Ltd. v. Metropolitan Life Insurance Co. (1990), 49 B.C.L.R.(2d) 183.
[35]   Lloyd v. Grace, Smith & Co. Ltd., [1912] A.C. 716.
[36]   Fridman, *The Law of Agency* (5th ed.) at pp. 280-1.
[37]   See Avery v. Salie (1972), 25 D.L.R.(3rd) 495.

Breach of Warranty of Authority

There is no contract when a person holds herself out to be an agent but has no authority, actual or apparent, and the named principal does not ratify. The situation may arise because the alleged agent has acted fraudulently; a rogue may give the name of a reputable party as principal for the purpose of obtaining goods on credit. The unfortunate seller may not be able to recover the goods if the false agent has absconded with them. The seller will have an action in tort for deceit against the fraudulent agent, but for the seller to succeed the culprit must not only be apprehended but must also have personal resources available to satisfy a court judgment.

An agent may act innocently without any real authority when, unknown to her, her principal has become bankrupt or insane or has died. No contract between a third party and the principal can be formed after the principal has lost contractual capacity or ceased to exist. And no contract is formed between the agent and the third party either, because the agent has acted *as agent*. The remedy of the third party lies not in the ineffectual contract, but in an action against the agent for *breach of warranty of authority*. It does not matter that, when the agent acted for the principal, she was unaware of the principal's misfortune (or demise). Accordingly, an agent should communicate with her principal frequently enough to be assured of his continued well-being.

Jurists have not always agreed on whether breach of warranty of authority is a tort or a wrong to be redressed within the law of contract. If the remedy is contractual, it is not related to the abortive contract between the third party and the principal: rather, it is regarded as a breach of a separate *implied* contract between the agent and the third party in which, in return for the third party agreeing to contract with the principal, the agent impliedly promises that she has authority to act.

We have seen that an agent may be liable if she acts in anticipation of a ratification that she never receives, or if she contracts on behalf of a non-existent principal. These are two further instances of breach of warranty of authority.

We must be careful to distinguish breach of warranty of authority from breach of the agency agreement. *Breach of warranty of authority* is a wrong for which a third party may sue an agent. *Breach of the agency agreement* is a wrong for which a principal may sue the agent, or the agent sue the principal, as the case may be.

TERMINATING AN AGENCY RELATIONSHIP

Frequently an agent performs services for her principal, or at least keeps time available to act as agent and is to that extent unavailable for employment. In this respect, she is akin to an employee. Courts are increasingly willing to infer that a principal-agent relationship contains elements of an employer-employee relationship as well. When such an inference is drawn each party is entitled to reasonable notice before termination becomes effective,[38] as will be discussed in the next chapter.

In the absence of evidence of an employment relationship, an agent's authority may be terminated on any of the following occasions:

---

[38] See Martin-Baker Aircraft Co. v. Canadian Flight Equipment, [1955] 2 Q.B. 556.

(a) at the end of a time specified in the agency agreement;

(b) at the completion of the particular project for which the agency was formed;

(c) upon notice by either the principal or the agent to the other that he or she wishes to end the agency;

(d) upon the death or insanity of either the principal or the agent;

(e) upon the bankruptcy of the principal; and

(f) upon an event which makes performance of the agency agreement impossible.

Where no specific time is fixed for an agency relationship, it is implied that either party may bring the relationship to an end by notice to the other. In other words, an option clause is implied that may be used to discharge the contract by agreement and without breach. If, however, the agreement is for a specified time, premature withdrawal by either principal or agent without the consent of the other constitutes a breach of contract.

Occasionally, an agency agreement may be discharged by frustration. An example of an agency that becomes impossible to perform occurs when an owner of goods has engaged an auctioneer to sell them, and the goods are destroyed by fire before their sale.

When an agency arrangement ends for any reason other than the bankruptcy, death, or insanity of the principal, the principal may be bound by the former agent continuing to act within her apparent authority. In his own interest, a principal ought to bring the termination to the attention of all third parties likely to be affected. This precaution is especially important when a partnership is dissolved, and will be discussed in Chapter 29.

Questions for Review

1. Give examples of common business relationships to which the law of principal and agent applies.

2. In what four ways can an agency relationship be established?

3. Does an express agreement for agency have to be in writing? In what circumstances is the *form* of the agency agreement important?

4. How does the need for ratification arise?

5. In what circumstances may a principal be unable to ratify a contract made earlier for it?

6. What is the meaning of the rule of estoppel? Whose interest is protected by the legal recognition of agency by estoppel?

7. What is the test for determining whether a third party can enforce against a principal a contract made by an agent who has exceeded her real authority?

8. When a principal acquiesces in a misrepresentation by his agent and has to pay damages to the third party for the tort of deceit, may the principal recoup the loss by suing his agent?

9. When an agency by necessity has been established, need the third party prove the consent of the principal in order to succeed? In what situations does the law recognize the possibility of an agency by necessity?

10. In what way may an agent disobey her principal so that the principal will suffer a loss? What is the nature of the principal's remedy against the agent?

11. Is vicarious performance generally permissible in agency agreements?

12. In what ways may an agent act in bad faith?

13. In what respect does the authority usually given to a real estate agent differ from the authority given to most other types of agent?

14. Is it possible for an agent to avoid liability to the third party even when she has not identified her principal?

15. The right of an undisclosed principal to intervene and enforce a contract against the third party is in apparent conflict with a general principle of law that we have considered in an earlier chapter. What is this principle?

16. What requirement must be satisfied before an undisclosed principal can sue the third party?

17. How may an agent become liable to a third party for not having kept in touch with her principal?

18. What is the difference between breach of warranty of authority and breach of the agency agreement?

19. In what respect may a consignee act within her apparent authority but beyond her real authority?

Problems

Problem 1

On July 2, Curran, a sales representative for the Bright Lighting Company obtained a written order from Watts for a generator suitable for his farmhouse. A few hours later when Watts was working in the fields, Curran drove past, and Watts called to him. Curran came to the fence, and Watts told him: "I've been thinking about the generator. You'll have to countermand that order. I can't afford it."

Curran then told Watts that he had already mailed Watts' written order to the offices of the Bright Lighting Company, and insisted that it was now too late for Watts to do anything about it. Watts replied that he did not care; as far as he was concerned, "the deal is off".

On July 10, the copy of Watts' purchase order was stamped "O.K. for shipment" in the offices of the Bright Lighting Company, and on July 12 Bright Lighting Company wrote to Watts acknowledging receipt of his order. The equipment was shipped to Watts on July 30, and refused by him. It was afterwards sold by the railroad company for storage.

Bright Lighting Company then sued Watts on the contract it claimed to have with him. Discuss the main arguments that could be made by each side and the probable result.

Problem 2

Dan Roberts, a real estate agent acting for Murray Smith in the sale of a house, knowingly made a false representation to a prospective purchaser, Anna Yeung, that a second kitchen in the house had been installed in conformity with city regulations. In fact, Smith had received a letter from the city building inspector stating that no building or plumbing permit had been obtained for the installation of the second kitchen, and that the installation constituted a violation of a city zoning by-law because the building was situated in a one-family-dwelling district; the letter further advised Smith that all stoves and sinks must be removed within 30 days. Smith had given a copy of this letter to Roberts and in no way authorized the false representation that Roberts subsequently made to Yeung. The parties signed a contract of sale and Yeung paid a deposit, but when she later learned the facts concerning the kitchen she refused to pay the balance and take possession of the house. Smith brought an action against Yeung for specific performance, claiming that he had not authorized the false assertion made by Roberts. Yeung counterclaimed for a rescission of the contract and damages for deceit. Who should succeed and why?

Problem 3

On January 10, Abbott signed an exclusive listing agreement with York Realty Ltd., real estate agents, for the sale of her residence in Toronto. The agreement gave exclusive authority to York Realty until the following July 10 to sell the property at a price of $250 000. It read in part:

will get paid if offer has to be above 250,000.

1. If an offer to purchase the said property is obtained from a purchaser in accordance with the price and terms of payment thereof, herein set out, I hereby agree to pay you a commission of 6% of the price set out in such offer whether or not I accept such offer.

will pay as long as it sells during listing period

2. If any sale is effected during the currency of this authority from any source whatsoever and at any price, I agree to pay you the above commission on the price agreed upon in such sale.

3. All inquiries from any source whatsoever shall be referred to you and all offers submitted to me shall be brought to your attention before accepting or rejecting same.

York Realty made efforts to sell the property but had not succeeded when Abbott received a notice of expropriation of the property by the Municipality of Metropolitan Toronto pursuant to By-Law No. 5905, passed May 3. The purpose of the expropriation was to acquire land necessary for the construction of a new expressway. A price of $200 000 was determined by arbitration, and Abbott then delivered to the Municipality the deed to the property, as required by the law.

York Realty Ltd. claimed commission of $12 000 (6% of $200 000) and when Abbott refused to pay, sued her. Discuss the defence or defences available to Abbott, and state whether you think the action should succeed. (For reference, see *Oxford Realty Ltd. v. Annette (or Annett)* (1961), 29 D.L.R. (2nd) 299.)

Cases

Case 1

A young people's group at a Saskatoon church decided to include a sleighing party in their winter program of social activities. The secretary consulted the yellow pages of the telephone directory and under "Sleigh Rides" found an advertisement for Kelly's Pavilion on the outskirts of the city. She then made arrangements with a booking office in the city, as designated in the advertisement, by paying a ten-dollar deposit at the office, the balance to be paid at the time of the party. The person in charge of the office had requested the secretary to make the ten-dollar cheque payable to "Kelly's Pavilion".

On the evening of the sleigh ride the group turned up at Kelly's Pavilion but could not locate anyone on the premises. After some searching they found a barn on adjacent property and met Dinsmore, the person who was to conduct the sleigh ride. Each member of the group paid the fee to Dinsmore, who then backed out a two-ton truck and fastened a sleigh to it. The surface was very slippery, and several of the members of the party had to push to get the truck going. Once the truck was moving, the driver, fearing it might get stuck again, took the party around the field at speeds between 25 and 40 kph. As the sleigh went around a turn at high speed one of the group, Lambert, fell off, and the runner went over her foot. She needed medical attention and lost wages because she was unable to go to work for some weeks.

Lambert sued Kelly's Pavilion for damages for breach of the implied contractual term to carry her safely. In defence, the owner of Kelly's Pavilion claimed that Dinsmore was not its employee; that the property from which Dinsmore operated had formerly been used by the Pavilion but had since been leased by it to Dinsmore; and that Kelly's Pavilion continued to operate as booking agent for his sleighing parties only as a convenience. The booking office applied the deposits it received for sleigh rides against the rent due from Dinsmore.

Should this action succeed? Outline the reason or reasons for your conclusion.

Case 2

J.J. Muti is the proprietor of Beau Brummel, a successful men's wear shop. Muti founded the business in 1961 and expanded it over the next twenty years. In 1981, his health deteriorated and he became content to maintain the business at its current level. He was also fortunate to hire J.J. Krabuff, an able assistant who gradually took over more and more of Muti's duties. In 1990 Muti promoted Krabuff to manager, and had a second office built at the back of the premises for him. The office was next to Muti's and people often remarked on the coincidence of having two "J.J.'s" in adjoining offices. By 1994, Muti's absences became longer as he convalesced from illness and spent winters in the south. Krabuff acquired the habit of working in Muti's more luxurious office, where the most important business records were kept. Muti did not object; Krabuff merely reverted to his own office whenever Muti spent time at Beau Brummel. Although Krabuff ran the business on a day-to-day basis, paying staff and other expenses, making deposits at the bank and reordering stock, Muti still made the major decisions about large orders, especially in selecting new high-fashion stock for each season.

On February 15, when Muti was vacationing in the Caribbean, a sales representative of Paolo Leather Goods of Milan, Italy visited Beau Brummel. He asked a clerk whether he could see the "boss". The clerk took the representative to Krabuff who was seated in Muti's office. The Paolo agent offered Krabuff the exclusive dealership for their leather-wear for the entire region, provided he would buy a preliminary order of $50 000 worth of goods. The agent said that three other retailers in the area were after the same deal but he felt Beau Brummel was the best outlet for his firm's high-quality clothing. Krabuff hesitated, concerned about the size of the first order, but finally agreed and placed the order from the representative's samples.

Two weeks later Muti returned and, on learning of the order, was very upset; two years earlier he had had a heated dispute with Paolo and vowed never to buy from the firm again. In addition, he felt it was the wrong time to make a financial commitment for so large an order. He cabled Milan at once to cancel the order, but received a reply that it was too late and the goods were in production. Muti rejected the goods when they arrived and Paolo sued for the price.

At the trial, the Paolo representative was questioned in cross-examination by Muti's lawyer as follows:

Q. Had you ever met Mr. Krabuff before?
A. No sir.
Q. Did he represent himself as owner?
A. No sir. I thought he owned the store.

Q. How did you come to that conclusion?

A. Well he was sitting in the big, fancy office, smoking a cigar, when I asked to see the boss. Nobody else was there. Who else could he be?

Q. I'm asking the questions. Mr. Krabuff never said, "I am the owner", or "boss" or even "manager", or anything like that?

A. No sir, but any person would naturally think ...

Q. Would you think a store manager would have authority to make such a contract?

A. Well, I'm not exactly sure. It might depend on the kind of store.

Q. What about this kind of store?

A. I suppose not, if he was only manager.

Should Paolo Leather Goods succeed in their action for the price? Explain.

Case 3

The firm of Howard & Sodhi, engineers, was retained by Hopeful Gold Mines Ltd. as its mining and engineering consultant. For a monthly fee of $1500 plus any related travelling expenses, Hopeful Gold Mines was entitled to three days per month of the services of either Howard or Sodhi, on request. The services were to take the form of a professional opinion on the quality of ore samples submitted to Howard & Sodhi from time to time, and on the engineering feasibility of economically extracting ore from any particular property designated by Hopeful Gold Mines. Howard & Sodhi had, in all, about twenty-five clients for whom they would do varying amounts of consulting work during the course of a month. Sodhi was also a director of Hopeful Gold Mines.

Two months after the agreement was made, a prospector, Watkins, told Howard about his discovery of some mining claims. After assaying samples of ore from these claims Howard & Sodhi decided that the claims merited further investigation. The claims were adjacent to an area in which Hopeful Gold Mines already had some mining interests under development. Howard arranged to make a trip into the area, and before leaving phoned the president of Hopeful Gold Mines to say that he would be going there "for other clients". Howard also said that he would, "if possible, try to stake some claims in the same approximate area" for Hopeful Gold Mines. The president agreed, and authorized Howard to investigate the area on behalf of Hopeful Gold Mines.

No claims were staked for Hopeful Gold Mines as a result of this trip, but Howard & Sodhi on their own did incorporate a new company, Yellow Gold Mines Ltd., to purchase Watkins' rights in the claims and to exploit the property. In addition to the usual monthly bill for $1500 retainer, Howard charged Hopeful Gold Mines with one-half his travelling expenses on the trip.

When these facts came to light, Hopeful Gold Mines sued Howard & Sodhi for damages. Evidence was adduced to show that Howard had not in fact been retained by "other clients" for the purpose of making the trip in question. State whether such an action would succeed.

Case 4

Jickles was a new Canadian whose business experience was limited to the successful operation of a small retail shop in eastern Europe. In late 1992, he entered into a franchising agreement with Snacks Unlimited, Ltd., to operate three shops in Winnipeg.

Under the contract, each shop was to make and sell milkshakes, hot dogs, and hamburgers, the ingredients to be of a specified high quality and the products made to uniform standards. The premises were also to be equipped and maintained according to a prescribed format and the shops would have the decor and distinctive sign of "Snacks Unlimited". Large sales were anticipated since prospective customers of the stores would already be acquainted with the products through the national and local advertising programs of Snacks Unlimited, and would be familiar with other franchised stores operating in the same manner.

The franchising agreement signed by Jickles required him to:

(a) buy his store equipment from Snacks Unlimited, on which both parties understood there was to be a profit for the latter;

(b) take a sub-lease from Snacks Unlimited for the three shops, on which a mark-up on the rent would accrue to Snacks Unlimited;

(c) deposit in advance the sum of $40 000 interest-free as prepaid rent;

(d) pay a franchise fee of 2% on gross sales, of which 1% would be allocated to advertising by Snacks Unlimited;

(e) wherever possible, buy supplies from sources indicated by Snacks Unlimited.

Jickles was persuaded by representations made to him that these terms were a reasonable price to pay for the lower costs of his supplies owing to the mass purchasing power of the franchising organization.

As was typical with such contracts, every aspect of the relationship was to be controlled by the franchisor, Snacks Unlimited, which would find the real estate, negotiate the lease, arrange the purchase of equipment, select the personnel, arrange the advertising and supervise the operation. Snacks Unlimited undertook not to franchise any other shop within two miles in any direction from any of Jickles' shops. Jickles was supplied with a *Confidential Manual of Operating Procedure* that specified the standards of cleanliness, lighting, maintenance, repairs, employee uniforms, and demeanour required in each shop. The agreement concluded with the words, "The relationship between the parties is only that of independent contractors. No partnership, joint venture or relationship of principal and agent is intended."

Jickles operated his three shops successfully during 1993, showing a net profit of $85 000 on gross sales of $1 500 000. In the fall of 1993 Jickles was made aware, quite by accident, that the companies from whom he was required to purchase his supplies were paying a rebate of between 5% and 20% to Snacks Unlimited. On the question of whether he had paid prices higher than the prevailing market prices for comparable supplies, it was difficult to generalize: for some materials this was true; for others he paid much the same price and in some instances even a somewhat lower price. In any event, Snacks Unlimited had instructed all the suppliers to have no dealings or negotiations with its franchisees that might indicate the true nature of the arrangements made with them for rebates.

Jickles sued Snacks Unlimited for an accounting of these undisclosed profits and rebates and an order requiring them to be paid over to him.

Discuss the merits of Jickles' case and indicate with reasons whether his action should succeed.

CHAPTER 23

THE CONTRACT OF EMPLOYMENT

Development of the Law Governing Employment

Relationship of Master and Servant

Employer's Liability

Notice of Termination of Individual Employment Contracts

Grounds for Dismissal without Notice

Wrongful Dismissal

Employee Welfare Legislation

Collective Bargaining

Labour Disputes

Implications of the Collective Agreement for the Individual Employee

Legal Status of Trade Unions

DEVELOPMENT OF THE LAW GOVERNING EMPLOYMENT

Before the middle of the 19th century, the law relating to employment was almost entirely composed of common law rules defining *the relationship of master and servant*. This law developed in an early business environment where the employer (master) had a separate contract with each of his employees (servants); welfare legislation and trade unions were unknown. The individual contract of employment is still the most common employment relationship, and the law of master and servant continues to be important. Nevertheless, the economic and social changes of the last hundred or more years have affected the common law in two significant respects. First, statutes have been passed to prescribe minimum standards of working conditions; we shall refer to this branch of the law as *employee welfare legislation*. Second, the emergence of trade unions has produced the phenomenon of the collective agreement and a whole separate body of law, that we may call *the law of collective bargaining*, to govern the relationship between employers and trade unions. In this chapter we shall discuss the master-servant relationship at common law, employee welfare legislation, and collective bargaining.

We begin with a note of caution. In our treatment of welfare legislation and collective bargaining we cannot cite all the relevant statutes in the space available, and in any event it might be dangerous to do so: this part of the law frequently changes and statutes may soon become obsolete. The purpose of the chapter is simply to acquaint the reader with the general approach of the law in another main area of business administration. For further discussion of specific labour problems, the reader should consult the works that have been specially prepared in this field, cited from time to time in footnotes.[1]

RELATIONSHIP OF MASTER AND SERVANT

Compared with Agency

The relation of master and servant, or, in current language, that of employer and employee, is established by a contract that gives one party (the employer) authority to direct and control the work of the other party (the employee). The services that are contracted for may or may not include making contracts with third parties as agent for the employer.

The distinction between agent and employee, then, is one of function. The same person is often both an employee and an agent. In some instances, the terms of employment may be such that an employee's chief duty is to make contracts with third parties on behalf of the employer: for example, a purchasing agent for a company has a duty to order goods on the company's credit and authority to do so within the limits of her agency. She is nonetheless also a company employee and subject to the direction of its senior officers. Other employees may have very limited duties as agents of their employer: the driver of a delivery truck is an

---

[1] See, especially, Adams, *Canadian Labour Law*. Toronto: Canada Law Book, 1985.

employee who may act as an agent when taking the truck into a garage for servicing, thereby binding the employer to pay the charges. In many types of employment, an employee has no occasion to enter into contracts on behalf of the employer and no authority, express or implied, to do so — a stenographer or lathe operator, for instance. Indeed, as we noted at the beginning of the preceding chapter, the functions may be completely separate, as when a business engages an agent who is not an employee at all.

In the last chapter we learned that when an agency agreement is of indefinite duration, an agent may have no recourse against a principal that terminates the agreement without notice. An employee, as we shall see, often has a right of action for damages for wrongful dismissal in comparable circumstances.

Both principals and employers may be liable in tort for the acts of their agents and employees respectively. However, for various reasons, some historical and some related to the different functions of agents and employees, the scope of liability of an employer may be wider than the corresponding liability of a principal; in any event the basis for vicarious liability is not the same for principals and employers. Accordingly, when a third party is injured it may be important to establish whether the wrongdoer was acting as an employee or as an agent of a firm.

Compared with an Independent Contractor

An independent contractor undertakes to do a specified task such as building a house. The contract between the parties does not create an employer-employee relationship because the contractor is not subject to the supervision of the person engaging him. His job is to produce a specified result, and the means he employs are his own affair.

It is not always easy to distinguish between an independent contractor and an employee. Occasionally the two functions are combined in a single person: the owner of a building may hire a building contractor to do certain repairs for a fixed price, but the agreement may also require the repairs to be made under the supervision of the owner. Such circumstances may make it difficult to decide whether the person doing the work is primarily an independent contractor or an employee.

When a firm undertakes work as an independent contractor, liabilities incurred by it in the course of accomplishing its task are almost entirely its own.

ILLUSTRATION

Imperial Contractors contracted with Parkinson Corp. to erect an administration building. During the construction work, Miss Chance, a passerby on the sidewalk far below, is injured by a falling brick. The accident is attributable to the inadequate protection for pedestrians provided by Imperial Contractors. Imperial Contractors and not Parkinson Corp. would generally be liable for the injury so caused.

On the other hand, Parkinson does have a duty to take reasonable care to hire a competent contractor; also, if by the nature of the work undertaken, the possibility of damage to adjoining property is apparent — for example, through blasting with dynamite[2] — or if the work is inherently dangerous to third parties, Parkinson has an obligation to see to it that the contractor takes reasonable precautions to avoid such damage.

---

[2] Aikman v. Mills & Co., [1934] 4 D.L.R. 264.

As we shall see in Chapter 34, a business engaging a building contractor may have to follow certain procedures in paying the contractor in order to avoid having its land and buildings subject to liens filed by employees of the contractor or by subcontractors such as suppliers of materials. Apart from this complication, a person engaging an independent contractor is not generally responsible for the contractor's obligations.[3]

The Relationship at Common Law

In defining the relationship of master and servant, the courts have developed rules about the employer's liability to third persons, the required notice to terminate the relationship, grounds for dismissal, and assessment of damages for wrongful dismissal. These rules are part of the common law as it continues to apply to individual employment contracts, and we shall now deal with them in turn.

EMPLOYER'S LIABILITY

Liability in Contract

Parties to a contract often understand that they will not perform personally — indeed a corporation cannot do so — and that either employees or an independent contractor will perform. The promisor still remains liable for satisfactory performance, as when a construction firm undertakes to erect a building according to specifications, although it hires a subcontractor to put up the structural steel and the subcontractor does defective work. So too will it be liable for breach of contract should its own employees do improper work.

Liability in Tort

In our discussion of vicarious liability in Chapter 4, we noted that a business is liable in damages to a third party for the consequences of any tort an employee may commit in the course of employment. The employer need not have authorized the wrongful act: it is liable even though it has forbidden such conduct. All the injured party need establish is that the employee caused the damage while engaged at work. If, however, the harm results while the employee is not engaged in the employer's work, as when he takes time off from his duties to attend to some personal matter, the employer is not liable: the employee alone is liable. Nor is the employer liable if the employee delegates the work to someone else without the employer's consent.

ILLUSTRATIONS

(a) Adair is employed by Magnum Computers as a sales agent. While driving a company van on her rounds, she negligently collides with another vehicle. She has committed a tort in the course of her employment; the owner of the damaged car may sue both Magnum Computers and Adair.

(b) Adair injures a pedestrian as a result of negligent driving while using the company van to take her family to the theatre after hours, without permission or knowledge of her employer. In the words of a Nova Scotia judgment in a similar case, Adair has "departed from

---

[3] See Vic Priestly Landscaping Contracting Ltd. v. Elder (1978), 19 O.R. (2d) 591 at 601-5.

the course of h[er] employment and ... embarked upon an independent enterprise — 'a frolic of h[er] own' — for purposes wholly unconnected with h[er] master's business."[4] She alone is liable: Magnum Computers is not.

(c) While delivering a computer, Adair becomes embroiled in an argument with a customer about the quality of the product. She strikes the customer; the customer falls and injures himself. Is Magnum Computers vicariously liable to the customer for the assault?

Of the three illustrations, (c) is the most difficult to resolve. As one judge put it, "Before the employer can be held liable the blow complained of must be closely connected with a duty being carried out in the authorized course of employment and not delivered at a time when the servant has divested himself of his character as a servant".[5] We must ask whether the unauthorized and wrongful act of the employee is "so connected with the authorized act as to be a mode of doing it" or whether it is "an independent act."[6]

If having conversations about her employer's product at the time of delivery is an authorized incident of Adair's employment so as to be a way of carrying out her duties, her employer is also liable for the assault; but if her conversation is an independent act, Adair alone is liable. The court will hear evidence of trade practice in this matter before reaching its decision.

When an employer has been held liable for the negligence of an employee, it has a right to be indemnified by the employee;[7] it may, if it deems it worthwhile, sue the employee.

Notice of Termination of Individual Employment Contracts

When an employee has been hired for a stated period and that time has elapsed, no notice is necessary on the part of either employer or employee. Neither party has any right to expect anything more than the cessation of employment at the end of the specified time: each has been, as it were, on notice ever since the employment contract was formed, as for example, where a student accepts summer employment to terminate on the Friday before Labour Day.[8]

Employers and employees often make no agreement about when the employment relationship is to end, and do not expressly agree on the length of notice required to terminate employment. They may intend the hiring to be by the week, the month, or some other length of time, renewable for successive periods and possibly lasting for many

---

4 Hall v. Halifax Transfer Co. Ltd. (1959), 18 D.L.R. (2d) 115, per MacDonald, J., at 120.
5 Wenz v. Royal Trust Co., [1953] O.W.N. 798, per Aylen, J., at 800.
6 Salmond, *The Law of Torts* (20th ed.), p. 457, Heuston and Buckley, ed. London: Sweet & Maxwell Limited, 1992.
7 Finnegan v. Riley, [1939] 4 D.L.R. 434.
8 See, for example: Employment Standards Act, R.S.O. 1990, c. E-14, s. 57(10)(a).

years; or as more often happens, they may simply regard the employment as a general or indefinite hiring.

In the absence of an express term about notice in a contract of employment, the common law rule is that reasonable notice shall be given. Sometimes a court can determine the length of reasonable notice from evidence of an established customary practice followed by the particular employer for the type of employee in question. In other circumstances, the court must ask what type of hiring the parties intended when they made the employment contract. In general, the minimum reasonable notice for a weekly hiring is one clear work week, and for a monthly hiring, one clear work month.[9] If the hiring is general or indefinite, reasonable notice depends on all the circumstances of the employment; until recent years it usually varied between three and six months and was occasionally as long as one year.[10] Executive compensation settlements have in the recent past been for as much as several years' salary. In most provinces and at the federal level as well, the minimum length of required notice is specifically set down by statute and any attempt by an employer to impose a term reducing the length of notice is void.[11] Since the provisions are minimum requirements only, customary notice periods in a particular trade or express contractual terms may require substantially longer periods of notice.

When no other evidence about the intention of the parties is available, the court may infer a weekly or a monthly hiring from the mere fact that the employee receives pay by the week or the month. A court is, however, perfectly free to find other considerations that outweigh any inferences one might draw from the length of the pay period. The court may, for example, rule that a hiring is indefinite even though the employee is paid by the week. As stated in *Lazarowicz v. Orenda Engines Ltd.*:

> Upon all the circumstances of this case I have come to the conclusion that the plaintiff, despite the fact that his wages were stated to be a weekly sum only, was employed upon a general or indefinite hiring only, and for these reasons: Firstly, the plaintiff was a graduate engineer....At the time he was employed by the defendant corporation [he] had been employed...at a monthly salary of $450. He was secure in that position and there seems little reason to conclude that he would have left that position to accept one with the defendant company if he were to be merely a weekly servant. A more important circumstance is the actual work performed by the plaintiff....The evidence...shows that he was in a position of some considerable importance, requiring a great deal of mechanical and technical experience.[12]

An employer is not in breach of the employment contract if in dismissing the employee without notice it tenders an additional amount of pay for a period equal to the length of time required for reasonable notice. In the *Lazarowicz* case, the court held that

---

9   The notice required to terminate a weekly or monthly hiring is similar to the notice required to terminate a weekly or monthly tenancy. For a fuller explanation see Chapter 27 under "Termination and Renewal of a Tenancy".

10   See Bardal v. The Globe and Mail Ltd. (1960), 24 D.L.R. (2d) 140; Duncan v. Cockshutt Farm Equipment Ltd. (1956), 19 W.W.R. 554; Campbell v. Business Fleets Ltd., [1954] 2 D.L.R. 263.

11   See, for example: Labour Standards Act, R.S.S. 1978, c. L-1, ss. 43-44; Labour Standards Code, R.S.N.S. 1989, c. 246, s. 72; Employment Standards Act, R.S.O. 1990, c. E-14, s. 57, as applied in Machtinger v. HOJ Industries Ltd. (1992), 91 D.L.R. (4th) 491 (S.C.C.).

12   (1960), 22 D.L.R. (2d) 568, per Robertson, C.J.O., at 573. (Affirmed on appeal: (1962), 26 D.L.R. (2d) 433.)

reasonable notice in the circumstances was three months; since the employee had been given only one week's salary in lieu of notice, it held that the employee was entitled to the balance of three months' salary.

An employee who decides to leave voluntarily has a contractual obligation to give the employer the same amount of notice as he himself would be entitled to receive for dismissal. If he does not do so the employer may, if it considers it worthwhile, sue the employee for damages equal to the loss caused by this breach of contract.

An employee is justified in leaving without giving the usual notice if he can show that he was obliged to work under dangerous conditions that the employer refused to correct. Here the employer has broken the contract, freeing the employee from his obligations, for it is an implied term in the contract that the employer will maintain a safe place to work. Again, an employee has grounds for leaving immediately if he is ordered to do an illegal act.

$\mathcal{G}$ROUNDS FOR DISMISSAL WITHOUT NOTICE

The Contractual Basis

The requirement of notice does not apply when an employer can show that it has dismissed the employee *for cause*. Dismissal for cause derives from the general law of contract: when an employee's conduct amounts to a breach of the contract of employment, the employer may be entitled to consider itself discharged from any further obligations and to terminate the contract at once. Of course, in contract law generally, not every petty breach would have this result.[13] However, in view of the frequently unequal bargaining power between an employer and an individual employee, there is a danger that an employer can impose its idea of what an important breach is. In response to this problem, the common law has tended to classify the kinds of breach that are sufficient grounds for dismissal without notice, and the collective bargaining process has developed the idea further. In some jurisdictions, employees have gained additional protection by statute.[14]

Misconduct

In the times of Henry VIII and Elizabeth I the law treated any violence by a servant against the person of his or her master as a minor form of treason, and visited the employee with the grisly methods of execution reserved for that most heinous of offences.[15] Even wishful thinking by an employee was hazardous while witchcraft remained an offence. This attitude of the law, demanding of employees the utmost in subjection and loyalty, lingered on until as late as the end of the 19th century a strike was regarded as a form of conspiracy.

Today, misconduct against an employer, while it may be grounds for a dismissal, is not a crime in itself. An employee guilty of such grossly immoral conduct as might bring the

---

[13] See Chapter 16 ("The Effect of Breach").

[14] See, for example, Employment Standards Act, R.S.O. 1990, c. E-14, s. 57(10)(c).

[15] See Smith, *The Law of Master and Servant* (6th ed.), p. 390, E.M. Smith, ed. London: Sweet & Maxwell Limited, 1906. We have followed the classification of grounds for dismissal outlined by Smith at pp. 102-15.

employer's business into public disrepute, disturb the morale of other employees, or cause the employer direct financial loss, may be summarily dismissed by the indignant employer. Conviction for a crime, especially when it involves moral turpitude such as stealing or embezzlement, may also be grounds for summary dismissal.

A firm is entitled to repose confidence in its employees, and, depending upon the nature of the employment, evidence of a lack of integrity is often grounds for instant dismissal. An employee's deception need cause no financial loss to his employer: it is enough that the employer can no longer trust him.

Disobedience

Wilful disobedience of a reasonable and lawful order from an employer is grounds for immediate dismissal without notice. The offence is broad enough to include situations where the employee does not directly disobey but acts in a manner inconsistent with the usual devotion to duty expected of employees of that kind. In the old case of *Ridgway v. Hungerford Market Co.*[16] a clerk entered in a company minute book a protest, in his own handwriting, against a resolution of the directors calling a meeting to appoint his successor. He was dismissed at once and forfeited the right to any reasonable notice that would normally have been implied in the directors' resolution.

Incompetence

The degree of skill an employer may demand depends partly on the representations of the employee when seeking the position and partly on the degree of skill ordinarily to be expected of an employee of that category and rate of pay. If an employee accepts a position on the understanding that he is capable of doing a particular kind of work and it becomes apparent that he cannot in fact do this work satisfactorily, the employer may then dismiss him without notice. The strict application of this principle is found in the words of an English judge:

> It appears to us that there is no material difference between a servant who will not, and a servant who cannot, perform the duty for which he was hired.[17]

On the other hand, incompetence as a cause for dismissal becomes more difficult to justify the longer an employee has been retained.[18]

Illness

Permanent disability or constantly recurring illness entitles an employer to consider the contract at an end, independently of any terms in the contract requiring notice. An employer cannot, however, recover damages from an employee for breach of contract in these circumstances: the contract is discharged by frustration, and not by breach.

---

[16] (1835), 111 E.R. 378.
[17] Harmer v. Cornelius (1858), 141 E.R. 94, per Willes, J., at 99.
[18] See Duncan v. Cockshutt Farm Equipment Ltd. (1956), 19 W.W.R. 554; Bardal v. The Globe and Mail Ltd. (1960), 24 D.L.R. (2d) 140.

Effect of Dismissal

Any of the four grounds for dismissal set out above permits an employer to treat the contract of employment as discharged. Misconduct, disobedience, or incompetence amount to discharge by the employee's breach, whereas illness discharges the contract by frustration. Discharge for any one of these personal failures of performance by an employee relieves the employer of the duty to give notice but it must nevertheless pay the dismissed employee any wages earned until the time of dismissal.

Adverse Economic Conditions

Ordinarily, an employer does not have the right to dismiss employees without notice because of adverse economic conditions. As we have noted, reasonable terms of notice are implied by law. An employee might expressly agree to give his employer the right to dismiss him in adverse economic conditions without notice, and an agreement to this effect would exclude an implied requirement for such notice. However, where a right to notice is provided by statute, even an express agreement to give it up is ineffective and the statute takes precedence, requiring the employer to give notice or wages in lieu of notice.

Neither does an employer have the right to temporarily lay off employees without notice for economic reasons. Yet some statutes now permit an employer to do so for periods as long as three months, under conditions prescribed by regulation.[19]

$\mathcal{W}$RONGFUL DISMISSAL

Damages

For an employee to succeed in an action against her employer for damages for wrongful dismissal, she must show that the employer has broken the contract. The employer has broken the contract if it fails to give the employee the notice to which she was entitled. An employer often defends its actions either by showing that the employee was dismissed for cause, or that adequate notice was in fact given. If the employer's defence fails, the court is left with the task of assessing damages.

The measure of damages for wrongful dismissal is merely a special application of the rules for assessing damages in contracts generally. In Chapter 17, we saw that the purpose of an award of damages is to place an injured party in the position it would have been in if the contract had been completed. In the context of an employment contract, we must ask what amount of damages will compensate the employee for failure to receive the required notice of termination.

In assessing damages, the first task for the court is to decide what length of time would have been reasonable notice in the circumstances. As we have noted, the court has considerable discretion when the contract is for a general or indefinite hiring:

> There can be no catalogue laid down as to what is reasonable notice in particular classes of cases. The reasonableness of the notice must be decided with reference to each particular case, having regard to the character of the employment, the length of service of the servant,

---

[19]   Canada Labour Code, R.S.C. 1985, c. L-2 and Canada Labour Standards Regulation, C.R.C. 1978, c. 986, s. 30; Employment Standards Act, R.S.O. 1990, c. E-14, ss. 57-58 and Rev. Reg. of Ont. 1990, Reg. 327.

the age of the servant and the availability of similar employment, having regard to the experience, training and qualifications of the servant.[20]

The next step in assessing damages for wrongful dismissal is to multiply the employee's rate of pay and the value of fringe benefits by the length of reasonable notice. We must remember that a party injured by breach of contract is expected to act reasonably in order to mitigate her loss. Accordingly, we must then ask whether the employee has made a serious attempt following her dismissal to obtain reasonably comparable work elsewhere. If the employer shows that the employee had such an opportunity to work elsewhere but declined it, the court will reduce the award of damages by the amount the employee might have earned during the required term of notice. However, a dismissed employee is not required to take any work simply to mitigate her loss; if the only work available is substantially below what she might reasonably expect on the basis of her qualifications and experience she may refuse it without fear that the court will reduce an award of damages.

Finally, we must ask whether the damage that flows naturally from the employer's breach may include losses other than salary and fringe benefits. The employee may have incurred travelling expenses in seeking other employment, or even become physically ill. As we noted in Chapter 17, courts in recent decisions have been willing to give damages for pain and suffering caused by wrongful dismissal.

Sometimes an employer has such a general dissatisfaction with or mistrust of an employee that it dismisses him apparently without cause. If the employer should later discover that there were in fact specific grounds for dismissing the employee without notice, it could, until recently, use these grounds to defeat an action by the employee for wrongful dismissal.[21] However, there is an increasing tendency to view an employee's interest in a job as being something more than merely contractual; in particular, the growing remedy of reinstatement, discussed in the next section, suggests that the interest is almost a proprietary one. This view has been put forward to claim that before an employee can be dismissed — and thus deprived of an "interest" in his job — he is entitled to a fair hearing. Accordingly, before dismissing an employee the employer should be required to confront him with a charge of misconduct and give the employee an opportunity to clear himself, or at least to explain his acts and minimize their significance.[22]

Reinstatement

The emphasis on damages for wrongful dismissal as the sole remedy of employees implicitly denies the availability of other remedies such as *reinstatement* — a form of specific performance by which the court orders the employer to continue to employ the aggrieved employee. We noted in Chapter 17 the great reluctance of courts to order specific performance of contracts of service against an employee. The courts are also unlikely to award reinstatement based on common law principles alone.[23] However, the impersonal nature of most employment in large industrial enterprises has diminished

---

[20] Bardal v. The Globe and Mail Ltd., per McRuer, C.J.H.C., supra, note 10 at 145.

[21] The courts admit such evidence even if it comes to light after the action has been started. See, for example: Lake Ontario Portland Cement v. Groner (1961), 28 D.L.R. (2d) 589; Aspinall v. Mid-West Collieries Ltd., [1926] 3 D.L.R. 362.

[22] See: Reilly v. Steelcase Canada Ltd. (1979), 26 O.R.(2nd) 725; Pulsifer v. GTE Sylvania Canada Ltd. (1983), 56 N.S.R.(2nd) 424; Pilato v. Hamilton Place Convention Centre (1984), 45 O.R.(2nd) 652.

[23] For an exception arising out of unusual circumstances, see Hill v. Parsons, [1971] 3 All E.R. 1345.

the strength of argument against reinstatement based on the personal nature of services. Unions have long bargained for arbitration procedures in cases of dismissal and for reinstatement in appropriate cases. Reinstatement has become the norm as the remedy for wrongful dismissal under collective agreements. Another example of the use of reinstatement occurs at universities; professors who have been wrongfully dismissed are ordinarily entitled to reinstatement.

Similar protection has become available to non-union employees in industries within the legislative jurisdiction of the federal Parliament. The Canada Labour Code provides that

> "…any [dismissed] person (a) who has completed twelve consecutive months of continuous employment by an employer, and (b) who is not a member of a group of employees subject to a collective agreement, may make a complaint…" [24]

If an adjudicator decides that the person has been "unjustly dismissed", he may order the employer to reinstate the person in its employ. This provision, first introduced in 1978, has been used with increasing frequency as the availability of alternative jobs for dismissed employees has declined. The Québec Labour Standards Act and the Nova Scotia Act create a similar right in employees, but in Québec only after four years of uninterrupted service with one employer, and in Nova Scotia only after ten years.[25] Specialists in the field expect to see this type of legislation in other provinces in the near future.

Employee Welfare Legislation

History

In the social upheaval that followed the industrial revolution and before the emergence of trade unions, employers had nearly all the advantage in bargaining: often, workers had either to accept the proposed terms of employment or see their families starve. The movement for reform in working conditions stressed the economic inequality between employer and employee. Reformers urged that society had a duty to protect the weaker contracting party. The arguments of the reformers, however, went directly against 19th century ideas on freedom of contract as a pillar of a larger political philosophy of *laissez faire*. The freedom of contract doctrine asserted that society functions most efficiently when contracting parties are left free to exact whatever terms their bargaining power will command, and that a society will come closest to realizing its economic potential when individuals are left to their own resources in resolving their conflicts of interest without the intervention of any outside arbiter.

The reform movement therefore had to proceed against formidable opposition by the proponents of freedom of contract. Nevertheless, the pressures of a changing society were irresistible: they resulted in a series of acts of Parliament commencing a little before the middle of the 19th century. These statutes marked a new role for the state — active intervention on the side of the employees.

---

[24] R.S.C. 1985, c. L-2, s. 245.
[25] Labour Standards Act, R.S.Q. 1991, c. N-1.1, ss. 124-28; Labour Standards Code, R.S.N.S. 1989, c. 246, ss. 71(1) and 26(2)(a).

Initially, the reform statutes specified the minimum age of workers, maximum hours of work, the presence of safety devices for machinery, the maintenance of safe premises in which to work, and the definition of the liability of employers when an employee was injured in the course of employment. These statutes were only a beginning. A review of the statute law we are to consider briefly in this section illustrates the degree to which our legislatures have qualified the freedom of contract between individual employers and employees.

To the extent that employees are now represented by trade unions, the disparity in bargaining power between employer and employees has been largely redressed. There remain, however, important categories of work in which employees typically are not unionized. In these types of work, employees still negotiate contracts of employment on an individual basis with their employers. Accordingly, legislation enacted for the welfare and protection of employees continues to afford a minimum standard of working conditions for many people.

Legislative Jurisdiction

In Canada, the activities of a comparatively small but very important group of businesses bring them under federal jurisdiction, and for them the rights and duties of employers and employees are governed by federal labour legislation. These industries include shipping, air transport, inter-provincial transportation systems, telegraphs, radio, banking, and the operations of federal Crown corporations.[26] The remainder of our economic activity, comprising the bulk of what we think of as industrial and commercial enterprise, is subject to provincial rather than federal legislation.

Employee Rights

Human Rights

Enhancing the rights of employees through human rights legislation began in the 1970s, and preceded the Canadian Charter of Rights and Freedoms. However, the process was accelerated by the words in s. 15 of the Charter, "Every individual…has the right to the equal protection and equal benefit of the law…without discrimination based on race, national or ethnic origin, colour, religion, sex, age or mental or physical disability." S. 28 emphasized that Charter rights "are guaranteed equally to male and female persons."

As we noted in Chapter 2, the Charter has not been applied to the private sector but human rights legislation passed by every province and the federal Parliament does apply to the private sector. Most complaints under the legislation relate to employment. The wording varies considerably but, generally speaking, the acts make it an offence to engage in:

> "a discriminatory practice…to refuse to employ or continue to employ an individual, or… to differentiate adversely…on a prohibited ground"[27], that is, on the basis of "race, national or ethnic origin, colour, religion, age, sex, marital status, family status, disability and conviction for which a pardon has been granted."[28]

Human rights legislation has had a considerable educational effect on both public and private sector employers. To employers who are sensitive to the issues of non-discrimination,

---

[26] Constitution Act, 1867, s. 91.
[27] Canadian Human Rights Act, R.S.C. 1985 c. H-6, s.7 (a) and (b).
[28] *Ibid.*, s. 3 (1).

there is little or no additional cost of doing business. Indeed, it has been argued that employers who seek the most competent people and comply with the legislation by ignoring the personal characteristics, listed above, of prospective employees benefit from the law in terms of increased efficiency.

Pay Equity

Pay equity legislation is directed toward redressing gender discrimination in remuneration. There are two ways of assessing the wage gap between men and women. The more traditional is through the principle of "equal pay for equal work". The law prohibits differential pay for substantially the same kind of work performed in the same establishment, the performance of which requires substantially the same skill, effort and responsibility, and performed under similar working conditions.[29]

The second approach requires a focus, not on the similarity of the male and female jobs, but on their *comparative value* to the employer — the concept of "equal pay for work of equal value" or "comparable worth".[30] The legislation requires employers to pay employees performing jobs traditionally done by women the same as those performing jobs done by men if the jobs are of equal or comparable value. The main task is to attribute a meaning to the word "value". It must mean something more than current market value of work, for if women are being hired at a traditionally lower wage than men receive, then an employer can argue that the market shows it can hire women at that lower wage: according to this argument, they are already being paid what they are "worth". Instead, the effort and training of the worker must be taken into account. Thus, while a secretary's job may require less physical effort and she may have better working conditions than a groundskeeper, her job may require more responsibility, more mental effort and greater skills training. Assessing the relative value of different kinds of work can be the subject of much debate.

Once a job evaluation results in a finding that one group of employees is paid too little in comparison with another, almost invariably it is unacceptable to reduce the wages of the more highly paid group. The pressure to increase the wages of the lower paid group may substantially raise the labour costs of an employer; thus the employer is likely to contest the finding because of perceived rises in costs.

Under traditional legislative reform, someone must file a complaint in order to trigger enforcement of the legislation's general prohibitions. An important difficulty with implementing pay equity results from reliance on a complaints system because such a system assumes that violations are the exception, not the rule; it is effective only if breaches of the legislation are infrequent. However, if wage discrimination is *systemic* and pervasive throughout the economy, then a complaints system of enforcement may easily be overwhelmed. To overcome this problem, the most recent pay equity legislation is based on systemic discrimination. It abandons the complaint system of enforcement in favour of a regulatory model that not only prohibits wage discrimination but also places positive

---

[29] In most jurisdictions, pay equity legislation distinguishes between the public and private sectors. At present, the standard of "equal pay for equal work" applies in Alberta and British Columbia in both sectors, and to private sector employers in Manitoba, New Brunswick, Newfoundland, Nova Scotia, Prince Edward Island, and Saskatchewan.

[30] This standard applies to both sectors in areas of federal jurisdiction and in Quebec. See *Canadian Pay Equity Compliance Guide* (North York: CCH Canadian Litd., 1990).

obligations on employers to scrutinize their pay practices and ensure that these practices comply with the legislation.

At present, the latest regulatory model applies to the public sectors in Manitoba, New Brunswick, Newfoundland, Nova Scotia, and Prince Edward Island, and in Ontario to the public sector and also to private sector employers who employ ten or more persons. Throughout the rest of Canada, the complaints system alone remains in force.

Employment Equity

The newest development in employment rights goes beyond requiring employers to treat equally individual applicants for jobs, regardless of personal characteristics. Employers will be required to strive toward making their workforce reflect the various under-represented classes of disadvantaged persons in the general population.

At the time of writing, the Ontario legislature has passed Bill 179 (December 1993) to be proclaimed into law during 1994. The Act will apply to all public sector employment and to private sector employers with more than 50 employees.

Employers will be required to conduct a "workforce analysis", that is, to obtain relevant information about the personal characteristics of their current employees, in order to determine under-representation of designated groups — women, visible minorities, aboriginals and disabled persons. In addition to information from their current employees, employers must seek the same information from job applicants before determining whether certain applicants should be given preference. Employers will be required to review their formal and informal hiring policies in order to remove all systemic discrimination against the designated groups, and to set goals and timetables for achieving representation based on the working-age population within each employer's community. Finally they must prepare a plan to implement their goals, including monitoring systems to assess their progress.

There has been vigorous debate about intrusiveness in obtaining information about the personal characterisitics of both employees and job applicants, and also about the weight employers will be required to give to the designated characteristics in making hiring decisions. Since we have no other examples of similar legislation, we must await its implementation.

Regulation of Working Conditions

Each of the provinces has enacted a variety of statutes prohibiting child labour, regulating the hours of work of young persons, and providing for the health and safety of employees while at work. Provinces may appoint inspectors to determine that these requirements are complied with. Other statutes specify a minimum age at which children may leave school and accept full-time employment.

For many years, Canadians have accepted manadatory retirement schemes as desirable and humane social institutions: workers were expected to leave their jobs, usually at age 65, and enjoy retirement on an adequate pension. However, increasing good health and life expectancy have meant that many people on approaching their 65th year, who feel vigorous and enjoy their work, wish to continue working for a few more years. Moreover, rapid inflation since the 1960s has led to an unexpected diminution of pensions available to many people reaching retirement age; they feel they must continue to work to maintain a reasonable standard of living. On the other hand, employers and others — especially young people seeking work — want employees to retire at the established compulsory retirement age. Some employers have insisted that they do so.

Since section 15 of the Charter of Rights and Freedoms guarantees "equal protection and benefit of the law without discrimination...based on...age", a number of employees wishing to remain in their jobs have challenged mandatory retirement provisions. They claim that basing mandatory retirement solely upon a particular age, without regard to the health or competence of an employee, is arbitrary and discriminatory and therefore offends the Charter. A similar argument was made successfully under the Manitoba Human Rights Code in 1981, before the Charter was made part of the Constitution; the court held that a mandatory retirement provision at the University of Manitoba offended the provincial Code and was void.[31] The province of Québec abolished compulsory retirement by statute in 1982.[32] The federal government in the autumn of 1985 abolished mandatory retirement in its civil service. Defenders of mandatory retirement schemes claim that, because the schemes are socially desirable, under section 1 of the Charter they are valid because they are a "reasonable limit prescribed by law" and "can be demonstrably justified in a free and democratic society". Human rights statutes, such as those of British Columbia and Ontario, prohibit discrimination based on age but only between the ages of 18 and 65 years, thus allowing mandatory retirement at 65. The Supreme Court of Canada allowed such schemes in a group of four decisions dealing with complaints made by employees of hospitals, community colleges and universities.[33] The issue is a good example of the important effects that the Charter can have not only upon individuals but also on the workplace and society generally.

A number of statutes provided special rules affecting women in respect to both working hours and working conditions; some have been repealed in the name of equality between the sexes, and it is yet to be seen how the remainder will be judged in relation to the guarantees of equality in section 15 of the Charter of Rights and Freedoms.

All provinces as well as the federal government provide by statute for minimum-wage rates, and grant discretionary power to designated government agencies to fix a minimumwage that varies with the industry. The legislation provides for limited working hours, with some exceptions, of eight hours a day and a maximum of 44 or 48 hours a week. These statutes also require overtime rates if the number of hours worked exceeds the specified maximum.

All but two provinces have given formal statutory sanction to agreements among employers and employees in a particular trade or industry within a specified geographic zone, when all agree to minimum rates of wages, and maximum hours of work and days

---

[31] McIntyre v. University of Manitoba (1981), 119 D.L.R.(3rd) 352, followed by Newport v. Government of Manitoba (1982), 131 D.L.R.(3rd) 564. Both cases held that s. 6(1) of the Human Rights Code, S.M. 1974, c. 65, made mandatory retirement provisions void.

[32] Abolition of Compulsory Retirement Act, S.Q. 1982, c. 12.

[33] McKinney v. University of Guelph, [1990] 3 S.C.R. 229; Harrison v. University of British Columbia [1990] 3 S.C.R. 451; Stoffman v. Vancouver General Hospital, [1990] 3 S.C.R. 483; Douglas/Kwantlen Faculty Association v. Douglas College, [1990] 3 S.C.R. 570. Provincial human rights codes, and the federal Human Rights Act, apply to *all* employment contracts within their jurisdiction, both in the public and private sectors. In contrast, s. 15 of the Charter applies to all employment contracts made in the *public sector*— contracts made by governments at all levels, by crown corporations, school boards, community colleges, etc.; it does not bind the *private sector*, including universities (see McKinney case), even though they may receive more than three-quarters of their funding from governments.

of labour.[34] This sanction is subject to the provisions of other statutes dealing with hours of work, minimum wages, and working conditions. The agreements must be reached at a properly convened conference of the employers and employees affected. Recognition of agreements of this kind is an important qualification of the negative attitude of the law towards restraint of trade.

All provinces now provide for annual vacations with pay. The most frequent requirement is for employers to grant their employees one week's paid vacation after one year of work. Some provinces also provide for public holidays with pay.

Unemployment Insurance

The Unemployment Insurance Act[35] established an unemployment insurance fund to which employers and employees must contribute according to a published schedule of rates. Coverage is very wide, with only such limited exceptions as persons over 65 years of age, or those receiving retirement pensions, employed by a spouse, employed by provincial governments, foreign governments, and international organizations.[36] Employees contribute to the fund through payroll deductions made by their employer. The employer must account for all employee contributions and, along with its own contributions, regularly remit them to the government. Unemployment insurance benefits are payable out of the fund to workers who have contributed in the past and are currently unemployed. These benefits are not available in a number of circumstances, one of which is loss of work caused by a labour dispute in which the employee is on strike. Other employees, not on strike but "locked out" because a plant or business is shut down by a strike, remain eligible for benefits.

Workers' Compensation

While the common law recognized that an employer could be liable to an employee for injury sustained in the course of employment, it was notoriously difficult for the employee to recover damages. The employer might defend the action successfully if it could show that the injury resulted from the contributory negligence of the employee, the negligence of a fellow employee, or the fact that the employee had assumed a risk of injury as a customary incident of the type of work he had contracted to do.

The doctrine of *contributory negligence* prevented an employee from recovering damages if the evidence showed that he was partly responsible for the accident, even in a small degree. Nor was an employer liable for injury to an employee caused by the negligence of a fellow employee (or *fellow servant*), provided the employer took reasonable care to hire competent workers: the usual result was that the employer escaped liability for the negligence of one employee that caused injury to another. Finally, the defence of *assumed risk*, broadly interpreted, might itself defeat almost any action by an employee, for it could be argued that every risk is a risk an employee assumes in accepting a particular employment.

---

[34] See, for example: Municipal Act, R.S.B.C. 1979, c. 290, ss. 919-27; Industrial Standards Act, R.S.O. 1990, c. 216; Labour Standards Code, R,S.N.S. 1989, c. 246, ss. 44-47.

[35] Unemployment Insurance Act, R.S.C. 1985, c. U-11.

[36] *Ibid.*, s. 3(2)

An action at common law also suffered from the fact that the burden lay with the employee to prove negligence on the part of the employer; he might find it exceedingly difficult to do so, especially if he suffered shock from his injury. In addition, the dependants of an employee who had been killed rather than injured in the course of employment had no cause of action — the right to sue for personal injury caused by a tort died with the injured person at common law. It was not until the latter part of the last century that legislation was enacted in England to permit action against an employer by the relatives of an employee killed while on the job. The legislation also clarified and extended the liability of employers; but the burden of proof remained with an employee or the dependants to prove negligence on the part of the employer. Similar statutes were passed in the Canadian provinces.

The final step was the enactment of the Workmen's Compensation Act. This statute made substantial improvement in the rights of injured employees, or of their immediate dependants in the event of death caused by accident while at work. The Act was passed in England in 1906 and later enacted in each of the provinces of Canada with various modifications.[37] Each of these Acts creates a Workers' Compensation Board to hear employees' claims. They also establish a fund to which employers subject to the Act must contribute regularly and out of which claims are paid. Payment out of the fund replaces any personal action against an employer. To succeed, an employee need only show that the injury was caused by an accident in the course of employment. The defences of contributory negligence, negligence of a fellow servant, and assumed risk no longer apply. An employee's claim will fail only if it is shown that the accident was caused substantially by wilful misconduct. Even then, the employee or the dependants will recover if the accident has caused death or serious disablement. The requirement of proving negligence on the part of the employer, so long a barrier to compensation for injury, no longer exists. The major advantage is that the costs and hazards of litigation are avoided. Also, since an employee claims recovery from a compensation board and not from his employer, he need not fear prejudicing his future with the employer by making the claim.

Coverage varies somewhat among the provinces. Generally included are workers in the following industries: construction, mining, manufacturing, lumbering, fishing, transportation, communications and public utilities. Industries are classified according to the degree of hazard. Exemptions may include casual employees and employees of small businesses employing fewer than a stated number of workers. For employees excluded from the usual workers' compensation benefits, several provinces have added a second part to their legislation defining the employer's liability for injuries caused by defective plant and equipment or by the negligence of other employees, and granting employees a right to damages in spite of contributory negligence on their part. In other jurisdictions, the common law rules still apply to casual employees and to those in small businesses.

An area of growing concern and controversy closely akin to occupational safety is occupational health. There are several reasons for the increasing prominence of health standards in the workplace. First, the general concern over environmental hazards to health has made the public much more sensitive to the special problems of the work environment: if a chemical dispersed in the atmosphere can harm people at a great distance, how much more dangerous is it for the workers who handle it and are directly exposed? Second, improvement in the general level of public health has drawn attention

---

[37] See, for example: Workers' Compensation Act, R.S.B.C. 1979, c. 437; R.S.N.S. 1989, c. 508; R.S.O. 1990, c. W-11.

to the fact that persons in particular occupations suffer to a greater degree than the general public from certain illnesses. Third, improvement in the quality of medical records and the sophistication of medical diagnosis has made it easier to connect certain diseases with some occupations. This last aspect has received great prominence in reference to industries where large numbers of workers can be seen to have very high incidences of specific ailments twenty or thirty years after starting work.

Many questions concerning occupational health in the workplace remain unanswered. Should the general system of workers' compensation be responsible for research into potential health hazards, for policing work conditions in plants, and for financial aid to affected workers? Should special legislation be enacted to make industries legally responsible for specific illnesses (keeping in mind that it may be very difficult to prove in a court that the workplace actually caused a particular illness)? Should certain industrial activities such as the processing of asbestos be banned completely (as has been done in some European countries)? Will other economic activities wither away because of the costs of imposing liability for their consequences? Could the country lose its comparative advantage in international trade by imposing such high standards of health on certain industries that they cannot compete with those in countries requiring lower standards? How economically important would be the lost jobs? It is likely that these and other questions relating to occupational health will be debated extensively over the next few years, and that there will be no easy answers to them — socially, economically, or legally.

COLLECTIVE BARGAINING

The process of establishing conditions of employment through negotiations between a business and the bargaining agent for its employees is known as *collective bargaining*. For those industries within federal jurisdiction, a federal statute regulates collective bargaining.[38] Statutes passed by each of the provinces regulate all other industries.[39] These acts state that all employees are free to belong to trade unions and that membership in a trade union does not provide the employer with grounds for dismissing an employee. The acts also require employers to recognize the representative union as the bargaining agent for employees for the purpose of determining the general terms of their employment.

If an employer is unwilling to recognize a trade union voluntarily, as often happens, the union may have to apply to be certified before it can proceed to bargain for the employees. *Certification* is an acknowledgment by an administrative tribunal (called in some provinces a labour relations board) that a particular union commands sufficient membership to justify its role as exclusive bargaining agent for the employees. The arrangement has the practical advantages of confining the negotiations to a single representative of the employees and avoiding the confusion of rival unions claiming the right to act as bargaining agents for a group of employees. We must distinguish between a bargaining agent and a bargaining unit: a *bargaining agent* is a union that has the exclusive right to bargain with the employer on behalf of the bargaining unit; the *bargaining unit* includes a specified group of employees eligible to join the union, whether they join or not.

---

[38] The Canada Labour Code, R.S.C. 1985, c. L-2.
[39] See, for example: Industrial Relations Act, S.B.C. 1979, c. 212; Labour Relations Act, S.O. 1992, c. 21; Trade Union Act, R.S.N.S. 1989, c. 475.

When an employer and union conclude their bargaining, they place the terms agreed upon in a contract called a *collective agreement*. The terms usually include a definition of the employees covered, an acknowledgment by the employer that the contracting union is their recognized bargaining agent, an outline of the steps that both parties must take in settling grievances, seniority provisions in the promotion and laying off of employees, wage rates, hours, vacation periods and other fringe benefits, the duration of the collective agreement, and the means by which it may be amended or renewed. Often there is a clause acknowledging that the maintenance of discipline and efficiency of employees is the sole function of the management of the company, subject to the right of an employee to lodge a grievance. The agreement almost invariably forbids strikes or lockouts as long as it continues to operate; indeed, most provinces require that such a term be included. The employees covered do not generally include those employed in a confidential capacity, those who have managerial responsibilities such as the authority to hire or discharge others, or those employed as guards or security police in the protection of business property. Some provinces have also excluded certain professional groups such as engineers, although the tendency in recent years has been to include more of the professions.

The terms of a collective agreement generally prescribe in detail the procedure for dismissing employees, displacing the common law rules for notice of dismissal and grounds for dismissal. To the extent also that the collective agreement prescribes working conditions above the level required by existing legislation, it replaces employee welfare legislation as a protection for the interests of workers.

Experience has shown that frequently the most difficult collective agreement to reach is the first one after certification: the union is new and its local members are inexperienced (even if they have advice from other union officials); management is unaccustomed to working with a union; often there has been some hostility and bitterness between employer and employees during the certification campaign. In response to the problem, first British Columbia in 1973, followed by the federal government, Québec, Manitoba and Ontario, passed legislation providing for "first contract arbitration".[40] If the parties cannot reach agreement on a contract within the time specified in the Act, then the provincial or federal labour board concerned may, after hearing the parties in an arbitration, impose a first contract upon them.

$\mathcal{L}$ABOUR DISPUTES

Types of Disputes

We may identify four major types of disputes affecting trade unions: jurisdictional disputes; recognition disputes; interest disputes; and rights disputes.

A *jurisdictional dispute* is a disagreement between competing unions for the right to represent a particular group of employees; the type of work they do may have two aspects, each of which seems to bring it within the terms of reference of a different trade union. Such a simple operation as drilling a hole through both metal and wood might raise a question of whether the worker should belong to the metalworkers' or the woodworkers' union.

---

[40] R.S.B.C. 1979, c. 137.5 as amended; R.S.Q. 1991, c. C-27, s. 93.1; R.S.M. 1987, c. L-10, s. 75; S.O. 1992, c. 21, s. 41.

A *recognition dispute* arises between an employer and a union when the employer insists on negotiating employment contracts directly with its employees and resists a union demand that it be recognized as the employees' bargaining agent.

An *interest dispute* arises when an employer and a union cannot reach agreement about the particular terms to be included in a collective agreement.

A *rights dispute* is a difference of opinion between employer and union on the interpretation of terms in a collective agreement already in existence.

Legislative Regulation

As we noted at the outset, the regulation of labour disputes is a field of study in its own right, and we cannot do more than indicate a few of the basic methods used. For an adequate treatment of the law, one must consult recognized works in the field; a few are listed in the bibliography at the end of this book.

Statutes have now provided machinery that either eliminates or minimizes the need to resort to strike action in each of the four main types of dispute mentioned above. Certification procedure, briefly considered in the preceding section, has done much to resolve jurisdictional disputes and is the only legal means of settling recognition disputes.

Our provincial statutes require both employer and employees to follow a series of procedures designed to aid in the settlement of interest disputes: first, they require a genuine attempt over a specified period to bargain in order to reach agreement;[41] second, if the parties fail to agree, they must submit to *conciliation procedure*, that is, bargain further with the help of a conciliation officer or board; finally, if the parties still fail to agree, the employer cannot declare a lockout or the union begin strike action until a further specified *cooling-off* period has elapsed.

For the fourth type of dispute, a rights dispute, the law imposes *arbitration procedure*: the parties are bound to accept the interpretation placed on the collective agreement by an arbitrator. In conciliation procedure the parties are not bound to accept the solution proposed by the conciliation officer, but in arbitration procedure the decision of the arbitrator is binding.

In summary, we can see that only in interest disputes does the possibility of lawful strike action exist, and then only after the prescribed conciliation procedure and cooling-off period. A strike is "illegal" if the preliminary grievance procedures set down by statute have not been followed or, even when they have been followed, the strike is not conducted according to carefully defined rules. The conduct of a strike by the union must be free of compulsion, intimidation, or threat. Furthermore, a strike may become unlawful if it is undertaken with an intent to injure another and not with the intent of furthering the trade interest of the strikers.

Although strikers are entitled to picket at or near the place of the employer's business, they must do so peaceably and only for the purpose of obtaining or communicating information. Statements made on placards or in literature distributed at the scene of the picketing must be correct and factual. Mr. Chief Justice McRuer of the Ontario Supreme Court outlined the scope of these rights as follows:

---

[41] In Canada, an employer need not bargain with a union that has not been certified and with which it has not previously made a collective agreement. In the United States, an employer must bargain with a union representing the majority of its employees, whether it is certified or not.

It is one thing to exercise all the lawful rights to strike and the lawful rights to picket; that is a freedom that should be preserved and its preservation has advanced the interests of the labouring man and the community as a whole to an untold degree over the last half-century. But it is another thing to recognize a conspiracy to injure so that benefits to any particular person or class may be realized. Further, if what any person or group of persons does amounts to a common law nuisance to another what is being done may be restrained by injunction.[42]

IMPLICATIONS OF THE COLLECTIVE AGREEMENT FOR THE INDIVIDUAL EMPLOYEE

The parties to a collective agreement are the employer and the representative union: generally, each party is a large organization or institution and the individual employee does not actively participate in negotiating the terms of employment. Since nearly all the bargaining is done by the union, comparatively little ground is left for an employee to negotiate with the employer at the time of making his or her individual contract of employment.

Labour unions have, of course, been a means by which workers collectively have achieved a bargaining power that they cannot have individually, and unions have secured many improvements in conditions of work. On the other hand, the process is one that necessarily subordinates individual employee preferences to the collective objectives of an organization. An individual's terms of employment are determined by virtue of his or her status as a member of the bargaining unit, rather than by virtue of any personal bargaining efforts:

> ...contract becomes largely the technique of group manipulation and use. Professional managements speak for the large corporation, and professional labor leaders speak for workers; the contract thus arrived at becomes a contribution to a code of administrative behavior by which the individual's personal right to contract is considerably diminished. As a working proposition, then, we are prepared to assert that contract is meaningful today more in terms of its use by organizations and less in terms of its use by individuals.[43]

The Province of Québec has a unique piece of legislation that takes this process a stage further: the terms of a collective agreement may apply even to workers who are not members of the bargaining unit for which the union was entitled to negotiate.[44] Under the legislation, when a union has bargained for a certain rate of pay with one or more large employers within the industry, the parties may apply to the Minister of Labour for a decree extending the provisions of the collective agreement to all other employers and employees within the industry or trade in the province or a region of the province. To succeed, the application must establish that the collective agreements already written have acquired a preponderant significance and importance for establishing conditions of labour within the industry or region. The effect is to establish a minimum wage law within the area covered by the decree, and to extend the terms of the collective agreement to workers not represented in the formation of the contract.

---

[42] General Dry Batteries of Canada Ltd. v. Brigenshaw, [1951] O.R. 522, per McRuer, C.J.H.C., at 528.

[43] Eells and Walton, *Conceptual Foundations of Business*, pp. 207-8. Homewood, Ill.: Richard D. Irwin Inc., 1961.

[44] Collective Agreement Decrees Act, R.S.Q. 1991, c. D-2.

Not only do unions have the dominant role in bargaining on behalf of individual workers, often workers do not have the freedom to choose whether to belong to the union. In *Bonsor v. Musicians' Union*[45] the plaintiff, who had been wrongfully expelled from the union and found it impossible to earn a livelihood as a musician without being a member, testified as follows:

> I would like to tell his lordship that if I could earn my living forthwith without being a member of this so-called Musicians' Union I would not want to join it, but I have got to join it in order to work because it is a closed shop. I will always pay my subscriptions, but I will not take any active part in union matters. I will be a member by force because I am forced to be a member.[46]

After quoting the above statement of the plaintiff, Denning, L.J. commented:

> When one remembers that the rules are applied to a man in that state of mind, it will be appreciated that they are not so much a contract as we used to understand a contract, but they are much more a legislative code laid down by some members of the union to be imposed on all members of the union. They are more like by-laws than a contract.[47]

Trade unions are, of course, only one of the modern institutions that have this effect on contract. Contracts between existing businesses that restrict competition by fixing prices or output effectively diminish the freedom of contract of the consuming public; we have considered the law dealing with this problem in Chapter 9. In addition, as we have seen, many financial institutions (insurance companies and finance companies, for example) present those to whom they sell their services with a standard form contract containing the printed terms of the agreement set down in advance on a take-it-or-leave-it basis, thereby diminishing the opportunity for the other contracting party to bargain for terms it would prefer.

*L*EGAL STATUS OF TRADE UNIONS

We touched briefly on the legal status of trade unions when discussing capacity to contract in Chapter 8. We noted that trade unions are recognized as legal entities before labour relations boards in order to bind them to the board's rulings; but this recognition is for a limited purpose, and we must not infer from the fact that unions have a separate existence before an administrative tribunal that they necessarily have comparable standing before the courts. We noted also that the technique of representative action provides a possible means by which unions may sue or be sued in the courts.

For various reasons, our legislatures have avoided the otherwise obvious path of requiring trade unions to come within existing companies legislation, and so conferring on them a corporate existence comparable with that of other business organizations.

---

45 [1954] Ch. 479. (The dissenting judgment of Denning, L.J., was approved on appeal to the House of Lords: [1956] A.C. 105.)

46 *Ibid.*, at 485.

47 *Ibid.*

Nevertheless, the legislatures seem to be moving in that direction and when there is no decisive statutory authority, the courts are able to cite the reasoning in the famous *Taff Vale* case, a decision handed down by the House of Lords in 1901.[48] In that case, a trade union was held to be a "quasi-corporate" body that could be sued. The decision held the union liable in damages for the plaintiff's loss as a result of a strike in which two agents of the union "put themselves in charge…and…illegally watched and beset men to prevent them from working for the company, and illegally ordered men to break their contracts." On these facts the court interpreted the strike as a conspiracy in restraint of trade under the then existing law of England. It next dealt with the question whether, even given an admitted wrong, the union as such could be sued for damages. It decided in the affirmative. Although the result of the *Taff Vale* case was nullified shortly afterwards by an act of Parliament,[49] and although this act was adopted by the provinces of Canada, the *judicial reasoning* concerning the legal personality of trade unions survived and persisted.

The Supreme Court of Canada in 1960 made extensive use of the *Taff Vale* decision in the case of *International Brotherhood of Teamsters v. Thérien*.[50] Thérien was the owner of a Vancouver trucking business and had been doing business with City Construction Company for some years when the company entered into a collective agreement with the Teamsters' Union requiring, as one of its terms, that all employees should be union members (a *closed-shop agreement*). Thérien agreed then to hire only union members for the operation of his trucks, but declined to join the union personally because he wished to maintain his relationship as an independent contractor in dealings with City Construction Company, and because in the capacity of an employer in his own right he claimed that he was forbidden by the Labour Relations Act of British Columbia from participating in union activities. The union took a different view, however, and as a result of union threats to picket City Construction Company, the general manager of that company informed Thérien that the company must dispense with his services. Thérien suffered a significant loss of business as a result, and brought action against the union claiming damages for the wrongful conduct of the union. The union defended on the grounds that it was not a legal entity and so could not be sued and, second, that in any case it had not been guilty of conduct that might constitute a tort.

On the first argument of the union the court noted that the union had been certified as a bargaining agent under the terms of the Labour Relations Act, and stated:

> It is necessary for the exercise of the [statutory] powers given that such unions should have officers or other agents to act in their names and on their behalf. The Legislature, by giving the right to act as agent for others and to contract on their behalf, has given them two of the essential qualities of a corporation in respect of liability for tort since a corporation can only act by its agents.[51]

---

[48] Taff Vale Railway Co. v. Amalgamated Society of Railway Servants, [1901] A.C. 426.

[49] See Trade Disputes Act, 1906, 6 Ed., c. 47, s. 1, declaring that actions of a trade union in furtherance of its interests would not thenceforth be interpreted as a restraint of trade.

[50] (1960), 22 D.L.R. (2d) 1. This decision has been followed in a Manitoba case: Dusessoy's Supermarket St. James Ltd. v. Retail Clerks Union Local No. 832 (1961), 34 W.W.R. 577.

[51] International Brotherhood of Teamsters v. Thérien, supra, per Locke, J., at 11.

The court quoted with approval the remarks of Lord Halsbury in the *Taff Vale* case:

> If the Legislature has created a thing which can own property, which can employ servants, and which can inflict injury, it must be taken, I think, to have impliedly given the power to make it suable in a Court of Law for injuries purposely done by its authority and procurement.[52]

Having identified the union as a suable legal entity, the court then found that the union had threatened to resort to picketing instead of following the grievance procedure set out in the collective agreement, and that the consequence of this conduct was the injurious termination of Thérien's arrangement with City Construction Company. It awarded damages to Thérien and ordered an injunction restraining the union from interfering with him in the operation of his business.

The *Thérien* decision is only one of a succession of Canadian cases developing the common law on the subject of the legal status of trade unions. It does not apply, of course, in provinces whose statutes specifically define the circumstances in which trade unions may be sued. In particular, Ontario has a statutory provision that restricts the possibility of an action against a trade union for torts.[53]

Questions for Review

1. Explain the following terms: collective agreement, vicarious liability, independent contractor, arbitration, assumed risk, conciliation, certification, "illegal" strike.
2. Give two reasons why it may be important to ascertain whether an agent may also be an employee.
3. What are the arguments for and against the use of specific performance as a remedy for breach of a contract of employment?
4. What are some of the torts an employee might be guilty of in the course of employment?
5. What conditions must be satisfied before an employer is liable for a tort committed by an employee against a third person?
6. An employee is laid off because there has been a sharp decline in the market for the employer's products. Is the employee entitled to notice?
7. On what grounds is a business justified in dismissing its employee without notice?
8. An employee leaves her position without giving notice to her employer. What factors should the employer consider before commencing legal action against the employee?
9. Quality Meat Packers Ltd. have major factories and warehouses from coast to coast. How does this fact complicate the company's collective bargaining with its employees?
10. In what respects has an employee's freedom to contract with an employer been qualified by modern developments in the law?
11. Why was it difficult, before the passing of the Workers' Compensation Act, for an employee injured at work to obtain a remedy against his employer?
12. How has the Workers' Compensation Act removed these difficulties?

---

[52] Taff Vale Railway Co. v. Amalgamated Society of Railway Servants, supra, note 46 per Halsbury, L.C., at 436.
[53] Rights of Labour Act, R.S.O. 1990, c. R-33. For legislation expressly making unions suable entities, see Industrial Relations Act, R.S.B.C. 1979, c. 212, s. 147; Labour Relations Act, R.S.M. 1987, c. L-10, s. 127; Industrial Relations Act, R.S.N.B. 1973, c. I-4, s. 114(2); Trade Union Act, S.S. 1983, c. T-17, s. 29, as amended.

13. What is collective bargaining? What are some of the usual terms of a collective agreement?
14. What kinds of labour disputes are there?
15. Under what circumstances may the form of an employment contract affect its enforceability? What statute is relevant?
16. Discuss the social justification for the doctrine of vicarious liability.
17. In *Addis v. Gramophone*, [1909] A.C. 488, Atkinson, L.J. made the following, often-quoted comment at pp. 493-4:

> I have been unable to find any case decided in this country [England] in which any countenance is given to the notion that a dismissed employee can recover in the shape of exemplary damages for illegal dismissal, in effect damages for defamation, for it amounts to that .... I have always understood that damages for breach of contract were in the nature of compensation, not punishment.

Is it the employer's or the employee's point of view that is represented in these comments of Lord Atkinson? How might contemporary social values affect this view? Explain.

18. In Victorian times Sir Henry Maine, a legal historian, stated that as society progressed, human relationships changed from a basis of status to that of contract. Many modern writers see in recent developments a return to a condition of status, such as that evolving for employees. It can be argued that a return to status is a return to a more rigid class society, with all its implications of a lower class akin to medieval serfdom. To what extent is this gloomy picture accurate? Comment on the validity of the argument.

Problems

Problem 1

MacDougall delivered milk on one of the routes of Farmers' Dairy. The dairy had the following notice to its drivers posted in its general office:

> To comply with a request from the insurance company our drivers are not permitted to take a rider or helper on their trucks unless authorized by the company. If these instructions are disobeyed Farmers' Dairy Ltd. will not accept responsibility in case of accident.

In addition, the company had signs placed on both the windshield and back window of each of its trucks stating "NO RIDERS".

One Saturday morning MacDougall asked a customer, Mrs. Brown, if her son Ted would like to help him deliver milk. The youngster persuaded his mother to let him go, as he had helped MacDougall once before and had a good time, and MacDougall had given him a drink of chocolate milk.

At one of the stops on the route the boy was getting into the truck with his hand on the door and one foot on the running-board when MacDougall started the truck suddenly. The boy was thrown to the ground and injured by the truck. His parents sued Farmers' Dairy Ltd. for damages for the medical expenses incurred. Should they succeed? (See *Hamilton v. Farmers' Ltd.*, [1953] 3 D.L.R. 382.)

Problem 2

In 1979 Able was hired by Cranbrook Collieries Ltd. as mine manager. In addition to his monthly salary he was given an allowance of $50 a month for coal to heat his house, since the house was not in the vicinity of the mine. About two years later Able was dismissed, on the grounds that he was often absent from his work and did not give proper supervision to the mining operation. Able argued that it was an incident of his position that he should be away from the mine from time to time for the purpose of consulting equipment suppliers and seeking new employees. Able brought an action against Cranbrook Collieries Ltd. for damages for wrongful dismissal.

During the trial, one of the teamsters employed by the mine testified that Able had instructed him to take coal to his house secretly, and that he had done so regularly without knowledge of any other employee of the mine. This fact was unknown to the directors of Cranbrook Collieries at the time they dismissed Able.

Should Able's action succeed? (See *Lake Ontario Portland Cement v. Groner* (1961), 28 D.L.R. (2d) 589.)

Problem 3

Rushmore operates a fleet of trucks under the name of Supersonic Delivery Service. His business consists of picking up parcels on request from small shops and delivering them to the shops' customers. One day Rushmore received a request from Jones Tool & Die Co. to deliver 20 iron pipes to Wilson at 149 Restful Vista Drive. He sent one of his drivers, Hastie, to pick up the pipes and deliver them. In error, Hastie delivered the pipes to 149 Wistful Vista, the home of McGee. Not finding anyone home there, Hastie left the pipes in an unlocked garage at the back of the house.

When McGee returned home at night, she opened the garage door to put her car inside, and groping for the light switch, tripped over the pipes and sustained a serious back injury. What, if anything, is the nature of McGee's claim? (See *Turner v. Thorne* (1960), 21 D.L.R.(2d) 29.)

Problem 4

C.W. Jonas was a porter employed by the Great East-West Railway Company. The passenger train on which he was working had discharged its passengers and was standing in a railway station. It was struck by another train as a result of the negligent operation of the railway and Jonas was severely injured. He sued the Great East-West Railway Company for damages for negligence.

In defence, the railway company produced its copy of an employment contract signed by Jonas. The contract included the following clause:

> The employee, C.W. Jonas, agrees that in consideration of employment and wages by the Great East-West Railway Company, he will assume all risks of accident or casualty incident to such employment and service whether caused by the negligence of the Company or of its employees or otherwise, and will forever release, acquit, and discharge the said Company from all liability therefor. The said employee waives all rights to workmen's compensation that might otherwise arise under this contract.

Without rendering a decision, discuss any public policy considerations inherent in a legal dispute of this kind.

Problem 5

Devellano operated a retail food supermarket that bought 60% of its merchandise from Prairie Wholesale Grocers Limited. As a result of a wage dispute the employees of Prairie Wholesale Grocers who were members of the Office & Shop Clerks Union went on strike. An official of that union then telephoned Devellano to enlist her support and apply economic pressure on Prairie Wholesale Grocers by reducing purchases from it. When Devellano refused, members of the union picketed her supermarket. They stopped cars on their way into the parking lot of the supermarket to distribute leaflets, intimating, inaccurately, that Devellano's store was controlled by Prairie Wholesale Grocers. The placards used while picketing contained the words "Devellano's Supermarket" and "Strike" in large letters, although none of Devellano's own employees were on strike. As a result, Devellano lost customers and sued the union for damages and an injunction to restrain the picketing of her premises. Discuss the defences available to the union and state whether they would succeed. (See *Dusessoy's Supermarkets St. James Ltd. v. Retail Clerks Union Local No. 832* (1961) 34 W.W.R. 577.)

Problem 6

Lucy Anang was hired as a chemist by the Plastic Toy Co. The contract of employment contained a term that, following termination of her employment with the company, she would not work for any competitor in the province for a period of five years nor at any time in the future disclose to anyone any information about secret processes used by Plastic Toy Co. Anang had worked in the laboratory of the company for a period of about three years when she was given two months' notice of dismissal.

After her dismissal Anang tried to earn a living as a consulting chemist. The plant supervisor at Plastic Toy then learned that she was disclosing certain information about manufacturing processes to one of the company's chief competitors. Specifically, it appeared that she had disclosed secret processes related to the production of equipment used in the colouring of toys, processes of value to the company.

Plastic Toy Co. sued Anang for damages and for an injunction restraining her from disclosing further information. One of Anang's defences was that no injunction could be granted to deprive her of the right to practice her profession as a chemist. What is the likelihood that the action will succeed?

Suppose instead that Anang had left Plastic Toy Co. because she had received an offer of a higher salary from a competitor of Plastic Toy. The management of Plastic Toy had no evidence that she disclosed any of its secret processes to her new employer, but was concerned that she might do so. Is it likely that Plastic Toy could obtain an injunction restraining Anang from working for its competitor? What conflicting policy issues must the court resolve? (For reference see *Reliable Toy Co. and Reliable Plastics Co. v. Collins*, [1950] 4 D.L.R. 499 and review Chapter 9 under the section "Agreements between Employee and Employer".)

Cases

Case 1

In August 1968, the directors of Universal Printing Co., publishers of an evening newspaper with a large circulation, approached Bell to persuade him to become their assistant advertising manager. They explained to him that if he accepted he would probably succeed the present advertising manager upon his retirement. At the time Bell held a responsible position with a Toronto advertising agency and was 43. During the discussions Bell emphasized that his present position was a very satisfactory one, that it was important at his age that his employment should be permanent, and that he would not consider a change that did not offer the prospect of a position lasting for the balance of his working life.

After careful consideration Bell accepted the position offered at a salary of $24 000 a year. He was promoted to advertising manager in 1976, and in the period from August 1968, to July 1982, his salary was increased regularly until it reached $4500 a month. In addition, every year he received a discretionary Christmas bonus of two weeks' salary approved by the directors plus a special distribution pursuant to a profit-sharing plan confined to selected employees and made under the sole direction of the principal shareholder of Universal Printing Co. Ltd. Bell's receipts under the profit-sharing plan were $13 600 in 1979, $12 400 in 1980 and $10 000 in 1981.

In August 1982, the President of the Universal Printing Co. Ltd., T. G. Dodds, called Bell into his office and after some opening pleasantries about Bell's prowess in golf, told Bell that he thought another advertising manager he had in mind could produce better results for the company. Dodds told Bell that if he could see his way clear to resigning forthwith he might have three months' salary in lieu of notice. Bell replied that he could not afford at this stage in his career to admit the incompetence implied in a resignation, and refused. Later in the afternoon his secretary brought him the following letter:

August 8, 1982

Dear Mr. Bell:

This is to confirm the notice given to you today of the termination of your employment with Universal Printing Co. Ltd. as of this date. Enclosed is a cheque for your salary to date. Your pension plan has been commuted to a paid-up basis that will pay you $250 a week commencing at age 65.

T. G. Dodds.

Bell at once made efforts to secure other employment, and by December 8, 1982, found a position with an advertising agency at a salary of $18 000 a year. If he had remained a further year with Universal Printing Co. Ltd., the paid-up value of his pension would have increased by $3500.

Bell brought an action against Universal Printing Co. Ltd. for damages for wrongful dismissal. What amount of damages, if any, should he recover? Are there any additional facts you would like to know?

Case 2

In September, Knowles, the owner of a professional hockey club, began negotiations with Meyer, a professional hockey player, for Meyer's services for the following two years. The two agreed orally to a salary of $3000 a week for Meyer during the training and playing seasons. At the time, Meyer asked whether players would be covered by workers' compensation insurance if injured. Knowles replied that the club's lawyer had advised that players were not covered but that in any event he was having written contracts drawn up by the lawyer in which a clause would provide that every player would be insured against injury and that if a player were disabled he would be looked after.

Written contracts were subsequently prepared and presented to all the players (including Meyer) for signing. The contracts in their written form specified the agreed salary for each individual player, and outlined the usual conditions regarding the player's obligations to the club, but there was no reference to insurance protection against injury or to the employer's obligation in the event a player were disabled.

Meyer played for the team for six weeks and then received a serious injury to his eye during a hockey game. He was immediately taken to the hospital. At the end of the game, Knowles announced to Meyer's teammates in the dressing room that he would pay Meyer's salary to the end of the season.

Knowles paid Meyer's salary to the date of his injury and refused to pay any additional sum. Meyer brought an action for damages claiming $45 000 representing his salary for the remaining fifteen weeks of the playing season; $500 for the cost of an artificial eye; and $100 000 general damages as compensation for the loss of his eye.

Discuss the issues raised by these facts and explain whether Meyer's action is likely to succeed.

CHAPTER 24

NEGOTIABLE INSTRUMENTS

History

In the last section of Chapter 14, we outlined the special nature of negotiable instruments; that section should be reread before proceeding with the present chapter.

Negotiable instruments began as a form of bill of exchange, a document made by a merchant or "banker" in one city instructing a colleague elsewhere to make a payment to a certain person or to the bearer of the document. They were probably used by the merchants of ancient Greece and Rome, and the practice was passed on to the medieval Islamic world. Later they came into wide use to meet the needs of merchants in the great age of discovery and trade.

By means of a bill of exchange a merchant in London, for instance, who had bought goods from a merchant coming from Hamburg, could arrange for the goods to be paid for by a banker in Hamburg, making it unnecessary for the Hamburg merchant to carry coins or bullion back with him. The London merchant could pay an appropriate sum to a London firm dealing in bills of exchange, and this firm would draw a bill on its agent in Hamburg instructing him to pay the Hamburg merchant in local currency on a certain date. The Hamburg merchant would accept the bill in exchange for his goods.

With trade taking place in both directions, the credits collecting in Hamburg would be set off by similar credits in London through goods sold by English merchants to others in Hamburg. In place of purely bilateral settlements, money-changing firms and merchants later learned to set off credits on a multilateral basis among several of the great trading cities. At regular intervals, usually at annual fairs held in the trading cities, they would get together and tally the paper they had honoured and pay each other any difference owing. The money-changers were able to charge fees because of the savings that merchants could make in not having to transport gold back and forth. Today, this form of setting off credits still exists in a much more sophisticated form through "clearing house" arrangements.

The rules governing negotiable instruments developed as part of the Law Merchant,[1] but as economic activity increased, the ordinary courts also adopted the rules. Eventually, a very large and complex body of case law developed around the subject. In the latter part of the 19th century, the British Parliament codified the rules in the Bills of Exchange Act, 1882. In Canada, the subject of negotiable instruments is within federal jurisdiction. Our Bills of Exchange Act[2] follows the English act closely.

While the law governing negotiable instrument is rather technical, it functions efficiently and causes few problems. We shall limit our discussion to a broad outline of what the law aims to do and how it accomplishes its purpose.

---

[1] *Supra*, Ch. 3, "The Sources of Law".

[2] The Bills of Exchange Act, R.S.C. 1985, c. B-4. When a footnote mentions a section only, the reference will be to this Act.

Nature and Uses of Negotiable Instruments

As Personal Property

Negotiable instruments are a kind of personal property called *choses in action*. We encountered this concept in earlier chapters, particularly Chapter 14, and in this chapter will consider the characteristics that distinguish negotiable instruments from other types of choses in action.

Every negotiable instrument contains an express or implied promise made by one or more parties to pay its amount. In the absence of evidence to the contrary, the promisee is presumed to have given good consideration for it. Thus, a negotiable instrument is normally a self-contained contract with all the necessary written evidence of its terms stated on its face. As a practical matter, a negotiable instrument usually arises out of an earlier contract in which one side satisfies its promise to pay for goods or services by giving a negotiable instrument. Delivery of the instrument is only a *conditional discharge* because if the debtor dishonours it the promisee's rights revive under the original contract. Promisees usually choose to sue on the negotiable instrument rather than on the original contract because it is generally simpler to do so.

Types of Instruments

The Bills of Exchange Act governs three common types of negotiable instrument: bills of exchange (or drafts), promissory notes, and cheques. Other kinds of instruments possessing the special quality of negotiability exist, but disputes concerning them have to be resolved by reference to the common law and not to the statute. For instance, bearer bonds have been held also to be negotiable instruments.

Following U.S. practice, there is a growing tendency to treat share certificates as negotiable instruments. Jurisdictions using the certificate of incorporation system, explained in Chapter 30, state expressly that a share certificate whose transfer is not restricted by words printed on its face is a negotiable instrument.[3]

We shall confine our discussion to the three common forms of negotiable instruments governed by the Bills of Exchange Act.

Bill of Exchange (Draft)

A bill of exchange (see Figure 1) is a written order by one party, the *drawer*, addressed to another party, the *drawee*, to pay a specified sum of money to a named party, the *payee* or to bearer, at a fixed or determinable future time or on demand. A bill of exchange originates with a creditor (drawer) that calls upon its debtor to acknowledge indebtedness and to agree to pay according to the terms stated in the instrument. A drawer sometimes designates itself as a payee; at other times it may direct that some other person or business to whom it owes money shall be the payee instead. The drawer expects the debtor (drawee) to consent by signing the instrument together with the word "accepted" and the date; the drawee becomes an *acceptor*. However, a bill of exchange may circulate among a

---

[3] Canada Business Corporation Act, S.C. 1985, c. c-44, s. 48(3).

number of holders as an item of valuable personal property even before it has been accepted. It has value for a holder because the drawer, by drawing and delivering it, has made an implied promise guaranteeing its payment.[4] Its subsequent acceptance adds the express promise of the acceptor.

An acceptor may indicate that the bill be paid out of its bank account. The drawer (or a subsequent holder) may then leave the instrument with its own bank for collection and deposit it in its account; that bank will present the bill to the acceptor's bank for payment out of the acceptor's account. After the amount is deducted from the acceptor's account, the cancelled bill of exchange is returned to the acceptor as evidence of payment just as cancelled cheques are returned.

Figure 1   A Bill of Exchange (Accepted Time Draft)

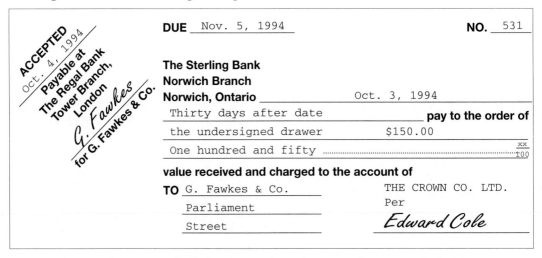

There are three types of bill of exchange, depending upon the time at which they are to be paid:

(a) *Demand drafts*, payable immediately upon presentation without the addition of any days of grace. The cheque is the leading example of a demand draft, and we treat it separately below.

(b) *Sight drafts*, in which the drawee is ordered to pay "at sight". In Canada, three days of grace for making payment are allowed after presentment for acceptance.

(c) *Time drafts*, payable a stipulated number of days, months, or other period "after date" (after the date stated on the instrument) or "after sight" (after present-ment for acceptance). Three days of grace should be added in fixing the matu-rity of a time draft. A bill payable at a given time after sight is a time draft, not a sight draft.

Presentment for acceptance is necessary whenever a bill is payable at sight or after sight, so that the time at which payment is due may be determined.[5]

---

[4] S. 129.
[5] S. 74.

Sight drafts can be used as a collection device. Instead of employing a collection agency to recover its slow accounts, a business may draw sight drafts on recalcitrant customers and have the drafts presented for acceptance and payment through the bank. The drawees will have a new incentive to accept and pay, not wishing to become known to the bank as poor credit risks.

Time drafts can be used as a means of finance for the business drawing them. By discounting them at a bank or by pledging them as security for a bank loan, the drawer can obtain cash in advance of the time when payment is due from the customer. Instead of waiting to be paid until the credit term granted to a customer expires, a business may draw a time draft on the customer immediately following the sale, and discount or pledge the draft. As we shall see in Chapter 33, however, there are other means of achieving this result. For example, a business may borrow from a bank by conditionally assigning its accounts receivable, it may sell its accounts to a factor, or it may assign them to a finance company.

Drafts and bills of lading often complement one another when goods sold on credit are shipped to the buyer by common carrier. Their joint use permits the seller to withhold possession of the goods from the purchaser when they reach their destination until the purchaser accepts a draft drawn on it for the price. The purchaser may examine the goods but cannot obtain possession from the carrier until the seller or its agent transfers the bill of lading to the purchaser.

Promissory Note

A promissory note (see Figure 2) is a written promise by one party, the *maker*, to pay a specified sum of money to another party, the *payee*, at a fixed or determinable future time or on demand. The maker is usually a debtor of the payee, and takes the initiative in preparing the instrument, though it may do so at the urging of the payee.

Figure 2 A Promissory Note

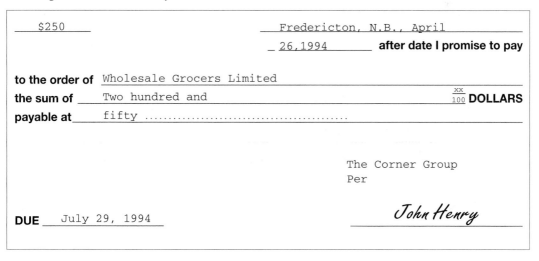

Unlike a bill of exchange, a promissory note is not presented for acceptance. From the outset, it contains an express promise to pay. To a subsequent holder, a promissory note that has been endorsed by the payee has the same effect as an accepted bill of exchange. The Bills of Exchange Act applies both to *accepted* bills and to notes, but the provisions relating to the *acceptance* of bills of exchange do not apply to promissory notes.

A maker of a note may word it so that it will be payable out of the maker's bank account at maturity; it is then paid through its bank and returned cancelled to the maker.

Cheque

A cheque (see Figure 3) is a bill of exchange drawn against a bank and payable on demand. From the point of view of the holder, a cheque contains the implied promise of its drawer that the drawer has funds on deposit at the bank sufficient to meet its amount, or that the amount is within the terms of a line of credit granted by the bank. For this reason it is sometimes convenient to think of the drawer of a cheque as a "promisor". The bank on which the cheque is drawn is called the *drawee bank*.

Figure 3   A Cheque

SUPERIOR PRODUCTS LIMITED		**No. 80013**
Calgary, Alberta		April 26, 1994

To
THE STERLING BANK
 Lethbridge, Alberta

Pay to the
order of _____ C. B. BOWEN & CO. LTD. _____ $ 400.00

FOUR HUNDRED _____ **DOLLARS**

.... XX/100

SUPERIOR PRODUCTS LIMITED
J. B. Riches
J. B. Walker

Since a cheque is payable on demand, the payee does not present it to a bank for acceptance, but cashes it or deposits it to the credit of its own account. The Bills of Exchange Act nowhere expressly authorizes the acceptance of cheques, nor does it refer specifically to the current banking practice of "certifying" cheques.[6] *Certification* amounts to an undertaking by the bank to pay the amount of the cheque to its holder when later presented for payment and, to ensure this result, the bank forthwith deducts the amount of the cheque from the drawer's account. Certification takes the form of the bank's stamped acknowledgement, with date, on the face of the cheque.

Occasionally a supplier will refuse to release goods until paid by certified cheque. The buyer prepares a cheque payable to the supplier, has the drawee bank certify it and then delivers it to the supplier. A payee may receive the cheque uncertified and before releasing

---

[6]   See Falconbridge, *The Law of Negotiable Instruments in Canada*, p. 43. Toronto: The Ryerson Press, 1955.

the goods will have the bank certify it; if the payee is returning to another city, such a cheque is safer to hold than cash — a thief would have to forge an endorsement before being able to cash it. In addition, certification at the request of the holder also forestalls any attempt by the drawer to stop payment on the cheque: since the payee could have cashed it instead of having it certified, the act of certifying makes the drawee bank liable directly to the payee.[7]

For most practical purposes, certification of a cheque is comparable to the acceptance of other types of bills of exchange.[8] The bank concerned is the drawee to whom the instrument is addressed, and once having undertaken certification it assumes a liability to the holder for the amount of the cheque.

The drawer may "postdate" a cheque by giving it a date later than the time when it is delivered to the payee. A cheque is an order addressed to a bank, and the bank must follow the instructions given to it on the face the cheque: the bank is therefore not entitled to pay the instrument before its date. While a cheque is by definition payable "on demand", a holder's right to demand payment is not effective until the date arrives; in the meantime the instrument operates like a time draft, though without the benefit for the drawer of three days of grace. Postdating is a convenience for a drawer who expects to be unavailable at the time a debt is due and who does not wish to pay in advance. It is common for a drawer to give a series of postdated cheques to meet instalment payments.

A drawer of a cheque may learn that the payee is in serious breach of their contract. Before the cheque has had time to be charged against its account, the drawer may countermand or "stop payment" by instructing its bank not to pay the cheque. The bank may require the drawer to agree that it will not hold it responsible if, through its inadvertence, the cheque is paid out of the drawer's account in spite of the countermand.

Even a cheque certified at the request of its drawer and not yet delivered to the payee may be countermanded and the amount returned to the drawer's account at the bank. Since the bank has a liability on the certified cheque, it will reject the countermand unless the cheque is surrendered by the drawer for cancellation or the drawer agrees to indemnify the bank should the bank be sued for refusing to honour the cheque.

Although payments can be made from current bank accounts by means of sight drafts, time drafts, and promissory notes, in recent years cheques have largely superseded them. This development is due to the practice of paying accounts once each month. Suppliers that once relied heavily upon the acceptance of drafts as immediate acknowledgements of indebtedness now depend upon the credit-worthiness of their buyers. The business community has gradually learned the limits to which its members may trust one another, and has adapted its use of banking facilities in the new context. A good credit reputation is a prized business resource, and its reputation is quickly lost when a business issues cheques that prove to be "n.s.f." (not sufficient funds). The comparative simplicity of payment by cheque has proved to be justified in all but a few instances. There are still a few trades in which the routine use of sight and time drafts persists by tradition, and in the field of international trade, where the parties are often unknown to one another and have to deal at great distance, drafts retain an

---

[7] When a cheque is certified at the request of the holder, the drawer is entirely discharged by its implied promise that the bank will honour the cheque. See Crawford and Falconbridge, *Banking and Bills of Exchange*, (8th ed.) B. Crawford, ed. p. 1791. Toronto: Canada Law Book Inc., 1986.

[8] The difference between certification and acceptance is confined to the circumstance where the drawee bank fails, and even then relates only to certification at the request of the holder (rather than of the drawer).

advantage. The promissory note, particularly the demand note, survives as the common method by which a borrower provides evidence of its indebtedness for a bank loan.

Most people have become accustomed to expect payment, including their wages, by cheque. The old pay envelopes have almost entirely disappeared, and employers now issue paycheques, often deposited directly in employees' personal bank accounts. The risks inherent in handling large amounts of cash on pay day are eliminated. Cheques also afford an easy and relatively safe method of making payments by mail.

A cheque, even one certified by a bank, is not legal tender. Strictly speaking, a creditor is entitled to payment in Bank of Canada notes and in coins up to the designated amounts for each denomination. However, to insist upon payment in cash would be inconvenient to both parties, and if a creditor refused a reasonable tender of payment by cheque and sued for payment in cash, court costs would likely be awarded against it.

$\mathcal{P}$REREQUISITES FOR LIABILITY

Until an instrument is delivered, the drawer, acceptor, or maker, as the case may be, has no liability, and even after signing it may reconsider and tear it up before delivering it. A drawee has no liability in respect of a bill of exchange before accepting and delivering it.

Delivery may be "actual", the instrument being issued directly by the promisor to the payee, or it may be "constructive", simply by notice to the payee that the instrument is complete and ready for delivery.[9] Once an instrument has been delivered, the term "negotiation" describes any subsequent transfer of it by the payee to a new holder as well as any later transfers to other holders.

$\mathcal{N}$EGOTIABILITY

Meaning of Negotiability

Negotiability is the special quality possessed by negotiable instruments as a distinct class of assignable contract. As noted in Chapter 14, their transfer is distinguished from ordinary assignments of contracts by three features:

(a) A negotiable instrument may be transferred (or assigned) from one holder to another without the promisor being advised about each new holder; the promisor becomes liable to each successive holder in turn.

(b) An assignee may sometimes acquire a better right to sue on the instrument than its predecessor (assignor) had.

(c) A holder may sue in its own name any other party liable on the instrument without joining any of the remaining parties.

The above legal qualities give a high degree of transferability to negotiable instruments. Ease of transfer enables negotiable instruments to meet business needs, because on their face they are sufficiently reliable for transferees to accept them without hesitation.

---

[9] S. 38.

For negotiable instruments to acquire these desirable qualities they must meet the following criteria:

(a) The promise or order must be set out in writing — otherwise the transferee would hold no evidence of the promise.

(b) The obligation must be for a money payment only, requiring no further inquiry into its value. Other types of obligation — to render services or transfer ownership of a chattel — would require a prospective assignee to investigate the value of what is being promised.

(c) The money promised must be a "sum certain". It may be repayable in instalments or with interest and still be a "sum certain".[10] But a promise to pay "the balance owing to you for services rendered" is insufficient because it is not possible from the face of the instrument to quantify the value of the promise.

(d) The promise or order must be unconditional so that the holder need not look outside the instrument to learn the implications of some qualifying phrase such as, "if the goods are delivered in good condition" or "subject to an allowance for poor material". A contract subject to a condition, though it may be valid between the immediate parties, lacks the certainty needed for a negotiable instrument: any attempt to transfer rights under it would be a mere assignment.

(e) The negotiable instrument must be payable at a fixed or determinable future time or on demand.[11] The value of a contractual right can be appraised only when it indicates the time at which it is to be performed.

(f) Negotiation must be of the whole instrument, not for part of the amount.

(g) The negotiable instrument must be signed by the drawer (or authorized signing officers of a drawer business)[12] if it is a draft or cheque, or by the maker if a promissory note.

Consequences when a Document is not Negotiable

Suppose *A* Co. draws a bill on *B* Ltd. payable to *C* Inc. and *B* Ltd. refuses to accept. Does drawing the bill nevertheless serve as notice to *B* Ltd. that it must now pay *C* Inc. instead of *A* Co.? The Bills of Exchange Act states that the act of presenting an instrument for acceptance does not of itself amount to notice of an assignment of the stated sum.[13] Accordingly, if *B* Ltd. refuses to accept, it owes nothing to *C* Inc.

Although a document may not amount to a negotiable instrument (where, for example, the order or promise is conditional), it may still be enforceable between the parties

---

10 Ss. 27 and 186. Problems arise where the instrument provides for payment of a fixed sum plus a variable or "floating" rate of interest, for example, "prime rate plus 2%". The Supreme Court of Canada has held that the sum must be capable of being ascertained by numerical calculation from the information contained in the instrument itself: *MacLeod Savings & Credit Union Ltd. v. Perrett*, [1981] 1 S.C.R. 78. The courts have had difficulty in applying this test with consistency.

11 It is hard to justify the uncertainty introduced by the definition of "determinable future time" in s. 23(b), *viz.*, "on or at a fixed period after the occurrence of a specified event which is certain to happen *though the time of happening is uncertain*" (italics added). It seems that a promissory note payable "at my death" would be a valid negotiable instrument. The provision is of little practical importance in business.

12 The signer is personally liable unless he states that he signs in a representative capacity: s. 51. The usual practice for a corporation is for its name to be printed on the instrument and for the officer to sign "per *X*" or "*X*, director". For an interesting case, see *Allprint Co. Ltd. v. Erwin* (1982), 136 D.L.R.(3rd) 587.

13 S. 126.

and be capable of assignment as an ordinary contractual right. In these circumstances, the Bills of Exchange Act does not apply and the parties' rights are subject to the general rules governing contractual assignments. Accordingly, a holder of the instrument cannot enforce the promise until the condition is met.

Methods of Negotiation

By Endorsement and Delivery

An order instrument is one expressed to be payable "to A", "to A or order", or "to the order of A". To negotiate it, A must endorse as well as deliver it to a new holder. Endorsement may take a number of forms, which we shall examine below, but essentially it is the signature (traditionally on the reverse side of the instrument) of the payee.

A party that purchases an order instrument without the proper endorsement on it acquires a very limited legal right, probably confined to recourse against the transferor, and has no rights against any prior parties.[14] In any event, a new holder cannot acquire a better legal right than the transferor until it has obtained the transferor's endorsement on the instrument. A new holder has a right to require the transferor to make the needed endorsement.[15]

By Delivery Only

Endorsement is not necessary for an instrument in "bearer" form. It is in bearer form when initially it is made payable "to bearer", or "to A Co. or bearer", or when no payee has been named and a space is left blank for the insertion of a name. It is also in bearer form when it is payable to an abstraction (for example, "Pay to Petty Cash"). Moreover, an order instrument becomes a bearer instrument when the specified payee endorses it without any qualifying words. Unless and until a subsequent payee endorses it payable to order, it may be negotiated by delivery alone.

An order instrument is safer because any attempt to negotiate it dishonestly amounts to the criminal offence of forgery.[16] The Bills of Exchange Act makes forgery one of the exceptions to the rule that a holder may acquire a better right than the transferor had. Forgery is a defence to the parties liable on an order instrument. By contrast, because a bearer instrument may be negotiated by delivery only, a thief may successfully negotiate it without resorting to forgery. Thus, even if a bearer instrument was lost or stolen at some previous time, its holder can require the party liable to pay, provided he can show that he acquired the instrument without knowledge of the loss or theft.[17]

Businesses rarely prepare negotiable instruments in bearer form, although as noted above, order instruments may be converted into bearer form by their holders. An employee, for example, may endorse her paycheque before taking it to the bank. If her endorsement is simply her signature, she has converted the cheque into a bearer instrument and it becomes subject to the risks discussed above.

---

[14] See Crawford and Falconbridge, *op. cit.*, p. 1503.
[15] S. 60.
[16] The Criminal Code, R.S.C. 1985, c. C-46, s. 374.
[17] Megrah and Ryder (eds.), *Byles on Bills of Exchange* (26th ed.), pp. 228 and 431. London: Sweet & Maxwell, 1988.

Bank notes were formerly promissory notes in bearer form, but now they simply state that they are legal tender and are freely negotiable by virtue of the Bank of Canada Act.[18]

ENDORSEMENT

Types of Endorsement

Endorsement in Blank

The payee on an order instrument signs his name — and nothing else — by way of endorsement, thus making it payable to bearer.

Special Endorsement

The payee specifies the next person to whom payment is to be made. For example:

> Pay to Prometheus
>   (*signed*) I. Zeus.

Restrictive Endorsement

By endorsing an instrument "for deposit only", the payee makes it non-negotiable. There is a risk that, if an instrument is stolen from a payee, the thief may forge the payee's endorsement and sell the instrument to a new holder, for example, by cashing it at a bank. Once it is endorsed "for deposit only", an instrument can only be deposited to the credit of the payee's account at the bank; it is no longer possible for a thief to cash the stolen instrument.

Conditional Endorsement

The payee specifies a party to whom payment is next to be made, provided he has lived up to the terms of a contract between them as, for example, "pay to the order of Bacchus if sober". Such a condition differs from a condition written into the instrument by a drawer, acceptor, or maker because it does not make the original promise in the instrument conditional. The party primarily liable may disregard a conditional endorsement in making payment, but the endorser may recover from the endorsee (Bacchus) if the condition was not satisfied.

Qualified Endorsement

The payee transfers rights in a way that denies liability as an endorser, for example, "Jane Bond, without recourse". Anyone giving value for the instrument is on notice that no remedy is available against Ms. Bond, should the party primarily liable default: as we shall see, in the absence of a qualified endorsement, an endorser normally is liable to subsequent endorsees. Manufacturers or wholesalers that "factor" their accounts receivable sometimes use a qualified endorsement. A factor may be willing to purchase drafts drawn on customers and endorsed over to it "without recourse"; the factor bears the risk of collection, without recourse to its client (the manufacturer or wholesaler).

---

18 The Bank of Canada Act, R.S.C. 1985, c, B-2, s. 25.

Anomalous Endorsement

Suppose a party to a negotiable instrument is not sufficiently creditworthy to persuade a prospective holder to buy it. For instance, a purchaser starting up a new business wishes to pay for goods by draft but the seller is unwilling to accept the purchaser's signature alone. The purchaser then obtains the signature of his sister; as a person with a recognized credit standing she signs the instrument solely to add her liability, as endorser, to that of her brother who is primarily liable. The endorsement is "anomalous" or exceptional because it is not added for the purpose of negotiating the instrument; the endorser was not a holder in her own right.

Bills, endorsed in this manner, are frequently called "accommodation bills". The acceptor or endorser usually signs to accommodate the drawer, that is, to make it easier for the drawer to obtain credit on the bill. An anomalous endorser contributes to negotiability because of her good credit standing.

Purposes of Endorsement

An endorsement may be the means of

    (a) transferring title to an instrument payable to order;
    (b) giving increased security to the payee (or subsequent holder);
    (c) identifying the party entitled to payment; or
    (d) acknowledging a partial payment.

We examined the first of these purposes above when we looked at the methods of negotiation and the types of endorsement. Most endorsements serve simply as the method of transferring ownership in the instrument.

We have also seen that an anomalous endorsement can make a negotiable instrument more marketable because the endorsement makes the endorser liable if the party with primary liability defaults. This is so even though the endorser has never owned the instrument and has not negotiated it to someone else.[19] An anomalous endorsement is a means of guaranteeing a debt, with the endorser in the role of guarantor.[20]

A holder of a negotiable instrument has no claim against the drawer if an intermediate holder has forged a signature. When a bank has cashed a cheque containing an endorsement forged by the person cashing it, the bank becomes a holder with no right to claim the amount from the drawee customer's account. To protect itself, a bank may occasionally require an endorsement from someone known to it for the purpose of identifying the person seeking to cash a cheque. For instance, it may require an endorsement in the following form:

> T. Smith is hereby identified
>   (*signed*) R. Jones.

As endorser, Jones is not liable for payment as are other endorsers should the party primarily liable default. Her liability is limited to the loss that would follow from having identified someone as T. Smith who later proved not to be that person.

---

[19] S. 130. The endorser is liable to the payee even though the payee has not himself endorsed. *Robinson v. Mann* (1901) 31 S.C.R. 484. Also, *Byles on Bills of Exchange* (26th ed.), p. 204.

[20] The same effect may be had without endorsement if both the guarantor and debtor sign in the first instance as joint makers of a promissory note.

If the maker of a note is to pay her debt by instalments, it is up to her to see that every time she makes a partial payment she obtains an endorsement on the instrument by its holder for the amount paid. Otherwise she remains liable for the full face amount of the instrument if it is subsequently negotiated to a holder who is unaware of the partial payments. An example of this type of endorsement is

> May 14, 1990.
> Received in part payment, $175.00
> (*signed*) B. Brown.

As an alternative arrangement the debtor may make a series of separate notes bearing the dates of the various instalments and require the surrender of the related note on the occasion of paying each instalment.

LIABILITY OF PARTIES

An Endorser

"Dishonour" is the failure by the party primarily liable to pay the instrument according to its terms. If the instrument is a draft, dishonour may take the form of either the drawee's refusal to accept or, if he accepts, of his later refusal to pay.[21] We have noted that an endorser is liable to any holder for the amount of the instrument, should the party primarily liable dishonour it, but this statement needs elaboration. If an endorser does not receive prompt notice of the dishonour from the holder, the endorser will be freed from liability.

In the rare event that an order instrument is negotiated several times, a particular endorser's liability extends to any *subsequent* endorser as well as the current holder; he has no liability to *prior* endorsers — indeed, they are liable to him. The holder has a choice of endorsers to require payment from when the instrument is dishonoured, provided each of them has received the necessary notice of dishonour.[22] In turn, an endorser who is held liable has recourse against any prior endorser but not against any subsequent one.[23] If the party primarily liable is unable to pay, the ultimate loser will be the first endorser (or the drawer if the instrument is a draft).

When an instrument contains a forged endorsement, the drawer and any endorser prior to the forgery are freed of liability. The only holder who can recover from an endorser in these circumstances is one who has satisfied the conditions for qualifying as a "holder in due course", as explained later. When such a holder suffers a loss arising from a forged endorsement or the forged signature of the drawer, unless the forger can be caught and made to pay, the loss will ultimately be borne by the person who acquires the instrument immediately following the forgery.[24]

---

[21] S. 132(a).
[22] Alternatively, the holder may sue all the endorsers as co-defendants in a single action and leave them to work out their individual liability among themselves.
[23] S. 100. Each endorser has, after receiving notice of dishonour, the same period for giving notice to earlier endorsers that the holder had after dishonour.
[24] S. 132(b).

ILLUSTRATION

A knew that C maintained an account at the B Bank. A drew a cheque on the B Bank payable to herself, forging C's signature as drawer. A then endorsed the cheque with her own signature and cashed it at a hotel operated by D. D endorsed the cheque and deposited it in the hotel account at the X Bank. The X Bank presented the cheque for payment to the B Bank through the bank clearing system. The B Bank recognized the forgery and refused to pay the cheque out of C's account. The cheque was then returned to the X Bank.

The X Bank is entitled to recover the amount that it had previously credited to D's account in respect of the cheque. The X bank is the holder (in fact, a holder in due course) and D, as the endorser immediately after the forgery, is liable.[25] In this illustration there is no other endorser between D and A, the perpetrator of the fraud. The loss must fall upon D unless A can be apprehended and the funds recovered from her.

An endorser also warrants to any later party that he had a good title to the instrument.[26]

Finally, unless a holder "duly presents" the instrument for payment, endorsers will not have any liability to him. Accordingly, an instrument payable on demand must be presented for payment within a reasonable time after its endorsement, and an instrument that is not payable on demand must be presented on the day it falls due.[27]

A Drawer

The drawer of a draft undertakes that on due presentment the draft will be accepted and paid according to its terms, and that if it is dishonoured the drawer will compensate the holder or any endorser who is compelled to pay it.[28] The drawer of a cheque undertakes that the cheque will be paid from his account on demand: if there are insufficient funds in his account, he is liable to the holder or to any endorser from whom the holder may recover. Because the parties to a cheque do not ordinarily contemplate a formal acceptance of it by the drawee bank, the drawer of the cheque becomes for practical purposes "the party primarily liable" comparable to the acceptor of a draft or the maker of a note.

A bank follows the instructions of its customer in disposing of the funds on deposit with it. Its authority to pay a cheque ends when its customer stops payment or when it receives notice of the customer's death.[29] While a holder cannot then hold the bank liable, his rights against the drawer remain unaffected by the countermand. A drawer who stops payment in fact dishonours the instrument, and may be sued by the holder. The death of the drawer makes the amount of the cheque a charge against the drawer's estate, and it becomes one of the debts the personal representative (executor or administrator) must settle.

---

[25] S. 49(1) and (2).
[26] S. 132(c).
[27] S. 85.
[28] S. 129.
[29] S. 167.

Notice of Dishonour

We have noted that neither an endorser nor a drawer will be liable in the absence of prompt, express notice of dishonour from the holder.[30] It is not enough for the holder to show that the endorser or drawer heard about the dishonour from some other source.[31] Notice must be given not later than the business day next following the dishonour.[32] If notice is mailed, the time limit applies to the time of depositing it in the post office and not to the time it is received.[33]

No special form of notice is required as long as it conveys the essential message. In two instances, however, a special form of notice of dishonour known as *protest* is prescribed. Protest is required if the instrument is drawn or payable or accepted in Québec[34] or outside Canada.[35] The services of a notary public, or justice of the peace where no notary public is available, are required to confirm the dishonour, prepare a notice of the protest in prescribed form[36] and deliver it to the endorsers and drawer within the same time as for a notice of dishonour generally.[37] The holder is responsible for contacting a notary public and is entitled to be reimbursed the notary's fee by the endorser or drawer to whom the notice of protest is delivered.[38] An endorser may waive the right to any notice of dishonour, and avoid the expense of the fee, by including the words, "No Protest" in his endorsement.[39]

A Transferor by Delivery

The term "transferor by delivery" describes anyone who negotiates an instrument in bearer form. Since no endorsement is required, a transferor by delivery is not liable on the instrument as an endorser.[40] He has no liability if the party primarily liable simply proves financially incapable of paying it. He is liable only to the one person to whom he negotiates the instrument, his *immediate transferee*, and then only for such loss as that transferee would sustain if the instrument were not genuine, that is, if the instrument is not what the transferor represented it to be or he was aware that it was valueless, or if he had no right to transfer it.[41]

An Acceptor or Maker

By accepting a bill, a drawee undertakes to pay it according to the terms of his acceptance.[42] Similarly, the maker of a promissory note undertakes to pay it according to its

---

30 S. 105(1)(b).
31 S. 98. See also Crawford and Falconbridge, op. cit., p. 1576.
32 S. 96. Under some circumstances a delay in giving notice may be excused (s. 104).
33 S. 102(2).
34 S. 113.
35 S. 111.
36 The prescribed forms are set out at the end of the Act.
37 S. 125.
38 S. 123.
39 S. 105(1)(b).
40 S. 136(2).
41 S. 137.
42 S. 127.

terms.[43] On the death of either the maker or acceptor, his liability passes to his personal representative.

Statute of Limitations

We have seen that the holder of a negotiable instrument must duly present the instrument for payment and, when necessary, give the required notice of dishonour in order to establish his legal rights against all prior parties to the instrument. He must then also prosecute his legal rights, by court action if necessary, within six years (five in Québec) because thereafter an action on a negotiable instrument is barred by the Statute of Limitations.[44] The period of six or five years dates from the maturity of the instrument, the time of the most recent payment made in respect of it, or the date of any written acknowledgment from which a promise to pay may be implied, whichever date is the latest. The lapse of this period of time does not, however, extinguish the liability of the parties completely. Chapter 34 contains a discussion of how such a liability may be revived.

$\mathcal{H}$OLDER IN DUE COURSE

In Chapter 10 we learned that an innocent purchaser of goods can often retain them even when the transferor, who had obtained them fraudulently, would have had to surrender them to the original vendor. We have also noted that a transferee of a negotiable instrument may be able to enforce payment when the transferor himself could not do so. Certain defences that might be successful against the transferor will fail against a transferee. Thus negotiation more closely resembles a transfer of title to goods than an assignment of a chose in action. Negotiable instruments are an exception to the general principle governing assignment of choses in action that an assignee takes no greater rights than the assignor had. For this reason, a negotiable instrument may become more valuable when it is transferred. The greater rights available to innocent third-party holders of negotiable instruments encourage reliance on these instruments and make them useful tools of commerce.

For the holder of a negotiable instrument to acquire something more than the transferor himself had, the holder must satisfy four conditions.[45]

(a) The holder must have taken the instrument complete and regular on its face.

(b) He must have acquired it before it was overdue and without notice of any prior dishonour.

(c) He, or someone through whom he claims, must have given consideration ("value") for the instrument.[46]

(d) He must have taken the instrument in good faith and without notice of any defect in the title of the person who negotiated it.

---

[43]   S. 185. If the party seeking payment is a "holder in due course" as defined below, the maker of a note cannot refuse to pay on the grounds that the payee whom he has named in his note either does not exist or lacks capacity to endorse.

[44]   See, for example: Limitation Act, R.S.B.C. 1979, c. 236, ss. 3 and 4; Limitations Act, R.S.O. 1990, c. L-15, s. 2(1)(e); Limitation of Actions Act, R.S.N.S. 1989, c. 258, s. 2(1)(e).

[45]   S. 55.

[46]   S. 56 requires that he shall have taken the instrument "for value" but s. 53 states that where value has been given at any time for a bill, the holder is deemed to be a holder for value.

A holder who satisfies these conditions is known as a *holder in due course*.[47]

Over the years, business experience has shown that the concept of negotiability has a convenience far outweighing the cost of its occasional abuse. In any event, the possibility of abuse is greatly reduced by confining the legal advantage to a holder in due course.

The rule that a person cannot be a holder in due course if he has taken the instrument with knowledge of its previous dishonour, or in bad faith, or with notice of a defect of title in the transferor, has one purpose. It deprives a holder of any advantage in conspiring with a transferee to take the instrument from him with a view to outflanking the defences of the party liable. The transferee does not qualify as a holder in due course and can be defeated by any of the defences that the party liable might have used against the transferor: the transferee can gain nothing by the manoeuver.

When the instrument is a time draft or note, a prospective holder of it can tell at a glance whether it is overdue or not. If it is already due, an obvious question to ask is why the present holder is trying to negotiate it instead of presenting it for payment. A prospective holder will have more difficulty deciding whether a demand draft is overdue. If it has been outstanding for an "unreasonable" length of time (which varies with the circumstances), it is deemed to be overdue,[48] and a new holder does not then become a holder in due course.

An outstanding demand note may have a different significance from a demand draft. A demand note is sometimes given as evidence of long-term indebtedness and may remain outstanding a long time without necessarily raising doubts about its collectability. Consequently, the criterion of an unreasonable length of time used in other areas of the law may be unsuitable in determining whether a demand note is overdue.[49]

An important benefit of the concept of a holder in due course is that banks are willing to discount drafts and cash cheques drawn on other banks with relatively little delay and at much reduced risk to themselves, since they acquire the instruments in the capacity of a holder in due course. If the law did not recognize the concept, banks would be reluctant to purchase negotiable instruments and hold them as assets; they would first have to make exhaustive inquiries to be sure that valuable consideration was given for an instrument and that it was free of fraud, illegality, duress, or undue influence. Banks would not risk acquiring instruments that might be subject to such defences when the time came to collect from the party primarily liable.[50]

DEFENCES

Meaning of Defence

The term "defences" is a legal description for the various arguments that a party liable on an instrument may put up against a holder who is demanding payment. There are two aspects to consider in determining whether a defence will succeed: (a) the status of the

---

[47] A subsequent holder will succeed to the rights of a holder in due course whether or not he himself satisfies all the essential conditions, unless he was a party to fraud or illegality affecting the instrument: s. 56.

[48] S. 69(2).

[49] S. 182. See also Crawford and Falconbridge, *op. cit.*, pp. 1510-11.

[50] As an additional protection a bank will require the endorsement of the person from whom it acquires the instrument; but recourse against endorsers is at best a second resort that banks naturally wish to avoid.

holder relative to the party liable; and (b) the type of defence of the party liable. We shall examine these aspects in the context of a legal action in which the plaintiff is the holder of the instrument and the defendant an acceptor, maker, drawer, or endorser.

Types of Holders

We must first determine the relationship between the holder and the party alleged to be liable on the instrument. When a holder has had direct dealings with that party, the two of them are *immediate parties*. If they have not had direct dealings with one another and yet are parties to the same instrument, they are *remote parties*. Since a holder in due course must acquire the instrument by negotiation from the payee or from a subsequent endorser, he is *always* a part remote from the acceptor of a draft, maker of a note, or drawer of a cheque.

ILLUSTRATION

A draws a cheque in favour of *B*. *B* endorses it to the order of *C*. *C* endorses it to the order of *D*. *D* is the present holder of the cheque.

A and B, B and C, and C and D are immediate parties. The remote parties are A and C, A and D, and B and D. Whether the present holder, D, is a holder in due course will depend upon whether he satisfies the four essential conditions.

Types of Defences

A holder's chance of success in collecting from an immediate party is no better than his contractual rights under the agreement between them. The negotiable instrument does not increase the holder's rights. Against an immediate party, the party liable can use a line of *mere personal defences*, usually not available against remote parties.

By contrast, a remote party who is a holder in due course has the best chance of success in collecting payment. The party liable has a greatly reduced list of possible defences, termed *real defences*, with which to resist the demands of a holder in due course.

If a remote party fails to meet the standards of a holder in due course, his position lies between an immediate party and a holder in due course, because he is subject not only to real defences but also to *defect of title* defences. He is not, however, subject to mere personal defences.

Mere Personal Defences

All the defences — real, defect of title, and mere personal — are available to the defendant when the contestants are immediate parties, but the mere personal defences, apart from the exception noted in the next paragraph, are available *only* when they are immediate parties. Defences good only against an immediate party are (a) lack of consideration, and (b) the right of set-off.

(a) When a promisor makes a gift of a negotiable instrument it is, of course, a gratuitous promise not yet performed. As with such promises generally, the promisor may plead lack of consideration and refuse to perform.[51] She may use the defence of lack of consideration where she gave the instrument to pay the price stated in the contract, and the underlying contract proves void or voidable for reasons of mistake, provisions in a statute (as with wagers), or public policy.[52] The Bills of Exchange Act makes it clear that an antecedent debt or liability constitutes valuable consideration for the instrument.[53]

(b) When a buyer receives goods she often pays for them with a negotiable instrument. If the goods are deficient in quality or quantity, the defences available to her against enforcement of the instrument will depend on whether the supplier has transferred the negotiable instrument.

ILLUSTRATION

May Dental Supplies Ltd. sells $500 worth of supplies to Dr. Nichols and receives a cheque in payment. Shortly afterwards, Dr. Nichols discovers that the shipment is short of several items worth in total $225, so that the dental supply company is in default.

Dr. Nichols then tells the supplier that she has stopped payment of the cheque at her bank. The supplier sues her on the instrument, Dr. Nichols can use the defence of set-off and the supplier can recover only $275 by court action. Here the parties are immediate parties.

Suppose instead that the supplier has already deposited Dr. Nichols' cheque and it has been charged against Dr. Nichols' account at her bank. The defence of set-off is lost to Dr. Nichols. The bank where Dr. Nichols keeps her account, having paid the supplier's bank, is entitled to keep the full $500 it has taken from her account. The dentist and her own bank are remote parties in respect of the transaction. By her act of drawing and delivering her cheque, the dentist has "cast her instrument upon the world" and has become accountable to any subsequent holder for its full amount should the payee succeed in negotiating it for value to a third party.[54] Dr. Nichol's only recourse is to claim a refund from the supplier.

The defence of set-off provides an illustration of the difference between the effect of an ordinary assignment of a debt and the negotiation of a negotiable instrument. In the law of negotiable instruments the defence is good between immediate parties but is lost when the party seeking to enforce the instrument is a remote party to the defendant. In an ordinary assignment the defence of set-off remains available against an assignee.

---

[51] While it is unlikely that a negotiable instrument would change hands more than once without consideration being given at some stage, if no party has given "value" for it, the party liable can continue to plead a lack of consideration, even when the plaintiff is a remote party. In order to enforce payment against the maker of a gratuitous instrument, the holder or *someone through whom he claims* (that is, a prior party) must have given value for the instrument.

[52] Lack of consideration is a reason for refusing to honour a negotiable instrument. It is a different matter if the promisor has already honoured the instrument and then seeks to recover its amount in a separate action. Thus, if a person pays a wager or makes a gift of money by cheque, he cannot recover the amount by court action unless he can offer additional reasons such as duress or undue influence.

[53] S. 53. See also English Law Revision Committee, *Sixth Annual Report*, pp. 17-18.

[54] In practice, the bank where May Dental Supplies Ltd. deposited the cheque would not sue Dr. Nichols if it found she had countermanded the cheque at her own bank. It is much easier for this bank to charge the amount back to May Dental Supplies Ltd., as it is entitled to do on the strength of the dental-supply company's endorsement at the time of deposit.

Defect of Title Defences

We have seen that a holder in due course must have taken the instrument without knowledge of any defect in title and, when he has done so, defences based on such defects will fail. Generally speaking, when an instrument is regular on its face, there is no defence against a holder in due course.[55] But if a holder takes the instrument *with* knowledge of one or more defects, or when there is an irregularity on the face of the instrument, he is *not* a holder in due course and a defence based on a defect will be successful.[56] Such defects are:

(a) incapacity to contract as a result of drunkenness or insanity;[57]
(b) discharge of the instrument by payment, or renunciation of a holder's rights in it;
(c) absence of delivery when the instrument was complete at the time;
(d) fraud, duress, undue influence, illegality;
(e) want of authority in an agent to complete the instrument on behalf of the party primarily liable.

Incapacity as a Result of Drunkenness or Insanity

We are already familiar with this type of defence as it applies to contracts generally, as discussed in Chapter 8. The defence is confined to drunkenness and insanity. Only if the subsequent holder was aware of the incapacity at the time the instrument was negotiated to him will the defence be effective. This type of incapacity must be distinguished from the incapacity of a minor as discussed under "Real Defences".

Discharge or Renunciation

The payment of an instrument on or after its maturity discharges it fully,[58] but if it remains regular on its face and does not appear to be overdue (as with a draft or time note) or to have been outstanding for an unreasonable length of time (as with a cheque), a holder in due course can still enforce the instrument.[59] If a holder takes the instrument with the knowledge that it has already been paid, he is not a holder in due course and cannot enforce it.

If a party paying an instrument fails to cancel it, he takes the risk that it will find its way into the hands of a holder in due course and he will be liable to pay it again. The usual way to cancel an instrument is by writing or stamping the word "paid" (with the date) across its face.

A holder's renunciation of his right to payment operates to discharge an instrument.[60] Any remote party who takes the instrument with notice of its renunciation cannot enforce it. However, if a holder later ignores his renunciation and negotiates the instrument to an innocent holder, the new holder can enforce it.

---

[55] These observations restate conditions (b) and (d), under the heading "The Holder in Due Course".
[56] Ss. 55 and 57(2).
[57] Depending upon the circumstances, insanity might instead be interpreted as a real defence. See Falconbridge and Crawford, *op. cit.*, pp. 1348-51.
[58] S. 138.
[59] There cannot be a holder in due course of an instrument paid before its maturity if it has been plainly cancelled. By definition, a holder in due course must take the instrument "complete and regular on the face of it".
[60] Ss. 141(2) and (3); 142(2) and 145(1).

Absence of Delivery

We have noted that delivery is a necessary step in establishing the liability of the party primarily liable. Suppose the treasurer of a business expects to be on a business trip when goods are to be delivered and paid for. She signs a completed negotiable instrument before leaving and delivers it to the supplier subject to the condition that it must not be used in any way until the supplier delivers the goods. The defence of "absence of delivery" includes such circumstances where there is physical delivery to a payee, but subject to a condition that must be satisfied.[61] If the condition is not satisfied, neither the payee nor any subsequent holder who acquires the instrument with knowledge of the defect can enforce payment. However, one who acquires it without notice of the defect may be able to enforce payment.

Fraud, Duress, Undue Influence, Illegality

These defences were discussed in detail as they relate to the law of contracts in Chapters 9 to 11. When a party has signed a negotiable instrument, for example, after being defrauded, he will have a good defence against a holder who takes the instrument with knowledge of the circumstances.

ILLUSTRATION

Conn offered to sell Mark a shipment of pure silk men's ties for $2000. After examining several samples Mark agreed and drew a cheque in favour of Conn for $2000 in full payment. In fact, virtually all the ties were made of polyester and worth only a fraction of the price. Conn had deliberately defrauded Mark. Brad, a friend of Conn, was present during the sale and was aware of Conn's deceitfulness. He paid Conn $1500 in cash in return for the endorsed cheque. However, before Brad was able to take it to the bank, Mark, on advice from the police, directed his bank to refuse payment.

Although Brad is a remote party he is not a holder in due course because he took the instrument with notice of the defect (Conn's fraud). Mark, therefore, has a good defence against the holder, Brad.

Want of Authority to Complete a Signed Instrument

Want of authority may arise when a party has signed an instrument but left some of the details blank, and then delivers it with instructions for completing it. No problem arises if the person in possession completes it in strict compliance with instructions; the instrument then has the same effect as though the party liable had completed it. As in agency law, the defence of want of authority will fail with respect to both an immediate transferee and any subsequent holder, if the agent had apparent authority to sign on behalf of the principal.[62]

Any abuse of authority, however, creates a defect of title, and the party liable may refuse payment to the party guilty of the abuse and to any holder who takes the instrument with notice of the defect. Since however, a holder in due course can enforce the instrument in the form in which it was completed,[63] it is risky to leave it to someone else to fill in the details.

---

[61] S. 39(1)(b).
[62] See explanation of the creation of an agency by estoppel in Chapter 22.
[63] S. 31.

Real Defences

Categories

The following defences are good against any holder, even a holder in due course:

     (a) incapacity to contract because of infancy;

     (b) cancellation of the instrument;

     (c) absence of delivery where the instrument is incomplete when taken;

     (d) fraud as to the nature of the instrument;

     (e) a forged signature on the instrument;

     (f) want of authority, in someone who has represented himself as an agent, to sign on behalf of the party liable;

     (g) alteration of the instrument.

Incapacity Because of Infancy

The incapacity to contract of a person under age is a real defence even when the instrument is given in payment for necessaries. A minor cannot be sued successfully on his negotiable instrument. A supplier may sue the minor for a reasonable price of necessary goods, but this remedy has to be distinguished from an action on the instrument itself. While no holder will have any recourse against a minor who is a prior party on the instrument, the holder's recourse against other parties is not affected.[64]

Cancellation

When cancellation is apparent on the instrument itself, the party liable has a good defence against everyone.[65] If a cancellation, made before maturity, is not apparent, an artful and dishonest holder may negotiate the instrument for value. The party liable may then find that he must honour his instrument a second time — in favour of a holder in due course.

Absence of Delivery of an Incomplete Instrument

We have noted that absence of delivery when an instrument is complete at the time is a mere defect of title defence and of no avail against a holder in due course. So too is a mere abuse of authority by an agent of the signer when the instrument has been delivered to him only for the purpose of completing it and transferring the property in it to someone else.[66] However, if an instrument is *both incomplete and undelivered* when it is intercepted by the wrongdoer, the signer will have a real defence, good against all holders. "Absence of delivery" requires *both* (a) prior abuse of signing authority or abuse of an incomplete document supplied by the signer for a special purpose only, *and* (b) failure to satisfy a condition to which the delivery of the instrument was subject — for example, a failure to supply specified goods.

---

[64] See Crawford and Falconbridge, *op. cit.*, pp. 1344-45. But see Soon v. Watson (1962), 33 D.L.R. (2d) 429, where an infant was held liable on a note. No authority is cited in the judgment and the law remains uncertain.

[65] S. 142.

[66] S. 39(1)(b).

ILLUSTRATION

X told *Y*, his employer, that the bank had asked him to procure a new specimen of his employer's signature for its files. *X* persuaded *Y* to give him *Y*'s signature on a blank piece of paper. *X* then completed the paper in the form of a demand note payable to the order of himself with *Y*'s signature in the space for the maker of the note. *X* told an acquaintance, *Z*, that *Y* was away on a trip and that he needed money at once for a family emergency. *Z* discounted the note for *X* and shortly afterwards presented it for payment to *Y*, who refused to pay it.

First, *Y* gave no authority to *X* to convert the paper into a complete negotiable instru-ment; the "instrument" was incomplete at the time, consisting of nothing but a signa-ture on a piece of paper. Second, there was an absence of delivery; the "note" was not delivered to *Z* by *X* as an authorized agent of *Y*. *Y* had given the specimen signature to *X* for the special purpose of supplying it to the bank. As a result, and despite his care-lessness, *Y* has a real defence, good against any holder, even a holder in due course such as *Z*. *Z*'s only recourse is to sue *X* (if he can be apprehended and has sufficient assets to satisfy a court judgment). In addition to his fraud, *X* would be liable to *Z* on the strength of his endorsement.

Fraud

As noted in the preceding section, fraud is usually a defect of title defence, giving the victim no protection against a holder in due course. Even when the instrument itself was misrepresented to him and he was not found to be negligent, the promisor is very likely to be held liable except in one instance: if he is a blind or illiterate person[67] he may suc-cessfully plead the real defence of *non est factum*, as discussed in Chapter 10.

Forged Signature

A forged signature may be that of either the party primarily liable or of an endorser. Either type of forgery is a real defence for persons who have assumed liability on the instrument *prior* to the forgery. Apart from situations of estoppel, as discussed below, the real defence of forgery provides the alleged drawer of a cheque with grounds for refusing to honour the instrument attributed to him. Since the funds out of which his cheque is to be paid are on deposit at the bank named as drawee on the cheque, the bank is necessarily involved as a result of the forgery.

Insofar as the *drawer's* signature is concerned, a bank is supposed to know the signa-tures of all its customers[68] and for this purpose keeps their specimen signatures on file. It has an obligation to detect a forgery of the drawer's signature and to restore any amount it mistakenly pays out of the drawer's account.

In Canada, a bank may be unable to recover money paid on an instrument bearing a *forged endorsement*.[69] To understand a bank's liability in this respect we must distinguish between a presenting bank and a drawee bank. A *presenting bank* is any bank where a payee or a subsequent endorsee presents a cheque to receive payment; a *drawee bank* is the bank where the drawer keeps his account. With a forged endorsement, the presenting bank and not the drawee bank has the primary obligation to detect the forgery. For this

---

[67] And perhaps persons unable to read the majority language (English or French) in their region of Canada.
[68] Bank of Montreal v. The King (1908), 38 S.C.R. 258.
[69] S. 48(1) and (3).

reason a presenting bank takes special precautions when asked to cash a cheque for a person who has no account there or who is not otherwise known to it.

(a) *A* drew a cheque on the Merchants Bank payable to the order of *B* and delivered the cheque to *B*. *X* stole the cheque from *B*, presented it for payment at a branch of the Crown Bank and forged *B*'s signature.

The Crown Bank would refuse to cash the instrument for *X* unless *X* could produce identification papers purporting to show that he is the payee, *B*. If the Crown Bank were persuaded to cash the cheque for *X*, the loss would fall upon it and would probably come to light along the following lines: the Crown Bank would stamp its name and the date on the cheque and clear it to the Merchants Bank branch against which it is drawn; the Merchants Bank would charge the amount against *A*'s account there; *B*, discovering the loss of the cheque, would ask *A* for a duplicate; *A* would then ascertain that the cheque charged against his account bore the forged endorsement of *B*; *A* (because of his real defence) would require the Merchants Bank to restore the amount to his account; the Merchants Bank would recover the amount from the Crown Bank because the Crown Bank's stamp on the cheque acts as its implied guarantee of the authenticity of prior endorsements, such as *X*'s forgery of *B*'s signature.

(b) The circumstances are the same as in (a) except that, instead of taking the cheque to the Crown Bank, *X* persuaded a druggist, *C*, to cash it for him. *C* then deposited the cheque in his account at the Crown Bank after endorsing it as required by the bank.

The Crown Bank, when all the facts are ascertained, may recover the amount from *C* on the strength of his liability as endorser.[70] It would normally recover the amount by charging it against *C*'s account.

Limits to the Defence of Forgery

A bank's liability for cheques bearing a forged endorsement does not extend to cheques where the payee is "fictitious or non-existing". As noted under "Methods of Negotiation", such a cheque is treated as being payable to bearer[71] and the bank as bearer would become entitled to enforce it against the drawer. In *Royal Bank v. Concrete Column Clamps*,[72] a dishonest payroll clerk of the drawer company fraudulently secured the signature of a company officer on a number of paycheques, some payable to former employees and some to fictitious persons. He subsequently forged endorsements and cashed all the cheques. The Supreme Court of Canada held that the bank could be held liable only for those fraudulent cheques made payable to former employees (existing persons) and that the drawer company would have to bear the loss for the remaining cheques made payable to fictitious persons.[73]

---

[70] Banks normally require their customers to endorse the cheques they present for cash or deposit, even if the cheques are in bearer form. However, even if *C* had not endorsed, he would, as a transferor by delivery, have warranted to the Crown Bank (his immediate transferee) that he had a right to transfer the cheque; he would not have this authority because of *X*'s forgery.

[71] S. 20(5).

[72] (1976), 74 D.L.R. (3d) 26.

[73] For a criticism of this decision, see B. Geva, "The Fictitious Payee and Payroll Padding", 2 *Canadian Business Law Journal* (1978), p. 418. See also, Fok Cheong Shing Investments Ltd. v. Bank of Nova Scotia, [1982] 2 S.C.R. 488.

Where the drawer of a cheque has a right to recover funds deducted from his account because the endorsement was forged, he must advise the bank of the forgery within a reasonable time, not to exceed one year from the time he learns of it.[74] The Act does not specify a similar time limit for notice when the signature of the drawer himself has been forged, but he has a duty to inform any holder or prospective holder of the facts as soon as he learns of them. If he does not do so, he may be estopped from using the real defence of forgery.[75] Although not a party to the instrument, he must take reasonable steps to avoid a loss for those who would be deceived by the forgery of his signature.

Want of Authority to Sign an Instrument

When someone purporting to be an agent signs a negotiable instrument without any real or apparent authority, the party described as principal can deny liability on the grounds that the instrument is not his; it is a form of forgery.[76]

We must distinguish want of authority *to sign* from want of authority *to complete an already signed instrument* (for example, to fill in the amount on behalf of the party liable). As we have seen, an instrument completed in an unauthorized manner may be negotiated to a holder in due course who may then require the party liable to pay.

Alteration

To provide a real defence, an alteration of a negotiable instrument must be apparent to the naked eye. No holder who takes an instrument bearing an apparent alteration can expect to recover from any party *prior* to the alteration, but he may recover from a party who *subsequently* endorsed the instrument for the altered amount. If, however, the alteration is not apparent, the instrument may be negotiated to a holder in due course who can sue parties prior according to the original terms of the instrument, as well as parties subsequent to the alteration for the altered sum.[77]

The drawer of a cheque owes a duty to his bank to prepare it in such a way as to make its alteration difficult; if he leaves spaces blank or otherwise invites alteration, he, not the bank, must absorb any loss resulting from alteration.[78]

CONSUMER BILLS AND NOTES

The modern concept of negotiability is a highly refined one, developed over the centuries and adapted to the convenience of business. Its advantages have had to be restricted, however, because of certain abuses. A select committee of the Ontario Legislature described a common abuse as follows:

---

[74] S. 48.

[75] *Ibid.*, which establishes forgery as a real defence and also recognizes that a party liable may be estopped from using that defence. A party may be estopped if it fails to take reasonable precautions to prevent forgery: Canadian Pacific Hotels Ltd. v. Bank of Montreal (1982), 139 D.L.R.(3rd) 575.

[76] In Don Bodkin Leasing Ltd. v. Toronto-Dominion Bank (1993), 10 B.L.R. (2d) 94, a bank that had paid almost $1 million on forged cheques was held not liable to its customer. Although the cheques had been forged by the customer's accountant who had no actual authority, he did have apparent authority.

[77] S. 144.

[78] Crawford and Falconbridge, *op. cit.*, p. 989.

Cases were brought to the Committee's attention where the seller in an instalment sales transaction misrepresented to the purchaser, in some cases dishonestly and fraudulently, the terms of the contract. Yet the purchaser was compelled to pay the whole debt because the discounter of the promissory note (the finance company) which formed part of the contract was a holder in due course with no knowledge, or provable knowledge, of the representations made.

The promissory note is a statement of obligation by which the signer promises to pay the holder an amount of money, but there is nothing in the note to the effect that there is any contractual obligation which must be fulfilled by the vendor of the goods or services before the money is payable...

If the paper was negotiated and had been bought by a finance company, a dissatisfied customer's refusal to pay because of the dealer's failure to fulfil his promise was no defence in an action on the note. Even if the dissatisfied customer went to court, the court, if it held that the finance company was a holder in due course, had to find in favour of the finance company and the disillusioned customer had to pay not only the purchase price but court and legal costs. The customer had a right of action against the dealer for non-performance, but this remedy was valueless with "fly-by-night" dealers.[79]

In some circumstances, the courts had held that a finance company and dealer were so closely related as to preclude the finance company from claiming to be a holder in due course.[80] In most cases, however, where no special relationship existed between conditional seller and finance company, the courts felt unable to restrict the rights ordinarily afforded to a holder in due course. As a result, Parliament amended the Bills of Exchange Act to remove the protection otherwise accorded to a holder in due course in consumer credit arrangements where a finance company acts in concert with a seller of goods on the instalment plan. After defining a consumer transaction, the statute states:

Every consumer bill or consumer note shall be prominently and legibly marked on its face with the words "consumer purchase" before or at the time the instrument is signed by the purchaser or by anyone signing to accommodate the purchaser [that is, a guarantor].[81]

The penalties for failure to comply with this section are severe: the instrument is void in the hands of either the seller or the finance company[82] (although they might negotiate it to an innocent holder in due course). In addition, everyone who normally participates in obtaining such an instrument without the appropriate marking is guilty of an offence and subject to a fine.[83] Most important, even when the instrument is properly marked on its face,

the right of the holder of a consumer bill or consumer note...to have the whole or any part thereof paid by the purchaser or...[a guarantor] is subject to any defence or right of set-off, other than counterclaim, that the purchaser would have had in an action by the seller on the consumer bill or consumer note.[84]

---

[79] Ontario, *Final Report of the Select Committee of the Ontario Legislature on Consumer Credit*, Sessional Paper No. 85, pp. 19-21.

[80] See Federal Discount Corporation Ltd. v. St. Pierre (1962), 32 D.L.R. (2d) 86, and Range v. Corporation de Finance Belvédère (1969), 5 D.L.R. (3d) 257.

[81] S. 190(1).

[82] Ibid., s. 190(2).

[83] Ibid., s. 192.

[84] Ibid., s. 191.

Thus, a buyer on consumer credit can now raise against a finance company that sues him as holder of his promissory note all the personal defences formerly available only against the seller.

Future Developments

A revolution in the use of negotiable instruments may result from the greater application of computer techniques now coming into operation. The ability to make almost instantaneous adjustments to individual account balances by "on-line" connections with a centrally-located computer could eliminate the use of cheques as a method of payment in many transactions. The actual physical transfer of paper representing written promises will likely be significantly reduced, and the holder in due course will become a less common phenomenon.

Questions for Review

1. A student insists that a cheque cannot be a form of draft because it originates with a debtor and not with a creditor. Is her reasoning correct?
2. Describe briefly the respective uses of demand drafts, sight drafts, and time drafts in commercial practice.
3. We sometimes refer to negotiable instruments as "a special class of promises in writing", yet a bill of exchange and a cheque take the form of an order to pay. Can these two views be reconciled?
4. Explain why a promise cannot take the form of a negotiable instrument if it is conditional.
5. What is meant by the "negotiation" of a negotiable instrument? In what ways may it take place?
6. "The act of endorsing and delivering a negotiable instrument payable to order differs from an ordinary assignment of contractual rights in three important respects." Explain this statement.
7. Abby drew a draft on James ordering him to pay Thomas "the amount of my account furnished". James accepted, writing, "Correct for, say, $750". Is this a negotiable instrument?
8. Gower has drawn a time draft on Cohen payable three months after sight to Jenkins. The draft is complete and regular with the possible exception of a clause that Cohen, the drawee, is "to pay the amount of this draft out of money due me on December 31 for professional services rendered". If Cohen refuses to accept the draft, does he owe its amount in future to Gower or to Jenkins?
9. Under what circumstances does an instrument, negotiable in its origin, cease to be negotiable?
10. You are the maker of a note in which you undertake to pay $500 to a moneylender on demand. Subsequently you pay an instalment of $200 to the moneylender on this liability. What steps should you take to ensure that you will not have to pay a further $500 at some later time?
11. Contrast the liability of an ordinary endorser and a transferor by delivery as to (a) the parties to whom each is liable; and (b) the scope of their liability.

12. You are a holder of a bill of exchange drawn by Richter on Ward, payable to MacDonald or order, accepted by Ward, and endorsed in blank by MacDonald. Upon presentment by you to Ward for payment, payment is refused. What is your legal position? What steps should you take to protect your rights?

13. The endorsements appearing on the back of each of three negotiable instruments are reproduced below. An asterisk following a name indicates an actual signature. Identify each of the endorsements by type and explain its effect for the parties concerned:

    (a) Pay to John Factor, Without Recourse
        The Synthetic Textile Co. Ltd.
        per Terry Lean,*/Manager.
        John Factor*

    (b) Pay to James Hawkins,
        S. Trelawney*
        For deposit only,
        James Hawkins*

    (c) Pay to Archibald Grosvenor only
        No Protest
        Reginald Bunthorne*
        Archibald Grosvenor*
        Archibald Grosvenor is hereby identified,
        Ralph Rackstraw*

14. An infant is a party to a negotiable instrument given by her in payment for necessary goods. What is her liability on the instrument?

15. In what circumstances may a remote holder of a negotiable instrument not be a holder in due course?

16. Describe the liability to the present holder of an "n.s.f." cheque or a person who has negotiated it to him in bearer form, without endorsing it.

17. *P* drew a cheque for $100 in favour of *Q*. *P* has his account at the *R* Bank. In drawing this cheque, *P* left a blank space before the words "one hundred" and *Q* added the words "two thousand and". The *R* Bank paid *Q* $2100 and the latter left the country with the proceeds. May *P* insist that the *R* Bank make good his loss of $2000? Why or why not?

18. Ayer drew a draft on Coole with the drawer named as payee. Coole accepted it, and Ayer then endorsed it to the order of Winter. Before Winter had endorsed it, the instrument was stolen and Winter's signature was forged by way of endorsement. The party guilty of the forgery succeeded in negotiating the bill to Frost who took it innocently and who in turn negotiated it to Holder. Examine the position of each of the parties to the instrument with respect to its enforceability.

19. *X* delivered $50 000 worth of goods to *Y* Ltd. and drew a draft on it for that amount payable in 90 days. *Y* Ltd. accepted and *X* then discounted the draft at his bank for the sum of $49 200 credited to his account. *Y* Ltd. dishonoured the draft at maturity. Describe *X*'s liability and rights.

20. On October 1, S.W. Martin made a note for $125 payable to the order of his son, Martin Jr., as a birthday present. The note was due October 31, following. Martin Jr. misplaced the note and his father refused to pay its amount until it was found. Martin Jr. did not locate the note until January 2, by which time his father had died. Martin

Jr. presented the note for payment to the executor of his father's estate, who refused to honour it. Give reasons why he should or should not be entitled to payment.

Problems

Problem 1

On April 28, the University of Penticton made a note payable to the Baroque Construction Co. Ltd., three months after date. The amount of the note was expressed simply as "the balance due to you for construction of our Arts Building". On May 2 following, the Baroque Construction Co. Ltd. sold the note to a private financier, R. Jay, for $47 500, having shown him accounts and vouchers indicating a balance of $50 000 due from the university. On July 31, R. Jay presented the note to the treasurer of the university for payment and was advised by him that the construction contract with the Baroque Construction Co. Ltd. contained a guarantee clause and that serious defects had developed in the foundation of the Arts Building. The treasurer stated that the university was not prepared to pay the note for this reason. R. Jay countered with the argument that the defective work was not the slightest concern of his, and that the proper officer of the university had signed the note. He then sued the University of Penticton on its note. Should he succeed? Give reasons.

Problem 2

Nan Jordan received a shipment of linen from Percy Bale, who carried on business in another city. Bale delivered the shipment personally and received a cheque in full payment from Jordan. Bale immediately went to Jordan's bank, but rather than cash the cheque simply had it certified so that it would be much simpler to take the amount home. The following day Jordan discovered that there was a substantial shortage in the shipment. She telephoned her bank at once to stop payment. The bank refused because Bale had certified the cheque. Jordan insisted that the bank must accept her order to stop payment regardless of certification. Is she right? Explain. What other remedies are available to her?

Problem 3

Elston owned all the issued common shares of Ham Ltd., a company incorporated in Ontario. In addition, Elston lent the company $160 000 of his personal funds and obtained in return a promissory note of the company payable to his order.

For personal reasons Elston subsequently had to borrow money on his own account from the Atlas Bank. To secure this loan he transferred the Ham Ltd. promissory note to the bank, but without endorsing it.

The Atlas Bank gave no notice to Ham Ltd. that it was the transferee. Two months after the bank acquired the note, Elston sold his shares in Ham Ltd. to new owners who had no knowledge of the existence of the note. At the same time Elston gave Ham Ltd. a general release of all claims he had against it in terms wide enough to include the company's obligation to him on the $160 000 note.

Elston defaulted on his personal loan from the Atlas Bank and the bank then demanded payment of the note from Ham Ltd. Ham Ltd. refused to pay, and the Atlas Bank brought an action against it for $160 000.

Give reasons whether or not this action should succeed. (See *Aldercrest v. Hamilton* [1970] 3 O.R. 529.)

Problem 4

On January 12, Waters was informed by the St. Lawrence Bank, where he maintained a current account, that a note for $3150 signed by him and made payable out of his account was due one week later. Waters knew that he had never made such a note but did not notify the bank because he assumed there must have been some mistake that was no concern of his.

Subsequently the note was paid, as it appeared, on Waters' forged signature and Waters insisted that the bank should add the $3150 back to his account. The bank refused and Waters sued it.

Outline the legal argument that Waters would use, and the defence of the St. Lawrence Bank. Explain also how your decision can be justified in terms of business practice.

Problem 5

As accountant at a branch of the Crown Bank, Cole misappropriated rent of $3000 due to the bank. When the bank inspector discovered these facts the bank notified the Flin Flon Fidelity & Guarantee Co., which had previously bonded Cole for the bank, and claimed the $3000. The bonding company told Cole that it was not its idea to prosecute if it could avoid it, and a possible way out would be for Cole to get his friends to come to his assistance. Cole then prevailed on his friend Smith to sign a promissory note payable 12 months after date in favour of the bonding company. When Smith dishonoured his note at maturity, the bonding company sued him. Should it succeed? Would the result be different if the bonding company had discounted Smith's note at its bank and Smith had refused to pay the bank at its maturity? (See *U.S. Fidelity and Guarantee Co. v. Cruikshank & Simmons* (1919), 49 D.L.R. 674.)

Problem 6

VanWyck drew a cheque payable to Lockhart, but decided not to send it until he had examined the goods purchased from Lockhart to see whether they were satisfactory. VanWyck's clerk, Anderson, inadvertently gave the cheque to Lockhart without first getting permission from VanWyck. (Anderson normally had nothing to do with the preparation or delivery of VanWyck's negotiable instruments.) Lockhart endorsed the cheque for value to Snider, who took it without notice of the circumstances. When Snider attempted to cash the cheque, she discovered that VanWyck had requested his bank to stop payment on it. Snider sued both VanWyck and Lockhart for the amount. State with reasons the rights of the respective parties and the probable result of the action.

Problem 7

Andrews, a clerk, placed on the desk of his employer, Barton, a number of mimeographed circular letters that required the employer's signature at the foot. Andrews arranged the letters so that, except for the first copy, no more was visible than the blank space for the signature at the bottom. One sheet in the pile was not a copy of the letter but a completed form of promissory note for $1000 payable to the order of Andrews. Having by this ruse obtained Barton's signature as maker of the note, Andrews negotiated it to Cartier. Cartier, not knowing about Andrew's fraud, paid $990 for it since 30 days remained until its maturity date. When Cartier later presented the note for payment, Barton refused to pay it. Cartier then sued Barton on the note. Who should succeed? Give reasons for your decision, citing any relevant cases.

Problem 8

Taylor mentioned to Gilbert, a real estate broker, that he was thinking of selling his house if he could get $185 000 for it. Gilbert suggested that Taylor sign an exclusive selling agreement but Taylor refused, saying that he would gladly pay Gilbert a commission if she produced a purchaser. Gilbert then spent considerable time and money in advertising Taylor's house and showing it to prospective buyers. Two weeks later, when Gilbert telephoned Taylor to ask whether she could bring a prospective buyer to the house, Taylor said he had changed his mind about selling and not to bother. Angered by what she considered to be unfair treatment, Gilbert threatened to sue Taylor for her expenditures unless Taylor would pay her $400. Taylor said, "All right, just to get rid of you I'll put a cheque in the mail today." He mailed the cheque. The following day he had second thoughts and requested his bank to stop payment. Gilbert sued Taylor on the cheque. Should she succeed?

PART FIVE

PROPERTY

The two preceding Parts — Chapters 6 to 24, comprising more than half of this book — have been devoted to the law of contract generally and with special types of contract that are of particular concern to businesses. The emphasis on contracts should not be surprising, since the making of contracts, for the buying and selling of goods and services, is fundamental to the conduct of business.

As we have seen, a consequence of the formation of a contract is the creation of a right to have the contract performed or to be compensated for its non-performance. We have noted (in Chapter 14) that certain contractual rights may be regarded as a form of property, called a chose in action. Two examples of property created by a contract are insurance policies and negotiable instruments, discussed in Chapters 20 and 24.

Not all types of property, however, originate in a contract. An important example of property is an interest in land, or real estate as it is frequently called. One may acquire such property by gift or inheritance. A person may also acquire property by a creative act: for example, copyright is a form of property that results from the act of creating a work of art or literature. As we shall see, any of these property interests may subsequently be transferred to other persons.

Traditionally, in the common law system, property is divided into real property and personal property; civil law systems recognize a corresponding though not identical distinction between immoveables and moveables. Real property refers to interests in land; all other forms of property are personal property. Personal property may in turn be sub-divided into choses in possession, such essentially tangible things as automobiles, furniture, jewellery and machinery, and choses in action, that is intangible or incorporeal "things," their essence being an enforceable legal right against another person.

We shall discuss several of these forms of property in the next four Chapters. Chapter 25 deals with "Intellectual Property" — a subject of increasing concern to modern business and in particular with trademarks, copyright, patents and industrial designs. Chapters 26–28 are concerned with the various interests in real property, including leases and mortgages.

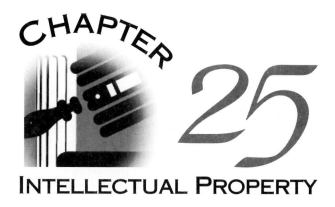

CHAPTER 25

INTELLECTUAL PROPERTY

The Nature of Intellectual Property

The terms *industrial property* and *intellectual property* have been used more or less inter-changeably, though until recently "industrial property" usually referred to trademarks, patents, and industrial designs, and the more lofty "intellectual property" described copyright — the work of authors and artists. As a comprehensive description neither term is entirely sat-isfactory. Industrial property conjures up images of tangible assets, such as machines and smokestacks, rather than intangible rights to which it is intended to refer; intellectual property hardly seems an appropriate description of some well-known trade names. Nevertheless, the word "intellectual" does better convey the notion that the various types of property included in the description are essentially the product of mental activity. Today the single term "intellec-tual property" normally encompasses all of these forms of property.

The feature common to trademarks, copyright, patents, and industrial designs — apart from the fact that they are all forms of intangible property — is that they are all con-cerned with ideas or inventions of which individuality or originality is an essential fea-ture. But not all ideas, information, or knowledge qualify as "property": confidential information, trade secrets, and what is commonly referred to as "know how", though in some ways protected by law, are not regarded as forms of property.

The proposition that ideas should receive legal protection as a form of property has not always been accepted. In particular, most socialist countries and many developing countries initially were strongly opposed, though in recent years they have generally been obliged to concede protection in order to attract foreign investment, especially in the more technologically advanced sectors. Nevertheless, while many countries have signed international agreements to harmonize intellectual property laws, the scope and extent of protection still varies considerably from one country to another.

Advocates of greater protection claim that creators, such as writers, inventors, and designers, have a moral right to the rewards arising from their efforts, and furthermore, that without protection, creativity is discouraged. Thus, it has been said:

> In most countries it is generally accepted that creators are entitled to a degree of protection for their works, on the grounds that a creator should benefit from the fruits of his labour. If creators are guaranteed a minimum of protection, they will be encouraged to create new works, thereby enriching the cultural life and fabric of the country and adding to the store of information.[1]

By contrast, opponents of protection claim that ideas and inventions, or at least some ideas and inventions, especially those concerning matters such as health, medicine, food production, and education, properly belong to the whole world. They point to the heavy social costs of protection — not only higher prices and payment of royalties and licence fees, but also inefficient use of resources resulting from restrictions on the use of new techniques and from the exercise of monopoly power. Thus excessive protection, as much as lack of protection, may hinder economic and social progress. The problem, especially for a country such as Canada, which is both an exporter and importer of cultural and technological innovation, is to find the right balance.

---

[1]   *Copyright in Canada: Proposals for a Revision of the Law*, p. 2. Ottawa: Consumer and Corporate Affairs Canada, 1977.

FORMS OF INTELLECTUAL PROPERTY

We have noted that there are four distinct types of intellectual property: trademarks, copyright, patents, and industrial designs. Each category comprises a particular type of property, protected according to its own rules. In addition, as we shall see in the final part of this chapter, there are some recently introduced statutory rights that do not fit easily into any of these categories. As a result, we are presented with a very complicated subject: some property rights are protected solely by statute, whereas others are also protected by common law rules; for some interests, registration is essential, while for others rights exist independently of registration; some types of intellectual property may fall within two different categories, yet others may fall into gaps between the categories so that no protection is provided at all. In addition, since intellectual property is essentially concerned with knowledge, information, and above all, innovation, it is inextricably linked to technological progress. In the fields of information and communication technology, progress has been especially fast. New methods of storing, presenting, and transmitting information and ideas are constantly being devised, and some of these techniques do not fit neatly into the traditional categories of intellectual property that were established a hundred or more years ago.

Before examining these four categories in greater detail, a word of warning is necessary: of all the different areas of law, intellectual property law is one of the most complex and technical, and perhaps the most specialized. The registration of trademarks and patents, for example, is normally dealt with by a small and select body of experts. For this reason, this chapter does not provide a detailed account of the law. Nonetheless, the subject is one of such increasing importance in business that we need to have a general understanding of which intellectual property rights may be protected, and how to protect those rights and avoid infringing the rights of others.

TRADEMARKS

Passing-off

At common law a person commits the tort of *passing-off* by misrepresenting goods, services, or a business in such a way as to deceive the public into believing that they are the goods, services, or business of some other person, thus causing damage to that person.[2] The main purpose of a passing-off action is to protect the other trader from what is, in effect, a misappropriation of goodwill.

Goodwill is not an easy concept to describe. It refers to an important asset of a successful business. A useful approach is to consider it as the difference between the market value of a business as a going concern and its break-up value, that is to say, the sum that could be obtained by selling off all of its fixed assets and inventory. The difference in the two sums can be attributed to the income of the business based on its reputation and established relationships with customers and clients. The name of the business, any mark

---

[2] For a detailed consideration of the common law, and of the law of trademarks generally, see *Hughes on Trade Marks*, R.T. Hughes and T.P. Ashton, eds. Toronto: Butterworths, 1984.

clearly associated with it, or some "get-up" such as a particular method of packaging or presenting its goods, all form part of that reputation and thus part of the goodwill.

Four distinct elements generally comprise the tort of passing-off. First, the plaintiff's goods, services, or business must enjoy a reputation that is of some value worth protecting.

Second, the defendant must have misrepresented its goods, services, or business as those of the plaintiff.

Third, there must either be actual confusion or a likelihood of confusion in the public's mind between the goods, services, or business of the plaintiff and those of the defendant. It is not necessary to prove that the defendant intended to create such confusion, or to cause damage to the plaintiff: the tort can be committed accidentally.

Fourth, the plaintiff must have suffered damage in consequence of the passing-off; in practice damage is presumed once the misrepresentation and the confusion, or likelihood of confusion, are proved.

Section 7 of the *Trade Marks* Act

In addition to the common law, section 7 of the Trade Marks Act[3] provides statutory causes of action that are closely related to, though not identical to, the action of passing-off. Section 7 prohibits:

    (a) making a false or misleading statement tending to discredit the business, wares, or services of a competitor;

    (b) directing public attention to one's wares, services or business in such a way as to cause or be likely to cause confusion in Canada between those wares, services or business and the wares, services or business of another;

    (c) passing-off other wares or services as and for those ordered or requested;

    (d) making, in association with wares or services, of any description that is false in a material respect and likely to mislead the public as to their character, quality, origin, or mode of production; or

    (e) doing any other act or adopting any other business practice contrary to honest industrial or commercial usage in Canada.

Section 7 appears to give wider protection in some respects than does the common law. Unfortunately, there is some doubt about the constitutional validity of section 7;[4] as we shall see, this doubt makes it difficult for a trademark holder to determine the best way to enforce its rights.

Business Names

The name of an established business is normally an important asset and part of the goodwill of the business. The choice of a business name is important, not only in order to provide the right sort of image for a business but also to avoid inadvertently becoming involved in potentially expensive proceedings for passing-off, or for infringing another person's trademark.

---

[3] Trade Marks Act, R.S.C. 1985, c. T-13.
[4] See the decision of the Supreme Court of Canada in McDonald v. Vapor Canada Ltd., [1977] S.C.R. 134. See also Seiko Time Canada Ltd. v. Consumers Distributing Co. Ltd. (1980), 29 O.R. (2d) 221; Asbjorn Horgard A/S v. Gibbs/Nortrac Industries Ltd., [1987)] F.C. 544.

Two types of business names can be distinguished: those of unincorporated businesses and those of corporations. In the case of unincorporated businesses, there is no general rule requiring the registration of business names. Most provinces have legislation that requires at least some unincorporated businesses to register; in Ontario, an individual who carries on business under a name *other* than his or her own name is required to register, as must a partnership unless the firm name consists solely of the names of the individual partners.[5] But the legislation is far from comprehensive and tends not to be strictly enforced; thus when we have selected a name, we cannot be sure, simply by making a search of the relevant provincial register, that no other business with the same, or a confusingly similar, name does not already exist.

The registration of corporate names is much more strictly regulated. Before a corporation can be incorporated certain information must be provided, including the name of the proposed corporation.[6] The appropriate government office must first approve the name and will refuse to register the corporation if it falls within certain prohibited categories (in particular, those that falsely suggest an association with the government or with certain professional bodies, or that are scandalous or obscene); if it is not sufficiently distinctive; or if it is likely to be confused with the name of some other corporation or other business entity.[7] In order to avoid the inconvenience and delay caused by the rejection of a chosen name, intending incorporators normally first make a "name search" to check that no existing corporation is registered with a similar name; of course, the government office responsible for registration also makes its own check.[8]

The fact that a corporation has been incorporated under a particular name does not, however, give it the right to carry on business under that name if to do so would infringe upon the registered trademark of some other business entity or would amount to the tort of passing-off. Thus, approval of the application to register does not of itself afford protection to a corporation. The approval may be challenged by some other corporation and the new corporation may be ordered to change its name.[9] Confusion may also exist with the name of an existing *unincorporated* business, which may not be registered at all. In addition, there may be confusion with the registered trademark of another business where the trademark is not the same as the name of its owner. It is sometimes advisable, therefore, when incorporating to make a search of the Trade Marks Register as well as the register of corporate names.[10]

Registered Trademarks

As we have seen, business names and trademarks are protected at common law through the passing-off action, without the need for any registration. Nevertheless, registration of

---

5 Business Names Act, R.S.O. 1990, c. B-17, s. 2.
6 See, for example, Canada Business Corporations Act, R.S.C. 1985, c. C-44, s. 6.
7 *Ibid.*, s. 12.
8 Records of corporations are now computerized which greatly facilitates such checks. If the name is not important to the incorporators, the problem can be avoided by using a "number name".
9 See Canadian Motorways Ltd. v. Laidlaw Motorways Ltd., [1974] S.C.R. 675. At the time of the 1988 Winter Olympic Games in Calgary, a number of companies were required to remove the word "Olympic" from their names to avoid infringement of the trademark of the International Olympic Committee.
10 It may also happen that two companies, one incorporated provincially and the other federally, could operate in the same province using confusingly similar names. For this reason, both provincial and federal registers should be searched.

trademarks does secure certain advantages over and above those that exist under the common law.

The Trade Marks Act gives the owner of a valid registered trademark the exclusive right to its use throughout Canada in respect of the wares and services for which it was registered.[11] No unauthorized person may then sell, distribute, or advertise any wares or services in association with a confusing trademark or trade name (s. 20), or otherwise use the mark in a manner that is likely to have the effect of depreciating the value of the goodwill attached to it (s. 22). An exception to this exclusive right arises when, after a trademark has been registered, it is discovered that some other person has been using a confusing trademark before the registered owner. When the mark has been registered for less than five years, the prior user may bring proceedings to have the registration expunged, on proof that the prior use has not been abandoned (s. 17(1)). However, when the registration occurred more than five years before the proceedings commenced, it will not be expunged unless the prior user shows that the registered owner had actual knowledge of the prior use when adopting the mark (s. 17(2)). If the registered owner had no such knowledge the court may make an appropriate order to allow the prior user to continue to use the mark, perhaps restricted to a given geographic area or in a modified form (s. 21).

Registration confers other advantages on the owner; normally it applies to the whole of Canada so that the right of exclusive use is not restricted to the area in which its owner actually does business and has established a reputation. A trademark that has been registered in Canada may also be registered in other countries that adhere to the International Convention for the Protection of Industrial Property. Procedurally, the registering of a trademark creates a presumption that it is valid and distinctive and is indeed owned by the registered owner.

A trademark registration is valid for a period of fifteen years, and may be renewed. Thus unlike copyright, patents, and industrial designs, a trademark can be preserved indefinitely. The Registrar may from time to time request evidence that the trademark is still being used, and if it has been abandoned or is not renewed at the end of the fifteen-year period, it may be expunged from the register.[12]

When a registered mark is used there is no need to indicate that it is registered, but it has become common practice, on labels and in advertisements, to so indicate by use of the symbol "R", or "TM", frequently accompanied by words such as "… is the registered trademark of XYZ Inc."

Registration

The Mark

A trademark is defined as:

   (a) a mark that is used by a person for the purpose of distinguishing or so as to distinguish wares or services manufactured, sold, leased, hired or performed by him from those manufactured, sold, leased, hired or performed by others;
   (b) a certification mark;
   (c) a distinguishing guise; or
   (d) a proposed trade mark.[13]

---

[11] Trade Marks Act, R.S.C. 1985, c. T-13, s. 19.
[12] Ibid., ss. 45, 46.
[13] Ibid., s. 2.

Although the Act does not define the word *mark*, it is generally accepted that virtually any visual characteristics of goods or their presentation that serve to distinguish them from goods that do not have the same trade connection can fairly be described as a "mark".[14] A trademark may be and frequently is part of a business name, but that name is not itself a trademark. For example, the word "Ford" is a trademark of the Ford Motor Company, but the full name is not.

A *certification mark* is a special type of trademark used to identify goods or services that conform to a particular standard, a typical example being the "Good Housekeeping Seal of Approval" mark. The owner of the certification mark may register it and licence its use to other persons whose goods or services meet the defined standards.

A *distinguishing guise* usually refers to the shaping of goods or of their containers, or to a mode of wrapping or packaging that is distinctive—a Coca Cola bottle, for example.

A *proposed trade mark*, as the name implies, is a mark that the owner proposes to use; the advantage of applying to register such a mark is that it can be protected without its actual use having been first established. Although the United States also permits registration of a proposed trademark, most countries require actual use before any rights may be acquired.

In order for a trademark to be registered it must satisfy a number of additional conditions. In particular, the mark must *not* be:

(a) a word that is primarily merely the name or surname of an individual who is living or has died within the preceding 30 years,
(b) clearly descriptive or deceptively misdescriptive of the character or quality of the wares or services, or of their place of origin;
(c) the name of any of the wares or services in connection with which it is used;
(d) likely to be confused with a registered trade mark; or
(e) a mark which is prohibited by s. 9 or s. 10 of the Trade Marks Act.[15]

These prohibitions serve a number of purposes. Given the exclusive nature of trademark rights, prohibitions (a), (b), and (c) seem primarily designed to ensure that the names of people and places, and descriptive words that are in common usage, are not in effect taken out of circulation through registration by giving a monopoly of use to the registered owner. The intention of prohibition (d) is to carry out the main purpose of the Act: trademarks are designed to be distinctive, and such distinctiveness would be lost if two or more persons were allowed to register confusingly similar marks.[16] Finally, sections 9 and 10 prohibit registration of marks that suggest an association with royalty, the government, certain international organizations or professional groups, or that are scandalous or obscene. Selecting and designing a suitable trademark is a difficult operation. Ideally, the mark will be distinctive and eye-catching and will quickly become associated in the public mind with the goods or services of its owner. On the one hand, it must be original so that it does not offend against condition (d) by being confusingly similar to some other registered mark. To this end, the normal practice is to make a search of the records of the

---

[14] *Kerly's Law of Trade Marks and Trade Names* (11th ed.), p. 5, T.A. Blanco White and R. Jacob, eds. London: Sweet & Maxwell, 1983.

[15] Trade Marks Act, R.S.C. 1985, c. T-13, s. 12.

[16] There is an exception to prohibition (d) where the same person seeks to register a number of related trademarks: *ibid.*, s. 15.

Canadian Trade Marks Office for other marks that are visually or phonetically similar to the mark being proposed for registration; in some cases it may also be advisable to make searches in the United States. On the other hand, the proposed mark should not be one that is likely to be rejected under one of conditions (a), (b), (c) or (e). In practice, the application to register is normally prepared and filed by a specialist trademark agent, who will give advice on the likelihood of an application being accepted; such advice is important, since the case law on this subject is extremely complicated.

ILLUSTRATIONS

(a) A mark consisting of the name of a historical figure, such as "William Shakespeare" or "John A. MacDonald" would probably be acceptable, even though it is very likely that there are living persons with those names. Similarly, fictitious names, such as "Captain Kirk" or "Darth Vadar", are registrable because the public would not identify the names with living individuals. In one instance, a coined name, "Marco Pecci", was held to be registrable in the absence of evidence that such an individual actually existed, despite the possibility that there might somewhere be a person of that name.[17]

(b) Words, especially adjectives, that are merely descriptive (or misdescriptive) of the quality of the goods are not acceptable. "Instant" or "Super" would be rejected though "Kold One" has been accepted when applied to beer[18] and, more recently, the word "Golden" was held not to be descriptive of a beer and therefore acceptable.[19]

(c) The use of a place name as descriptive of the quality or origin of goods is normally not permitted. The mark "Toscano", applied to wine, was disallowed since that is the Italian name for wine from a famous region.[20] In another case, however, a producer was permitted to register the mark "Oberhaus" in relation to wine, despite the fact that there is in Germany a small village called Oberhausen where wine is produced. It was considered unlikely that the Canadian wine-buying public would know of the place.[21]

The Owner

Registration alone does not make a person (whether an individual or corporation) the owner of a trademark; that person must already be the owner at the time of registration. This is so, even in the case of applications based upon proposed use, for the mark will be registered only after the applicant has filed a declaration that it has commenced to use the mark in Canada.

The application to register may be based upon any one of the following grounds:

(a) the mark has been previously used or made known in Canada;

[17] Gerhard Horn Investments Ltd. v. Registrar of Trade Marks, (1983) 2 F.C. 878.
[18] Registrar of Trade Marks v. Provenzano (1978), 40 C.P.R. (2d) 288.
[19] Molson Cos. v. John Labatt Ltd. (1984), 1 C.P.R. (3d) 494.
[20] Jordan & Ste. Michelle Cellars Ltd. v. Gillespies & Co. (1985), 6 C.P.R. (3d) 377. In that case, the words were also misdescriptive, since the wine was Canadian.
[21] Stabilisierungsfonds für Wein v. T.G. Bright & Co. (1985), 4 C.P.R. (3d) 526.

    (b) the mark has been registered and used abroad, in a country that is a party to the convention; or

    (c) it is proposed to use the mark in Canada.[22]

Generally, the mere advertising of a trademark is not sufficient to constitute "use"; the goods or services to which the mark relates must have been sold or performed. However, advertising alone may be sufficient to amount to "making known" the mark in Canada.

Opposition Proceedings

The initial obstacle in registering a trademark is to satisfy the Registrar that the chosen mark is eligible for registration. If there is no objection by the Registrar, or an objection has been overcome,[23] the Trade Marks Office issues a notice that the application has been approved for advertisement in the Trade Marks Journal and, subsequently, the application must be advertised. Once the trademark has been advertised, any person may, within two months, file a notice of opposition.[24] Registration may be opposed on any of the following grounds:

    (a) the application did not comply with the various formal requirements for filing;

    (b) the mark is not registrable;

    (c) the applicant is not the person entitled to registration; or

    (d) the mark is not distinctive.[25]

The opponent must specify the ground or grounds upon which the opposition is based in sufficient detail to enable the applicant to reply to the objection. However, the onus of satisfying the Registrar that the trademark should be registered still rests on the applicant. This is so, even though the Registrar has in effect already reached a preliminary decision in favour of the application by permitting it to be advertised. Opposition proceedings are determined in the first place by Hearing Officers, with appeal to the Trial Division of the Federal Court.

An objection that the mark is not registrable includes all the elements set out in section 12 of the Act—that the mark is primarily merely a name of an individual or that it is descriptive of the character or quality of the goods or their place of origin, or that it comes within the categories of prohibited use. The motivation behind a challenge is usually to prevent a business competitor from gaining an advantage by being granted the exclusive right to use the mark. The other common reason is that the objector claims already to have rights, whether registered or not, to the use of a mark that is identical or confusingly similar. Determining what is, or is not, "confusing" depends very much upon the nature of the business concerned and of the goods or services supplied.

---

[22] Trade Marks Act, R.S.C. 1985, c. T-13, s. 16.

[23] If the Registrar refuses registration, the owner may appeal against that decision to the courts.

[24] Trade Marks Act, s. 38(1), as amended by the Miscellaneous Statute Law Amendment Act, 1991, S.C. 1992, c.1., s. 134.

[25] Ibid., ss. 37, 38 (2)(d).

The use of a trademark comprising the words "Dutch Boy", for ice cream sold in southern Ontario, was held not to be confusing with another mark containing the same words used for pickled herrings sold in Western Canada.[26] And "Playboy", in connection with magazines and hotels, was held not to be confusing with the same name for hair stylists.[27]

Remedies for Infringement

As we have seen, a trademark may be infringed at common law by passing-off, and a registered trademark may in addition be infringed by any unauthorized use of that mark, or a confusingly similar mark, by some other person.[28] The infringement may be accidental or deliberate; it is not necessary to show an intention to damage the goodwill of the owner of the mark,[29] though such an intention may persuade a court to award punitive damages.

The trademark owner may bring an action for infringement in the appropriate provincial court, in which case common law as well as statutory remedies are available, but a successful judgment can be enforced only within that province. On the other hand, if an action is brought in the Federal Court, the judgment is enforceable anywhere in Canada. However, the Federal Court has jurisdiction only to hear actions brought under the Trade Marks Act. At first glance, this would not seem to cause any difficulty since, as we have seen, section 7 of the Act purports to provide even greater protection to trademark owners, whether registered or not, than does the common law. However, because the constitutional validity of section 7 is in doubt, the owner will have to decide whether to pursue both statutory and common law remedies in a provincial court, and obtain only limited territorial protection, or to rely solely on the other provisions of the Act and sue in the Federal Court.

Whether the action is one at common law, for passing-off, or a statutory action, the remedies that the court may order are essentially the same. If there is injury to the goodwill of the owner, then damages may be awarded; if the defendant has profited from the infringement, an account of profits may be ordered. In any event, the defendant may be restrained from further infringement by an injunction and may be required to deliver up or dispose of infringing materials. The court may also order the defendant to allow the plaintiff to search for and seize offending wares, and relevant books and records,[30] and in a statutory action, may impose a ban upon further imports of offending products.[31]

Assignment, Licensing, and Franchising

At common law, a trademark was considered to be a part of the goodwill of a business and therefore inseparable from the business itself. Consequently, the owner

---

[26] Oshawa Holdings Ltd. v. Fjord Pacific Marine Industries Inc. (1981), 55 C.P.R. (3d) 289.

[27] Playboy Enterprises Inc. v. Germain (1978), 39 C.P.R. (2d) 32.

[28] For a comprehensive study of infringement of trademarks, see D.J.A. Cairns, *Remedies for Trademark Infringement*. Toronto: Carswell, 1988.

[29] Even a "spoof" upon a trademark may be actionable: see Source Perrier S.A. v. Fira-Less Marketing Co. Ltd. (1983), 70 C.P.R. (2d) 61.

[30] This is the so-called "Anton Piller relief": see Anton Piller K.G. v. Manufacturing Processes Ltd., [1976] Ch. 55.

[31] The power to ban imports has been restricted by the North American Free Trade Agreement Implementation Act, S.C. 1993, c. 44, s. 234.

could not assign a trademark except where the transferee also took over the business. Nor was it possible to retain the use of a trademark while granting a licence to another person to use it as well; the essence of a trademark is its distinctiveness, a quality that is lost once it is used by two or more different persons. Section 48 of the Trade Marks Act substantially modifies these rules so that the owner may now transfer a trademark (a) whether or not it is registered, (b) either as part of or separately from the goodwill of the business, and (c) in respect of either all or some of the goods and services in association with which it has been used. An owner may also license the use of a registered trademark, the licensee being permitted to use the mark under conditions prescribed by the licence (s. 50).

Special care must be taken when assigning or licensing a trademark to ensure that the rights of either or both parties are not lost. Generally, when a business is sold the rights in a trademark with which it is associated pass to the purchaser; thus, a transfer of the business operates to assign the trademark. If the mark is registered, the fact of the assignment may be entered on the register, but an assignment may be valid even if unregistered. If a mark is unregistered the new owner may seek to register it after having commenced to use it. A more difficult situation occurs when an owner keeps the business but assigns the trademark, perhaps because the business is to discontinue production of the particular line of goods with which the mark is associated. An example occurs when a foreign company, that has previously marketed its goods in Canada and has established rights to a trademark here, forms a subsidiary company in Canada to take over the manufacture or distribution of its goods. The difficulty arises because, in the eyes of the public, the trademark may remain distinctive of the goods of the previous owner rather than those of the new owner, who consequently will not immediately have an established right to it.[32]

When licensing a trademark, the owner often desires to continue to use the mark and also to permit concurrent use by one or more other businesses, usually in return for payment of a fee or royalty. The former system, whereby licensed users could be registered, has been abandoned and it is now sufficient to give notice to the public that use is under licence; in that case use by the licensee is then deemed to be that of the registered owner itself so as to preserve the distinctiveness of the mark.[33] A licensee cannot transfer the right to use a mark, and a breach of any of the terms of the licence will normally constitute an infringement of the trademark.

Although a *franchise agreement* is usually much broader in scope than the licensing of a trademark, the franchiser will in most cases require that the franchisee market goods or services under the franchiser's trademark. Franchisers normally insist on strict conditions in the franchise agreement, relating to such matters as quality control, purchasing of supplies and equipment, advertising, and the use of trademarks, trade names, designs, and the like. Breach of the agreement by a franchisee normally terminates its right to use the trademark, so that continued use would amount to infringement.

---

[32] See Wilkinson Sword (Canada) Ltd. v. Juda, [1968] 2 Ex. C.R. 137.

[33] Trade Marks Act, s. 50, as amended by the Intellectual Property Law Improvement Act, S.C. 1993, c. 44, s. 69. See Linehan, "Trade Mark Licensing Agreements under the new Amendments", (1993) 10 *Canadian Intellectual Property Rev.* 537.

COPYRIGHT

Statutory Origin

Unlike the law of trademarks, copyright is entirely the creature of statute; there is no common law action for infringement of copyright. Copyright is a comparatively modern concept. It was unknown in the ancient world and began to be considered only after the invention of the printing press in the 15th century. Even then, it took a couple of centuries to evolve; the first known copyright law was the Statute of Queen Anne, adopted in England in 1709.[34] For many years copyright was associated almost exclusively with the written word, though its scope was later extended to cover drawings, paintings, and musical scores. In recent years, with the advent of motion pictures, sound recording, radio and television broadcasting, and the like, it has become a central feature of several major industries.

In Canada, the law of copyright is governed by the Copyright Act,[35] originally adopted in 1924 and substantially amended in 1988 and 1993.

International Treaties

Canada is a signatory to the Convention of Berne, an agreement to which more than sixty countries adhere. An author who is a citizen of a Convention country has copyright protection in Canada, and Canadian authors enjoy protection in other Convention countries. Canada also adheres to the Universal Copyright Convention. The Universal Copyright Convention enables a citizen of a contracting state to enjoy the same copyright protection in another contracting state as does a national of that state. Thus, a Canadian national can obtain protection in the United States simply by following the American practice of marking the work with the symbol ©, or the word "copyright", followed by the name of the copyright owner and the year of first publication. Similar benefits are also provided by a number of reciprocal agreements that Canada has entered into with other countries, and the Copyright Act itself extends far beyond the boundaries of Canada, since it applies to the original works of all British subjects or residents within Her Majesty's Realms and Territories, and thus gives protection in Canada to citizens of the United Kingdom and the Commonwealth countries.

Nature of Copyright

What is commonly referred to as "copyright" is really a collection of distinct rights conferred by statute. The basic rights of the owner of copyright are:

— the right to produce or reproduce the work in question, or any substantial part of it, in any material form;
— the right to perform or deliver the work in public; and
— the right to publish an unpublished work.

---

[34] 8 Anne, c. 19. There were some statutes in the previous century dealing with the licensing of printers.
[35] R.S.C. 1985, c. C-42, as amended by S.C. 1988, c. 15. For a comprehensive study of the subject, see *Hughes on Copyright and Industrial Design*, R.T. Hughes ed. Toronto: Butterworths, 1984.

There are also a number of more specific rights:

— the right to translate the work;
— the right to convert the work from one form into another (e.g., to convert a novel into a play, or vice-versa);
— the right to make a recording or film of the work;
— the right to communicate the work by radio communication (including television);
— the right to exhibit the work in public; and
— the right to authorize any of the above.[36]

The essence of copyright is perhaps better understood, however, when expressed in terms of limits; its importance lies in the power of the author or owner of the copyright to restrain others from doing any of those things that only the author or owner has the right to do. In all works in which it exists, copyright arises automatically and without any registration simply by the act of creation, whether the work is published or not. The author or creator of the work is the original owner and may assign the copyright. Thus, copyright may be owned by the author of a book or by the firm that publishes it, by the composer of a piece of music or by the recording company, or it may be owned by some person not connected in any way with the creation or production process, such as a relative or creditor of the author. However, there are other rights, generally referred to as *moral rights*, that are personal to the author or creator and that cannot be assigned. These include:

— the right to integrity of the work;
— the right to prevent its being distorted or mutilated;
— the right to prevent it from being used in association with some product, service, cause or institution; and
— where the work is copied, published, or performed, the right to be associated with the work as author by name or pseudonym, or to remain anonymous.[37]

Thus, the author of a play is entitled to have the authorship properly attributed to her when it is performed or, if she wishes to remain anonymous or use an alias, the right not to have her true identity revealed. And an artist who paints a picture is entitled not to have it defaced.

ILLUSTRATION

A sculptor who created a group of flying geese, to be displayed in a shopping centre, is entitled not to have them decorated with red ribbons at Christmas time.[38] This is so whether or not he still owns the copyright.

We have noted that copyright exists in unpublished as well as published works. However, there can be no copyright in any work unless and until it has been created. Thus, there is no copyright in a mere idea, but only in the expression of an idea in a material form. As was stated in one leading case:

---

[36] Copyright Act, R.S.C. 1985, c. C-42, s. 3(1).
[37] *Ibid.*, ss. 14.1 and 28.2 (as amended by S.C. 1988, c. 15).
[38] Snow v. Eaton Centre Ltd. (1982), 70 C.P.R. (2d) 105.

> It is…an elementary principle of copyright law that an author has no copyright in ideas but only in his expression of them. The law of copyright does not give him any monopoly in the use of the ideas with which he deals or any property in them, even if they are original. His copyright is confined to the literary work in which he has expressed them.[39]

Thus, a playwright could "borrow" the plot from another person's novel, provided the play was expressed entirely in his own words. Such conduct might be considered to be unprofessional, and to amount to *plagiarism*, but it would not by itself constitute an infringement of copyright.

Works in which Copyright Exists

Copyright exists in every original *literary, dramatic, musical,* and *artistic work.*[40] It must be emphasized that the requirement of *originality* applies to each of these four categories. "Originality" is used here in the sense that the work must have originated from the author; there is no requirement that it must be particularly imaginative, novel, or skilful.

Literary Works

The Copyright Act gives a very broad meaning to "literary work". The expression includes any work that is reduced to writing or printing, and includes maps, charts, plans, tables, and compilations. As well as the obvious items such as books, and magazine and newspaper articles, the term has been held to include income tax tables, street directories, examination papers, insurance forms, parts catalogues, and the like. From this list it is apparent that, for the purposes of the Act, literary merit is not an essential element of a "literary work". Machine drawings and sketches have sometimes been treated as literary works, though it is more common for them to be classified as artistic works; the actual classification is usually unimportant.

Amendments to the Act made in 1988 added computer programs to the list of protected literary works.[41] Prior to that year, the situation in Canada regarding computer programs had been somewhat uncertain. A program is usually first written in a computer "language", such as BASIC or FORTRAN. This "source code" is humanly readable. It is then translated into an "object code", consisting of a series of "0's" and "1's", readable by the computer. The object code may in turn be embodied in a "chip". It is reasonably clear that the humanly readable source code qualifies as a literary work. However, in *Apple Computer Inc. v. Macintosh Computers Ltd.*[42] the defendants were accused of copying the plaintiff's chips and, in doing so, substantially reproducing the programs embodied in the chips. The defendants argued that the program is merely a "specification" and that by copying the chip the defendants were simply carrying out the specification, just as is done when one makes a pie from a recipe. The plaintiffs responded that the defendants' conduct should more properly be compared to copying the recipe itself. The Supreme Court of Canada agreed and held that copyright subsists in computer programs embodied in a chip, or in other machine-readable form, and that the copying of a

---

[39]   Moreau v. St. Vincent (1950), Ex. C.R. 198, per Thorson, P., at 202.
[40]   Copyright Act, R.S.C. 1985, c. C-42, s. 5(1).
[41]   *Ibid.* as amended by S.C. 1988, c. 15, s. 1(2)(3).
[42]   (1990), 71 D.L.R. (46) 95. See the detailed review of the issues raised in this case by Hayhurst, "Recent Developments in Canadian Law: Intellectual Property", (1987) 19 *Ottawa Law Review* 137, at 196.

chip constitutes an infringement of the copyright in the program itself. The 1988 amendment reinforces this position, defining "computer program" to mean instruction or statements expressed, fixed, embodied, or stored in any manner, for use directly or indirectly in a computer in order to bring about a specific result. The new provisions contain certain exemptions, permitting the making of single copies for a specific purpose, such as making a back-up copy or reproducing the program in another form in order to render it compatible with a particular computer.

Dramatic Works

A "dramatic work" is defined to include any piece for recitation, choreographic work, or entertainment in "dumb show", the scenic arrangement or acting form of which is fixed in writing or otherwise, and any cinematographic production where the arrangement or acting form or the combination of incidents represented give the work an original character.[43] The category is sufficiently wide to include not only the older forms of drama, such as plays, operas, and ballets, but also most new forms of entertainment. The key words in the definition are "fixed in writing or otherwise". The text of a play, or the libretto and score of a musical comedy, are protected since they are fixed in written form. But so also are films, video recordings of dramatic works, or a sound recording of an interview or of a poetry reading.

Although an event such as a street riot or a plane crash, or perhaps even a football game, occurs independently of a person making a record of it, and is not itself a "dramatic work", recording such an event, for example on film, can constitute the dramatic work of the photographers and film editors; copyright can subsist in such a film, and to copy the film would constitute an infringement of copyright. Before 1988, a "live" broadcast of such an event was considered not to be protected by copyright, because it was not "fixed".[44] This rule has been amended, in part to comply with Canada's obligations under the Free Trade Agreement with the United States, and in large measure to deal with a number of problems relating to cable retransmissions of television signals. The amendment states that it shall be an infringement of copyright to communicate a work to the public by any form of telecommunication unless the retransmission complies with the Broadcasting Act.[45] The new rule deals with the problem of "live" broadcasts by providing that a work is considered to be "fixed" even if it becomes fixed simultaneously with its transmission.

Musical Works

A "musical work" is defined as any combination of melody and harmony, or either of them alone, that is printed, reduced to writing, or otherwise graphically produced or reproduced. The important word here is "graphically", for copyright extends only to the music in written or notational form; a performance of a musical work is not within the definition. However, separate protection is given to records or other "contrivances" that

---

43 Copyright Act. R.S.C. 1985, c. C-42, s. 2.
44 Canadian Admiral Corp. v. Rediffusion Inc. [1954] Ex. C.R. 382. In the leading Australian case of Victoria Park Racing and Recreation Co. Ltd. v. Taylor (1957), 58 C.L.R. 479, it was held that no copyright was infringed when the defendants broadcast a radio commentary on horseraces organized by the plaintiffs from a platform erected on land adjoining the racetrack.
45 Canada-United States Free Trade Agreement Implementation Act, S.C. 1988, c. 65, s. 64.

mechanically reproduce sound.[46] The contrivance or recording is itself regarded as a work in which copyright subsists, whether or not the work being performed also has its own copyright. Thus, a recording of a live performance by a jazz pianist or trumpeter, in which a new work is improvised, is protected by copyright even though the music itself was never reduced to written or graphic form. A recording of a symphony by Beethoven is similarly protected, even though any copyright in the symphony itself would long ago have expired.

Artistic Works

An "artistic work" is defined by the Copyright Act to include paintings, drawings, maps, charts, plans, photographs, engravings, sculptures and artistic craftsmanship, and architectural works of art, which in turn are defined as any building or structure, or model of such building or structure. For architectural works, copyright is restricted to the artistic character and design and does not extend to the processes or methods of construction.[47] Some overlap exists between "artistic" works and "literary" works, since the definition of the latter also includes maps, charts, and plans.

We should note that a *trademark* of distinctive design may also qualify as an artistic work and be protected by copyright. In addition, plans and drawings of machinery or other devices may be protected by copyright as artistic works, and at the same time may depict or describe an invention protected by *patent*. It is frequently difficult to determine whether a particular piece of work is an artistic work, protected by copyright, or an *industrial design*, which may receive a different form of protection.

Excluded Works

Copyright was never intended to protect mass-produced items, and until 1988 the Copyright Act expressly excluded designs capable of being registered under the Industrial Design Act, where those designs were intended to be used as models or patterns to be reproduced by some industrial process. The Act now provides that there is no copyright in three-dimensional articles that are functional, or in drawings or plans for such articles.[48] However, as noted earlier, an artistic work may take a three-dimensional form, such as a sculpture or an architect's model, and have the benefit of copyright.

Public policy in Canada does not appear to prohibit copyright in works that are obscene, immoral, or otherwise offensive, but as a matter of public policy the courts would likely refuse to grant damages to an author of such a work whose copyright was infringed.

The Protection of Copyright

Duration of Copyright

Generally, a work is protected by copyright during the life of its author and for a further period of fifty years after the author's death.[49] However, the Copyright Act prescribes different terms for the following:

---

[46] Copyright Act, R.S.C. 1985, c. C-42, s. 5.
[47] *Ibid.*, s. 2, as amended.
[48] S.C. 1988, c. 15, s. 11.
[49] Copyright Act, R.S.C. 1985, c. C-42, s. 6. The deceased author's estate or an assignee of the copyright, for example, a publisher, may use the protection. If the author is unknown, the term is fifty years from the date of first publication.

(a) *photographs and phonograph records* are protected for fifty years from the making of the original negative, plate, or master tape;

(b) *posthumous works* — works not published before the death of the author — are protected for fifty years from the date of first publication;

(c) *jointly authored* works are protected for fifty years after the death of the last surviving author; and

(d) *Crown copyright* persists for fifty years from the date of first publication.

Ownership of Copyright

In general, copyright belongs initially to the author or creator of a work. Copyright in a work may be jointly owned by two or more authors, such as the joint authors of a book. However, it is also possible for separate copyrights to exist in different parts of the same complete work; for example, the writer of the lyrics of a song may hold copyright in the words (as a literary work) and the composer may hold copyright in the music.

There are a number of exceptions to the general rule. When photographs have been commissioned, copyright belongs to the person who ordered the photograph to be taken rather than to the photographer, unless otherwise agreed. Works that have been prepared or published by or under the direction of the government belong to the Crown, subject to contrary agreement. Most important is the rule that where the author of a work was employed by some other person and the work was made *in the course of employment*, copyright belongs to the *employer* — again, unless otherwise agreed. Thus, copyright in an examination paper or a set of lecture notes would normally belong to the university or college, rather than to the teacher who authored them.

As mentioned earlier, and as discussed in the next section, copyright may be assigned by the original owner to some other person. The Act provides that, when an author has assigned a work, copyright in it reverts automatically to the author's estate twenty-five years after the death of the author. This rule cannot be varied by agreement. However, the rule applies only in cases of sole authorship where the original copyright belonged to the author.

Assignment and Licensing

An owner of copyright may assign it, as an item of property, for value or by way of gift, or it may pass under the will or intestacy of the owner. The so-called "moral rights" of an author, as already noted, are not capable of being assigned. An owner may also assign only part of a copyright in a work, or may divide it territorially. For example, one person might own the copyright in Canada and another in the United States; copyright could even be divided between Western and Eastern Canada. Authors often assign the copyright in a book to their publishing company in return for the payment of a royalty — for example, 10% of total sales revenue. The parties may attach a variety of conditions to an assignment, dealing with such matters as publication in other countries, translations, and reproduction in other forms.

Sometimes, an author may retain the copyright in a work but give the publisher a licence to print or reproduce and sell it, again normally in return for a royalty.

Licences may also be much more restricted: an author may grant a licence for the single performance of a play or musical work, on a specified date at a particular theatre, or for the reproduction of an extract from a work in some other work, for example, in an anthology of poetry, a collection of essays, or a set of teaching materials.

In some circumstances, a person wishing to perform or reproduce a copyrighted work may do so without obtaining the consent of the owner by paying a prescribed royalty. This may be done, for example, when the author has been dead for twenty-five years and copyright has reverted to the author's estate, or when the author cannot be traced.

A special arrangement is available for musical and musical-dramatic works. An author may assign the performing rights of the work to a *Performing Rights Society*; there are three such societies in Canada at present. In turn, the society grants licences for performance for a fee, pays part of the fee to the author and retains the remainder to cover the society's costs. A Copyright Board has authority to regulate the rates set by these collectives.

Registration

As we have seen, copyright comes into existence automatically on the creation of a work. Registration of copyright is not necessary, but the Act provides for registration[50] and it does confer certain advantages on the registered owner. In particular, the certificate of registration creates a presumption that copyright subsists in the work and that the person registered is the owner of the copyright. Still, the advantages to be gained from registration are relatively small and the practice is not widely used except by performing rights societies.

Infringement of Copyright

What Constitutes Infringement?

Copyright consists of a number of exclusive rights vested in the owner. An infringement occurs when another person, without the consent of the owner, does an act that only the owner has the right to do. Thus, the unauthorized public performance, publication, or reproduction of a copyrighted work constitutes an infringement, as does the translation of a work or its conversion into some other form, or recording, broadcasting, or exhibiting it in public. A person who purports to authorize some other person to do any of those acts, without the owner's consent, is also guilty of infringing copyright.

It is not necessary for the entire work to be copied to constitute an infringement of copyright; the unauthorized copying of a substantial part is sufficient. What amounts to a "substantial part" is a question of fact and of degree. A quotation of a few lines from a written work, especially if attributed to its author, does not constitute an infringement, but the quotation of several pages might. The offending copy need not be identical to the original work, and one cannot avoid liability simply by arranging the copied work in a different format or by making a few changes.

---

[50] *Ibid.*, s. 54.

ILLUSTRATION

A club compiled and published lists of information relating to forthcoming horse races — times of races, distances, the horses in each race, the jockeys and weights, and similar information. A publisher used these lists to compile a news sheet, though the information was arranged in a different sequence and set out differently. The news sheet infringed the club's copyright.[51]

A person may also infringe copyright by reproducing a work in an altogether different form. For example, making a three-dimensional object from a designer's drawings may infringe the copyright in those drawings.[52]

The person who actually makes the copy is not the only one who may be liable for infringement of copyright. A theatre owner who permits her theatre to be used by a group of actors or musicians for a performance that infringes the author's copyright is as guilty of infringement as are the performers. Also, a bookseller who imports and sells a "pirated" edition of a copyrighted book is as guilty as the illegal publisher. It is an infringement of copyright to authorize a person to do something that the owner of the copyright has the sole right to do. Thus a person who buys a book and lends it to a friend for the purpose of photocopying it infringes the copyright in the book as much as does the friend. However, to manufacture and sell tape recorders that have a facility for "dubbing" prerecorded tapes onto blank tapes has been held not to constitute authorizing an infringement.[53]

"Fair Dealing" and Other Permitted Uses

Certain acts that would otherwise amount to infringements of copyright are expressly permitted by the Copyright Act.[54] The most important exemption allows the fair use of copyright works for the purpose of private study, research, criticism, review, or newspaper summary. While the exemption does not allow the reproduction of the entire work, it is unclear to what extent, for example, a teacher may photocopy part of a book or article and distribute copies to her students. The Act permits the infrequent use of short passages from a work in a collection of material for school use. Other exemptions allow the public reading of reasonable extracts from works, newspaper reports of public political speeches, and the performance of musical works by church or educational bodies for religious, educational, or charitable purposes.

Remedies for Infringement

The usual civil remedies are available in cases of infringement of copyright:

    (a) *damages* for profit or income lost by the owner, or for conversion of the owner's property;[55]

---

51   See British Columbia Jockey Club v. Standen (1983), 146 D.L.R. (3d) 693.
52   Hanfstaengl v. H.R. Baines & Co., [1985] A.C. 20; Bayliner Marine Corp. v. Doral Boats Ltd. (1985), 5 C.P.R. (3d) 289.
53   CBS Songs Ltd. v. Amstrad Consumer Electronics, [1988] 2 All E.R. 484.
54   Copyright Act, R.S.C. 1985, c. C-45, ss. 27, 28.
55   Improper copies are deemed to be the property of the copyright owner. Punitive damages may be awarded in appropriate cases.

(b) *account* for profits made by the defendant as a result of the infringement (normally an alternative to damages);

(c) *injunction*, to restrain the defendant from further infringement and to require the delivering-up of any offending copy.

Of course, many infringements of copyright go unpunished. While it may be a breach of copyright to photocopy a book or article other than for purposes of study or research, or to videotape a television broadcast of a copyrighted work for later viewing,[56] it is most unlikely that the offences will be discovered or, if they are, that it will be worthwhile for the owner to sue the offender.

$\mathcal{P}$ATENTS

At common law, an inventor had no inherent right to the fruits of his or her creation and no law was broken by merely making use of another's invention. Thus, like copyright, but unlike trademarks, the law of patents is entirely based upon statute. However, a patent differs fundamentally from copyright: while copyright comes into existence *automatically* as a result of the act of creation, a patent exists only by virtue of being granted by the appropriate government body.

In England, the law of patents is usually traced back to the Statute of Monopolies[57] of 1623; it gave the sovereign the sole right to issue *letters patent* for the exclusive "working or making of any manner of new manufacture". Even today, the issue of patents in the United Kingdom remains a matter of royal prerogative. The law of patents evolved slowly in Britain, the first general statute being adopted only 1852; by that time a substantial body of patent law had already evolved in the United States, following the adoption of a federal patent law in 1790.

Patent legislation was introduced as early as 1824 and 1826, in Lower and Upper Canada respectively. The first federal Patent Act[58] was adopted in 1869, based largely upon the existing American legislation. This American influence prevailed until just a few years ago. The current Patent Act,[59] originally enacted in 1935, was substantially amended in 1987,[60] in part to bring Canada's law into conformity with international practice under the Patent Cooperation Treaty. The 1987 amendments changed a number of the specifically American features of our law. These amendments came into effect on October 1, 1989; patents granted or applied for prior to that date remain subject to the earlier law. Further substantial amendments, notably in respect of pharmaceutical products, were introduced in 1992.[61]

The concept of a patent is now almost universally recognized. Well over one hundred countries belong to the Paris Union and adhere to the International Convention for the

---

[56] Tom Hopkins Int'l. Inc. v. Wall Redekop Realty Ltd. (1984), 1 C.P.R. (3d) 348.

[57] 21 Jac. 1, c. 3. The Statute of Monopolies apparently never applied in Canada.

[58] S.C. 1869, c. 11.

[59] R.S.C. 1985, c. P-4. For a comprehensive study of the current law, see *Hughes and Woodley on Patents*, R.T. Hughes and J.H. Woodley, eds. Toronto: Butterworths, 1984. References to the Act, in this chapter, are to the provisions as amended, unless otherwise stated.

[60] R.S.C. 1985, c. 33 (3d. Supp.).

[61] S.C. 1993, c. 2.

Protection of Industrial Property, which dates back to 1883, and over forty nations have signed the Patent Cooperation Treaty of 1970. Canada belongs to both.[62]

The Nature of Patents

An inventor, or the legal representative of an inventor, may obtain a patent that gives the applicant exclusive property in the invention for a period of twenty years.[63] This property comprises the "exclusive right, privilege and liberty of making, constructing and using the invention and selling it to others to be used".[64]

In return for this right, the inventor must make the invention public, by filing an adequate description of the invention, so that others will be able to duplicate the invention freely when the statutory period of monopoly has expired.[65] Thus, an inventor has a choice: he can keep the invention entirely secret and continue to exploit it indefinitely, but run the risk that some other person will sooner or later stumble upon the same invention or will unravel the secret; or he can reveal it and enjoy exclusive rights for a limited period only. Given the speed at which technological advances are now being made, and the perhaps over-generous period of protection, applying for a patent would seem advisable for inventions that are likely to prove lucrative. However, obtaining a patent is a complex and fairly expensive business and if an invention is likely to have only a short productive life, secrecy may be the better option. The alternatives of registering the invention as an industrial design or relying upon copyright protection of the plans or specifications should also be considered. But it must be remembered that while copyright provides protection for a much longer period, the protection is more limited, since it extends only to the method of expressing and not to the idea itself.

Patentable Inventions

Only "inventions" qualify for patent protection. What qualities must they have? The Act defines an invention as "any new and useful art, process, machine, manufacture or composition of matter, or any new and useful improvement in any art, process, machine, manufacture or composition of matter".[66] Thus, three elements in the definition must be present for an invention to be patentable. It must be:

    (a) an art, process, machine, manufacture, or composition of matter or an improvement to such;
    (b) new; and
    (c) useful.

As well, inherent in the notion of an invention is the requirement that it is something that possesses the quality of ingenuity and is not simply an obvious step any person with ordinary skill in the field may have taken.

Art, Process, Machine, Manufacture, or Composition of Matter

For an invention to be patentable, it must fall within one of these categories. The word "art" refers to the manual or productive arts, as distinct from the fine arts. A "process"

---

[62] See Patent Cooperation Treaty, Can. T.S. 1990, No. 22, entered into force January 2, 1990.
[63] Patent Act, R.S.C. 1985, c. P-4, s. 27. Prior to October 1989 the relevant period was seventeen years.
[64] *Ibid.*, s. 42.
[65] Pioneer Hi-Bred Ltd. v. Commissioner of Patents (1989), 60 D.L.R. (4th) 223.
[66] *Ibid.*, s. 2.

means a method of manufacture or operation designed to produce a particular result, for example, a new process for the chemical cleaning of fabrics. "Machine" and "manufacture" are given their usual meanings, and a "composition of matter" refers to such things as chemical formulae that produce new compounds and substances.

A patent will not be issued solely for a scientific principle or abstract theorem, or for a mathematical formula.[67] For these purposes, a computer program is equated to a mathematical formula and is *not* by itself patentable,[68] though a patent may be granted for an invention that involves the use of a computer program as an essential part to achieve a particular result.

The Canadian treatment of inventions relating to food and drugs has recently undergone a number of important changes. Until the 1987 reforms, no patent might be issued for any "substance" intended for food or medicine, but the process for producing it could be patented. A patent may now be issued in respect of "substances" themselves, prepared or produced by microbiological processes and intended for food or medicine, as well as for the particular method by which the substance is prepared or produced.[69]

For pharmaceutical products protected by patent in other countries, a system of compulsory licensing existed that allowed Canadian firms to manufacture or import drugs upon payment of a low royalty to the patentee. This system led to the development of a thriving generic drug industry in Canada, to the economic benefit of the Canadian consumer but to the detriment of foreign pharmaceutical companies. It also arguably acted as a deterrent to research and development of pharmaceutical products within Canada. It became a controversial issue that featured prominently in the debates on the Free Trade Agreement between Canada and the United States and in the subsequent NAFTA negotiations; American pressure has in part been responsible for the changes that have been made in the law.

The 1987 provisions introduced a temporary system, under which the controversial compulsory licensing system was abandoned and replaced by a system under which the patentee of a newly developed drug was protected against importation into Canada for a period of ten years, and against manufacture in Canada for seven years. In an attempt to guard against unreasonable increases in drug prices resulting from the abolition of compulsory licenses, a Patented Medicine Prices Review Board was established with the power to roll back excessive drug prices. The 1992 amendments go further, treating all medicines the same regardless of their place of manufacture and extending full twenty-year protection to pharmaceutical patents. Compulsory licensing is permitted only in restrictive circumstances, but the powers of the Review Board have been strengthened in an effort to prevent excessive price increases.[70]

Novelty

An essential element of an invention is that it be "new". A patent will not be granted for a machine or process that is already known or in use, even if it has not been patented by some other person.

Until 1989, Canada was one of the few countries — along with the United States — to apply a "first-to-invent" system; that is to say, if two or more persons applied for a patent

---

67 Patent Act, R.S.C. 1985, c. P-4, s. 27(3).

68 Schlumberger Canada Ltd. v. Commissioner of Patents, [1982] 1 F.C. 845.

69 Patent Act, R.S.C. 1985, c. P-4, s. 39(1).

70 For a review of these developments see Horton, "Pharmaceuticals, Patents and Bill C-91", (1993) 10 *Canadian Intellectual Property Rev.* 145.

for the same invention, only the first inventor was considered the true inventor and entitled to the patent. The new law adopts the more common "first-to-file" system; in cases of
conflicting applications, the application with the earlier filing date prevails.

An invention for which a patent is claimed must be one that has not been disclosed to
the public anywhere in the world before the filing date. There is an exception to this rule
when the inventor himself makes the disclosure, but even then he must file the application within one year of making the disclosure.[71]

Utility

For an invention to qualify as "useful" it must possess industrial value, for example, by
making a process easier, cheaper, or faster. Also implied is that it be usable; that is to say,
it should be reproducible and operable, so that a skilled worker, by following the specifications published in the patent, should be able to reproduce the invention and obtain the
desired result.

Ingenuity

An invention requires an element of ingenuity; as we have noted, it must be more than
an obvious step. As has been said:

> The question to be answered is whether at the date of invention… an unimaginative skilled
> technician, in light of his general knowledge and the literature and information on the sub-
> ject available to him on that date, would have been led directly and without difficulty to the
> invention.[72]

In reaching such a conclusion, the patent office or court must be careful not to be
influenced by hindsight: great inventions often seem deceptively simple and obvious in
retrospect.

Obtaining a Patent

Only the inventor, or the legal representatives of the inventor, may apply for the grant of a
patent.[73] "Legal representatives" include not only heirs and executors, but also persons
claiming through the inventor. If an inventor has assigned the rights to an invention to
another person or to a corporation, the assignee may apply. An employer usually owns
inventions made by its employees, and thus is entitled to apply for a patent.

Applications for patents are made to the Commissioner of Patents and are processed by
the Patent Office, located in Hull, Québec. Individual inventors may pursue their own
applications, but any other applicants must use the services of a registered *patent agent*. In
practice, making an application is a highly complex and specialized matter and is almost
invariably handled by a patent agent. The agent first makes a search of the register of
patents, and frequently also a search at the U.S. Patent Office, to ensure that no patent has
already been granted in respect of the invention. The next major task is to draft the application, in a form prescribed by the Patent Rules. The most important part of the application
has two elements: (a) the *specification*, providing a full description of the invention, its use,

---

[71] *Ibid.*, s. 27.
[72] Beecham Canada Ltd. v. Proctor & Gamble Co. (1982), 61 C.P.R. (2d) 1, at 27, per Urie, J.A.
[73] Patent Act, R.S.C. 1985, c. P-4, ss. 2, 27.

operation, or manufacture; and (b) the *claim*, setting out the features claimed to be new and in respect of which the applicant claims an exclusive right. Particular care must be taken to ensure that the claim is sufficiently broad to obtain the maximum benefit from the invention. At the same time it must not be excessively wide, so as to include matters that are obvious or already known, and thus render the claim invalid.

When an application has been filed, a further application may be made, within seven years, for the claim to be examined.[74] The Patent Office then appoints an Examiner to consider the application. The Examiner makes searches of patents, and frequently of technical publications, to ensure that the claimed invention is indeed novel and otherwise complies with the requirements of the Patent Act. The Examiner scrutinizes the specification and claim to ensure that complete disclosure has been made and that the invention is described in a way that would enable other persons to utilize it once the period of protection has elapsed. During this stage the applicant may make amendments to the application in order to satisfy objections raised by the Examiner. When the process is complete, the Examiner determines whether or not a patent shall be granted. An appeal from a rejection of the application goes to the Patent Appeal Board and then to the courts.

When the application is successful, the Patent Office issues a "Notice of Allowance", and on payment of a fee (which is additional to the application fee) it issues the patent. Since 1989, the Act requires that a further yearly fee be paid in order to maintain the patent. The fees, however, are relatively modest: for an applicant that qualifies as a "small entity"[75] the total fees to obtain a patent and to maintain it for the full twenty-year period could be less than $2500. The cost of protection for a five-year period could be as little as $500. However, the services of a skilled patent agent will cost considerably more than the fees paid to the Patent Office.

Enforcement and Protection of Patent Rights

As we have seen, patent rights may now be preserved for a period of 20 years, so long as the yearly maintenance fee is paid. A patent confers on its owner the exclusive right of constructing and using the invention and selling it to others to be used. An owner may assign patent rights to others, or grant a licence for their limited or exclusive use. An assignment must be in writing and registered with the Patent Office, as must a grant of an exclusive licence.[76]

Any unauthorized act that interferes with the full enjoyment of the exclusive rights conferred by the patent is an infringement. The usual remedies of damages, injunction, and accounting for profit are available to the patentee and to anyone (for example, an assignee or licensee) claiming under him. An action to protect or enforce a patent right may be brought in the Federal Court or in the appropriate provincial court.

The granting of a patent is a serious matter, since giving an exclusive right to use and exploit an invention, for a period of up to twenty years, in effect creates a monopoly. The result is to confer a considerable advantage over business competitors and sometimes, if the patentee chooses not to exploit the invention, to deprive the public of the use of the

---

[74]   *Ibid.*, s. 35.
[75]   A "small entity" means an individual inventor, or a business concern whose gross annual revenue does not exceed $2 million and which meets a number of other conditions: Patent Rules, C.R.C. 1978, c. 1250, as amended. The fees payable by other applicants are twice as high.
[76]   *Ibid.*, s. 50(2). The grant of a limited licence need not be registered.

invention. There are many stories — most of them probably fabrications — of large corporations buying up inventions (such as everlasting light bulbs) that threaten their business in order to suppress the invention.

Patent legislation attempts to protect the public in three major ways. First, it seeks to ensure that only genuine inventions qualify for the grant of a patent and it disallows claims that are too broad in scope. One of the most important functions of the patent examiner is to enforce these policies. In addition, third parties, such as business competitors or rival researchers, may challenge the validity of a patent by bringing an *action for impeachment* in the Federal Court. The Attorney General of Canada may also bring such an action. For patent applications filed after October 1, 1989, an alternative form of challenge is available: any person may apply to the Commissioner of Patents for re-examination of any claim of a patent. Upon receiving such a request, the Commissioner establishes a Re-examination Board to examine the request.

Another form of protection allows the Attorney General, or any interested person, to apply to the Commissioner of Patents when it is alleged that patent rights are being abused. An abuse occurs, for example:

— if the patent is capable of being worked in Canada but is not being worked on a reasonable scale;

— if its working in Canada is being hindered by the patentee importing articles from abroad;

— if demand for the patented article in Canada is not being met to a reasonable extent;

— if the patentee is hindering the creation of new industries or damaging the public interest by refusing to grant licences; or

— if any trade, industry or person engaged therein is unfairly prejudiced.[77]

The aim of patent law is not only to encourage new inventions by protecting them, but also to encourage the working of those inventions in Canada without undue delay. Thus, a patentee cannot simply hold a patent for the purpose of blocking trade; if it does not exploit the invention itself in a reasonable manner, it must sell it or grant a licence on reasonable terms. Where there is abuse, some other person who wishes to make use of the invention may apply for the grant of a *compulsory licence*, which may be ordered on terms that allow the applicant to work the patent while giving the patentee a fair return. Normally this arrangement involves the payment of a stipulated rate of royalty on products manufactured under the licence. In the case of foods and medicines, a special system of compulsory licensing has been established so that a licence may be granted even in cases where there has been no abuse of the patent.

The Competition Act provides a further form of protection of the public interest. It prohibits the exploitation of a patent in such a way as to unduly restrain trade or prevent or lessen competition, and authorizes the Federal Court to grant appropriate relief.[78]

---

[77] *Ibid.*, s. 65.
[78] R.S.C. 1985, c. C-34, as revised by S.C. 1986, c. 26.

*I*NDUSTRIAL DESIGNS

Industrial designs comprise a fourth type of intellectual property, registrable under the Industrial Design Act.[79] Originally enacted in 1868, the Act has been amended on a number of occasions. Despite the amendments, the Act remains a somewhat archaic and rather unsatisfactory piece of legislation.

The Industrial Design Act permits the proprietor of an industrial design to register it and obtain exclusive rights to its use in Canada for a term of five years, with the possibility of renewing the registration for one further term of five years. At common law there is no property in an industrial design, except insofar as it may qualify for protection as a trademark. Protection is consequently dependant upon registration. A proprietor may apply to register a design with the Commissioner of Patents, in Hull. Application must be made within one year of the first publication of the design.[80] "Publication" in this sense means making the design available to the public, for example, by selling an article to which the design has been applied. The only person entitled to apply for registration is the "proprietor", who is usually the designer, but if a client or customer commissioned and paid for the design, that person is considered to be the proprietor. If the design was produced by an employee in the normal course of employment, the employer will normally be the proprietor.

Until the Act was amended in 1988, it contained no definition of an industrial design. The Act now states that "industrial design" means:

> features of shape, configuration, pattern or ornament and any combination of those features that, in a finished article, appeal to and are judged solely by the eye.[81]

Features that are solely utilitarian or functional are not protected, nor is any method or principle of manufacture or construction protected. For many years it was thought that the Act referred only to designs placed on an article, such as a decorative design on a dinner service, a crest or emblem on a sports shirt, or a design on a roll of wallpaper. More recently, however, it has been held to apply also to the design of the shape of the article *itself*, insofar as the design is ornamental and not dictated by the function of the article. Thus, the shape of a stacking chair, or of a knife handle, may be registered. In order to secure registration some degree of originality is also required.

Registration gives the proprietor the exclusive right to apply the design to any article for the purpose of sale. However, in order to protect the design each article to which the design is applied must be marked with the name of the proprietor, the word "Registered" or its abbreviation, "Rd", and the year of registration. A proprietor may assign or grant a licence for the use of a registered design, but the assignment or licence must be recorded on the register in order to preserve the exclusive right.

During the existence of the exclusive right, no other person may apply the design, or any imitation of it, to any article for the purpose of sale without the written consent of

---

[79] R.S.C. 1985, c. I-9, as amended by S.C. 1988, c. 15.
[80] S.C. 1992, c. 1, ss. 47-52. Previously actual registration had to occur within one year of first publication in Canada. The NAFTA Implementation Act, s. 162, introduces the concept of "worldwide novelty".
[81] R.S.C. 1985, C. I-9, S. 2 (as amended).

the proprietor.[82] The usual remedies of damages, injunction, and account for profits are available to the proprietor and, in addition, the Act prescribes a number of summary offences, punishable by fine, for infringement of industrial design rights.

As we have seen, both industrial designs and patents may be protected only by prompt registration. Normally, it will not be difficult to decide whether a design qualifies for patent protection or should be registered as an industrial design. Industrial designs are essentially ornamental, whereas a patentable invention must be useful. In cases of doubt, the advice of a qualified patent agent should be sought.

The same design or logo that may be applied to an article as an industrial design may also be considered a trademark. Similarly, the ornamental shape of a container or wrapper may be registered as an industrial design as well as be protected under trademark law as a "distinguishing guise". Protection as a trademark is clearly superior, since property rights in a trademark are not dependent upon registration and are not limited to a maximum period of ten years. However, the two forms of protection do not conflict: a proprietor may register an industrial design and still claim protection for the design as a trademark.

The situation with respect to copyright is more complex. The Copyright Act originally refused copyright protection for designs capable of being registered under the Industrial Design Act. An exception was made for designs that were not used or intended to be used as models or patterns to be multiplied by any industrial process. This provision was revised in 1988,[83] though the intention of the new provision remains essentially similar. Now, if the design is applied to a useful article and the article is reproduced in a quantity of more that fifty, some other person does not infringe copyright in the design simply by reproducing the article. Thus, protection for the design can only be secured by registering it under the Industrial Design Act.[84]

CONFIDENTIAL INFORMATION, TRADE SECRETS, AND KNOW-HOW

The description "intellectual property" should properly be restricted to the four forms — trademarks, copyright, patents, and industrial designs — that we have discussed in this chapter. Mere ideas or knowledge, however valuable, are not regarded as "property" in the strict sense of the word. Thus, the Supreme Court of Canada has ruled that confidential information is not property that can be the subject of theft under the Criminal Code.[85] Such information may nevertheless have commercial value: a secret manufacturing process — if it *can* be kept secret — may be more valuable not patented than patented; and a uniquely efficient way of operating a business, though not capable of being patented at all, may be worth millions in extra profits to its owner. Similarly, a list of customers or clients may constitute an important part of the goodwill of a business. And information can be valuable to people other than its owner; although not property in the strict sense, information can still be sold to others as, for example, where data is made available to subscribers to a computerized data-retrieval service.

---

[82] *Ibid.*, s. 11.
[83] *Ibid.*, ss. 64, 64.1, as amended by S.C 1988, c. 15, s. 11.
[84] See Bayliner Marine Corp. v. Doral Boats Ltd. (1986), 10 C.P.R. (3d) 289.
[85] R. v. Stewart [1988] 1 S.C.R. 963.

The possessor of confidential information, trade secrets, or know-how is not entirely without legal protection, though such protection normally arises out of a contractual or fiduciary relationship rather than from any proprietary interest. Thus, a seller may supply machinery or equipment to a buyer and at the same time license the buyer to use the seller's know-how, or some secret process; it is usual to stipulate in the contract that the buyer will not divulge the secret to anyone else. Similarly, some types of contracts of employment include a restrictive covenant restraining the employee, if she leaves the employment, from making use of the employer's confidential information or divulging it to someone else. In addition, employees, company directors, partners, and parties to a joint venture stand in a *fiduciary relationship* to their employers, corporations, or co-partners. To misuse or divulge confidential information acquired in the course of such a relationship constitutes a breach of trust, which might be restrained by injunction or punished by an award of damages or an accounting for profits made as a result of the breach.[86]

TECHNOLOGICAL CHANGE AND INTELLECTUAL PROPERTY LAW

Although a number of important statutory changes have been made recently, the basic principles of the statutes governing Canadian intellectual property law are generally well over a century old. Yet few aspects of society have changed so much as those that are affected by intellectual property law. Firms and nations now spend vast amounts on research and development, aware that inventiveness is the key to competitiveness in the international economy. Entertainment, of which copyright is the raw material, is a multi-billion-dollar industry. In corporate mergers and takeovers, trademarks and brand names are frequently valued in millions. Information, it seems, knows no frontiers: of the total number of patents now registered each year in the United States, approximately one half are registered by foreign inventors. Intellectual property has become internationalized.

New technologies have created new problems, not all of which are easily solved by analogy to old situations. That this is so is illustrated by two recent statutes, enacted to protect the rights of plant breeders and the designers of integrated circuits, respectively. The Plant Breeders' Rights Act[87] provides exclusive rights, similar to patent rights, in respect of new varieties of plants. To qualify, a plant variety must be clearly distinguishable from all other commonly known varieties of the species, be both stable and homogeneous, and be of a variety not yet sold in Canada. Application is made to a Commissioner of Plant Breeders' Rights, who may require or conduct such tests as are necessary to establish the novelty of the variety. A grant is for a term of eighteen years, subject to a payment of an annual fee, and confers the exclusive right to sell, produce and use the variety. The Integrated Circuit Topography Act[88] also provides exclusive rights similar to patent rights in the "topography" or design of integrated circuits (semiconductor chips) and in the circuits that incorporate such designs themselves. Registration is required, and protection is for a period of ten years.

---

[86] See Lac Minerals Ltd. v. International Corona Resources Ltd. (1989), 61 D.L.R. (4th) 14. Misuse of confidential information by corporate directors or officers is discussed further in Chapter 31.
[87] S.C. 1990, c. 20.
[88] S.C. 1990, c. 37.

New technologies have not only given rise to the creation of new types of intellectual property and new rights; the ways in which existing rights may be exercised, and infringed, is also changing. The advent of sound recording and television, not to mention direct broadcasting by satellite, cable transmission, and computer data-banks, have greatly widened the concept of "publication". At the same time, tape and video recorders and photocopiers have made it very easy to infringe intellectual property rights. New questions are constantly being raised, to which simple answers cannot be given; for example, to what extent does copyright law apply to material accessible through e-mail? As was observed at the beginning of this chapter, intellectual property law raises important issues of public policy. We conclude by quoting the Economic Council of Canada:

> ...new technology and the movement towards an increasingly knowledge-based economy and society are throwing up issues of such scale and significance that no part of the existing policy structure can remain unaffected.[89]

Questions For Review

1. Should ideas be protected as a form of property?
2. What are the essential elements in the tort of passing-off?
3. Define "goodwill".
4. What precautions should the incorporators of a new corporation take to ensure that the name chosen for their corporation is not likely to be confused with a trademark or name of some other existing corporation or business?
5. What are the advantages of registering a trademark?
6. What is a certification mark and how does it differ from a normal trademark?
7. On what grounds may the proposed registration of a trademark be opposed?
8. What terms and conditions are normally included in a franchise agreement?
9. What rights does an owner of copyright possess?
10. In relation to copyright, what are "moral rights"?
11. In what ways can a person become the owner of copyright?
12. What function is performed by a Performing Rights Society?
13. What is an industrial design and in what ways does it differ from (a) a trademark, (b) a work protected by copyright, and (c) a patented invention?
14. By what means may the creator of a new computer program protect his or her innovation?
15. What are the principal advantages and disadvantages of obtaining a patent for an invention?
16. What special considerations apply to the granting of patents for new medicines and medical treatments?
17. What constitutes an abuse of patent rights, and what is its effect?
18. By what means may confidential information be protected?

---

[89] *Report on Intellectual and Industrial Property.* Ottawa: Economic Council of Canada, 1971.

Problems

Problem 1

A small brewery in Queensville, Ontario, has developed a new brand of beer with a flavour that is similar to German lager beer. A competition is held among the employees of the brewery to find a suitable name for the new brew and the winning name is "Loewenberg". The company applies to register the name "Loewenberg" as a registered trademark.

The application is opposed by a rival brewing company, which contends that the name is not registrable because:

(a) "Loewenberg" is the name of a place; in fact there are three villages by that name, two in Germany and one in Austria;
(b) "Loewenberg" is also the name of a person, there being eleven persons of that name in the Toronto phone directory alone;
(c) "Loewenberg" is the name of a small chain of footwear stores in British Columbia; and
(d) there is a well known brand of beer in Germany, by the name of "Loewenbrau", and the two names are confusingly similar.

Discuss whether any of these grounds of opposition should prevent registration.

Problem 2

Shamrock Homes Inc. is a major construction company that specializes in the construction of large residential developments. Brendan, their chief engineer, has worked out an entirely new method of planning a development, requiring the construction of a factory in which prefabricated components for houses are manufactured and assembled to speed up the construction of houses. The factory is specially designed to be converted into a shopping mall when all the houses are completed. Shamrock estimates that the new method reduces construction costs by as much as 15%.

The company wishes to patent this new method, fearing that competitors will easily be able to copy it otherwise. Give your opinion as to whether the method is patentable. (See *Re Application for Patent of North Oakland Development Co.* (1982), 82 C.P.R. (2d) 282.)

Problem 3

Dolphin Marine Ltd. is a well established firm with an excellent reputation for building racing boats. It has recently produced a new 12-metre model, the DM35X, with a fibreglass hull of novel design, which has been highly successful in a number of important races.

Kopikat Inc. is a small firm that has been building catamarans for a number of years with little success, either sporting or financial. Kenny, the controlling shareholder and president of Kopikat, buys one of the new Dolphin models, constructs a mould of the hull, and commences to produce a racer with a hull identical to the DM35X and with other features that are very similar. Kopikat is planning to market it at a price $8000 lower than the DM35X.

Has Kopikat infringed any right of Dolphin?

Cases

Case 1

Susan, an accountant, purchased a new computer program from Verbasure Inc. for $280. The program is contained on one 5-1/4 inch diskette, and is accompanied by a twenty-page instruction manual.

Susan copied the diskette onto the hard disc in her office computer. She also made another copy on a 3-1/2 inch diskette for use on her lap-top model.

While she was using the program at home one weekend her son, Timothy, a high school student, asked if he could try the program out on his own computer. He said it was similar to a program that the school was proposing to use in one of the computer science courses, but possessed some more advanced features.

Susan knew that Timothy often copied her programs, and had warned him on a number of occasions that if he did so, he must not take the copy out of the house.

A few weeks later, Susan received a phone call from the principal of Timothy's school. The school had negotiated a special arrangement with Verbasure, which had agreed to supply a number of copies of the program at a special rate for use in the computer science course. However, they had discovered that Timothy was selling diskettes containing the program, together with photocopies of the instruction manual, to fellow students for $25 each.

Discuss the potential liability of Susan (a) for making extra copies for herself, and (b) for the copies made by Timothy.

Case 2

McCoy's Restaurants Ltd. is a large firm incorporated under the Canada Business Corporations Act. It operates a chain of some sixty restaurants across Canada under the name of "McCoy's", and is very well known nationally due to its extensive advertising campaigns.

Angus McCoy recently bought a restaurant, previously known as "Sam's Diner", situated at a busy truck stop near Brandon, Manitoba. He formed a company under the name of Angus McCoy (Brandon) Ltd., incorporated under the Manitoba Business Corporations Act, and renamed the restaurant "The Real McCOY's". The decor and furnishings of Angus's restaurant are not at all like those of the McCoy chain, but the external appearance bears some similarity.

The president of McCoy's Restaurant Ltd. is angry because she has been planning to open a branch in that particular location. She alleges that Angus is attempting to deceive the public, is trading on her company's reputation, and is benefitting from its advertising. She has written to Angus, insisting that he change the name of his company and of his restaurant, otherwise McCoy's Restaurants will commence legal proceedings.

Angus maintains that no one is confused, that he chose the name "The Real McCOY's" deliberately to distinguish his restaurant from those of the chain, and that, since the principal owners of McCoy's Restaurants Ltd. are called Angelotti and Zbigniewsky, respectively, they are the ones who are trading under false colours.

Advise Angus what legal actions might be taken against him and whether or not they might succeed.

CHAPTER 26

INTERESTS IN LAND AND THEIR TRANSFER

THE NATURE OF INTERESTS IN LAND

The Meaning of Real Property

We usually refer to land as *real property*, an important term that needs some explanation. The word *property* itself has two closely related meanings. The more common one defines property as "everything which is the subject of ownership...everything that has exchangeable value or which goes to make up wealth..."[1] By this definition, property means *the thing itself*, whether it be a piece of land, a piece of cheese, or a bill of lading, a share certificate, or the tangible things these documents represent. The lesser-known meaning of property is not the thing itself but *the legal interest* in the thing — the right or rights that the law will recognize and protect. Property in this sense has been called "ownership, the unrestricted and exclusive right to a thing; the right to dispose of a thing in every legal way, to possess it, to use it, and to exclude everyone else from interfering with it".[2] A common synonym for the term "property" in the sense of ownership is the word *title*: the expressions "ownership *of* a thing", "title *to* a thing", and "property *in* a thing" are used interchangeably. Although the first meaning of property — the thing itself — is of general importance in law, it is in the second sense that we use the word in the present chapter.

Historically, the word "real" referred to the kind of remedy a party could get in court when property rights had been interfered with. Certain types of interests in land gave the owner a remedy by way of *real action* — a right to repossess the interest interfered with — rather than a remedy by way of *personal action*, a right to money damages but not a right to have the interest back again. Real actions were available only when one of a carefully defined class of interests was interfered with; but in time the term "real property" came to refer to interests in land generally, whether or not a real action would lie for the recovery of the interest, and we shall so use the term.

The law of real property has special concepts and terms of its own, and we must take great care to use the terms accurately. The reasons for this special terminology are partly historical and partly attributable to the peculiar qualities of land. Land is permanent, except on the rare occasions when a piece of it slides into the sea and is lost, or is permanently flooded by a large hydro development, as occurred along the St. Lawrence Seaway. Otherwise a given piece of land exists perpetually: it remains long after its temporary owners are gone, and it has a fixed location. An interest in land recognized by law may affect that land and the people concerned with it long after the temporary owner who created the interest has died. Thus, if the owner of land grants to a city the right to lay water-mains across the land and maintain and repair them, the right could affect a subsequent owner who would like to tear up the pipes and erect a building. If over many years successive owners of the land were to grant away more of their rights, eventually there would be a complex bundle of rights held by various persons. Each subsequent owner would own the land minus the rights granted away. In this manner, land may easily be the subject of many complicated interests.

---

[1] Black, *Law Dictionary* (6th ed.), p. 1216, St. Paul: West Publishing Co., 1990.
[2] *Ibid.*

The Definition of Land

The word *land* has a special meaning in the law of real property. Ordinarily, when we think of land, we think of the surface and its contours. For everyday usage this concept is sufficient, but a purchaser who buys land must know more accurately what the term includes. In law, land includes not only the surface but all that is under the surface, including the minerals, oil, or whatever else is present within the boundaries of the lot, and everything above the surface including the buildings on the land and the column of air as well. It used to be said that land included all the earth to the centre of the globe and all the air up to the heavens. For all practical purposes, the owner of land today does have ownership extending below the surface as far as people can penetrate with mine shafts and oil wells. But it is a different matter with the column of air above the land: various statutes, international treaties concerning air travel, and municipal by-laws limiting the use of land have cut down ownership of the column of air considerably. Aircraft may pass freely over the land at a safe height, and the owner is often restricted in the height of buildings that may be erected.

Perhaps most important to remember is that land includes all things permanently affixed to it — trees, buildings, fences. Thus, when *A* transfers his house and lot to *B*, the document describes the land only, according to its location and dimensions, but it is nevertheless presumed that everything affixed to the land goes with it. Lawyers do not draw a distinction between land and buildings as do businesses and accounts. Although for business purposes we report the depreciation of buildings but not of land, the two are lumped together in law when ascertaining ownership or transferring the title to land.

The Use of Land

Land, as we have noted, has special qualities distinguishing it from goods and chattels: it is virtually indestructible and has a fixed location. The owner of a chattel may do as he pleases with it — he may even destroy it, and no one has the legal right to interfere. Land has never been regarded in this manner when it is situated in a community where people live quite close to one another. From very early times, communal governments have assumed the power to regulate and prohibit dangerous activities in populous areas. If a landowner sets off explosives or lights fires that spread sparks onto a neighbour's lands, the danger is obvious. Accordingly, community regulations limit a landowner's right to use his land for dangerous activities.

There are further restrictions on the use of land that seriously affect an owner's freedom of activity. The courts have long recognized that a user of land may be restrained from committing the tort of *nuisance*. A nuisance is an activity that interferes with the ordinary comfort and enjoyment of land of other persons in the vicinity. The interference may take the form of smoke, noxious vapours, noise, polluted water, or other harmful liquids flowing in streams or percolating through the earth — things that escape from the land of the user and affect other persons' lands. A person who has sustained injury from a nuisance may obtain money damages for the loss and also obtain an injunction from the court restraining the offender from continuing the conduct responsible for the nuisance.

Community regulation has grown rapidly in recent years. Early regulations covered only such nuisances as fire and health hazards, but the increased density and size of urban centres and the growing complexities of city life have forced municipal governments into large-scale regulation of the use of land. Zoning by-laws prescribe the use and type of buildings that may be erected in various districts of a municipality; building regulations prescribe minimum standards of quality for materials and the size of all parts of structures erected within an area; planning by-laws set out requirements for roadways and for water and sewage services, and often prescribe the amounts of land a land developer must give to the municipality for use as school and park areas. Growing public awareness and concern about long-term environmental hazards, such as those created by chemicals formerly considered safe, has led to the passage in all jurisdictions of environmental assessment and protection legislation. Another area of concern has been the protection of historical, architectural, and archeological buildings and sites, a concern reflected in "heritage" statutes. Consequently, we are witnessing the growth of a large body of public law, imposing various limits on the use owners may make of their land. These restrictions are especially important for industrial enterprises and redevelopment projects in urban centres.

The Development of Strict Rules in Land Law

In feudal times land was the most valuable asset because it contained the principal sources of wealth — crops, animals, timber, and serfs. Before industry or merchant trade, land represented the wealth of the country. In England, the king learned early to utilize a system of landholding to consolidate his strength. In feudal England no one *owned* land except the Crown. A lord *held* land from the Crown, subject to certain rights and duties. So long as the lord performed his duties, he and his heirs continued to hold the land. In turn, each lord granted portions of his estate to vassals, who held the land from the lord subject to various rights and duties. The vassals often granted their land to sub-vassals subject to further rights and duties. In later feudal times these relationships became extremely intricate and technical. The king objected to the complexities because they made it difficult for him to enforce his own feudal rights and collect taxes. Parliament passed statutes and the courts handed down decisions to cut down the number of interests in land. Gradually, a strict set of legal rules grew up for recognizing a limited number of interests in land. If a holder of land tried to create a type of interest not already recognized by the courts, the interest would be void. In contrast with the law of contract where rules generally grew to meet business convenience and fairness, rules for the recognition of classes of interests in land often had no relation to convenience or fairness; rather they were rules, arbitrarily made, for the purpose of limiting the number of interests in land and keeping them within manageable proportions. Even so, the variety of interests that can arise in relation to just one piece of land is great. Many if not most of the old rules have been repealed or modernized by various statutes, but comparatively speaking, the old concepts have been very slow to die in this field of the law.

The strictness of the courts is understandable when we consider how imaginative and resourceful were the medieval landowners and their lawyers in developing concepts of land ownership. They carved up ownership in two main ways: (a) according to the time during which the holder of the interest would have the right to exclusive possession of the land — interests called *estates in time*, and (b) according to the kind of use permitted or restricted upon the land — called *interests less than estates*. We shall discuss these interests in the following two sections.

$\mathcal{E}$STATES IN TIME

Freehold Estates

Fee Simple Estate

This estate, usually referred to as the fee simple, is the greatest interest a person can own in land and is as close to the idea of complete ownership as English law comes. Thus, when we speak of a person owning land, we mean that he holds the fee simple in it. The holder of the fee simple holds it for all time present and future, subject only to its return to the government in the event of his dying without having relatives to inherit it and without having made a will giving it to some person. He may grant the whole of the fee simple away; he may grant away a lesser interest keeping the rest for himself; or he may grant the whole of it in various portions to different persons.

ILLUSTRATIONS

(a) *A*, the holder of the fee simple in Black-acre, may grant it to an older brother *B* for the rest of *B*'s life. At *B*'s death it returns to *A*, or to *A*'s heirs if *A* dies before *B*.

(b) *A* may grant Blackacre to a brother for life, with the rest of the fee simple going to a niece, *C*, at the brother's death.

The holder of a fee simple may carve up the estate in other ways and grant the portions to other persons; the above illustrations serve merely as examples.

Life Estate

A life estate is an estate in land for the life of one person — usually for the life of the person who holds the estate, but not necessarily: a person may hold an estate, measured by the life of *another* person. Thus *A* may grant Blackacre to *B* for the rest of *A*'s own life; if *A* dies within a few months, the life estate ends and *B* retains no interest in Blackacre. This type of life estate, however, is quite rare. The more usual life estate, for the life of the person to whom the interest is given, often arises under the terms of a will. Thus, for example, the owner of a fee simple may by the terms of her will give a life estate in the family home to her husband; or a widow may give a life estate to her eldest child. In either of these situations she may also direct that the rest of the fee simple pass, let us say, to the grandchildren.

The balance of the fee simple, after a life estate has been carved out, is called either a *reversion* or a *remainder*. It is called a reversion when the grantor of the life estate reserves the balance of the fee simple for herself and her heirs (that is, it *reverts* to the grantor or her heirs after the life estate ends). It is called a remainder when it goes to some third person. The balance of the estate in Illustration (a) above is a reversion and in Illustration (b) a remainder.

Unfortunately, life estates create many problems. First, it is very difficult to sell land subject to a life estate: very few people will buy only the remaining years of a life tenant's interest, an uncertain period of time; similarly, they will rarely buy a reversion or remainder, because it is impossible to tell how long the life tenant will live, thus delaying a purchaser's right to make use of the land. Only if both the *life tenant* and the *remainderman* join in the sale and together grant the whole of the fee simple will it be relatively easy to sell the land. Second, a life tenant is limited in the changes he can make on the land without the consent of the remainderman: he cannot tear down buildings or cut down trees without the permission of the remainderman even if he wishes to replace them with something more valuable; he must leave the land to the remainderman substantially as he received it. On the other hand, he is under no duty to make repairs, and may let buildings decay. Third, he cannot compel the remainderman to contribute anything to the cost of substantial repairs and maintenance needed on the land though they will ultimately be of great benefit to the remainderman in preserving its value.

Life estates were much more common until the end of the 19th century when land was still perhaps the most important measure of the wealth of individuals. In our society today, land is no longer so major a portion of a person's wealth. Assets in the form of shares and bonds, bank accounts, life insurance, jewellery, and automobiles may add up to a larger portion. This change in the form of wealth has led to a different method of providing a life income for a surviving dependant. Instead of creating a *life estate in land,* a person may give a *life interest* in a sum of money. She directs in her will that a portion of her assets be liquidated into a fund of money and invested, and the income to be paid to the dependant for life. On the dependant's death, the principal sum is paid to those who would formerly have been remaindermen of real property.

Rights in the Matrimonial Home

For many centuries a widow's principal security on the death of her husband was a right to *dower*, that is, a right to a life interest in one-third of the real property held by her husband in fee simple during their married life. As we have just noted, that form of financial security no longer makes practical sense. Legislation has reformed and expanded property rights of spouses to include assets nominally held in the name of the other spouse, both during their joint lives and after death of one of them.

Dower has now been abolished in all provinces, but the new legislation still recognizes the special interest that a spouse has in the family home. Statutory rights go much farther than the ancient right to dower, and include the right to refuse consent to change of the family home or to its sale (a sale without consent is void), as well as a life estate in the *whole* of the family home to the surviving spouse.

The legislation varies greatly from province to province and has been changing so frequently in recent years that it would not be useful to attempt a summary. However, some of the main features are as follows: in some provinces, the claim to a matrimonial home must be registered in the land registry office; in others it arises as soon as husband and wife establish a home within the meaning of the statute; in some provinces with older legislation, the right accrues only to the wife and not to either spouse; some legislation protects only one matrimonial home while others make it a question of fact whether a couple also has a second family home such as a cottage.

Claims to the matrimonial home are so important that no transaction involving residential property should be entered into without taking into account the relevant matrimonial property legislation.

Leasehold Estates

A leasehold estate is an interest in land for a definite period of time — a week, a month, a year, a hundred years, or any other specific period. Here we find the great distinction between a freehold and a leasehold estate: a freehold estate is either for an *infinite* time (the fee simple) or an *indefinite* time (the life estate), whereas the leasehold is for a definite time. In a leasehold estate, the person to whom the interest is granted is called the *lessee* or *tenant* and the grantor of the interest is called the *lessor* or *landlord*.

Historically, leaseholds have always been considered lesser estates than freeholds. This was so even though it was obvious that leases for one hundred years would almost invariably last longer than a life tenancy, a freehold estate. A leasehold interest must be derived from a freehold interest and cannot last longer than the freehold from which it is derived.

ILLUSTRATION

By will *T* gives *A* a life estate in Blackacre with the remainder after *A*'s death to *X* in fee simple. *A* leases Blackacre to *B* Co. Ltd. for one hundred years. Several months later *A* dies. *X*, the remainderman, can take pos-session of Blackacre and put *B* Co. Ltd. out. *X* is not bound by the lease because *A* could not create a leasehold interest in Blackacre to last longer than *A*'s own life estate.

The above result is an application of the rule that a person cannot grant to another a greater interest than he himself holds.[3]

Leasehold interests share an important characteristic with freehold interests: a lease gives a lessee the right to exclusive possession of the land described in the lease. Thus a lessee has the right to keep all persons off the leased land including the lessor himself, unless the lessor has reserved the right to enter the property for inspection and repairs. The law concerning leasehold interests is the meeting-place of the strict concepts of real property and the flexible concepts of contract. Leases play an important role in commerce and industry, and in finance as an alternative to the traditional method of borrowing money on the security of mortgages. Leaseholds are discussed more fully in Chapter 27 ("Landlord and Tenant") and Chapter 33 ("Legal Devices for Securing Credit").

Concurrent Interests in Estates

Two or more persons may become owners of the same estate in land at the same time. They are concurrent holders of the estate whether it be a fee simple, a life estate, or a leasehold estate. In the absence of any special agreement between them or of special terms set out in the grant by which they acquired the interests, concurrent holders are deemed to be *tenants in common*. Tenants in common hold equal shares in the estate; that is, each is entitled to the same rights over the property and an equal share of the income. Each interest is an *undivided* interest: one tenant cannot fence off a portion of the property for her exclusive use — each is entitled to the use of the whole property. However, tenants in common may agree expressly to hold unequal shares, transfer the share of one to another, or divide and fence the property into exclusive lots. In addition, a tenant in common may transfer her interest to any third party without the consent of the others: the transferee becomes a tenant in

---

[3] In 1877 England passed the Settled Estates Act creating an important exception to the rule. The statute was later enacted only in British Columbia and Ontario. Under the statute a life tenant may lease his estate for a term not exceeding 21 years, and the lease will be valid against the remainderman. If the life tenant dies, the lessee pays the rent to the remainderman for the balance of the lease, and may stay in possession. The statute also provides that the rent bargained for by the life tenant must be the best reasonably obtainable.

common with them. When a tenant in common dies, her interest goes to her heirs, who continue to hold the interest with the other tenants in common.

Another form of concurrent interest is the *joint tenancy*. A joint tenancy arises only when expressly created in the grant of the estate or afterwards by an express agreement between the holders of the estate. The feature that distinguishes a joint tenancy from a tenancy in common is the *right of survivorship*. Under the right of survivorship the interest of a deceased joint tenant passes immediately on his death to the surviving tenant or tenants instead of to the heirs of the deceased tenant. Thus, if A, B, and C own Blackacre in joint tenancy, upon C's death his interest will pass to A and B, who will continue to own Blackacre in joint tenancy between them; C's interest does not go to his heirs.

A joint tenant may destroy the right of survivorship at any time before his death without the consent of the other joint tenants. By a procedure called *severance*, he turns his joint tenancy into a tenancy in common with the other tenant or tenants. If there are two or more other tenants remaining, they continue as joint tenants with each other but are tenants in common with the one who has severed his joint tenancy. The most common method of severance is by a joint tenant's granting his interest to a third party; the grant automatically turns the interest transferred into a tenancy in common with the remaining interests. There are other ways to sever a joint tenancy, such as giving a mortgage on one's share. However, a joint tenant cannot sever his share by disposing of it in his will: the courts have held that a will speaks only at the moment a testator has died, and at that moment his share has already passed to the surviving joint tenant or tenants.

Husband and wife often take title to their family home in joint tenancy. On the death of either spouse the survivor automatically receives full title to the property. Joint tenancy is an advantage to the survivor because the house does not form part of the deceased partner's estate, thus becoming entangled in problems of *probate* (administration and settling of a deceased person's estate). Legal fees and probate costs are significantly reduced. Formerly, a capital gains tax advantage was available for not having family real property owned in joint tenancy where the family owned two properties (for example a city residence and a country residence or cottage) and each spouse could separately own one of the properties. Since now only one principal residence is allowed per couple as a capital gains tax exemption, joint ownership of a family home by husband and wife has become an attractive and popular arrangement.

Condominiums

Condominiums are a modern response to a shortage of housing and recreational areas in large urban centres; it is claimed that they provide the occupiers with the satisfaction of home ownership and communal access to recreational areas that they could not hope to purchase for their own exclusive use.

Nearly all the common law provinces have enacted legislation permitting the granting of an estate in fee simple in individual units of multiple-unit developments, such as high-rise apartments, row housing or groups of single-family semi-detached, duplex, or similar residences.[4] The legislation is not restricted to residential housing and applies equally to the development of commercial and industrial buildings. An owner of a unit is entitled to exclusive possession of that unit and also obtains an undivided part ownership, in

---

[4] See, for example: Condominium Act, R.S.B.C. 1979, c. 61; R.S.O. 1990, c. C-26; R.S.N.S. 1989, c. 85.

common with other unit owners, of *common elements* including structures and areas external to the unit such as entrances, stairs and elevators, and communal facilities such as laundries, recreation rooms, garages, swimming pools, tennis courts, playgrounds and so forth. Each unit can be bought and sold, mortgaged and passed to successors on death. It is separately assessed and taxed and may be sold for unpaid taxes. Such transfers do not affect the ownership of other units. A purchaser acquires a unit subject to several important conditions: in a multiple-unit building he must, like a tenant, allow entry to make necessary repairs to services; contribute to the operation, upkeep and in some degree to the restoration of the common property; and insure his own unit. In addition, he becomes a member of the *condominium corporation* charged with responsibility for management of the property as a whole and given statutory powers for that purpose, and he is subject to the rules and regulations governing the development. Although the corporation is not the owner of the common elements, it may own one or more units and thus share in that ownership. For example, it may own units rented to janitorial and supervisory staff as well as for its own offices.

The legislation has done away with the technical difficulties that the common law found in granting ownership of a freehold entirely separated from the ground by other units of freehold. However, condominium law does leave a number of practical problems that necessarily arise in complex high-rise buildings. For example, the definition of a unit is a matter of critical importance: does a unit-owner's property extend beyond the surface of the walls of the rooms? If a piece of plaster a centimetre thick is knocked out of the wall, is the damage to the property of the unit-owner or to the common elements and thus the corporation's responsibility to repair? If the description of a unit included ownership of, let us say, the space 8 centimetres beyond the surface of the wall, and plumbing in that space immediately behind the plaster failed, would the unit-owner be responsible for repairs even if the plumbing served an adjoining unit and not his own? We can see that it may be a serious disadvantage to own much of the area beyond the surface of the inner walls. Responsibility for repairs and maintenance is generally in the hands of the corporation, but where services are within the unit, it is important to set out clearly where responsibility lies.

The equivalent of condominium ownership has long existed in many parts of the world, especially where buildings are expected to have a very long life, often calculated in hundreds of years. A modern apartment building of low quality, constructed for rental accommodation, may have an expected life of only 40 to 50 years. Its conversion to a condominium may have pitfalls for an unwary buyer who purchases a rapidly deteriorating asset. For example, if such an apartment building, already 15 years old, were converted to a condominium and a purchaser bought a unit with an instalment mortgage over a 25-year period, the building might well be in a state of great disrepair by the time the buyer had paid the mortgage off. Instead of acquiring an appreciating asset, as is usually the case with the purchase of a residential home, the condominium unit-owner might find that the unit had lost a substantial part of its value. Accordingly, it is important for a prospective purchaser of a unit to take great care in assessing the quality of construction in a condominium building.

In a good-quality rental apartment building, a competent landlord is interested in maintaining this asset in good condition, and will have the necessary management and technical expertise to do so. In a condominium, when the last unit has been sold the purchasers of condominium units become the owners of the complex. If the entrepreneur who built the condominium retains no further interest, the tasks of maintaining the condominium in a good state of repair, paying its bills and having generally efficient management become the collective responsibility of unit-owners through the condominium corporation. Ordinarily, it would not be possible for individual owners to run a large development, and they would authorize the corporation to hire an expert to oversee the operation. Frequently the entrepreneur, while still controlling the condominium corporation as the owner of the unsold units, will arrange a management contract for, let us say, five years. Thus, even after selling off the last unit, the entrepreneur may stay on as manager at a substantial fee. Accordingly, it is important for a prospective buyer of a unit to assess the reputation of the entrepreneur and the quality of management he is likely to provide for the condominium development. Even when management is in competent hands, a unit-owner cannot sit back as a house-owner ordinarily can and attend to her own property. She must remain concerned about the sound management of the condominium corporation on a continuing long-term basis.

The financing and sale of condominium units are more complicated than those of privately-owned residences because of the continuing obligation of a unit-owner to pay charges levied by the condominium corporation and because of the relationship between a master mortgage of all the common elements, including the ground on which the condominium development is located, and the mortgages of the individual units. So too the nature and amount of insurance required for a condominium presents special problems. If a high-rise apartment building is destroyed by fire, the apportionment of loss between each unit and common elements and the responsibility for subsequent reconstruction present considerable difficulty. The most common method of dealing with the problem is through an "insurance trust". A trustee insures the entire building for the benefit of both the condominium corporation and every individual unit owner; each pays part of the premium proportionate to its interest.

We can see then, that while there are many attractive features in the development of condominiums, there are also new problems confronting prospective purchasers that must be weighed against the advantages.

An alternative to condominiums is co-operative housing. In a co-operative housing development a member merely buys a share in the co-operative organization and, by virtue of his equity in it, becomes entitled to occupy one of the units in the development. A risk of this type of home ownership, however, is that the whole co-operative venture may flounder because of bad management and insolvency: all members are affected equally by the failure, and may lose their equity investment even though they may personally have been honouring their obligations and paying the required contributions for taxes and upkeep. Financing a share in co-operative housing presents difficulties of its own. A member buys an equity share and has rights to occupy a unit that are similar to a leasehold interest. The method of borrowing money on the value of a share in a co-operative, combined with the right to occupy a unit, is more complicated than a straight loan by way of mortgage on a private residence, but on the other hand a share is often available to prospective tenants who have less capital than is usually required to buy a condominium unit. A co-operative venture usually requires a high degree of commitment to a community project, and more direct involvement in management than is typical of condominium ownership. A high level of involvement in the management of the co-operative is probably the best assurance of sound management and survival.

*I*NTERESTS LESS THAN ESTATES

Easements

In addition to estates in land divided according to time, there are other interests distinguished by the use or benefit they confer upon the holder. None of these interests gives the right of exclusive possession as do freehold and leasehold estates.

At the beginning of this chapter we referred to an example of a landowner granting a right to a city to lay water-mains over her land and to maintain and repair them. This right belongs to the class of interests called easements. An *easement* is a right enjoyed by one landowner over the land of another, for a special purpose rather than for the general use and occupation of land. The most common type of easement is a *right of way*: The holder of a right of way may pass back and forth over the land of another in order to get to and from his own land. He does not have the right to remain on the other's land or bring things on the land and leave them there or to obstruct others from using the land, but he can maintain an action against anyone who interferes with his right to pass. Other examples of easements are the right to string wires and cables across land, to hang eaves of a building over another's land, to drain water or waste materials from one piece of land over a watercourse on another's land. Once granted, an easement attaches to the land and binds subsequent owners — they cannot interfere with the exercise of the easement. Similarly, purchasers from the owner of the land benefiting from the easement acquire the former owner's easement rights.

As essential requirement of an easement is that there must be a *dominant tenement* (a piece of land that is to benefit from the easement) and a *servient tenement* (the land subject to the easement). The location of the dominant tenement has presented difficulties. It has long been decided that the dominant tenement need not directly adjoin the servient tenement, but it must be reasonably close to it. This qualification is vague, but the law has not been able to devise a more exact definition. It is highly unlikely that if Blackacre is 30 kilometres from Whiteacre, the owner of Blackacre can acquire a right of way over Whiteacre; but it is not clear what the answer would be if one kilometre separated the lands and if it were shown that the proposed easement would be of great benefit to the use and enjoyment of Blackacre.

The term "easement" is sometimes used to describe certain statutory rights such as the right granted a telephone company to run wires and cables either underground or overhead on poles. The telephone company has the right to leave wires where they have been installed and to inspect and repair them when necessary — rights very similar to easements. But often the telephone company owns no land in the area. The nearest land that could be considered a dominant tenement may be many kilometres away. Strictly speaking, the right is not an easement: it owes its existence to a statute. If a telephone company were to attempt to buy an easement to lay cables over long distances without the authority of a statute, no easement would come into existence because there would be no dominant tenement reasonably close by. Although it might have contractual rights against the person who sold the right, the company would have no real property interest in the cables. A subsequent purchaser of the lands would not be bound to let the company use the land or even to let it take the cables away.

An adjoining landowner may acquire an easement without a written grant from the owner of the servient tenement. The method by which the adjoining owner may do so is called *prescription*. In medieval England, a custom grew that if an individual habitually exercised a right over the land of another for a very long time and if that right *could* have been granted to him as an easement, it was presumed that he had received a grant of easement at one time but had subsequently lost the grant. This fiction was merely a convenient way of permitting a person to rely on a right he had exercised for a very long time. From this fiction developed a rule that if a person continuously exercised a right, openly, notoriously, without fraud or deceit, without using force or threats against the owner of the land, and at no time acknowledged the right of the owner in writing or paid for the use of the land, he would acquire an easement by prescription after 20 years. The right had to be exercised continuously, that is without interruption by the owner's exerting his rights of ownership through exacting a fee or keeping the prospective easement holder off the land.

An easement by prescription is as valid as an easement by grant and is fully recognized in the four Atlantic provinces and in parts of Manitoba and Ontario. Easements by prescription are not recognized in the three westernmost provinces or in those parts of Manitoba and Ontario covered by *land titles* registration, a system of recording interests in land that will be discussed in the last section of this chapter. In areas where easements by prescription may arise, a landowner must guard against them. One great danger is that a former owner of the land may have permitted the exercise of a right for many years. The presription period continues to run from the moment that the right was exercised regardless of a transfer of ownership of the land. Thus, there may be only a small part of the 20 years to go when the current owner obtains title. While a prospective easement may seem inoffensive to the current owner, there is a risk that the easement may later reduce the market value of the land.

ILLUSTRATION

X obtains an easement by prescription over a ten-foot strip of Servacre by using it as a right of way to his garage on Domacre for over 20 years. During this period Servacre contains only a single family dwelling. Later it becomes suitable for erecting a large apartment building, but municipal building regulations for the construction of apartments require that the ten-foot strip be used for a parking area. Without the ten-foot strip there would be insufficient parking area to comply with the regulations. The owner of Servacre will be unable to develop the property or sell it to another party interested in developing it unless and until a release of the easement can be bought from the owner of Domacre.

Covenants

Often, an owner of land wishes to sell part of it yet control or restrict the use of that part he proposes to sell. We can understand her motives: she may wish to see the property kept in good repair so that the area does not deteriorate; she may wish to prevent the carrying on of a noisy business that would interfere with her privacy; she may wish the purchaser to improve the land by planting trees and shrubs, to enhance the beauty of the area. She may, of course, require the purchaser to do any or all of these things as part of the consideration for the sale of the land. If the purchaser does not abide by his promise, the vendor has her normal contractual remedies for breach.

But if the purchaser resells the land to a third party, there is no privity of contract between the vendor and the third party, and the third party need not fear a contractual action by the vendor if he chooses to ignore his predecessor's promise. The vendor has a remedy only if the purchaser's promise has created *an interest in land* that the law recognizes as binding upon all subsequent holders. Recognition of such interests would create further complexities.

ILLUSTRATION

V, owner of Blackacre and Whiteacre, sells Whiteacre to P. As part of the consideration he obtains a promise that P and all subsequent owners of Whiteacre will keep in repair all buildings on both Whiteacre and Blackacre. So long as P owns Whiteacre, he is bound by his promise. Subsequently P sells Whiteacre to A, who is aware of that promise. A refuses to carry it out, and V sues A for breach. The court would have no difficulty dismissing the promise to repair buildings on Blackacre as not binding A: A has no connection with P's promise insofar as it affects Blackacre — he has no interest in that land nor was he a party to the contract between V and P. Thus, A is not bound to repair the buildings on Blackacre.

The promise concerning Whiteacre is more troublesome. It may seem reasonable for V, who still owns adjoining lands, to require Whiteacre to be kept in good repair so that the area will remain at high market value. The courts have held, however, that it is too onerous to subject subsequent owners to such positive duties, and that as a matter of public policy it would be dangerous to permit the creation of interests in land requiring a subsequent owner to personally perform promises in perpetuity. Lands might eventually be tied up by an interminable series of such promises or covenants for the benefit of surrounding lands.

In spite of constant discouragement from the courts over the centuries, vendors continued to extract promises from purchasers, some highly desirable and some injurious and spiteful. In the middle of the last century one of these covenants was questioned in the English Court of Chancery in the famous case of *Tulk v. Moxhay*.[5] The court decided that it was too onerous to require a subsequent holder to act positively in order to carry out covenants (as in the above illustration), but if the covenant were purely *negative*, that is, if the holder were required to refrain from certain conduct or certain use of the land, then the court would hold the covenant valid and enforceable. These negative covenants became known as *covenants running with the land*, or *restrictive covenants*. Restrictive covenants are subject to a rule similar to that concerning easements — there must be a piece of land subject to the covenant and another piece that receives the benefit of the covenant. A covenant recognized by the courts as running with the land is enforceable *by* any subsequent holder of the land benefiting from it *against* any subsequent holder of the land subject to it.

There are a number of rules governing the types of conduct that may be regulated by restrictive covenants, how the benefits of the covenants may be transferred, and

---

[5] (1848), 41 E.R. 1143.

how they may be enforced.[6] Covenants found to be highly unreasonable or against public policy will not be enforced by the courts against subsequent holders.

Suppose an owner of land subject to a restrictive covenant acts quickly in defiance of it, for example, by erecting a high wall or cutting a doorway through an existing wall, before an aggrieved adjacent owner manages to obtain an injunction. Is the adjacent owner without remedy? The court may exercise its discretion, especially when a deliberately provocative breach of covenant has occurred, to grant a *mandatory injunction* requiring the wrongdoer to tear down the prohibited wall, or block the doorway and restore the wall. If it is too late to restore the damage, as when the wrongdoer has cut down a row of hundred-year-old oak trees, the court may award damages in lieu of an injunction.

Restrictive covenants are widely used in residential areas to regulate the uses to which land may be put. Typical restrictive covenants prohibit the use of land for other than residential purposes, limit building on the land to one-family dwellings, require minimum frontage per house, and specify minimum distances at which buildings may be erected from the sidelines of lots or from street lines.

If over the years the character of an area has changed and a once reasonable covenant has become unduly restrictive, an affected landowner may apply to the court to have the covenant terminated. The court will require that the owner of the land for whose benefit the covenant was made be served with notice and given an opportunity to defend the covenant.

Restrictive covenants that regulate land use over an entire neighbourhood or a shopping centre are referred to as *building-scheme covenants*. In a building scheme each owner mutually agrees with all other owners to be bound by the covenant in return for the promise of all neighbouring owners to be similarly bound. In order to have the court remove the covenant for the benefit of one owner, all adjoining owners must be served with notice and given a chance to state their opinions. As a result, it may be very difficult to have a restrictive covenant under a building scheme terminated.

Covenants are gradually being replaced by municipal regulations in the form of zoning and building by-laws, especially in newly-developed areas. Nevertheless, covenants still play an important role in older settled parts of our cities and towns; sometimes they unduly restrict the development of an area.

Other Interests

There are several other interests in land that are less than estates, but we leave most of them to be described in treatises on real property. One interest deserves special mention — the right to take minerals, oil, and gas from under the surface of land occupied by others. The right to remove materials is usually found in an agreement commonly called a *lease*. An oil, gas, or mineral lease bears little if any similarity to a true leasehold interest. Rather, it comprises several interests in land combined in one agreement between the parties. To the extent that the agreement permits the lessee to occupy a portion of the surface area of the land (often only a very small proportion of the area from which the

---

[6] See Preston and Newsome, *Restrictive Covenants Affecting Freehold Land* (7th ed.), London: Sweet & Maxwell Limited, 1982. An Ontario court has held that for a restrictive covenant to be enforceable, not only must the party seeking to enforce it (the covenantee) own land to be benefited by the covenant but the land must also be identified in the instrument creating the covenant. Re Sekretov and City of Toronto (1973), 33 D.L.R. (3d) 257. For statutory authority to modify or discharge a restrictive covenant see, for example: Conveyancing and Law of Property Act, R.S.O. 1990, c. C-34, s. 61(1).

oil, gas, or mineral is taken) it is similar to a true lease. To the extent that it grants the right to travel back and forth over the owner's land, lay pipes and move equipment, it is similar to an easement. To the extent that it permits removal of materials extracted from the ground (previously the real property of the owner and now the personal property of the lessee), it is similar to an ancient interest in land known as a *profit à prendre*. The law concerning mineral, oil, and gas leases has become highly specialized in recent years. It will suffice to know that such agreements are more than mere leases and that they form a highly developed field of study of their own.

A "licence" given to another person by an owner to use his land is not, strictly speaking, an interest in land at all. Thus, if *B* gives his friend, *A*, permission to hold a garage sale on his front lawn, *A* becomes a "licensee" on *B*'s land during the garage sale; she is not a trespasser. However, she has no "right" to remain on *B*'s land and if he should revoke permission, something he may do at any time, *A* would have only a reasonable minimum time to remove her goods and herself from *B*'s lawn. Suppose *B* had charged *A* $25 for the use of the lawn for one full day. Revocation of permission to use the lawn for that day would be a breach of contract; if the breach were sufficiently serious *A* might well obtain an injunction preventing *B* from removing her and her goods until the end of the day. An injunction — or any other remedy — would be a contractual right enforceable against *B*; it would not be enforceable against a purchaser of *B*'s land. If *B* sold his land before the day of the sale, *A*'s only remedy would then be for damages against him. Nevertheless, contractual licences between enterprises that have entered into long-term and stable relations can have substantial business value, and they do create rights binding between the original parties. Their relative simplicity when contrasted with the formalities of creating an interest in land has made licences a useful business tool.

◯dverse Possession

Suppose that twenty years ago *A* stole ten dollars from a corner store. Had he been caught at the time, he might well have been charged with theft. But if twenty years later this fact is discovered and throughout that time *A* has been a law-abiding person, almost everyone will feel that it would be morally, if not legally, wrong to pursue the matter. Similarly, if someone had left several pieces of furniture with a friend while she travelled around the world, the friend would probably return them without question a few months later. But if the owner did not ask for their return until a dozen years later, her friend would probably have come to think of the pieces of furniture as his own and resent having to part with them. This desire to leave things undisturbed, as they have been for a very long time, finds its expression in the law of *limitations*. The policy of the law is that a person who has a right of action against another must pursue it within a definite period of time or lose the right: he must not keep the other party in indefinite jeopardy of being sued.[7] In Chapter 34 we shall discuss when a creditor who does not sue to collect a debt within the time permitted will lose that right to sue. Limitation statutes are not concerned with the merits of the plaintiff's claim: they require only that he pursue his claim within a definite time or abandon it.

---

[7] In matters of criminal law, in theory at least, a person should be prosecuted and punished regardless of the time that has elapsed since he committed an offence. The state is the prosecutor, and limitation statutes generally do not apply to it.

Limitation rules apply to interests in land. They might arise as an issue, for example, in the following circumstances:

(a) A occupies land owned by B. He treats it as his own and improves it. His family continues to occupy the land for many years after his death. After several generations, the heirs of B try to dispossess the heirs of A.

(b) A mistakenly puts up a fence that encloses not only his own land but part of B's land. He erects a costly building covering a portion of B's land that he had enclosed. Years later the mistake comes to light, and B insists on the destruction of the building so that he may get his land back.

These circumstances present difficult problems for the court. In each case B owned the land; but to dispossess A or his successors would work hardship and injustice. In medieval times, when there were many large estates and absentee landowners, squatters who entered and stayed on their lands for long periods were very common. In recent times, with speedy means of transport and communication and with accurate surveys available, the number of squatters has become smaller. Even so, disputes frequently occur, and modern statutes in England and the five eastern common law provinces set out limitation periods beyond which an owner loses the right to regain possession of his land.[8] By adverse possession an occupier of land can *extinguish the title* of the owner; the possessor becomes in effect the owner of the land.

The three westernmost provinces and parts of Manitoba and Ontario have a modern land titles system governing the recording of interests in land. In the belief that this advanced system of registration, combined with modern methods of surveying, can eliminate almost all errors, and with a policy of having all interests in land recorded exclusively in the official registry, all these jurisdictions have provided by statute that the title of the registered owner cannot be extinguished by adverse possession.[9] But the attitude of people towards reviving long-dormant claims, as we have discussed above, has caused resistance to the new rules. There have been cases where the courts of some of these jurisdictions were unwilling to accept the full implications of the statutory provisions. In some cases they have avoided the provisions, and in effect recognized possessory interests.[10]

Of course, most instances of possession of the land of another are not adverse possession but rather are the result of an arrangement between owner and occupier. The most common example is that of a tenant in possession under a lease. The terms of the lease govern the relations between landlord and tenant: though the lease may run many years longer than the time needed for adverse possession to destroy an owner's title to land, the lease continues to govern their relations, not the statutory rules on limitation periods.[11] But if the tenant were to stop paying rent due under the lease and ignore his other obligations, treating the land as if it were his own, he would then be in adverse possession, and the limitation period would begin to run from the time of his breach. The landlord could, of course,

---

8 See, for example: Limitations Act, R.S.O. 1990, c. L-15, s. 4 (10 years); Limitations of Actions Act, R.S.N.S. 1989, c. 258, s. 10 (20 years).

9 See, for example: Land Titles Act, R.S.A. 1980, c. L-5, s. 64(1); Real Property Act, R.S.M. 1987, c. R-30, s. 61(2).

10 See Sinclair v. McLellan, [1919] 2 W.W.R. 782; Boyczuk v. Perry, [1948] 1 W.W.R. 495.

11 The Supreme Court of Canada has recently confirmed this rule: Bovey v. Ganonoque (Town), [1992] 1 S.C.R. 5.

sue the tenant for breach of the lease and have him evicted; but if he failed to pursue his remedies within the time set out in the statute, he would lose all his rights. Here then, we see the elements needed for adverse possession: the possessor stays in exclusive possession using the land like an owner and ignoring the claims of other persons including the owner.

A further element of adverse possession is that it must be *open and notorious* — a person who furtively creeps into a deserted house each night and sleeps there for a period equal to the limitation period would not extinguish the title of the owner. A court takes various facts into account in deciding whether a person has established possession that is both exclusive, and open and notorious.[12] By showing that he has paid the municipal taxes, made improvements to the property, fenced the property, or performed other acts normally done by an owner, a possessor may strengthen his claim of adverse possession.

Adverse possession ceases to be effective if it is interrupted by the owner before the limitation period has elapsed. Thus, if the owner demands and receives rent from the possessor in acknowledgement of the owner's superior rights to the land, the adverse possession is terminated. However, if the possessor remains in possession after the rent period expires, a new limitation period will begin; but it must run the full duration to extinguish the owner's title — it is not added to the previous period. When the owner has not interrupted possession, the adverse possessor may pass possession directly to another person, and the limitation period continues to run against the owner from the time of the entry into adverse possession by the first possessor.

Unless another person establishes adverse possession, the law presumes the owner of land to be in possession of it. This rule has two consequences: first, an owner's title is not prejudiced merely by the fact that he has not occupied the land or leased it to a tenant — land abandoned for an indefinite period remains the property of the owner; second, when an adverse possessor abandons land before the limitation period has expired, the law regards possession as returned to the owner — the limitation period must start afresh if the possessor returns, or if someone else goes into adverse possession.

$\mathcal{T}$HE TRANSFER OF INTERESTS IN LAND

An interest in land may be transferred in any one of several ways. If the holder of an interest dies *intestate* (without leaving a will), the interest passes according to statutory rules of inheritance to the holder's heir or heirs; that is, the interest passes automatically to the closest relatives. If, for example, a widow holds a fee simple in Blackacre and at her death she is survived by two daughters, they will become the owners of the fee simple.

A person need not allow her wealth to go automatically according to the rules of intestate succession. She may dispose of her property by *will* according to her wishes and the claims she feels she should satisfy. Thus, a second way that land may be transferred is by will.

The most common way of disposing of interests in land is by transfers between living persons. The methods used to transfer land have developed over hundreds of years; by the middle of the 19th century, a comparatively uniform method had been evolved in the use of a *grant*. It contains a description of the grantor, the grantee, and the interest being transferred, and is signed and sealed by the grantor before a witness. Since the document is under seal, it is often called a *deed of conveyance* — frequently shortened to *deed*. We

---

[12]   See, for example: Wallis's Ltd. v. Shell-Mex and BP, [1974] 3 All E.R. 575

should recall, however, that every document under seal is a deed, and many deeds are not concerned with transfers of land at all. The equivalent of a grant under the land titles system, used in some areas as described in the next section, is called a *transfer* and is effective without being made under seal.

The holder of an interest in land may be compelled to transfer it against her will. A creditor may obtain judgment against her in court and eventually have the land sold in order to satisfy the debt. A common type of compulsory transfer of land is *expropriation*. When a public body such as the federal government or a local school board requires land for its activities, it may proceed under statute to force the transfer of land to itself. It must, of course, pay compensation for taking the land, and if the parties cannot agree upon a price the statute provides for arbitration or judicial proceedings to determine the price to be paid.

The most important method of transfer is by voluntary grant in performance of a contract for the sale of land. A holder of an interest may grant the whole of it or only part, reserving the rest of it to himself. When he grants only part of it, the balance remains his. For example, when a landlord grants a lease for five years he retains the *reversion*, and possession returns to him at the end of the lease. Again, if the holder of a fee simple grants a life estate, the reversion stays with the holder and his heirs. When a person grants an easement over his land, he retains the remaining interest in the land (the servient tenement).

Often the transferor of an interest wishes to transfer almost all his interest, retaining only a small part for himself. In these circumstances, the *form* of the grant changes: he conveys away his whole interest except that he expressly reserves the part he wishes to keep. Thus, if A owns both Blackacre and Whiteacre and wishes to sell Whiteacre but retain an easement over it in order to get to and from Blackacre, A will grant Whiteacre at the same time reserving a right-of-way over it. Such *reservations* are quite common in grants of land.

In summary, a transfer of an interest in land can have two results: first, if it is a transfer of the *whole interest*, then the interest remains unaltered but is in the hands of another person; second, if it is a transfer of only *part of an interest*, the interest is divided into two parts and there are two holders — the grantee with the interest he has obtained under the grant, and the grantor with the interest he has retained because he did not transfer it by the grant.

THE RECORDING OF INTERESTS IN LAND

Our discussion of interests in land shows that they are varied and complex and also that they may be transferred in a variety of ways. How is a prospective purchaser to discover what interest a vendor really holds in the land he proposes to sell and what claims others have? Ordinarily, under the terms of a contract to sell land, the vendor sets out the interest he is selling and gives the purchaser the right to examine all the title documents in order to ascertain whether the vendor really has the interest claimed. In England, until recent times, owners of land kept all the title documents to their land going back many years, often centuries. The system worked quite well, but it placed a very high value on these title documents as evidence of an owner's interest. Thus, an accidental loss or destruction of the documents could create serious problems in proving ownership. And, of course, such documents deteriorated through handling over the years.

In Canada and the United States a more reliable method of ascertaining title has developed. Each transfer of an interest in land is recorded in a public registry office. The usual practice is for a grantor to deliver to the grantee the original document and a duplicate copy. The grantee in turn files both of them with the registrar. The original is then recorded (formerly by hand or typewriter, but now on microfilm or computer storage systems), assigned a number, and filed away. The duplicate is stamped and certified by the registrar, the number of the original is recorded on it and it is returned to the grantee. Registry office records are stored in a fireproof structure — both the original document and the microfilm of it — and in addition the purchaser receives the duplicate copy of the original. Thus the danger of loss or destruction of a record of transfer is virtually eliminated. This method has now come into use in many parts of England also.

Generally, there is a registry office for each regional political division within a province or state. For example, each county or district within a province usually has a land registry office located in the county or district town, the seat of regional government. Under the protection of provincial statutes, a purchaser *searches* (examines) the title to the particular piece of land she is buying only in the local registry office. Any person with an interest in the land is protected only if that interest is registered. If the interest is not registered he takes the risk that a *bona fide purchaser*, that is, a purchaser who buys the land without knowledge of an unregistered claim, will buy free of that claim. In turn, the new owner must register her interest in order to protect it.

Before the introduction of the registry system, if V granted a fee simple in Blackacre to X and subsequently V made a second grant of the same interest to P who did not know of the first grant, X would have title to Blackacre and P would have nothing. For when V granted Blackacre to X, he sold all that he had — he had nothing more to give to P. Accordingly, the grant to P was a nullity. But under the registry system, if P registers her deed before X registers his, P will effectively cut out X and obtain title to Blackacre. The result of this rule is of course that purchasers register their grant immediately on receiving them. Prospective purchasers rely on records in the registry office: they buy interests according to these records and need not worry about other interests that may have been granted but not recorded.

Reflecting the rules of the statutes of limitations, some registry systems limit to forty years the period in the records that a purchaser must search for evidence of good title.[13]

---

[13] Registry Act, R.S.O. 1990, c. R-20, s. 4; Limitations of Actions Act, R.S.N.S. 1989, c. 258, s. 20.

ILLUSTRATION

X is considering the purchase of Red Oaks from Y. The records in the registry office show that A sold Red Oaks to B in 1910, but B's name does not appear again. The next entry on the record is a grant in 1933 by M to N, and from then on there is a continuous chain of title to the present holder, Y.

X need not worry about the transfer from A to B. In all probability B transferred title to M, and M neglected to register the grant, but it is not necessary to establish this link. The fact that M conveyed the land to N more than forty years ago and that there is no subsequent difficulty with the title establishes a title upon which X, as an intending purchaser, can rely.

Searching the title to a piece of land under the registry system can be a laborious and sometimes a hazardous task. An error in one of the documents that has gone undetected may later be discovered and disclose an outstanding interest, creating serious consequences for the current owner. If harm results through the negligence of a lawyer, he or she must compensate the client. Lawyers take out liability insurance to compensate clients in case such an error occurs.

The risks inherent in this system of registration encouraged the adoption of a newer system in the mid-19th century. The new system is called the *land titles* or the *Torrens* system, named after an officer in the Australian marine shipping-registry department. He adopted the system of ship registration directly for land registration. The distinctive feature of the system is that as each new transaction concerning a piece of land is submitted for registration, the land titles office carefully examines and approves the document before recording it. At the time of recording, the office brings all outstanding interests in the land up to date and certifies them as being correct. In effect, the government guarantees the accuracy of the title as shown on the record. There are variations from jurisdiction to jurisdiction in the methods of recording and in the type of guarantee given by the government. The great advantage of the system is that a purchaser need not search through forty or more years of records to discover the state of the title. The land titles office will give him a complete statement, valid to the moment the statement is issued.

As we have seen, the land titles system attempts to do away with the risks of adverse possession and to give absolute and concise information on the state of the title. The older registry system makes no attempt to do this: its purpose is simply to give a complete record of all title documents and let the searcher judge their validity. The registry system exists in the older settled parts of Canada — the four Atlantic provinces and throughout most of southern Ontario and parts of Manitoba. The land titles system is used in the three westernmost provinces, most of Manitoba, throughout most of northern Ontario, and in a number of southern Ontario districts.

We must not assume that a careful search of the recorded documents will assure a purchaser that the land is free from all other claims. We have already noted that in the provinces using the registry system, a purchaser cannot rely on the records because the vendor's title may have been extinguished by adverse possession. The purchaser should personally inspect the property to see if there is evidence of a third party that appears to be asserting a right of exclusive possession over the whole or any part of the lands. Otherwise the interest purchased may already have been extinguished. Nor is adverse possession the only possible source of trouble: there are other claims against lands not ordinarily recorded under either the registry or the land titles system. Two such claims are arrears of municipal tax on the land and, in some provinces, arrears of tax against corporations accruing while they hold the land. If any of these claims comes to light after a purchaser has paid the vendor, he must satisfy them in order to protect his interest in the land. Thus, a prospective purchaser should obtain evidence from the municipality of any taxes outstanding and evidence from the provincial government of any arrears of corporation taxes. This information cannot be obtained from the registry or land titles office but only from the government concerned.

A further claim may arise if the vendor is a judgment debtor at the time of the sale. The vendor may have been sued successfully by a creditor that has registered its judgment with the sheriff for the county or district. If a claim of this kind is outstanding (unpaid) at the time the land is sold, the judgment creditor may still require the sheriff to *levy execution*, that is, seize and hold a sale of the land in order to realize the amount due under the judgment. The purchaser will then have to pay the debt to save the land. Accordingly, a purchaser should also make a search for executions in the sheriff's office to ensure that there are none before completing the sale. Various other claims against a vendor, such as debts owed to public bodies for fines or taxes, may be registered in the sheriff's office, according to each province's own rules. In order to facilitate a search for these claims the sheriff's office and the land registry office are often in the same building, or special facilities are provided in the registry office to search the execution records.

Another hazard to a purchaser may be created by a tenant in possession of the land. In most jurisdictions, short-term leases, usually for three years or less, need not be registered or even be in writing and are valid against purchasers that buy the interest of the landlord. Thus, a purchaser must inspect the property to see whether there are any tenants, and if there are, it should obtain an acknowledgement from them of the type of tenancy they claim to hold. If the vendor assures the purchaser that the tenant is only a monthly tenant that can be given one month's notice to vacate, the purchaser may later discover that the tenant has a two-year lease. The purchaser would be unable to put the tenant out even though it had bought the premises for the purpose of obtaining possession for itself and carrying on business there. But if the purchaser obtains a signed acknowledgement from the tenant that he is a monthly tenant only, the court would not permit the tenant to claim later that he had a lease for two years. A purchaser may thus rely upon a signed statement of the tenant.

We can see that the sale of an interest in land is a complex transaction requiring careful examination of the records at the local registry or land titles office, the offices of municipal and provincial governments, the local sheriff's office, and an inspection of the land itself. We should remember that a sale of land is completed and title passed to a purchaser when she obtains delivery of the deed. The purchaser becomes full owner of her newly acquired property at that moment in time. Prompt registration or recording of land titles gives protection against subsequent fraudulent acts by an unscrupulous vendor.

Questions for Review

1. Distinguish between real property and personal property.
2. What two different legal meanings may the term "property" have?
3. *P* purchases a house from *V*, with possession three months hence. The deed of conveyance describes only the land on which the house is situated and includes no description of any house. Is *V* entitled to move the house from its foundations and have it delivered to his own land before the closing date for the sale of the land?
4. Distinguish between a remainder and a reversion.
5. Distinguish the circumstances under which an easement may be obtained by prescription and a title may be extinguished by adverse possession. Need the required period of time be the same?
6. What quality must a restrictive covenant have in common with an easement if it is to be enforceable?
7. Distinguish between a restrictive covenant in a grant, a building-scheme covenant and a zoning by-law.
8. How does the existence of a life estate hamper the sale of land?
9. In whose interest is it to register a grant of land? Why?
10. Kolev's neighbours are having a party and making noise at night. What rights has Kolev?
11. In what ways may title to land be acquired?
12. Gartner planted a weeping willow tree near the boundary of his lot. The tree has grown and is now weeping on Smith's adjoining lot. Has Smith any rights? Would the age of the tree make any difference?
13. What are rights in the matrimonial home? How did they evolve?
14. Describe the basic distinction between the land titles system and the registry system.
15. Is a purchaser sufficiently assured of obtaining a good title to land by searching in the registry office? Why?
16. Why is a telephone company's use of land for its cable often not an easement? What is the significance of the fact that no easement is created?
17. "...we conceive of the land as property, something that is specifically owned. But such ownership expresses only a practical relationship among men: the land itself is common to everyone. What we think of as property we actually hold in trust." (From *Survival Day Bulletin*, 1971.)
    (a) Discuss some of the respects in which the law recognizes an obligation to others in the use of property (both real and personal) that we own.
    (b) Explain the basis of the argument that individual owners should retain considerable discretion in using their property free from restriction.

Problems

Problem 1

Artois owned a row of a dozen retail stores in a new shopping district. He took great pride in the fact that they were all designed with colonial-style façades for their full three storeys. He occupied one store himself and ran a profitable antique business. He rented the other eleven stores. Several years later, Artois needed money for a new venture; he decided to sell all the stores and lease back the one he occupied himself. The shopping district was prosperous, and he had no trouble selling them. From each purchaser he obtained the following covenant inserted in each grant: "The Grantee covenants on behalf of himself and his assignees not to erect neon or other lighted signs either on the face of the building or at right angles to it, and further covenants not to let the façade fall into disrepair or to become unsightly."

Three of the stores adjacent to each other were purchased by Brougham, Crawford, and Dugan respectively. Several years later each received an offer to purchase his store from Super Duper Discount Stores Ltd. The price was very high, and all three accepted the offers. A few days after completion of the sales, Super Duper moved into possession and began to erect a large neon sign over the stores and to remove the colonial façade. Artois arrived and was horrified. He demanded that the work stop at once. The manager of Super Duper refused, and Artois immediately brought an action for injunction to restrain both the erection of the neon sign and the removal of the colonial façade, for an order to restore the façade and to obey the terms of the covenant, and for damages. At the trial Super Duper admitted that it was aware of the covenant when it bought the stores but claimed that there was no privity of contract with Artois and accordingly that no part of the covenant was binding.

Who should succeed? Why? (See *Haywood v. Brunswick Building Society* (1881) 8 Q.B.D. 403; *Clegg v. Hands* (1890) 44 Ch. D. 503.)

Problem 2

Peter Green owned and operated Green's General Hardwares as well as the lands and buildings where he carried on business. His younger brother John worked for him as manager, as did his daughter, Susan. Peter died leaving a will in which he gave the business and real property to John for life, with the remainder to Susan at John's death. John and Susan could not agree on how to run the business: John wanted to push sales and expansion as quickly as possible; Susan feared that such action would make the business unstable — she preferred to build more slowly, consolidating the gains of the business. The dispute became heated, and John fired Susan. Within a few years the business was in serious financial difficulty; John had allowed several buildings, including a warehouse, to fall into disrepair. Susan sought by court action to force John to keep the buildings in good repair. Should she succeed? Why?

John died and left a will giving his whole estate including the business and buildings to his wife. Who is entitled to the business and why?

Problem 3

Ferrand owned a summer cottage near Fredericton, New Brunswick. He sold it and delivered a grant to Simpson in exchange for $35 000 cash on June 10. On June 11, Simpson received a telephone call to return home to Newfoundland where her mother was seriously ill; Simpson departed at once without registering her grant to the cottage. When Ferrand learned this he called an acquaintance, Entwistle, and asked him whether he was interested in buying the cottage at a bargain price of $26 000. Entwistle had offered Ferrand that amount several months before and Ferrand had refused. Entwistle eagerly accepted the offer on June 20 and paid Ferrand. On the same day, Entwistle received a grant to the cottage and registered it without knowledge of its prior sale to Simpson. Ferrand then absconded with the money from both sales.

Several weeks later, Simpson returned to find Entwistle occupying the cottage. When Entwistle refused to move, Simpson brought an action to have Entwistle put out and herself declared the owner.

Registry Act, R.S.N.B. 1973, c. R-6, contains the following provision:

> 19. All instruments may be registered in the registry office in the county where the lands lie, and if not so registered, shall… be deemed fraudulent and void against subsequent purchasers for valuable consideration whose conveyances are previously registered.

Will Simpson succeed in her action? Would the result be different if Entwistle had heard that Simpson had purchased the cottage before he paid Ferrand the $26 000? Give reasons.

Problem 4

Broum and Vulkan were joint tenants of a large property, Homicide Heights, until Broum shot and killed Vulkan while they were hunting together on the property. Broum was subsequently convicted of criminal negligence as a result of this "accident". Later, when he sought to sell the whole property for $500 000 to a firm of real estate speculators, Mrs. Vulkan protested. Explain briefly whether she would have legal grounds for complaining. (See *Shobelt v. Barber* (1967) 60 D.L.R. (2d) 519.)

Problem 5

For over thirty years Montgomery owned two farms: Green Gables, on which he lived, and Wildwood. The two were separated by a farm owned by Cavendish. Montgomery continually used a road across the Cavendish farm to go to and from Green Gables and Wildwood. The access to the road was through a gate on the boundary of the Cavendish property. During most of these years Montgomery gave Cavendish a large turkey for New Year's, presumably as a gesture of good will and appreciation for the use of the road.

Three years ago Montgomery sold Wildwood to Radoja. Radoja made relatively little use of the road over the Cavendish property (going across twice yearly to visit Montgomery with mortgage payments) until last year, when she also bought Green Gables. The old road then became valuable to Radoja as the most convenient access between her two properties. In the meantime, however, the Cavendish family had extended their lawn across the roadway and Radoja's suddenly increased use of the road led to a dispute about her rights.

Cavendish sought a court injunction to restrain Radoja's use of the alleged right-of-way. Indicate, with reasons, whether the court will grant the injunction.

Case

Running southerly from Halifax along the Atlantic is a provincial highway approximately a thousand feet from the shoreline, where Essex Oil Ltd. has owned a service station on the east side of the road since 1953. The Essex Oil property extends about 300 metres along the east side of the highway and 100 metres east to a right-of-way owned by the province for a proposed scenic highway that would run closer to the seacoast parallel to the existing highway. The oil company's land was unfenced except along the existing highway, beside the station. On the other side of the provincial right-of-way and running down to the Atlantic shore is the Webster Trailer Court and Campsite, a business that was operating there for some years before Essex Oil opened its station.

The province continually deferred construction of the new road, and the right-of-way, a strip about 50 metres wide, lay vacant. The trailer court obtained a licence from the province to use the right-of-way but made no request of Essex Oil Ltd. to use that portion of its land not occupied for the business of the service station. Beginning in 1954, without any communication with Essex Oil, Webster's employees cut the grass on both the provincial right-of-way and the oil company's land, cleared litter, planted flowers, and painted the fence on the far side of the oil company's land, adjacent to the existing road. The employees converted the whole of this land into a playground for guests, putting up tennis courts and a baseball diamond, and during the winter flooding part of the land for a skating rink.

Finally, in 1973, some 19 years after the trailer court had begun to make use of this land, the province announced that it had abandoned all plans to build a road on the proposed site. Essex Oil Ltd. then decided to dispose of its unused land and wrote to Webster Trailer Court and Campsite, offering to sell the land for $25 000.

Mr. Webster, owner of the trailer court, consulted his solicitor, who checked the title deed and confirmed that the disputed land belonged to Essex Oil Ltd. The solicitor also advised him, however, that if the trailer court were to remain in possession for another two months it would have been using the land for 20 years and would then, under Nova Scotia law, have obtained title by adverse possession and without any payment to Essex Oil Ltd.

The Webster Trailer Court and Campsite did not reply to Essex Oil's offer and continued to make use of the land for the enjoyment of its guests. Essex Oil Ltd. wrote again in three weeks and received no reply. A week later, the local manager of Essex Oil Ltd. attempted to reach Mr. Webster by telephone. His secretary said he was out of town for another four weeks, but had left word that on his return he would be glad to discuss the offer in the oil company's first letter.

The full 20-year period had elapsed by only two or three days when the management of Essex Oil Ltd. became suspicious of what was going on and immediately had a fence constructed around the unfenced sides of its strip of land, right across a number of tennis courts and through the baseball diamond. It had no sooner done so than it received a letter from the Webster Trailer Court and Campsite solicitor stating that his client had a "possessory title" to the disputed land. Webster Trailer Court and Campsite then brought an action against Essex Oil Ltd. for a court order to the effect that it had acquired title to the land.

Discuss the validity of the plaintiff's case and the nature of the argument, if any, that might be offered by the defendant.

CHAPTER 27

LANDLORD AND TENANT

THE NATURE OF THE RELATIONSHIP

Definition of a Tenancy

A leasehold interest is created when a landlord (lessor) grants, and a tenant (lessee) accepts, a term. A *term* is an interest in land for a definite period. The landlord thus divides the interest in the land between himself and the tenant by giving a term to the tenant and retaining the reversion. At the end of the term, the tenant must give up the land: the right to possession reverts to the landlord. The word *lease* is used both as a short form for leasehold interest, and to refer to the agreement between landlord and tenant creating the leasehold.

As we have seen in the preceding chapter, a leasehold interest is an estate in land. When parties create a leasehold, certain rights and duties automatically accrue to both the landlord and the tenant. But the requirements of land law for creating an estate are strict, and do not take into account the intentions of the parties; even when they clearly intend to create a leasehold interest, but fail to fulfil these requirements, no estate in the land comes into being, and the usual rights and duties between landlord and tenant do not arise. The consequences may be serious for either party but especially for a would-be tenant: she may be evicted by the owner at once; she has no right herself to evict strangers; she cannot acquire further interests in land such as easements, which may be annexed only to a freehold or a leasehold estate. For these reasons the essentials for the creation of a leasehold interest deserve emphasis. They are, first, that the tenant must obtain the right to exclusive possession, and second, that the tenancy must be for a definite or ascertainable period of time.

When reading this chapter it will be important to bear in mind that most provinces now distinguish *residential tenancies* as a special class of tenancy in their landlord and tenant legislation. They do so in an effort to recognize the special importance of basic shelter for individuals who lease apartments and houses as their place of residence. We shall deal separately with these amendments in the concluding section of this chapter under the heading "Residential Tenancies". The discussion through the major part of the chapter will therefore apply to *commercial tenancies*; its relevance for residential tenancies must be qualified by reference to the specific statutory amendments that we discuss in the final section.

Exclusive Possession

Exclusive possession defines the historic distinction between estates in land and lesser interests in land. It distinguishes control over the land from a mere right to use the land in common with others. A person who has a right to use land in common with others may have an easement, as we have discussed in the preceding chapter, or may be merely a *licensee*. A licensee enters upon land with the consent of the owner, as for example when he goes fishing in a farmer's stream; he is on the land lawfully, not as a trespasser, but he has no interest in the land. He does not have the right to put others off the land or to object if the activity of others interferes with his use and enjoyment of it. Moreover, in some circumstances the owner may put him off the land even when the owner has given him a contractual right to be there. The rights of a contractual licensee can be quite complicated and are better left for a treatise on land law.[1] A tenant's right to exclusive possession gives her far greater power than a contractual licensee. She may keep anyone off the land, and her landlord has no right to put her off the land until the term ends. A tenant may keep even the landlord from entering the land unless she has given the landlord the right to enter for a specific purpose, such as to view the state of repair of the property and to make repairs. The right to exclusive possession of land gives a tenant the ability to acquire other lesser rights — a tenant may acquire an easement over adjoining land for the duration of her tenancy in the same manner as may the holder of a fee simple.

There have been numerous cases about what constitutes exclusive possession. The main problem is whether a person has exclusive possession when under the terms of the lease others are given limited rights to use or access over the land. Thus, if a business contemplates obtaining a lease that reserves to the landlord or other persons the right to make special use of the premises at the same time, it exposes itself to serious risk. It should obtain legal advice about the matter. Generally, it is not wise under the terms of a lease to grant a right for the use of the premises to a third person or the landlord, except that the landlord may be given the right to enter for the limited purpose of inspecting the premises and making repairs.

Definite or Ascertainable Period

A lease must begin on a fixed date, and it must end on a fixed or ascertainable date; the final date need not be stated if the period itself is definite. Thus, a lease that begins on March 1 of a certain year to run for a week, a month, a year, five years, or 500 years is a valid leasehold interest because the date of expiry can always be worked out accurately. If the parties attempt to create a term for an uncertain period, the term is void and no leasehold interest comes into existence. It has been held that a lease "for the duration of the war" or "until the tenant becomes insolvent" is void. However, parties who wish to have a lease of such a nature, can accomplish their purpose by a comparatively simple change in the wording. The requirement of certainty is satisfied if a lease must end *at the latest* upon a certain date, but may be brought to an end *at an earlier date* upon the happening of a particular event. Thus we may have a valid lease from A to B for 100 years that is to be terminated earlier if and when "hostilities between country *X* and country *Y* should formally come to an end", or "should *B* become insolvent". This requirement illustrates the strict formalism that remains part of land law.

CLASSES OF TENANCIES

Term Certain

A term certain is a tenancy that expires on a specific day, the term ending without any further act by either the landlord or the tenant. A lease of a restaurant at a summer resort "from May 24 to September 15" of a particular year or a long-term lease of a cold-storage

---

[1] For example, Burn (ed.) *Cheshire and Burn's Modern Law of Real Property* (14th ed.), pp. 555-75. London: Butterworths, 1988.

plant "from March 1, 1980 to February 29, 1992" are examples of typical commercial leases for a term certain. The tenant is expected to vacate before the end of the last day of the tenancy unless it has made new arrangements with the landlord. If it stays on without making any arrangements, it becomes an *overholding tenant* and may be put out by the landlord. If, however, the landlord accepts further rent without protesting, a new tenancy may be created, as explained below.

Periodic Tenancy

A periodic tenancy is a leasehold interest that renews itself automatically on the last day of the term for a further term of the same duration, unless either the landlord or the tenant serves notice, as discussed later in this chapter, to bring the tenancy to an end. A periodic tenancy may be created by a formal agreement, but in Canada it arises more often in an informal way when a tenant moves into possession and pays an agreed rent to the landlord at regular intervals as agreed between them, either in writing or orally. If, for example, a business pays rent on the first day of each month, the tenancy renews itself for another month without further agreement between the parties. A periodic tenancy also comes into existence when a tenant remains in possession after its tenancy for a term certain has expired, and pays further rent to the landlord. The most common type of periodic tenancies are weekly, monthly, and yearly. The yearly tenancy is often called a *tenancy from year to year.*

We may note here the contrast between a term certain and a periodic tenancy: a term certain ends automatically unless the parties make an arrangement to continue it; a periodic tenancy renews automatically unless either of the parties serves notice to end it. We shall discuss the requirements of notice below, under "Termination and Renewal of a Tenancy".

Tenancy at Will

A tenancy at will is not a true leasehold interest because it does not last for a definite period, nor does the tenant have any right to exclude the landlord and remain on the premises. The tenant is there merely at the landlord's will, and the landlord may demand possession at any time without notice. The tenant does, however, have a reasonable time to gather up possessions and leave.

On the other hand, a tenant at will is under no obligation to remain in possession and pay rent; it may vacate possession at any time without notice. Such a tenancy may exist when the owner of real property allows a prospective purchaser to occupy the premises pending the conveyance of the title to it, or when a landlord permits a tenant to remain on a day-to-day basis pending the wrecking of the building to make way for new construction. A tenancy at will may be gratuitous, or the landlord may exact a payment without turning the arrangement into a leasehold.

Tenancy at Sufferance

A tenancy at sufferance is not a tenancy at all. The typical example is that of an overholding tenant, which entered into possession rightfully under its lease but now stays in possession wrongfully after the term has expired. Since it came into possession lawfully, it is not treated as a *trespasser* unless the landlord orders it to leave and it refuses. (Ordinarily, a trespasser is one who enters without consent or lawful right on the lands of another or who, having entered lawfully, refuses to leave when ordered to do so by the owner.) We should contrast the position of a tenant at sufferance with that of a tenant at will. Although a tenant at will has no estate in the land and can be put out by the landlord, it is nonetheless there lawfully, by agreement. A tenant at sufferance has no agreement with the landlord: its occupation of the land is merely suffered by the landlord until the landlord acts to put it out.

COVENANTS

Payment of Rent

The covenant to pay rent is more easily understood if we remember the nature of a leasehold interest. A leasehold is quite simply a specific period carved out of the fee simple and sold for a fixed sum. Very often leases recognize this fact by stating the total rent to be paid during the whole of the lease, and then setting out how this sum is to be paid. The transaction is similar to an instalment purchase of a chattel. For example, the tenant may promise to pay the sum of $120 000 to lease a suite of offices for five years in 60 monthly instalments of $2000 per month. Thus, when the leasehold is transferred to the tenant, it becomes the holder or owner of that period of five years somewhat like the purchaser of a car on instalments becomes the owner of an interest in the car; each is to pay for the purchase over the succeeding few years.[2] We may carry the analogy further: if the car is destroyed, the buyer must still pay for it. Similarly, if leased premises are destroyed — in the absence of a specific term in the lease dealing with the problem — the tenant is still liable for the rent; it has purchased a leasehold interest consisting of a certain geographically defined area, and must pay for it whether or not the building and amenities continue to exist for the full term. It appears, then, that the doctrine of frustration has no application to commercial leaseholds, with perhaps the exception of leasehold interests above the ground floor in a multi-storey building. If, for example, a ten-storey building burns down, can the landlord insist that a firm on the ninth floor continue to be liable for rent because it could employ a surveyor to show it exactly where its office suite used to be, and so it may still use the space if it wishes? To the present time, there are no decisions on this problem, but probably the tenant would be released from its obligation to pay rent. A leading treatise states:

> If the subject-matter [of a lease] is destroyed entirely, it is submitted that the lease comes automatically to an end....There being no such thing in law as a [lease]...of a volume of space above the surface of the earth... it is submitted that no [lease]...of part of a building without any of the soil upon which the building stands, can survive such a destruction of the building as leaves no physically defined subject matter....[3]

In addition, it is generally the duty of the landlord to provide access to leased premises on upper floors by means of staircases or elevators, and failure to do so might in itself relieve the tenant from liability to pay rent.

---

[2] We shall discuss the nature of a purchaser's interest in an instalment plan purchase in detail in Chapter 33.
[3] Blundell & Wellings, *Woodfall's Law of Landlord and Tenant* (27th ed.), pp. 966-7. London: Sweet & Maxwell Limited, 1968.

When a tenant leases only a portion of the landlord's building, the landlord usually retains control over heating and repairs and maintenance. In these circumstances it is usual to state in the lease that liability to pay rent shall be suspended if the leased premises are substantially destroyed by fire or other cause, and not by the tenant's own negligence. Such a provision is not automatically implied, however, and unless it is expressly stated in the lease, the tenant remains liable for the rent — subject to our discussion above concerning leases of premises above the ground floor.

A tenant's covenant to pay rent is independent of any express promise by the landlord to make repairs to the property, and the tenant is not excused from paying rent on the grounds that the landlord has not performed her part of the bargain. A tenant is not, however, liable for further rent when the acts of the landlord amount to an eviction, as we shall see when we consider the covenants of "repairs" and "quiet enjoyment" below.

The terms of the covenant to pay rent are binding on both parties. During the term, the landlord cannot increase the rent unless express provision has been made, as in the case where the parties agree that the landlord may increase the rent by an amount equal to any increase in property taxes. If the landlord wishes to increase the rent, he cannot do so until the term expires: he may, of course, bargain for an increase in any subsequent lease.

Assignment and Subletting

A tenant may wish to assign the balance of the term of a tenancy before it expires. For example, a firm's business may have become so successful that it requires larger premises, or it may be offered a large sum for goodwill to sell the business as a going concern provided, of course, that it assigns the balance of the lease to the purchaser so that the business may continue at the same location. A tenant, as owner of a leasehold interest, has (subject to the terms of the lease) the right to assign it, just as the owner of a fee simple or a chattel has the right to sell or transfer those forms of property. A tenant does not, however, terminate its contractual obligations to the landlord by assigning: the landlord may still hold it accountable for performance of those obligations if, after the assignment, the assignee does not perform them. For this reason a tenant always makes it a term of the assignment of its tenancy that the assignee shall carry out all of the tenant's covenants in the lease and indemnify it against any loss caused by default in that respect.

A landlord leasing premises is often concerned with the reputation of the tenant as well as with its ability to pay the rent: it may be a matter of prestige, for instance, to have the head office of a large Canadian corporation as a tenant in a new building in order to encourage other prospective tenants of good quality. A landlord may also be concerned about the type of business to be carried on for one or more of several reasons: the prestige or reputation of the building; unprofitable competition with the business of other tenants or with that of the landlord himself — a problem often arising in large business blocks and shopping centres; noise, fumes, or traffic interfering with other tenants; the wear and tear certain businesses may inflict upon the premises. Various combinations of these reasons may determine whether or not a landlord will accept a particular tenant. Yet if a tenant were free subsequently to assign to whomever it pleased it might, by assigning, defeat the landlord's objectives. For this reason, a landlord almost invariably requires a tenant to covenant that it will not assign the lease without leave (permission) from the landlord.

Now, if a landlord were free to grant leave or withhold it as he chose, the tenant might be placed in a difficult position. A landlord could arbitrarily refuse to give consent to an assignment that is in no way harmful to her. Accordingly, tenants often stipulate that the words "but such consent shall not be unreasonably withheld" be added to the covenant. In the provinces of Manitoba, New Brunswick, Ontario, Prince Edward Island, and Saskatchewan, these words are implied by statute as part of the covenant unless they are expressly excluded.[4] It is both harsh and unusual for them to be expressly excluded; a tenant should be cautious about entering into a lease in the provinces mentioned above when the landlord excludes the implied words, or in the other provinces when the landlord refuses to permit the addition of these words to the covenant requiring her consent to an assignment.

A sublease differs from an assignment as follows: an assignment is a transfer of the *whole* of the remainder of the tenant's term to the assignee; so long as the assignee performs all its covenants, the tenant has no further right or interest in the lease. A sublease is a transfer of *part only* of the tenant's term to the subtenant. If the term given the subtenant expires just one day before the expiration of the main lease (leaving the tenant with a reversion of one day), the tenancy of the subtenant is created not by an assignment but by a sublease, and the tenant becomes the landlord of its subtenant. The sublease may differ materially from the main lease in the rent payable, in any of the covenants given by either party, and in the extent of the premises sublet (the subtenant may hold only a portion of the premises leased to the tenant). In a sublease, just as in an assignment, the tenant remains liable to the landlord to perform all the covenants under the main lease. The discussion concerning the requirement of consent of the landlord for assignment applies equally to subleases — the covenant usually refers to subletting as well as to assignment.

Restriction on Use of Premises

We have noted that a landlord is usually concerned with both the reputation of a tenant and the use to which the premises are to be put. Once a landlord has accepted a tenant, she can do nothing about the tenant's manner of conducting its affairs. She may, however, exercise control over the uses that the tenant may make of the premises, for example, by exacting a covenant restricting the use to particular trades. Such covenants are enforceable against the tenant's assignees and subtenants.

A tenant may, of course, be equally interested that the landlord should not rent adjoining premises to a competing business. It often obtains a covenant from the landlord to that effect. If, however, the landlord should commit a breach by renting adjoining premises to an innocent third party unaware of the covenant, the tenant will not be able to take action against the third party. Its remedy will be limited to an action for damages against the landlord.

Even in the absence of an express covenant, there is an implied covenant by the tenant to treat the premises in a tenant-like manner, that is, use them only for those purposes for

---

[4] The right to assign a leasehold interest, when it is subject to consent that may not be unreasonably withheld, is now considered to be a major term of the lease. If a landlord unreasonably withholds consent, his doing so will be a major breach; the tenant may end the relationship by cancelling the lease without further liability: Lehndorff Canadian Pension Properties Ltd. v. Davis Management Ltd. (1989), 59 D.L.R. (4th) 1 (B.C.C.A.)

which they are reasonably intended. Thus, a tenant could not turn a cold-storage plant into a glue factory, or a restaurant into a hotel. In other words, a tenant may be prevented from carrying on activities for which the premises were not intended and which would cause excessive wear and tear.

Fitness for Occupancy

A leading writer on the subject of landlord and tenant, in commenting upon the existence of implied covenants of fitness for leased premises, has said: "One is reminded here of the chapter on the subject of snakes in the treatise on Iceland referred to by Dr. Johnson. Speaking generally, there is no covenant of fitness at all on the part of the lessor. The lessee takes the…premises as he finds them and at his own risk."[5] Until recent years, unless a tenant was given an express covenant in the lease concerning the fitness of the premises for its particular use, or unless the landlord made a misrepresentation, thus giving the tenant the usual remedies in contract and tort for misrepresentation, the tenant was responsible for its own investigation of the premises and had to take them as it found them.[6] However, courts have suggested that the course of dealing between the parties may create an implied covenant that the premises will be fit for the lessee's purposes as disclosed to the lessor, much as the implied condition of fitness arises in a sale of goods.[7]

As we noted in Chapter 14, a landlord is not liable to a tenant or the tenant's customers, family, or guests for injuries caused by the unsafe condition of the premises, unless the landlord was, or ought to have been, aware of the dangerous condition when the lease was entered into and failed to warn the tenant who was unaware of the danger until a mishap occurred. If, however, the landlord covenants to make repairs and the tenant sustains a loss because the landlord fails to do so after receiving notice of the danger, the landlord will be liable for the loss. In all other circumstances the tenant, as the party in exclusive possession of the property, bears any responsibility that arises from injuries caused to persons on the property.

Repairs

As a general rule, a landlord is not liable to make repairs to the property unless she expressly covenants to do so. Quite apart from law, of course, a landlord has an economic incentive to maintain her property in rentable condition. In some circumstances, she may be liable to repair structural defects that develop, particularly if failure to repair would amount to an indirect eviction of the tenant and consequently a breach of the covenant for quiet enjoyment, as we shall see in the next subsection. For example, if the failure of a landlord to repair a leak in the roof of an office building results in the soaking and eventual crumbling of the ceiling and walls in an office suite, the tenant has an action against the landlord even where no covenant to repair has been given. When rented premises are in a large building, the landlord is responsible to the tenants for the maintenance of corridors, stairways, and elevators.

---

[5] Foa, *Outline of the Law of Landlord and Tenant* (4th ed.), p. 71. London: The "Law Times" Office, 1928. (In the book to which Dr. Johnson referred, the chapter on snakes contained one brief sentence: "There are no snakes in Iceland.")

[6] Long before the recent legislation affecting residential tenancies, the courts had made an exception to this common law rule: they held that when a landlord rents premises as a furnished house or furnished apartment, he gives an implied warranty that they will be in a habitable state at the beginning of the lease.

[7] Telex (A/Asia) Proprietary Ltd. v. Thomas Cook & Sons (A/Asia) Proprietary Ltd., [1970] 2 N.S.W.R. 257 (C.A.).

A tenant also is not liable to make repairs to the premises unless it has expressly covenanted to do so. This rule is subject to two exceptions. First, the tenant must not make such use of the premises as will cause excessive wear, as we have already noted. Second, it is liable for committing *waste*. Waste may be either *voluntary* — as when a tenant pulls down part of a building or otherwise damages it, or makes alterations that reduce its value — or *permissive*, that is negligent, as when a tenant is aware of some small damage such as a leak in the roof and realizes that more serious harm will result if it does not correct the problem, and yet neglects to do so. The law concerning permissive waste is complex and rather uncertain, but fortunately of little consequence today, since parties to a lease generally make an express agreement about which of them shall keep the leased premises in good repair.

When a tenant leases an entire building or property, the landlord frequently obtains a covenant from it to keep the property in good repair, reasonable wear and tear excepted. As tenant, it thus agrees to make such repairs as are necessary to keep the property in the same condition as when the lease began, except for normal depreciation. The tenant is not liable for rot caused by faulty construction or for deterioration in the property due to a normal and progressive action of the forces of nature. Unless the lease exempts the tenant, however, the tenant's covenant to repair includes liability to make good any loss by fire or storm. Often a tenant exempts itself from liability in this respect by qualifying the covenant to repair with the words "loss by fire, lightning, and tempest excepted".

When a tenant leases only part of a building, the landlord usually undertakes to provide various services such as heat, water, and elevator service and also to keep the premises in good repair. We should note that there is an important difference between a covenant to repair on the part of the tenant and on the part of the landlord: a tenant is in possession of its premises and should be aware of their falling into disrepair — it is in breach of the covenant the moment it permits the premises to fall into disrepair, and it is not up to the landlord to remind her tenant. The landlord, not being in possession of the tenant's premises, is not presumed to be aware of any state of disrepair in them and her duty to repair does not arise until the tenant gives her notice. A landlord who undertakes to repair the premises often reserves the right to go on the premises at reasonable hours and inspect and view the state of repair. Reserving this right, however, does not place any duty upon her to make inspections or to repair until she has received notice from the tenant.

Quiet Enjoyment

The whole purpose of a tenant in acquiring a lease is to obtain possession and to "enjoy" the premises during the term of the lease. Accordingly, the landlord covenants to give quiet enjoyment either impliedly, simply by granting the lease, or expressly, in a specific covenant for that purpose. The covenant has two aspects: first, it is an assurance against the consequences of the landlord's having a defective title at the time she gives the lease; and second, it is a covenant that the landlord will not, subsequent to the making of the lease, herself interfere, or permit anyone obtaining an interest in land from him to interfere with the tenant's enjoyment of the premises.

(a) Greer owns a large tract of land including certain warehouses. A mining company survey shows valuable ore deposits; she grants the company a long-term mining lease, and the company undertakes extensive mining excavations. Subsequently, she leases the warehouses to Atkins Inc., which wishes to use them to store heavy machinery. Atkins discovers that the mining operations have undermined the foundations of the warehouses, making them unsafe for use. Since the mining company is conducting its activities properly, and Greer cannot prevent its operations because she had validly granted it a mining lease before granting Atkins Inc. its lease, Greer's title was defective; therefore, she committed a breach of her covenant to Atkins Inc. for quiet enjoyment.

(b) Mendoza leases a suite of offices to McAdam and McCollum, a firm of practising accountants. Subsequently, he leases the area on the floor directly above to a machine shop. The machineshop operations create noise and heavy vibrations, making it impossible for the accountants to carry on any aspect of their practice with adequate care. Mendoza is in breach of his covenant.

The courts have held that breach of the covenant of quiet enjoyment requires physical interference with the enjoyment of the premises, and that mere interference with the comfort or convenience of the lessee through some personal annoyance is not in itself sufficient. In an unreported Ontario appeal case[8] a residential tenant argued that his liability for rent had been abrogated by the landlord's default in the covenant for quiet enjoyment. The landlord had made a contract to reroof the apartment and the reroofing had caused considerable temporary disruption to the tenant; in addition, a large pet snake apparently owned by another tenant was allowed to roam over the lawns. The court ruled that at most the tenant would have been entitled to claim for damages, but not to treat the conduct as a breach of the covenant for quiet enjoyment.

Insurance

In the absence of an express provision, neither landlord nor tenant is under a duty to insure the premises for the benefit of the other. In most cases, of course, the landlord will insure the premises to protect her own investment. If the leased property consists of an entire building or group of buildings that pass into the complete control of one tenant, especially if the lease is for a very long term, the rent may be set on the understanding that full responsibility for the premises passes to the tenant and that it will insure them. The question of insurance is closely tied to the problem of what should happen to the tenancy in case of the complete destruction of the premises by fire, flood, or storm. Unfortunately, parties often fail to consider these possibilities very carefully. Failure to make proper provision can lead to great hardship, particularly for the tenant. A lease stating that if the premises are substantially destroyed, the liability to pay rent is suspended until the building is repaired, may not be a benefit to the tenant; indeed, such a clause may place a tenant at the mercy of a capricious or simply undecided landlord. While the landlord decides what to do, the tenant, although not paying rent, is temporarily out of

---

[8]   Greenbranch Investments Ltd. v. Goulborn and Goulborn (November 20, 1972).

business. If it leases premises elsewhere, it may find when the building is repaired that it is liable to pay rent for both locations. A fair term of a lease should state that the repairs must be made within a certain time and that if they are not made within that time, the tenant then has the option of terminating the lease rather than waiting until the premises are restored. A further variation gives the tenant the right to make the repairs itself and deduct the costs from future rent.

The complexity of liability and insurance problems increases when there is a large number of business tenants, each with its own employees, as in a large office building or a shopping mall. Who is liable for the loss if an employee should negligently cause a fire that substantially destroys a mall? Providing insurance protection and allocating risk through the use of exemption clauses requires great expertise.[9]

Provision of Services and Payment of Taxes

Once more, a distinction must be made between tenancies for a whole building and those for a suite or a portion of a building. When a tenancy is for a portion of a building only and the landlord retains control over the building as a whole, it is usual for him to covenant to provide a reasonable amount of heat during the colder months of the year, water, sometimes electric power, and occasionally even telephone service. When the tenancy is for the whole of the building, it is usual for the tenant to provide all these things itself.

Generally, property taxes are paid by the landlord when the tenant leases only a portion of the building. If it leases the whole of the building, the taxes may be paid by either party. As long as the agreement is clear, it is not important who pays: if it is the landlord, the rent is that much higher; if the tenant, then it is that much lower. In the absence of an agreement on the matter it is the landlord's duty to pay the taxes.

$\mathscr{R}$EMEDIES FOR BREACH OF COVENANT

Remedies of the Landlord

Damages and Rent

A landlord may sue for damages caused by a tenant's breach of any covenant other than the covenant to pay rent. The right to recover rent requires further discussion. Suppose, without excuse, that a tenant abandons the premises and pays no further rent. According to long established rules concerning interests in land, the landlord is then in a predicament. On the one hand, by leaving the premises vacant and insisting on her rights under the lease, she can claim the entire rent due under it. But the tenant may be impecunious at the time and unable to pay the full amount due. (In land law, apart from any statutory provisions to the contrary, there is no duty to mitigate damages as there is in contract law.) On the other hand, the landlord may occupy the premises or lease them to another tenant at a lower rent in order to reduce her loss, but she will then be presumed to have accepted the *surrender* by the tenant, freeing it from further obligations to pay rent.

---

[9] See Greenwood Shopping Plaza Ltd. v Beattie, [1980] 2 S.C.R. 228, where employees were held personally liable and could not take advantage of an exemption clause as third parties. The subsequent Supreme Court decision in London Drugs v. Kuehne & Nagel International Ltd. (1992) 97 D.L.R. (4th) 261, appears to overturn, or at least limit, the restrictive view taken in the Greenwood case.

While a lease creates an interest in land, it is also a contract between the parties. The courts could look to the principles of contract law for a solution, but it was not until recently that they conceded this possibility: they now give the landlord a way out by stating that if she wishes both to resume possession and to continue to hold the tenant liable for rent, she must inform the tenant that she regards it to be in breach and will hold it responsible for any loss during the remainder of the tenancy even if she relets the premises to a new tenant at a lower rent. Thus a landlord may now mitigate her losses without losing her rights against the defaulting tenant. But if the landlord chooses not to mitigate, it has become unclear whether the tenant still remains liable for the full rent. To clarify the law with respect *only* to residential tenancies, Ontario and several other provinces amended their landlord and tenant laws, as follows:

> Where a tenant abandons the premises in breach of the tenancy agreement, the landlord's right to damages is subject to the same obligation to mitigate his damages as applies generally under the rule of law relating to breaches of contract.[10]

Does this amendment lead to the implication that no similar rule exists for commercial tenancies? In 1971, the Supreme Court of Canada affirmed the rule that a landlord has no duty to mitigate if she chooses not to do so.[11] However, a number of recent cases have left the law in the area confused, some holding that a landlord is always expected to mitigate losses,[12] and others holding that a landlord need only mitigate if she chooses to sue for damages rather than for rent paid with the premises left empty.[13]

Under the Bankruptcy and Insolvency Act, a landlord has priority over other creditors in the event of the tenant's bankruptcy to the amount of three months' rent in arrears.[14] For rents due in excess of this sum, she ranks only as a general creditor. The purpose of the three months' preference is to encourage landlords to be a little more patient with a defaulting commercial tenant. Inability to pay rent may be only temporary, but eviction will close the business down, probably causing greater hardship to both the tenant and other creditors of the tenant. Provincial landlord and tenant acts recognize the right of a trustee in bankruptcy to repudiate an outstanding lease without further liability or, with proper notice, to continue to use the premises for so long as may serve the purpose of liquidation and to pay rent at the rate specified in the lease.[15]

Eviction

This remedy is sometimes called the landlord's right of re-entry. The right of re-entry for failure to pay rent is a term implied by statute if not expressly included in the lease. The period for which rent must be in arrears before a landlord is entitled to re-enter and evict

---

[10] Residential Tenancy Act, S.B.C. 1984, c. 15, s. 48(5) and (6); Landlord and Tenant Act, S.M. 1987, c. L-70, s. 94; R.S.O. 1990, c. L-7, s. 90.

[11] Highway Properties Ltd. v. Kelly, Douglas & Co. Ltd. (1971), 17 D.L.R. (3d) 710.

[12] See for example, Smith v. Busler, [1988] B.C.J. No. 2793 (B.C.S.C.); Globe Convestra Ltd. v. Vucetic (1990), 15 R.P.R. (2d) 220 (Ont. Gen. Div.)

[13] See, for example, 607190 Ontario Inc. v. First Consolidated Holdings Corp. (1990), 60 O.A.C. 285 (Div. Ct.); Transco Mills Ltd. v. Percan Enterprises Ltd., (1993) B.C.L.R. (2d) 254 (B.C.C.A.).

[14] R.S.C. 1985, c. B-3, s. 136(1)(f), as amended by S.C. 1992, c. 27. In the absence of bankruptcy proceedings, a landlord's priority under provincial legislation is usually greater than three months.

[15] See, for example: Commercial Tenancy Act, R.S.B.C. 1979, c. 54, s. 32; Landlord and Tenant Act, R.S.O. 1990, c. L-7, ss. 38(2) and 39(1); R.S.M. 1987, c. L-70, ss. 46(2) and 47(1).

the tenant varies considerably from province to province and is longer in the case of residential tenancies. Before evicting a tenant in default, the landlord must follow the procedure laid down in the legislation of the province.

Leases often provide that the landlord may re-enter and evict the tenant for breach of any of the other covenants in the lease. Since eviction amounts to a *forfeiture*, that is, to the penalty of forfeiting the remainder of term to the landlord, the court is very reluctant to permit eviction for breach of any covenant other than one relating to payment of rent, use of the property, or assignment of the lease. The court grants relief against forfeitures either under the general principles of equity or under various statutory reliefs found in provincial legislation.[16] Generally speaking, so long as the tenant subsequently makes good its breach, the court will restrain the landlord from evicting it and will declare the lease to be valid under its original terms.

Distress

The landlord has a power of distress or the right to *distrain* for rent; that is, she may seize assets of the tenant found on the premises and sell them to realize arrears of rent. Usually, the landlord authorizes a bailiff to distrain on the property of the tenant. The right to distrain does not arise until the day after the rent is due and a demand for payment has been made. A landlord cannot prevent the tenant from removing goods from the premises even as late as the day the rent is due; she may, however, object if the tenant is clearly removing the goods in order to avoid the landlord's power of distress. If the tenant removes the goods in spite of the landlord's objection or later removes them fraudulently to prevent the landlord from asserting her rights, after the right has arisen, the landlord may follow the goods and have them seized in another location, provided that they have not been sold in the meantime to an innocent purchaser. The time limit within which a landlord may seize goods in this fashion varies from province to province. It should be noted that a landlord cannot exercise the right of eviction and simultaneously or subsequently exercise a right of distress. The right to distrain is limited to situations where the relationship of landlord and tenant still exists.

Certain personal property is exempt from seizure: necessary household furniture, a limited supply of food and fuel, and mechanic's tools. If a landlord by mistake seizes the goods of third parties such as customers or consignors, they must be released later on proof of ownership. The landlord may also seize equipment or appliances, purchased on the instalment plan and not fully paid for, but before selling them she must first pay the balance owing to the seller.[17] A lease may contain a term by which a commercial tenant "contracts out" of its right to exemptions should the landlord distrain for rent; the result, in the words of the Ontario Law Reform Commission, is that "a successful seizure can leave the tenant with nothing but the clothes on his back."[18]

---

[16] Courts of Justice Act, R.S. O. 1990, c. C-43, s. 98; Law and Equity Act, R.S.B.C. 1979, c. 224, s. 21.

[17] The priority of a landlord may be superior to that of a chattel mortgagee, that is, of a different type of secured creditor. Chattel mortgages are discussed in Chapter 33, "Legal Devices for Securing Credit."

[18] *Interim Report on Landlord and Tenant Law Applicable to Residential Tenancies*, p. 14. Toronto: Ontario Law Reform Commission, 1968. We shall see in our discussion below that many of the provinces have now abolished the remedy of distress for residential (though not for commercial) tenancies.

Injunction

If a tenant proposes or has undertaken a use of the premises that would be in breach of a covenant restricting use, the landlord may obtain an injunction ordering the tenant to cease the prohibited use. The landlord may obtain an injunction against certain types of use even when they are not prohibited under the terms of the lease, if they are inconsistent with the general design and ordinary use to which the property would be put. For example, a landlord could obtain an injunction to prevent a house ordinarily used as residential property from being turned into a hospital.[19]

Generally speaking, wherever a landlord may obtain an injunction, she also has the right to re-enter the property and evict the tenant. Which of these remedies she chooses depends largely on the circumstances, and in particular, on whether the lease is an otherwise desirable one from the point of view of the landlord.

Remedies of the Tenant

Damages

A tenant may recover from the landlord for damages arising from breach by the landlord of any of her covenants. A landlord, believing the tenant has committed a breach, may wrongfully infringe the tenant's rights. For instance, she may evict the tenant, mistakenly believing that the tenant was in arrears of rent and had been served with notice. The wrongful eviction by the landlord is a breach of the covenant for quiet enjoyment. Similarly, if a landlord distrains upon more goods than were reasonably necessary to satisfy a claim for arrears of rent, the tenant may recover damages. The landlord or her bailiff, in attempting to distrain upon the goods of the tenant, must not enter the premises illegally, that is by use of force, or the landlord will be subject to an action for damages for trespass. A tenant may thus prevent an exercise of the power of distress by keeping the premises continually locked; but in these circumstances the threat of distress can be a continuing harassment to the tenant.

If a landlord has expressly covenanted to keep the premises in good repair or rebuild if they are destroyed, her failure to do so will be a breach not only of the covenant to repair but also of the covenant for quiet enjoyment.

Injunction

A tenant may also obtain an injunction to restrain a landlord from continuing breach of the covenant of quiet enjoyment. The court will not grant an injunction, however, where it would be futile to do so. Thus, while a court will grant an injunction against a landlord for interfering with quiet enjoyment caused by a continuing nuisance, such as vibrations, noise, or fumes escaping from the landlord's premises, it would not grant an injunction to prevent an activity that had already destroyed the usefulness of the tenant's premises, as where vibration had so damaged the structure that it was condemned as unsafe for occupation. The tenant's remedy would be in vacating the premises and seeking damages.

An important covenant often given by a landlord to a retail tenant is a promise not to lease premises in the same building or shopping centre to a competing business. When a

---

[19]   McCuaig v. Lalonde (1911), 23 O.L.R. 312.

breach occurs, the remedy most often sought by an aggrieved tenant is an injunction restraining the landlord and second tenant from carrying on the competing business.

Termination of the Lease

When a landlord's breach of the covenant of quiet enjoyment has made the premises unfit for the tenant's normal use and occupation, the tenant, in addition to any other remedy, may terminate the lease and vacate the premises. Upon so doing, it ceases to have any further liability to the landlord. The landlord's breach must render the entire premises unfit for the tenant's use, thus amounting to a total eviction, before the tenant obtains this option. If the landlord's interference is only with part of the premises or only a nuisance or inconvenience, rather than amounting to a total eviction, the tenant remains bound to pay the rent and cannot terminate the lease. Its remedies are then an action for damages for the injury suffered and an injunction to restrain further breach. Even in residential tenancies where tenants have been given greater rights than in commercial tenancies, the courts have not supported tenants who collaborated to withhold rent in the face of the landlord's neglect to complete promised amenities in a new apartment building (elevators, garage, parking lots, pool, sauna, laundry room, landscaping and so forth).[20]

TERMINATION AND RENEWAL OF A TENANCY

Surrender

As we noted under "Classes of Tenancies" above, a commercial tenancy for a term certain expires automatically without notice. Although not required by law, a landlord sometimes serves a reminder on the tenant that the lease is about to expire and that it must vacate on the date of expiry. Upon vacating the premises, the tenant surrenders them to the landlord.

A surrender may also take place during the term of a tenancy by agreement between landlord and tenant. The agreement may be express, as when a tenant no longer desires to keep the premises and pays the landlord a sum of money to release it from obligations for the balance of the term. Alternatively, a landlord may bargain for the tenant's surrender of the remainder of its term when the landlord needs vacant possession in order to sell the property or wishes to make substantial alterations or demolish the building. Occasionally, a tenant may abandon the premises without making an agreement to surrender to the landlord. As we have seen, a landlord may, by her conduct, be presumed to have treated an abandonment as a surrender of the premises when she re-rents to another tenant or takes possession of the premises herself to make use of them for her own purposes. It may often be difficult to decide from the circumstances whether the landlord has accepted an abandonment and thus released the tenant from further obligation to pay rent. Since abandonment is usually committed by an impecunious tenant, the landlord's right of action against it often has little practical value.

---

[20] C. Jowell, "Comments — Landlord and tenant relations — rent-withholding in Ontario", (1970) 48 *Can. Bar Rev.* 323 at p. 328, and reference to In the Matter of Vivene Developments Ltd. v. Jack K. Tsuji, an unreported case, transcript, County Court Reporters, Toronto, March, 1969, cited by Jowell.

Forfeiture

In our earlier discussion of the remedies of a landlord, we noted that breach of certain of the tenant's covenants (such as failure to pay rent) would entitle the landlord to evict the tenant and thus impose a forfeiture of the lease. Once such a forfeiture takes place, the relationship of landlord and tenant is terminated. The former tenant has no further obligations under the lease, although it may be liable in damages for any injury suffered by the landlord because of its breach of a covenant before forfeiture. Similarly, if a landlord has attempted to impose forfeiture by improperly evicting the tenant — entitling the tenant to consider its obligations under the lease at an end — the relationship of landlord and tenant is terminated, but the tenant may still maintain an action for damages based on the landlord's breach of covenants.

Termination by Notice to Quit

A periodic tenancy renews itself automatically unless either the landlord or the tenant serves *notice to quit* on the other party, that is, serves notice of an intention to bring the tenancy to an end. Notice to quit served by a tenant is sometimes called notice of intention to vacate. In weekly, monthly, or quarter-yearly tenancies, the length of notice required to bring the tenancy to an end is *one clear period of tenancy*. In other words, one party must give the other notice *on or before the last day of one tenancy period* for the tenancy to come to an end *on the last day of the next period*.

ILLUSTRATION

West Side Corp. rents a small warehouse from Bernstein on a monthly basis, commencing March 1, at a rent of $1250 per month. The following September, West Side buys a warehouse building with possession available on November 1. West Side must serve Bernstein with notice to quit on or before September 30 if it wishes to terminate the tenancy on October 31. October is

then a clear month. If, however, it does not serve notice until after September 30 — say, on October 3 — October is no longer a clear month, and West Side Corp. is not able to terminate the tenancy until November 30, by serving notice to quit any time in October. In these circumstances, November will be the clear month.

The English rule that six clear months' notice is necessary to terminate a yearly tenancy at the end of the first year or any succeeding year of the tenancy applies to commercial leases in all provinces except New Brunswick, Nova Scotia and Prince Edward Island. In these provinces only three clear months' notice is required.

ILLUSTRATION

Bok leases the Greenbrier summer hotel, located in the Muskoka district of Ontario, from O'Brien at a yearly rental of $30 000, commencing April 1, 1988. The yearly tenancy will renew itself automatically each April 1

unless either party gives six clear months' notice before April 1, that is, on or before September 30 of the preceding year. If Bok wishes to vacate the property by March 31, 1992, he must serve notice on or before

ILLUSTRATION (CONTINUED)

September 30, 1991. If he serves notice on October 1, 1991, it is too late; the tenancy will automatically renew itself on April 1, 1992 and continue to March 31, 1993. Thus, the maximum time that may elapse between giving notice and terminating the tenancy may be 18 months less a day, that is from October 1, 1991 to March 31, 1993.

We have already noted that if a tenant remains in possession after the expiration of a term certain, it becomes a tenant at sufferance and may be evicted by the landlord at any time on demand. If, however, the landlord accepts further rent from the tenant, a periodic tenancy then arises on all the terms of the original lease except those repugnant to a periodic tenancy. An example of a repugnant term would be a covenant by the landlord to redecorate the premises every three years during a term certain of 12 years. This covenant would not become part of a subsequent periodic tenancy.

Generally speaking, if a periodic tenancy arises after the expiry of a *term certain expressed in years* (for example, a lease for five years at an annual rental of $8400 payable in instalments of $700 per month), then the periodic tenancy created will be a *yearly tenancy*. If instead the term certain is stated as a *term of months* (say, a lease for eight months at a monthly rent of $700), then the periodic tenancy created will be a *monthly* one; similarly, if the term certain is expressed in terms of weeks or quarter-years, a succeeding periodic tenancy will be weekly or quarter-yearly respectively. The wording used to describe the term in the original lease may be ambiguous and can result in a difficult question of interpretation about whether a succeeding periodic tenancy created by the payment of rent is a yearly, monthly, or weekly tenancy. Suppose, for example, in the original lease a term certain is granted for one and a half years at a monthly rent of $700, and the tenant remains in possession and continues to pay rent after the expiry of the original term. Is the term thus created one expressed in years or months? There has been conflict in the Canadian cases.[21] If such a problem should arise, it is best to seek legal advice at once: if the periodic tenancy following the original lease is held to be a yearly one, it may be impossible for either party unilaterally to bring the tenancy to an end for a period of up to 18 months; whereas if the periodic tenancy is a monthly one, the maximum period of notice would be just under two months.

The above requirements for a valid notice to quit are those that ordinarily apply, but the parties to a lease may agree to vary them to suit their own needs. Thus, landlord and tenant may agree that some period less than six months, say two months, is sufficient notice for either party to terminate a yearly tenancy. Similar variations may be agreed upon for any type of tenancy.

Renewal

A lease for a term certain, particularly a lease of premises for a retail store, often provides for a renewal at the option of the tenant. The reason a prospective tenant asks for such an option makes good business sense: in taking the risk of operating a retail outlet in a particular area, it may not want to be burdened with a long-term lease for fear that the venture

---

[21] See Williams and Rhodes, *The Canadian Law of Landlord and Tenant* (6th ed.), pp. 4:11-13. Toronto: The Carswell Company Limited, 1988.

may prove unprofitable. On the other hand, if it takes only a short-term lease and the venture proves to be a success, it cannot count on successfully negotiating for a new lease at the expiry of the original lease. An option permits it to terminate the tenancy at the end of the original lease if it does not wish to continue, yet it has the security of exercising the option if business proves successful. A typical option arrangement would be an initial lease for three or perhaps five years, with an option for a further five or ten years. Landlords are usually quite willing to grant options provided they receive some protection against inflation and sufficient notice to obtain a new tenant if the option is not exercised.

The various forms of protection a landlord may seek are numerous. In general, a landlord will require that the rent in any renewal be increased by the amount of any increase in taxes that occurs during the original lease, and sometimes will also require either a fixed increase in rent or a series of percentage increases at various intervals during the term of the renewal, commonly tied to the consumer price index or some other measure of the rate of inflation. A landlord will usually require notice of at least three months from the tenant that it intends to exercise the option, and probably six months if the renewal is for a long period, such as ten years.

Fixtures

As we noted in Chapter 26 in our introduction to real property, land includes everything fixed to it. Trees, fences, and buildings form part of the land, but they are distinguished from the land itself in that they are called fixtures. Technically, then, an oil derrick, a grain elevator, a stand of timber, and a large office building are all fixtures, although in the everyday language of business they are not commonly called fixtures. An object that is affixed to a fixture (such as a furnace installed in a building) is itself a fixture. It is in this more restricted sense that the word is commonly used, and may become the source of disagreement.

Whether an object is held to be a fixture may determine who is its owner. Generally, an object permanently affixed to a building becomes a part of the building and of the real property itself. In a sale of land the vendor cannot remove fixtures that were attached at the time of the contract of sale; they belong to the purchaser. Similarly, because fixtures belong to the landlord a tenant cannot remove them. The question of what is or is not a fixture does not often arise in a sale of land: usually the purchaser and vendor agree between them what fixtures remain with the land; if the vendor wishes to take certain fixtures away, it expressly reserves that right in the agreement of sale and the sale price may be adjusted accordingly. In landlord and tenant, however, a problem may arise *after* the lease begins: the tenant may attach objects to the premises for its own benefit without any agreement with the landlord. The question then arises whether it may take them away when it vacates the premises.

The result would be very harsh if a tenant temporarily attached very valuable objects to the building, unaware of the consequences of so doing, and later discovered it could not remove them under any circumstances; and the landlord might well reap an unjust benefit. Understandably, the law has developed more flexible rules in these circumstances than in a sale of land. To apply the rules we must decide, first, whether the object has become a fixture and, second, if it has, whether it belongs to those classes of fixtures that may be removed by a tenant.

To determine whether an object has become a fixture, we may ask a number of questions. Has the object been fastened to the building with the intention that it become a fixture? What use is to be made of it? How securely and permanently is it attached? How much damage, if any, will be caused to the building by its removal? A picture hanging on a hook in the wall is quite obviously not attached. A partition nailed and bolted to the walls of the building is quite clearly a fixture. But what would we conclude about: a table that has been bolted to the floor to prevent delicate machinery on it from being jarred; machinery bolted to the floor to prevent vibration; a display stand tacked to a wall so that it will not topple over; a neon sign held in place by guy wires bolted to the roof of the building? Ordinarily, objects not bolted or anchored in any way but merely resting on their own weight are presumed not to be fixtures. Objects affixed even comparatively flimsily create a presumption that they are fixtures, although this presumption may be rebutted by asking what a reasonable person would intend when attaching the object, for instance the display stand mentioned above. When objects are held not to be fixtures they may be removed by the tenant at any time. If the tenant should inadvertently forget to remove them from the premises when the lease expires, they still remain the property of the tenant, and may be claimed afterwards.

Even when it is decided that an object was affixed in such a manner that it has become a fixture, the tenant may still have the right to remove it if it can show either (a) that it was attached for the convenience of the tenant or for the better enjoyment of the object, as when it is purely ornamental, or (b) that it was a *trade fixture*, that is, an article brought onto the premises for the purpose of carrying on some trade or business, including manufacturing. Both these classes of fixtures are commonly called *tenant's fixtures*. A tenant may remove them before the end of its tenancy, provided that in doing so it does not cause permanent damage to the structure of the building and it repairs what damage is done. If, however, a tenant leaves without removing its fixtures and the term expires, they are presumed to become part of the premises and the property of the landlord. We might add that tenant's fixtures include only those fixtures brought onto the premises by the tenant itself. Fixtures installed by the landlord or left by preceding tenants are the landlord's property from the time of installation or from the beginning of the tenancy, and may not be removed.

From the above discussion, we should conclude that it is difficult to state precise and predictable tests to determine in every circumstance whether objects attached to the premises by a tenant remain its property or become a part of the building. The problem can often be avoided in advance by making an express agreement concerning fixtures. If the parties expressly agree that a particular object, that would otherwise undoubtedly be a fixture, is to remain the property of the tenant, the agreement is conclusive: a difficult decision based on implications arising from the facts will never have to be made. It is, of course, wise to make such an agreement in writing.

ORAL LEASES

When a tenant is in possession under a short-term lease of three years or less, the lease need not be in writing in order to satisfy the Statute of Frauds in most jurisdictions, although, of course, a written lease is wise in any event.[22] Leases of longer than three years are usually unenforceable if they are not in writing. If, for example, a tenant enters into an oral lease for five years and the landlord later changes his mind and refuses to let the tenant into possession, the tenant is without remedy. If, however, the tenant is already in possession and has paid rent, the doctrine of part performance as discussed in Chapter 12 under the Statute of Frauds will apply; under the rules of equity the court will order the landlord to give the tenant its lease in the terms originally agreed between them. A landlord too may obtain specific performance and hold the tenant bound to a long-term lease if, after taking possession, the tenant should wish to avoid the lease and vacate the premises.

TRANSFER OF THE LANDLORD'S INTEREST

As we noted at the beginning of this chapter, a landlord grants away a present right to possession of his land for a term and reserves to himself the right to possession at the end of the term, that is, the reversion. He also receives the benefit of the tenant's covenants. When a landlord sells land subject to a lease, he parts with both the reversion and the benefits of the covenants given by the tenant. Accordingly, a purchaser acquires the whole interest in the land subject to the outstanding lease, and succeeds to both the rights and duties of the former landlord. We may well ask, "How can a purchaser receive both the rights and duties of the landlord when the tenant was not a party to the sale and there is no privity of contract between purchaser and tenant?" The answer is that between the tenant and the new landlord who has purchased the reversion there is *privity of estate*. The doctrine of privity of estate is much older than the doctrine of privity of contract. It dates from feudal times, from the relationship between lord and vassal. Although the archaic aspects of this doctrine have been abolished, privity of estate between a new landlord and the tenant has been retained and is eminently sensible: neither landlord nor tenant can destroy the stability of the relationship by claiming that the original contract of lease does not bind them. Their respective interests in the land create the relationship between them.

The creation of privity of estate with a new landlord does not bring to an end privity of contract with the former landlord. Although a landlord may sell his reversion, he still remains personally liable on his covenants to his tenant, in particular the covenant for quiet enjoyment. Thus, if the new landlord should interfere with the covenant for quiet enjoyment in an irreparable manner, the tenant, if it chose, could sue the original landlord in contract. It might well have to do this if the new landlord had subsequently become insolvent or had little in the way of assets. The doctrine of privity of estate is a concept of real property and does not apply to personal property, with the possible exception of ships.[23]

---

22. The enforceability of oral short-term leases may depend upon the amount of rent to be paid. See, for example: Statute of Frauds, R.S.O. 1990, c. S-19, s. 3, and R.S.N.S. 1989, c. 442, s. 3; Carter v. Irving Oil Co. [1952] 4 D.L.R. 128, per MacDonald, J., at 131; Williams and Rhodes, *The Canadian Law of Landlord and Tenant* (6th ed.), pp. 2:1-2.

23. See Lord Strathcona Steamship Co. v. Dominion Coal Co., [1926] A.C. 108; Port Line Ltd. v. Ben Line Steamers Ltd., [1958] 2 Q.B. 146. See also "Contracts Concerning Land" in Chapter 14 under "Exceptions to the Privity of Contract Rule".

The leasehold estate acquired by a tenant, like other interests in real property, is valid against parties that subsequently acquire an interest in the land. Thus, if after leasing his land the landlord borrows against it under a mortgage, the mortgagee's (that is, the creditor's) title will be subject to the rights of the tenant. In the event of default by the mortgagor (the landlord-borrower) the mortgagee may claim the reversion, but is not entitled to evict the tenant. So long as the tenant observes the terms of the lease, the mortgagee is bound by it and cannot obtain possession except as provided under the lease. On the other hand, if a tenant obtains a leasehold interest in property already mortgaged — unless the mortgagee concurred in the lease at the time it was given — the tenant is, in theory at least, at the mercy of the mortgagee in the event that the landlord defaults. However, the best interest of the mortgagee will almost always be to collect the rent rather than put the tenant out and try to obtain a new tenant. The risk to a tenant is greater if the lease is a long-term one, and at the time of default the value of the premises for leasing purposes has increased substantially beyond the current rent. For this reason, it is wise for a tenant to obtain the concurrence of the mortgagee before entering into a long-term lease.

To protect its interest, a tenant should register a long-term lease in the land registry office. Otherwise the interest may be destroyed if the landlord fraudulently sells to a bona fide purchaser who has no notice of the tenancy. The need for registration varies from province to province. In some provinces, leases as short as three years must be registered, while in others, only leases over seven years need be. Leases under three years need not be registered in any province.

LEASEBACKS

In Great Britain, it has long been common practice for the owner of a fee simple to grant a long-term lease and retain the reversion, whereas in similar circumstances in North America he would sell the fee simple outright. Several factors have contributed to this difference, but perhaps the main one is the strictly limited amount of land available in Great Britain and the significance accordingly attached to retaining the ultimate reversion. In North America, where until recently land has been relatively cheap and almost unlimited, it has not been valued so highly. In England, leases for 21 years, 49 years, or 99 years are very common, and sometimes leases for as long as 999 years are granted. For practical purposes, the longer the term of the lease, the more the position of the tenant approximates that of an owner in fee simple: only the remote reversionary interest of the landlord or his heirs and the regular payment of rent serve to remind the tenant of its status.

In North America, the supply of land no longer appears limitless; particularly is this so in and around large cities. A lease is a flexible and adaptable tool of finance, especially to the investor desiring a secure, long-term income. For these reasons, the use of relatively long-term leases of commercial properties has grown rapidly throughout North America. An established company with a good record of earnings is often able to arrange with a financial institution, usually an insurance company, to finance its acquisition of a new building by a long-term leasing device known as a *leaseback*, which forms part of a larger transaction. The business and the insurance company arrange the entire transaction in advance. First, the business obtains a short-term loan, usually from a bank, to finance construction of the building. As soon as the building is completed, the business sells it to

(financial institution)

the insurance company and pays off its bank loan. The insurance company then leases the building back to the business. The lease is usually for a period of 20 or 25 years, with the lessee business receiving an option to renew for two or three additional five-year periods. The lessee business acts very much as the owner of the property rather than as a tenant, paying for all repairs, maintenance, insurance, and property taxes during the currency of the lease.

The leaseback device has several advantages for the lessee business. First, the business need not go through the relatively more expensive and elaborate procedure of issuing securities in the capital market as a means of financing its expansion. The arrangements for a leaseback are relatively simple, once a willing financial institution is found to undertake the project. Second, a leaseback may be more advantageous than buying the property and mortgaging it, because a mortgagee will not generally provide the full value of the project, leaving the company to raise the balance, whereas under a leaseback a financial institution provides the whole amount required. Third, the lessee business may be able to claim a larger deduction for expenses in computing its taxable income than it could claim as capital cost allowance and interest on borrowed funds, had it purchased the building instead and financed it by a bond issue or a mortgage.

From the point of view of a lessor financial institution, rented property represents an investment of funds which, in addition to providing regular rental revenue that includes the amortization of the cost of the property, also gives the lessor the reversionary interest and possession of the entire property at the expiration of the lease. In addition, if the lessee business gets into financial difficulty, the legal formalities in evicting it are simpler and quicker than for a mortgagee foreclosing on a mortgage. This advantage is seldom a major concern, however, since the leasebacks are confined in practice to large businesses with good earning records. Under leasebacks, any improvements in the building constructed by the tenant and any inflation in land values accrue to the benefit of the landlord at the expiration of the lease.

Sometimes a leaseback includes an option for the lessee business to purchase the premises at the end of the term or the last renewal of the term. The price at which the option may be exercised by the lessee may be determined in a variety of ways; it may be simply a specified sum of money, or it may be calculated by a formula taking into account, for example, whether the option is exercised at the end of the original term or the end of a renewal.

The leaseback, as compared with other leases, is a relatively long, detailed, and complex document, often carefully setting out the rights a tenant has in making alterations and adding fixtures to the building, as well as in the types of trade it may carry on. Sometimes the lessor may impose restrictions on the future borrowing of the lessee business, as a means of insuring that it will not enter into obligations so great as to impair its ability to pay the rent.

RESIDENTIAL TENANCIES

Since 1969, most provinces have enacted legislation that reflects the changing attitude in Canada toward housing. Rapid urbanization since World War II has caused Canadian cities to grow very quickly and has raised dramatically the cost of buying housing. The cities have also attracted the vast majority of immigrants as well as Canadians from declining rural areas. Much of this influx has been met by rental accommodation, especially in high-rise apartment buildings, as the newcomers to the cities have not had adequate capital to invest in the purchase of private homes. The typical city tenant now lives in a large apartment complex, knows few of his neighbours and is remote from his corporate landlord. He has come to regard himself as a consumer of housing and to think of his relation with his landlord as based on a contract for services rather than an acquisition of an estate in land. The new legislation reflects this view by repealing a number of the rules of landlord and tenant law that differ from the rules of contract law. Generally, it limits a landlord's remedies to the provisions of the statute. It does so, however, only for residential tenancies, and does not affect the leasing of premises for business purposes. We shall briefly review major changes in residential tenancy law.

The landlord in a residential tenancy is prohibited from requiring any security deposit in excess of one month's rent, and even that sum may only be applied to the payment of rent for the last rent period under the tenancy agreement; the landlord must also pay interest on the amount of the deposit at a specified rate.[24] Formerly, landlords used security deposits to reimburse themselves for damage to the premises during a tenancy agreement; and if a landlord refused to return any or all of the deposit the burden lay with the tenant to sue for it. While the abolition of security deposits removes the landlord's advantage, the benefit may be illusory in a time of chronic housing shortages. Landlords may simply raise their rent by an amount adequate to cover the risks met formerly by security deposits.

The amending legislation has abolished the landlord's remedy of distress.[25] This change was made in response to criticism by the Ontario Law Reform Commission, which described distress as "an extra-judicial remedy for the recovery of rent", and complained that in many leases a tenant was required to waive his usual rights to retain necessary goods against an exercise of this remedy.[26]

The doctrine of frustration is now declared to apply to residential tenancies.[27] It replaces the common law rule that a contract for a leasehold estate in land contained an absolute promise by the tenant to pay rent and keep the property in repair; as we noted in Chapter 15, a tenant was liable to pay rent for the balance of the term even when the premises became uninhabitable through no fault of his own, and also to restore the property if it was destroyed for any reason during the tenancy. It should be noted, however, that this requirement for restoration of the property was customarily expressly excluded in leases in multi-storey buildings.

Several other changes complement the recognition of the possibility of frustration. Formerly, the failure of a landlord to perform its own covenants, even if they were major terms, did not release the tenant from the obligation to pay rent unless the landlord's breach amounted to an eviction of the tenant. The new legislation makes a number of promises or covenants in a residential lease interdependent, so that breach by one party

---

[24] The Landlord and Tenant Act, R.S.O. 1990, c. L-7, s. 82. The protection afforded tenants with respect to security deposits varies considerably from province to province. See, for example: Residential Tenancy Act, S.B.C. 1984, c. 15, ss. 15-17; R.S.N.S. 1989, c. 401, s. 12 as amended, S.N.S. 1992, c. 27.

[25] S.B.C. 1984, c. 15, s. 48(1); S.M. 1987, c. L-70, s. 88; R.S.O. 1990, c. L-7, s. 84.

[26] See *Interim Report on Landlord and Tenant Law Applicable to Residential Tenancies*, Chapter 2, Ontario Law Reform Commission, 1968, and preceding discussion in this chapter under "Remedies of the Landlord".

[27] S.B.C. 1984, c. 15, s. 46 (2); S.M. 1987, c. L-70, s. 90; R.S.O. 1990, c. L-7, c. 86.

of a condition entitles the other to regard himself as freed from his own obligations.[28] We have already noted that when a tenant wrongfully breaks his lease by abandoning his residence and failing to pay the rent, the landlord's right to damages is subject to an obligation to mitigate damages by re-renting the property as quickly as she reasonably can. In addition, a landlord may not arbitrarily or unreasonably withhold consent to an assignment or subletting.[29]

The legislation makes the landlord liable for maintaining residential premises in a good state of repair fit for habitation, and states that the tenant's knowledge of the lack of repair before the lease is irrelevant.[30] Formerly, a residential tenant was deemed to have accepted the property in its state at the time of entering into the lease. The landlord had no liability for repairs or injury caused even by hidden dangers about which the tenant could not reasonably have known: the landlord was liable for repairs only when renting furnished premises.

The legislation also makes provision for any local municipality to establish a residential landlord and tenant advisory bureau to receive complaints and mediate or arbitrate disputes between the parties.[31]

Finally, termination by notice to quit has been changed to require notice even for a term certain tenancy that would otherwise end without any act by either landlord or tenant.[32] In the absence of notice to quit, a tenancy is deemed to continue as a periodic tenancy. In addition, the notice has been lengthened in some provinces. In Ontario, probably because the shortage of rental accommodation in the large cities is so widespread, legislative protection of tenants is highest. All tenancies other than weekly tenancies require at least 60 clear days' notice prior to the termination date[33] and weekly tenancies require 28 days, on the part of both landlord and tenant.[34] Landlords are precluded from terminating tenancies and evicting tenants[35] except for a serious breach of the lease by a tenant; or because at the end of the current lease the landlord wishes to repossess the premises for occupation by himself or his immediate family; or because the premises are going to be torn down or substantially altered in order to be used for different purposes such as conversion to commercial premises.[36]

Questions for Review

1. Define lessor; leasehold estate; reversion; power of distress; fixture; overholding tenant; leaseback; forfeiture.
2. What is the significance of the statement that a landlord's promise to make repairs is independent of the tenant's promise to pay rent?

---

[28]   S.B.C. 1984, c. 15, s. 49; R.S.O. 1990, c. L-7, ss. 87 and 94; S.M. 1987, c. L-70, ss. 91 and 98.
[29]   S.B.C. 1984, c. 15, s. 12(2); S.M. 1987, c. L-70, ss. 82 and 93.
[30]   S.B.C. 1984, c. 15, s. 8; S.M. 1987, c. L-70, s. 98.
[31]   S.B.C. 1984, c. 15, Part 7; R.S.M. 1987, c. L-70, s. 85; R.S.O. 1990, c. L-7, s. 124.
[32]   For example: R.S.O. 1990, c. L-7, ss. 101 and 102; S.B.C. 1984, c. 15, s. 27(2).
[33]   R.S.O. 1990, c. L-7, ss. 99-102.
[34]   *Ibid.*, s. 98. See also R.S.N.S. 1989, c. 401, s. 10(1)(c) as amended, S.N.S. 1992, c. 27. Nova Scotia requires the landlord to give four weeks' notice but the tenant need give only one week's notice.
[35]   S.B.C. 1984, c. 15, s. 27; R.S.O. 1990, c. L-7, ss. 107(1) and 110(3).
[36]   S.B.C. 1984, c. 15, s. 29(4) and R.S.O. 1990, c. L-7, s. 105. Both require 120 days' notice in case of demolition but in any event not before expiration of the current lease. In Ontario, notice of forfeiture is required under s. 106 even for non-payment of rent.

3. Should a leasehold interest be shown as an asset (with an equal and offsetting liability) on the balance sheet of a business? If so, at what amount?
4. What are the two elements of the landlord's covenant to provide the tenant with quiet enjoyment of the premises?
5. Give an example of a tenancy for a term certain and of a periodic tenancy.
6. What is the importance of determining whether a periodic tenancy is weekly, monthly, or yearly?
7. Distinguish between an assignment and a subletting.
8. By what term do we describe the relationship between a purchaser of the landlord's interest and the tenant?
9. Gunz obtains a lease of a warehouse for a term certain of five years. During the term of the lease the landlord, Brown, mortgages the land to Sweetwater Mortgage Company. At the expiration of the lease Gunz and Brown enter into another lease for a further five years. Is there any difference in the position of Gunz during the first term and the second term insofar as the mortgage is concerned?
10. What remedies may a landlord have when a tenant is in breach of a covenant that restricts the use of the premises?
11. In what way may a tenant be in a difficult position when the premises burn down, even if the lease states that the rent is suspended until the premises are rebuilt?
12. What difference usually occurs in a covenant to provide services when a tenant rents the whole of a building rather than only a portion of it?
13. What alternatives are available to a tenant under a lease for a term certain when it finds it is not able to use the premises for the full term?
14. Which of the covenants usually found in a lease are given exclusively by the tenant? exclusively by the landlord? by either party?
15. What two essentials must be satisfied for the successful creation of a leasehold interest? In what ways may a would-be tenant be prejudiced if it does not succeed in acquiring a leasehold interest?
16. What incident in the relation of landlord and tenant distinguishes a tenancy at sufferance from a periodic tenancy?
17. If a tenant wrongfully vacates the premises before the expiration of the lease, is it always liable for rent for the balance of the term? Does it matter whether the tenancy is residential or commercial?
18. Outline the arguments for and against the landlord's right to distrain for rent.
19. What public policy underlies a distinction between residential and commercial tenancies?

Problems

Problem 1

Ms. Bone, the owner of a downtown block of stores, rented one of them to Mr. Bull, who opened a retail china shop on the premises. Bull's tenancy was from year to year. He had a number of display cases built with glass doors to keep their fragile contents out of the reach of curious customers. The cases were secured to the wall by one-inch nails. Bull also purchased and installed heavy-duty air-conditioning equipment, which was connected to the water supply and anchored to the floor.

Several years later, Bull was adjudged bankrupt on a petition of his creditors. At the time he owed Bone $3600 for three months' rent. The trustee in bankruptcy remained in possession of the store pending liquidation of the business assets. The trustee claimed the display cases and air-conditioner for the benefit of Bull's general creditors, but Bone claimed them as lessor of the store.

Discuss the respective rights of Bone and of the trustee in bankruptcy.

Problem 2

Kruger leased a warehouse to Pool Co. Ltd. for a term certain of eight months at a rent of $3000 per month, commencing January 1 and expiring August 31. Pool did not move out on August 31 and tendered its cheque for $3000 to pay the rent for September. It was accepted by Kruger. On October 1, Pool's manager appeared at Kruger's office with another cheque for $3000. Kruger said he had inspected the warehouse and was disappointed by the rough treatment the building was receiving from Pool's employees. When the manager replied that he could hardly expect otherwise in a busy operation, Kruger stated it was not worth his while to rent it under those conditions unless he received at least $4000 per month. The manager refused to pay that much and tendered the company's cheque for $3000. Kruger refused the cheque and ordered Pool to "clear out of the warehouse at once". The manager left and mailed the cheque to Kruger, who simply held it and did not cash it. On November 1, Kruger called Pool by telephone and asked if the company would pay $4000. The manager replied, "No." Kruger said that he was at the end of his patience and had given Pool a full month to change its mind. He sent a bailiff to evict Pool that very day, cashed its cheque for the previous month, and sent it a demand for "the $1000 still owing".

Pool was forced to move its stock to a more expensive warehouse at once and suffered some damage to its goods when they were moved into the street by the bailiff. It sued Kruger for losses of $8000 caused by the eviction. Should it succeed? Give reasons for your opinion.

Problem 3

Horner agreed orally to rent part of a building from Saxe to operate a retail music store. The only terms discussed by the parties were that the rent would be $1500 per month and that Horner could have possession on May 1. When Horner first inspected the property she commented that the plaster on the ceiling appeared to be in a dangerous condition. Saxe assured her that it had been that way for some time "without anything happening".

In September of the same year, a customer in Horner's store was injured by falling plaster. He sued Horner and was awarded damages of $7500. Horner refused to pay further rent to Saxe until the damages were made up to her, claiming that the premises had been in a dangerous condition at the time she rented them and that she had drawn this condition to Saxe's attention.

Two months later Saxe sued Horner for $3000 arrears of rent. Horner counterclaimed for damages of $7500. Discuss the probable outcome of this action. Does it matter that the parties never expressly agreed upon any specific length of term for the lease?

Problem 4

Three years ago, Kazakis leased a farm from a widow, Mrs. Barnsworthy, under a fifteen-year lease. While tilling a new field that he had just brought under cultivation with a great deal of hard work, Kazakis's plough struck an object that on examination and careful extraction proved to be an ancient boat built by prehistoric inhabitants of the area, of considerable archeological interest and value. A large metropolitan museum offered him $10 000 for it. At this point Mrs. Barnsworthy intervened, insisting she was entitled to the money, and the museum refused to proceed with the purchase until the two parties could settle the matter. Which of them should be entitled to the money, and why?

Problem 5

Upp and Adam, the owners of a chain of variety stores, submitted to Carnival Shopping Centre Ltd. a signed offer to lease space in the Carnival's shopping centre. The offer stated that the lease should contain a clause protecting the variety store against competition in the shopping centre, should provide for expansion of its warehouse, and should contain all those clauses "to be found in the usual form of shopping centre leases". The general manager of Carnival accepted by adding his signature to the document.

In the months following the signing of the agreement, the parties had many discussions about the amount of warehouse space that would be made available and the rent that would be charged for it. Finally, some six months after the offer was signed, the solicitor for Carnival sent a form of lease to Upp and Adam for them to sign. They replied that they did not wish to proceed with the lease. Carnival sued them for breach of contract.

Should this action succeed? (See *Causeway Shopping Centre Ltd. v. Thompson & Sutherland Ltd.* (1965) 50 D.L.R. (2d) 362; *Friesen v. Braun* [1950] 2 D.L.R. 250.)

Cases

Case 1

John Perini purchased a house and then called on his widowed daughter-in-law, whom he admired, and said, "Mary, I want you to look at the house I have bought for you. You won't have to worry about rent any more." Mary was very pleased, and moved into the house with her children within a few days. During the first three years after he purchased the house, Perini frequently visited his daughter-in-law and grandchildren in the house but then moved into a senior citizens' home where, except for a few special family occasions at the house, they came to visit him.

Perini died fourteen years after he had purchased the house. Mary had always paid the municipal taxes and looked after the house but paid no rent to her father-in-law. Perini regularly paid the fire insurance premiums himself under a policy that specified that any claims would be paid to him as the insured. He never conveyed the title to Mary, apparently because he had once bought a house for another member of his family who had soon after sold it, wasted the proceeds, and returned to him destitute, asking for money.

An officer of the trust company that was executor for Perini's estate found the duplicate copy of the deed in Perini's name, among his papers. The executor then claimed the house from Mary as part of the Perini estate to be given to other beneficiaries under the will. Mary did not understand the legal arrangements; she could only state that she believed the house had been bought in her name and that she had lived in it continuously from the time of its purchase. She needed the house for her family and resisted the executor's demand. The trust company, as executor for the estate, sued her for possession of the property.

During the trial the court was referred to the Limitations Act of the province. The sections referred to read in part as follows:

4. No person shall make entry...or bring an action to recover any land or rent, but within ten years next after the time at which the right to make such entry... or to bring such action ...first accrued to the person making or bringing it.

5. Where a person is in possession...as tenant at will, the right of the person entitled subject thereto...to make an entry...or to bring an action to recover the land or rent shall be deemed to have first accrued either at the determination of the tenancy, or at the expiration of one year after the commencement of the tenancy, at which time the tenancy shall be deemed to have determined.

8. No person shall be deemed to have been in possession of any land within the meaning of this Act merely by reason of having made an entry thereon.

Express an opinion, with reasons, about the probable outcome of this action.

Case 2

Frost Investments Limited owned three adjoining buildings downtown that it rented to various tenants as office space. All three buildings were heated centrally from a single heating plant in Building No. 1. The Generous Loan Company occupied offices in Building No. 3 under a lease in which the lessor, Frost, covenanted to maintain the heat continuously above 60 degrees from October 1 to May 24, except for weekends. In January a serious fire occurred in Building No. 2 breaking the heating connections between Buildings No. 1 and No. 3. The damage was so serious that Frost decided to demolish Building No. 2 and rebuild.

In the meantime, Generous Loan Company suffered a significant drop in business because of temperatures well below 60 degrees in its offices. It eventually vacated the premises and leased other quarters at a higher rent. It then sued Frost claiming damages of $1750 for the additional amount of rent it had to pay the new landlord for what otherwise would have been the balance of the term of its lease with Frost, and $6000 for its estimated loss of profits. Frost counterclaimed for rent for the balance of the term of the lease, seven months at $2150 per month. What do you think the decision should be?

Case 3

Tagom rented a service station from Oil Can Limited for a term of 12 months commencing July 1, at a rent of $975 per month payable on the first day of each month. The lease contained the following clause:

> If the lessee shall hold over after the term...the resulting tenancy shall be a tenancy from month to month and not a tenancy from year to year, subject to all the terms, conditions and agreements herein contained insofar as same may be applicable to a tenancy from month to month.

On May 28 of the following year, Oil Can sent Tagom a notice stating that he must give vacant possession on the expiry of the lease. On June 30, Oil Can representatives visited Tagom and asked him what he intended to do. He replied that he would not leave the premises "peacefully". Tagom remained in possession on July 1, and sent a cheque by registered mail to Oil Can as rent for that month. Although the area superintendent had given instructions to the accounting department not to accept any rent from Tagom, a junior clerk deposited it in the company bank account. Soon afterwards, a senior officer discovered the error, informed Tagom that the act of the clerk in accepting the cheque had been inadvertent and against instructions, and delivered a refund cheque from the company to Tagom for $975. Tagom returned the cheque.

Was a new tenancy created or could Oil Can obtain a court order for immediate possession? (See *Imperial Oil Ltd. v. Robertson* (1960) 21 D.L.R. (2d) 535.)

CHAPTER 28

MORTGAGES OF LAND

THE CONCEPT OF THE MORTGAGE

The history of the word "mortgage" helps us to understand its meaning. Mortgage is derived from the Norman French words *mort*, meaning dead or passive, and *gage*, meaning pledge. In the Middle Ages the Church condemned the lending of money for interest as the sin of usury. Nevertheless, even in a simple economy some form of credit was often needed, and people simply would not lend money and assume the risk that it might not be repaid unless they received some benefit for taking the risk. To evade the usury laws an individual would lend money on the condition that the borrower would pledge his land as security. The lender would actually take possession of the borrower's land (a *"live"* gage rather than a mortgage) and retain it until the loan was repaid. Meanwhile he would be entitled to keep any of the crops or rents earned from the land. These benefits derived from the land would be the equivalent of interest, but since the lender was in possession he was considered to be entitled to the benefits: the courts did not consider the transaction usurious. If the borrower did not repay the debt on the appointed day, he lost all right to claim his land — it became the land of the lender absolutely.

This ancient form of live gage was very cumbersome, first because it meant that the borrower had to give up possession of his land (the best means he might have of earning the money for repayment), and second because the lender had to take possession in order to obtain the benefits (an arrangement that might be inconvenient or impossible for him). As England grew commercially, so did the need for more sophisticated means of obtaining credit; the law changed to meet these needs. Eventually, the lender was permitted to exact interest on the loan without going into possession, that is, to take his security as a *mort* gage.[1] He had a right to the interest as well as to the principal sum as a debt owed by the borrower. The lender retained the right to go into possession and take the land absolutely upon default by the borrower. This latter right, the right to take the land absolutely, was the cause of the main development in the law of mortgages.

THE DEVELOPMENT OF MORTGAGE LAW

Harshness of the Common Law

Under the common law, a mortgage is a conveyance of an interest in land (usually the fee simple) by the *mortgagor* (the borrower) to the *mortgagee* (the lender) as security for a debt, with a condition that if the debt is repaid by an appointed day the conveyance becomes void and the interest in the land reverts to the mortgagor. If the appointed day passes without the debt being repaid, the condition then expires, and the mortgagee owns the interest absolutely. The common law courts construed the condition strictly: if a mortgagor was delayed by a storm or by illness and arrived with the money the day after the final day for payment, it was too late — the mortgagee could take possession of and keep the land. Moreover, the mortgagee was still entitled to repayment of the debt: he could sue the unfortunate mortgagor and collect the debt even while retaining the land.

---

[1] For a more detailed history of mortgages, see Rayner and McLaren, *Falconbridge on Mortgages* (4th ed.), pp. 3-7. Toronto: Canada Law Book Company Limited, 1977.

The gross unfairness of this position was soon remedied by the court of equity: if the mortgagor appealed to that court, it would restrain the mortgagee from suing for the debt unless he agreed to reconvey the land to the mortgagor on payment of the full sum owing. At this point in the development of the law a defaulting mortgagor did not, at least, lose his money as well as his land. He could keep one or the other, depending on whether the mortgagee chose to keep the land and not sue for the debt, or to sue for the debt on condition that he would reconvey the land.

The Mortgagor's Right to Redeem

A mortgagor was still in an unfair position, because the choice lay with the mortgagee. If the mortgagor had borrowed only a small sum of money on the security of land worth many times as much, it would be small comfort to know that he would not be sued but that the mortgagee would keep his land instead. Thus if a mortgagor, delayed by a severe storm, arrived the morning after the last day to pay off his mortgage, he could not demand the return of an estate worth many thousands of pounds even though he had borrowed only a few hundred pounds and now tendered payment. The court of equity eventually granted a remedy in these cases of hardship as well. If the mortgagor petitioned the court and pleaded hardship and also tendered payment of the debt in full, the court would acknowledge his interest in the land and permit him to *redeem* it; it would order the mortgagee to reconvey the land to him. This right of redemption obtained by the mortgagor from a court of equity has become known as the *equity of redemption*; it is often called simply the *equity*. We see here the derivation of the modern business term "equity" meaning the interest of the proprietors of a business in its total assets after allowing for creditors' claims.

The Mortgagee's Right to Foreclose

Gradually, over a long period, the chancery courts entertained petitions of hardship based on weaker and weaker excuses, longer and longer after the day for payment had passed, until finally they accepted almost any excuse provided full payment was tendered. The scales were then tipped in favour of the mortgagor. A mortgagee who was quite willing to accept payment for a long time after the due date might finally despair of ever obtaining payment and begin to improve the land, treating it as his own. Years later, the mortgagor could appear and force him to reconvey upon tendering the full amount of the debt. In a turnabout, mortgagees now began to appeal to the chancery courts for a declaration that the mortgagor had had every reasonable opportunity to redeem and that if he did not do so within a fixed time set by the court his right to redeem would be forever foreclosed. The mortgagee could then safely treat the land as his own. By the 19th century, the foreclosure period became generally accepted as six months from the date of the hearing in the case.

   In practice, a mortgagee rarely takes possession until after it has obtained foreclosure, unless it believes that the mortgagor has no intention of trying to redeem and will allow the premises to become dilapidated. There are three main reasons for not going into possession: first, a mortgagee generally wants its money rather than the mortgagor's property, and it would prefer to encourage the mortgagor to pay off the debt; second, its possession would be uncertain, since the mortgagor might at any moment tender payment and demand possession; third, it must account for any benefits it receives from occupation of the land and deduct it from the amount owing if the mortgagor tenders payment, thus losing any material advantage gained from taking possession.

The Consequences of These Developments

In summary then, under rules developed by the courts and apart from statutory reforms, a mortgage is a conveyance of an interest in land as security for a debt. If the debt is repaid as promised, the mortgage is discharged and the mortgagor has the title to the land returned to him. If he defaults, the land becomes the property of the mortgagee subject to the right of the mortgagor to redeem. Most mortgages today call for repayment, not in a lump sum on the last day, but in a series of instalment payments of principal and accrued interest. Mortgages almost always contain an *acceleration clause*, which states that upon default of any instalment, the whole of the principal sum of the mortgage and accrued interest immediately falls due; default accelerates the maturity date, and the mortgagee may pursue all its remedies.

Upon default the mortgagee may put the mortgagor out and take possession itself. It may also ask the court for an order of foreclosure. The mortgagor may repay the loan at any time before the deadline specified in the court order and obtain the return of his land, but if he does not do so, the land becomes the mortgagee's absolutely.

Even after the final day for redemption the mortgagee may successfully sue the mortgagor for the debt until the period prescribed by the Statute of Limitations runs out,[2] provided of course it can still reconvey the land to the mortgagor.[3] Following foreclosure, once the mortgagee has sold the land to a third party it loses the right to sue for any deficiency, even though the mortgagor may subsequently become very wealthy. The courts presume that by selling the land the mortgagee has elected to accept the receipts of the sale in full satisfaction of the debt. On this basis it may also retain any profit made on the sale.

Under the land titles system (covering the areas discussed in Chapter 26 above) mortgages are called *charges*.[4] Charges are not, strictly speaking, conveyances of the legal title. Rather, they are liens upon the land, for which the ordinary remedy is to force a sale of the land and then apply the proceeds toward repayment of the debt. We discuss the mortgagee's remedy of sale more fully below.

As in earlier times, real estate mortgages still frequently arise out of a private transaction between two individuals. However, a very large proportion of mortgage lending to individual borrowers is now done by financial institutions — insurance companies, trust companies, and banks, for example — which have assumed the role of corporate mortgagees.[5]

---

[2] The limitations periods vary from six to thirty years among the provinces. The matter is complicated by the number of parties that may be involved in a mortgage transaction and the variety of problems that may arise.

[3] Except in Manitoba and Saskatchewan, where a final order of foreclosure extinguishes the right to sue on the personal covenant of the mortgagor: Mortgage Act, R.S.M. 1987, c. M200, s. 16; Limitation of Civil Rights Act, R.S.S. 1978, c. L-16, s. 6.

[4] Since 1984, mortgages throughout Ontario, including those regions under the registry system, have been converted to charges: Land Registration Reform Act, R.S.O. 1990, c. L-4, s. 6.

[5] The reverse situation, where the mortgage borrower is a corporation and the lenders individuals (bondholders), is also common, as we shall see in our discussion of the nature of corporate securities in Chapter 30 and of floating charges as security devices in Chapter 33.

RIGHTS OF THE MORTGAGEE AND MORTGAGOR UNDER COMMON LAW AND EQUITY

Although the courts of common law and equity are merged, the interests of the mortgagee and mortgagor are still interpreted according to the remedies available before the merger. In the absence of statutory reform,[6] a mortgagee is considered to be the holder of the *legal* title, and the mortgagor to have the *equitable* title; that is, his interest is recognized by equity and will be enforced against the mortgagee under the circumstances we have already described. The remedies of a mortgagee upon default by the mortgagor are as follows: (a) it may sue the mortgagor on his personal covenant to repay, just as a creditor may sue any debtor who is in default; (b) it may dispossess the mortgagor and occupy the land itself (or put in a tenant); (c) it may sell the land, as explained below; (d) it may proceed with an action for foreclosure and eventually destroy the mortgagor's right to redeem; and (e) subsequent to foreclosure it may again sue on the covenant to pay the debt, always provided it is willing and able to reconvey the land. A mortgagee frequently chooses a combination of these remedies.

The remedies of a mortgagor after default are as follows: (a) he may repay the mortgage loan together with interest and all expenses incurred by the mortgagee up to and including the date of the order of foreclosure and obtain a reconveyance of his land; (b) he may obtain an accounting for any benefits received by the mortgagee and deduct these from the amount owing on redemption; and (c) if sued on his covenant to repay after foreclosure, he may require the mortgagee to prove that it is ready and able to reconvey the land upon repayment. We may note that a mortgagor may obtain relief against the consequences of an acceleration clause: if he pays all prior accrued payments, performs all other terms of which he may have been in default and pays all costs incurred by the mortgagee, a court will permit him to continue to make regular payments under the original terms of the mortgage.[7]

THE MORTGAGEE'S REMEDY OF SALE UPON DEFAULT

As we have seen, once a mortgagee forecloses and disposes of the land, it no longer has any right to demand payment. Two alternative remedies have developed, however, whereby the land may be sold and the mortgagee still maintain an action to recover the balance of the debt if the sale has not produced a sufficient price to repay the debt completely. These two remedies may be described as follows.

Sale by the Court

A mortgagee may request to have the land sold under the supervision of the court (or in some of the western provinces, under the supervision of the registrar of titles), the sale to

---

6 Despite these reforms and the fact that the mortgagor who gives a charge on his land retains legal title, the old terminology concerning legal and equitable title remains in common use.

7 Mortgages Act, R.S.O. 1990, c. M-40, ss. 22-23.

be either by tender or by auction. Some jurisdictions permit the mortgagee or its agent to bid; others prohibit such bidding. The sale must be advertised for a specified period and carried out according to provincial statutes and regulations. In some jurisdictions the court or registrar sets a reserve price below which no tenders will be accepted. The reserve price is not disclosed: when the tenders are opened, the highest one is accepted if it is over the reserve price. If no bid is above the reserve price, then the land remains unsold and the mortgagee may resort to its other remedies.

When a sale produces a successful bid, the mortgagee is entitled to recover the principal sum owing, accrued interest, and expenses of the court action and the sale. If the sale produces a smaller sum, the mortgagee may obtain judgment against the mortgagor for the deficiency. If the sale is for a larger sum, the surplus is returned to the mortgagor or his other secured creditors of the land.

In some jurisdictions, when a mortgagee starts a foreclosure action and the mortgagor believes that the land is worth more than his mortgage debt, the mortgagor or a subsequent secured creditor may request the court to hold a sale. We shall return to this topic when we discuss provincial variations later in this chapter.

Sale by the Mortgagee

Many mortgages, and in some jurisdictions the statutes governing mortgages, give the mortgagee a contractual *power of sale* that may be exercised privately without court action or supervision, although advance notice to the mortgagor is generally required. A mortgagee may exercise its power of sale at any time after default, subject to any statutory period of grace. By executing a proper grant and declaring that the grant is made in pursuance of a power of sale, it may validly transfer the title to the land to any third party. The sale must, however, be a genuine sale and not amount to a fraud upon the mortgagor. A mortgagee may not sell to itself either directly or through an agent. Whenever a mortgagee exercises a power of sale, it is under a duty to take reasonable steps to obtain a fair price for the land. If the mortgagor can show that the mortgagee sold for an unreasonably low price, the court will reduce the deficiency accordingly or give the mortgagor judgment for any surplus he should have received. If the mortgagee is a private lender, she may sell the land to a company of which she is a shareholder or officer, but such sales will be jealously scrutinized by the court and may be easily upset if there is any evidence of taking unfair advantage by selling at an unreasonably low price.

The same rules concerning the proceeds of a sale apply here as in a sale by the court: if there is a deficiency, the mortgagee may still sue the mortgagor for the sum; if there is a surplus, it must return it to the mortgagor or to the remaining secured creditors.

Sale by a Mortgagor of His or Her Interest

Financial Arrangements

A mortgage transaction is, as we can see, a sophisticated credit arrangement. When it concerns but two parties, it is reasonably straightforward. The transaction becomes more complex, however, with the addition of a third party to the relationship.

A, the owner of Blackacre, mortgages it to *B* Trust Co. for $50 000. Subsequently she sells Blackacre to *X* for $80 000. How is the price to be paid by *X*? There are three possibilities. First, *X* may pay *A* the full $80 000 and obtain an undertaking from *A* that she will pay off the mortgage to *B* Trust Co. Second, *X* may pay $30 000 to *A* for *A*'s equity of redemption and a further $50 000 to *B* in full payment of the mortgage. Third, *X* may pay *A* $30 000, as above, and accept Blackacre *subject to the mortgage*; that is, he will himself assume responsibility for paying off the mortgage. We can see that the third possibility is really a variation of the second: instead of paying the mortgage off at once, *X* simply pays it off as it falls due.

In circumstances like those in the above illustration the first possibility rarely occurs, because *X* takes the risk that *A*'s creditors might obtain the purchase money through court action or *A* might abscond so that the funds never reach *B* Trust Co., leaving *X* to pay *B* in order to redeem the mortgage. He might end up paying $130 000 for Blackacre instead of $80 000. The second possibility does not occur very frequently either, for two reasons: first, by the terms of the mortgage the mortgagor may not have the right to pay off the mortgage before the due date; second, purchasers rarely pay the full purchase price for land. Land transactions are almost invariably financed by a credit arrangement, usually in the form of a mortgage. Therefore, it is often most convenient for *X* simply to pay $30 000 to obtain Blackacre and to *assume* the mortgage liability for making payments.

In some circumstances, especially where the mortgagor (vendor) has significantly reduced the first mortgage by instalment payments, the purchaser may arrange through a financial institution for a new mortgage for a larger sum of money. He would use the proceeds of the new mortgage to pay off the existing mortgage and use the balance towards the cash portion of the purchase price.

Effect of Default by the Purchaser

What would happen if the purchaser, *X*, should then default on payment? The fact that *A* has sold her equity of redemption to *X* does not affect *B*'s rights as mortgagee holding the legal title to Blackacre; it retains all its rights against the land. It may also recover from *A*, the mortgagor, on her covenant to repay the debt. If it sues *A*, what rights does *A* have upon paying off the mortgage? *A* may successfully sue *X* for the full sum of money she was required to pay to *B*. One reason for this result is that, as part of his purchase price for Blackacre, *X* assumed the mortgage and agreed to pay it off. The law implies that the promise to pay off the mortgage includes a promise to indemnify *A*, that is, save *A* from any liability under it. A second reason is that by paying off the mortgage *A* has in effect purchased the mortgagee's rights. She becomes *subrogated* to the mortgagee's rights and is in effect the mortgagee to whom *X* is now a mortgagor. At this point *A* may invoke all the remedies against *X* that *B* Trust Co. might itself have utilized against the land and the mortgagor.

Instead of suing *A*, may the mortgagee *B* sue the purchaser *X* directly? There is no contract between *B* and *X* giving *B* this right. Nor do the courts recognize any privity of estate between a mortgagee and the purchaser of the equity as they do in landlord and tenant.

Under common law rules, *B* may successfully sue *X* only if it can obtain an assignment of *A*'s right to indemnity discussed in the preceding paragraph. As a practical matter *A* will often agree to assign her right in order to avoid having the mortgagee sue her on her covenant in the mortgage. In Ontario, the Mortgages Act gives the mortgagee a statutory right to sue the purchaser *X* directly, without obtaining an assignment from *A*, the mortgagor, while *X* holds the equity.[8] If he sells it to yet another purchaser *Y*, then *Y* becomes liable to pay the mortgage, and *X* is released from his statutory obligation to the mortgagee.

SECOND MORTGAGES

A prospective purchaser often finds he does not have sufficient money to buy the equity in land already subject to a mortgage, or sometimes the owner of land already subject to a mortgage may wish to raise an additional sum by using his equity as security. Although there is only one legal title to the land and it is already held by the mortgagee, the mortgagor or his successor may nevertheless mortgage the equity and still retain an equity of redemption; equitable title may be divided up as many times as the holder of the equity wishes to do so and can find creditors willing to take an interest in the remaining equity as security for the debts owed to them. Second mortgages (that is, mortgages of the equity of redemption) are quite common. Less common are third and fourth mortgages (further mortgages of the equity of redemption).

ILLUSTRATION

V offers Hillcroft for sale for $230 000 subject to a mortgage for $150 000 to *M* Co. Ltd. *P* would like to buy Hillcroft, but she has only $55 000 in cash, and she needs $80 000. She arranges to borrow $25 000 from her business associate *M2* and to give *M2* a second mortgage on Hillcroft. Having made these arrangements *P* accepts *V*'s offer to sell, and they arrange a *closing date* (a date for completing the transaction).

On the closing day the following transactions take place: (a) *V* delivers a transfer of Hillcroft to *P*; (b) *P* delivers a mortgage of Hillcroft to *M2*; (c) *M2* gives *P* $25 000; (d) *P* gives *V* the total sum of $80 000 and also assumes the first mortgage made by *V* with *M* Co. Ltd. These transactions usually take place simultaneously in the office of one lawyer or in the registry office; each party trades the necessary documents and sums of money and immediately registers the transfer and mortgage. The net result of the transaction is as follows: *P* holds the equity in Hillcroft subject to the first mortgage to *M* Co. Ltd. for $150 000 and the second mortgage to *M2* for $25 000. She is indebted in the sum of $175 000.

A second mortgagee has rights similar to those of a first mortgagee except that his interest is in the equity of redemption, not the legal title, and he ranks behind the first mortgagee in priority of payment. Thus, in the illustration, if *P* defaults payment on both mortgages, the first mortgagee may start an action for foreclosure. The second mortgagee may decide to stand by and do nothing. If the first mortgagee completes the foreclosure

---

[8] Mortgages Act, R.S.O. 1990, c. M-40, s. 20(2), (3).

against the equity in Hillcroft, the interest of both *P* and the second mortgagee is destroyed. The second mortgagee loses his security in Hillcroft and is left with only a right of action for debt against *P*, who may be insolvent. If the first mortgagee proceeds with a sale under power of sale or sale by the court, the proceeds will be paid, *first*, to satisfy the first mortgage debt and expenses of the sale, and *second*, to satisfy the second mortgage debt. The second mortgagee will be paid only to the extent that there is any surplus after paying off the first mortgagee. Of course, the sale may bring in more money than the total amount owed on both mortgages, and the excess will go to *P*.

When the first mortgagee begins a foreclosure action, the second mortgagee may redeem, that is, pay off the first mortgage himself and receive an assignment of it. But then he will have invested an additional sum in the land: in our illustration above *M2* would have to pay about $150 000. With *P* insolvent, *M2* would have little hope of collecting by suing for the debt. He may in turn commence a foreclosure action, and in effect buy Hillcroft for about $175 000 (which may or may not be a good buy depending on the current real estate market); or he may proceed with either of the two remedies of sale, taking the risk that a sale may not bring in enough to pay off the sums he has invested.

A second mortgage invariably provides that default on the first mortgage is also immediate default on the second mortgage, that is, a breach of the mortgagor's obligation to protect the second mortgagee's interest in the land, and he may immediately act upon the usual remedies. In the absence of such protection a second mortgagee might find himself in the following position:

(a) payment of the second mortgage is not yet due and thus there is no default on it;
(b) the first mortgage, having an earlier due date, is in default and the first mortgagee promptly pursues one of its remedies against the land — foreclosure, sale by court, or exercise of the power of sale;
(c) the result of either of these remedies would be to destroy the second mortgagee's interest in the land.

In a sale either by the court or by the first mortgagee, to the extent that the sale brought in more than the debt due on the first mortgage the second mortgagee would receive compensation, but he might well recover only a part of the debt. To avoid these risks a second mortagagee may himself act promptly to pursue his remedies.

When a mortgagor places successive mortgages upon his equity, each ranks in priority according to its creation in time. Each subsequent mortgage gives all the usual remedies to the mortgagee, subject to the prior rights of any earlier mortgagee. Each subsequent mortgagee takes a greater risk as creditor for several reasons: first, the land is subject to a greater financial debt and any drop in price will injure the security of the latest mortgagee first; second, a succession of mortgages on one piece of land usually indicates financial instability and poor management on the part of the borrower; third, failure by a subsequent mortgagee to act reasonably promptly in case of default may result in the destruction of its secured interest in the land, if a prior mortgagee exercises its power of sale; fourth, the cost of redeeming prior mortgages may be too high — in order to prevent foreclosure of its interest a subsequent mortgagee may have to lay out more money than it can afford.[9]

---

[9] Subsequent mortgagees frequently demand additional security, such as mortgages on other lands or personal property, before advancing a mortgage loan.

Sometimes a mortgagor defaults on only the second mortgage, or if he has defaulted on the first as well, the first mortgagee may be quite satisfied with the adequacy of its security and is willing to "sit tight" and see what the subsequent mortgagees and creditors intend to do. The first mortgagee need not worry since it has the prime interest in the land and no one can affect its position. In this situation, the second mortgagee may proceed with foreclosure or a sale, and thus destroy the interest of the mortgagor in the equity of redemption without affecting the first mortgagee. If the second mortgagee forecloses, he becomes the sole holder of the equity of redemption, subject to the prior interest of the first mortgagee. Similarly, when the second mortgagee proceeds by sale, the purchaser obtains the whole of the equity of redemption clear of the mortgagor's interest, though of course still subject to the first mortgage. In either case the new holder of the equity of redemption must make satisfactory arrangements with the first mortgagee; he may redeem the first mortgage or else assume the obligations under it by agreement with the first mortgagee.

$\mathscr{M}$ORTGAGEE'S RIGHTS COMPARED WITH RIGHTS OF OTHER CREDITORS

A creditor firm that has no security other than its debtor's promise is a *general creditor*, and its claim ranks as a general claim; a creditor that has one or more forms of collateral security is a *secured creditor* and has a prior claim against one or more of the assets of the debtor. If the debtor becomes insolvent, the general creditors must wait until the claims of the secured creditors have been satisfied out of the assets against which they have their claims. When the sale of an asset brings in more than the amount owing the secured creditor, the excess becomes available for the settlement of general claims. Here we may see the relation of the mortgagee's remedy of sale to other creditors' claims: as we noted earlier in this chapter, after a sale of the mortgaged land by the mortgagee any surplus is returned to the mortgagor; if the mortgagor is insolvent, the surplus goes to his creditors. At other times the particular security realizes less than the amount of the secured creditor's claim, and to the extent of the deficiency it then ranks as a general creditor along with all the general creditors.

ILLUSTRATION

(a) Harper is the proprietor of a successful small retail business with a building worth about $320 000. He has mortgaged the building for $250 000 to Commerce Trust Co. Unfortunately his area suffers a serious recession when a large local industry closes, he has meagre working capital, and cannot weather the indefinite loss in sales. He becomes insolvent and is declared bankrupt. A trustee is appointed, and in due course the building is sold; the remainder of Harper's assets are also sold. The following is a statement of Harper's financial position after all the assets are liquidated:

ILLUSTRATION

Assets		Liabilities	
Bank balance from		Commerce Trust Co.	$247 000
sale of building	$270 000	General Creditors	$85 000
sale of other assets	$ 38 000		
TOTAL	$308 000	TOTAL	$332 000

The assets would distributed as follows:

Commerce Trust Co.	$247 000
General Creditors	$61 000
	$308 000

We see that the mortgagee receives 100 cents on the dollar of debt owed to it from the sale of the building. In addition the sale produces a surplus of $23 000. This sum is added to the $38 000 realized from all other assets, and is paid out rateably to the general creditors. Here they receive $\frac{61\,000}{85\,000}$ of each dollar of indebtedness — about 72 cents on each dollar.

(b) Suppose, however, that the sale of the building brings a much smaller sum because of the depressed market — say, $200 000. The assets and liabilities are now as follows:

Assets		Liabilities	
Bank balance from:		Commerce Trust Co.	$247 000
sale of building	$200 000	General Creditors	$85 000
sale of other assets	$38 000		
TOTAL	$238 000	TOTAL	$332 000

The assets would now be distributed as follows:

Creditors

	Secured	General	Total
Commerce Trust Co.	$200 000		
plus $\frac{47\,000}{132\,000}$ x 38 000		$13 530	$213 530
General Creditors			
$\frac{85\,000}{132\,000}$ x 38 000		$24 470	$24 470
	$200 000	$38 000	$238 000

Note: We obtain the figure of $132 000 by adding the deficiency of $47 000 on the mortgage debt to the total unsecured debt. In these circumstances the mortgagee receives a total of over $213 000 from a debt of $247 000 — about 86 cents on each dollar of debt. On the other hand the general creditors suffer much more severely: they receive about $\frac{24\,500}{85\,000}$ of each dollar of indebtedness — about 29 cents on each dollar. We may note that their position is worsened by the fact that the mortgagee joined them to rank as a general creditor for that portion of the debt unsatisfied by the sale of the building, thus dividing the assets among a larger group of claims.

THE MORTGAGE AS A CONTRACT AND AS A TRANSFER OF AN INTEREST IN LAND

The Mortgage as a Contract

A mortgage document — as well as transferring an interest in land to the mortgagee — is a contract containing a number of important terms, the most important being the personal covenants of the mortgagor to pay off the debt and of the mortgagee to discharge its interest in the land upon repayment. It is useful to set out the more important covenants of each party. The mortgagor covenants

(a) to pay the debt and accrued interest, either at maturity date or in instalments as agreed by the parties,[10]
(b) to keep the property adequately insured in the name of the mortgagee;
(c) to pay taxes on the land and buildings;
(d) to keep the premises in a reasonable state of repair.

The mortgagee covenants

(a) to execute the necessary discharge of the mortgage upon repayment in full;
(b) to leave the mortgagor in possession and not interfere with his use and enjoyment of the mortgaged premises so long as the mortgagor observes all his covenants.

The mortgagor signs the mortgage, but the mortgagee merely accepts the document without signing it. The mortgagee's promises are set out as provisos — some are simply implied by the principles of mortgage law — and its acceptance of the document binds it to the terms. We can see that contractual obligations form a large part of a mortgage transaction.

The Mortgage as a Transfer of an Interest in Land

A mortgage is both a transfer of an interest in land in the same way as a grant is, and also a contract containing terms that govern the transfer. As a transfer, it must comply with the usual requirements by adequately describing the parties and the land being transferred, and must be in the proper form required for registration in the registry office of the jurisdiction. Our discussion in the preceding chapter concerning the recording of interests in land applies equally to interests created by mortgage. Thus, if a mortgagee fails to register its mortgage, a subsequent purchaser from the mortgagor, unaware of the mortgage, will acquire title free from it upon registering his own grant. Similarly a subsequent mortgagee, unaware of the first mortgage, will establish priority over the first mortgage if it registers first. We are concerned here only with establishing the mortgagee's interest in the land: failure to register does not wipe out its other rights as a creditor against the mortgagor. Failure to register may result in the complete loss of the land as security where there is a transfer to an innocent purchaser, or to loss of priority against another secured creditor of the mortgagor that registers its claim first.

Assignment

When a mortgagee is a private lender, he may wish to obtain cash by selling the mortgage rather than by waiting for the mortgage debt to fall due in order to collect. The mortgage may be a sound investment, having good security and a reliable debtor, or it may be a risky investment. In either case, the mortgagee may sell his mortgage at the best price he can get for it. The sale of a mortgage is a transaction involving both its contractual and real property aspects. The mortgagee *assigns* his rights to the covenants made by the mortgagor, and *grants* or transfers his interest in the land to the purchaser (assignee) of the mortgage. Sometimes, in order to obtain a higher price, an assignor-mortgagee guarantees

---

[10] Except in Alberta and Saskatchewan, where a mortgagor cannot be sued personally for the mortgage debt. See the section dealing with provincial variations, below.

payment — that is, if the mortgagor defaults in payment the assignor, on the assignee's demand, will pay off the mortgage and take back an assignment of it. In most sales, however, a mortgagee sells the mortgage outright, and the purchaser takes the risk of default together with all the usual remedies of a mortgagee.

A purchaser of a mortgage, as an assignee of contractual rights, is bound by the usual rules of assignment in contract. As we have seen in Chapter 14, the debtor, in this case the mortgagor, is not bound by the assignment until receiving notice of it, and the assignee takes the mortgage subject to the equities and the state of the mortgage account between mortgagor and mortgagee.

Discharge of Mortgages

When a mortgagor, or a subsequent purchaser of her equity, pays off the whole of the mortgage debt at maturity of the loan, she is entitled to a discharge from the mortgagee. A discharge operates both as an acknowledgment that the debt has been paid in full and as a reconveyance of the legal title from the mortgagee to the holder of the equity. To protect herself, the holder of the equity of redemption registers the discharge in the land registry office; by registering she conclusively becomes the holder of the legal title. A fraudulent mortgagee cannot then successfully exercise a power of sale and grant the legal title to an innocent purchaser on the pretence that the mortgage is unpaid and in arrears. A fraudulent mortgagee has been known to do just that and to deprive a mortgagor of the land when the mortgagor has neglected to obtain a discharge and register it.[11] In areas under the land titles system, a discharge from the mortgagee operates to dissolve the charge upon the mortgagor's land.

A mortgage usually contains a contractual term permitting the mortgagor to repay the mortgage and to obtain a discharge even before the debt matures. The term permitting such repayment may have various conditions attached to it. Often a mortgagee requires a period of notice, usually three months, before it need accept the money; such a requirement gives it time to find a new borrower so that the money received does not lie idle earning no interest until it finds a new investment. A mortgagee often requires payment of a bonus, for example three months' interest, in lieu of notice, or it may require both notice and a bonus. Certain types of mortgages, particularly second mortgages and short-term mortgages, permit repayment "at any time without notice or bonus". Mortgages containing such a term are usually called *open mortgages*.

Flexible mortgage-prepayment clauses often contain various other prepayment possibilities. A mortgagor may be permitted to prepay part of the debt rather than all of it, simply to make good use of extra earnings and to reduce the interest payable on the mortgage loan. A mortgage may also permit the mortgagor to prepay a specified portion of the mortgage debt and to obtain a partial discharge, that is, a discharge of a definite portion of the mortgaged lands. Partial discharges are common when the mortgagor is a land developing company. It may own a large piece of undeveloped land and wish to sell off a part free from any encumbrance, or it may wish to erect a large building on a particular part of the land and require financing in the form of a large new mortgage, which it cannot obtain except as a first mortgage. These various methods of prepaying part or all of a mortgage debt play an important role in the credit financing of land development.

---

[11]   Dicker v. Angerstein (1876), 3 Ch. D. 395.

$\mathcal{P}$ROVINCIAL VARIATIONS

The remedies available to mortgagees and mortgagors developed, as we have seen, over a long period. The various provinces of Canada adopted existing English law at the date each province obtained its first legislative body; the dates range from 1758 in Nova Scotia to 1870 in Alberta, Manitoba and Saskatchewan. Accordingly, the variations in the mortgage law adopted by each province may be considerable. Subsequent to its adoption of the English law, each province developed its own procedures and made statutory amendments to meet its own needs. The needs differed widely according to the economy of the province and the character of business within it. The result is a rather confused and sometimes inconsistent pattern of remedies for both mortgagee and mortgagor. We present here a brief summary of the main variations among these remedies.

In Alberta, British Columbia and Saskatchewan, a mortgagee's right to sue on the covenant to repay has been restricted by statute. A mortgagee may sue only mortgagors that are corporations and have waived the statutory protection.[12] In all provinces, a mortgagee may request the court or registrar to hold a sale of mortgaged land, and except in Nova Scotia, may sell under a power of sale if it is provided for either by statute or under the terms of the mortgage. In British Columbia, in that portion of Manitoba under the registry system, and in Ontario, New Brunswick, Prince Edward Island, and Newfoundland, a mortgagee may foreclose the equity of redemption in the manner we have already discussed. In Alberta, Saskatchewan, and that portion of Manitoba under the land titles system, the usual remedy is sale by the court: if the sale does not produce any satisfactory bids then the mortgagee may proceed to foreclose, but foreclosure appears to be a rare remedy in practice. In Nova Scotia, although the court issues an order of "foreclosure and sale", foreclosure is not really permitted: the court must hold a sale.

With the exception of New Brunswick, those provinces permitting a mortgagee to start an action for foreclosure also allow the mortgagor to request the court to hold a sale, provided he deposits a sum of money (usually under $100) as security for the costs of the sale in the event of its producing no acceptable bids. A mortgagor may thus prevent the mortgagee from acquiring the mortgagor's interest in the land; this right of the mortgagor can be an important protection when the land is worth substantially more than the mortgage debt. We should remember, however, that if the market value of the land does exceed the mortgage debt by a significant amount, the mortgagor, unless he is considered a bad personal credit risk, should be able to refinance the land by obtaining an extension of his mortgage or arranging for a new mortgage and paying off his old mortgagee to whom he has defaulted. In any event, he should be able to sell the equity of redemption at its market value. In all jurisdictions a mortgagor has the right to redeem the land by paying off the entire debt before foreclosure or sale.

---

[12] Law of Property Act, R.S.A. 1980, c. L-8, s. 41, (as amended by S.A 1982, c. 24) and s. 43, (as amended by S.A. 1983, c. 97 and S.A. 1984, c. 24); Property Law Act, R.S.B.C. 1979, c. 340, s. 28; Limitation of Certain Civil Rights Act, R.S.S. 1978, c. L-16, s. 2. See National Trust Co. v. Mead, [1990] 2. S.C.R. 410.

Reverse Mortgages

A recent development in Canadian law has been the adoption from Europe of the concept of the *reverse mortgage*. It can be a benefit mainly to senior citizens who are retired and have been described as "house rich and cash poor".[13] Typically, a homeowner purchased a house many years earlier and during her career paid off the mortgage debt on the property; she owns it without debt. However, her employment did not make provision for a generous retirement pension and she now has a meagre income. Meanwhile her house has increased substantially in market value.

Using the reverse mortgage concept, she may give a mortgage on her house, and receive a monthly payment based on the market value of the property, prevailing interest rates, and actuarial calculations of her life expectancy. She remains in possession of the house while the principal and interest on the reverse mortgage accrue; no repayment is due until she sells the house or dies. When one of these two events occur, and if the market value of the house is greater than the accrued debt, the lender pays the excess to the owner or her estate. If the value of the house is less than the accrued debt then the lender absorbs the deficiency.

As our population ages and the number of persons who may find themselves in the financial position we have just described increases, the reverse mortgage seems likely to become more common. Financial institutions may well begin to promote this new area. There are wide variations in the design of reverse mortgages and at present no systems of regulation.

Concern has been expressed that seniors should seek advice before undertaking a reverse mortgage, and consider alternatives such as selling the house and buying or renting smaller accommodation.

A Typical Real Estate Transaction

The Circumstances

A real estate transaction can best be understood by following a typical sale in some detail from start to finish. We shall use for an example a fictional piece of land in Oshawa, Ontario. John Vincent owns the land and building on Main Street described in his grant as Lot 27, Plan 7654 in the City of Oshawa. The building fronting on Main Street consists of a large store at ground level and three suites of offices on the second floor. Vincent occupies the store himself and runs a men's wear shop. The offices are rented to three tenants, one to Dr. A. McAvity, dentist, the second to Happy Auto Insurance Company, and the third to C. McCollum, chartered accountant. Business has been poor; Vincent is 70 years old and wishes to retire. He has advertised without success to find a buyer of his business. He has received many inquiries about purchasing the building, a prime location, but no one is interested in buying his rather old-fashioned stock and fixtures. He has finally decided to run a selling-out sale and then sell the building.

---

[13] For a useful discussion of the reverse mortgage, see Mary Beggan, "Reverse Mortgages: Ahead of Our Time", 99:5 *Canadian Banker* 45.

The Offer to Purchase

Hi-Style Centres Ltd., a firm selling women's wear, operates a chain of stores and is anxious to have an outlet in Oshawa. It approaches Vincent with the proposal that he rent the store to them. Vincent has decided to leave Oshawa and retire to Victoria, B.C., and wishes to break all business connections in the East. He says he would consider an offer to purchase but not to rent. Hi-Style makes two offers to purchase, both rejected by Vincent as too low. It now makes a third offer which Vincent is considering seriously. The essential terms are:[14]

(a) Hi-Style offers to buy the premises for $645 000, payable as follows: tender $25 000 as a deposit by certified cheque attached to the offer; assume the first mortgage of about $375 000 held by the Grimm Mortgage Company; give back to Vincent a second mortgage of $125 000 (interest and other terms set out in detail); pay the balance on *closing date* (completion date).

(b) The sale is to be closed 60 days after the date of the offer.

(c) Hi-Style may search the title and submit *requisitions* (questions concerning claims against Vincent's title) within 20 days of acceptance of the offer. Vincent promises to deliver a copy of the survey of the lot which he has in his possession for examination by Hi-Style. If serious claims against Vincent's title are raised and Vincent cannot answer them satisfactorily, the contract will be terminated and the deposit returned to Hi-Style. If no requisitions are submitted within 20 days, it is presumed that Hi-Style accepts Vincent's title as satisfactory.

(d) Vincent is to remain in possession and the building is to remain at his risk until closing. He promises to keep the building insured to its full insurable value. He also undertakes to give possession of the building in substantially the same condition as it was at the time of making the contract. If the building is destroyed or seriously damaged, Hi-Style may elect to take over the premises and to receive the proceeds of all insurance, or it may elect to terminate the contract, with Vincent to suffer the loss, if any.

(e) Vincent is to pay all taxes and insurance until closing and deduct from the amount due at closing all outstanding current expenses, such as accrued water and electric bills, unpaid taxes, and insurance. He will transfer all insurance policies to Hi-Style, provided the insurance companies are willing to accept Hi-Style as a satisfactory risk, and Hi-Style will pay for the prepaid unexpired portion of such policies. Alternatively, Hi-Style may arrange its own insurance to commence on the day of closing.

(f) Vincent warrants that two of his three suites of offices are leased to tenants as stated at rents of $1250 monthly per suite under leases expiring two years after date of closing for Suite No. 1, and two years four months after closing for Suite No. 2; Suite 3 is rented as a monthly tenancy only at $900. He will deliver the original of

---

14 An offer to purchase may also include other terms, the importance of which varies according to the circumstances, in particular the nature of the property. For example the vendor might be required to give a warranty that the heating plant conforms to regulations; to produce a certificate of inspection of boiler or gas installations; to warrant that the premises do not violate existing zoning by-laws; to identify all encroachments or easements in respect of which the property is either a servient or a dominant tenement; and to allow the prospective purchaser access to the premises for the purpose of checking the land survey.

the two leases and assignments of the leases on closing, an acknowledgment from the third tenant that she is only a monthly tenant, and signed notices to the tenants that Hi-Style is the new landlord to whom they are to pay their rent.

(g) The offer is open for two days and acceptance must be communicated to the office of the lawyer for Hi-Style in Oshawa before 5:00 p.m. on the second day.

Preparations for Completing the Transaction

Vincent has two copies of the offer. He decides to accept it and sends one signed copy to Hi-Style's lawyer, Harmon, retaining the other copy for his own lawyer, Vale. He also sends a copy of the survey of his lot to Harmon. The manager of Hi-Style has taken the careful step of having Harmon draw up the offer in the first place. Thus Harmon is familiar with its terms; in particular, she has made a special note in her file of the last day to submit requisitions concerning title to the land, as well as the date of closing the transaction.

Harmon now takes the following steps: (1) She sends a junior member of her law firm to the registry office to search the title to the lot and also compare the survey received from Vincent with the plan of the whole area as filed in the registry office, to make sure there are no discrepancies in the boundaries of the lot and to learn whether there are any outstanding claims registered for unpaid corporation taxes. (2) She writes to the city tax department asking for a certificate showing the state of real property taxes, both arrears and current, and encloses the small fee usually required for the certificate. (3) She writes to the Grimm Mortgage Company and asks them to prepare and forward a mortgage statement showing what the exact amount outstanding on the mortgage, including accrued interest, will be on the date of closing. (4) She examines the zoning by-law and checks with the office of the building inspector for any outstanding work orders and deficiency notices under municipal by-laws. (5) She asks her client to examine the premises carefully to confirm that the building is occupied by the tenants and by Vincent as stated in the contract and that there are no other persons who appear to be exercising an adverse claim over any part of the premises. In the case of valuable commercial property on main streets, the boundaries are very important, especially if demolition and reconstruction are even remotely contemplated. Harmon advises Hi-Style to hire a surveyor to make a new survey and compare it with the old, thus checking whether adjacent owners are in possession of any part of the lot and have perhaps extinguished Vincent's title to portions they have occupied. (6) She checks with the sheriff's office for any claims that may be filed there against the vendor.

Within a few days Vincent's lawyer, Vale, prepares a *draft deed,* that is, a copy of the grant that Vincent will later sign for delivery on closing. He sends a copy to Harmon, who examines it and approves of its content. Harmon prepares a draft copy of the second mortgage to be given by Hi-Style to Vincent on closing and sends it to Vale. To avoid any confusion about names or initials and the description of the land to be conveyed, both lawyers check very closely to see that all details are described in identical terms in the following documents: the grant received by Vincent when he originally bought the land; the first mortgage by Vincent to Grimm Mortgage Company; the draft deed by Vincent to Hi-Style; and the draft second mortgage from Hi-Style to Vincent.

Harmon finds that Vincent's title to the land is in good order and that there are no outstanding corporation taxes or municipal taxes except for the current year. She receives a mortgage statement from Grimm Mortgage Company, and it agrees with the statement made by Vincent concerning the amount outstanding. A few weeks before the date of closing, Vale prepares a document called a *statement of adjustments* (see below) setting out all the items, both credits and debits, that must be adjusted between the parties to arrive at the correct amount to be paid by Hi-Style to Vincent on the date of closing. The closing date is to be April 15.

Re: Lot 27, Plan 7654, in the City of Oshawa
Hi-Style Centres Ltd. purchase from Vincent

STATEMENT OF ADJUSTMENTS

1. SALE PRICE			$645 000.00
2. Deposit paid by purchaser		$ 25 000.00	
3. First mortgage to Grimm Mortgage Company to be assumed by purchaser	$373 580.60		
Plus interest, April 1 to 15 at 10.5%	$1 612.03		
		$375 192.63	
4. Second mortgage back to vendor		$125 000.00	
5. Unpaid taxes for current year, $5695.00, charged to vendor to April 15 — 3 1/2 months		$1 661.04	
6. Rent received in advance:			
Suite #1: 1 1/2 months	1 875.00		
Suite #2: 1 1/2 months	1 875.00		
Suite #3: 1/2 month	450.00		
		$4 200.00	
7. Union Hartford Fire Insurance Policy no. 8953744, three years, expires Nov. 1, current year. Amount: $450 000 Premium: $1870. Unexpired portion:			$1 012.92
8. Full tank of furnace oil — 2000 litres @ 43.4¢			$868.00
9. BALANCE DUE ON CLOSING		$115 827.25	
		646 880.92	$646 880.92

The Closing

On the morning of April 15, Vale and Harmon meet at the registry office. Harmon checks again with the sheriff's office to search for executions and finds none. She also brings her search of the title up to date to make sure no new documents have been registered against it. She gives Vale the properly executed mortgage for $125 000 made out in duplicate, and a certified cheque for $115 827.25. On behalf of the vendor Vale delivers the following documents to Harmon:

(a) properly executed grant in duplicate;
(b) original copy of leases to Suites No. 1 and No. 2;
(c) properly executed assignments of each lease;
(d) acknowledgment of tenant in Suite No. 3 that she is a monthly tenant at a rent of $900 payable in advance;
(e) notice signed by Vincent to each tenant of Suites No. 1, No. 2, and No. 3 informing them of the change of ownership and requesting them to pay all future rent to Hi-Style;
(f) current tax bill.

He also hands to Harmon, for the purpose of inspection, a certified copy of the insurance policy on the building and a transfer noting both the interest of Hi-Style as purchaser and Vincent as second mortgagee. Vale will subsequently send these to the insurance company himself. After trading documents, Harmon registers the grant from Vincent to Hi-Style, and Vale registers the second mortgage from Hi-Style to Vincent.

Vale agrees not to release the funds he has received until Vincent delivers possession to Hi-Style. The mechanics of delivering possession to a purchaser sometimes cause great friction and even court action. To avoid such friction the vendor should arrange to be completely out of the premises by the time the deal is closed and deliver the keys to the purchaser. If this is not done, the purchaser may understandably be very upset and demand that the money not be released. Once anger replaces common sense both vendor and purchaser may become obstinate, and the vendor's lawyer holding the cheque is caught between them. In the present case, however, all goes smoothly: Vincent vacates the premises the day before and delivers the keys to Vale who now hands them over to Harmon. On returning to her office, Harmon calls the manager of Hi-Style to tell her that the keys are available. The manager picks up the keys, goes to the building, and finds the store vacant. She calls Harmon and informs her that Hi-Style is now in possession. Harmon calls Vale and tells him that he may release the cheque to Vincent. The sale has now been effected.

After the Closing

Each lawyer, however, has several things to do yet besides submitting a bill. Vale will write to Grimm Mortgage Company to inform it of the sale and name the purchaser. He will also write to the city tax office to inform them of the change of ownership. He will write to the insurance company enclosing the copy of the policy and the transfer, and request the return of the policy with an endorsement noting the change of ownership and the interest of the second mortgagee in the property. He will also request that a copy of the policy be sent to the purchaser.

Harmon will communicate with Vale to see that all these things have been completed. She will also write to Grimm Mortgage Company and to the city tax office asking each of them to send all further notices to the head office of Hi-Style. She will write to each of the tenants to inform them of the change of ownership, enclosing Vincent's notice and giving them the address at which Hi-Style would like the rent to be paid.

Only after all these things have been done, when the lawyers are able to return all the documents to their respective clients and to make a full written report of all details, will the transaction be complete.

It is important to stress that each sale of land is a separate and distinctive transaction: the terms should be tailored to meet the specific requirements of the parties in the circumstances. Perhaps we see the greatest degree of standardization in contracts for the sale of similar houses in a subdivision. Even there, however, significant variations in such standard contracts occur because of special credit arrangements, extra features installed by the builder or arrangements for completion of the house after possession. In the sale of commercial property, the variations are far greater: often, possession does not pass to the purchaser on closing, as where the whole premises are already rented to tenants and are purchased for their investment value, or where the vendor stays on as a tenant. Sometimes when the sale of a business is involved, the purchaser covenants to buy goods from the vendor, or the vendor covenants to refrain from opening a competing business in the same neighbourhood. Our fictional illustration set out above is not a model for other transactions, nor does it deal with every detail that might arise in the circumstances. Rather it is intended to give a picture and an understanding of a typical real estate transaction.

Questions for Review

1. How did equity first mitigate the harsh common law rule by which a mortgagor lost his land and still owed the debt?
2. Describe the equity of redemption.
3. What is foreclosure? How does it protect a mortgagee?
4. Describe the two possible types of sale on default of a mortgagor.
5. Who receives the surplus after a sale?
6. What is a second mortgage? Under what circumstances does it commonly arise?
7. State two reasons why we rarely find a mortgagee in possession before foreclosure.
8. What is a closing date?
9. Distinguish between a general creditor and a secured creditor.
10. What is priority of payment?
11. Name two duties of a mortgagor in addition to her obligation to pay off the mortgage debt.
12. Name two duties of a mortgagee.
13. In what circumstances would a mortgagor ask the court to sell her land rather than permit the mortgagee to foreclose?
14. Why should the lawyer for a purchaser of real property search for executions in the sheriff's office?
15. What interest does a mortgagee have in seeing that the mortgaged property is adequately insured? What constitutes adequate insurance from a mortgagee's point of view?

16. What possible financial arrangements may a purchaser make when acquiring land subject to an existing mortgage?

Problems

Problem 1

Four years ago Azoic Wholesalers Ltd. purchased a warehouse building for $465 000. To finance the purchase the company paid $50 000 in cash, gave a 12% first mortgage to the Reliable Insurance Company for $265 000, and an 16% second mortgage of $150 000 to the vendor. The vendor subsequently sold the second mortgage to Sharpe Realties Ltd. for $135 000. All documents were duly registered. For the next few years Azoic Wholesalers Ltd. managed to pay interest on both mortgages and somewhat reduce the principal.

Azoic Wholesalers Ltd. subsequently became insolvent and was declared bankrupt. A trustee in bankruptcy was appointed, and all the assets of the company were sold. The following statement shows its financial condition after all assets were liquidated:

Azoic Wholesalers Ltd.
STATEMENT OF CONDITION AT DATE OF DISTRIBUTION

Assets		Liabilities	
Bank balance from:		Reliable Insurance Co.	
sale of building	$365 000	(first mortgage)	$252 000
sale of all other assets	$58 000	Sharpe Realties Ltd.	
		(second mortgage)	$143 000
Total available cash	$423 000		
Deficiency of assets	$81 000	General creditors	$109 000
	$504 000		$504 000

Calculate how the available cash will be distributed to the various creditors.

Problem 2

Fedorkow purchased a 200-acre farm on the St. John River in New Brunswick for $90 000. He paid $12 000 cash and gave back a mortgage of $78 000 to the vendor, Bowes. The mortgage was payable over a fifteen-year period with interest at $9\frac{1}{2}$% in instalments of about $630 per month. Within a year, Bowes fell ill and decided to retire to a warm climate. She sold the mortgage to Manor Mortgage Co. with only a slight discount on the amount then outstanding because she personally guaranteed payment by Fedorkow.

A year later Fedorkow received an offer to purchase his frontage on the St. John River, an area of about 10 acres, for $32 000. He visited the offices of Manor Mortgage Co. and asked if they would be interested in giving a discharge of the mortgage over the 10 acres. Manor Mortgage Co. agreed to do so provided Fedorkow would give a $1000 bonus and a further $12 000 in reduction of the mortgage debt. The parties carried out the arrangement, and the 10 acres was discharged from the mortgage, leaving the mortgage on the remainder of the farm. Subsequently, Fedorkow defaulted on the mortgage, having also let the farm fall into disrepair. Manor Mortgage Co. sued Bowes as guarantor of the mortgage debt for the balance of $31 560 then outstanding.

Should Manor Mortgage Co. succeed? (See *Farmers' Loan Co. v. Patchett* (1903), 6 O.L.R. 255, and *Molson's Bank v. Heilig* (1895), 26 O.R. 276.)

Problem 3

Burton owned the premises and business of Burton's Hardware, subject to a mortgage he had given to Milton as security for a loan of $25 000. Burton suffered severe business losses and finally became insolvent. Milton foreclosed and took possession of the property that had been left in a severely dilapidated condition and with taxes in arrears by Burton. The municipal tax department served Milton with a demand to pay tax arrears of $5850; otherwise the premises would be sold at a tax sale. Milton was undecided whether it was worthwhile paying the tax arrears and delayed making a decision. Meanwhile she became occupied with another large business transaction. The municipality finally proceeded with the sale after giving Milton adequate notice. At the sale Ponsby bought the premises for $5850.

Several years later Burton re-established himself in business and became very successful. Milton sued Burton on his personal covenant for the mortgage debt. In argument before the court Burton claimed that Milton must return the mortgaged premises before she would be entitled to payment of the debt. In reply Milton stated that the premises were lost because of the arrears of taxes that accrued while Burton was in possession, and thus it was Burton's failure to perform his covenant to pay taxes that caused the property to be lost. Burton conceded that this argument might well have been sound if the property had been sold while he was in possession, but not after foreclosure.

Discuss the merits of each argument, and state whether the mortgagee should succeed. (See *Dowker v. Thompson*, [1941] 2 D.L.R. 141.)

Problem 4

Bauer, a wealthy enterpreneur, bought Sunnydell Acres, a rather rundown farm, with a view to making it into a model dairy farm. He arranged a mortgage with Farm Mortgage Corp. for $80 000 and proceeded to renovate the farm. He found it difficult to run the farm because of a farm-labour shortage and decided finally to buy additional automatic equipment. For this purpose he arranged a second mortgage on Sunnydell with Meyer for $19 000.

A short time afterwards, Bauer's entire herd fell ill with a fatal cattle disease. He abandoned Sunnydell and returned to the city. Farm Mortgage Corp. foreclosed and sold the farm to Jones. Meyer, the second mortgagee, then sued Bauer on his personal covenant for the second mortgage debt. In defence Bauer claimed that Meyer could not sue unless he could reconvey Sunnydell to him in return for payment.

Should Meyer succeed? What difference, if any, is there between the position of Milton in Problem 3 and Meyer in the present case?

Problem 5

Lawlor purchased a small house from Cloutier at a price of $80 000. She paid $15 000 in cash and gave Cloutier a first mortgage for the balance. A year later, when Lawlor had reduced the principal amount of the mortgage to $52 000, she suffered financial reverses that made it impossible for her to continue to repay mortgage principal as required. Cloutier brought an action against Lawlor and on May 15 obtained an order for foreclosure with the deadline for payment by Lawlor specified as November 15.

On July 10, the insurance of $50 000 on the house expired and Lawlor renewed it while she was seeking to refinance with a new mortgagee. A few weeks later the house was seriously damaged by fire; the insurance adjuster appraised the loss at $35 000.

Both Cloutier and Lawlor immediately claimed the insurance money. The insurance company refused to pay Cloutier on the grounds that the insurance policy contained no mortgage clause that would have assigned to him rights in any claim "insofar as his interest may appear". The insurance company also refused to pay any part of the loss to Lawlor on the grounds that she had no insurable interest in the property.

Discuss the validity of the claims of Cloutier and Lawlor. Assume that there is no evidence to show that the fire was other than accidental in its origin. (For reference, see *Hanson v. Queensland Insurance Company, Limited* (1966) 56 W.W.R. 215.)

Cases

Case 1

Three years ago, the Lister Company Ltd. borrowed $200 000 from the Hi-Rise Bank. The Lister Company was in the textile business and gave a real estate mortgage on one of its buildings as collateral security for the bank loan: the mortgage provided security in the land, building, and fixtures in the building.

The company was later adjudged bankrupt on a petition of its creditors. A question arose about whether certain expensive machinery in the mortgaged building was in fact a fixture against which the bank would retain priority in liquidation. The trustee in bankruptcy, representing the general creditors, claimed it was not a fixture, so that the proceeds from its sale would be applied to all creditors' claims and not solely to that of the bank as mortgagee.

An officer of the bank and the trustee in bankruptcy went personally to inspect the machine, but were unable to agree whether it could be described as being "permanently" affixed. The bank then started legal action to have its claim as mortgagee of the machine confirmed. At this point, the trustee offered as a compromise to recognize the bank's priority to the extent of $20 000, a sum much less than the probable resale value of the machine; the bank accepted the offer and withdrew its action.

A few days later the bank learned that at the time it took the mortgage on the building the machine in question had been affixed to a cement floor in the plant in a permanent way, but that the building had since been renovated and the machine was reattached much less securely to the new floor. Neither the bank nor the trustee had this information when they contracted to substitute $20 000 in cash for the mortgage claim. The trustee refused to waive the agreement, however, and the Hi-Rise Bank brought an action asking the court for rescission of that contract and an order acknowledging its claim as a secured creditor with respect to the machine.

Discuss the nature of the argument on which the bank would base its claim and indicate whether its action should succeed. (For reference, see *Huddersfield Banking Co. v. Henry Lister & Son, Ltd.,* [1895] 2 Ch. 273; *Fairgrief v. Ellis*, [1935] 2 D.L.R. 806.)

Case 2

Victor Contractors Ltd. financed the construction of a high-rise apartment tower in Hamilton by receiving "draws" on first mortgage financing as work progressed. Rail Canada Pension Fund held the first mortgage for $10 700 000. The mortgage contained the following clause:

> The Mortgagor [Victor Contractors Ltd.] covenants and agrees with the Mortgagee [Rail Canada Pension Fund] that, except with the prior consent of the Mortgagee (which consent shall not be unreasonably withheld), it will not enter into any agreement for the sale, transfer or other disposition of the mortgaged premises.

On May 31, Victor Contractors agreed to sell the apartment building to Steel City Developers Corp. for $16 000 000. Steel City Developers paid a deposit of $75 000 and agreed to assume the existing first mortgage. The closing date was December 1, with the balance due on closing. The contract included the following clause:

> This Agreement is conditional upon the Vendor [Victor Contractors Ltd.] being able to obtain within thirty days following this date the consent of the first mortgagee [Rail Canada Pension Fund] to this sale and to the assumption of the first mortgage obligations by the Purchaser [Steel City Developers Corp.].

When Victor Contractors requested consent from Rail Canada Pension Fund, its manager stated that he would have to be satisfied with the financial capability of Steel City Developers and wished to see its audited financial statements. The secretary-treasurer of Steel City Developers refused to produce the statements on the grounds that her company had a firm policy of never disclosing its financial affairs to anyone except its bank because this policy gave it an advantage over its competitors.

With matters at an impasse, the solicitors for Steel City Developers finally wrote on June 28th, informing Victor Contractors that since, as vendor, it had been unable to obtain the consent of the first mortgagee as required, "This Agreement is now null and void." In reply, Victor Contractors wrote, "It is clear that your letter of June 28th written on behalf of your client constituted a wrongful renunciation of the contract of sale and purchase."

Victor Contractors then sued Steel City Developers for specific performance or, alternatively, for damages for breach of contract. Steel City Developers counterclaimed for the return of the deposit of $75 000.

Outline what you consider to be the main issue that the court will have to resolve in this case and offer with reasons an opinion about the probable outcome. Why would Rail Canada Pension Fund have insisted upon a right to satisfy itself of the financial capability of any purchaser of the apartment building?

PART SIX

BUSINESS ORGANIZATIONS: THEIR FORMS, OPERATIONS AND RESPONSIBILITIES

Business may be carried on in one of three forms — sole proprietorship, partnership, or corporation. By definition, only an individual may carry on business as a sole proprietor; similarly, it requires two or more persons to carry on business as a partnership. By contrast, a corporation is the most flexible business form: an individual may incorporate a business and be the sole owner (shareholder); a small group of persons may establish a corporation to carry on business; a very large enterprise, with thousands of shareholders, could not carry on business except by means of a corporation.

Chapter 29 is devoted mainly to the law of partnership, but we also discuss briefly the place of sole proprietorships.

While there is no separate body of law regulating sole proprietorships and no special formalities are required to begin operations, they remain subject to many regulations of general application to businesses. For example, the owner may be required to obtain a licence in order to carry on a particular type of business. In most provinces, if business is carried on under any name other than the actual name of the sole proprietor, that name must be registered. By contrast, each province regulates partnerships under its Partnership Act. These acts govern not only the relationship among partners but also their relations with the rest of the community.

The much more complex law of corporations is the subject of Chapters 30, 31, and 32. In Chapter 30, we examine the nature and significance of corporations and their formation and composition. In Chapter 31, we concern ourselves with the relations between directors and shareholders, and the management of a corporation's internal affairs.Chapter 32 deals with the external business relations of a corporation — with its customers, its creditors, its potential investors and the general public. Environmental protection laws have become increasingly important in the conduct of business and we focus upon this area as a useful example of government regulation.

CHAPTER 29

SOLE PROPRIETORSHIPS AND PARTNERSHIPS

CHOOSING THE APPROPRIATE FORM OF BUSINESS ORGANIZATION

Almost all businesses in Canada are carried on in one of the following forms: sole proprietorship, partnership — including limited partnership — or corporation. A few businesses are carried on by cooperatives, trusts, and other types of unincorporated association but because of their limited importance we shall not consider them.

A sole proprietorship or a partnership may come into existence without formality, that is, simply by the actions of the individual or group setting up a business. However, a corporation may only be formed under a statute in a prescribed manner and registered with the designated government department. Although for many years the procedure for incorporation was expensive and cumbersome, now a corporation can be formed quickly and for a few hundred dollars. In addition, almost all provinces currently permit a corporation to be created with a single shareholder, so that corporations are viable alternatives not only to partnerships but also to sole proprietorships. Accordingly, when an individual or a group of persons contemplate establishing a business, an initial decision must be made whether or not to incorporate. At this point careful legal, accounting, and management advice should be sought. Many small businesses decide to incorporate at the outset while others make the decision to do so later, or they remain unincorporated. There are now more than 800 000 corporations registered in Canada, representing close to one-third of all businesses, many of them small and medium-sized enterprises.

In the next chapter we shall consider the reasons why a person, or group of persons, might decide to incorporate their business. The subject of this chapter is those businesses that carry on without incorporating.[1]

SOLE PROPRIETORSHIPS

An individual who sets up a business has, merely by her act, created a "sole proprietorship"; no formalities are necessary. While there is no distinct body of law regulating sole proprietorships, they are subject to many regulations that apply to all forms of business: laws regarding public health and safety, zoning and, of course, taxation, apply to all businesses, whether sole proprietorships, partnerships, or corporations. A sole proprietor may have to obtain a licence to carry on a particular type of business. For example, a municipal licence is normally required before one may start business as an electrician, plumber, restaurateur, or taxi-driver. Provincial licensing and registration may be required for a car dealer, insurance broker, or employment agency. The proprietor must keep proper accounts for income tax purposes; she must make payroll deductions for employee income tax, unemployment insurance, and Canada Pension Plan; she must meet health and safety regulations for her staff, including compliance with workers compensation standards, and in hiring staff, she must be conscious of human rights.

---

[1] We should point out here that a corporation may be a member of a partnership, along with other individuals or corporations.

In most provinces, statutes require that if business is carried on under a name other than the actual name of the owner, whether the owner is a sole proprietor, a partnership or a corporation, the name must be registered.[2]

$\mathcal{P}$ARTNERSHIPS

Although partnerships may be established without formality, their affairs are governed by a well-developed body of laws. This is because until the present century, partnership was the accepted way for two or more persons to carry on an enterprise, and problems concerning almost every aspect of partnership arose and became the subject of legal decisions, starting about the middle of the 18th century. By the 1880s, there was a virtually complete body of rules that were well settled, but the maze of decisions on detailed points made it difficult to discover the broader principles. To remedy this situation, the British Parliament in 1890 passed the Partnership Act,[3] which brought together the multitude of cases under more general principles and codified the law as the experts in the field then believed it to be. The English Act has been adopted in substantially the same form by all the common law provinces.

The Act has remained virtually unchanged from its original form for several reasons: first, this area of the law had reached maturity, and its principles were highly developed by the time the Act was passed; second, the Act, which was substantially the work of Sir Frederick Pollock, the recognized authority in the field of partnership law, was well drawn and readily comprehensible to the intelligent business person; third, the corporation was rapidly emerging as the dominant form of business organization, thus relieving any pressure to adapt the partnership form to changing business requirements. These factors probably account for the fact that there have been comparatively few cases on the interpretation of the Act. The Act itself is an accurate representation of the state of partnership law today. Two of the leading textbooks on the subject are rather slim volumes, yet are quite adequate as commentaries on the statute.[4]

$\mathcal{T}$HE NATURE OF PARTNERSHIP

Advantages and Disadvantages

A partnership may be formed by two or more persons, who may be natural persons (individuals) or legal persons (corporations). There are obvious advantages in carrying on a venture, whether in business or any other field, as a joint undertaking. Working together, members of a group may pool their knowledge and skills, and their physical and financial resources. There are also obvious disadvantages: disagreements may lead to stalemates; dishonesty or incompetence of one member may lead to losses suffered by other members; when a group wishes to make important decisions, it may lose valuable time in arranging a meeting. None of these problems exists when a person acts solely on

---

[2] See, for example, Business Names Act, R.S.O. 1990, c. B-17, s.2 (2).

[3] 53 & 54 Vict., c. 39 (United Kingdom).

[4] Drake, C.D., *Law of Partnership* (3rd. ed.). London: Sweet & Maxwell, 1983; Underhill, *The Principles of the Law of Partnership* (12th ed.), Ivamy and Jones, ed. London: Butterworth & Co. Ltd., 1986.

his or her own behalf. Generally speaking, however, the advantages of group activity outweigh the disadvantages, at least in the minds of people who contemplate a joint undertaking. As a result, they often agree to carry out common goals in partnership with each other. Under our system of law, the word "partnership" refers exclusively to joint business enterprises carried on for profit. It does not refer to other associations, such as charitable enterprises, joint trustees of an estate, or public boards.

The Partnership Concept of Business

"Partnership is the relation which subsists between persons carrying on a business in common with a view of profit."[5] To a business person this definition of partnership, contained in the various partnership acts, is extremely important because of the consequences that may follow from a finding that he or she is a partner. (We shall discuss these consequences in a later subsection.) Whether two or more persons are partners depends upon all the circumstances of a case. Normally a formal written partnership agreement is drawn up and is signed by all the partners. However, business people may be found to be partners in carrying on a business even though they have not consciously so agreed. Naturally the element of agreement is a very important one, and if two persons expressly agree to form a partnership, this is ordinarily conclusive; but in the absence of an express agreement they may still be held to be partners if they have acted as such. In any event, the courts insist upon looking at the substance of the relationship, and are not necessarily guided by what the parties may themselves choose to call it.

Since the term *partnership* applies only to business, it is important too to discover whether the activity carried on amounts to a business. The term *business* is a nebulous one. It may be said to include "every trade, occupation, or profession", but it does not include every activity carried on for a profit. For instance, owning property and collecting rent from tenants need not amount to carrying on a business. Hence the joint ownership of property does not of itself make the owners partners. Similarly, if a group of investors forms a syndicate to hold a portfolio of securities, this arrangement does not amount to carrying on a business unless the investors engage in the trade of buying and selling shares, rather than merely retaining them for investment income.

The Fact of Partnership

Not every business relationship makes the parties to the relationship partners with each other. In the first place, isolated or even intermittent transactions carried on jointly do not by themselves establish the parties as partners. Thus, if two merchants in the Atlantic provinces pooled an order of goods purchased in Montreal so that they could fill one freight car and obtain a lower freight rate, such an arrangement would not make them partners. Business people may carry on a venture with common interests in its success, yet even when these interests are of a substantial and continuing nature the venture may not be a partnership. Generally, the sharing of gross receipts does not create a partnership: if an owner of a theatre were to rent it to a drama group and one of the terms of the contract of rental was that she would receive ten per cent

---

[5] The Partnership Act, 1890, s. 1(1). The same wording is used in Canadian versions of the statute. See, for example: R.S.B.C. 1979, c. 312, s. 2; R.S.O. 1990, c. P-5, s. 2; R.S.N.S. 1989, c. 334, s. 4. In subsequent footnotes of this chapter, references to B.C., Ontario and N.S. will be to these statutes.

of the gross receipts, such an arrangement would not make the owner a partner in the venture of producing a play.

On the other hand, a receipt of a share of the profits of the business is evidence tending to establish a partnership, though it is not by itself conclusive. In particular it is insufficient evidence if the sharing of profits is part of an arrangement to (a) repay a debt owed; (b) pay an employee or agent of the business as part of his remuneration; (c) pay a widow, widower or child of a deceased partner an annuity; (d) repay an advance of money made as a loan by which the lender is to receive a rate of interest varying with the profits; (e) pay the seller of a business an amount for goodwill varying with the profits. None of the above payments by itself makes the recipient of the payment a partner in the business.[6]

Apart from the above specific situations, it is virtually impossible to imagine circumstances in which the only evidence available would be the fact that a person is sharing in the profits of a business. A person receiving a share of profits has usually contributed property or money to the business. Even though partners often share profits according to a ratio that is not based on capital contribution, nonetheless the courts consider profit-sharing that coincides with the ratio of capital contribution strong evidence of partnership. Another important factor is whether the person receiving the profits has taken part in the management of the business. Evidence showing that she has taken some active role in the business, particularly in making decisions on important matters, when added to the fact that she has shared in the profits, will usually suffice to establish her as a partner. A person may also find herself liable as a partner by estoppel if she allows a third party to rely on a representation made by her or by anyone else that she is a partner in the firm and as a result of that representation the third party advances credit to the firm. The situations that may arise are, of course, limitless: the above discussion is intended to illustrate only some of the questions that arise most frequently.

The Liability of a Partner

What is the significance of deciding that a particular venture is a partnership and identifying a person as a partner in the venture? The significance lies primarily in the partner's personal liability to outsiders who have dealt with the partnership. Generally speaking, a person who is held to be a partner becomes personally responsible for the debts and liabilities of the partnership.

Probably the greatest risk of liability to which a partner subjects himself results from the contractual obligations of the partnership. "Every partner is an agent of the firm and his other partners for the purpose of the business of the partnership, and the acts of every partner who does any act for carrying on in the usual way business of the kind carried on by the firm of which he is a member, bind the firm and its partners",[7] unless the authority of the partner has been restricted by an agreement with the other partners and the third party knows of this restriction. Any acts done by a partner within the scope of his usual authority and relied upon by an outsider bind the firm and all the partners. Thus, a restriction placed upon the authority of a partner has the same effect as a restriction placed upon the authority of an agent by his principal: it does not affect outsiders who do not have knowledge of the restriction.

---

[6] B.C., s. 4; Ont., s. 3; N.S., s. 5.
[7] B.C., s. 7; Ont., s. 6; N.S., s. 8.

The liability of a firm, and of its partners, is not restricted to contracts. The Act also makes them liable for "any wrongful act or omission of any partners acting in the ordinary course of the business of the firm", and for any misapplication of funds that have been placed in the care of the partnership.[8] A firm may consequently be liable for the negligence or other torts of its members, and for breaches of trust committed by any of them.

Every partner is liable jointly with the other partners for all the debts and obligations of the firm incurred while he is a partner.[9] When the liabilities of a partnership exceed its assets, a creditor or injured party, having obtained judgment against the partnership and exhausted its assets in trying to satisfy judgment, may look to the personal assets of any partner or partners until the judgment has been satisfied. Accordingly, it is important for a person advancing credit to a firm to determine whether it is a partnership, and if so who are the partners. Because of the potential liability, it is crucial for anyone considering entering into a partnership to choose partners very carefully.

In principle, a person is liable only for the obligations of a partnership created while he is a member of the firm. Hence, "a person who is admitted as a partner into an existing firm does not thereby become liable to the creditors of the firm for anything done before he became a partner", and "a partner who retires from a firm does not thereby cease to be liable for partnership debts or obligations incurred before his retirement."[10] The only way he may free himself from his obligations is by novation between the partners remaining in the firm, its creditors, and himself.[11]

Even after retiring from a partnership, a partner may be liable by estoppel to third parties who reasonably believe he is still a member of the firm and advance credit to the firm in reliance on his membership. A retiring partner may free himself from this liability by carrying out the requirements of the Partnership Act.[12] An advertisement in the official gazette of the province is adequate notice to persons generally who had not dealt with the firm before the retiring partner left the firm, but all persons who have dealt with the firm on a fairly regular basis before the partner's retirement should receive actual notice of the retirement if the retiring partner is to be fully protected. It is customary, therefore, to send notices to all those persons who have dealt with the firm more or less recently, depending on the nature of the business. Estoppel does not apply when a partner dies. His estate is not liable for credit extended to the firm after his death, even though the creditors do not know he has died.[13]

Does a Partnership Have a Separate Personality?

In the next chapter, on corporation law, we shall discuss in considerably more detail the significance of the separate personality of a group. It has been established as a matter of law that a corporation does have a separate personality of its own. In the law of partnership the position is somewhat confused and doubtful. Perhaps the most widely-held view is a strict one, that a partnership has no independent existence and merely represents the collective rights and duties of all the partners.

---

[8] B.C., ss. 11, 12; Ont., ss. 11, 12; N.S., ss. 12, 13. See Public Trustee v. Mortimer (1985), 16 D.L.R. (4th) 404; Korz v. St. Pierre (1988), 43 D.L.R. (4th) 528.
[9] B.C., ss. 10, 13; Ont., ss. 10, 13; N.S., ss. 12, 15.
[10] B.C., s. 10; Ont., s. 10; N.S., s. 12.
[11] See Chapter 15 under "Discharge by Agreement" (Substituted Agreement).
[12] B.C., s. 39; Ont., s. 36; N.S., s. 39. See also the discussion of registration of partnerships, below.
[13] Ibid.

In actual practice, however, and in some of its legal implications, a partnership does have a semi-separate existence of its own. For example, partnership creditors have first call against partnership assets before the personal creditors of an individual partner. This is so because until the creditors of the partnership have been paid, it is impossible to identify and distribute the share of an individual partner. If, after these creditors are paid, no assets remain, then the partner has no share for personal creditors to seize.

Another instance of separate existence occurs in the rule that a deceased partner's personal creditors have first call against the personal assets of her estate.[14] Thus, if the partnership assets are insufficient to pay off the partnership creditors, they must wait for the personal creditors to be paid out of the personal estate of the deceased partner before they can take what is left in order to satisfy their debt. Under the Bankruptcy and Insolvency Act, this rule applies also to the estate of a living partner who becomes bankrupt.[15]

Third, real property held by a partnership is treated according to the usual rules governing real property as far as the partnership is concerned, but insofar as the individual partners are concerned, their interest in the real property is considered personal property.

Fourth, a partnership may bring an action in the name of the firm without naming all the partners as plaintiffs, and an outside party may sue a partnership in its firm name without naming all the partners as defendants. Thus, for the purposes of court action, the partnership may be treated as a separate entity. It is, in fact, wise to sue a partnership in the firm name rather than in the names of the individual partners: all the provincial acts have incorporated a rather anomalous rule, developed in the case law prior to the acts, that partners are liable only *jointly* for contractual debts and obligations of their firm. The significance of this rule is that only *one* cause of action arises from the obligation. If by carelessness or ignorance of the facts a plaintiff brings action against some of the partners and obtains judgment against them, her rights will be exhausted: if their assets are insufficient to satisfy the judgment and she later discovers that there are other partners, she will not be able to sue those others for the deficiency. This risk is eliminated if she sues the defendants in the firm name, as all provinces now permit a plaintiff to do. Once the assets of the firm are exhausted, she may go against the personal assets of any of the partners. We should note that the rule concerning joint liability does not apply to actions based upon tort or breach of trust; in either of these cases a plaintiff may bring a subsequent action against partners who were not parties to the original action. Such liability is called *joint and several liability.*

Finally, as an accounting matter, a partnership is treated as a separate entity with its own assets, liabilities, and financial statements.

THE RELATION OF PARTNERS TO ONE ANOTHER

The Partnership Act sets out a number of terms that will be implied if certain matters are not expressly covered in a partnership agreement. Unfortunately, although all the provinces have adopted the English act, they have rearranged the sections to conform to

---

[14] B.C., s. 10; Ont., s. 10; N.S., s. 11.
[15] R.S.C. 1985, c. B-3, s. 142.

their customary way of setting down statutes, so that the section numbers differ from one province to another. Generally speaking, the sections concerned with the relations of partners to one another start at about section 20 and embrace the succeeding dozen sections. For convenience we shall use the numbering of the Manitoba Act as representative of the general scheme.[16] The main terms that are implied are summarized below, with explanatory comment where necessary. It is important to remember that the parties to a partnership agreement *may, and frequently do, vary these terms* either at the time of the original agreement or later by unanimous consent.

S. 23(1) "All property and rights and interests in property originally brought into the partnership stock or acquired, whether by purchase or otherwise, on account of the firm or for the purposes or in the course of the partnership's business are called... 'partnership property' and must be held and applied by the partners exclusively for the purposes of the partnership, and in accordance with the partnership agreement." A partner is therefore not entitled to use the property for private purposes. All property bought with money belonging to the firm is deemed to have been bought on account of the firm and is available only for the use of the firm.

S. 27(a) "All partners are entitled to share equally in the capital and profits of the business and must contribute equally towards the losses..." Partners commonly vary this term: they contribute different proportions of capital and share profits based on other criteria such as time spent on partnership business.

S. 27(b) If a partner incurs expenses or personal liabilities "in the ordinary and proper conduct of the business of the firm", or in doing anything to preserve the business or property of the firm, the firm must indemnify him for these expenses or liabilities.

S. 27(c) If a partner contributes to the partnership a sum of money or other valuable consideration in excess of what he has agreed to subscribe under the partnership agreement, he is entitled to interest at the rate of five per cent on the value of the excess contribution while it remains with the firm. Excess contributions are usually called "advances"; where there is an express agreement that a partner will make an advance, a different rate of interest may be fixed.

S. 27(e) "Every partner may take part in the management of the partnership business." In small partnerships, this implied term is occasionally varied. For example, a parent who takes a child into partnership may wish to reserve the management of the firm to himself. Very large partnerships, such as large law firms, often have two or three classes of partners, and it may be that only the senior partners take part in the management of the firm.

S. 27(f) "No partner shall be entitled to remuneration for acting in the partnership business." This term is often varied according to the circumstances of the partnership arrangement. Sometimes, one partner is the managing partner who hopes to derive his livelihood from the partnership business, whereas the other partner or partners are merely investing partners. Their partnership agreement will likely state that the managing partner is to be "paid a salary". Entitlement to this "salary" is normally considered as a first call on the partnership profits. The agreement may state that the sum shall be deducted from his share of the profits, or more usually that it be his prior share before any further division of profits among all the partners. If at the end of a firm's financial year there are no profits, "salary" received during the year by a partner, unlike that of an

---

[16] R.S.M. 1987, c. P-30.

employee, would constitute an advance on profits and be repayable to the firm.

Normally, partners are not willing and able to wait until some time after the end of the firm's accounting year, when the year's profits have been ascertained, before enjoying any of the fruits of their labour. It is common, therefore, to provide that a partner may "draw" up to a specified amount each month out of his prospective share of profits. Such an amount will be considered merely an advance on his share of the projected profits, repayable to the firm to the extent that it exceeds his share of the actual profits.

S. 27(g) "No person may be introduced as a partner without the consent of all existing partners." Two common variations occur: where there are senior and junior partners, and the consent of only the senior partners is required; where a partner has reserved the right to have a son or daughter join the firm at a later date.

S. 27(h) "Any difference arising as to ordinary matters connected with the partnership business may be decided by a majority of the partners, but no change may be made in the nature of the partnership business without the consent of all existing partners." In case of a serious disagreement this provision can be troublesome. The minority may insist that the particular decision did not concern an ordinary matter but affected the nature of the partnership business. It may be advisable, therefore, to spell out clearly which matters may only be decided unanimously.

S. 27(i) "The partnership books are to be kept at the place of business of the partnership or the principal place if there is more than one and every partner may, when he thinks fit, have access to and inspect and copy any of them."

S. 31 "Partners are bound to render true accounts and full information of all things affecting the partnership to any partner or his legal representative." The only circumstances under which this term and the previous one might be varied would be in a partnership having several classes of partners. It is possible that by express agreement the most junior group of partners might not have access to all the books and records of the partnership. Even such a reservation, however, would be restricted to a narrow class of information.

S. 32(1) "Every partner must account to the firm for any benefit derived by him without the consent of the other partners from any transaction concerning the partnership or from any use by him of the partnership property, name or business connection."

S. 33 "Where a partner without the consent of the other partners carries on any business of the same nature as and competing with that of the firm, he must account for and pay over to the firm all profits made by him in that business." These terms are varied occasionally according to the circumstances of the partnership. For example, an entrepreneur might be carrying on a retail business in the downtown area and subsequently enter into a partnership to carry on a similar business in a suburban shopping centre. Since the two businesses might well be considered "of the same nature and competing with" each other, the partner owning the downtown business would require, as a term of the partnership agreement, that the partners in the suburban business consent to his continuing the downtown business.

S. 34(1) A partnership is, by its very nature, a personal relationship between the partners. A person enters into a partnership with another in the belief that the other person has the desired qualities for the business venture. As one would expect, therefore, no partner may assign his share in the partnership, either absolutely or by way of mortgage, so as to permit the assignees to take over his duties or "to interfere in the management or administration of the partnership business or affairs, or to require any accounts of the partnership transactions, or to inspect the partnership books." An assignee may, however, "receive the share of profits to which the assigning partner would otherwise be entitled and the assignee must accept the account of profits agreed to by the partners."

Termination of Partnership

Implied Statutory Rules

The dozen sections of the Partnership Acts following those just discussed provide a further series of implied terms dealing with the dissolution of the firm. In addition, two sections found in the earlier group are related to dissolution and are discussed briefly below:

S. 29 "Where no fixed term is agreed upon for the duration of the partnership, any partner may determine the partnership at any time on giving notice of his intention so to do to all other partners." The notice so given may be oral or in writing. If the partnership was originally formed by deed, however, a notice in writing is necessary.

S. 30 "Where a partnership entered into for a fixed term is continued after the term has expired and without any express new agreement, the rights and duties of the partners remain the same as they were at the expiration of the term so far as is consistent with the incidents of a partnership at will." A *partnership at will* is one having no fixed term. Thus, if the partners continue to act in the same manner as they acted during the term of the agreement, it is presumed that the partnership simply continues. Without such continuing conduct, however, the partnership is dissolved by the expiration of a fixed term. Similarly, if it was entered into for a single venture or undertaking, it expires by the termination of that venture or undertaking.

S. 36(1) "Subject to any agreement between the partners, every partnership is dissolved as regards all the partners by the death or bankruptcy or insolvency of any partner." This term, perhaps more than any other, is varied by the partnership agreement. Even in a simple partnership between two persons, their agreement should provide for some means of ascertaining the value of the partnership upon the death or insolvency of either of them so that the remaining partner may save the business from collapse and may buy out the share of the deceased or insolvent partner. In a partnership having large assets and many members, the operation of this implied term dissolving the partnership could be disastrous. Accordingly, the partnership agreement usually provides that the partnership will continue in existence upon the death or insolvency of any partner. Various kinds of arrangements may form a part of the partnership agreement to provide for buying out the share of a deceased partner, often by the use of life insurance schemes. The problem is primarily financial rather than legal. These arrangements must take into account the ability of the remaining partners to pay for the share of the deceased or insolvent partner, methods for ascertaining the value of that share, and the tax consequences of a particular method.

S. 36(2) "A partnership may, at the option of the other partners, be dissolved if any partner suffers his share of the partnership property to be charged under this act for his separate debts." Thus, if one of the partners does assign or charge his interest in the partnership to his creditors, the remaining partners may choose to dissolve the partnership.

Dissolution by Law

A partnership is essentially a contractual arrangement that is dissolved by any event that makes it unlawful for the business of the firm to be carried on or for members of the firm to carry it on in partnership. The results here are in keeping with the general law of contract concerning illegality.

Even when there is disagreement amongst the partners concerning dissolution, or where dissolution at a specific time would be contrary to the terms of the partnership agreement, the court may on an application by one or more partners order the partnership dissolved under the following circumstances:

S. 38(a) "Where a partner is found…[mentally incompetent]…or is shown to the satisfaction of the court to be of permanently unsound mind…" In these circumstances, the application may be made on behalf of the incompetent partner as well as by any other partner.

S. 38(b) "Where a partner, other than the partner suing, becomes in any other way permanently incapable of performing his part in the partnership contract."

S. 38(c) "Where a partner, other than the partner suing, has been guilty of such conduct as, in the opinion of the court, regard being had to the nature of the business, is calculated to prejudicially affect the carrying on of the business." For example, if a partner in a brokerage firm was convicted of theft, his partner could apply successfully to the court to have the partnership dissolved even though the partnership was by agreement to continue for a fixed term.

S. 38(d) "Where a partner, other than the partner suing, wilfully or persistently commits a breach of the partnership agreement, or otherwise so conducts himself in matters relating to the partnership business that it is not reasonably practicable for the other partner or partners to carry on the business in partnership with him."

S. 38(e) "Where in any case circumstances have arisen which in the opinion of the court, render it just and equitable that the partnership is dissolved." This latter provision is a general catch-all clause, giving courts a wide discretion to prevent serious injustice to partners when unforeseen circumstances arise.

S. 40 "Where a partnership has been dissolved or a partner has retired…any partner may publicly give notice of the dissolution or retirement and may require the other partner or partners to concur for that purpose in all necessary or proper acts, if any, which cannot be done without his or their concurrence." Thus, if one partner brings about the dissolution of a partnership, either under the provisions of the agreement or by order of the court, he may require the other partners to do all necessary acts to make the dissolution effective. For example, he could require other signing partners to sign cheques or any other documents necessary to discharge liabilities to creditors and to free the assets of the partnership so that they might be liquidated and divided amongst the partners.

S. 42 "On the dissolution of a partnership every partner is entitled as against the other partners in the firm and all persons claiming through them in respect of their interest as partners, to have the property of the partnership applied in payment of the debts and liabilities of the firm and to have the surplus assets after such payment applied in payment of what may be due the partners respectively…"

S. 47 "In settling accounts between the partners after a dissolution of partnership the following rules shall, subject to any agreement, be observed:

(a) Losses including losses and deficiencies of capital are to be paid first out of profits, next out of capital, and lastly, if necessary, by the partners individually in the proportion in which they were entitled to share in the profits.

(b) The assets of the firm including the sums if any contributed by the partners to make up losses and deficiencies of capital, are to be applied in the following manner and order:

(i) in paying the debts and liabilities of the firm to persons who are not partners therein.

(ii) in paying to each partner rateably what is due from the firm to him for advances as distinguished from capital.

(iii) in paying to each partner rateably what is due from the firm to him in respect to capital.

(iv) the ultimate residue, if any, is to be divided among the partners in the proportion in which profits are divisible."

The above provisions are usually strictly adhered to. In some special circumstances where, let us say, a relatively poor partner has invested the whole of his assets in a rather risky partnership venture, the partners might possibly provide between themselves that if liabilities exceeded the assets of the partnership itself upon dissolution, the balance would be borne wholly by the wealthier partner. With this rather limited exception, however, the above rules would apply in almost all cases.[17]

The Partnership Agreement

As we have seen, parties may be held by the courts to be partners simply by their conduct. As a result, third parties have little interest in the terms of a partnership agreement: unless a third party is made aware of the internal arrangements of the partnership, she is entitled to assume that the usual rules as codified in the Partnership Act apply. A partnership is bound by a contract made with a third party provided it was within the usual authority of the partner making the contract, and it is liable for torts committed against third parties within the usual rules of agency and master and servant.

The significance of a partnership agreement lies in the relations of partners among themselves. A partnership agreement may be wholly oral and yet be valid and enforceable provided it does not come within one of the sections of the Statute of Frauds. The Statute of Frauds affects a contract of partnership only if by its terms it extends beyond one year and performance has not begun. Once a partnership begins to operate, the statute has no effect.[18] As we know, of course, an oral agreement is subject to the flaws of memory of the parties to the agreement, and if only for certainty it is worthwhile to have a written record of it.

We have seen that the Partnership Act sets out a number of implied terms in the absence of any provision in the agreement to the contrary. Generally speaking, partners may agree to whatever terms they wish, provided the terms are not illegal and do not

---

[17] See *Garner v. Murray*, [1904] 1 Ch. 57, for an interpretation of this section when partners make unequal capital contributions or share losses unequally and one of them with a deficiency of capital is insolvent.

[18] *Burdon v. Barkus* (1862), 45 E.R. 1098. As noted in Chapter 12, the Statute of Frauds has been abolished in some provinces.

offend public policy. Business partnerships, like marriages, can be perilous ventures, and probably because dissolution of a partnership is somewhat easier, a higher proportion of them break up after a very short time. The reasons for dissolution are extremely varied. Many are dissolved because the business venture has proved unprofitable, others because the venture has proved very profitable and the partners have gone on to form a corporation. Still others dissolve because of a conflict of personalities that the parties cannot resolve. A large portion of profitable partnerships are destroyed by misunderstanding or mistrust. The failure to decide important issues in advance often leads to the kind of misunderstanding and mistrust that in turn creates an eventually irreparable breach between the parties.

The main purpose of a partnership agreement is therefore to set out, as carefully and as clearly as possible, the objects of the partnership, the responsibilities of each of the partners, the capital contributions of each to the firm, the time and energy that each will devote to its business, the respective shares of profits and losses that each partner will take, procedures for settling disagreements (usually by arbitration), and provisions for dissolution or for one or more of the partners to buy out the other partners.

In order to draft an effective partnership agreement, the parties must be candid with each other from the very outset and they must deal with the most probable events that might upset the partnership or change its course of action. A well-drafted, carefully-thought-out partnership agreement is of itself no guarantee of a successful partnership. The other elements — a sound business idea, reasonably good luck, mutual trust and good faith, and diligence of application — must be present for a partnership to succeed: a well-drawn agreement simply minimizes one major hazard.

If only because of subjective bias, it is virtually impossible for partners to draft their own agreement. The usual problems of ambiguous words and unconscious interpretations favourable to oneself can create the same misunderstandings that arise in the law of contracts. In addition, individual partners are unaware of many of the pitfalls that accumulated experience in business and learning in partnership law may avoid. For these reasons a partnership agreement is, perhaps more than any other type of agreement, one that should be drafted with expert advice and assistance. If the parties to the agreement are investing large sums in the venture, then each should have her own legal counsel to help protect her investment.

THE JOINT VENTURE

The joint venture (sometimes called a "consortium") is an agreement that two or more parties (often corporations) make to contribute a part of their respective resources (particular assets and expertise) to a specific project. Sometimes a project requires a greater capital outlay than any one corporation, even a large one, may be prepared to put at risk. A joint venture spreads the risk among the participants. In the oil and gas industry, large corporations have found it practical to undertake exploration expenditures jointly to discover and develop oil and gas reserves, as in the Arctic and Atlantic continental shelf explorations. Inevitably most of their efforts result in dry holes, but a single discovery may result in the location of large recoverable reserves and provide a handsome return to each of the participants. Rather than devote their exploration budgets individually to a few projects with a high probability of failure in each, the corporations have preferred to spread the risk in this way.

Legally, a joint venture may take a variety of forms. Its simplest form is just a contractual relationship among the participants for a specific undertaking. In other cases it is like a partnership and may have a semi-separate existence of its own for the purpose of suing and being sued. As in a partnership, it is normal for a joint venture to establish a separate accounting entity for the allocation of contributions and the distribution of revenues. An alternative method is for the parties to incorporate a separate corporation (a joint subsidiary) for the venture with each participant holding shares in it.

Participants typically regard a joint venture as an extension of their own operations and a collaboration with other parties rather than as a separate business, though this is less likely to be so when they incorporate a separate corporation to carry on the venture. A venture is for a specific project or series of explorations, and of limited duration. Normally, profits are not retained jointly for investment in other projects, but are distributed to each of the participants in proportions set down in the joint-venture agreement. The parties may also try to limit their liability by providing that their only contribution will be those things specifically set out in the agreement, that the agreement shall not be construed as a partnership, and that their liability will not be joint and several. Such restrictions may not be effective against outsiders if it is subsequently determined that the venture was as a matter of fact a partnership.[19]

Participants may also try to limit the authority of members to act as agents for one another in the operation of a joint venture and may identify one of themselves (or an independent party) as the "operator" of the joint venture. Whether such an arrangement will be effective to limit the agency of each participating member remains a question of fact to be determined by the court if a dispute arises with an outside third party.

Co-venturers in a joint venture are in a fiduciary relationship with each other with respect to the purposes of the undertaking. They are much like partners with a continuing duty of utmost good faith in the conduct of the affairs of their joint enterprise.

$\mathcal{R}$EGISTRATION OF PARTNERSHIPS

Almost all provinces require the filing, in a local registry office, of a declaration giving such essential information as the names and addresses of each partner and the name under which they intend to carry on business, the time during which the partnership has existed, and an acknowledgment that the persons named in the declaration are its only members. Declarations must also be filed when there is any change in membership, in a partnership's name, or when a firm is dissolved. However, registration requirements do not necessarily apply to all partnerships. For example, in Nova Scotia partnerships engaged in farming or fishing are not required to register.[20]

Penalties for failure to carry out the requirements of the statute vary from province to province. Generally there are fines for failure to register within a pre-

---

[19]   Lansing Building Supply (Ontario) Ltd. v. Ierullo (1990), 71 O.R. (2d) 173.
[20]   Partnerships and Business Names Registration Act, R.S.N.S. 1989, c. 335, s.2(a). Prior to 1990, only partnerships for trading, manufacturing and mining had to register in Ontario.

scribed period, and in Ontario, for example, the Act states, "no partnership in respect of which a declaration has not been filed as required by this Act and no member thereof is capable of maintaining any action or other proceeding in any court in Ontario in respect of any contract made in connection with the business carried on by the partnership."[21] This rule is not as severe as it at first seems; a partnership may register late on payment of a prescribed penalty, and may then commence proceedings. The records of the declaration of partnership are open to the public and may be examined upon payment of a small fee.

The purposes of this registration system are quite clear. It provides the minimum of essential information about a partnership and particularly about the names of partners in the firm, thus enabling a plaintiff to serve each partner with notice of an action if she wishes to do so. It is also helpful to prospective creditors or other suppliers in checking the accuracy of information given by a member of the partnership concerning the membership of the firm.

*L*IMITED PARTNERSHIPS

All provinces have either a Limited Partnership Act or a set of provisions in their Partnership Act permitting the carrying on of business under certain very restricted conditions, with limited liability. These Acts came into force at about the same time that the private limited company (discussed in the next chapter) also became available for general use. Since for most business ventures, incorporating a company is a more useful way to obtain limited liability, very little use has been made of limited partnerships.

The major requirement for the formation of a limited partnership is that there must be one or more general partners. A *general partner* has unlimited liability, while the remaining *limited partners* may have a liability limited to the amount paid by each of them to the limited partnership as capital. That is, they stand to lose what they have invested in the business but are not liable to contribute further.

All the Acts prohibit a limited partner from taking an active part in the management of the partnership. If she does so, she becomes liable as a general partner. The words of prohibition vary considerably in each of the statutes.[22] A limited partner would be "taking an active part" if she were personally to transact any business for the firm or be employed for that purpose as an agent or as a lawyer; but she can examine the records of the firm, inquire into its progress, and advise on its management without incurring the liability of a general partner. The result is that a limited partner who attempts to take part in the management of the firm does so at a considerable personal risk. She may find herself in the dilemma that if she does not interfere, the business may fail completely; yet if she chooses to exercise some control in order to save the business, she will incur unlimited liability. For this reason more than any other, limited partnerships have been rarely used.

The limited partnership provisions set out more stringent regulations for registration than are demanded of ordinary partnerships. Failure to comply with requirements of detailed essential information also results in the loss of limited liability.

---

[21] Business Names Act, R.S.O. 1990, c. B-17, s. 7.
[22] See, for example: Partnership Act, R.S.M. 1970, c. P30, s. 63(1).

Questions for Review

1. What purpose did the codification of partnership law serve? Why has the statute remained essentially unchanged?
2. In what sense is a partner an agent?
3. What is the main value of a partnership agreement?
4. What are two main characteristics that make a joint undertaking a partnership?
5. Why might a person be anxious to disclaim being a partner in a firm?
6. A partner's duty of good faith is similar to that of an agent. State two situations where this duty would arise.
7. Jones and Chang enter into a partnership agreement that they write on the back of a postcard. Does this document constitute the whole of the agreement between them?
8. What is partnership by estoppel?
9. Fry, a partner in the firm of Potter, Skillet, and Fry, assigns her interest in the firm to Cook without the consent of her partners. What are Cook's rights? What are the partners' rights?
10. Why is it advantageous to sue a partnership in the firm name?
11. Grey and Burton have formed a limited partnership. Burton is a limited partner. Describe Grey's position. What types of conduct should Burton avoid if he is to continue to enjoy limited liability?
12. Name two important instances of joint undertakings for profit that are not partnerships.
13. In what circumstances will unanimous approval rather than a simple majority be required for a business decision of a partnership?
14. What type of partnership results when a group of partners continue to carry on business together after their agreement has expired?
15. What are the main forms that a "joint venture" may take?

Problems

Problem 1

Kuli owned a tobacco farm and entered into an agreement with Magory whereby Magory would:

    (1) work the land for Kuli for one year;
    (2) be given possession of a house on the land during that period;
    (3) receive from Kuli half the necessary supplies for the land and provide the other half himself;
    (4) market the crop and give half the proceeds to Kuli.

Were Kuli and Magory partners?

Problem 2

Hallvorson and Bowes agreed to form a partnership to carry on a restaurant business. Hallvorson agreed to pay in $15 000 as his capital contribution. The parties started operation of the restaurant before Hallvorson paid in his $15 000. Both parties worked diligently at the business for several months, all the while arguing about the respective capital contribution of each. During this period only Bowes had contributed capital.

Finally Bowes ordered Hallvorson to leave. Hallvorson sued for a declaration that he was a partner even though he had not contributed his capital share.

What should be the result?

Problem 3

A, B, and C carried on the business of building contractors in partnership without a written agreement. A was the founder of the business and still managed it. The success of the firm had been due throughout its existence to the capacity and personal qualities of A, who financed it and skilfully ran it. By oral agreement, each partner had the right to periodically draw such sums from the profits of the firm as were necessary for his living expenses, such withdrawals to approximate the proportionate interest of each partner. There was no express agreement concerning the sharing of profits.

A, without the knowledge of B and C, invested excess funds of the firm in property entirely unrelated to the business of the firm, the profits of which he claimed for himself. These investments in no way interfered with the operations of the firm's business, and he eventually replaced the funds he had taken.

What are B's and C's rights?

Problem 4

Wright carried on business as a stockbroker in Toronto. By agreement with Wright, Randolph, a New York broker, transacted on the New York Stock Exchange such business as he saw fit to accept for Wright's clients, and charged rates agreed upon with Wright. Wright and Randolph shared the fees realized from these transactions equally. A creditor of Randolph started an action against him and joined Wright as Randolph's partner.

What is the position of Wright?

CHAPTER 30

THE NATURE OF A CORPORATION AND ITS FORMATION

THE NATURE OF A CORPORATION

The corporation or limited company has become the dominant feature of the modern business world. Not only is it the main instrument of big business, it also rivals sole proprietorship and partnership as a means of carrying on smaller enterprises.

A corporation is a person in the eyes of the law; that is, it is a legal person. To understand the nature of a corporation we must first comprehend the idea of a legal person. A legal person is an entity recognized by the legal system as having rights and duties under that system. At first glance it might seem obvious that each human being is a legal person and that only human beings can have rights and obligations. But this is an oversimplification. The law need not recognize every natural person as a legal person: when slavery existed, a slave was not considered a legal person but a chattel with no rights or duties. He had no right to complain about mistreatment; he could not sue either his master or anyone else. Nor could his master sue him if he disobeyed. The master could physically punish him, sometimes even kill him, just as he could punish or kill his dog. Today all human beings are recognized as legal persons in civilized countries, but we do assign varying statuses and capacities to them, sometimes virtually divesting them of legal personality, as in the case of a person who has been judged insane.

We have said that legal personality need not coincide with human personality. Not only may it be withheld from human beings, but it may also be granted to entities or bodies other than human beings. Legal personality has been granted to inanimate objects, such as idols (in India, for example) and funds (in European countries). These objects have rights and duties under the law, but, of course, they can neither insist on these rights nor carry out their duties except through human agents.

For our purposes, the most important non-human legal person is the corporation. The corporation evolved from the need to look after the common interests of a group of natural persons. People argued about whether a group, be it a group of nuns in a convent or merchants carrying on a business, could have a "personality" distinct from each of the individual members, a group personality with a separate existence of its own. Scholars from the Middle Ages onward engaged in deep philosophical and political controversy about the nature of the state as a group personality and about the nature of lesser groups within the state. The political controversy still continues today, but the legal principle is firmly established, in both common law and civil law countries, that a corporation may be created as a separate and distinct legal person apart from its members.[1]

There are numerous types of corporations: government corporations created to carry on special activities — the Bank of Canada, the Canadian Broadcasting Corporation, Central Mortgage and Housing Corporation, Canadian National Railway; municipal corporations to run local government; charitable corporations — the Red Cross, the Heart Foundation, the Ford Foundation; educational institutions; and business corporations, the most numerous type of all. For the purposes of this book, we are concerned only with business corporations.

---

[1]   See Bonham and Soberman, "The Nature of Corporate Personality", in *Studies in Canadian Company Law*, Ziegel, ed. Vol. 1, Ch. 1.

The Significance of Separate Corporate Existence

The significance of the separate legal personality of a business corporation can best be understood when compared with partnership, under the subheadings below.

Limited Liability

As we have seen, each partner is liable for the debts of the partnership to the limit of his or her personal assets. A corporation is liable for its own debts, but the liability of its shareholders is limited to the amount of the price of the shares they have purchased from the corporation. If, as is usual, a shareholder has paid the full price, he or she can lose no more in the event that creditors seize the corporation's assets. It is for this reason, the limited liability of their *shareholders*, that business corporations are referred to as limited companies — something of a misnomer since the corporation itself is liable to the full extent of its assets.

Limited liability is widely regarded as one of the main advantages of incorporation. However, the benefit of limited liability is sometimes over-estimated since, for a small corporation to obtain credit, its directors or shareholders are often required to give personal guarantees or to pledge their own property as collateral security. In addition, as we shall see in the next two chapters, when shareholders become directors — as they often do in smaller enterprises — they are subject to a wide and increasing range of liability to other shareholders, to those doing business with the corporation and to society as a whole.

Transfer of Ownership

A partner cannot retire from a partnership and release herself from her liabilities unilaterally. She must bargain for her release with both her partners and her creditors; she may even be liable for debts contracted after her retirement, unless she has given notice to persons who habitually deal with the partnership and has fulfilled the other requirements of the Partnership Act. Since a shareholder has no liability for corporate debts even while he retains his shares, creditors of the corporation have no interest and no say in what he does with his shares. The shareholder may sever all connections with the corporation simply by transferring his shares to another person.[2] Anyone may buy the shares and is entitled to all the rights of a shareholder upon registration of the transfer at the corporation's office.

Management

A partnership is unsuitable for a venture involving a large number of investors. Each partner, as agent of the partnership, may enter into contracts on behalf of the partnership, and as the number of partners increases the risk of unwise and perhaps ruinous contracts is correspondingly greater. This state of affairs would discourage many prospective investors, especially when added to the perils of unlimited liability for partnership debts. In contrast, shareholders have no authority to bind their corporation to contractual obligations — only

---

[2] Subject to restrictions placed on transfer of shares in private or closely held corporations. See the section "Widely Held and Closely Held Corporations" below.

officers of the corporation may do so. A partnership usually requires unanimity on major business decisions, a requirement that could stalemate a firm with a large number of partners. In a corporation, management is delegated to an elected board of directors that normally reaches decisions by simple majority votes. Major decisions that are referred back to the shareholders do not require unanimity, but at most a two-thirds or three-quarters majority, depending on the issue and on the requirements of the corporation law statutes in the jurisdiction.

Continuous Existence

We have seen that in the absence of special provisions in the partnership agreement, the death or bankruptcy of a partner dissolves a partnership. Even when provisions are made in advance to continue the partnership and to pay off the share of the deceased or bankrupt partner, the procedure is often cumbersome and expensive. A corporation, by contrast, exists independently of any of its shareholders.[3] A person's shares may be transferred by gift or by sale, by creditors seizing them, by will or by statute transmitting them to the personal representative on death, yet none of these events affects the existence of the corporation. A corporation continues in existence perpetually unless it is dissolved by order of a court or by a voluntary resolution of its shareholders, or it is struck off the register for failure to comply with statutory regulations.

Loyalty

A partner owes a duty of loyalty to the partnership, usually making it a breach for her to carry on another business independently and on her own behalf without the consent of all the other partners, or to enter into contracts with the partnership on her own behalf. A shareholder owes no such duty to the corporation: he may carry on any independent business himself and may trade freely with the corporation as if he were a stranger.

Separation of Ownership and Management

The separation of ownership and management ranks with limited liability as a primary feature of the business corporation. These two features permit the raising of large amounts of capital: they enable an investor to invest a specific sum of money and receive a regular return on it, without either taking any additional risk beyond the sum invested or having to take an active part in management of business affairs. Of course, the investor may choose to take an active role in the corporation by running for office, or he may sell his interest if he becomes dissatisfied with the operation of the corporation; but it is primarily the possibility that he may limit his risk and take no active part that has made corporate investment so attractive to investors generally.

Although at one time the leading shareholders in a corporation were usually its managers as well, there has been a steadily increasing separation between those who invest and those who manage.[4] The separation is, however, less pronounced in Canada than in

---

[3] It survives even the death of all its shareholders: Re Noel Tedman Holdings Pty. Ltd., [1967] Qd.R. 561 (Queensland Supreme Court)

[4] For a detailed study of this subject see Berle and Means, *The Modern Corporation and Private Property*. New York: The Macmillan Company, 1932.

the United States because many large Canadian corporations are wholly-owned subsidiaries of foreign parent corporations.

Limitations on Separate Corporate Existence

Convenience and Abuse

One can easily fall into the habit of thinking of a corporation as a real creature independent of the law, but it is a mistake to do so. We must remember that a corporation, insofar as it may enter into legal relations, is simply a creature of the legal system with no existence apart from that system. A legal system that has granted recognition to a corporation may also withdraw it, whenever necessary to protect interests considered more important. Thus, while the corporate form with its limited liability may be a tempting instrument for sharp dealing and fraud, the law does not assist such activity; when necessary it ignores the separate existence of a corporation and goes behind the "corporate veil" to hold the individuals controlling the corporation personally responsible for their acts. On the other hand, if the law were to ignore separate corporate personality on any slight pretext, it would be perilous to rely upon the advantages of incorporation, and this most useful tool of commerce would become ineffective. We are confronted here by conflicting interests of society: the desire for a reliable and useful tool of business and the desire to do justice and prevent the tool from being improperly employed. In the main, the attitude of the courts has been to accept corporate personality at face value and to go behind it only as a last resort. The courts have proceeded cautiously — many would say timidly — treating each case on its own particular merits. As a result, it is difficult to state consistent general principles that determine when the courts will look behind the corporate veil and when they will refuse to do so. We shall examine the basic position taken by the courts and discuss several areas where they have gone beyond the corporate entity to deal directly with the controllers of an enterprise.

Salomon's Case

The classic case on the existence of the corporation as a separate entity came before the House of Lords in 1897 in *Salomon v. Salomon & Co. Ltd.*[5]

Salomon had carried on a successful business as a shoe manufacturer for many years. In 1892 he formed a corporation in which he held almost all the shares (the few remaining shares being held by members of his family) and sold his business to the corporation. Unfortunately a series of strikes in the shoe industry eventually drove the corporation into insolvency, and a trustee was appointed to wind it up. The trustee claimed that the corporation was merely a sham, that Salomon was the true owner of the business and the true debtor — as such he should pay off all debts owed by the corporation. The lower courts supported the trustee's position, but the House of Lords decided in favour of Salomon. The Lords said that either the corporation was a true legal entity or it was not. Since there was no fraud nor any intention to deceive, all transactions having been fully

---

[5]   [1897] A.C. 22.

disclosed to the parties and the statutory regulations complied with, the corporation was duly created and was solely responsible for its own debts.

The decision was important because it recognized the separate legal personality of the so-called "one-man company" at the time when it was becoming a common form of doing business. Many writers believed (and some still do) that the court had gone too far in giving independent existence to the corporation. Nevertheless, as a leading writer on the subject has said, "Since the *Salomon* case, the complete separation of the company and its members has never been doubted."[6]

Some later cases have carried the logic of *Salomon's* case to absurd lengths. For example, it has been held that the owner of a business who transferred all its assets to a corporation of which he was the sole owner, but neglected to transfer the benefit of the fire insurance policy on the assets as well, could recover nothing when those assets were destroyed by fire.[7] The scholastic logic, worthy of medieval philosophers, stated that the assets were owned by the corporation (true) and a shareholder has no direct ownership in them, but only in the corporation itself (also true), and therefore has no insurable interest in the assets! This decision was followed for a number of years by Canadian courts, but has now been rejected by the Supreme Court of Canada.[8] The court accepted that a shareholder, even one who owns all the shares of a corporation, does not own its assets, but rejected the contention that he has no insurable interest in those assets. If they are destroyed, his shares will diminish in value; consequently, he should be entitled to insure against their destruction.

For the most part, the principle of separate legal personality has worked well in the commercial world, but when application of the *Salomon* decision leads to absurd results, courts should refuse to follow it: the sections below illustrate the movement away from "strict logic" in the application of the rule.

Taxation

The corporate entity bestows certain legitimate tax advantages, the details of which are better dealt with in a book on taxation. It should be noted here that, to prevent tax avoidance, the income tax acts of almost every country including Canada have provisions that disregard the "separateness" of the corporation from its controlling shareholders and related companies for some purposes. Under Canadian tax law, a corporation is charged a lower rate of tax on its first $200 000 of active business income[9] than on taxable income exceeding that amount. Since the owners of a corporation might be tempted to incorporate several more companies, split the assets and the profits among them, and thus multiply the number of times they could take advantage of the low rate on the first $200 000, our tax law permits the $200 000 to be claimed just once on behalf of a whole group of "associated corporations", however many there may be.[10] It is interesting to note some of the statutory descriptions of associated corporations: where one of the corporations controls the other; where both of the corporations are controlled by the same person or group of persons; and where the persons in control of two corporations are "related"

---

6 Gower, *Principles of Modern Company Law* (5th ed.), p. 88. London: Sweet & Maxwell Ltd., 1992.
7 Macaura v. Northern Assurance Co., [1925] A.C. 619.
8 Kosmopoulos v. Constitution Insurance Co. of Canada (1987), 34 D.L.R.(4th) 208.
9 Income Tax Act. R.S.C. 1985, c.1 (5th Supp.), s. 125(1),(2).
10 *Ibid.*, s. 125(3).

(within the wide meaning given by the Act) to each other.[11] For taxation purposes, then, the fact that the shareholders of two corporations are "related" makes the two corporations "associated" for the purpose of the lower tax rate. Similarly, the Income Tax Act may disregard corporate separateness in a sale of assets between a controlling shareholder and a corporation, or between two related corporations, in order to prevent tax avoidance through the manipulation of the sale price.[12] As we shall see in Chapter 34, the Bankruptcy and Insolvency Act contains somewhat similar provisions to protect creditors from fraud.

Residence

It is often important to ascertain where a corporation "resides" in order to decide whether a particular rule or statute applies to it. The concept of corporate residence has not been clearly developed; in fact, the criteria for determining the issue may vary according to the type of problem concerned. Thus, a corporation may he held to reside in country *A* under one statute and in country *B* under another.

Neither the place of incorporation nor the place of its head office necessarily determines a corporation's place of residence, although both may be important. We may look behind these formal attributes to examine such matters as the principal place of operations and of management, as well as the residence of the controlling shareholders — in other words, the human factors behind the corporate facade. These elements are frequently contradictory and do not easily lead to a clear decision about a corporation's place of residence. Generally, however, when the place of incorporation and head office coincide, the presumption is that a corporation is resident in that place.

The place of residence is important in matters of taxation: a non-resident corporation generally pays taxes only on income earned within the jurisdiction, whereas a resident corporation pays taxes on its whole income wherever earned. Residence may also be crucial for other purposes: for example, in the leading case of *Daimler v. Continental Tyre,*[13] a company incorporated and carrying on business mainly in England was declared to be an enemy alien and therefore unable to bring an action in the English court because almost all of its shareholders were German nationals residing in Germany, which was then at war with England. Thus, it was the residence of the controlling shareholders that determined the residence and therefore the enemy character of the company. We may note that the company was still recognized as a legal entity — it was not considered a sham — but because of its enemy character it lost its rights during hostilities, as would a natural person who was an enemy alien.

Agency

Just as a corporation employs agents, so it may in turn act as an agent for others. Some corporations regularly engage in the business of acting as agents for others: investment dealers, shipping agents, auctioneers, foreign buying agents, and many others may be incorporated. The question arises whether a corporation may be said to act as agent for its own shareholders, that is, to carry on a business transaction directly on behalf of its

---

[11] *Ibid.,* s. 256(1).
[12] *Ibid.,* ss. 69 and 251.
[13] [1916] 2 A.C. 307.

shareholders rather than for its own benefit. An express agreement making the corporation an agent for its shareholders is perfectly valid, for in such cases the shareholders clearly wish the corporation to act for them.

It is more difficult to establish such an agency relationship when it has to be inferred from the circumstances. We should note that sometimes it is the shareholders who hope to benefit from the claim that the corporation acted as their agent;[14] at other times the government or another outsider wishes to hold the shareholders liable as principals. *Salomon's* case was an example of the latter situation, and there the court rejected a claim by the creditors that even if the corporation did exist independently, it acted not for itself but as Salomon's agent. Sometimes the courts have accepted the claim and at other times have rejected it. Although it is difficult to extract a clear principle from the later decisions, it seems fair to say that when the transactions very clearly indicate that the corporation was acting as an agent for the shareholders, the court will so hold.

Perhaps the most striking example of how far the courts will go occurred in *Re F. G. (Films) Ltd.*[15] A British film company was incorporated with a very small capital, no employees, and no business offices. Its principal shareholder was an American citizen who held 90% of the shares. The British company proceeded to "hire" a U.S. film-producing corporation, of which the American was president, to produce a film in India. The U.S. corporation provided all the capital, cast, and management. The British company then attempted to register the film as one made by a British company to obtain certain advantages in showing films at British cinemas. Not only did the court refuse to hold that the U.S. corporation was the agent of the British company, but, looking at all the surrounding circumstances of the British company, its incorporators, its capital, and its operations, the court declared that in fact the reverse was true: the British company was acting as agent of its U.S. shareholder and the U.S. film corporation for purposes of registering the film. Accordingly, the court decided that the film was produced by the U.S. corporation.

Fraud

A court will not lightly impute fraud in any transaction, for to do so is to place a serious stigma on the person so accused and perhaps induce a criminal prosecution against him. Once the court believes that fraud has been demonstrated, however, it will disregard all formal blocks in its way to hold the defrauder liable. The court will not accept the technical objection that the corporation as a separate entity, rather than its shareholders, has committed the fraud.

Patton v. Yukon Consolidated Gold Co.[16] illustrates the courts' policy in dealing with fraud. The defendant, Treadgold, while acting as agent for a corporation he had helped promote, the Yukon company, bought the assets of North Fork Company for Yukon at a high price. Treadgold owned virtually all the shares in North Fork, but did not disclose this interest to the directors of Yukon. When Yukon later sued him for breach of duty as an agent, he defended by stating that North Fork was an entirely separate entity from himself, that it was North Fork, not Treadgold, that sold its assets to the Yukon company, and that he was therefore under no duty to disclose his position as shareholder in that

---

[14] Smith, Stone & Knight Ltd. v. Birmingham Corporation, [1939] 4 All E.R. 116.
[15] [1953] 1 W.L.R. 483.
[16] [1934] 3 D.L.R. 400.

company. The court dismissed his contention, held that the whole scheme was one devoted "to make a secret profit for himself", and accordingly held him liable to repay all the profits made by North Fork.

There are other areas where the courts disregard the corporate entity. The above examples serve only to illustrate some of the more important instances.

Methods of Incorporation

Royal Charter

The oldest method of incorporation is by royal charter granted by the sovereign as part of the prerogative. The first corporations were incorporated by this method in 16th-century England. A charter, when issued by the Crown, signified the birth of the corporation — from the moment of issue the corporation was in existence. Until the 19th century, all corporations were created by charter, including many famous names in the development of England's empire. Some of these are still in existence, the best known to Canadians being the Hudson's Bay Company founded in 1670. A few royal charters are still issued today to universities, learned societies, and charitable institutions, but none to business corporations.

Special Acts

At the end of the 18th century, Parliament began to pass special statutes to create corporations for large projects that were virtually impossible to finance in any other way. These projects were usually concerned with the public interest — railroads, canals, waterworks, and other public utilities. Today, special acts are still used to create such corporations as the Bell Telephone Company and the Canadian Pacific Railway, and also to create special government corporations like Central Mortgage and Housing Corporation, the Canadian Broadcasting Corporation and Air Canada.

Parliament and the provincial legislatures have also passed statutes setting out procedures for the incorporation of businesses in which the public has a special interest. In those fields where specific safeguards and procedures are required for the protection of the public, no one may carry on business without complying with the statutory provisions. Thus, all banks must be incorporated under the federal Bank Act, and trust and loan companies either under federal acts regulating these businesses or relevant provincial statutes.

General Acts

The Memorandum and Letters Patent Systems

Today, almost all business corporations are incorporated under the provisions of a statute of general application. Under a statute of this type any group of persons who comply with its requirements may form a corporation. In Canada we have had a unique development, in that different types of general acts have evolved. In 1862, a new system was introduced in England which depended on Parliament rather than on the royal prerogative, and this system was adopted by five provinces: it now remains in force in only two — British Columbia and Nova Scotia. The system requires applicants to register a document that sets out the fundamental terms of their agreement, called a *memorandum of association*. If the memorandum and certain other prescribed documents comply with the statute and the registration fee is paid, the authorized government office issues a *certificate of incorporation* and the corporation comes into existence. We shall call corporations incorporated in this manner memorandum corporations.

Originally, the other five provinces and the federal government employed a different system under their general acts, but it remains in force only in Québec and Prince Edward Island. There the incorporating document is called the *letters patent*, an offspring of the royal charter, but issued under the authority of the Crown's representative in each jurisdiction rather than directly by the Crown.

Under the letters patent system, a general statute regulates the conditions under which the Crown representative — a government agency — may issue letters patent. Although in theory the granting of letters patent is discretionary, in practice, the steps taken by applicants do not differ greatly from those for registering a memorandum under the English system. Since the great majority of corporations operating in Canada were at one time incorporated by letters under either federal, Ontario or Québec acts, and since their business operations and the sale of their securities extend throughout the country, one still encounters these corporations frequently in all parts of Canada.

The Articles of Incorporation System

In 1970, Ontario passed a substantially different Business Corporations Act, creating a new method of incorporation adapted from a system in use in the United States. In 1975, the federal Parliament adopted the same system in its new statute, although many of the provisions of the federal act were quite different from those of the Ontario version. The Canada Business Corporations Act[17] has become the model for the new system: Manitoba, Saskatchewan, New Brunswick, Alberta, Ontario and Newfoundland have followed with acts based on the federal scheme, although with local variations. Under the articles of incorporation system, persons who wish to form a corporation sign and deliver *articles of incorporation* to a government office and in turn are issued with a certificate of incorporation. The system combines features of both the memorandum and letters patent systems. Unfortunately, the terminology chosen is unnecessarily confusing in the Canadian business and legal context; the new statutes have adopted terms used in various parts of the United States, in particular the word "articles", which has a different meaning in those Canadian provinces still using the memorandum system, as well as in Britain and most Commonwealth countries.

As the articles of incorporation system is now the most widely used one in Canada, our discussion will focus on it. However, we must keep in mind the three different methods of incorporation; wherever the differences have important consequences we shall point them out.

3 methods of incorporation:
memorandum corporation system.
letters patent system
articles of incorporation system

---

[17] 1985, c. C-44.

Widely Held and Closely Held Corporations

When the first general statutes permitting incorporation of business enterprises were passed in England and Canada in the mid-19th century, the legislators believed limited companies would be used primarily for large undertakings having many shareholders. These acts required at least seven incorporators to sign the original application to establish the corporation. By the turn of the century it had become evident that incorporation was also a useful and fully effective tool for family businesses — as in *Salomon's* case. It had also become evident that the big publicly held corporations needed to be restrained from misleading investors. Various statutory requirements were created to ensure the disclosure and publication of a corporation's financial position, both in soliciting prospective investors and in reporting to shareholders. These regulations seemed inappropriate for the small family business, as did the need to have at least seven shareholders, the latter being merely a technical requirement that could be satisfied by giving one share each to six employees or relatives while the true controlling shareholder held all the remaining shares.

These facts were recognized in 1908 when the British Parliament enacted provisions to permit the formation of private companies. These companies were distinguished from all other companies, which we shall call widely held corporations, by the following characteristics:

    (a) the right to transfer shares had to be restricted in some manner;
    (b) the number of shareholders was limited to fifty;
    (c) any invitation to the public to buy shares was prohibited.

In addition, the number of shareholders required was reduced to three.

Provisions for the incorporation of private companies exist in substantially the same form in Prince Edward Island and Nova Scotia as they do in the English act.[18] Statutes of provinces employing the articles of incorporation system do not maintain a formal distinction between public and private corporations,[19] and permit even a single shareholder to form a corporation (as does the British Columbia Act). A corporation in those provinces may still restrict the right to transfer shares but none of these acts specifies the type of restriction, and it can take almost any form. In practice, the most common restriction is to require the consent of the board of directors to any transfer, but there are other varieties, such as giving the right of first refusal to existing shareholders or directors before a shareholder can sell to an outsider, or giving a major shareholder the right of veto. Requiring the consent of directors gives them the discretion to approve or reject a proposed member of the corporation, much as partners determine whether they will admit a new partner. Thus, a restriction on the transfer of shares frequently represents the

---

[18] Nova Scotia's recognition of private companies, oddly, is found in The Securities Act, R.S.N.S. 1989, c. 418, s. 1(1)(ag). This section simply defines a private company. The Companies Act does not refer to private companies.

[19] The statutes do, however, distinguish between corporations offering their shares to the public and those whose shares may not be traded and are restricted to a small group of shareholders. For a brief discussion of corporations whose shares are traded, see Chapter 32, under "Securities Legislation".

wishes of the majority, who want to be able to choose their fellow members in a small enterprise on the basis of competence and trust as they could in partnership. Because of the restrictions on the transfer of shares, shares in private companies and closely held corporations are never quoted on stock exchanges or traded by brokers.

As suggested, the main use of the closely held corporation is to incorporate small- and medium-sized business enterprises where the number of investors is small. Closely held corporations have often been described as incorporated partnerships. Although the description is apt, we must not be misled by it: a closely held corporation is a true limited company with the same legal significance and corporate independence as the widely held corporation. In fact, when a large corporation creates a subsidiary or branch, it often does so by incorporating a closely held corporation. Many large English and U.S. corporations operate wholly-owned subsidiaries in Canada that are closely held: all the shares are held by the parent corporation abroad, except for a few that may be held here by corporate officers. A number of these subsidiaries rival our own large public corporations in size, but apart from these important exceptions, widely held corporations are generally much larger than closely held ones.

The vast majority of corporations are closely held — over 90% in Canada; and closely held corporations are important in a wide cross-section of economic activity. It may therefore seem surprising that they are largely neglected as a subject of study in business administration. The literature of economics, finance, accounting and management directs its attention to widely held corporations in the securities market and the related need for financial disclosure. There is a popularly-held image of large corporations operating in a world of capital markets, proxy battles, take-over bids, conglomerates, inter-corporate directorships, professional "organization men" and classic organization charts. Until recently, at least, closely held corporations have been permitted the luxury of operating in an atmosphere of relative privacy. Their low profile may explain why much less is known and written about them. In a closely held corporation, as we have noted, the owners or a significant proportion of them are usually the managers as well, thus focusing questions of management and ultimate decision-making within a small group. We shall examine the legal implications of this characteristic of closely held corporations in the next chapter.

The Constitution of a Corporation

The Charter (Articles of Incorporation)

Almost all commercial corporations are incorporated under a general act and, as we have seen, most are now incorporated under the articles of incorporation system. The articles of incorporation are often referred to as the "charter" of the corporation; they set out essential information about the corporation such as its name, registered office, any restrictions on the business it may carry on, the shares and classes of shares it may issue and on the transfer of those shares. The precise requirements for such essentials vary from one province to another. In those provinces that have not adopted the articles of incorporation system, the corresponding "charter" document is the letters patent or the memorandum of association.

Occasionally, to suit the special requirements of a closely held corporation, matters not usually found in a charter will be placed there: they are often included when a compromise arrangement has been made between two groups. For example, if two corporations merge, the shareholders of the smaller corporation may wish to have some special privileges entrenched in the charter of the new corporation. Matters directly dealt with in a charter are comparatively difficult to alter. They give considerable protection to the shareholders who benefit from them, but tend to tie the corporation down. In order to change rights placed in the charter, a special amending procedure must be followed, resulting in the issue of an amending document.[20] In most circumstances, the charter is an unsuitable instrument for reflecting special arrangements among the shareholders. Instead, shareholders enter into a separate shareholders' agreement outside the corporate constitution, setting out how they will exercise their powers. This topic will be discussed further in the following chapter.

By-Laws

Incorporators generally keep the incorporating documents as short as possible to gain flexibility in the operation of the corporation. The corporation still needs detailed operating rules for its day-to-day affairs; the skeleton provided by the incorporating document must be filled out and given muscle in order to act. Under both the articles of incorporation and letters patent systems these operating rules are called *by-laws*, but for a memorandum corporation they are called *articles of association*. We shall refer to them as by-laws, since what we say about by-laws generally applies to the articles of association, but with this important exception: all articles of association are specially entrenched and cannot be amended except by a special resolution at a shareholders' meeting, requiring a three-quarters majority. By-laws are more flexible, requiring confirmation by only a simple majority of shareholders, although corporations acts do specify some matters that must be dealt with by special resolution requiring an increased majority, normally two-thirds.

Another difference is that under the memorandum system, *both* the memorandum *and* articles of association must be registered and they form part of the corporate constitution; under the other two systems it is not strictly necessary to have by-laws at all. Of course, it is normal and convenient to have them and they may be amended, or new by-laws adopted, as and when required with a minimum of formality. Usually, the directors amend by-laws or adopt new ones, but they need confirmation at the next general meeting of shareholders to remain valid. Under the articles of incorporation system, shareholders themselves have the power to propose and adopt by-laws.

By-laws fall into two main categories. The first category provides general operating rules for the business of a corporation; such by-laws are usually passed at the first meeting of the shareholders. The first by-laws are often quite long and elaborate, dealing with such matters as the number and qualification of directors; their term of office; the place and required notice for meetings of directors; the quorum necessary (that is, the minimum number who must be present) before a meeting of directors can act on behalf of the corporation; the categories of executive officers; provisions for voting by proxy, for the allotment of shares, and for the declaration of dividends. The following brief excerpts from general by-laws will illustrate the matters usually looked after:

---

[20] The procedures for altering letters patent or a memorandum tend to be more cumbersome than those under the newer articles of incorporation system.

The affairs of the Corporation shall be managed by a board of five (5) directors.

The qualifications of a director shall be the holding of at least one share in the capital stock of the Corporation provided, however, that any person who is an officer or director of any other corporation which is a shareholder of the Corporation may hold office as a director of the Corporation.

Three of the directors shall form a quorum for the transaction of business.

Questions arising at any meeting of directors shall be decided by a majority of votes. In the event of an equality of votes the Chairman of the meeting in addition to an original vote shall have a second or casting vote.

The remuneration to be paid to the directors shall be such as the board of directors shall from time to time determine and such remuneration shall be in addition to the salary paid to any officer or employee of the Corporation who is a member of the board of directors.

Shares in the Corporation's capital stock shall be allotted by resolution of the board of directors on such terms and conditions and to such persons as the directors shall deem advisable.

The directors may from time to time by resolution declare dividends and pay the same out of the funds of the Corporation available for that purpose, subject to the provisions (if any) of the articles of incorporation or articles of amendment of the Corporation.

An advantage in having detail of this nature relegated to a general by-law is that it may later be altered with approval of the shareholders without the formality of having the charter changed.

A second purpose of by-laws is to give the directors express authority from the shareholders to carry out those transactions that require shareholder approval, according to statute or the corporation's own charter. It is not important whether approval is given in the form of a "by-law" or by a "resolution" of the shareholders. The particular matters requiring this type of approval vary from province to province, but most statutes now do not make it necessary (unless the corporation's own charter so requires) for a by-law to be passed in order to confer any particular power on the directors. Nevertheless, although directors may have the power to borrow money on the security of the corporation's assets without special authorization, it is common for them to ask the shareholders to confirm a major loan transaction, because creditors may insist upon such confirmation in the form of a by-law or resolution.

Capital

The word "capital" has different meanings in different contexts. In letters patent and memorandum jurisdictions, when a corporation is incorporated, its charter places an upper limit on the number and money value of shares it may issue. This limit is called the "authorized capital". A corporation need not issue all its share capital: many retain a portion of their authorized capital and never issue it to shareholders. The *issued and paid-up capital* of a corporation is the part that has been subscribed and paid for by the shareholders.

In articles of incorporation jurisdictions the concept of authorized capital has been removed. A corporation may state the maximum number of shares that can be issued if it so wishes, or it can leave matters open-ended. A corporation must, however, still keep a "stated capital account" disclosing the consideration received for each share issued.

The issued capital of a corporation is the result of a series of contracts — contracts of subscription — between the corporation and its shareholders. We should bear in mind that there are several ways of becoming a shareholder: by being one of the original applicants for incorporation; by buying additional shares issued by a corporation subsequent to its incorporation; or by acquiring shares already issued to another share-holder, either by gift or by purchase. The first two ways result from contracts between the shareholder and the corporation; the transactions increase the issued capital as shown in the accounts of the corporation. The third way is the result of a transfer to which the corporation is not a party at all; the terms, including the price, are arrived at independently of the corporation and do not affect its accounts.

Until the early part of the 20th century, all shares had a nominal or *par value,* that is, a fixed value placed upon them like a bank note or a bond. Usually, these shares were in large denominations such as $100, $500, or $1000, and were issued by the corporation at their par value. Within a short time after issue, however, a share rarely had a market price identical with its par value. If the corporation had fared well and was declaring large dividends, or had excellent prospects, its shares would be in high demand and command a premium price on the market, often several times their par value; if the corporation had suffered losses or was a poor earner, its shares might bring only a fraction of their par value on the market. Accordingly, within a short time after being issued, par value provided little or no indication of a fair price for shares. In addition, par value created a hardship. A corporation was prohibited from issuing its shares at a discount other than for the payment of commission. If a corporation's shares were selling on the market at, say, half their par value and the corporation required additional capital in order to improve its position, investors would not purchase a new issue at par. In order to make a more successful issue, the corporation was compelled to reduce the par value of the shares to a more realistic figure and to reduce its capital accordingly by obtaining an amendment to its charter.

In the United States, the idea evolved of issuing *no par value* shares, that is, shares that represent a specific proportion of the issued capital of the corporation, rather than a fixed sum of money.

ILLUSTRATIONS

(a) Rigid Rods Ltd. was incorporated under the memorandum system with an authorized share capital of $10 000 000, divided into 100 000 shares of $100 nominal value. In its initial share issue it offered 50 000 shares at the par value of $100. They were all sold, giving the corporation an issued and paid-up capital of $5 000 000.

The market for steel rods slumped; the corporation suffered losses so that its shares now sell on the market for $60. The directors wish to raise a further $3 000 000, but the Act prevents them from issuing the remaining shares for less than them from issuing the remaining shares for less than their nominal value $100. However, if they tried to ask that price no one would buy them. Before

they can raise further capital they will have to arrange for the corporation to amend its charter to reduce the par value of the shares, with shareholder approval.

(b) Pliable Plastics Inc. was incorporated under the articles of incorporation system. Its articles contain no restriction on the total number of shares that may be issued and its shares have no par value. Initially, it issued 50 000 shares at $100 each, giving it a stated capital of $5 000 000. The directors wish to raise a further $3 000 000. If the current market price of the shares has fallen to $60, they can raise $3 000 000 by issuing 50 000 new shares. On the other hand if the market price has risen to $120, they will need to issue only 25 000.

The advantages of no par value shares, in particular the fact that they may be issued from time to time at prices that correspond to the current appraisal of their worth by investors, resulted in their adoption by all the jurisdictions in the United States and soon afterwards they were permitted in Canada. The articles of incorporation system has now abolished par value shares entirely.

Until the introduction of the articles of incorporation system, virtually all preferred shares were issued with a par value. They paid a preferred dividend expressed as a percentage of par value and the corporation could redeem them at par value: for example 8% on a par value of $100. With the abolition of par value, preferred shares are stated now to have a redemption price, say, of $100, with a preferred dividend expressed simply as a sum — $8.

THE CAPACITY OF A CORPORATION

We have discussed the nature and significance of a corporation having an existence separate and distinct from its shareholders, and examined the various ways in which a corporation may be created. We have now to discuss the capacity of a corporation to perform acts and enter into binding obligations on its own behalf. In Chapter 8 we noted that the capacity of a natural person may vary considerably according to his status, as for example, the capacity of an infant, lunatic, alien or soldier; in some instances his capacity to enter into obligations by contract or to incur liability for negligent or other acts is more limited than that of the normal adult citizen.

Although corporations cannot act on their own volition, but only through their agents or organs, the courts do treat corporations, whenever practical, as having the same capacity as a human being. Not all corporations have the same capacity; as we are about to see, there are different statuses among corporations as there are among human beings. As we noted in Chapter 8, for example, municipal corporations are usually quite strictly limited in their capacity. Any attempt to act outside that capacity is *ultra vires*, that is, a nullity, and has no legal effect. Corporations formed by memorandum of association had somewhat similar limitations on their capacity: the objects for which a corporation was formed were required to be stated in its memorandum and any contract outside the scope of those objects was *ultra vires* and void.

The *ultra vires* doctrine has now been abolished throughout Canada. However, memorandum and letters patent jurisdictions (except for Nova Scotia) still require charters to contain a clause setting out a corporation's objects, and all jurisdictions permit incorporators, if they wish, to set out in the charter restrictions upon the activities of the corporation. Making a contract that exceeds the objects, or that contravenes a restriction, constitutes misconduct by the management. Consequently, a shareholder may bring an action against the officers responsible for the breach, and where possible ask for an injunction to restrain their misconduct. (In the case of a major breach, a shareholder may ask to have the corporation wound up.) However, such remedies do not affect the rights of outsiders who have contracted with the corporation unless they knew that the contract was contrary to the objects or to a restriction.

◁Nature of Corporate Securities

From the Point of View of their Holders

The classic distinction between shares and bonds (or debentures) has long been that a holder of a share is an investor and owner of an interest in the corporation while a holder of a bond is a creditor. In the business world today, there is no such clearcut distinction between shareholder and bondholder. In the language of modern business the true "equity" owner of a business, the person who takes the greatest risk, is the common shareholder. From this end of the scale, we proceed by degrees to the person who is a mortgagee or bondholder at the other end of the scale, where the holder takes the least risk. In between we may have varying types of preferred shareholders and unsecured creditors. Often when deciding to invest in the bonds of a corporation rather than its preferred stock, an individual does not believe that she has made the choice between becoming a creditor and becoming an investor. She believes in both instances that she is an investor, but that she enjoys a higher security in the one form of investment than in the other. Her investment decisions are primarily determined by economic considerations, or perhaps by convenience. For example, she may choose to buy bonds instead of shares because they have a maturity date and she will not have to worry about selling them on the market; or because the bonds promise a more certain return than dividends and "growth". Alternatively, she may choose preferred shares for tax reasons, because she can still claim a dividend tax credit while realizing something like an interest form of return.

We have seen in Chapter 14 that share and bond certificates are a type of personal property subject to different rules of transfer and ownership from those that apply to sales of goods. We noted further in Chapter 24 that these choses in action may in some circumstances be treated as negotiable instruments. Thus, bond certificates in bearer form may be considered as a type of negotiable instrument at common law. Articles of incorporation statutes expressly treat share certificates in bearer form as a type of negotiable instrument. These developments have followed stock market custom in Canada and current practices in the United States.

In theory, if bonds and shares are to serve the purposes of a capital market they should be readily transferable (that is, "liquid") and this purpose is promoted when the hazards of owning them are minimal. When bonds and shares are treated as negotiable instruments, an innocent holder for value may often acquire a better title than his predecessor had, as for example when he purchases bonds or share certificates that have been stolen.

In practice, giving bond and share certificates negotiability has aggravated the problem of forged and stolen certificates, particularly in recent years in the United States. Since an innocent holder for value can obtain good title to a stolen certificate, looser practice has developed in accepting these certificates. Two unfortunate results have flowed from this development: first, there has been an increased temptation to indulge in theft, as it is easy to sell stolen certificates; second, it has become easier to pass off forged (and therefore worthless) certificates on purchasers. The innocent holder of a forged negotiable instrument, as we have seen, obtains no title, since he or she is subject to the real defence of forgery.

At this point it is very difficult to foresee where future developments with respect to negotiability will lead.

From the Point of View of the Corporation

The line between shareholder and bondholder is nonetheless a distinct and important one in its legal consequences for a corporation. First of all, since bondholders are creditors, interest paid to them is a debt of the corporation. It must be paid whether the corporation has earned profits for the year or not. Shareholders are not creditors, and receive dividends only when the directors declare them. One consequence, especially important for taxation, is that interest payments are normally an expense of doing business and are deducted before income can be calculated; dividends, on the other hand, are payable from profits after income tax has been calculated. Second, bonds are usually secured by a mortgage on the real property of the corporation (debentures, by a "floating charge" on the assets in general — see discussion of these devices in Chapter 33 under "Floating Charges"). If a corporation becomes insolvent, its bondholders receive their money back not only before the shareholders but also before the general creditors: they are secured creditors, and the trustee acting for them can sell the corporation's assets to satisfy the debt owed to them. Third, bond or debenture holders do not have a direct voice in the management of the corporation unless it is in breach of the terms of the trust deed or indenture under which the securities were created. Only when a corporation gets into financial difficulty or is in breach of the trust deed may the trustee, acting on behalf of the bond or debenture holders, step in and take part in management. It is true, however, that bondholders do exert an indirect form of control over management through the restrictive clauses commonly written into bond indentures. While it is probably unwise for bondholders to place extensive restrictions on the future decisions of management in this way, bond indentures may include formulae placing a ceiling on the further long-term borrowing and leasing in which the corporation may engage, on the amount of dividends it may pay, and even, in smaller corporations, on the salaries of officers.

Preferred shareholders are in an intermediate category. Depending on the rights provided for them in the description of preferred shares in the corporation's charter, they do not normally have a right to vote unless the payment of dividends to them has fallen in arrears. In this respect they are more like creditors than investors. Nevertheless, payment of preferred dividends is not a contractual commitment of a corporation, as is bond interest. Furthermore, a preferred shareholder must enforce his or her rights as an individual and is not dependent upon a trustee taking action, as a bondholder normally is.

In the latter part of the 19th century, the capital structures of corporations tended to become complex. Often they included three or more kinds of shares and several priorities of bonds. The related securities were in large denominations, that is, of a relatively high par value. The tendency since the turn of the century has been towards a simplification of capital structures, although recent developments in tax law and estate planning may be reversing this tendency. Today, most larger corporations have, in addition to an issue of common shares, one or more classes of bonds or debentures and possibly a class of preferred shares. It is also important to note that once a corporation has been successfully established a large proportion of subsequent financing will be through retained earnings.

The Rights and Privileges of Security Holders

The various combinations of rights and privileges that may attach to either preferred or common shares are extensive. They depend on the financial position of a corporation, the advice of the investment house acting as its underwriter, and to some extent on the bias of the incorporators or of management. Among corporations already in operation and requiring further financing, managers will differ in their assessment of the risk to the corporation that a particular balance of financing in the capital structure will create: some have a greater aversion to debt than others, and some dislike equity financing because of its potential, real or imagined, for disturbing the present balance in voting power. All these factors influence not only the method of financing chosen, but also the rights that may attach to the various securities issued. In itself, modern corporate legislation places few constraints on the financing of corporations, and leaves it to incorporators or management to determine the rights and privileges of each class of security and to set them out clearly.

Problems of interpretation arise in the drafting of rights for various classes of shareholders just as they do in the drafting of statutes, contracts and wills. Two questions with respect to preferred shareholders' rights to dividends are particularly important. The first is whether the rights are *cumulative*: if the full preferred dividend is not paid in one year, do the arrears accumulate so that they are paid in a subsequent year or on winding up the corporation, before the common shareholders are entitled to anything? The second is whether, on winding up, their rights are *participating*: if after the preferred shareholders have been fully paid, do they still participate in any remaining surplus along with the common shareholders? The courts have considered these and similar questions, but most of their decisions date from the time when all shares had par values and share rights were described rather differently. It may well be unwise to rely on those cases today. This uncertainty makes it all the more important to draft class rights with the greatest care, stating expressly what those rights are.

Questions For Review

1. Distinguish a legal person from a natural person.
2. Describe the effect of a finding that corporations are "associated" for taxation purposes.
3. What is a royal charter?
4. What kinds of corporations are incorporated by special act?
5. From whom does a letters patent corporation derive its existence? How does a memorandum corporation differ?
6. Are articles of incorporation more like letters patent or a memorandum of association? Why?
7. What arguments did the creditors use in attempting to show that Salomon should be held liable?
8. Distinguish between a charter and by-laws.
9. What are the two main purposes of by-laws?
10. What are the main characteristics of a closely held corporation?
11. Under what circumstances might a corporation require an amendment to its charter?
12. What are the special rights that normally attach to preferred shares?
13. Why are par values for shares misleading?

Problems

Problem 1

Parliament passes a statute declaring that it is against the public interest for any railway company to transport coal mined by itself because such activity tends to restrict competition. Rocky Mountain Railway Company subsequently purchases all the shares of Albert Collieries Limited. Albert Collieries has always shipped its coal on the Rocky Mountain line and continues to do so. The Department of Justice has started an action to obtain an injunction against further shipments of Albert coal on the Rocky Mountain line.

Summarize the arguments for each side. Who should win?

Problem 2

Arthurs, Boulez, and Coombes were the directors and sole shareholders of Driftwood Products Limited. After several years of hard work and considerable success all three decided to take a vacation together and leave their office manager in charge. They flew to the Bahamas for three weeks of sun and fishing. While they were away, the manager instructed the company lawyer to sue a debtor who was long overdue in payment of his account. Several days after the action was started, it was learned that all three shareholders had been killed when their fishing boat overturned in a storm. The debtor has suggested defending the action by claiming that the creditor corporation ceased to exist when all three shareholders were killed.

Explain the ways in which this contention may be answered.

Problem 3

Ilona Sunac holds a patent on her design of a special oil burner jet, which is claimed to save 25% to 30% of the fuel consumption of conventional jets for the same heat output. With the advice of her accountant and lawyer, she has gathered a small group of investors to develop and market the device. In return for transferring her patent rights to the new corporation, she will receive an interest worth about $175 000 and will be appointed research director at a substantial salary. The other investors will contribute $300 000 in cash as working capital. Her co-investors have suggested that she take $100 000 worth of common shares and 12% debentures worth $75 000. A friend, however, has offered his opinion that Ilona would be better off taking all $175 000 in shares, so that she will maximize her profits through the growth of the corporation. Discuss the issues raised by the advice Ilona has received.

Cases

Case 1

Macbeth, the owner of 20 hectares located on the outskirts of Niagara Falls, decided to sell, and on January 2 signed an exclusive listing agreement with Ross, a real-estate broker. Macbeth agreed to pay Ross a commission of 5% on the sale of the property, which he listed at $350 000.

On January 19, Ross filed articles of incorporation for a new corporation, Burnam Wood Properties Ltd., of which he was the sole shareholder. He appointed his friend Lennox as general manager.

Several weeks later, Ross introduced Macbeth to Lennox as general manager of Burnam Wood but said nothing to suggest that he, Ross, had any interest in the corporation. Within a few days Lennox submitted an offer on behalf of the corporation to purchase Macbeth's property for $240 000. Macbeth rejected the offer but made a counter-offer to sell at $290 000. Burnam Wood accepted the counter-offer, and the deal was closed on March 15, when Macbeth paid Ross his commission of $14 500.

Shortly afterwards, Burnam Wood entered into negotiations with another corporation, Castle Hall Developments Ltd., and sold the 20 hectares to it for $450 000, realizing a quick profit of $160 000.

On April 24 following, Macbeth learned of the resale by Burnam Wood and also learned about Ross' share ownership in the Burnam Wood company. Macbeth immediately sued Ross and Burnam Wood jointly for recovery of the real-estate commission of $14 500 and for the $160 000 profit realized on the second sale by Burnam Wood Properties Ltd. to Castle Hall Developments Ltd.

Examine the validity of Macbeth's claim and offer an opinion about its chances for success.

Case 2

In 1980, Banquo, Douglas and Macduff incorporated Dunsinane Dining Ltd., to open and run a restaurant specializing in Scottish cuisine. The corporation issued 100 shares, 40 each to Banquo and Douglas and 20 to Macduff, and the three became directors of the corporation. Because Banquo and Macduff believed in totally abstaining from drinking alcohol, they insisted on inserting in the corporation's articles of incorporation the following restriction:

> The corporation shall at no time engage in the buying or selling of alcoholic beverages of any kind.

Banquo died recently and his nephew Fleance inherited his shares and was also appointed to the vacant seat on the board of directors. Fleance and Douglas decided that the restaurant would be much more profitable if it were able to serve liquor. As the majority on the board, they applied for and obtained a liquor permit for the corporation and have ordered a large supply of fine Scottish malt whiskies.

Macduff is deeply offended and wishes to prevent the contract from being performed and insists on the restriction in the articles being observed. Advise him about the steps he may take.

CHAPTER 31

THE INTERNAL AFFAIRS OF CORPORATIONS

THE BUSINESS AND AFFAIRS OF A CORPORATION

The Canada Business Corporations Act (CBCA),[1] and the corresponding provincial statutes, draw a broad distinction between two aspects of a corporation's activities. Section 102 states that "the directors shall manage the *business* and *affairs* of a corporation" [italics added]. The difference between these two terms is explained in section 2 (1), where "affairs" are defined as "the relationships among a corporation...and the shareholders, directors and officers...but *does not include the business carried on* [by the corporation]..." [italics added]. The distinction, which is helpful in understanding the complex activities of corporations, is between:

(a) *the affairs:* the internal arrangements, among those responsible for running a corporation and its main beneficiaries — the shareholders — which we discuss in this chapter, and

(b) *the business:* the external relations, between a corporation and those who deal with it as a business enterprise — its customers, suppliers, and employees — as well as relations with government regulators and society as a whole; discussed in Chapter 32.

There is at least one major area, the sale of securities, where the distinction becomes blurred: an invitation to the public to invest in a corporation is directed toward those who are not yet part of its internal relations, but if they accept an offer to buy shares they will subsequently become involved in its "affairs." Because of the strong public interest in regulating the sale of securities to keep a stable and efficient market, we shall discuss distribution of securities in Chapter 32.

THE STRUCTURE OF THE MODERN BUSINESS CORPORATION

Business corporations differ from one another as much in their size and composition as do municipalities, trade unions, and governments. These variations are necessary if corporations are to perform their widely differing functions in society; corporations should not all be cast in the same mould. Modern legislation tries to take these needs into account and is reasonably flexible in permitting widely differing corporate structures although, as we shall see, flexibility is restricted by a belief that certain elements are essential to all corporations.

The two basic organs common to all corporations are the general body of shareholders and the board of directors. In closely held corporations, such as family companies or "incorporated partnerships", it often happens that most, or even all, of the shareholders are also directors. But although in practice the distinction between shareholders and directors may sometimes become blurred — for example, when they get together to discuss business,

---

[1] R.S.C. 1985, c. C-44. Unless otherwise stated, statutory references in this chapter are to that Act.

does the group constitute a directors' meeting or a shareholders' meeting? — it remains important legally.

In a large corporation, by contrast, the board of directors may have as many as fifteen or twenty members. Generally, in such cases the board will appoint a *managing director* (often called the president) or a smaller committee of directors (the *management committee* or *executive committee*) to direct the affairs and business of the corporation, and to supervise its full-time officers and employees; the director or committee refers only the more important policy matters to the less frequent meetings of the full board. In turn, the board of directors usually calls no more than the required annual meeting of shareholders, at which it reports to them on the state of the corporation's affairs and holds elections for the coming year. Thus we see that the directors function, at the business level, in somewhat the same manner as a cabinet of government functions at the political level.

IRECTORS

The Role of the Directors

As we have seen, section 102 of the CBCA provides that *the directors shall manage the business and affairs of the corporation.* In addition to the general power of management, the Act confers a number of specific powers on the directors. The most important of these are:

(a) to issue shares — subject to the corporation's constitution, the directors may issue shares at such times, to such persons and for such consideration as they may determine (s. 25);

(b) to declare dividends — the directors determine whether, or to what extent, profits should be distributed to the shareholders or retained in the corporation;

(c) to adopt by-laws governing the day-to-day affairs of the corporation — the directors may adopt new by-laws or amend existing ones; although they must submit them for approval at the next meeting of shareholders, the by-laws remain effective until then (s. 103);

(d) to call meetings of shareholders (s. 133) — the directors must call an annual general meeting each year, but may call additional meetings whenever they wish.

A corporation is required to have one or more directors.[2] A corporation whose shares are issued to the public must have not fewer than three directors, at least two of whom must be "outsiders"; that is, they must not be officers or employees of the corporation.

Where a corporation has more than one director, decisions of the board of directors are normally taken by majority vote, unless the corporate constitution requires a higher special majority or unanimity. Usually, the by-laws make provision for the holding of meetings of the board, the election of a chairperson, rules on voting, quorums, and like matters.

Shareholders, as such, play little or no part in management. As we shall see later in this Chapter, shareholders have certain rights, the most important being to vote at meetings. But generally, once the shareholders have voted to elect a board of directors they

---

[2] Even a corporation with only a single shareholder must have one or more directors, though there is no reason why the shareholder should not also be the sole director. The articles of incorporation are required to state the number of directors which the corporation is to have; s. 6(1)(e).

have no further power to participate in management. If they do not like the way the directors are running the corporation's business and affairs, they cannot interfere; legally their only course is to dismiss them and elect new directors in their place.[3] It is consequently of vital importance that the shareholders should select competent and trustworthy individuals as their directors.

Appointment and Removal of Directors

Any individual may be appointed director of a corporation, unless she is under the age of eighteen, has been found to be of unsound mind, or has the status of bankrupt (s. 105). However, a majority of the directors of a corporation must be resident Canadians.[4] Unless required by the articles of incorporation, a director need not hold shares in the corporation.

A corporation's first directors are appointed at the time of incorporation and hold office until the first meeting of shareholders,[5] which must be held not less than eighteen months after the corporation comes into existence (s. 133). Subsequently, directors are elected, re-elected, or replaced, on a regular basis; normally this occurs at the annual general meeting of the corporation, but elections may be held at any time at a special meeting called for that purpose. Casual vacancies on the board — for example where a director dies or becomes seriously ill — may normally be filled by the remaining directors.

Directors are elected by ordinary resolution of the shareholders (s. 106(3)); that is, a simple majority vote is sufficient. The effect of this rule is that a single shareholder, or a group of shareholders, holding anything more than 50 percent of the total votes, say 500 out of 999 shares, is able to elect the entire board of directors. Conversely, complete equality between two competing groups can lead to deadlock — as sometimes happens when two equal partners incorporate their business. An exception to this rule may be made by providing, in the articles of incorporation, that directors be elected by a system of cumulative voting — a form of proportional representation designed to ensure that any substantial minority of shareholders will be represented on the board.[6] Such systems, however, are quite rare in Canadian corporations.

As we have already mentioned, once they have elected the board of directors the shareholders have virtually no say in the management of the corporation's business and affairs. At one time, the position of the directors could be even more strongly entrenched — for example by providing in the corporate constitution that they should hold office for life, or that an incumbent director might be replaced only by a special majority or unanimous vote of the shareholders. This type of provision is no longer permitted. A director's term of office may now not exceed three years,[7] and even during that term a special meeting may be called to vote on the removal of a director (s. 109).

---

3   If dissatisfied shareholders hold a sufficient proportion of the shares, they need not wait until the next meeting called by the directors; they may requisition a meeting (s. 143) to elect a new board. See the subsequent discussion, under "Statutory Safeguards: A Voice in the Affairs of the Corporation."

4   S. 105(3). A landed immigrant counts as "Canadian", but only until one year after she becomes eligible to apply for citizenship.

5   When forming a corporation under the CBCA, the incorporators must file a notice stating the names and addresses of the first directors, and signed by them; s. 106(1),(2).

6   For example, a group representing 20 percent of all shareholders would be able to elect one director out of five; see s. 107.

7   The Act provides that the term of office may not expire later than the close of the third annual meeting following the election; s. 106(3). Strictly, this means that a term could last for as long as 45 months; see s. 133(a).

Moreover, except where cumulative voting is provided for, an ordinary resolution (simple majority) is sufficient for the removal of any director, and the articles may not prescribe a greater majority (s. 6(4)).

DUTIES OF DIRECTORS

To the Shareholders

As in public office, the concentration of such great power in the hands of a few persons may tempt them to use it for their own interests and against the interests of those for whom they should be acting. One might conclude that their first duty is to those shareholders who have elected them. However, this is not so. Just as the first duty of an elected member of Parliament is to the country as a whole rather than to his or her constituency, so too, the courts have stated, the first duty of a director is owed to the corporation as a whole. This statement raises the philosophic argument about whether the corporation is entirely separate from the shareholders.

To the present time, both English and Canadian courts have tended to treat the shareholders and the corporation as entirely separate entities, and have held that the duties of the directors are owed almost exclusively to the corporation. No general duty is owed by the board of directors to the shareholders. Thus, if the directors receive a takeover bid in which the proposed purchaser makes an offer to buy shares in the corporation, the directors, in the absence of statutory provisions, are under no legal duty to forward this offer to the shareholders for their consideration.[8] They may reject the offer out of hand or they may accept an offer on behalf of their own share interest even though the same offer is not made to the other shareholders. Only if the directors offer to act on behalf of the other shareholders, thereby creating an agency relationship, will they be under the duties of an agent.[9] Under securities legislation enacted in most of the provinces since 1966, directors are now required to issue a *directors' circular* to the shareholders setting out, among other things, their own interests, their own intentions with respect to an offer, and details of any arrangements made with the offeror corporation concerning their continuance in office or compensation for loss of office. However, the legislation does not apply to all corporations; in particular, take-overs of small private ("non-issuing") corporations are generally not regulated.

United States courts have been willing to employ equitable principles to place a duty upon the board of directors towards the general body of shareholders, and have held that, when negotiating the sale of a controlling block of shares, the directors are dealing in the assets of the corporation: in these circumstances, they are under a duty to act in the best interests of the shareholders generally. Thus, if majority shareholders obtain higher than the market price for their own block of shares because it represents control, they may be required to apportion the excess among all the shareholders.[10] This point of view has been adopted in provincial securities legislation,[11] but has been rejected in cases where the legislation does not apply.[12]

---

8 Percival v. Wright [1902] 2 Ch. 421.
9 Allen v. Hyatt (1914), 17 D.L.R. 7.
10 Perlman v. Feldman, 219 F. 2d 173 (1955).
11 See, for example, Securities Act, R.S.O. 1990, c. S-5, s. 95.
12 See Bell v. Source Data Control Ltd. (1989), 53 D.L.R.(4th) 580.

To the Corporation

In contrast to the paucity of decisions on directors' duties towards shareholders, a large body of case law has developed on their duties towards the corporation itself. Although the judgments are complicated by the inherent complexity of corporate relations, some fairly clear general principles have evolved. These may be conveniently broken down into three groups: (a) the duties of care and skill; (b) the duty to disclose an interest in contracts with the company; and (c) the duty to refrain from abuse of corporate opportunity.

Care and Skill

In a general sense, the duties of care and skill required of a director towards a corporation are quite minimal. We have not as yet developed standards for a professional class of directors; it is therefore difficult to assign to a director any special degree of skill, competence, or expertise such as we demand of a doctor, accountant, lawyer, or engineer.[13]

A director is bound to exercise reasonable care, that is, not to be negligent in carrying out duties. In this respect no greater diligence is required of a director than is required of the average person; he is placed under no higher standard. According to the CBCA, "Every director and officer of a corporation in exercising his powers and discharging his duties shall...exercise the care, diligence and skill that a reasonably prudent person would exercise in comparable circumstances" (s. 122(1)). A director is safe in his ignorance, at least as long as he is not deliberately ignorant. Accordingly, if he fails to attend a meeting at which something occurs that may amount to a breach of duty by the directors who do attend, he will not incur any liability himself.[14] There is no duty upon him to attend the meetings of the directors regularly, nor to examine the books of the corporation, nor to search carefully into its financial position. A director is entitled to rely on information received from the officers of the corporation, such as its president and treasurer, and on professional advice from accountants and lawyers.[15] However, he may not wilfully close his eyes to mistakes and misconduct. If he acquiesces in such matters, he may be liable in damages to the corporation for any losses that result.

The CBCA and corresponding provincial statutes also make directors liable to their corporation when they vote at meetings of the board on specified matters that cause financial losses to the corporation, such as the improper redemption of shares or payment of a dividend. (s. 118(2)). In addition, if their corporation should become insolvent the directors are personally liable to all employees of the corporation (rather than to the corporation itself) for up to six months unpaid wages for services performed while they were directors.[16] Directors may also become liable for failure to comply with other statutes; for example, in the event that the corporation is insolvent, the federal government may

---

[13] However, as we shall see in the next chapter, the standard of care for directors in complying with environmental regulations appears to be rising substantially.

[14] In some circumstances, for example, where a corporation pays a dividend when it does not have sufficient assets available, the directors are personally liable for their decision. Only a director who expressly dissents from the decision is relieved from responsibility. Even one who was not present at the meeting when the decision was taken is liable unless he records his dissent as soon as he becomes aware of the decision; s. 123.

[15] *Dovey v. Corey*, [1901] A.C. 477. See also s. 123(4).

[16] S. 119. This section is unique, in that liability for unpaid wages is unqualified; it is no excuse that a director acted with proper care and skill in carrying out his duties.

collect from the directors income tax that the corporation was required to withhold from wages and salaries of employees.[17]

To Disclose an Interest in Contracts with the Corporation

In contrast to the standards of care and skill, the duty of good faith towards the corporation imposes a high standard of conduct on a director. The CBCA requires that directors and officers shall "act honestly and in good faith with a view to the best interests of the corporation" (s. 122(1)).

Perhaps the most important duty is to disclose any interest that the director may have in contracts made with the corporation. This interest may arise where a director sells his own property to the corporation, or buys property from the corporation, or it may arise in more indirect ways: a director may be a shareholder in another corporation that is selling to or buying from his corporation, or the person making a contract with his corporation may be acting as agent or trustee for him or for a member of his family. The problem arises frequently among related corporations. The relationship may be that of parent company and subsidiary, or it may merely be that one or more directors of one corporation are shareholders and perhaps directors of a second corporation.

ILLUSTRATION

Brown holds a large number of shares in each of World Electric and Universal Shipbuilding, and is a director of each of these corporations. Universal Shipbuilding requires expensive turbo-generator sets for two large ships under construction. World Electric is one of several manufacturers of turbo-generators. Brown is faced with an obvious conflict of interest: can she encourage or even support a contract between the two corporations? On one side, it is in Brown's interest to see Universal Shipbuilding obtain the equipment at the lowest possible price. On the other side, it is in her interest to see World Electric get the contract and obtain the highest possible price.

The courts have evolved a set of rules to look after this situation. In virtually every jurisdiction these rules have been codified and form a part of corporation legislation.[18] Generally, a director who has an interest in a contract must disclose this fact at a meeting of the board of directors that considers the contract, and must not vote on the matter. If, after learning of the interest, the remaining independent members of the board still wish to go through with the contract, then a subsequent vote of them alone will create a binding contract. Failure by a director to disclose her interest gives the director's corporation the right to rescind the contract upon learning of her interest in it. Alternatively, it may affirm the contract on the terms in which it was made.[19]

Sometimes almost all the directors of a corporation are interested in a contract, and the remaining independent directors are not enough to form a quorum. In these circum-

---

17 Income Tax Act, R.S.C. 1985, c. 1 (5th Supp.), s. 227. 1. A director may raise the defence of due diligence, showing that he had used reasonable care in the circumstances.

18 For example, CBCA, s. 120.

19 A similar duty, to make full disclosure to an independent board of directors, is imposed upon a promoter who enters into a contract with a new corporation that he has played a role in establishing; see Erlanger v. New Sombrero Phosphate Co. (1873), 3 App. Cas. 1218.

stances, the contract should be presented to a general meeting of the shareholders for their ratification after full disclosure has been made to them. This practice is generally followed, for without this subsequent ratification the contract probably remains subject to rescission.

To Refrain from Abuse of Corporate Opportunity

In the preceding paragraphs we discussed the duty that arises when a director has an interest in a contract proposed to be made with the corporation. In this section we shall discuss, primarily, a director's duty to the corporation in a transaction he makes with a third person as a means of acquiring an interest in a property or venture. In other words, we are dealing here with contracts a director makes with persons other than the corporation. If it appears in the particular circumstances that it was a director's duty to acquire property for the corporation, or to give the corporation the chance of first refusal, and if instead he acquires title to the property for himself, then he has intercepted an opportunity belonging to the corporation and has committed a breach of duty. Under the principles of equity, he is regarded as a trustee of the property; that is, he holds the formal legal title in trust for the true beneficial owner in equity, the corporation. We shall discuss the ways in which this duty may arise and the remedies available to the corporation in case of breach.

The duty of a director to acquire property on behalf of a corporation arises chiefly in two situations. The first situation occurs when he has received a mandate to act as agent either in the purchase of a specific piece of property or in the purchase of a class of property generally. In these circumstances he is under a duty ordinarily placed upon any agent to acquire property for his principal. If a director buys property for himself after he has received an express mandate to acquire such property for the corporation, there is no difficulty in finding him guilty of a breach. In the absence of an express mandate there may be a difficult question whether, in all the circumstances of the case, the director received an implied mandate to act as agent.

The second situation occurs when a director receives information about a profitable venture or an opportunity to buy property at an advantageous price. If this opportunity has arisen because of his corporate office, that is, if he has received the information as a director of the corporation, then it is his duty to give the corporation first chance at acquiring an interest in the venture or property. If the corporation decides not to acquire the property, the director is probably free to do so. But he makes a dangerous decision if he assumes that the corporation would not want the property anyway, or that it would be disadvantageous for the corporation to acquire the property, and then acquires it in his own name without consulting the corporation. Here again, it may be very difficult for a court to decide whether in the circumstances the information came to the director personally, because he is a person with expert knowledge in a particular field, or in his role as a director of the corporation. Nevertheless, once the court decides that the opportunity belonged to the corporation, the result is quite clear: purchasing on his own behalf is a breach of duty.

A subsequent sale to the corporation of property held by a director, without disclosure of his interest in it (as when his interest is indirect, through a second corporation), may be strong evidence of a scheme to sell that property to the corporation from the very date of its acquisition. Purchasing property with the intention of reselling it to the corporation is tantamount to acquiring it as an agent of the corporation in the first place.

The position of a director who acquires an interest in property or a venture while under a duty to act for the corporation is the same as that of any agent who acquires an interest on behalf of his principal: although he may have formal or legal ownership of the property, he holds it for the benefit of the principal, the beneficial or equitable owner. On discovery of the transaction the corporation may force the director to transfer the interest to it while reimbursing him for his cost of acquiring the interest; he is not entitled to any profit. If, when the corporation discovers the transaction, the director has already sold the property to a bona fide purchaser, then he must disgorge to the corporation any profits that he made as a result of the transactions.[20] If the corporation itself had innocently bought the property, it may elect either to rescind the contract, if that is possible, and obtain the full purchase price back, or to keep the property and recover the profits made by the director.

Professor Beck has specified the standard that ought to be applied by directors in governing their conduct vis-a-vis the corporation, as follows:

> The modern doctrine of corporate opportunity is simply an extension of Equity's old rule that a fiduciary must not use his position to appropriate for himself benefits which he ought to have acquired, if at all, for his principal. In corporate terms, the test should be whether the opportunity was so closely associated with the existing and prospective activities of the corporation that the directors should fairly have acquired it for, or made it available to the corporation. If an affirmative answer is given to the question posed, a showing of good faith should, as in all cases of fiduciary duty, be no defence.[21]

The duty to refrain from abuse of corporate opportunity is imposed not only on directors of a corporation but also on its other officers and senior employees who owe it a fiduciary duty.[22]

Insider Trading

In addition to the three categories of directors' duties considered above, there is a fourth type of conduct for which English and Canadian courts were reluctant to impose liability, but where the legislatures have intervened to create a duty — that of insider trading.

Insider trading occurs when a director or officer of a corporation, or some other person (for example, a major shareholder of the corporation), buys or sells the corporation's shares or other securities, making use of confidential inside information in order to make a profit or avoid a loss.

---

[20] Canada Safeway Ltd. v. Thompson, [1951] 3 D.L.R. 295; [1952] 2 D.L.R. 591.
[21] Beck, "The Saga of Peso Silver Mines: Corporate Opportunity Reconsidered", (1971) 49 *Can. Bar Rev.* 72. For a judicial formulation of this standard see Canadian Aero Service Ltd. v. O'Malley *et. al.* (1973), 40 D.L.R. (3d) 371 (Supreme Court of Canada).
[22] See MacMillan-Bloedel v. Binstead (1983), 22 B.L.R. 255.

ILLUSTRATION A

The directors of a small family company are approached by a large public corporation, which offers to buy all the shares of the family company at a price considerably above that at which the shares had previously been valued. The next day, one of the directors is approached by a member of the family who is a shareholder and who offers to sell some of her shares to him. Without disclosing to her the proposed takeover, he buys the shares at a price well below that of the offer.

ILLUSTRATION B

The directors of a mining corporation receive a confidential report from their surveyor that very valuable mineral deposits have just been discovered. One of the directors immediately instructs her broker to buy as many of the corporation's shares as possible on the stock exchange, before the good news is released and forces up the price.

ILLUSTRATION C

The directors of a corporation learn that their major customer has just declared bankruptcy, owing the corporation a large sum of money. Default on the account by their customer is likely to result in the corporation showing a substantial loss in the forthcoming half-yearly accounts. One of the directors promptly sells his shares just before the news becomes public and the shares drop in value.

In each of these cases, a director has made use, for his own benefit, of information that came to him in his capacity as a director. Such behaviour is widely perceived as improper and unfair.

At common law, however, there were two problems in holding the director liable. First, as we have seen, the courts have consistently held that a director's duty is owed to the corporation and not to individual shareholders. Absent fraud, or other special circumstances — as where directors could be regarded as acting as trustees for the shareholders in negotiating a takeover — a director owed no duty to disclose confidential information to a shareholder.[23] Second, no harm appeared to be done to the corporation; in the illustrations above, the confidential information affected the value of the corporation's shares, but in no sense could it have been used for the corporation's benefit.[24]

In the absence of the courts declaring insider trading a breach of duty owed to shareholders the legislatures have stepped in to fill the void. As we shall see later in this chapter and in Chapter 32, securities legislation has made insider trading a criminal offence, punishable by fines and/or imprisonment, and imposes strict disclosure requirements

---

[23] Percival v. Wright, Allen v. Hyatt, *supra* nn. 8, 9.

[24] An argument can be made that the information was a form of property that belonged to the corporation and, having been used for the personal benefit of the director, he should have to account for that benefit. That argument has been accepted by courts in the United States, but has not been successful in Canada or England.

whenever a director, or other insider, trades in the securities of his own corporation. These provisions apply principally to corporations whose securities are publicly traded. However, section 131(4) of the CBCA provides that, even in the case of a private company, an insider who, for his own benefit or advantage, makes use of specific, confidential, price-sensitive information in connection with a transaction in securities of his own corporation, or any of its affiliates, is liable

(a) to compensate any person for any direct loss suffered as a result of the transaction, and

(b) to account to the corporation for any benefit or advantage obtained.[25]

For the purposes of the legislation, "insider" includes a director or officer, an employee, any shareholder who holds more than ten percent of the corporation's securities, and a "tippee" — that is, a person who knowingly receives confidential information from an insider.

$\mathcal{R}$IGHTS OF SHAREHOLDERS

Sources of Shareholders' Rights

In large, widely held corporations, shareholdings are widely distributed, frequently with no single shareholder or group holding more than five per cent of the voting stock. No majority or even controlling group of shareholders can be discerned; only in exceptional circumstances can a group be mobilized to try to overturn the rule of the existing managers. In such corporations management is largely self-perpetuating, even when it is inefficient and perhaps incompetent. It should be noted too that in large corporations management — the senior executive officers — operates almost entirely independently of the board of directors. The chief executive officer is often a director and president of the corporation, but may provide only a tenuous link between senior management and the board. Those decisions that are referred to the board are usually rubber-stamped when the president speaks in their favour.

Paradoxically, such managers are probably supported in their position by a sensible piece of practical advice to individual investors: "If you don't like the management, sell!" In other words, "Do not get into costly corporate struggles; cut your losses by getting out and re-investing in a corporation more to your liking." This advice is a guiding principle that leaves poor managers in control until their corporation's misfortunes become manifestly public knowledge — at which time it may be too late to salvage one's investment. In such circumstances, the take-over bid may turn out to be the shareholders' best protection. Poorly managed corporations — especially those in which the rate of return to investors is low in relation to the value of the business or assets — become obvious targets for take-overs. It is this threat rather than any fear of a successful shareholders' revolt that tends to keep corporate managers on their toes.

In closely held corporations, the problem is radically different. The usual problem is a serious disagreement among the principal shareholders, who are usually also directors and senior employees of the corporation. In the absence of careful contractual arrangements

---

[25] Broadly similar provisions are included in some provincial statutes; see for example Business Corporations Act, R.S.O. 1990, c. B-16, s. 138.

providing safeguards, a minority shareholder in a closely held corporation may find himself "locked in" and "frozen out" at the same time.

The minority shareholder is "locked in" in the sense that he probably cannot sell his shares except at a small fraction of what he believes they should be worth. There are two reasons for this unhappy state of affairs: first, in most closely held corporations the transfer of shares is restricted, usually requiring the consent of the board of directors. It is the dominating majority on the board who have made the minority shareholder's life miserable, and they may be unwilling to agree to the transfer of his shares except to someone of their own choosing. Second, even if the minority shareholder is free to sell the shares, he will have great difficulty in finding a buyer who would consider acquiring a minority position in a private corporation.

The minority shareholder may be "frozen out" in the following manner: first, the majority directors may fire him from his job with the corporation, or at the very least refuse to renew his employment contract when it expires; second, they may remove him from the board of directors, or re-elect someone else in his place at the next election; and third, they may increase salaries to themselves, so that the corporation itself earns no apparent profit. Even if a profit is shown, it may be retained by the corporation, since dividends are payable only at the discretion of the board of directors. Thus, it can happen that a minority shareholder with his life savings invested in a corporation may find himself deprived of his salary-earning position, his directorship, and his prospect of any dividends on his investment; and he may also be without a marketable security — even though he has a substantial share interest in the corporation.

In these circumstances the majority shareholders may not have broken any law, and no remedy exists at common law. However, a number of statutory provisions empower the courts to give relief to minority shareholders. We shall discuss these, as well as ways of avoiding the problem by use of shareholders' agreements, under "Rescuing the 'Locked-in' Shareholder", below.

Apart from these special remedies, the statutes seek to protect shareholders in two main ways: disclosure of the corporation's affairs, and the right to a voice in the corporation's affairs. A third category of shareholder rights — financial entitlements to profits and assets on winding up — has developed from two sources: interpretation of the incorporating statute and interpretation of the corporate constitution.

Statutory Safeguards: Disclosure

The Financial Statement

The importance of disclosure derives from the assumptions that the cold light of publicity offers investors an opportunity to evaluate the effectiveness of management and that in extreme cases publicity is an effective deterrent to high-handed behaviour or misconduct in management.

Of the several types of disclosure, perhaps the most important takes the form of the annual financial statement of the corporation, which must be presented to the shareholders at the annual general meeting. All corporations acts require that a certain minimum of information be part of the financial statement, though requirements vary significantly. Generally speaking, the basic items required are the income statement, showing the results of operations for the financial year; the balance sheet, showing the corporation's assets and sources of assets as of the financial year-end (including details of changes in share capital during the year); a statement of changes in financial position, analyzing changes in working capital; a statement of retained earnings showing changes during the year, including the declaration of dividends; and a statement of contributed surplus. The annual financial statement should be in comparative form, showing corresponding data for the preceding financial year. In addition, some statutes require that shareholders be sent comparative interim quarterly financial statements.

To assist in the analysis and evaluation of the financial statement, the acts provide for the appointment of an independent auditor by the shareholders: smaller closely held corporations may dispense with this requirement, but only if the shareholders unanimously agree to do so. The auditor represents the shareholders' interests and must be an independent person not in the employ of the corporation. She has the duty to investigate all the records and accounts of the corporation so that she may check on the fairness of the financial statement well in advance of the annual general meeting of shareholders. Her task is to present to the shareholders her opinion of the financial statement issued by the directors. She must state whether in her opinion the statement fairly presents the financial position and results of operations of the corporation in accordance with generally accepted accounting principles.[26] Both the auditor's report and the financial statement must be sent to all shareholders well before the corporation's annual general meeting; the period usually specified is at least twenty-one days before the meeting.[27] These items are included in the corporation's *annual report* to shareholders.

The financial statement is prepared from the *books of account*. Only the auditor, as representative of the shareholders, and the directors have the right to examine these books; shareholders as such do not have access to them. If a shareholder suspects that something is wrong, he may communicate his information to the auditor in the hope that the auditor will make use of it, but the auditor has no duty to undertake a special examination at the request of a shareholder. Or again, a shareholder may communicate with a director who would be sympathetic to his point of view and who may be willing to check the information against the books of account. As a last resort, a shareholder may, in all jurisdictions except Prince Edward Island, apply to a court for the appointment of an inspector.

Appointment of Inspector

All the jurisdictions (again with the exception of Prince Edward Island) have statutory provisions for applying to the courts to appoint an inspector to investigate the affairs of the corporation and to audit its books. The statutes give inspectors sweeping powers of inquiry, and the remedy can be a very effective one. In some jurisdictions there are a number of obstacles that undermine this effectiveness: in particular, a substantial proportion of shareholders may be required to join in the application, and the applicant may be required to give security to cover the costs of an investigation, which may be very high. However, the CBCA, and most of the provincial acts based on it, now permit a single shareholder to apply; the acts state that the applicant is not required to give security for costs (s. 229).

---

[26] See section 5400, *CICA Handbook* (Canadian Institute of Chartered Accountants) for a complete statement of the form and content of the auditor's report.

[27] CBCA, s. 159.

A concerned shareholder may choose either of two options: he may request the Director — a government official appointed to supervise the affairs of corporations — to apply to the court to order an investigation, or he may apply directly to the court himself. In either event, it is necessary to make out a *prime facie* case, that is, produce sufficient evidence of the probability of serious mismanagement to warrant further investigation.

Documents of Record

The second major requirement of disclosure is the statutory provision that a corporation must maintain certain *documents of record* at its head office for the inspection of any shareholder during usual business hours. The documents of record to which the shareholders have access include minute books of the proceedings at meetings of the shareholders; a register of all transfers of shares, including the date and other particulars of each transfer; a copy of the corporation's charter; a copy of all by-laws (or articles) and special resolutions; a register of shareholders; and a register of the directors. These documents may often be useful to a minority group of shareholders attempting to collect evidence to support a claim of misconduct or ineffectiveness on the part of the directors. In particular, the share register permits a dissentient group to obtain the names and addresses of all other shareholders so that they may communicate with them, explain their complaints, and attempt to enlist their support.

Another document of record is the minute book of the proceedings at meetings of the board of directors. Unlike the other documents of record, however, directors alone, not the shareholders, have a right of access to it.

Record of Insider Trading

Since the early 1930s, United States federal securities legislation has required directors and officers to report their own trading in their corporation's securities, so that shareholders may learn whether they are making use of confidential information in order to traffic profitably in the shares of the corporation. Until 1966, disclosure requirements for directors and officers of Canadian companies were minimal. Only the Ontario and federal acts required directors to disclose information and this was of a very limited scope and usefulness. In 1966, Ontario substantially amended the disclosure requirements of the Corporations Act and passed a new Securities Act,[28] requiring detailed information on dealings by insiders to be filed with the provincial Securities Commission, which publishes a report each month. The Act was substantially revised in 1978 and again in 1987, giving greater administrative supervision to the Commission. Most of the other provinces have enacted securities acts similar to the Ontario provisions; we shall return to the subject of securities legislation in the next chapter.

Statutory Safeguards: A Voice in the Affairs of the Corporation

Notice and Attendance at Meetings

Disclosure alone, of course, is not a sufficient safeguard for the shareholder. Shareholders must be able to do something about unsatisfactory management. If they wish to voice

---

[28] See now, R.S.O. 1990, c. S-5.

their objections, they need a forum to do so. The forum provided under all the statutes is the general meeting of shareholders. The corporation may hold other meetings of shareholders in the course of the year, but it is required by statute to hold at least one annual general meeting.[29] Shareholders are entitled to advance notice of all meetings, and, as we have seen, they are entitled to receive copies of the financial statement before the annual general meeting. They may attend the meetings, question the directors, and make criticisms of the management of the corporation.

The Right to Requisition Meetings

Occasions may arise where the shareholders wish to call a meeting and the board of directors refuses to do so. All the provinces provide in their statutes that the shareholders themselves may call the meeting. Unfortunately, these provisions require a comparatively large proportion of the shareholders to petition in order to compel the calling of the meeting, a requirement virtually impossible to meet in large corporations where even a relatively large group of shareholders may hold a very small percentage of the total shares.[30] The right to requisition a special meeting is therefore rather limited in large corporations, but is still especially valuable in the smaller closely held companies.

The Right to Vote

The right to attend meetings and to criticize must ultimately be backed by some form of sanction in the hands of the shareholders. This sanction is found in the right to vote. The collective power of the shareholders is exercised through the passing — or defeating — of resolutions; an ordinary resolution, which is adopted by a simple majority of votes cast, and a special resolution, which requires a two-thirds majority.[31] The CBCA sets out a number of matters that must be approved by either an ordinary or a special resolution, the most important being:

(a) the approval of alterations to the articles of incorporation (s. 173);
(b) the approval of certain other fundamental changes, such as amalgamation with another corporation (s. 183) or the sale of all, or substantially all, of the corporation's property (s. 189);
(c) the approval of any amendments made by the directors to the by-laws (s. 103);
(d) the election of the auditor (s. 162); and
(e) the election, or removal, of directors (ss. 106, 109).

Items (a) and (b) require a special resolution; the other items, and any other matters that might be put on the agenda, may be effected by ordinary resolution.[32] Except in the relatively rare case where a fundamental change is proposed in the corporate constitution, or in the nature of its business, the most important matter voted upon by the shareholders

---

[29] CBCA, s. 133. The Act requires that an annual meeting be held not more than fifteen months after the previous annual meeting; thus it is possible for a calendar year to pass without a meeting.

[30] The CBCA, s. 143, requires a requisition to be made by five percent of the shareholders, and this is also the requirement in the other articles of incorporation jurisdictions and in British Columbia; Company Act, R.S.B.C. 1979, c. 59, s. 171. Prince Edward Island stipulates the impossibly high figure of 25 percent; Companies Act, R.S.P.E.I. 1974, c. C-5, s. 30.

[31] S. 2. In memorandum companies a special resolution requires a three-quarters majority.

[32] Unless the articles provide for a system of cumulative voting; see *supra*.

is the election of directors since, as we have seen, it is the directors who control the management of the corporation's affairs.

However, not all shareholders necessarily have the right to vote. A corporation's shares may be divided into different classes, with different voting rights. Common shares almost invariably carry the right to vote; preferred shares usually carry a right to vote only in specified circumstances, such as when preferred dividends are in arrears. The founders of a corporation may create several classes of shares and weight the voting heavily in favour of a small group of shares held by themselves. For example, they could give class A shares one hundred votes per share and class B, issued to a broader group of shareholders, only one vote per share. It would be virtually impossible for a publicly-listed corporation to have such a share structure today: securities commissions, stock exchanges, and underwriters would very probably refuse such an issue, and without their concurrence a public offering is impossible. Virtually all common stock offered on the market today carries one vote per share. By contrast, in closely held corporations there is no restriction upon the different rights that may be attached to various classes of shares, provided at least one class has voting rights; within a particular class, however, all shares must enjoy the same rights.[33]

Class rights, which may relate not only to voting but also to other matters such as rights to priority in payment of dividends or to receive the surplus on liquidation of the corporation,[34] must be set out in the articles of incorporation. Consequently, they may only be varied by special resolution of the shareholders. Additionally, to alter the rights of a particular class requires approval by the votes of two-thirds of that class and of any other class that may be adversely affected (s. 176).

Proxies

In most widely held corporations, only a small proportion of shareholders manage to attend the annual general meeting. All corporations statutes permit a shareholder who will not be present to assign his voting right to any shareholder who will be present at the meeting. He does this by signing a proxy form in the name of the person to whom he wishes to assign his vote. Most jurisdictions now go further and require all corporations, except the smallest closely held ones, to send a proxy form, the contents of which are prescribed in detail, to all shareholders at the same time as notice of a meeting is given.

In the event of a proxy fight between two groups of shareholders — usually the board of directors and a dissentient group — each group solicits all the shareholders by mail in order to persuade them to give their proxy forms to the group making the solicitation. The dissentient group may go to the corporation's head office to obtain lists of all the shareholders from the share register in order to make their solicitations. Here the board of directors has a great advantage: as a matter of practice, they include proxy forms, offering one of themselves as the proposed proxy, with the mailed notice of the annual general meeting.[35] In this manner, the costs of compiling the list and addressing and mailing the notices are borne by the corporation, whereas a group of dissentient shareholders, in order to solicit proxy forms, must bear all these costs themselves. In very large corporations, the

---

[33] S. 24. See Re Bowater Canadian Industries and R. L. Crain Inc. (1988), 46 D.L.R.(4th) 161.

[34] We encountered the concept of preferred shares in Chapter 30.

[35] This advantage is only partly offset by disclosure requirements and by compelling management to provide shareholders with a means to nominate a different proxy.

costs may be prohibitive for a dissentient group. The larger the corporation, the more difficult it is to dislodge an incumbent board of directors, but there have been a few instances of dissatisfied shareholders voting out the entire board of directors and, in turn, removing the senior management of large corporations.

Pre-Emptive Rights

One of the more important powers given to the board of directors is the power to issue shares. The issue of new shares involves two possible risks for existing shareholders. First, the issue of shares to some other person will necessarily reduce the proportion of the total number of shares that a shareholder holds in the corporation. Thus a shareholder who holds 51 percent (or 34 percent) of all the corporation's shares would find that she could no longer secure the adoption of an ordinary resolution (or prevent the passing of a special resolution) if sufficient new shares were issued to someone else. Second, there is the risk of "stock watering"; if new shares are issued for a price that is less than the value of the existing shares, the value of those shares will be diluted.

ILLUSTRATION

A owns 34 out of the total of 100 shares issued by *XYZ* Inc. It is estimated that the assets of *XYZ* Inc. are worth approximately $1 million. A majority of the directors wish to raise additional capital and resolve to issue 20 new shares to *T*, at a price of $5000 per share. As a result, *A* will now own only 28.3 percent of the total shares, and can no longer block the adoption of a special resolution. Further, *A's* shares, previously worth $10 000 each, will be worth only $9167.

United States courts have for many years been concerned with maintaining the proportionate holdings of shares of shareholders. They have declared that at common law a shareholder has a pre-emptive right to retain her proportionate holdings in a corporation, but this right is subject to various qualifications. Accordingly, when a corporation proposes to issue more shares it must normally offer each shareholder a proportion of the new issue equal to the proportion she holds in the already-issued shares. A shareholder who has 3% of the issued shares of a corporation is entitled to purchase a further 3% of any new issue. A right of pre-emption is consequently very important in retaining the balance of power in the corporation. It also ensures that, if the new shares are issued at a price that is less than the value of the existing shares, the existing shareholders are not prejudiced, at any rate if they exercise their right of pre-emption. Any reduction in the value of their existing shares will be exactly balanced by the gain they receive in buying the new shares at an under-value.

A general principle of pre-emption has not been recognized by Canadian courts. In limited circumstances, however, the courts have recognized rights somewhat similar to pre-emptive rights. Thus, although the directors have the right to issue authorized share capital of the corporation at their discretion, they must issue shares only for the purpose of raising capital or for purposes that are in the best interest of the corporation. If they have a bona fide intention to raise capital, they may distribute the shares to whomever they wish upon payment of a fair price. But if directors issue shares not for the benefit of the corporation but to affect voting control, they may be restrained from making the issue, or it may subsequently be declared void. For example, if directors were to issue shares to themselves for the purpose of out-voting at a general meeting shareholders who, up to that point, had a majority of the issued shares, the extra share issue could be prevented by court action. This rule has been stated by Mr. Justice Rose:

> ...No one would think of saying that directors may never allot shares of an authorized issue without first offering to the existing shareholders the shares which they propose to allot; but the allotment here proposed differs radically from the usual allotment from time to time, as opportunity offers, of the shares of an issue which has been determined upon as a means of providing the company with the requisite working capital...[Here] no shares had been issued for a long time; the company had been carrying on a successful business with the capital which it had; the readily saleable assets were apparently worth three or four times the par value of the issued shares; each shareholder was justified in considering that he had an interest in those assets proportionate to his holding of the issued shares; to do something which would alter those proportions, to do it without giving to each shareholder an opportunity of protecting his interest and to do it not in the usual course of the company's business, but for the purpose of shifting from one body of shareholders to another the power of electing directors and so of controlling the company's policy, was, I think, beyond the power of the directors.[36]

While not required to do so, a corporation may voluntarily recognize its shareholders' pre-emptive right. When it proposes to issue further shares it may first issue *subscription rights* or *share rights* to all present shareholders. These rights are granted in a document from the corporation and give each shareholder one right for each share held. The shareholder has then an option to purchase a new share at a specified price for, let us say, every five subscription rights. A shareholder owning 50 shares will then receive 50 rights entitling her to buy 10 shares at a specified price per share. Subscription rights are normally made transferrable, and if the market value of the existing shares exceeds the specified price for the new shares by a significant sum, the rights themselves will have a market value; they may be sold to anyone who wishes to purchase them and exercise the option.

Rights to Dividends and Return of Capital

The general purpose of any investment is to obtain a total return greater than the capital sum invested. The total return may include either or both of two elements: an increase in the market value of the shares, and earnings distributed regularly to the investor. Investors in common stock are often concerned with more than the annual distribution of profits. They may be satisfied with smaller dividends if there is a capital appreciation in the corporation's assets or if a significant part of the profits is retained within the business and has the effect of increasing the value of the shares.

Preferred shares are in a different category. Except in rare cases, they are preferred as to capital, that is, on winding up their stated redemption value is returned to preferred shareholders before anything is paid to common shareholders, but they will receive no more than that sum regardless of the increase in the net assets of the corporation. The

---

[36] Bonisteel v. Collis Leather Co. Ltd. (1919), 45 O.R. 195 at 200. But for a more recent broadening of directors' discretion, see Teck Corporation v. Millar *et al.* (1973), 33 D.L.R. (3d) 288, esp. pp.328-331.

preferred shareholder is, therefore, primarily interested in the regular distribution of profits in the form of dividends.

Whether dividends are declared is a matter entirely within the discretion of the board of directors; shareholders have no right to be paid a dividend even when the corporation makes large profits. There can be no discrimination, however, in the payment of dividends among shareholders of the same class; each is entitled to such dividends as are declared in proportion to the number of shares of that class held. In addition, directors are bound to pay dividends in the order of preference assigned to the classes of shareholders. Thus, they could not pay the common shareholders a dividend without first paying the whole of any preferred dividends owing to preference shareholders.

On the dissolution of a corporation, provided it has assets remaining after paying off all its creditors, shareholders are entitled to a proportionate share of the remaining net assets. The distribution of these net assets among the various classes of shareholders must also be made in accordance with the respective priorities of each class. The rights of various shareholders on dissolution have been discussed in the preceding chapter, in the section "Nature of Corporate Securities".

THE PROTECTION OF MINORITY SHAREHOLDERS[37]

Duties of Directors and Shareholders Contrasted

We have seen that directors of corporations are under strict duties of good faith. In contrast, a shareholder owes no positive duty to act for either the welfare of the corporation itself or the welfare of her fellow shareholders.[38] Her obligation ends when she has paid the full purchase price for her shares. She may leave her share certificates lying in some forgotten corner, and never trouble to attend meetings or to return proxy forms. In this respect she is much like a property owner. Unless a statute places an obligation upon her to comply with some public duty — for example, filing income tax returns concerning her dividends — she is free to do nothing about her interest in the corporation. If she attends shareholders' meetings and votes she is free, generally, to exercise her vote in whatever way she pleases and for whatever purposes she desires. By voting in favour of or against a particular resolution, she may cause the corporation to suffer a loss or may even harm her fellow shareholders; the attitude of the courts is that as a part owner of the corporation she may take into account whatever factors she wishes and vote her shares accordingly. This seems to be so even where the shareholder is herself a director of the corporation. Although a director owes a duty, in exercising her powers and duties, to act honestly and in good faith with a view to the best interests of the corporation (s. 122), when she votes as a shareholder she is entitled to consider her own personal interests.[39]

---

[37] See MacIntosh, "Minority Shareholder Rights in Canada and England: 1860-1987", (1989) 27 *Osgoode Hall L.J.* 561.

[38] Unlike some U.S. courts, Canadian courts have consistently held that majority shareholders owe no duty to the minority; see, for example, Brant Investments Ltd. v. Keeprite Inc. (1991), 3 O.R. (3d) 289.

[39] See North-West Transportation v. Beatty (1887), 12 App. Cas. 589.

Possible Oppression of Minority Rights

At the very least, the above statement of a shareholder's freedom to use her vote means that the courts will not substitute their judgment for hers when her actions are based upon business considerations. The courts' presumption is in favour of the shareholder from the beginning: they will not interfere even when they think that the shareholder's decision is irresponsible. If carried to an extreme, this view would permit completely unreasonable decisions that are deliberately intended to injure other shareholders. A controlling group of shareholders — through their ability to determine the composition of the board of directors, to approve its actions or decline to do anything about its misdeeds, and (if they have a two-thirds majority) even to amend the corporation's constitution — could ensure that the affairs of the corporation were managed entirely for their own benefit and to the detriment of the minority. As we saw, when we considered the dilemma of the "frozen-in" shareholder, these things can happen without any law being broken.

ILLUSTRATION A

A,B,C, and *D* are the equal shareholders and directors of a corporation, Traviata Trattoria Ltd. The articles of incorporation restrict the business of the corporation to the operation of one or more restaurants. Contrary to *D*'s wishes, *A, B*, and *C* decide to sell the restaurant to a property developer and to invest the proceeds in a casino business. They use their votes to pass two special resolutions; (1) approving the sale of the restaurant (substantially the only asset of the corporation), and (2) amending the articles to remove the restriction on the business that may be carried on by the corporation.

In this example, no wrong has been done to the corporation and the majority has acted within its rights. Nevertheless, *D* may justifiably feel aggrieved since the whole basis upon which he became a shareholder in the corporation has been changed.

ILLUSTRATION B

Sixty percent of the shares of Figaro Ltd. are held by Almaviva Inc., a large public corporation, and forty percent by its original founder, Susanna. Following a disagreement over company policy with Susanna, Almaviva uses its majority voting power to appoint three of its own directors to be directors of Figaro. The new directors subsequently sell an important piece of Figaro's property to Bartolo Ltd., a corporation wholly controlled by Almaviva. The sale is at a gross undervalue.

Here, the directors of Figaro have probably been in breach either of their duty of care and skill or their duty to act in good faith and in the interests of their corporation. The corporation, Figaro, has been injured, since the value of its assets has been reduced, but the loss falls entirely on its minority shareholder, Susanna, since the majority shareholder, Almaviva gains more as shareholder of the purchaser, Bartolo (100% of the undervalue), than it loses as shareholder of the vendor, Figaro (60% of the undervalue). Consequently,

Almaviva, as controlling shareholder of Figaro, will not complain about any breach of duty by its directors.

ILLUSTRATION C

The shares in Jenufa Ltd. are held in equal proportions by *A*, her husband *B*, and his two sons by a previous marriage, *C* and *D*, all of whom had until recently been directors. After an acrimonious divorce, *B*, *C*, and *D* use their majority voting power to remove *A* from the board. Subsequently, they greatly increase their own salaries as full-time officers of the corporation, which consequently reduces the corporation's profits. Instead of distributing the remaining profits as dividends, they decide to reinvest them in a fund to provide for the long-term capital needs of the corporation. They also refuse to consent to *A* transferring her shares to any third party.

In this case, *A* is locked-in and frozen-out, as we have described earlier in this chapter. But the corporation has not been injured and, unless it can be shown that *B*, *C*, and *D* acted in bad faith, there may have been nothing improper in their actions.

Under traditional principles of company law, the aggrieved minority shareholders in the above illustrations received very little assistance from the courts. However, special statutory remedies that have been introduced during the past two or three decades, have greatly improved the situation of the minority. In examining the more important of these, we shall concentrate upon the remedies provided in the CBCA and in the statutes of those provinces that have adopted the articles of incorporation system.[40]

The Appraisal Remedy

In some situations, where the majority shareholders make fundamental changes to the corporation, s. 190 now offers a procedure whereby a dissenting shareholder need no longer go along with the change; he may elect instead to have his shares bought out by the corporation. If a price cannot be agreed, the court will fix a fair price. However, the appraisal remedy is limited to specific actions by the majority.[41]

While the remedy can be important in closely-held corporations, where no ready market exists for minority shareholdings, the procedure is a complicated one, and the dissenter must comply with every step prescribed by the Act in order to take advantage of it. If instead, the shareholder can show that his interests have been "unfairly disregarded" he is more likely to resort to the "Oppression Remedy" discussed below. A dissenter in a widely-held corporation would normally just sell his shares on the market.

Wrongs Done to the Corporation — the Derivative Action

When a corporation has suffered an injury, as in Illustration B or, for example, where directors have made a secret profit for themselves by exploiting a "corporate opportunity",

---

[40] Corresponding provisions are contained in the British Columbia statute, but the remaining provinces have not introduced such far-reaching reforms.

[41] S. 190(1) sets out the actions of the majority that permit a dissenting shareholder to be paid fair value for his shares. The most important are: changing any restrictions on the issue, transfer or ownership of shares in the corporation or on the business the corporation may carry on; "amalgamating", that is, merging the corporation with one or more other corporations into a single corporation; and selling, leasing, or exchanging substantially all of the corporation's property.

the corporation may sue the wrongdoer in the same manner as may a natural person. Ordinarily, an action must be started by its officers or board of directors. However, if the directors are the wrongdoers they are hardly likely to commence an action against themselves. Unless an aggrieved minority shareholder is permitted to bring an action in the name of the corporation, the wrong will go unremedied and the controlling directors will get away with their ill-gotten gain. No legal system can permit such oppressive conduct to continue without a remedy — at least in theory. Thus, at common law a minority shareholder was permitted to start an action on behalf of the corporation in the name of himself and all other aggrieved shareholders — a representative or class action derived from the injury to the corporation, and frequently called a derivative action.

Unfortunately, the courts had great difficulty with the concept of a mere shareholder suing in the name of the corporation. They surrounded this right with procedural requirements that had the effect of almost stifling any theoretical right to a remedy. In particular, the complaining shareholder could be required to deposit a substantial sum of money with the court as security for costs in the event of losing the case. Yet if the action succeeded, any damages awarded would go to the corporation and he would benefit only to the extent that the value of his shares thus increased.

The modern statutory derivative action (s. 239) overcomes most of these procedural barriers. It permits a shareholder to obtain leave from the court to bring an action in the name and on behalf of the corporation: to do so he need only establish that the directors will not bring the action themselves, that he is acting in good faith, and that it appears to be in the interests of the corporation or its shareholders that the action be commenced. If he establishes these things, then the court may make an order to commence the action. The acts prohibit the court from requiring the shareholder to give security for costs. Indeed, "the court may at any time order the corporation...to pay to the complainant interim costs, including legal fees and disbursements..." (s. 242(4)), and may make "an order requiring the corporation...to pay reasonable legal fees incurred by the complainant in connection with the action" (s. 240(d)). In other words, the court is directed to look to the welfare and ability of the shareholder to pursue the action.

Another important innovation introduced by the statutory derivative action is that, instead of any damages recovered in a successful action automatically going to the official plaintiff — the corporation — the court may direct "that any amount adjudged payable by a defendant in the action shall be paid, in whole or in part, directly to former and present shareholders of the corporation...instead of to the corporation..." (s. 240(c)). Thus in our Illustration B, above, Susanna could receive direct compensation for her loss, rather than being compensated only indirectly through an increase in the assets of the corporation.

Decisions of the courts applying the statutory derivative action indicate that the position of minority shareholders has been much improved and many of the former defects have been removed.[42] Nevertheless, the remedy has been somewhat overshadowed by the oppression remedy, discussed below.

---

[42] See, for example, Re Canadian Hidrogas Resources Ltd. (1979), 8 B.L.R. 104; Re Bellman and Western Approaches Ltd. (1981), 130 D.L.R. (3d) 193.

Rescuing the "Locked-in" Shareholder — Winding-Up and the Oppression Remedy

We have briefly described the plight of the locked-in minority shareholder under common law rules: his former business associates have frozen him out of the corporation but have been scrupulously careful not to break any rules or to be guilty of harming the corporation itself. In a partnership, the rules of equity give considerable protection to a minority member; he is entitled to an accounting of profits and to receive his share of them regularly; if the impasse is total between the partners he can insist on a dissolution and sale of the assets and receipt of his proportionate part of the proceeds. Since the other partners cannot continue to use the partnership assets for their sole benefit, they must either face dissolution and sale or else offer him a reasonable settlement. Not so in a closely held corporation: in the absence of contractual protection through a private agreement among the shareholders, a minority shareholder has none of the rights of a partner.

Company law statutes have, however, followed partnership law in one important respect: they give the courts discretion to make an order winding up a company where it is "just and equitable" to do so.[43] Because of the drastic nature of the remedy the courts have been reluctant to use it if the corporation is flourishing or is fairly large.[44] Typically, the remedy is available where the corporation is a small family business or an "incorporated partnership", where there is deadlock, where relations between the participants have broken down, or where a "partner" has been frozen out.[45] In these cases, the remedy has proven quite effective, since the mere threat of its use has often been sufficient to persuade the majority to reach a compromise.

More recently however, beginning with the English act of 1948,[46] an alternative remedy — often called the *oppression remedy* — has been introduced and widely adopted in Canada.[47] It provides far greater flexibility since it allows a court, where the complainant has been treated unfairly or oppressively, to make any order it considers just and appropriate to remedy the situation. Typically, it is the remedy sought where a minority shareholder is "frozen-out", as in our Illustration C,[48] but it has also been applied in cases of deadlock or breakdown in the relations between shareholders or directors, which formerly might have led to a just and equitable winding-up:[49] in a few cases, the oppression remedy has been used where a wrong has been done to the corporation, and a minority shareholder has suffered in consequence, even though a derivative action would seem to be more appropriate in such circumstances.[50] Thus it is possible that Susanna, in our Illustration B, might seek an oppression remedy rather than bring a derivative action.[51] To justify the making of an order under section 241, a complainant must show that the

---

[43] See CBCA, s. 214(1)(b)(ii). The "just and equitable winding-up" rule has been a feature of English and Canadian company law statutes since around the end of the nineteenth century.

[44] Re R.C. Young Insurance Ltd. [1955] O.R. 598.

[45] For a good example, see Ebrahimi v. Westbourne Galleries Ltd. [1973] A.C. 360.

[46] Companies Act 1948, s. 210.

[47] It was first introduced in British Columbia; see now R.S.B. 1979, c. 59, s. 185. The corresponding provision in the CBCA is s. 241.

[48] Re Ferguson and Imax Systems Corp. (1983), 150 D.L.R.(3d) 718; Daniels v. Fielder (1989), 52 D.L.R.(4th) 424.

[49] Eiserman v. Ara Farms (1989), 52 D.L.R. (4th) 498; Tilley v. Hailes (1992), 7 O.R.(3d) 257.

[50] See, for example, Journet v. Superchef Food Industries Ltd. (1984), 29 B.L.R. 206.

[51] For discussion of this issue see MacIntosh, "The Oppression Remedy: Personal or Derivative?", (1991) 70 *Can. Bar Rev.* 29.

action complained of has been "oppressive or unfairly prejudicial or...unfairly disregards the interests" of the complainant. However, the courts have emphasized on occasions that the conduct need not be wrongful or in bad faith, though this will be a factor to take into account.[52]

Section 241(3) allows the court to make any order it thinks fit. By far the most common remedy granted has been to require the majority to buy out the minority interest at a fair price, but a wide range of other orders may be made. Because of its great flexibility, and the absence of technical obstacles, the oppression remedy is quickly becoming the most widely used shareholder remedy in Canada; it has largely replaced both the derivative action and "just and equitable" winding up.

Shareholder Agreements

Their Difficulties and Advantages

Although the oppression remedy has greatly increased the protection given to the minority shareholder, he still must depend on the court exercising its discretion in his favour — and it may well refuse to do so if the majority have complied with the corporation's charter and are not in breach of their duties to the corporation. Thus, a shareholder is still in a less secure position than is a partner. This is a factor to be considered if a group of, say, three equal partners propose to transform their business into a corporation. It may make good business sense to incorporate because of the nature of the business, its growth and tax position. Yet each of the three partners, if aware of the dangers of being a minority shareholder at odds with the other two, might well hesitate to give up the protection of partnership law. Fortunately it is possible to devise an employment contract with the corporation and a concurrent agreement among the shareholders themselves — outside the constitution of the corporation — that approximates the protection available to partners. The process is not simple because, as we have seen, directors owe their primary duty to the corporation: they must not fetter their duty to exercise their discretion "bona fide in the best interests of the corporation", however inappropriate that duty may be when applied to a closely held corporation in which the directors themselves hold all the shares. Thus, subject to an important exception to be discussed below, any agreement among shareholders must be restricted to their role as shareholders and must not impinge on their role as directors.[53] This danger can be avoided in a well-drafted shareholder agreement. Each employment and shareholder agreement must be custom-tailored to the needs of an individual business, just as in partnership, but it may be useful to examine briefly the chief elements normally used to protect minority shareholders.

Right to Employment

Each shareholder may enter into a long-term employment contract with the corporation with a salary subject to increases at an agreed rate. There may be a provision that after a preliminary financial statement each year, he will receive an employee's profit-sharing bonus equal to a specified proportion of the corporate profits before taxes.

---

[52] Brant Investments Ltd. v. Keeprite Inc., *supra* n. 38; Westfair Foods Ltd. v. Watt (1991), 79 D.L.R. (4th) 48.
[53] Motherwell v. Schoof [1949] 4 D.L.R. 812.

Right to Participate in Management

The shareholders mutually promise to elect each other to the board of directors at each annual meeting and not to nominate or vote for any other person. They may agree not to sell their shares to an outsider without giving the right of first refusal proportionately to the remaining shareholders. They may also promise not to vote for any major change in the corporation's capital structure or in the nature of its business except by unanimous agreement.

The Right to a Fair Price for a Share Interest

The shareholders may agree to a regular method of revaluation of their shares (usually on an annual basis). If one of them commits a major breach of the shareholder agreement and remains unwilling to remedy it, on notice he can be required to sell his interest to the others at the appraised value. In addition, if any shareholder is wrongfully expelled or dismissed by the others, who remain unwilling to reinstate him, he may require them to buy out his interest at the appraised value. This provision may also state that in the event of a dispute about appraisal a named person, usually the auditor, will arbitrate and assess the value of the interest.

There can be many refinements to shareholder agreements; the above provisions are intended to illustrate their general nature. Anyone who finds that his would-be fellow shareholders object to an agreement of this type ought to consider seriously whether it is wise to proceed further in the proposed venture.

Unanimous Shareholder Agreement

Articles of incorporation statutes formally recognize unanimous shareholder agreements and expressly permit them to govern relationships among shareholders in a closely-held corporation in much the same manner as in a partnership. Although these agreements have yet to be interpreted by the courts, it is probable that the courts will apply the same equitable principles as are used in construing partnership agreements. The CBCA states that "an agreement among all the shareholders...that restricts in whole or in part the powers of the directors to manage the business and affairs of the corporation is valid" (s.146(2)), and that a shareholder who is party to such an agreement "has all the rights, powers and *duties* of a director...to the extent that the agreement restricts the discretion or powers of the directors,...and the *directors are thereby relieved of their duties and liabilities* to the same extent"(s. 146(5))[italics added].

The Act also states that "a transferee of shares subject to an unanimous shareholder agreement is deemed to be a party to the agreement" (s. 146(4)). Thus, on the sale of a share interest in a closely held corporation that is subject to such an agreement, the transferee not only receives an assignment of rights as a shareholder but is also bound to carry out the duties of the transferor. A unanimous shareholder agreement must be "noted conspicuously" on the face of a share certificate in order to bind subsequent transferees (s. 49(8)).

These provisions modify the common law rule that no agreement may fetter the discretion of directors. However, only unanimous agreements have special status under the Acts: if all shareholders are not a party to the agreement, the special status will not come about. Accordingly, these agreements cannot be utilized in corporations using employee profit-sharing schemes where employees receive a share interest, unless the employees also are made parties to the agreement.

The CBCA refers to unanimous shareholder agreements at more than a dozen places and treats them almost as if they were part of the corporate constitution, rather like by-laws.[54] It appears that the CBCA, and corresponding provincial acts, have created the opportunity to develop a new, flexible device for business planning in closely held corporations.

Questions for Review

1. Do the directors owe their duties to the shareholders or to the corporation? Why is it possible to distinguish between the shareholders and the corporation?
2. What types of duties do directors have? What are the remedies the corporation has for breach of each of these duties?
3. What main categories of shareholders' rights does this chapter discuss?
4. Distinguish between the books of account and the documents of record in relation to (a) content, and (b) shareholders' rights.
5. What is the point of a statutory requirement that directors must disclose their transactions in shares of the corporation?
6. What practical difficulties stand in the way of a shareholder who has reason to believe that the affairs of the corporation warrant a special investigation?
7. What is the value of a shareholder's right to attend a general meeting?
8. What is a proxy? Why is the proxy important to shareholders? What is a proxy battle? How may a group of dissentient shareholders utilize the proxy system? In what respect do the directors have an advantage over minority shareholders in a proxy battle?
9. In what ways might a majority group of shareholders act to the detriment of the remaining shareholders? What recourse does the minority group have?
10. Describe two main ways in which the rights of shareholders differ from the rights of bondholders.
11. What is meant by a derivative action?
12. In what ways may a director be guilty of insider trading?
13. Who is an "insider"?
14. How are the directors of a corporation appointed?
15. What is the difference between an ordinary resolution and a special resolution? When is a special resolution needed?
16. What is the appraisal remedy? When is it available?

Problems

Problem 1

Messrs. Forrest, Moss and Pine jointly purchased a piece of land located in Calgary for $1 000 000, with a view to erecting a large apartment building. They then incorporated

---

[54] See for example s. 103(1): "Unless the articles, by-laws *or a unanimous shareholder agreement* otherwise provide, the directors may, by resolution, make, amend, or repeal any by-laws that regulate the business or affairs of the corporation." [italics added]

Forest Park Apartments Ltd. and appointed themselves its directors. Forrest was a member of a small investment club composed of fifteen wealthy Calgarians; he told his fellow members about the projected building and persuaded them collectively to invest $7 000 000 in common shares of Forest Park — 70 000 shares issued at $100 each.

Shortly afterwards, a meeting of the directors passed a resolution to buy the land from Forrest, Moss and Pine by allotting them 20 000 shares in the corporation. Several weeks after the transaction was completed, Foley, who as an investment club member had purchased 5000 shares, learned the details and complained to the directors. They stated that in their opinion the land was worth at least $2.5 million and that the corporation had obtained it at a bargain price. Foley was still dissatisfied and threatened to start an action against them. What would be the substance of her complaint, and what remedies would she request? Would she succeed?

Problem 2

Collins Co. Ltd., incorporated in Ontario, has issued 700 shares at $100 each. The corporation has five directors who among them hold all 700 of the issued shares, 360 being held by one of them named Bonner.

Albi, the treasurer and one of the directors of the corporation, reported to a directors' meeting that she had received several requests from other directors that more shares be issued. She stated that in her opinion the corporation could make use of additional capital and proposed that a further 300 shares should be issued at $150, which would represent a fair price. All the directors agreed. The chairman then asked each director to state how many shares he or she would like. All except Bonner asked for varying amounts, from 60 to 100 shares. Bonner stated he did not care how many shares he received just so long as he received the same proportion of the new issue as his present holdings represented in the issued shares; if 300 were to be issued, he wanted $\frac{360}{700} \times 300$ shares, that is, 154 shares. Albi then introduced a motion that each director should be permitted to buy 60 shares. Bonner objected that he would then hold only 420 out of 1000 issued shares and would lose voting control, a primary object of his initial investment. Despite these objections, the resolution was passed, four to one, authorizing the issue of 60 shares to each director.

Bonner brought an action to restrain the board from making the issue on the grounds that it deprived him of his controlling interest. Discuss.

Problem 3

O'Mara and Zimmerman had been for about twenty years president and vice-president, respectively, as well as directors of Dominion Air Surveys Ltd. The business of the corporation was topographical mapping and geophysical exploration, and O'Mara and Zimmerman were each professionally qualified geophysicists enjoying widely respected reputations.

Five years ago, a controlling interest in Dominion Air Surveys Ltd. was acquired by Eagle Air Services Ltd. of Boston. With the change in ownership, O'Mara and Zimmerman began to feel less secure in their position, and their misgivings grew as it became clearer that their former authority to make independent decisions for the corporation was being eroded by head office. As a hedge against the loss of their positions, they formed another corporation, Blue Sky Photogrammetry Ltd. with objects almost identical to those of their present employer, Dominion Air Surveys Ltd.

In 1972, the Canadian government invited tenders on some extensive aerial survey work to be undertaken in the Caribbean area as a project of the Canadian International Development Agency. To help Dominion Air Surveys make an expert submission of a tender, O'Mara recommended the purchase of an aerodist (an airborne electronic distance-measuring device) for $75 000 and when the purchase was approved by head office, he and Zimmerman proceeded to use the device to gain a clear idea of the work that would be involved in the C.I.D.A. project. They then submitted a well-documented tender on behalf of Dominion Air Surveys Ltd. Two other corporations also submitted tenders at this time.

About three weeks later, and before any tender had been accepted, O'Mara and Zimmerman resigned their positions as officers and directors of Dominion Air Surveys Ltd. and devoted their time to the preparation of another tender, this one to be submitted by their newly formed corporation, Blue Sky Photogrammetry Ltd. Blue Sky's tender proved to be successful, in part because the Canadian government was impressed with the professional qualifications of O'Mara and Zimmerman and also because it was anxious to avoid political criticism for awarding the contract to any corporation owned outside Canada (as were the three others submitting tenders). O'Mara and Zimmerman then undertook the work for their new corporation, earning a substantial profit for it, as well as acquiring a basis for obtaining other new business.

Dominion Air Surveys Ltd. brought an action against O'Mara and Zimmerman alleging breach of their fiduciary duty as directors and asking damages of $150 000, the amount estimated to be the profit made on the C.I.D.A. contract.

Offer, with specific legal reasons, an opinion about the outcome of this action. (See *Canadian Aero Services Ltd. v. O'Malley* (1974), 40 D.L. R. (3d) 371.)

Cases

Case 1

Town Malls Inc. owned a valuable corner lot at the edge of a downtown shopping area in Edmonton. It had also acquired adjoining lots along the north side of its corner lot on a rather run-down street that seemed ripe for redevelopment. However, in order to build a new shopping mall Town needed to acquire several lots along the east side of the corner lot on the avenue opposite some of the city's best shops. Town's director in charge of acquisitions, Anne Bamhatra, sent a letter to Sylvan Devco Inc., the owner of the desired lots, asking if they would consider selling.

Geraldine Crain, president of Sylvan, replied that she was not interested in selling but would consider joining Town in a venture to develop the mall together. Each would continue to own its portion of the mall but they would jointly hire a firm of achitects to develop a plan, would invite joint construction tenders, and would agree on common rental rates and use a single agency for the purpose.

Town held a directors' meeting where the proposal was discussed. Town's president, Harold Kinder, said he thought it was a very sound idea to share the risk in uncertain economic times. The board then voted in favour of pursuing the proposal in principle. As chair of the meeting, Kinder did not vote but all the other directors voted yes. Negotiations proceeded over the following few months. Bamhatra and Kinder were the chief negotiators for Town; Crain and another director acted for Sylvan. The deal was signed and the corporations sent joint invitations to several firms of architects.

A week later, Bamhatra attended a luncheon where she learned from a friend of the Kinder family that the principal shareholders in Sylvan were Kinder's sister-in-law (15%), his first cousin (25%), and a friend holding shares (20%) in trust for Kinder's wife who was in poor health and confined to a wheelchair. Kinder had not mentioned these family connections to Sylvan at any meetings of Town's directors. Kinder has worked as a full-time salaried executive officer of Town for eight years, and also holds a 20% share interest in the corporation.

Bamhatra was perplexed by the news she obtained at the luncheon. She and her fellow directors owned 60% of the shares in Town. Discuss what actions she and her colleagues might take.

NOTE: The CBCA, s. 120 states:

> (1) A director or officer of a corporation who...is a party to a material contract...or...has a material interest in any person who is a party to a material contract...with the corporation, shall disclose...the nature and extent of his interest.
>
> (2) The disclosure required by subsection (1) shall be made...at a meeting at which the proposal is first considered.
>
> (5) A director referred to in subsection (1) shall not vote on any resolution to approve the contract...
>
> (8) Where a director or officer...fails to disclose...a court may on the application of the corporation...set aside the contract on such terms as it thinks fit.

Case 2

Normin Inc. is a large mining corporation, incorporated under the Canada Business Corporations Act, the shares of which are publicly traded and are listed on the Toronto Stock Exchange. It has recently been conducting extensive exploration on land acquired in the Canadian Arctic.

Late in the afternoon of March 31, Normin's chief executive officer, Baffin, received a fax from the mineralogist in charge of the explorations. The fax, headed "Highly Confidential", informed Baffin that a giant deposit of tin had been discovered. It appeared that it would be fairly easy to extract and would be extremely profitable.

Baffin at once informed as many of the directors and senior officers as he could contact. After some discussion they agreed to prepare a press release the next morning. However, on the evening of March 31:

(a) One of the directors, Banks, telephoned his broker, Charles, and without giving any reason instructed Charles to buy as many Normin shares on his account as he could, provided the price did not exceed $30 per share. The following morning, Normin shares opened on the exchange at $28.75. Charles bought 10 000 shares for Banks, at prices between $28.75 and $29.50.

(b) Another director, Melville, contacted her brother, Parry, and offered to buy his shares in Normin. Parry had acquired the shares some years before, but had since lost interest in the investment and had several times asked Melville if she would like to buy them. Melville offered to pay $29 per share, and Parry accepted and transferred his 15 000 shares to his sister.

(c) Hudson, a senior executive of Normin, told his bridge partner, Frobisher, that she should tell no one, but should buy Normin shares as soon as possible. Frobisher bought 2000 shares on the exchange, the following morning, at $29.25 per share.

At midday on April 1, the press release was published, giving details of the find. Trading on the exchange became brisk, and by the end of the day the price of Normin shares had reached $47.50.

Discuss the possible liability of any of the individuals mentioned, and the remedies, if any, which Parry and other shareholders who sold their shares before midday on April 1 might have.

Case 3

As of last summer, Mr. C. Chaplin was a director and vice-president of Pan Metal Mines Ltd. A new group had acquired majority control in the corporation in January; prior to that time Chaplin had been in effective control, serving both as general manager in charge of exploration policy and as chief financial officer. In the latter capacity, he had raised $750 000 for the corporation last year. After control changed hands, he remained as vice-president, and was paid a salary at the annual rate of $100 000.

At each meeting of its directors Pan Metal Mines Ltd. entertains several offers from prospectors who wish to sell their claims. At a meeting of the board of directors on March 10 last, the directors discussed an offer from a prospector known as Lucky Longfellow, who was prepared to sell a group of claims about five miles from the corporation's own property for $200 000 cash and shares in a new corporation that would be formed to take over the property. The members of the board eventually decided to reject Longfellow's offer by a vote of four against the proposal and three in favour. Chaplin was one of those who voted against accepting the offer. In arguing against acceptance, he had noted that the corporation did not, as of that time, have the required $200 000 in cash.

On April 21 following, Chaplin was approached personally by Longfellow and a geologist, McGee, who persuaded him to join a group of three others to acquire the same claims from Longfellow. A new corporation, Hiawatha Mines Ltd., was formed in June and Chaplin and the others each purchased 50 000 new shares at $1 each from the company. Longfellow received $150 000 in cash out of the proceeds of this issue of shares, plus an additional 50 000 new shares, as consideration for transferring his claims. Shortly afterwards, Hiawatha Mines made a public issue of a further 400 000 shares. When the corporation was formed, the parties had no more information about the prospect of finding ore on the property in sufficient quantity to justify a mining operation than they had had when Longfellow presented his proposal to Pan Metal's board of directors. However, as a result of encouraging tests of ore taken from the property in late July, the market price of Hiawatha shares rose to $2.50.

On August 16, the newly-appointed president of Pan Metal Mines, O.R. Murrow, sent Chaplin a memorandum stating, "It is imperative that all officers of this corporation make full disclosure of their interest in any other mining companies." At the next meeting of the board of directors on August 20, Chaplin disclosed his interest in Hiawatha Mines Ltd. Murrow asked him if he was prepared to turn over to Pan Metal Mines his interest in Hiawatha, at cost. Chaplin demurred and after a heated debate refused. The board of directors then passed a motion on a 6 to 1 vote rescinding Chaplin's appointment as vice-president, to take effect immediately, with no further salary to be paid.

Chaplin looked for other employment and three months later managed to secure a position at $2000 a month; in the process he learned to his sorrow that his reputation in the mining business had been seriously damaged as a result of his dismissal by Pan Metal

Mines Ltd. He brought an action against that corporation for damages for wrongful dismissal, and the corporation counterclaimed for the profit he had made on his shares in Hiawatha, then selling for $4.

Discuss the nature of the issues raised by these facts and offer a decision. (For references, see *Peso Silver Mines Ltd. (N.P.L.) v. Cropper* (1966), 56 D.L.R. (2d) 117, affirmed S.C.C. 58 D.L.R. (2d) 1; *Canadian Aero Service Ltd. v. O'Malley* (1974), 40 D.L.R. (3d) 371.)

Case 4

Shakespeare Farms Ltd. is a small, privately-owned corporation, incorporated under the Canada Business Corporations Act. It has four shareholders — Lear, a widower, and his three daughters, Cordelia, Goneril and Regan. They each own 25 shares for a total of 100 issued shares. Lear, Goneril and Regan are the directors; Cordelia is still a student and has been abroad for the past two years.

Some years ago, Lear transferred his farm to the corporation and had the shares issued to himself and the daughters. The farm is the corporation's sole asset; Lear continues to operate it with help from Goneril and Regan. He lives in the farm house, which he rents from the corporation for a nominal amount.

A few weeks ago the corporation received an offer from a developer to buy the land. Goneril and Regan wish to accept the offer, since they think the price is an excellent one. Lear is appalled, both because the farm has been in his family for many generations and because he will lose his home if the land is sold.

Following an acrimonious meeting of the three directors, at which it was resolved (by two votes to one) to sell the farm, Goneril and Regan gave notice to call a meeting of shareholders. Notice was sent to Cordelia at her last-known address, but she did not reply nor did she return to Canada in order to attend the meeting. A special resolution approving the sale of the farm was passed, by 50 votes to 25.

Lear has also learned that Goneril and Regan intend to use their control of the board of directors to force through a resolution that the proceeds of sale of the farm are to be used by the corporation to buy a fashion boutique.

Advise Lear if there is anything he can do to prevent these plans being carried through.

CHAPTER 32

THE EXTERNAL RESPONSIBILITIES OF A CORPORATION

THE CHANGING NATURE OF BUSINESS RESPONSIBILITIES

The classic 19th-century view of management obligations was centred almost entirely on the corporation: the duty of directors was to protect its capital and to produce profits for its ultimate beneficiaries, the shareholders. Since there were very few restrictions on the activities of business enterprises their liabilities arose mainly through contract and tort in carrying on business. In the early part of the 20th century, duties owed by enterprises — and as we shall see, owed also by their directors and officers — began to expand, first to their employees in terms of health and safety, reasonable hours of work, and adequate notice of termination. Recognition also grew of a more general responsibility owed toward the community in which enterprises were located — and eventually toward society as a whole — to refrain from carrying on hazardous activities that might harm neighbours, and to ensure the safety of products in the hands of consumers.

Today, even to operate a small corner store the proprietor will find that she must comply with a large number of regulations, as we noted in Chapter 29. In addition, tort liability has become so broad that a proprietor must also be sure to have adequate insurance, so that she can compensate a customer who slips on the floor or who claims he was made ill by a carton of tainted milk. At the level of the small business, both government regulation and general tort liability tend to resolve themselves into issues of higher overhead costs — the time taken to make sure every detail is looked after, including careful keeping of accounts — and paying premiums for insurance against those risks that inevitably occur. However, it is manufacturing, natural resource, and transportation enterprises that now feel the major effects of the vast increase in regulation. Current regulatory schemes are the result not only of the increased complexity of our society but also of the greater awareness of the harmful consequences of various types of conduct, especially for the environment.

In this chapter we shall discuss the liability of corporations at common law and under various regulatory schemes — liability, both for enterprises themselves and for their directors and senior officers.

LIABILITY OF A CORPORATION FOR ACTS OF ITS AGENTS

Generally speaking, a corporation is liable for the acts of its agents under the ordinary rules of agency. An officer of a corporation acting within his or her usual authority but without express authority may bind it to contracts made with third parties. A corporation may ratify acts made by unauthorized agents on its behalf. The duties of agent to principal and principal to agent also remain the same.

What is the effect upon an innocent third party if the act has been performed in an irregular manner — if, for instance, the confirmation of a by-law by the shareholders requires a minimum period of notice to the shareholders in advance of the meeting, and a lesser period was actually given? It was held that in the absence of notice of the irregularity or of suspicious circumstances, everything that appears regular on its face may be relied upon by an outsider and will bind the company.[1] The propriety of the internal processes of a company is often referred to as *indoor management*,[2] and is simply a variation of the question of apparent authority in agency law generally: an innocent third party may rely on the regularity of a corporate act, just as he may rely on the apparent authority of an agent, if it is reasonable for him to do so in the circumstances.

Certain corporate documents — the charter and in some jurisdictions the articles of association — are filed in a government office and are available to the public for examination on payment of a small fee, in a manner similar to the registration of title documents concerning land. At one time, the public was deemed to have notice of the contents of these documents whether they had read them or not. Hence, if the documents prohibited either the corporation or one of its officers from carrying out certain acts, a third party could not rely upon what otherwise might be the officer's apparent authority to perform those acts. The rule created a wholly unfair burden that could lead to substantial injustice. Happily the rule has been abolished by statute. Of course, a contracting third party who actually has read or knows the contents of a restriction will be bound by it, but in saying this we are merely restating the common law rule of agency: a third party who knows of an express restriction between the principal and agent cannot claim to rely on an apparent authority that ignores the restriction.

Pre-Incorporation Contracts

We have noted in Chapter 22 that, at common law and apart from statute, a corporation cannot ratify a contract made on its behalf before it came into existence. This rule applies in the four provinces using either the memorandum or letters patent system of incorporation. If a contract is made in the name of a company even one day before it comes into existence the contract is of no effect and a new contract will have to be negotiated between the parties to carry out their original intent. The liability of an agent who purports to act for a non-existent corporation arises under breach of warranty of authority as discussed in Chapter 22.

Articles of incorporation jurisdictions have largely remedied the deficiencies of the common law. Their acts provide that:

> A corporation may, within a reasonable time after it comes into existence, by any action or conduct signifying its intention to be bound thereby, adopt a written contract made before it came into existence in its name or on its behalf, and upon such adoption
>
> (a) the corporation is bound by the contract and is entitled to the benefits thereof as if the corporation had been in existence at the date of the contract and had been a party thereto; and
>
> (b) a person who purported to act in the name of or on behalf of the corporation ceases...to be bound by or entitled to the benefits of the contract.[3]

If the corporation does not adopt the pre-incorporation contract, the acts expressly make the person who signed the contract bound by it and entitled to any benefits

---

[1] Royal British Bank v. Turquand (1856), 119 E.R. 886.
[2] This rule receives statutory recognition in articles of incorporation jurisdictions: see Canada Business Corporations Act, R.S.C. 1985, c. C-44, s. 18.
[3] *Ibid.*, s. 14(2). There are some variations from province to province. For example, Ontario does not restrict the rule solely to written contracts.

under it.[4] In neither event then can the contract be considered a nullity. The acts also seek to prevent unfair manipulation by a corporation and a contractor. For example, a contractor may make a contract on behalf of a corporation that he himself will subsequently incorporate and control and to which he plans to give virtually no assets. If, after incorporation, he decides that the contract is a bad bargain, he might cause the corporation to adopt the contract and thereby seemingly escape any personal liability as its agent-contractor. To prevent this abuse, the acts go on to state:

> ...whether or not a written contract made before the coming into existence of a corporation is adopted by the corporation, a party to the contract may apply to a court for an order fixing obligations under the contract as joint or joint and several or apportioning liability between or among the corporation and a person who purported to act in the name of or on behalf of the corporation and upon such application the court may make any order it thinks fit.[5]

The acts also state that a promoter acting on behalf of a corporation before it comes into existence may avoid personal liability and waive any benefits under the contract when the contract includes an express term that the promoter will not be bound by the agreement.[6]

PROTECTION OF CREDITORS

Implications of Limited Liability

We have seen that when a sole trader or partnership becomes insolvent, the creditors may seize whatever assets are available, and that if a deficiency remains they may seize the personal assets of the trader or partners. In these forms of business organization, a debtor's liability is not limited to her business assets: her personal assets may be seized as well. In addition, unless she eventually receives a discharge from the courts in bankruptcy proceedings, any property she acquires for many years to come may also be seized, and judgment creditors may garnishee her salary or wages.

In a limited company, however, a creditor's rights are limited to the assets held by the corporation. If these assets are inadequate, it has no further remedy against the shareholders. Accordingly, a creditor's only protection is the fund of assets owned by the corporation itself. For this reason, legislatures and courts have tried to evolve rules to assure creditors that these assets will not be wasted.

Except for such financial institutions as banks, insurance companies, and trust and loan companies, the law requires no minimum of issued capital for corporations. Legally, a corporation may carry on business with a share capital of $1. Of course, a corporation would find it difficult to obtain credit with only a nominal equity investment, but even so, such a corporation might become liable to pay a large sum of money as a result, say, of the negligent conduct of one of its officers or employees.

It is not possible to devise legal rules that will protect creditors from the risk of extending credit to a corporation whose management runs it badly and impairs its capital

---

[4] *Ibid.*, s. 14(1).
[5] *Ibid.*, s. 14(3).
[6] *Ibid.*, s. 14(4).

through business losses. The primary concern of the law with respect to capital is with corporations that once had a capital (or "equity") base substantial enough to persuade creditors to extend large amounts of credit; when subsequently such corporations suffer a substantial impairment of that capital, it may be important to know how the impairment took place. The rules that have evolved are designed to prevent the kinds of decisions that will deliberately impair a corporation's ability to meet its obligations. These rules are essentially of two kinds: rules that prohibit any payment by the company to its shareholders that renders the corporation's liquid assets insufficient to pay the then outstanding claims of creditors, or any such payment when the corporation is already insolvent;[7] and rules that prohibit the "return of capital" to shareholders (for example, by declaring excessive dividends) even when the corporation might still be left with sufficient liquid assets to pay its creditors. We will consider these two types of rules briefly in turn.

The Solvency Test

After a corporation has received assets from shareholders by an issue of share capital, subsequent transactions with those shareholders will be confined largely to payments of dividends, and in certain circumstances to the redemption or re-purchase by the corporation of its own shares. If payments by the corporation in either of these instances were to have the effect of rendering the corporation insolvent, the directors might become personally liable to the corporation for the deficiency. They would be equally liable, of course, for authorizing such transactions after the corporation had become insolvent. Their liability in this respect is, in most jurisdictions, set out specifically in a provision of the corporations act.[8]

The effectiveness of this test depends upon the definition of insolvency that is used. For the purposes of the corporations acts, two factors must be considered: a corporation is deemed insolvent if the realizable value of its assets has become less than its total liabilities, or if it is unable to pay its debts as they become due.[9]

The Maintenance of Capital Test

The creditors of a limited company have a second line of defence, albeit one to which less importance is now attached than formerly. This protection consists of a number of provisions in the corporations acts designed to ensure that the original and subsequent infusions of assets in the form of shareholder "capital" will be preserved — or at least not deliberately depleted. (As we have noted, no corporations act can ensure that this "contributed capital" will be preserved in the face of losses from company operations.)

The theory underlying provisions for the maintenance of capital requires more than a solvency test; it requires that assets paid into the corporation by shareholders be preserved as far as possible within the corporation as a "capital fund". It recognizes that the assets provided to a business by its shareholders may, as part of a total package of resources available to management, be depleted by business losses and thus become inadequate to pay creditors in full.

---

7 Directors who approve such payments may be personally liable for them: *Ibid.*, s. 118.
8 *Ibid.*, ss. 42 and 118(2)(c).
9 *Ibid.*, s. 42. The federal Bankruptcy and Insolvency Act provides, additionally, an "after the fact" test that permits a trustee in bankruptcy to apply for a court inquiry in respect of dividends paid within 12 months preceding bankruptcy to determine whether the dividend rendered the company insolvent, and that authorizes the court to give judgment to the trustee against the directors, jointly and severally, in the amount of such dividend. R.S.C. 1985, c. B-3, s. 101.

Hence, the theory requires that the additional amount of assets provided by shareholders be as far as possible maintained and available for absorbing business reverses so that creditors may still be paid in full. The maintenance of capital test therefore goes beyond the solvency test.

For example, a company might, depending on the composition of its assets, have assets just equal to its liabilities and be able to pay its creditors as their claims fall due. It could have reached that precarious financial condition by having deliberately paid back to shareholders the money they had invested in the company; the company would still satisfy the solvency test but would have violated the maintenance of capital test. Suppose, on the other hand, it had reached that condition because of business losses: while it would not have deliberately impaired its capital fund, the prior existence of the fund (now exhausted) has at least avoided insolvency to date. The case for a maintenance of capital requirement was succinctly explained by Adam Smith:

> Traders and other undertakers may, no doubt, with great propriety, carry on a very consider-
> able part of their projects with borrowed money. In justice to their creditors, however, their
> own capital ought, in this case, to be sufficient to ensure, if I may say so, the capital of those
> creditors; or to render it extremely improbable that those creditors should incur any loss,
> even though the success of the project should fall very much short of the expectation of the
> projectors.[10]

His argument applies to all forms of business organization but seems particularly cogent when the business is a corporation with limited liability.

The accounting system is designed to provide a signal whenever a transaction results in an impairment of capital. Thus, a dividend payment that has the effect of creating a negative balance in the retained earnings account — indicating disbursements to shareholders of more assets than have accrued to date in the form of profits — would impair the capital fund. Similarly, a reduction in the share capital account, recording a redemption or purchase by the company of its own shares, signals a possible impairment of the capital fund (depending upon whether the reduction exceeds accumulated retained earnings).

Needless to say, this accounting test assumes a particular meaning of "capital fund". We are not here thinking of particular assets or classes of assets; we are thinking of the capital fund as a source of assets. If we translate all types of assets into dollar amounts, add them together and then deduct from that total the dollar amount of all liabilities and retained earnings to date, we necessarily come to a dollar figure that is an abstract idea — the capital fund. Once a company begins operations, capital of this kind can no longer be related directly to the very assets contributed by shareholders in exchange for their shares or to any specific assets into which those original assets have since been converted in the course of business. The closest we can come to describing this concept of capital is as an *equity* or *interest* in an aggregate of business assets: capital in a financial sense. Its amount depends critically, however, on accounting conventions used in measuring the assets reported on the balance sheet.

We can see that the attempt to protect the capital fund as a form of security for creditors has drawn on both legal and accounting theory. The resulting "model", however, has become something of a patchwork. Practical considerations have, as discussed below, compromised the strict principle against impairment of the capital fund.

---

[10] Smith, A., *The Wealth of Nations*, pp. 291-3, as reprinted, New York: Random House, 1937.

Implications of the Maintenance of Capital Test

Dividends

Suppose a corporation had originally issued $5 000 000 in shares. After several years of operations it finds itself, after deducting its liabilities, left with net assets of just $5 000 000, that is, an amount equal to its original issued capital. If it were now to declare and pay a dividend to its shareholders, the result would be as much a reduction of the capital fund as if it had returned part of its capital to them directly. In these circumstances, it would be unlawful to declare a dividend.[11] Similarly, if the company had suffered successive losses, resulting in the reduction of its net assets to an amount below the capital paid in by shareholders, the same rule would prevent the company from paying any dividends until it had earned enough profits to restore the deficiency in its capital fund. The one instance in which some of our corporations acts have specifically authorized the payment of dividends out of capital is the payment of dividends by a corporation with wasting assets (for example, a mine) out of funds derived from the operations of the company.[12] For other companies, it is possible to take the formal step of reducing a company's stated capital by writing an existing deficit off against it; the company would then start with a clean slate, and could pay dividends out of current earnings.

Return of Capital

A reduction of stated capital must be distinguished from an actual return of capital to the shareholders. A reduction generally does no more than recognize a state of affairs that has occurred: the company's net assets have decreased in value. As such it is not objectionable. By contrast, a return of capital — like the payment of a dividend when there are no profits or capital gain out of which to pay it — reduces the funds available to meet the claims of creditors and, if the company should subsequently become insolvent, would give a preferred repayment to shareholders before the creditors' claims are met.

The statutes in both letters patent and memorandum jurisdictions had very strict rules about maintenance of capital, expressed in four related prohibitions. A company could not:

(i) return any part of its capital to its shareholders except with the consent of its creditors or by leave of the court;

(ii) purchase its own shares (apart from redeeming preferred shares as provided in the company charter), or enable a subsidiary company to hold shares in the parent company;

(iii) give financial help of any kind to someone, and in particular, lend money, for the purpose of buying shares;

(iv) issue shares at a discount (that is, at a price less than their par value), except to discount the usual commission paid to brokers for selling shares.

The rules were vigorously applied by the courts and could sometimes cause unreasonable hardship. Although some or all of the rules remain in force in a few jurisdictions, they have mostly been repealed or replaced with more practical rules better suited to business needs. In articles of incorporation jurisdictions, a corporation may repay capital

---

[11] 1985, c. C-44, s. 42.
[12] See, for example: Business Corporations Act, R.S.O. 1990, c. B–16, s. 39. However, several acts, including the the Canada Business Corporations Act, do not contain any comparable provision.

to its shareholders provided that it will still be able to satisfy both parts of the solvency test.[13] This rule is reasonable, since shareholders may have contributed substantially more capital than, as it turns out, the corporation really needs; so long as creditors are amply protected there is no reason to insist that excess — and unutilized — capital remains in the corporation.

Corporations may also redeem or purchase their own shares for a number of specified reasons, subject to solvency requirements to protect creditors.[14] Since the prohibition against a corporation holding its own previously issued shares has been relaxed, the rule against giving financial help to any person to buy shares has also become unnecessary.[15]

Finally, the rule prohibiting the issue of shares at less than their par value has necessarily disappeared with the introduction of no-par value shares — a development that we have already discussed. Of course directors remain under a duty to try to obtain a fair price when they issue shares.

Loans to Shareholders, Directors and Employees

The old rules against return of capital were reinforced by a prohibition against corporations making loans of any kind to its shareholders, directors, or employees. The idea behind the prohibition was that any loans might amount to an indirect return of capital, at any rate when made to shareholders, and might deprive the corporation of liquidity. A common exception was to permit loans to employees to help them buy housing or to buy shares in their corporate employer under a share purchase plan. Articles of incorporation jurisdictions have relaxed the rules considerably: loans to shareholders, directors, and employees are prohibited only if they would endanger a corporation's solvency, or reduce the value of its assets — not counting such loans as an asset — to less than the amount of its stated capital.[16]

$\mathcal{P}$ROTECTION OF CURRENT AND PROSPECTIVE INVESTORS

Securities Legislation

In Canada, securities legislation is substantially within provincial jurisdiction,[17] in contrast with the United States where the related controls are divided between federal and

---

[13] See Canada Business Corporations Act, R.S.C., 1985, c. C-44, s. 38.

[14] *Ibid.*, ss. 30 - 37.

[15] It remains illegal, of course, to lend money for this purpose if to do so would make the corporation insolvent: *Ibid.*, s. 44(1).

[16] *Ibid.*, s. 44. The section seems to produce the strange result that a loan may be made to an employee for a house or share purchase, or to a parent or subsidiary company, even when the loan would put the corporation in a position where it was unable to pay its debts as they fell due.

[17] Federally incorporated companies, in addition to being subject to provincial securities acts, must file any prospectus with the federal government; *Ibid.*, s. 193. In 1971, the securities regulatory authorities in the provinces of Alberta, British Columbia, Manitoba, New Brunswick, Ontario, Prince Edward Island, Québec, and Saskatchewan agreed to a number of "National Policies" which include, for example, an agreed procedure by which an underwriter may clear a prospectus in more than one province. In addition, the five westernmost provinces (British Columbia to Ontario) agreed upon a further number of "Uniform Act Policies".

state jurisdictions. Each Canadian province has a Securities Act or Securities Fraud Prevention Act, under which a government board, known as a *securities commission* in most of the provinces, is created. The securities commission operates as the enforcing agency charged with ensuring that the requirements of the Act are complied with.

Two main objectives of securities legislation are common to all provinces: to prevent and punish fraudulent practices in the securities industry; and to require full disclosure of financial information to prospective buyers of shares and bonds offered for the first time to the public. These objectives are related to the policy of increasing the efficiency of the capital market, first by maintaining the confidence of investors, and second by providing information for rational investment decisions. A basic purpose of securities legislation is to make the capital market an efficient medium for allocating available funds among competing investment opportunities; according to this theory, improving investors' ability to make intelligent choices gives the most deserving projects a priority.

Traditionally, our securities legislation has used two devices for achieving the objectives described above: registering or licensing those engaged in various aspects of the securities business; and requiring the issuer of securities to the public to file a prospectus with the securities commission.

The registering of persons engaged in the securities business is an important device for ensuring a reasonable measure of ethical conduct. Licensing is on an annual basis, and each securities commission has authority under its provincial statute to revoke, suspend, or refuse to renew the licence of anyone when in its opinion such action is in the public interest. Operating without a licence is a criminal offence. Depending upon the jurisdiction, a licence may be required of persons engaged in a wide variety of activities. Those affected include brokers (who buy and sell securities as agents), investment dealers (who buy and sell securities as principals), broker-dealers (who may act as either principal or agent in the promotion of companies), securities issuers (companies issuing their securities directly to the public without the intermediate services of investment dealers), salespeople employed by any of these businesses, and investment counsel and securities advisers.

The *filing* of a prospectus with a securities commission is not merely a formality. The commission will refuse to file a prospectus if, after a thorough review of the contents, its staff concludes that the prospectus is misleading or omits required data, and no one may issue securities to the public unless and until the prospectus has been filed. Prospectus requirements are an attempt to ensure that prospective investors have access to the pertinent facts about a company before deciding whether or not to invest in it. In many instances, an investor is entitled to a copy of the prospectus before buying securities, and may rescind the contract of subscription if he or she does not receive the prospectus and acts to repudiate the contract within a specified period. The minimum detail required in the prospectus is prescribed by statute, or in regulations appended to the act, and is too comprehensive to set out here in full. It is sufficient to note that the prospectus must, among other things, include a full description of the securities to be offered (either shares or bonds) with a statement of their voting rights, preference, conversion privileges, and rights on liquidation, if any; the nature of the business carried on; the names, addresses, and occupations of the directors; the proposed use of the proceeds from the issue of securities; details of any share options to be given by the company;[18] the remuneration of the underwriter; the dividend record of the company; the particulars of property and services to be paid for out of the proceeds of the issue; and recent audited financial statements.

The enactment of revised securities acts in the various provinces, commencing in 1966, has ushered in a new era of public control over the securities industry in Canada. In addition to licensing and prospectus provisions, the legislation has introduced important forms of control largely inspired by experience in the United States since the establishment of the Securities and Exchange Commission in 1934.[19] One of the most important innovations gives the securities commission control over the stock exchanges within the province (in Ontario, for example, over the Toronto Stock Exchange).[20] The significance of the provision is that control by the regulatory body now extends not only to issues of new securities but also to trading in already outstanding securities: the act specifies the minimum of financial information that must be disclosed, on a regular basis, to shareholders of all companies whose shares are traded on the stock exchange.[21] In addition, the legislation contains provisions designed to make the proxy a more effective means of registering shareholders' opinions[22] and to give shareholders who have received a takeover bid for their shares sufficient information and time to assess the merits of the bid.[23] Takeover provisions include a requirement for disclosure of the number of shares in the offeree company held by the offeror company and its officers, details of recent trading in those shares, and terms of any agreement between the offeror and the officers of the offeree company.[24] As we noted earlier in our discussion of "Statutory Safeguards: Disclosure", the legislation also requires publication of insiders' transactions in their company's shares,[25] authorizes actions against insiders and makes insider trading a statutory offence.[26] The efficacy of many aspects of securities regulation has been seriously questioned by some economists and finance theorists.[27]

Corporate Reorganization, Mergers, and Winding Up

The fields of corporation law subsumed under this heading are complex, often technical, and always difficult. They are fields requiring the talents of experts, both financial and legal. Needless to say, no one faced with the problem of making a decision in one of the above areas should undertake a course of action without expert assistance from beginning to end of the project. The problems involved usually concern creditors' rights, the effects of taxation, the relevance of combines legislation, and the rights of various classes of share-

---

[18] A share option is a right to subscribe for shares in the company at a fixed price within a specified time, given by a company as consideration for the payment of money, the rendering of services (often the services of directors), or any other valuable consideration. The option becomes valuable at any time before expiry that the market price exceeds the option price.

[19] It is not possible to do justice to this important area in the present chapter. For a complete discussion see Alboini, *Ontario Securities Law.* Toronto: Richard De Boo, 1980.

[20] Securities Act, R.S.O. 1990, c. S–5, s. 23.

[21] *Ibid.,* ss. 75 to 83.

[22] *Ibid.,* ss. 84 to 88.

[23] *Ibid.,* ss. 89 to 105.

[24] The contents of the takeover bid are described in s. 98 and in regulations under the Act.

[25] *Ibid.,* ss. 106 to 109.

[26] *Ibid.,* ss. 76, 122(1)(c) and 134.

[27] See, for example, articles in Manne (ed.), *Economic Policy and the Regulation of Corporate Securities;* Posner, *Economic Analysis of Law,* (2nd ed.), pp. 331-34. Boston: Little Brown and Company, 1977.

holders, in addition to the general economic consequences for the corporations involved and the adaptability of the legal devices available under the statute law of the jurisdiction.

$\mathcal{P}$ROTECTION OF THE PUBLIC INTEREST: ENVIRONMENTAL REGULATION

The Role of Regulation

We have already noted how a number of areas of regulation to which businesses are subject have expanded in recent years. Apart from the benefits that may be secured to organized employees through collective agreements under a carefully regulated system of labour relations, individual employees are protected by workers compensation legislation, employment standards acts and, most recently, by human rights codes and pay equity legislation, as noted in Chapter 23. The increasing complexity of consumer products and the inability of distributers and retailers to assure the quality and safety of products has, of necessity, led to increased liability for producers through safety, health and labelling standards and consumer protection legislation, discussed in Chapter 19. There are other important areas of regulation, including the Competition Act to prohibit collusive business arrangements contrary to the public interest, and protection of the environment. Regulatory schemes now play an important role in many business decisions.

Environmental regulation has evolved rapidly in recent years and provides a helpful example of the growing responsibilities of business and the consequences of failure to comply with regulatory requirements. For the remainder of this chapter we shall focus on business and the environment.

Concern about the Environment: Rapid Growth in Regulation

More than in any other area, public concern about the environment has generated rapidly increasing government regulation of business. Major environmental disasters, such as the running aground of the *Exxon Valdez* off the coast of Alaska and the Bhopal chemical spill in India, and the worldwide concern about the "greenhouse effect" and depletion of the earth's ozone layer, have made the public much more aware of the dangers associated with many activities in industry, in transportation, and in the field of natural resources such as logging. A few regulatory schemes began many years ago, in order to prevent the most obviously harmful disregard of the environment. In the 19th century there were laws prohibiting the dumping of dangerous substances into our rivers, lakes, and harbours. However, at that time, and indeed until quite recently, there was limited appreciation of the cumulative effects of pollution; governments made very little effort to enforce the early schemes and offending industries often ignored them entirely.

Increased awareness has made enforcement a major public issue. In the last few years there has been an enormous growth in regulatory schemes generally, and particularly in those designed to limit or eliminate environmental pollution. There are now 29 federal statutes dealing with the environment and many sets of regulations under these acts. In addition, each province has its own legislation. The total volume of regulations in Canada is immense: one law publisher has produced a complete set of Canadian regulations together with a digest of recent cases; the materials fill six, thick loose-leaf volumes![28] Municipalities also pass by-laws to provide local environmental protection and to restrict activities deemed to be harmful. As a result, a large proportion of enterprises must now seek professional advice about which regulatory schemes may apply to their industry.

The Nature of Liability

To help us in discussing regulatory schemes generally, we should first note an important distinction between:

(a) *civil liability* — liability toward a plaintiff, typically to pay damages for harms done through committing a tort or breaking a contract; and

(b) *criminal liability* — conviction for an offence, typically punished by imprisonment or payment of a fine.

Schemes of government regulation resemble traditional criminal law because, in order to protect the public interest, they almost invariably prohibit certain kinds of conduct and punish those who ignore the prohibitions.

While environmental regulations are not primarily concerned with punishing wrongdoers they nevertheless derive their standards from criminal law.[29] Accordingly, we shall begin by describing the elements that, traditionally, the prosecution must prove in order to obtain a conviction.

In general, the prosecution must prove beyond a reasonable doubt, not only that an accused actually committed the offence with which he is charged, but also that he was "at fault": it must establish that the accused had *mens rea* (a guilty mind), that is, a guilty intention or guilty knowledge. The offence of "possession of stolen goods" provides a useful example: a person who is found to be in possession of stolen goods has not committed an offence, if he did not know that they were stolen, even if he were naive about their source. Only when a court is persuaded that the accused knew the goods were stolen will he be found guilty.

As we move away from the traditional criminal offences, toward what are sometimes called regulatory offences, such as careless driving, we find that the courts — and, as we shall see, more and more often the statutes that create new offences — broaden the definition of *mens rea*; it may be enough to show that if any ordinary person would or *should* have realized that his conduct was an offence, the wrongdoer will be convicted. For instance, if a

---

[28] Roger Cook & Alastair Lucas, *Canadian Environmental Law*, 2nd. ed. Toronto: Butterworths, 1991. The following statutes are examples of the diverse areas covered: R.S.C. 1985, Atomic Energy Control Act, c. A-16; Fisheries Act, c. F-14; Northern Inland Waters Act, c. N-25; Canada Wildlife Act, c. W-9; R.S.N.S. 1989, Ozone Layer Protection Act, c. 331; Pest Control Products Act, c. 341; B.C. Environmental Management Act, 1981, c. 14; Transport of Dangerous Goods Act, 1985, c. 17.

[29] Some statutory regulations also create civil liability, so that a wrongdoer may have to compensate a party harmed by its breach. See, for example, liability for "insider trading", discussed in Chapter 31, above. S. 131 of the Canada Business Corporations Act (CBCA), makes "insiders" (usually directors or employees of a corporation) who use confidential information to profit from a transaction in the corporation's securities, liable to compensate any person who suffered a loss, and accountable to the corporation for the profits. In addition, such regulations almost invariably authorize the appropriate government agency to prosecute and to exact punishment. S. 251 of the CBCA makes a person who contravenes s. 131 "guilty of an offence punishable on summary conviction."

person drove his car at 100 km per hour through a crowded shopping area in a city, he would very likely be convicted of a provincial offence of "careless driving" or even the more serious Criminal Code offence of "dangerous driving", despite his own belief that he was not endangering anyone.

The broader definition of the guilty mind principle as applied in the careless driving case results from public policy concerns — the need for deterrence; for reasons of road safety we do not want people who drive dangerously to avoid conviction easily. Consequently, for a number of offences, the courts now hold there is a *presumption* that the accused, in committing the wrongful act, had the requisite guilty mind in a broad sense — that he was careless and did not make a diligent effort to avoid the breach. However, the accused can overcome the presumption by persuading the court that he acted with reasonable care in the circumstances.

As early as the middle of the 19th century, the courts went even further. They held that for certain regulatory schemes where public health and safety was paramount, no *mens rea* at all was required for a conviction; it was enough for the prosecution simply to prove that the accused had committed the wrongful act. As a result, under some statutes, but very few, accused persons may be convicted without any proof of *mens rea*, for example, a driver in a new vehicle with a faulty speedometer who is unaware that he is exceeding the speed limit.[30]

The issue of whether the prosecution must establish that the accused had a guilty mind within the narrower traditional definition of intention or actual knowledge, or within a broader definition, or indeed, whether there is need to establish a guilty mind at all, remains a controversial and vexing problem in criminal law. In a 1978 case in which a municipal government was charged with breach of an environmental regulation, the Supreme Court of Canada divided criminal offences into three classes, which may be summarized as follows:[31]

1. *Mens rea offences*, where the prosecution must demonstrate the existence of a "guilty mind", consisting of some positive state of mind such as intent, knowledge, or recklessness.
2. *Offences of strict liability*, where there is no necessity for the prosecution to prove the existence of *mens rea*; the doing of the prohibited act raises a presumption that an offence has been committed, leaving it open to the accused to avoid liability by proving that he took all reasonable care.
3. *Offences of absolute liability*, where it is not open to the accused to excuse himself by showing that he was free of fault. Simply doing the act makes one guilty of the offence.

It is generally agreed that the third class remains a very limited one; our courts are reluctant to punish an accused where no evidence of carelessness has been presented. Indeed, the Supreme Court of Canada has decided that an absolute liability offence is unconstitutional when conviction may lead to an accused being imprisoned.[32]

---

[30] See R. v. Hickey (1976) 70 D.L.R. (3d) 689 (C.A.). At least in some provinces, exceeding the speed limit is still considered such an offence. R.S.B.C. 1979, c. 288, s. 151; R.S.O. 1990, c. H-8, s. 128 (14).
[31] See, R. v. City of Sault Ste Marie, (1978) 85 D.L.R. (3d) 161 (S.C.C.).
[32] Reference re s. 94(2) of the B.C. Motor Vehicle Act, [1985] 2 S.C.R. 486, per Lamer, J., at 514.

Liability of Corporations

We have seen earlier in this chapter that corporations may incur *civil liability* as principals for the acts or omissions of their agents and employees. Corporations are also liable to be *punished under criminal law*, subject to the principles we have just discussed. However, the characteristics of corporations present special problems:

(a) as we have seen, most offences require the prosecution to prove both that the accused actually committed the offence and also that at the very least he has been negligent — but a corporation has neither a physical body with which to carry out the offence, nor a "mind" of its own that could be considered negligent;

(b) if convicted, a guilty person's punishment is often imprisonment — but a corporation cannot be imprisoned.

The consequences of (b) merely limit sanctions against a corporation to fining it, or to ordering it to desist from certain conduct, or in some cases to dissolving the corporation, a relatively painless form of capital punishment. The prosecution may also lay charges personally against directors and senior officers of a corporation, a topic to which we shall soon return.

With regard to (a), the courts did not find it easy to apply the principles of criminal law to corporations. First, there was the question of whether a corporation could "commit" an offence, that is, whether it could actually carry out an act, since it has no physical presence — no hand to "pull the trigger". Nevertheless, for the very limited number of *absolute liability* offences, the courts seemed to ignore this issue and simply convicted a corporation when an agent or employee committed the offence in the course of her employment. However, for crimes that required a guilty mind, until early in this century the courts generally held that a corporation could not itself be guilty even when it was clear that the individuals involved were acting for the corporation. The individuals who committed offences might be convicted, but not the corporation.

A leading case in 1915 altered this principle and allowed courts to come to the conclusion that a corporation could commit an act requiring a guilty mind, at least in some circumstances. In *Lennard's Carrying Company*[33] a ship owner was sued for damages under a statute that stated an owner would not be liable for harm caused by its vessel "without his actual fault". Speaking for the House of Lords, Viscount Haldane found that a Mr. Lennard was "the active director" of the corporation, and that it was "impossible...to contend...that he did not know or can excuse himself for not having known" that the ship was unseaworthy. He went on to call the director, "the active spirit", the "directing mind and will", and "*the very ego and centre of the personality* of the corporation". Viscount Haldane then made an important statement of policy:

> [Mr. Lennard's] action must, *unless a corporation is not to be liable at all,* have been an action which was the action of the company itself... [emphasis added].

Accordingly, although the owner was a corporation, the House of Lords found that it was "actually" at fault and therefore liable. While this was a civil case and not a criminal prosecution, it was seen as opening the door for courts to find the actions of senior officers and directors of corporations to be those of the corporation itself, both with regard to the actual committing of the acts and the required guilty or negligent mind.

---

[33] Lennard's Carrying Company Ltd. v. Asiatic Petroleum Company Ltd., [1915] A.C. 705.

A further problem arises when the wrongful act is committed not by a senior officer or director, but by a person lower down in the hierarchy. Canadian courts have generally tended to find an act committed by an employee who has significant responsibilities, such as being the head of an important department or a branch, to be an act of the corporation itself.[34] But the courts would not hold the act of a low-level employee, for example, of a clerk who cheated a customer — in the absence of evidence that a senior employee was aware of and permitted the conduct — to be the act of the corporation itself. However, drawing the line between those employees and officers whose acts will be identified as acts of the corporate employer and those whose acts will not be so identified is not an easy task; commentators have been critical of various decisions reached by the courts.[35]

Personal Liability of Directors and Senior Officers

It is often said that simply holding corporations liable, especially for environmental offences, is not in itself a strong enough deterrent to assure effective enforcement of regulatory schemes:

(a) a large corporation with sufficient assets might consider the penalty merely a "licence"; it pays the fine and carries on with its activities; the corporation's managers thus often pass the costs on to the ultimate consumer through higher prices, or to the corporation's innocent shareholders through lower dividends;

(b) at the other extreme, a corporation may be merely a "shell" with virtually no assets to pay its fine; those who control the enterprise walk away from it and start up a similar activity using a new corporation.

Accordingly, a strong argument has been made that effective deterrence requires that as well as the corporation, the individuals responsible for the offence be punished directly. Hence, directors and senior officers have more and more been held personally liable for offences found to have been committed by their corporation. In addition, particularly in the United States, the generally accepted view today is that criminal sanctions (imprisonment) are necessary as a deterrent. As has been recently said:

> Corporations who were not deterred by civil sanctions fear criminal prosecutions, and the threat of jail sends a clear message to corporate executives that they are not immune to criminal sanctions. As noted by Joseph Block, Chief Executive of the Environmental Crimes Division of the Department of Justice, "[I]ncarceration is one cost of business that you can't pass to the consumer."[36]

Even when it is agreed that, in addition to the corporation, its human actors ought to be held liable for breaches, problems remain in attempting to prosecute individuals. In complex organizations, where responsibility is diffused among a number of persons, each in charge of a narrow, perhaps ill-defined task, it is often difficult to identify with any certainty who is "responsible", that is, who can — and should — be convicted of committing an

---

[34] See, R. v. Waterloo Mercury Sales Ltd. (1974), 18 C.C.C. (2d) 248, (Alberta), where a used-car sales manager, who was neither a director nor a signing officer of the corporation, illegally turned back the odometers on used cars. His company was found guilty.

[35] See, for example, T. Asplund's Annotation to Canadian Dredge and Dock Company Ltd. v. R. (1985) 45 C.R. (3d) 289.

[36] See, Nelson Smith, "No Longer Just a Cost of Doing Business..." 53 *Louisiana Law Review* 119 (1992), at p. 126.

offence. The task is particularly difficult when, in order to obtain a conviction, the prosecution must prove beyond a reasonable doubt that the accused was the person who committed the offending act. (Of course, whenever a director or officer of a corporation has been found personally to have committed an offence, the courts do not hesitate to find the wrongdoer guilty and to punish accordingly.)

These two factors, a belief that human agents and not just corporations should be made liable, and that it is often difficult to obtain convictions, have led legislatures:

(a) to enact express provisions making senior officers and directors liable; and
(b) to make the grounds for individual liability much broader, as we shall see below, under "Who Should be Found Liable?"

As a recent Canadian book on the subject states, "An impressive number of statutes expressly impose personal liability upon officers and directors for offences by the corporation."[37]

THE BASIS FOR LIABILITY IMPOSED ON ENTERPRISES AND THEIR HUMAN AGENTS

What Standard of Skill and Care Must Be Met?

When an offence such as improper disposal of hazardous wastes occurs, a presumption arises that the activity was carried on negligently. An enterprise as well as any of its directors and officers charged with an offence can overcome the presumption by showing that they used "due diligence" in carrying out their duties. The challenge for the accused is to meet what is generally acknowledged to be a steadily rising standard of due diligence. The enterprise must demonstrate that it has "an effective system to prevent offences, monitor the results of the system and improve the system if problems occur".[38] Since science and technology are advancing steadily, it is difficult to rely on yesterday's standards. Each enterprise whose activities may pose a risk must show that it reviews its current monitoring system frequently, and makes reasonable efforts to keep up to date on technological change in the field.

Another aspect of the problem relates to the expertise of directors and senior officers. Are they held to higher standards of care and skill if they have expertise in the area where a hazardous activity is carried on? Suppose a senior officer is an engineer with long experience in the field. Would she be expected to take precautions against a risk that an accountant would be unlikely to be aware of? A common-sense view would say yes, and there is some support for it in a 1983 case, *R. v. Placer Developments Ltd.*,[39] where the accused corporation allowed diesel fuel to escape into fishing waters. The court seemed to expect greater diligence from the company's experienced senior officers:

> The accused was required to possess, and did possess sufficient expertise to be aware of the potential risk to the environment posed by a fuel system in northern mining camps...[T]he

---

[37] Thompson, McConnell & Huestis, *Environmental Law and Business in Canada*. Aurora: Canada Law Book, 1993, at p. 299. In an accompanying footnote, the authors point out that, "there are at least 80 federal statutes of this type, 62 in British Columbia, 98 in Alberta, 45 in Manitoba, 126 in Ontario and 19 in New Brunswick."

[38] *Ibid.*, at p. 304.

[39] 13 C.E.L.R. 42 (Y.T. Terr. Ct.).

accused had the opportunity and knowledge in the field, through their employees Mr. Morganti with thirty-two months field experience and Mr. Goddard with twenty-five years experience, to influence the offending conduct on the site.[40]

On the other hand, the court suggested that even if the accused firm did not possess that expertise it would still be liable for the offence:

> The greater the likelihood of harm, the higher the duty of care... *Anyone choosing to become involved* in activities posing danger to the public or to the environment *assumes an obligation* to take whatever measures may be necessary to prevent harm... Unless equipped with appropriate professional skills, no one ought to undertake any activity involving a danger to the public... Mining in the north requires not only an expert knowledge of mining, but equally important, an expert appreciation of the special problems caused by remote operations in northern environments [italics added].[41]

These observations appear to suggest that the accused corporation was caught in one of two ways: either it failed to employ the expertise *it ought to have known* that it needed in order to manage the hazardous activity, or if it did employ the necessary expertise, then the person having that expertise *failed to use the professional care and skill attributed to him*. Perhaps an unskilled employee who had been sent to the site would not be found personally liable because he could not have been expected to anticipate the risk, but the employer enterprise would be caught by its failure to send an employee with the necessary skills to carry out the task.

A recent decision of the Supreme Court of Canada suggests that, at least in the absence of explicit regulatory standards for specific categories of persons, a standard must not vary according to the special knowledge and training of an individual. In *Regina v. Creighton*,[42] Madam Justice McLachlin, for the majority of the Court, at page 670, stated:

> The first concept is the notion that the criminal law may properly hold people engaged in risky activities to a minimum standard of care, judged by what *a reasonable person in all the circumstances* would have done. This notion posits a *uniform standard for all persons* engaging in the activity, *regardless of their background, education* or psychological disposition [italics added].

She then stated, "The second concept is the principle that the morally innocent not be punished..." These two statements may be in conflict. On the one hand, there appears to be a uniform standard, but on the other, we ought not to punish the innocent, presumably even if they do not meet the standard.[43] The law in this area is changing quickly, making it all the more important for enterprises whose activities involve any significant environmental risks to make diligent efforts to comply with standards of care as described below.

---

[40] *Ibid.*, at 49.
[41] *Ibid.*, at 52.
[42] 105 D.L.R. (4th), 632.
[43] At pages 678 and 679, Madam Justice McLachlin went on to say:

> We see then that the care required by some activities is greater than the care required by others...*The standard flows from the circumstances of the activity. It does not vary with the experience or ability of the actual accused.*
>
> A person may fail to meet an elevated *de facto* standard of care in either of two ways. *First, the person may undertake an activity requiring special care when he or she is not qualified to give that care.* Absent special excuses like necessity, this may constitute culpable negligence. An untrained person undertaking brain surgery might violate the standard this way. *Second, a person who is qualified may negligently fail to exercise the special care required by the activity.* A brain surgeon performing surgery in a grossly negligent way might violate the standard in this second way. *The standard is the same, although the means by which it is breached may differ.*

Who Should be Found Liable?

We have already noted that, apart from the liability of an enterprise itself, any person who actually commits an offence is personally liable, even when he was acting within the scope of his authorized activities and a senior officer acquiesced or ordered him to perform. The issues become more difficult when legislatures enact regulations to make senior officers and directors liable because they are considered to be in charge of an activity, even though they have not participated directly in the offence. The task is to find appropriate language, sufficient to capture those who should bear the blame and yet absolve those who were innocent. With this purpose in mind, our legislatures have tended to use two phrases: the first makes liable those who "cause or *permit*" a hazardous substance to be discharged;[44] the second makes liable, "any officer, director or agent…who directed, authorized, assented to, *acquiesced in* or participated in the commission of an offence"[45] [italics added].

So, who are these persons? In order to "permit" or "acquiesce in" an activity such as disposing of hazardous materials, one must have a significant role in controlling those who actually carry it out. Permitting or acquiescing has no meaning if the person charged is merely one who learned about the activity but could do nothing to affect it. Accordingly, the prosecution must first persuade a court that a person charged had effective powers and responsibility. A senior officer and director who is personally in charge of a hazardous procedure (that is, she is the person to whom those performing the activity report on a regular basis), presents a clear case of effective control and responsibility for the activity.

But what of an "outside" director — a person who was elected to the board because of his experience in financial services and who faithfully attends board meetings twice a year? He reads all the material sent to him and asks probing and useful questions at meetings. However, when it comes to environmental concerns he relies on the reports and assurances given by the senior officer, the "inside" director, who is in charge. Should the outside director also be considered to share in control? Did he "permit" or "acquiesce in" an offence that occurred under the supervision of the inside director?

Since the law is not intended to punish innocent and reasonably diligent people, it would seem that ordinarily an outside director *in his particular circumstances* ought not to be held personally liable for the offence. This view seems to be confirmed by the current case law: virtually all of the charges brought under Canadian legislation have been against inside directors. However, in many situations there is not a clear-cut division between insider and outsider: for instance, did the outsider receive any reports that disclosed questionable practices to a reasonable person in his position? Were answers to his questions evasive? What should an outsider do when he feels uneasy with the information provided?

We should also note that not all insiders are in control of an operation, or directly involved in it, simply because they are directors and senior officers within the enterprise. Should an inside director who learns second-hand about a potential problem in another

---

Just as the adoption of a *uniform standard of care* which is blind to personal characteristics of the accused…precludes lowering the standard for deficiencies of experience and temperament, *so it precludes raising the standard for special experience or training*…[italics added].

This analysis may present substantial difficulties for courts to determine liability in situations where a person without special training could not reasonably be expected to foresee a risk, while another person with expertise in the field would be expected to foresee that same risk.

44 See, for example: Fisheries Act, R.S.C. 1985, c. F-14, s. 36(3); Health Act, R.S.B.C. c. 55, s. 11.
45 Canadian Environmental Protection Act, R.S.C. 1985, c. 16 (4th Supp.), s. 122.

branch of the enterprise be expected to undertake a personal investigation, outside her normal responsibilities? These questions remain very difficult and depend on the particular facts. As a result it may be a number of years before the courts provide clear guidance as to what they find to be sufficient control for a person to be convicted of an offence.

In *R. v. Bata Industries Ltd.*,[46] the corporation's premises contained a large, toxic, chemical-waste storage site with many decaying, rusting, and uncovered containers; soil samples revealed concentrations of various dangerous chemicals. The prosecution charged Bata Industries with permitting the discharge of liquid industrial waste that could impair the quality of the groundwater and contaminate the environment. Charges were also laid against three directors. All the defendants argued that they had shown due diligence in carrying out their duties. Ormston, J., found that Bata Industries did not establish a proper system to prevent the escape of toxic substances and did not take reasonable steps to ensure the effective operation of even their faulty system. The corporation was found guilty.

With respect to the directors, the court provided a useful summary of the questions that should be asked in assessing a director's defence of having shown "due diligence" in his particular circumstances:

(a) Did the board of directors establish a pollution prevention "system"... i.e., was there supervision or inspection?

(b) Did each director ensure that the corporate officers have been instructed to set up a system sufficient within the terms and practices of the industry of ensuring compliance with environmental laws, to ensure that the officers report back periodically to the board...?

(c) The directors are responsible for reviewing the environmental compliance reports provided by the officers...but are justified in placing *reasonable* reliance on reports...

(d) The directors should substantiate that the officers are promptly addressing environmental concerns brought to their attention by government agencies or other concerned parties including shareholders.

(e) The directors should be aware of the standards of their industry and other industries which deal with similar environmental pollutants or risks.

(f) The directors should immediately and personally react when they have notice the system has failed.

In the *Bata* case, Thomas Bata was found to be "the director with the least personal contact with the plant" where the offence occurred. His responsibilities were at other plants and "he attended on site...once or twice a year to review the operation and performance goals..." Although Mr. Bata did not personally review the operation when he was on site:

> He responded to the matters brought to his attention promptly and appropriately. He had placed an experienced director on site and was entitled in the circumstances to assume that ... [the on-site director] was addressing the environmental concerns ... He was entitled to rely upon his system ... *unless he became aware the system was defective.*[47] [italics added].

Accordingly, Mr. Bata was acquitted.

---

[46] (1992), 9 O.R. (3d) 329, at 362.
[47] *Ibid.*, at 364.

In contrast, another director, Douglas Marchant, was found to have more responsibility than Mr. Bata but less than a third director who was held to be "on-site". Mr. Marchant came to the facility once a month and toured the plant. The court found that the problem was brought to his "*personal attention*" and that:

> ... *he had personal knowledge.* There is no evidence that he took any steps after having knowledge to view the site and assess the problem ... [D]ue diligence requires him to exercise a degree of supervision and control that "demonstrated that he was exhorting those whom he may be normally expected to influence or control to an accepted standard of behaviour": ... [the court cites *R. v. Sault Ste. Marie...*].

Mr. Marchant was found guilty.

From this example, we can see that a finding of guilt will depend on the degree of involvement of a director in the particular circumstances of each case.

What Should Be the Punishment?

A further question is: what punishment should a court impose? Generally, corporations are fined according to the seriousness of the breach and the harm caused.[48] Directors and officers receive somewhat smaller fines, but in extreme cases, they may be sentenced to prison terms.[49] To give an appreciation of the courts' approach we provide the example that follows.

In *R. v. Varnicolor Chemical Ltd.,*[50] the defendant corporation reprocessed and disposed of industrial wastes. Waste material escaped from its toxic disposal site into the groundwater, and moved towards a river that was a source of drinking water for down-river communities. The corporation took no action to clean up the spill; rather it was the Ministry of the Environment that did so at an estimated cost of $2.5 million. Both the corporation and one of its directors, Severin Argenton, were charged with offences. The defendant was, "the only officer and director to take an active part in the operations and actual management of...[Varnicolor]. He was clearly, at all relevant times, the sole directing mind of the company..." Accordingly, his actions were the actions of the corporation. Mr. Argenton pleaded guilty. Charges against the corporation were stayed. The court discussed in detail the criteria for sentencing Mr. Argenton.

It stated that the purposes in sentencing are: (a) to protect the public; (b) to deter and rehabilitate offenders; (c) to promote compliance with the law; and (d) to express public disapproval of the act. It summarized the factors that should affect the severity of a sentence as follows:

1. *The nature of the environment affected*: The concern is both with the sensitivity of the environment affected and the gravity of the risk. In this case, the drinking water of residents in the area would be contaminated.

---

[48]   See discussion in R. v. Canadian Pacific Forest Products Ltd., B.C. J. No. 1339, June 2, 1992 (unreported), where, on appeal, a fine of $500 000 was reduced to $76 000.

[49]   For a case in which both a fine ($76 000) and a jail sentence (30 days) were imposed, see R. v. Romaniuk (1993) Sask. Rep. 129 (Q.B.).

[50]   (1992), 9 C.E.L.R. (N.S.) 176.

2. *The extent of the damage actually inflicted*: Here, there was a high cost of cleanup.
3. *The deliberateness of the offence*: In considering this factor, the court stated:

> Not only was Mr. Argenton involved on site in the operations of the company, but he was as well involved in the negotiations which preceded the issuance of the certificate of approval by the Ministry...for the Varnicolor site...Therefore, as a result of this active involvement and in-depth knowledge of the business operations, it is clear that Mr. Argenton was uniquely in a position to be aware...of...the requirements of the Ministry.
>
> Mr. Argenton has indicated that he found these requirements to be unclear and ambiguous; However, it was at all time open to...[him] to seek clarification...There is no indication...that he made any attempts to do so.
>
> In a number of respects, Mr. Argenton acted in defiance of the requirements...
>
> Such violations are in effect a breach of trust on the part of the person to whom such a certificate has been granted and, as such, jail terms are an appropriate penalty to ensure compliance with the law by both the person being sentenced and society in general:[51]

4. *The attitude of the defendant*: In this case, Mr. Argenton did not voluntarily report the escape of toxic waste, nor did he show a co-operative attitude.
5. *Attempts to comply with the regulations*: There was no evidence of a cleanup at the site by Varnicolor or by Mr. Argenton, and indeed, the corporation had become inactive.

The maximum sentence under the Environmental Protection Act was twelve months. The court found that the conduct of the defendant amounted to a serious breach of the Act, and sentenced him to eight months in jail. We can see then, that the courts are prepared in egregious cases to imprison those who ignore environmental regulations.

The Business Consequences

What conclusions can we draw from these developments and how will they affect the conduct of business? Clearly, there is a public consensus that protecting the environment is a high priority; in response to public concern legislatures have created extensive regulatory schemes. Meeting the standards under these schemes imposes substantial costs on many businesses, especially on resource industries and manufacturing and transportation enterprises. The most important challenge is to meet the requirements effectively and efficiently.

How may this be done? First, businesses need to review their practices to learn whether any of their activities, especially disposing of waste materials, create a concern about health or safety or the breach of regulations. They must seek the best advice available and keep up to date with current technology; they are expected to take every reasonable precaution to meet the latest standards.

Second, once they are well informed about the risks, they will review their insurance coverage with a view to obtaining the maximum risk protection that is available and affordable. The cost of insurance coverage leads to the third stage: if after obtaining the best advice for implementing safety systems and obtaining insurance, a particular business activity ceases to be competitive, then it becomes necessary to decide whether to continue that branch of operations.

---

[51] *Ibid.*, at 180-181.

Questions for Review

1. What is meant by "constructive notice" of a company's constitution?
2. How do corporation statutes attempt to ensure the maintenance of capital?
3. What are the purposes of securities legislation? What are the legal devices for achieving these purposes?
4. Are breaches of regulations more closely related to civil law or criminal law? Explain.
5. In criminal law, what elements must the prosecution prove in order to obtain a conviction?
6. What is a "strict liability" offence?
7. What special problems does prosecuting corporations present to legislatures and courts?
8. Describe the argument made for holding directors and senior officers of corporations personally liable for offences.
9. Describe briefly the standard of skill and care imposed in environmental offences.
10. Is it necessary to participate directly in committing an offence in order to be found guilty? Explain.
11. What circumstances might lead a court to impose a jail sentence on a director?
12. Explain briefly the elements in environmental regulation that affect business decisions.

Problems

Problem 1

Igor Gilbert carried on business in Winnipeg as a sole proprietor manufacturing precision nylon gears. His products were of high quality and attracted the attention of Corbin Industries Limited, a large manufacturer of precision tools. Corbin Industries negotiated with Gilbert and finally arranged that Gilbert incorporate a company, Gilbert Gears Limited, and sell 90% of the shares to Corbin Industries for $450 000. Gilbert retained 10% of the stock and stayed on as a director and general manager of the new company on a salary-plus-share-of-profits basis.

Gilbert Gears was incorporated under the Business Corporations Act of Manitoba. Its by-laws provided that two directors must sign any contract in which the value of goods and services exceeded $10 000. It is customary in the trade for contracts of much larger amounts to be made with the signature of the general manager alone.

Gilbert continued to run the business as a one-man show, much to the chagrin of Corbin Industries. Finally he signed a contract to provide $250 000 worth of gears within two months to Eager Instrument Corporation, a competitor of Corbin Industries. The contract, if performed, would have tied up the entire production of Gilbert Gears and prevented it from filling emergency orders for Corbin Industries, which was the parent company's prime reason for buying into the enterprise. On the instructions of Corbin Industries, Gilbert Gears Limited called a special meeting of its board of directors, and passed a resolution dismissing Gilbert as general manager and declaring the contract with Eager Instrument Corporation invalid on the grounds that the by-laws prohibited such a contract unless signed by two directors. Eager Instrument Corporation sued Gilbert Gears Limited for breach of contract. Who would succeed?

Problem 2

The general manager and president of Vanguard Corp. Ltd., John Lenzner, engaged Eva Andrews, a real-estate agent specializing in the sale of industrial property, to sell Vanguard's large warehouse in Regina. The terms of the written agreement included a promise by Vanguard to pay Andrews a commission of $20 000 on completion of the sale if a price of $350 000 were obtained.

Andrews obtained an offer to purchase the warehouse at $350 000 signed for Patel Industries Ltd. by its president. The offer had been prepared on an ordinary residential offer-to-purchase form. Lenzner accepted on behalf of Vanguard, but inserted the following: "Subject to negotiation of final details and preparation of a formal contract in consultation with our respective solicitors."

At this stage, two directors of Vanguard learned of the transaction and protested that under the by-laws of that company a transaction involving this amount of money must be approved by the board of directors. At a meeting called to consider the matter, the directors refused to approve the transaction and after further discussion with Patel Industries the parties agreed to call the deal off.

When Vanguard refused to pay the commission to Andrews she brought an action against it for $20 000. She alleged first that the acceptance of the offer to purchase entitled her to the commission; and second, that in any event her agency agreement with Vanguard contained an implied term that it would do nothing to prevent the satisfactory completion of a transaction at the required price so as to deprive her of the agreed commission.

Evaluate these arguments and indicate whether the action should succeed. (For references, see *Friesen v. Braun*, [1950] 2 D.L.R. 250; *Luxor (Eastbourne) Ltd. v. Cooper*, [1941] 1 All E.R. 33.)

Problem 3

Gigantic Forestry Inc., one of Canada's largest pulp and paper enterprises with twelve mills in various locations across the country, operates a pulp mill on the Grizzly River in British Columbia. It has a government permit to discharge up to 18 200 kilograms of suspended solids per day into the river. The main suspended solids consist of lime mud, ash, wood bark, clay, sand, and pulp fibre. Gigantic was charged with exceeding the permitted levels of discharge and pleaded guilty. There had been a previous conviction eighteen months earlier, with a fine of $50 000 against the corporation. Two directors, described below, were also charged.

On February 27, Gigantic discharged suspended solids at a level significantly in excess of its permit. The spill resulted from a mechanical failure causing an overflow of lime mud from the storage tank into an emergency spill pond. The pond being near to capacity when the emergency occurred overflowed to the river. The suspended solid emission was 35 483 kilograms per day, almost double the permitted level.

Aggravating factors are: (1) Prior to the spill, Gigantic had prepared a "response manual" to deal with spills but no specific guidelines were in place to deal with this type of event. Since then guidelines have been created including reduction of production in relevant areas and, if machinery cannot be repaired, shutting down production completely. (2) The emergency spill pond had not been cleaned for five or six days. (3) The high-level alarm in the storage tank was not working that evening.

On the day of the spill, during the day shift, it was noted that the mud filter drive tripped out three times. The night-shift supervisor checked the filter at approximately 19:45 hours that day, just after the start of his shift. The filter drive was not working. Millwrights were called and they set to work to repair the mud filter drive at 20:30 hours, and by 04:25 hours the next day, February 28, mud was again being pumped from the storage tank to the mud filter.

Initially during the shutdown of the mud system, mud continued to flow from the mud washer to the storage tank. The night-shift supervisor instituted procedures to minimize the flow of mud from the mud washer to the storage tank. He had noted a large amount of clear liquid in the pond when he came on shift. The shift supervisor then made certain that everything was done to minimize the overflow of the storage tank to the pond. The shift supervisor's judgment that mud was not escaping from the pond to the river was unfortunately incorrect. To the recollection of the plant people interviewed following this incident, this was the first time the pond had overflowed to the river.

Jason Blinkov is a director and president of Gigantic. He resides in Vancouver where the corporation has its head office and visits the Grizzly River site several times a year, but spends most of his workdays in Vancouver or visiting the other eleven mills. His assistant, Bryan Crowe, is in charge of environment control systems at all twelve mills and regularly prepares detailed reports on each plant for Blinkov to review. Melissa Charbonneau is a director and manager of the Grizzly River mill. She lives in a nearby town and spends most of each day at the mill. The supervisors report to her at least once each month and are instructed to report any problems immediately. She had not personally examined the storage tank or emergency spill pond for several months before the spill. At 22:00 hours on the day of the spill, the night-shift supervisor telephoned Charbonneau and told her of the problem. She said she would examine the situation the following morning.

The court fined Gigantic $200 000. Should either or both directors, Blinkov and Charbonneau be found guilty, and if so, suggest what the penalty might be.

PART SEVEN

CREDIT TRANSACTIONS

Modern businesses rarely operate without buying goods and services on credit. Credit may be long-term, as when a corporation raises a part of its capital by issuing bonds or debentures, or it may be short-term, as when a business purchases supplies to be paid for within thirty days.

A reputable business generally has little difficulty obtaining credit to purchase its normal day-to-day needs. For purchases of more substantial items such as heavy equipment or large computers, the firm granting credit may require security beyond the buyer's contractual promise to pay; the creditor may require collateral security in the form of a mortgage of the buyer's land, as discussed in Chapter 28. More often, a buyer will give collateral in the form of a security interest in other types of property — the items purchased from the creditor, other chattels, or stocks and bonds.

In Chapter 33, we discuss the different legal devices for securing credit. A growing number of provinces have adopted comprehensive legislation called Personal Property Security Acts, regulating diverse kinds of credit arrangements. Some provinces still retain a variety of separate statutes governing such different forms as conditional sales, chattel mortgages, and floating charges created by corporations.

In addition, special rules apply to certain types of bank loans under the federal Bank Act. The relationships and conflicts that might arise among these different forms of security is one of the issues we consider in this chapter.

Unhappily, some businesses inevitably fail. They may become insolvent and be unable to meet the claims of all their creditors. In Chapter 34, we consider the rights of creditors when a business does become bankrupt — an area under federal legislation — and we also examine the protection given to creditors by provincial legislation, in particular, statutes dealing with bulk sales and mechanics' liens.

CHAPTER 33

LEGAL DEVICES FOR SECURING CREDIT

Secured Transactions

The Meaning of Collateral Security

The best security for a debt is the good reputation and the earning power of the debtor — the true basis for most loans and accounts receivable. Over and above a debtor's willingness and ability to pay back the debt, various legal devices exist to give a creditor "backup" or "collateral" assurance that debts owing will be recovered. Most of these devices are agreed to in advance as terms in the contract by which they are created; they are often called *consensual security interests*, and typically give a creditor *collateral security*, that is, a right to take possession of and to sell specified assets of the debtor in satisfaction of the debt. Security agreements can be very widely drawn, and new legislation makes it theoretically possible to cover virtually all existing and future property owned by a debtor.

There are also security interests that arise as a normal consequence of a transaction, not because the parties to a credit transaction have bargained for them, but because of rules of the common law or express statutory provisions. They may be described as *non-consensual security interests*. We have examined examples of such interests as rights of lien and resale available to unpaid sellers of goods and repair services in earlier chapters[1] and will examine others in the next chapter.[2] In this chapter our main concern is with consensual security interests.

We should note that an *unsecured creditor*, that is, a general creditor with no security interest in any of the debtor's assets, may ultimately acquire an interest rather like a security interest through a court action to collect an overdue debt. When a creditor obtains judgment for the amount of the debt and the debtor fails to pay, the creditor can then obtain an execution order authorizing the seizure and sale of certain of the debtor's assets.[3] By contrast, a secured creditor need not invoke the rather lengthy judicial machinery required to obtain an execution order, but can proceed on its own to enforce its rights over the security. In this sense, a security interest provides a creditor with a self-help remedy. More important, as we shall see, an unsecured judgment creditor generally has no right to seize any assets already subject to a security interest of another creditor; the secured creditor has *priority*.

Security Practices

For sound business reasons, suppliers generally do not require collateral security when extending credit to customers: unsecured transactions are simpler and cheaper to record; their risk is small because trade credit is usually short-term; and competition may make it unwise for a supplier to risk alienating customers by demanding security. If a supplier loses only a small proportion of its sales revenue by defaults in payment, it may well be

---

[1] See Chapter 19 for an explanation of an unpaid seller's rights of lien and resale and Chapter 21 for similar rights available to warehousing and repair service businesses and common carriers.
[2] See Chapter 34, in the section "Administration and Settlement of a Bankrupt's Affairs" for priority of claims set out in the Bankruptcy and Insolvency Act and in the section "Mechanics' Liens" for a discussion of liens available to workers and suppliers of materials in construction projects.
[3] See the discussion of "Methods of Enforcing Judgment" in Chapter 17.

better off accepting the loss than incurring added administrative costs and perhaps losing sales by requiring security for each sale, and then having to take possession of and sell the secured assets if default occurs.[4]

In any event, collateral security is not a good substitute for a sound debtor; suppliers or lenders would be unlikely to extend credit at all if they thought it probable that they would have to use their remedies to recover the secured assets. (Pawnbrokers may be an exception.) Indeed, the significance of security for a creditor is minimal so long as the debtor business remains healthy. Security is nonetheless a risk-reducing device, because it establishes a creditor's priority relative to other creditors in the event of a debtor's insolvency.

Even when a debt is stated to be payable "on demand", the debtor must normally be given time to raise the funds to repay the debt; if the creditor seizes property without giving reasonable notice it may be liable in damages.[5] Unfortunately, however, when a debtor's financial position has deteriorated to the point that a creditor decides it must act, the secured assets in the possession of the debtor may already be in a rapidly deteriorating condition or even in the process of mysteriously disappearing; other creditors may also have designs on them. Accordingly, security agreements frequently require a debtor to waive any right to notice of the creditor's intention to exercise security rights. After a creditor takes possession, however, statutes generally require the creditor to give notice to the debtor of the time and place at which the goods are to be sold in order to satisfy the debt.[6]

Provincial Variations

Section 92 of the Constitution Act, 1867, assigns "Property and Civil Rights in the Province" to provincial jurisdiction. The legislatures of the various provinces have dealt with legal arrangements for securing credit in quite different ways. Since businesses in any of the provinces often seek a national market for their goods and services, the effect of having to comply with widely varying provincial laws adds to the cost of doing business. In contrast, nearly all of the states in the United States have sought to reduce this economic cost by adopting a Uniform Commercial Code on a state-by-state basis. Several provinces and the Yukon have also attempted a more uniform approach, as we shall see in the subsequent section on "Personal Property Security Legislation". Nevertheless, Canadian law in this area remains a patchwork of diverse, and sometimes conflicting, provincial and federal legislation.[7]

This chapter does not attempt to offer a comprehensive review of all the law affecting credit devices in each of the provinces; instead, it seeks to illustrate the main kinds of legal risks that exist for businesses and the ways in which some jurisdictions have attempted to deal with legal questions raised by the granting of secured credit.

---

[4] Note that part of the loss from incurring bad debts may be recouped by claiming it as a deduction in calculating taxable income.

[5] Ronald Elwyn Lister Ltd. v. Dunlop Canada Ltd. (1982), 135 D.L.R.(3d) 1; Kavcar Investments Ltd. v. Aetna Financial Services Ltd. (1989), 62 D.L.R.(4th) 277. At least ten days notice must be given before enforcing security in the property of an insolvent debtor; see Chap. 34, below.

[6] See, for example: Conditional Sales Act, R.S.N.S. 1989, c. 84, s. 14(3); Personal Property Security Act, R.S.O. 1990, c. P-10, s. 63(5); R.S.M. 1987, c. P-35, s. 58(5); S.S. 1979-80, c. P-6.1, s. 59(4).

[7] See Ziegel, "Can Canadian Commercial Law be Rehabilitated?," (1992) 20 *C.B.L.J.* 322.

Credit Devices

Devices Previously Considered

In this chapter we shall be concerned with collateral security in the form of personal property rather than real property. Nonetheless, the concept of priority in relation to land mortgages and to other creditors' claims explained in Chapter 28 remains relevant, and readers may find it helpful to review the section entitled "The Mortgagee's Rights Compared with the Rights of Other Creditors" in that chapter. Historically, the law affecting credit devices has been drawn from a combination of real estate mortgage law and the law of the sale of goods.

Earlier chapters have also dealt with such consensual security devices as guarantees, conditional assignment of accounts receivable (book debts), and pledges. Leases and consignments are two other types of transactions that we have already encountered; since they may indirectly create a form of secured credit, we should now reconsider them from this point of view.

Leases

We have examined leases of equipment as an instance of bailment for hire or use in Chapter 21, and leases of land as a temporal interest or estate in real property in Chapter 27. Leases may also serve as a type of security device. This use of a lease is clearer when the business retaining the ownership interest in the leased asset (the lessor) recovers in rent over the term of the lease an amount that substantially reimburses it for the cost of the asset, and when the length of the lease approaches the useful economic life of the rented asset. Frequently, the party paying the rent (the lessee) may also be given an option to buy the asset for a relatively small sum at the expiration of the lease. The effect of such *financing leases* is much the same as if the lessor company lent the lessee the money to buy the asset and the lessee undertook to repay the borrowed money in regular instalments. The major difference is that the lessor remains the owner of the asset. Financing leases can therefore be regarded as a disguised method of borrowing and buying that at the same time provides a security interest for the lessor. They are, in fact, an old device that has been coming back into fashion. At the turn of the century, leases of consumer durables were quite common and were called *conditional hire-purchase contracts*. A close parallel exists between a lease and an instalment purchase (conditional sale) contract: the hirer (lessee) undertakes to pay rent for a specified period and at the end of that period can elect to buy it, applying rent already paid towards the purchase price.[8]

Businesses frequently acquire photocopiers, computers and motor vehicles by means of leases; the decision whether to buy or lease is influenced by taxation, among other factors. Consumers, too, are urged to acquire more expensive durables by leasing them; from a marketing point of view, leases may have a psychological advantage to the extent that consumers may believe that they are making less of a commitment when leasing than when buying outright.

---

[8] In some instances a lease with an option to purchase is treated as a conditional sale for purposes of conditional sales legislation: International Harvester Credit Corp. of Canada Ltd. v. Leedahl, [1978] 3 W.W.R. 649.

Consignments

We distinguished briefly between a consignment of goods and a sale of goods in the opening section of Chapter 18. A consignment may also amount to an indirect type of secured credit. As we have seen, retailers of expensive items such as jewellery or oriental carpets may not have sufficient capital to carry inventory for display and sale to customers. They may instead bring in a stock of goods shipped on consignment by a manufacturer or wholesale distributor. The arrangement is based on a *consignment contract* in which a retail business (consignee) acknowledges that the merchandise remains the property of the manufacturer or wholesale distributor (consignor). The retailer agrees to become an insurer of the goods to the amount of their wholesale price, and — as agent of the consignor for the purpose of selling the goods — to be accountable for all money received on the sale of the merchandise up to its wholesale price. Goods held on consignment are not part of a retailer's inventory and are not, therefore, generally available for the payment of other creditors' claims. Nevertheless, the consignor provides financing in the form of goods rather than money, and, by the terms of the consignment contract, the consignee "owes" the consigned merchandise (to the value of its wholesale price) to the consignor.

Personal property security law, discussed later in this chapter, expressly recognizes that leases and consignments may create a "security interest".[9]

Other Credit Devices

Among the more important forms of security we have yet to consider are those created by conditional sale contracts, chattel mortgages and floating charges, and by section 427 of the federal Bank Act. The sections to follow on "Conditional Sales" and "Chattel Mortgages" will complete our discussion of the relationship between a debtor and a secured creditor as the principal parties in the formation of a security device; the remainder of the chapter is largely devoted to the additional legal problems that arise when third parties are affected by the existence of a security device.

CONDITIONAL SALES

Nature of the Security

Contracts for the sale of goods, especially expensive durable goods, frequently take place on credit with provision for the seller to retain a security interest in the goods sold. A familiar form of transaction provides that the transfer of title to the buyer is conditional upon the buyer's completion of a series of scheduled instalment payments. In the meantime, the buyer has possession of the goods and the seller retains the title to them as security for the full payment of the purchase price. In our discussion it will be helpful to refer to the parties as the *conditional seller* and the *conditional buyer*.

During the term of a conditional sale contract, a conditional buyer makes regular instalment payments and has possession of the goods as a bailee for value. Ordinarily, a bailee for value is under a duty to take as good care of the article as a prudent person would take of his or her own property (as with a bailment for hire and use). A conditional

---

[9] Personal Property Security Act, s. 2, para. (nn) (Ont. and Sask.); s. 2(a)(ii) (Man.).

seller, however, often places the conditional buyer under a higher duty by making her responsible for damage to the article whether caused by her or not; that is, the conditional sale contract places the conditional buyer under strict liability.

Remedies of a Conditional Seller

The essential feature of a conditional sale agreement, as it is of a financing lease or indeed, of a mortgage of land, is the creation of a debt: the conditional buyer promises to pay a sum of money. She also makes subsidiary promises to help protect the value of the security — to keep the property in good condition, and for large and expensive chattels like automobiles and mobile homes, to keep them insured for at least the value of the debt. But the most important obligation is to repay the debt, and it is this obligation on which the conditional buyer most often defaults.

What are a conditional seller's remedies on default? First, as a creditor, the conditional seller has the ordinary contractual remedy of suing the debtor for the unpaid balance of the debt. Second, a conditional seller invariably makes it a term of the agreement that it may retake possession of the goods on default by the buyer. *Repossession*, as it is commonly called, does not affect the ownership of the goods since the seller has retained title from the outset. A conditional seller is not entitled to use force in recovering goods by self-help. It may be sued by the buyer for trespass or assault in attempting to assert its rights without regard for the buyer's property or person. When a conditional seller encounters resistance in retaking possession, therefore, it should not persist. The proper course of action is to obtain a court order authorizing the necessary steps in acquiring possession. In some provinces, in fact, a seller is not entitled to repossess goods except by court process. A conditional buyer who resists in the face of the court order is then guilty of contempt of court.

A majority of the provinces permit a conditional seller not only to repossess the goods upon a conditional buyer's default but also to sue the buyer for any deficiency arising because the amount still owed by the buyer exceeds the amount realized on resale of the goods.[10] In other provinces a conditional seller has to make a choice — either to sue the conditional buyer for the amount owing or to repossess the goods, but not both.[11] Moreover, consumer protection legislation in some provinces provides that a term in the conditional sale contract allowing the conditional seller to repossess and resell the goods on default is unenforceable after the conditional buyer has paid a certain proportion (for example, two-thirds) of the purchase price.[12]

Rights of the Conditional Buyer

Does a conditional buyer acquire an accumulating equity, entitled to protection, as she pays progressively more instalments toward total payment of the price agreed upon? We can answer this question by asking in turn whether a conditional buyer would be left

---

[10] For example: Conditional Sales Act, R.S.N.S. 1989, c. 84, s. 14(3); Personal Property Security Act, R.S.O. 1990, c. P-10, s. 63(5)(f).

[11] For example: Personal Property Security Act, S.B.C. 1989, c. 36, s. 58; Conditional Sales Act, R.S. Nfld. 1990, c. C-28, s. 13(3).

[12] For example: Consumer Protection Act, R.S.O. 1990, c. C-31, s. 23; Personal Property Security Act, S.B.C. 1989, c. 36, s. 58(3). However, a court may still grant the right to repossess and resell on special application by the conditional seller.

with any rights once she had defaulted and the conditional seller had repossessed the goods. Does the conditional buyer have a right to redeem (recover) the goods by paying the debt within a given period following default? Does she have a right to an accounting for any surplus if the conditional seller realizes more from the resale of the goods than the conditional buyer still owes? And would she remain liable for any deficiency after resale of the goods?

Unfortunately, the various provincial legislatures have given diverse answers to these questions. Some provinces permit a conditional buyer to redeem within specified periods upon payment of the instalments in arrears plus interest and costs incurred by the seller in repossessing.[13] Other provinces require a conditional buyer who has defaulted to pay the whole unpaid balance of the price — not merely the amounts in arrears — when an acceleration clause is included in the conditional sale contract.[14] In most jurisdictions a conditional buyer has a statutory right to receive any surplus realized by a conditional seller that repossesses and resells the goods for more than the amount owed by the buyer plus costs of reselling.[15] The right hardly balances a conditional buyer's corresponding liability for a deficiency should the proceeds of resale be inadequate, since the resale of used goods seldom brings in more than the amount owing on them. Possession and resale of chattels is notoriously "value destructive".

Trade Practice

In the business world, a conditional sale contract serves two main functions as a security device: first, it gives the secured party a right, with or without the help of the courts, to look to the goods in satisfaction of the debtor's obligation; and second, it gives the secured party priority in the goods over the interests of third parties, especially other creditors.

In consumer transactions, security devices are used primarily to give a secured creditor a right to repossession. This right is analogous to the threat of a big stick in the closet; the fear of repossession, while its effect is not statistically measurable, doubtless often provides an incentive to a conditional buyer to perform the contract and avoid the sanction. When a right of repossession is actually exercised, it is most likely to be used against expensive durable goods such as automobiles, boats or mobile homes. Even then, the realizable value for the secured creditors will probably be disappointing. It is common for goods in the hands of a defaulting debtor to have deteriorated considerably before repossession.

Many merchants who sell goods on the instalment plan do not finance the credit transactions themselves. Instead, they sell or assign their conditional sale agreements to finance companies that collect the instalments and administer the contracts. A finance company acquires, as assignee, an asset in the form of a *retail instalment account receivable*; in return, the merchant gains, as assignor, revenue in the form of cash (less a discount) very quickly after it makes a credit sale. Thus, it requires less capital to operate. Under the terms of most conditional sale assignments to finance companies, however, conditional sellers remain liable for payment if their conditional buyers should default. When

---

[13] For example: Personal Property Security Act, s. 62(1) (Sask.), s. 63(1) (Man.).
[14] For example: Personal Property Security Act, R.S.O. 1990, c. P-10, ss. 59 and 66; Conditional Sales Act, R.S.N.S. 1989, c. 84, s. 14(1).
[15] For example: Personal Property Security Act, R.S.O. 1990, c. P-10, s. 64.

an assignee has recourse to the assignor for payment if an assigned account proves uncollectable, the arrangement is known as *recourse financing*.

Conditional sale contracts play an important role in financing wholesale purchasers as well as retail purchasers: a retail merchant or dealer may finance its purchases of stock-in-trade from a manufacturer by buying them from the manufacturer under a conditional sale contract. This practice is common in the automobile business. As a conditional seller, the manufacturer acquires an asset in the form of a *wholesale instalment account receivable*, which it almost invariably assigns to a finance company. As an assignee, the finance company stands in the position of the manufacturing company, with title in the goods withheld from the dealer or merchant (the conditional buyer) until the account is paid in full.

Rights of an Assignee of a Conditional Sale Contract

We may recall from Chapter 14 that an assignee of a conditional seller takes "subject to the equities", that is, subject to personal defences that the buyer has against the conditional seller. For example, a buyer might protest that the goods were defective, or that the seller was not honouring its warranty or had been guilty of a misrepresentation. The buyer might then successfully resist action by an assignee finance company to recover the balance owing. To avoid this result, finance companies required conditional sellers to obtain promissory notes from their conditional buyers for the total amount due under the contract. Conditional sellers then endorsed these notes in favour of finance companies and sent them to the companies along with a copy of the assigned conditional sale contract. Until the courts and legislatures intervened, this practice put consumers at a disadvantage: a finance company had the rights of a holder in due course (see Chapter 24) and did not need to worry about the personal defences of a conditional buyer. The use of promissory notes to make finance companies holders in due course was widely criticized, principally because the practice placed consumers at the tactical disadvantage of having to take the initiative in trying to enforce their rights against sellers. Consumers with complaints had to seek redress in the courts against their conditional sellers, not being in the position of simply withholding payment as a means of self-help.

The Supreme Court of Canada in a 1969 decision limited the right of finance companies to sue as holders in due course, making them subject to the defences that would have been available to conditional buyers against their conditional sellers — at least in those cases where finance companies had received copies of the conditional sale contracts out of which the promissory notes arose and could thus be considered to have a special interest in the transactions.[16] Growing concern for consumer protection led to a 1970 amendment to the Bills of Exchange Act expressly removing the protection of a holder in due course in consumer sales.[17] As a result, the use of promissory notes has become less common, since they no longer improve the position of assignee finance companies.

A conditional seller usually assigns all its conditional sale contracts to the same finance company. It would be tempting for the finance company to collaborate with the conditional seller in designing a standard form conditional sale contract with terms to meet their common interests at the expense of consumers. The contract might well include a type of exempting clause by which conditional buyers agreed that an assignee acquired

---

[16] Range v. Corporation de Finance Belvédère (1969), 5 D.L.R. (3d) 257.
[17] See now, R.S.C. 1985, c. B-4.

rights against buyers free from any of the buyers' personal defences against sellers — a result similar to that which a promissory note formerly produced. Such a term is sometimes called a *cut-out clause*. Consumer Protection Acts seek to make these clauses ineffective.[18]

CHATTEL MORTGAGES

Nature of the Security

Chartered banks utilize chattel mortgages as an important device for securing credit in the field of consumer financing. Banks now dominate the field and it may well be that a larger volume of credit is now provided on the security of chattel mortgages than on conditional sale contracts. Many consumers have learned to obtain credit by borrowing from financial institutions and using the proceeds for their purchases; accordingly, less credit is now extended by the selling businesses themselves. Banks are not restricted to chattel mortgages in the kinds of collateral they may require in granting personal or consumer loans; when lending money for the purchase of a new car a bank may, for example, obtain a guarantee of a third party, a pledge of shares or bonds, or a conditional assignment of the cash surrender value of a life insurance policy. However, when a consumer borrows to finance a purchase of goods from a bank and gives a chattel mortgage, the effect may not seem much different from buying the goods under a conditional sale contract. The consumer will make regular payments to a financial institution in either situation (assuming the conditional seller would assign the contract to a finance company), and under either device the credit grantor may repossess the goods purchased if the consumer defaults. However, the goods that comprise the collateral may differ: in a conditional sale, it is the very goods purchased; in a chattel mortgage, the debtor (chattel mortgagor) may give security in a variety of other personal property and even in property acquired after the chattel mortgage has been executed (*after-acquired property*). While a mortgagee may borrow money to finance the purchase of a specific asset, the security need not be confined to that asset. In any event, we should note that a chattel mortgagee and a seller of goods are ordinarily entirely separate parties; the borrower has no legal excuse to refuse to pay instalments to the mortgagee because of a seller's breach of the contract of sale. This situation is in contrast to the defences a buyer may have against an assignee finance company when an assignor seller has committed a similar breach.

A chattel mortgage that includes after-acquired property is a very flexible device. It may cover inventories that fluctuate during its term, as some goods are bought and added to inventory while others are sold and subtracted from inventory. The mortgage does not transfer title to specific goods to the creditor, and buyers acquire good title to goods sold by the debtor in the ordinary course of business. The creditor's security interest remains as a suspended priority against general creditors; if the debtor defaults the secured creditor may then seize the property covered by the chattel mortgage and sell it to satisfy the debt.

A chattel mortgage may also cover goods not yet in a deliverable state, such as inventories of goods in production and growing crops. In some provinces the extent to which growing crops can be used as security is subject to special rules — priority may depend

---

18 For example: Consumer Protection Act, R.S.O. 1990, c. C-31, s. 31; R.S.B.C. 1979, c. 65, s. 3(1); R.S.N.S. 1989, c. 92, ss. 21, 25, 28.

upon the money borrowed being used to purchase seed, or necessaries such as groceries, or for repairs to farm equipment.[19]

The terms of chattel mortgages vary with the type of goods used as security. When a mortgage is on stock-in-trade, the mortgagor may be required to covenant to keep the realizable value of inventories in excess of a stated amount. When a mortgage is on particular assets, the mortgagor usually covenants not to sell or dispose of the goods without the prior consent of the mortgagee, and not to permit them to be seized to satisfy the claims of other creditors. Any default in these covenants gives the mortgagee the power to seize the assets. A chattel mortgage usually differs from a real estate mortgage since a chattel mortgagee ordinarily prohibits the sale of the mortgaged property without consent, but a land mortgagee usually does not. A chattel mortgagor usually covenants to keep the mortgaged goods insured against loss by theft and damage by fire, to pay the insurance premiums, and to make the insurance payable to the mortgagee "insofar as his interest may appear".

It is helpful to contrast a chattel mortgage with a pledge. In a chattel mortgage, the borrower retains possession of the property and the lender's security interest is in the title to specific goods or in after-acquired property. By contrast, a pledge is a form of bailment: the lender takes possession of the assets or of documents evidencing the borrower's ownership, while the title remains with the borrower.

Remedies of a Chattel Mortgagee

A chattel mortgagee has remedies similar to those of a conditional seller. First, as a creditor it may sue on the mortgagor's covenant to pay the debt. Second, it may take possession of the mortgaged goods upon default by the mortgagor. If the mortgagor refuses to give up possession voluntarily, the mortgagee may follow the same procedure as a conditional seller in repossessing goods. So long as the goods remain in the possession of the mortgagee, the mortgagor may redeem them by paying the balance of the debt with interest and costs.

A chattel mortgagee invariably reserves the right upon default to resell the goods to a third party. In exercising its right of sale, it must act reasonably and fairly to obtain a good price for them. If it fails to do so, it may be accountable to the mortgagor for the difference between the price it obtained and what would have been a fair price for the goods. If on selling at a fair price, the mortgagee obtains less than the debt outstanding, it may obtain judgment against the mortgagor for the deficiency, but if there is any surplus it must return that surplus to the mortgagor.

A chattel mortgagee, like a mortgagee of real property, may foreclose the interest of the mortgagor by court proceedings and have the chattel declared to be its property absolutely. In contrast with a real estate mortgagee, however, a chattel mortgagee seldom resorts to this measure.

Business Uses of a Chattel Mortgage

A vendor often uses a chattel mortgage in the sale of a business as a going concern where office equipment, machinery, or vehicles are included in the sale transaction. If the purchaser does not have all the cash required, the vendor may agree to take a chattel mort-

---

[19] Personal Property Security Act, s. 34(6) (Sask.) and s. 34(1) (Man.).

gage on specific equipment or machinery, or on the stock-in-trade, as security for the unpaid balance. In other words, the vendor receives its price partly in cash and partly in a promise to pay secured by a chattel mortgage.

Another common use of the chattel mortgage occurs in the sale of a building with equipment, such as a furnished office building, a hotel, or an apartment building in which each suite has a refrigerator and stove. Frequently the price includes both real property and equipment in the building. Not only may the vendor take back a real estate mortgage for the unpaid balance of the purchase price, but it may also take back a concurrent chattel mortgage on all moveable equipment. By so doing, the vendor obtains better security for the debt should it become necessary to foreclose or sell. In addition to prohibiting the mortgagor from disposing of any of the equipment, the chattel mortgage avoids any question about whether certain equipment is a fixture; a real estate mortgage would cover only fixtures, but with a concurrent chattel mortgage covering furniture and equipment the question becomes irrelevant.

We have seen earlier that real estate mortgages frequently originate in a purchase of real property; the vendor "takes back" a mortgage as part of the consideration offered by the purchaser. In contrast, commercial sellers of goods and equipment seldom take back chattel mortgages; they usually prefer to sell on short-term credit, leaving it to buyers to borrow longer-term capital from financial institutions. When commercial sellers do find it necessary to offer longer-term financing to buyers, they prefer using conditional sale contracts or leasing the assets.

Bills of Sale

A bill of sale is a written contract of sale in which a seller acknowledges the transfer of ownership of specified goods to a buyer for a stated price. It provides evidence of ownership for a buyer who does not acquire immediate possession and leaves the goods for the time being with the seller. Used in this way, a bill of sale is a document evidencing title rather than a credit device. The buyer may resell the goods simply by written assignment of the bill of sale.

A bill of sale may also be used as an instrument of credit much like a chattel mortgage. A person wishing to borrow money may be able to "sell" the title to goods for cash, while still retaining possession and use of them; the "buyer" is in fact a lender who obtains title to goods as security for repayment of the sum lent (the price of the goods). The true intention of the bill of sale can readily be inferred from a term providing for a transfer of the title back to the original owner upon repayment in full of the price. The courts regard such a bill of sale as a chattel mortgage; in those provinces that have not introduced personal property security legislation, chattel mortgages are normally regulated by the Bills of Sales Act.

$\mathcal{E}$FFECT OF SECURITY INTERESTS ON INNOCENT PURCHASERS FOR VALUE

Implications of the Separation of Possession and Ownership

The existence of security arrangements typically separates possession of property from formal legal ownership of it. For example, a consignor ships goods to a consignee while retaining title under a consignment contract; a conditional seller gives possession of goods to a conditional buyer while retaining title under a conditional sale contract; a mortgagee acquires title but leaves possession of the goods with a mortgagor under a chattel mortgage. Since possession of goods usually creates an appearance of ownership to a third party, the effect (intended or unintended) of a credit device may be to mislead an innocent third person; a debtor left in possession of goods may appear to own assets that he in fact does not own.

The Common Law

A third party may innocently buy goods that a seller appears to own, but because of a security arrangement, does not. Under the common law, a seller cannot transfer title to goods that it does not own; a creditor, whose existence is not known to the buyer, may have legal title to the goods and subsequently assert its right to repossess them from the buyer. The buyer is thus unaware of the risk that he does not acquire title and may lose the goods.

Legislative Intervention

Legislatures have frequently been more sympathetic to the interests of innocent third parties than have the courts of common law. Long ago legislatures attempted some protection for innocent third parties by providing that a mercantile agency holding goods on consignment, and thus clothed by its principal with an appearance of ownership, may nevertheless give buyers good title to the goods. These statutes also provided that an agency may for its own financing purposes effectively use consigned goods as security, even when its principal has prohibited such use.[20] Legislatures have extended this protection to third parties by recognizing that a conditional seller similarly clothes a conditional buyer with an appearance of ownership. The Sale of Goods Act, in referring to sales generally, states:

> Where a person having bought or agreed to buy goods, obtains, with the consent of the seller, possession of the goods or documents of title to the goods, the delivery or transfer by that person...of the goods or documents of title, under a sale, pledge or other disposition thereof to a person receiving the same in good faith and without notice of any lien or other right of the original seller in respect of the goods, has the same effect as if the person making the delivery or transfer were a mercantile agent in possession of the goods or documents of title with the consent of the owner.[21]

In other words, a conditional seller gives a conditional buyer the same power to transfer title as if the buyer were a mercantile agent; a seller is prevented by the Sale of Goods Act from denying the validity of any disposition of goods to an innocent third party. The Sale of Goods Act seems to say that a conditional seller can never repossess the goods from an innocent purchaser for value.

In practice, however, the Act may be qualified by the interpretation of its own words. When can a purchaser be said to have received goods "in good faith and without notice of any lien or other right"? Suppose the purchaser has a means, however inconvenient, of

---

20 For example: The Factors Act, R.S.O. 1990, c. F-1, s. 2.
21 For example: Sale of Goods Act, R.S.B.C. 1979, c. 370, s. 30(2); R.S.O. 1990, c. S-1, s. 24(2); R.S.N.S. 1989, c. 408, s. 28(3).

discovering whether a security interest exists and does not take the opportunity to find out. Can he claim to be "without notice"? In other words, how "innocent" must an innocent purchaser be to retain the goods against a secured creditor of the seller? Most provinces provide a means for secured creditors to make details of security devices available to the public by filing or registering a copy of the contract or instrument or a summary of it at a public office. Thus, prospective purchasers and other third parties often have the means of learning whether goods in which they are considering acquiring an interest are already subject to a security interest. In the following subsection we shall examine the effect of registration on the rights of an otherwise innocent purchaser who does not take the trouble to search a public registry.

Effect of Registration

A statute providing for registration of security interests may or may not state what the effect of registration is for a purchaser of the secured property.[22] Suprisingly, some legislatures seem to have been reluctant to set out a definitive rule; we are left to conclude that registration has no effect — that because of the Sale of Goods Act provision, an innocent purchaser can acquire a good title even when a conditional seller has registered its security interest in the goods. However, registration even in these jurisdictions may still be worthwhile: it can have the advantage for the conditional seller of protecting its security interest at least against the general creditors of a defaulting debtor if not against an innocent purchaser.

ILLUSTRATION

Peng purchases a video cassette recorder (VCR) from Federchuk's Stereo Stores Ltd. under a conditional sale agreement. He makes a down payment and agrees to pay the balance plus finance charges in 18 equal monthly instalments. Two months later Peng sells the recorder to Tse without disclosing the existence of the conditional sale contract. Can Federchuk's gain possession of the VCR from Tse despite the fact that she is an innocent purchaser?

(a) Let us assume that these transactions occur in a province whose statute provides that registration or "perfection" of a security interest in goods protects a secured creditor's title against an innocent purchaser. Federchuk's would be able to recover the VCR from Tse if it had properly registered its security interest before Peng resold the machine to Tse, since she would then have had the opportunity to find out about the security interest before making the purchase. She is not in a stronger position because of her ignorance. Federchuk's claim takes priority.

(b) Let us assume instead that the transactions occur in a province whose statute says nothing about the effect of registration on innocent purchasers for value. The Sale of Goods Act governs and Tse can keep the VCR. Federchuk's has no means of protecting its security interest against such purchasers. Although the resale deprives the conditional

---

[22] Personal property security acts commonly make a properly registered security agreement effective as against third parties, but they also make exceptions for specified classes of bona fide transferees: see, for example, R.S.O. 1990, c. P-10, ss. 9(1), 25 and 28. Contrast the Conditional Sales Act, R.S.N.S. 1989, c. 84, s. 3(1).

seller of its remedy of taking possession, Federchuk's may still sue Peng for the unpaid balance under the contract, or alternatively, for the tort of conversion of goods which it owned.

(c) The result in (b) depends on Tse being both a purchaser and innocent. She cannot defeat Federchuk's title if she fails to meet either of these tests. Thus, if Peng had given her the VCR as a gift, even if she was unaware of the conditional sale agreement, Federchuk's could still recover it from her. Similarly, if Federchuk's can produce evidence to show that although Tse paid for the recorder, she was aware that Peng had bought it "on time", then Federchuk's could recover it. She would no longer have the protection of the Sale of Goods Act as an innocent buyer because she had "notice of [a]...right of the original seller". Indeed, on the latter facts, Tse is guilty along with Peng of the tort of conversion by being a party to his wrongdoing. Moreover, if Tse is not an innocent purchaser, it does not matter which type of provincial statute exists, or even whether Federchuk's has registered the conditional sale contract; she cannot legally resist Federchuk's recovery of the VCR.

Originally most provinces had one statute dealing with conditional sales and another dealing with chattel mortgages. The personal property security legislation now adopted by a majority of provinces deals with nearly all forms of security interest in a single statute, and provides a common method of registration for all types. In the illustration on the previous page, much the same effect would be achieved if, instead of buying on credit by means of a conditional sale, Peng had borrowed the money from a bank, given a chattel mortgage as security, and used the proceeds of the loan to buy the VCR. The bank would then have been in a position analogous to Federchuk's for the purposes of registration and of maintaining its rights of repossession against third parties. However, we must take care to note that some provinces have different rules about the effects of registration of conditional sales and chattel mortgages.

Ontario, the four Western provinces and the Yukon now have computerized central registration systems. In some of the other provinces, however, registration is on a local basis and constitutes notice only in the district in which the security interest is registered. The real need is for a national registration system to protect the interests both of secured creditors and innocent purchasers.[23]

The Mercantile Agency Rule

There is one common type of business transaction in particular in which a conditional seller clothes a conditional buyer with an appearance of ownership: as we noted in our discussion of trade practices, manufacturers of certain goods often sell them to dealers or merchants under wholesale conditional sale contracts. Suppose that a retail business in a province whose statute provides that registration protects a secured creditor finances its inventories under a wholesale conditional sale contract registered by the manufacturer. Is the retailer able to give a good title to its customers when it does not itself have title? A negative answer would fly in the face of consumer expectations. This type of financing arrangement invites consumers to rely on a merchant's apparent ownership of its inventories.

---

[23] A uniform system of personal property security was proposed by the Canadian Bar Association and the Uniform Law Conference in 1982: see Ziegel, "The Uniform Personal Property Security Act 1982", (1982-83) 7 C.B.L.J. 494.

Hence provincial statutes provide that when a conditional seller delivers goods to a conditional buyer which resells them *in the ordinary course of business*, a retail buyer acquires a good title to the goods.[24] Should the dealer fail to meet its obligations, the manufacturer or a finance company holding a registered wholesale instalment account receivable cannot seize the goods from the retail buyer.

Unprotected Buyers in Private Sales

We should note that the above rule *does not* protect buyers of goods from someone who is not a regular seller of those goods. An unfortunate buyer may find that the conditional seller or its assignee can lawfully seize the goods purchased. The buyer's only remedy is to sue the seller for breach of an implied promise to convey good title. Unfortunately, a seller's warranty in a private sale is likely to be of little value — certainly of less value than would be the warranty of an established business selling goods as a mercantile agent. A business is more likely to have sufficient assets to satisfy a court judgment.

Accordingly, it can be argued that an innocent purchaser in a private sale needs more protection than she would have in a sale by a regular dealer. Yet she has less protection; in this respect it seems that the law is unsatisfactory.

Registration Practices

Security legislation does not "require" registration in the sense that failure to comply is an offence. If a secured creditor (or its assignee) chooses not to register its interest, it simply takes a risk that third parties may acquire interests prevailing over its own. Why might a creditor choose not to register? The answer turns on the nature of the creditor's business. Suppose that a creditor's business is primarily one of selling relatively low-value goods to many different customers. If it does not find it worthwhile to trace goods wrongfully disposed of by a debtor and then to sue in order to recover them from an innocent purchaser, it may decide to save the trouble and expense of registering the security interest in the first place. In practice, disputes do not often arise between a secured creditor and a subsequent transferee of goods. Accordingly, except for more expensive consumer durable goods, retail conditional sellers (or finance companies as their assignees) may decide not to register conditional sale contracts.

On the other hand, sales by a manufacturer or wholesaler often involve taking a security interest in assets of a debtor business that has other creditors as well. For instance, a truck manufacturer may sell an expensive fleet of vehicles under a conditional sale agreement to a large retail business. The retail business purchases stock-in-trade from suppliers who also provide credit. If the business should become insolvent, a dispute may arise over the truck manufacturer's claim to repossess the vehicles and thus to deprive the other creditors of an important asset from which to realize their own claims. Risk of this kind of dispute provides the main incentive for registration, as we shall see in the following section. In most provinces, registration of a security interest is essential for a creditor to maintain priority against other creditors.[25]

---

[24] For example: Personal Property Security Act, R.S.O. 1990, c. P-10, s. 28(1).
[25] For example, Personal Property Security Act, s. 20 (Alta., B.C. and Ont.), s. 22 (Man. and Sask.).

*E*FFECT OF SECURITY INTERESTS ON OTHER CREDITORS OF A DEBTOR

Priorities and Registration

We have learned that other creditors of a debtor may be affected by a security interest claimed by a particular creditor. Priorities among creditors become of crucial importance when the proceeds from a liquidation of all the assets of a debtor are insufficient to pay in full the claims of all creditors, as we have seen in our discussion of land mortgages. Information about the existence of security interests is therefore essential in making decisions about granting credit: a prospective creditor needs to know the extent to which an applicant has already given collateral security to other creditors before deciding whether to grant further credit of its own. If it decides to grant credit, it must determine what the rate of interest and length of term for repayment should be, considering all the risks.

Fraudulent Preferences

The secret creation of a security interest in conspiracy with a secured creditor can be a scheme by a debtor to deprive general creditors of assets in an impending collapse of the debtor's business. The federal Bankruptcy and Insolvency Act makes it an offence to give a fraudulent preference to a creditor.[26] Some provinces go further and require that registration of a chattel mortgage be accompanied by an *affidavit of bona fides*.[27] The affidavit is a sworn declaration by the chattel mortgagee that the mortgage instrument was "executed in good faith and for the express purpose of securing the payment of money...and not for the purpose of protecting the goods...against the creditors of the said mortgagor." The mortgagee will be guilty of an offence if the affidavit is shown to have been false. This provision is intended to make it more difficult for an insolvent debtor to give a fraudulent preference to a particular creditor, or to a friend or family member, by mortgaging valuable goods to that person at less than a fair value, thus putting them out of the reach of general creditors.

Effect of Assignment of Book Debts on General Creditors

In this chapter we have thus far examined two of the ways in which a security interest may arise: as a result of a sale of goods on credit, and as a result of a loan to purchase goods. In these circumstances a debtor's increased liabilities are offset by the newly acquired secured assets. A third use of security devices arises when an existing creditor requires additional collateral as a condition for leaving a loan outstanding. For this purpose businesses often provide a conditional assignment of book debts to a bank or other creditor. As we saw in Chapter 14, an assignment of this kind is conditional in two respects: first, the amount of the accounts receivable used as security fluctuates with the state of accounts between the borrowing business (assignor) and its customers; second, the assignment is only a potential one as long as the borrowing business keeps its loan

---

[26] R.S.C. 1985, c. B-3, ss. 95, 198(b).
[27] Bills of Sale Act, R.S.N.S. 1989, c. 39, s. 8. No affidavits are required in jurisdictions in which a Personal Property Security Act is in force.

with the bank in good standing: the security arrangement does not materialize in an actual assignment, with notice to the borrowing business' customers, unless the borrowing business defaults on its loan. Should default occur, however, the lending institution, as assignee, may realize directly on the book debts owed to the assignor in priority to the assignor's general creditors. Thus, an assignment of book debts may seriously prejudice the position of those general creditors, and prospective general creditors need a means of ascertaining whether an assignment has been made. Again, registration of a creditor's security interest in a public office provides the necessary information.

All provinces have provisions dealing with assignment of book debts, either in a separate statute[28] or as part of a single omnibus statute covering all forms of personal property security.[29] The legislation declares an assignment to be ineffective against creditors of an assignor and against subsequent assignees of the book debts unless the assignment is properly registered.[30] The object is to assure prospective creditors of a business that, unless there is registered public notice to the contrary, the assets of the business in the form of accounts receivable will be available to meet their claims. Registration provides public notice that those accounts are not available.

While registration of an assignment may provide information to assist the decisions of a prospective creditor, it does nothing for existing creditors whose decisions to give the debtor credit have already been made. The effect of an assignment is to deprive them of a part of the assets to which they might otherwise have been able to look for payment of their claims; knowledge of the assignment does not help them. Thus, when a major creditor such as a bank insists on obtaining and registering an assignment of book debts, unless the assignment provides a significant benefit to the debtor in exchange, the assignee obtains its new priority at the expense of the remaining creditors, for whom no relief seems to be available.

In jurisdictions retaining a separate statute to deal exclusively with assignments of book debts, registration requirements apply to assignments of accounts receivable in general, that is, to assignments that embrace future book debts arising out of later business activities of an assignor as well as of all existing book debts. However, an assignment of specific debts already due from individual customers or "growing due", that is, accruing in specific contracts such as conditional sale agreements, are not considered to be assignments of books debts requiring registration in order to protect the interest of assignees. These debts no longer form part of the assets of the assignor; they have been sold in exchange for some benefit which itself should be reflected in the financial position of the assignor. Nevertheless, in provinces that have replaced a separate assignment of book debts act with personal property security legislation, no exception is made for specific debts already due. The Acts apply to every assignment "intended as security" and to "every assignment of book debts not intended as security." An unconditional assignment of an existing debt consequently does not have to be registered unless the debt is characterized as a "book debt".

---

[28] For example: Assignment of Book Debts Act, R.S.N.S. 1989, c. 24, s. 4.

[29] Personal property security acts expressly apply to assignments of book debts: s. 2 (Sask., Man.).

[30] An assignment of book debts is also void as against a trustee in bankruptcy unless it has been properly registered: Bankruptcy and Insolvency Act, R.S.C. 1985, c. B-3, s. 54.

FLOATING CHARGES

It is common for a corporation to borrow money for a long term by issuing mortgage bonds to the public, using its land and buildings as security. Each certificate issued to a bondholder is evidence of an interest in a *trust deed*, an elaborate form of mortgage on the lands and buildings of the corporation. The parties to a trust deed are the borrowing corporation (as mortgagor) and a trustee for the bondholders (as mortgagee); the bondholders themselves are beneficiaries of the mortgagee's rights, and the trustee administers these rights for their benefit. Generally, a trust company acts as trustee for the bondholders.

Mortgage bonds issued by Canadian corporations frequently provide additional security over and above the mortgage of real property through the creation of a floating charge. A *floating charge* adds those remaining corporate assets not already mortgaged or pledged to the security. When a trust deed includes a provision for a floating charge, the trustee for the mortgage bondholders also has access to business assets, including chattels and choses in action, ahead of the unsecured creditors of the corporation.

A floating charge nicely complements a mortgage of real property because it provides security over the whole of the assets as a working unit. If the corporation defaults in the payment of its bond obligations, the trustee may then more easily place the corporation in the hands of a receiver and manager who can operate it in the interest of the bondholders. A sale of the mortgaged lands and buildings on default by the corporation is often an ineffective remedy for the bondholders; if the buildings and fixtures are of a highly specialized nature, they will have relatively small realizable value on a forced sale. Such value as they possess is best realized through continued operation of the corporation. On the other hand, one of the criticisms of a floating charge is that it is too pervasive a type of security and operates to the great disadvantage of the remaining creditors.

Canadian corporations sometimes issue bonds secured by a floating charge alone and without a mortgage of specific assets. Such bonds are referred to technically as *floating charge debentures* or *contingent debentures*, although they are commonly called simply *debentures*. Strictly speaking the term "debenture" alone describes corporate bonds that are just a promise to repay the stipulated sum, and are not secured either by a mortgage or a floating charge. The term refers also to bonds issued by municipalities, where the assurance of repayment is in the municipal taxing power rather than in a security interest in tangible assets.

All provinces require mortgages and floating charges contained in trust deeds to be registered. As with conditional sales and chattel mortgages, failure to register makes the trust deed void against creditors and subsequent purchasers or mortgagees.

Statutory registration requirements vary from province to province. Some are found in corporations acts, while others are in separate acts.[31] In jurisdictions that have adopted personal property security legislation, the interests that are secured by floating charges fall within the general scope of the legislation and are protected by registration in the normal way (see below).[32]

---

[31]   For example: Corporations Securities Registration Act, R.S.N.S. 1989, c. 102.

[32]   In Ontario it was for some time unclear whether a floating charge on a corporation's assets needed to be registered under the Corporate Securities Registration Act (CSRA), the Personal Property Security Act (PPSA), or both. Since 1989, registration under the PPSA alone is required and the CSRA is repealed. However, charges registered under the CSRA prior to October 10, 1989 remain protected: S.O. 1989, c. 16, s. 84; R.S.O. 1990, c. P-10, s. 78.

$\mathcal{P}$ERSONAL PROPERTY SECURITY LEGISLATION

Jurisdiction and Application

At the time of writing, British Columbia, Alberta, Saskatchewan, Manitoba, Ontario and the Yukon have each enacted a statute — the Personal Property Security Act — that deals globally with various types of security interest by a common system of registration. Each of these provinces has repealed its statutes dealing separately with conditional sale contracts, chattel mortgages and assignments of book debts. Instead, a single act now applies "to every transaction...that in substance creates a security interest";[33] it governs not only conditional sale contracts, chattel mortgages and assignments of book debts but also floating charges, pledges, leases and consignments intended as security and other less common forms. It does not apply, however, to non-consensual security interests; nor does it apply to interests in real property. It should also be noted that the legislation, though adopting the same basic principles, is by no means identical from one province to another.

Purpose

Two principal benefits may be gained from rules that are consistent from one type of security device to another. First, the remedies of both debtor and creditor in the event of default should be uniform, and in particular, legislation should recognize and protect a buyer's remaining equity in the security in the same way regardless of the security device used. Second, third parties should have a single form of warning of the existence of a security interest for all types of security.

The personal property security acts recognize that all security devices have the same purpose — to secure repayment by the debtor. They set out to establish a single unified system with common rules for the following purposes:

(a) to define a secured party's remedies against the debtor;
(b) to create one system of registration for all secured interests;
(c) to define priorities between a secured party on the one hand, and third party purchasers, subsequent secured parties and general creditors on the other.

The diversity of existing security interests makes it impossible to set out a simple system of priorities, but the legislation does attempt to develop a consistent set of principles for ascertaining priorities.

The acts establish a centralized registration system within each province for recording security interests. By using computer facilities to record and revise security information and by enlarging the geographic area over which a search can be made, a very large data base is established and maintained. The system does not distinguish the particular form of security interest registered; all are reduced to a common form of *financing statement*. The legislation does not, however, prohibit businesses from using their old contract forms to create security interests or from continuing to refer to them by such traditional labels as "conditional sale contracts" or "chattel mortgages".

---

[33] Personal Property Security Act, R.S.O. 1990, c. P-10, s. 2.

Registration Goals and Concepts

When parties create a security interest, they stake a claim that may often prejudice the interest of others. The degree to which legislatures and courts should support security interests at the expense of innocent third parties is an important policy question.[34] We see here two conflicting goals: that of encouraging lenders to advance credit by lessening their risks through security devices; and that of encouraging others to engage in trade by enabling them to rely on the certainty of title in transactions. If security interests are to be protected by the law, then an effective early warning system alerting third parties to those interests, whatever their form, should be an important corollary. Accordingly, beyond mere creation of a security interest by the agreement of creditor and debtor alone, the legislation requires two further events: first, the security interest must attach to the asset; and second, it must be perfected.

Attachment occurs only upon performance of the security agreement by both debtor and creditor. A security interest cannot attach to an asset until the debtor has acquired an ownership interest in it. Nor does a security interest attach until the creditor has performed its part of the bargain by giving the value promised to the debtor.

Perfection of a security interest may occur when the secured party takes possession of the assets — as in a pledge — thus ending any false impression of ownership given by the debtor's possession. Perfection occurs most often, however, when a secured party files a financing statement within the registration system. The financing statement gives details of the security interest and provides public notice of the creditor's interest.[35]

The three stages of creation, attachment and perfection are necessary to protect the security against competing interests of third parties. Thus, suppose that *X* Co. borrows money from *Y* Bank in order to buy a truck, gives *Y* Bank a chattel mortgage on the truck, and takes delivery of it. The security interest is created by the loan contract and chattel mortgage; the interest attaches when *Y* Bank hands over the money to *X* Co. and *X* Co. uses it to obtain delivery of the truck from the dealer. The interest is perfected when *Y* Bank registers a financing statement.

Suppose that one secured party finds itself competing for priority with another claiming security in the same asset. The legislation assigns priority to the creditor that *first perfects* its interest;[36] in practice this generally means that priority goes to the first to register. Thus a creditor that first creates and attaches its interest may nevertheless lose its priority if it delays perfecting that interest and a subsequent creditor perfects first. The subsequent creditor might even be aware of the unperfected security interest of the first creditor and, by registering its own interest first, perfects it and obtains priority.[37]

The system adopts an insurance method from the land titles system of recording interests in land; the provincial government maintains a fund to reimburse losses caused by incorrectly processed information. The central registry office provides a guaranteed cer-

---

[34] For a review of this question, see Goode, "Is the Law too Favourable to Secured Creditors?" (1983-4) 8 C.B.L.J. 53.

[35] The two alternatives are not available for every form of security interest. A security interest in negotiable instruments is perfected only by possession (holding) of the instrument and a security interest in book debts is perfected only by registration.

[36] Personal Property Security Act, R.S.O. 1990, c. P-10, s. 30.

[37] See BMP & Daughters Investment Corp. v. 941242 Ontario Ltd. (1992), 7 B.L.R.(2d) 270.

tificate of search.[38]A search under this system is made against the name of a particular debtor, whereas under the land titles system it is made against a described parcel of land.

After-Acquired Property

The legislation recognizes that assets subsequently acquired by a debtor can be added to a security interest already created, and permits the use of chattel mortgages to cover after-acquired goods such as inventories.[39] However, in consumer transactions the security interest of sellers or creditors is confined to the goods financed and does not extend to any other assets of the consumer.

The Personal Property Security Act recognizes not only inventories as an acceptable form of security interest but also permits *proceeds* from the sale of inventory in the course of business — cash or accounts receivable — to join the security interest.[40] In doing so, it acknowledges a long-standing security practice in the financing of inventories.

Purchase-Money Security Interests

The legislation attempts to clarify the priorities among secured creditors who claim competing interests in the same assets. Suppose one creditor takes security in after-acquired property and a subsequent creditor supplies new assets to the same debtor, taking back its own security interest in them. Although the new assets become after-acquired property of the debtor, a good case can be made for giving the one who supplies later credit a priority over existing creditors; otherwise a business in financial straits will find it difficult to obtain the additional credit it needs to rehabilitate itself and survive. In any event, the debtor's assets have been increased by the value of the assets financed by credit, so that the first creditor has not had its security diminished.

In recognition of this problem, the acts give special priority to a *purchase-money security interest*. This interest arises when a seller (for example, a conditional seller) *reserves* a security interest in the very goods sold to the debtor and when a lender (for example, a chattel mortgagee) finances a debtor's acquisition of the very assets used as collateral.[41] The rule is a necessary qualification to a system that makes it easy to include after-acquired assets and their proceeds in a security interest.

Relations among competing priorities are potentially very complex, especially for the financing of business inventories. Fortunately, in practice a business probably has only a single source of financing for its inventories, so the need to establish priorities is unlikely to arise. In financing other business assets, however, competition is more likely between one secured creditor claiming a charge on after-acquired assets and another claiming a purchase-money security interest, as when a corporation gives a floating charge over all its assets and then acquires new equipment under a conditional sale contract. In these circumstances, the legislation gives priority to the interest of the conditional seller.

---

[38] R.S.O. 1990, c. P–10, ss. 43 and 44.

[39] *Ibid.,* s. 12.

[40] Consequently, a secured creditor will be able to trace the proceeds into the debtor's bank account: Massey-Ferguson Industries Ltd. v. Bank of Montreal (1983), 4 D.L.R. (4th) 96.

[41] R.S.O 1990, c. P-10, s. 33.

Leases and Consignments as Security Interests

The acts recognize that both leases and consignments of goods can be used as forms of security.[42] On the other hand, the legislation also recognizes that these arrangements are frequently used quite apart from any intention to create a security interest. Accordingly, the registration provisions in Manitoba and Ontario apply only to leases and consignments "intended as security". The application of registration requirements to a particular transaction will thus turn on whether the parties truly "intended" to create a security interest. The Ontario decision in *Re Stephanian's Persian Carpets Ltd.*,[43] illustrates the point.

Anglo-Oriental Rugs Ltd. was a wholesale distributor delivering expensive carpets to retailers under consignment contracts giving the retailer (consignee) an unrestricted right to return consigned carpets at any time prior to their sale, and requiring the retailer to account to Anglo-Oriental for the proceeds of each rug sold up to its whole-sale cost. The arrangement was described as "usual and customary in...the sale of oriental rugs throughout the world". For a number of years Anglo-Oriental and Stephanian's did business on this basis. Anglo-Oriental did not register consignment contracts as security interests under the Personal Property Security Act. When Stephanian's became bankrupt, the trustee in bankruptcy claimed fourteen carpets on consignment from Anglo-Oriental for the benefit of general creditors. The trustee argued that the consignment contract had been intended to create a security interest, not perfected by registration, and was therefore subordinate to the interest of the trustee. The court held on the facts that the consignment of rugs had not been intended as security; the fact that unsold rugs remained in the inventory of Stephanian's did not provide any "security" to Anglo-Oriental, since the rugs belonged to them in any event. As a result, registration was not required to protect their ownership and the court ordered the trustee to return the rugs to Anglo-Oriental.

By contrast, in *Standard Finance Corp. v. Coopers & Lybrand Ltd.*,[44] a lease of a photo-copier, with an option for the lessee to purchase the machine for ten percent of its original price at the end of the term of the lease, was held to have been intended as a security agreement rather than as a true lease. The lessor had no real interest in retaining title to the copier at the end of the term, since it would already have received the full price in rent and would not be able to re-lease the used machine. Since the agreement had not been registered the lessor's interest was subordinate to that of the trustee in bankruptcy when the lessee became insolvent.

As the above cases illustrate, it is not always easy to determine whether a lease or consignment is intended as security. The three western provinces and the Yukon have taken the alternative course and require the registration of all chattel leases and consignments, regardless of intent.[45]

---

[42] *Ibid.*, s. 2(a)(ii).
[43] (1980) 1 P.P.S.A.C. 119.
[44] (1984), 26 B.L.R. 175.
[45] For example, S.A. 1988, c. P-4.05, s. 3; S.B.C. 1989, c. 36, s. 2(1).

Criticisms[46]

As we have seen, the acts set out general rules to replace detailed rules specific to each type of security interest, and so make it easier to resolve questions of priority claims in many instances. The acts themselves are complex and technical, and present a number of problems of interpretation. As already mentioned, problems exist in the case of transactions such as leases and consignments. Nor can the legislation remove all uncertainty as to whether a security interest has in fact been created and thus needs to be perfected. The most serious problem, however, is caused by the great diversity of legal rules that persists across Canada. First, some provinces have adopted personal property security legislation while others retain a number of separate statutes each dealing with a different type of security interest. Second, where the newer legislation has been adopted, it differs from province to province. Third, the newer legislation neither covers the entire field nor excludes other laws. In particular a serious conflict exists between provincial laws and the federal Bank Act.

Types of Security for Bank Loans

Loans under the Bank Act

History

The right to lend to primary producers against the security of their natural products has long been a distinctive feature of Canadian banking practice and, in fact, antedates Confederation. The production of raw materials dominated the early Canadian economy. Typically the producers — usually small-scale farmers — have always required short-term financial assistance to help defray costs through the growing season; farmers must wait several months to recoup costs through sales of their produce, and generally they lack sufficient capital to finance themselves in the meantime. Appropriate financing is a short-term *self-liquidating loan,* that is, a loan that must be repaid from the proceeds from sale of the very goods whose production the loan is financing. Over the years, successive revisions of the Bank Act have expanded the types of assets that may serve as security and the types of borrowers who may qualify for this type of bank loan, but their underlying self-liquidating character remains substantially the same.

Types of Borrower

S. 427 of the current federal Bank Act,[47] which came into effect in 1992, is the successor to s. 178 of the previous Bank Act, that in turn replaced section 88 of an earlier act in 1980. It is common to encounter, in the literature on this subject, the expression "section 178 loan", or even "section 88 loan". S. 427 empowers Canadian chartered banks to lend to the following types of borrower:

---

[46] For a discussion of the problems see Ziegel and Cuming, "The Modernization of Canadian Personal Property Security Law" (1981) 31 *U.T.L.J.* 249; Ziegel, "The New Provincial Chattel Security Law Regimes", (1991) 70 *Can.Bar Rev.* 681.

[47] Bank Act, S.C. 1991, c. 46.

(a) wholesale or retail purchasers or shippers of, or dealers in:

(i) products of agriculture, the forest, the quarry and mine, the sea, lakes and rivers; and

(ii) wares and merchandise whether manufactured or not;

(b) manufacturers;

(c) aquaculturalists;

(d) farmers;

(e) fishermen.

Types of Security

The types of security that banks are authorized to take varies with the type of borrower and have become quite diverse. At the retail and wholesale level, a bank may take primary produce or manufactured items of inventory held in stock pending resale. Thus, a grain-elevator company may borrow under s. 427 to permit it to pay farmers on receipt of their grain for storage. Manufacturers may borrow under the section on the security of inventories of raw materials, goods being processed and finished goods; a significant proportion of loans is to manufacturing companies. When lending to farmers, a bank may accept as security crops growing or produced on the farm, livestock or agricultural equipment. The section permits advances to a farmer for the purchase of seed, fertilizer or pesticides, with future crops serving as security for the loan; the purchase of feed with the livestock as security; the purchase of agricultural equipment with the equipment itself as security; and repairs, improvements and additions to farm buildings on the security of agricultural equipment. Fishermen may obtain loans on the security of fishing vessels, equipment, supplies or products of the sea. Similarly, forestry producers can borrow on the security of fertilizer, pesticide, forestry equipment or forest products.

The security taken by a bank is neither a pledge nor a chattel mortgage. It is not a pledge because the borrower does not physically transfer the assets to the bank as security; indeed, the security may not even be in existence when the loan is made — it may be a crop yet to be grown. Nor does the security amount to a transfer of ownership, because the bank does not acquire title to the property as security: to realize the security the bank must have a power of attorney from the borrower.

Rights of a Lending Bank

A borrower under section 427 signs an agreement containing the following promises: to keep the property insured and free from claims; to account to the bank for the proceeds of sales; to give the bank a right to take possession in the event of default or neglect; to grant a power of attorney to the bank; and to consent to the sale of the security without notice or advertisement if the borrower defaults. While the loan is in good standing the borrower must apply the money realized from the sale of the goods towards a reduction of the loan. As a further assurance that the proceeds from sales are applied against the loan, a bank frequently takes a conditional assignment of the borrower's accounts receivable. If the borrower defaults and the bank takes possession of the goods in the borrower's hands and sells them, the bank is entitled to retain out of the proceeds whatever amount will repay the balance owing on the loan plus costs;[48] any surplus belongs to the borrower, and any deficiency represents a debt still due.

To protect its security against a borrower's unsecured creditors and subsequent purchasers or mortgagees in good faith, a bank must insist that the borrower file a standard form of notice expressing an intention to give this type of security. Filing of a notice of intention constitutes constructive notice of the bank's interest to other persons dealing with the borrower and preserves the bank's authority.[49] The place for filing is the local or nearest office of the Bank of Canada.[50] In order to protect the value of the security itself, a bank may also require borrowers other than farmers or fishermen to submit at frequent intervals a statement showing the current value and location of the goods comprising the security.

Other Forms of Collateral Security for Bank Loans

The Bank Act also authorizes chartered banks to employ many of the devices for securing credit that we have considered earlier in this chapter. In addition to, or instead of, security under s. 427 a bank may require any of the following types of security as a condition for granting credit:

(a) An assignment of a warehouse receipt, representing title to goods while held in storage, or of an order bill of lading representing title to goods while in the course of transit.

(b) A pledge of shares and bonds, accompanied by a power of attorney signed by the borrower authorizing the bank to sell them as the borrower's agent if need be.

(c) A pledge of drafts drawn by the borrower against his customers.

(d) An assignment of book debts.

(e) An assignment of cash surrender value of a life insurance policy.

(f) A chattel mortgage.

(g) A real estate mortgage.[51]

(h) A guarantee by a third party.

While the right is not expressly granted by the Bank Act, Canadian judicial decisions permit a bank, in addition to holding collateral security provided by the borrower, to exercise a right of lien on other personal property belonging to the borrower in the bank's possession.[52] A bank may apply against a loan drafts that the borrowing business has left with it for collection.[53] It may apply in settlement of the loan any deposit balances kept with it by the borrowing business if it has not previously earmarked these balances for some particular purpose.[54] A bank lien does not extend to property left with the bank for safe-keeping.[55]

---

[48] Employees of the borrower take priority over the bank to the extent of three months' arrears of wages. Bank Act, S.C. 1991, c. 46, s. 427(7).

[49] See Royal Bank of Canada v. Lions Gate Fisheries Ltd. (1991), 76 D.L.R.(4th) 289.

[50] S. 427(4),(5).

[51] Normally a mortgage loan is limited to 75% of the value of the property; further restrictions apply to loans made on the security of residential (as opposed to commercial) property: s. 425.

[52] Re Williams (1903), 7 O.L.R. 183.

[53] Merchants Bank v. Thompson (1912), 26 O.L.R. 183.

[54] Riddell v. Bank of Upper Canada (1859), 18 U.C.R. 139.

[55] Leese v. Martin (1873), L.R. 17 Eq. 224.

Conflicts between the Bank Act and Provincial Legislation

As the preceding sections have shown, banks may utilize a wide range of security devices: they can take advantage of the provisions of s. 427 of the Bank Act, or can use the more common forms of security such as chattel mortgages and floating charges. The range of options available, however, can pose a dilemma for banks and can lead to conflicting claims between them and other creditors. One problem is that a degree of overlap exists between s. 427 of the Bank Act and the credit devices more generally available. For example, while s. 427 does not extend to all forms of property that can be the subject of a security interest under personal property security acts, it is unclear to what extent security interests under s. 427 fall within the scope of the provincial acts and are protected by registering under those acts.[56] Second, the Bank Act and the provincial acts each have their own system of registration, and can result in conflict between creditors, each claiming priority under a different scheme.[57] Third, since the Bank Act is federal legislation but other personal property security legislation is within provincial jurisdiction, neither level of government can resolve the problems alone. Although the operation of s. 427 cannot be made subject to provincial legislation,[58] the respective spheres of operation of the different laws remains unclear.

ℬANK CREDIT CARDS

Since the 1960s Canadian chartered banks have participated in the growing international practice of issuing credit cards to customers. Customers use the cards to make purchases from retail sellers who have agreed in advance with the bank to accept cards as a means of payment. While no security is required by banks from cardholders, the arrangement does provide a form of credit security for retailers. Banks in effect guarantee the credit of cardholders to retailers, and pay retailers the price of goods and services sold to cardholders, less a percentage commission. Sellers are thus relieved of concern about collecting customers' accounts. A credit cardholder may owe the bank for a variety of purchases from different retailers and can elect to finance them by paying the bank in instalments.

A consumer who pays for goods or services with a bank credit card is in the same position with respect to breaches of contract by a seller as if she had paid cash. Sometimes this may be a disadvantage, since a consumer who has not yet paid for goods or services is more likely to have his complaint adjusted by the seller; in a more serious dispute the buyer on credit need not take the initiative to enforce his rights — simply refusing to pay is an effective bargaining tool. A credit card buyer does not have this remedy: banks insist that they are lenders to cardholders and not assignees of contracts from sellers. Thus, the cardholder must pay the bank and pursue remedies directly against the seller.

---

[56] See Rogerson Lumber Co. Ltd. v. Four Seasons Chalet Ltd. and Bank of Montreal (1980), 113 D.L.R.(3d) 671; Re Bank of Nova Scotia and International Harvester Credit Corp. of Canada Ltd. (1990), 73 D.L.R.(4th) 385. For full discussion of this issue see Cuming, "The Position Paper on Revised Bank Act Security", (1992) 20 *C.B.L.J.* 336.

[57] For example, Bank of Montreal v. Pulsar Ventures Inc. and City of Moose Jaw, [1988] 1 W.W.R. 250.

[58] Bank of Montreal v. Hall, [1990] 1 S.C.R. 121.

Questions for Review

1. In what sense may a lease be used by the lessor as a security device?
2. What is the difference between a consensual security interest and a non-consensual one?
3. If there were no statute requiring registration of a conditional sale and an innocent purchaser acquired second-hand goods from a conditional buyer in a private sale, who would have title to them, the purchaser or the conditional seller?
4. If a person, without checking the public records, purchases second-hand goods already subject to a registered conditional sale, and the conditional seller repossesses them, what recourse, if any, has the purchaser?
5. Conditional sale agreements invariably contain a term prohibiting the buyer from moving the goods from the provincial jurisdiction. Why?
6. Distinguish between a chattel mortgage and a pledge.
7. To what extent may a mortgagee's control over mortgaged property differ in a chattel mortgage and a land mortgage?
8. Why should a lender under a chattel mortgage give public notice when a lender under a pledge need not?
9. What is the advantage for bondholders of a corporation in having a floating charge included in the trust deed?
10. Why would a province pass legislation prohibiting the mortgaging of crops yet to be grown, except to finance seed or necessaries?
11. May a secured creditor ever perfect its security interest without registering a financing statement in a public registry office? (Assume a personal property security jurisdiction.)
12. Does registration of a security interest provide equally valuable information to prospective creditors and existing creditors of the debtor?
13. An automobile dealer acquires a number of cars for its inventory under a wholesale conditional sale contract with the manufacturer of the cars. The dealer fails to keep up its instalment payments to the manufacturer but in the meantime sells one of the cars to a consumer. By what argument might the manufacturer claim it is entitled to recover the car from the consumer? Will it be permitted to do so?
14. For each of the following situations, describe the most suitable device that may be employed for securing credit or for obtaining priority:
    (a) The proprietor of a flour mill in Windsor has purchased grain stored in a public elevator in Thunder Bay. The proprietor of the mill now requires money to pay for the grain purchased.
    (b) X wants to buy a new car. He has no money in the bank but has a steady job and some life insurance.
    (c) A large, well-established retail store with a satisfactory earnings record requires the temporary use of an additional $500 000.
    (d) A small corporation, with barely adequate capital, is obliged for competitive reasons to extend 90 days' credit to customers, but for the purpose of paying its own accounts it requires customers' money more promptly.
    (e) Y has heard about an extraordinarily good buy in some mining stock. She has insufficient money in the bank.

(f) A farmer wishes to make improvements to his farm buildings and has insufficient funds for the purpose.

(g) A furniture manufacturer has sold finished stock to a retail furniture dealer on credit. Before the furniture in question reaches the retail store, the manufacturer learns that the retail dealer is insolvent.

15. In a province having a separate act dealing with assignment of books debts, under what circumstances may an assignment be "void as against general creditors of the assignor"? What reasoning lies behind the rule?

16. In personal property security jurisdictions the concept of a purchase-money security interest is recognized. How may this concept be helpful in business?

17. Provincial statutes providing for registration or perfection of security interests do not make failure to comply an offence. Why not?

18. Statutory provisions for registration or perfection of security interests may be the result of a policy against secret liens. What is the objection to secret liens? What costs are incurred in discouraging them?

19. Why do banks insist that credit card transactions are loans to their card holders and not assignments to banks of sellers' accounts receivable?

Problems

Problem 1

Mechanical Industries Ltd. was adjudged bankrupt on a petition of its trade creditors. As of the date of the judgment the company had assets of an estimated realizable value of $540 000 including accounts receivable of $150 000. The liabilities are as follows:

Current Liabilities

Trade creditors	$610 000
Bank Loan	240 000
Note payable—shareholder	500 000
Total current liabilities	$1 350 000

The bank loan is a demand loan for which the security is a general assignment of accounts receivable. At the time the bank made the loan it agreed that the assignment was conditional — that it would not require the customers of Mechanical Industries Ltd. to pay their accounts to the bank unless the loan was in default.

What steps should the bank have taken to protect its security? Assuming it has taken these steps, what amount will it receive on liquidation? Assuming it failed to take these steps, what amount will it receive?

Problem 2

Carter was employed for years as a truck driver for a large road-haulage firm. He decided to go into business for himself and spent his savings to buy a new $100 000 truck. Within a few weeks he discovered that he had made a mistake buying the truck for cash; he needed capital to modernize his garage where he stored the truck and kept a small office. Ready Finance Co. lent Carter $50 000 on the security of a chattel mortgage on the truck.

Carter had business difficulties and defaulted on his third payment to the finance company when the balance owing was $44 000. The company seized the truck and sold it for $36 000 and is now suing Carter for the deficiency of $8 000. Carter is convinced that the company has acted improperly.

What facts would be relevant to ascertain whether he is correct? If he is correct, what recourse does Carter have?

Problem 3

Holmes purchased a refrigerator and stove from Watts Electric Ltd. under a conditional sale agreement. Watts Electric Ltd. discounted the contract with Domestic Finance Co. Neither Watts Electric nor Domestic Finance registered the agreement.

Several months later Holmes sold the appliances to Fischer for cash without disclosing that there was still an unpaid balance owing to Domestic Finanace, and left the province. After Holmes defaulted payment, Domestic Finance discovered that Fischer had possession of the appliances and repossessed them. Fischer then sued Domestic Finance for wrongful seizure of the appliances.

State the arguments for the plaintiff and the defendant. What should the decision be?

Problem 4

Avila purchased a second-hand Cadillac from Better Buy Motors Ltd. under a conditional sale agreement. She used the car for several months in her work as a sales representative and paid her instalments regularly. When she had only two instalments left to pay, the car was towed out of her driveway and delivered to Fancy Finance Corp., on instructions of that company. Avila had never heard of Fancy Finance before. It informed her that it had "repossessed" the car under a prior, properly registered chattel mortgage which it held, and that the chattel mortgagor had fraudulently sold the car to Better Buy Motors.

Examine the nature of Avila's rights and indicate against whom they are available. What factors should be taken into account in assessing her loss?

Problem 5

Oliver purchased a used car from Hardy Motors Ltd. for $5500 and paid $3800 in cash as a down payment on the understanding that he should have 30 days in which to pay the balance. The manager of Hardy Motors Ltd. stated that 30-day credit was unusual for this type of purchase and that he would still have to get Oliver's signature on a conditional sale agreement "as a matter of form". Oliver signed the agreement which included a term that Oliver should pay the balance of the purchase price over 24 months in monthly instalments of $89.50 each. The manager told Oliver that he would hold the conditional sale agreement for 30 days so that Oliver would have that time in which to raise the balance of the purchase price.

Hardy Motors Ltd. was in financial trouble. In breach of its understanding with Oliver the company at once discounted (assigned) the conditional sale contract with Vanguard Finance Co. The finance company informed Oliver of the assignment and requested payment to it of the monthly instalments specified in the conditional sale agreement. Oliver ignored the notice, and before the expiration of the 30 days paid the balance of $1700 directly to Hardy Motors Ltd. Soon after Hardy Motors Ltd. was adjudged bankrupt, and the manager absconded with the cash assets of the business. Vanguard Finance seized the car from Oliver, who then sued the finance company for wrongful seizure, asking for a court order for return of the car to him.

Should Oliver's action succeed?

Cases

Case 1

Camp purchased a prefabricated summer cottage on the instalment plan from Green Lumber Limited. The purchase price was $55 000, of which she paid $27 000 down in cash. She then signed a conditional sale contract for $28 000 plus a finance charge of $8 000. The contract required the amount of $36 000 to be paid in equal monthly instalments of $600 for the next five years. Camp also gave her promissory note for $36 000 made payable to Green Lumber.

The conditional sale contract signed by Camp contained the following clause:

> Purchaser takes notice that this agreement together with Vendor's title to property in and ownership of the goods and said note are to be forthwith assigned and negotiated to Income Finance Corporation which Corporation shall not be affected by any equities existing between Vendor and Purchaser and that all payments are to be made to said Corporation.

Income Finance Corporation had recently advertised a special feature of the financing services it could provide where the money was to be devoted to home improvements or buildings. It had published an advertisement which read:

> You get automatic life insurance (arranged through Perpetual Life Insurance Company) covering the balance owing up to an amount of $30 000 — no extra cost, no physical examination. You receive a certificate containing provisions and details of the policy.

Perpetual Life is a subsidiary of Income Finance Corporation. The premium cost of insurance coverage on Camp's life was included in the finance charge of $8 000.

Green Lumber assigned the conditional sale contract and endorsed Camp's note to the Income Finance Corporation immediately following the sale. Camp died after she had paid only six of the monthly instalments. Income Finance Corporation then claimed the balance owing from the executor of Camp's estate. The executor protested that the proceeds of the life insurance policy were by the conditional sale contract to be applied in liquidation of the debt in the event of Camp's death; he produced a "Life Insurance (Family Protection) Certificate" found among Camp's papers to prove the point. The finance company replied that no legal relation with respect to the contract of insurance existed either between the deceased and itself or between the deceased and Perpetual Life, and it brought action against Camp's estate for the balance due under the conditional sale agreement.

Discuss the merits of the finance company's argument and indicate whether its action should succeed.

Case 2

Dowdy formed a company called Economy Cabs Limited and, as president and general manager, arranged for the purchase of three used cars from Vintage Motors Ltd., a firm of automobile dealers. The price for all three cars was $27 550 and the purchase was financed and arranged as follows: Economy Cabs Limited gave its promissory note for $27 550 to Vintage Motors; in a covering letter, Economy Cabs undertook to repay the holder of the note by monthly instalments of $1000 with the whole amount of the balance to become immediately due on default in any monthly instalment; Vintage Motors endorsed the note and discounted it with the Bank of Southern Canada. Under a separate conditional sale contract between Vintage Motors and Economy Cabs, Vintage retained title and right to repossession and resale of the cars as security for the payment of the purchase price.

After the financing had been completed, Dowdy mailed to Vintage Motors the following statement:

> This is to inform you that in view of the accommodation that you kindly arranged through the Bank of Southern Canada for $27 550 on behalf of Economy Cabs Limited, I give you my personal guaranty that I will see that this indebtedness is paid off according to the arrangements made.
>
> (signed) "U.R. Dowdy"

Dowdy soon found that to attract adequate business Economy Cabs would have to purchase newer cabs to replace the old ones. Only six months after starting business, it traded in one of its cabs on a newer one from Vintage Motors. After an allowance on the cab traded in, the net effect of the transaction was to increase its indebtedness by $8200. At this time, its liability on the original promissory note had been reduced by $6000 (six payments of $1000) to $21 550, each part payment being acknowledged by an endorsement of the bank on the note. Economy Cabs signed a new note for $29 750 in favour of Vintage Motors, which discounted the additional borrowing with the Bank of Southern Canada by endorsing the new note and substituting it for the original one. The bank cancelled the original note and returned it to Economy Cabs. A new conditional sale contract was also drawn up to cover the new amount of debt and the existing cabs.

Four months later, Economy Cabs Limited became insolvent and made no further payments to the bank. Its cabs had a resale value, in total, of about $21 000. The Bank of Southern Canada demanded from Vintage Motors an immediate settlement of the balance of $25 750 on the strength of its endorsement on the note. In turn, Vintage Motors demanded reimbursement from Dowdy, and when he refused to pay, brought an action against him.

Describe the nature of the defences available to Dowdy and indicate to what extent, if any, he would be liable.

CHAPTER 34

CREDITORS' RIGHTS

Statutory Arrangements for the Protection of Creditors

In Chapter 17 we examined two of the most important methods by which a creditor's rights may be enforced — levying execution against the goods of the debtor, and garnishing his wages. These methods work more or less satisfactorily where the debtor has sufficient assets or income to satisfy the debt and where there is only one creditor. We also considered, in Chapter 33, the rights of a secured creditor to recover what is owing by taking possession of the debtor's property that constitutes the security for the debt, and selling it. We noted that where there are a number of creditors, with conflicting claims, problems of priorities arise.

The great majority of businesspersons are honest, and pay their debts reasonably promptly if they are able to do so — resorting to legal procedures to collect money owed by solvent debtors is comparatively unusual. But in some cases a debtor's financial position may become so hopeless that it is unwise or impossible for him to continue to carry on business, as when he becomes insolvent. A person becomes insolvent when he is unable to pay his debts as they fall due or when his liabilities exceed his realisable assets. When a debtor finds himself in that condition, at least some of his creditors will share the loss with him.

A number of statutes have as their main purpose the protection of creditors' claims. These acts set out the right of creditors both against their debtor and against each other. In this chapter, our main concern will be with the ways in which the Bankruptcy and Insolvency Act, the Bulk Sales Act, and the Mechanics' Lien Act assist in this purpose.

Bankruptcy

Jurisdiction over bankruptcy is assigned to the federal Parliament under the Constitution Act, 1867. The first federal Bankruptcy Act was adopted in 1919 and remained in force for some thirty years until replaced by the Bankruptcy Act of 1949. That Act remains the basis of our current bankruptcy law, though it has been substantially amended on a number of occasions, most notably in 1992, when it was re-named the Bankruptcy and Insolvency Act.[1] In the period prior to 1919 some provinces passed legislation governing procedures for "assignments" and prohibiting certain types of fraudulent conduct by debtors,[2] but no legal machinery existed for the compulsory division of an insolvent debtor's property among his creditors, nor was there any means for giving an honest debtor a formal discharge from his obligations once all his assets had been distributed to his creditors; they could continue to pursue him for payment, subject only to limitations statutes.

---

[1] Bankruptcy and Insolvency Act, R.S.C. 1985, c. B-3, as amended by S.C. 1992, c. 27. Unless otherwise stated, statutory references in this part of the Chapter are to that act.

[2] Some provincial legislation remains in effect; see for example the Assignments and Preferences Act, R.S.O. 1990, c. A-33. In case of a conflict between provincial and federal legislation dealing with insolvency, the latter prevails: British Columbia v. Henfrey Samson Belair Ltd. (1989), 59 D.L.R.(4th) 726.

The Bankruptcy and Insolvency Act performs a number of functions.[3] First, it establishes a uniform practice in bankruptcy proceedings throughout the country and attempts to do so as inexpensively as possible. Second, it provides for an equitable distribution of the debtor's assets among his various creditors. Third, it provides a framework for preserving and reorganizing his business or affairs by working out an arrangement with the agreement of his creditors, and thus avoiding a total liquidation of a debtor's estate, if possible. Fourth, it provides for the release of an honest but unfortunate debtor from his obligations and so permits him to make a fresh start free of debts.

Policy Issues

It is helpful in bankruptcy law to distinguish the public interest from that of the parties to a bankruptcy proceeding, even though their interests often coincide. Business confidence and respect for the law are reinforced if creditors are able to recover what is lawfully owing to them. But their interests may diverge from that of society generally in a number of ways. The chief concern of most creditors is to recover promptly as much as possible of what is owed to them. They will normally have little interest in whether a debtor's business can be saved and turned around. Bankruptcy law, however, contains provisions whereby creditors may be encouraged, and sometimes compelled, to accept an arrangement designed to save a business. Similarly, a creditor normally wishes to preserve the possibility of recovering in full what is owed, even if this is not possible in the debtor's present financial circumstances. However, it is in the public interest to allow an honest but unfortunate debtor to be discharged from his debts once he has paid as much as is possible and to give him a fresh start. It is important to keep economic initiative alive, rather than to stifle it on account of a past misfortune.

In other circumstances, where a debtor has virtually no assets available to meet his debts, the natural instinct of his creditors may be simply to cut their losses[4] and not waste time and money in a fruitless attempt to recover something. One of the aims of bankruptcy legislation, however, is to promote an atmosphere of confidence in business relations, and confidence would be undermined were bankruptcy frauds to go unpunished. The Act consequently contains provisions to punish dishonest debtors and to prevent them from re-engaging in business activities.

There are, of course, limits to what even well drafted legislation can achieve. In many situations, the damage done to creditors' claims by the time bankruptcy occurs is largely irreparable. The best protection for creditors is their own astuteness in granting credit. Careful creditors check the credit rating of prospective borrowers and, where appropriate, require collateral security. To assist prospective creditors by making more information available to them, the Act requires certain information to be filed concerning bankrupt debtors and the directors and officers of bankrupt corporations.

Government Supervision

The Act creates the position of Superintendent of Bankruptcy,[5] who keeps a record of all bankruptcy proceedings in Canada and has a general supervisory function over all bankrupt

---

[3] For a detailed account of bankruptcy law, see Houlden and Morawetz, *Bankruptcy and Insolvency Act 1992*, Toronto: Carswell, 1993.

[4] To some extent creditors "share" their losses with the government, by claiming a deduction for bad debts in calculating taxable income.

[5] S. 5.

estates. The Superintendent is responsible for investigating the character and qualifications of persons applying for licences to act as trustees and has the power to suspend or cancel a trustee's licence. He or she may issue directives to trustees or receivers regarding the administration of a bankrupt estate, may intervene in any court proceeding, and may investigate situations where a bankruptcy offence may have been committed.[6]

For the purposes of administration, the Act makes each province and territory a bankruptcy district; each district may be divided into two or more divisions, according to the size of the province. For each division, one or more official receivers is appointed. Official receivers are officers of the court and are required to report to the Superintendent all bankruptcies originating in their divisions.[7]

The Act designates the highest trial court in each province or territory as the court for hearing bankruptcy proceedings.[8] Usually a particular judge or judges of the provincial court are designated to deal with bankruptcy matters, and their courts are commonly referred to as the Bankruptcy Court, though strictly speaking no separate bankruptcy tribunal exists. The courts hear creditors' petitions for the bankruptcy of their debtors and determine whether a debtor should be discharged after his affairs have been wound up.

The actual administration of a debtor's estate is placed in the hands of a licensed trustee, who is appointed by the court or, in the case of a voluntary assignment in bankruptcy, by the official receiver. In either case, in appointing the trustee regard must be paid to the wishes of the creditors, who retain the power to appoint a substitute trustee.[9] The creditors also appoint one or more (but not exceeding five) inspectors to instruct and supervise the trustee.[10]

Persons to Whom the Act Applies

The Act applies, in general, to debtors who are individuals, partnerships and corporations — apart from banks, insurance companies, and trust, loan or railway companies.[11]

The application of bankruptcy law to corporations is somewhat problematic since, as we saw in Chapter 30, the principle of limited liability means that the shareholders of a corporation are not liable for its debts. The corporation is liable for its own debts to the full extent of its assets, but these may be very few. Notions of punishment and rehabilitation have little meaning for a bankrupt corporation. A group of individuals may form a corporation with a very small capital sum and, if it becomes bankrupt, they lose very little (unless they have personally guaranteed its debts). To make a fresh start in business they may simply form a new corporation. The worst abuses — for example, where the assets of a corporation are "creamed off" by the payment of excessive dividends or by redeeming shares — are governed by provisions that allow such transactions to be reviewed and set aside. Further, where a corporation commits a bankruptcy offence, any director or officer who authorised, participated in, or acquiesced in the offence is liable to punishment for the offence.[12]

---

6 S. 10(1).
7 S. 12.
8 S. 183.
9 S. 14.
10 S. 116.
11 S. 2.
12 S. 204. An individual who is a bankrupt is not permitted to be a director of a corporation; see, for example, Canada Business Corporations Act, s. 105(1).

The Act, as its new title indicates, applies to insolvent persons as well as to bankrupts. An insolvent person is defined, for the purposes of the Act, as a person who is not bankrupt, whose liabilities to creditors amount to $1000, and who

   (a) is unable to meet his obligations as they generally become due;

   (b) has ceased paying his current obligations in the ordinary course of business as they generally become due; or

   (c) has debts due and accruing due, the aggregate of which exceed the realizable value of his assets.[13]

A bankrupt is defined as a person who has made an assignment or against whom a receiving order has been made; that is, a formal legal step must be taken in order to declare a person bankrupt.

The Act thus distinguishes between two basic types of person — those who are potential candidates for bankruptcy and those who have been declared bankrupt. Within the latter category, a further distinction is made between debtors who voluntarily declare bankruptcy and those who are forced into bankruptcy by their creditors.

Yet another important distinction is drawn in the Act between commercial debtors and "consumer debtors". It defines a consumer debtor as an insolvent natural person (i.e. an individual) whose aggregate debts, excluding any debt secured by the person's principal residence, do not exceed $75 000.[14] Thus, despite the name, the true distinction is not between non-business and business debtors but rather between small, individual, debtors and others.

The relevance of the distinctions — between insolvent persons and bankrupts, and between commercial and consumer debtors — will be considered when we discuss the various procedures provided for under the Act.

Procedures under the Act

The Act makes provision for three distinct types of procedure, applicable in different circumstances and each with its own special consequences:

   (a) a proposal — a procedure to avoid formal liquidation of the debtor's estate, at least temporarily, by allowing the debtor time to attempt to re-organize and save a viable business or, in the case of a consumer debtor, to re-organize his affairs;

   (b) an assignment — a voluntary application by a debtor to institute bankruptcy proceedings; and

   (c) a receiving order — initiated by creditors to have their debtor declared bankrupt by the court.

We shall examine each of these procedures in turn.

Proposals

The Act makes provision for two types of proposal — commonly referred to as commercial proposals (Division I) and consumer proposals (Division II) — the latter being a simplified

---

[13] S. 2.
[14] S. 66.11.

procedure available to individual consumer debtors. For corporations, an alternative method of avoiding liquidation is by means of a compromise and arrangement with the creditors, approved by the court, under the Companies' Creditors Arrangement Act.[15] That Act and the Bankruptcy and Insolvency Act are distinct statutes and provide alternative procedures,[16] though many of their provisions are broadly similar.

Commercial Proposals

A Division I proposal may be made by an insolvent person, a liquidator of an insolvent person's property, or by a receiver in relation to an insolvent person; a proposal may also be made by a bankrupt, or by the trustee of a bankrupt's estate, provided the estate has not yet been wound up.[17]

A proposal constitutes an offer made by the debtor to his creditors, providing for the orderly repayment of his debts, or of some part of his debts,[18] over a period of time. If the proposal is accepted by a sufficient proportion of the creditors, application may be made to the court to have it declared binding upon all the creditors.

Where a proposal is made before bankruptcy, the debtor files a copy of the proposal with the official receiver in the debtor's district. The proposal must be accompanied by a statement showing the debtor's financial position, verified by affidavit of a licensed trustee. An insolvent person can gain additional time by filing a notice of intention with the official receiver, stating his intention to make a proposal.[19] If the debtor has already been made bankrupt, the proposal and statement of financial position are delivered to the existing trustee. Such a proposal must be approved by the inspectors (appointed by the creditors to supervise the trustee), before any further action is taken.

The next stage is to obtain approval for the proposal at a meeting of the creditors. One of the most important changes introduced in the 1992 amendments was to bring secured creditors within the scope of the Act. Now, a proposal may be made to secured creditors, or to one or more classes of secured creditors, as well as to unsecured creditors. Acceptance of a proposal requires the approval of a majority in number, and two-thirds in value, of the unsecured creditors, and a similar proportion of each class of secured creditors. Secured creditors not included in the proposal, or whose class have rejected the proposal, continue to enjoy the protection provided by their security.

If the proposal is accepted by a sufficient proportion of creditors, the next step is for the trustee to apply to the court for approval. Although the court will be reluctant to refuse approval to a proposal that is acceptable to the majority of creditors, it must be satisfied that the terms of the proposal are reasonable and for the benefit of the general body of creditors.[20] In particular, it may withhold approval if the proposal fails to provide reasonable security for repayment of at least fifty cents on the dollar to unsecured creditors, or if the debtor has been guilty of a bankruptcy offence.

---

[15] R.S.C. 1985, c. C-36. Although a federal statute, this act applies to both federally and provincially incorporated corporations.
[16] See Bankruptcy and Insolvency Act, s. 66(2).
[17] S. 50(1).
[18] Certain debts, notably those to the Crown and to employees, must be paid in full; s. 60 (1.1), (1.3).
[19] S. 50.4.
[20] S. 59(2).

Once approved by the court, the proposal is binding on all unsecured creditors and on all secured creditors of a class that has given its approval. Unless the proposal provides to the contrary, the debtor retains control of his property. However, monies payable under the proposal must be paid to the trustee for distribution to the creditors. Where the debtor defaults in the performance of any provision of the proposal the trustee is required to notify all creditors and the official receiver. Application may then be made, by any creditor or by the trustee, to have the proposal annulled.[21] The effect of annulment is that the debtor is deemed to have made an assignment (see below).

Consumer Proposals

An insolvent individual who owes no more than $75 000, not counting any debt secured by mortgage on a principal residence, may make a proposal to his creditors for the reduction or extension of time for the payment of his debts.[22] It should be noted that the provisions do not apply to individuals who have already been declared bankrupt; bankrupt consumers are subject to the general provisions of the Act, though they presumably may make a proposal under Division I.

A Division II proposal must be prepared with the assistance of an "administrator" — a licensed trustee or other person appointed by the Superintendent to administer consumer proposals. The administrator is responsible for investigating the debtor's financial affairs and for providing counselling. Procedures are simplified, and a formal meeting of creditors is not required unless requested by creditors representing 25 percent in value of the proven debts. Where no meeting is requested, the proposal is deemed to be accepted by the creditors. A proposal that has been accepted, or deemed to be accepted, does not require approval of the court.

An important consequence of filing a consumer proposal is that the debtor also obtains protection against lease terminations, acceleration of instalment payments, or having utilities shut off.[23]

Assignments

By making an assignment an insolvent person may voluntarily declare himself bankrupt. A debtor who is no longer able to meet his debts as they fall due may prefer to initiate bankruptcy proceedings himself, rather than wait for his creditors to do so. By making an assignment he puts an end to an unsatisfactory situation and makes possible his earlier rehabilitation. Also, to continue to carry on a business once he knows he is insolvent might well involve him in the commission of a bankruptcy offence, and thus prejudice his eventual discharge.[24]

A debtor makes an assignment by filing a petition with the official receiver, accompanied by a sworn statement of his property and of his debts and creditors.[25] When the official receiver files the petition, she appoints a trustee, who becomes responsible for the administration of the debtor's estate and to whom the debtor's property is assigned. From that point

---

[21] S. 63.
[22] S. 66.12.
[23] S. 66.34.
[24] S. 173(1)(c).
[25] S. 49(1),(2). As we saw above, a person who defaults on a proposal may also be deemed to have made an assignment.

on, the debtor ceases to have any right to dispose of or deal with his property.

The estate of a bankrupt who has made an assignment is administered in the same manner as one administered under a receiving order; the procedure will be dealt with in the next section of this Chapter. However, a special simplified form of summary administration is provided in the case of an individual bankrupt who has made an assignment and whose realizable assets, after deducting the claims of secured creditors, do not exceed $5000 in value.[26]

Receiving Orders

A creditor, or group of creditors, may file a petition with the court in the judicial district where the debtor is located, to have the debtor declared bankrupt, provided the creditor (or group) is owed not less than $1000, and the debtor has committed an act of bankruptcy within the previous six months.[27] A secured creditor may initiate a petition, but to the extent that it makes a claim in bankruptcy it is considered to have abandoned its security.[28]

It should be noted that, unlike the rules for making proposals and assignments, there is no requirement that the debtor be insolvent; it is sufficient that he has committed an act of bankruptcy. An act of bankruptcy, as we shall see in the next section of this Chapter, may be committed by a person who is not insolvent. However, in the great majority of cases where a receiving order is made, the debtor is likely to be insolvent.

Subject to a few exceptions, a petition may be filed in respect of any debtor, whether an individual, partnership, or corporation. No petition may be made against an *individual* who is engaged solely in fishing, farming or the tillage of the soil, or against a wage earner who does not earn more than $2500 a year and does not carry on any business on his own account.[29]

Bankruptcy proceedings are considered penal in nature, and the burden of proving the facts alleged is on the petitioning creditors, who must comply with all the formalities required by the Act. The petition may be opposed by the debtor, who may dispute the existence of the debt or of an alleged act of bankruptcy. And even where the petitioning creditors succeed in establishing facts that would justify the making of a receiving order, the court has a general discretion to refuse to make the order or to grant a stay of proceedings. For example, it may decline to make an order if it considers that, given a fair chance, the debtor will be able to meet his obligations within a reasonable period. It may also decline to make an order where the debtor has no assets to divide among the creditors and there is no likelihood that he will have assets in the future.

Where a receiving order is made, its effect is to vest the bankrupt's property in the trustee appointed by the court to administer the estate.

Acts of Bankruptcy

We have noted that before creditors can succeed in having their debtor adjudged bankrupt and a receiving order issued, they must prove that he has committed an act of

---

[26] S. 49(6).
[27] S. 43.
[28] S. 43(2).
[29] S. 48. Such an individual may, however, make a voluntary assignment. A corporation engaged in farming or fishing may be petitioned.

bankruptcy. The Bankruptcy Act sets out in detail the various types of conduct that constitute an act of bankruptcy by a debtor.[30] In summary they are as follows:

(i) Assignment of assets to a trustee — if a debtor makes an assignment of his property to a trustee for the benefit of his creditors, whether it is an authorized assignment or not, and the arrangement is not satisfactory to the creditors, they may cite the assignment as an act of bankruptcy and petition to have a receiving order issued. They might choose to do so, for example, when the debtor has transferred his assets to a trustee who is not acceptable to them.

(ii) A fraudulent transfer of assets to a third party other than a trustee — a transfer of property by a debtor in anticipation of bankruptcy in order to withhold assets from distribution to creditors is a fraudulent transfer. As we shall see when discussing "Powers and Duties of the Trustee" below, any attempt to deprive creditors of access to assets by transferring them to a third person (including the debtor's spouse or child) is void if the transfer takes place within a specified period prior to bankruptcy.

(iii) A fraudulent preference — any payment by a debtor that has the effect of settling the claim of one creditor in preference to the outstanding claims of other creditors is a fraudulent preference.

(iv) An attempt by the debtor to abscond, with intent to defraud creditors.

(v) A failure to redeem goods seized under an execution issued against the debtor[31] — as we have seen in Chapter 17, a creditor may sue a debtor, obtain judgment, and seek to satisfy the judgment by having the debtor's assets seized. When a debtor's assets are few, a seizure may well benefit the judgment creditor to the disadvantage of other creditors; accordingly, if a debtor fails to take steps to prevent the sale of his property under an execution order, he commits an act that entitles his creditors to apply to the court for his bankruptcy. If they do so, all the debtor's property, including the property subject to the execution order, is put in the hands of a licensed trustee for distribution to all the creditors.[32]

(vi) Presentation at a meeting of creditors of (a) a statement of assets and liabilities disclosing the debtor's insolvency, or (b) a written admission by the debtor that he is unable to pay his debts.

(vii) An attempt to remove or hide any of his property, with intent to defraud creditors.

(viii) Notice to any of the creditors that the debtor is suspending payment of his debts.

(ix) Default in any proposal that the debtor has previously persuaded the creditors to accept as a means of forestalling bankruptcy proceedings.

(x) A failure to meet liabilities generally as they become due.

The most common of these acts of bankruptcy are failing to pay debts as they become due, and failing to redeem goods seized under an execution.

---

[30] S. 42.

[31] More specifically, a debtor commits an act of bankruptcy if he permits an execution to remain unsatisfied for fourteen days after seizure by the sheriff, or until within four days of the time fixed for the sale by the sheriff, or in a variety of other circumstances set out in section 42(1)(e).

[32] It is possible that, instead of petitioning for a receiving order, all the debtor's major creditors might choose to obtain individual judgments and execution orders. In Ontario, the Creditors Relief Act, R.S.O. 1990, c. C-45 provides for a scheme of rateable distribution of the proceeds of sale among execution creditors.

ADMINISTRATION AND SETTLEMENT OF A BANKRUPT'S AFFAIRS

Powers and Duties of the Trustee

The appointment of a trustee is the first step in establishing creditor control. The trustee takes possession of the assets of the bankrupt debtor and of all books and documents relating to his affairs. He becomes in effect a temporary manager of the business, subject to the supervision of inspectors appointed by the creditors. He may carry on the business, or alternatively, sell the assets. He can do such things as employ a lawyer, borrow further money for the business by pledging or mortgaging its remaining free (unsecured) assets, and negotiate with creditors for the acceptance by them of specific assets in lieu of money settlement of their claims. He may even engage the bankrupt debtor himself to assist in the administration of the bankrupt estate. To do these things he must have specific authority from the inspectors.[33] The principal duties of a trustee, however, are to recover all property that under bankruptcy law should form part of the debtor's estate, and to apply that property in satisfaction of the claims of creditors.[34]

Recovery of Property

As stated above, a trustee takes possession of those assets of the debtor in the debtor's posession, and also seeks to recover any other assets, such as collecting debts owed to the debtor. In addition, there may be property that the debtor disposed of and that by law should form part of his bankrupt estate to be available to satisfy the claims of creditors. Thirteen sections of the Act under the heading "Settlements and Preferences" are needed to set out the complex rules for the recovery of property.[35]

Settlements

The term "settlement" refers to gifts of property made by the debtor before becoming bankrupt. The intention of the rules is to prevent a person who is insolvent, or on the verge of insolvency, from successfully giving his property away — usually to members of his family or to friends — to the detriment of his creditors. In general, any gratuitous transfer of property by a debtor that occurred within a year before his bankruptcy becomes void and recoverable by the trustee. It is even possible for the trustee to impeach a transfer of property made as long as five years before the bankruptcy, but the burden is then on the trustee to show that at the date of the transfer the debtor was unable to pay his debts in full without the aid of such property.[36] In realizing the assets of the debtor, the trustee in bankruptcy may demand the property, or its value, from the party who received it.

A trustee may recover payments of money by the debtor to or for the benefit of a spouse or child, and transfers of property under a marriage contract, if made within six months preceding bankruptcy or at any time when the debtor was unable to pay his

---

[33] S. 30.
[34] S. 16(3), 25.
[35] Ss. 91 to 101.2 inclusive.
[36] S. 91(1) and (2). In practice it is almost impossible for a trustee to establish the exact financial status of a bankrupt debtor at a time as long as a year or more before the bankruptcy.

debts without the aid of that money or property.[37] A settlement may be attacked not only under the provisions of the Bankruptcy Act but also under provincial laws dealing with fraudulent conveyances;[38] it is not unusual for a trustee in bankruptcy to pursue both kinds of remedies.

Preferences

A debtor may choose to pay one creditor before he pays another, that is, to give *preference* to the claim of the first creditor over the second — perhaps because he depends on the prompt services or delivery of goods from the first creditor.[39] A solvent debtor is entitled pay his creditors in any order he chooses. By contrast, in bankruptcy the guiding principle is that creditors of the same class should be treated equally. A debtor facing imminent bankruptcy may, in breach of this principle, attempt unfairly to favour certain creditors over others. The Act deals with this situation by providing that:

(i) a payment of money or a transfer of property to a creditor,

(ii) by an insolvent debtor within three months preceding bankruptcy,

(iii) with a view to giving that creditor preference over other creditors,

amounts to a *fraudulent preference* and is recoverable.[40] The time limit extends to twelve months where the creditor who received the preference is a related person.[41] The provisions are intended to nullify transactions that would otherwise defeat the legitimate claims of creditors; they do not invalidate payments made in good faith to creditors who were unaware of the impending bankruptcy, nor other transfers of property such as the sale of inventory or other business assets in the normal course of business.[42]

Reviewable Transactions

A third source of potential abuse is that category of transactions where a debtor has enterered into a contract with a relative or a corporation in which he has a major interest. Since he was not dealing at *arm's length* with that other party, there is a risk that the interests of his creditors may have been harmed: the debtor may have sold property at an undervalue, or bought at an excessive price; the effect is as if he had made a gift of the difference between the sum actually received or paid and the fair market value of the property. Under the Act, transactions that were not at arm's length are reviewable; if entered into by the debtor within twelve months preceding bankruptcy, the trustee may apply to the court for an inquiry into whether or not the debtor gave or received, as the case may be, fair market value for the property or services that were the subject of the transaction.[43] Persons related to each other are deemed not to deal at arm's length. The Act defines "related" broadly, so that it includes not only personal relationships through

---

[37] S. 92, 93. The onus is upon the recipient to show that the transferor was solvent at the time.

[38] See, for example, Fraudulent Conveyances Act, R.S.O. 1990, c. F-29.

[39] Another reason, if the debtor is a corporation, is that the directors may have given personal guarantees of one or more of the debts.

[40] S. 95.

[41] S. 96.

[42] S. 97.

[43] Ss. 3 and 100. A similar inquiry may be made where a bankrupt corporation has paid dividends to its shareholders or has redeemed shares: s. 101.

blood, marriage or adoption, but also the relationship between a corporation and its controlling shareholders or between two or more corporations with a common controlling person or group.[44] If the price paid in the transaction was conspicuously greater or less than fair market value, the court may award the difference gained by the other party to the trustee in bankruptcy.

Payment of Claims

Having taken possession of all of a bankrupt's property, the trustee's duty is to apply the property in payment of the lawful claims against the bankrupt estate. In appropriate cases the trustee may distribute *liquidating dividends* (payments on account) to the creditors from time to time as required by the inspectors and as realization of the debtor's assets permits. In doing so he must, of course, be careful to take account of the claims of the secured and preferred creditors.

Two of the more important changes introduced by the reforms of 1992 concern the rights of unpaid sellers and of secured creditors; these have been mentioned already, in chapters 19 and 33 respectively. An unpaid seller now has a right to repossess goods sold and delivered to a bankrupt in relation to his business.[45] The supplier must make a demand within thirty days of the delivery of the goods, and the goods must still be in the possession of the purchaser, be identifiable, and be in the same condition as when sold. The claim ranks above any other claim to the goods, except that of a bona fide purchaser of the goods for value without notice of the supplier's right. A supplier who repossesses goods cannot subsequently claim against the bankrupt for any deficiency in respect of those goods. An additional priority is created for farmers, fishermen and aquaculturalists who have supplied their products to a bankrupt and have not been paid. The claims of such suppliers extends not only to the goods supplied, but are secured by a charge on the entire inventory of the purchaser; this charge ranks above any other claim against that inventory, except that of an unpaid seller of specific goods.[46]

ILLUSTRATION

F, a farmer, supplied vegetables to *G*, a wholesale greengrocer. *H*, a dealer in garden supplies, sold some bags of fertilizer to *G*. Neither has been paid. Within 30 days of delivering their goods, *F* and *H* both learn that *G* has become bankrupt and they immediately demand the return of their goods. The vegetables have been sold by *G*, but the fertilizer remains in his inventory.

Because the vegetables are no longer in *G*'s possession, *F* has lost his right, as an unpaid seller, to repossession. However, since he is a farmer he has a charge on all of *G*'s inventory for the amount owed to him. This charge takes priority over other claims against *G*'s inventory, including those of a secured creditor who has a general charge on inventory. However, it does not take priority over *H*'s claim to repossess the fertilizer, since *H* can claim as an unpaid seller in respect of the specific goods supplied.

---

[44] S. 4.
[45] S. 81.1.
[46] S. 81.2.

The 1992 amendments also bring secured creditors within the scope of the Act. Secured creditors, as we have seen, may be included in a proposal made by an insolvent person and may also be affected by the rights of unpaid sellers and of agricultural suppliers. The act now requires a secured creditor to give at least ten days notice to an insolvent person before enforcing its security,[47] and contains provisions governing the conduct of a receiver, appointed by a secured creditor, insofar as that conduct relates to the administration of a bankrupt estate.[48]

Subject to these provisions, however, a secured creditor is entitled to enforce its security to obtain payment of what is owing. A secured creditor must pay to the trustee any surplus if the security it holds is worth more than the debt owing to it. When the trustee and secured creditor cannot agree on the value of the security, it may be necessary to sell it and pay the secured claim out of the proceeds.[49] The bankrupt estate is entitled to any surplus for the benefit of other creditors. When the value of the security is less than the secured debt, the creditor receives the full value of the security and in addition ranks as a general claim along with other unsecured creditors for the deficiency. When the trustee and secured creditor agree on the value of the secured assets without having to sell them, the creditor may accept the security in settlement of its account, either by paying any excess value to the trustee or by making a claim against the trustee as a general creditor for the deficiency.

Out of the free assets remaining after payment or settlement of secured claims, the trustee must next pay the *preferred creditors*. Preferred creditors are listed in section 136 of the Act. The following is a summary of preferred claims, in the order of their priority:

(a) When the bankrupt debtor is deceased, his reasonable funeral and legal expenses related to his death.
(b) Expenses and fees of the licensed trustee in bankruptcy and his legal costs.
(c) A levy for the purpose of defraying the expense of the supervision of the Superintendent in Bankruptcy.
(d) Up to six months' arrears of wages of employees of the bankrupt debtor to the extent of $2000 for each employee. (The Act postpones all claims for wages by spouses, former spouses, parents, children, brothers, sisters, uncles and aunts of the debtor, until all other claims have been satisfied.)[50]
(e) Municipal taxes levied within the two years preceding bankruptcy.
(f) Arrears of rent due to the landlord for a period of three months preceding bankruptcy.
(g) The costs of the first execution or attachment creditor. (A creditor obtains an execution order against tangibles, such as land or goods, and an attachment against choses in action, such as accounts receivable or bank deposits.)
(h) Indebtedness of the bankrupt under the Canada Pension Plan, the Unemployment Insurance Act and the Income Tax Act for amounts required to be deducted from employees' salaries.[51]
(i) Claims for certain injuries sustained by employees.

---

[47] S. 244.
[48] Ss. 245–247.
[49] Ss. 127–134.
[50] Ss. 137(2) and 138.
[51] Before the 1992 amendments priority was given to various other claims of the Crown. These now rank as unsecured claims; ss. 86-88.

After settling the secured and preferred claims, the trustee pays the general or unsecured creditors rateably to the extent of the funds remaining.

To rank as a claim against the bankrupt estate, all creditors must "prove" their debts. They do so by submitting declarations to the trustee outlining the details of their accounts and specifying the vouchers or other evidence by which they can substantiate these claims. The declaration states whether or not the claim is a secured or preferred claim.

Because the assets are almost certainly insufficient to satisfy all the claims in full, the priority of claims is important. A trustee must act with great care in the administration and liquidation of the debtor's affairs; he may be personally liable to creditors for losses caused them by his failure to pay the claims in the proper order of priority, or for any breach of trust.

Duties of the Bankrupt Debtor

Following a receiving order or authorized assignment, the debtor must submit himself for examination by the official receiver to explain his conduct, the causes of his bankruptcy, and the disposition of his property. He must submit a sworn statement of his affairs to the trustee, together with a list of the names and addresses of his creditors and the security held by them, attend the first meeting of creditors and give the information they require. He must also deliver up possession of his property to the trustee, cooperate with the trustee, and "aid to the utmost of his power in the realization of his property and the distribution of the proceeds among his creditors."[52]

Bankruptcy Offences

A bankrupt debtor, and any other person who commits an offence listed in the Act, is liable to imprisonment or to a substantial fine. These offences include failing to perform any of the duties we have considered above, making a fraudulent disposition of his property before or after bankruptcy, giving untruthful answers to questions put to him at an examination, concealing, destroying, or falsifying books or documents, and obtaining any credit or property by false representations before or after bankruptcy.[53]

Discharge of the Bankrupt Debtor

As we have noted, an important object of our bankruptcy legislation is to clear an honest but unfortunate debtor of outstanding debts and to leave him free to resume business life. The discharge of a bankrupt debtor usually cancels the unpaid portion of his debts remaining after they have been reduced by payment of liquidating dividends, and gives the debtor a clean slate with which to start business again.[54]

The discharge of a debtor is an official act of the court. In deciding whether to grant or refuse a debtor's application for discharge, the court consults the report of the trustee.[55] One of the more important reasons why a court may refuse or suspend the debtor's discharge is that his assets have proved to be insufficient to pay the unsecured creditors at least 50 cents on the dollar; he may still obtain a discharge, however, if he can show that

---

[52] S. 158(k).
[53] S. 198.
[54] The Act specifies in s. 178 those types of debts that are not released by an order of discharge — for example, fines, alimony, liabilities for goods supplied as necessaries of life.
[55] Ss. 170-172.

he cannot justly be held responsible for this circumstance. Other reasons for refusing to give a discharge are that the bankrupt debtor neglected to keep proper books; that he continued to trade after he knew he was insolvent; that he failed to account satisfactorily for any loss or deficiency of assets; that he caused the bankruptcy by rash speculation or extravagant living; that within three months preceding bankruptcy he gave an undue preference to a creditor; that he was bankrupt or made a proposal to his creditors on a previous occasion; that he is guilty of any bankruptcy offence or has failed to perform his duties, as explained above. Other related reasons are set out in the Act.[56]

Until obtaining his discharge, a bankrupt debtor is liable to fine or imprisonment if without disclosing his status he obtains credit of $500 or more for a purpose other than the supply of necessaries for himself and his family, or if he recommences business and fails to disclose to those with whom he deals that he is an undischarged bankrupt.[57]

OTHER METHODS OF LIQUIDATION

We have seen that the Bankruptcy and Insolvency Act provides a means for liquidating insolvent corporations, partnership firms, and sole proprietorships. There are, in addition, a variety of ways in which the affairs of a solvent corporation may be wound up, but it is shareholders rather than the corporation or creditors who initiate proceedings.

Each of the provinces has a separate statute or a part in its corporations act to provide a means of winding up solvent corporations with provincial charters.[58] The legislation may authorize the shareholders to appoint a liquidator, who may be a director, officer, or employee of the corporation, to wind up the affairs of the corporation without recourse to the court, or alternatively it may authorize them to apply to the court for a winding-up order and the appointment of a liquidator.

In addition, the federal Winding-Up Act[59] outlines a procedure by which the shareholders of a solvent, federally-incorporated corporation may petition the court to issue a winding-up order. The court may issue a winding-up order if the capital of the corporation has been impaired to the extent of 25%, or if a substantial proportion of the shareholders petition for winding-up because of a lack of integrity or responsibility on the part of the corporation's management.

A corporation may also surrender its charter, apart from proceedings under either the Bankruptcy Act or a Winding-Up Act. For example, the Canada Business Corporations Act permits dissolution, if a corporation has no property and no liabilities, by special resolution of the shareholders. "Articles of dissolution" are then sent to the director of the federal government office that regulates federally-created corporations and he issues a certificate of dissolution.[60] A corporation may wish to dissolve in this way

---

[56] S. 173.

[57] S. 199.

[58] See, for example: Company Act, R.S.B.C. 1979, c. 59, Part 9, Division 3; Corporations Act, R.S.M. 1987, c. 225, Part XVI; Business Corporations Act, R.S.O. 1990, c. B-16, Part XVI; Companies Winding-Up Act, R.S.N.S. 1989, c. 82.

[59] R.S.C. 1985, c. W-10. In theory, the Act may also be used by creditors, but priority of the Bankruptcy and Insolvency Act makes this procedure obsolete.

[60] R.S.C. 1985, c. C-44, s. 210. Some provincial statutes also provide for dissolution of corporations formed under their acts. See, for example: Business Corporations Act, R.S.M. 1987, c. 225, Part XVII; R.S.O. 1990, c. B-16, s. 239.

when it has sold all its assets to another corporation and distributed the proceeds to its shareholders, and when the purchasing corporation has with the consent of creditors assumed all its liabilities.

Bulk Sales

Unencumbered Assets as a Security for General Creditors

In general, a prospective creditor has two main sources to which it may look for assurance of repayment of the credit it is asked to provide: the existing assets of the applicant, and the money generated from future operations of the applicant's business. The second source is primarily a matter for financial analysis that requires an estimate of future cash receipts and payments to determine whether the predicted cash flows can comfortably meet the required repayment. The first of these sources of repayment is more directly a matter for the law. In the preceding chapter, we examined how systems of registration may assist prospective creditors in ascertaining the extent to which the assets of a prospective debtor have already been encumbered. We noted that a debtor who uses assets as collateral for obtaining secured credit removes them from the reach of any present or future unsecured creditor. It is only the remaining unencumbered assets that are available to satisfy the claims of the unsecured creditors.

The Nature of a Bulk Sale

A debtor may also remove even these assets from the reach of creditors, directly and irrevocably, by a bulk sale. A bulk sale, as defined by provincial statutes, is a sale of essentially all the stock-in-trade of a business or of the fixtures, goods, and chattels with which a person carried on business. It is a sale of such a large portion of the assets as will seriously impair continued operations of the business. Often a seller makes a bulk sale incidental to the sale of the business as a going concern. On the other hand, a sale of goods in the ordinary course of business, even though a large sale, is not a bulk sale.

Bulk Sales Act

Each common law province has enacted a Bulk Sales Act. The object of the statute is to protect the creditors of a person making a bulk sale. The statute proceeds on the premise that creditors are entitled to regard the assets of a debtor's business as security for the amounts owing them. If a bulk sale merely caused a change in the composition of the business assets — inventory or equipment exchanged for cash — the creditors would have no cause for concern: the business would be at least as capable of paying its debts as formerly. The danger for creditors is, however, that the proceeds of the sale may not be retained within the business. The seller, for example, may abscond with the money or apply it in ways such that the creditors cannot recover it. The solution proposed by the Act is a shrewd one. It places the onus on the buyer in a bulk sale to take certain prescribed steps to inform the seller's creditors of the proposed sale, to obtain their consent to the transaction without having their accounts paid, or, if they demand the payment of their accounts, to make sure to pay the necessary portion of the purchase money to the creditors before paying the balance to the seller.

What sanctions does the Act impose to ensure the compliance of the buyer? It gives the creditors a remedy against a buyer who fails to fulfil the statutory requirements. The sale is voidable and the buyer becomes liable to the seller's creditors for the value of the goods. Creditors must act promptly, however, if they wish to attack a sale; they lose their remedies if they wait beyond the time limit set out in the Act.

A buyer can avoid the possibility of being held liable to creditors of the seller when the purchase price agreed on is greater than the outstanding claims of all the creditors. All the buyer need do is personally see that the creditors are paid in full out of the purchase money, before paying the balance to the seller.

When, however, a buyer settles on a purchase price that is less than the total claims of the creditors, she cannot safely pay the price either to the seller, or to a trustee appointed by the seller to receive the purchase price for distribution to the creditors. In these circumstances, she must obtain consent to the terms of the transaction from the minimum proportion of the creditors set out in the Bulk Sales Act.[61] Even when the required proportion of creditors consent to a bulk sale, the sale may be upset by proceedings under the Bankruptcy and Insolvency Act if the creditors are to be paid less than one hundred cents on the dollar. If, for example, a dissenting minority of creditors believe the sale is at an unreasonably low price, they may apply for a receiving order on the grounds that the seller's assignment to a trustee for the benefit of the creditors is an act of bankruptcy. The relation between the provincial Bulk Sales Act, and the federal Bankruptcy and Insolvency Act is complicated and technical, and requires the advice of qualified experts in the field.

Bulk sales legislation makes it difficult for the owner of a business to dispose of stock-in-trade without the payment or concurrence of trade creditors. What happens, however, if the owner decides to mortgage his stock-in-trade instead of selling it? By executing a chattel mortgage, a debtor can deprive his trade creditors of access to an asset in the same way as if he had sold it. The Bulk Sales Act does not apply to a chattel mortgagee; he is not obliged to comply with the Act to protect his security. The only protection for creditors when a chattel mortgage is given and duly registered is the prohibition of fraudulent preferences under the Bankruptcy and Insolvency Act. The risk remains, of course, that the mortgagor may dissipate the consideration received before the creditors can recover it.

The Ontario Act

The Bulk Sales Act of Ontario provides a good illustration of the law affecting this type of transaction: it is helpful to summarize briefly its provisions. At the outset, the Act gives a discretion to the court on the application of a seller to exempt a sale in bulk from the application of the Act if the court is satisfied that the sale is advantageous to the seller and will not impair his ability to pay creditors in full.[62] When the seller obtains such an order, the buyer may pay him directly without risk.

The Act then states the circumstances in which a buyer may, without resort to the court, pay the purchase money directly to the seller and still be assured of obtaining a valid title to the goods and equipment. They are as follows:

---

[61] See, for example, R.S.O. 1990, c. B-14, s. 8(2); R.S.N.S. 1989, c. 48, s. 6.
[62] R.S.O. 1990, c. B-14, s. 3. Note, however, that a creditor of the seller may still demand particulars of the sale in writing under s. 7.

(a) when the buyer obtains from his seller a detailed statement of creditors showing that the aggregate claims of the unsecured creditors as a group and the
secured creditors as a group each do not exceed $2500; or

(b) when the seller provides the buyer with an affidavit that before the sale he has
paid all his creditors in full or that he has made adequate provision for giving
security for payment in full after the completion of the sale.[63]

In either of these instances, the buyer may reasonably rely on the seller's representation if
he has no knowledge to the contrary.

As a further protection for creditors, the Ontario Act requires public notice of a bulk
sale, as do some of the other provinces. The onus is on a buyer to see that the relevant
documents and prescribed statements and affidavits are filed within five days after the
sale in the office of the clerk of the county or district court in the area where the seller's
stock or equipment is located.[64]

If a seller does not fulfil any one of the requirements set out above, then the buyer
must follow the more formal requirements of the Act. She must first obtain evidence from
the seller that his creditors have been advised of the details of the proposed bulk sale and
have agreed to it. More specifically, she must obtain from the seller written consent to the
sale by at least 60% of the seller's unsecured creditors in number and amount of claims in
excess of $50. She must also obtain an affidavit from the seller that the seller has sent the
following documents to his creditors at least 14 days before the sale: a copy of the proposed bulk sales contract; a statement of his affairs; a statement showing all creditors and
the amount due to each one.[65] This advance disclosure gives the creditors an opportunity,
if they so wish, to petition for a receiving order against the seller, and so avoid the bulk
sale. Assuming they do not, the buyer may then pay the purchase money to a trustee
appointed by the seller with the consent of a prescribed majority of his creditors, or to a
trustee appointed by a judge.[66] If creditors wish to challenge a bulk sale on the grounds
that the buyer has failed to comply with the provisions of the Act, they must do so within
six months.[67]

MECHANICS' LIENS

The Nature of a Mechanic's Lien

We noted in Chapter 21 that a bailee who makes repairs or improvements on goods bailed
with her obtains a possessory lien on the goods for the value of her services. She may keep
them in her possession until the bailor or the owner pays the amount due her. In addition,
in some provinces a bailee may sell the goods to satisfy her claim. By contrast, when a
person extends credit by performing work or supplying materials in the construction of a
building or other structure affixed to land, it is physically impossible for him to exercise a

---

[63] S. 8(1).
[64] S. 11(1).
[65] S. 8(2).
[66] S. 9.
[67] S. 19.

possessory lien. In any event, under the law of real property, when goods are affixed permanently to land they become fixtures: the supplier of the goods is not permitted to sever them from the property. In these circumstances, a creditor has no recourse at common law except to sue for the debt owing and obtain judgment and an order for execution against the land — a rather cumbersome process and not practical where the debt is small.

In all provinces of Canada, persons who have extended credit in the form of goods and services to improve land have a statutory remedy under mechanics' lien legislation. Although the title and wording of the acts vary from province to province,[68] each act provides substantially the same protection for creditors. Its basic purposes are to give creditors who have provided work and material for the improvement of land an interest in the land as security for payment and "to prevent multiplicity of actions for small claims, in which the cost would be enormously out of proportion to and in excess of the sums claimed...."[69]

The provisions of mechanics' lien acts operate in two somewhat different ways which can best be understood by an example.

ILLUSTRATION

Ostrakh owns a valuable piece of land zoned for an apartment building. She has an architect prepare plans for a ten-storey, 80-unit apartment block and arranges to finance the project by giving a large mortgage to the Eagle Insurance Co. Ostrakh then hires Arden Construction Co. Ltd. to erect the building for an agreed price. Arden in turn subcontracts the special tasks of supplying and erecting the structural steel, installing the plumbing and heating systems and the electrical wiring, and supplying and installing elevators, to various firms specializing in these trades.

Here we have two types of contracts: a master contract between the owner of the property and her main contractor, Arden Construction, and a series of sub-contracts between the main contractor and specialized trades. In respect to the master contract, Ostrakh is personally liable for the whole amount of the contract price as a contractual debt; Arden Construction has a mechanic's lien, that is, an interest in Ostrakh's land and building as it is erected, for the total value of work and materials (to the maximum of the contract price) provided by Arden Construction and its subcontractors. In turn, the subcontractors and suppliers have a right of action against Arden Construction for the value of the work and materials supplied for the project under the terms of the subcontracts. There is, however, no privity of contract between Arden Construction's subcontractors and suppliers and Ostrakh. Nevertheless, the Mechanics' Lien Act also gives liens against Ostrakh's land to the subcontractors and suppliers. The value of these liens is limited by the Act to a specified proportion of the price due from Ostrakh to Arden Construction under the master contract. This proportion, called a *holdback*, varies somewhat from

---

[68] In Alberta and British Columbia the statute is called the "Builders' Lien Act", and in Ontario, since 1983, the "Construction Lien Act".

[69] McPherson v. Gedge (1884), 4 O.R. 246, per Wilson C.J., at 257.

province to province but is generally from 10 to 20 per cent.[70] Where the value of the work and materials exceeds the holdback, the subcontractors and suppliers have no security in Ostrakh's land for the excess sum.

Ostrakh fully protects against liens of the subcontractors and suppliers by retaining the holdback during construction and for a specified period afterwards. If Arden Construction should become insolvent during this period, Ostrakh would pay the holdback into court for the benefit of the lienholders. The court would then supervise the payment of this money amongst the lienholders, and neither Ostrakh personally nor her land would be subject to their claims.

A mechanics' lien is available only to creditors that participate directly as workers or supply material for use directly in the construction work. In *Brooks-Sanford Co. v. Theodore Tieler Construction Co.*, the court said:

> While the objects and policy [of the Mechanics' Lien Act]...is to prevent an owner from obtaining the benefits of the labour and capital of others without compensation, it is not the intention to compel him to pay his contractor's indebtedness for that which does not go into or benefit his property.[71]

The courts have held that an architect who prepares the plans for a building comes within this definition and is entitled to a lien. Some provincial statutes give a lien to a lessor who rents equipment for use on the contract site for the price of the rental of the equipment.[72] On the other hand, a party that sells tools or machinery to a contractor is not entitled to a lien against a building constructed with the use of the tools or machinery it has supplied; the tools and machinery remain the property of the contractor and can be used in other projects as well.[73] Nor can suppliers obtain a lien against property where the contractor has ordered materials for the building and has had them delivered to its own premises, unless the supplier can prove that the supplies were later used in the construction of the building. Where, however, a supplier delivers the goods directly to the building site, it obtains a lien immediately, whether the materials are eventually used in the structure or not.[74] The reason for this provision is that a supplier that delivers materials to the building site reasonably assumes that they will be used there and relies upon the property as security for its claim.

Suppliers of materials may, if they choose, waive their right of lien by contract. They may find an advantage in doing so when the effect is to persuade a mortgagee to lend additional funds for the completion of a project: the suppliers may then realize their claims out of the proceeds of a sale of the completed building.

Provincial legislatures seem to have acknowledged that the bargaining power of wage-earners (or at least of those who receive low rates of pay) may be unequal to that of builders and contractors who employ them, and that these wage-earners may not fully understand the nature of their rights. As a result, the various provincial acts contain a

---

[70] See, for example: Builders' Lien Act, R.S.B.C. 1979, c. 40, s. 20(1), as amended by S.B.C. 1984, c. 16, s. 1; Construction Lien Act, R.S.O. 1990, c. C-30, s. 1(1); Mechanics' Lien Act, R.S.N.S. 1989, c. 277, s. 13(2). (Subsequent references to these particular acts in footnotes will be simply to B.C., Ont. and N.S. followed by section number.)

[71] (1910), 22 O.L.R. 176, per Moss, C.J.O., at 180.

[72] This type of lien is available in Ontario, Alberta, Newfoundland and Saskatchewan: see, for example, Ont. s. 1(1) and 14(1).

[73] Crowell Bros. v. Maritime Minerals Ltd., [1940] 2 D.L.R. 472.

[74] B.C., s. 4; Ont. s. 15; N.S., s. 6(1).

provision that a term in a contract of employment waiving the employee's right of lien is void. However, in some provinces this provision does not apply to employees whose wages exceed a specified amount per day.

Provincial acts give wage-earners a priority for approximately one month's arrears of wages over all other liens derived through the same contractor or subcontractor.[75] This priority recognizes the fact that wages often provide the sole means of subsistence of wage-earners, while suppliers of materials and lessors of equipment probably carry on business with several construction projects at once, and usually have larger capital funds to depend on if a single contractor or owner defaults in payment.

Procedures under a Mechanics' Lien Act

A mechanic's lien arises immediately upon work being done or materials being supplied for the improvement of property or (in some provinces) upon the supply of rented equipment for use on a contract site. To make a lien legally actionable, the lienholder must register it. It may be registered during the performance of the work or services or supply of material or within a specified period of time after completion or abandonment of performance. The specified period is, for example, 31 days in British Columbia, and 45 days in Nova Scotia and Ontario.[76] If a lien is not registered within the time specified it ceases to exist. Registration gives a lienholder a period within which it must commence a legal action — usually 90 days after the work has been completed or the materials have been placed or furnished, or after the expiry of the period of credit.[77] For this purpose provinces have interpreted "completion of the contract" to mean "substantial performance of the contract".[78] Registration also gives a contractor or subcontractor a lien against the property itself.

In most of the provinces, an action brought by one lien claimant is deemed to be brought on behalf of all other lien claimants, and it is unnecessary even to name other lien claimants as participants since they must be served with notice of the trial.[79]

A lien may be registered against land in the same way and same place as are other interests in land. Registration provides public notice of a lienholder's claim and establishes the lienholder's priority over unsecured creditors of the owner of the property and over subsequent mortgagees and purchasers of an interest in the property. After registration, a lien expires unless the lienholder brings an action to enforce the claim within the prescribed time and registers a certificate stating that the action has been started, or unless another lienholder starts an action within this period.

A mechanic's lien does not give a lienholder the right personally to take possession of or to sell land and buildings to realize a claim. In fact, if the lienholder is a subcontractor and if the owner pays the statutory holdback into court, the lienholder's rights are limited to its share in this fund: it has no rights against the land and buildings of the owner. Even if an owner fails to pay the statutory holdback into court, the lienholder's claim against the land is limited to the amount the owner should have paid into court. To realize its claim against the land, a lienholder, whether a main contractor or a subcontractor, must first bring an action and obtain a court order appointing a trustee. The trustee then has

---

[75] B.C., s. 6(4); Ont., s. 81; N.S., s. 16.
[76] B.C., s. 22(4); Ont., s. 31; N.S., s. 24.
[77] B.C., s. 25(1) (one year); Ont., s. 36; N.S., s. 26(1).
[78] B.C., s. 1; Ont., s. 2.
[79] Ont., ss. 50(3) and 59; N.S., ss. 34(4) and (5).

the power to manage the property and to sell it for the benefit of the lienholder and other creditors. If eventually the trustee does sell the property, he must pay the proceeds to satisfy, first, the claims for municipal taxes; second, those of mortgagees who have prior registered mortgages; third, lienholders' claims for wages regardless of the order in which they filed their liens; fourth, all other lienholders' claims regardless of the order in which they filed their liens; fifth, subsequent mortgagees or other persons who have a secured interest in the land; and, finally, if there are any proceeds left, claims of the general creditors of the owner.[80] After all creditors are paid, any balance remaining belongs to the owner.

During the construction of a building and for the specified statutory period afterwards, the owner may safely make progress payments to the contractor for all amounts except the statutory holdback.[81] However, if the owner receives notice from subcontractors or suppliers that liens are outstanding and unlikely to be paid by the contractor, she should cease payments to the contractor at once and ascertain the extent of the liens. If there is some doubt whether the holdback is sufficient to satisfy the claims for liens, she should seek legal advice immediately; as soon as she has knowledge of these claims, she loses the protection of the Mechanics' Lien Act to the extent that she continues to make payments to the contractor. On the other hand, she must not make the error of wrongfully withholding payment due to a solvent contractor because of an unfounded claim for a lien.

In some jurisdictions, all money received by contractors and subcontractors on account of the contract price are deemed to be trust funds held for the benefit of those who have performed work or services or furnished materials. The contractor or subcontractor, accordingly, cannot divert those funds to its own use until all of the claims against it are satisfied.[82]

Once the statutory period has elapsed and no claims have been registered, the owner may pay the amount withheld to the contractor and so complete her obligations under the contract.

Practical Application of Mechanics' Liens

An owner of land usually finances a construction project by mortgaging the land to a mortgagee who advances the mortgage money as work progresses on the building. Some mechanics' lien acts require a mortgagee to withhold from the mortgage advances an amount equal to the sum that the owner should withhold from the contractor. Even if the act does not have such requirements, it is sensible for a mortgagee to do so to protect the mortgagor (owner), who is liable to subcontractors and suppliers for the amount of the holdback if the contracting firm does not pay its accounts.

When a tenant contracts to have a building erected on his landlord's property or, perhaps more commonly, to have improvements made to existing buildings, a mechanic's lien is not enforceable against the landlord's interest in the property unless the lienholder can establish that the work was undertaken either expressly or impliedly at the request of the landlord.

---

[80] The problem of priorities, particularly those respecting lienholders as opposed to prior and subsequent mortgagees, is complex and technical. See Macklem and Bristow, *Construction and Mechanics' Liens in Canada* (5th ed.), Chapter 8. Toronto: Carswell, 1985.

[81] B.C., s. 20(3); Ont., s. 22(1); N.S., s. 13(5).

[82] Ont., s. 7(4).

We should note that the party that takes the greatest risk in the construction industry is the general contractor. Most large contracts are awarded by tender to the lowest bidder with a sound reputation. In this highly competitive business, contractors often cut their margin both for errors and profit to a very small sum in order to win a contract. Bad luck in the form of unexpectedly difficult foundation work, bad weather delaying the project, a breakdown of essential equipment, an accident seriously injuring key personnel, or a labour dispute, may leave a contractor in a deficit position. Mismanagement or inadvertence, such as making a mistake in calculating an important cost figure in the contract or underestimating the cost of subcontracts, may also bring failure to a contractor.

Even when her contractor is in financial difficulty, an owner incurs no liability herself if she follows the procedures of the mechanics' lien act. The subcontractors, on the other hand, take the risk that the holdback will not be sufficient to pay their claims. Where the subcontract is for a large sum of money, they generally protect themselves by receiving progress payments from the contractor: they do not let themselves get too far ahead in the work without being paid a proportion of the price.

Contractors often undertake to construct buildings on land owned by themselves, especially residential buildings. Usually a builder erects such a building with a view to selling it soon after its completion. If bad luck or mismanagement should cause his insolvency, his "subcontracts" with specialized trades are really main contracts with himself as owner. Accordingly, the land is subject to liability for the total value of the liens, and the holdback provisions do not apply. Often a builder will have obtained mortgage money on the land; the mortgagee will have priority over the lienholders for the money already advanced to the builder before the liens arise. When a mortgagor becomes insolvent, his mortgagee usually stops making progress payments immediately. If the lienholders and mortgagee can come to an agreement, the mortgagee may advance the rest of the money to permit the completion of the building, thus making it easier to sell and realize sufficient funds to pay off the lienholders, and perhaps to obtain a sound buyer who will manage the property successfully and honour the mortgage commitments.

$\mathcal{L}$IMITATIONS OF CREDITORS' RIGHTS

The Effect of Limitations Statutes

We noted in Chapter 15 that a promisee who has a right of action against a promisor who defaults payment on a debt or who is in breach of contract must begin an action within a prescribed period or lose the right to sue. In the common law provinces the remedy for breach of ordinary contracts is barred when six years have elapsed from the time the right of action arose.[83] A plaintiff must start court proceedings within the six-year period or lose the right to resort to the courts. Such limitations on actions are justified as being in the public interest: the opportunity for litigation should end after a certain defined period because, first, a person who neglects to pursue a claim leaves the other party in a state of uncertainty which ought not to continue perpetually; and second, as the years pass it becomes more difficult to adduce the evidence concerning

---

[83] See, for example: Limitation Act, R.S.B.C. 1979, c. 236, s. 3, as amended, S.B.C. 1987, c. 22; Limitation Act, R.S.O. 1990, c. L-15, s. 45(1)(g); Limitation of Actions Act, R.S.N.S. 1989, c. 258, s. 2(1)(e).

the facts of the case — memories may fade and witnesses die, and important records may be lost.

It is important to ascertain when a right of action "arises" in order to calculate the limitation period. A right of action does not arise until there has been a breach or default. Thus, in a contract for the sale of goods on credit, the seller's right of action does not arise at the time of the making of the contract or even at the time of the delivery of the goods, but only when the price falls due and the buyer fails to pay. A trade account receivable often comprises a number of charges for goods or services invoiced at different times in the past and since paid in part. A customer (debtor) is entitled to specify the particular purchases against which a payment on account is to be applied, but in the absence of such instructions the supplier (creditor) is entitled to treat each payment as discharging the oldest outstanding purchases and so to keep the debt current.

Ways in Which the Limitation Period is Extended

We noted in Chapter 26 in our discussion of adverse possession that if at any time after the statutory limitation period begins, a person in adverse possession acknowledges the owner's right by paying rent, he ceases to be an adverse possessor. The limitation period stops running; an entirely new limitation period begins to run if the tenant remains in possession after the period for which he has paid rent expires. In a similar manner, the limitation period for an action for breach of contract starts over again if the debtor makes a part payment or delivers a written promise to pay; the creditor has six years to bring its action from the time of the making of the part payment or delivery of the written promise.

An important difference exists, however, between limitation periods regarding possession of land and limitations of actions in contract. When a limitation period runs out against the owner of land, her title is extinguished — it is completely gone. When a limitation period against a contractual right of action expires, the debt is not extinguished — only the legal remedy is barred. The statute has provided the debtor with a shield, but he may, if he chooses, throw it aside. If the debtor makes a new promise to pay the debt, he is bound by his promise and may be sued upon it. In these circumstances the creditor sues not on the original claim but on the new promise to pay. We see here a modification of the doctrine of consideration: the still-existing but statute-barred debt provides good consideration for the subsequent promise of the debtor. Since the creditor's right of action is derived from the new promise, the creditor has no greater rights than the new promise bestows. Thus, if the debtor promises to pay the debt out of the proceeds of a particular transaction if it should produce a profit, or if he promises to pay only half the sum in satisfaction of the whole debt, the creditor's rights are limited to suing on those terms.[84]

To be enforceable by a creditor, limitations statutes required a promise to pay a statute-barred debt to be in writing; the creditor could not sue on an oral promise alone. Although this requirement appeared in early limitation acts in England, courts of equity ignored it when the oral promise was accompanied by a part payment of the debt; they permitted the creditor to sue on the oral promise. This exception to the requirement of writing is now formally recognized in most of the limitations statutes.[85]

---

[84] See *Phillips v. Phillips* (1844), 67 E.R. 388, per Sir James Wigram, V.C., at 396.

[85] See, for example: *Limitation Act*, R.S.B.C. 1979, c. 236, s. 5(2)(a)(ii); *Limitations Act*, R.S.O. 1990, c. L-15, s. 50.

A debtor need not make an express promise to pay; his promise to pay may be implied from the circumstances of the part payment. Generally speaking, a presumption of a new promise to pay arises from the mere fact of making a part payment without other evidence to contradict the presumption. But if a debtor should say, "Take this — it is all you are going to get", then, of course, no such presumption arises, and the creditor has no right of action for the balance. The reasoning applies as well to a written acknowledgment of a debt. A written acknowledgment is not an express promise to pay, but usually such a promise is implied in the debtor's acknowledgment. The terms of the acknowledgment itself or the surrounding circumstances may, however, contradict such an implication — as when a debtor writes to a creditor, stating: "I know I owe you $1000, but the debt is barred by the Limitations Act. Since I believe you overcharged on the contract price anyway, I have no intention of paying this balance." Quite clearly, no implied promise to pay arises from such a statement.

Limitations in Other Types of Actions

The limitation period for actions on negotiable instruments is the same as for ordinary contracts, six years. When a cause of action arises from breach of a promise under seal, the limitation period is considerably longer, usually twenty years, but it may vary according to the subject-matter of the promise. For example, the personal covenant of a mortgagor in a mortgage of land is discharged after ten years in some provinces.

Each province has a general limitations statute governing limitation periods for a number of different classes of actions. In addition, numerous other statutes, both federal and provincial, prescribe limitation periods for various rights of action under them. Some of these statutes extinguish the cause of action; others only bar recourse to the courts. The limitation periods vary from a few days to many years, according to the purposes that the statute serves. For this reason, when considering starting an action or defending one under the provisions of a statute, a lawyer first checks to see if a limitation period may affect the rights of the parties.

Questions for Review

1. Explain each of the following terms: void assignment; receiving order; preferred creditor; lienholder; holdback; authorized assignment; licensed trustee; liquidating dividend; undischarged bankrupt; insolvent person; bulk sale.
2. What are the purposes of the present federal bankruptcy legislation? In what ways does the Bankruptcy and Insolvency Act attempt to accomplish these purposes?
3. Why is a creditor likely to be concerned on learning that another creditor has obtained an execution order against the debtor?
4. What is the difference between a receiving order and an assignment under the Bankruptcy and Insolvency Act?
5. What steps may an insolvent person take to avoid bankruptcy?
6. Describe briefly three acts of bankruptcy. What is the legal significance of a debtor committing an act of bankruptcy?
7. What is the difference between an act of bankruptcy and a bankruptcy offence?
8. What is the value to a bankrupt debtor of obtaining a discharge from a court?
9. Upon its debtor becoming bankrupt, when may a secured creditor retain the assets it holds as security?

10. Should a licensed trustee pay preferred creditors before settling with secured creditors?
11. What are the duties of a bankrupt debtor?
12. What procedure should a buyer of a business follow when the seller discloses that the sale price is insufficient to pay all the seller's creditors in full?
13. Why is it important for a buyer in a bulk sale to comply with the Bulk Sales Act?
14. What is the difference in effect of a limitation period expiring against an interest in land and one expiring against a right of action for breach of contract?
15. What is the difference in the security of a supplier of materials for use in the construction of a building when (a) the building is being built by a contracting firm on land it owns, and (b) the building is being built by a contractor engaged by the owner of the land?
16. What types of creditors are normally protected by mechanics' lien legislation?
17. How are the rights of an unpaid seller of goods protected by the Bankruptcy and Insolvency Act?

Problems

Problem 1

Doba, a contractor, laid a cement floor in Brown's garage. Brown refused to pay for the work on the grounds that the grade on the floor did not drain water properly whenever water got into the garage. Two years after the floor was built, in response to a demand for payment, Brown wrote as follows, "We have discussed this matter many times, and you should know by now that I will never pay for this work until you correct the grade of my garage floor." Doba did not do further work to change the grade. Five years after receiving the letter quoted above, Doba sued Brown for the price originally agreed.

Should Doba succeed? Discuss the nature of Brown's possible defences.

Problem 2

Martin's creditors obtained a receiving order against him and had a trustee appointed to realize his assets. In the course of his duties the trustee was unable to account for the disappearance of certain assets which once appeared on Martin's books. Martin disclaimed any knowledge of them. Upon further investigation the trustee discovered that two months prior to the receiving order, Martin deposited $2000 cash in his wife's savings account and gave $3000 worth of merchandise to a creditor, Jensen, in settlement of a business debt of $2700.

Discuss the consequences of this discovery for each of the following persons: (a) Mrs. Martin, (b) Jensen, (c) Martin himself.

Problem 3

At various times between 1984 and 1988, Kelly Sands had acted as lawyer for Waters & Co. Ltd., representing it in a series of real estate transactions and in the incorporation of a subsidiary. Sands' total fees for these services had accumulated to $8000. Following an interview with company management on August 5, 1988, the treasurer gave Sands the company's cheque for $5000. The cheque was dated August 5 but at the treasurer's request Sands agreed not to cash it until the end of the month when the company's cash flow position would be better able to handle it.

Sands cashed the cheque on September 2 but did nothing to collect the balance of her account. She died in June 1994. In the course of winding up her estate, her executrix sought to recover the balance of $3000. When Waters & Co. Ltd. failed to pay, the executrix issued a writ on August 26, 1994.

Should this action succeed? Is there any additional information you would like?

Problem 4

Frontenac Manufacturing Co. Ltd. engaged Acme Construction Co. Ltd. to construct a new plant. Acme estimated that it would require 60 000 bricks for the job and ordered that quantity at $71 per thousand from Mason Builders' Supplies Ltd. Mason delivered the bricks to Acme's warehouse. Subsequently Acme found that it had miscalculated and needed only 40 000 bricks for the Frontenac building; it used the remaining 20 000 bricks on another job. Acme failed to pay Mason and became insolvent. Mason registered a lien against Frontenac's new building claiming $4260 from the holdback.

Should Mason succeed? What change in procedure in the sale of the bricks between Mason and Acme would affect the result?

Cases

Case 1

Pavlovic awarded a contract to Dawson Bros., builders, for the erection of a house on Pavlovic's land. The price of the house was $72 000. Pavlovic was a man of substance, whereas Dawson Bros. was a new contracting firm of no financial standing.

Dawson Bros. ordered lumber from Hill Lumber Co. to be used in the construction of the Pavlovic house. Before Hill supplied the lumber, its manager wrote to Pavlovic as follows: "We are furnishing building material to Dawson Bros. for the construction of your residence. We would ask you to see that this material is paid for before settling with Dawson Bros. in full; otherwise we will have to protect ourselves in the usual manner." Hill Lumber began deliveries to Dawson Bros., but, not receiving a reply from Pavlovic, refused to complete the deliveries unless Pavlovic promised to become personally responsible for the whole amount. Pavlovic then gave the required undertaking in writing, and Hill made deliveries to Dawson to the value of $23 200.

While the house was being built, Pavlovic made progress payments from time to time to Dawson Bros. In making the payments he withheld 15% of the value of the house to its then-current stage of construction, as estimated by the architect; this was the percentage specified in the Mechanics' Lien Act of the province. To keep Dawson Bros. going on with the construction work, Pavlovic paid out of the money held back some $4500 for the workers' wages and electrical and plumbing services. Finally, when the house was nearly finished, Dawson Bros. abandoned the contract. By this time, Pavlovic had made progress payments totalling $59 000 and the architect's estimate of value was $70 000. It cost Pavlovic a further $3800 in wages to complete the building on his own.

Dawson Bros. had paid Hill Lumber Co. $5200 on account when it abandoned the contract. Hill Lumber Co. then sought the balance of its account, $18 000, from Pavlovic. He refused to pay, claiming that he was liable for only the balance of the money he had held back in making his progress payments to Dawson Bros., viz., $6000. Pavlovic paid the $6000 into court. Hill Lumber Co. duly registered a mechanic's lien against Pavlovic's house and brought an action against him for $18 000, asking also for a court order that if the requested judgment for $18 000 was not satisfied by Pavlovic, the house should be sold and the judgment satisfied out of the proceeds.

What should the result of the action be?

Case 2

The N.S.F. Manufacturing Co. Ltd. was adjudged bankrupt on a petition of its creditors, and the trustee in bankruptcy realized the following amounts from the sale of its business assets:

Cash in bank	$ 1 000
Accounts receivable	7 000
Inventories	36 000
Land and buildings	52 000
	$96 000

The liabilities of the business were as follows at the time of the receiving order:

Bank loan secured under section 427	
of the Bank Act	$20 000
Trade accounts payable	34 800
Municipal taxes payable	1 200
Wages payable (five months at $600	
per month for one employee)	3 000
First mortgage on land and buildings	31 000
Second mortgage on land and buildings	24 000
	$114 000

The expenses of liquidation were $1600. The trustee's fee was $1800.

How many cents on the dollar will the general creditors receive? Show the order in which the trustee in bankruptcy should make payments to the various types of creditors. Assume that all secured creditors had taken the necessary steps to protect their security.

Case 3

The Canadian Goldentone Corporation Ltd., manufacturers of stereo components and television picture tubes, purchased substantial quantities of electrical parts from Koyle Electric Ltd. during the past four years. During this period Koyle Electric Ltd. assigned individually and for value all its accounts receivable to A.S.B. Factors, Inc., who then undertook their collection. All of the invoices of Koyle Electric to Canadian Goldentone were stamped with a notification that the sum shown as owing had been assigned to A.S.B. and directed that payment be made to A.S.B.

In November last, Koyle Electric contracted to buy from Canadian Goldentone a number of stereo tuners to be used as prizes in a sales promotion contest; the total price was $4900, payable 60 days after delivery. Canadian Goldentone delivered the tuners. At the time, it owed Koyle Electric $14 700, representing a number of individual purchases for which it had already been invoiced. In the following month Koyle Electric made an authorized assignment under the Bankruptcy Act, its management having conceded that the company had become insolvent. Canadian Goldentone had made no further purchases of parts from Koyle Electric after it sold Koyle the stereo tuners.

Realizing that if it had to file a claim against the bankrupt estate of Koyle Electric Ltd. it would probably realize much less than the $4900 owing to it for the stereo tuners, Canadian Goldentone proposed to set this amount off against its account payable of $14 700 and to pay the factor, A.S.B., the net amount of $9800. A.S.B. Factors Inc. refused, however, to accept the tender of $9800 and sued Canadian Goldentone Corporation Ltd. for the full amount of $14 700.

Should A.S.B. succeed? Give reasons. (See *L.F. Dommerich & Co. Inc. v. Canadian Admiral Corporation Ltd.* (1962), 34 D.L.R. (2d) 530).

Case 4

Rena Jones incorporated an Ontario corporation, Jones Cement Ltd., in 1992. On January 2, 1993, she went to a finance company, Financial Acceptance Corporation (F.A.C.) and asked for a loan on some equipment that Jones Cement Ltd. then owned. She stated that there were no *liens,* charges or *writs of execution* outstanding against Jones Cement Ltd. or against any of its assets. F.A.C. decided to grant the loan if Ms. Jones' guaranteed payment personally. On January 10, 1993, Ms. Jones went to F.A.C.'s office and signed on behalf of Jones Cement Ltd. a *chattel mortgage* for $90 000 on the equipment. There were still no liens, charges or writs of execution against the company. Ms. Jones was also asked to sign the chattel mortgage as guarantor. The guarantee was on the same document, and was under seal: it was a personal guarantee in which Ms. Jones agreed to pay any sums not paid to F.A.C. by Jones Cement Ltd. (This is a standard business practice.)

On May 1, 1993, everything went wrong and Jones Cement Ltd. filed an *assignment in bankruptcy.* F.A.C. claimed in the bankruptcy as a secured creditor relying upon its chattel mortgage.

The trustee in bankruptcy would not allow the claim, alleging that F.A.C. had not filed a *financing statement* and therefore had not properly registered the chattel mortgage. The Court upheld the trustee's position and F.A.C. was forced to file a proof of claim in the bankruptcy as an unsecured creditor. If F.A.C. had been a secured creditor it would have been able to recover the full amount of the loan, i.e., $90 000. However, as an unsecured creditor, F.A.C. received only $12 000.

After receiving the $12 000, F.A.C's solicitors wrote to Ms. Jones demanding payment of the remaining $78 000, stating that they were relying on the guarantee signed by Ms. Jones. When Ms. Jones refused to pay, F.A.C. served her with a statement of claim at her home in Mississauga. She entered an appearance to the action and subsequently filed a statement of defence. At the spring assizes the trial came on before Keensight, J. at the Brampton sittings.

Ms. Jones' defence was that she had relied on F.A.C. to register the chattel mortgage properly and that because of its neglect to do so, F.A.C. could not transfer a right to full recovery to her by way of subrogation. F.A.C.'s position was that the guarantee was a separate and distinguishable contract and did not gain its validity from the proper or improper registration of the chattel mortgage.

After hearing all the evidence and arguments from both sides, Keensight, J. reserved his decision.

    (a) Briefly define each term and phrase italicized in the case, and explain its use or significance.

    (b) Discuss the defences put forward by Ms. Jones and state, with reasons, whether you think the action against her would succeed or fail.

PART EIGHT

INTERNATIONAL TRANSACTIONS

Our final Chapter deals with matters that do not fit readily under the headings of previous Parts of this book. Certainly, international business transactions are primarily contractual in nature, and we might have included them in Part Four, under the title "Special Types of Contracts". However, as we shall see, when a business operates internationally it must be concerned with far more than just its contractual relationships with its customers and suppliers. International business is extensively regulated by governments, so that the legal relationship between an importer or exporter and the governments of the countries concerned in the transaction is often at least as important as is that between the private parties involved. International business consequently has both a private law and a public law dimension. But there is yet a third dimension to consider — international law: the treaties and agreements made between governments are also an important factor in international business.

The conduct of international business generally involves a wide variety of legal issues. To understand them, it is useful to consider how firms become "international", or "multinational". The establishment of international business operations can be viewed as a progression. Initially, investors establish a firm in a single locality and it begins to market its products in that locality. Gradually, as it prospers, it expands its sphere of operations, selling its goods or services further from home, until it comes to be seen as a substantial regional, or national, undertaking. At some later point it will find a customer for its products in another country and at that time its operations become international and the firm engages in foreign trade.

At first, its foreign market may be restricted to one or two customers. In time, however, as its reputation grows, the firm may find it worthwhile to appoint an agent in the other country or to establish a representative office there. Gradually, its activities expand, from seeking customers and providing information, to supplying spare parts and repairs and maintenance services.

Another important step occurs when the firm commences other activities abroad, such as processing its products. Initially those activities may be quite modest ones, like labelling, packaging or simple assembly of components. Eventually, however, the operations may develop into full-scale manufacturing and a branch plant or a subsidiary may be established. Our original firm has graduated from foreign trade to foreign investment and has become a multinational enterprise .

In this Chapter we deal both with foreign trade and with foreign investment, examining the private relationships between parties to contracts, the public relationships between those parties and the governments concerned, and the international relationships among governments. The final section of the Chapter is devoted to a topic of increasing concern to business everywhere — the resolution of international business disputes.

The topics dealt with in this Chapter are complex and wide-ranging. Each of them has been the subject of voluminous treatises and we cannot hope to do more than provide a brief overview. Our principal aim is to make our readers aware of some of the most important issues and of the problems that may arise when business becomes international.

CHAPTER 35

INTERNATIONAL BUSINESS
TRANSACTIONS

Canadian Business in a Global Economy

Thus far our book has been concerned with law and business administration in Canada. But neither law nor business is restricted to a purely national dimension. Increasingly, the world is becoming a single giant marketplace in which firms from different countries compete against and sometimes cooperate with each other.

For Canada, more than for most other countries, the international dimension of business is especially important. In 1993, for example, Canada's exports of goods totalled approximately $181 billion, or roughly one-quarter of the nation's gross domestic product. Imports of goods totalled $169 billion, so Canada enjoyed a substantial trade surplus,[1] only partly offset by a deficit in commercial services. Among the world's trading nations, Canada ranked eighth in exports of merchandise (after Germany, the United States of America, Japan, France, the United Kingdom, Italy, and the Netherlands), and twelfth in exports of services. To put these figures in perspective, the world's largest exporters, Germany and the U.S.A., with far larger populations, only export approximately three times as much as Canada, and Japan little more than double.[2]

Canada's largest trading partner is the United States, which takes three-quarters of our exports and provides two-thirds of our imports; in turn, Canada is also the largest trading partner of the U.S., exporting more to the U.S. than does Japan. But Canada also has substantial trading relations with countries as diverse as Japan, the United Kingdom, Germany, Korea, China, the Netherlands, France, and Russia. Traditionally, Canada has been seen as an exporter of raw materials and minerals (and indeed remains the world's second largest exporter in those categories), but in more recent years we have also become an important exporter of manufactured goods, chemicals, and transport and telecommunications equipment.

Perhaps of equal importance is the fact that, of the world's major industrialized economies, Canada stands in eighth place as an exporter of investment capital. By the end of 1993, the total stock of Canadian direct investment abroad amounted to $115 billion, while foreign direct investment in Canada totalled $146 billion, the greater proportion of it coming from the United States.[3] Canadian corporations actively carry on business in all parts of the globe, just as foreign-owned corporations are prominent in Canada.

Law and International Business

Foreign trade and foreign investment result in a wide variety of legal relationships. Contractual relationships of many different types arise: sale of goods and services, carriage of goods, bailment, insurance, agency, and employment. Questions regarding the law of negotiable instruments, of intellectual property, of partnerships and corporations,

---

[1] For further data on Canada's international trade, see *Exports: Merchandise Trade 1993* and *Imports: Merchandise Trade 1993*, Ottawa: Statistics Canada, International Trade Division, 1994.
[2] *International Trade 90-91*, Geneva: GATT Secretariat, 1992.
[3] *Canada's International Investment Position*, Ottawa: Statistics Canada, 1993.

of secured transactions and of creditors' remedies are raised. There is, however, an additional complication: international business transactions, by definition, involve parties in two or more different countries. The question must consequently be asked, "which country's law applies to the situation?" This is a question of *private law* — of the law that generally governs transactions between private parties, such as a seller and buyer of goods.

In addition, questions of *public law* commonly arise,[4] since virtually every government regulates foreign trade and investment to some extent, with the result that we must also consider legal relationships between private persons and governments. Finally, governments frequently make bilateral agreements (such as double taxation treaties, investment protection treaties, or the Canada-US Free Trade Agreement) or multilateral agreements (such as the General Agreement on Tariffs and Trade, the North American Free Trade Agreement, or the International Convention for the Protection of Industrial Property). Thus, questions of *public international law*, involving relations between states, also arise.

In this Chapter we shall examine some of the more important legal questions that arise in connection with foreign trade and with foreign investment, considered from the perspectives of private law, public law, and international law. The Chapter will conclude with a brief description of the methods that exist for resolving international business disputes.

Foreign Trade

Export Contracts[5]

Export contracts — they might equally well be termed "import contracts" — generally fall into one of two categories: contracts for the international sale of goods and contracts for the supply of services abroad. Goods or services may be supplied in one of three main ways. The supplier may deliver directly to the customer in the other country; delivery may be made through the supplier's own marketing organization established in the other country; or the customer may accept delivery in the supplier's home country, and himself arrange to ship the goods home. Whichever method is adopted, the contract between supplier and customer constitutes the essence of the transaction. The following discussion will concentrate upon the most common type of export transaction — contracts for the international sale of goods.

The Contract of Sale

Much of what has been written in earlier chapters of this book with respect to the law of contracts and, in particular, to contracts for the sale of goods, applies equally to export contracts as it does to contracts with a purely domestic scope. However, contracts with an international element commonly present special problems. What distinguishes an international contract from a purely domestic one is the simple fact that the goods are to be delivered to, or services supplied to, a customer in another country.

---

[4] For the distinction between private and public law, see Chapter 3.

[5] For a comprehensive study of this subject, see C.M. Schmitthoff, *Export Trade*, 9th ed. London: 1990, Stevens & Sons. A specifically Canadian perspective is provided by J.G. Castel, A.L.C. de Mestral and W.C. Graham, *The Canadian Law and Practice of International Trade,* Toronto: 1991, Emond Montgomery Publications Ltd.

The usual transaction for the international sale of goods involves a number of parties and often consists of several distinct though related contracts. In addition to the basic agreement for sale of the goods, the parties normally arrange for the transportation of the goods, by land, sea, or air, for their insurance during shipment and, frequently, for the financing of the transaction. Thus carriers, insurers, banks, or finance houses may be involved as well as the buyer and seller. Since export transactions require special expertise, the parties commonly employ the services of specialist *export houses* or *freight forwarders*, who make the arrangements for shipment, insurance, and financing.

The Proper Law of the Contract

As we have noted, an export contract by definition involves two or more countries. A question that frequently arises is "Whose law governs the contract or its various component parts?"

ILLUSTRATION

A Canadian manufacturer sells goods to a Hungarian customer. The goods are to be shipped by a German airline, insured by a British insurance company, and financed by a Swiss merchant bank.

Several contracts make up the entire transaction, and each one could be governed by a different law. To determine which law applies, it is necessary to refer to a body of principles known as the *conflict of laws*, or *private international law*. The question is vital, since the laws of the different countries may vary considerably with respect to such matters as the rights of unpaid vendors or carriers, the terms to be implied as to quality or fitness of the goods, or the circumstances in which a contract will be frustrated. Canadian courts, and the courts of most other countries, hold that the proper law of the contract is the law that the parties intended to govern.[6] The clearest method of establishing the proper law is for the parties themselves to make express provision.[7] A contract might state that it is subject to the law of Ontario, or of England, or Switzerland. The choice of law need not be that of the location of one of the parties or be related to the place where the contract is to be performed; sometimes the parties choose a "neutral" law.

Where the parties do not expressly stipulate the proper law, the court will attempt to determine the intention of the parties from the surrounding circumstances. For example, if the contract states that any dispute is to be submitted to arbitration in a particular country, or that the courts of a particular country shall have jurisdiction, then it is probable that they also intended the law of that country to govern the contract.[8] An intention may also be inferred from the use of particular legal terminology or the form of the document. Where the court cannot draw such an inference it will apply the system of law that it considers to be most closely connected with the contract. In making this determination, it will have regard to all the circumstances and pay special attention to such factors as the

---

[6] For detailed consideration of this issue, see J.G. Castel, *Introduction to Conflict of Laws*, 2nd ed. Toronto: 1986, Butterworths.

[7] Vita Foods Products Inc. v. Unus Shipping Co. Ltd. [1939] A.C. 277.

[8] Hamlyn & Co. v. Talisker Distillery [1984] A.C. 202.

place where the contract was made, the place where it is to be performed, the subject matter of the contract, and the place of business of the parties.[9] And since the contract may comprise a number of distinct elements, it is possible that different laws may apply to different parts.[10]

Contractual Terms

Another difficulty is that different terms or expressions may have different meanings in different legal systems or to parties from different countries. In practice the problem is not so severe as it might seem; over the centuries a widely accepted standard terminology has evolved. Initially, the meaning of terms such as "F.O.B." and "C.I.F.", which we encountered in Chapter 18, became largely standardized through mercantile custom. More recently, a set of standard terms (known as "Incoterms"), adopted by the International Chamber of Commerce, have come to be widely used; the original Incoterms were first published in 1936, and the current version dates from 1990.

Another important development has been the publication, and widespread adoption, of standard form contracts, published by various trade associations and by international bodies such as the United Nations Economic Commission for Europe (UNECE). Other international organizations, such as the International Institute for the Unification of Private Law (UNIDROIT) and the United Nations Commission on International Trade Law (UNCITRAL) have encouraged the harmonization of national commercial laws or the adoption of uniform laws. One significant result was the adoption, in 1980, of the Vienna Convention on Contracts for the International Sale of Goods, since implemented in Canada.[11] The standardization of terms and practices has been important in reducing disputes; the terms are familiar to commercial arbitrators, with the result that a common international standard of interpretation has emerged. The process of standardization is an ongoing one, continually evolving in order to keep up with developments such as containerization and electronic data processing.

The Documentation

An export sale normally requires at least four documents. These are:

(1) the contract of sale;
(2) the bill of lading;
(3) the insurance policy or certificate; and
(4) the invoice.

We have already discussed the contract of sale. Bills of lading were considered in Chapter 18, and insurance policies are dealt with in Chapter 20. A *bill of lading*, as we have seen, is an acknowledgment by the carrier that the goods have been delivered for shipment; it operates as a document of title to the goods, facilitating the financing of the transaction. The *insurance policy*, similarly, is evidence that the goods are insured against loss or

---

[9] Imperial Life Assurance Co. of Canada v. Colmenares [1967] S.C.R. 443.
[10] M.W. Hardy Inc. v. A.V. Pound & Co. Ltd. [1956] A.C. 588.
[11] International Sale of Goods Contracts Convention Act, S.C. 1991, c. 13. It has also been adopted by several of the provinces; see for example, International Sale of Goods Act, S.N.S. 1988, c. 13; R.S.O. 1990, c. I-10.

damage during transit and is usually necessary in order to obtain financing. The *invoice* is of special importance in international sales of goods and must be correct in every respect, since it provides information not only for the parties to the transaction but also for the customs authorities of the country of importation. The invoice states the names and addresses of the buyer and seller, the date of the order, a full description of the goods sold, details of packaging, and the price (on the basis of which customs duty is normally calculated). It must conform to the requirements of the importing country, which may insist upon the production of additional documents, such as certificates of value, origin, quality, or inspection. In recent years these traditional forms of documentation have begun to be replaced by computerized communications: bodies such as the Comité Maritime International have devised uniform sets of rules dealing with *electronic data exchange* in international business transactions.[12]

Shipment and Insurance

Since it is the shipment of goods to another country that distinguishes the international sale of goods from purely domestic transactions, shipping arrangements are an essential element of an export sale. The parties may agree that the buyer will collect the goods from the seller's factory and make its own arrangements for transportation, or that the seller will deliver the goods to the buyer's premises in the other country, or that each will be responsible for some stage of the transportation. Usually, too, the goods will be insured against loss or damage during transit and either the buyer or the seller may assume responsibility for arranging insurance. The contract price reflects whether it is the seller or the buyer who arranges and pays for shipment and insurance, and up to which stage of the journey. A seller may quote a price *ex works* (i.e. at the factory gate); if it is agreed to deliver the goods to the buyer's own premises, the total price will be correspondingly higher. And as we saw in Chapter 18, the precise arrangements for shipment may determine the point at which title to the goods, or the risk of loss, passes from the seller to the buyer.

Over the centuries a number of standard terms have evolved to describe the more common types of arrangements for shipment. Examples of these terms (with the corresponding Incoterm abbreviations) are:

- EXW (Ex Works);
- FOB (Free on Board);
- CIF (Cost, Insurance and Freight); and
- DDP (Delivery Duty Paid).

These terms broadly correspond to the various stages of shipment and the extent of the obligations undertaken by the seller. Thus, in EXW contracts, the seller's responsibility is only to make the goods available to the buyer at the seller's own works or warehouse. The buyer bears the cost, and the risk, of transportation, though the seller is still obliged to furnish the necessary invoice and to provide all reasonable assistance to obtain any export licence or other authorization necessary for exporting the goods.

---

[12] See Kindred, "Trading Internationally by Electronic Bills of Lading", (1992) 7 *Banking and Finance Law Rev.* 264.

Under an FOB contract, the buyer arranges shipment and the seller's obligation is to deliver the goods to the carrier named by the buyer. The seller's responsibility ends when the goods are safely on board the ship or aircraft. Other variants are the FCA (Free to Carrier) and FAS (Free Alongside Ship) contracts, where the seller's duty is, respectively, to deliver to the first carrier (for example, where the goods are collected by the carrier and loaded into a container for shipment to a cargo terminal), and to deliver to a specified pier or warehouse at the port of shipment.

A CIF contract represents a major extension of the seller's obligations. Here, the seller assumes responsibility for shipping the goods to the country of destination. The seller is responsible not only for shipment to the port of destination but also for insuring the goods.[13] A final category of contracts extends the obligations of the seller still further, with the seller bearing the risks and costs of transporting the goods to an agreed destination, and sometimes (as in a DDP contract) even paying the import duties.

As new methods of goods transportation are developed, so also are new types of contractual terms. The use of pallets, of roll-on/roll-off ferries and, especially, of containers, has revolutionized the carriage of goods and, in turn, has led to the development of new legal terms, such as FCL and LCL. Where the consignment comprises a full container load (FCL), shipment may be made door-to-door in a sealed container; if there is less than a full container load (LCL), the goods are consolidated with the goods of other exporters in a "groupage container" and are loaded, and separated, at a container freight station.

Payment

A basic element in any contract of sale is the payment of the price. In an international contract the currency used to denominate the price and to make payment is important. The price may be denominated in one currency but paid in some other currency, and it is even becoming common to denominate the price in a "non-currency", such as the ECU or SDR, which cannot be used for making payment.[14] Generally, a seller does not mind in which currency the price is paid, so long as that currency is freely convertible. However, it will state the price in a stable currency, especially if there is to be a substantial time lag between contract and payment and, if the buyer's country imposes *exchange controls*, or does not permit its currency to be freely converted — as is often the case in developing countries — the seller will also require actual payment to be made in a "hard" currency. An exporter or importer may also "hedge" against the risk of currency fluctuations by using a method of *foreign exchange risk management*, such as borrowing in foreign currency or taking an option to buy or sell foreign currency.[15]

Financing

Financing is especially important in international sales, partly because the time between the goods leaving the seller and reaching the buyer tends to be longer than in domestic

---

[13] Under a CFR (Cost and Freight) contract, the seller pays carriage but the buyer arranges its own insurance.

[14] The ECU (European Currency Unit) and SDR (Special Drawing Rights) are not really currencies at all, but are used for determining rates of exchange. Thus an ECU can be translated into a corresponding number of francs, marks, pounds, or dollars.

[15] See further P. Raworth, *Legal Guide to International Business Transactions,* Toronto: 1991, Carswell, at 112-15.

sales, and partly because the amounts involved in international sales tend to be larger. A seller would like to receive payment as soon as its goods leave the factory or warehouse, whereas the buyer would prefer to postpone payment until the goods have been safely delivered. To accommodate both preferences normally requires the services of a banker.

For a long time the *bill of exchange* (see Chapter 24) was the most important method of payment in export sales. In recent years, other methods of financing have been devised, the most important of which are the *collection arrangement* and the *letter of credit*. Under a collection arrangement the seller employs the services of its bank to collect payment, by depositing the documents with the bank and receiving credit for the price (less the bank's charges). By contrast, a buyer obtains a letter of credit from its bank and uses it to pay the seller.[16] More recently, banks and finance houses have developed other highly flexible methods of financing — such as non-recourse finance, factoring, and financial leasing — methods that require more detailed explanation and are beyond the scope of this book.[17]

Countertrade

Earlier in this Chapter we referred to exchange controls. A number of developing countries and countries in the formerly-socialist bloc found it necessary to impose exchange controls or restrictions on the convertibility of their currencies, especially after the debt crisis of the 1970s. In order to protect their balance of payments, governments in those countries permitted firms to import goods, and to obtain the hard currency to pay for them, only if in turn they were able to earn hard currency by exporting their own products. These restrictions led to the development of the practice known as "countertrade". In its simplest form, countertrade is a form of barter: a seller agrees to accept, instead of money, payment in goods produced or procured by the buyer. In one well-known example, an American firm sold insulating material in China and received silk carpets in return. Another increasingly common arrangement is for a Western corporation that sells machinery to a firm in a developing country to agree to accept part of that firm's production as the price; thus it might sell modern cutting and sewing equipment and receive finished clothing in return. The variety of forms of countertrade is virtually unlimited, but it should be emphasized that countertrade involves greater risks than do simple sales, since the "seller" will have to find a way of disposing of the goods acquired in exchange.

Export of Services

The "export" of services can take a number of forms. A buyer may come to a seller, as where a foreign tourist stays in a hotel or attends a concert in Canada. Transactions of this nature generally do not involve any element of foreign law. Or a seller might go to a buyer, as where a Canadian bank or insurance company opens a branch in another country to serve customers there. It is also possible for services to be "transmitted" to customers in other countries. Data, legal or financial advice, or technological expertise may be supplied to customers in other countries. Property in one country may be insured by an insurance company in another country. Banks may lend money to foreign clients. Approximately 20 percent of the total worldwide volume of exports is now comprised of services. Much of what has been said in relation to the international sale of goods applies

---

[16] An alternative method is for the buyer to obtain a banker's guarantee. (See Chapter 20).
[17] For full consideration, see Schmitthoff (n.5), Chap. 24.

equally to the provision of services — for example, the importance of determining the proper law of the contract, and the problems of payment. Of particular importance, in contracts involving the transfer of technology, are the local rules governing the protection of intellectual property. A Canadian corporation that licenses a patent or a trademark, or supplies "know-how", to an enterprise in another country will be concerned to ensure that its rights are protected by the laws of that country and that its trade secrets do not become public knowledge.[18]

Establishing an Overseas Marketing Organization

As the volume of a firm's export business grows it may consider establishing a marketing organization in those countries where it does substantial business. At first, a firm may find it sufficient to appoint or employ an *agent* in the other country to solicit business, transmit orders, or provide information to prospective customers. Such an arrangement obviously raises questions of agency law, but more important, it may be a key factor in determining whether the exporter is considered to be carrying on business in the other country and as a result becomes subject to its laws — especially its tax laws. An alternative strategy is to enter into a *sole distributorship* agreement with a firm in the other country. Again, special attention must be given to the protection of trademark or patent rights. Finally, a firm may decide to establish a more permanent presence in the other country, in the form of a branch plant or subsidiary corporation. We shall deal with this stage later, under the heading "Foreign Investment".

Government Regulation of International Trade

Ever since foreign trade first began, governments have sought to regulate it by controlling exports and imports and by imposing customs duties. Countries consider trade relations a matter of national importance and although many countries, such as Canada and most of its major trading partners, are broadly committed to the principle of free trade they still maintain numerous barriers that a would-be exporter must overcome. A particular concern of governments is to preserve a reasonable balance of trade with other countries; consequently the tendency is to encourage exports and discourage imports.

Export Promotion

Governments provide a variety of services to their own producers in order to assist them to compete in the global market. An important function of Canadian embassy staff abroad is to collect commercial information and disseminate it to Canadian business. More tangible support, mostly in the form of insurance, guarantees, and financial services, is provided by the Export Development Council, a crown corporation whose purpose is to facilitate and develop Canada's export trade, and by other specialist bodies such as the Canadian Wheat Board. Government support is especially important with respect to exports to less-developed countries, by providing loan guarantees and long-term credit. International aid programs may also provide indirect assistance to exporters; for example, programs funded by the Canadian International Development Agency (CIDA) frequently require a substantial Canadian content.

---

[18] The protection of intellectual property was considered in Chapter 25.

Export Controls

Although the general policy of most countries is to encourage exports, restrictions upon exports remain common. Export controls in Canada date back to the Export Act of 1897,[19] which regulated the export of a number of commodities, notably lumber. The federal government introduced further controls for reasons of national security during the war of 1914-18, and created a more comprehensive system following the Second World War and the commencement of the "Cold War" in 1947, by the Export and Import Permits Act.[20] The Act introduced a system of licensing for exports of certain listed products and for most exports to listed countries. Among the listed products are armaments, munitions, and other strategic materials; listed countries were mostly confined to members of the then Communist bloc.

Further regulations, and other statutes, have added to the lists both of products and of countries; restrictions have been imposed on the export of certain types of cultural property and of some energy and agricultural products, and from time to time countries such as South Africa, Iran, Libya, Iraq, and Serbia have joined the list of proscribed countries. Canadian membership in NATO has also led to restrictions on exports of high-tech products to Communist and some other countries on the "COCOM list". More recently, the Special Economic Measures Act[21] contains a general power to make orders and regulations restricting or prohibiting the exportation by Canadians of goods, whether from Canada or anywhere else in the world, to designated foreign states or to persons in such states. An added problem, which has probably affected Canada more than any other country, has been the extra-territorial application of American legislation; the legislation is intended to prevent the re-export (from Canada and other countries) of products originating in the U.S. to countries such as Cuba, and also prohibits dealings with those countries by foreign subsidiaries of American corporations.

Import Duties

Customs duties on imports have been in existence almost as long as international trade itself. Originally these duties provided an important source of revenue for many countries; indeed, in 1867 customs duties constituted the major part of federal revenue. The growth of other sources of Government revenue, especially income tax, and the world-wide movement to tariff reduction, have steadily reduced the fiscal importance of import duties; their most important function nowadays is to protect domestic products against competition from cheaper imports.

Two statutes contain most of Canada's import duty legislation: the Customs Act[22] and the Customs Tariff Act.[23] The first deals with the administration of the system by Revenue Canada (Customs and Excise), and provides the basis for regulations that classify products and determine their dutiable value and country of origin. The latter Act sets out the rates of duty (tariff) imposed on each category of products. The setting of tariffs is no longer determined unilaterally by governments, but is largely regulated by international

---

[19] S.C. 1897, c. 17: see now R.S.C. 1985, c. E-18.
[20] S.C. 1947, c. 17; now R.S.C. 1985, c. E-19.
[21] S.C. 1992, c. 17, s. 4.
[22] R.S.C. 1985 (2nd Supp.), c. 1.
[23] R.S.C. 1985 (3rd.Supp.), c. 41.

agreements, such as the GATT and the NAFTA. For goods imported into Canada various preferences are granted, notably for products coming from Commonwealth, Caribbean, and less-developed countries and from our NAFTA partners, Mexico and the United States. Determining the origin of goods consequently becomes very important, since goods may be manufactured in one country, from raw material or components originating in another country, and may be routed via a third country.[24]

Import Restrictions

With the decline in the importance of import duties over the years, the existence of *non-tariff barriers* has become more significant as an obstacle to international trade. Countries often impose restrictions on imports; sometimes they are overt, in other instances they are less visible. By Canadian law, some goods (for example, narcotics) may not be imported at all; others may be imported only under licence and subject to particular conditions. Generally, Canada adopts a relatively liberal policy toward imports from other countries and adheres to the principles established by the GATT. Nevertheless, Canada does impose import *quotas* on certain products,[25] particularly textiles and agricultural products. A wide variety of other statutes impose restrictions on imports in order to protect public health, public safety, the environment, and for other reasons of public policy. Other countries impose their own restrictions and a Canadian manufacturer wishing to export its products must always check to ensure that the products will be allowed to enter the other country. Frequently, national rules on the marketing of products are just as important as restrictions on importation: there is little point exporting products to a country if they cannot legally be resold there. National health and safety standards and labelling requirements must be complied with, and they are sometimes formulated in such a way that, although ostensibly they apply to domestic and imported products alike, in practice they discriminate against imports.

Dumping and Subsidies

The desire to promote exports, by producers themselves and by their governments, sometimes leads to two types of practice that are generally regarded as unfair — *dumping* and *export subsidization*. Dumping occurs where a firm sells goods abroad at prices lower than those at which similar goods sell in the domestic market. In effect, the firm uses the profits on its domestic sales to subsidize its exports and undercut its competitors. Subsidization occurs where the government of a country provides special benefits, financial or otherwise, to its producers in order to assist them to export. Benefits may take a wide variety of forms, such as reduced freight charges, income tax rebates, or unusually favorable credit terms or guarantees.

Dumping and export subsidization, by reducing the price of imported goods, may be regarded as a benefit to the consumers of the importing country. Not surprisingly, those practices are resented by domestic manufacturers of competing products. Where domestic competition exists, and it appears that material injury has been or is likely to be

---

[24] The dispute between Canada and the U.S. regarding the origin of Honda cars manufactured in Canada, using components made in Japan, and sold in the U.S., is a good example.

[25] See Export and Import Permits Act, R.S.C. 1985, c. E-19. Other restrictions are contained in the Customs Act (*supra* n. 22) and the Special Import Measures Act, R.S.C. 1985, c. S-15.

caused to domestic producers of similar goods, importing countries often impose counter-measures to nullify the benefits of foreign subsidies. Counter-measures take the form of *anti-dumping duties* and *countervailing duties,* designed to increase the cost of imports by the amount of the margin of dumping or of the export subsidy. In Canada such duties are imposed under the Special Import Measures Act.[26] Many Canadian exporters have encountered difficulties with the corresponding measures imposed by the United States.[27] We shall return to this issue later, when considering the impact of the Free Trade Agreement and of the NAFTA.

The International Law of Trade

In theory, national governments are free to adopt whatever measures they choose to regulate imports into, and exports from, their own territories. Of course, in doing so they are aware that other countries may retaliate; if Country A imposes restrictions on imports from Country B, it can hardly expect Country B to accept Country A's exports freely. The international law of trade is based to a large extent upon the principle of reciprocity, an approach generally followed in negotiating agreements between states, sometimes on a multilateral basis and sometimes bilaterally. Canada is a party to many such agreements, two of which — the GATT and the North American Free Trade Agreement (NAFTA) — are of particular importance.

The GATT

The General Agreement on Tariffs and Trade (GATT) is the principal instrument that lays down agreed rules for international trade. It came into force on January 1, 1948, with nine members, one of which was Canada. By the end of 1992, a total of 104 countries were members, with a further 28 having applied for membership. GATT membership includes all of the major Western industrialized nations, most of the countries of the former socialist bloc and many less-developed countries, which together account for over 90 percent of total world trade.

The original intention of the GATT was to establish an International Trade Organization (ITO), as a part of the United Nations Organization. This object was only partly achieved, since the ITO as such did not come into existence, but the GATT is nevertheless far more than just a treaty, or collection of treaties. It has its own Secretariat (in Geneva), a Council of Members, and the capacity to establish Tribunals (or Panels) to adjudicate disputes between member countries. Over the years its scope has been extended and its rules augmented by agreements reached in a series of "rounds", the most recent being the so-called "Uruguay Round", commenced in 1986 and finally concluded in December, 1993.

Probably the most serious shortcoming of the GATT was that it applied only to the international trade in goods, and even then did not apply to most agricultural products or to textiles.[28] The Uruguay Round extended GATT arrangements to include trade in farm products, textiles, some services and to the protection of intellectual property rights. It

---

[26] *Supra,* n. 25.
[27] For an interesting example, see IPSCO Inc. & IPSCO Steel Inc. v. United States & Lone Star Steel Co. 899 F.2d. 1192 (U.S. Court of Appeals), and the commentary by McConnell, (1991) 70 *Can.Bar Rev.* 180.
[28] Trade in textiles was in part governed by the Multifibre Agreement (MFN) of 1974.

also extended its application to include TRIMs (*trade-related foreign investment measures*), and considerably strengthened the mechanisms available for the settlement of disputes. Disagreements still remain with respect to cultural exports (e.g. films), maritime trade and financial services. Begining in 1995, the GATT is intended to be known as the "World Trade Organization".

In addition to providing a forum for negotiations and for the resolution of trade disputes, the most important functions of the GATT have been (1) harmonizing customs tariffs, and (2) establishing a body of rules governing trade between contracting states. Probably the greatest single achievement of the GATT has been the progressive reduction and, in some cases, elimination of customs duties. Member states now impose import duties according to a uniform agreed schedule. In addition, the GATT sets out a code of rules governing international trade, the fundamental principle of which is that of non-discrimination. That principle, in turn, has two elements: first, goods originating from one contracting state should not be treated more or less favourably than goods from another state — that is to say, all should receive *most-favoured-nation* (MFN) treatment;[29] second, goods from other contracting states should, once the appropriate tariff has been paid, be treated no less favourably than corresponding domestic goods — that is to say, they should receive *national treatment*. In accordance with these basic principles, the GATT generally prohibits quotas and other forms of non-tariff barriers, export subsidies and, except under strict conditions, the imposition of anti-dumping duties and countervailing duties. The GATT also establishes rules on such matters as the transportation of goods, customs procedures and valuation.

The GATT has had a two-way impact upon Canadian law and the laws of the other contracting states. First, it imposes a positive duty to enact laws to implement obligations agreed to within the GATT framework. Thus, for example, Canada has implemented the GATT tariff schedule through the Customs Tariff Act. Second, it imposes a negative duty not to apply laws that are contrary to the obligations it has undertaken pursuant to the GATT. Consequently, insofar as Canada imposes anti-dumping and countervailing duties, it may do so only within the limits prescribed by the GATT.

North American Free Trade

An exception to the MFN-principle, recognised in the GATT, permits the creation of regional *free-trade areas,* within which customs duties may be eliminated entirely. The most important and best known of such areas is the European Economic Community (EEC), a customs and economic union of twelve West-European states. In 1988 another free trade area was created, with the signing of the Canada-United States Free Trade Agreement. This agreement, which came into force at the beginning of 1989,[30] provides for the phasing out of tariffs in trade between the two nations over a period of ten years. Four years later, on December 17, 1992, the leaders of Canada, Mexico and the United States signed the North American Free Trade Agreement (NAFTA), bringing into existence the world's largest free

---

[29] By way of exception, reduced rates of duty are applied to many goods coming from less-developed countries.
[30] It takes effect in Canada by virtue of the Canada-United States Free Trade Agreement Implementation Act, S.C. 1988, c. 65.

trade area, with more than 360 million consumers.[31] The NAFTA also contains a clause permitting other countries on the American continent to join, and Chile has already announced its intention to apply for membership.

Although the NAFTA is based upon essentially the same principles as the GATT, in many respects it goes considerably further in liberalizing trade and investment. All tariffs on goods between the three countries are to be eliminated, in three stages, by the year 2008. The NAFTA streamlines customs procedures and eliminates user fees. Agricultural products are within the scope of the NAFTA, which provides for the progressive elimination of import barriers, export subsidies and domestic support. Special rules apply to energy and natural resources: export restrictions will generally not be permitted. Services, including financial services, are dealt with in the agreement, with providers of services entitled to receive national treatment[32] in the other member countries. Government procurement — the purchase of goods and services by governments — is partly opened to competition. Of major significance are the rules on intellectual property; all principal intellectual property rights — copyright, patents and trademarks — are recognised and protected and laws are to be harmonized to secure broadly equivalent protection in each country.[33] Finally, the NAFTA is not restricted to trade in goods and services; it also contains provisions relating to investment.

$\mathcal{F}$OREIGN INVESTMENT

Forms of Foreign Investment

A distinction is commonly drawn between *portfolio investment* and *direct investment*. Portfolio investment is essentially "passive" investment, normally in government or corporate bonds or listed securities. Foreign direct investment (FDI), by contrast, occurs as part of active business operations. It can be defined as

> investment made to acquire a lasting interest in an enterprise operating in an economic environment other than that of the investor, the investor's purpose being to have an effective voice in the management of the enterprise.[34]

It may involve the acquisition of property, such as a factory or hotel, or of all or a substantial part of the shares[35] in an existing corporation in the "host" country. FDI may also involve the establishment of an entirely new business ("greenfields" investment), and also includes the reinvestment of earnings in the host country.

---

[31] The NAFTA is implemented in Canada by the North American Free Trade Agreement Implementation Act, S.C. 1993, c. 44, and came into effect on January 1, 1994. The Canada-U.S. agreement is effectively superseded, being suspended during the operation of the NAFTA.

[32] Or MFN treatment, if that is better.

[33] This has required changes to be made in Canadian laws, such as those governing the compulsory licensing of pharmaceutical patents; see Chapter 25.

[34] United Nations, *World Investment Directory 1992*, New York: 1992, UNCTC.

[35] To be classified as direct, rather than portfolio, investment the acquisition must normally be of at least 10 percent of the shares of the host country corporation.

Normally, FDI is conducted through the establishment of

(a) a branch;

(b) a subsidiary; or

(c) a joint venture.

Where it establishes a *branch* the investor carries on business in the host country in its own name, the foreign branch being an integral part of its global business, with the assets of the branch owned directly by the foreign investor. By contrast, a *subsidiary* is a separate corporation, incorporated in the host country and owning assets there. The parent investor owns the shares in the subsidiary, but not the assets. The distinction can sometimes be very important; for example, some countries do not allow foreign ownership of land, but permit a local corporation to do so, even if a majority of its shares are held by foreigners. A *joint venture* is formed by two or more parties, at least one of which is normally from the host country: it can take the form either of a type of partnership (contractual joint venture) or of a jointly-owned subsidiary corporation (equity joint venture).[36] Canadian investors overseas generally prefer the subsidiary or equity joint venture forms, principally for tax reasons, and some host countries permit foreign investment only in those forms.

Government Regulation of Foreign Investment

A firm wishing to invest and carry on business in another country must, of course, comply with the laws of that country. For example, a foreign corporation that carries on business in Canada through a branch may be required by the laws of the province where the branch is located to obtain a licence and to register certain information.[37] If it wishes to incorporate a subsidiary in Canada it may be required to have a majority of directors who are resident Canadians.[38] In the same way, a Canadian firm seeking to establish a branch or subsidiary abroad will have to comply with the local laws. Some countries do not permit foreign corporations to conduct business through a branch. Others do not allow foreigners to own a majority of the shares in a domestic corporation, thus making a joint venture (with a local partner) the only feasible method of carrying on business.

Many countries have a somewhat contradictory attitude towards foreign investment. On the one hand, they see foreign investment as desirable because it brings much-needed capital into the economy, creates employment, opens up export markets, and introduces modern technology and management skills. On the other hand, they regard it with suspicion as a form of economic imperialism, likely to cause social and environmental damage, to stifle the development of local business, and to exert undue political influence. Consequently they seek both to attract foreign investment and to control it, by a mixture of incentives and restrictions. They offer inducements such as tax holidays, but at the same time exclude foreign investors from participating in certain activities (such as finance, communications and transportation), forbid them to own real estate, or require them to meet specific conditions with regard to matters such as creating jobs or utilizing domestic raw materials.

---

[36] Joint ventures are discussed in Chapter 29.

[37] See, in Ontario, Part VIII of the Corporations Act, R.S.O. 1990, c. C-38, and the Corporations Information Act, R.S.O. 1990, c. C-39.

[38] See, for example, Canada Business Corporations Act, R.S.C. 1985, c. C-44, s. 105(3).

Like many other countries, Canada subjects certain types of inward direct investment to review and to prior general authorization. Prior to 1985, Canada took a rather restrictive attitude to foreign investment, reflecting concern over the high level of foreign ownership of Canadian industry and resources. The Foreign Investment Review Agency (FIRA) could refuse to authorise investment it considered not to be in the national interest, or it could attach conditions to an investment. In 1985, FIRA was replaced by a new agency, Investment Canada[39] which, although it retains most of the powers of FIRA, has adopted a more positive approach to the promotion of foreign investment. As a general rule, Investment Canada does not review the establishment of a new business, requiring only that it be notified. The same is true of the acquisition of an existing Canadian business if its assets are less than $5 million.[40] The acquisition of larger businesses requires authorization, and must be "of significant benefit to Canada"; in practice, authorization is almost always granted.

However, a more restrictive approach is taken in some sectors. All acquisitions or investments to establish a new business in cultural sectors such as book publishing and film making are subject to review, regardless of the amount involved. A variety of federal, and in some cases provincial, statutes restrict foreign ownership of banking and financial services, insurance, transport undertakings, fishing and fish processing, oil, gas and uranium. The existence of public monopolies, such as the post office, electricity and liquor sales, further restricts the potential for foreign investment.

Foreign Investment and International Law

As we noted in our discussion of Foreign Trade, prior to the conclusion of the Uruguay Round the GATT applied only to the international trade in goods, and consequently had no general application to foreign investment. However, certain types of investment rules can clearly have an impact upon trade. If, in granting approval to a foreign investment, a host country attaches conditions (usually called *performance requirements*), for example that the investor must use local raw materials or components, or that it must export a stipulated percentage of its total production, those conditions will interfere with the investor's freedom to trade. The legality of such *trade-related investment measures* (TRIMs) was considered by a Panel of the GATT, in a complaint referred to it in 1982.[41] The United States, at the request of a number of American corporations that had invested in Canada, complained that conditions imposed by FIRA, requiring the investors to buy components and materials from local Canadian sources, was in effect imposing restrictions on the importation of similar goods. The Panel upheld the complaint, ruling against Canada.[42] The agreements reached in the Uruguay round will considerably extend the application of the GATT to investment rules.

---

[39] Investment Canada Act, S.C. 1985, c. 20.

[40] The review threshold is $150 million for investment by Mexican and U.S. investors, by virtue of the NAFTA; see below.

[41] United States v. Canada: Administration of the Foreign Investment Review Act, report of February 7, 1984 (Case No.108, GATT Doc.L/5308).

[42] The Panel rejected a further complaint that export requirements constituted a form of export subsidy. Such measures, however, may now be contrary to the GATT as a consequence of the changes adopted in the Uruguay Round.

Probably the greatest fear of a potential foreign investor is that its assets might be expropriated by the host country government, or nationalized without adequate compensation. Expropriation has been one of the more controversial issues in international law; some industrialized countries would like to see expropriation entirely prohibited, whereas many developing countries consider the power to nationalize to be essential to their economic development. The United Nations has tended towards the latter position, and has declared that every state has the right to nationalize, expropriate or transfer ownership of foreign-owned property, but that appropriate compensation must be paid.[43] The 1985 Convention establishing the Multilateral Investment Guarantee Agency (MIGA), under the auspices of the World Bank, provides some protection against the consequences of expropriation, but probably of greater importance are the numerous bilateral *investment protection treaties*, entered into between capital-importing and capital-exporting countries. These treaties usually provide that foreign investment should receive national treatment, that is, it should be treated no less favourably than a comparable domestic enterprise would be, that it should be given full legal protection and be protected against arbitrary or discriminatory measures that interfere with its management and operation, and that investors should have the right to repatriate their capital and profits. In addition, it is usual to provide that a host country may not expropriate or nationalize the property of an investor from the other country "except for a public purpose, under due process of law, in a non-discriminatory manner", and that any such expropriation "must be accompanied by prompt, adequate and effective compensation".[44]

Finally, we should note that the NAFTA significantly relaxes the general rules of the Investment Canada Act as they apply to Mexican and US investment in Canada.[45] In particular, the threshold for review and approval of acquisitions is to be progressively raised (except in some cultural and transportation sectors), from $5 million to $150 million. Performance requirements, regarding such matters as exporting or local sourcing of goods or services, will not be permitted and, as a general principle, investors will be entitled to national treatment, or to MFN treatment if that is better.[46] Canadian investment in Mexico and in the United States will enjoy similar privileges and protection.

$\mathcal{T}$HE RESOLUTION OF INTERNATIONAL BUSINESS DISPUTES

Like any other business activities, foreign trade and foreign investment can give rise to diverse disputes. They may be based in private law, as for example between parties to an international contract for the sale of goods. Or disputes may be primarily about public or administrative law, between governments on the one hand and importers or investors on the other. In addition, questions of public international law may arise where it is alleged

---

[43] United Nations Charter of Economic Rights and Duties of States, adopted December 12, 1974.

[44] See, for example, article VI of the "Agreement between the Government of Canada and the Government of the Republic of Poland for the Promotion and Reciprocal Protection of Investments", signed in Warsaw on April 6, 1990 (Canada Treaty Series 1990, No.43).

[45] The Act has been amended by S.C. 1993, c. 35 and c. 44.

[46] Sometimes a country may impose restrictions upon its own investors that do not apply to foreign investors: in such a case, MFN treatment may be more favourable than national treatment.

that one state is in breach of its treaty obligations to another. An aggrieved party may bring such a dispute before a national court, an arbitrator, or some form of international tribunal.

Judicial Proceedings

In principle, Canadian courts, and those of most other countries, are open to the world, in the sense that one need not be a Canadian citizen or resident in order to be able to sue or be sued in them. Nevertheless, a number of problems may arise in disputes with an international element.

ILLUSTRATION

A Canadian manufacturer contracts to sell electrical equipment to a Korean construction company, delivery to be made at a construction site in Saudi Arabia. The price is stated to be payable in Swiss Francs. The manufacturer ships the equipment to Saudi Arabia but the Korean company refuses to take delivery, claiming that the goods do not meet the contract specification.

The Canadian firm wishes to sue for the price; perhaps the Korean party will claim damages. But in which country should the action be brought? In Canada, Korea, Saudi Arabia, Switzerland, or perhaps somewhere entirely different? What if the contract has stipulated that it is governed by the laws of New York State? In determining these questions, a number of issues must be considered.

Jurisdiction

The question whether or not a court will consent to hear an action is essentially one for the court itself to decide. Courts do not encourage "forum shopping" — that is, allowing a plaintiff to seek out a jurisdiction most likely to view its claim favourably. Courts insist that the issue must have some "connecting factor" with the country in which a party seeks to bring the action. Moreover, even when it finds that there is a connecting factor, the court might decide that there are much stronger connecting factors with some other country, or that it would be more appropriate for the action to be brought in another country.

Standing

Although the parties need not be residents or citizens of a country in order to have access to its courts, some restrictions may apply. For example, a foreign corporation that has not been licensed or registered in Canada cannot be a plaintiff in Canadian courts. A further problem arises where the defendant is not present, or does not have an establishment within the jurisdiction and cannot be served with the writ or originating process. Although courts may give leave to serve the process outside the jurisdiction, they are generally reluctant to try actions against absent defendants unless there is a very strong connection between the cause of action and the country concerned.

Choice of Law

We have already discussed the question of the proper law of the contract. It is important to recall that it is not unusual, in international trade disputes, for the court of one country to apply the law of another. Thus, in our illustration, if the contract had stipulated that the law of New York was to apply, that clause might in itself be adequate reason for a Canadian court to decline jurisdiction to a Canadian plaintiff. Even so it might be possible for the Korean party to sue a Canadian defendant in a Canadian court for damages for non-performance, in which case the court would determine the rights of the parties according to New York law.

Enforcement of Foreign Judgments

Even if a plaintiff persuades a court to accept jurisdiction in a dispute of an international nature, and succeeds in obtaining a judgment against the defendant, the matter does not necessarily end there. If the defendant has assets within the jurisdiction, judgment may be levied against those assets by court order. But, to return to our example, a Canadian judgment against the Korean contractor, or a Korean judgment against the Canadian manufacturer, might be of little value if the losing party has no assets in the country where judgment is granted. The question then arises whether a Korean judgment may be enforced in Canada, and vice versa. Unfortunately, this is a complex legal issue, often without a clear answer. At common law a local judgment, provided it is for a sum of money, is considered to be a debt, and a creditor can ask a Canadian court to enforce payment.[47] But a foreign judgment debt will normally only be recognised so long as the foreign court was exercising proper jurisdiction according to the standards of the local courts (the "forum"). Ordinarily, the standards require that: there was a "real and substantial connection" between the substance of the action and the country in which judgment was granted; the judgment was not obtained by fraud; and it does not offend against natural justice or public policy.[48]

Commercial Arbitration

The difficulties and uncertainties surrounding international litigation have increasingly led the parties in international commercial contracts to make express provision for binding arbitration arranged privately, outside the court system. Rather than risk a dispute being heard before the "home" court of the other party, parties often consider it preferable to provide for a hearing before a "neutral" body, quite possibly in a third country. The agreement sometimes names one or more persons to act as arbitrator, but more commonly it nominates an "institutional" arbitrator. Over the years a number of specialist institutions have been established, the International Chamber of Commerce being probably the best known.

---

[47] Most Canadian provinces have adopted legislation providing for the enforcement of foreign judgments on a reciprocal basis. However, only a few reciprocal agreements with other countries have been entered into, the ones with the United Kingdom being the most important; see, for example, Reciprocal Enforcement of Judgments (U.K.) Act, R.S.O. 1990, c. R-6.

[48] Morguard v. de Savoye, (1990), 76 D.L.R.(4th) 256. That case concerned the recognition by a British Columbia court of an Alberta judgment. However, the principles enunciated by the Supreme Court of Canada have subsequently been applied to judgments by foreign courts; see, for example, Moses v. Shore Boat Builders Ltd. (1993), 106 D.L.R.(4th) 654, in which the judgment of an Alaskan court was held to be enforceable against a B.C. boat builder.

Arbitration associations exist in major commercial centres such as London, New York and Hong Kong, and countries such as Sweden and Switzerland are also popular arbitration venues, because of their long-standing traditions of neutrality. In Canada, arbitration centres exist in Quebec City and Vancouver.

One major advantage of arbitration, as opposed to litigation, is that the arbitrators normally have greater experience of international commerce than one would expect to find among judges of the regular courts. Other advantages are the non-public nature and confidentiality of the proceedings, especially important where the dispute concerns trade secrets, and usually costs are lower and decisions are speedier. Most modern commercial arbitration employs standard procedures, such as those adopted in the UNCITRAL model, that are generally better adapted to international disputes than are regular court procedures.

Perhaps the greatest advantage of commercial arbitration, as opposed to litigation, lies in the relative ease with which awards may be enforced. Unlike litigation, arbitration is consensual: the parties to the original contract have agreed to submit any dispute to arbitration and to abide by the award. As a result, there is no valid reason for a court to refuse to enforce such an award should one of the parties fail to comply with it. In the past decade Canada has enacted legislation, at both the federal and provincial levels, to implement the 1958 United Nations Convention on the Recognition and Enforcement of Foreign Arbitral Awards and to adopt the 1985 UNCITRAL Model Law on International Commercial Arbitration.[49]

Inter-Nation Disputes

Generally, governments cannot be compelled to appear as defendants before the courts of another country, or to submit to arbitration. An individual or corporation that wishes to challenge the actions or decisions of a government — for example, the refusal of an import licence, or the expropriation of an investment — may normally do so only in the courts of that country.

However, where a complainant alleges that a state is in breach of a treaty obligation owed to one or more other states, a number of procedures exist for the resolution of the dispute. For example, bi-lateral investment protection treaties usually provide that the parties agree to submit to binding arbitration any dispute concerning the expropriation of assets or payment of proper compensation, such arbitration to be conducted by the International Centre for the Settlement of Investment Disputes (ICSID), or according to the UNCITRAL rules.[50] Most important from a Canadian perspective are the procedures provided for under the GATT and the NAFTA.

The GATT

Since its inception in 1948, the GATT has contained a mechanism for the resolution of disputes between states that are parties to the agreement. The mechanism was revised and strengthened as a result of the Uruguay Round of negotiations.

---

[49] Commercial Arbitration Act, R.S.C. 1985, c. 17 (2nd Supp.); United Nations Foreign Arbitral Awards Convention Act, S.C. 1986, c. 21; International Commercial Arbitration Act, S.B.C. 1986, c. 14; R.S.O. 1990, c. I-9.

[50] See, for example, the Canada-Poland Treaty, *supra* n.44, art. IX.

We should note that only states that are contracting parties may raise a complaint against another contracting party. Private persons have no standing as such, though an individual or firm that considers it has been injured by an action of a foreign government in violation of the GATT may request its own government to bring proceedings.

The GATT contains two types of proceedings for the settlement of disputes. Article XXII provides for consultation between the parties and, if necessary, a conciliation procedure — essentially a diplomatic solution. Alternatively, under Article XXIII, a contracting state that considers that the proper operation of the GATT is being "nullified or impaired" by the actions of another contracting state may request the Council of the GATT to appoint a Panel to adjudicate the dispute. After hearing the submissions of the parties, the Panel makes "recommendations", which may require an offending state to remove a provision of law or an administrative practice found to be contrary to the GATT or, in certain cases, to compensate an injured party. Since 1948, over one hundred cases have been submitted to GATT Panels, more than 95 percent of these involving four parties — Canada, the European Community, Japan and the United States. Up to 1990, Canada had been the object of 15 complaints (8 of these brought by the U.S.) and had itself initiated 19 complaints (11 against the U.S.). Among more recent disputes are those by the U.S. in respect of Canadian countervailing duties on grain corn and in respect of provincial rules on the marketing of alcoholic beverages, and by Canada against the U.S. in respect of countervailing duties on Canadian pork and on softwood lumber.

The NAFTA

The NAFTA contains dispute resolution provisions that are rather similar to those of the GATT, though the NAFTA may have a number of advantages, in particular more effective implementation. When a dispute arises under both the NAFTA and the GATT, the complainant may choose under which set of procedures it should be settled.[51]

In the event of a dispute, Chapter 20 of the NAFTA[52] provides for the holding of consultations at the request of either party. Should no mutually satisfactory agreement be reached, the dispute is then referred to a Free Trade Commission. If in turn the Commission fails to find an acceptable solution, either party may request the Commission to appoint an Arbitral Panel. A Panel is comprised of five members, two of whom are appointed by each of the parties from lists of experts in trade law or practice, with a chairperson selected by agreement or by lot. The Panel hears the submissions of the parties and produces a report, published by the Commission. The parties must implement the report within thirty days; if a party fails to do so, an aggrieved party may withdraw benefits in retaliation.

Chapter 19 of the NAFTA, which is based upon the chapter of the same number in the Canada-United States Agreement, contains separate provisions for the resolution of disputes concerning the imposition of anti-dumping and countervailing duties; such disputes occur frequently and are often more important, at least in financial terms, than the general disputes that are dealt with under Chapter 20. Currently, each country applies its own anti-

---

[51] There are a few exceptions, where the NAFTA procedures must be used.
[52] Chapter 20 is the successor of Chapter 18 of the Canada-US Free Trade Agreement. Among recent disputes resolved under that chapter are those against Canada, in respect of rules requiring the landing in Canada of West Coast salmon caught by U.S. fishing boats, and against the U.S. concerning the minimum size requirements for importation of lobsters.

dumping and countervail laws, but the parties are entitled to ensure that those laws are correctly applied. The nature of a complaint, consequently, is that the country imposing the anti-dumping or countervailing duty has incorrectly, or improperly, applied its own law. The complaint procedure has already been used on a number of occasions.[53] In the longer term the parties are required to establish common rules on subsidies and on anti-competitive practices such as dumping.

Questions for Review

1. How are direct investment and portfolio investment distinguished?
2. Why is it that an international sale of goods may involve a number of separate contracts?
3. What is meant by the "proper law of the contract"? Which factors are taken into account in determining the proper law?
4. What are "Incoterms"? Give some examples.
5. What are the functions of bilateral investment protection treaties?
6. Explain (a) anti-dumping duties, and (b) countervailing duties. How are disputes concerning such duties resolved under the North American Free Trade Agreement?
7. What are the main advantages of commercial arbitration, as opposed to litigating disputes in the courts?
8. What are TRIMs? Give examples.
9. Distinguish between a contractual joint venture and an equity joint venture. What factors might lead an investor to establish a joint venture in another country?
10. What is "countertrade"?
11. Distinguish between national treatment and most-favoured nation treatment.
12. Why might a country impose restrictions upon exports?
13. What is "foreign exchange risk management"?
14. What are "non-tariff barriers"? Give examples.
15. By what means do countries seek to promote exports? Are such means permitted by the GATT?
16. What is the role of Investment Canada?

Problems

Problem 1

ABC Inc., a manufacturing company located in Hamilton, Ontario, agrees to sell machine tools to a customer in Belgium. The contract price is stated to be "$50 000, FOB the S.S. Lusitania in Halifax, Nova Scotia." ABC Inc. arranges for the goods to be shipped from its factory and loaded on the Lusitania by Titanic Transporters Ltd., an Ontario shipper. ABC Inc. does not insure the goods, believing that Titanic's insurance provides adequate coverage.

---

[53] For example, under the Canada-U.S. Agreement the Panel has ruled upon countervailing duties imposed by the U.S. Department of Commerce with respect to the importation of live pigs from Canada (ruling of May 19, 1992, 5 TCT 8088), and of findings of dumping by Revenue Canada against U.S. beer manufacturers (ruling of August 6, 1992, 5 TCT 8198).

(a) What, if any, will be the liability of ABC Inc. if the goods are:
   1. damaged in a road accident, caused by the negligence of Titanic's driver, en route to Halifax?
   2. damaged due to the negligence of a crane operator while being loaded onto the Lusitania?
   3. lost at sea in mid-Atlantic?
(b) What difference would it make if the price had been stated "CIF Antwerp"?

Problem 2

XYZ Ltd., a large Canadian mining corporation, entered into an agreement three years ago with the government of the Republic of Utopia to develop the mining and processing of the rich zinc deposits in that country. A joint-venture corporation, Cantopia Ltd., was established (under the law of Utopia), in which XYZ held 49 percent of the shares and the government of Utopia held the remainder. XYZ invested $25 million in the project, in the form of machinery, technology, and capital to finance the operation of mines and smelters; the Utopian government's contribution to the project took the form of a lease, at nominal rent, of a large tract of land where valuable deposits had been discovered. It was agreed that Cantopia would mine the zinc, process it, and export it through XYZ's world-wide marketing organization. Profits would be shared in the ratio 49/51 percent.

Recently, following a military coup, the new government of Utopia enacted a law requiring all mining enterprises to sell their total output to the newly established National Resources Corporation, wholly owned by the Utopian government, at prices to be established by a government agency. Under the prices established for zinc, it has become impossible for Cantopia to operate at a profit.

Are there any steps that XYZ can take to protect its investment?

Problem 3

Canadian production of widgets is almost entirely in the hands of three corporations — Altawidge Ltd., Ontwidge Ltd., and Scotiawidge Ltd. All three corporations export a substantial volume of their products to the United States.

Two years ago, as a result of increased competition from Malaysian widget producers, two of the Canadian corporations — Ontwidge and Scotiawidge — experienced financial difficulties. As a result, the governments of Ontario and Nova Scotia stepped in to help save the widget industry. They provided long-term, low-interest loans to the corporations and granted other benefits, such as research grants and exemption from property taxes. By contrast, Altawidge has received no government support, but has been able to compete with its rivals because its operations are more advanced technologically.

Recently, there have been complaints from widget producers in the United States that they have lost a substantial share of the American market to imports from Canada and Malaysia. They allege that widget production in both countries is heavily subsidized. As a result of these complaints, the U.S. Department of Commerce has introduced a countervailing duty of 17 cents for each widget imported from Canada. The effect of the duty is to make Canadian widgets more expensive in the U.S. than domestically-produced widgets.

Altawidge has in turn complained that, whether or not the Nova Scotia and Ontario producers receive an improper subsidy, their own products enjoy no such benefit and should not be subjected to the duty.

Discuss the issues raised and suggest what steps might be taken to resolve the dispute.

$\mathcal{B}$IBLIOGRAPHY

1. General References

Allen, C.K. *Law in the Making* (7th ed.). London: Oxford University Press, 1964.

Black, H.C. *Black's Law Dictionary* (5th ed.). St. Paul, Minn.: West Publishing Co., 1979.

Denning (Lord). *The Discipline of Law*. London: Butterworth & Co., 1979.

Jackson, R.M. *The Machinery of Justice in England* (7th ed.). Cambridge: Cambridge University Press, 1977.

Lloyd, D. *The Idea of Law* (rev. ed.) Harmondsworth: Penguin, 1974.

Plucknett, T. *A Concise History of the Common Law*. London: Butterworth & Co., 1956.

Posner, R.A. *Economic Analysis of Law* (2nd ed.). Boston: Little, Brown and Company, 1977.

Stuart, D. *Canadian Criminal Law: a Treatise* (2nd ed.). Toronto: Carswell Company, 1987.

Waddams, S. *Introduction to the Study of Law* (4th ed.). Toronto: Carswell Company, 1992.

2. Social Context

Friedmann, W. *Law in a Changing Society*. New York: Columbia University Press, 1972.

Hart, H.L.A. *The Concept of Law*. London: Oxford University Press, 1961.

Hazard, L. *Law and the Changing Environment*. San Francisco: Holden-Day, 1971.

Hogg, P.W. *Constitutional Law of Canada* (3rd ed.). Toronto: Carswell Company, 1992.

Lederman, W.R. *Continuing Canadian Constitutional Dilemmas*. Toronto: Butterworth & Co., 1981.

Russell, P.H. *Leading Constitutional Decisions* (3rd ed.). Ottawa: Carleton University Press, 1982.

Schur, E.M. *Law and Society: A Sociological View*. New York: Random House, 1968.

3. Torts

Fleming, J.G. *The Law of Torts* (8th ed.). Sydney: Law Book Co., 1992.

_____. *An Introduction to the Law of Torts* (2nd ed.). Oxford: Clarendon Press, 1985.

Hart, H.L.A. and A.M. Honoré. *Causation in Law* (2nd ed.). Oxford: Oxford University Press, 1985.

Linden, A.M. *Canadian Tort Law* (5th ed.). Toronto: Butterworth & Co., 1993.

Waddams, S.M. *Products Liability* (3rd ed.). Toronto: Carswell Company, 1993.

4. Contracts

Corbin, A.L. *Corbin on Contracts* (1 vol. ed.). St. Paul: West Publishing Co., 1952.

Flavell, C.J.M. *Canadian Competition Law*. A Business Guide. Toronto: McGraw-Hill Ryerson Ltd., 1979.

Fridman, G.H.L. *The Law of Contract in Canada* (3rd ed.). Toronto: Carswell Company, 1994.

Furmston, M.P. *Cheshire and Fifoot's Law of Contract* (12th ed.). London: Butterworth & Co., 1991.

Guest, A.G. *Anson's Law of Contract* (26th ed.). Oxford: Clarendon Press, 1984.

Nozick, R.S. *Competition Act, 1992.* Toronto: Carswell Company, 1991.

Palmer, G.E. *Mistake and Unjust Enrichment.* Columbus: Ohio State University Press, 1962.

Prichard, J.R., W.T. Stanbury and T.A. Wilson. *Canadian Competition Policy.* Toronto: Butterworth & Co., 1979.

Swan, J. and B.J. Reiter. *Contracts, Cases, Notes & Materials* (4th ed.). Toronto: Emond-Montgomery Publications Ltd., 1991.

Treitel, G.H. *The Law of Contract* (8th ed.). London: Stevens & Sons Ltd., 1991.

Waddams, S.M. *The Law of Contracts* (3rd ed.). Toronto: Canada Law Book Company, 1993.

Williston, S. *Treatise on the Law of Contract* (3rd ed.). W.H.E. Jaeger, ed. Mount Kisco, N.Y.: Baker, Voorhis, 1957.

5. Special Types of Contracts

Agency

Fridman, G.H.L. *The Law of Agency* (5th ed.). London: Butterworth & Co., 1983.

Bailment

Paton, G.W. *Bailment in the Common Law.* London: Stevens & Sons Ltd., 1952.

Tyler, E.L.G. and N.E. Palmer. *Crossley Vaines' Personal Property* (5th ed.). London: Butterworth & Co. 1973.

Employment

Adams, G.W. *Canadian Labour Law.* Toronto: Canada Law Book Company, 1985

Arthurs, H.W., D.D. Carter and H.J. Glasbeek. *Labour Law and Industrial Relations* in Canada. Toronto: Kluwer/Butterworth & Co., 1981.

Insurance and Guarantee

Crawford, B. *et al. Cases on the Canadian Law of Insurance.* Toronto: Carswell & Company, 1983.

MacGillivray, E.J. *MacGillivray and Parkington on Insurance Law Relating to All Risks other than Marine* (8th ed.), M. Parkington, ed. London: Sweet & Maxwell Ltd., 1988.

McGuiness, K.P. *The Law of Guarantee.* Toronto: Carswell Co., 1986.

Sale of Goods

Atiyah, P.S. *The Sale of Goods* (8th ed.). London: Pitman & Sons Ltd., 1990.

Fridman, G.H.L. *Sale of Goods in Canada* (3rd ed.). Toronto: Carswell Company, 1986.

Guest, A.G., ed. *Benjamin's Sale of Goods* (4th ed.) London: Sweet & Maxwell Ltd., 1992.

6. Property

General

Burn, E.H., ed. *Cheshire & Burn's Modern Law of Real Property* (14th ed.). London: Butterworth & Co., 1988.

Megarry, R. and H.W.R. Wade. *The Law of Real Property* (7th ed.). London: Butterworth & Co., 1992.

Mendes da Costa, D. and R.L. Balfour. *Property Law* (2nd ed.). Toronto: Emond-Montgomery, 1990

Preston, C.H.S. and G.H. Newsom. *Restrictive Covenants Affecting Freehold Land* (7th ed.). London: Sweet & Maxwell Ltd., 1982.

Sinclair, A.M. *Introduction to Real Property Law* (3rd ed.). Toronto: Butterworth & Co., 1987.

Intellectual Property

Cairns, D.J.A. *Remedies for Trademark Infringement.* Toronto: Carswell Company, 1988.

Hughes, R.T. *Hughes on Copyright and Industrial Design.* Toronto: Butterworth & Co., 1984.

Hughes, R.T. and T.P. Ashton. *Hughes on Trade Marks.* Toronto: Butterworth & Co., 1984.

Hughes, R.T. and J.H. Woodley. *Hughes and Woodley on Patents.* Toronto Butterworth & Co., 1984.

Landlord and Tenant

Lamont, D.H. *Residential Tenancies* (4th ed.). Toronto: Carswell Company, 1983.

Rhodes, F.W. *Williams' The Canadian Law of Landlord and Tenant* (6th ed.). Toronto: Carswell Company, 1988.

Blundell & Wellings, *Woodfall's Law of Landlord and Tenant* (27th ed.). London: Sweet & Maxwell Ltd., 1968.

Mortgages

Falconbridge, J.D. *The Law of Mortgages* (4th ed.), W.B. Rayner and R.H. McLaren, eds. Agincourt, Ont.: *Canada Law Book Company,* 1977.

7. Forms of Business Organization

Corporations

Gower, L.C.B. et al. *Gower's Principles of Modern Company Law* (5th ed.). London: Stevens & Sons Ltd., 1992.

Welling, B. *Corporate Law in Canada* (2nd ed.). Toronto: Butterworths, 1991.

Ziegel, J.S., ed. *Studies in Canadian Company Law, Vol. 1.* Toronto: Butterworth & Co., 1967.

_____. *Studies in Canadian Company Law, VoL 2.* Toronto: Butterworth & Co., 1973.

Environment

Cook, R. and Lucas, A., *Canadian Environmental Law* (2nd ed.). Toronto: Butterworth & Co., 1991

Thompson, McConnell, and Huestis, *Environmental Law and Business in Canada.* Aurora: Canada Law Book, 1993.

Partnership

Drake, C.D. *Law of Partnership* (3rd ed.). London: Sweet & Maxwell Ltd., 1983.

Underhill, A. *Principles of the Law of Partnership* (12th ed.). H. Ivamy, ed. London: Butterworth & Co., 1986.

8. Credit Transactions

General

Dunlop, C.R.B. *Creditor-Debtor Law in Canada* (2nd ed.). Toronto: Carswell Company, 1994.

Laskin, J.B. *et al. Debtor and Creditor* (2nd ed.). Toronto: Emond-Montgomery, 1982.

Bankruptcy

Canada. *Report of the Committee on Bankruptcy and Insolvency Legislation, Canada 1970.* Ottawa: Information Canada, 1970.

Houlden, L.W., and C.H. Morawetz. *Bankruptcy and Insolvency Act, 1994.* Toronto: Carswell Company, 1993.

Limitations of Actions

Weaver, E.L. *Limitations*, A.E. Laverty, ed. Toronto: Canadian Law List Publishing Co., 1939.

Mechanics' Liens

Macklem, D.N. and Bristow, D.I. *Construction and Mechanics' Liens in Canada* (6th ed.). Toronto: Carswell Company, 1990.

9. International Business

Schmitthoff, C.M. *Export Trade* (9th ed.). London: Stevens and Sons, 1990.

Castel, J.G., de Mestral, A.L.C. and Graham, W.C. *The Canadian Law and Practice of International Trade.* Toronto: Edmond Montgomery Publications Ltd., 1991.

Castel, J.G. *Introduction to Conflict of Laws* (2nd ed.). Toronto: Butterworth & Co., 1986.

Raworth, P. *Legal Guide to International Business Transactions.* Toronto: Carswell Company, 1991.

A

Aboriginal peoples
 and the constitution, 35
 contractual capacity of, 181
Absent fraud, 708
Absolute privilege, 93
Acceleration clause, 407, 637
Acceptance of an offer
 in bilateral contracts, 142–43
 by long-distance communication, 139–41
 communication to offeror, 137
 conditional, by an agent, 466
 incomplete agreements, 143–44
 moment of acceptance, 138–39
 positive nature, 136–37
Acceptor, 517
 liability of, 529–30
Accord and satisfaction, 309–310
Act of God, 312–13, 452
Action
 capacity to start an, 58–59
 duty of care in tort law, 80–81
 frivolous and vexatious, 65–66
 for the price, 396
Adequate notice, 337–338
Administrative law, 52–53
Administrator, 298
Advances, excess partnership contributions, 668
Adverse possession, 594–96
Advertising, and "use" of trademark, 557
Advocates, 70
Affidavit of bona fides, 772
After-acquired property
 as chattel mortgage, 765
 personal property security legislation, 777
Agency
 by estoppel, 468–70
 by express agreement, 465
 by necessity, 470–71
 by ratification, 466–68
 defined, 464
 implied authority of wife, 180–81
 nature of, 464–65
 officers of corporations as agents, 179
Agency agreement, 464
 breach of, 479
 termination of, 479–80
Agent
 breach of faith, 473
 breach of warranty of authority, 479

commission, 474–75
defined, 464
del credere, 465
duties of, 471–74
duty of diligence, 471
liability on contracts made for principal, 476–78
limits of apparent authority, 468–70
mercantile, 470
personal performance, 472
Agreement, discharge by, 308–309
Agreement to sell, as type of contract of sale, 373
Agricultural products, 829
Alberta
 adverse possession of land, 593
 articles of incorporation system, 687
 computerized system for registering security interest, 770
 "equal pay for equal work" approach to pay equity, 498n. 29
 Frustrated Contracts Act, 318
 mortgage debt, 645n. 10
 mortgage law, 647
 Personal Property Security Act, 775
Alteration, as real defence, 539
Alternative dispute resolution (ADR), 67–68
 arbitration, 67
 mediation, 67
Anarchists, 10, 11, 12
Annual general meeting, 710, 713
Annual report, 711
Anti-dumping duties, 830, 831
Anti-Inflation Act, 26
Anticipatory breach, 333
Appeals, 64
Apportionment of loss legislation, 85
Appraisal remedy, 719
Aquaculturalists
 as creditors, 799
 as debtors, 795
Arbitration, 67
 "first contract," 504
Arbitration procedure, 505
Argenton, Severin, 749–50
Aristotle, 14–15
Article of incorporation system, number of directors stated, 701n
Articles of association, 690
Articles of incorporation system, 687
 concept of authorized capital, 691